CHAPTERS 12–26

FOURTH EDITION

Accounting

■ **CHARLES T. HORNGREN**
Stanford University

■ **WALTER T. HARRISON, JR.**
Baylor University

■ **LINDA SMITH BAMBER**
University of Georgia

Annotations by
Betsy Willis   Becky Jones
Baylor University

PRENTICE-HALL
Upper Saddle River, New Jersey 07458

To Betsy Willis and Becky Jones for their wisdom on learning and teaching over a 10-year period and to Michael Bamber for his insight on business practices and ethical issues in management accounting.

Executive Editor: *Annie Todd*
Executive Editor: *Deborah Hoffman Emery*
Development Editor: *Bruce Kaplan*
Senior Editorial Assistant: *Jane Avery*
Assistant Editor: *Natacha St. Hill*
Editor in Chief: *P.J. Boardman*
Director of Development: *Stephen Deitmer*
Executive Marketing Manager: *Beth Toland*
Book Production: *Progressive Publishing Alternatives*
Production Editor: *Carol Lavis*
Managing Editor: *Bruce Kaplan*
Senior Manufacturing Supervisor: *Paul Smolenski*
Manufacturing Manager: *Vincent Scelta*
Design Director: *Pat Smythe*
Interior Design: *Lorraine Castellano*
Cover Design: *Deborah Chused*
Composition: *TSI Graphics*
Cover Art/Photo: *Marjorie Dressler*

Printed in the United States of America
10 9 8 7 6 5 4 3 2

ISBN 0-13-082307-4

Prentice Hall International (UK) Limited, London
Prentice Hall of Australia Pty. Limited, Sydney
Prentice Hall of Canada Inc., Toronto
Prentice Hall Hispanoamericano, S.A., Mexico
Prentice Hall of India Private Limited, New Delhi
Prentice Hall of Japan, Inc., Tokyo
Simon & Schuster Asia Pte. Ltd., Singapore
Editora Prentice Hall do Brasil, Ltda., Rio de Janeiro

Charles T. Horngren Series in Accounting

- **AUDITING: AN INTEGRATED APPROACH, 7E**
  Arens/Loebbeck

- **KOHLER'S DICTIONARY FOR ACCOUNTANTS, 7E**
  Copper/Ljiri

- **FINANCIAL STATEMENT ANALYSIS, 2E**
  Foster

- **GOVERNMENTAL AND NONPROFIT ACCOUNTING: THEORY AND PRACTICE, 5E**
  Freeman/Shoulders

- **FINANCIAL ACCOUNTING, 3E**
  Harrison/Horngren

- **COST ACCOUNTING; A MANAGERIAL EMPHASIS, 9E**
  Horngren/Foster/Datar

- **ACCOUNTING, 4E**
  Horngren/Harrison/Bamber

- **CASES IN FINANCIAL REPORTING, 2E**
  Hirst/McAnally

- **PRINCIPLES OF FINANCIAL AND MANAGEMENT ACCOUNTING: A SOLE PROPRIETORSHIP APPROACH, 2E**
  Horngren/Harrison/Robinson

- **INTRODUCTION TO FINANCIAL ACCOUNTING, 7E**
  Horngren/Sundem/Elliot

- **INTRODUCTION TO MANAGEMENT ACCOUNTING, 11E**
  Horngren/Sundem/Stratton

- **BUDGETING, 6E**
  Welsch/Hilton/Gordon

Photo Credits

About the Authors

Charles T. Horngren is the Edmund W. Littlefield Professor of Accounting, Emeritus, at Stanford University. A graduate of Marquette University, he received his MBA from Harvard University and his Ph.D. from the University of Chicago. He is also the recipient of honorary doctorates from Marquette University and DePaul University.

A Certified Public Accountant, Horngren served on the Accounting Principles Board for six years, the Financial Accounting Standards Board Advisory Council for five years, and the Council of the American Institute of Certified Public Accountants for three years. For six years, he served as a trustee of the Financial Accounting Foundation, which oversees the Financial Accounting Standards Board and the Government Accounting Standards Board.

Horngren is a member of the Accounting Hall of Fame.

A member of the American Accounting Association, Horngren has been its President and its Director of Research. He received its first annual Outstanding Accounting Educator Award.

The California Certified Public Accountants Foundation gave Horngren its Faculty Excellence Award and its Distinguished Professor Award. He is the first person to have received both awards.

The American Institute of Certified Public Accountants presented its first Outstanding Educator Award to Horngren.

Horngren was named Accountant of the Year, Education, by the national professional accounting fraternity, Beta Alpha Psi.

Professor Horngren is also a member of the Institute of Management Accountants, where he has received its Distinguished Service Award. He was a member of the Institute's Board of Regents, which administers the Certified Management Accountant examinations.

Horngren is the author of other accounting books published by Prentice-Hall: *Cost Accounting: A Managerial Emphasis*, Ninth Edition, 1997 (with George Foster and Srikant Datar); *Introduction to Financial Accounting*, Seventh Edition, 1999 (with Gary L. Sundem and John A. Elliott); *Introduction to Management Accounting*, Eleventh Edition, 1999 (with Gary L. Sundem and William O. Statton); and *Financial Accounting*, Third Edition, 1998 (with Walter T. Harrison, Jr.).

Horngren is the Consulting Editor for the Charles T. Horngren Series in Accounting.

Walter T. Harrison, Jr. is Professor of Accounting at the Hankamer School of Business, Baylor University. He received his B.B.A. degree from Baylor University, his M.S. from Oklahoma State University, and his Ph.D. from Michigan State University.

Professor Harrison, recipient of numerous teaching awards from student groups as well as from university administrators, has also taught at Cleveland State Community College, Michigan State University, the University of Texas, and Stanford University.

A member of the American Accounting Association and the American Institute of Certified Public Accountants, Professor Harrison has served as Chairman of the Financial Accounting Standards Committee of the American Accounting Association, on the Teaching/Curriculum Development Award Committee, on the Program Advisory Committee for Accounting Education and Teaching, and on the Notable Contributions to Accounting Literature Committee.

Professor Harrison has lectured in several foreign countries and published articles in numerous journals, including *The Accounting Review, Journal of Accounting Research, Journal of Accountancy, Journal of Accounting and Public Policy, Economic Consequences of Financial Accounting Standards, Accounting Horizons, Issues in Accounting Education*, and

Journal of Law and Commerce. He is coauthor of *Financial Accounting, Third Edition, 1998* (with Charles T. Horngren) published by Prentice Hall. Professor Harrison has received scholarships, fellowships, research grants or awards from Price Waterhouse & Co., Deloitte & Touche, the Ernst & Young Foundation, and the KPMG Peat Marwick Foundation.

Linda Smith Bamber is Professor of Accounting at the J.M. Tull School of Accounting at the University of Georgia. She graduated summa cum laude from Wake Forest University, where she was a member of Phi Beta Kappa. She is a certified public accountant. For her performance on the CPA examination, Professor Bamber received the Elijah Watt Sells Award in addition to the North Carolina Bronze Medal. Before returning to graduate school, she worked in cost accounting at RJR Foods. She then earned an MBA from Arizona State University, and a Ph.D. from The Ohio State University.

Professor Bamber has received numerous teaching awards from The Ohio State University, the University of Florida, and the University of Georgia, including selection as Teacher of the Year at the University of Florida's Fisher School of Accounting.

She has lectured in Canada and Australia in addition to the U.S., and her research has appeared in numerous journals, including *The Accounting Review, Journal of Accounting Research, Journal of Accounting and Economics, Journal of Finance, Contemporary Accounting Research, Auditing: A Journal of Practice and Theory, Accounting Horizons, Issues in Accounting Education,* and *CPA Journal.* She provided the annotations for the *Annotated Instructor's Edition* of Horngren, Foster, and Datar's *Cost Accounting: A Managerial Emphasis,* Seventh, Eighth, and Ninth Editions.

A member of the Institute of Management Accounting, the American Accounting Association (AAA), and the AAA's Management Accounting Section and Financial Accounting and Reporting Section, Professor Bamber has chaired the AAA New Faculty Consortium Committee, served on the AAA Council, the AAA Research Advisory Committee, the AAA Corporate Accounting Policy Seminar Committee, the AAA Wildman Medal Award Committee, the AAA Nominations Committee, and has chaired the Management Accounting Section's Membership Outreach Committee. She served as Associate Editor of *Accounting Horizons,* and will serve as editor of *The Accounting Review* from 1999 to 2002.

PRENTICE HALL
BUSINESS PUBLISHING

cross

training

Charles T.
Horngren Stanford University

Walter T.
Harrison, Jr. Baylor University

Linda Smith
Bamber University of Georgia

fourth edition

accounting

exercise. motivation. stamina. commitment.

Teaching introductory accounting today is a lot like training athletes. It requires a careful warmup, focus on specific topics and ideas, regular doses of motivation, and a cooling-off period when "the big picture" is clearly evident. Helping your students develop and master these skills is what **ACCOUNTING 4/E** is all about.

- **Exercise** - always key to any athlete's performance, we offer a wealth of assignment material, now including new Daily Exercises, Team Projects, and Internet Exercises.
- **Motivation** - your students will see how accounting principles are actually used in a variety of well-known companies including NIKE, Dell Computer, and McDonald's through a unique series of On Location! Videos, in-text Internet Tours, and new Decision Guidelines.
- **Stamina** - an athlete has to start and finish the race strongly. So too must a principles text offer balanced, comprehensive coverage of both financial and managerial topics. New coauthor Linda Smith Bamber has added her talents and expertise to the management accounting chapters.
- **Commitment** - as athletes commit to a regular training regimen and you commit to your students, we commit to providing you with the best available text and package. Prentice Hall, our publisher, commits to giving you the best service available by providing forums like PHASE (Prentice Hall Accounting Seminars for Educators) and customer services like the toll-free Accounting and Taxation Hotline (1-800-227-1816).

We believe that **ACCOUNTING 4/E** offers an unprecedented teaching and learning system for your accounting students. We invite you to learn more about how our new training program can challenge your students to "just do it." If you have any suggestions or questions, we'd like to hear from you.

Going the Distance.

Charles T. Horngren
Stanford University

Walter T. Harrison, Jr.
Baylor University

Linda Smith Bamber
University of Georgia

Chapter 1
ACCOUNTING AND THE BUSINESS ENVIRONMENT
1. Prologue on Careers in Accounting.
2. Expanded focus on the statement of cash flows throughout the text.

Chapter 2
RECORDING BUSINESS TRANSACTIONS
1. The accounting equation shows the link between the journal entry and the ledger accounts, and from Chapter 1 to Chapter 2.

Chapter 3
MEASURING BUSINESS INCOME: THE ADJUSTING PROCESS
1. T-accounts show transaction effects on the accounting equation.

Chapter 4
COMPLETING THE ACCOUNTING CYCLE
1. New visuals for the work sheet.
2. Classified balance sheet provided for the sole proprietor running example.

Chapter 5
MERCHANDISING OPERATIONS AND THE ACCOUNTING CYCLE
1. Clear separation of the perpetual and the periodic inventory systems.
2. New visuals, speedbumps, and learning tips.
3. New section on accrual accounting and cash flows for a merchandising entity.

Chapter 6
ACCOUNTING INFORMATION SYSTEMS: SPECIAL JOURNALS, CONTROL ACCOUNTS, AND SUBSIDIARY LEDGERS
1. Streamlined coverage of accounting systems.
2. New section on the general journal's role in an accounting information system.
3. New coverage of the credit memorandum and the debit memorandum.

Chapter 7
INTERNAL CONTROL, MANAGING CASH, AND MAKING ETHICAL JUDGMENTS
1. Revised focus on controlling and managing cash.
2. New section on how owners and managers use the bank reconciliation.
3. New emphasis on cash budgeting.

Chapter 8
ACCOUNTS AND NOTES RECEIVABLE
1. Streamlined section on accounting for uncollectible receivables.
2. New section on reporting receivables transactions on the statement of cash flows.

Chapter 9
ACCOUNTING FOR MERCHANDISE INVENTORY
1. New material on cost of goods sold and gross margin; ethical issues in inventory accounting; and reporting inventory transactions on the statement of cash flows.

Chapter 10
ACCOUNTING FOR PLANT ASSETS, INTANGIBLE ASSETS, AND RELATED EXPENSES
1. New sections on capitalizing the cost of interest, research and development costs, and ethical issues in accounting for plant assets and intangibles.
2. New material on reporting plant asset transactions on the statement of cash flows.

Chapter 11
CURRENT LIABILITIES AND PAYROLL ACCOUNTING
1. New coverage of accounting for notes payable issued at a discount, and unearned revenue.
2. New summary of payroll liabilities.
3. New section on ethical issues in reporting current and contingent liabilities.

Chapter 12
ACCOUNTING FOR PARTNERSHIPS
1. New section on the different types of partnerships: general, limited, and S corporations.
2. New visuals throughout the chapter.

Chapter 13
CORPORATE ORGANIZATION, PAID-IN CAPITAL, AND THE BALANCE SHEET
1. New section on ethical considerations in accounting for the issuance of stock.
2. Streamlined coverage of accounting for income taxes by corporations.

Chapter 14
RETAINED EARNINGS, TREASURY STOCK, AND THE INCOME STATEMENT
1. Accounting equation added to help students learn that stock dividends and stock splits do not affect total stockholders' equity.
2. New section on reporting comprehensive income covers FASB Statement 130.

Chapter 15
LONG-TERM LIABILITIES
1. New graphs show the movements of interest expense and bond carrying amount over the life of a bond issue.
2. New section on reporting long-term liability transactions on the statement of cash flows.

Chapter 16
ACCOUNTING FOR INVESTMENTS AND INTERNATIONAL OPERATIONS
1. New section on short-term trading investments.
2. Moved section on preparing consolidated financial statements to an appendix.
3. New section on reporting comprehensive income (FASB Statement 130) and on reporting investment transactions on the statement of cash flows.

Chapter 17
PREPARING AND USING THE STATEMENT OF CASH FLOWS
1. New coverage on how the statement of cash flows is prepared from the income statement plus the comparative balance sheet.
2. Expanded coverage of the indirect method of reporting cash flows from operating activities.
3. New section on using cash-flow information in investment and credit analysis.

Chapter 18
FINANCIAL STATEMENT ANALYSIS
1. New section on benchmarking versus an industry average and benchmarking versus a key competitor.
2. New section on Economic Value Added.

Chapter 19

INTRODUCTION TO MANAGEMENT ACCOUNTING

1. New introductory chapter covers service plus merchandising and manufacturing companies.
2. New second half of the chapter covers modern business environment topics such as the shift towards a service economy, competing in the global marketplace, and quality.
3. New section on ethics, with two dilemmas for students to solve and inclusion of the standards of Ethical Conduct for Management Accountants.

Chapter 20

JOB COSTING

1. New separate chapter provides a more complete treatment of job costing.
2. New introductory section contrasts job costing and process costing.
3. New section on job costing in a non-manufacturing company.

Chapter 21

PROCESS COSTING

1. New time lines diagram process cost accounting and show the difference between FIFO and Weighted Average Costing.

Chapter 22

COST-VOLUME-PROFIT ANALYSIS AND THE CONTRIBUTION MARGIN APPROACH TO DECISION MAKING

1. New comparison of variable costing and absorption costing shows how managers use these methods.

Chapter 23

THE MASTER BUDGET AND RESPONSIBILITY ACCOUNTING

1. New section on budgeting for a service company.
2. New section on the allocation of indirect costs to departments.

Chapter 24

FLEXIBLE BUDGETS AND STANDARD COSTS

1. New section on common pitfalls to avoid in price and efficiency variance computations.
2. Streamlined overhead variance analysis.

Chapter 25

ACTIVITY-BASED COSTING AND OTHER TOOLS FOR COST MANAGEMENT

1. Expanded coverage of activity-based costing with a running example contrasting the traditional system and an activity-based costing system; a discussion of when activity-based costing is most likely to pass the cost-benefit test; and a new section on warning signs to identify a broken cost system.
2. Quality discussion expanded with NEW assignment material.

Chapter 26

SPECIAL BUSINESS DECISIONS AND CAPITAL BUDGETING

1. New - Two themes are now woven through the shorter-term decisions: focus on relevant information and use a contribution margin approach.

Seeing is believing. When your students see how well-known companies like NIKE use accounting each and every day, they'll appreciate the importance of being well trained in class. Using **ACCOUNTING 4/E**, *your students will benefit from the Daily Exercises, Team Projects, and other valuable learning assignment materials. Our On Location! Custom Case Videos are linked to chapter-opening stories to help you motivate your students. Each video profiles a company, showing how today's leading businesses employ accounting information to drive business decisions.*

on location!

Cross-training sure works for NIKE. Five "On-Location" segments were shot at NIKE headquarters in Beaverton, OR.

- **Accounting and Its Environment**
- **Accounting Cycle**
- **How Accounting Systems Support Management**
- **Accounting for Endorsement Contracts**
- **Performance Evaluation and the Role of Accounting**

On Location companies include McDonald's, General Motors, May Department Stores, Home Depot, and more.

your students' performance

guarantee

Just like beginning athletes question the value of a good warm-up, your non-major students may wonder how accounting is relevant to their field of study.

Our Decision Guidelines make procedures relevant by showing the student **who** is likely to use the information and **how** it will be used.

DECISION	GUIDELINE		
Has a transaction occurred?	If the event affects the entity's financial position and can be reliably recorded - Yes		
	If either condition is absent - No		
Where to record the transaction?	In the journal, the chronological record of transactions		
What to record for each transaction?	Increases and/or decreases in all the accounts affected by the transaction		
How to record an increase/decrease in the following accounts?	Rules of debit and credit:		
		Increase	Decrease
Asset		Debit	Credit
Liability		Credit	Debit
Owners' equity		Credit	Debit
Revenue		Credit	Debit
Expense		Debit	Credit
Where to store all the information for each account?	In the ledger, the book of accounts and their balances		
Where to list all the accounts and their balances?	In the trial balance		
Where to report the Results of operations?	In the income statement		
	(revenue - expenses = net income or net loss)		
Financial position?	In the balance sheet		
	(assets = liabilities + stockholders' equity)		

NEW!! Thinking It Over segments ask students to reflect on concepts they have just learned; in-text answers provide immediate feedback

NEW!! Working It Out exercises give students additional practice putting concepts and techniques to work; again, in-text answers provide immediate feedback

Concept Links point students back to previous discussion of topics for those who want, or need, the review

Infographics help students understand concepts by providing interesting visual displays of often difficult material: one picture is worth a thousand words

Concept Highlights provide summaries of key concepts that students can use for review

Mid-Chapter and End-of-Chapter Summary Problems help students work with key chapter material discussed up to that point, while fully worked-out solutions let them test their understanding

SELECTED EXERCISES AND PROBLEMS ARE LINKED TO PRENTICE HALL SPREADSHEET STUDENT SOFTWARE AND PHAS GENERAL LEDGER SOFTWARE PACKAGES. WRITING ASSIGNMENTS ARE INCLUDED IN THE END-OF-CHAPTER MATERIAL IN EVERY CHAPTER.

Extensive market research told us accounting instructors want a greater variety of different problems and exercises. So we added New assignment material to each chapter.

New **Daily Exercises** *include a whole new set of assignments on single topics, perfect for day-to-day drills.*
New **Team Projects** *provide collaborative learning cases in every chapter*
New **Internet Exercises** *are featured in nearly every chapter and are often tied to the chapter-opening story, and in some cases, the accompanying "On Location!" video.*
Mid-Chapter and End-of-Chapter Summary Problems *are provided with worked-out solutions*
Group A & B Problems *provide homework alternatives*
Decision Cases *have been expanded from the previous edition*
Ethical Cases *appear in each chapter*

Our problems

are your **solutions**

DAILY EXERCISE • CHAPTER 5

DE 5-18 Contrasting accounting income and cash flows (Objective 4)

Lands' End, the catalog merchant, reported the following for the year ended January 31, 1997 (as adapted, with amounts in millions):

Cash payments for financing activities	$ 28
Cash payments to suppliers	$ 573
Cash collections from customers	$1,118
Cost of sales	$ 609
Selling, general, and administrative expenses	$ 424
Cash payments for investing activities	$ 18
Net sales revenue	$1,119

As an investor, you wonder which was greater, Lands' End (a) gross margin, or (b) the company's excess of cash collections from customers over cash payments to suppliers. Compute both amounts to answer this real-world question.

DE 5-19 Computing cost of goods sold in a periodic inventory system (Objective 6)

At January 31, 1996, The May Department Stores Company had merchandise inventory of $2,134 million. During the year May purchased inventory costing $8,472 million, including freight in. At January 31, 1997, May's inventory stood at $2,380 million.

1. Compute May's cost of goods sold as in the periodic system.

2. Compare your cost-of-goods-sold figure to Exhibit 5-1, page xxx. The two amounts should be equal. Are they?

INTERNET EXERCISE • CHAPTER 17

Statement of Cash Flows — Compaq

This innovative company started operations at the beginning of the personal computer revolution in 1982. During their first year, Compaq had sales of $111 million — a U.S. business record. Now it is a Fortune 100 company and the number one supplier of PCs in the world with sales exceeding $20 billion.

The computer industry is highly competitive, especially for PC manufacturers, as many customers consider the PC to be a commodity. Numerous PC manufacturers have come and gone, but Compaq has strengthened its leadership position year after year. The Statement of Cash Flows demonstrates the Company's financial strength.

REQUIRED:

1. Go to http://www.compaq.com. This is Compaq's home page where visitors can purchase a computer over the Internet as well as read Compaq's webzine and learn about the company.

2. Click Inside Company and then Investor Relations to find Compaq's corporate information. The financial statements are located in the section SEC documents.

3. The Statement of Cash Flows provides sources and uses of cash by Compaq.

a. Does Compaq use the Direct or Indirect method in calculating Cash provided by Operating Activities?

b. For the most recent year, what is Net Income and Cash Provided by Operating Activities? These are measures of Compaq's operating activities. Why are these two numbers different?

c. Compare the differences between Cash Received from Customers and Cash Paid to Suppliers and Employees for the past three years. Given the competitive environment of the PC market, what are possible reasons for this trend?

d. Why does Compaq report a "Reconciliation of net income to net cash provided by (used by) operating activities" at the end of the Statement of Cash Flows?

e. Did Compaq have any material non-cash transactions? Explain.

f. Compare Compaq's Purchases of Property, Plant, and Equipment to its Depreciation and Amortization for the past three years. Comment on Compaq's expected future growth opportunities as it relates to this data.

The NIKE Annual Report financials are included in an end-of-text appendix. The entire NIKE Annual Report is shrink-wrapped to the text so students can identify with a real Annual Report. Financial Statement Cases, based on NIKE, are at the end of financial accounting chapters.

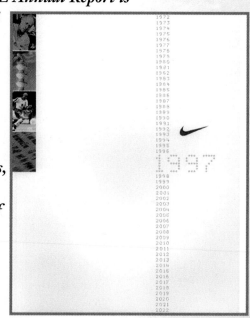

accounting made easy

CD-ROM

This self-paced computerized tutorial program teaches students accounting procedures and concepts in short, self-paced units; pretests student understanding; and then ties all the material together with case studies at the end. The CD-ROM is available in two levels:

Level 1 covers accounting basics such as business organization, accounting information, financial statements, the accounting equation, general ledger, and basic business transactions.

Level 2 focuses on accounting procedures to cover the following areas: recording transactions, posting transactions, adjustments, and completing the accounting cycle.

- Easy-to-use instructions are given in the program

- Self-paced software program allows students to learn accounting procedures on their own

- Dialogue boxes refer the students back to the appropriate topic in **ACCOUNTING 4/E** when they give incorrect answers

- On-screen and audio responses provide instant feedback

- All concepts are tied together by a comprehensive, end-of-module case

CAREER PATHS IN ACCOUNTING CD-ROM

Winner of the New Media INVISION Gold Award in Education

This CD-ROM provides students with a dynamic, interactive job-search tool. It includes workshops in career planning, resume writing, and interviewing skills. Students can learn the latest market trends, facts about the accounting profession, and the skills they need to land a job. The CD also provides salary information, video clips on specific jobs, and profiles and interviews with accounting professionals.

ACCOUNTING 4/E
software specifically designed for students:

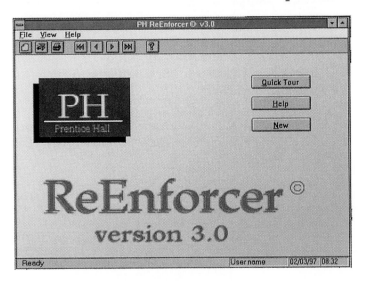

PH Re-Enforcer Tutorial Software 3.0 for Windows. *This enhanced interactive tutorial allows students to work through accounting problems to reinforce concepts and skills covered in the text. Users can work through multiple choice questions, short exercises, vocabulary games, and case problems using multimedia graphics and a computer tutorial based on objective and/or difficulty level.*

A Teacher's Edition allows instructors to edit, change, and add existing or additional material.

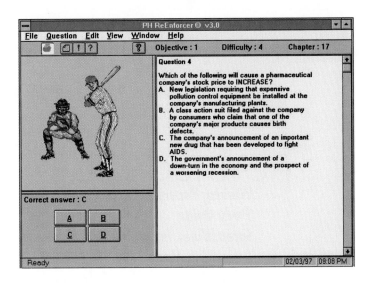

Also available:

- *Prentice Hall Accounting Software (PHAS): A General Ledger Package*
- *New, Improved Spreadsheet Templates*

  Quick Tours are part of the Prentice Hall Accounting Software (PHAS) 2.0 and the PH Re-Enforcer Tutorial Software 3.0. The Quick Tours provide students with quick and easy practice drills that demonstrate how to use the program.

- *Prentice Hall's Software Training Video teaches students and instructors how to use Prentice Hall's software products.*

Surfing for Success in Business *introduces students to the Internet and more specifically, the many useful ways to extract and use accounting information from the World Wide Web.*

The Presentation Manager *is a user-friendly program that organizes the Instructor's Manual, custom Video footage, PowerPoint slides, Teaching Transparencies, PHAS General Ledger Program, and the PH ReEnforcer© Tutorial Software under one convenient instructional tool. This powerful resource can help instructors create a powerful classroom presentation.*

our core

teaching aids

Instructor's Manual and Video Guide
On Location! Video Library
Accounting Tutorial Videos
Teaching Transparencies
Solution Transparencies
PHLIP Website support for both instructors and students
Solutions Manual
Test Item File - Prentice Hall Custom Test Software
PH Professor: A Classroom Presentation on PowerPoint

For The Student

Working Papers
Study Guide
Spreadsheet Templates with Solutions
Accounting Made Easy CD-ROM
PHAS: General Ledger Software
PH Re-Enforcer
Accounting Tutorial Videos
PHLIP Website support

Plus...

New Tutorial Video Library by Beverly Amer, Northern Arizona University, provides detailed instruction on important topics in accounting principles, while demonstrating key concepts with sample problems from the book. Tied to the text, these video segments are perfect for students who miss class or need additional review.

REVIEWERS OF ACCOUNTING, 4/E

Frank Aquilino, Montclair State University
John R. Blahnik, Lorain County Community College
Thomas M. Bock, Berkeley College (NYC)
Marianne Bradford, University of Tennessee
Kathleen M. Brenan, Ashland University
Robert C. Brush, Cecil Community College
Eric Carlsen, Kean College of New Jersey
Betty Chavis, California State University, Fullerton
Siu N. Chung, Los Angeles Valley College
Marilynn Collins, John Carroll University
Robert D. Collmier, Bloomfield College
Joan E. Cook, Milwaukee Area Technical College
David Erlach, Queens College of CUNY
William E. Faulk, Northwestern Michigan College
Mary A. Flanigan, Longwood College
James S. Gale, Northern Virginia Community College
Kathleen H. Gandy, Catonsville Community College
George F. Gardner, Bemidji State University

Sally W. Gilfillan, Longwood College
Jane Green, Valley College
Steven C. Hall, Widener University
Douglas S. Hamilton, Berkeley College (West Paterson, NJ)
William H. Harvey, Henry Ford Community College
Daniel G. Hertz, Montana State University
Jay Hollowell, Commonwealth College
Patricia H. Holmes, Des Moines Area Community College
Zachary E. Holmes, Oakland Community College
Richard C. Jarvies, Fayetteville Technical Community College
Betty T. Johns, Dundalk Community College
Thomas Kam, Hawaii Pacific University
N. Leroy Kauffman, Western Carolina University
Frank J. Kopczynski, University of New Hampshire
William G. Lasher, Jamestown Community College

Heidi H. Meier, Cleveland State University
Barbara A. Moreira, Berkeley College (Waldwick, NJ)
Harold Moreland, Pacific Lutheran University
M. Salah Negm, Prince George's Community College
Linda Hayden Overstreet, Hillsborough Community College
Frank N. Paliotta, Berkeley College (NYC)
LaVonda Ramey, Schoolcraft College
Carla Rich, Pensacola Junior College
Victoria S. Rymer, University of Maryland
Wayne M. Schell, Christopher Newport University
Richard W. Schrader, North Dakota State University
Robert Shepherd, San Jose State University
Sue Singer, Western Maryland College
Carolyn Streuly, Marquette University
Kim Tarantino, California State University, Fullerton
Robert R. Wennagel, College of the Mainland
Beulah Winfrey, College of the Ozarks

Our thanks to you and your colleagues who contributed to the development of Accounting, 4/E...

Focus Group Participants
John Blahnik, Lorain County Community College
Kay Carnes, Gonzaga University
Joan E. Cook, Milwaukee Area Technical College
Judith M. Cook, Grossmont College
Michael Farina, Cerritos College
Bob Garrett, American River College
Shirley Glass, Macomb Community College
Janet Grange, Chicago State University
William Harvey, Henry Ford Community College
Sherry Hellmuth, Elgin Community College
Anthony W. Jackson, Governor's State College
Sam Lanzafame, Bryant & Stratton
Lawrence Lease, Shasta College
Dennis Ludden, Moraine Valley Community College
Dan Lux, Salt Lake Community College
Linda Spotts Michael, Maple Woods Community College
LaVonda Ramey, Schoolcraft College
Mary Ston, Oakland Community College
George Tutt, Spokane Community College
Karen Walton, John Carroll University
Martin E. Ward, DeVry Institute of Technology

Special thanks to Thelma Blake and Terry L. Sofsky, students at Harford Community College in Maryland, for giving extensive student feedback.

SUPPLEMENT AUTHORS/REVIEW

Instructor's Manual and Video Guide
Betsy Willis, Baylor University
Becky Jones, Baylor University
Beverly Amer, Northern Arizona University

Solutions Manual
Charles T. Horngren, Stanford University
Walter T. Harrison, Jr., Baylor University
Linda Smith Bamber, University of Georgia

Test Item File
Alice B. Sineath, Forsyth Technical Community College

Working Papers
Ellen Sweatt, DeKalb College

PH Professor: A Classroom Presentation on PowerPoint
Olga Quintana, University of Miami

On Location! Video Library
Accounting Tutorial Videos
Beverly Amer, Northern Arizona University

Solutions Transparencies
Charles T. Horngren, Stanford University
Walter T. Harrison, Jr., Baylor University
Linda Smith Bamber, University of Georgia

Study Guide
Stephen Schaefer, Contra Costa Community College

Spreadsheet Templates with Solutions
Albert Fisher, Community College of Southern Nevada

Technical Reviewers
John R. Blahnik, Lorain County Community College
Carolyn Streuly, Marquette University
Barbara Mull, Harford Community College

Solutions Manual Technical Reviewers:
Thomas Hoar, Houston Community College
Kathleen Brenan, Ashland University
Carolyn Streuly, Marquette University

PowerPoint Reviewers:
Jean Insinga, Middlesex Community College
Anita Ellzey, Harford Community College

Test Item File Reviewers:
Thomas M. Carment, Northeastern State University
Richard C. Jarvies, Fayetteville Technical Community College
Thomas Hoar, Houston Community College

CONTRIBUTIONS

ENSURING QUALITY

Contributors to the First, Second, and Third Editions

Salvador D. Aceves, Napa Valley College
John Blahnick, Lorain County Community College
Nina Brown, Tarrant County Junior College
Kurt H. Buerger, Angelo State University
Glenn Bushnell, DeAnza College
Eric Carlson, Kean College of New Jersey
Wallace P. Carroll, J. Sargeant Reynolds Community College
Darrel W. Davis, University of Northern Iowa
S. T. Desai, Cedar Valley College
James Emig, Villanova University
Kevin Feeney, Southern Connecticut State University
Carl J. Fisher, Foothill College
Jessica Frazier, Eastern Kentucky University
Marilyn Fuller, Paris Junior College
Roger Gee, San Diego Mesa College
Lucille Genduso, Nova University
James Genseal, Joliet Junior College
Barbara Gerrity, Berkeley School of Westchester
Gloria Grayless, Sam Houston State University
Ann Gregory, South Plains College

Deborah Halik, Ivy Technical College
Jim Hansen, North Dakota State University
Saad Hassanein, Marymount University
Jimmie Henslee, El Centro College
Cynthia Holloway, Tarrant County Junior College
Andrew Hrechek, Seton Hall University
Jean Insinga, Middlesex Community College
Tyronne James, Southern University of New Orleans
Fred Jex, Macomb Community College
Mary Thomas Keim, California State University - Bakersfield
Nancy L. Kelly, Middlesex Community College
Randy Kidd, Penn Valley Community College
Raymond L. Larson, Appalachian State University
Cathy Larson, Middlesex Community College
Linda Lessing, SUNY College of Technology - Farmingdale
Lola Locke, Tarrant County Junior College
Catherine Lumbattis, Southern Illinois University
Paul Mihalek, University of Hartford
Graham Morris

Bruce Neumann, University of Colorado - Denver
Alfonso R. Oddo, Niagara University
Linda Overstreet, Hillsborough Community College
Robert Palmer, Troy State University
Patrick M. Premo, St. Bonaventure University
Karen Russom, North Harris College
Sherry Shively, Johnson County Community College
Kathleen Simione, Quinnipiac College
Dorothy Steinspair, Middlesex Community College
Gracelyn Stuart, Palm Beach Community College
Diane Tanner, University of North Florida
Katherene Terrell, University of Central Oklahoma
Cynthia Thomas, Central Missouri State University
John Vaccaro, Bunker Hill Community College
Paul Waite, Niagara Community College
Martin Ward, DeVry Institute of Technology
James Weglin, North Seattle Community College
Bill Wempe, Wichita State University
Dale Westfall, Midland College
Joseph Zernik, Ivy Technical College

English-as-a-Second-Language Reviewer

Zhu Zhu, Phoenix College

Focus Group Participants

Richard Ahrens, Los Angeles Pierce College
Charles Alvis, Winthrop University
Juanita Ardevany, Los Angeles Valley College
Patricia Ayres, Arapahoe Community College
Carl Ballard, Central Piedmont Community College
Maria Barillas, Phoenix College
Dorcus Berg, Wingate College
Angela Blackwood, Belmont Abbey College
Gary R. Bower, Community College of Rhode Island
Jack Brown, Los Angeles Valley College
Virginia Brunell, Diablo Valley College
James Carriger, Ventura College
Stan Carroll, New York City Technical College
Janet Cassagio, Nassau Community College
Lester Chadwick, University of Delaware
Stanley Chu, Borough of Manhattan Community College
Kerry Colton, Aims Community College
Shaun Crayton, New York City Technical College
Susan Crosson, Santa Fe Community College
Donald Daggett, Mankato State University
Joneal W. Daw, Los Angeles Valley College
Lyle E. Dehning, Metropolitan State College
Wanda DeLeo, Winthrop University
Jim Donnelly, Bergen Community College
Bruce England, Massasoit Community College
Dave Fellows, Red Rocks Community College

Roger Gee, San Diego Mesa College
Martin Ginsberg, Rockland Community College
Earl Godfrey, Gardner Webb University
Edward S. Goodhart, Shippensburg University
Jean Gutmann, University of Southern Maine
Ralph W. Hernandez, New York City Technical College
Carl High, New York City Technical College
Mary Hill, University of North Carolina - Charlotte
Jean Insinga, Middlesex Community College
Bernard Johnson, Santa Monica College
Diane G. Kanis, Bergen Community College
John Keelan, Massachusetts Bay Community College
Mary Thomas Keim, California State University - Bakersfield
Cynthia Kreisner, Austin Community College
Raymond L. Larson, Appalachian State University
Cathy Larson, Middlesex Community College
Linda Lessing, SUNY College of Technology - Farmingdale
Angela Letourneau, Winthrop University
Frank Lordi, Widener University
Audra Lowray, New York City Technical College
Grace Lyons, Bergen Community College
Edward Malmgren, University of North Carolina - Charlotte
Paola Marocchi, New York City Technical College
Larry McCarthy, Slippery Rock University
Linda Spotts Michael, Maple Woods Community College
Greg Mostyn, Mission College

Kitty Nessmith, Georgia Southern University
Lee Nicholas, University of Northern Iowa
Terry Nunnelly, University of North Carolina - Charlotte
Alfonso R. Oddo, Niagara University
Al Partington, Los Angeles Pierce College
Lynn Mazzola Paluska, Nassau Community College
Juan Perez, New York City Technical College
Ronald Pierno, University of Missouri
Geraldine Powers, Northern Essex Community College
Harry Purcell, Ulster County Community College
John Ribezzo, Community College of Rhode Island
Rosemarie Ruiz, York University
Stephen Schaefer, Contra Costa College
Parmar Sejal, Bergen Community College
Lynn Shoaf, Belmont Abbey College
Walter J. Silva, Roxbury Community College
Leon Singleton, Santa Monica College
David Skougstad, Metropolitan State College
Paul Sunko, Olive-Harvey College
Chandra Taylor, New York City Technical College
Phillip Thornton, Metropolitan State College
John L. Vaccaro, Bunker Hill Community College

Prentice Hall Accounting and Taxation Services Hotline:

When you call Prentice Hall's unique Accounting and Taxation Services Hotline you'll be able to speak directly to one of our Accounting and Taxation Service Specialists, Monday through Friday, during normal business hours (E.S.T.). Otherwise, you may leave a message and your call will be returned promptly. Our specialists can provide you with information on text instock dates, supplements, software, and much more. Plus, they'll process your Accounting and Taxation orders. Keep this toll-free number on hand — it's your direct link to satisfaction for all your adoption needs!

Accounting and Taxation Service Hotline Number
1-800-227-1816

Accounting and Taxation Service Hotline E-Mail:
christopher_smerillo@prenhall.com

Accounting Software Technical Support Line:
1-800-875-4118

The Prentice Hall Accounting Seminars for Educators (PHASE):

Prentice Hall sponsors a series of seminars for professors to get together, share information, and learn from the experts. Contact your local Prentice Hall sales representative, or e-mail the Accounting and Taxation Hotline for information concerning upcoming seminar dates and locations.

The Prentice Hall Accounting Faculty Directory

Compiled by James R. Hasselback. Published by Prentice Hall since 1978, this has become the most frequently cited reference in professional and academic material. This listing of the Deans and Accounting Faculty from over 900 four-year schools presents their names, addresses, telephone/fax/e-mail, as well as degree and area of specialization, and is updated annually.

Beth Toland
Executive Marketing Manager

Annie Todd
Executive Editor

P.J. Boardman
Editor in Chief

Deborah Hoffman Emry
Executive Editor

Eve Adams
Advertising Art Director

Jane Avery
Senior Editorial Assistant

Elaine Oyzon-Mast
Editorial Assistant

Robert Prokop
Senior Marketing Assistant

Bruce Kaplan
Development Editor

Stephen Deitmer
Director of Development

Pat Smythe
Design Manager

Natacha St. Hill
Assistant Editor

Iain MacDonald
Accounting Sales Director

Kris King
Sales Director

Dana Simmons
Sales Director

Julia Meehan
Event Marketing Manager

Janet Ferruggia
Marketing Communications Director

Brian Kibby
Director of Marketing

Contents

14 Retained Earnings, Treasury Stock, and the Income Statement 582

15 Long-Term Liabilities 624

PART FIVE

Management Accounting and Product Costing   816

Accounting for Partnerships

After studying this chapter, you should be able to

1. Identify the characteristics of a partnership
2. Account for partners' initial investments in a partnership
3. Allocate profits and losses to the partners by different methods
4. Account for the admission of a new partner to the business
5. Account for the withdrawal of a partner from the business
6. Account for the liquidation of a partnership
7. Prepare partnership financial statements

Blake Willis's accounting practice grew rapidly. After three years, the firm's revenue topped $150,000, and net income reached $90,000. After taking the business this far while working alone, Willis faced a tough decision. Should he continue as a sole proprietorship, or would it be better to incorporate the business? He decided instead to take on a partner and form a partnership.

Willis's closest friend at The University of Georgia, Ann Campi, had recently moved back to Savannah, Georgia. Like Willis, Campi had majored in accounting at Georgia. For the past three years, she had worked as a consultant for an accounting firm in Washington, D.C. Together, the pair formed the partnership of Willis & Campi, Certified Public Accountants. Willis would specialize in tax matters, and Campi would attract consulting clients.

The partnership form of business introduced some complexities that Willis's proprietorship had avoided. How much cash should Campi contribute to the business? She was buying into the client base developed by Willis. How should the partners divide profits and losses? How should a partner who leaves the firm be compensated for his or her share of the business? Willis and Campi had to iron out these and many other details.

A **partnership** is an association of two or more persons who co-own a business for profit. This definition derives from the Uniform Partnership Act, which nearly every state in the United States has adopted to regulate partnership practice.

Forming a partnership is easy. It requires no permission from government authorities and involves no legal procedures. When two persons decide to go into business together, a partnership is automatically formed.

A partnership brings together the assets, talents, and experience of the partners. Business opportunities closed to an individual may open up to a partnership. Suppose neither Willis nor Campi has enough money individually to buy a small office building in which to practice. They may be able to afford it together in a partnership. They may pool their talents and know-how. Their partnership can thus offer a fuller range of accounting services than either person could offer alone.

Partnerships come in all sizes. Many partnerships have fewer than ten partners. Some medical and law firms have 20 or more partners. The largest CPA firms have over 1,500 partners. Exhibit 12-1 lists the eight largest CPA firms in the United States, the number of partners in each firm, and their revenues in 1996.

Characteristics of a Partnership

Objective 1

Identify the characteristics of a partnership

Starting a partnership is voluntary. A person cannot be forced to join a partnership, and partners cannot be forced to accept another person as a partner. Although the partnership agreement may be oral, a written agreement between the partners reduces the chance of a misunderstanding. The following characteristics distinguish partnerships from sole proprietorships and corporations.

THE WRITTEN PARTNERSHIP AGREEMENT A business partnership is like a marriage. To be successful, the partners must cooperate. But business partners do not vow to remain together for life. Business partnerships come and go. To make certain that each partner fully understands how the partnership operates and to lower the chances that any partner might misunderstand how the business is run, partners may draw up a **partnership agreement,** also called the **articles of partnership.** This agreement is a contract between the partners, so transactions involving the agreement are governed by contract law. The articles of partnership should make the following points clear:

1. Name, location, and nature of the business
2. Name, capital investment, and duties of each partner
3. Method of sharing profits and losses among the partners
4. Withdrawals of assets allowed to the partners
5. Procedures for settling disputes between the partners
6. Procedures for admitting new partners
7. Procedures for settling up with a partner who withdraws from the business
8. Procedures for liquidating the partnership—selling the assets, paying the liabilities, and disbursing any remaining cash to the partners

LIMITED LIFE A partnership has a life limited by the length of time that all partners continue to own the business. If Blake Willis of the chapter opening story withdraws from the business, the partnership of Willis & Campi will cease to exist. A new partnership may emerge to continue the same business, but the old partnership will have been dissolved. **Dissolution** is the ending of a partnership. The addition of a new partner dissolves the old partnership and creates a new partnership.

MUTUAL AGENCY **Mutual agency** in a partnership means that every partner can bind the business to a contract within the scope of the partnership's regular business op-

Margin definitions

Partnership. An association of two or more persons who co-own a business for profit.

Partnership Agreement. The contract between partners that specifies such items as the name, location, and nature of the business; the name, capital investment, and duties of each partner; and the method of sharing profits and losses among the partners. Also called **articles of partnership.**

Dissolution. Ending of a partnership.

Mutual Agency. Every partner can bind the business to a contract within the scope of the partnership's regular business operations.

Rank 1996	Firm	City	Number of Partners	1996 Revenue (Billions)
1	Arthur Andersen & Co., S.C.	Chicago	1,575	$4.5
2	Ernst & Young	New York	1,933	3.6
3	Deloitte & Touche	Wilton, Conn.	1,556	2.9
4	KPMG Peat Marwick	New York	1,515	2.5
5	Coopers & Lybrand	New York	1,241	2.1
6	Price Waterhouse	New York	963	2.0
7	Grant Thornton	New York	285	0.8
8	McGladrey & Pullen	Davenport, Iowa	388	0.3

Source: Accounting Today, March 17–April 6, 1997, page 28.

erations. If Ann Campi enters into a contract with a business to provide accounting service, then the firm of Willis & Campi—not just Campi—is bound to provide that service. If Campi signs a contract to purchase lawn services for her home, however, the partnership will not be bound to pay. Contracting for personal services is not a regular business operation of the partnership.

UNLIMITED LIABILITY Each partner has an **unlimited personal liability** for the debts of the partnership. When a partnership cannot pay its debts with business assets, the partners must use their personal assets to meet the debt. Proprietors also have unlimited personal liability for the debts of their business.

Suppose the Willis & Campi firm has had an unsuccessful year and the partnership's liabilities exceed its assets by $20,000. Willis and Campi must pay this amount with their personal assets. Because each partner has unlimited liability, if a partner is unable to pay his or her part of the debt, the other partner (or partners) must make payment. If Campi can pay only $5,000 of the liability, Willis must pay $15,000.

Unlimited liability and mutual agency are closely related. A dishonest partner or a partner with poor judgment may commit the partnership to a contract under which the business loses money. In turn, creditors may force *all* the partners to pay the debt from personal assets. Hence, a business partner should be chosen with care.

Partners can avoid unlimited personal liability for partnership obligations by forming a *limited partnership*. In this form of business organization, one or more *general partners* assume the unlimited liability for business debts. In addition, the partnership has another class of owners, *limited partners*, who can lose only as much as their investment in the business. In this sense, limited partners have limited liability similar to the limited liability enjoyed by the stockholders of a corporation. Some of the large accounting firms in Exhibit 12-1 have reorganized as limited partnerships.

CO-OWNERSHIP OF PROPERTY Any asset—cash, inventory, machinery, and so on—that a partner invests in the partnership becomes the joint property of all the partners. Also, each partner has a claim to his or her share of the business's profits.

NO PARTNERSHIP INCOME TAXES A partnership pays no income tax on its business income. Instead, the net income of the partnership is divided and becomes the taxable income of the partners. Suppose Willis & Campi, Certified Public Accountants, earned net income of $200,000, shared equally by the partners. The firm would pay no income tax *as a business entity*. Willis and Campi, however, would each pay income tax as individuals on their $100,000 shares of partnership income.

PARTNERS' OWNER'S EQUITY ACCOUNTS Accounting for a partnership is much like accounting for a proprietorship. We record buying and selling goods and services, collecting and paying cash for a partnership just as we do for a proprietorship. But because a partnership has more than one owner, the partnership must have more than one owner's equity account. Every partner in the business—whether the firm has two or 2,000 partners—has an individual owner's equity account. Often these accounts carry the name of the particular partner and the word *capital*. For example, the owner's equity account for Blake Willis would read "Willis, Capital." Similarly, each partner has a

> **Unlimited Personal Liability.** When a partnership (or a proprietorship) cannot pay its debts with business assets, the partners (or the proprietor) must use personal assets to meet the debt.

■ Daily Exercise 12-1

Partnership Advantages	Partnership Disadvantages
Versus Proprietorships:	1. Partnership agreement may be difficult to formulate. Each time a new partner is admitted or a partner withdraws, the business needs a new partnership agreement.
1. Can raise more capital.	
2. Brings together the expertise of more than one person.	
3. 1 + 1 > 2 in a good partnership. If the partners work well together, they can add more value than by working alone.	2. Relationships among partners may be fragile.
	3. Mutual agency and unlimited personal liability create personal obligations for each partner.
Versus Corporations:	
4. Less expensive to organize than a corporation, which requires a charter from the state.	
5. No taxation of partnership income, which is taxed to the partners as individuals.	

EXHIBIT 12-2
Advantages and Disadvantages
of Partnerships
■ **Daily Exercise 12-2**

withdrawal account. If the number of partners is large, the general ledger may contain the single account Partners' Capital, or Owners' Equity. A subsidiary ledger can be used for individual partner accounts.

Exhibit 12-2 lists the advantages and disadvantages of partnerships (compared with proprietorships and corporations).

> **Learning Tip:** A partnership is really a "multiple proprietorship." Most features of a proprietorship also apply to a partnership—in particular, limited life and unlimited liability.

Different Types of Partnerships

There are two basic types of partnerships: general partnerships and limited partnerships.

General Partnerships

General Partnership. A form of partnership in which each partner is an owner of the business, with all the privileges and risks of ownership.

A **general partnership** is the basic form of partnership organization. Each partner is an owner of the business with all the privileges and risks of ownership. The general partners share the profits, losses, and the risks of the business. The partnership *reports* its income to the governmental tax authorities (the Internal Revenue Service in the United States), but the partnership itself pays *no* income tax. The profits and losses of the partnership pass through the business to the partners, who then pay personal income tax on their income.

Limited Partnerships

Limited Partnership. A partnership with at least two classes of partners: a general partner and limited partners.

A **limited partnership** has at least two classes of partners. There must be at least one *general partner,* who takes primary responsibility for the management of the business. The general partner also takes the bulk of the risk of failure in the event the partnership goes bankrupt (liabilities exceed assets). In real-estate limited partnerships, the general partner often invests little cash in the business. Instead, the general partner's contribution is his or her skill in managing the organization. Usually, the general partner is the last owner to receive a share of partnership profits and losses. But the general partner may earn all excess profits after satisfying the limited partners' demands for income.

The *limited partners* are so named because their personal obligation for the partnership's liabilities is limited to the amount they have invested in the business. Usually, the limited partners have invested the bulk of the partnership's assets and capital. They therefore usually have first claim to partnership profits and losses, but only up to a specified limit. In exchange for their limited liability, their potential for profits usually has an upper limit as well.

Limited Liability Partnership. A form of partnership in which each partner's personal liability for the business's debts is limited to a certain amount. Also called **LLP's.**

Most of the large accounting firms are organized as **limited liability partnerships, or LLPs,** which means that each partner's personal liability for the business's debts is limited to a certain amount. The LLP must carry a large insurance policy to protect the public in case the partnership is found guilty of malpractice. Medical, legal, and other firms of professionals can also be organized as LLPs.

S CORPORATIONS An **S Corporation** is a corporation that is taxed in the same way that a partnership is taxed. Therefore, S corporations are often discussed in conjunction with partnerships. This form of business organization derives its name from Subchapter S of the U.S. Internal Revenue Code.

S Corporation. A corporation taxed in the same way as a partnership.

An ordinary (Subchapter C) corporation is subject to double taxation. First, the corporation pays corporate income tax on its income. Then, when the corporation pays dividends to the stockholders, they pay personal income tax on their dividend income. An S corporation pays no corporate income tax. Instead, the corporation's income flows through directly to the stockholders (the owners), who pay personal income tax on their share of the S corporation's income. The one-time taxation of an S corporation's income is an important advantage over an ordinary corporation. Thus from a tax standpoint, an S corporation operates like a partnership.

To qualify as an S corporation, the company can have no more than 75 stockholders, all of whom must be citizens or residents of the United States. Accounting for an S corporation resembles that of accounting for a partnership because the allocation of corporate income follows the same procedure used by partnerships.

Initial Investments by Partners

Let's see how to account for the multiple owner's equity accounts—and learn how they appear on the balance sheet—by examining how to account for the startup of a partnership.

Objective 2

Account for partners' initial investments in a partnership

Partners in a new partnership may invest assets and liabilities in the business. These contributions are entered in the books in the same way that a proprietor's assets and liabilities are recorded. Subtraction of each partner's liabilities from his or her assets yields the amount to be credited to that partner's capital account. Often the partners hire an independent firm to appraise their assets and liabilities at current market value at the time a partnership is formed. This outside evaluation assures an objective accounting for what each partner brings into the business.

Assume that Dave Benz and Joan Hanna form a partnership to manufacture and sell computer software. The partners agree on the following values based on an independent appraisal:

Benz's contributions

- Cash, $10,000; inventory, $70,000; and accounts payable, $85,000 (The appraiser believes that the current market values for these items equal Benz's values.)
- Accounts receivable, $30,000, less allowance for doubtful accounts of $5,000
- Computer equipment—cost, $800,000; accumulated depreciation, $200,000; current market value, $450,000

Hanna's contributions

- Cash, $5,000
- Computer software: cost, $18,000; market value, $100,000

The partnership records receipt of the partners' initial investments at the current market values of the assets and liabilities because, in effect, the partnership is buying the assets and assuming the liabilities at their current market values. The partnership entries are as follows:

Benz's investment

June 1	Cash	10,000	
	Accounts Receivable	30,000	
	Inventory	70,000	
	Computer Equipment	450,000	
	Allowance for Doubtful Accounts		5,000
	Accounts Payable		85,000
	Benz, Capital ($560,000 − $90,000)		470,000
	To record Benz's investment in the partnership.		

BENZ AND HANNA Balance Sheet June 1, 19X5				
Assets			**Liabilities**	
Cash		$ 15,000	Accounts payable	$ 85,000
Accounts receivable	$30,000			
Less Allowance for				
doubtful accounts	(5,000)	25,000	**Capital**	
Inventory..............................		70,000	Benz, capital	470,000
Computer equipment		450,000	Hanna, capital	105,000
Computer software		100,000	Total liabilities	
Total assets		$660,000	and capital..	$660,000

EXHIBIT 12-3
Partnership Balance Sheet

Hanna's investment

June 1	Cash	5,000	
	Computer Software	100,000	
	Hanna, Capital...		105,000
	To record Hanna's investment in the partnership.		

The initial partnership balance sheet reports the amounts shown in Exhibit 12-3. Note that the asset and liability sections on the balance sheet are the same for a proprietorship and a partnership.

- ■ Daily Exercise 12-3
- ■ Daily Exercise 12-4

Sharing Partnership Profits and Losses

Objective 3

Allocate profits and losses to the partners by different methods

Allocating profits and losses among partners is one of the most challenging aspects of managing a partnership. If the partners have not drawn up an agreement or if the agreement does not state how the partners will divide profits and losses, then, by law, the partners must share profits and losses equally. If the agreement specifies a method for sharing profits but not losses, then losses are shared in the same proportion as profits. For example, a partner who was allocated 75% of the profits would likewise absorb 75% of any losses.

In some cases, an equal division is not fair. One partner may perform more work for the business than the other partner, or one partner may make a larger capital contribution. In the preceding example, Joan Hanna might agree to work longer hours for the partnership than Dave Benz to earn a greater share of profits. Benz could argue that he should share in more of the profits because he contributed more net assets ($470,000) than Hanna did ($105,000). Hanna might contend that her computer software program is the partnership's most important asset and that her share of the profits should be greater than Benz's share. Agreeing on a fair sharing of profits and losses in a partnership may be difficult. We now discuss options available in determining partners' shares.

Sharing Based on a Stated Fraction

Partners may agree to any profit-and-loss-sharing method they desire. They may, for example, state a particular fraction of the total profits and losses that each individual partner will share. Suppose the partnership agreement of Lou Cagle and Justin Dean allocates two-thirds of the business profits and losses to Cagle and one-third to Dean. If net income for the year is $90,000 and all revenue and expense accounts have been closed, the Income Summary account has a credit balance of $90,000:

- ■ Daily Exercise 12-5

Income Summary	
	Bal. 90,000

The entry to close this account and allocate the profit to the partners' capital accounts is

Dec. 31	Income Summary......................................	90,000	
	Cagle, Capital ($90,000 × 2/3).........		60,000
	Dean, Capital ($90,000 × 1/3)..........		30,000
	To allocate net income to partners.		

Consider the effect of this entry. Does Cagle get cash of $60,000 and Dean cash of $30,000? No. The increase in the partners' capital accounts cannot be linked to any particular asset, including cash. Instead, the entry indicates that Cagle's ownership in *all* the assets of the business increased by $60,000 and Dean's by $30,000.

If the year's operations resulted in a net loss of $66,000, the Income Summary account would have a debit balance of $66,000. In that case, the closing entry to allocate the loss to the partners' capital accounts would be

Dec. 31	Cagle, Capital ($66,000 × 2/3)...........	44,000	
	Dean, Capital ($66,000 × 1/3)............	22,000	
	Income Summary		66,000
	To allocate net loss to partners.		

■ Daily Exercise 12-6

Just as a profit of $90,000 did not mean that the partners received cash of $60,000 and $30,000, so the loss of $66,000 does not mean that the partners must contribute cash of $44,000 and $22,000. A profit or loss will increase or decrease each partner's capital account, but cash may not change hands.

Sharing Based on Capital Contributions

Profits and losses are often allocated in proportion to the partners' capital contributions in the business. Suppose that Jenny Aycock, Erika Barber, and Sue Cordoba are partners in ABC Company. Their capital accounts have the following balances at the end of the year, before the closing entries:

Aycock, Capital	$ 40,000
Barber, Capital	60,000
Cordoba, Capital.................	50,000
Total capital balances	$150,000

Assume that the partnership earned a profit of $120,000 for the year. To allocate this amount on the basis of capital contributions, compute each partner's percentage share of the partnership's total capital balance by dividing each partner's contribution by the total capital amount. These figures, multiplied by the $120,000 profit amount, yield each partner's share of the year's profits:

Aycock:	($40,000/$150,000) × $120,000 =	$ 32,000
Barber:	($60,000/$150,000) × $120,000 =	48,000
Cordoba:	($50,000/$150,000) × $120,000 =	40,000
	Net income allocated to partners =	$120,000

The closing entry to allocate the profit to the partners' capital accounts is

Dec. 31	Income Summary	120,000	
	Aycock, Capital................................		32,000
	Barber, Capital.................................		48,000
	Cordoba, Capital		40,000
	To allocate net income to partners.		

After this closing entry, the partners' capital balances are

Aycock, Capital ($40,000 + $32,000)	$ 72,000
Barber, Capital ($60,000 + $48,000)	108,000
Cordoba, Capital ($50,000 + $40,000)	90,000
Total capital balances after allocation of net income	$270,000

Sharing Based on Capital Contributions and on Service

One partner, regardless of his or her capital contribution, may put more work into the business than the other partners do. Even among partners who log equal service time, one person's superior experience and knowledge may command a greater share of income. To reward the harder-working or more valuable person, the profit-and-loss-sharing method may be based on a combination of contributed capital *and* service to the business. The Chicago-based law firm Baker & McKenzie, for example, which has nearly 500 partners, takes seniority into account in determining partner compensation.

Assume that Debbie Randolph and Nancy Scott formed a partnership in which Randolph invested $60,000 and Scott invested $40,000, a total of $100,000. Scott devotes more time to the partnership and earns the larger salary. Accordingly, the two partners have agreed to share profits as follows:

1. The first $50,000 of partnership profits is to be allocated on the basis of partners' capital contributions to the business.
2. The next $60,000 of profits is to be allocated on the basis of service, with Randolph receiving $24,000 and Scott receiving $36,000.
3. Any remaining amount is to be allocated equally.

If net income for the first year is $125,000, the partners' shares of this profit are computed as follows:

	Randolph	Scott	Total
Total net income			$125,000
Sharing of first $50,000 of net income, based on capital contributions:			
Randolph ($60,000/$100,000 × $50,000)	$30,000		
Scott ($40,000/$100,000 × $50,000)		$20,000	
Total			50,000
Net income remaining for allocation			75,000
Sharing of next $60,000, based on service:			
Randolph	24,000		
Scott		36,000	
Total			60,000
Net income remaining for allocation			15,000
Remainder shared equally:			
Randolph ($15,000 × 1/2)	7,500		
Scott ($15,000 × 1/2)		7,500	
Total			15,000
Net income remaining for allocation			$ –0–
Net income allocated to the partners	$61,500	$63,500	$125,000

On the basis of this allocation, the closing entry is

■ **Daily Exercise 12-7**

Dec. 31	Income Summary	125,000	
	Randolph, Capital		61,500
	Scott, Capital		63,500
	To allocate net income to partners.		

Sharing Based on Salaries and on Interest

Partners may be rewarded for their service and their capital contributions to the business in other ways. In one sharing plan, the partners are allocated salaries plus interest on their capital balances. Assume that Randy Lewis and Gerald Clark form an oil-exploration partnership. At the beginning of the year, their capital balances are $80,000 and $100,000, respectively. The partnership agreement allocates annual salaries of $43,000 to Lewis and $35,000 to Clark. After salaries are allocated, each partner earns 8% interest on his beginning capital balance. Any remaining net income is divided equally. Partnership profit of $96,000 will be allocated as follows:

	Lewis	Clark	Total
Total net income			$96,000
First, salaries:			
Lewis	$43,000		
Clark..		$35,000	
Total..			78,000
Net income remaining for allocation			18,000
Second, interest on beginning capital balances:			
Lewis ($80,000 × 0.08).................................	6,400		
Clark ($100,000 × 0.08)		8,000	
Total..			14,400
Net income remaining for allocation			3,600
Third, remainder shared equally:			
Lewis ($3,600 × 1/2)	1,800		
Clark ($3,600 × 1/2)......................................		1,800	
Total..			3,600
Net income remaining for allocation			$ –0–
Net income allocated to the partners...............	$51,200	$44,800	$96,000

In the preceding illustration, net income exceeded the sum of salary and interest. If the partnership profit is less than the allocated sum of salary and interest, a negative remainder will occur at some stage in the allocation process. Even so, the partners use the same method for allocation purposes. For example, assume that Lewis and Clark Partnership earned only $82,000:

■ **Daily Exercise 12-8**

	Lewis	Clark	Total
Total net income			$82,000
First, salaries:			
Lewis	$43,000		
Clark..		$35,000	
Total..			78,000
Net income remaining for allocation			4,000
Second, interest on beginning capital balances:			
Lewis ($80,000 × 0.08).................................	6,400		
Clark ($100,000 × 0.08)		8,000	
Total..			14,400
Net income remaining for allocation			(10,400)
Third, remainder shared equally:			
Lewis ($10,400 × 1/2)	(5,200)		
Clark ($10,400 × 1/2).....................................		(5,200)	
Total..			(10,400)
Net income remaining for allocation			$ –0–
Net income allocated to the partners...............	$44,200	$37,800	$82,000

A net loss would be allocated to Lewis and Clark in the same manner outlined for net income. The sharing procedure would begin with the net loss and then allocate salary, interest, and any other specified amounts to the partners.

Thinking It Over Are these salaries and interest amounts business expenses in the usual sense? Explain your answer.

Answer: No, partners do not work for their own business to earn a salary, as an employee does. They do not loan money to their own business to earn interest. Their goal is for the partnership to earn a profit. Therefore, salaries and interest in partnership agreements are simply ways of expressing the allocation of profits and losses to the partners. For example, the salary component of partner income rewards service to the partnership. The interest component rewards a partner's investment of cash or other assets in the business. But the partners' salary and interest amounts are *not* salary expense and interest expense in the partnership's accounting or tax records.

We see that partners may allocate profits and losses on the basis of a stated fraction, contributed capital, service, interest on capital, or any combination of these factors. Each partnership shapes its profit-and-loss-sharing ratio to fit its own needs.

Partner Drawings

Like anyone else, partners need cash for personal living expenses. Partnership agreements usually allow partners to withdraw cash or other assets from the business. Drawings from a partnership are recorded exactly as for a proprietorship. Assume that both Randy Lewis and Gerald Clark are allowed a monthly withdrawal of $3,500. The partnership records the March withdrawals with this entry:

Mar. 31	Lewis, Drawing...	3,500	
	Clark, Drawing	3,500	
	Cash..		7,000
	Monthly partner withdrawals of cash.		

During the year, each partner's drawing account accumulates 12 such amounts, a total of $42,000 ($3,500 × 12) per partner. At the end of the period, the general ledger shows the following account balances immediately after net income has been closed to the partners' capital accounts. Assume these beginning balances for Lewis and Clark at the start of the year and that $82,000 of profit has been allocated on the basis of the preceding illustration.

Lewis, Capital		Clark, Capital	
	Jan. 1 Bal. 80,000		Jan. 1 Bal. 100,000
	Dec. 31 Net. inc. 44,200		Dec. 31 Net. inc. 37,800

Lewis, Drawing		Clark, Drawing	
Dec. 31 Bal. 42,000		Dec. 31 Bal. 42,000	

The drawing accounts must be closed at the end of the period, exactly as for a proprietorship: The closing entry credits each partner's drawing account and debits each capital account. ◀▥▥

◀▥▥ ◀▥▥ ◀▥▥ We covered this closing entry in Chapter 4, page 147.

Learning Tip: The amount of the drawings does not depend on the partnership's income or loss for the year.

Admission of a Partner

A partnership lasts only as long as its partners remain in the business. The addition of a new member or the withdrawal of an existing member dissolves the partnership. We turn now to a discussion of how partnerships dissolve—and how new partnerships arise.

Often a new partnership is formed to carry on the former partnership's business. In fact, the new partnership may retain the dissolved partnership's name. Price Waterhouse, for example, is an accounting firm that retires and hires partners during the year. Thus the former partnership dissolves and a new partnership begins many times. But the business retains the name and continues operations. Other partnerships may dissolve and then re-form under a new name. Let's look now at the ways that a new member may gain admission into an existing partnership.

Admission by Purchasing a Partner's Interest

A person may become a member of a partnership by gaining the approval of the other partner (or partners) for entrance into the firm *and* by purchasing a present partner's interest in the business. Let's assume that Roberta Fisher and Benitez Garcia have a partnership that carries these figures:

Cash	$ 40,000	Total liabilities	$120,000
Other assets	360,000	Fisher, capital	110,000
		Garcia, capital	170,000
Total assets	$400,000	Total liabilities and capital	$400,000

Business is going so well that Fisher receives an offer from Barry Dynak, an outside party, to buy her $110,000 interest in the business for $150,000. Fisher agrees to sell out to Dynak, and Garcia approves Dynak as a new partner. The firm records the transfer of capital interest in the business with this entry:

Apr. 16	Fisher, Capital	110,000	
	Dynak, Capital		110,000
	To transfer Fisher's equity in the business to Dynak.		

The debit side of the entry closes Fisher's capital account because she is no longer a partner in the firm. The credit side opens Dynak's capital account because Fisher's equity has been transferred to Dynak. The entry amount is Fisher's capital balance ($110,000) and not the $150,000 price that Dynak paid Fisher to buy into the business. The full $150,000 goes to Fisher, including the $40,000 difference between her capital balance and the price received from Dynak. In this example, the partnership receives no cash because the transaction was between Dynak and Fisher, not between Dynak and the partnership. Suppose Dynak pays Fisher less than Fisher's capital balance. The entry on the partnership books is not affected. Fisher's equity is transferred to Dynak at book value ($110,000).

The old partnership has dissolved. Garcia and Dynak draw up a new partnership agreement with a new profit-and-loss-sharing ratio and continue business operations. If Garcia does not accept Dynak as a partner, Dynak gets no voice in management of the firm. However, under the Uniform Partnership Act, the purchaser shares in the profits and losses of the firm and in its assets at liquidation.

Admission by Investing in the Partnership

As Ann Campi did in our chapter opening story, a person may be admitted as a partner by investing directly in the partnership rather than by purchasing an existing partner's interest. The new partner contributes assets—for example, cash, inventory, or equipment—to the business. Assume that the partnership of Robin Ingel and Michael Jay has the following assets, liabilities, and capital:

Cash	$ 20,000	Total liabilities	$ 60,000
Other assets	200,000	Ingel, capital	70,000
		Jay, capital	90,000
Total assets	$220,000	Total liabilities and capital	$220,000

Laura Kahn offers to invest equipment and land (Other Assets) with a market value of $80,000 to persuade the existing partners to take her into the business. Ingel and Jay agree to dissolve the existing partnership and to start up a new business, giving Kahn one-third interest—[$80,000/($70,000 + $90,000 + $80,000) = 1/3]—in exchange for the contributed assets. Notice that Kahn is buying into the partnership at book value because her one-third investment ($80,000) equals one-third of the new partnership's total capital ($240,000). The entry to record Kahn's investment is

July 18	Other Assets	80,000	
	Kahn, Capital...		80,000
	To admit L. Kahn as a partner with a one-third interest in the business.		

After this entry, the partnership books show

Cash...	$ 20,000	Total liabilities.......................	$ 60,000
Other assets		Ingel, capital..........................	70,000
($200,000 + $80,000).........	280,000	Jay, capital..............................	90,000
		Kahn, capital	80,000
Total assets............................	$300,000	Total liabilities and capital	$300,000

■ Daily Exercise 12-9
■ Daily Exercise 12-10

Kahn's one-third interest in the partnership does not necessarily entitle her to one-third of the profits. The sharing of profits and losses is a separate element in the partnership agreement.

ADMISSION BY INVESTING IN THE PARTNERSHIP—BONUS TO THE OLD PARTNERS

The more successful a partnership, the higher the payment the partners may demand from a person entering the business. Partners in a business that is doing quite well might require an incoming person to pay them a bonus. The bonus increases the current partners' capital accounts.

Suppose that Hiro Nagasawa and Ralph Osburn's partnership has earned above-average profits for ten years. The two partners share profits and losses equally. The partnership balance sheet carries these figures:

Cash...	$ 40,000	Total liabilities.......................	$100,000
Other assets...........................	210,000	Nagasawa, capital.................	70,000
		Osburn, capital......................	80,000
Total assets............................	$250,000	Total liabilities and capital	$250,000

The partners agree to admit Glen Parker to a one-fourth interest with his cash investment of $90,000. Parker's capital balance on the partnership books is only $60,000, computed as follows:

Partnership capital before Parker is admitted ($70,000 + $80,000)	$150,000
Parker's investment in the partnership...	90,000
Partnership capital after Parker is admitted...	$240,000
Parker's capital in the partnership ($240,000 × 1/4)	$ 60,000
Bonus to the old partners ($90,000 – $60,000)...	$ 30,000

■ Daily Exercise 12-11

In effect, Parker had to buy into the partnership at a price ($90,000) above the book value of his one-fourth interest ($60,000). Parker's extra investment of $30,000 creates a *bonus* for the existing partners. The entry on the partnership books to record Parker's investment is

Mar. 1	Cash	90,000	
	Parker, Capital		60,000
	Nagasawa, Capital ($30,000 × 1/2)		15,000
	Osburn, Capital ($30,000 × 1/2)		15,000
	To admit G. Parker as a partner with a one-fourth interest in the business.		

Parker's capital account is credited for his one-fourth interest in the partnership. The *bonus* is allocated to the partners on the basis of their profit-and-loss ratio.

The new partnership's balance sheet reports these amounts:

Cash ($40,000 + $90,000)	$130,000	Total liabilities	$100,000
Other assets	210,000	Nagasawa, capital ($70,000 + $15,000)	85,000
		Osburn, capital ($80,000 + $15,000)	95,000
		Parker, capital	60,000
Total assets	$340,000	Total liabilities and capital	$340,000

■ Daily Exercise 12-12

Working It Out Mia and Susan are partners with capital balances of $25,000 and $75,000, respectively. They share profits and losses in a 30:70 ratio. Mia and Susan admit Tab to a 10% interest in a new partnership when Tab invests $20,000 in the business.

1. Journalize the partnership's receipt of cash from Tab.
2. What is each partner's capital in the new partnership?

Answers

1.	Cash	20,000	
	Tab, Capital		12,000
	Mia, Capital ($8,000 × 0.30)		2,400
	Susan, Capital ($8,000 × 0.70)		5,600
	To admit Tab with a 10% interest in the business.		

Partnership capital before Tab is admitted ($25,000 + $75,000)	$100,000	
Tab's investment in the partnership	20,000	
Partnership capital after Tab is admitted	$120,000	
Tab's capital in the partnership ($120,000 × 1/10)	$ 12,000	
Bonus to the old partners ($20,000 − $12,000)	$ 8,000	

2. Partners' capital balances:

Mia, capital ($25,000 + $2,400)	$ 27,400
Susan, capital ($75,000 + $5,600)	80,600
Tab, capital	12,000
Total partnership capital	$120,000

ADMISSION BY INVESTING IN THE PARTNERSHIP— BONUS TO THE NEW PARTNER

A potential new partner may be so important that the existing partners offer him or her a partnership share that includes a bonus. A law firm may strongly desire a former governor or other official as a partner because of the person's reputation and connections. A restaurant owner may want to go into partnership with a famous sports personality, movie star, or model. The growing chain Planet Hollywood, for example, opened its first restaurant in 1991 in New York City. Planet Hollywood, whose majority owner is Robert Earl, has prospered

"Planet Hollywood, whose majority owner is Robert Earl, has prospered with the help of celebrity partners Sylvester Stallone, Arnold Schwarzenegger, Bruce Willis, and Don Johnson."

with the help of celebrity partners Sylvester Stallone, Arnold Schwarzenegger, Bruce Willis, and Don Johnson.

Suppose that Allan Page and Olivia Franco have a law partnership. The firm's balance sheet appears as follows:

■ Daily Exercise 12-13

Cash..................................	$140,000	Total liabilities......................	$120,000
Other assets.........................	360,000	Page, capital..........................	230,000
		Franco, capital.......................	150,000
Total assets.........................	$500,000	Total liabilities and capital	$500,000

Page and Franco admit Martin Schiller, a former attorney general, as a partner with a one-third interest in exchange for his cash investment of $100,000. At the time of Schiller's admission, the firm's capital is $380,000 (Page, $230,000, plus Franco, $150,000). Page and Franco share profits and losses in the ratio of two-thirds to Page and one-third to Franco. The computation of Schiller's equity in the partnership is

Partnership capital before Schiller is admitted ($230,000 + $150,000)	$380,000
Schiller's investment in the partnership	100,000
Partnership capital after Schiller is admitted	$480,000
Schiller's capital in the partnership ($480,000 × 1/3).................................	$160,000
Bonus to the new partner ($160,000 − $100,000).......................................	$ 60,000

In this case, Schiller bought into the partnership at a price ($100,000) below the book value of his interest ($160,000). The bonus of $60,000 went to Schiller from the other partners. The capital accounts of Page and Franco are debited for the $60,000 difference between the new partner's equity ($160,000) and his investment ($100,000). The existing partners share this decrease in capital as though it were a loss, on the basis of their profit-and-loss ratio. The entry to record Schiller's investment is

Aug. 24	Cash...	100,000	
	Page, Capital ($60,000 × 2/3)	40,000	
	Franco, Capital ($60,000 × 1/3)...................	20,000	
	Schiller, Capital		160,000
	To admit M. Schiller as a partner with		
	a one-third interest in the business.		

The new partnership's balance sheet reports these amounts:

Cash		Total liabilities	$120,000
($140,000 + $100,000).......	$240,000	Page, capital	
Other assets..........................	360,000	($230,000 − $40,000).........	190,000
		Franco, capital	
		($150,000 − $20,000).........	130,000
		Schiller, capital......................	160,000
Total assets..........................	$600,000	Total liabilities and capital	$600,000

Working It Out John and Ron are partners with capital balances of $30,000 and $40,000, respectively. They share profits and losses in a 25:75 ratio. John and Ron admit Lou to a 20% interest in a new partnership when Lou invests $10,000 in the business.

1. Journalize the partnership's receipt of cash from Lou.
2. What is each partner's capital in the new partnership?

Answers

1. Cash.. 10,000
     John, Capital ($6,000 × 0.25)... 1,500
     Ron, Capital ($6,000 × 0.75)... 4,500
          Lou, Capital.. 16,000
     To admit Lou with a 20% interest in the business.

Partnership capital before Lou is admitted ($30,000 + $40,000)..........	$70,000
Lou's investment in the partnership......................................	10,000
Partnership capital after Lou is admitted.................................	$80,000
Lou's capital in the partnership ($80,000 × 0.20)........................	$16,000
Bonus to the new partner ($16,000 – $10,000).............................	$ 6,000

2. Partners' capital balances:

John, capital ($30,000 – $1,500)..........	$28,500
Ron, capital ($40,000 – $4,500)	35,500
Lou, capital	16,000
Total partnership capital.....................	$80,000

Withdrawal of a Partner

Objective 5

Account for the withdrawal of a partner from the business

A partner may withdraw from the business for many reasons, including retirement or a dispute with the other partners. The withdrawal of a partner dissolves the old partnership. The partnership agreement should contain a provision to govern how to settle with a withdrawing partner. In the simplest case, illustrated on page 517, a partner may withdraw and sell his or her interest to another partner in a personal transaction. The only entry needed to record this transfer of equity debits the withdrawing partner's capital account and credits the purchaser's capital account. The dollar amount of the entry is the capital balance of the withdrawing partner, regardless of the price paid by the purchaser. The accounting when one current partner buys a second partner's interest is the same as when an outside party buys a current partner's interest.

If the partner withdraws in the middle of an accounting period, the partnership books should be updated to determine the withdrawing partner's capital balance. The business must measure net income or net loss for the fraction of the year up to the withdrawal date and allocate profit or loss according to the existing ratio. After the books have been closed, the business then accounts for the change in partnership capital.

The withdrawing partner may receive his or her share of the business in partnership assets other than cash. The question arises as to what value to assign the partnership assets—book value or current market value? The settlement procedure may specify an independent appraisal of assets to determine their current market value. If market values have changed, the appraisal will result in revaluing the partnership assets. Thus the partners share in any market value changes that their efforts caused.

Suppose that Keith Isaac is retiring in midyear from the partnership of Green, Henry, and Isaac. After the books have been adjusted for partial-period income but before the asset appraisal, revaluation, and closing entries, the balance sheet reports the following:

Cash	$ 39,000	Total liabilities......................	$ 80,000
Inventory..............................	44,000	Green, capital.......................	54,000
Land.....................................	55,000	Henry, capital.......................	43,000
Building $95,000		Isaac, capital	21,000
Less Accum. depr. (35,000)	60,000	Total liabilities and	
Total assets	$198,000	capital...............................	$198,000

An independent appraiser revalues the inventory at $38,000 (down from $44,000) and the land at $101,000 (up from $55,000). The partners share the differences between these assets' market values and their prior book values on the basis of their profit-and-loss ratio. The partnership agreement has allocated one-fourth of the profits to Susan

Green, one-half to Charles Henry, and one-fourth to Isaac. (This ratio may be written 1:2:1 for one part to Green, two parts to Henry, and one part to Isaac.) For each share that Green or Isaac has, Henry has two. The entries to record the revaluation of the inventory and land are

July 31	Green, Capital ($6,000 × 1/4)...............................	1,500	
	Henry, Capital ($6,000 × 1/2)...............................	3,000	
	Isaac, Capital ($6,000 × 1/4)	1,500	
	Inventory ($44,000 – $38,000)......................		6,000
	To revalue the inventory and allocate the loss to the partners.		
31	Land ($101,000 – $55,000)...................................	46,000	
	Green, Capital ($46,000 × 1/4).....................		11,500
	Henry, Capital ($46,000 × 1/2).....................		23,000
	Isaac, Capital ($46,000 × 1/4)		11,500
	To revalue the land and allocate the gain to the partners.		

After the revaluations, the partnership balance sheet reports the following:

Cash..................................	$ 39,000	Total liabilities		$ 80,000
Inventory.................................	38,000	Green, capital		
Land	101,000	($54,000 – $1,500 + $11,500)...		64,000
Building $95,000		Henry, capital		
Less Accum. depr. .... (35,000)	60,000	($43,000 – $3,000 + $23,000)...		63,000
		Isaac, capital		
		($21,000 – $1,500 + $11,500)...		31,000
Total assets	$238,000	Total liabilities and capital		$238,000

The books now carry the assets at current market value, which becomes the new book value, and the capital accounts have been adjusted accordingly. As the balance sheet shows, Isaac has a claim to $31,000 in partnership assets. How is his withdrawal from the business accounted for?

Withdrawal at Book Value

If Keith Isaac withdraws by receiving cash equal to the book value of his owner's equity, the entry will be

July 31	Isaac, Capital..	31,000	
	Cash..		31,000
	To record withdrawal of K. Isaac from the business.		

■ **Daily Exercise 12-14**

This entry records the payment of partnership cash to Isaac and the closing of his capital account upon his withdrawal from the business.

Withdrawal at Less than Book Value

The withdrawing partner may be so eager to leave the business that he or she is willing to take less than his or her equity. This situation has occurred in real-estate and oil-drilling partnerships. Assume that Keith Isaac withdraws from the business and agrees to receive partnership cash of $10,000 and the new partnership's note for $15,000. This $25,000 settlement is $6,000 less than Isaac's $31,000 equity in the business. The remaining partners share this $6,000 difference—which is a bonus to them—according to their profit-and-loss ratio. However, because Isaac has withdrawn from the partnership, a new agreement—and a new profit-and-loss ratio—must be drawn up. In forming a new partnership, Henry and Green may decide on any ratio that they see fit. Let's assume they agree that Henry will earn two-thirds of partnership profits and losses and Green one-third. The entry to record Isaac's withdrawal at less than book value is

July 31	Isaac, Capital	31,000	
	Cash		10,000
	Note Payable to K. Isaac		15,000
	Green, Capital ($6,000 × 1/3)		2,000
	Henry, Capital ($6,000 × 2/3)		4,000
	To record withdrawal of K. Isaac from the business.		

Isaac's account is closed, and Henry and Green may or may not continue the business as a new partnership.

■ Daily Exercise 12-15

Withdrawal at More than Book Value

The settlement with a withdrawing partner may allow him or her to take assets of greater value than the book value of that partner's capital. Also, the remaining partners may be so eager for the withdrawing partner to leave the firm that they pay him or her a bonus to withdraw from the business. In either case, the partner's withdrawal causes a decrease in the book equity of the remaining partners. This decrease is allocated to the partners on the basis of their profit-and-loss ratio.

The accounting for this situation follows the pattern illustrated for withdrawal at less than book value—with one exception. The remaining partners' capital accounts are debited because the withdrawing partner receives more than his or her book equity.

■ Daily Exercise 12-16

Working It Out Linda is withdrawing from the partnership of Linda, Jacob, and Karla. The partners share profits and losses in a 1:2:3 ratio for Linda, Jacob, and Karla, respectively. After the revaluation of assets, Linda's capital balance is $50,000, and the other partners agree to pay her $60,000. Journalize the payment to Linda and her withdrawal from the partnership.

Answer

Linda, Capital...	50,000	
Jacob, Capital [($60,000 − $50,000) × 2/5]........................	4,000	
Karla, Capital [($60,000 − $50,000) × 3/5]........................	6,000	
Cash		60,000
To record withdrawal of Linda from the business.		

Death of a Partner

Like any other form of partnership withdrawal, death of a partner dissolves a partnership. The partnership accounts are adjusted to measure net income or loss for the fraction of the year up to the date of death, then closed to determine the partners' capital balances on that date. Settlement with the deceased partner's estate is based on the partnership agreement. The estate commonly receives partnership assets equal to the partner's capital balance. The partnership closes the deceased partner's capital account with a debit. This entry credits a payable to the estate.

Alternatively, a remaining partner may purchase the deceased partner's equity. The deceased partner's equity is debited, and the purchaser's equity is credited. The amount of this entry is the ending credit balance in the deceased partner's capital account.

Objective 6

Account for the liquidation of a partnership

Liquidation of a Partnership

Admission of a new partner or withdrawal or death of an existing partner dissolves the partnership. However, the business may continue operating with no apparent change to outsiders such as customers and creditors. In contrast, business **liquidation** is the process of going out of business by selling the entity's assets and paying its liabilities. The final step in liquidation of a business is the *distribution of the remaining cash to the owners*. Before

Liquidation. The process of going out of business by selling the entity's assets and paying its liabilities. The final step in liquidation of a business is the distribution of any remaining cash to the owner(s).

the business is liquidated, its books should be adjusted and closed. After closing, only asset, liability, and partners' capital accounts remain open.

Liquidation of a partnership includes three basic steps:

1. Sell the assets. Allocate the gain or loss to the partners' capital accounts on the basis of the profit-and-loss ratio.
2. Pay the partnership liabilities.
3. Disburse the remaining cash to the partners on the basis of their capital balances.

In practice, the liquidation of a business can stretch over weeks or months. Selling every asset and paying every liability of the entity takes time. After the 80 partners of Shea & Gould, one of New York's best-known law firms, voted to dissolve their partnership, the firm remained open for an extra year to collect bills and pay off liabilities.

To avoid excessive detail in our illustrations, we include only two asset categories—Cash and Noncash Assets—and a single liability category—Liabilities. Our examples assume that the business sells the noncash assets in a single transaction and pays the liabilities in a single transaction.

Assume that Jane Aviron, Elaine Bloch, and Mark Crane have shared profits and losses in the ratio of 3:1:1. (This ratio is equal to 3/5, 1/5, 1/5, or a 60%, 20%, 20% sharing ratio.) They decide to liquidate their partnership. After the books are adjusted and closed, the general ledger contains the following balances:

Cash	$ 10,000	Liabilities	$ 30,000
Noncash assets	90,000	Aviron, capital	40,000
		Bloch, capital	20,000
		Crane, capital	10,000
Total assets	$100,000	Total liabilities and capital	$100,000

Sale of Noncash Assets at a Gain

Assume that the Aviron, Bloch, and Crane partnership sells its noncash assets (shown on the balance sheet as $90,000) for cash of $150,000. The partnership realizes a gain of $60,000, which is allocated to the partners on the basis of their profit-and-loss-sharing ratio. The entry to record this sale and allocation of the gain is

Oct. 31	Cash	150,000	
	Noncash Assets		90,000
	Aviron, Capital ($60,000 × 0.60)		36,000
	Bloch, Capital ($60,000 × 0.20)		12,000
	Crane, Capital ($60,000 × 0.20)		12,000
	To sell noncash assets at a gain.		

The partnership must next pay off its liabilities:

Oct. 31	Liabilities	30,000	
	Cash		30,000
	To pay liabilities.		

In the final liquidation transaction, the remaining cash is disbursed to the partners. *The partners share in the cash according to their capital balances.* (In contrast, *gains and losses* on the sale of assets are shared by the partners on the basis of their profit-and-loss-sharing ratio.) The amount of cash left in the partnership is $130,000—the $10,000 beginning balance plus the $150,000 cash sale of assets minus the $30,000 cash payment of liabilities. The partners divide the remaining cash according to their capital balances:

Oct. 31	Aviron, Capital ($40,000 + $36,000)	76,000	
	Bloch, Capital ($20,000 + $12,000)	32,000	
	Crane, Capital ($10,000 + $12,000)	22,000	
	Cash		130,000
	To disburse cash in liquidation.		

	Cash	+	Noncash Assets	=	Liabilities	+	Capital Aviron (60%)	+	Bloch (20%)	+	Crane (20%)
Balance before sale of assets......	$ 10,000		$ 90,000		$ 30,000		$ 40,000		$ 20,000		$ 10,000
Sale of assets and sharing of gain........	150,000		(90,000)				36,000		12,000		12,000
Balances.....................	160,000		–0–		30,000		76,000		32,000		22,000
Payment of liabilities..	(30,000)				(30,000)						
Balances.....................	130,000		–0–		–0–		76,000		32,000		22,000
Disbursement of cash to partners	(130,000)						(76,000)		(32,000)		(22,000)
Balances.....................	$ –0–		$ –0–		$ –0–		$ –0–		$ –0–		$ –0–

EXHIBIT 12-4
Partnership Liquidation—Sale of Assets at a Gain

A convenient way to summarize the transactions in a partnership liquidation is given in Exhibit 12-4.

■ **Daily Exercise 12-17**
■ **Daily Exercise 12-18**

After the disbursement of cash to the partners, the business has no assets, liabilities, or owners' equity. All the balances are zero. By the accounting equation, partnership assets *must* equal partnership liabilities plus partnership capital.

> **Learning Tip:** Upon liquidation, gains on the sale of assets are divided according to the *profit-and-loss ratio*. The final cash disbursement is based on *capital balances*.

Sale of Noncash Assets at a Loss

Liquidation of a business often includes the sale of noncash assets at a loss. When this occurs, the partners' capital accounts are debited as they share the loss in their profit-and-loss-sharing ratio. Otherwise, the accounting follows the pattern illustrated for the sale of noncash assets at a gain.

Thinking It Over The liquidation of the Dirk & Cross partnership included the sale of assets at a $150,000 loss. Lorraine Dirk's capital balance of $45,000 was less than her $60,000 share of the loss. Allocation of losses to the partners created a $15,000 deficit (debit balance) in Dirk's capital account. Identify ways that the partnership could deal with the negative balance (a capital deficiency) in Dirk's capital account.

Answer: Two possibilities are
1. Dirk could contribute assets to the partnership in an amount equal to her capital deficiency.
2. Joseph Cross, Dirk's partner, could absorb her capital deficiency by decreasing his own capital balance.

Partnership Financial Statements

Partnership financial statements are much like those of a proprietorship. However, a partnership income statement includes a section showing the division of net income to the partners. For example, the partnership of Leslie Gray and DeWayne Hayward might report its statements for the year ended December 31, 19X6, as shown in Panel A of Exhibit 12-5. A proprietorship's statements are presented in Panel B for comparison.

Objective 7

Prepare partnership financial statements

Large partnerships may not find it feasible to report the net income of every partner. Instead, the firm may report the allocation of net income to active and retired partners and average earnings per partner. For example, Exhibit 12-6 shows how the CPA firm Main Price & Anders reported its earnings.

(dollars in thousands)

PANEL A—Partnership

GRAY & HAYWARD CONSULTING Income Statement Year Ended December 31, 19X6		
Revenues		$ 460
Expenses		(270)
Net income		$ 190
Allocation of net income:		
To Gray	$114	
To Hayward	76	$ 190

PANEL B—Proprietorship

GRAY CONSULTING Income Statement Year Ended December 31, 19X6	
Revenues	$ 460
Expenses	(270)
Net income	$ 190

GRAY & HAYWARD CONSULTING Statement of Owners' Equity Year Ended December 31, 19X6	Gray	Hayward
Capital, December 31, 19X5 .	$ 50	$ 40
Additional investments	10	—
Net income	114	76
Subtotal	174	116
Drawings	(72)	(48)
Capital, December 31, 19X6 .	$102	$ 68

GRAY CONSULTING Statement of Owners' Equity Year Ended December 31, 19X6	
Capital, December 31, 19X5	$ 90
Additional investment	10
Net income	190
Subtotal	290
Drawings	(120)
Capital, December 31, 19X6	$170

GRAY & HAYWARD CONSULTING Balance Sheet December 31, 19X6	
Assets	
Cash and other assets	$170
Owners' Equity	
Gray, capital	$102
Hayward, capital	68
Total capital	$170

GRAY CONSULTING Balance Sheet December 31, 19X6	
Assets	
Cash and other assets	$170
Owner's Equity	
Gray, capital	$170

Concept Highlight

EXHIBIT 12-5
Financial Statements of a
Partnership and a
Proprietorship

■ Daily Exercise 12-19
■ Daily Exercise 12-20

MAIN PRICE & ANDERS Combined Statement of Earnings Year Ended August 31, 19X7	
Dollar amounts in thousands	
Fees for professional services	$914,492
Earnings for the year	$297,880
Allocation of earnings:	
To partners active during the year—	
Resigned, retired, and deceased partners	$ 19,901
Partners active at year end	253,270
To retired and deceased partners—retirement and death benefits	8,310
Not allocated to partners—retained for specific	
partnership purposes	16,399
	$297,880
Average earnings per partner active at year end (1,336 partners)	$ 223

EXHIBIT 12-6
Reporting Net Income for a
Large Partnership

The following Decision Guidelines feature summarizes the main points of accounting for partnerships.

DECISION GUIDELINES — Accounting for Partnerships

DECISION	GUIDELINES
How to organize the business?	A partnership offers both advantages and disadvantages in comparison with proprietorships and corporations. (See Exhibit 12–2, page 510.)
On what matters should the partners agree?	See the list on page 508, under the heading "The Written Partnership Agreement."
At what value does the partnership record assets and liabilities?	Current market value on the date of acquisition, because, in effect, the partnership is buying its assets at their current market value.

How are partnership profits and losses shared among the partners?	• Equally if there is no profit-and-loss-sharing agreement.
	• As provided in the partnership agreement. Can be based on the partners'
	  a. Stated fractions
	  b. Capital contributions
	  c. Service to the partnership
	  d. Salaries and interest on their capital contributions

What happens when a partner withdraws from the partnership?	The old partnership ceases to exist. The remaining partners may or may not form a new partnership.
How are new partners admitted to the partnership?	• *Purchase a partner's interest.* The old partnership is dissolved. The remaining partners may admit the new partner to the partnership. If not, the new partner gets no voice in the management of the firm but shares in the profits and losses of the partnership. Close the withdrawing partner's Capital account, and open a Capital account for the new partner. Carry over the old partner's Capital balance to the Capital account of the new partner. • *Invest in the partnership.* Buying in at book value creates no bonus to any partner. Buying in at a price above book value creates a bonus to the old partners. Buying in at a price below book value creates a bonus for the new partner.

How to account for the withdrawal of a partner from the business?	• First, adjust and close the books up to the date of the partner's withdrawal from the business.
	• Second, appraise the assets and the liabilities at their current market value.
	• Third, account for the partner's withdrawal
	  a. At book value (no change in remaining partners' Capital balances)
	  b. At less than book value (increase the remaining partners' Capital balances)
	  c. At more than book value (decrease the remaining partners' Capital balances)

What happens if the partnership goes out of business?	Liquidate the partnership, as follows:
	  a. Adjust and close the partnership books up to the date of liquidation.
	  b. Sell the partnership's assets. Allocate gain or loss to the partners' Capital accounts based on their profit-and-loss ratio.
	  c. Pay the partnership liabilities.
	  d. Disburse any remaining cash to the partners based on their Capital balances.

How do partnership financial statements differ from those of a proprietorship?	• The partnership income statement reports the allocation of net income or net loss to the partners. • The partnership balance sheet (or a separate schedule) reports the Capital balance of each partner. • The statement of cash flows is the same for a partnership as for a proprietorship.

The partnership of Taylor & Uvalde is considering admitting Steven Vaughn as a partner on January 1, 19X8. The partnership general ledger includes the following balances on that date:

Cash	$ 9,000	Total liabilities	$ 50,000
Other assets	110,000	Taylor, capital	45,000
		Uvalde, capital	24,000
Total assets	$119,000	Total liabilities and capital	$119,000

Ross Taylor's share of profits and losses is 60%, and Thomas Uvalde's share is 40 percent.

REQUIRED (ITEMS 1 AND 2 ARE INDEPENDENT)

1. Suppose that Vaughn pays Uvalde $31,000 to acquire Uvalde's interest in the business. Taylor approves Vaughn as a partner.
   a. Record the transfer of owner's equity on the partnership books.
   b. Prepare the partnership balance sheet immediately after Vaughn is admitted as a partner.

2. Suppose that Vaughn becomes a partner by investing $31,000 cash to acquire a one-fourth interest in the business.
   a. Compute Vaughn's capital balance, and record his investment in the business.
   b. Prepare the partnership balance sheet immediately after Vaughn is admitted as a partner. Include the heading.

3. Which way of admitting Vaughn to the partnership increases its total assets? Give your reason.

■ SOLUTION

REQUIREMENT 1

a.

Jan. 1	Uvalde, Capital	24,000	
	Vaughn, Capital		24,000
	To transfer Uvalde's equity in the partnership to Vaughn.		

b. The balance sheet for the partnership of Taylor and Vaughn is identical to the balance sheet given for Taylor and Uvalde in the problem, except that Vaughn's name replaces Uvalde's name in the title and in the listing of Capital accounts.

REQUIREMENT 2

a. Computations of Vaughn's capital balance:

Partnership capital before Vaughn is admitted ($45,000 + $24,000)	$69,000
Vaughn's investment in the partnership	31,000
Partnership capital after Vaughn is admitted	$100,000
Vaughn's capital in the partnership ($100,000 × 1/4)	$ 25,000

Jan. 1	Cash	31,000	
	Vaughn, Capital		25,000
	Taylor, Capital [($31,000 – $25,000) × 0.60]		3,600
	Uvalde, Capital[($31,000 – $25,000) × 0.40]		2,400
	To admit Vaughn as a partner with a one-fourth interest in the business.		

b.

TAYLOR, UVALDE, & VAUGHN Balance Sheet January 1, 19X8				
Cash ($9,000 + $31,000)	$ 40,000	Total liabilities	$ 50,000
Other assets	110,000	Taylor, capital ($45,000 + $3,600)	48,600
		Uvalde, capital ($24,000 + $2,400)	26,400
		Vaughn, capital	25,000
Total assets	$150,000	Total liabilities and capital	$150,000

REQUIREMENT 3

Vaughn's investment in the partnership increases its total assets by the amount of his contribution. Total assets of the business are $150,000 after his investment, compared with $119,000 before. In contrast, Vaughn's purchase of Uvalde's interest in the business is a personal transaction between the two individuals. It does not affect the assets of the partnership regardless of the amount Vaughn pays Uvalde.

Summary of Learning Objectives

1. *Identify the characteristics of a partnership.* A *partnership* is a business co-owned by two or more persons for profit. The characteristics of this form of business organization are its *ease of formation, limited life, mutual agency, unlimited liability,* and *no partnership income taxes.* In a *limited partnership,* the limited partners have limited personal liability for the obligations of the business.

A written *partnership agreement,* or *articles of partnership,* establishes procedures for admission of a new partner, withdrawals of a partner, and the sharing of profits and losses among the partners. When a new partner is admitted to the firm or an existing partner withdraws, the old partnership is *dissolved,* or ceases to exist. A new partnership may or may not emerge to continue the business.

2. *Account for partners' initial investments in a partnership.* Accounting for a partnership is similar to accounting for a proprietorship. However, a partnership has more than one owner. Each partner has an individual capital account and a withdrawal account.

3. *Allocate profits and losses to the partners by different methods.* Partners share net income or loss in any manner they choose. Common sharing agreements base the *profit-and-loss ratio* on a stated fraction, partners' capital contributions, and/or their service to the partnership. Some partnerships call the cash drawings of partners *salaries* and *interest,* but these amounts are not ex-

penses of the business. Instead, they are merely ways of allocating partnership net income to the partners.

4. *Account for the admission of a new partner to the business.* An outside person may become a partner by purchasing a current partner's interest or by investing in the partnership. In some cases, the new partner must pay the current partners a bonus to join. In other situations, the new partner may receive a bonus to join.

5. *Account for the withdrawal of a partner from the business.* When a partner withdraws, partnership assets may be reappraised. Partners share any gain or loss on the asset revaluation on the basis of their profit-and-loss ratio. The withdrawing partner may receive payment equal to, greater than, or less than his or her capital book value, depending on the agreement with the other partners.

6. *Account for the liquidation of a partnership.* In *liquidation,* a partnership goes out of business by selling the assets, paying the liabilities, and disbursing any remaining cash to the partners.

7. *Prepare partnership financial statements.* Partnership *financial statements* are similar to those of a proprietorship. However, the partnership income statement commonly reports the allocation of net income to the partners, and the balance sheet has a Capital account for each partner.

Accounting Vocabulary

articles of partnership
(p. 508)
dissolution   (p. 508)
general partnership
(p. 510)

limited partnership
(p. 510)
limited liability partnership
(p. 510)
liquidation   (p. 523)

LLP's   (p. 510)
mutual agency   (p. 508)
partnership   (p. 508)
partnership agreement
(p. 508)

S Corporation   (p. 511)
unlimited personal liability
(p. 509)

Questions

1. What is another name for a partnership agreement? List eight items that the agreement should specify.
2. Ron Montgomery, who is a partner in M&N Associates, commits the firm to a contract for a job within the scope of its regular business operations. What term describes Montgomery's ability to obligate the partnership?
3. If a partnership cannot pay a debt, who must make the payment? What term describes this obligation of the partners?
4. How is the income of a partnership taxed?
5. Identify the advantages and disadvantages of the partnership form of business organization.
6. Rex Randall and Ken Smith's partnership agreement states that Randall gets 60% of profits and Smith gets 40 percent. If the agreement does not discuss the treatment of losses, how are losses shared? How do the partners share profits and losses if the agreement specifies no profit-and-loss-sharing ratio?
7. What determines the amount of the credit to a partner's Capital account when the partner contributes assets other than cash to the business?
8. Do partner withdrawals of cash for personal use affect the sharing of profits and losses by the partner? If so, explain how. If not, explain why not.
9. Name two events that can cause the dissolution of a partnership.
10. Briefly describe how to account for the purchase of an existing partner's interest in the business.
11. Jeff Malcolm purchases Nona Brown's interest in the Brown & Kareem partnership. What right does Malcolm obtain from the purchase? What is required for Malcolm to become Paula Kareem's partner?
12. Sal Assissi and Cal Carter each have capital of $75,000 in their business. They share profits in the ratio of 55:45. Kathy Denman acquires a one-fifth share in the partnership by investing cash of $50,000. What are the capital balances of the three partners immediately after Denman is admitted?
13. When a partner resigns from the partnership and receives assets greater than his or her capital balance, how is the excess shared by the other partners?
14. Distinguish between dissolution and liquidation of a partnership.
15. Name the three steps in liquidating a partnership.
16. The partnership of Ralls and Sauls is in the process of liquidation. How do the partners share (a) gains and losses on the sale of noncash assets, and (b) the final cash disbursement?
17. Compare and contrast the financial statements of a proprietorship and a partnership.
18. Summarize the situations in which partnership allocations are based on (a) the profit-and-loss-sharing ratio, and (b) the partners' capital balances.

Daily Exercises

Partnership characteristics
(Obj. 1)

DE12-1 Sandy Saxe and Ira Weiss are forming a business to imprint T-shirts. Saxe suggests that they organize as a partnership in order to avoid the unlimited personal liability of a proprietorship. According to Saxe, partnerships are not very risky.

Saxe explains to Weiss that if the business does not succeed, each partner can withdraw from the business, taking the same assets that he or she invested at its beginning. Saxe states that the main disadvantage of the partnership form of organization is double taxation: First, the partnership pays a business income tax; second, each partner also pays personal income tax on his or her share of the business's profits.

Correct the errors in Saxe's explanation.

Partnership characteristics
(Obj. 1)

DE12-2 After studying the characteristics of a partnership, write two short paragraphs, as follows.

1. Explain the *advantages* of a partnership over a proprietorship and a corporation.
2. Explain the *disadvantages* of a partnership over a proprietorship and a corporation.

A partner's investment in a partnership
(Obj. 2)

DE12-3 Val Dierks invests a building in a partnership with Lena Marx. Dierks purchased the building in 1997 for $300,000. Accumulated depreciation to the date of forming the partnership is $80,000. A real estate appraiser states that the building is now worth $400,000. Dierks wants $400,000 capital in the new partnership, but Marx objects. Marx believes that Dierks's capital contribution into the partnership should be measured by the book value of his building.

Marx and Dierks seek your advice. Which value of the building is appropriate for measuring Dierks's capital, book value or current market value? State the reason for your answer. Give the partnership's journal entry to record Dierks's investment in the business.

Investments by partners
(Obj. 2)

DE12-4 Duane Warner and Eli Broad are forming the partnership Sun Florida Development to develop a theme park near Panama City. Warner contributes cash of $2 million and land valued at $30 million. When Warner purchased the land in 1996, its cost was $8 million. The partnership will assume Warner's $3 million note payable on the land. Broad invests cash of $10 million and construction equipment that he purchased for $7 million (accumulated depreciation to date, $3 million). The equipment's market value is equal to its book value.

1. Before recording any journal entries, compute the partnership's total assets, total liabilities, and total owners' equity immediately after organizing.
2. Journalize the partnership's receipt of assets and liabilities from Warner and from Broad. Record each asset at its current market value with no entry to accumulated depreciation.
3. Use your journal entries to prove the correctness of total owners' equity from requirement 1.

Partners' profits, losses, and capital
balances
(Obj. 3)

DE12-5 Examine the Benz and Hanna balance sheet in Exhibit 12-3, page 512. Note that Benz invested far more in the partnership than Hanna. Suppose the two partners fail to agree upon a profit-and-loss-sharing ratio. For the first month (June 19X5), the partnership lost $20,000.

1. How much of this loss goes to Benz? How much goes to Hanna?
2. Assume the partners withdrew no cash or other assets during June. What is each partner's capital balance at June 30? Prepare a T-account for each partner's capital to answer this question.

Partners' profits, drawings, and capital
balances; closing entries
(Obj. 3)

DE12-6 ◄▥ *Link Back to Chapter 4 (Closing Entries).* Return to the Benz and Hanna balance sheet in Exhibit 12-3, page 512. The partnership earned $115,000 during the year ended May 31, 19X6, its first year of operation. The partners share profits and losses based on their capital balances at the beginning of the year. During the first year, Benz withdrew $80,000 cash from the business and Hanna's drawings totaled $60,000.

1. Journalize the entries for (a) partner withdrawals of cash, (b) closing the business's profits into the partners' capital accounts at May 31, 19X6, and (c) closing the partners' drawing accounts.
2. Post to the partners' capital accounts after inserting their beginning amounts. What is the amount of total partnership capital at May 31, 19X6?

Allocating partnership profits based on
capital contributions and service
(Obj. 3)

DE12-7 Day, Flagg, and Garcia have capital balances of $20,000, $30,000, and $50,000, respectively. The partners share profits and losses as follows:
a. The first $40,000 is divided based on the partners' capital balances.
b. The next $40,000 is based on service, equally shared by Day and Garcia.
c. The remainder is divided equally.

Compute each partner's share of the business's $110,000 net income for the year.

DE12-8   Susan Lin and Chan Tran have capital balances of $30,000 and $40,000, respectively. The partners share profits and losses as follows:

Allocating partnership profits based on salaries and interest
(Obj. 3)

a.   Lin receives a salary of $15,000 and Tran a salary of $10,000.
b.   The partners earn 8% interest on their capital balances.
c.   The remainder is shared equally.

Compute each partner's share of the year's net income of $50,000.

DE12-9   Study the Ingel and Jay partnership balance sheet near the bottom of page 517. Christa Lee pays $125,000 to purchase Michael Jay's interest in the partnership.

Admitting a partner who purchases an existing partner's interest
(Obj. 4)

1.   Journalize the partnership's transaction to admit Lee to the partnership. What happens to the $35,000 difference between Lee's payment and Jay's capital balance?
2.   Must Robin Ingel accept Christa Lee as a full partner? What right does Lee have after purchasing Jay's interest in the partnership?

DE12-10   Return to the partnership balance sheet of Ingel and Jay near the bottom of page 517. Anthony Klaiber invests cash of $40,000 to acquire a one-fifth interest in the partnership.

Admitting a partner who invests in the business
(Obj. 4)

1.   Does Klaiber's investment provide a bonus to the partners? Show calculations to support your answer.
2.   Journalize the partnership's receipt of the $40,000 from Klaiber.

DE12-11   Study the partnership balance sheet of Nagasawa and Osburn on page 518. Suppose Beth Quixote invests $190,000 to purchase a one-half interest in the new partnership of Nagasawa, Osburn, and Quixote (NOQ).
   Journalize the partnership's receipt of cash from Quixote.

Admitting a new partner; bonus to the existing partners
(Obj. 4)

DE12-12   This exercise uses the data given in Daily Exercise 12-11. After recording the partnership's receipt of cash from Quixote in Daily Exercise 12-11, prepare the balance sheet of the new partnership of NOQ Partners at June 30, 19X9. Include a complete heading.

Preparing a partnership balance sheet
(Obj. 7)

DE12-13   Refer to the partnership balance sheet of Page and Franco near the top of page 520. Assume Haenni invests $120,000 to acquire a 30% interest in the new partnership of Page, Franco, and Haenni.
   Journalize the partnership's receipt of cash from Haenni.

Admitting a new partner; bonus to the new partner
(Obj. 4)

DE12-14   Examine the Green, Henry, and Isaac balance sheet near the bottom of page 521.

Withdrawal of a partner
(Obj. 5)

1.   The partners share profits and losses as follows: 25% to Green, 50% to Henry, and 25% to Isaac. Suppose Susan Green is withdrawing from the business, and the partners agree that no appraisal of assets is needed. How much in assets can Green take from the partnership? Give the reason for your answer, including an explanation of why the profit-and-loss-sharing ratio is not used for this determination.
2.   Henry and Isaac plan to form a new partnership to continue the business. If Green demands cash for her full settlement upon withdrawing from the business, how can Henry and Isaac come up with the cash to pay Green? Identify two ways.

DE12-15   Return to the Green, Henry, and Isaac partnership balance sheet near the bottom of page 521. Suppose Henry is retiring from the business and the partners agree to revalue the assets at their current market value. A real-estate appraiser issues his professional opinion that the current market value (replacement cost) of the building is $150,000, and that the building is half used up. The book values of all other assets approximate their current market value.
   Journalize (a) the revaluation of the building and its accumulated depreciation, (b) borrowing $40,000 on a note payable in order to pay Henry, and (c) payment of $40,500 to Henry upon his retirement from the business on July 31.

Withdrawal of a partner at more than book value; asset revaluation
(Obj. 5)

DE12-16   This exercise uses the data given in Daily Exercise 12-15 with one modification. Assume Henry is retiring from the partnership and agrees to take cash of $60,500.
   Journalize the payment of $60,500 to Henry upon his withdrawal from the partnership.

Withdrawal of a partner at less than book value   *(Obj. 5)*

DE12-17   Use the data in Exhibit 12-4, page 525. Suppose the partnership of Aviron, Bloch, and Crane liquidates by selling all noncash assets for $80,000.
   Complete the liquidation schedule as shown in Exhibit 12-4.

Liquidation of a partnership at a loss
(Obj. 6)

DE12-18   This exercise builds on the solution to Daily Exercise 12-17. After completing the liquidation schedule in Daily Exercise12-17, journalize the partnership's (a) sale of noncash assets for $80,000 (use a single account for Noncash Assets), (b) payment of liabilities, and (c) disbursement of cash to the partners. Include an explanation with each entry.

Liquidation entries for a partnership
(Obj. 6)

DE12-19 This exercise uses the Green, Henry, and Isaac balance sheet, after revaluation of inventory and land, given in the middle of page 522. Furthermore, assume Isaac has withdrawn from the partnership at less than book value, as recorded at the top of page 523.

Prepare the balance sheet of the new partnership of Green and Henry on July 31.

DE12-20 The partnership of Teter and Lund had these balances at September 30, 19X8:

Cash	$20,000	Service revenue..........	$140,000
Liabilities	40,000	Teter, capital	30,000
Lund, capital..........	10,000	Total expenses............	50,000
Other assets	60,000		

Teter gets two-thirds of profits and losses, and Lund one-third.

Prepare the partnership's income statement for the year ended September 30, 19X8.

Exercises

E12-1 Lana Kendall, a friend from college, approaches you about forming a partnership to export software. Since graduating, Kendall has worked for the Export-Import Bank, developing important contacts among government officials and business leaders in Eastern Europe. Kendall believes she is in a unique position to capitalize on the growing market in Eastern Europe for American computers. With expertise in finance, you would have responsibility for accounting and finance in the partnership.

REQUIRED

Discuss the advantages and disadvantages of organizing the export business as a partnership rather than a proprietorship. Comment on how partnership income is taxed.

E12-2 Sylvester Gato has been operating an apartment-location service as a proprietorship. He and Tim Vanderploeg have decided to reorganize the business as a partnership. Gato's investment in the partnership consists of cash, $13,100; accounts receivable, $10,600, less allowance for uncollectibles, $800; office furniture, $2,700, less accumulated depreciation, $1,100; a small building, $55,000, less accumulated depreciation, $27,500; accounts payable, $3,300; and a note payable to the bank, $10,000.

To determine Gato's equity in the partnership, he and Vanderploeg hire an independent appraiser. This outside party provides the following market values of the assets and liabilities that Gato is contributing to the business: cash, accounts receivable, office furniture, accounts payable, and note payable—the same as Gato's book value; allowance for uncollectible accounts, $2,900; building, $71,000; and accrued expenses payable (including interest on the note payable), $1,200.

REQUIRED

Make the entry on the partnership books to record Gato's investment.

E12-3 Beth Vines and Chad Horton form a partnership, investing $40,000 and $70,000, respectively. Determine their shares of net income or net loss for each of the following situations:

a. Net loss is $52,000, and the partners have no written partnership agreement.
b. Net income is $44,000, and the partnership agreement states that the partners share profits and losses on the basis of their capital contributions.
c. Net loss is $77,000, and the partnership agreement states that the partners share profits on the basis of their capital contributions.
d. Net income is $110,000. The first $60,000 is shared on the basis of partner capital contributions. The next $45,000 is based on partner service, with Vines receiving 30% and Horton receiving 70 percent. The remainder is shared equally.

E12-4 Beth Vines withdrew cash of $52,000 for personal use, and Chad Horton withdrew cash of $50,000 during the year. Using the data from situation (d) in Exercise 12-3, journalize the entries to close (a) the income summary account, and (b) the partners' drawing accounts. Explanations are not required. Indicate the amount of increase or decrease in each partner's capital balance. What was the overall effect on partnership capital?

E12-5 Jason Kraft is admitted to a partnership. Prior to his admission, the partnership books show Grant Boyd's capital balance at $100,000 and Alison Terrell's capital balance at $50,000. Compute each partner's equity on the books of the new partnership under the following plans:

a. Kraft pays $80,000 for Terrell's equity. Kraft's payment is not an investment in the partnership but instead goes directly to Terrell.
b. Kraft invests $50,000 to acquire a one-fourth interest in the partnership.
c. Kraft invests $90,000 to acquire a one-fourth interest in the partnership.

E12-6 Make the partnership journal entry to record the admission of Kraft under plans (a), (b), and (c) in Exercise 12-5. Explanations are not required.

Recording the admission of a new partner
(Obj. 4)

E12-7 After the books are closed, Brandon & Holmes's partnership balance sheet reports capital of $60,000 for Brandon and $80,000 for Holmes. Brandon is withdrawing from the firm. The partners agree to write down partnership assets by $30,000. They have shared profits and losses in the ratio of one-third to Brandon and two-thirds to Holmes. The partnership agreement states that a withdrawing partner will receive assets equal to the book value of his owner's equity.

Withdrawal of a partner
(Obj. 5)

1. How much will Brandon receive? Holmes will continue to operate the business as a proprietorship.
2. What is Holmes's beginning capital on the proprietorship books?

E12-8 Lana Brown is retiring from the partnership of Brown, Green, and White on May 31. The partner capital balances are Brown, $36,000; Green, $51,000; and White, $22,000. The partners agree to have the partnership assets revalued to current market values. The independent appraiser reports that the book value of the inventory should be decreased by $8,000, and the book value of the land should be increased by $32,000. The partners agree to these revaluations. The profit-and-loss ratio has been 5:3:2 for Brown, Green, and White, respectively. In retiring from the firm, Brown receives $25,000 cash and a $25,000 note from the partnership.

Withdrawal of a partner
(Obj. 5)

Journalize (a) the asset revaluations, and (b) Brown's withdrawal from the firm.

REQUIRED

E12-9 Marsh, Ng, and Orsulak are liquidating their partnership. Before selling the noncash assets and paying the liabilities, the capital balances are Marsh, $23,000; Ng, $14,000; and Orsulak, $11,000. The partnership agreement divides profits and losses equally.

Liquidation of a partnership
(Obj. 6)

1. After selling the noncash assets and paying the liabilities, the partnership has cash of $48,000. How much cash will each partner receive in final liquidation?
2. After selling the noncash assets and paying the liabilities, the partnership has cash of $45,000. How much cash will each partner receive in final liquidation?

REQUIRED

E12-10 Prior to liquidation, the accounting records of Pratt, Qualls, and Ramirez included the following balances and profit-and-loss-sharing percentages:

Liquidation of a partnership
(Obj. 6)

		Noncash				Capital		
	Cash	+ Assets	= Liabilities	+	Pratt (40%)	+	Qualls (30%)	+ Ramirez (30%)
Balances before sale of assets	$8,000	$57,000	$19,000		$20,000		$15,000	$11,000

The partnership sold the noncash assets for $73,000, paid the liabilities, and disbursed the remaining cash to the partners. Complete the summary of transactions in the liquidation of the partnership. Use the format illustrated in Exhibit 12-4.

E12-11 The partnership of Foust, Gray, and Hart is dissolving. Business assets, liabilities, and partners' capital balances prior to dissolution follow. The partners share profits and losses as follows: Cory Foust, 25%; Betty Gray, 55%; and Clyde Hart, 20 percent.

Liquidation of a partnership
(Obj. 6)

Create a spreadsheet or solve manually—as directed by your instructor—to show the ending balances in all accounts after the noncash assets are sold for $136,000 and for $90,000. Determine the unknown amounts:

	A	B	C	D	E	F
1			**FOUST, GRAY, AND HART**			
2			**Sale of Noncash Assets**			
3			**(For $136,000)**			
4						
5		Noncash		Foust	Gray	Hart
6	Cash	Assets	Liabilities	Capital	Capital	Capital
7	$ 6,000	$126,000	$77,000	$12,000	$37,000	$6,000
8	136,000	(126,000)		?	?	?
9						
10	$142,000	$ 0	$77,000	$?	$?	$?
11						
12				($A8–$B7)*.25		
13						
14						
15			**(For $90,000)**			
16		Noncash		Foust	Gray	Hart
17	Cash	Assets	Liabilities	Capital	Capital	Capital
18	$ 6,000	$126,000	$77,000	$12,000	$37,000	$6,000
19	90,000	(126,000)		?	?	?
20						
21	$ 96,000	$ 0	$77,000	$?	$?	$?
22						
23				($A19–$B18)*.25		
24						

Identify two ways the partners can deal with the negative ending balance in Hart's capital account.

CHALLENGE EXERCISE

Preparing a partnership balance sheet
(Obj. 7)

E12-12 On October 31, 19X9, Jill Justine and Don Gabriel agree to combine their proprietorships as a partnership. Their balance sheets on October 31 are as follows:

	Justine's Business		Gabriel's Business	
	Book Value	Current Market Value	Book Value	Current Market Value
Assets				
Cash	$ 3,700	$ 3,700	$ 4,000	$ 4,000
Accounts receivable (net)............	22,000	20,200	8,000	6,300
Inventory.....................................	51,000	46,000	34,000	35,100
Plant assets (net)	121,800	103,500	53,500	57,400
Total assets................................	$198,500	$173,400	$99,500	$102,800
Liabilities and Capital				
Accounts payable	$ 23,600	$ 23,600	$ 9,100	$ 9,100
Accrued expenses payable...........	2,200	2,200	1,400	1,400
Notes payable	55,000	55,000		
Justine, capital.............................	117,700	?		
Gabriel, capital			89,000	?
Total liabilities and capital..........	$198,500	$173,400	$99,500	$102,800

Prepare the partnership balance sheet at October 31, 19X9.

Beyond the Numbers

Partnership issues
(Obj. 1, 5)

BN12-1 The following questions relate to issues faced by partnerships.

1. The text suggests that a written partnership agreement should be drawn up between the partners in a partnership. One benefit of an agreement is that it provides a mechanism for

resolving disputes between the partners. List five areas of dispute that might be resolved by a partnership agreement.

2. The statement has been made that "If you must take on a partner, make sure the partner is richer than you are." Why is this statement valid?

3. Willis, Boone, & Hill is a law partnership. Andrew Hill is planning to retire from the partnership and move to Canada. What options are available to Hill to enable him to convert his share of the partnership assets to cash?

ETHICAL ISSUE

Cindy Nguyen and Dan Tiedeman operate The Party Center, a party supply store in Charlotte, North Carolina. The partners split profits and losses equally, and each takes an annual salary of $50,000. To even out the work load, Tiedeman does the buying and Nguyen serves as the accountant. From time to time, they use small amounts of store merchandise for personal use. In preparing for a large private party at her home, Nguyen took engraved invitations, napkins, placemats, and other goods that cost $1,000. She recorded the transaction as follows:

Cost of Goods Sold..........	1,000	
Inventory..................		1,000

1. How should Nguyen have recorded this transaction?
2. Discuss the ethical dimensions of Nguyen's action.

Problems (GROUP A)

P12-1A Elizabeth Palomin and John Arendale are discussing the formation of a partnership to install payroll accounting systems. Palomin is skilled in systems design, and she is convinced that her designs will draw large sales volumes. Arendale is a super salesperson and has already lined up several clients.

Writing a partnership agreement (Obj. 1)

Write a partnership agreement to cover all elements essential for the business to operate smoothly. Make up names, amounts, profit-and-loss-sharing percentages, and so on as needed.

REQUIRED

P12-2A On June 30, Abe Treacy and Megan Kell formed a partnership. The partners agreed to invest equal amounts of capital. Treacy invested his proprietorship's assets and liabilities (credit balances in parentheses).

Investments by partners (Obj. 2, 7)

	Treacy's Book Value	Current Market Value
Accounts receivable.............................	$ 7,200	$ 7,200
Allowance for doubtful accounts	(–0–)	(1,050)
Inventory...	22,340	24,100
Prepaid expenses	1,700	1,700
Office equipment..................................	45,900	27,600
Accumulated depreciation.....................	(15,300)	–0–
Accounts payable.................................	(19,100)	(19,100)

On June 30, Kell invested cash in an amount equal to the current market value of Treacy's partnership capital. The partners decided that Treacy would earn two-thirds of partnership profits because he would manage the business. Kell agreed to accept one-third of the profits. During the remainder of the year, the partnership earned $60,000. Treacy's drawings were $35,200, and Kell's drawings were $23,000.

1. Journalize the partners' initial investments.
2. Prepare the partnership balance sheet immediately after its formation on June 30.
3. Journalize the December 31 entries to close the Income Summary account and the partners' drawing accounts.

REQUIRED

P12-3A Englewood Consulting Associates is a partnership, and its owners are considering admitting Hilda Newton as a new partner. On March 31 of the current year, the capital accounts of the three existing partners and their shares of profits and losses are as follows:

Admitting a new partner (Obj. 4)

	Capital	Profit-and-Loss Share
Jim Zook.................	$ 40,000	15%
Richard Land..........	100,000	30
Jennifer Lim	160,000	55

Journalize the admission of Newton as a partner on March 31 for each of the following independent situations:

1. Newton pays Lim $145,000 cash to purchase Lim's interest in the partnership.
2. Newton invests $60,000 in the partnership, acquiring a one-sixth interest in the business.
3. Newton invests $60,000 in the partnership, acquiring a one-fifth interest in the business.
4. Newton invests $40,000 in the partnership, acquiring a 10% interest in the business.

Computing partners' shares of net income and net loss
(Obj. 3, 7)

P12-4A Larry Collins, Elinor Davis, and Paul Chiu have formed a partnership. Collins invested $15,000, Davis $18,000, and Chiu $27,000. Collins will manage the store, Davis will work in the store half-time, and Chiu will not work in the business.

1. Compute the partners' shares of profits and losses under each of the following plans:
   a. Net loss is $42,900, and the articles of partnership do not specify how profits and losses are shared.
   b. Net loss is $60,000, and the partnership agreement allocates 40% of profits to Collins, 25% to Davis, and 35% to Chiu. The agreement does not discuss the sharing of losses.
   c. Net income is $92,000. The first $40,000 is allocated on the basis of salaries, with Collins receiving $28,000 and Davis receiving $12,000. The remainder is allocated on the basis of partner capital contributions.
   d. Net income for the year ended January 31, 19X8, is $180,000. The first $75,000 is allocated on the basis of partner capital contributions, and the next $36,000 is based on service, with Collins receiving $28,000 and Davis receiving $8,000. Any remainder is shared equally.

2. Revenues for the year ended January 31, 19X8, were $870,000, and expenses were $690,000. Under plan (d), prepare the partnership income statement for the year.

Withdrawal of a partner
(Obj. 4, 5)

P12-5A Personal Financial Services is a partnership owned by three individuals. The partners share profits and losses in the ratio of 28% to Dan Smythe, 38% to Max Lark, and 34% to Emily Spahn. At December 31, 19X7, the firm has the following balance sheet:

Cash		$ 12,000	Total liabilities	$ 75,000
Accounts receivable	$ 22,000			
Less allowance for uncollectibles	(4,000)	18,000	Smythe, capital	83,000
Building	$310,000		Lark, capital	50,000
Less accumulated			Spahn, capital	62,000
depreciation	(70,000)	240,000	Total liabilities and	
Total assets		$270,000	capital	$270,000

Lark withdraws from the partnership on December 31, 19X7, to establish his own consulting practice.

Record Lark's withdrawal from the partnership under the following plans:

1. Lark gives his interest in the business to Terry Boyd, his nephew.
2. In personal transactions, Lark sells his equity in the partnership to Bea Patell and Al Bruckner, who each pay Lark $40,000 for half his interest. Smythe and Spahn agree to accept Patell and Bruckner as partners.
3. The partnership pays Lark cash of $15,000 and gives him a note payable for the remainder of his book equity in settlement of his partnership interest.
4. Lark receives cash of $10,000 and a note for $70,000 from the partnership.
5. The partners agree that the building is worth only $280,000 and that its accumulated depreciation should remain at $70,000. After the revaluation, the partnership settles with Lark by giving him cash of $14,100 and a note payable for the remainder of his book equity.

Liquidation of a partnership
(Obj. 6)

P12-6A The partnership of Monet, Blair, & Trippi has experienced operating losses for three consecutive years. The partners—who have shared profits and losses in the ratio of Mindy Monet, 10%; Burt Blair, 30%; and Toni Trippi, 60%—are considering the liquidation of the business. They ask you to analyze the effects of liquidation under various possibilities regarding the sale of the noncash assets. They present the following condensed partnership balance sheet at December 31, end of the current year:

Cash..............................	$ 27,000	Liabilities......................................	$131,000
Noncash assets..........................	202,000	Monet, capital	21,000
		Blair, capital..................................	39,000
		Trippi, capital	38,000
Total assets	$229,000	Total liabilities and capital	$229,000

REQUIRED

1. Prepare a summary of liquidation transactions (as illustrated in Exhibit 12-4) for each of the following situations:
   a. The noncash assets are sold for $212,000.
   b. The noncash assets are sold for $182,000.
2. Make the journal entries to record the liquidation transactions in requirement 1b.

P12-7A ◀▥ *Link Back to Chapter 4 (Closing Entries).* BP&O is a partnership owned by Bell, Pastena, and O'Donnell, who share profits and losses in the ratio of 5:3:2. The adjusted trial balance of the partnership (in condensed form) at September 30, end of the current fiscal year, follows.

Liquidation of a partnership (Obj. 6)

BP&O Adjusted Trial Balance September 30, 19XX		
Cash	$ 10,000	
Noncash assets.............................	177,000	
Liabilities.....................................		$135,000
Bell, capital		57,000
Pastena, capital		44,000
O'Donnell, capital........................		21,000
Bell, drawing................................	45,000	
Pastena, drawing...........................	37,000	
O'Donnell, drawing	18,000	
Revenues.......................................		211,000
Expenses	181,000	
Totals	$468,000	$468,000

REQUIRED

1. Prepare the September 30 entries to close the revenue, expense, income summary, and drawing accounts.
2. Insert the opening capital balances in the partner capital accounts, post the closing entries to the capital accounts, and determine each partner's ending capital balance.
3. The partnership liquidates on September 30 by selling the noncash assets for $132,000. Using the ending balances of the partner capital accounts computed in requirement 2, prepare a summary of liquidation transactions (as illustrated in Exhibit 12–4).

Problems (GROUP B)

P12-1B Dolores Sanchez and Leticia Gaitan are discussing the formation of a partnership to import dresses from Guatemala. Sanchez is especially artistic, so she will travel to Central America to buy merchandise. Gaitan is a super salesperson and has already lined up several large stores to which she can sell the dresses.

Writing a partnership agreement (Obj. 1)

Write a partnership agreement to cover all elements essential for the business to operate smoothly. Make up names, amounts, profit-and-loss-sharing percentages, and so on as needed.

REQUIRED

P12-2B Jo Ringle and Mel LeBlanc formed a partnership on March 15. The partners agreed to invest equal amounts of capital. LeBlanc invested his proprietorship's assets and liabilities (credit balances in parentheses):

Investments by partners (Obj. 2, 7)

	LeBlanc's Book Value	Current Market Value
Accounts receivable..............................	$ 12,000	$ 12,000
Allowance for doubtful accounts	(740)	(1,360)
Inventory	43,850	31,220
Prepaid expenses	2,400	2,400
Store equipment....................................	36,700	26,600
Accumulated depreciation.....................	(9,200)	(–0–)
Accounts payable...................................	(22,300)	(22,300)

On March 15, Ringle invested cash in an amount equal to the current market value of LeBlanc's partnership capital. The partners decided that LeBlanc would earn 70% of partnership profits because he would manage the business. Ringle agreed to accept 30% of profits. During the period ended December 31, the partnership earned $80,000. Ringle's drawings were $32,000, and LeBlanc's drawings were $36,000.

REQUIRED

1. Journalize the partners' initial investments.
2. Prepare the partnership balance sheet immediately after its formation on March 15.
3. Journalize the December 31 entries to close the Income Summary account and the partners' drawing accounts.

Admitting a new partner
(Obj. 4)

P12-3B   Red River Resort is a partnership, and its owners are considering admitting Greg Lake as a new partner. On July 31 of the current year, the capital accounts of the three existing partners and their shares of profits and losses are as follows:

	Capital	Profit-and-Loss Ratio
Ellen Urlang..........	$48,000	1/6
Amy Sharp..............	64,000	1/3
Bob Hayes	88,000	1/2

REQUIRED

Journalize the admission of Lake as a partner on July 31 for each of the following independent situations.

1. Lake pays Hayes $50,000 cash to purchase one-half of Hayes's interest.
2. Lake invests $50,000 in the partnership, acquiring a one-fifth interest in the business.
3. Lake invests $40,000 in the partnership, acquiring a one-eighth interest in the business.
4. Lake invests $30,000 in the partnership, acquiring a 15% interest in the business.

Computing partners' shares of net income and net loss
(Obj. 3, 7)

P12-4B   Robin Dewey, Kami Karlin, and Dean DeCastro have formed a partnership. Dewey invested $20,000; Karlin, $40,000; and DeCastro, $60,000. Dewey will manage the store, Karlin will work in the store three-quarters of the time, and DeCastro will not work in the business.

REQUIRED

1. Compute the partners' shares of profits and losses under each of the following plans:
   a. Net income is $87,000, and the articles of partnership do not specify how profits and losses are shared.
   b. Net loss is $47,000, and the partnership agreement allocates 45% of profits to Dewey, 35% to Karlin, and 20% to DeCastro. The agreement does not discuss the sharing of losses.
   c. Net income is $104,000. The first $50,000 is allocated on the basis of salaries of $34,000 for Dewey and $16,000 for Karlin. The remainder is allocated on the basis of partner capital contributions.
   d. Net income for the year ended September 30, 19X4, is $91,000. The first $30,000 is allocated on the basis of partner capital contributions. The next $30,000 is based on service, with $20,000 going to Dewey and $10,000 going to Karlin. Any remainder is shared equally.
2. Revenues for the year ended September 30, 19X4, were $572,000, and expenses were $481,000. Under plan (d), prepare the partnership income statement for the year.

Withdrawal of a partner
(Obj. 4, 5)

P12-5B   Airborne Systems is a partnership owned by three individuals. The partners share profits and losses in the ratio of 30% to Eve Koehn, 40% to Earl Neiman, and 30% to Ivana Marcus. At December 31, 19X6, the firm has the following balance sheet:

Cash		$ 25,000	Total liabilities	$103,000
Accounts receivable	$ 16,000			
Less allowance for				
uncollectibles	(1,000)	15,000		
Inventory		92,000	Koehn, capital...	38,000
Equipment........................	130,000		Nieman, capital...	49,000
Less accumulated			Marcus, capital...	42,000
depreciation	(30,000)	100,000	Total liabilities and	
Total assets........................		$232,000	capital	$232,000

Koehn withdraws from the partnership on this date.

Record Koehn's withdrawal from the partnership under the following plans:

REQUIRED

1. Koehn gives her interest in the business to Lynn Albelli, her cousin.

2. In personal transactions, Koehn sells her equity in the partnership to Matt Bullock and Shelley Jones, who each pay Koehn $15,000 for half her interest. Neiman and Marcus agree to accept Bullock and Jones as partners.

3. The partnership pays Koehn cash of $5,000 and gives her a note payable for the remainder of her book equity in settlement of her partnership interest.

4. Koehn receives cash of $20,000 and a note payable for $20,000 from the partnership.

5. The partners agree that the equipment is worth $150,000 and that accumulated depreciation should remain at $30,000. After the revaluation, the partnership settles with Koehn by giving her cash of $10,000 and inventory for the remainder of her book equity.

P12-6B The partnership of Whitney, Kosse, & Itasca has experienced operating losses for three consecutive years. The partners—who have shared profits and losses in the ratio of Fran Whitney, 15%; Walt Kosse, 60%; and Emil Itasca, 25%—are considering the liquidation of the business. They ask you to analyze the effects of liquidation under various possibilities regarding the sale of the noncash assets. They present the following condensed partnership balance sheet at December 31, end of the current year:

Liquidation of a partnership
(Obj. 6)

Cash	$ 7,000	Liabilities	$ 63,000
Noncash assets	163,000	Whitney, capital	24,000
		Kosse, capital	66,000
		Itasca, capital	17,000
		Total liabilities and	
Total assets	$170,000	capital	$170,000

REQUIRED

1. Prepare a summary of liquidation transactions (as illustrated in the Exhibit 12-4) for each of the following situations:
   a. The noncash assets are sold for $175,000.
   b. The noncash assets are sold for $141,000.

2. Make the journal entries to record the liquidation transactions in requirement 1b.

P12-7B ◀▥ *Link Back to Chapter 4 (Closing Entries).* RMG & Company is a partnership owned by Ryan, Morales, and Goldberg, who share profits and losses in the ratio of 1:3:4. The adjusted trial balance of the partnership (in condensed form) at June 30, end of the current fiscal year, follows.

Liquidation of a partnership
(Obj. 6)

RMG & COMPANY
Adjusted Trial Balance
June 30, 19XX

Cash	$ 24,000	
Noncash assets	116,000	
Liabilities		$100,000
Ryan, capital		22,000
Morales, capital		41,000
Goldberg, capital		62,000
Ryan, drawing	14,000	
Morales, drawing	35,000	
Goldberg, drawing	54,000	
Revenues		108,000
Expenses	90,000	
Totals	$333,000	$333,000

REQUIRED

1. Prepare the June 30 entries to close the revenue, expense, income summary, and drawing accounts.

2. Insert the opening capital balances in the partners' capital accounts, post the closing entries to the capital accounts, and determine each partner's ending capital balance.

3. The partnership liquidates on June 30 by selling the noncash assets for $100,000. Using the ending balances of the partners' capital accounts computed in requirement 2, prepare a summary of liquidation transactions (as illustrated in Exhibit 12–4).

Applying Your Knowledge

DECISION CASE

Settling disagreements among partners *(Obj. 3)*

Becky Jones invested $20,000 and Imelda Nichols invested $10,000 in a public relations firm that has operated for ten years. Neither partner has made an additional investment. They have shared profits and losses in the ratio of 2:1, which is the ratio of their investments in the business. Jones manages the office, supervises the 16 employees, and does the accounting. Nichols, the moderator of a television talk show, is responsible for marketing. Her high profile generates important revenue for the business. During the year ended December 19X4, the partnership earned net income of $87,000, shared in the 2:1 ratio. On December 31, 19X4, Jones's capital balance was $150,000, and Nichols's capital balance was $100,000.

REQUIRED

Respond to each of the following situations.

1. What explains the difference between the ratio of partner capital balances at December 31, 19X4, and the 2:1 ratio of partner investments and profit sharing?
2. Nichols believes that the profit-and-loss-sharing ratio is unfair. She proposes a change, but Jones insists on keeping the 2:1 ratio. What two factors may underlie Nichols's unhappiness?
3. During January 19X5, Jones learned that revenues of $18,000 were omitted from the reported 19X4 income. She brings this omission to Nichols's attention, pointing out that Jones's share of this added income is two-thirds, or $12,000, and Nichols's share is one-third, or $6,000. Nichols believes that they should share this added income on the basis of their capital balances—60%, or $10,800, to Jones and 40%, or $7,200, to herself. Which partner is correct? Why?
4. Assume that the 19X4 $18,000 omission was an account payable for an operating expense. On what basis would the partners share this amount?

FINANCIAL STATEMENT CASE

KPMG Peat Marwick is an international accounting firm. Summary data from the partnership's *1997 Annual Report* follow.

(Dollars in millions, except where indicated)	Years Ended June 30				
	1997	**1996**	**1995**	**1994**	**1993**
Revenues					
Assurance	$1,234	$1,122	$1,064	$1,093	$1,070
Consulting	1,007	775	658	473	349
Tax	743	628	567	515	557
Total Revenues	$2,984	$2,525	$2,289	$2,081	$1,976
Operating Summary					
Revenues	$2,984	$2,525	$2,289	$2,081	$1,976
Personnel Costs	1,215	1,004	887	805	726
Other Costs	1,212	1,030	967	898	829
Income to Partners	$ 557	$ 491	$ 435	$ 378	$ 421
Statistical Data					
Average Number of Partners	1,494	1,428	1,413	1,449	1,453

REQUIRED

1. What percentages of total revenues did KPMG earn by performing assurance services (similar to audit), consulting services, and tax services during 1993? What were the percentages in 1997? Which type of services grew the most from 1993 to 1997?
2. Compute the average revenue per partner in 1997. Assume each partner works 2,000 hours per year. On average, how much does each partner charge a client for one hour of time?
3. How much net income did each KPMG partner earn, on average, in 1997? For people who enjoy accounting, consulting, and tax work, do you see why accounting is a popular major in college?

Team Project

Visit a business partnership in your area, and interview one or more of the partners. Obtain answers to the following questions and ask your instructor for directions. As directed by your instructor, either (a) prepare a written report of your findings, or (b) make a presentation to your class.

1. Why did you organize the business as a partnership? What advantages does the partnership form of organization offer the business? What are the disadvantages of the partnership form of organization?

2. Is the business a general partnership, or is it a limited partnership?

3. Do the partners have a written partnership agreement? What does the agreement cover? Obtain a copy if possible.

4. Who manages the business? Do all partners participate in day-to-day management, or is management the responsibility of only certain partners?

5. If there is no written agreement, what is the mechanism for making key decisions?

6. Have you ever admitted a new partner? If so, when did it occur? What are the partnership's procedures for admitting a new partner?

7. Has a partner ever withdrawn from the business? If so, when? What are the partnership's procedures for settling up with a withdrawing partner?

8. If possible, learn how the partnership divides profits and losses among the partners.

9. Ask for any additional insights that the partner whom you interview can provide about the business.

Internet Exercise ANDERSON WORLDWIDE

The world largest accounting firms are organized as partnerships. Known as the Big Six (or Five or Four or Three—depending on the results of recent mergers), these firms provide more than the traditional auditing and tax work. Today, these accounting firms call themselves professional services firms and they provide every conceivable business service: from business process reengineering to identifying CEO candidates for its clients. What began as green-eye shaded accountants pouring over a client's accounting records has evolved into a $20+ billion industry.

The largest of the accounting firms is Arthur Andersen. Founded in Chicago by its namesake, Arthur Andersen, back in 1913, the firm has expanded to over 50,000 people in 76 countries.

1. Go to **http://www.arthurandersen.com.** This is the home page for Arthur Andersen.

2. Click on **About Arthur Andersen.** This section allows you to learn more about the firm as well as the history of accounting. Note, to fully enjoy the history of accounting pages, your Web browser needs to have the Shockwave for Director plug-in. After exploring this section, answer the following questions:

   a. Why does Arthur Andersen *not* publish financial statements? In fact, none of the large accounting firms publish financial statements.

   b. What are the two main groups that comprise Andersen Worldwide? How much in revenues did Andersen Worldwide earn last year?

   c. Which business does Arthur Andersen cite as the most important?

   d. How do accounting professors across the country rank Arthur Andersen?

CHAPTER 13

Corporate Organization, Paid-in Capital, and the Balance Sheet

LEARNING OBJECTIVES

After studying this chapter, you should be able to

1. Identify the characteristics of a corporation
2. Record the issuance of stock
3. Prepare the stockholders' equity section of a corporation's balance sheet
4. Account for cash dividends
5. Use different stock values in decision making
6. Evaluate a company's return on assets and return on stockholders' equity
7. Account for a corporation's income tax

Based in Glendale, California, IHOP Corporation develops, franchises, and operates International House of Pancakes family restaurants. There are almost 600 IHOPs in 35 states, Canada, and Japan—with big concentrations of IHOP restaurants in California, New York, New Jersey, Florida, and Texas.

IHOP still serves up stacks of great pancakes, but now you can buy the stock as well. When IHOP Corp. went public, the company offered 6.2 million shares at $10 each. The shares got off to a strong start and have performed well. IHOP's stock lately has traded at about $36 per share. *Sources:* Adapted from "Stacked Stock," *Forbes*, July 6, 1992, p. 128, and "Looking at IHOP: Not Just Pancakes," *New York Times*, November 6, 1992.

What does it mean to "go public," as IHOP did? A corporation *goes public* when it issues its stock to the general public. A common reason for going public is to raise money for expansion. By offering its stock to the public, a company can hope to raise more money than if the stockholders are limited to a few insiders. In its public offering of stock, IHOP hoped to receive cash of $62 million (6.2 million shares of stock at $10 each). The investors who bought IHOP's stock at $10 have done well. IHOP stock is now worth over $36 per share. The opportunity to profit from buying a good stock makes corporations an attractive form of business organization.

Objective 1

Identify the characteristics of a corporation

Corporations: An Overview

The corporation is the dominant form of business organization in the United States. International House of Pancakes is an example. Although proprietorships and partnerships are more numerous, corporations transact more business and are larger in terms of total assets, sales revenue, and number of employees. Most well-known companies, such as NIKE, CBS, General Motors, and IBM, are corporations. Their full names include *Corporation* or *Incorporated* (abbreviated *Corp.* and *Inc.*) to indicate that they are corporations—for example, CBS, Inc., and General Motors Corporation.

Characteristics of a Corporation

Why is the corporate form of business so attractive? We now look at the features that distinguish corporations from proprietorships and partnerships, and some of the advantages and disadvantages of corporations.

Charter. Document that gives the state's permission to form a corporation.

SEPARATE LEGAL ENTITY A corporation is a business entity formed under state law. The state grants a **charter,** which is a document that gives a business the state's permission to form a corporation. Neither a proprietorship nor a partnership requires state approval to do business, because in the eyes of the law the business is the same as the owner(s).

Stockholder. A person who owns the stock of a corporation. Also called **shareholder.**

From a legal perspective, a corporation is a distinct entity, an artificial person that exists apart from its owners, who are called **stockholders** or **shareholders.** The corporation has many of the rights that a person has. For example, a corporation may buy, own, and sell property. Assets and liabilities in the business belong to the corporation rather than to its owners. The corporation may enter into contracts, sue, and be sued.

Stock. Shares into which the owners' equity of a corporation is divided.

The owners' equity of a corporation is divided into shares of **stock.** The corporate charter specifies how much stock the corporation can issue (sell).

CONTINUOUS LIFE AND TRANSFERABILITY OF OWNERSHIP Most corporations have *continuous lives* regardless of changes in the ownership of their stock. The stockholders of IHOP or any corporation may transfer stock as they wish. They may sell or trade the stock to another person, give it away, bequeath it in a will, or dispose of it in any other way. The transfer of the stock does not affect the continuity of the corporation. In contrast, proprietorships and partnerships terminate when their ownership changes.

◄||||| ◄||||| ◄||||| We introduced the idea of mutual agency, which applies only to partnerships, in Chapter 12, page 508.

NO MUTAL AGENCY *Mutual agency* is an arrangement whereby all owners act as agents of the business. A contract signed by one owner is binding for the whole company. Mutual agency operates in partnerships but *not* in corporations. ◄||||| A stockholder of IHOP Corp. cannot commit the corporation to a contract (unless he or she is also an officer in the business). For this reason, a stockholder need not exercise the care that partners must in selecting co-owners of the business.

Limited Liability. No personal obligation of a stockholder for corporation debts. A stockholder can lose no more on an investment in a corporation's stock than the cost of the investment.

LIMITED LIABILITY OF STOCKHOLDERS Stockholders have **limited liability** for corporation debts. That is, they have no personal obligation for corporation liabilities. The most that a stockholder can lose on an investment in a corporation's stock is the amount invested. In contrast, proprietors and partners are personally liable for all the debts of their businesses.

The combination of limited liability and no mutual agency means that persons can invest limited amounts in a corporation without fear of losing all their personal wealth if the business fails. This feature enables a corporation to raise more capital from a wider group of investors than proprietorships and partnerships can.

SEPARATION OF OWNERSHIP AND MANAGEMENT   Stockholders own the business, but a *board of directors*—elected by the stockholders—appoints corporate officers to manage the business. Thus stockholders may invest $1,000 or $1 million in the corporation without having to manage the business or disrupt their personal affairs.

Management's goal is to maximize the firm's value for the stockholders' benefit. However, the separation between owners—stockholders—and management can create problems. Corporate officers may decide to run the business for their own benefit and not to the stockholders' advantage. Stockholders may find it difficult to lodge an effective protest against management policy because of the distance between them and management.

CORPORATE TAXATION   Corporations are separate taxable entities. They pay a variety of taxes not borne by proprietorships or partnerships, including an annual franchise tax levied by the state. The franchise tax is paid to keep the corporate charter in force and enables the corporation to continue in business. Corporations also pay federal and state income taxes.

Corporate earnings are subject to **double taxation.** First, corporations pay income taxes on corporate income. Then, stockholders pay personal income tax on the cash dividends (distributions) they receive from corporations. Proprietorships and partnerships pay no business income tax. Instead, the tax falls solely on the owners.

> **Double Taxation.** Corporations pay their own income taxes on corporate income. Then, the stockholders pay personal income tax on the cash dividends that they receive from corporations.

GOVERNMENT REGULATION   Because stockholders have only limited liability for corporation debts, outsiders doing business with the corporation can look no further than the corporation itself for any claims that may arise against the business. To protect persons who loan money to a corporation or who invest in its stock, both federal agencies and the states monitor corporations. This *government regulation* consists mainly of ensuring that corporations disclose the information that investors and creditors need to make informed decisions. For many corporations, government regulation is expensive.

Exhibit 13-1 summarizes the advantages and disadvantages of the corporate form of business organization.

■ Daily Exercise 13-1

Organization of a Corporation

The process of creating a corporation begins when its organizers, called the *incorporators*, obtain a charter from the state. The charter includes the authorization for the corporation to issue a certain number of shares of stock, which are shares of ownership in the corporation. The incorporators pay fees, sign the charter, and file required documents with the state. The corporation then comes into existence. The incorporators agree to a set of **bylaws,** which act as the constitution for governing the corporation.

The ultimate control of the corporation rests with the stockholders. The stockholders elect the members of the **board of directors,** which sets policy for the corporation and appoints the officers. The board elects a **chairperson,** who usually is the most powerful person in the corporation. The board also designates the **president,** who is the chief operating officer in charge of day-to-day operations. Most corporations also have vice presidents in charge of sales, manufacturing, accounting and finance, and other key areas. Often, the president and one or more vice presidents are also elected to the board of directors. Exhibit 13-2 shows the authority structure in a corporation.

> **Bylaws.** Constitution for governing a corporation.
>
> **Board of Directors.** Group elected by the stockholders to set policy for a corporation and to appoint its officers.
>
> **Chairperson.** Elected by a corporation's board of directors, usually the most powerful person in the corporations.
>
> **President.** Chief operating officer in charge of managing the day-to-day operations of a corporation.

Advantages	Disadvantages
1. Can raise more capital than a proprietorship or partnership	1. Separation of ownership and management
2. Continuous life	2. Corporate taxation
3. Ease of transferring ownership	3. Government regulation
4. No mutual agency of stockholders	
5. Limited liability of stockholders	

EXHIBIT 13-1
Advantages and Disadvantages of a Corporation

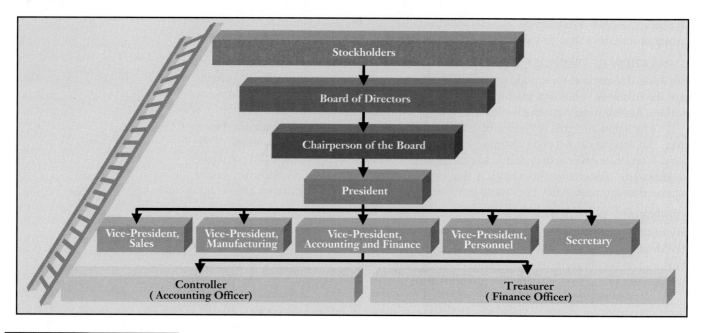

EXHIBIT 13-2
Authority Structure in a
Corporation

■ **Daily Exercise 13-2**

Capital Stock

A corporation issues *stock certificates* to its owners in exchange for their investments in the business. Because stock represents the corporation's capital, it is often called *capital stock.* The basic unit of capital stock is called a *share.* A corporation may issue a stock certificate for any number of shares it wishes—one share, 100 shares, or any other number—but the total number of *authorized* shares is limited by charter. Exhibit 13-3 depicts an actual stock certificate for 288 shares of Central Jersey Bancorp common stock. The certificate shows the company's name, the stockholder's name, the number of shares, and the par value of the stock (discussed later in this chapter).

Outstanding Stock. Stock in the hands of stockholders.

Stock in the hands of a stockholder is said to be **outstanding.** The total number of shares of stock outstanding at any time represents 100% ownership of the corporation.

EXHIBIT 13-3
Stock Certificate

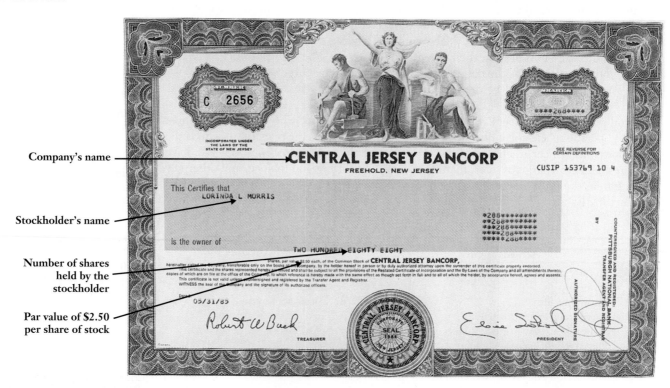

Company's name

Stockholder's name

Number of shares held by the stockholder

Par value of $2.50 per share of stock

Stockholders' Equity

The balance sheet of a corporation reports assets and liabilities in the same way as a proprietorship or a partnership. However, owners' equity of a corporation—called **stockholders' equity**—is reported differently. State laws require corporations to report the sources of their capital. The two most basic sources of capital are

- **Paid-in capital** (also called **contributed capital**), which represents investments by the stockholders in the corporation
- **Retained earnings,** which is capital that the corporation has earned through profitable operations

Exhibit 13-4 outlines a summarized version of the balance sheet of Wal-Mart Stores, Inc., to show how to report these categories of stockholders' equity.

Stockholders' Equity. Owners' equity of a corporation.

Paid-in Capital. A corporation's capital from investments by the stockholders. Also called **contributed capital.**

Retained Earnings. A corporation's capital that is earned through profitable operation of the business.

Paid-in Capital Is Received from the Stockholders

Common stock is paid-in capital. It is regarded as the permanent capital of the business because it is *not* subject to withdrawal by the stockholders. An investment of cash or any other asset in a corporation increases the corporation's assets and stockholders' equity. Wal-Mart's entry for receipt of $20,000 cash and issuance of Wal-Mart stock to a stockholder is

Common Stock. The most basic form of capital stock. In a corporation, the common stockholders are the owners of the business.

Oct. 20	Cash...................................	20,000	
	Common Stock..........		20,000
	Issued stock.		

Retained Earnings Are Earned from the Customers

Profitable operations produce income, which increases stockholders' equity through a separate account called Retained Earnings. At the end of the year, the net income (or net loss) balance of the Income Summary account is closed to Retained Earnings. For example, if Wal-Mart's net income is $3,000 million, Income Summary will have a $3,000 million credit balance. Wal-Mart's closing entry will debit Income Summary to transfer net income to Retained Earnings as follows (in millions of dollars):

Dec. 31	Income Summary...............................	3,000	
	Retained Earnings.......................		3,000
	To close *net income* to Retained Earnings.		

If operations produce a net *loss* rather than net income, the Income Summary account will have a debit balance. Income Summary must be credited to close it. With a $60,000 loss, the closing entry is

Dec. 31	Retained Earnings...............................	60,000	
	Income Summary.......................		60,000
	To close *net loss* to Retained Earnings.		

NEGATIVE RETAINED EARNINGS IS CALLED A DEFICIT A large loss may cause a debit balance in the Retained Earnings account. This condition—called a Retained

Assets	$39,604	Liabilities		$22,461
		Stockholders' Equity		
		Paid-in capital:		
		Common stock..........................		375
		Retained earnings.......................		16,768
		Total stockholders' equity..........		17,143
		Total liabilities and		
Total assets..........	$39,604	stockholders' equity.......................		$39,604

EXHIBIT 13-4
Summarized Balance Sheet of Wal-Mart Stores, Inc. (Amounts in Millions)

■ Daily Exercise 13-3

Deficit. Debit balance in the Retained Earnings account.

Earnings **deficit**—is reported on the balance sheet as a negative amount in stockholders' equity. HAL, INC., which owns Hawaiian Airlines, Inc., reported this deficit:

Stockholders' Equity	(in millions)
Paid-in capital: Common stock..........	$ 50
Deficit...	(193)
Total stockholders' equity	$(143)

HAL's deficit was so large that it produced a negative amount of stockholders' equity. This situation is unusual for a going concern.

Corporations May Pay Dividends to the Stockholders

Dividends. Distributions by a corporation to its stockholders.

Legal Capital. The portion of stockholders' equity that cannot be used for dividends.

If the corporation has been profitable and has sufficient cash, a distribution of cash may be made to the stockholders. Such distributions—called **dividends**—are similar to a withdrawal by the owner from a proprietorship or by a partner from a partnership. Dividends decrease both the assets and the retained earnings of the business. Most states prohibit the practice of using paid-in capital for dividends. Accountants use the term **legal capital** to refer to the portion of stockholders' equity that *cannot* be used for dividends.

Some people think of Retained Earnings as a fund of cash. It is not, because Retained Earnings is an element of stockholders' equity. *Remember that cash and other property dividends are paid out of assets, not out of retained earnings.*

Stockholders' Rights

The ownership of stock entitles stockholders to four basic rights, unless specific rights are withheld by agreement with the stockholders:

1. *Vote.* The right to participate in management by voting on matters that come before the stockholders. This is the stockholder's sole right to a voice in the management of the corporation. A stockholder is entitled to one vote for each share of stock owned.

2. *Dividends.* The right to receive a proportionate part of any dividend. Each share of stock in a particular class receives an equal dividend.

3. *Liquidation.* The right to receive a proportionate share (based on number of shares held) of any assets remaining after the corporation pays its liabilities in liquidation.

4. *Preemption.* The right to maintain one's proportionate ownership in the corporation. Suppose you own 5% of a corporation's stock. If the corporation issues 100,000 new shares of stock, it must offer you the opportunity to buy 5% (5,000) of the new shares. This right, called the *preemptive right*, is usually withheld from the stockholders.

Classes of Stock

Corporations issue different types of stock to appeal to a wide variety of investors. The stock of a corporation may be either common or preferred and either par or no-par.

Common and Preferred Stock

Every corporation issues *common stock*, the most basic form of capital stock. Unless designated otherwise, the word *stock* is understood to mean "common stock." Common stockholders have the four basic rights of stock ownership, unless a right is specifically withheld. For example, some companies issue Class A common stock, which usually carries the right to vote, and Class B common stock, which may be nonvoting. (Classes of common stock may also be designated Series A, Series B, and so on.) The general ledger has a separate account for each class of common stock. In describing a corporation, we would say the common stockholders are the owners of the business.

Investors who buy common stock take the ultimate risk with a corporation. The corporation makes no promises to pay them. If the corporation succeeds, it will pay dividends to its stockholders, but if net income and cash are too low, the stockholders may receive no dividends. The stock of successful corporations increases in value, and investors enjoy the benefit of selling the stock at a gain. But stock prices can decrease, leaving the investors holding worthless stock certificates. Because common stockholders take a risky investment position, they demand increases in stock prices, high dividends, or both. If the corporation does not deliver, the stockholders sell the stock, and its market price falls.

Preferred stock gives its owners certain advantages over common stockholders. These benefits include the priority to receive dividends before the common stockholders and the priority to receive assets before the common stockholders if the corporation liquidates. Corporations pay a fixed amount of dividends on preferred stock. Investors usually buy preferred stock to earn those dividends.

Owners of preferred stock also have the four basic stockholder rights, unless a right is specifically denied. Often the right to vote is withheld from preferred stockholders. Companies may issue different classes of preferred stock. (Class A and Class B or Series A and Series B, for example). Each class is recorded in a separate account. Preferred stock is rarer than you might think. A recent survey of 600 corporations revealed that only 145 of them (24%) had some preferred stock outstanding (Exhibit 13-5). All corporations have common stock. Exhibit 13-6 summarizes the similarities and differences among common stock, preferred stock, and long-term debt.

Par Value, Stated Value, and No-Par Stock

Stock may be par-value stock or no-par stock. **Par value** is an arbitrary amount assigned by a company to a share of its stock. Most companies set the par value of their common stock quite low to avoid legal difficulties from issuing their stock below par. Most states require companies to maintain a minimum amount of stockholders' equity for the protection of creditors, and this minimum is often called the corporation's legal capital. For corporations with par-value stock, *legal capital* is the par value of the shares issued.

The common stock par value of Kimberly Clark, best known for its Kleenex tissues, is $1.25 per share. Of 600 million shares of stock, Kimberly Clark has issued 284.3 million shares. J.C. Penney's common stock par value is 50¢ per share, and Sprint Corporation's common stock par value is $2.50 per share. Par value of preferred stock is often higher; some preferred stocks have par values of $25 and $10. Par value is used to compute dividends on preferred stock, as we shall see.

No-par stock does not have par value. Kimberly Clark has 20 million shares of preferred stock authorized with no par value. But some no-par stock has a **stated value**, which makes it similar to par-value stock. The stated value is an arbitrary amount that accountants treat as though it were par value.

Issuing Stock

Large corporations such as Coca-Cola, Xerox, and British Petroleum need huge quantities of money to operate. They cannot expect to finance all their operations through

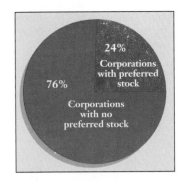

"The common stock par value of Kimberly Clark, best known for its Kleenex tissues, is $1.25 per share."

EXHIBIT 13-5
Preferred Stock

Preferred Stock. Stock that gives its owners certain advantages over common stockholders, such as the priority to receive dividends before the common stockholders and the priority to receive assets before the common stockholders if the corporation liquidates.

Par value. Arbitrary amount assigned to a share of stock.

■ **Daily Exercise 13-4**

Stated Value. Similar to par value.

Objective 2

Record the issuance of stock

EXHIBIT 13-6
Comparison of Common Stock, Preferred Stock, and Long-Term Debt

	Common Stock	Preferred Stock	Long-Term Debt
Investment risk	High	Medium	Low
Corporate obligation to repay principal	No	No	Yes
Dividends/interest	Dividends	Dividends	Tax-deductible interest expense
Corporate obligation to pay dividends/interest	Only after declaration	Only after declaration	At fixed dates
Fluctuations in market value under normal conditions	High	Medium	Low

borrowing. They need capital that they raise by issuing stock. The charter that the incorporators receive from the state includes an **authorization of stock**—that is, a provision giving the state's permission for the business to issue (to sell) a certain number of shares of stock. Corporations may sell the stock directly to the stockholders or use the service of an *underwriter*, such as the brokerage firms Merrill Lynch and Dean Witter. An underwriter agrees to buy all the stock it cannot sell to its clients.

The corporation need not issue all the stock that the state authorizes. Management may hold some stock back and issue it later if the need for additional capital arises. The stock that the corporation issues to stockholders is called *issued stock*. Only by issuing stock—not by receiving authorization—does the corporation increase the asset and stockholders' equity amounts on its balance sheet.

The price that the stockholder pays to acquire stock from the corporation is called the *issue price*. Often, the issue price far exceeds the stock's par value because the par value was intentionally set quite low. The company's earnings record, prospects for success, and general business conditions determine the stock's issue price. Investors will not pay more than market value for the stock. In the following sections, we show how companies account for the issuance of stock.

Issuing Common Stock

Companies often advertise the issuance of their stock to attract investors. The *Wall Street Journal* is the most popular medium for the advertisements, which are also called *tombstones*. Exhibit 13-7 is a reproduction of IHOP's tombstone, which appeared in the *Wall Street Journal*, with the data given in the chapter opening story.

The lead underwriter of IHOP's public offering was The First Boston Corporation. Twenty-one other domestic brokerage firms and investment bankers sold IHOP's stock to their clients. Outside the United States, six investment bankers assisted with the offering. Altogether, IHOP hoped to raise approximately $62 million of capital. As it turned out, IHOP issued only 3.2 million of the shares and received cash of approximately $32 million.

ISSUING COMMON STOCK AT PAR Suppose IHOP's common stock carried a par value of $10 per share. The stock issuance entry of 3.2 million shares would be

Jan. 8	Cash (3,200,000 × $10)	32,000,000	
	Common Stock		32,000,000
	Issued common stock at par.		

The amount invested in the corporation, $32 million in this case, is paid-in capital, or contributed capital, of IHOP. The credit to Common Stock records an increase in the corporation's paid-in capital.

ISSUING COMMON STOCK AT A PREMIUM Many corporations set par value at a low amount, then issue common stock for a price above par value. The amount above par is called a *premium*. IHOP's common stock has a par value of $0.01 (1 cent) per share. The $9.99 difference between issue price ($10) and par value ($0.01) is a premium. This sale of stock increases the corporation's paid-in capital by the full $10, the total issue price of the stock. Both the par value of the stock and the premium are part of paid-in capital.

A premium on the sale of stock is not gain, income, or profit to the corporation, because the entity is dealing with its own stockholders. This situation illustrates one of the fundamentals of accounting: *A company neither earns a profit nor incurs a loss when it sells its stock to, or buys its stock from, its own stockholders.*

With a par value of $0.01, IHOP's entry to record the issuance of the stock is

■ **Daily Exercise 13-5**

July 23	Cash (3,200,000 × $10)	32,000,000	
	Common Stock (3,200,000 × $0.01)		32,000
	Paid-in Capital in Excess of Par—		
	Common (3,200,000 × $9.99)		31,968,000
	Issued common stock at a premium.		

EXHIBIT 13-7
Announcement of Public
Offering of IHOP Stock

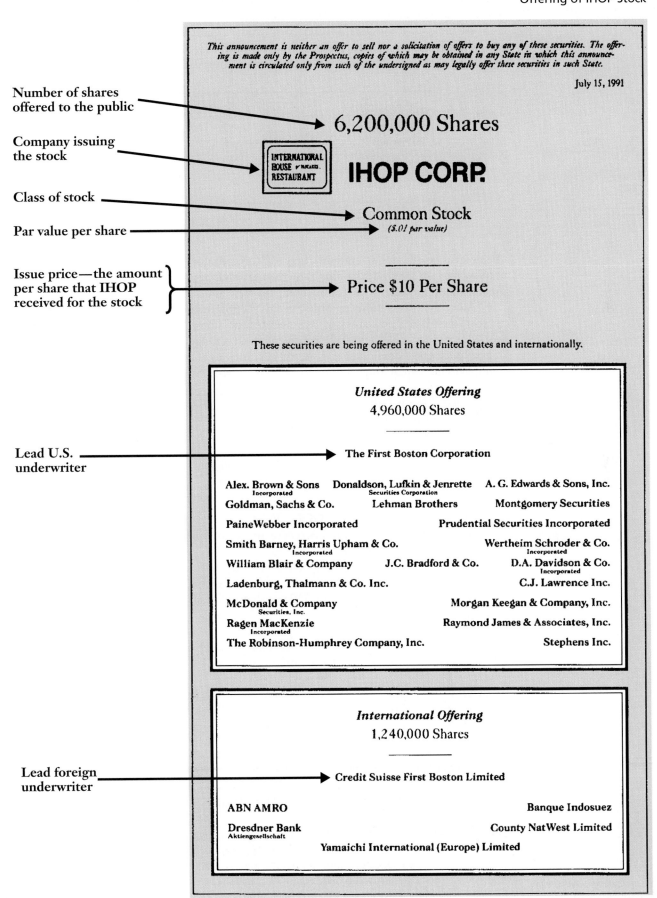

Number of shares
offered to the public

Company issuing
the stock

Class of stock

Par value per share

Issue price—the amount
per share that IHOP
received for the stock

Lead U.S.
underwriter

Lead foreign
underwriter

This announcement is neither an offer to sell nor a solicitation of offers to buy any of these securities. The offering is made only by the Prospectus, copies of which may be obtained in any State in which this announcement is circulated only from such of the undersigned as may legally offer these securities in such State.

July 15, 1991

6,200,000 Shares

IHOP CORP.

INTERNATIONAL HOUSE of PANCAKES RESTAURANT

Common Stock

($.01 par value)

Price $10 Per Share

These securities are being offered in the United States and internationally.

United States Offering

4,960,000 Shares

The First Boston Corporation

Alex. Brown & Sons Incorporated	Donaldson, Lufkin & Jenrette Securities Corporation	A. G. Edwards & Sons, Inc.
Goldman, Sachs & Co.	Lehman Brothers	Montgomery Securities

PaineWebber Incorporated   Prudential Securities Incorporated

Smith Barney, Harris Upham & Co. Incorporated   Wertheim Schroder & Co. Incorporated

William Blair & Company   J.C. Bradford & Co.   D.A. Davidson & Co. Incorporated

Ladenburg, Thalmann & Co. Inc.   C.J. Lawrence Inc.

McDonald & Company Securities, Inc.   Morgan Keegan & Company, Inc.

Ragen MacKenzie Incorporated   Raymond James & Associates, Inc.

The Robinson-Humphrey Company, Inc.   Stephens Inc.

International Offering

1,240,000 Shares

Credit Suisse First Boston Limited

ABN AMRO   Banque Indosuez

Dresdner Bank Aktiengesellschaft   County NatWest Limited

Yamaichi International (Europe) Limited

Account titles that could be used in place of Paid-in Capital in Excess of Par—Common are *Additional Paid-in Capital—Common* and *Premium on Common Stock*. Since both par value and premium amounts increase the corporation's capital, they appear in the stockholders' equity section of the balance sheet.

At the end of the year, IHOP Corp. would report stockholders' equity on its balance sheet as follows, assuming that the corporate charter authorizes 40,000,000 shares of common stock and the balance of retained earnings is $26,000,000.

■ Daily Exercise 13-6
■ Daily Exercise 13-7

Stockholders' Equity	
Paid-in capital:	
Common stock, $0.01 par, 40 million shares authorized, 3.2 million shares issued	$ 32,000
Paid-in capital in excess of par	31,968,000
Total paid-in capital	32,000,000
Retained earnings	26,000,000
Total stockholders' equity	$58,000,000

We determine the dollar amount reported for common stock by multiplying the total number of shares *issued* (3.2 million) by the par value per share. The *authorization* reports the maximum number of shares the company may issue under its charter.

All of the transactions recorded in this section include a receipt of cash by the corporation as it issues new stock to its stockholders. These transactions are different from the vast majority of stock transactions reported each day in the financial press. In those transactions, one stockholder sells his or her stock to another investor, and the corporation makes no formal journal entry because its paid-in capital is unchanged.

Working It Out IHOP Corp. actually had total liabilities of $92 million on the balance sheet date just given. What was IHOP's debt ratio?

Answer: The debt ratio is 0.61:

$$\frac{\text{Total liabilities}}{\text{Total assets}} = \frac{\$92,000,000}{\$92,000,000 + \$58,000,000} = 0.61$$

ISSUING NO-PAR COMMON STOCK When a company issues stock that has no par value, there can be no premium. A recent survey of 600 companies revealed that they had 69 issues of no-par stock.

When a company issues no-par stock, it debits the asset received and credits the stock account. Glenwood Corporation, which manufactures skateboards, issues 3,000 shares of no-par common stock for $20 per share. The stock issuance entry is

Aug. 14	Cash (3,000 × $20)	60,000	
	Common Stock		60,000
	Issued no-par common stock.		

Regardless of the stock's price, Cash is debited and Common Stock is credited for the amount of cash received. There is no Paid-in Capital in Excess of Par for true no-par stock.

Glenwood Corporation's charter authorizes Glenwood to issue 10,000 shares of no-par stock, and the company has $46,000 in retained earnings. The corporation reports stockholders' equity on the balance sheet as follows:

Stockholders' Equity	
Paid-in capital:	
Common stock, no-par, 10,000 shares authorized, 3,000 shares issued	$ 60,000
Retained earnings	46,000
Total stockholders' equity	$106,000

ISSUING NO-PAR COMMON STOCK WITH A STATED VALUE Accounting for no-par stock with a stated value is identical to accounting for par-value stock. The premium account for no-par common stock with a stated value is entitled Paid-in Capital in Excess of Stated Value—Common.

■ Daily Exercise 13-8

ISSUING COMMON STOCK FOR ASSETS OTHER THAN CASH When a corporation issues stock in exchange for assets other than cash, it records the assets received at their current market value and credits the capital accounts accordingly. The assets' prior book value does not matter because the stockholder will demand stock equal to the market value of the asset given. Kahn Corporation issued 15,000 shares of its $1 par common stock for equipment worth $4,000 and a building worth $120,000. Kahn's entry is

Nov. 12	Equipment..	4,000	
	Building..	120,000	
	Common Stock (15,000 × $1)...............		15,000
	Paid-in Capital in Excess of Par—		
	Common ($124,000 – $15,000).........		109,000
	Issued common stock in exchange for equipment		
	and a building.		

Working It Out How did this transaction affect Kahn Corporation's cash? Total assets? Paid-in capital? Retained earnings? Total stockholders' equity?

■ Daily Exercise 13-9

Answer

	Cash	Total Assets	Paid-in Capital	Retained Earnings	Total Stockholders' Equity
Effect	None	Increase $124,000	Increase $124,000	None	Increase $124,000

Issuing Preferred Stock

Accounting for preferred stock follows the pattern we illustrated for common stock. The charter of Brown-Forman Corporation, a distilling company, authorizes issuance of 1,177,948 shares of 4%, $10 par preferred stock. [The 4% refers to the annual cash dividend rate on the stock. Each Brown-Forman preferred stockholder receives an annual cash dividend of $0.40 ($10 par × 0.04). Note that the dividend is computed based on the *par value*.] Assume that on July 31 the company issued all the shares at a price equal to the par value. The issuance entry is

July 31	Cash..	11,779,480	
	Preferred Stock (1,177,948 × $10)		11,779,480
	Issued preferred stock at par.		

If Brown-Forman had issued the preferred stock at a premium, the entry would have also credited an account titled Paid-in Capital in Excess of Par—Preferred. A corporation lists separate accounts for Paid-in Capital in Excess of Par on Preferred Stock and on Common Stock to differentiate the two classes of equity.

Accounting for no-par preferred stock follows the pattern illustrated for no-par common stock. When reporting stockholders' equity on the balance sheet, a corporation lists preferred stock, common stock, and retained earnings—in that order.

Ethical Considerations in Accounting for the Issuance of Stock

Issuance of stock for *cash* poses no serious ethical challenge. The company simply receives cash and issues the stock to the shareholders, giving them stock certificates as evidence of their purchase.

Issuing stock for assets other than cash can pose an ethical challenge, however. The company issuing the stock often wishes to record a large amount for the noncash asset received (such as land or a building) and for the stock that it is issuing. Why? Because large asset and stockholders' equity amounts on the balance sheet make the business look more prosperous and more creditworthy. The motivation to look good can inject a subtle bias into the amount recorded for stock issued in return for assets other than cash.

As we discussed on page 553, a company is supposed to record an asset received at its current market value. But one person's perception of a particular asset's market value can differ from another person's perception. One person may appraise land at a market value of $400,000. Another may honestly believe the land is worth only $300,000. A company receiving land in exchange for its stock must decide whether to record the land received and the stock issued at $300,000, at $400,000, or at some amount in between.

The ethical course of action is to record the asset at its current fair market value, as determined by a good-faith estimate of market value from independent appraisers. It is rare for a public corporation to be found guilty of *understating* the asset values on its balance sheet, but companies have been embarrassed by *overstating* their asset values. Investors who rely on the financial statements may be able to prove that an overstatement of asset values caused them to pay too much for the company's stock. In this case, a court of law may render a judgment against the company. For this reason, companies often tend to value assets conservatively in order to avoid an overstatement of their book value.

Donations Received by a Corporation

Corporations occasionally receive gifts, or *donations*. For example, city council members may offer a company free land to encourage it to locate in their city. Cities in the southern United States have lured some companies away from the North with such offers. The free land is a donation. For example, J.C. Penney Co. and American Airlines moved corporate headquarters from New York City to the Dallas–Fort Worth area because of concessions granted by the Texas cities. Also, a stockholder may make a donation to the corporation in the form of cash, land or other assets, or stock.

A donation increases the corporation's assets, but the donor (giver) receives no ownership interest in the company in return. A donation increases the corporation's revenue and thus affects income and retained earnings. The corporation records a donation by debiting the asset received at its current market value and by crediting Revenue from Donations, which is reported as Other Revenue on the income statement. But a donation received from a government entity is recorded as a credit to Donated Capital. For example, American Airlines would debit Land and credit Donated Capital for the value of any land it receives from a city or county government. Donated capital is a separate category of paid-in capital listed on the balance sheet after Common Stock and Paid-in Capital in Excess of Par.

■ Daily Exercise 13-10

Objective 3

Prepare the stockholders' equity section of a corporation's balance sheet

Review of Accounting for Paid-in Capital

Let's review the first half of this chapter by showing the stockholders' equity section of Medina Corporation's balance sheet in Exhibit 13-8. All amounts are assumed for the il-

EXHIBIT 13-8
Part of Medina Corporation's Balance Sheet

■ Daily Exercise 13-11

■ Daily Exercise 13-12

■ Daily Exercise 13-13

Stockholders' Equity	
Paid-in capital:	
Preferred stock, 5%, $100 par, 5,000 shares authorized, 400 shares issued	$ 40,000
Paid-in capital in excess of par—preferred	14,000
Common stock, $10 par, 20,000 shares authorized, 4,500 shares issued	45,000
Paid-in capital in excess of par—common	72,000
Donated capital	20,000
Total paid-in capital	191,000
Retained earnings	85,000
Total stockholders' equity	$276,000

lustration. Note the two sections of stockholders' equity: paid-in capital and retained earnings. Also observe the order of the equity accounts:

- Preferred stock at par value
- Paid-in capital in excess of par on preferred stock
- Common stock at par value
- Paid-in capital in excess of par on common stock
- Donated capital

Many companies combine several accounts, such as Paid-in Capital in Excess of Par—Common, plus Donated Capital, and report the sum as **Additional Paid-in Capital** on the balance sheet. However, they are careful not to include Paid-in Capital in Excess of Par—Preferred because that paid-in capital belongs to the preferred stockholders.

Additional Paid-in Capital. The sum of paid-in capital in excess of par—common plus donated capital and other accounts combined for reporting on the balance sheet.

Thinking It Over Examine Medina Corporation's stockholders' equity in Exhibit 13-8, and answer these questions.

1. How much did Medina's preferred stockholders pay into the corporation?
2. How much did the common stockholders pay into Medina Corporation?
3. What did the stockholders get for their payments into the company?
4. How does the donated capital differ from the other paid-in capital accounts?

Answers

1. $54,000 ($40,000 + $14,000)
2. $117,000 ($45,000 + $72,000)
3. The stockholders received stock, which represents their ownership in the assets of the corporation.
4. Donated capital represents a donation to the company for which the donor received no ownership interest in the assets of the company. The stock accounts and the paid-in capital in excess of par represent what the stockholders paid for their ownership in the company's assets.

Now review the Decision Guidelines feature to solidify your understanding of stockholders' equity as it is reported on the balance sheet.

DECISION GUIDELINES	Reporting Stockholders' Equity on the Balance Sheet
DECISION	**GUIDELINES**
What are the two main segments of stockholders' equity?	• Paid-in capital • Retained earnings
Which is more permanent, paid-in capital or retained earnings?	Paid-in capital is more permanent because corporations use their retained earnings for declaring dividends to the stockholders.
How are paid-in capital and retained earnings	
• Similar?	• Both represent the stockholders' equity (ownership) in the assets of the corporation.

• Different?	• Paid-in capital and retained earnings come from different *sources:*
	  a. Paid-in capital comes from the corporation's stockholders, who invested in the company.
	  b. Retained earnings comes from the corporation's customers. It was earned by the company's profitable operations.

What are the main categories of paid-in capital?	• Preferred stock
	• Common stock
	• Paid-in capital in excess of par on
	  a. Preferred stock
	  b. Common stock
	• Donated capital

1. Test your understanding of the first half of this chapter by answering whether each of the following statements is true or false:

   a. A stockholder may bind the corporation to a contract.

   b. The policy-making body in a corporation is called the board of directors.

   c. The owner of 100 shares of preferred stock has greater voting rights than the owner of 100 shares of common stock.

   d. Par-value stock is worth more than no-par stock.

   e. Issuance of 1,000 shares of $5 par-value stock at $12 increases contributed capital by $12,000.

   f. The issuance of no-par stock with a stated value is fundamentally different from issuing par-value stock.

   g. A corporation issues its preferred stock in exchange for land and a building with a combined market value of $200,000. This transaction increases the corporation's owners' equity by $200,000 regardless of the assets' prior book value.

2. The brewery Adolph Coors Company has two classes of common stock. Only the Class A common stockholders are entitled to vote. The company's balance sheet included the following presentation:

Shareholders' Equity	
Capital stock	
Class A common stock, voting, $1 par value, authorized and issued 1,260,000 shares......................	$ 1,260,000
Class B common stock, nonvoting, no-par value, authorized and issued 46,200,000 shares....................	11,000,000
	12,260,000
Additional paid-in capital	2,011,000
Retained earnings	872,403,000
	$886,674,000

REQUIRED

1. Record the issuance of the Class A common stock. Assume that the additional paid-in capital amount is related to the Class A common stock. Use the Coors account titles.

2. Record the issuance of the Class B common stock. Use the Coors account titles.

3. Rearrange the Coors stockholders' equity section to correspond to the following format:

Shareholders' Equity	
Paid-in capital:	
Class A common stock.......................................	$
Paid-in capital in excess of par—Class A common stock	
Class B common stock.......................................	
Total paid-in capital	
Retained earnings...	
Total shareholders' equity.....................................	$

4. What is the total paid-in capital of the company?

5. How did Coors withhold the voting privilege from the Class B common stockholders?

■ **SOLUTIONS**

1. Answers to true/false statements:

   a. False   b. True   c. False   d. False

   e. True   f. False   g. True

2. a. Cash 3,271,000

      Class A Common Stock... 1,260,000

      Additional Paid-in Capital... 2,011,000

      To record issuance of Class A common stock at a premium.

b. Cash.. 11,000,000

       Class B Common Stock 11,000,000

       To record issuance of Class B common stock.

c. Shareholders' Equity

    Paid-in capital:

Class A common stock, voting, $1 par value, authorized and issued 1,260,000 shares	$ 1,260,000
Paid-in capital in excess of par—Class A common stock	2,011,000
Class B common stock, nonvoting, no par value, authorized and issued 46,200,000 shares...	11,000,000
Total paid-in capital..	14,271,000
Retained earnings..	872,403,000
Total shareholders' equity...	$886,674,000

d. Total paid-in capital is $14,271,000, as shown in the answer to (c).

e. The voting privilege was withheld from stockholders by specific agreement with them.

Accounting for Cash Dividends

Corporations share the company's wealth with their owners, the stockholders, through dividends. Corporations declare dividends from retained earnings and pay the dividends with cash. The corporation must have enough retained earnings to declare the dividend and enough cash to pay the dividend.

Dividend Dates

A corporation must declare a dividend before paying it. The board of directors alone has the authority to declare a dividend. The corporation has no obligation to pay a dividend until the board declares one, but once declared, the dividend becomes a legal liability of the corporation. Three relevant dates for dividends are

1. *Declaration date.* On the declaration date, the board of directors announces the intention to pay the dividend. The declaration creates a liability for the corporation. Declaration is recorded by debiting Retained Earnings and crediting Dividends Payable.

2. *Date of record.* The corporation announces the record date, which follows the declaration date by a few weeks, as part of the declaration. The corporation makes no journal entry on the date of record because no transaction occurs. Nevertheless, much work takes place behind the scenes to properly identify the stockholders of record on this date because the stock is being traded continuously. Only the people who own the stock on the date of record receive the dividend.

3. *Payment date.* Payment of the dividend usually follows the record date by two to four weeks. Payment is recorded by debiting Dividends Payable and crediting Cash.

Dividends on Preferred and Common Stock

Declaration of a cash dividend is recorded by debiting Retained Earnings and crediting Dividends Payable as follows:[1]

Objective 4
Account for cash dividends

June 19   Retained Earnings XXX

              Dividends Payable   XXX

              Declared a cash dividend.

Payment of the dividend, which usually follows declaration by a few weeks, is recorded by debiting Dividends Payable and crediting Cash:

July 2   Dividends Payable XXX

              Cash.................................   XXX

             Paid the cash dividend.

■ **Daily Exercise 13-14**

---

[1]In Chapters 1–4, we debited the Dividends account, which is closed to Retained Earnings. Many businesses debit Retained Earnings directly, as shown here.

Case A: Total dividend of $150,000	
Preferred dividend (9,000 shares × $1.75 per share).............	$ 15,750
Common dividend ($150,000 – $15,750).............................	134,250
Total dividend	$150,000
Case B: Total dividend of $20,000	
Preferred dividend (9,000 shares × $1.75 per share).............	$ 15,750
Common dividend ($20,000 – $15,750)..............................	4,250
Total dividend	$ 20,000
Case C: Total dividend of $8,000	
Preferred dividend (the full $8,000 goes to preferred because the annual preferred dividend is $15,750)	$ 8,000
Common dividend (none because the total dividend did not cover the preferred dividend for the year)............	-0-
Total dividend	$ 8,000

If Pine Industries' annual dividend is large enough to cover the preferred dividend for the year (Cases A and B), the preferred stockholders receive their regular dividend, and the common stockholders receive the remainder. But if the year's dividend falls below the amount of the annual preferred dividend (Case C), the preferred stockholders receive the entire dividend, and the common stockholders receive nothing that year.

Dividends Payable is a current liability. When a company has issued both preferred and common stock, the preferred stockholders receive their dividends first. The common stockholders receive dividends only if the total declared dividend is large enough to pay the preferred stockholders first.

In addition to its common stock, Pine Industries, Inc., has 9,000 shares of preferred stock outstanding. Preferred dividends are paid at the annual rate of $1.75 per share. Exhibit 13-9 shows the division between preferred and common for three amounts of the total annual dividend declared by Pine Industries.

This example illustrates an important relationship between preferred stock and common stock. To an investor, the preferred stock is safer because it receives dividends first. However, the earnings potential from an investment in common stock is much greater than from an investment in preferred stock. Preferred dividends are usually limited to the specified amount, but there is no upper limit on the amount of common dividends.

When a company has more than one class of preferred stock or common stock, the division of dividends among the various classes of stock follows this same pattern: the preferred stock with the most senior rights gets the first dividends, and so on.

We noted that preferred stockholders enjoy the advantage of priority over common stockholders in receiving dividends. The dividend preference is stated as a percentage rate or a dollar amount. For example, preferred stock may be "6% preferred," which means that owners of the preferred stock receive an annual dividend of 6% of the par value of the stock. If par value is $100 per share, preferred stockholders receive an annual cash dividend of $6 per share (6% of $100). The preferred stock may be "$3 preferred," which means that stockholders receive an annual dividend of $3 per share regardless of the preferred stock's par value. The dividend rate on no-par preferred stock is stated in a dollar amount per share.

■ **Daily Exercise 13-15**

Dividends on Cumulative and Noncumulative Preferred Stock

The allocation of dividends may be complex if the preferred stock is *cumulative*. Corporations sometimes fail to pay a dividend to their preferred stockholders. This occurrence is called *passing the dividend*, and the passed dividends are said to be *in arrears*. The owners of **cumulative preferred stock** must receive all dividends in arrears plus the current year's dividend before the corporation pays dividends to the common stockholders.

Cumulative Preferred Stock.
Preferred stock whose owners must receive all dividends in arrears before the corporation pays dividends to the common stockholders.

The preferred stock of Pine Industries is cumulative. Suppose the company passed the 19X4 preferred dividend of $15,750. Before paying dividends to its common stockholders in 19X5, the company must first pay preferred dividends of $15,750 for both 19X4 and 19X5, a total of $31,500. *Preferred stock is cumulative in the eyes of the law unless it is labeled as noncumulative.*

Assume that Pine Industries passes its 19X4 preferred dividend. In 19X5, the company declares a $50,000 dividend. The entry to record the declaration is

Sep. 6	Retained Earnings...	50,000	
	Dividends Payable, Preferred ($15,750 × 2).........		31,500
	Dividends Payable, Common		
	($50,000 – $31,500)...		18,500
	Declared a cash dividend.		

If the preferred stock is *noncumulative*, the corporation is not obligated to pay dividends in arrears. Suppose that the Pine Industries preferred stock was noncumulative and the company passed the 19X4 preferred dividend of $15,750. The preferred stockholders would lose the 19X4 dividend forever. Of course, the common stockholders would not receive a 19X4 dividend either. Before paying any common dividends in 19X5, the company would have to pay the 19X5 preferred dividend of $15,750.

Having dividends in arrears on cumulative preferred stock is *not* a liability for the corporation. (A liability for dividends arises only after the board of directors declares the dividend.) Nevertheless, a corporation must report cumulative preferred dividends in arrears. This information alerts common stockholders as to how much in cumulative preferred dividends must be paid before any dividends will be paid on the common stock. This information gives the common stockholders an idea about the likelihood of receiving dividends and satisfies the disclosure principle.

Dividends in arrears are often disclosed in notes, as follows (all dates and amounts assumed). Observe the two references to Note 3 in this section of the balance sheet. The "6%" after "Preferred stock" is the dividend rate.

Preferred stock, 6%, $50 par, 2,000 shares issued (Note 3)	$100,000
Retained earnings (Note 3)...	414,000

Note 3—Cumulative preferred dividends in arrears. At December 31, 19X2, dividends on the company's 6% preferred stock were in arrears for 19X1 and 19X2, in the amount of $12,000 (6% × $100,000 × 2 years).

Convertible Preferred Stock

Convertible preferred stock may be exchanged by the preferred stockholders, if they choose, for another class of stock in the corporation. For example, the Pine Industries preferred stock may be converted into the company's common stock. A note to Pine's balance sheet describes the conversion terms as follows:

> The . . . preferred stock is convertible at the rate of 6.51 shares of common stock for each share of preferred stock outstanding.

If you owned 100 shares of Pine's convertible preferred stock, you could convert it into 651 (100 × 6.51) shares of Pine common stock. Under what condition would you exercise the conversion privilege? You would do so if the market value of the common stock that you could receive from conversion exceeded the market value of the preferred stock that you presently hold. This way, you as an investor could increase your personal wealth.

Different Values of Stock

There are several different *stock values* in addition to par value. Market value, redemption value, liquidation value, and book value are used for various investor decisions.

Market Value

A stock's **market value,** or *market price*, is the price for which a person could buy or sell a share of the stock. The issuing corporation's net income, financial position, and future prospects and the general economic conditions determine market value. Daily newspapers

Convertible Preferred Stock. Preferred stock that may be exchanged by the preferred stockholders, if they choose, for another class of stock in the corporation.

Market Value. Price for which a person could buy or sell a share of stock.

report the market price of many stocks. Corporate annual reports report the high and the low market values of the company's common stock for each quarter of the year. *In almost all cases, stockholders are more concerned about the market value of a stock than about any of the other values discussed next.* In the chapter opening story, IHOP's most recent stock price was quoted at 36, which means that the stock could be sold for, or bought for, $36 per share. The purchase of 100 shares of IHOP stock would cost $3,600 ($36.00 × 100), plus a commission. If you were selling 100 shares of IHOP stock, you would receive cash of $3,600 less a commission. The commission is the fee an investor pays to a stockbroker for buying or selling the stock. The price of a share of IHOP stock has fluctuated from $10 at issuance to a recent high of $44.75.

> **Learning Tip:** If you buy stock in IBM from another investor, IBM gets no cash. The transaction is a sale between investors. IBM records only the change in stockholder name.

Redemption Value

Preferred stock that requires the company to redeem (pay to retire) the stock at a set price is called *redeemable preferred stock*. The company is *obligated* to redeem the preferred stock. The price the corporation agrees to pay for the stock, which is set when the stock is issued, is called the *redemption value*. Some preferred stock is *callable*, which means that the company may call (pay to retire) the stock if it wishes. The preferred stock of Pine Industries, Inc., is "callable at the option of the Company at $25 per share."

Beginning in 2001, Pine is "required to redeem annually 6,765 shares of the preferred stock ($169,125 annually)." Pine's annual redemption payment to the preferred stockholders will include this redemption value plus any dividends in arrears. In the year 2000, Pine Industries' preferred stock ceases to be owners' equity and becomes a liability. Starting in 2001, Pine must start paying off the preferred stock as though it were debt.

■ Daily Exercise 13-16

Thinking It Over Suppose you are a banker and Pine Industries asks you for a large long-term loan in the year 2000. If you overlook Pine's obligation to pay off its preferred stock, what error are you likely to make in evaluating the loan request?

Answer: By ignoring Pine's obligation to pay off its preferred stock, you may lend money to Pine on too-favorable terms. For example, you may be willing to lend more money to Pine Industries than the company is able to pay back. Or you may give Pine too much time to pay you back. In either case, you run the risk of failing to collect the loan.

Liquidation Value

The *liquidation value*, which applies only to preferred stock, is the amount the corporation agrees to pay the preferred stockholder per share if the company liquidates. Dividends in arrears are added to liquidation value in determining the payment to the preferred stockholders if the company liquidates. Some companies report their preferred stock at its liquidation value on the balance sheet. Consider the BF Goodrich Company, which makes chemicals and aerospace components and sells tires under the Michelin label. BF Goodrich has 2.2 million shares of convertible preferred stock that is stated at "a liquidation value of $50 per share." The balance in BF Goodrich's preferred stock account is thus $110 million (2.2 million shares × $50).

Book Value

Book Value. Amount of owners' equity on the company's books for each share of its stock.

The **book value** of a stock is the amount of owners' equity on the company's books for each share of its stock. Corporations often report this amount in their annual reports. If the company has only common stock outstanding, its book value is computed by dividing total stockholders' equity by the number of shares *outstanding*. A company with stockholders' equity of $180,000 and 5,000 shares of common stock outstanding has a book value of $36 per share ($180,000/5,000 shares).

If the company has both preferred and common stock outstanding, the preferred stockholders have the first claim to owners' equity. Ordinarily, preferred stock has a specified liquidation or redemption value. The book value of preferred stock is its redemption value plus any cumulative dividends in arrears on the stock. Its book value *per share* equals the sum of redemption value and any cumulative dividends in arrears divided by the number of preferred shares *outstanding*. After the corporation figures the book value of the preferred shares, it computes the common stock book value per share. The corporation divides the common equity (total stockholders' equity minus preferred equity) by the number of common shares outstanding.

The company balance sheet reports the following amounts:

Stockholders' Equity	
Paid-in capital:	
Preferred stock, 6%, $10 par, 5,000 shares authorized,	
5,000 shares issued (redemption value $13 per share).........	$ 50,000
Paid-in capital in excess of par—preferred..............................	14,000
Common stock, $1 par, 20,000 shares authorized,	
15,000 shares issued...	15,000
Paid-in capital in excess of par—common..............................	172,000
Donated capital	40,000
Total paid-in capital..	291,000
Retained earnings...	122,000
Total stockholders' equity	$413,000

Suppose that four years' (including the current year) cumulative preferred dividends are in arrears. The book-value-per-share computations for this corporation are as follows:

Preferred

Redemption value (5,000 shares × $13).......................	$ 65,000
Cumulative dividends ($50,000 × 0.06 × 4).................	12,000
Stockholders' equity allocated to preferred	$ 77,000
Book value per share ($77,000/5,000 shares).............	$ 15.40

Common

Total stockholders' equity...	$413,000
Less stockholders' equity allocated to preferred.........	(77,000)
Stockholders' equity allocated to common	$336,000
Book value per share ($336,000/15,000 shares)..........	$ 22.40

■ **Daily Exercise 13-17**

If the preferred stock has no specified redemption value, then we would use the sum of par value plus paid-in capital in excess of par–preferred, $64,000, plus cumulative dividends to compute the book value of the preferred stock.

BOOK VALUE AND DECISION MAKING   How is book value per share used in decision making? Companies negotiating the purchase of a corporation may wish to know the book value of its stock. The book value of stockholders' equity may figure into the negotiated purchase price of a corporation whose stock is not publicly traded. Also, a corporation may buy out a retiring executive or other stockholder, agreeing to pay the book value of the person's stock in the company.

Some investors have traditionally compared the book value of a share of a company's stock with the stock's market value. The idea was that a stock selling below its book value was underpriced and thus a good buy. The relationship between book value and market value is far from clear. Some investors believe that a company whose stock sells at a price below book value must be experiencing financial difficulty.

Book value is a product of the accounting system, which is based on historical costs. Market value, conversely, depends on investors' subjective outlook for dividends and increases in the stock's value. Exhibit 13-10 contrasts the book values and ranges of market

■ **Daily Exercise 13-18**

EXHIBIT 13-10
Book Value and Market Value for Three Companies

	Year-End Book Value	52-Week Market-Value Range
IHOP Corp.	$11.55	$19.25–$ 37.38
Toys "Я" Us	12.57	$24.38–$ 37.63
IBM	40.47	$56.25–$109.44

values for the common stocks of three well-known companies. For all three companies, the market value of stock exceeds its book value—a mark of success.

Evaluating Operations: Rate of Return on Total Assets and Rate of Return on Common Stockholders' Equity

Objective 6

Evaluate a company's return on assets and return on stockholders' equity

Investors and creditors are constantly evaluating managers' ability to earn profits. Investors search for companies whose stocks are likely to increase in value. Investment decisions often include a comparison of companies. But a comparison of IHOP's net income with the net income of a new company in the restaurant industry simply is not meaningful. IHOP's profits may run into the millions of dollars, which far exceed a new company's net income. To compare companies of different size, investors use some standard profitability measures, including rate of return on total assets and rate of return on stockholders' equity.

Return on Assets

Rate of Return on Total Assets. The sum of net income plus interest expense divided by average total assets. This ratio measures the success a company has in using its assets to earn income for the persons who finance the business. Also called **return on assets.**

The **rate of return on total assets,** or simply **return on assets,** measures a company's success in using its assets to earn income for the persons who are financing the business. Creditors have loaned money to the corporation and thus earn interest. The stockholders have invested in the corporation's stock and therefore own the company's net income. The sum of interest expense and net income is the return to the two groups that have financed the corporation's assets, and this is the numerator of the return-on-assets ratio. The denominator is average total assets. Return on assets is computed as follows, using data from the 1996 annual report of IHOP Corp. (dollar amounts in thousands of dollars):

$$\text{Rate of return on total assets} = \frac{\text{Net income} + \text{Interest expense}}{\text{Average total assets}}$$

$$= \frac{\$18,604 + \$11,691}{(\$252,057 + \$328,889)/2} = \frac{\$30,295}{\$290,473} = 0.104$$

Net income and interest expense are taken from the income statement. Average total assets is computed from the beginning and ending balance sheets.

Investors use return on assets to compare companies in terms of how well their management earns a return for the people who finance the corporation. By relating the sum of net income and interest expense to average total assets, they have a standard measure that describes the profitability of all types of companies. Brokerage companies such as Merrill Lynch and Paine Webber often single out particular industries as likely sources of good investments. For example, brokerage analysts may believe that the health-care industry is in a growth phase. These analysts would identify specific health-care companies whose profitabilities are likely to lead the industry and so be sound investments. Return on assets is one measure of profitability.

What is a good rate of return on total assets? There is no single answer to this question because rates of return vary widely by industry. For example, high technology companies earn much higher returns than do utility companies, groceries, and manufacturers of consumer goods such as toothpaste.

Return on Equity

Rate of Return on Common Stockholders' Equity. Net income minus preferred dividends, divided by average common stockholders' equity. A measure of profitability. Also called **return on equity.**

Rate of return on common stockholders' equity, often called **return on equity,** shows the relationship between net income and average common stockholders' equity. The numerator is net income minus preferred dividends. Preferred dividends are subtracted because the preferred stockholders have the first claim on the company's net income. The denominator is average *common stockholders' equity*—total stockholders' equity minus preferred equity. IHOP's rate of return on common stockholders' equity for 1996 is computed as follows (dollar amounts in thousands of dollars):

$$
\begin{array}{c}
\text{Rate of return} \\
\text{on common} \\
\text{stockholders'} \\
\text{equity}
\end{array}
= \frac{\text{Net income} - \text{Preferred dividends}}{\text{Average common stockholders' equity}}
$$

$$
= \frac{\$18,604 - \$0}{(\$108,297 + \$129,357)/2} = \frac{\$18,604}{\$118,827} = 0.157
$$

■ **Daily Exercise 13-19**

IHOP Corp. has no preferred stock, so preferred dividends are zero. With no preferred stock outstanding, average *common* stockholders' equity is the same as average *total* equity—the average of the beginning and ending amounts.

IHOP's return on equity (15.7%) is higher than its return on assets (10.4%). This difference results from the interest-expense component of return on assets. Companies such as IHOP borrow at one rate (say, 7%) and invest the funds to earn a higher rate (say, 16%). Borrowing at a lower rate than the return on investments is called *using leverage*. During good times, leverage produces high returns for stockholders. However, too much leverage can make it difficult to pay the interest on the debt. The company's creditors are guaranteed a fixed rate of return on their loans. But because the stockholders have no guarantee that the corporation will earn net income, their investments are riskier. Consequently, stockholders demand a higher rate of return than do creditors, which explains why *return on equity should exceed return on assets*. If return on assets is higher than return on equity, the company is in trouble. Interest expense should always be lower than the amount the company earns on its investments.

Investors and creditors use return on common stockholders' equity in much the same way they use return on total assets—to compare companies. The higher the rate of return, the more successful the company. IHOP's 15.7% return on common stockholders' equity would be considered good in most industries. Investors also compare a company's return on stockholders' equity with interest rates available in the market. If interest rates are almost as high as return on equity, many investors will lend their money to earn interest. They choose to forgo the extra risk of investing in stock when the rate of return on equity is too low.

■ **Daily Exercise 13-20**

Accounting for Income Taxes by Corporations

Corporations pay income tax in the same way that individuals do. Corporate and personal tax rates differ, however. At this writing, the federal tax rate on most corporate income is 35 percent. Most states also levy their own income taxes on corporations, so most corporations have a combined federal and state income tax rate of approximately 40 percent.

To account for income tax, the corporation measures for each period:

- Income tax expense, an expense on the income statement
- Income tax payable, a liability on the balance sheet

Accounting for income tax by a corporation follows the general principles that govern accounting for all other transactions. Let's return to IHOP Corp. In 19X6, IHOP reported income before tax (also called pretax accounting income) of approximately $30 million on its income statement. IHOP's combined income tax rate was 40 percent. Assume IHOP's income tax expense and income tax payable are the same. Then IHOP would record income tax for the year as follows (amounts in millions):

Objective 7

Account for a corporation's income tax

19X6		
Dec. 31	Income Tax Expense ($30 × 0.40)..........	12
	Income Tax Payable	12
	Recorded income tax for the year.	

IHOP's 19X6 financial statements would report these figures (adapted, in millions):

Income statement		Balance sheet	
Income before income tax..........	$ 30	Current liabilities:	
Income tax expense....................	(12)	Income tax payable..........	$12
Net income................................	$ 18		

Early in 19X7, IHOP would pay its income tax payable when the company files its 19X6 income tax return with the Internal Revenue Service.

In general, income tax expense and income tax payable can be computed as follows:[2]

$$\text{Income tax expense} = \text{Income before income tax (from the income statement)} \times \text{Income tax rate}$$

$$\text{Income tax payable} = \text{Taxable income (from the income tax return filed with the IRS)} \times \text{Income tax rate}$$

The income statement and the income tax return are entirely separate documents:

- The income statement reports the results of operations that we have been working with throughout this course.
- The income tax return is filed with the Internal Revenue Service to determine how much tax the company must pay the government.

For most companies, income tax expense and income tax payable differ. Certain items of revenue and expense enter into the determination of income at different times for the purposes of measuring income for accounting purposes and for measuring taxable income for income tax purposes. The most important difference between income before income tax and taxable income occurs when a corporation uses the straight-line method to compute depreciation for the financial statements and an accelerated depreciation method for the tax return and the payment of taxes. The tax depreciation method is called the *modified accelerated cost recovery system*, abbreviated as MACRS. ◀▥ For any one year, MACRS depreciation listed on the tax return may differ from accounting depreciation on the income statement.

◀▥◀▥◀▥ We learned in Chapter 10, page 434, that the MACRS depreciation method is similar to the double-declining-balance method.

Continuing with the IHOP illustration, suppose for 19X7 that IHOP Corp. has

- Pretax accounting income of $40 million on the income statement
- Taxable income of $35 million on the company's income tax return

IHOP will record income tax for 19X7 as follows (dollar amounts in millions and an income tax rate of 40%):

19X7			
Dec. 31	Income Tax Expense ($40 × 0.40)	16	
	Income Tax Payable ($35 × 0.40)		14
	Deferred Tax Liability		2
	Recorded income tax for the year.		

IHOP's 19X7 financial statements would report these figures (adapted, in millions):

Income statement		Balance sheet	
Income before income tax..........	$ 40	Current liabilities:	
Income tax expense....................	(16)	Income tax payable.............	$14
Net income................................	$ 24	Long-term liabilities:	
		Deferred tax liability..........	2*
		*Assumes the beginning balance of Deferred tax liability was zero.	

[2]The authors thank Jean Marie Hudson for suggesting this presentation.

Early in 19X8, IHOP would pay its income tax payable of $14 million because this is a current liability. Deferred tax liability, however, is usually long-term, and the company may pay this liability over a longer period.

■ **Daily Exercise 13-21**

The Decision Guidelines feature provides an overview of the second half of the chapter.

DECISION GUIDELINES	Dividends, Stock Values, Evaluating Operations, & Accounting for Income Tax
DECISION	**GUIDELINES**
Dividends Whether to declare a cash dividend?	• Must have enough retained earnings to declare the dividend. • Must have enough cash to pay the dividend.
What happens with a dividend?	• The corporation's board of directors declares the dividend. Then the dividend becomes a liability of the corporation. • The date of record fixes who will receive the dividend. • Payment of the dividend occurs later.
Who receives the dividend?	• Preferred stockholders first receive their dividends at a specified rate. • Common stockholders receive the remainder.
Stock Values How much to pay for a stock?	Its market value.
What unique values apply to preferred stock?	• Redemption value—the amount the corporation must pay to redeem (retire) the stock • Liquidation value—the amount the corporation agrees to pay if the company liquidates
What is book value's role in decision making?	Sometimes used to help determine the market value of a stock that is not traded on a stock exchange.
Evaluating Operations How to evaluate the operations of a corporation?	There are many ways. Two measures that relate earnings to the amount that stockholders have invested include • Rate of return on assets • Rate of return on common stockholders' equity For a healthy company, return on stockholders' equity should exceed return on assets.
Accounting for Income Tax What are the three main accounts?	• Income tax expense • Income tax payable, a current liability • Deferred tax liability, usually a long-term liability
How to measure • Income tax expense?	$\dfrac{\text{Income before income tax}}{\text{(from the income statement)}} \times \text{Income tax rate}$
• Income tax payable?	$\begin{array}{c}\text{Taxable income (from the income}\\ \text{tax return filed with the}\\ \text{Internal Revenue Service)}\end{array} \times \text{Income tax rate}$
• Deferred tax liability?	Difference between income tax expense and income tax payable for any one year

1. Use the following accounts and related balances to prepare the classified balance sheet of Whitehall, Inc., at September 30, 19X4. Use the account format of the balance sheet.

Common stock, $1 par, 50,000 shares authorized, 20,000 shares issued	$ 20,000	Long-term note payable	$ 73,000
		Inventory	85,000
Dividends payable	4,000	Property, plant, and equipment, net	225,000
Cash	9,000	Revenue from donations	18,000
Accounts payable	28,000	Accounts receivable, net	23,000
Retained earnings	75,000	Preferred stock, $3.75, no-par, 10,000 shares authorized, 2,000 shares issued	24,000
Paid-in capital in excess of par—common	115,000	Accrued liabilities	3,000

2. The balance sheet of Trendline Corporation reported the following at March 31, 19X6, the end of its fiscal year. Note that Trendline reports paid-in capital in excess of par or stated value after the stock accounts.

Stockholders' Equity	
Preferred stock, 4%, $10 par, 10,000 shares authorized (redemption value, $110,000)	$100,000
Common stock, no-par, $5 stated value, 100,000 shares authorized	250,000
Paid-in capital in excess of par:	
Common stock	231,500
Retained earnings	395,000
Total stockholders' equity	$976,500

REQUIRED

1. Is the preferred stock cumulative or noncumulative? How can you tell?
2. What is the total amount of the annual preferred dividend?
3. How many shares of preferred and common stock has the company issued?
4. Compute the book value per share of the preferred and the common stock. No prior year preferred dividends are in arrears, but Trendline has not declared the current-year dividend.

■ SOLUTION

WHITEHALL, INC.
Balance Sheet
September 30, 19X4

Assets		Liabilities	
Current:		**Current:**	
Cash	$ 9,000	Accounts payable	$ 28,000
Accounts receivable, net	23,000	Dividends payable	4,000
Inventory	85,000	Accrued liabilities	3,000
Total current assets	117,000	Total current liabilities	35,000
Property, plant and equipment, net	225,000	Long-term note payable	73,000
		Total liabilities	108,000

Stockholders' Equity		
Paid-in capital:		
Preferred stock, $3.75, no-par, 10,000 shares authorized, 2,000 shares issued	$ 24,000	
Common stock, $1 par, 50,000 shares authorized, 20,000 shares issued	20,000	
Paid-in capital in excess of par—common	115,000	
Total paid-in capital	159,000	
Retained earnings	75,000	
Total stockholders' equity		234,000
Total liabilities and stockholders' equity		$342,000

Total assets	$342,000

1. The preferred stock is cumulative because it is not specifically labeled otherwise.
2. Total annual preferred dividend: $4,000 ($100,000 × 0.04).
3. Preferred stock issued: 10,000 shares ($100,000/$10 par value).
   Common stock issued: 50,000 shares ($250,000/$5 stated value).
4. Book values per share of preferred and common stock:

Preferred:
Redemption value	$110,000
Cumulative dividend for current year ($100,000 × 0.04)	4,000
Stockholders' equity allocated to preferred	$114,000
Book value per share ($114,000/10,000 shares)	$ 11.40

Common:
Total stockholders' equity	$976,500
Less stockholders' equity allocated to preferred	(114,000)
Stockholders' equity allocated to common	$862,500
Book value per share ($862,500/50,000 shares)	$ 17.25

Summary of Learning Objectives

1. Identify the characteristics of a corporation. A corporation is a separate legal and business entity. *Continuous life*, the *ease of raising large amounts of capital and transferring ownership*, and *limited liability* are among the advantages of the corporate form of organization. An important disadvantage is *double taxation*. Corporations pay *income taxes*, and stockholders pay tax on dividends. *Stockholders* are the owners of the corporations. They elect a *board of directors*, which elects a chairperson and appoints the officers to manage the business.

2. Record the issuance of stock. Corporations may issue different classes of stock: *par value, no-par value, common*, and *preferred*. Stock is usually issued at a *premium*—an amount above par value.

3. Prepare the stockholders' equity section of a corporation's balance sheet. The balance sheet carries the capital raised through stock issuance under the heading Paid-in Capital or Contributed Capital in the stockholders' equity section.

4. Account for cash dividends. Only when the board of directors declares a *dividend* does the corporation incur the liability to pay dividends. Preferred stock has priority over common stock as to dividends, which may be stated as a percentage of par value or as a dollar amount per share. In addition, preferred stock has a claim to dividends in arrears if it is *cumulative. Convertible* preferred stock may be exchanged for the corporation's common stock.

5. Use different stock values in decision making. A stock's *market value* is the price for which a share may be bought or sold. *Redemption value, liquidation value*, and *book value*—the amount of owners' equity per share of company stock—are other values that may apply to stock.

6. Evaluate a company's return on assets and return on stockholders' equity. *Return on assets* and *return on stockholders' equity* are two standard measures of profitability. A healthy company's return on equity will exceed its return on assets.

7. Account for a corporation's income tax. Corporations pay income tax and must account for the income tax expense and income tax payable. A difference between the expense and the payable creates another account, Deferred Tax Liability.

Accounting Vocabulary

additional paid-in capital
  (p. 555)
authorization of stock
  (p. 550)
board of directors
  (p. 545)
book value (p. 560)
bylaws (p. 545)
chairperson (p. 545)
charter (p. 544)
common stock (p. 547)
contributed capital
  (p. 547)

convertible preferred stock
  (p. 559)
cumulative preferred stock
  (p. 558)
deficit (p. 548)
dividends (p. 548)
double taxation (p. 545)
legal capital (p. 548)
limited liability (p. 544)
market value (p. 559)
outstanding stock
  (p. 546)
paid-in capital (p. 547)

par value (p. 549)
preferred stock (p. 549)
president (p. 545)
rate of return on common
  stockholders' equity
  (p. 562)
rate of return on total assets
  (p. 562)
retained earnings (p. 547)
return on assets (p. 562)
return on equity (p. 562)
shareholder (p. 544)
stated value (p. 549)

stock (p. 544)
stockholder (p. 544)
stockholders' equity
  (p. 547)

Questions

1. Why is a corporation called a creature of the state?
2. Identify the characteristics of a corporation.
3. Explain why corporations face a tax disadvantage.
4. Briefly outline the steps in the organization of a corporation.
5. How are the structures of a partnership and a corporation similar, and how are they different?

6. Name the four rights of a stockholder. Is preferred stock automatically nonvoting? Explain how a right may be withheld from a stockholder.

7. Dividends on preferred stock may be stated as a percentage rate or a dollar amount. What is the annual dividend on these preferred stocks: 4%, $100 par; $3.50, $20 par; and 6%, no-par with $50 stated value?

8. Which event increases the assets of the corporation: authorization of stock or issuance of stock? Explain.

9. Suppose H. J. Heinz Company issued 1,000 shares of its 3.65%, $100 par preferred stock for $120. How much would this transaction increase the company's paid-in capital? How much would it increase Heinz's retained earnings? How much would it increase Heinz's annual cash dividend payments?

10. Give two alternative account titles for Paid-in Capital in Excess of Par—Common Stock.

11. How does issuance of 1,000 shares of no-par stock for land and a building, together worth $150,000, affect paid-in capital?

12. Rank the following accounts in the order they would appear on the balance sheet: Common Stock, Preferred Stock, Retained Earnings, Dividends Payable. Also, give each account's balance sheet classification.

13. Briefly discuss the three important dates for a dividend.

14. Mancini, Inc., has 3,000 shares of its $2.50, $10 par preferred stock outstanding. Dividends for 19X1 and 19X2 are in arrears, and the company has declared no dividends on preferred stock for the current year, 19X3. Assume that Mancini declares total dividends of $35,000 at the end of 19X3. Show how to allocate the dividends to preferred and common if preferred is (a) cumulative, or (b) noncumulative.

15. As a preferred stockholder, would you rather own cumulative or noncumulative preferred? If all other factors are the same, would the corporation rather the preferred stock be cumulative or noncumulative? Give your reason.

16. How are cumulative preferred dividends in arrears reported in the financial statements? When do dividends become a liability of the corporation?

17. Distinguish between the market value of stock and the book value of stock. Which is more important to investors?

18. How is book value per share of common stock computed when the company has both preferred stock and common stock outstanding?

19. Why should a healthy company's rate of return on stockholders' equity exceed its rate of return on total assets?

20. Explain the difference between the income tax expense and the income tax payable of a corporation.

Daily Exercises

Characteristics of a corporation
(Obj. 1)

DE13-1 Suppose you are forming a business and you need some outside money from other investors. Assume you have decided to organize the business as a corporation that will issue stock to raise the needed funds. Briefly discuss your most important reason for organizing as a corporation rather than as a partnership. If you had decided to organize as a partnership, what would be your most important reason for not organizing as a corporation?

Authority structure in a corporation
(Obj. 1)

DE13-2 Consider the authority structure in a corporation, as diagrammed in Exhibit 13-2, page 546.

1. What group holds the ultimate power in a corporation?
2. Who is the most powerful person in the corporation?
3. Who is in charge of day-to-day operations?
4. Who manages the accounting?
5. Who has primary responsibility for the corporation's cash?

Similarities and differences between the balance sheets of a corporation and a proprietorship
(Obj. 1)

DE13-3 Examine the summarized balance sheet of Wal-Mart Stores, Inc., in Exhibit 13-4, page 547. Suppose Wal-Mart Stores were a proprietorship owned by Sam Walton. How would the Wal-Mart proprietorship balance sheet differ from the one given in Exhibit 13-4? How would the proprietorship balance sheet be similar to the one given in Exhibit 13-4?

Characteristics of preferred and common stock
(Obj. 1)

DE13-4 Answer the following questions about the characteristics of a corporation's stock.

1. Which stockholders are the real owners of a corporation?
2. Which right clearly distinguishes a stockholder from a creditor (who has lent money to the corporation)?
3. What privileges do preferred stockholders enjoy that common stockholders do not have?
4. Which class of stockholders would expect to reap greater benefits from a highly profitable corporation? Why?

Effect of a stock issuance on net income
(Obj. 2)

DE13-5 Study IHOP's July 23 stock issuance entry given on page 550, and answer these questions about the nature of the IHOP transaction.

1. IHOP received $32,000,000 for the issuance of its stock. The par value of the IHOP stock was only $32,000. Was the excess amount of $31,968,000 a profit to IHOP? If not, what was it?
2. Suppose the par value of the IHOP stock had been $1 per share, $5 per share, or $10 per share. Would a change in the par value of the company's stock affect IHOP's net income? Give the reason for your answer.

DE13-6 The Coca-Cola Company reported the following on its balance sheet at December 31, 1997 (adapted, amounts in millions, except for par value):

Issuing stock and interpreting stockholders' equity (Obj. 2)

Common stock, $0.25 par value	
Authorized: 5,600 shares	
Issued: 3,443 shares	$ 861
Paid-in capital in excess of par	1,527
Retained earnings	17,869

1. Assume Coca-Cola issued all of its stock during 1997. Journalize the company's issuance of the stock for cash.
2. Was Coca-Cola's main source of stockholders' equity paid-in capital or profitable operations? How can you tell?

DE13-7 At December 31, 1997, The Coca-Cola Company reported the following on its comparative balance sheet, which included 1996 amounts for comparison (adapted, with all amounts except par value in millions):

Issuing stock and analyzing retained earnings (Obj. 2)

	December 31, 1997	1996
Common stock $0.25 par value		
Authorized: 5,600 shares		
Issued: 3,443 shares in 1997	$ 861	
3,433 shares in 1996		$ 858
Paid-in capital in excess of par	1,527	1,058
Retained earnings	17,869	15,127

1. How much did Coca-Cola's total paid-in capital increase during 1997? What caused total paid-in capital to increase? How can you tell?
2. Journalize Coca-Cola's issuance of stock for cash during 1997.
3. Did Coca-Cola have a profit or a loss for 1997? How can you tell?

DE13-8 Steitz Corporation has three classes of stock: Common, $1 par; Preferred Class A, $10 par; and Preferred Class B, no-par.
Journalize Steitz's issuance of

Issuing stock (Obj. 2)

a. 1,000 shares of common stock for $40 per share
b. 1,000 shares of class A preferred stock for a total of $25,000
c. 1,000 shares of class B preferred stock for $18 per share

Explanations are not required.

DE13-9 This exercise shows the similarity and the difference between two ways to acquire plant assets.
Case A—Issue stock and buy the assets in separate transactions:

Issuing stock to finance the purchase of assets (Obj. 2)

Data Warehouse, Inc., issued 10,000 shares of its $5 par common stock for cash of $700,000. In a separate transaction, Data Warehouse then used the cash to purchase a warehouse building for $600,000 and equipment for $100,000. Journalize the two transactions.

Case B—Issue stock to acquire the assets:

Data Warehouse issued 10,000 shares of its $5 par common stock to acquire a warehouse building valued at $600,000 and equipment worth $100,000. Journalize this transaction.

Compare the balances in all accounts after making both sets of entries. Are the account balances similar or different?

DE13-10 Suppose Lands' End received two donations as follows:

Accounting for receipt of two donations (Obj. 3)

a. Land worth $8,400,000 received from the city of Dodgeville, Wisconsin
b. A company recreation center valued at $2,000,000 received from the founder of the company

1. Journalize Lands' End's receipt of both donations.
2. Which donation affected the company's
   a. Total assets?
   c. Total stockholders' equity?
   b. Total paid-in capital?
   d. Net income?
   Was each effect an increase or a decrease?

Preparing the stockholders' equity section of a balance sheet
(Obj. 3)

DE13-11 The financial statements of Landa Computer, Inc., reported the following accounts (adapted, in millions except for par value):

Net sales	$1,031.5	Paid-in capital in excess of par	$ 26.2
Accounts payable	62.4	Cost of goods sold	588.0
Retained earnings....................	166.2	Common stock $0.01 par,	
Other current liabilities	52.3	40.2 shares issued......................	0.4
Operating expenses.................	412.9	Inventory.......................................	165.0
Donated capital	8.4	Long-term debt	7.6

Prepare the stockholders' equity section of the Landa Computer balance sheet. Net income has already been closed to Retained Earnings.

Using stockholders' equity data
(Obj. 3)

DE13-12 ◀▥ *Link Back to Chapter 1 (Accounting Equation, Income Statement).*
Use the Landa Computer data in Daily Exercise 13-11 to compute Landa's

a. Net income   b. Total liabilities   c. Total assets

Reporting stockholders' equity on the balance sheet
(Obj. 3)

DE13-13 Telex Corporation began operations in 19X3 with a charter that authorized the company to issue 10,000 shares of 5%, $10 par preferred stock and 100,000 shares of no-par common stock. During 19X3 through 19X8, Telex issued 3,000 shares of the preferred stock for $25 per share, and 50,000 shares of its common stock for $6 per share. At December 31, 19X8, Telex had retained earnings of $110,000. During 19X9, Telex earned net income of $70,000 and declared cash dividends of $15,000.
     Show how Telex Corporation reported stockholders' equity on its balance sheet at December 31, 19X9.

Accounting for cash dividends
(Obj. 4)

DE13-14 Augusta Company earned net income of $90,000 during the year ended December 31, 19X6. On December 15, Augusta declared the annual cash dividend on its 6% preferred stock (10,000 shares with total par value of $100,000) and a $0.50 per share cash dividend on its common stock (50,000 shares with total par value of $250,000). Augusta then paid the dividends on January 4, 19X7.
     Journalize for Augusta Company:

a. Declaring the cash dividends on December 15
b. Closing net income to Retained Earnings on December 31, 19X6
c. Paying the cash dividends on January 4, 19X7

Did Retained Earnings increase or decrease during 19X6? By how much?

Dividing cash dividends between preferred and common stock
(Obj. 4)

DE13-15 Refer to the stockholders' equity of Medina Corporation in Exhibit 13-8, page 554. Answer these questions about Medina's dividends.

1. How much in dividends must Medina declare each year before the common stockholders receive cash dividends for the year?
2. Suppose Medina declares cash dividends of $10,000 for 19X5. How much of the dividends go to preferred? How much goes to common?
3. Is Medina's preferred stock cumulative or noncumulative? How can you tell?
4. Suppose Medina passed the preferred dividend in 19X6 and 19X7. In 19X8, Medina declares cash dividends of $10,000. How much of the dividends go to preferred? How much goes to common?

Similarities and differences between preferred stock and common stock
(Obj. 5)

DE13-16 For the following list of characteristics of capital stock, indicate whether each characteristic applies to preferred and common stock:

a. Stated dividend
b. Voting rights
c. Preemptive right
d. Priority to receive assets in the event of liquidation
e. Cumulative
f. Callable
g. Redemption value

DE13-17 Refer to the stockholders' equity of Medina Corporation in Exhibit 13-8, page 554. Medina's preferred stock has a redemption value of $150 per share, and Medina has not declared preferred dividends for three years (including the current year). Compute the book value of Medina's (a) preferred stock, and (b) common stock.

Book value per share of preferred and common stock
(Obj. 5)

DE13-18 Answer the following questions about various stock values.

Explaining the use of different stock values for decision making
(Obj. 5)

1. Suppose you are an investor considering the purchase of Coca-Cola common stock as an investment. You have called your stockbroker to inquire about the stock. Which stock value are you most concerned about and why?

2. Suppose you are the general manager of a small company that is considering going public, as IHOP Corp. did in the chapter opening story. Which stock value are you most concerned about and why?

3. How is the book value of a stock used in decision making?

DE13-19 Give the formula for computing (a) rate of return on total assets, and (b) rate of return on common stockholders' equity. Then answer these questions about the rate-of-return computations.

Computing and explaining return on assets and return on equity
(Obj. 6)

1. Why is interest expense added to net income to compute return on assets?

2. Why are preferred dividends subtracted from net income to compute return on common stockholders' equity?

DE13-20 The Coca-Cola Company has earned extraordinarily high rates of return on its assets and its stockholders' equity in recent years. Coca-Cola's 1996 financial statements reported the following items—with 1995 figures given for comparison (adapted, in millions):

Computing return on assets and return on equity for a leading company
(Obj. 6)

	1996	1995
Balance sheet		
Total current assets	$ 5,910	$ 5,450
Total long-term assets	10,251	9,591
Total assets	$16,161	$15,041
Total liabilities	$10,005	$ 9,649
Total stockholders' equity (all common)	6,156	5,392
Total liabilities and equity	$16,161	$15,041
Income statement		
Net sales	$18,546	
Cost of goods sold	6,738	
Gross margin	11,808	
Selling, administrative, and general expenses	7,893	
Interest expense	286	
All other expenses, net	137	
Net income	$ 3,492	

Compute Coca-Cola's rate of return on total assets and rate of return on common stockholders' equity for 1996. Do these rates of return look high or low?

DE13-21 Pappadeaux Pizza had income before income tax of $100,000 and taxable income of $80,000 for 19X9, the company's first year of operations. The income tax rate is 40 percent.

Accounting for a corporation's income tax
(Obj. 7)

1. Make the entry to record Pappadeaux's income taxes for 19X9.

2. Show what Pappadeaux Pizza will report on its 19X9 income statement starting with income before income tax. Also show what Pappadeaux will report for current and long-term liabilities on its December 31, 19X9, balance sheet. Assume the beginning balance of Deferred Tax Liability was zero.

Exercises

E13-1 Kathy Whittle and Angela Lane are opening a limousine service to be named K & A Transportation Enterprises. They need outside capital, so they plan to organize the business as a corporation. They come to you for advice. Write a memorandum informing them of the steps in forming a corporation. Identify specific documents used in this process, and name the different parties involved in the ownership and management of a corporation.

Organizing a corporation
(Obj. 1)

Issuing stock
(Obj. 2)

E13-2 Exhibition Software completed the following stock issuance transactions:

June 19 Issued 1,000 shares of $1.50 par common stock for cash of $10.50 per share.
July 3 Sold 300 shares of $4.50, no-par Class A preferred stock for $12,000 cash.
　　11 Received inventory valued at $23,000 and equipment with market value of $11,000. Issued 3,300 shares of the $1.50 par common stock.
　　15 Issued 1,000 shares of 5%, no-par Class B preferred stock with stated value of $50 per share. The issue price was cash of $60 per share.

REQUIRED

1. Journalize the transactions. Explanations are not required.
2. How much paid-in capital did these transactions generate for Exhibition Software?

Issuing stock and preparing the stockholders' equity section of the balance sheet
(Obj. 2, 3)

E13-3 The charter for Greenlawn, Inc., authorizes the company to issue 100,000 shares of $3, no-par preferred stock and 500,000 shares of common stock with $1 par value. During its start-up phase, Greenlawn completed the following transactions:

July 6 Issued 500 shares of common stock to the promoters who organized the corporation, receiving cash of $15,000.
　　12 Issued 300 shares of preferred stock for cash of $18,000.
　　14 Issued 800 shares of common stock in exchange for land valued at $24,000.
　　31 Earned a small profit for July and closed the $4,000 net income into Retained Earnings.

REQUIRED

1. Record the transactions in the general journal.
2. Prepare the stockholders' equity section of the Greenlawn balance sheet at July 31.

Recording issuance of stock
(Obj. 2)

E13-4 The balance sheet of Baldridge Corporation, as adapted, reported the following stockholders' equity. Baldridge has two separate classes of preferred stock, labeled Series A and Series B. All dollar amounts, except for per-share amounts, are given in thousands.

Stockholders' Equity	
Preferred stock, $1 par, authorized 4,000,000 shares (Note 7)	
Series A	$ 50
Series B	370
Common stock, $0.10 par, authorized 20,000,000, [issued and] outstanding	
9,000,000 shares	900
Capital in excess of par	75,000

Note 7. Preferred Stock:	Shares [Issued and] Outstanding
Series A..........	50,000
Series B..........	370,000

REQUIRED

The Series A preferred stock was issued for $5 cash per share, the Series B preferred was issued for $10 cash per share, and the common was issued for cash of $72,370. Make the summary journal entries to record issuance of all the Baldridge stock. Explanations are not required. After you record these entries, what is the balance of Capital in Excess of Par?

Recording issuance of no-par stock
(Obj. 2)

E13-5 Oriental Rug Co., located in Memphis, Tennessee, imports European furniture and Oriental rugs. The corporation issued 5,000 shares of no-par common stock for $10 per share. Record issuance of the stock if the stock (a) is true no-par stock, and (b) has stated value of $2 per share.

Stockholders' equity section of a balance sheet
(Obj. 3)

E13-6 The charter of Elsimate Company authorizes the issuance of 5,000 shares of Class A preferred stock, 1,000 shares of Class B preferred stock, and 10,000 shares of common stock. During a two-month period, Elsimate completed these stock-issuance transactions:

Jan. 23 Issued 1,000 shares of $1 par common stock for cash of $12.50 per share.
Feb. 2 Sold 300 shares of $4.50, no-par Class A preferred stock for $20,000 cash.
　　12 Received inventory valued at $25,000 and equipment with market value of $16,000 for 3,300 shares of the $1 par common stock.
　　17 Issued 1,000 shares of 5%, no-par Class B preferred stock with stated value of $50 per share. The issue price was cash of $60 per share.

REQUIRED

Prepare the stockholders' equity section of the Elsimate balance sheet for the transactions given in this exercise. Retained earnings has a balance of $46,000.

E13-7 Lynn Corp. recently organized. The company issued common stock to an attorney in exchange for his patent with a market value of $40,000. In addition, Lynn received cash both for 2,000 shares of its $50 par preferred stock at $80 per share and for 26,000 shares of its no-par common stock at $15 per share. The city of Atlanta donated 50 acres of land to the company as a plant site. The market value of the land was $400,000. Retained earnings at the end of the first year was $70,000. Without making journal entries, determine the total paid-in capital created by these transactions.

Paid-in capital for a corporation
(Obj. 2)

E13-8 Colleen Kennedy, Inc., has the following selected account balances at June 30, 19X7. Prepare the stockholders' equity section of the company's balance sheet.

Stockholders' equity section of a balance sheet
(Obj. 3)

Inventory	$112,000	Common stock, no-par with	
Machinery and equipment	109,000	$1 stated value, 500,000 shares	
Preferred stock, 5%, $20 par,		authorized, 120,000 shares	
20,000 shares authorized,		issued	$120,000
5,000 shares issued	100,000	Accumulated depreciation—	
Paid-in capital in excess		machinery and equipment	62,000
of par—preferred stock	88,000	Retained earnings	119,000
		Cost of goods sold	81,000

E13-9 Mannheim Corporation has the following stockholders' equity:

Dividing dividends between preferred and common stock
(Obj. 4)

Preferred stock, 7%, $10 par, 100,000 shares authorized, 20,000 shares issued...........................	$ 200,000
Common stock, $0.50 par, 500,000 shares authorized, 300,000 shares issued.........................	150,000
Paid-in capital in excess of par—common..............	600,000
Total paid-in capital...	$ 950,000
Retained earnings...	150,000
Total stockholders' equity....................................	$1,100,000

First, determine whether preferred stock is cumulative or noncumulative. Then compute the amount of dividends to preferred and to common for 19X8 and 19X9 if total dividends are $10,000 in 19X8 and $60,000 in 19X9.

E13-10 The following elements of stockholders' equity are adapted from the balance sheet of Baldridge Corporation. All dollar amounts, except the dividends per share, are given in thousands.

Computing dividends on preferred and common stock
(Obj. 4)

Stockholders' Equity	
Preferred stock, cumulative, $1 par (Note 7)	
Series A, 50,000 shares issued..	$ 50
Series B, 370,000 shares issued...	370
Common stock, $0.10 par, 9,000,000 shares issued............................	900

Note 7. Preferred Stock:	**Designated Annual Cash Dividend per Share**	
	Series A...........	$0.20
	Series B...........	1.30

The Series A preferred has preference over the Series B preferred, and the company has paid all preferred dividends through 19X4.

Compute the dividends to both series of preferred stock and to common for 19X5 and 19X6 if total dividends are $0 in 19X5 and $1,100,000 in 19X6.

REQUIRED

E13-11 The balance sheet of Gamma Corporation reported the following:

Book value per share of preferred and common stock
(Obj. 5)

Redeemable preferred stock; 100 shares issued and outstanding, redemption value $6,000	$ 4,800
Common stockholders' equity, 10,000 shares issued and outstanding.........	216,000
Total stockholders' equity	$220,800

Assume that Gamma has paid preferred dividends for the current year and all prior years (no dividends in arrears). Compute the book value per share of the preferred stock and the common stock.

E13-12 Refer to Exercise 13-11. Compute the book value per share of the preferred stock and the common stock if three years' preferred dividends (including dividends for the current year) are in arrears. The preferred stock dividend rate is 6 percent. Round book value to the nearest cent.

Book value per share of preferred and common stock; preferred dividends in arrears
(Obj. 5)

E13-13 DuBois Furniture, Inc., reported these figures for 19X7 and 19X6:

	19X7	19X6
Income statement:		
Interest expense	$ 17,400,000	$ 7,100,000
Net income	12,000,000	18,700,000
Balance sheet:		
Total assets	351,000,000	317,000,000
Preferred stock, $1.30, no-par,		
100,000 shares issued and outstanding	2,500,000	2,500,000
Common stockholders' equity	164,000,000	151,000,000
Total stockholders' equity	166,500,000	153,500,000

Compute rate of return on total assets and rate of return on common stockholders' equity for 19X7. Do these rates of return suggest strength or weakness? Give your reason.

E13-14 Temple Construction Company was chartered in Texas during 19X0. Temple has income before income tax of $420,000 in 19X0. Taxable income is $380,000 for 19X0. Texas has no corporate income tax, and the federal income tax rate is 35 percent. Record Temple's income tax for the year. Show what Temple will report on its 19X0 income statement starting with income before income tax. Also show what Temple will report for current and long-term liabilities on its December 31, 19X0, balance sheet.

CHALLENGE EXERCISE

E13-15 Wal-Mart Stores, Inc., reported these comparative stockholders' equity data (amounts in millions except par value):

	January 31,	
	19X2	19X1
Common stock ($0.10 par value)	$ 115	$ 114
Capital in excess of par value	626	416
Retained earnings	6,249	4,836

During 19X2, Wal-Mart completed these transactions:

a. Net income, $1,608.
b. Cash dividends declared and paid, $195.
c. Issuance of stock for cash, $211.

1. Give the journal entries to show how Wal-Mart accounted for these 19X2 transactions.
2. For each stockholders' equity account, start with the January 31, 19X1, balance and work toward the balance at January 31, 19X2 to show how your journal entries accounted for the changes in the Wal-Mart accounts.

Beyond the Numbers

BN13-1 Answering the following questions will enhance your understanding of the capital stock of corporations.

1. Why do you think capital stock and retained earnings are shown separately in the shareholders' equity section?
2. Lynn Liu, major shareholder of L-S, Inc., proposes to sell some land she owns to the company for common shares in L-S. What problem does L-S, Inc., face in recording the transaction?
3. Preferred shares generally are preferred with respect to dividends and on liquidation. Why would investors buy common stock when preferred stock is available?
4. What does it mean if the liquidation value of a company's preferred stock is greater than its market value?
5. If you owned 100 shares of stock in Carta Corporation and someone offered to buy the stock for its book value, would you accept the offer? Why or why not?

ETHICAL ISSUE

Note: This case is based on an actual situation.

George Campbell paid $50,000 for a franchise that entitled him to market Success Associates software programs in the countries of the European Common Market. Campbell intended to sell individual franchises for the major language groups of western Europe—German, French, English, Spanish, and Italian. Naturally, investors considering buying a franchise from Campbell asked to see the financial statements of his business.

Believing the value of the franchise to be greater than $50,000, Campbell sought to capitalize his own franchise at $500,000. The law firm of McDonald & LaDue helped Campbell form a corporation chartered to issue 500,000 shares of common stock with par value of $1 per share. Attorneys suggested the following chain of transactions:

a. A third party borrows $500,000 and purchases the franchise from Campbell.
b. Campbell pays the corporation $500,000 to acquire all its stock.
c. The corporation buys the franchise from the third party, who repays the loan.

In the final analysis, the third party is debt-free and out of the picture. Campbell owns all the corporation's stock, and the corporation owns the franchise. The corporation's balance sheet lists a franchise acquired at a cost of $500,000. This balance sheet is Campbell's most valuable marketing tool.

1. What is unethical about this situation?
2. Who can be harmed? How can they be harmed? What role does accounting play?

REQUIRED

Problems (GROUP A)

P13-1A Barry Camp and Mark Wible are opening an Office Depot store in a shopping center in Santa Fe, New Mexico. The area is growing, and no competitors are located nearby. Their most basic decision is how to organize the business. Camp thinks the partnership form is best. Wible favors the corporate form of organization. They seek your advice.

Organizing a corporation
(Obj. 1)

Write a memo to Camp and Wible to make them aware of the advantages and the disadvantages of organizing the business as a corporation. Use the following format for your memo:

REQUIRED

Date: _____
To: **Barry Camp and Mark Wible**
From: **Student Name**
Subject: **Advantages and disadvantages of the corporation form of business organization**

P13-2A The partners who own Engell & Blatt wished to avoid the unlimited personal liability of the partnership form of business, so they incorporated the partnership as E&B Exploration, Inc. The charter from the state of Louisiana authorizes the corporation to issue 10,000 shares of 6%, $100 par preferred stock and 250,000 shares of no-par common stock. In its first month, E&B Exploration completed the following transactions:

Journalizing corporation transactions and preparing the stockholders' equity section of the balance sheet
(Obj. 2, 3)

Jan. 3   Issued 5,100 shares of common stock to Engell and 3,800 shares to Blatt, both for cash of $10 per share.
    7   Received land valued at $160,000 as a donation from the city of Lafayette.
  12   Issued 1,000 shares of preferred stock to acquire a patent with a market value of $110,000.
  22   Issued 1,500 shares of common stock to other investors for $15 cash per share.

1. Record the transactions in the general journal.
2. Prepare the stockholders' equity section of the E&B Exploration, Inc., balance sheet at January 31. The ending balance of Retained Earnings is $40,300.

REQUIRED

P13-3A Kluzewski Corporation was organized in 19X8. At December 31, 19X8, Kluzewski's balance sheet reported the following stockholders' equity:

Issuing stock and preparing the stockholders' equity section of the balance sheet
(Obj. 2, 3)

Preferred stock, 5%, $10 par, 50,000 shares authorized, none issued..............	$ —
Common stock, $2 par, 100,000 shares authorized, 10,000 shares issued........	20,000
Paid-in capital in excess of par—common.......................................	30,000
Retained earnings (Deficit)...	(5,000)
Total stockholders' equity	**$45,000**

Answer the following questions, making journal entries as needed.

REQUIRED

1. What does the 5% mean for the preferred stock? After Kluzewski issues preferred stock, how much in cash dividends will Kluzewski expect to pay on 1,000 shares?

2. At what price per share did Kluzewski issue the common stock during 19X8?

3. Were first-year operations profitable? Give your reason.

4. During 19X9, the company completed the following selected transactions. Journalize each transaction. Explanations are not required.
   a. Issued for cash 5,000 shares of preferred stock at par value.
   b. Issued for cash 1,000 shares of common stock at a price of $7 per share.
   c. Issued 20,000 shares of common stock to acquire a building valued at $140,000.
   d. Net income for the year was $50,000, and the company declared no dividends. Make the closing entry for net income.

5. Prepare the stockholders' equity section of the Kluzewski Corporation balance sheet at December 31, 19X9.

Stockholders' equity section of the balance sheet
(Obj. 3)

P13-4A Stockholders' equity information for two independent companies, The Yankee Group, Inc., and Alltell Corp. is as follows:

• **The Yankee Group, Inc.** The Yankee Group is authorized to issue 50,000 shares of $5 par common stock. All the stock was issued at $12 per share. The company incurred a net loss of $41,000 in 19X1. It earned net income of $60,000 in 19X2 and $90,000 in 19X3. The company declared no dividends during the three-year period.

• **Alltell Corp.** Alltell's charter authorizes the company to issue 10,000 shares of $2.50 preferred stock with par value of $50, and 120,000 shares of no-par common stock. Alltell issued 1,000 shares of the preferred stock at $54 per share. It issued 40,000 shares of the common stock for a total of $220,000. The company's retained earnings balance at the beginning of 19X3 was $72,000, and net income for the year was $90,000. During 19X3, the company declared the specified dividend on preferred and a $0.50 per share dividend on common. Preferred dividends for 19X2 were in arrears.

REQUIRED

For each company, prepare the stockholders' equity section of its balance sheet at December 31, 19X3. Show the computation of all amounts. Entries are not required.

Analyzing the stockholders' equity of an actual corporation
(Obj. 3, 4)

P13-5A The purpose of this problem is to familiarize you with financial statement information. U and I Group, which makes food products and livestock feeds, included the following stockholders' equity on its year-end balance sheet at February 28, 19X8:

Stockholders' Equity	($ Thousands)
Voting Preferred stock, 5.5% cumulative—par value $23 per share; authorized 100,000 shares in each class:	
Class A—issued 75,473 shares	$ 1,736
Class B—issued 92,172 shares	2,120
Common stock—par value $5 per share; authorized 5,000,000 shares; issued 2,870,950 shares	14,355
Paid-in Capital in Excess of Par—Common............................	5,548
Retained earnings	8,336
	$32,095

REQUIRED

1. Identify the different issues of stock U and I has outstanding.

2. Give the summary entries to record issuance of all the U and I stock. Assume that all the stock was issued for cash. Explanations are not required.

3. Assume that preferred dividends are in arrears for 19X8.
   a. Write Note 5 of the February 28, 19X8, financial statements to disclose the dividends in arrears.
   b. Record the declaration of a $450,000 dividend on February 28, 19X9. An explanation is not required.

Preparing a corporation balance sheet; measuring profitability
(Obj. 3, 6)

P13-6A ◀ᴍ *Link Back to Chapter 1 (Accounting Equation).* The following accounts and related balances of Borzhov, Inc., are arranged in no particular order.

Accounts receivable, net..........	$46,000	Interest expense.........................	$ 6,100
Paid-in capital in excess of par—common....................	19,000	Property, plant, and equipment, net	261,000
Accrued liabilities	26,000	Common stock, $1 par,	
Long-term note payable..........	42,000	500,000 shares authorized,	
Inventory.................................	81,000	236,000 shares issued.............	236,000

Dividends payable	$ 9,000	Prepaid expenses	$ 10,000
Retained earnings	?	Revenue from donation	6,000
Accounts payable	31,000	Common stockholders' equity,	
Trademark, net	9,000	June 30, 19X1	222,000
Preferred stock, $0.10, no-par,		Net income	31,000
10,000 shares authorized		Total assets, June 30, 19X1	404,000
and issued	27,000	Cash	13,000

REQUIRED

1. Prepare the company's classified balance sheet in the account format at June 30, 19X2. Use the accounting equation to compute Retained Earnings.

2. Compute rate of return on total assets and rate of return on common stockholders' equity for the year ended June 30, 19X2.

3. Do these rates of return suggest strength or weakness? Give your reason.

P13-7A AIG Financial Services has 10,000 shares of $3.50, no-par preferred stock and 50,000 shares of no-par common stock outstanding. AIG declared and paid the following dividends during a three-year period: 19X1, $20,000; 19X2, $100,000; and 19X3, $215,000.

Computing dividends on preferred and common stock
(Obj. 4)

REQUIRED

1. Compute the total dividends to preferred stock and to common stock for each of the three years if
   a. Preferred is noncumulative.
   b. Preferred is cumulative.

2. For case (1b), record the declaration of the 19X3 dividends on December 28, 19X3, and the payment of the dividends on January 17, 19X4.

P13-8A The balance sheet of Elsimate, Inc., reported the following:

Analyzing the stockholders' equity of an actual corporation
(Obj. 4, 5)

Stockholders' Investment [same as stockholders' equity]	
Redeemable nonvoting preferred stock, no-par (redemption value, $358,000)	$320,000
Common stock, $1.50 par value, authorized 75,000 shares;	
issued 36,000 shares	54,000
[Additional] paid-in capital	231,000
Retained earnings	119,000
Total stockholders' investment	$724,000

Notes to the financial statements indicate that 8,000 shares of $2.60 preferred stock with a stated value of $40 per share were issued and outstanding. Preferred dividends are in arrears for three years, including the current year. The additional paid-in capital was contributed by the common stockholders. On the balance sheet date, the market value of the Elsimate common stock was $7.50 per share.

REQUIRED

1. Is the preferred stock cumulative or noncumulative? How can you tell?
2. What is the amount of the annual preferred dividend?
3. Which class of stockholders controls the company? Give your reason.
4. What is the total paid-in capital of the company?
5. What was the total market value of the common stock?
6. Compute the book value per share of the preferred stock and the common stock.

P13-9A The accounting (not the income tax) records of MRI Intelligence Systems, Inc., provide the income statement for 19X3.

Computing and recording a corporation's income tax
(Obj. 7)

Total revenue		$680,000
Expenses:		
Cost of goods sold	$290,000	
Operating expenses	180,000	
Total expenses before tax	470,000	
Income before income tax		$210,000

The operating expenses include depreciation of $40,000 computed under the straight-line method. In calculating taxable income on the tax return, MRI uses the modified accelerated cost recovery system (MACRS). MACRS depreciation was $50,000 for 19X3. The corporate income tax rate is 35 percent.

1. Compute taxable income for the year.
2. Journalize the corporation's income tax for 19X3.
3. Prepare the corporation's single-step income statement for 19X3.

Problems (GROUP B)

Organizing a corporation
(Obj. 1)

P13-1B Helen Monroe and Rita Cheng are opening a Shoney's Restaurant in Columbia, South Carolina. There are no competing family restaurants in the immediate vicinity. Their most fundamental decision is how to organize the business. Monroe thinks the partnership form is best for their business. Cheng favors the corporate form of organization. They seek your advice.

REQUIRED

Write a memo to Monroe and Cheng to make them aware of the advantages and the disadvantages of organizing the business as a corporation. Use the following format for your memo:

Date:	_____
To:	**Helen Monroe and Rita Cheng**
From:	**Student Name**
Subject:	**Advantages and disadvantages of the corporate form of business organization**

Journalizing corporation transactions and preparing the stockholders' equity section of the balance sheet
(Obj. 2, 3)

P13-2B The partnership of Sanchez & Mundo needed additional capital to expand into new markets, so the business incorporated as Tiempo Grande, Inc. The charter from the state of Arizona authorizes Tiempo Grande to issue 50,000 shares of 6%, $100-par preferred stock and 100,000 shares of no-par common stock. In its first month, Tiempo Grande completed the following transactions:

Dec. 2 Issued 9,000 shares of common stock to Sanchez and 12,000 shares to Mundo, both for cash of $5 per share.
8 Received a parcel of land valued at $112,000 as a donation from the city of Tucson.
10 Issued 400 shares of preferred stock to acquire a patent with a market value of $50,000.
27 Issued 12,000 shares of common stock to other investors for cash of $96,000.

REQUIRED

1. Record the transactions in the general journal.
2. Prepare the stockholders' equity section of the Tiempo Grande, Inc., balance sheet at December 31. The ending balance of Retained Earnings is $57,100.

Issuing stock and preparing the stockholders' equity section of the balance sheet
(Obj. 2, 3)

P13-3B Manitowoc, Inc., was organized in 19X7. At December 31, 19X7, Manitowoc's balance sheet reported the following stockholders' equity:

Preferred stock, 6%, $50 par, 100,000 shares authorized, none issued..............	$ —
Common stock, $1 par, 500,000 shares authorized, 60,000 shares issued	60,000
Paid-in capital in excess of par—common	40,000
Retained earnings—Deficit	(25,000)
Total stockholders' equity..	$75,000

REQUIRED

Answer the following questions, making journal entries as needed.

1. What does the 6% mean for the preferred stock? After Manitowoc issues preferred stock, how much in cash dividends will Manitowoc expect to pay on 1,000 shares?
2. At what price per share did Manitowoc issue the common stock during 19X7?
3. Were first-year operations profitable? Give your reason.
4. During 19X8, the company completed the following selected transactions. Journalize each transaction. Explanations are not required.
   a. Issued for cash 1,000 shares of preferred stock at par value.
   b. Issued for cash 2,000 shares of common stock at a price of $3 per share.
   c. Issued 50,000 shares of common stock to acquire a building valued at $100,000.
   d. Net income for the year was $65,000, and the company declared no dividends. Make the closing entry for net income.
5. Prepare the stockholders' equity section of the Manitowoc, Inc., balance sheet at December 31, 19X8.

Stockholders' equity section of the balance sheet
(Obj. 3)

P13-4B The following summaries for Omega Fotographic, Inc., and Homeowners Insurance Company provide the information needed to prepare the stockholders' equity section of the company balance sheet. The two companies are independent.

- **Omega Fotographic, Inc.**   Omega Fotographic is authorized to issue 50,000 shares of $1 par common stock. All the stock was issued at $12 per share. The company incurred net losses of $50,000 in 19X1 and $14,000 in 19X2. It earned net income of $23,000 in 19X3 and $71,000 in 19X4. The company declared no dividends during the four-year period.
- **Homeowners Insurance Company.**   Homeowners Insurance Company's charter authorizes the company to issue 50,000 shares of 5%, $10 par preferred stock and 500,000 shares of no-par common stock. Homeowners Insurance issued 1,000 shares of the preferred stock at $15 per share. It issued 100,000 shares of the common stock for $400,000. The company's retained earnings balance at the beginning of 19X4 was $120,000. Net income for 19X4 was $60,000, and the company declared the specified preferred dividend for 19X4. Preferred dividends for 19X3 were in arrears.

For each company, prepare the stockholders' equity section of its balance sheet at December 31, 19X4. Show the computation of all amounts. Entries are not required.

REQUIRED

P13-5B   The purpose of this problem is to familiarize you with financial statement information. Bethlehem Steel Corporation, a large steel company, reported the following stockholders' equity on its balance sheet at December 31, 19X5:

Analyzing the stockholders' equity of an actual corporation (Obj. 3, 4)

Stockholders' Equity	($ Millions)
Preferred stock—	
Authorized 20,000,000 shares in each class; issued:	
$5.00 Cumulative Convertible Preferred Stock, at $50.00 stated value, 2,500,000 shares.....................................	$ 125
$2.50 Cumulative Convertible Preferred Stock, at $25.00 stated value, 4,000,000 shares.....................................	100
Common stock—$8 par value—	
Authorized 80,000,000 shares; issued 48,308,516 shares.................	621
Retained earnings	529
	$1,375

Note that Bethlehem reports no Paid-in Capital in Excess of Par or Stated Value. Instead, the company reports those items in the stock accounts.

REQUIRED

1. Identify the different issues of stock Bethlehem has outstanding.
2. Which class of stock did Bethlehem issue at par or stated value, and which class did it issue above par or stated value?
3. Assume preferred dividends are in arrears for 19X5.
   a. Write Note 6 of the December 31, 19X5, financial statements to disclose the dividends in arrears.
   b. Journalize the declaration of a $60 million dividend at December 31, 19X6. An explanation is not required.

P13-6B   ◀━ *Link Back to Chapter 1 (Accounting Equation).* The following accounts and related balances of Columbia Manufacturing are arranged in no particular order.

Preparing a corporation balance sheet; measuring profitability (Obj. 3, 6)

Common stock, $5 par, 100,000 shares authorized, 22,000 shares issued	$110,000	Retained earnings........................	$?
		Inventory......................................	181,000
Dividends payable.....................	3,000	Property, plant, and equipment, net.........................	278,000
Total assets, November 30, 19X6...............	581,000	Prepaid expenses	13,000
		Patent, net....................................	37,000
Net income..................................	36,200	Accrued liabilities	17,000
Common stockholders' equity, November 30, 19X6.............	383,000	Long-term note payable..............	104,000
		Accounts receivable, net.............	102,000
Interest expense.........................	12,800	Preferred stock, 4%, $10 par, 25,000 shares authorized, 3,700 shares issued.................	37,000
Additional paid-in capital— common..............................	140,000	
Accounts payable	31,000	Cash..	32,000

REQUIRED

1. Prepare the company's classified balance sheet in the account format at November 30, 19X7. Use the accounting equation to compute Retained Earnings.
2. Compute rate of return on total assets and rate of return on common stockholders' equity for the year ended November 30, 19X7.
3. Do these rates of return suggest strength or weakness? Give your reason.

P13-7B Nevada Airline Corporation has 5,000 shares of 5%, $10 par value preferred stock and 100,000 shares of $1.50 par common stock outstanding. During a three-year period, Nevada declared and paid cash dividends as follows: 19X1, $1,500; 19X2, $15,000; and 19X3, $26,000.

REQUIRED

1. Compute the total dividends to preferred stock and to common stock for each of the three years if
   a. Preferred is noncumulative.
   b. Preferred is cumulative.
2. For case (1b), record the declaration of the 19X3 dividends on December 22, 19X3, and the payment of the dividends on January 14, 19X4.

P13-8B The balance sheet of Oak Manufacturing, Inc., reported the following:

Stockholders' Investment [same as stockholders' equity]	($ Thousands)
Cumulative preferred stock..	$ 45
Common stock, $1 par, authorized 40,000,000 shares; issued 16,000,000 shares...	16,000
[Additional] paid-in capital...	176,000
Retained earnings	(77,165)
Total stockholders' investment..	$114,880

Notes to the financial statements indicate that 9,000 shares of $1.60 preferred stock with a stated value of $5 per share were issued and outstanding. The preferred stock has a redemption value of $25 per share, and preferred dividends are in arrears for two years, including the current year. The additional paid-in capital was contributed by the common stockholders. On the balance sheet date, the market value of the Oak Manufacturing common stock was $7.50 per share.

REQUIRED

1. Is the preferred stock cumulative or noncumulative? How can you tell?
2. What is the amount of the annual preferred dividend?
3. What is the total paid-in capital of the company?
4. What was the total market value of the common stock?
5. Compute the book value per share of the preferred stock and the common stock.

P13-9B The accounting (not the income tax) records of Solomon Energy Corporation provide the income statement for 19X7.

Total revenue................................	**$930,000**
Expenses:	
Cost of goods sold	$430,000
Operating expenses	270,000
Total expenses before tax	700,000
Income before income tax............	**$230,000**

The operating expenses include depreciation of $50,000 computed on the straight-line method. In calculating taxable income on the tax return, Solomon uses the modified accelerated cost recovery system (MACRS). MACRS depreciation was $80,000 for 19X7. The corporate income tax rate is 40 percent.

REQUIRED

1. Compute taxable income for the year.
2. Journalize the corporation's income tax for 19X7.
3. Prepare the corporation's single-step income statement for 19X7.

Applying Your Knowledge

DECISION CASE

Ron Buck and Sue Ladd have written a spreadsheet program that they believe will rival Excel and Lotus. They need additional capital to market the product, and they plan to incorporate the business. They are considering alternative capital structures for the corporation. Their primary goal is to raise as much capital as possible without giving up control of the business. The partners plan to invest the software program and receive 110,000 shares of the corporation's common stock. The partners have been offered $110,000 for the rights to the software program.

The corporation's plans for a charter include an authorization to issue 5,000 shares of preferred stock and 500,000 shares of $1 par common stock. Buck and Ladd are uncertain about the most desirable features for the preferred stock. Prior to incorporating, the partners are discussing their plans with two investment groups. The corporation can obtain capital from outside investors under either of the following plans:

- **Plan 1.** Group 1 will invest $105,000 to acquire 1,000 shares of $5, no-par preferred stock and $70,000 to acquire 70,000 shares of common stock. Each preferred share receives 50 votes on matters that come before the stockholders.
- **Plan 2.** Group 2 will invest $160,000 to acquire 1,400 shares of 6%, $100 par nonvoting, noncumulative preferred stock.

Assume that the corporation is chartered.

REQUIRED

1. Journalize the issuance of common stock to Buck and Ladd. Explanations are not required.
2. Journalize the issuance of stock to the outsiders under both plans. Explanations are not required.
3. Assume that net income for the first year is $150,000 and total dividends are $30,000. Prepare the stockholders' equity section of the corporation's balance sheet under both plans.
4. Recommend one of the plans to Buck and Ladd. Give your reasons.

FINANCIAL STATEMENT CASE

CASE 1. The NIKE, Inc., financial statements appear in Appendix A. Answer the following questions about the company's stock.

Analyzing stockholders' equity
(Obj. 2, 3)

REQUIRED

1. How can you tell from NIKE's balance sheet that NIKE treats its Redeemable Preferred Stock as a liability and not as stockholders' equity? Why is the preferred stock a liability?
2. Examine NIKE's balance sheet. Which stockholders' equity account increased the most during the year ended May 31, 1997 (fiscal year 1997)? Did this increase occur because of paid-in capital that NIKE received from its stockholders? If so, explain. If not, identify what caused the big increase in stockholders' equity.
3. During fiscal year 1997, NIKE's stockholders converted $1,000 of NIKE's Class A Common Stock into NIKE's Class B Common Stock. Make NIKE's journal entry to record this transaction. Only the two stock accounts were affected.
4. Did NIKE issue any Class B Common Stock during fiscal year 1997 over and above the stock that NIKE issued for the conversion of Class A common into Class B common? How can you tell?

Team Project

Competitive pressures are the norm in business. Lexus automobiles (made in Japan) have cut into the sales of Mercedes-Benz (a German company), Jaguar Motors (a British company), General Motors' Cadillac Division, and Ford's Lincoln Division (both U.S. companies). Dell, Gateway, and Compaq computers have siphoned business away from Apple and IBM. Foreign steelmakers have reduced the once-massive U.S. steel industry to a fraction of its former size.

Indeed, corporate downsizing has occurred on a massive scale. During the past few years, each company or industry mentioned here has pared down plant and equipment, laid off employees, or restructured operations.

REQUIRED

1. Identify all the stakeholders of a corporation and the stake each group has in the company. A *stakeholder* is a person or a group who has an interest (that is, a stake) in the success of the organization.
2. Identify several measures by which a corporation may be considered deficient and which may indicate the need for downsizing. How can downsizing help to solve this problem? Discuss how each measure can indicate the need for downsizing.
3. Debate the downsizing issue. One group of students takes the perspective of the company and its stockholders, and another group of students takes the perspective of other stakeholders of the company.

CHAPTER 14

Retained Earnings, Treasury Stock, and the Income Statement

After studying this chapter, you should be able to

1. Account for stock dividends
2. Distinguish stock splits from stock dividends
3. Account for treasury stock
4. Report restrictions on retained earnings
5. Identify the elements of a corporation's income statement
6. Prepare a statement of stockholders' equity

Murray Weintraub, chief financial analyst for Sledd & Co. Investment Bankers, is evaluating May Department Stores' operations. Net earnings for 1996 are essentially unchanged from 1995, but net earnings from continuing operations have grown. Which 1996 income figure—net earnings of $755 million (line 12 in Exhibit 14-1) or net earnings of $749 million from continuing operations (line 8)—should Weintraub use to evaluate May's operations during 1996?

The answer depends on the decision Weintraub will make. If he wants to measure how well the company has performed in light of all its activities, then he should look at net income (line 12). But if he wants to predict the level of income the company can expect to earn in the future, he should consider only those aspects of its operations that May can repeat from year to year. Murray Weintraub and his staff are probably more interested in net earnings from continuing operations than in net income. Most sophisticated investors and lenders concentrate their analysis on income from continuing operations, which can be expected to generate income for the company in the future.

THE MAY DEPARTMENT STORES COMPANY Statement of Earnings (partial, adapted)		
(Dollars in millions)	1996	1995
1 Revenues	$12,000	$10,952
2 Cost of sales	8,226	7,461
3 Selling, general, and administrative expenses	2,265	2,081
4 Interest expense, net	277	250
5 Total cost of sales and expenses	10,768	9,792
6 Earnings from continuing operations before income taxes	1,232	1,160
7 Provision for income taxes	483	460
8 **Net Earnings from Continuing Operations**	749	700
9 Net earnings from discontinued operation	11	55
10 Net earnings before extraordinary loss	760	755
11 Extraordinary loss related to early extinguishment of debt, net of income taxes	(5)	(3)
12 **Net earnings**	$ 755	$ 752

I n this chapter, we discuss continuing operations, discontinued operations, and other operating activities reported on the corporate income statement. We explain special gains and losses that affect net income but differ from basic revenues and operating expenses on corporate income statements. First, however, we continue the discussion of stockholders' equity that we began in Chapter 13. Here we go more deeply into retained earnings, dividends, and treasury stock transactions, which are important to corporations.

Retained Earnings and Dividends

We have seen that the equity section on the corporate balance sheet is called *stockholders' equity* or *shareholders' equity*. The paid-in capital accounts and retained earnings make up the stockholders' equity section.

Retained Earnings is the corporate account that carries the balance of the business's net income less its net losses from operations and less any declared dividends accumulated over the corporation's lifetime. *Retained* means "held onto." Retained Earnings is the shareholders' claim against total assets arising from accumulated income. Successful companies grow by reinvesting the assets they generate from profitable operations.

A debit balance in Retained Earnings, which arises when a corporation's expenses exceed its revenues, is called a *deficit*. This amount is subtracted from the sum of the credit balances in the other equity accounts on the balance sheet to determine total stockholders' equity. In a recent survey, 84 of 600 companies (14%) had a retained earnings deficit (Exhibit 14-2).

At the end of each accounting period, the Income Summary account—which carries the balance of net income for the period—is closed to the Retained Earnings account. Assume that the following amounts are drawn from a corporation's temporary accounts:

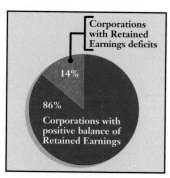

Income Summary					
Dec. 31, 19X6	Expenses	750,000	Dec. 31, 19X6	Revenues	850,000
			Dec. 31, 19X6	Bal.	100,000

This final closing entry transfers net income from Income Summary to Retained Earnings:

19X6			
Dec. 31	Income Summary	100,000	
	Retained Earnings		100,000
	To close net income to Retained Earnings.		

Working It Out Assume that the beginning balance of Retained Earnings was $720,000. What will Retained Earnings's balance be after this net income?

Answer

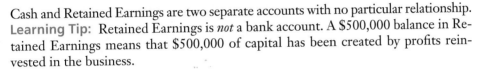

Retained Earnings

Jan. 1, 19X6	Bal.	720,000
Dec. 31, 19X6	Net inc.	100,000
Dec. 31, 19X6	Bal.	820,000

Remember that the account title includes the word *earnings*. *Credits to the Retained Earnings account arise only from net income.* When we examine a corporation's financial statements and want to learn how much net income the corporation has earned and retained in the business, we turn to Retained Earnings. Its balance is the cumulative, lifetime earnings of the company less its cumulative losses and dividends.

The Retained Earnings account is not a reservoir of cash waiting for the board of directors to pay dividends to the stockholders. Instead, Retained Earnings is an owners' equity account representing a claim on all assets in general and not on any asset in particular. In fact, the corporation may have a large balance in Retained Earnings but not have the cash to pay a dividend. Why? The company may have used its cash to purchase a building or other asset or to pay off liabilities.

- To *declare* a dividend, the company must have an adequate balance in Retained Earnings.
- To *pay* the dividend, it must have the cash.

Cash and Retained Earnings are two separate accounts with no particular relationship. **Learning Tip:** Retained Earnings is *not* a bank account. A $500,000 balance in Retained Earnings means that $500,000 of capital has been created by profits reinvested in the business.

Stock Dividends

A **stock dividend** is a proportional distribution by a corporation of its own stock to its stockholders. Stock dividends are fundamentally different from cash dividends because stock dividends do not transfer the assets of the corporation to the stockholders. Cash dividends are distributions of the asset cash, but stock dividends

- Affect *only* the accounts within stockholders' equity
- Have *no* affect on total stockholders' equity
- Increase the stock account and decrease Retained Earnings

Because both Common Stock and Retained Earnings are elements of stockholders' equity, total stockholders' equity is unchanged. There is merely a transfer from one stockholders' equity account to another, and no asset or liability is affected by a stock dividend.

The corporation distributes stock dividends to stockholders in proportion to the number of shares they already own. For example, suppose you owned 300 shares of Xerox Corporation common stock. If Xerox distributed a 10% common stock dividend, you would receive 30 (300 × 0.10) additional shares. You would now own 330 shares of the stock. All other Xerox stockholders would receive additional shares equal to 10% of their prior holdings. You would all be in the same relative position after the dividend as you were before.

Stock Dividend. A proportional distribution by a corporation of its own stock to its stockholders.

Objective 1

Account for stock dividends

Reasons for Stock Dividends

In distributing a stock dividend, the corporation gives up no assets. Why, then, do companies issue stock dividends? A corporation may choose to distribute stock dividends for these reasons:

1. *To continue dividends but conserve cash.* A company may want to keep cash in the business in order to expand, buy inventory, pay off debts, and so on. Yet the company may wish to continue dividends in some form. To do so, the corporation may distribute a stock dividend. Stockholders pay tax on cash dividends but not on stock dividends.

2. *To reduce the market price of its stock.* Distribution of a stock dividend may cause the market price of a share of the company's stock to decrease because of the increased supply of the stock. Suppose the market price of a share of stock is $50. Doubling the number of shares of stock outstanding by issuing a stock dividend would drop the stock's market price by approximately half, to $25 per share. The objective is to make the stock less expensive and thus more attractive to a wider range of investors.

Recording Stock Dividends

The board of directors announces stock dividends on the declaration date. The date of record and the distribution date then follow. (This is the same sequence of dates used for a cash dividend.) The declaration of a stock dividend does *not* create a liability because the corporation is not obligated to pay assets. (Recall that a liability is a claim on *assets*.) Instead, the corporation has declared its intention to distribute its stock. Assume that Louisiana Lumber Corporation has the following stockholders' equity prior to a stock dividend:

Stockholders' Equity	
Paid-in capital:	
Common stock, $10 par, 50,000 shares	
authorized, 20,000 shares issued..........................	$200,000
Paid-in capital in excess of par—common	70,000
Total paid-in capital	270,000
Retained earnings	85,000
Total stockholders' equity......................................	$355,000

The entry to record a stock dividend depends on its size. Generally accepted accounting principles distinguish between *small stock dividends* (less than 25% of the corporation's issued stock) and *large stock dividends* (25% or more of issued stock).

SMALL STOCK DIVIDEND—LESS THAN 25% Assume that Louisiana Lumber Corporation declares a 10% (*small*) common stock dividend on November 17. The company will distribute 2,000 (20,000 × 0.10) shares in the dividend. On November 17, the market value of its common stock is $16 per share. GAAP requires small stock dividends to be accounted for at market value. Therefore, Retained Earnings is debited for the market value of the 2,000 dividend shares. Common Stock Dividend Distributable is credited for par value, and Paid-in Capital in Excess of Par—Common is credited for the remainder. Louisiana Lumber makes the following entry on the declaration date:

Nov. 17	Retained Earnings (20,000 × 0.10 × $16).............	32,000	
	Common Stock Dividend Distributable		
	(20,000 × 0.10 × $10).................................		20,000
	Paid-in Capital in Excess of		
	Par—Common		12,000
	To declare a 10% common stock dividend.		

The accounting equation for this transaction shows that a stock dividend affects neither assets, liabilities, nor total stockholders' equity.

Assets	=	Liabilities	+	Stockholders' Equity
				−32,000
0	=	0		+20,000
				+12,000

On the distribution date, the company records issuance of the dividend shares as follows:

Dec. 12	Common Stock Dividend Distributable	20,000	
	Common Stock		20,000
	To issue common stock in a stock dividend.		

Again, there is no effect on assets, liabilities, or total stockholders' equity.

Assets	=	Liabilities	+	Stockholders' Equity
0	=	0		−20,000
				+20,000

Common Stock Dividend Distributable is an owners' equity account. It is reported in the stockholders' equity section of the balance sheet immediately after Common Stock and before Paid-in Capital in Excess of Par—Common.

The following tabulation shows the changes in the stockholders' equity of Louisiana Lumber caused by the stock dividend:

Stockholders' Equity	Before the Stock Dividend	After the Stock Dividend	Change
Paid-in capital:			
Common stock, $10 par,			
50,000 shares authorized,			
20,000 shares issued................	$200,000		
22,000 shares issued................		$220,000	Up by $20,000
Paid-in capital in excess of			
par—common........................	70,000	82,000	Up by $12,000
Total paid-in capital.................	270,000	302,000	Up by $32,000
Retained earnings.....................	85,000	53,000	Down by $32,000
Total stockholders' equity	$355,000	$355,000	Unchanged

Note that the increase in Common Stock and Paid-in Capital in Excess of Par exactly offsets the decrease in Retained Earnings. Total stockholders' equity is unchanged from $355,000.

LARGE STOCK DIVIDEND—25% OR MORE   A *large* stock dividend significantly increases the number of shares available in the market and thus is likely to decrease the stock price significantly. Because of the drop in market price per share, a large stock dividend is not likely to be perceived as a dividend. GAAP does not require that large stock dividends be accounted for at a specific amount. A common practice is to use the par value of the dividend shares.

Suppose Louisiana Lumber declares a 50% common stock dividend. The declaration entry is

Dec. 7	Retained Earnings (20,000 × 0.50 × $10 par)	100,000	
	Common Stock Dividend Distributable		100,000
	To declare a 50% common stock dividend.		

The company records issuance of the dividend shares on the payment date by this entry:

Dec. 22	Common Stock Dividend Distributable	100,000	
	Common Stock		100,000
	To issue common stock in a stock dividend.		

As before, total stockholders' equity is unchanged by a stock dividend.

Working It Out A corporation issued 1,000 shares of its $15 par common stock as a stock dividend when the stock's market price was $25 per share. Record the declaration and distribution. Assume that the 1,000 shares issued are (1) 10% of the outstanding shares, and (2) 100% of the outstanding shares.

Answer

(1) *Date of declaration (small stock dividend):*

Retained Earnings (1,000 × $25)	25,000	
Common Stock Dividend Distributable (1,000 × $15).........		15,000
Paid-in Capital in Excess of Par—Common		10,000

Common Stock Dividend Distributable	15,000	
Common Stock		15,000
(2) *Date of declaration (large stock dividend):*		
Retained Earnings (1,000 × $15)	15,000	
Common Stock Dividend Distributable		15,000
Date of distribution:		
Common Stock Dividend Distributable	15,000	
Common Stock		15,000

■ **Daily Exercise 14-3**

Stock Splits

Stock Split. An increase in the number of outstanding shares of stock coupled with a proportionate reduction in the par value of the stock.

A large stock dividend may decrease the market price of the stock. A stock *split* also decreases the market price of stock—with the intention of making the stock more attractive. A **stock split** is an increase in the number of authorized, issued, and outstanding shares of stock, coupled with a proportionate reduction in the stock's par value. For example, if the company splits its stock 2 for 1, the number of outstanding shares is doubled and each share's par value is halved. Most leading companies in the United States—IBM, Ford Motor Company, Giant Food, Inc., and others—have split their stock.

The market price of a share of IBM common stock has been approximately $100. Assume that the company wishes to decrease the market price to approximately $25. That is, IBM decides to split the common stock 4 for 1 to reduce the stock's market price from $100 to $25. A 4-for-1 stock split means that the company would have four times as many shares of stock outstanding after the split as it had before and that each share's par value would be quartered. Assume that IBM had 140 million shares of $5 par common stock issued and outstanding before the split:

IBM Stockholders' Equity (Adapted) Before 4-for-1 Stock Split	(In millions)	After 4-for-1 Stock Split	(In millions)
Common stock, $5 par, 187.5 million shares authorized, 140 million shares issued	$ 700	Common stock, $1.25 par, 750 million shares authorized, 560 million shares issued	$ 700
Capital in excess of par	6,800	Capital in excess of par	6,800
Retained earnings	11,630	Retained earnings	11,630
Other	3,293	Other	3,293
Total stockholders' equity	$22,423	Total stockholders' equity	$22,423

After the 4-for-1 stock split, IBM would have 750 million shares authorized and 560 million shares (140 million shares × 4) of $1.25 par ($5/4) common stock issued and outstanding. Total stockholders' equity would be exactly as before the stock split. Indeed, the balance in the Common Stock account does not even change. Only the par value of the stock and the number of shares authorized, issued, and outstanding change. Compare the figures in red in the preceding stockholders' equity presentations for IBM.

Because the stock split affects no account balances, no formal journal entry is necessary. Instead, the split is recorded in a *memorandum entry* such as the following:

Aug. 19   Split the common stock 4 for 1. Called in the outstanding $5 par common stock and distributed four shares of $1.25 par common stock for each old share previously outstanding.

■ **Daily Exercise 14-4**
■ **Daily Exercise 14-5**

A company may engage in a reverse split to decrease the number of shares of stock outstanding. For example, IBM could split its stock 1 for 4. After the split, par value would be $20 ($5 × 4), shares authorized would be 46.875 million (187.5 million/4), and shares issued and outstanding would be 35 million (140 million/4). Reverse splits are unusual.

Event	Effect on Total Stockholders' Equity
Declaration of *cash* dividend	Decrease
Payment of *cash* dividend	No effect
Declaration of *stock* dividend	No effect
Distribution of *stock* dividend	No effect
Stock split	No effect

Source: Adapted from material provided by Beverly Terry.

Similarities and Differences between Stock Dividends and Stock Splits

Both stock dividends and stock splits increase the number of shares of stock owned per stockholder. Also, neither stock dividends nor stock splits change the investor's total cost of the stock owned or the company's total stockholders' equity.

Objective 2

Distinguish stock splits from stock dividends

Consider Avon Products, Inc., whose beauty products are sold in 119 countries primarily by independent sales representatives. Assume that you paid $3,000 to acquire 150 shares of Avon common stock. If Avon distributes a 100% stock dividend, your 150 shares increase to 300, but your total cost is still $3,000. Likewise, if Avon distributes a 2-for-1 stock split, your shares increase to 300, but your total cost is unchanged. Neither type of stock action creates taxable income for the investor.

Stock dividends and stock splits differ in that a stock *dividend* shifts an amount from retained earnings to paid-in capital, leaving the par value per share unchanged. A stock *split* affects no account balances whatsoever. Instead, a stock split changes the par value of the stock. It also increases the number of shares of stock authorized, issued, and outstanding.

■ **Daily Exercise 14-6**

Exhibit 14-3 summarizes the effects of dividends and stock splits on total stockholders' equity.

Treasury Stock

Objective 3

Account for treasury stock

Stock that a corporation has issued and later reacquired is called **treasury stock.**[1] In effect, the corporation holds the stock in its treasury. Corporations may purchase their own stock for several reasons:

Treasury Stock. A corporation's own stock that it has issued and later reacquired.

1. The company has issued all its authorized stock and needs the stock for distributions to officers and employees under bonus plans or stock purchase plans.
2. The purchase helps support the stock's current market price by decreasing the supply of stock available to the public.
3. The business is trying to increase net assets by buying its shares low and hoping to sell them for a higher price later.
4. Management wants to avoid a takeover by an outside party.

Treasury stock is like unissued stock: Neither treasury stock nor unissued stock is outstanding in the hands of shareholders. The company does not receive cash dividends on its treasury stock, and treasury stock does not entitle the company to vote or to receive assets in liquidation. The difference between unissued stock and treasury stock is that treasury stock has been issued and bought back by the company itself. Unissued stock has never been issued.

The purchase of treasury stock decreases the company's assets and its stockholders' equity. The size of the company literally decreases, as shown on its balance sheet. Purchasing treasury stock is consistent with a corporate strategy of downsizing.

The Treasury Stock account has a debit balance, which is the opposite of the other owners' equity accounts. Therefore, *Treasury Stock is a contra stockholders' equity account.*

---

[1]In this text we illustrate the *cost* method of accounting for treasury stock because it is used most widely. Other methods are presented in intermediate accounting courses.

Purchase of Treasury Stock

We record the purchase of treasury stock by debiting Treasury Stock and crediting the asset given in exchange—usually Cash. Suppose that Jupiter Drilling Company had the following stockholders' equity before purchasing treasury stock:

Stockholders' Equity [*Before* Purchase of Treasury Stock]	
Paid-in capital	
Common stock, $1 par, 10,000 shares authorized, 8,000 shares issued	$ 8,000
Paid-in capital in excess of par—common	12,000
Total paid-in capital	20,000
Retained earnings	14,600
Total stockholders' equity..	$34,600

On November 22, Jupiter purchases 1,000 shares of its $1 par common as treasury stock, paying cash of $7.50 per share. Jupiter records the purchase of treasury stock as follows:

Nov. 22	Treasury Stock, Common (1,000 × $7.50)	7,500	
	Cash		7,500
	To purchase 1,000 shares of treasury stock at $7.50 per share.		

The accounting equation shows that the purchase of treasury stock decreases both Jupiter's assets and its stockholders' equity by the full cost of the treasury stock.

$$\begin{array}{ccccc} \text{Assets} & = & \text{Liabilities} & + & \begin{array}{c}\text{Stockholders'}\\\text{Equity}\end{array} \\ \hline -7{,}500 & = & 0 & - & 7{,}500 \end{array}$$

Treasury stock is recorded at cost, without reference to the stock's par value. The Treasury Stock account is often reported beneath Retained Earnings on the balance sheet. Treasury Stock has a debit balance, which makes it a contra stockholders' equity account, so its balance is subtracted from the sum of total paid-in capital and retained earnings, as follows:

■ **Daily Exercise 14-7**

Stockholders' Equity [*After* Purchase of Treasury Stock]	
Paid-in capital:	
Common stock, $1 par, 10,000 shares authorized, 8,000 shares issued, 7,000 shares outstanding..............	$ 8,000
Paid-in capital in excess of par—common	12,000
Retained earnings	14,600
Subtotal	34,600
Less treasury stock, 1,000 shares at cost	(7,500)
Total stockholders' equity...	$27,100

The purchase of treasury stock does not decrease the number of shares issued. The Common Stock, Paid-in Capital in Excess of Par, and Retained Earnings accounts remain unchanged. However, total stockholders' equity decreases by the cost of the treasury stock. Also, shares of stock *outstanding* decrease from 8,000 to 7,000. To compute the number of outstanding shares, subtract the treasury shares (1,000) from the shares issued (8,000). Although the number of *outstanding shares* is not required to be reported on the balance sheet, this figure is important. Only outstanding shares have voting rights, receive cash dividends, and share in assets if the corporation liquidates.

Thinking It Over *Ethical Issue:* Treasury stock transactions have a serious ethical and legal dimension. A company buying its own shares as treasury stock must be extremely careful that its disclosures of information are complete and accurate. Otherwise, a stockholder who sold shares back to the company may claim that he or she was deceived into selling the stock at too low a price. What would happen if a company purchased treasury stock at $17 per share and one day later announced a technological breakthrough that would generate millions of dollars in new business?

Answer: The stock price would likely increase in response to the new information. If it could be proved that management withheld the information, a shareholder selling stock back to the company may file a lawsuit to gain the difference per share. The stockholder would claim that with knowledge of the technological advance, he or she would have held the stock until after the price increase.

Sale of Treasury Stock

A company may sell its treasury stock at a variety of prices.

SALE OF TREASURY STOCK AT COST   The company may sell its treasury stock at any price agreeable to the corporation and the purchaser. If the stock is sold for the same price that the corporation paid to reacquire it, the entry is a debit to Cash and a credit to Treasury Stock for the same amount.

SALE OF TREASURY STOCK ABOVE COST   If the sale price of treasury stock is greater than its reacquisition cost, the difference is credited to the account Paid-in Capital from Treasury Stock Transactions because the excess came from the company's stockholders. Suppose Jupiter Drilling Company resold 200 of its treasury shares for $9 per share (cost was $7.50 per share). The entry is

Dec. 7	Cash (200 × $9)...	1,800
	Treasury Stock, Common (200 × $7.50—	
	the purchase cost per share)	1,500
	Paid-in Capital from Treasury Stock	
	Transactions..	300
	To sell 200 shares of treasury stock above cost.	

Note that the sale of treasury stock increases both Jupiter's assets and its stockholders' equity by the full sale price of the treasury stock.

Assets	=	Liabilities	+	Stockholders' Equity
+1,800	=	0		+1,500
				+300

Paid-in Capital from Treasury Stock Transactions is reported with the other paid-in capital accounts on the balance sheet, beneath the Common Stock and Capital in Excess of Par accounts as follows:

Stockholders' Equity [*After* Purchase and Sale of Treasury Stock]	
Paid-in capital:	
Common stock, $1 par, 10,000 shares authorized,	
8,000 shares issued, 7,200 shares outstanding	$ 8,000
Paid-in capital in excess of par—common.....................................	12,000
Paid-in capital from treasury stock transactions...........................	300
Retained earnings...	14,600
Subtotal..	34,900
Less treasury stock, 800 shares at cost (of $7.50 per share)	(6,000)
Total stockholders' equity	$28,900

■ Daily Exercise 14-8
■ Daily Exercise 14-9

Observe that total stockholders' equity increased from $27,100 to $28,900. The $1,800 increase is the amount of cash received from sale of the treasury stock.

SALE OF TREASURY STOCK BELOW COST At times, the resale price of treasury stock is less than cost. The difference between these two amounts is debited to Paid-in Capital from Treasury Stock Transactions if this account has a credit balance, as in our example. Jupiter Drilling would record the sale of 400 shares of treasury stock at $5 per share with the following entry:

Dec. 23	Cash (400 × $5)..	2,000	
	Paid-in Capital from Treasury Stock Transactions		
	(from Dec. 7 entry on page 591)	300	
	Retained Earnings..	700	
	Treasury Stock, Common (400 × $7.50—		
	the purchase cost per share).................................		3,000
	To sell 400 shares of treasury stock below cost.		

Suppose this sale of treasury stock, at a price below cost, occurred when there was no prior balance in Paid-in Capital from Treasury Stock Transactions. In that case, the full amount of the difference between the sale price ($2,000) and the cost of the treasury stock ($3,000) is debited to Retained Earnings as follows:

Dec. 23	Cash (400 × $5)..	2,000	
	Retained Earnings..	1,000	
	Treasury Stock, Common (400 × $7.50)		3,000
	To sell 400 shares of treasury stock below cost.		

Treasury Stock Transactions: A Summary

Treasury stock transactions take place between the business and its owners, the stockholders, so

- Neither the purchase nor the sale of treasury stock creates a gain or a loss, and thus treasury stock transactions have no effect on net income.
- Sale of treasury stock above cost increases paid-in capital, not income.
- Sale of treasury stock below cost decreases paid-in capital or retained earnings, but does not create a loss.

". . . The Limited, Inc. purchased $500 million of its own stock."

Does this mean that a company cannot increase its net assets by buying treasury stock low and selling it high? Not at all. Management often buys treasury stock because it believes that the market price of its stock is too low. For example, The Limited, Inc., purchased $500 million of its own stock. Suppose The Limited holds the stock as the market price rises and resells the stock for $....600 million. Net assets of the company increase by $100 million. Exhibit 14-4 summarizes The Limited's financial position before and after the sale of treasury stock.

Retirement of Stock

A corporation may purchase its own common stock or preferred stock and *retire* it by canceling the stock certificates. Retirements of preferred stock occur more often than retirements of common stock, as companies seek to avoid having to pay the dividends on the preferred stock. The retired stock cannot be reissued. Retiring stock, like purchasing treasury stock, decreases the corporation's outstanding stock. Unlike a treasury stock purchase, stock retirement decreases the number of shares issued. In retiring stock, the corporation removes the balances from all paid-in capital accounts related to the retired shares, such as Capital in Excess of Par.

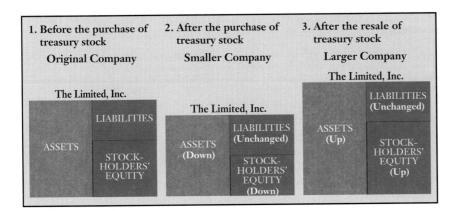

A corporation may repurchase shares for retirement for a price that is below the stock's issue price (par value plus any capital in excess of par). This difference between repurchase price and issue price increases Paid-in Capital from Retirement of Stock. This new layer of paid-in capital created by a retirement of stock (preferred or common) belongs to the common stockholders. If the corporation must pay more than the stock's issue price, the excess decreases Retained Earnings.

Retiring stock, like purchasing treasury stock, is a transaction that does not affect net income. No gain or loss arises from stock retirement because the company is doing business with its owners.

Review the first half of the chapter by studying the following Decision Guidelines feature.

■ **Daily Exercise 14-11**

DECISION GUIDELINES — Accounting for Retained Earnings, Dividends, and Treasury Stock

DECISION	GUIDELINES	
How to record:		
• Declaration of a small stock dividend? (20–25%)	Retained Earnings .... Common Stock Dividend Distributable.............................. Paid-in Capital in Excess of Par	Market value Par value Excess
• Declaration of a large stock dividend? (25% or more)	Retained Earnings .... Common Stock Dividend Distributable	Par value Par value
• Stock split?	Memorandum only: Split the common stock 2 for 1. Called in the outstanding $10 par common stock and distributed two shares of $5 par for each old share outstanding (amounts assumed).	

What are the effects of stock dividends and stock splits on:	Effects of	
	Stock Dividend	Stock Split
• Number of shares of stock authorized?	No effect	Increase
• Shares issued?	Increase	Increase
• Shares outstanding	Increase	Increase
• Par value per share?	No effect	Decrease
• Total assets and total liabilities	No effect	No effect
• Total stockholders' equity	No effect	No effect
• Common Stock account	Increase	No effect
• Retained Earnings account	Decrease	No effect

(continued)

How to record:

- Purchase of treasury stock?

Treasury Stock.......................... Cost	
Cash	Cost

- Sale of treasury stock
  - At cost?

Cash................................ Amt received	
Treasury Stock	Cost

   Above cost?

Cash................................ Amt received	
Treasury Stock	Cost
Paid-in Capital from	
Treasury Stock Transactions....	Excess

   Below cost?

Cash................................ Amt received	
Paid-in Capital from Treasury	
Stock Transactions.................. Amt up to	
prior bal.	
Retained Earnings...................... Excess	
Treasury Stock	Cost

or

Cash.. Amt received	
Retained Earnings..................... Excess	
Treasury Stock	Cost

Effects of

What are the effects of the purchase and sale of treasury stock on:	Purchase of Treasury Stock	Sale of Treasury Stock
• Total assets?	Decrease by full amount of payment	Increase by full amount of cash receipt
• Total stockholders' equity?	Decrease by full amount of payment	Increase by full amount of cash receipt

Restrictions on Retained Earnings

Objective 4

Report restrictions on retained earnings

Dividends, purchases of treasury stock, and retirements of stock require payments by the corporation to its stockholders. These outlays decrease the corporation's assets, so fewer assets are available to pay liabilities. Therefore, a corporation's creditors seek to restrict its dividend payments and treasury stock purchases. For example, a bank may agree to loan $500,000 only if the borrowing corporation limits dividend payments and purchases of treasury stock.

To ensure that corporations maintain a minimum level of stockholders' equity for the protection of creditors, state laws restrict the amount of treasury stock that a corporation may purchase. Restrictions on dividends and treasury stock purchases often focus on the balance of retained earnings.

Companies usually report their retained earnings restrictions in notes to the financial statements. The following disclosure by RTE Corporation, a manufacturer of electronic transformers, is typical:

> **NOTES TO CONSOLIDATED FINANCIAL STATEMENTS**
> **NOTE F—LONG-TERM DEBT**
>
> The ... loan agreements ... restrict cash dividends and similar payments to shareholders. Under the most restrictive of these provisions, retained earnings of $4,300,000 were unrestricted as of December 31, 19X3.

With this restriction, the maximum dividend that RTE Corporation can pay its stockholders is $4,300,000.

Appropriations of Retained Earnings

Appropriations are restrictions on Retained Earnings that are recorded by formal journal entries. A corporation may *appropriate*—segregate in a separate account—a portion of Retained Earnings for a specific use. For example, the board of directors may appropriate part of Retained Earnings for building a new manufacturing plant or for meeting possible future liabilities. A debit to Retained Earnings and a credit to a separate account—Retained Earnings Appropriated for Plant Expansion—records the appropriation. This appropriated Retained Earnings account appears directly above the regular Retained Earnings account on the balance sheet.

Appropriation of Retained Earnings. Restriction of retained earnings that is recorded by a formal journal entry.

Retained earnings appropriations are rare. Corporations generally disclose any retained earnings restrictions in the notes to the financial statements as illustrated in the preceding section.

Variations in Reporting Stockholders' Equity

■ **Daily Exercise 14-12**

Accountants and other business people may use terminology and formats in reporting stockholders' equity that differ from our general examples. We use a more detailed format in this book to help you learn the components of the stockholders' equity section. Companies assume that readers of their statements already understand the details they omit.

One of the most important skills you will learn in this course is the ability to understand the financial statements of real companies. Thus we present in Exhibit 14-5 a side-by-side comparison of our general teaching format and the format that you are

Concept Highlight

EXHIBIT 14-5
Formats for Reporting Stockholders' Equity

General Teaching Format		Real-World Format	
Stockholders' equity		**Stockholders' equity**	
Paid-in capital:		Preferred stock, 8%, $10 par, 30,000	
Preferred stock, 8%, $10 par, 30,000 shares authorized and issued....................................	$ 300,000	shares authorized and issued...........................	$ 310,000
Paid-in capital in excess of par—preferred	10,000	Common stock, $1 par, 100,000 shares authorized, 60,000 shares issued	60,000
Common stock, $1 par, 100,000 shares authorized, 60,000 shares issued	60,000	Additional paid-in capital...................................	2,160,000
		Retained earnings (Note 7)...............................	1,565,000
Paid-in capital in excess of par—common	2,140,000	Less treasury stock, common (1,400 shares at cost)	(42,000)
Paid-in capital from treasury stock transactions, common....................................	9,000		$4,053,000
Paid-in capital from retirement of preferred stock..	4,000	*Note 7—Restriction on retained earnings.*	
Donated capital...	7,000	At December 31, 19XX, $400,000 of retained earnings is restricted by the company's board of directors to absorb the effect of any contingencies that may arise. Accordingly, possible dividend declarations are restricted to a maximum of $1,165,000 ($1,565,000 – $400,000).	
Total paid-in capital..	2,530,000		
Retained earnings appropriated for contingencies..	400,000		
Retained earnings—unappropriated.....................	1,165,000		
Total retained earnings.......................................	1,565,000		
Subtotal..	4,095,000		
Less treasury stock, common (1,400 shares at cost)...	(42,000)		
Total stockholders' equity	$4,053,000		

more likely to encounter in real-world balance sheets. Note the following points in the real-world format:

1. The heading Paid-in Capital does not appear. It is commonly understood that Preferred Stock, Common Stock, and Additional Paid-in Capital are elements of paid-in capital.

2. Preferred stock is often reported in a single amount that combines its par value and premium.

3. For presentation in the financial statements, all additional paid-in capital—from capital in excess of par on common stock, treasury stock transactions, and stock retirement—appears as a single amount labeled Additional Paid-in Capital. Additional Paid-in Capital belongs to the common stockholders, and so it follows Common Stock in the real-world format.

4. Often, total stockholders' equity ($4,053,000 in Exhibit 14-5) is not specifically labeled.

Now that we have covered stockholders' equity in detail, we turn to the corporate income statement.

SUMMARY PROBLEM FOR YOUR REVIEW · MID-CHAPTER

Simplicity Pattern Co., Inc., a well-known maker of sewing patterns, reported the following shareholder's equity:

Shareholders' Equity	($ Thousands)
Preferred stock, $1.00 par value	
Authorized—10,000,000 shares	
Issued—None..	$ —
Common stock, 8 1/3 cents par value	
Authorized, 30,000,000 shares	
Issued 13,733,229 shares.......................................	1,144
Capital in excess of par value	48,122
Earnings retained in business	89,320
	138,586
Less treasury stock, at cost (1,919,000 common shares)..........	14,742
	$123,844

REQUIRED

1. What was the average issue price per share of the common stock?
2. Journalize the issuance of 1,200 shares of common stock at $4 per share. Use Simplicity's account titles.
3. How many shares of Simplicity's common stock are outstanding?
4. How many shares of common stock would be outstanding after Simplicity split its common stock 3 for 1?
5. Using Simplicity account titles, journalize the declaration of a stock dividend when the market price of Simplicity common stock is $3 per share. Consider each of the following stock dividends independently:
   a. Simplicity declares a 10% common stock dividend on the shares outstanding, computed in requirement 3.
   b. Simplicity declares a 100% common stock dividend on the shares outstanding, computed in requirement 3.
6. Journalize the following treasury stock transactions, assuming they occur in the order given:
   a. Simplicity purchases 500 shares of treasury stock at $8 per share.
   b. Simplicity sells 100 shares of treasury stock for $9 per share.
   c. Simplicity sells 100 shares of treasury stock for $5 per share.

■ **SOLUTION**

1. Average issue price of common stock was $3.59 per share
   [($1,144,000 + $48,122,000)/13,733,229 shares = $3.59].

2. Cash (1,200 × $4) 4,800
    Common Stock (1,200 × $0.08 1/3) 100
    Capital in Excess of Par Value 4,700
    To issue common stock at a premium.

3. Shares outstanding = 11,814,229 (13,733,229 shares issued minus 1,919,000 shares of treasury stock)

4. Shares outstanding after a 3-for-1 stock split = 35,442,687 (11,814,229 shares outstanding × 3)

5a. Earnings Retained in Business (11,814,229 × 0.10 × $3) 3,544,269
    Common Stock Dividend Distributable
      (11,814,229 × 0.10 × $0.08 1/3) 98,452
    Capital in Excess of Par Value 3,445,817
    To declare a 10% common stock dividend.

  b. Earnings Retained in Business (11,814,229 × $0.08 1/3) 984,519
    Common Stock Dividend Distributable 984,519
    To declare a 100% common stock dividend.

6a. Treasury Stock (500 × $8) 4,000
    Cash 4,000
    To purchase 500 shares of treasury stock at $8 per share.

  b. Cash (100 × $9) 900
    Treasury Stock (100 × $8) 800
    Paid-in Capital from Treasury Stock Transactions 100
    To sell 100 shares of treasury stock at $9 per share.

  c. Cash (100 × $5) 500
    Paid-in Capital from Treasury Stock.
      Transactions (balance from answer 6b) 100
    Earnings Retained in Business.. 200
      Treasury Stock (100 × $8) 800
    To sell 100 shares of treasury stock at $5 per share.

The Corporate Income Statement— Analyzing the Quality of Earnings

A corporation's net income (revenues plus gains minus expenses and losses) receives more attention than any other item in the financial statements. In fact, net income is probably the most important piece of information about a company. Net income measures the business's ability to earn a profit and indicates how successfully the company has managed its operations. To stockholders, the larger the corporation's profit, the greater the likelihood of dividends. To creditors, the larger the corporation's profit, the better it is able to pay its debts. Net income builds up a company's assets and owners' equity. It also helps to attract capital from new investors who hope to receive dividends from future successful operations.

    Suppose you are considering investing in the stock of The May Department Stores Company. You would examine May's income statement in Exhibit 14-1 (page 584). May's trend of income from continuing operations (which May sets in boldface type and labels as Net Earnings from Continuing Operations, line 8) is up during 1996. The trend of net income (which May labels as Net earnings, line 12) is essentially flat. May also reports a third income figure, net earnings before extraordinary loss (line 10). To understand the makeup of net income, let's examine the various types of income in detail. Exhibit 14-6 provides a comprehensive example that we will use in the following discussions. It is the income statement of Allied Electronics Corporation, a small manufacturer of precision instruments.

Objective 5

Identify the elements of a corporation's income statement

Continuing Operations

Income from a business's continuing operations helps investors make predictions about the business's future earnings. In the income statement of Exhibit 14-6, the topmost section reports income from continuing operations. This part of the business is expected to continue from period to period. We may use this information to predict that Allied Electronics Corporation will earn income of approximately $54,000 next year.

ALLIED ELECTRONICS CORPORATION
Income Statement
Year Ended December 31, 19X5

Continuing operations	Net sales revenue		$500,000
	Cost of goods sold		240,000
	Gross margin		260,000
	Operating expenses (detailed)		181,000
	Operating income		79,000
	Other gains (losses):		
	Loss on restructuring operations		(10,000)
	Gain on sale of machinery		21,000
	Income from continuing operations before income tax		90,000
	Income tax expense		36,000
	Income from continuing operations		54,000
Special items	Discontinued operations:		
	Operating income, $30,000, less income tax of $12,000	$18,000	
	Gain on disposal, $5,000, less income tax of $2,000	3,000	21,000
	Income before extraordinary item and cumulative effect of change in depreciation method		75,000
	Extraordinary flood loss, $20,000, less income tax saving of $8,000		(12,000)
	Cumulative effect of change in depreciation method, $10,000, less income tax of $4,000		6,000
	Net income		$ 69,000
Earnings per share	Earnings per share of common stock (20,000 shares outstanding):		
	Income from continuing operations		$2.70
	Income from discontinued operations		1.05
	Income before extraordinary item and cumulative effect of change in depreciation method		3.75
	Extraordinary loss		(0.60)
	Cumulative effect of change in depreciation method		0.30
	Net income		$3.45

EXHIBIT 14-6
Allied Electronics Corporation's
Income Statement

The continuing operations of Allied Electronics include three items deserving explanation. First, during 19X5, the company had a $10,000 loss on restructuring operations. Restructuring costs include severance pay to laid-off workers, moving expenses for employees transferred to other locations, and environmental cleanup expenses. The restructuring loss is part of continuing operations because Allied Electronics is remaining in the same line of business. But the restructuring loss is highlighted as an "other" item (unusual) on the income statement because its cause—restructuring—falls outside Allied's main business endeavor, which is selling electronics products.

Second, Allied had a gain on the sale of machinery, which is also outside the company's core business activity. This explains why the gain is reported separately from Allied's sales revenue, cost of goods sold, and gross margin.

Third, income tax expense has been deducted in arriving at income from continuing operations. The tax that corporations pay on their income is a significant expense. We use an income tax rate of 40% in our illustrations. The $36,000 income tax expense in Exhibit 14-6 equals the pretax income from continuing operations multiplied by the tax rate ($90,000 × 0.40 = $36,000).

Special Items

An income statement may include three categories of special gains and losses:

■ **Daily Exercise 14-13**

- Discontinued operations
- Extraordinary gains and losses
- Cumulative effect of a change in accounting principle

Discontinued Operations

Most large corporations engage in several lines of business. For example, General Mills, Inc., best known for its food products, also has retailing and restaurant operations. In addition to its retail stores, Sears, Roebuck & Co., has a real-estate development company (Homart) and an insurance company (Allstate). We call each identifiable division of a company a **segment of the business.**

A company may sell a segment of its business. For example, May Department Stores sold Payless, its chain of shoe stores. Such a sale is not a regular source of income because a company cannot keep selling its segments indefinitely. The sale of a business segment is viewed as a one-time transaction.

Financial analysts typically do not include income or loss on discontinued operations in predictions of future corporate income. The discontinued segments will not generate income for the company in the future.

The income statement carries information on the segment that has been disposed of under the heading Discontinued operations. This section of the income statement is divided into two components: (1) operating income or (loss) on the segment that is disposed of, and (2) any gain (or loss) on the disposal. It is necessary to separate discontinued operations into these two components because the company may operate the discontinued segment for part of the year. This is the operating income (or loss) component. Then, the disposal of the segment results in a gain (or loss). Income and gain are taxed at the 40% rate and reported by Allied Electronics Corporation as follows:

Discontinued operations:		
Operating income, $30,000, less income tax, $12,000	$18,000	
Gain on disposal, $5,000, less income tax, $2,000	3,000	$21,000

Trace this presentation to Exhibit 14-6.

In the normal course of business, companies dispose of old plant and equipment as they acquire new, more productive assets. Gains and losses on these asset dispositions are *not* reported as discontinued operations because they don't relate to a segment of the business that is being discontinued. Gains and losses on normal asset dispositions can be reported along with operating revenues and expenses or highlighted in an "Other" section of the income statement.

Extraordinary Gains and Losses (Extraordinary Items)

Extraordinary gains and losses, also called **extraordinary items,** are both unusual for the company and infrequent. Losses from natural disasters (such as earthquakes, floods, and tornadoes), and the taking of company assets by a foreign government (expropriation), are extraordinary. Gains and losses on the early retirement of debt are also extraordinary items, as reported by May Department Stores in Exhibit 14-1.

Extraordinary items are reported along with their income tax effect. During 19X5, Allied Electronics Corporation lost $20,000 of inventory in a flood. This flood loss, which reduced income, also reduced Allied's income tax. The tax effect of the loss is computed by multiplying the amount of the loss by the tax rate. The tax effect decreases the net amount of the loss in the same way that the income tax reduces the amount of net income. An extraordinary loss can be reported along with its tax effect on the income statement as follows:

Extraordinary flood loss	$(20,000)
Less income tax saving	8,000
Extraordinary flood loss, net of tax	(12,000)

Trace this item to the income statement in Exhibit 14-6. An extraordinary gain is reported in the same way as a loss, net of the income tax on the gain.

Segment of the Business. One of various separate divisions of a company.

Extraordinary Item. A gain or loss that is both unusual for the company and infrequent. Also called **extraordinary gains and losses.**

■ **Daily Exercise 14-14**

Gains and losses due to employee strikes, the settlement of lawsuits, discontinued operations, and the sale of plant assets are *not* extraordinary items. They are considered normal business occurrences. However, because they are outside the business's central operations, they are reported on the income statement as other gains and losses. Examples include the gain on sale of machinery and the restructuring loss in the Other gains (losses) section of Exhibit 14-6.

Cumulative Effect of a Change in Accounting Principle

Companies sometimes change from one accounting method to another, such as from double-declining-balance (DDB) to straight-line depreciation, or from first-in, first-out (FIFO) to weighted-average cost for inventory. ◀▦ An accounting change makes it difficult to compare one period's financial statements with the statements of preceding periods. Without detailed information, investors and creditors can be misled into thinking that the current year is better or worse than the preceding year when in fact the only difference is a change in accounting method. To help investors separate the effects of regular business operations from those effects generated by a change in accounting method, companies report the effect of the accounting change in a special section of the income statement. This section usually appears after extraordinary items.

We need to know what cumulative effect an accounting change would have had on net income of prior years. GAAP requires companies that change accounting methods to disclose the difference between net income actually reported under the old method and the net income that the company would have experienced if it had used the new method all along.

Suppose Allied Electronics Corporation changes from DDB to straight-line depreciation at the beginning of 19X5. The change in accounting method will affect cumulative amounts from previous years. If the company had been using straight-line depreciation every year, depreciation expense would have been less, and net income would have been $6,000 higher ($10,000 minus the additional income tax of $4,000). Exhibit 14-6 reports the cumulative effect of this accounting change. A change from straight-line to double-declining-balance usually produces a negative cumulative effect.

The company generally reports changes in inventory methods and changes in revenue methods in this same manner. Numerous exceptions make changes in accounting principle—usually a change in accounting method—a complicated area. Details are covered in later accounting courses.

 Working It Out Examine all the income tax amounts in Exhibit 14-6. How much was Allied Electronics' *total* income tax expense during 19X5?

Answer: **$46,000 = ($36,000 + $12,000 + $2,000 − $8,000 + $4,000)**
Observe in Exhibit 14-6 that income tax is reported along with each separate category of income or loss:

Category of Income or Loss	Income Tax Expense (Saving)
Income from continuing operations	$36,000
Discontinued operations ($12,000 + $2,000)..........	14,000
Extraordinary gains and losses	(8,000)
Cumulative effect of accounting change	4,000
Total income tax expense for 19X5	$46,000

Note that $36,000 is the company's income tax expense from continuing operations; $46,000 is *total* income tax expense.

Earnings per Share

The final segment of a corporate income statement presents the company's earnings per share, abbreviated as EPS. In fact, GAAP requires that corporations disclose EPS figures

◀▦ ◀▦ ◀▦ For a review of depreciation methods, see Chapter 10. For a review of inventory accounting methods, see Chapter 9.

■ **Daily Exercise 14-15**

on the income statement. **Earnings per share** is the amount of a company's net income per share of its *outstanding common stock*. EPS is a key measure of a business's success:

$$\text{Earnings per share} = \frac{\text{Net income} - \text{Preferred dividends}}{\begin{array}{c}\text{Weighted-average number of}\\\text{common shares outstanding}\end{array}}$$

Just as the corporation lists its different sources of income separately—from continuing operations, discontinued operations, and so on—it also lists the EPS figures based on different income sources separately. Consider the following EPS calculations for Allied Electronics Corporation:

Earnings per share of common stock (20,000 shares outstanding):	
Income from continuing operations ($54,000/20,000)	$2.70
Income from discontinued operations ($21,000/20,000)	1.05
Income before extraordinary item and cumulative effect of change in depreciation method ($75,000/20,000)	3.75
Extraordinary loss ($12,000/20,000)..	(0.60)
Cumulative effect of change in depreciation method ($6,000/20,000)..	0.30
Net income ($69,000/20,000)	$3.45

The final section of Exhibit 14-6 shows how the EPS figures are reported on the income statement.

WEIGHTED-AVERAGE NUMBER OF COMMON SHARES OUTSTANDING Computing EPS is straightforward if the number of common shares outstanding does not change during the accounting period. For many corporations, however, this figure varies during the year. Consider a corporation that had 100,000 shares outstanding from January through November, then purchased 60,000 shares as treasury stock. This company's EPS would be misleadingly high if computed using 40,000 (100,000 − 60,000) shares. To make EPS as meaningful as possible, corporations use the weighted average of the number of common shares outstanding during the period.

Let's assume that Diskette Demo Corporation had these shares of common stock outstanding for the following periods:

- January through May—240,000 shares
- June through August—200,000 shares
- September through December—210,000 shares

We compute the weighted-average number of common shares outstanding by considering the outstanding shares per month as a fraction of the year:

Number of Common Shares × Outstanding	Fraction of Year	Period during the Year		Weighted Average = Number of Common Shares Outstanding
240,000	× 5/12	(January through May)	=	100,000
200,000	× 3/12	(June through August)	=	50,000
210,000	× 4/12	(September through December)	=	70,000
		Weighted-average number of common shares outstanding during the year		220,000

The weighted-average (220,000) number of common shares outstanding would then be divided into net income to compute the corporation's EPS.

EFFECT OF PREFERRED DIVIDENDS ON EARNINGS PER SHARE Throughout our discussion of EPS, we have used only the number of shares of common stock outstanding. Holders of preferred stock have no claim to the business's income beyond the stated preferred dividend. But preferred dividends do affect the EPS figure. Recall that EPS is earnings per share of *common* stock. Recall also that dividends on preferred stock are paid first.

◄▥▥ ◄▥▥ ◄▥▥ Chapter 13, page 549, provides detailed information on preferred stock.

◄▥▥ Therefore, preferred dividends must be subtracted from income subtotals (income from continuing operations, income before extraordinary items and cumulative effect of accounting change, and net income) in the computation of EPS. Preferred dividends are not subtracted from income or loss from discontinued operations, and they are not subtracted from extraordinary gains and losses or the cumulative effect of accounting changes.

If Allied Electronics Corporation had 10,000 shares of preferred stock outstanding, each with a $1.00 dividend, the annual preferred dividend would be $10,000 (10,000 × $1.00). The $10,000 would be subtracted from each of the different income subtotals, resulting in the following EPS computations for the company:

■ **Daily Exercise 14-16**

Earnings per share of common stock (20,000 shares outstanding):	
Income from continuing operations ($54,000 − $10,000)/20,000.................	$2.20
Income from discontinued operations ($21,000/20,000)...............................	1.05
Income before extraordinary item and cumulative effect of	
change in depreciation method ($75,000 − $10,000)/20,000.....................	3.25
Extraordinary loss ($12,000/20,000)	(0.60)
Cumulative effect of change in depreciation method ($6,000/20,000)	0.30
Net income ($69,000 − $10,000)/20,000..	$2.95

EARNINGS PER SHARE DILUTION Some corporations make their preferred stock more attractive to investors by offering convertible preferred stock. Holders of convertible preferred may exchange the preferred stock for common stock. When preferred stock is converted to common stock, the EPS is *diluted*—reduced—because more common stock shares are divided into net income. Corporations with complex capital structures present two sets of EPS figures.

- EPS based on outstanding common shares (*basic* EPS)
- EPS based on outstanding common shares plus the number of additional common shares that would arise from conversion of the preferred stock into common stock (*diluted* EPS)

■ **Daily Exercise 14-17**

Thinking It Over What makes earnings per share so useful as a business statistic?

Answer: Earnings per share is useful because it relates a company's income to one share of stock. Stock prices are quoted at an amount per share, and investors usually consider how much they must pay for a certain number of shares. Earnings per share is used to help determine the value of a share of stock.

Combined Statement of Income and Retained Earnings

Some companies report income and retained earnings on a single statement. Exhibit 14-7 illustrates how Allied Electronics would combine its income statement and its statement of retained earnings.

Reporting Comprehensive Income

Comprehensive Income. Company's change in total stockholders' equity from all sources other than from the owners of the business.

As we have seen throughout this book, all companies report net income or net loss on their income statement. Companies with certain gains and losses are also required by FASB Statement 130 to report another income figure. **Comprehensive income** is the company's change in total stockholders' equity from all sources other than from the owners of the business. Comprehensive income includes net income plus some specific gains and losses. FASB Statement 130 includes two new components of comprehensive income:

- Unrealized gains or losses on certain investments
- Foreign-currency translation adjustments   } Chapter 16 explains these items.

602 Part 3 Accounting for Partnerships and Corporate Transactions

Income statement	Sales revenue..	$500,000
	Cost of goods sold..	240,000
	Gross margin	260,000
	Expenses (listed individually).....................................	191,000
	Net income for 19X5...	$ 69,000
Statement of retained earnings	Retained earnings, December 31, 19X4........................	130,000
		199,000
	Dividends for 19X5...	(21,000)
	Retained earnings, December 31, 19X5.......................	$178,000

Earnings per share of common stock (20,000 shares outstanding):

Income from continuing operations..	$2.70
Income from discontinued operations	1.05
Income before extraordinary item and cumulative effect of change in depreciation method	3.75
Extraordinary loss...	(0.60)
Cumulative effect of change in depreciation method	0.30
Net income	$3.45

EXHIBIT 14-7
Combined Statement of Income and Retained Earnings

■ **Daily Exercise 14-18**

These items do not enter into the determination of net income but instead are reported as other comprehensive income, as shown in Exhibit 14-8. Assumed figures are used for all items.

Earnings per share applies only to net income and its components as discussed earlier. Earnings per share is not reported for other comprehensive income.

Investors and creditors who believe net income is the best measure of operating performance can use net income to evaluate the company. Others who view comprehensive income as the best measure of the company's progress can use comprehensive income in their evaluations.

The Decision Guidelines feature on page 604 covers the major aspects of a corporate income statement.

Prior-Period Adjustments

What happens when a company makes an error in recording revenues or expenses? After the revenue and expense accounts are closed, the company's Retained Earnings account will absorb the effect of the error. The balance of Retained Earnings will be wrong until the error is corrected.

Corrections to the beginning balance of Retained Earnings for errors of an earlier period are called **prior-period adjustments.** The correcting entry includes a debit or credit to Retained Earnings for the error amount and a credit or debit to the asset or liability account that was misstated. The prior-period adjustment appears on the corporation's statement of retained earnings to indicate to readers the amount and the nature of the change in the beginning Retained Earnings balance.

Prior-period Adjustment. A correction to retained earnings for an error of an earlier period.

NATIONAL EXPRESS COMPANY
Income Statement
Year Ended December 31, 19X9

Revenues..	$10,000
Expenses (summarized)...........................	6,000
Net income...	4,000
Other comprehensive income:	
Unrealized gain on investments..........	1,000
Comprehensive income	$ 5,000

EXHIBIT 14-8
Reporting Comprehensive Income

DECISION	GUIDELINES	
What are the main sections of the income statement?	Continuing operations	• Continuing operations, including other gains and losses and income tax expense
	Special items	• Discontinued operations—gain or loss—less the income tax effect • Extraordinary gain or loss, less the income tax effect • Cumulative effect of change in accounting principle, less the income tax effect • Net income (or net loss) • Other comprehensive income (Exhibit 14-8)
What earnings per share (EPS) figures must a corporation report?	Earnings per share	• Earnings per share—applies only to net income (or net loss) and its components, not to other comprehensive income Must compute separate EPS figures for all amounts that apply, including • Income from continuing operations • Discontinued operations • Income before extraordinary item and cumulative effect of accounting change • Extraordinary gain or loss • Cumulative effect of accounting change • Net income (or net loss)
How to compute the EPS for net income?	$$EPS = \frac{\text{Net income} - \text{Preferred dividends}}{\text{Weighted-average number of common shares outstanding}}$$	

Assume that De Graff Corporation recorded income tax expense for 19X4 as $30,000. The correct amount was $40,000. This error resulted in

- Understating 19X4 expenses by $10,000, and
- Overstating net income by $10,000

A bill from the government in 19X5 for the additional $10,000 in taxes alerts the De Graff management to the mistake. De Graff's prior-period adjustment would be reported on the statement of retained earnings for 19X5, as follows. Observe that a prior-period adjustment appears as an adjustment of the beginning balance of Retained Earnings.

■ **Daily Exercise 14-19**

DE GRAFF CORPORATION
Statement of Retained Earnings
Year Ended December 31, 19X5

Retained earnings balance, December 31, 19X4, as originally reported	$390,000
Prior-period adjustment—debit to correct error in recording income tax expense of 19X4	(10,000)
Retained earnings balance, December 31, 19X4, as adjusted..........	380,000
Net income for 19X5..	114,000
	494,000
Dividends for 19X5	(41,000)
Retained earnings balance, December 31, 19X5	$453,000

	Common Stock	Additional Paid-in Capital	Retained Earnings	Treasury Stock	Total
ALLIED ELECTRONICS CORPORATION					
Statement of Stockholders' Equity					
Year Ended December 31, 19X5					
Balance, December 31, 19X4............	$ 80,000	$160,000	$130,000	$(25,000)	$345,000
Issuance of stock................................	20,000	65,000			85,000
Net income			69,000		69,000
Cash dividends.....................................			(21,000)		(21,000)
Stock dividends—8%	8,000	26,000	(34,000)		–0–
Purchase of treasury stock................				(9,000)	(9,000)
Sale of treasury stock........................		13,000		4,000	17,000
Balance, December 31, 19X5	$108,000	$264,000	$144,000	$(30,000)	$486,000

EXHIBIT 14-9
Statement of Stockholders' Equity

Statement of Stockholders' Equity

Objective 6

Prepare a statement of stockholders' equity

Most companies report a statement of stockholders' equity, which is more comprehensive than a statement of retained earnings. The statement of stockholders' equity is formatted exactly as a statement of retained earnings but with columns for each element of stockholders' equity. The **statement of stockholders' equity** thus reports the changes in all categories of equity during the period: the stock accounts, additional paid-in capital, retained earnings, treasury stock, and the total.

Exhibit 14-9 uses assumed figures for Allied Electronics Corporation to illustrate the statement of stockholders' equity. Negative amounts—debits—appear in parentheses.

Like the retained earnings statement, the statement of stockholders' equity is less important than the income statement or the balance sheet. However, it reports stock transactions, dividends, and the effects of treasury stock transactions in the interest of full disclosure.

Statement of Stockholders' Equity. Reports the changes in all categories of stockholders' equity during the period.

■ **Daily Exercise 14-20**

Reporting Stockholders' Equity Transactions on the Statement of Cash Flows

Many of the transactions discussed in this chapter are reported on the statement of cash flows. Stockholders' equity transactions are *financing activities* because the company is dealing with its owners, the stockholders—the most basic group of people who finance the company. The financing transactions that affect stockholders' equity and cash (and thus appear on the statement of cash flows) fall into three main categories: issuances of stock, repurchases of stock, and dividends.

1. Issuances of stock *include basic transactions in which a company issues its stock for cash.*

2. *As we discussed earlier in the chapter, a company can* repurchase its stock *as treasury stock, or it can buy the stock and retire it.* In both cases, the company pays cash to repurchase its own stock. A sale of treasury stock, like issuances of stock, increases the company's cash.

3. *Most companies pay* cash dividends *to their stockholders.* Dividend payments are a type of financing transaction because the company is paying its stockholders for the use of their money. In contrast, *stock dividends* are not reported on the statement of cash flows because stock dividends do not affect cash.

EXHIBIT 14-10
Reporting Financing Activities on the Statement of Cash Flows

Cash Flows from Financing Activities	
Proceeds from issuance of common stock	$76,000
Purchase of treasury stock	(7,000)
Proceeds from sale of treasury stock	14,000
Repurchase and retirement of preferred stock	(34,000)
Payment of cash dividends	(51,000)
Net cash outflow for financing activities	$ (2,000)

■ **Daily Exercise 14-21**

Exhibit 14-10 shows how to report stockholders' equity transactions as financing activities on the statement of cash flows. All amounts are assumed. Cash receipts appear as positive amounts and cash payments as negative amounts, denoted by parentheses. The term *proceeds* means cash receipt.

SUMMARY PROBLEM FOR YOUR REVIEW

The following information was taken from the ledger of Kraft Corporation:

Loss on sale of discontinued operations	$ 5,000	Common stock, no-par, 45,000 shares issued	$180,000
Prior-period adjustments—credit to Retained Earnings	5,000	Sales revenue	620,000
Gain on sale of plant assets	21,000	Interest expense	30,000
Cost of goods sold	380,000	Extraordinary gain	26,000
Income tax expense (saving):		Operating income, discontinued operations	25,000
Continuing operations	32,000	Loss due to lawsuit	11,000
Discontinued operations:		General expenses	62,000
Operating income	10,000	Preferred stock, 8%, $100 par, 500 shares issued	50,000
Loss on sale	(2,000)		
Extraordinary gain	10,000	Paid-in capital in excess of par—preferred	7,000
Cumulative effect of change in inventory method	(4,000)	Retained earnings, beginning, as originally reported	103,000
Treasury stock, common (5,000 shares at cost)	25,000	Cumulative effect of change in inventory method (debit)	(10,000)
Dividends	16,000		
Selling expenses	78,000		

REQUIRED

Prepare a single-step income statement and a statement of retained earnings for Kraft Corporation for the current year ended December 31. Include the EPS presentation and show your computations. Kraft had no changes in its stock accounts during the year.

SOLUTION

KRAFT CORPORATION
Income Statement
Year Ended December 31, 19XX

Revenue and gains:		
Sales revenue		$620,000
Gain on sale of plant assets		21,000
Total revenues and gains		641,000
Expenses and losses:		
Cost of goods sold	$380,000	
Selling expenses	78,000	
General expenses	62,000	
Interest expense	30,000	
Loss due to lawsuit	11,000	
Income tax expense	32,000	
Total expenses and losses		593,000
Income from continuing operations		48,000
Discontinued operations:		
Operating income, $25,000, less income tax, $10,000	15,000	
Loss on sale of discontinued operations, $5,000, less income tax saving, $2,000	(3,000)	12,000
Income before extraordinary item and cumulative effect of change in inventory method		60,000
Extraordinary gain, $26,000, less income tax, $10,000		16,000
Cumulative effect of change in inventory method, $10,000, less income tax saving, $4,000		(6,000)
Net income		$ 70,000
Earnings per share:		
Income from continuing operations [($48,000 − $4,000)/40,000 shares]		$1.10
Income from discontinued operations ($12,000/40,000 shares)		0.30
Income before extraordinary item and cumulative effect of change in inventory method [($60,000 − $4,000)/40,000 shares]		1.40
Extraordinary gain ($16,000/40,000 shares)		0.40
Cumulative effect of change in inventory method ($6,000/40,000)		(0.15)
Net income [($70,000 − $4,000)/40,000 shares]		$1.65

Computations:

$$EPS = \frac{Income - Preferred\ dividends}{Common\ shares\ outstanding}$$

Preferred dividends: $50,000 × 0.08 = $4,000
Common shares outstanding:
45,000 shares issued − 5,000 treasury shares = 40,000 shares outstanding

KRAFT CORPORATION
Statement of Retained Earnings
Year Ended December 31, 19XX

Retained earnings balance, beginning, as originally reported	$103,000
Prior-period adjustment—credit	5,000
Retained earnings balance, beginning, as adjusted	108,000
Net income for current year	70,000
	178,000
Dividends for current year	(16,000)
Retained earnings balance, ending	$162,000

Summary of Learning Objectives

1. Account for stock dividends. *Retained Earnings* carries the balance of the business's net income accumulated over its lifetime, less its declared dividends and any net losses. *Cash dividends* are distributions of corporate assets made possible by earnings. *Stock dividends* are distributions of the corporation's own stock to its stockholders.

2. Distinguish stock splits from stock dividends. Stock dividends shift amounts from retained earnings to paid-in capital. *Stock splits* do not change any account balance. Stock splits change the par value of the stock, whereas stock dividends do not. Both increase the number of shares outstanding and lower the market price per share of stock.

3. Account for treasury stock. *Treasury stock* is the corporation's own stock that has been issued and reacquired and is currently held by the company. The corporation may sell treasury stock for its cost or for more or less than cost.

4. Report restrictions on retained earnings. Retained earnings may be *restricted* by law or contract or by the corporation itself. An *appropriation* is a restriction of retained earnings that is recorded by formal journal entries.

5. Identify the elements of a corporation's income statement. The corporate *income statement* lists separately the various sources of income—*continuing operations*, which include other gains and losses; *discontinued operations*; and *extraordinary gains and losses*. The bottom line of the income statement reports *net income* or *net loss* for the period. *Income tax expense* and *earnings-per-share* figures also appear on the income statement, likewise divided into different categories based on the nature of income.

6. Prepare a statement of stockholders' equity. A statement of stockholders' equity reports the changes in all the equity accounts, including Retained Earnings.

Accounting Vocabulary

appropriation of retained earnings   (p. 595)
comprehensive income (p. 602)
earnings per share (EPS) (p. 601)

extraordinary gains and losses   (p. 599)
extraordinary item (p. 599)
prior-period adjustment (p. 603)

segment of the business (p. 599)
statement of stockholders' equity   (p. 605)
stock dividend   (p. 585)
stock split   (p. 588)

treasury stock   (p. 589)

Questions

1. Identify the two main parts of stockholders' equity.
2. Identify the account debited and the account credited from the last closing entry a corporation makes each year. What is the purpose of this entry?
3. Ametek, Inc., reported a cash balance of $73 million and a retained earnings balance of $162.5 million. Explain how Ametek can have so much more retained earnings than cash. In your answer, identify the nature of retained earnings and state how it ties to cash.
4. A friend of yours receives a stock dividend on an investment. He believes that stock dividends are the same as cash dividends. Explain why the two are not the same.
5. Give two reasons for a corporation to distribute a stock dividend.
6. A corporation declares a stock dividend on December 21 and reports Stock Dividend Payable as a liability on the December 31 balance sheet. Is this correct? Give your reason.
7. What percentage distinguishes a small stock dividend from a large stock dividend? What is the main difference in accounting for small and large stock dividends?
8. To an investor, a stock split and a stock dividend have essentially the same effect. Explain the similarity and difference to the corporation between a 100% stock dividend and a 2-for-1 stock split.
9. Give four reasons why a corporation might purchase treasury stock.
10. What effect does the purchase of treasury stock have on the (a) assets, (b) issued stock, and (c) outstanding stock of the corporation?
11. What is the normal balance of the Treasury Stock account? What type of account is Treasury Stock? Where is Treasury Stock reported on the balance sheet?
12. Revell, Inc., purchased treasury stock for $25,000. If Revell sells half the treasury stock for $15,000, what account should it credit for the $2,500 difference? If Revell later sells the remaining half of the treasury stock for $9,000, what accounts should be debited for the $3,500 difference?
13. What effect does the purchase and retirement of common stock have on the (a) assets, (b) issued stock, and (c) outstanding stock of the corporation?
14. Why do creditors wish to restrict a corporation's payment of cash dividends and purchases of treasury stock?
15. What are two ways to report a retained earnings restriction? Which way is more common?
16. Identify four items on the income statement that generate income tax expense. What is an income tax saving, and how does it arise?
17. Why is it important for a corporation to report income from continuing operations separately from discontinued operations and extraordinary items?
18. Give two examples of extraordinary gains and losses and four examples of gains and losses that are *not* extraordinary.
19. What is the most widely used of all accounting statistics?
20. What is the earnings per share of a company with net income of $5,500, issued common stock of 12,000 shares, and treasury common stock of 1,000 shares?
21. What account is affected by all prior-period adjustments? On what financial statement are prior-period adjustments reported?

Daily Exercises

DE14-1 Sprint Telex Company has 100,000 shares of $2.50 par common stock outstanding. Sprint declares a 5% stock dividend when the market value of its stock is $13 per share.

Recording a small stock dividend (Obj. 1)

1. Journalize Sprint's declaration of the stock dividend on March 19 and distribution of the dividend shares on April 2. Explanations are not required.
2. What was the overall effect of the stock dividend on Sprint Telex's total assets? On total stockholders' equity?

DE14-2 Pirelli Rubber Works has 20,000 shares of $1 par common stock outstanding. Pirelli issued this stock at a price of $10 per share. Pirelli declares a 50% stock dividend when the market value of its common stock is $62.50 per share.

Recording a large stock dividend and reporting stockholders' equity (Obj. 1)

1. Journalize Pirelli's declaration of the stock dividend on July 5 and distribution of the dividend shares on July 26. Explanations are not required.
2. Prepare the stockholders' equity section of Pirelli's balance sheet after issuance of the stock dividend. Retained Earnings had a balance of $60,000 before the dividend, and Pirelli's corporate charter authorizes the company to issue 100,000 shares of common stock.

DE14-3 ◀▥ *Link Back to Chapter 13 (Cash dividends).* Compare and contrast the accounting for cash dividends and stock dividends. In the space provided, insert either "Cash dividends," "Stock dividends," or "Both cash dividends and stock dividends" to complete each of the following statements:

Comparing and contrasting cash dividends and stock dividends (Obj. 1)

1. _____ decrease Retained Earnings.
2. _____ decrease both total assets and total stockholders' equity, resulting in a decrease in the size of the company.
3. _____ rearrange the account balances within stockholders' equity but have no effect on total stockholders' equity.
4. _____ have no effect on a liability.
5. _____ increase paid-in capital by the same amount that they decrease Retained Earnings.

DE14-4 Examine the table on Louisiana Lumber's stockholders' equity on page 586. Suppose Lousiana Lumber Company split its common stock 2-for-1 in order to decrease the market price of its stock. The company's stock was trading at $15 immediately before the split.

Accounting for a stock split (Obj. 2)

1. Prepare the stockholders' equity section of Louisiana Lumber's balance sheet after the stock split.
2. Which account balance changed after the stock split? Which account balances were unchanged?

DE14-5 Examine the table on Louisiana Lumber's stockholders' equity on page 586. Suppose Lousiana Lumber Company split its common stock 1 for 2 (a reverse stock split) in order to increase the market price of its stock. The company's stock was trading at $15 immediately before the split.

Accounting for a reverse stock split (Obj. 2)

1. Prepare the stockholders' equity section of Louisiana Lumber's balance sheet after the stock split.
2. Which account balances changed after the stock split? Which account balances were unchanged?

DE14-6 Forbes Waste Services has prospered during the past ten years, and the company's stock price has shot up to $78 recently. Forbes management wishes to decrease its stock price to the range of $19 to $20, which will be attractive to more investors. Should Forbes issue a 100% stock dividend or split the stock? If you propose a stock split, state the split ratio that will accomplish Forbes's objective. Show your computations.

Using a stock split or a stock dividend to decrease the market price of a stock (Obj. 2)

DE14-7 The table on Jupiter Drilling's stockholders' equity section before the purchase of treasury stock, appears on page 590. Suppose that Jupiter Drilling later purchases 500 shares of its common stock as treasury stock, paying cash of $5 per share.

Accounting for the purchase of treasury stock (Obj. 3)

1. Journalize the purchase of treasury stock.
2. Prepare the stockholders' equity section of Jupiter's balance sheet immediately after the purchase of treasury stock.
3. What effect does the purchase of treasury stock always have on total stockholders' equity? How did Jupiter's purchase of treasury stock affect the company's total stockholders' equity? Give the amount.

Accounting for the sale of treasury stock
(Obj. 3)

DE14-8 Return to the Jupiter Drilling Company situation in Daily Exercise 14-7. After purchasing the 500 shares of treasury stock for $5 per share, Jupiter later sold 400 of the treasury shares for $8 per share.

1. Journalize the sale of treasury stock.
2. Prepare the stockholders' equity section of Jupiter's balance sheet immediately after the sale of treasury stock.
3. What effect does the sale of treasury stock always have on total stockholders' equity? How did Jupiter's sale of treasury stock affect the company's total stockholders' equity? Give the amount.

Accounting for the purchase and sale of treasury stock (above cost)
(Obj. 3)

DE14-9 Equifax Associates, Inc., began operations in 19X9. After issuing its common stock to the public, Equifax completed the following treasury stock transactions during the year:

a. Purchased 2,000 shares of the company's $1 par common stock as treasury stock, paying cash of $6 per share.
b. Sold 1,000 shares of the treasury stock for cash of $8 per share.
c. Sold 700 shares of the remaining treasury stock at a price of $3 per share.

Journalize these transactions. Explanations are not required. Show how Equifax will report treasury stock on its balance sheet after all three transactions. In reporting the treasury stock, focus solely on the Treasury Stock account. You may ignore Paid-in Capital from Treasury Stock Transactions and Retained Earnings.

Accounting for the purchase and sale of treasury stock (below cost)
(Obj. 3)

DE14-10 Riddell Corporation began 19X8 with retained earnings of $95,000 and no paid-in capital from treasury stock transactions. During 19X8, Riddell earned net income of $40,000 and declared and paid cash dividends of $15,000. Riddell also completed the following treasury stock transactions:

a. Purchased 5,000 shares of the company's $2.50 par common stock as treasury stock, paying cash of $8 per share.
b. Sold 2,000 shares of the treasury stock at a price of $6 per share.

Journalize these transactions. Explanations are not required. Then show how Riddell will report retained earnings and treasury stock on its balance sheet at December 31, 19X8.

Accounting for the retirement of preferred stock
(Obj. 3)

DE14-11 Study Exhibit 14-5 on page 595. Suppose the corporation retired its preferred stock. What would be the amount of the company's total stockholders' equity if the cost to retire the preferred stock were (a) $310,000, (b) $270,000, or (c) $400,000?

Interpreting a restriction of retained earnings
(Obj. 4)

DE14-12 Study Exhibit 14-5, page 595. The company's board of directors is preparing to declare a cash dividend.

1. Assuming the company has plenty of cash to pay the dividend, what is the maximum amount of the cash dividend that the board of directors can declare? Explain how you arrived at your answer.
2. What is the nature of the retained earnings restriction in the exhibit? Why did the company restrict (appropriate) its retained earnings? Explain.

Preparing a complex corporate income statement
(Obj. 5)

DE14-13 List the major parts of a complex corporate income statement for Harley-Davis Corporation for the year ended December 31, 19X7. Include all the major parts of the income statement, starting with net sales revenue and ending with net income (not loss). You may ignore dollar amounts and earnings per share. Use Exhibit 14-6, page 598, as a guide.

Explaining the items on a complex corporate income statement
(Obj. 5)

DE14-14 Study the income statement of Allied Electronics Corporation in Exhibit 14-6, page 598. Answer these questions about the company's operations:

1. How much total markup did Allied earn on the sale of its products—before deducting any operating expenses? Name this item and give its amount.
2. Why are the loss on restructuring and the gain on sale of machinery reported as "Other gains (losses)"?
3. What dollar amount of net income would most sophisticated investors predict for Allied Electronics to earn during 19X6 and beyond? Name this item, give its amount, and state your reason.
4. How do the discontinued operations differ from the extraordinary loss?

Preparing a complex corporate income statement
(Obj. 5)

DE14-15 XTE Corporation accounting records include the following items, listed in no particular order, at December 31, 19X9.

Extraordinary gain	$ 5,000	Other gains (losses)	$ (2,000)
Cost of goods sold	71,000	Net sales revenue	182,000
Operating expenses	64,000	Loss on discontinued	
Accounts receivable	19,000	operations	(15,000)

Income tax of 40% applies to all items.

Prepare XTE's income statement for the year ended December 31, 19X9. Use Exhibit 14-6, page 598, as a guide. Omit earnings per share.

DE14-16 Return to the XTE Corporation data in Daily Exercise 14-15. XTE Corporation had 8,000 shares of common stock outstanding at December 31, 19X8. The company issued an additional 6,000 shares of common stock on August 31, 19X9. XTE declared and paid preferred dividends of $3,000 during 19X9.

Reporting earnings per share (Obj. 5)

Show how XTE Corporation reported earnings-per-share data on its 19X9 income statement.

DE14-17 A corporation has preferred stock outstanding, and the corporation issued additional common stock during the year.

Interpreting earnings per share data (Obj. 5)

1. Give the basic equation to compute earnings per share of common stock for net income.
2. List the income items for which the corporation must report earnings-per-share data.
3. What makes earnings per share so useful as a business statistic?

DE14-18 Use the XTE Corporation data in Daily Exercise 14-15. In addition, XTE Corporation had unrealized losses of $1,000 on investments and a $2,000 foreign-currency translation adjustment (a gain) during 19X9. Start with XTE Corporation's net income from Daily Exercise 14-15 and show how XTE could report other comprehensive income on its 19X9 income statement.

Reporting comprehensive income (Obj. 5)

Should XTE Corporation report earnings-per-share data for other comprehensive income?

DE14-19 Examine De Graff Corporation's statement of retained earnings on page 604. Suppose instead that De Graff had overpaid 19X4 income tax expense by $15,000. Show how De Graff would report this prior-period adjustment on the statement of retained earnings for 19X5.

Reporting a prior-period adjustment (Obj. 6)

DE14-20 ◀▥ *Link Back to Chapter 1 (Accounting Equation).* Use the statement of stockholders' equity in Exhibit 14-9, page 605, to answer the following questions about Allied Electronics Corporation.

Using the statement of stockholders' equity (Obj. 6)

1. At December 31, 19X5, Allied had total liabilities of $514,000. How much were the company's total assets?
2. How much cash did the issuance of common stock bring in during 19X5?
3. What was the cost of the treasury stock that Allied purchased during 19X5? What was Allied's cost of the treasury stock that Allied sold during the year? For how much did Allied sell the treasury stock during 19X5?
4. Was the stock dividend that Allied declared and distributed during 19X5 "large" or "small"? How can you tell? What was the par value of the stock that Allied distributed in the stock dividend? What was the market value of the stock distributed in the dividend?

DE14-21 ◀▥ *Link Back to Chapter 8 (Operating Cash Flows) and Chapter 10 (Investing Cash Flows).* During 19X9, Heimlich, Inc., completed the following cash transactions. Heimlich collected cash of $750,000 from customers during 19X9. The company issued common stock, receiving cash of $190,000, and then paid $160,000 to purchase equipment. Also during the year, Heimlich purchased treasury stock for $8,000 and later sold the treasury stock for $12,000. Heimlich paid cash dividends of $22,000 during 19X9.

Reporting stockholders' equity transactions on the statement of cash flows (Obj. 6)

1. Report cash flows from financing activities on Heimlich's 19X9 statement of cash flows.
2. Identify Heimlich's operating cash flows and investing cash flows for 19X9. Refer to Chapters 8 and 10 if needed.

Exercises

E14-1 Groesbeck, Inc., is authorized to issue 100,000 shares of $1 par common stock. The company issued 60,000 shares at $4 per share, and all 60,000 shares are outstanding. When the retained earnings balance was $150,000, Groesbeck declared and distributed a 50% stock dividend. Later, Groesbeck declared and paid a $0.30 per share cash dividend.

Journalizing cash and stock dividends and reporting stockholders' equity (Obj. 1)

1. Journalize the declaration and distribution of the stock dividend.
2. Journalize the declaration and payment of the cash dividend.
3. Prepare the stockholders' equity section of the balance sheet after both dividends.

REQUIRED

E14-2 The stockholders' equity for Maborn, Inc., on September 30, 19X4—end of the company's fiscal year—follows:

Stockholders' Equity	
Common stock, $10 par, 100,000 shares authorized,	
50,000 shares issued..	$500,000
Paid-in capital in excess of par—common..........................	50,000
Retained earnings..	140,000
Total stockholders' equity	$690,000

On October 12, the market price of Maborn's common stock was $16 per share and the company declared a 10% stock dividend. Maborn issued the dividend shares on October 30.

REQUIRED

1. Journalize the declaration and distribution of the stock dividend.
2. Prepare the stockholders' equity section of the balance sheet after the issuance of the stock dividend.

E14-3 Mad Dog Showbiz, Inc., had the following stockholders' equity at May 31:

Common stock, $2 par, 200,000 shares authorized,	
50,000 shares issued	**$100,000**
Paid-in capital in excess of par...................................	60,000
Retained earnings..	210,000
Total stockholders' equity...	**$370,000**

On June 7, Mad Dog split its $2 par common stock 4 for 1. Make the necessary entry to record the stock split, and prepare the stockholders' equity section of the balance sheet immediately after the split.

E14-4 Identify the effects of the following transactions on total stockholders' equity. Each transaction is independent.

a. A 10% stock dividend. Before the dividend, 500,000 shares of $1 par common stock were outstanding; market value was $7.625 at the time of the dividend.

b. Sale of 600 shares of $5 par treasury stock for $9.00 per share. Cost of the treasury stock was $6.00 per share.

c. A 3-for-1 stock split. Prior to the split, 60,000 shares of $4.50 par common were outstanding.

d. Purchase of 1,500 shares of treasury stock (par value $0.50) at $4.25 per share.

e. A 50% stock dividend. Before the dividend, 1,000,000 shares of $2 par common stock were outstanding; market value was $13.75 at the time of the dividend.

f. Issuance of 50,000 shares of $10 par common at $16.50.

E14-5 Journalize the following transactions of Larry's Shoes, a regional chain of men's shoe stores:

Jan. 19	Issued 20,000 shares of no-par common stock at $15 per share.
Apr. 22	Purchased 1,000 shares of treasury stock at $14 per share.
Oct. 11	Sold 200 shares of treasury stock at $16 per share.
Nov. 28	Sold 200 shares of treasury stock at $10 per share.

E14-6 Sax 10th Avenue, Inc., had the following stockholders' equity on November 30:

Stockholders' Equity	
Common stock, $5 par, 500,000 shares authorized,	
50,000 shares issued..	$250,000
Paid-in capital in excess of par	150,000
Retained earnings..	520,000
Total stockholders' equity	$920,000

On December 19, the company purchased 10,000 shares of treasury stock at $6 per share. Journalize the purchase of the treasury stock, and prepare the stockholders' equity section of the balance sheet at December 31.

E14-7 The agreement under which Hitari, Inc., issued its long-term debt requires the restriction of $150,000 of the company's retained earnings balance. Total retained earnings is $270,000, and total paid-in capital is $220,000.

Reporting a retained earnings restriction
(Obj. 4)

Show how to report stockholders' equity on Hitari's balance sheet, assuming the following:

REQUIRED

a. Hitari discloses the restriction in a note. Write the note.

b. Hitari appropriates retained earnings in the amount of the restriction and includes no note in its statements.

c. Hitari's cash balance is $185,000. What is the maximum amount of dividends Hitari can declare?

E14-8 Graz Corporation's accounting records contain the following information for 19X8 operations:

Preparing a multiple-step income statement
(Obj. 5)

Sales revenue....................................	$380,000
Operating expenses (including income tax).................	93,000
Cumulative effect of change in depreciation method (debit)	(7,000)
Cost of goods sold..........................	245,000
Loss on discontinued operations....	50,000
Income tax expense— extraordinary gain	6,000
Income tax saving—change in depreciation method	3,000
Income tax saving—loss on discontinued operations.........	20,000
Extraordinary gain	15,000

Prepare a multi-step income statement for 19X8. Omit earnings per share. Was 19X8 a good year, a fair year, or a bad year for Graz Corporation? Explain your answer in terms of the outlook for 19X9.

REQUIRED

E14-9 Bloomberg Corporation earned net income of $62,000 for the second quarter of 19X6. The ledger reveals the following figures:

Computing earnings per share
(Obj. 5)

Preferred stock, $5.00 per year, no-par, 1,600 shares issued and outstanding	$ 70,000
Common stock, $10 par, 52,000 shares issued	520,000
Treasury stock, common, 2,000 shares at cost.......................................	36,000

Compute Bloomberg's EPS for the quarter. Bloomberg Corporation had no changes in its stock accounts during the quarter.

REQUIRED

E14-10 Glenellen, Inc., had 40,000 shares of common stock and 10,000 shares of 5%, $10 par preferred stock outstanding on December 31, 19X8. On April 30, 19X9, the company issued 9,000 additional common shares and ended 19X9 with 49,000 shares of common stock outstanding. Income from continuing operations of 19X9 was $115,400, and loss on discontinued operations (net of income tax) was $8,280. The company had an extraordinary gain (net of tax) of $55,200.

Computing earnings per share
(Obj. 5)

Compute Glenellen's EPS amounts for 19X9, starting with income from continuing operations.

REQUIRED

E14-11 Pepper Upper, Inc., a soft-drink company, reported a prior-period adjustment in 19X9. An accounting error caused net income of prior years to be overstated by $3.8 million. Retained earnings at January 1, 19X9, as previously reported, stood at $395.3 million. Net income for 19X9 was $142.1 million, and dividends were $39.8 million.

Preparing a statement of retained earnings with a prior-period adjustment
(Obj. 6)

Prepare the company's statement of retained earnings for the year ended December 31, 19X9.

REQUIRED

E14-12 The Plaza Hotel Company, a large hotel chain, had retained earnings of $413.6 million at the beginning of 19X7. The company showed these figures at December 31, 19X7:

Preparing a combined statement of income and retained earnings
(Obj. 5, 6)

	($ Millions)
Net income..	$127
Cash dividends—preferred	2
common	85
Debit to retained earnings due to retirement of preferred stock.........	11

Beginning with net income, prepare a combined statement of income and retained earnings for The Plaza Hotel Company for 19X7.

REQUIRED

E14-13 During 19X8, Westec Resources earned income from continuing operations of $75,000. The company also sold its land development segment (discontinued operations) at a loss of $30,000 and had an extraordinary gain of $8,000 on an insurance settlement. Late in the year, Westec sold treasury stock for $9,000 that the company had purchased for $4,000 two years earlier. At year end, Westec had a foreign-currency translation adjustment (a loss) of $3,000.

1. Compute Westec's net income and comprehensive income for 19X8. All amounts are net of income taxes.

2. What would be the final earnings-per-share figure that Westec would report for 19X8? During the year, Westec had 20,000 shares of common stock (and no preferred stock) outstanding.

E14-14 At December 31, 19X8, FIRSTAR Corp. reported the following stockholders' equity:

Common stock, $5 par, 200,000 shares authorized,	
120,000 shares issued...	**$ 600,000**
Additional paid-in capital	**1,100,000**
Retained earnings	**1,700,000**
Treasury stock, 2,500 shares at cost.........................	**(78,000)**
	$3,322,000

During 19X9, FIRSTAR completed these transactions and events (listed in chronological order):

a. Declared and issued a 50% stock dividend. At the time, FIRSTAR's stock was quoted at a market price of $31 per share.

b. Sold 1,000 shares of treasury stock for $36 per share (cost of these shares was $31 per share).

c. Issued 500 shares of common stock to employees at $28 per share.

d. Net income for the year was $340,000.

e. Declared and paid cash dividends of $180,000.

Prepare FIRSTAR's statement of stockholders' equity for 19X9.

CHALLENGE EXERCISE

E14-15 Universal Syndicates, Inc., began 19X8 with 3 million shares of $1 par common stock issued and outstanding. Beginning paid-in capital in excess of par was $6 million, and retained earnings was $9 million. In March 19X8, Universal issued 100,000 shares of stock at $11 per share. In December, when the stock's market price was $12 per share, the board of directors declared and distributed a 10% stock dividend.

1. Make the journal entries for the issuance of stock for cash and for the declaration and the distribution of the 10% stock dividend.

2. Prepare the company's statement of stockholders' equity for the year ended December 31, 19X8.

Beyond the Numbers

BN14-1 The following accounting issues have arisen at Amtel Sportswear, Inc.:

1. The treasurer of Amtel wants to disclose a large loss as an extraordinary item because Amtel Sportswear produced too much product just before a very cool summer. Why do you think the treasurer wants to use that particular disclosure? Would such disclosure be acceptable?

2. Corporations sometimes purchase their own stock. When asked why they do so, Amtel management responds that the stock is undervalued. What advantage would Amtel gain by buying and selling its own stock under these circumstances?

3. Amtel earned a significant profit in the year ended November 30, 19X2, because land that it held was expropriated for a new highway. The company proposes to treat the sale of land to the government as operating revenue. Why do you think Amtel is proposing such treatment? Is this disclosure appropriate?

ETHICAL ISSUE ◀▥▥ *Link Back to Chapter 9 (Accounting Principles).*

Anadarko Petroleum Company is an independent oil producer in Anadarko, Oklahoma. In February, company geologists discovered a pool of oil that tripled the company's proven reserves. Prior to disclosing the new oil to the public, top managers of the company quietly bought most of Anadarko's stock as treasury stock. After the discovery was announced, Anadarko's stock price increased from $13 to $40.

1. Did Anadarko managers behave ethically? Explain your answer.
2. Identify the accounting principle relevant to this situation. Review Chapter 9 if necessary.
3. Who was helped and who was harmed by management's action?

REQUIRED

Problems (GROUP A)

P14-1A Faldo Golf, Inc., completed the following selected transactions during 19X6:

Journalizing stockholders' equity transactions
(Obj. 1, 3)

Feb. 6   Declared a cash dividend on the 10,000 shares of $2.25, no-par preferred stock. Declared a $0.20 per share dividend on the 10,000 shares of common stock outstanding. The date of record was February 17, and the payment date was February 20.

Feb. 20 Paid the cash dividends.

Mar. 21 Split common stock 3 for 1 by calling in the 10,000 shares of $15 par common and issuing new stock in its place.

Apr. 18 Declared a 50% stock dividend on the common stock to holders of record April 30, with distribution set for May 30. The market value of the common stock was $15 per share.

May 30   Issued the stock dividend shares.

June 18 Purchased 2,400 shares of the company's own common stock at $12 per share.

Nov. 14 Sold 800 shares of treasury common stock for $10 per share.

Dec. 22 Sold 700 shares of treasury common stock for $16 per share.

Record the transactions in the general journal.

REQUIRED

P14-2A The balance sheet of Parnevik, Inc., at December 31, 19X7, reported 500,000 shares of $1 par common stock authorized with 100,000 shares issued. Paid-in Capital in Excess of Par—Common had a balance of $300,000. Retained Earnings had a balance of $69,000. During 19X8, the company completed the following selected transactions:

Journalizing dividend and treasury stock transactions and reporting stockholders' equity
(Obj. 1, 2, 3)

Feb. 15 Purchased 5,000 shares of the company's own common stock for the treasury at $4 per share.

Mar. 8   Sold 2,000 shares of treasury common stock for $7 per share.

Sep. 28 Declared a 10% stock dividend on the *outstanding* common stock to holders of record October 15, with distribution set for October 31. The market value of Parnevik's common stock was $5 per share.

Oct. 31 Issued the stock dividend shares.

Nov. 5   Split the common stock 2 for 1 by calling in the 109,700 shares of old $1 par common stock and issuing twice as many shares of $0.50 par common. (Stock splits affect all authorized and issued stock, including treasury stock and stock that is outstanding.)

Dec. 31 Earned net income of $73,000 during the year.

1. Record the transactions in the general journal. Explanations are not required.
2. Prepare the stockholders' equity section of the balance sheet at December 31, 19X8.

REQUIRED

P14-3A Ballesteros Corporation is positioned ideally in its business. Located in Tucson, Arizona, Ballesteros is the only company between Texas and California with reliable sources for its imported gifts. The company does a brisk business with specialty stores such as Pier 1 Imports. Ballesteros's recent success has made the company a prime target for a takeover. An investment group from Denver is attempting to buy 51% of Ballesteros's outstanding stock against the wishes of Ballesteros's board of directors. Board members are convinced that the Denver investors would sell the most desirable pieces of the business and leave little of value.

Purchasing treasury stock to fight off a takeover of the corporation
(Obj. 3)

At the most recent board meeting, several suggestions were advanced to fight off the hostile takeover bid. The suggestion with the most promise is to purchase a huge quantity of treasury stock. Ballesteros has the cash to carry out this plan.

1. As a significant stockholder of Ballesteros Corporation, write a memorandum to explain to the board how the purchase of treasury stock would make it more difficult for the Denver group to take over Ballesteros. Include in your memo a discussion of the effect that purchasing treasury stock would have on stock outstanding and on the size of the corporation.

REQUIRED

2. Suppose Ballesteros management is successful in fighting off the takeover bid and later sells the treasury stock at prices greater than the purchase price. Explain what effect these sales will have on assets, stockholders' equity, and net income.

P14-4A The balance sheet of Arrow Electronic Corporation at December 31, 19X3, presented the following stockholders' equity:

Paid-in capital:	
Common stock, $1 par, 250,000 shares authorized,	
50,000 shares issued...	$ 50,000
Paid-in capital in excess of par—common	350,000
Total paid-in capital..	400,000
Retained earnings...	110,000
Total stockholders' equity..	$510,000

During 19X4, Arrow completed the following selected transactions:

Mar. 29	Declared a 50% stock dividend on the common stock. The market value of Arrow common stock was $5 per share. The record date was April 19, with distribution set for May 19.
May 19	Issued the stock dividend shares.
July 13	Purchased 2,000 shares of the company's own common stock at $6 per share.
Oct. 4	Sold 1,600 shares of treasury common stock for $8 per share.
Dec. 27	Declared a $0.20 per share dividend on the common stock outstanding. The date of record was January 17, 19X5, and the payment date was January 31.
31	Closed the $71,000 net income to Retained Earnings.

REQUIRED

1. Record the transactions in the general journal.
2. Prepare the retained earnings statement at December 31, 19X4.
3. Prepare the stockholders' equity section of the balance sheet at December 31, 19X4.

P14-5A The following information was taken from the ledger and other records of BellWestern Corporation at June 30, 19X5:

REQUIRED

General expenses.......................	$ 71,000	Selling expenses.........................	$ 87,000
Gain on discontinued		Common stock, no-par, 22,000	
operations	1,000	shares authorized and issued.	350,000
Cost of goods sold.....................	319,000	Preferred stock, 6%, $25 par,	
Interest expense	23,000	20,000 shares authorized,	
Sales returns	15,000	4,000 shares issued	100,000
Dividend revenue	19,000	Cumulative effect of change in	
Treasury stock, common		depreciation method (credit).	7,000
(2,000 shares).........................	28,000	Income tax expense (saving):	
Sales discounts..........................	7,000	Continuing operations	28,000
Extraordinary loss	27,000	Gain on discontinued	
Loss on sale of plant assets	10,000	operations..........................	400
Dividends declared and paid		Extraordinary loss.................	(10,800)
on common stock....................	12,000	Cumulative effect of change	
Sales revenue	589,000	in depreciation method......	3,000
Retained earnings, beginning ...	63,000		

REQUIRED

Prepare a single-step income statement, including earnings per share, for BellWestern Corporation for the fiscal year ended June 30, 19X5. Evaluate income for the year ended June 30, 19X5, in terms of the outlook for 19X6. Note that 19X5 was a typical year and BellWestern's managers hoped to earn income from continuing operations equal to 10% of net sales.

P14-6A Margaret Brown, accountant for Cascade Communication, Inc., was injured in a sailing accident. Another employee prepared the following income statement for the fiscal year ended June 30, 19X4:

CASCADE COMMUNICATION, INC.
Income Statement
June 30, 19X4

Revenues and gains:		
Sales		$733,000
Gain on retirement of preferred stock (issued for		
$70,000; purchased for $59,000)		11,000
Paid-in capital in excess of par—common		100,000
Total revenues and gains		844,000
Expenses and losses:		
Cost of goods sold	$383,000	
Selling expenses	103,000	
General expenses	74,000	
Sales returns	22,000	
Prior-period adjustment—understated		
income tax for fiscal year 19X3	4,000	
Dividends	15,000	
Sales discounts	10,000	
Income tax expense—continuing operations	32,000	
Total expenses and losses		643,000
Income from operations		201,000
Other gains and losses:		
Extraordinary gain	$ 30,000	
Operating income on discontinued segment	25,000	
Loss on sale of discontinued operations	(40,000)	
Total other gains		15,000
Net income		$216,000
Earnings per share		$ 10.80

The individual amounts listed on the income statement are correct. However, some accounts are reported incorrectly, and others do not belong on the income statement at all. Also, income tax has not been applied to all appropriate figures. The income tax rate on discontinued operations and on the extraordinary gain, is 40 percent. Cascade issued 24,000 shares of common stock in 19X1 and held 4,000 shares as treasury stock during the fiscal year 19X4. The retained earnings balance, as originally reported at June 30, 19X3, was $409,000.

REQUIRED

Prepare a corrected combined statement of income and retained earnings for fiscal year 19X4; include earnings per share. Prepare the income statement in single-step format.

P14-7A The capital structure of Kite Design Company at December 31, 19X2, included 5,000 shares of $2.50 preferred stock and 130,000 shares of common stock. Common shares outstanding during 19X3 were 130,000 January through February; 119,000 during March; 121,000 April through October; and 128,000 during November and December. Income from continuing operations during 19X3 was $371,885. The company discontinued a segment of the business at a gain of $69,160, and also had an extraordinary loss of $49,510. The board of directors of Kite Design Company has restricted $100,000 of retained earnings for expansion of the company's office facilities.

Computing earnings per share and reporting a retained earnings restriction (Obj. 4, 5)

1. Compute Kite's earnings per share for 19X3. Start with income from continuing operations. Income and loss amounts are net of income tax.

2. Show two ways of reporting Kite's retained earnings restriction. Retained earnings at December 31, 19X2, was $127,800, and Kite declared cash dividends of $264,500 during 19X3.

REQUIRED

P14-8A Lucent Technology, Inc., reported the following statement of stockholders' equity for the year ended September 30, 19X9:

(Dollar amounts in millions)	Common Stock	Additional Paid-in Capital	Retained Earnings	Treasury Stock	Total
LUCENT TECHNOLOGY, INC.				
Statement of Stockholders' Equity				
Year Ended September 30, 19X9				
Balance, October 1, 19X8.................	$173	$2,118	$1,706	$(18)	$3,979
Net income			520		520
Cash dividends			(117)		(117)
Issuance of stock					
(5,000,000 shares).........................	7	46			53
Stock dividend..................................	18	272	(290)		-0-
Sale of treasury stock		5		11	16
Balance, September 30, 19X9..........	$198	$2,441	$1,819	$ (7)	$4,451

REQUIRED

1. What is the par value of Lucent's common stock?
2. At what price per share did Lucent issue its common stock during the year?
3. What was the cost of treasury stock sold during the year? What was the selling price of the treasury stock sold? What was the increase in total stockholders' equity?
4. Lucent's statement of stockholders' equity lists the stock transactions in the order in which they occurred. What was the percentage of the stock dividend? Round to the nearest percentage.

Problems (GROUP B)

Journalizing stockholders' equity transactions
(Obj. 1, 3)

P14-1B Assume that Mickelsen Corp. completed the following selected transactions during the current year:

April 18 Declared a cash dividend on the 5%, $100 par preferred stock (1,000 shares outstanding). Declared a $0.20 per share dividend on the 100,000 shares of common stock outstanding. The date of record was May 2, and the payment date was May 23.

May 23 Paid the cash dividends.

June 10 Split common stock 2 for 1 by calling in the 100,000 shares of $10 par common and issuing new stock in its place.

July 30 Declared a 10% stock dividend on the common stock to holders of record August 21, with distribution set for September 11. The market value of the common stock was $15 per share.

Sep. 11 Issued the stock dividend shares.

Oct. 26 Purchased 2,500 shares of the company's own common stock at $14 per share.

Nov. 8 Sold 1,000 shares of treasury common stock for $17 per share.

Dec. 13 Sold 500 shares of treasury common stock for $13 per share.

REQUIRED Record the transactions in the general journal.

Journalizing dividend and treasury stock transactions and reporting stockholders' equity
(Obj. 1, 2, 3)

P14-2B The balance sheet of Infomax, Inc., at December 31, 19X6, reported 100,000 shares of no-par common stock authorized, with 30,000 shares issued and a Common Stock balance of $180,000. Retained Earnings had a credit balance of $133,500. During 19X7, the company completed the following selected transactions:

Mar. 15 Purchased 4,000 shares of the company's own common stock for the treasury at $5 per share.

Apr. 30 Declared a 20% stock dividend on the 26,000 shares of *outstanding* common stock to holders of record December 21, with distribution set for May 15. The market value of Infomax common stock was $10 per share.

May 15 Issued the stock dividend shares.

Oct. 8 Sold 2,800 shares of treasury common stock for $12 per share.

Dec. 19 Split the no-par common stock 2 for 1 by issuing two new no-par shares for each old no-par share previously issued. Prior to the split, the corporation had issued 35,200 shares. Stock splits affect all authorized and issued stock, including treasury stock as well as stock that is outstanding.

31 Earned net income of $117,000 during the year.

1. Record the transactions in the general journal. Explanations are not required.
2. Prepare the stockholders' equity section of the balance sheet at December 31, 19X7.

REQUIRED

P14-3B Dannon Corporation is ideally positioned in the clothing business. Located in Lansing, Michigan, Dannon is the only company with a distribution network for its imported goods. The company does a brisk business with specialty stores such as Bloomingdale's, I. Magnin, and Bonwit Teller. Dannon's recent success has made the company a prime target for a takeover. Against the wishes of Dannon's board of directors, an investment group from Omaha is attempting to buy 51% of Dannon's outstanding stock. Board members are convinced that the Omaha investors would sell off the most desirable pieces of the business and leave little of value.

Increasing dividends to fight off a takeover of the corporation (Obj. 1)

At the most recent board meeting, several suggestions were advanced to fight off the hostile takeover bid. One suggestion is to increase the stock outstanding by distributing a 100% stock dividend.

As a significant stockholder of Dannon Corporation, write a short memo to explain to the board whether distributing the stock dividend would make it more difficult for the investor group to take over Dannon Corporation. Include in your memo a discussion of the effect that the stock dividend would have on assets, liabilities, and total stockholders' equity—that is, the dividend's effect on the size of the corporation.

REQUIRED

P14-4B The balance sheet of Air Touch Instruments Corporation at December 31, 19X6, reported the following stockholders' equity:

Journalizing dividend and treasury stock transactions, reporting retained earnings and stockholders' equity (Obj. 1, 3)

Paid-in capital:	
Common stock, $10 par, 100,000 shares authorized, 20,000 shares issued..........................	$200,000
Paid-in capital in excess of par-common	300,000
Total paid-in capital	500,000
Retained earnings..	190,000
Total stockholders' equity	$690,000

During 19X7, Air Touch Instruments completed the following selected transactions:

Apr. 30 Declared a 10% stock dividend on the common stock. The market value of Air Touch Instruments' common stock was $24 per share. The record date was May 21, with distribution set for June 5.

June 5 Issued the stock dividend shares.

July 29 Purchased 2,000 shares of the company's own common stock at $21 per share.

Nov. 13 Sold 400 shares of treasury common stock for $22 per share.

27 Declared a $0.30 per share dividend on the common stock outstanding. The date of record was December 17, and the payment date was January 7, 19X8.

Dec. 31 Closed the $62,000 net income to Retained Earnings.

REQUIRED

1. Record the transactions in the general journal.
2. Prepare a retained earnings statement at December 31, 19X7.
3. Prepare the stockholders' equity section of the balance sheet at December 31, 19X7.

P14-5B The following information was taken from the ledger and other records of Penn Oil, Inc., at September 30, 19X6.

Preparing a detailed income statement (Obj. 5)

Cost of goods sold	$424,000	Interest expense	$ 11,000
Cumulative effect of change in depreciation method (debit)..	(3,000)	General expenses.......................	113,000
Loss on sale of plant assets	20,000	Preferred stock, $2, no-par, 10,000 shares authorized,	
Sales returns	9,000	5,000 shares issued	200,000
Gain on discontinued operations	5,000	Retained earnings, beginning ...	88,000
Income tax expense (saving):		Selling expenses.........................	136,000
Continuing operations	72,000	Common stock, $10 par, 25,000	
Gain on discontinued		shares authorized and issued	250,000
operations..........................	2,000	Sales revenue	860,000
Extraordinary loss..................	(12,000)	Treasury stock, common	
Cumulative effect of change in		(1,000 shares)........................	11,000
depreciation method	(1,000)	Interest revenue	4,000
Sales discounts...........................	18,000	Extraordinary loss	30,000

REQUIRED

Prepare a single-step income statement, including earnings per share, for Penn Oil, Inc., for the fiscal year ended September 30, 19X6. Evaluate income for the year ended September 30, 19X6, in terms of the outlook for 19X7. Assume that 19X6 was a typical year and that Penn Oil managers hoped to earn income from continuing operations equal to 10% of net sales. The number of shares of common stock outstanding was unchanged during fiscal year 19X6.

P14-6B   Dan Hollingsworth, accountant for Global Marine Corporation, was injured in a skiing accident. Another employee prepared the accompanying income statement for the fiscal year ended December 31, 19X3.

The individual amounts listed on the income statement are correct. However, some accounts are reported incorrectly, and others do not belong on the income statement at all. Also, income tax has not been applied to all appropriate figures. The income tax rate on discontinued operations and on the extraordinary loss, was 40 percent. Global Marine issued 52,000 shares of common stock in 19X1 and held 2,000 shares as treasury stock during 19X3. The retained earnings balance, as originally reported at December 31, 19X2, was $361,000.

GLOBAL MARINE CORPORATION
Income Statement
19X3

Revenue and gains:		
Sales..		$362,000
Gain on retirement of preferred stock		
(issued for $81,000; purchased for $71,000)..........		10,000
Paid-in capital in excess of par—common................		80,000
Total revenues and gains..		452,000
Expenses and losses:		
Cost of goods sold..	$105,000	
Selling expenses..	56,000	
General expenses...	61,000	
Sales returns	11,000	
Dividends	7,000	
Sales discounts..	6,000	
Income tax expense	20,000	
Total expenses and losses		266,000
Income from operations		186,000
Other gains and losses:		
Loss on discontinued operations	$ (3,000)	
Extraordinary flood loss..	(20,000)	
Prior-period adjustment—understated		
income tax for 19X2	(14,000)	
Total other losses..		(37,000)
Net income...		$149,000
Earnings per share		$ 2.98

Prepare a corrected combined statement of income and retained earnings for 19X3; include earnings per share. Prepare the income statement in single-step format.

P14-7B   The capital structure of Jacobs-Cathey Heating Contractors, Inc., at December 31, 19X6, included 20,000 shares of $1.25 preferred stock and 44,000 shares of common stock. Common shares outstanding during 19X7 were 44,000 January through May, 50,000 June through August, and 60,500 September through December. Income from continuing operations during 19X7 was $81,100. The company discontinued a segment of the business at a gain of $6,630, and also had an extraordinary gain of $33,660. Jacobs-Cathey's board of directors restricts $100,000 of retained earnings for contingencies.

1. Compute Jacobs-Cathey's earnings per share. Start with income from continuing operations. Income and loss amounts are net of income tax.

2. Show two ways of reporting Jacobs-Cathey's retained earnings restriction. Retained earnings at December 31, 19X6, was $107,000, and Jacobs-Cathey declared cash dividends of $29,000 during 19X7.

P14-8B Bahama Vacationland, Inc., reported the following statement of stockholders' equity for the year ended October 31, 19X4:

Using a statement of stockholders' equity (Obj. 6)

(Dollar amounts in millions)	Common Stock	Additional Paid-in Capital	Retained Earnings	Treasury Stock	Total
Balance, Nov. 1, 19X3	$427	$1,622	$904	$(117)	$2,836
Net income			336		336
Cash dividends			(194)		(194)
Issuance of stock (10,000,000 shares)	13	41			54
Stock dividend	22	113	(135)		-0-
Sale of treasury stock		9		19	28
Balance, Oct. 31, 19X4	$462	$1,785	$911	$ (98)	$3,060

Title: **BAHAMA VACATIONLAND, INC.** / **Statement of Stockholders' Equity** / **Year Ended October 31, 19X4**

Answer these questions about Bahama Vacationland's stockholders' equity transactions.

REQUIRED

1. What is the par value of the company's common stock?
2. At what price per share did Bahama Vacationland issue its common stock during the year?
3. What was the cost of treasury stock sold during the year? What was the selling price of the treasury stock sold? What was the increase in total stockholders' equity?
4. Bahama Vacationland's statement lists the stock transactions in the order they occurred. What was the percentage of the stock dividend? Round to the nearest percentage.

Applying Your Knowledge

DECISION CASE

Willamette Industries had the following stockholders' equity amounts on June 30, 19X8:

Analyzing cash dividends and stock dividends (Obj. 1)

Common stock, no-par, 100,000 shares issued...	$ 750,000
Retained earnings	830,000
Total stockholders' equity	$1,580,000

In the past, Willamette has paid an annual cash dividend of $1.50 per share. Despite the large retained earnings balance, the board of directors wished to conserve cash for expansion. The board delayed the payment of cash dividends and in July distributed a 10% stock dividend. During August, the company's cash position improved. The board declared and paid a cash dividend of $1.364 per share in September.

Suppose you owned 10,000 shares of Willamette common stock, acquired three years ago, prior to the 10% stock dividend. The market price of the stock was $30 per share before any of these dividends.

REQUIRED

1. How does the stock dividend affect your proportionate ownership in Willamette Industries? Explain.
2. What amount of cash dividends did you receive last year? What amount of cash dividends will you receive after the dividend action?
3. Immediately after the stock dividend was distributed, the market value of Willamette stock decreased from $30 per share to $27.273 per share. Does this decrease represent a loss to you? Explain.

4. Suppose Willamette announces at the time of the stock dividend that the company will continue to pay the annual $1.50 cash dividend per share, even after the stock dividend. Would you expect the market price of the stock to decrease to $27.273 per share as in requirement 3? Explain.

FINANCIAL STATEMENT CASES

Stock splits retained earnings, and earnings per share
(Obj. 2, 5)

REQUIRED

CASE 1. Use the NIKE, Inc., financial statements in Appendix A to answer the following questions.

1. During the year ended May 31, 1997, NIKE split both its Class A Common Stock and its Class B Common Stock.
   a. What was the split ratio? The statement of shareholders' equity provides the answer (the bottom panel gives details for the year ended May 31, 1997).
   b. How many shares of Class A Common Stock did NIKE have outstanding at May 31, 1997? How many Class B Common shares were outstanding at May 31, 1997?
   c. How does a stock split affect the stock accounts? Confirm your answer by studying NIKE's statement of shareholders' equity (the bottom panel gives details for the year ended May 31, 1997).

2. Prepare a T-account for Retained Earnings to show the beginning and ending balances and all activity in the account during the year ended May 31, 1997. The statement of shareholders' equity provides the data.

3. Show how NIKE computed net income *per share* for the year ended May 31, 1997.

Treasury stock, retained earnings, and earnings per share
(Obj. 3, 5)

REQUIRED

CASE 2. Obtain the annual report of a company of your choosing. Answer the following questions about the company. Concentrate on the current year in the annual report you select.

1. How many shares of common stock had the company issued through the end of the current year? How many shares were in the treasury? How many shares were outstanding on the date of the current balance sheet?

2. Compute average cost per share of treasury stock (common). Compare this figure to book value per share of common stock. Does it appear that the company was able to purchase treasury stock at book value? (*Note:* This question can be answered only if the company reports the cost of treasury stock.)

3. Prepare a T-account for Retained Earnings to show the beginning and ending balances and all activity in the account during the current year.

4. Show how to compute net income (or net loss) *per share* for the current year.

Team Project

REQUIRED

Obtain the annual reports (or annual report data) of five well-known companies. You can get the reports either from your college library or by mailing a request directly to the company (allow two weeks for delivery). Or you can visit the Web site for this book (http://www.prenhall.com/harrison/) or the SEC EDGAR database, which includes the financial reports of most well-known companies.

1. After selecting five companies, examine their income statements to search for the following items:
   a. Income from continuing operations
   b. Discontinued operations
   c. Extraordinary gains and losses
   d. Cumulative effects of accounting changes
   e. Net income or net loss
   f. Earnings-per-share data

2. Study the companies' balance sheets to see
   a. What classes of stock each company has issued.
   b. Which item carries a larger balance—the Common Stock account, or Paid-in Capital in Excess of Par (also labeled Additional Paid-in Capital)?
   c. What percentage of each company's total stockholders' equity is made up of retained earnings?
   d. Whether the company has treasury stock. If so, how many shares and how much is the cost?

3. Examine each company's statement of stockholders' equity for evidence of
   a. Cash dividends
   b. Stock dividends (Some companies use the term *stock split* to refer to a large stock dividend.)
   c. Treasury stock purchases and sales
4. As directed by your instructor, either write a report or present your findings to your class. You may be unable to understand *everything* you find, but neither can the Wall Street analysts! You will be amazed at how much you have learned.

Long-Term Liabilities

After studying this chapter, you should be able to

1. Account for basic bonds payable transactions by the straight-line amortization method
2. Amortize bond discount and premium by the effective-interest method
3. Account for retirement of bonds payable
4. Account for conversion of bonds payable
5. Show the advantages and disadvantages of borrowing

6. Account for lease and pension liabilities

APPENDIX LEARNING OBJECTIVES

A1. Compute the future value of an investment
A2. Compute the present value of a single future amount and the present value of an annuity
A3. Determine the cost of an asset acquired through a capital lease

> **❝** *[The upgrading of Chrysler bonds] cut our interest rate payments by half a point, or $5 million annually.* **❞**

In the early 1990s, Chrysler Corporation experienced some financial difficulty, and the automaker's bonds were downgraded to junk-bond status—that is, rated as highly risky. What was the result? Chrysler's interest expense shot up, and this increase hurt the company's profits. Since then Chrysler Corp. has worked hard to improve its bond rating. The company has enhanced product quality, redesigned its Jeep Grand Cherokee, and introduced the Neon subcompact and a new Ram pickup truck. Moody's Investor Service has taken note of these operational improvements and has upgraded the Chrysler bonds. The result? "It cut our interest rate payments by half a point, or $5 million annually," according to a Chrysler spokesperson. Not only will these savings greatly improve reported income, but the stock market responded to the bond-rating news by increasing the price of Chrysler stock.

hapters 13 and 14 covered two ways of financing operations: contributed capital (the stock accounts and additional paid-in capital) and profitable operations (retained earnings). This chapter discusses the third way to finance a company—long-term liabilities, including bonds payable (and notes payable), lease liabilities, and pension liabilities. The chapter appendix provides background on the valuation of long-term liabilities.

Before launching into accounting for bonds payable, let's compare stocks and bonds.

Stocks	*Bonds*
1. Stocks represent ownership (equity) of the corporation.	1. Bonds represent a debt (liability) of the corporation.
2. Shareholder is an owner of the corporation.	2. Bondholder is a creditor of the corporation.
3. Shareholder has the right to receive dividends, if declared.	3. Bondholder expects to receive interest.
4. Dividends are optional to the corporation.	4. Interest is a contractual obligation of the corporation.
5. Dividends are not an expense and are not tax-deductible by the corporation.	5. Interest is a tax-deductible expense of the corporation.
6. Corporation is *not* obligated to repay amount invested by the shareholders.	6. Corporation must repay the bonds payable at maturity.

Bonds: An Introduction

Large companies such as Chrysler Corporation cannot borrow billions from a single lender because no lender will risk that much money on a single company. Banks and other lenders diversify their risk by loaning smaller amounts to numerous customers. That way if a borrower cannot repay, the lender is not devastated.

How then do large corporations borrow a huge amount? They issue bonds payable to the public. **Bonds payable** are groups of notes payable issued to multiple lenders, called bondholders. Chrysler can borrow large amounts from thousands of individual investors, each buying a modest amount of Chrysler bonds.

Purchasers of the bonds receive a bond certificate, which carries the issuing company's name. The certificate also states the *principal*, which is the amount the company has borrowed from the bondholder. This figure, typically stated in units of $1,000, is also called the bond's face value, maturity value, or par value. The bond obligates the issuing company to pay the holder the principal amount at a specific future date, called the maturity date, which also appears on the certificate.

Bondholders lend their money to earn interest. The bond certificate states the interest rate that the issuer will pay the bondholder and the dates that the interest payments are due (generally twice a year). Some bond certificates name the bondholder (the investor). Exhibit 15-1 shows an actual bond certificate.

Issuing bonds usually requires the services of a securities firm, such as Merrill Lynch, to act as the *underwriter* of the bond issue. The **underwriter** purchases the bonds from the issuing company and resells them to its clients. Alternatively, the underwriter may sell the bonds for a commission, agreeing to buy all unsold bonds. This usually guarantees that the corporation can borrow the amount of money needed.

Types of Bonds

All the bonds in a particular issue may mature at a specified time **(term bonds),** or they may mature in installments over a period of time **(serial bonds).** Serial bonds are like installment notes payable.

Secured, or *mortgage*, *bonds* give the bondholder the right to take specified assets of the issuer (called collateral) if the company *defaults*—that is, fails to pay interest or principal. *Unsecured bonds*, called **debentures**, are backed only by the good faith of the borrower.

Bonds Payable. Groups of notes payable (bonds) issued to multiple lenders called bondholders.

Underwriter. Organization that purchases the bonds from an issuing company and resells them to its clients or sells the bonds for a commission, agreeing to buy all unsold bonds.

Term Bonds. Bonds that all mature at the same time for a particular issue.

Serial Bonds. Bonds that mature in installments over a period of time.

Debentures. Unsecured bonds, backed only by the good faith of the borrower.

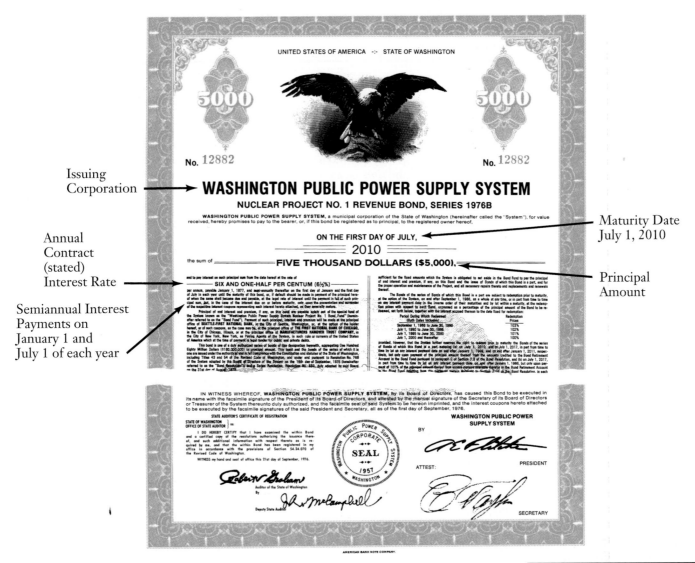

Issuing Corporation

Annual Contract (stated) Interest Rate

Semiannual Interest Payments on January 1 and July 1 of each year

Maturity Date July 1, 2010

Principal Amount

EXHIBIT 15-1
Bond (Note) Certificate

Bond Prices

A bond issued at a price above its maturity (par) value is said to be issued at a **premium,** and a bond issued at a price below maturity (par) value has a **discount.** As a bond nears maturity, its market price moves toward par value. On the maturity date, the market value of a bond exactly equals its par value because the company that issued the bond pays that amount to retire the bond.

After a bond is issued, investors may buy and sell bonds through the bond market just as they buy and sell stocks through the stock market. The most famous bond market is the New York Exchange, which lists several thousand bonds. Bond prices are quoted at a percentage of their maturity value. For example, a $1,000 bond quoted at 100 is bought or sold for $1,000, which is 100% of its par value. The same bond quoted at 101 1/2 has a market price of $1,015 (101.5% of par value, or $1,000 × 1.015). Prices are quoted to one-eighth of 1 percent. A $1,000 bond quoted at 88 3/8 is priced at $883.75 ($1,000 × 0.88375).

Exhibit 15-2 contains price information for the bonds of Ohio Edison Company, taken from *The Wall Street Journal.* On this particular day, 12 of Ohio Edison's 9 1/2%, $1,000 par-value bonds maturing in the year 2006 (indicated by 06) were traded. The bonds' highest price on this day was $795 ($1,000 × 0.795). The lowest price of the day was $785 ($1,000 × 0.785). The closing price (last sale of the day) was $795. This price was 2% higher than the closing price of the preceding day. What was the bonds' closing price the preceding day? It was 77 1/2 (79 1/2 − 2).

Premium. Excess of a bond's issue price over its maturity (par) value. Also called **bond premium.**

Discount (on a Bond). Excess of a bond's maturity (par value) over its issue price. Also called a **bond discount.**

■ **Daily Exercise 15-1**

EXHIBIT 15-2

Bond Price Information for
Ohio Edison Company (OhEd)

Bonds	Volume	High	Low	Close	Net Change
OhEd 9 1/2 06	12	79 1/2	78 1/2	79 1/2	+2

Present Value[1]

A dollar received today is worth more than a dollar received in the future. Why? Because you can invest today's dollar and earn income from it. Likewise, deferring your cash payments until later gives your money a longer period to grow. Money earns income over time, a fact called the *time value of money*. Let's examine how the time value of money affects the pricing of bonds.

Assume that a bond with a face value of $1,000 reaches maturity three years from today and carries no interest. Would you pay $1,000 to purchase the bond? No, because the payment of $1,000 today to receive the same amount in the future provides you with no income on the investment. You would not be taking advantage of the time value of money. Just how much would you pay today in order to receive $1,000 at the end of three years? The answer is some amount *less* than $1,000. Let's suppose that you feel $750 is a good price. By investing $750 now to receive $1,000 later, you earn $250 interest revenue over the three years. The issuing company sees the transaction this way: It pays you $250 interest for the use of your $750 for three years.

Present Value. Amount a person would invest now to receive a greater amount at a future date.

The amount that a person would invest *at the present time* to receive a greater amount at a future date is called the **present value** of a future amount. In our example, $750 is the present value of the $1,000 amount to be received three years later.

Our $750 bond price is a reasonable estimate. The exact present value of any future amount depends on (1) the amount of the future payment (or receipt), (2) the length of time from the investment to the date when the future amount is to be received (or paid), and (3) the interest rate during the period. Present value is always less than the future amount. We discuss the method of computing present value in the appendix that follows this chapter. We need to be aware of the present-value concept, however, in the discussion of bond prices that follows. If your instructor so directs you, please study the appendix now.

 Learning Tip: Present value is always less than future value. You should be able to invest today's money (present value) so that it will increase (future value). The difference between present value and future value is interest.

Bond Interest Rates

Bonds are sold at market price, which is the amount that investors are willing to pay at any given time. Market price is the bond's present value, which equals the present value of the principal payment plus the present value of the cash interest payments (which are made semiannually, annually, or quarterly over the term of the bond).

Two interest rates work to set the price of a bond:

Contract Interest Rate. Interest rate that determines the amount of cash interest the borrower pays and the investor receives each year. Also called the **stated interest rate.**

- The **contract interest rate,** or **stated interest rate,** is the interest rate that determines the amount of cash interest the borrower pays—and the investor receives—each year. The contract interest rate is set by the bond contract and does not change during the life of the bonds. For example, Chrysler's 9% bonds have a contract interest rate of 9 percent. Thus Chrysler pays $9,000 of interest annually on each $100,000 bond. Each semiannual interest payment is $4,500 ($100,000 × 0.09 × 1/2).

Market Interest Rate. Interest rate that investors demand in order to loan their money. Also called the **effective interest rate.**

- The **market interest rate,** or **effective interest rate,** is the rate that investors demand for loaning their money. The market interest rate varies, sometimes daily. A company may issue bonds with a contract interest rate that differs from the prevailing market interest rate. Chrysler may issue its 9% bonds when the market rate has risen to 10 percent. Will the Chrysler bonds attract investors in this market? No, because investors can earn 10% on other bonds of similar risk. Therefore, investors will purchase Chrysler bonds only at a price less than par value. The difference between the lower price and the bonds' face value is a *discount*. Conversely, if the market interest

■ **Daily Exercise 15-2**

[1]The chapter appendix covers present value in more detail.

			Issuance Price of Bonds Payable
Contract (stated) interest rate on a bond payable	=	Market interest rate	→ Par (face, or maturity) value
Example: 9%	=	9%	→ Par: $1,000 bond issued for $1,000
Contract (stated) interest rate on a bond payable	less than	Market interest rate	→ Discount (price below par)
Example: 9%	<	10%	→ Discount: $1,000 bond issued below $1,000
Contract (stated) interest rate on a bond payable	greater than	Market interest rate	→ Premium (price above par)
Example: 9%	>	8%	→ Premium: $1,000 bond issued above $1,000

rate is 8%, Chrysler's 9% bonds will be so attractive that investors will pay more than face value for them. The difference between the higher price and face value is a *premium*. Exhibit 15-3 shows how the contract (stated) interest rate and the market interest rate interact to determine the issuance price of bonds payable.

■ **Daily Exercise 15-3**
■ **Daily Exercise 15-4**

Issuing Bonds Payable to Borrow Money

Suppose Chrysler Corporation has $50 million in 9% bonds that mature in five years. Assume that Chrysler issues these bonds at par on January 1, 1999. The issuance entry is

```
1999
Jan. 1   Cash ............................................................  50,000,000
             Bonds Payable...................................                       50,000,000
         To issue 9%, 5-year bonds at par.
```

Chrysler, the borrower, makes a one-time entry similar to this to record the receipt of cash and the issuance of bonds. Afterward, investors buy and sell the bonds through the bond markets. The buy-and-sell transactions between investors do *not* involve the corporation that issued the bonds. It keeps no records of these transactions, except for the names and addresses of the bondholders. This information is needed for mailing the interest and principal payments.

Interest payments occur each January 1 and July 1. Chrysler's entry to record the first semiannual interest payment is

```
1999
July 1   Interest Expense ($50,000,000 × 0.09 × 6/12) ..........  2,250,000
             Cash ...............................................................                   2,250,000
         To pay semiannual interest on bonds payable.
```

At maturity, Chrysler will record payment of the bonds as follows:

```
2004
Jan. 1   Bonds Payable............................................  50,000,000
             Cash...............................................................                  50,000,000
         To pay bonds payable at maturity.
```

■ **Daily Exercise 15-5**

Issuing Bonds and Notes Payable Between Interest Dates

The foregoing entries to record Chrysler's bond transactions are straightforward because the company issued the bonds on an interest payment date (January 1). However, corporations often issue bonds between interest dates.

Assume that MGM Grand, Inc., which runs the MGM Grand Hotel and Theme Park in Las Vegas, issued $230 million of 12% notes payable due in the year 2008. Assume further that these notes were dated 1998 and carry the price "100 plus accrued interest from date of original issue." An investor purchasing the MGM Grand, Inc., notes after the issue date must pay market value *plus accrued interest*. The issuing company will pay the full semiannual interest amount to the bondholder who is holding the bonds at the next interest payment date. Companies do not split semiannual interest payments among two or more investors who happen to hold the bonds during a particular six-month interest period.

Now assume that MGM Grand, Inc., sold $100,000,000 of its notes on July 15, 1998, one month after the date of original issue on June 15. The market price of the notes on July 15 is the face value. MGM Grand receives one month's accrued interest in addition to the notes' face value. MGM Grand's entry to record issuance of the notes payable is as follows:

1998			
July 15	Cash...	101,000,000	
	Bonds Payable...		100,000,000
	Interest Payable ($100,000,000 ×		
	0.12 × 1/12)......................................		1,000,000
	To issue 12%, ten-year notes at par, one month after the original issue date.		

MGM Grand's entry to record the first semiannual interest payment is

1998			
Dec. 15	Interest Expense ($100,000,000 ×		
	0.12 × 5/12)..	5,000,000	
	Interest Payable...	1,000,000	
	Cash ($100,000,000 × 0.12 × 6/12)........		6,000,000
	To pay semiannual interest on notes payable.		

The debit to Interest Payable eliminates the credit balance in that account (from July 15). MGM Grand has now paid off that liability.

Note that MGM Grand pays a full six months' interest on December 15. After subtracting the one month's accrued interest received at the time of issuing the note, MGM Grand has recorded interest expense for five months ($5,000,000). This interest expense is the correct amount for the five months that the notes have been outstanding.

Selling bonds and notes between interest dates at market value plus accrued interest simplifies the borrower's accounting. MGM Grand, Inc., pays the same amount of interest on each note regardless of the length of time the investor has held the note. MGM Grand need not compute each noteholder's interest payment on an individual basis.

■ **Daily Exercise 15-6**

Issuing Bonds Payable at a Discount

Unlike stocks, bonds are often issued at a discount. We know that market conditions may force the issuing corporation to accept a discount price for its bonds. Suppose Chrysler issues $100,000 of its 9%, five-year bonds when the market interest rate is 9 1/2 percent. The market price of the bonds drops to 98, which means 98% of par value. Chrysler receives $98,000 ($100,000 × 0.98) at issuance and makes the following journal entry:

1999			
Jan. 1	Cash ($100,000 × 0.98).......................................	98,000	
	Discount on Bonds Payable	2,000	
	Bonds Payable...		100,000
	To issue 9%, five-year bonds at a discount.		

After posting, the bond accounts have the following balances:

Bonds Payable	Discount on Bonds Payable
100,000	2,000

Chrysler's balance sheet reports the following immediately after issuance of the bonds:

Long-term liabilities:		
Bonds payable, 9%, due 2004	$100,000	
Less: Discount on bonds payable	(2,000)	$98,000

Discount on Bonds Payable is a contra account to Bonds Payable. Subtracting its balance from Bonds Payable yields the carrying amount of the bonds. The relationship between Bonds Payable and the Discount account is similar to the relationship between Equipment and Accumulated Depreciation. Thus Chrysler's liability is $98,000, which is the amount the company borrowed. If Chrysler were to pay off the bonds immediately, Chrysler's required outlay would be $98,000 because the market price of the bonds is $98,000.

INTEREST EXPENSE ON BONDS PAYABLE ISSUED AT A DISCOUNT   We earlier discussed the difference between the contract interest rate and the market interest rate. Suppose the market rate is 9 1/2% when Chrysler issues its 9% bonds. The 1/2% interest-rate difference creates the $2,000 discount on the bonds. Investors are willing to pay only $98,000 for a $100,000, 9% bond when they can purchase similar bonds and earn 9 1/2% on the investment. Chrysler borrows $98,000 cash but must pay $100,000 cash when the bonds mature five years later.

What happens to the $2,000 balance of the discount account over the life of the bond issue? The $2,000 discount is additional interest expense to Chrysler. The $2,000 is a cost—beyond the stated 9% interest—that the business pays for borrowing the investors' money. The discount has the effect of raising the interest expense on the bonds to the market interest rate of 9 1/2 percent. Each accounting period over the life of the bonds, the discount is accounted for as interest expense through a process called amortization.

STRAIGHT-LINE AMORTIZATION OF BOND DISCOUNT   We amortize a bond discount by dividing it into equal amounts for each interest period. This method is called *straight-line amortization.* In our example, the initial discount is $2,000, and there are ten semiannual interest periods during the bonds' five-year life. Therefore, 1/10 of the $2,000 ($200) of bond discount is amortized each interest period. Chrysler's semiannual interest entry on July 1, 1999 is recorded as follows:[2]

1999			
July 1	Interest Expense	4,700	
	Cash ($100,000 × 0.09 × 6/12)		4,500
	Discount on Bonds Payable ($2,000/10)		200
	To pay semiannual interest and amortize discount on bonds payable.		

---

[2]Some accountants prefer to record the payment of interest and the amortization of the discount in two separate entries, as follows:

1999			
July 1	Interest Expense	4,500	
	Cash ($100,000 × 0.09 × 6/12)		4,500
	To pay semiannual interest.		
July 1	Interest Expense	200	
	Discount on Bonds Payable ($2,000/10)		200
	To amortize discount on bonds payable.		

Objective 1

Account for basic bonds payable transactions by the straight-line amortization method

Interest expense of $4,700 for the six-month period is the sum of

- The contract interest ($4,500, which is paid in cash), plus
- The amount of discount amortized ($200)

■ **Daily Exercise 15-7**

Discount on Bonds Payable is credited to amortize (reduce) its debit balance. Because Discount on Bonds Payable is a contra account, each reduction in its balance increases the carrying amount of the bonds payable. Ten amortization entries will decrease the discount balance to zero, and the carrying amount of bonds payable will have increased to the bonds' face value of $100,000. The entry to pay off the bonds at maturity is

2004				
Jan. 1	Bonds Payable...	100,000	
	Cash..		100,000
	To pay bonds payable at maturity.		

Issuing Bonds Payable at a Premium

Bonds issued at a premium are less common than bonds issued at a discount. To illustrate issuing bonds at a premium, let's change the Chrysler example. Assume that the market interest rate is 8% when the company issues its 9%, five-year bonds. Because 9% bonds are attractive in this market, investors pay a premium price to acquire them. If the bonds are priced at 104 (104% of par value), Chrysler receives $104,000 cash upon issuance. The entry is

1999				
Jan. 1	Cash ($100,000 × 1.04)	104,000	
	Bonds Payable		100,000
	Premium on Bonds Payable...........................		4,000
	To issue 9%, five-year bonds at a premium.		

After posting, the bond accounts have the following balances:

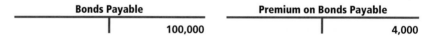

Bonds Payable	Premium on Bonds Payable
100,000	4,000

Chrysler's balance sheet reports the following immediately after issuance of bonds:

Long-term liabilities:		
Bonds payable, 9%, due 2004..........	$100,000	
Premium on bonds payable	4,000	$104,000

Premium on Bonds Payable is added to Bonds Payable to show the book value, or carrying amount, of the bonds. Chrysler's liability is $104,000, which is the amount that the company borrowed. Immediate payment of the bonds would require an outlay of $104,000 because that is the market price of the bonds at issuance. The investors would not give up the bonds for less than their market value.

INTEREST EXPENSE ON BONDS PAYABLE ISSUED AT A PREMIUM   The 1% difference between the 9% contract interest rate on the bonds and the 8% market rate creates the $4,000 premium. Chrysler borrows $104,000 cash but must pay only $100,000 at maturity. We treat the premium as a savings of interest expense to Chrysler. The premium cuts Chrysler's cost of borrowing and reduces Chrysler's interest expense to an effective interest rate of 8%, the market rate. We account for the premium much as we handled the discount. We amortize the bond premium as a decrease in interest expense over the life of the bonds.

STRAIGHT-LINE AMORTIZATION OF BOND PREMIUM   In our example, the beginning premium is $4,000, and there are ten semiannual interest periods during the bonds'

five-year life. Therefore, 1/10 of the $4,000 ($400) of bond premium is amortized each interest period. Chrysler's semiannual interest entry on July 1, 1999, is[3]

1999			
July 1	Interest Expense	4,100	
	Premium on Bonds Payable ($4,000/10)	400	
	Cash ($100,000 × 0.09 × 6/12)		4,500
	To pay semiannual interest and amortize premium on bonds payable.		

Interest expense of $4,100 is the remainder of the contract cash interest ($4,500) less the amount of premium amortized ($400). The debit to Premium on Bonds Payable reduces its credit balance.

■ **Daily Exercise 15-8**

 Thinking It Over Consider bonds issued at a discount. Which will be greater, the cash interest paid per period or the amount of interest expense? Answer the same question for bonds issued at a premium.

Answer: For bonds issued at a *discount*, interest expense will be greater than cash interest paid, by the amount of the discount amortized each period. Remember that the company received less than face value when it issued the bonds. But at maturity the company must pay the full face value back to the bondholders. This discount increases the company's interest expense above the amount of cash interest paid each period.

For bonds issued at a *premium*, interest expense will be less than the amount of cash interest paid, by the amount of the premium amortized for the period. This is because the premium amount received at issuance decreases the interest expense below the amount of cash interest paid each period.

Reporting Bonds Payable

Bonds payable are reported on the balance sheet at their maturity amount plus any unamortized premium or minus any unamortized discount. For example, at December 31, Chrysler in the preceding example has amortized Premium on Bonds Payable for two semiannual periods ($400 × 2 = $800). The Chrysler balance sheet would show these bonds payable as follows:

Long-term liabilities:		
Bonds payable, 9%, due 2004	$100,000	
Premium on bonds payable [$4,000 – ($2 × $400)]	3,200	$103,200

Over the life of the bonds, ten amortization entries will decrease the premium balance to zero. The payment at maturity will debit Bonds Payable and credit cash for $100,000.

Adjusting Entries for Interest Expense

Companies issue bonds when they need cash. The interest payments seldom occur on December 31 (or the end of the fiscal year). Nevertheless, interest expense must be accrued at the end of the period to measure income accurately. ◀▮ The accrual entry may often be complicated by the need to amortize a discount or a premium for only a partial interest period.

◀▮◀▮◀▮ The adjusting entry for bond interest expense is the same as the adjusting entries for other accrued liabilities as in Chapters 3 (page 104) and 11 (page 488) except for the addition of the amortization of the premium or discount.

---

[3] The payment of interest and the amortization of bond premium can be recorded in separate entries as follows:

1999			
July 1	Interest Expense	4,500	
	Cash ($100,000 × 0.09 × 6/12)		4,500
	To pay semiannual interest.		
July 1	Premium on Bonds Payable ($4,000/10)	400	
	Interest Expense		400
	To amortize premium on bonds payable.		

Xenon Corporation issued $100,000 of its 8%, ten-year bonds at a $2,000 discount on October 1, 1999. The interest payments occur on March 31 and September 30 each year. On December 31, Xenon records interest for the three-month period (October, November, and December) as follows:

```
1999
Dec. 31   Interest Expense ...............................................................   2,050
              Interest Payable ($100,000 × 0.08 × 3/12).................         2,000
              Discount on Bonds Payable ($2,000/10 × 3/12).........            50
          To accrue three months' interest and amortize discount
          on bonds payable.
```

Interest Payable is credited for the three months of cash interest that have accrued since September 30. Discount on Bonds Payable is credited for three months of amortization.

Xenon's balance sheet at December 31, 1999, reports Interest Payable of $2,000 as a current liability. Bonds Payable appears as a long-term liability, presented as follows:

Long-term liabilities:		
Bonds payable, 8%, due 2009......................................	$100,000	
Less: Discount on bonds payable ($2,000 – $50)..........	(1,950)	$98,050

Observe that the balance of Discount on Bonds Payable decreases by $50. The bonds' carrying amount therefore increases by $50. The bonds' carrying amount continues to increase over its ten-year life, reaching $100,000 at maturity, when the discount will be fully amortized.

The next semiannual interest payment occurs on March 31, 2000:

■ Daily Exercise 15-9
■ Daily Exercise 15-10

```
2000
Mar. 31   Interest Expense................................................................   2,050
          Interest Payable................................................................   2,000
              Cash ($100,000 × 0.08 × 6/12)......................................         4,000
              Discount on Bonds Payable ($2,000/10 × 3/12) .........            50
          To pay semiannual interest, part of which was accrued,
          and amortize three months' discount on bonds payable.
```

Amortization of a premium over a partial interest period is similar except that Premium on Bonds Payable is debited.

Take a few moments and review the first half of the chapter by studying the Decision Guidelines feature.

DECISION GUIDELINES	Accounting for Long-Term Liabilities—Part A
DECISION	**GUIDELINES**
Need to pay back principal amount	Type of bonds to issue:
• All at maturity? • In installments?	• Term bonds • Serial bonds
Are the bonds secured?	Then they are
• Yes • No	• Mortgage, or secured, bonds • Debenture, or unsecured, bonds

(continued)

DECISION GUIDELINES *(continued)*

How are bond prices

- Quoted?

- As a percentage of maturity value (Example: A $500,000 bond priced at $510,000 would be quoted at 102 ($510,000 ÷ $500,000 = 1.02.)

- Determined?

- Present value of the future principal amount to pay plus present value of the future interest payments (see chapter appendix)

What are the two interest rates used for bonds?

- *Contract (stated) interest rate* determines the amount of cash interest the borrower pays. This interest rate is set by contract and does not change during the life of the bonds.
- *Market (effective) interest rate* is the rate that investors demand for loaning their money. The market interest rate determines the borrower's true rate of interest expense. This rate varies, sometimes daily.

What causes a bond to be priced at

When the bonds are issued,

- Par (face, or maturity) value?

- Contract interest rate on the bond *equals the* Market interest rate

- A premium?

- Contract interest rate on the bond *greater than* the Market interest rate

- A discount?

- Contract interest rate on the bond *less than* the Market interest rate

What is the relationship between interest expense and interest payments when bonds are issued at

- Par (face, or maturity) value?
- A premium?
- A discount?

- Interest expense *equals* Interest payment
- Interest expense *less than* Interest payment
- Interest expense *greater than* Interest payment

How to report bonds payable on the balance sheet?

Par (face, or maturity) amount
$\begin{cases} \text{+ Premium on bonds payable} \\ \quad \text{or} \\ \text{− Discount on bonds payable} \end{cases}$

SUMMARY PROBLEM FOR YOUR REVIEW　　MID-CHAPTER

Assume that Alabama Power Company has outstanding an issue of 9% bonds that mature on May 1, 2019. The bonds are dated May 1, 1999, and Alabama Power pays interest each April 30 and October 31.

1. Will the bonds be issued at par, at a premium, or at a discount if the market interest rate is 8% at date of issuance? If the market interest rate is 10 percent?

2. Assume that Alabama Power issued $1,000,000 of the bonds at 104 on May 1, 1999.
   a. Record issuance of the bonds.
   b. Record the interest payment and amortization of premium or discount on October 31, 1999.
   c. Accrue interest and amortize premium or discount on December 31, 1999.
   d. Show how the company would report the bonds on the balance sheet at December 31, 1999.
   e. Record the interest payment on April 30, 2000.

REQUIRED

■ SOLUTION

If the market interest rate is 8%, 9% bonds will be issued at a *premium*. If the market rate is 10%, the 9% bonds will be issued at a *discount*.

REQUIREMENT 1

1999

a. May 1   Cash ($1,000,000 × 1.04)   1,040,000
          Bonds Payable..   1,000,000
          Premium on Bonds Payable   40,000
          To issue 9%, 20-year bonds at a premium.

b. Oct. 31   Interest Expense...   44,000
          Premium on Bonds Payable ($40,000/40).................   1,000
          Cash ($1,000,000 × 0.09 × 6/12).......................   45,000
          To pay semiannual interest and amortize premium
          on bonds payable.

c. Dec. 31   Interest Expense...   14,667
          Premium on Bonds Payable ($40,000/40 × 2/6)   333
          Interest Payable ($1,000,000 × 0.09 × 2/12)   15,000
          To accrue interest and amortize bond premium
          for two months.

d. Long-term liabilities:
          Bonds payable, 9%, due 2019........ $1,000,000
          Premium on bonds payable
          ($40,000 − $1,000 − $333) ....   <u>38,667</u> $1,038,667

2000

e. Apr. 30   Interest Expense...   29,333
          Interest Payable...   15,000
          Premium on Bonds Payable ($40,000/40 × 4/6).......   667
          Cash ($1,000,000 × 0.09 × 6/12).......................   45,000
          To pay semiannual interest, part of which was accrued,
          and amortize four months' premium on bonds payable.

■ SUPPLEMENT TO SOLUTION

Bond problems include many details. You may find it helpful to check your work. We verify the answers to the summary problem in this supplement.

     On April 30, 2000, the bonds have been outstanding for one year. After the entries have been recorded, the account balances should show the results of one year's cash interest payments and one year's bond premium amortization.

Fact 1:   Cash interest payments should be $90,000 ($1,000,000 × 0.09).

Accuracy check: Two credits to Cash of $45,000 each = $90,000. Cash payments are correct.

Fact 2:   Premium amortization should be $2,000 ($40,000/40 semiannual periods × 2 semiannual periods in 1 year).

Accuracy check: Three debits to Premium on Bonds Payable ($1,000 + $333 + $667) = $2,000. Premium amortization is correct.

Fact 3:   We can also check the accuracy of interest expense recorded during the year ended December 31, 1999.

                  The bonds in this problem will be outstanding for a total of 20 years, or 240 (that is, 20 × 12) months. During 1999, the bonds are outstanding for eight months (May through December).

                  Interest expense for eight months *equals* payment of cash interest for eight months minus premium amortization for eight months. Interest expense should therefore be ($1,000,000 × 0.09 × 8/12 = $60,000) minus [($40,000/240) × 8 = $1,333], or ($60,000 − $1,333 = $58,667).

Accuracy check: Two debits to Interest Expense ($44,000 + $14,667) = $58,667. Interest expense for 1999 is correct.

Effective-Interest Method of Amortization

The straight-line amortization method was explained first to introduce the concept of amortizing bond discount and premium. However, it has a theoretical weakness. Each period's amortization amount for a premium or discount is the same dollar amount over the life of the bonds. Over that time, however, the bonds' carrying amount continues to increase (with a discount) or decrease (with a premium). Thus the fixed dollar amount of amortization changes as a percentage of the bonds' carrying amount, making it appear that the bond issuer's interest rate changes over time. But in reality, the issuer locked in a fixed interest rate when the bonds were issued. The interest *rate* on the bonds does not change.

GAAP *(Accounting Principles Board Opinion No. 21)* requires that discounts and premiums be amortized using the *effective-interest method* unless the difference between the straight-line method and the effective-interest method is immaterial. In that case, either method is permitted. We will see how the effective-interest method keeps interest expense at the same percentage over the bonds' life. The total amount of bond discount or bond premium amortized over the life of the bonds is the same under both methods.

Effective-Interest Method of Amortizing Bond Discount

Assume that Bethlehem Steel Corporation issues $100,000 of its 9% bonds at a time when the market rate of interest is 10 percent. Assume also that these bonds mature in five years and pay interest semiannually, so there are ten semiannual interest payments. The issue price of the bonds is $96,149.[4] The discount on these bonds is $3,851 ($100,000 − $96,149). Exhibit 15-4 illustrates amortization of the discount by the effective-interest method.

EXHIBIT 15-4
Effective-Interest Method of Amortizing Bond Discount

PANEL A—Bond Data
Maturity value—$100,000
Contract interest rate—9%
Interest paid—4 1/2% semiannually, $4,500 ($100,000 × 0.045)
Market interest rate at time of issue—10% annually, 5% semiannually
Issue price—$96,149

PANEL B—Amortization Table

	A	B	C	D	E
End of Semiannual Interest Period	Interest Payment (4 1/2% of Maturity Value)	Interest *Expense* (5% of Preceding Bond Carrying Amount)	Discount Amortization (B − A)	Discount Account Balance (D − C)	Bond Carrying Amount ($100,000 − D)
Issue Date				$3,851	$ 96,149
1	$4,500	$4,807	$307	3,544	96,456
2	4,500	4,823	323	3,221	96,779
3	4,500	4,839	339	2,882	97,118
4	4,500	4,856	356	2,526	97,474
5	4,500	4,874	374	2,152	97,848
6	4,500	4,892	392	1,760	98,240
7	4,500	4,912	412	1,348	98,652
8	4,500	4,933	433	915	99,085
9	4,500	4,954	454	461	99,539
10	4,500	4,961*	461	–0–	100,000

*Adjusted for effect of rounding.

Notes
- *Column A* The semiannual interest payments are constant—fixed by the contract interest rate and the bonds' maturity value.
- *Column B* The interest expense each period is computed by multiplying the preceding bond carrying amount by the market interest rate. The effect of this *effective interest rate* determines the interest expense each period. The amount of interest each period increases as the effective interest rate, a constant, is applied to the increasing bond carrying amount (E).
- *Column C* The excess of each interest expense amount (B) over each interest payment amount (A) is the discount amortization for the period.
- *Column D* The discount balance decreases by the amount of amortization for the period (C), from $3,851 at the bonds' issue date to zero at their maturity. Balance of discount + bonds' carrying amount = bonds' maturity value ($100,000).
- *Column E* The bond's carrying amount increases from $96,149 at issuance to $100,000 at maturity.

---

[4]We compute this present value by using the tables that appear in this chapter's appendix.

The *accounts* debited and credited under the effective-interest amortization method and the straight-line method are the same. Only the *amounts* differ. We may take the amortization *amounts* directly from the table in Exhibit 15-4. We assume that the first interest payment occurs on July 1 and use the appropriate amounts from Exhibit 15-4, reading across the line for the first interest payment date:

■ Daily Exercise 15-11
■ Daily Exercise 15-12

July 1	Interest Expense (column B)..	4,807	
	Discount on Bonds Payable (column C)...................		307
	Cash (column A)...		4,500
	To pay semiannual interest and amortize discount on bonds payable.		

Exhibit 15-5, Panel A, diagrams the interest expense over the life of bonds payable issued at a discount. Panel B shows how the carrying amount of the bonds rises to the maturity date. All amounts are taken from Exhibit 15-4. Focus on the highlighted items to understand the main points of the exhibit.

EXHIBIT 15-5

Interest Expense and Bond Carrying Amount Both Increase for Bonds Payable Issued at a Discount

PANEL A—Interest Expense on Bonds Payable Issued at a Discount

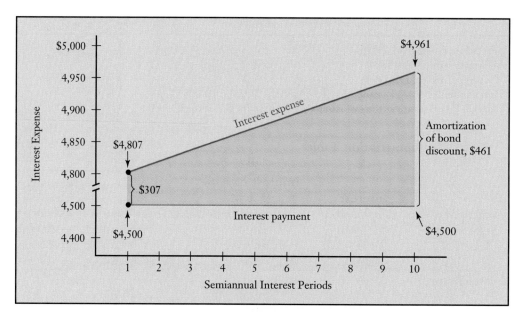

PANEL B—Carrying Amount of Bonds Payable Issued at a Discount

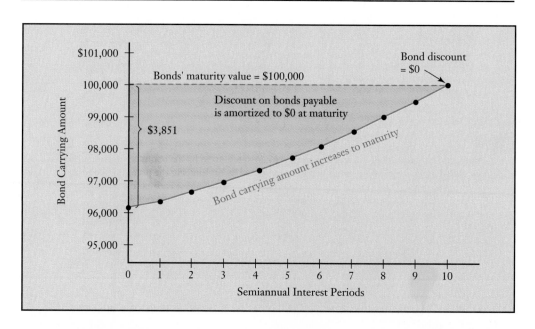

Thinking It Over Over the life of a bond issued at a *discount*, will the periodic amount of interest expense increase or decrease under the effective-interest amortization method?

Answer: The periodic amount of interest expense *increases* because the carrying amount of the bond *increases* toward maturity value. To see this, refer to columns B and E of Exhibit 15-4. The upward-sloping line in Exhibit 15-5, Panel A, illustrates the increasing amount of interest expense.

Effective-Interest Method of Amortizing Bond Premium

Let's modify the Bethlehem Steel example to illustrate the interest method of amortizing bond premium. Assume that Bethlehem Steel issues $100,000 of five-year, 9% bonds that pay interest semiannually. If the bonds are issued when the market interest rate is 8%, their issue price is $104,100.[5] The premium on these bonds is $4,100, and Exhibit 15-6 illustrates amortization of the premium by the effective-interest method.

EXHIBIT 15-6
Effective-Interest Method of Amortizing Bond Premium

PANEL A—Bond Data
Maturity value—$100,000
Contract interest rate—9%
Interest paid—4 1/2% semiannually, $4,500 ($100,000 × 0.045)
Market interest rate at time of issue—8% annually, 4% semiannually
Issue price—$104,100

PANEL B—Amortization Table

	A	B	C	D	E
End of Semiannual Interest Period	Interest *Payment* (4 1/2% of Maturity Value)	Interest *Expense* (4% of Preceding Bond Carrying Amount)	Premium Amortization (A − B)	Premium Account Balance (D − C)	Bond Carrying Amount ($100,000 + D)
Issue Date				$4,100	$104,100
1	$4,500	$4,164	$336	3,764	103,764
2	4,500	4,151	349	3,415	103,415
3	4,500	4,137	363	3,052	103,052
4	4,500	4,122	378	2,674	102,674
5	4,500	4,107	393	2,281	102,281
6	4,500	4,091	409	1,872	101,872
7	4,500	4,075	425	1,447	101,447
8	4,500	4,058	442	1,005	101,005
9	4,500	4,040	460	545	100,545
10	4,500	3,955*	545	–0–	100,000

*Adjusted for effect of rounding.

Notes

- *Column A* The semiannual interest payments are constant—fixed by the contract interest rate and the bonds' maturity value.
- *Column B* The interest expense each period is computed by multiplying the preceding bond carrying amount by the effective interest rate. The amount of interest decreases each period as the bond carrying amount decreases.
- *Column C* The excess of each interest payment (A) over the period's interest expense (B) is the premium amortization for the period.
- *Column D* The premium balance decreases by the amount of amortization for the period (C) from $4,100 at issuance to zero at maturity. Bonds' carrying amount – premium balance = bonds' maturity value ($100,000).
- *Column E* The bonds' carrying amount decreases from $104,100 at issuance to $100,000 at maturity.

[5]Again, we compute the present value of the bonds from the tables in this chapter's appendix.

Assuming that the first interest payment occurs on October 31, we read across the line in Exhibit 15-6 for the first payment date and get the appropriate amounts:

Oct. 31	Interest Expense (column B)...	4,164	
	Premium on Bonds Payable (column C)..........................	336	
	Cash (column A)...		4,500
	To pay semiannual interest and amortize premium on bonds payable.		

Thinking It Over How does the method of amortizing bond premium or discount affect the amount of cash interest paid on a bond?

Answer: The amortization method for bond premium or discount has *no effect* on the amount of cash interest paid on a bond. The amount of cash interest paid depends on the contract interest rate stated on the bond. That interest rate, and the amount of cash interest paid, are fixed and therefore remain constant over the life of the bond. To see this, examine column A of Exhibits 15-4 and 15-6.

At year end, it is necessary to make an adjusting entry to accrue interest and amortize the bond premium for a partial period. In our example, the last interest payment occurred on October 31. The adjustment for November and December covers two months, or one-third of a semiannual period. The entry, with amounts drawn from Exhibit 15-6, line 2, is as follows:

Dec. 31	Interest Expense ($4,151 × 1/3)..	1,384	
	Premium on Bonds Payable ($349 × 1/3)..........................	116	
	Interest Payable ($4,500 × 1/3).................................		1,500
	To accrue two months' interest and amortize premium on bonds payable for two months.		

The second interest payment occurs on April 30 of the following year. The payment of $4,500 includes

- Interest expense for four months (January through April)
- The interest payable at December 31
- Premium amortization for four months

The payment entry is as follows:

Apr. 30	Interest Expense ($4,151 × 2/3)..	2,767	
	Interest Payable..	1,500	
	Premium on Bonds Payable ($349 × 2/3)..........................	233	
	Cash		4,500
	To pay semiannual interest, some of which was accrued, and amortize premium on bonds payable for four months.		

If these bonds had been issued at a discount, procedures for these interest entries would be the same, except that Discount on Bonds Payable would be credited.

Exhibit 15-7, Panel A diagrams the interest expense over the life of bonds issued at a premium. Panel B shows how the carrying amount of the bonds falls to maturity. All amounts are taken from Exhibit 15-6. Focus on the highlighted items.

■ **Daily Exercise 15-13**

Thinking It Over For a bond issued at a *premium*, will the periodic amount of interest expense increase or decrease? Assume the effective-interest method.

Answer: The periodic amount of interest expense *decreases* because the carrying amount of the bond *decreases* toward maturity value. To see this, study columns B and E of Exhibit 15-6. The downward-sloping line in Exhibit 15-7, Panel A, illustrates the decreasing amount of interest expense.

PANEL A—Interest Expense on Bonds Payable Issued at a Premium

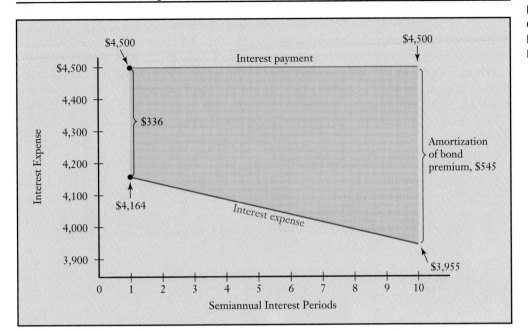

PANEL B—Carrying Amount of Bonds Payable Issued at a Premium

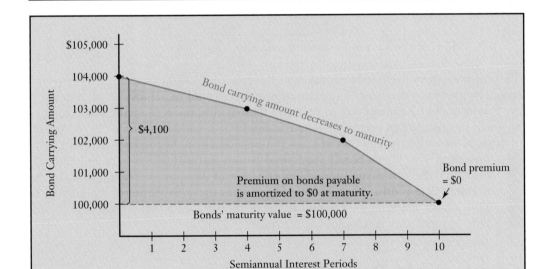

Retirement of Bonds Payable

Normally companies wait until maturity to pay off, or retire, their bonds payable. All bond discount or premium has been amortized, and the retirement entry debits Bonds Payable and credits Cash for the bonds' maturity value. But companies sometimes retire their bonds payable prior to maturity. The main reason for retiring bonds early is to relieve the pressure of making interest payments. Interest rates fluctuate. The company may be able to borrow at a lower interest rate and then use the proceeds from new bonds to pay off the old bonds, which bear a higher interest rate.

Some bonds are **callable,** which means that the bonds' issuer may *call,* or pay off, those bonds at a specified price whenever the issuer so chooses. The call price is usually a few percentage points above the par value, perhaps 104 or 105. Callable bonds give the issuer the benefit of being able to take advantage of low interest rates by paying off the bonds whenever it is favorable to do so. An alternative to calling the bonds is to purchase

Objective 3

Account for retirement of bonds payable

Callable Bonds. Bonds that the issuer may call or pay off at a specified price whenever the issuer wants.

them in the open market at their current market price. Whether the bonds are called or purchased in the open market, the journal entry is the same.

Air Products and Chemicals, Inc., a producer of industrial gases and chemicals, has $70 million of debentures outstanding with a discount of $350,000. Lower interest rates in the market may convince management to pay off these bonds now. Assume that the bonds are callable at 103. If the market price of the bonds is 99 1/4, will Air Products and Chemicals call the bonds or purchase them in the open market? The market price is lower than the call price, so market price is the better choice. Retiring the bonds at 99 1/4 results in an extraordinary gain of $175,000, computed as follows:

Par value of bonds being retired	$70,000,000
Less: Discount on bonds payable	(350,000)
Carrying amount of bonds payable	69,650,000
Market price ($70,000,000 × 0.9925)	69,475,000
Extraordinary gain on retirement of bonds payable	$ 175,000

The following entry records retirement of the bonds, immediately after an interest date:

June 30	Bonds Payable	70,000,000	
	Discount on Bonds Payable		350,000
	Cash ($70,000,000 × 0.9925)		69,475,000
	Extraordinary Gain on Retirement of Bonds Payable		175,000
	To retire bonds payable before maturity.		

■ Daily Exercise 15-14

The entry removes the bonds payable and the related discount from the accounts and records a gain on retirement. Any existing premium would be removed with a debit. If Air Products and Chemicals retired only half these bonds, the accountant would remove only half the discount or premium. GAAP identifies gains and losses on early retirement of debts as *extraordinary*, and they are reported separately on the income statement.

> **Learning Tip:** When bonds are retired before maturity, these steps must be followed: (1) Record partial-period amortization of discount or premium, if the retirement date is other than an interest payment date. (2) Write off the portion of Discount or Premium that relates to the portion of bonds being retired. (3) Compute extraordinary gain or loss on retirement.

Objective 4

Account for conversion of bonds payable

Convertible Bonds and Notes

Convertible Bonds. Bonds (or notes) that may be converted into the common stock of the issuing company at the option of the investor.

Many corporate bonds and notes payable may be converted into the common stock of the issuing company at the option of the investor. These bonds and notes, called **convertible bonds** (or **notes**), combine the receipts of interest and principal on the bonds with the opportunity for gains on the stock. The conversion feature is so attractive that investors accept a lower contract, or stated, interest rate than they would on nonconvertible bonds. The lower cash interest payments benefit the issuer. The issuance of convertible bonds payable is recorded like any other debt.

"Prime Western, Inc., which operates hotels, had convertible notes payable outstanding that were carried on Prime's books at $12.5 million."

If the market price of the issuing company's stock gets high enough, the bondholders will convert the bonds into stock. The corporation records conversion by debiting the bond accounts and crediting the stockholders' equity accounts. The carrying amount of the bonds becomes the book value of the newly issued stock. No gain or loss is recorded.

Prime Western, Inc., which operates hotels, had convertible *notes* payable outstanding that were carried on Prime's books at $12.5 million. Assume that the maturity value of the notes was $13 million. Also assume that Prime Western's stock rose significantly. The note-holders converted the notes into 400,000 shares of the company's $1 par common stock. Prime Western's entry to record conversion of its notes payable into stock is

May 14	Notes Payable	13,000,000	
	Discount on Notes Payable		
	($13,000,000 – $12,500,000)..............		500,000
	Common Stock (400,000 × $1)..............		400,000
	Paid-in Capital in Excess of		
	Par—Common..................................		12,100,000
	To record conversion of notes payable.		

■ Daily Exercise 15-15

The entry closes the notes (or bonds) payable account and its related discount or premium account. The carrying amount of the notes ($13,000,000 – $500,000) becomes the amount of increase in stockholders' equity ($400,000 + $12,100,000).

Current Portion of Long-Term Debt

Serial bonds and serial notes are payable in serials, or installments. The portion payable within one year is a current liability, and the remaining debt is long-term. At July 3, 19X3, Sara Lee Corporation had $1,590 million of long-term debt maturing in various amounts in future years. The portion payable in the next year was $426 million. Therefore, $426 million was a current liability at July 3, 19X3, and $1,164 million was a long-term liability. Sara Lee Corporation reported the following among its liabilities at July 3, 19X3:

	$ Millions
Current liabilities:	
Current maturities of long-term debt..........	$ 426
Long-term debt less current maturities...........	1,164

Mortgage Notes Payable

You have probably heard of mortgage payments. Many notes payable are mortgage notes, which actually contain two agreements:

- The *note* is the borrower's promise to pay the lender the amount of the debt.
- The **mortgage**—a security agreement related to the note—is the borrower's promise to transfer to the lender the legal title to certain assets if the debt is not paid on schedule.

The borrower is pledging these assets as security for the note. Often the asset that is pledged was acquired with the borrowed money. For example, most homeowners sign mortgage notes to purchase their residence, pledging that property as security for the loan. Businesses sign mortgage notes to acquire buildings, equipment, and other long-term assets. Mortgage notes are usually serial notes that require monthly or quarterly payments.

Mortgage. Borrower's promise to transfer the legal title to certain assets to the lender if the debt is not paid on schedule.

Advantage of Financing Operations (Raising Money) by Issuing Bonds versus Stock

Objective 5

Show the advantages and disadvantages of borrowing

Businesses have different ways to acquire assets. Management may decide to purchase or to lease equipment. The money to finance the asset may be financed by the business's

	Plan 1 Borrow $500,000 at 10%	Plan 2 Issue $500,000 of Common Stock
Net income before expansion	$300,000	$300,000
Project income before interest and		
income tax..	$200,000	$200,000
Less interest expense ($500,000 × 0.10).............	(50,000)	–0–
Project income before income tax.....................	150,000	200,000
Less income tax expense (40%).........................	(60,000)	(80,000)
Project net income	90,000	120,000
Total company net income	$390,000	$420,000
Earnings per share after expansion:		
Plan 1 ($390,000/100,000 shares)	$3.90	
Plan 2 ($420,000/150,000 shares)		$2.80

retained earnings, by a stock issue, a note payable, or a bond issue. Each financing strategy has its advantages, as follows:

Advantages of Financing Operations by	
Issuing Stock	**Issuing a Note or Bonds**
Creates no liabilities or interest expense, both of which must be paid even during bad years. Less risky to the issuing corporation.	Does not dilute stock ownership or control of the corporation. Usually results in higher earnings per share because interest expense is tax-deductible and ownership is not diluted.

◀▥◀▥◀▥ Earnings per share (EPS) is a company's net income per share of outstanding common stock (Chapter 14, page 601). EPS may be the most important figure on the income statement.

Exhibit 15-8 shows the earnings-per-share (EPS) advantage of borrowing. ◀▥ Suppose that a corporation with net income of $300,000 and with 100,000 shares of common stock outstanding needs $500,000 for expansion. Management is considering two plans for financing the expansion:

- Plan 1 is to borrow $500,000 at 10% (issue $500,000 of 10% bonds payable).
- Plan 2 is to issue 50,000 shares of common stock for $500,000.

■ **Daily Exercise 15-16**
■ **Daily Exercise 15-17**

Management believes the new cash can be invested in operations to earn income of $200,000 before interest and taxes.

The EPS figure is higher if the company borrows. The business earns more on the investment ($90,000) than the interest it pays on the bonds ($50,000). Earning more income on borrowed money than the related interest expense increases the earnings for common stockholders and is called **trading on the equity.** It is widely used in business to increase earnings per share of common stock.

Trading on the Equity. Earning more income on borrowed money than the related interest expense, thereby increasing the earnings for the owners of the business.

Borrowing has its disadvantages. Interest expense may be high enough to eliminate net income and lead to a cash crisis or even bankruptcy. Also, borrowing creates liabilities that accrue during bad years as well as during good years. In contrast, a company that issues stock can omit its dividends during a bad year.

Computer spreadsheets are useful in evaluating financing alternatives: issuing common stock, preferred stock, or bonds. This assessment is often called "what if" analysis—for instance, "what if we finance with common stock?" The answers to "what if" questions can be modeled on a spreadsheet to project the company's financial statements over the next few years.

Lease Liabilities

Lease. Rental agreement in which the tenant (lessee) agrees to make rent payments to the property owner (lessor) to obtain the use of the asset.

A **lease** is a rental agreement in which the tenant **(lessee)** obtains the use of an asset and agrees to make rent payments to the property owner **(lessor).** Leasing avoids having to make the large initial cash down payment that a purchase requires. Accountants divide leases into two types: operating leases and capital leases.

Lessee. Tenant in a lease agreement.

Lessor. Property owner in a lease agreement.

Operating Leases

Operating leases may be short-term or cancelable. Many apartment leases and car-rental agreements are for a year or less. These operating leases give the lessee the right to use the asset but provide the lessee with no continuing rights to the asset. The lessor retains the usual risks and rewards of owning the leased asset. To account for an operating lease, the lessee debits Rent Expense (or Lease Expense) and credits Cash for the amount of the lease payment. The lessee's books report neither the leased asset nor any lease liability (except perhaps a prepaid rent amount or a rent accrual at the end of the period).

Capital Leases

Most businesses use capital leasing to finance the acquisition of some assets. In a recent survey of 600 companies, 291 (48.5%) had one or more capital leases. For example, airlines lease airplanes, and grocery stores lease buildings. A capital lease is a long-term and noncancelable financing obligation that is a form of debt. How would you distinguish a capital lease from an operating lease? *FASB Statement No. 13* provides the guidelines. To be classified as a **capital lease,** a particular lease agreement must meet any *one* of the following criteria:

1. The lease transfers title of the leased asset to the lessee at the end of the lease term. Thus the lessee becomes the legal owner of the leased asset.

2. The lease contains a *bargain purchase option.* The lessee can be expected to purchase the leased asset and become its legal owner.

3. The lease term is 75% or more of the estimated useful life of the leased asset. The lessee uses up most of the leased asset's service potential.

4. The present value of the lease payments is 90% or more of the market value of the leased asset. In effect, the lease payments operate as installment payments for the leased asset.

Only those leases that fail to meet all these criteria may be accounted for as operating leases.

ACCOUNTING FOR A CAPITAL LEASE   Accounting for a capital lease is much like accounting for a purchase. The lessor removes the asset from its books. The lessee enters the asset into its own accounts and records a lease liability at the beginning of the lease term. Thus the lessee capitalizes the asset in its own financial statements even though the lessee may never take legal title to the property.

Safeway, the grocery chain, operates grocery stores in buildings that it leases from other companies. Suppose that Safeway leases a storage building, agreeing to pay $10,000 annually for a 20-year period, with the first payment due immediately. This arrangement is similar to purchasing the building on an installment plan. In an installment purchase, Safeway would debit Building and credit Cash and Installment Note Payable. The company would then pay interest and principal on the note payable and record depreciation on the building. Accounting for a capital lease follows this pattern.

"Safeway, the grocery chain, operates grocery stores in buildings that it leases from other companies."

Safeway records the building at cost, which is the sum of the $10,000 initial payment plus the present value of the 19 future lease payments of $10,000 each.[6] The company credits Cash for the initial payment and credits Lease Liability for the present value of the future lease payments. Assume that the interest rate on Safeway's lease is 10% and that the present value (PV) of the future lease payments is $83,650.[7] At the beginning of the lease term, Safeway makes the following entry:

---

[6]The chapter appendix explains present value.
[7]The formula for this computation appears in the chapter appendix.

```
19X1
Jan.  2     Building ($10,000 + $83,650)...........................................   93,650
                 Cash ...................................................................              10,000
                     Lease Liability (PV of future lease payments)..........              83,650
                 To acquire a building and make the first annual lease
                 payment on a capital lease.
```

Because Safeway has capitalized the building, the company records depreciation. Assume that the building has an expected life of 25 years. It is nevertheless depreciated over the lease term of 20 years because the lessee has the use of the building only for that period. No residual value enters into the depreciation computation because the lessee will have no residual asset when the building is returned to the lessor at the expiration of the lease. Therefore, the annual depreciation entry is as follows:

```
19X1
Dec. 31    Depreciation Expense ($93,650/20) .............................   4,683
                 Accumulated Depreciation—Building.....................              4,683
                 To record depreciation on leased building.
```

At year end, Safeway must also accrue interest on the lease liability. Interest expense is computed by multiplying the lease liability by the interest rate on the lease. The following entry credits Lease Liability (not Interest Payable) for this interest accrual:

```
19X1
Dec. 31    Interest Expense ($83,650 × 0.10) .................................   8,365
                 Lease Liability.......................................................              8,365
                 To accrue interest on the lease liability.
```

The balance sheet at December 31, 19X1 reports the following:

Assets		
Plant assets:		
Building...	$93,650	
Less: Accumulated depreciation	(4,683)	$88,967
Liabilities		
Current liabilities:		
Lease liability (next payment due on Jan. 2, 19X2)..........		$10,000
Long-term liabilities:		
Lease liability [beginning balance ($83,650) + interest		
accrual ($8,365) – current portion ($10,000)]		82,015

The lease liability is split into current and long-term portions because the next payment ($10,000) is a current liability and the remainder is long-term.

The January 2, 19X2, lease payment is recorded as follows:

```
19X2
Jan. 2     Lease Liability..................................................................   10,000
                 Cash ...................................................................              10,000
                 To make second annual lease payment on building.
```

Off Balance Sheet Financing

An important part of business is obtaining the funds needed to acquire assets. To finance operations a company may issue stock, borrow money, or retain earnings in the business. All three of these financing plans affect the right-hand side of the balance sheet. Issuing stock affects preferred or common stock. Borrowing creates notes or bonds payable. Internal funds come from profitable operations (represented by retained earnings) that generate cash.

Off balance sheet financing is the acquisition of assets or services with debt that is not reported on the balance sheet. A prime example is an operating lease. The lessee has the use of the leased asset, but neither the asset nor any lease liability is reported on the balance sheet. In the past, most leases were accounted for by the operating method. However, *FASB Statement No. 13* has required businesses to account for an increasing number of leases by the capital lease method. Also, *FASB Statement No. 13* has brought about detailed reporting of operating lease payments in the notes to the financial statements. Much useful information is reported only in the notes, so experienced investors study them carefully.

Off Balance Sheet Financing. Acquisition of assets or services with debt that is not reported on the balance sheet.

Pension and Postretirement Benefit Liabilities

Pension Liabilities

Most companies have a pension plan for their employees. A **pension** is employee compensation that will be received during retirement. Employees earn the pensions by their service, so the company records pension expense while employees work for the company. To record the company's payment into a pension plan, the company debits Pension Expense and credits Cash. Insurance companies and pension trusts manage pension plans. They receive the employer payments and any employee contributions, then invest those amounts for the employees' future benefit. The goal is to have the funds available to meet any obligations to retirees.

Pension. Employee compensation that will be received during retirement.

Pensions are perhaps the most complex area of accounting. As employees earn their pensions and the company pays into the pension plan, the assets of the plan grow. The obligation for future pension payments to employees also accumulates. At the end of each period, the company compares the fair market value of the assets in the pension plan—cash and investments—with the accumulated benefit obligation of the pension plan. The *accumulated benefit obligation* is the present value of promised future pension payments to retirees. If the plan assets exceed the accumulated benefit obligation, the plan is said to be *overfunded*. In this case, the asset and obligation amounts need be reported only in the notes to the financial statements. However, if the accumulated benefit obligation exceeds plan assets, the plan is *underfunded*, and the company must report the excess liability amount as a long-term pension liability in the balance sheet.

The pension plan of Mainstream Manufacturing & Sales, Inc., has assets with a fair market value of $3 million on December 31, 19X0. On this date, the accumulated pension benefit obligation to employees is $4 million. Mainstream's balance sheet will report Long-Term Pension Liability of $1 million. This liability will be listed along with Bonds Payable, Long-Term Notes Payable, Lease Liabilities, and other long-term liabilities.

■ **Daily Exercise 15-19**

Postretirement Benefit Liabilities

Many companies provide benefits, mainly for health care, to their retirees. As the employees work, the company accrues the expense and the liability of providing health benefits during retirement. This practice satisfies the matching principle. The long-term liability for postretirement benefits other than pensions can be substantial, as these figures show for several well-known companies:

(in millions)

Company	Liability for Postretirement Benefits Other than Pensions	Total Stockholders' Equity
IBM	$6,418	$21,628
The Dow Chemical Company	1,507	7,954
PepsiCo, Inc.	689	6,623

IBM's liability is almost 30% of total stockholders' equity. Dow's and PepsiCo's nonpension liabilities are a smaller percentage of stockholders' equity, but still significant.

Reporting Long-Term Liability Transactions on the Statement of Cash Flows

As we have seen, companies can finance their operations either with debt (liabilities, such as notes payable and bonds payable) or with stock. In a financing transaction, a company raises money by issuing stock or bonds payable. Financing transactions also include paying money back to the company's stockholders and lenders. Chapters 13 and 14 covered stockholder's equity transactions. Here we focus on the reporting of borrowing transactions on the statement of cash flows.

AMR Corporation, the parent company of American Airlines, finances most of its operations with debt. Let's examine AMR's financing activities as reported on its statement of cash flows. Exhibit 15-9 is an excerpt from AMR's cash-flow statement.

During 19X4, AMR Corporation borrowed $146 million by issuing long-term debt (notes payable and bonds payable; see line 1). The company borrowed an additional $200 million and paid it back during the same year (lines 2 and 3; these were short-term notes payable). Finally, AMR paid $549 million on long-term debt and capital lease obligations (line 4).

Observe that these borrowing and payback transactions are reported as Cash Flows from Financing Activities. Chapter 17 will cover financing activities in more detail.

 Working It Out Did AMR's long-term liabilities increase or decrease during 19X4? How can you tell?

Answer: AMR's long-term liabilities *decreased*. The company paid off more long-term debt and capital lease obligations ($549 million) than it borrowed ($146 million) during the year.

The Decision Guidelines feature provides a summary of the major points of the chapter's second half.

EXHIBIT 15-9
Statement of Cash Flows (partial, adapted) for AMR Corporation

■ Daily Exercise 15-20

AMR CORPORATION (Parent Company of American Airlines) Statement of Cash Flows (partial; adapted)	
(In millions)	Year Ended December 31, 19X4
Cash Flows from Financing Activities:	
1 Proceeds from issuance of long-term bonds (or notes) payable	$ 146
2 Other short-term borrowings	200
3 Payments on other short-term borrowings	(200)
4 Payments on long-term bonds (or notes) payable and capital lease obligations	(549)

DECISION GUIDELINES

Accounting For Long-Term Liabilities—Part B

DECISION	GUIDELINES
What happens to the bonds' carrying amount when bonds payable are issued at	
• Par?	• Carrying amount *stays* at par (face, or maturity) value during the life of the bonds.
• A premium?	• Carrying amount *falls* gradually to the bonds' maturity value on their maturity date.
• A discount?	• Carrying amount *rises* gradually to the bonds' maturity value on their maturity date.

(continued)

DECISION GUIDELINES *(continued)*

How to account for the conversion of convertible bonds payable into common stock?

Remove all the bonds payable (and related premium or discount) accounts and credit Common Stock at par, plus any excess to Paid-in Capital in Excess of Par.

What are the advantages of financing operations with

- Stock?

- Bonds (or notes) payable?

- Creates no liability or interest expense. Less risky to the issuing corporation.
- Does not dilute stock ownership or control of the corporation.
  Results in higher earnings per share—under normal conditions.

How to account for

- An operating lease?

- A capital lease?

- Debit lease (or rent) expense when making each lease payment.
- At the beginning of the lease period, record
  a. Asset (as though it were purchased).
  b. Lease liability—present value of future lease payments.

Each period thereafter, record

a. Lease payment as a debit to the Lease Liability account, a credit to Cash.
b. Depreciation expense on the asset.
c. Interest expense on the lease liability.

What are the main long-term liability transactions to report on the statement of cash flows?

Cash flows from financing activities:

Borrowing by issuing bonds
(or notes) payable .... Cash receipt
Paying back bonds (or notes)
payable .... (Cash payment)
Paying capital lease obligations........ (Cash payment)

SUMMARY PROBLEM FOR YOUR REVIEW

Trademark, Inc., has outstanding an issue of 8% convertible bonds payable that mature in 2019. Suppose the bonds were dated October 1, 1999, and pay interest each April 1 and October 1.

1. Complete the following effective-interest amortization table through October 1, 2001:   **REQUIRED**

   Bond data:

   - Maturity value—$100,000
   - Contract interest rate—8%
   - Interest paid—4% semiannually, $4,000 ($100,000 × 0.04)
   - Market interest rate at the time of issue—9% annually, 4 1/2% semiannually
   - Issue price—90 3/4

   Amortization table:

Semiannual Interest Date	A Interest Payment (4% of Maturity Amount)	B Interest Expense (4 1/2% of Preceding Bond Carrying Amount)	C Discount Amortization (B – A)	D Discount Account Balance (D – C)	E Bond Carrying Amount ($100,000 – D)
10-1-99					
4-1-00					
10-1-00					
4-1-01					
10-1-01					

2. Using the amortization table, record the following transactions:
   a. Issuance of the bonds on October 1, 1999.
   b. Accrual of interest and amortization of discount on December 31, 1999.
   c. Payment of interest and amortization of discount on April 1, 2000.
   d. Conversion of one-third of the bonds payable into no-par common stock on October 2, 2001.
   e. Retirement of two-thirds of the bonds payable on October 2, 2001. Purchase price of the bonds was 102.

■ SOLUTION

REQUIREMENT 1

Semiannual Interest Date	A Interest Payment (4% of Maturity Amount)	B Interest Expense (4 1/2% of Preceding Bond Carrying Amount)	C Discount Amortization (B – A)	D Discount Account Balance (D – C)	E Bond Carrying Amount ($100,000 – D)
10-1-99				$9,250	$90,750
4-1-00	$4,000	$4,084	$84	9,166	90,834
10-1-00	4,000	4,088	88	9,078	90,922
4-1-01	4,000	4,091	91	8,987	91,013
10-1-01	4,000	4,096	96	8,891	91,109

REQUIREMENT 2

1999
a. Oct. 1 Cash ($100,000 × 0.9075).. 90,750
        Discount on Bonds Payable... 9,250
            Bonds Payable 100,000
        To issue 8%, 20-year bonds at a discount.

b. Dec. 31 Interest Expense ($4,084 × 3/6) 2,042
            Discount on Bonds Payable ($84 × 3/6)........................... 42
            Interest Payable ($4,000 × 3/6).. 2,000
        To accrue interest and amortize bond discount for three months.

2000
c. Apr. 1 Interest Expense 2,042
        Interest Payable 2,000
            Discount on Bonds Payable ($84 × 3/6).......................... 42
            Cash.. 4,000
        To pay semiannual interest, part of which was accrued, and amortize three months' discount on bonds payable.

2001
d. Oct. 2 Bonds Payable ($100,000 × 1/3)...................................... 33,333
            Discount on Bonds Payable ($8,891 × 1/3).................... 2,964
            Common Stock ($91,109 × 1/3) 30,369
        To record conversion of bonds payable.

e. Oct. 2 Bonds Payable ($100,000 × 2/3).. 66,667
        Extraordinary Loss on Retirement Bonds 7,260
            Discount on Bonds Payable ($8,891 × 2/3)..................... 5,927
            Cash ($100,000 × 2/3 × 1.02)... 68,000
        To retire bonds payable before maturity.

Summary of Learning Objectives

1. Account for basic bonds payable transactions by the straight-line amortization method. A corporation may borrow money by issuing long-term notes and *bonds payable*. A bond contract specifies the maturity value of the bonds, the *contract interest rate*, and the dates for paying interest and principal. Bonds may be secured (*mortgage* bonds) or unsecured (*debenture* bonds).

Bonds are traded through organized markets, such as the New York Exchange. Bonds are typically divided into $1,000 units. Their prices are quoted at a percentage of face value. *Market interest rates* fluctuate and may differ from the contract rate on a bond. If a bond's contract rate exceeds the market rate, the bond

sells at a *premium*. A bond with a contract rate below the market rate sells at a *discount*.

Money earns income over time, a fact that gives rise to the *time-value-of-money concept*. An investor will pay a price for a bond equal to the present value of the bond principal plus the present value of the bond interest.

Straight-line amortization allocates an equal amount of premium or discount to each interest period.

2. Amortize bond discount and premium by the effective-interest method. In the *effective-interest method* of amortization, the market rate at the time of issuance is multiplied by the bonds' carrying amount to determine the interest expense each period and to compute the amount of discount or premium amortization.

3. _Account for retirement of bonds payable._ Companies may retire their bonds payable before maturity. _Callable_ bonds give the borrower the right to pay off the bonds at a specified call price, or the company may purchase the bonds in the open market. Any gain or loss on early extinguishment of debt is classified as _extraordinary_.

4. _Account for conversion of bonds payable._ _Convertible bonds_ and notes give the investor the privilege of trading the bonds in for stock of the issuing corporation. The carrying amount of the bonds becomes the book value of the newly issued stock.

5. _Show the advantages and disadvantages of borrowing._ A key advantage of raising money by borrowing versus issuing stock

is that interest expense on debt is tax-deductible. Thus borrowing is less costly than issuing stock. Borrowing's disadvantage results from the fact that the company _must_ repay the loan and its interest.

6. _Account for lease and pension liabilities._ A _lease_ is a rental agreement between the _lessee_ and the _lessor_. In an _operating lease_, the lessor retains the usual risks and rights of owning the asset. The lessee debits Rent Expense and credits Cash when making lease payments. A _capital lease_ is long-term, noncancelable, and similar to an installment purchase of the leased asset. In a capital lease, the lessee capitalizes the leased asset and reports a lease liability.

Companies also report a _pension liability_ on the balance sheet if the accumulated benefit obligation exceeds the market value of pension plan assets.

Accounting Vocabulary

bond discount   (p. 627)
bond premium   (p. 627)
bonds payable   (p. 626)
callable bonds   (p. 641)
capital lease   (p. 645)
contract interest rate
   (p. 628)
convertible bonds   (p. 642)
debentures   (p. 626)

discount (on a bond)
   (p. 627)
effective interest rate
   (p. 628)
lease   (p. 644)
lessee   (p. 644)
lessor   (p. 644)
market interest rate   (p. 628)
mortgage   (p. 643)

notes   (p. 642)
off balance sheet financing
   (p. 647)
operating lease   (p. 645)
pension   (p. 647)
premium   (p. 627)
present value   (p. 628)
serial bonds   (p. 626)

stated interest rate
   (p. 628)
term bonds   (p. 626)
trading on the equity
   (p. 644)
underwriter   (p. 626)

Questions

1. How do bonds payable differ from notes payable?
2. How does an underwriter assist with the issuance of bonds?
3. Compute the price to the nearest dollar for the following bonds with a face value of $10,000:
   a. 93   c. 101 3/8   e. 100
   b. 88 3/4   d. 122 1/2
4. In which of the following situations will bonds sell at par? At a premium? At a discount?
   a. 9% bonds sold when the market rate is 9%
   b. 9% bonds sold when the market rate is 10%
   c. 9% bonds sold when the market rate is 8%
5. Identify the accounts to debit and credit for transactions
   a. to issue bonds at _par_,
   b. to pay interest,
   c. to accrue interest at year end, and
   d. to pay off bonds at maturity.
6. Identify the accounts to debit and credit for transactions
   a. to issue bonds at a _discount_,
   b. to pay interest,
   c. to accrue interest at year end, and
   d. to pay off bonds at maturity.
7. Identify the accounts to debit and credit for transactions
   a. to issue bonds at a _premium_,
   b. to pay interest,
   c. to accrue interest at year end, and
   d. to pay off bonds at maturity.
8. Why are bonds sold for a price "plus accrued interest"? What happens to accrued interest when the bonds are sold by an individual?
9. How does the straight-line method of amortizing bond discount (or premium) differ from the effective-interest method?
10. A company retires ten-year bonds payable of $100,000 after five years. The business issued the bonds at 104 and called them at

103. Compute the amount of gain or loss on retirement. How is this gain or loss reported on the income statement?
11. Bonds payable with a maturity value of $100,000 are callable at 102 1/2. Their market price is 101 1/4. If you are the issuer of these bonds, how much will you pay to retire them before maturity?
12. Why are convertible bonds attractive to investors? Why are they popular with borrowers?
13. Describe how to report serial bonds payable on the balance sheet.
14. Contrast the effects on a company of issuing bonds versus issuing stock.
15. Identify the accounts a lessee debits and credits when making operating lease payments.
16. What characteristics distinguish a capital lease from an operating lease?
17. A business signs a capital lease for the use of a building. What accounts are debited and credited
   a. to begin the lease term and make the first lease payment,
   b. to record depreciation,
   c. to accrue interest on the lease liability, and
   d. to make the second lease payment?
18. Show how a lessee reports on the balance sheet any leased equipment and the related lease liability under a capital lease.
19. What is off balance sheet financing? Give an example.
20. Distinguish an overfunded pension plan from an underfunded plan. Which situation requires the company to report a pension liability on the balance sheet? How is this liability computed?
21. What two basic transactions affect long-term liabilities and are reported as cash flows from financing activities on the statement of cash flows?

Daily Exercises

Pricing bonds
(Obj. 1)

DE15-1 Compute the price of the following bonds:

a. $100,000 quoted at 97 1/2
b. $400,000 quoted at 102 5/8
c. $2,000,000 quoted at 89 3/4
d. $500,000 quoted at 110 3/8

Determining bonds payable amounts
(Obj. 1)

DE15-2 Washington Public Power Supply System (WPPSS) borrowed money by issuing the bond payable in Exhibit 15-1, page 627. Assume the issue price was 93 1/2.

1. How much cash did WPPSS receive when it issued the bond payable?
2. How much must WPPSS pay back at maturity? When is the maturity date?
3. How much cash interest will WPPSS pay each six months? Carry the interest amount to the nearest cent.

Bond interest rates
(Obj. 1)

DE15-3 Assume the WPPSS bond in Exhibit 15-1, page 627, was issued at a price of 93 1/2. Was the market interest rate at the date of issuance 6 1/2%, above 6 1/2%, or below 6 1/2 percent? How can you tell?

Determining bond prices at par,
discount, or premium
(Obj. 1)

DE15-4 Determine whether the following bonds payable will be issued at par value, at a premium, or at a discount:

a. Sparta Corporation issued 8% bonds when the market interest rate was 6 7/8 percent.
b. Athens Company issued bonds payable that pay cash interest at the contract rate of 7 percent. At the date of issuance, the market interest rate was 8 1/4 percent.
c. The market interest rate is 9 percent. Corinth, Inc., issues bonds payable with a stated rate of 8 1/2 percent.
d. Macedonia Corp. issued 7 1/2% bonds payable when the market rate was 7 1/2 percent.

Journalizing basic bond payable
transactions
(Obj. 1)

DE15-5 Suppose WPPSS issued the ten-year bond in Exhibit 15-1, page 627, when the market interest rate was 6 1/2 percent. Assume that the fiscal year of WPPSS ends on June 30. Journalize the following transactions for WPPSS. Include an explanation for each entry.

a. Issuance of the bond payable at par on July 1, 2000.
b. Payment of cash interest on January 1, 2001. (Round to the nearest dollar.)
c. Payment of the bonds payable at maturity. (Give the date.)

Issuing bonds payable between interest
dates and then paying the interest
(Obj. 1)

DE15-6 Assume WPPSS issued the ten-year bond in Exhibit 15-1, page 627, at par value on September 1, 2000, two months after the bond's original issue date of July 1, 2000. Assume that the fiscal year of WPPSS ends on June 30. Journalize the following transactions for WPPSS. Include an explanation for each entry.

a. Issuance of the bonds payable on September 1, 2000. (Carry amounts to the nearest cent.)
b. Payment of the first semiannual interest amount on January 1, 2001. (Carry amounts to the nearest cent.)

Issuing bonds payable at a discount;
paying interest and amortizing discount
by the straight-line method
(Obj. 1)

DE15-7 Washington Public Power Supply System did in fact issue the bond payable in Exhibit 15-1, page 627, to borrow money. Assume WPPSS issued the bond at a price of 88 on July 1, 2000. Also assume that WPPSS's fiscal year ends on June 30. Journalize the following transactions for WPPSS. Include an explanation for each entry.

a. Issuance of the bond payable on July 1, 2000.
b. Payment of interest and amortization of bond discount on January 1, 2001. (Use the straight-line method to amortize the discount. Round interest to the nearest dollar.)

Issuing bonds payable at a premium;
paying interest and amortizing
premium by the straight-line method
(Obj. 1)

DE15-8 Assume WPPSS issued the bond payable in Exhibit 15-1 at a price of 106 on July 1, 2000. Also assume that WPPSS's fiscal year ends on June 30. Journalize the following transactions for WPPSS. Include an explanation for each entry.

a. Issuance of the bond payable on July 1, 2000.
b. Payment of interest and amortization of bond premium on January 1, 2001. (Use the straight-line method to amortize the premium. Round interest to the nearest dollar.)

Issuing bonds payable, accruing interest,
and amortizing bond discount
(Obj. 1)

DE15-9 Return to the WPPSS bond in Exhibit 15-1, page 627. Assume that WPPSS issued the bond payable on July 1, 2000 at a price of 94. Also assume that WPPSS's accounting year ends on December 31. Journalize the following transactions for WPPSS. Include an explanation for each entry.

a. Issuance of the bonds on July 1, 2000.

b. Accrual of interest expense and amortization of bond discount on December 31, 2000. (Use the straight-line amortization method, and round the interest amount to the nearest dollar.)

c. Payment of the first semiannual interest amount on January 1, 2001.

DE15-10 Use the situation in Daily Exercise 15-9, and show how Washington Public Power Supply System would report interest payable and the bond payable on its balance sheet at December 31, 2000.

Reporting interest payable and bonds payable on the balance sheet
(Obj. 1)

DE15-11 AdTech, Inc., issued $500,000 of 7%, ten-year bonds payable at a price of 87 on March 31, 19X8. The market interest rate at the date of issuance was 9%, and the AdTech bonds pay interest semiannually.

Issuing bonds payable and amortizing discount by the effective-interest method
(Obj. 2)

1. How much cash did AdTech receive upon issuance of the bonds payable?

2. Prepare an effective-interest amortization table for the bond discount, through the first three interest payments. Use Exhibit 15-4, page 637, as a guide, and round amounts to the nearest dollar.

3. Record AdTech's issuance of the bonds on March 31, 19X8, and, on September 30, 19X8, payment of the first semiannual interest amount and amortization of the bond discount. Explanations are not required.

DE15-12 Mir Aerospace, Inc., issued $500,000 of 6%, five-year bonds payable to partially finance a space station. At the time of issuance, the market interest rate was 8%, so Mir received cash of $460,073. Mir pays interest annually.

Preparing a complete bond amortization table and using the table for relevant information
(Obj. 2)

1. Prepare Mir's effective-interest amortization table for the bonds. Use Exhibit 15-4, page 637, as a guide, and round amounts to the nearest dollar.

2. Use the amortization table to answer these questions about Mir's bonds payable and related interest expense:
   a. At what amount will Mir report the bonds payable at the end of Year 1? At the end of Year 3?
   b. How much cash interest will Mir pay for Year 1? Year 3? Year 5?
   c. How much interest expense will Mir record for Year 1? Year 5?

DE15-13 StopGap, Inc., issued $200,000 of 8%, ten-year bonds payable at at price of 115 on May 31, 19X7. The market interest rate at the date of issuance was 6%, and the StopGap bonds pay interest semiannually.

Issuing bonds payable and amortizing premium by the effective-interest method
(Obj. 2)

1. How much cash did StopGap receive upon issuance of the bonds payable?

2. Prepare an effective-interest amortization table for the bond premium, through the first three interest payments. Use Exhibit 15-6, page 639, as a guide, and round amounts to the nearest dollar.

3. Record StopGap's issuance of the bonds on May 31, 19X7, and, on November 30, 19X7, payment of the first semiannual interest amount and amortization of the bond premium. Explanations are not required.

DE15-14 Assume that Lowes, Inc., issued the bonds payable in Exhibit 15-6, page 639. Lowes has extra cash and wishes to retire the bonds payable immediately after making the sixth semiannual interest payment. The bonds are quoted in the market at a price of 98.

Accounting for the retirement of bonds payable
(Obj. 3)

1. What is Lowes' carrying amount of the bonds payable on the retirement date?

2. How much cash must Lowes pay to retire the bonds payable?

3. Compute Lowes' gain or loss on the retirement of the bonds payable. What type of gain or loss is this?

4. Journalize Lowes' transaction to retire the bonds payable.

DE15-15 ◀▦ Link Back to Chapter 4 (Debt Ratio). Oracle Design Corp. has $1,000,000 of convertible bonds payable outstanding, with a bond premium of $80,000 also on the books. The bondholders have notified Oracle that they wish to convert the bonds into stock. Specifically, the bonds may be converted into 200,000 shares of Oracle's $1 par common stock.

Accounting for the conversion of bonds payable
(Obj. 4)

1. What is Oracle's carrying amount of its convertible bonds payable prior to the conversion?

2. Journalize, on Oracle's books, the conversion of the bonds payable into common stock. No explanation is required.

3. How will the conversion affect Oracle's debt ratio?

DE15-16   Greenhill Financial Services of Boise, Idaho, needs to raise $1 million to expand company operations into Montana. Greenhill's president is considering the issuance of either

- Plan A: $1,000,000 of 8% bonds payable to borrow the money
- Plan B: 100,000 shares of common stock at $10 per share

Before any new financing, Greenhill expects to earn net income of $350,000, and the company already has 200,000 shares of common stock outstanding. Greenhill believes the expansion will increase income before interest and income tax by $200,000. Greenhill's income tax rate is 40 percent.

   Prepare an analysis similar to Exhibit 15-8, page 644, to determine which plan is likely to result in the higher earnings per share. Which financing plan would you recommend for Greenhill?

DE15-17   Return to the financing situation of Greenhill Financial Services in Daily Exercise 15-16. What other factors, besides the effect on earnings per share, should Greenhill consider in deciding how to raise the $1 million? Give the advantages of issuing (a) stock and (b) bonds.

DE15-18   MNA Associates, Inc., includes the following selected accounts in its general ledger at December 31, 19X7:

Bonds payable............................	$350,000	Current obligation under	
Equipment under		capital lease..............................	$ 8,000
capital lease.......................	114,000	Accounts payable........................	19,000
Interest payable (due		Long-term capital lease	
March 1, 19X8)	7,000	liability	42,000
Current portion of		Discount on bonds	
bonds payable........................	50,000	payable (all long-term)	6,000
Notes payable, long-term...........	60,000		

Prepare the liabilities section of MNA's balance sheet at December 31, 19X7, to show how MNA would report these items. Report a total for current liabilities.

DE15-19   Gateway Integrated Circuits has a pension plan for its employees. Gateway's pension plan has an accumulated benefit obligation of $3,000,000. This means that Gateway would have to pay $3,000,000 now if the company had to settle the plan's pension liability today. To offset this liability, Gateway has invested in a pension fund that holds investments in stocks, bonds, and real estate.

1.   The market value of the investments held by Gateway's pension fund is $3,200,000. Is the pension plan overfunded or underfunded? How much pension liability should Gateway report on its balance sheet?
2.   Assume instead that the market value of the investments in Gateway's pension fund is $2,500,000. Is the pension plan overfunded or underfunded? How much pension liability should Gateway report on its balance sheet?

DE15-20   Examine the excerpt from AMR Corporation's statement of cash flows in Exhibit 15-9, page 648. The statement of cash flows reports two basic types of long-term debt transactions as financing activities. What are they?

Exercises

E15-1   On February 1, Mesquite Grill Corp. issues 7%, 20-year bonds payable with a face value of $100,000. The bonds sell at 98 and pay interest on January 31 and July 31. Mesquite Grill Corp. amortizes bond discount by the straight-line method. Record (a) issuance of the bonds on February 1, (b) the semiannual interest payment on July 31, and (c) the interest accrual on December 31.

E15-2   Audi Motor Corporation issues 8%, 20-year bonds payable with a face value of $1,000,000 on March 31. The bonds sell at 101 1/2 and pay interest on March 31 and September 30. Assume that Audi amortizes bond premium by the straight-line method. Record (a) issuance of the bonds on March 31, (b) payment of interest on September 30, and (c) accrual of interest on December 31.

E15-3   Refer to the data for Audi Motor Corporation in Exercise 15-2. If Audi issued the bonds payable on June 30, how much cash would Audi receive upon issuance of the bonds?

E15-4   Ford, Inc., issues $400,000 of 9%, 20-year bonds payable that are dated April 30. Record (a) issuance of bonds at par on May 31, and (b) the next semiannual interest payment on October 31.

E15-5   Assume Toblerone Chocolate Co. is authorized to issue $500,000 of 7%, ten-year bonds payable. On January 2, when the market interest rate is 8%, the company issues $400,000 of the bonds and receives cash of $372,660. Toblerone amortizes bond discount by the effective-interest method.

1. Prepare an amortization table for the first four semiannual interest periods. Follow the format of Exhibit 15-4, Panel B.

2. Record the first semiannual interest payment on June 30 and the second payment on December 31.

REQUIRED

Preparing an effective-interest amortization table; recording interest accrual and payment and the related premium amortization
(Obj. 2)

E15-6 On September 30, 1999, the market interest rate is 7 percent. Template Software, Inc., issues $300,000 of 8%, 20-year bonds payable at 110 5/8. The bonds pay interest on March 31 and September 30. Template Software amortizes bond premium by the effective-interest method.

1. Prepare an amortization table for the first four semiannual interest periods. Follow the format of Exhibit 15-6, Panel B.

2. Record issuance of the bonds on September 30, 1999, the accrual of interest at December 31, 1999, and the semiannual interest payment on March 31, 2000.

REQUIRED

E15-7 Atlas Airlines, Inc., issued $600,000 of 8 3/8% (0.08375), five-year bonds payable when the market interest rate was 9 1/2% (0.095). Atlas pays interest annually at year end. The issue price of the bonds was $574,082.

Debt payment and discount amortization schedule
(Obj. 2)

Create a spreadsheet model to prepare a schedule to amortize the discount on these bonds. Use the effective-interest method of amortization. Round to the nearest dollar, and format your answer as follows:

REQUIRED

	A	B	C	D	E	F
1						
2						Bond
3		Interest	Interest	Discount	Discount	Carrying
4	Date	Payment	Expense	Amortization	Balance	Amount
5	1-1-X1				$	$574,082
6	12-31-X1	$	$	$		
7	12-31-X2					
8	12-31-X3					
9	12-31-X4					
10	12-31-X5					
		600000*.08375	+F5*.095	+C6–B6	600000–F5	+F5+D6

E15-8 Skytell Communications issued $500,000 of 8% bonds payable at 97 on October 1, 19X0. These bonds mature on October 1, 19X8, and are callable at 101. Skytell pays interest each April 1 and October 1. On October 1, 19X5, when the bonds' market price is 104, Skytell retires the bonds in the most economical way available.

Recording retirement of bonds payable
(Obj. 3)

Record the payment of the interest and amortization of bond discount at October 1, 19X5, and the retirement of the bonds on that date. Skytell uses the straight-line amortization method.

REQUIRED

E15-9 Magnetic Imaging Company issued $400,000 of 8 1/2% bonds payable on July 31, 19X3, at a price of 98 1/2. After five years, the bonds may be converted into the company's common stock. Each $1,000 face amount of bonds is convertible into 40 shares of $20 par stock. The bonds' term to maturity is 15 years. On July 31, 19X9, bondholders exercised their right to convert the bonds into common stock.

Recording conversion of bonds payable
(Obj. 4)

1. What would cause the bondholders to convert their bonds into common stock?

2. Without making journal entries, compute the carrying amount of the bonds payable at July 31, 19X9. Magnetic Imaging uses the straight-line method to amortize bond premium and discount.

3. All amortization has been recorded properly. Journalize the conversion transaction at July 31, 19X9.

REQUIRED

E15-10 Riviera Industries reported the following at September 30:

Recording early retirement and conversion of bonds payable
(Obj. 3, 4)

Long-term liabilities:
Convertible bonds payable, 9%, eight years to maturity....... $300,000
Less: Discount on bonds payable .... (6,000) $294,000

1. Record retirement of half of the bonds on October 1 at the call price of 102.

2. Record conversion of the remainder of the bonds into 4,000 shares of Riviera's $5 par common stock on October 1. What would cause the bondholders to convert their bonds into stock?

REQUIRED

E15-11 Gulfstream Avionics Company is considering two plans for raising $1,000,000 to expand operations. Plan A is to borrow at 9%, and plan B is to issue 100,000 shares of common stock. Before any new financing, Gulfstream has net income of $600,000 and 100,000 shares of common

Analyzing alternative plans for raising money
(Obj. 5)

stock outstanding. Management believes the company can use the new funds to earn additional income of $420,000 before interest and taxes. The income tax rate is 40 percent.

REQUIRED

Reporting long-term debt and pension liability on the balance sheet
(Obj. 6)

REQUIRED

Analyze Gulfstream's situation to determine which plan will result in higher earnings per share. Use Exhibit 15-8 as a guide.

E15-12 The chief accounting officer of Delta Electronics Corporation is considering how to report long-term notes payable and pension liabilities.

1. Delta's bookkeeper has assembled the following for long-term notes payable:

Long-term Notes Payable	
Total	$537,000
Less—Current portion	(22,000)
Discount on notes payable	(1,000)
	$514,000

None of the discount is related to the current portion of long-term notes payable. Show how Delta's balance sheet should report these liabilities.

2. Delta's pension plan has assets with a market value of $800,000. The plan's accumulated benefit obligation is $870,000. What amount of long-term pension liability, if any, will Delta report on its balance sheet?

Journalizing capital lease and operating lease transactions
(Obj. 6)

E15-13 A capital lease agreement for equipment requires Allegiance Signal Company to make ten annual payments of $9,000, with the first payment due on January 2, 19X5. The present value of the nine future lease payments is $51,831.

REQUIRED

1. Journalize the following transactions of Allegiance Signal Company:

   19X5
   Jan. 2   Beginning of lease term and first annual payment.
   Dec. 31   Depreciation of equipment.
         31   Interest expense on the lease liability. The interest rate is 10 percent.

2. Journalize the January 2, 19X5, lease payment if this is an operating lease.

CHALLENGE EXERCISES

Analyzing bond transactions
(Obj. 1, 2)

E15-14 This (partial and adapted) advertisement appeared in *The Wall Street Journal*.

A *subordinated* debenture gives rights to the bondholder that are more restricted than the rights of other bondholders.

Answer these questions about Mark IV Industries' debenture bonds payable:

1. Suppose Mark IV Industries issued these bonds payable at their offering price on March 31, 1998. Describe the transaction in detail, indicating who received cash, who paid cash, and how much.
2. Why is the contract interest rate on these bonds so high?
3. Compute Mark IV Industries' annual cash interest payment on the bonds.
4. Compute Mark IV Industries' annual interest expense under the straight-line amortization method.
5. Prepare an effective-interest amortization table for Mark IV Industries' first two interest payments on September 30, 1998 and March 31, 1999. Use Exhibit 15-4 as a guide and show all amounts in thousands. The market rate of interest on the bonds is 13.65% per year.
6. Compute Mark IV Industries interest expense for the first full year ended March 31, 1999, under the effective-interest method. Use the amortization table you prepared for requirement 5.

E15-15 Refer to the bond situation of Mark IV Industries in Exercise 15-14. Assume Mark IV Industries issued the bonds at the advertised price and that the company uses the effective-interest amortization method and reports financial statements on a calendar-year basis.

Analyzing bond transactions
(Obj. 1, 2)

1. Journalize the following bond transactions of Mark IV Industries. Show all amounts in thousands of dollars.

  1998
  Mar. 31   Issuance of the bonds.
  Sep. 30   Payment of interest expense and amortization of discount on bonds payable.
  Dec. 31   Accrual of interest expense and amortization of discount on bonds payable.

2. What is Mark IV Industries' carrying amount of the bonds payable at
  a. September 30, 1998?   b. December 31, 1998?   c. March 31, 1999?

Beyond the Numbers

BN15-1 ◀▥ *Link Back to Chapter 4 (Debt Ratio).* The following questions are not related.

Questions about long-term debt
(Obj. 6 and Appendix to Chapter 15)

1. IMAX Corporation obtains the use of most of its theater properties through leases. IMAX prefers operating leases over capital leases. Why is this a good idea? Consider IMAX's debt ratio.
2. IMAX likes to borrow for longer periods when interest rates are low and for shorter periods when interest rates are high. Why is this a good business strategy?
3. IMAX needs to borrow $2 million to open new theaters. IMAX can borrow $2 million by issuing 8%, 20-year bonds at a price of 96. How much will IMAX actually be borrowing under this arrangement? How much must IMAX pay back at maturity?

ETHICAL ISSUE

LTV, manufacturer of aircraft and aircraft-related electronic devices, borrowed heavily during the 1970s to exploit the advantage of financing operations with debt. At first, LTV was able to earn operating income much higher than its interest expense and was therefore quite profitable. However, when the business cycle turned down, LTV's debt burden pushed the company to the brink of bankruptcy. Operating income fell to levels below interest expense.

Is it unethical for managers to saddle a company with a high level of debt? Or is it just risky? Who could be hurt by a company's taking on too much debt? Discuss.

Problems (GROUP A)

Journalizing bond transactions (at par) and reporting bonds payable on the balance sheet
(Obj. 1)

P15-1A The board of directors of NetCore Communications authorizes the issue of $3 million of 8%, 20-year bonds payable. The semiannual interest dates are March 31 and September 30. The bonds are issued on April 30, 19X7, at par plus accrued interest.

1. Journalize the following transactions:
  a. Issuance of the bonds on April 30, 19X7.   c. Accrual of interest on December 31, 19X7.
  b. Payment of interest on Sept. 30, 19X7.   d. Payment of interest on March 31, 19X8.
2. Check your recorded interest expense for 19X7, using as a model the supplement to the summary problem on page 636.
3. Report interest payable and bonds payable as they would appear on the NetCore balance sheet at December 31, 19X7.

P15-2A On March 31, 19X6, Univar Corp. issues 7 3/4%, ten-year notes payable with a face value of $400,000. The notes pay interest on March 31 and September 30, and Univar amortizes premium and discount by the straight-line method.

1. If the market interest rate is 8 1/2% when Univar issues its notes, will the notes be priced at par, at a premium, or at a discount? Explain.

2. If the market interest rate is 7% when Univar issues its notes, will the notes be priced at par, at a premium, or at a discount? Explain.

3. Assume that the issue price of the notes is 101. Journalize the following note payable transactions:
   a. Issuance of the notes on April 1, 19X6.
   b. Payment of interest and amortization of premium on September 30, 19X6.
   c. Accrual of interest and amortization of premium on December 31, 19X6.
   d. Payment of interest and amortization of premium on March 31, 19X7.

4. Check your recorded interest expense for the year ended March 31, 19X7, using as a model the supplement to the review problem on page 636.

5. Report interest payable and notes payable as they would appear on the Univar balance sheet at December 31, 19X6.

P15-3A Charleston Chicken's balance sheet reported the following data on September 30, Year 1, end of the fiscal year (amounts rounded):

LONG-TERM DEBT	
5% debenture bonds payable due Year 14, net of discount of $37,200 (effective interest rate of 8%)	**$112,800**

Charleston amortizes bond discount by the effective-interest method.

1. Answer the following questions about Charleston's long-term debt:
   a. What is the maturity value of the 5% debenture bonds?
   b. What is the carrying amount of the 5% debenture bonds at September 30, Year 1?
   c. What is Charleston's annual cash interest payment on the 5% debenture bonds?

2. Prepare an amortization table through September 30, Year 3, for the 5% debenture bonds. Charleston pays interest annually on September 30.

3. Record the September 30, Year 3, interest payment and amortization of the discount on the 5% debenture bonds.

4. What is Charleston's carrying amount of the 5% debenture bonds at September 30, Year 3, immediately after the interest payment?

P15-4A On December 31, 19X1, Visioneer Corp. issues 8%, ten-year convertible bonds with a maturity value of $500,000. The semiannual interest dates are June 30 and December 31. The market interest rate is 9%, and the issue price of the bonds is 94. Visioneer amortizes bond premium and discount by the effective-interest method.

1. Prepare an effective-interest method amortization table for the first four semiannual interest periods.

2. Journalize the following transactions:
   a. Issuance of the bonds on December 31, 19X1. Credit Convertible Bonds Payable.
   b. Payment of interest on June 30, 19X2.
   c. Payment of interest on December 31, 19X2.
   d. Retirement of bonds with face value of $100,000 July 1, 19X3. Visioneer purchases the bonds at 96 in the open market.
   e. Conversion by the bondholders on July 1, 19X3, of bonds with face value of $200,000 into 50,000 shares of Visioneer $1 par common stock.

3. Prepare a balance sheet presentation of the bonds payable that are outstanding at December 31, 19X3.

P15-5A Journalize the following transactions of Audré Cosmetics, Inc.:

19X1
Jan. 1 Issued $1,000,000 of 8%, ten-year bonds payable at 97.
      1 Signed a five-year capital lease on machinery. The agreement requires annual lease payments of $16,000, with the first payment due immediately. The present value of the four future lease payments is $48,590.
July 1 Paid semiannual interest and amortized discount by the straight-line method on our 8% bonds payable.

Dec. 31   Accrued semiannual interest expense and amortized discount by the straight-line method on our 8% bonds payable.

     31   Recorded depreciation on leased machinery.

     31   Accrued interest expense at 12% on the lease liability.

19X11

Jan.   1   Paid the 8% bonds at maturity.

P15-6A   Research indicates that consumers prefer upscale restaurants. To capitalize on this trend, Samurai Steakhouses, Inc., is embarking on a massive expansion. Plans call for opening 20 new restaurants within the next two years. Each restaurant is scheduled to be 30% larger than the company's existing locations and feature upgraded menus. Management estimates that company operations will provide $3 million of the cash needed for expansion. Samurai must raise the remaining $1.5 million from outsiders. The board of directors is considering obtaining the $1.5 million either through borrowing or by issuing common stock.

Financing operations with debt or with stock
(Obj. 5)

REQUIRED

1.   Write a memo to company management. Discuss the advantages and disadvantages of borrowing and of issuing common stock to raise the needed cash. Use the following format for your memo:

Date: _____

To: Management of Samurai Steakhouses, Inc.

From: Student Name_____

Subject: Advantages and disadvantages of borrowing versus issuing stock to raise $1.5 million for expansion

Advantages and disadvantages of borrowing:
Advantages and disadvantages of issuing stock:

2.   How will what you learned in this problem help you manage a business?

P15-7A   The accounting records of Pinelli Tire Company include the following items:

Reporting liabilities on the balance sheet
(Obj. 6)

Equipment acquired under capital lease.................	$187,000	Accumulated pension benefit obligation..................	$419,000
Pension plan assets (market value)	382,000	Bonds payable, long-term	300,000
Interest payable.........................	13,000	Mortgage note payable, long-term	82,000
Interest expense.......................	57,000	Accumulated depreciation,	
Bonds payable, current portion	75,000	equipment	46,000
Capital lease liability, long-term...............................	81,000	Capital lease liability, current......................................	18,000
Discount on bonds payable (all long-term)..........	7,000	Mortgage note payable, current.....................................	23,000
Interest revenue.......................	5,000		

Show how these items would be reported on the Pinelli Tire Company balance sheet, including headings and totals for current liabilities, long-term liabilities, and so on. Note disclosures are not required.

REQUIRED

Problems   (GROUP B)

P15-1B   The board of directors of Xena Production Company authorizes the issue of $6 million of 7%, ten-year bonds payable. The semiannual interest dates are May 31 and November 30. The bonds are issued on June 30, 19X5, at par plus accrued interest.

Journalizing bond transactions (at par) and reporting bonds payable on the balance sheet
(Obj. 1)

REQUIRED

1.   Journalize the following transactions:
     a.   Issuance of the bonds on June 30, 19X5.
     b.   Payment of interest on November 30, 19X5.
     c.   Accrual of interest on December 31, 19X5.
     d.   Payment of interest on May 31, 19X6.

2.   Check your recorded interest expense for 19X5, using as a model the supplement to the review problem on page 636.

3.   Report interest payable and bonds payable as they would appear on the Xena balance sheet at December 31, 19X5.

Issuing bonds, amortizing premium or discount by the straight-line method, and reporting the bonds payable on the balance sheet
(Obj. 1, 2)

REQUIRED

P15-2B On March 1, 19X4, Lucerne Republic Corp. issues 8 1/2%, 20-year bonds payable with a face value of $400,000. The bonds pay interest on February 28 and August 31. Lucerne amortizes premium and discount by the straight-line method.

1. If the market interest rate is 7 3/8% when Lucerne issues its bonds, will the bonds be priced at par, at a premium, or at a discount? Explain.

2. If the market interest rate is 8 7/8% when Lucerne issues its bonds, will the bonds be priced at par, at a premium, or at a discount? Explain.

3. Assume that the issue price of the bonds is 96. Journalize the following bond transactions:
    a. Issuance of the bonds on March 1, 19X4.
    b. Payment of interest and amortization of discount on August 31, 19X4.
    c. Accrual of interest and amortization of discount on December 31, 19X4.
    d. Payment of interest and amortization of discount on February 28, 19X5.

4. Check your recorded interest expense for the year ended February 28, 19X5, using as a model the supplement to the review problem on page 649.

5. Report interest payable and bonds payable as they would appear on the Lucerne balance sheet at December 31, 19X4.

Analyzing a company's long-term debt and journalizing its transactions
(Obj. 2)

P15-3B Arclight Control Company's balance sheet reported the following data on September 30, Year 1, end of the fiscal year (amounts rounded):

> **LONG-TERM DEBT:**
>
> **6.00% debenture bonds payable due Year 20 with an effective**
> **interest rate of 8.00%, net of discount of $39,200......................... $160,800**

Arclight amortizes discount by the effective-interest method.

REQUIRED

1. Answer the following questions about Arclight's long-term debt:
    a. What is the maturity value of the 6.00% debenture bonds?
    b. What is the carrying amount of the 6.00% debenture bonds at September 30, Year 1?
    c. What is Arclight's annual cash interest payment on the 6.00% debenture bonds?

2. Prepare an amortization table through September 30, Year 3, for the 6.00% debenture bonds. Arclight pays interest annually on September 30.

3. Record the September 30, Year 3 interest payment and amortization of the discount on the 6.00% debenture bonds.

4. What is Arclight's carrying amount of the 6% debenture bonds at September 30, Year 3, immediately after the interest payment?

Issuing convertible bonds at a premium, amortizing by the effective-interest method, retiring bonds early, converting bonds, and reporting the bonds payable on the balance sheet
(Obj. 2, 3, 4)

P15-4B On December 31, 19X1, Marquis, Inc., issues 9%, ten-year convertible bonds with a maturity value of $300,000. The semiannual interest dates are June 30 and December 31. The market interest rate is 8%, and the issue price of the bonds is 106. Marquis amortizes bond premium and discount by the effective-interest method.

REQUIRED

1. Prepare an effective-interest method amortization table for the first four semiannual interest periods.

2. Journalize the following transactions:
    a. Issuance of the bonds on December 31, 19X1. Credit Convertible Bonds Payable.
    b. Payment of interest on June 30, 19X2.
    c. Payment of interest on December 31, 19X2.
    d. Retirement of bonds with face value of $100,000 on July 1, 19X3. Marquis pays the call price of 102.
    e. Conversion by the bondholders on July 1, 19X3, of bonds with face value of $150,000 into 10,000 shares of Marquis's $10 par common stock.

3. Prepare the balance sheet presentation of the bonds payable that are outstanding at December 31, 19X3.

Journalizing bonds payable and capital lease transactions
(Obj. 1, 6)

P15-5B Journalize the following transactions of Lincoln Properties, Inc.:

19X1
Jan. 1 Issued $400,000 of 8%, ten-year bonds payable at 97.
       1 Signed a five-year capital lease on equipment. The agreement requires annual lease payments of $20,000, with the first payment due immediately. Assume that the present value of the four future lease payments is $60,750.
July 1 Paid semiannual interest and amortized discount by the straight-line method on our 8% bonds payable.
Dec. 31 Accrued semiannual interest expense, and amortized discount by the straight-line method on our 8% bonds payable.

Dec. 31 Recorded depreciation on leased equipment.
   31 Accrued interest expense at 12% on the lease liability.
19X11
Jan. 1 Paid the 8% bonds at maturity.

Financing operations with debt or with stock
(Obj. 5)

P15-6B Two businesses are considering how to raise $10 million.

Oshkosh Corporation is in the midst of its most successful period since it began operations in 1972. For each of the past ten years, net income and earnings per share have increased by at least 15 percent. The outlook for the future is equally bright, with new markets opening up and competitors unable to manufacture products of Oshkosh's quality. Oshkosh Corporation is planning a large-scale expansion.

Fond du Lac Company has fallen on hard times. Net income has remained flat for five of the last six years, with this year falling by 10% from last year's level of profits. Top management has experienced unusual turnover, and the company lacks strong leadership. To become competitive again, Fond du Lac Company desperately needs $10 million for expansion.

REQUIRED

1. Propose a plan for each company to raise the needed cash. Which company should borrow? Which company should issue stock? Consider the advantages and the disadvantages of raising money by borrowing and by issuing stock, and discuss them in your answer. Use the following memorandum headings to report your plans for the two companies:
   - Plan for Oshkosh Corporation to raise $10 million (including the advantages and disadvantages of borrowing and issuing stock)
   - Plan for Fond du Lac Corporation to raise $10 million (including the advantages and disadvantages of borrowing and issuing stock)
2. How will what you learned in this problem help you manage a business?

Reporting liabilities on the balance sheet
(Obj. 6)

P15-7B The accounting records of Fleet Rentals, Inc., include the following items:

Capital lease liability,		**Accumulated depreciation,**	
long-term	$ 73,000	building	$108,000
Accumulated pension		**Mortgage note payable,**	
benefit obligation	207,000	long term.............................	67,000
Building acquired under		**Capital lease liability,**	
capital lease	290,000	current	9,000
Bonds payable, long-term	160,000	**Interest expense**	47,000
Premium on bonds		**Pension plan assets**	
payable (all long-term)..........	13,000	(market value)	190,000
Interest payable	14,200	**Bonds payable, current**	
Interest revenue.......................	5,300	portion	20,000

REQUIRED

Show how these items would be reported on Fleet Rentals' balance sheet, including headings and totals for current liabilities, long-term liabilities, and so on. Note disclosures are not required.

Applying Your Knowledge

DECISION CASE

Analyzing alternative ways of raising $5 million
(Obj. 5)

Business is going well for Trinitron Robotics. The board of directors of this family-owned company believes that Trinitron could earn an additional $1,500,000 income before interest and taxes by expanding into new markets. However, the $5 million that the business needs for growth cannot be raised within the family. The directors, who strongly wish to retain family control of the company, must consider issuing securities to outsiders. They are considering three financing plans.

Plan A is to borrow at 8 percent. Plan B is to issue 100,000 shares of common stock. Plan C is to issue 100,000 shares of nonvoting, $3.75 preferred stock ($3.75 is the annual cash dividend paid on each share of preferred stock). Trinitron presently has net income of $6,000,000 and 1,000,000 shares of common stock outstanding. The company's income tax rate is 40 percent.

REQUIRED

1. Prepare an analysis similar to Exhibit 15-8 to determine which plan will result in the highest earnings per share of common stock.
2. Recommend one plan to the board of directors. Give your reasons.

FINANCIAL STATEMENT CASES

Analyzing long-term debt
(Obj. 1)

CASE 1. The NIKE, Inc., income statement, balance sheet, and statement of cash flows in Appendix A provide details about the company's long-term debt. Use those data to answer the following questions.

1. How much cash did NIKE borrow on long-term debt and notes payable during the year ended May 31, 1997? The statement of cash flows provides the data.

2. Examine the statement of cash flows for the year ended May 31, 1997. Journalize all transactions that affected long-term debt and notes payable during the year.

3. Journalize in a single entry NIKE's interest expense for the year ended May 31, 1997. Assume that NIKE paid 90% of its interest expense and accrued the remainder at year end.

Analyzing long-term debt
(Obj. 1)

CASE 2. Obtain the annual report of a company of your choosing. Answer the following questions about the company. Concentrate on the current year in the annual report you select.

1. Examine the statement of cash flows. How much long-term debt did the company pay off during the current year? How much new long-term debt did the company incur during the year? Journalize these transactions, using the company's actual account balances.

2. Prepare a T-account for the Long-Term Debt account to show the beginning and ending balances and all activity in the account during the year. If there is a discrepancy, insert this amount in the appropriate place. Note: Do not expect to be able to explain all details in real financial statements!

3. Study the notes to the financial statements. Is any of the company's retained earnings balance restricted as a result of borrowings? If so, indicate the amount of the retained earnings balance that is restricted and the amount that is unrestricted. How will the restriction affect the company's dividend payments in the future?

4. Journalize in a single entry the company's interest expense for the current year. If the company discloses the amount of amortization of premium or discount on long-term debt, use the real figures. If not, assume the amortization of discount totaled $700,000 for the year.

Team Project

Note: This project uses the chapter appendix.

Alcenon Corporation leases the majority of the assets that it uses in operations. Alcenon prefers operating leases (versus capital leases) in order to keep the lease liability off its balance sheet and maintain a low debt ratio.

Alcenon is negotiating a ten-year lease on an asset with an expected useful life of 15 years. The lease requires Alcenon to make ten annual lease payments of $20,000 each, due at the end of the period, plus a down payment that is due at the beginning of the lease term. The interest rate in the lease agreement is 10 percent. The leased asset has a market value of $135,800. The lease agreement specifies no transfer of title to the lessee and includes no bargain purchase option.

Write a report for Alcenon's management to explain how much the down payment must be for Alcenon to be able to account for this lease as an operating lease. Use the following format for your report:

Date:	_____
To:	Alcenon Management
From:	<u>Student Name</u>
Subject:	Required amount of the down payment on a lease in order to account for the lease as an operating lease

Internet Exercise CHRYSLER CORP.

Balancing on the brink of bankruptcy during the 1970s, Chrysler received an unprecedented $1 billion loan from the U.S. government. Through drastic measures and changes, including selling their international divisions, Chrysler managed to reverse its fortunes. Chrysler repaid the $1 billion loan early which contributed to its selection by Forbes as the 1996 Company of the Year. Today Chrysler is a thriving company earning record sales and profits.

Now instead of borrowing from the U.S. government, Chrysler borrows from more traditional sources. An examination of Chrysler's financial statements reveals much about the Company's ability to borrow and repay its loans.

1. Go to Chrysler's home page at **http://www.chrysler.com.** This is the gateway to view Chrysler's automotive history, price a vehicle, or check to see what is on the drawing board for tomorrow's cars and trucks.

2. Click on **Service Center** to see the drop-down menu of options. Select **News.**

3. Click on **Investor Relations** and select **Annual Report**. From the options provided, select *the most recent HTML version of the annual report*. Review the **Financial Section** which contains the **Consolidated Financial Statements** and *Notes* to answer the following questions.

   a. Refer to the financial statement reporting liabilities. For the most recent year, calculate total current liabilities and total long-term liabilities. (*Hint:* Current liabilities + long-term liabilities = total liabilities.)

   b. For the two years of financial information presented, calculate the debt ratio (total liabilities/total assets). Comment on the trend and in general what the trend indicates regarding risk.

   c. Which financial statement reports interest costs incurred during the accounting period? Which financial statement reports interest costs paid during the accounting period? For the past three years, list the amount of interest costs incurred.

   d. Refer to the Statement of Cash Flows. Which type of activity reports borrowing and repayment of debt? For the most recent year, list the amount of *proceeds under long-term borrowings and revolving lines of credit*. For the most recent year, list the amount of *payments on long-term borrowings and revolving lines of credit*. Did Chrysler Corporation borrow or repay more debt this year? Calculate this difference.

   e. Refer to the Note reporting detail on Debt. (In 1997 this was note # 7.) What is a debenture? When do the Chrysler debenture bonds mature? What rate of interest is reported for the debentures for the past two years? Comment on the trend and whether it's considered favorable or unfavorable. What factors may account for this trend?

APPENDIX to Chapter 15

Time Value of Money: Future Value and Present Value

The following discussion of future value lays the foundation for present value but is not essential. For the valuation of long-term liabilities, some instructors may wish to begin at the bottom of page 666.

The term *time value of money* refers to the fact that money earns interest over time. Interest is the cost of using money. To borrowers, interest is the expense of renting money. To lenders, interest is the revenue earned from lending. When funds are used for a period of time, we must recognize the interest. Otherwise we overlook an important part of the transaction. Suppose you invest $4,545 in corporate bonds that pay 10% interest each year. After one year, the value of your investment has grown to $5,000. The difference between your original investment ($4,545) and the future value of the investment ($5,000) is the amount of interest revenue you will earn during the year ($455). If you ignored the interest, you would fail to account for the interest revenue you have earned. Interest becomes more important as the time period lengthens because the amount of interest depends on the span of time the money is invested.

Let's consider a second example, but from the borrower's perspective. Suppose you purchase a machine for your business. The cash price of the machine is $8,000, but you cannot pay cash now. To finance the purchase, you sign an $8,000 note payable. The note requires you to pay the $8,000 plus 10% interest one year from date of purchase. Is your cost of the machine $8,000, or is it $8,800 [$8,000 plus interest of $800 ($8,000 × 0.10)]? The cost is $8,000. The additional $800 is interest expense and not part of the cost of the machine. If you ignored the interest, you would overstate the cost of the machine and understate the amount of interest expense.

Future Value

Objective A1

Compute the future value of an investment

The main application of future value is the accumulated balance of an investment at a future date. In our first example above, the investment earned 10% per year. After one year, $4,545 grew to $5,000, as shown in Exhibit 15A-1. If the money were invested for five years, you would have to perform five such calculations. You would also have to consider the compound interest that your investment is earning. Compound interest is the interest you earn not only on your principal amount but also on the interest to date. Most business applications include compound interest. The following table shows the interest revenue earned each year at 10%:

End of Year	Interest	Future Value
0	—	$4,545
1	$4,545 × 0.10 = $455	5,000
2	5,000 × 0.10 = 500	5,500
3	5,500 × 0.10 = 550	6,050
4	6,050 × 0.10 = 605	6,655
5	6,655 × 0.10 = 666	7,321

Earning 10%, a $4,545 investment grows to $5,000 at the end of one year, to $5,500 at the end of two years, and so on. Throughout this discussion, we round off to the nearest dollar.

EXHIBIT 15A-1
Future Value

Present Value		Future Value
Time 0 $4,545	Roll forward (accumulate)	1 year $5,000
	Present value × (1 + Interest rate) = Future value	
	$4,545 × 1.10 = $5,000	

Future-Value Tables

The process of computing a future value is called *accumulating* because the future value is *more* than the present value. Mathematical tables ease the computational burden. Exhibit 15A-2, Future Value of $1, gives the future value for a single sum (a present value), $1, invested to earn a particular interest rate for a specific number of periods. Future value depends on three factors: (1) the amount of the investment, (2) the length of time between investment and future accumulation, and (3) the interest rate.

The heading in Exhibit 15A-2 states $1. Future-value tables and present-value tables are based on $1 because unity (the value 1) is so easy to work with. Observe the Periods column and the interest-rate columns 4% through 16 percent. In business applications, interest rates are always stated for the annual period of one year unless specified otherwise. In fact, an interest rate can be stated for any period, such as 3% per quarter or 5% for a six-month period. The length of the period is arbitrary. For example, an investment may promise a return (income) of 3% per quarter for six months (two quarters). In that case, you would be working with 3% interest for two periods. It would be incorrect to use 6% for one period because the interest is 3% compounded quarterly, and that amount differs somewhat from 6% compounded semiannually. Take care in studying future-value and present-value problems to align the interest rate with the appropriate number of periods.

Let's use Exhibit 15A-2. The future value of $1.00 invested at 8% for one year is $1.08 ($1.00 × 1.080, which appears at the junction under the 8% column and across from 1 in the Periods column). The figure 1.080 includes both the principal (1.000) and the compound interest for one period (0.080).

Suppose you deposit $5,000 in a savings account that pays annual interest of 8 percent. The account balance at the end of one year will be $5,400. To compute the future value of $5,000 at 8% for one year, multiply $5,000 by 1.080 to get $5,400. Now suppose you invest in a ten-year, 8% certificate of deposit (CD). What will be the future value of the CD at maturity? To compute the future value of $5,000 at 8% for 10 periods, multiply $5,000 by 2.159 (from Exhibit 15A-2) to get $10,795. This future value of $10,795 indicates that $5,000 earning 8% interest compounded annually, grows to $10,795 at the end of ten years. In this way, you can find any present amount's future value at a particular future date. Future value is especially helpful for computing the amount of cash you will have on hand for some purpose in the future.

EXHIBIT 15A-2
Future Value of $1

Period	4%	5%	6%	7%	8%	9%	10%	12%	14%	16%
1	1.040	1.050	1.060	1.070	1.080	1.090	1.100	1.120	1.140	1.160
2	1.082	1.103	1.124	1.145	1.166	1.188	1.210	1.254	1.300	1.346
3	1.125	1.158	1.191	1.225	1.260	1.295	1.331	1.405	1.482	1.561
4	1.170	1.216	1.262	1.311	1.360	1.412	1.464	1.574	1.689	1.811
5	1.217	1.276	1.338	1.403	1.469	1.539	1.611	1.762	1.925	2.100
6	1.265	1.340	1.419	1.501	1.587	1.677	1.772	1.974	2.195	2.436
7	1.316	1.407	1.504	1.606	1.714	1.828	1.949	2.211	2.502	2.826
8	1.369	1.477	1.594	1.718	1.851	1.993	2.144	2.476	2.853	3.278
9	1.423	1.551	1.689	1.838	1.999	2.172	2.358	2.773	3.252	3.803
10	1.480	1.629	1.791	1.967	2.159	2.367	2.594	3.106	3.707	4.411
11	1.539	1.710	1.898	2.105	2.332	2.580	2.853	3.479	4.226	5.117
12	1.601	1.796	2.012	2.252	2.518	2.813	3.138	3.896	4.818	5.936
13	1.665	1.886	2.133	2.410	2.720	3.066	3.452	4.363	5.492	6.886
14	1.732	1.980	2.261	2.579	2.937	3.342	3.797	4.887	6.261	7.988
15	1.801	2.079	2.397	2.759	3.172	3.642	4.177	5.474	7.138	9.266
16	1.873	2.183	2.540	2.952	3.426	3.970	4.595	6.130	8.137	10.748
17	1.948	2.292	2.693	3.159	3.700	4.328	5.054	6.866	9.276	12.468
18	2.026	2.407	2.854	3.380	3.996	4.717	5.560	7.690	10.575	14.463
19	2.107	2.527	3.026	3.617	4.316	5.142	6.116	8.613	12.056	16.777
20	2.191	2.653	3.207	3.870	4.661	5.604	6.727	9.646	13.743	19.461

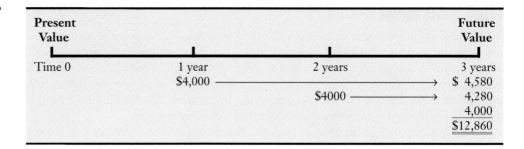

Future Value of an Annuity

In the preceding example, we made an investment of a single amount. Other investments, called annuities, include multiple investments of an equal periodic amount at fixed intervals over the duration of the investment. Consider a family investing for a child's education. The Dietrichs can invest $4,000 annually to accumulate a college fund for 15-year-old Helen. The investment can earn 7% annually until Helen turns 18—a three-year investment. How much will be available for Helen on the date of the last investment? Exhibit 15A-3 shows the accumulation—a total future value of $12,860.

The first $4,000 invested by the Dietrichs grows to $4,580 over the investment period. The second amount grows to $4,280, and the third amount stays at $4,000 because it has no time to earn interest. The sum of the three future values ($4,580 + $4,280 + $4,000) is the future value of the annuity ($12,860), which can be computed as follows:

End of Year	Annual Investment +	Interest	Increase = for the Year	Future Value of Annuity
0	—	—	—	0
1	$4,000	—	$4,000	$ 4,000
2	4,000 + ($4,000 × 0.07 = $280) =		4,280	8,280
3	4,000 + ($8,280 × 0.07 = $580) =		4,580	12,860

These computations are laborious. As with the Future Value of $1 table (a lump sum), mathematical tables ease the strain of calculating annuities. Exhibit 15A-4, Future Value of Annuity of $1, gives the future value of a series of investments, each of equal amount, at regular intervals.

What is the future value of an annuity of three investments of $1 each that earn 7 percent? The answer 3.215 can be found in the 7% column and across from 3 in the Periods column of Exhibit 15A-4. This amount can be used to compute the future value of the investment for Helen's education, as follows:

Amount of each periodic investment	×	Future value of annuity of $1 (Exhibit 15A-4)	=	Future value of investment
$4,000	×	3.215	=	$12,860

This one-step calculation is much easier than computing the future value of each annual investment and then summing the individual future values. In this way, you can compute the future value of any investment consisting of equal periodic amounts at regular intervals. Businesses make periodic investments to accumulate funds for equipment replacement and other uses—an application of the future value of an annuity.

Objective A2

Compute the present value of a single future amount and the present value of an annuity

Present Value

Often a person knows a future amount and needs to know the related present value. Recall Exhibit 15A-1, in which present value and future value are on opposite ends of the

Period	4%	5%	6%	7%	8%	9%	10%	12%	14%	16%
1	1.000	1.000	1.000	1.000	1.000	1.000	1.000	1.000	1.000	1.000
2	2.040	2.050	2.060	2.070	2.080	2.090	2.100	2.120	2.140	2.160
3	3.122	3.153	3.184	3.215	3.246	3.278	3.310	3.374	3.440	3.506
4	4.246	4.310	4.375	4.440	4.506	4.573	4.641	4.779	4.921	5.066
5	5.416	5.526	5.637	5.751	5.867	5.985	6.105	6.353	6.610	6.877
6	6.633	6.802	6.975	7.153	7.336	7.523	7.716	8.115	8.536	8.977
7	7.898	8.142	8.394	8.654	8.923	9.200	9.487	10.089	10.730	11.414
8	9.214	9.549	9.897	10.260	10.637	11.028	11.436	12.300	13.233	14.240
9	10.583	11.027	11.491	11.978	12.488	13.021	13.579	14.776	16.085	17.519
10	12.006	12.578	13.181	13.816	14.487	15.193	15.937	17.549	19.337	21.321
11	13.486	14.207	14.972	15.784	16.645	17.560	18.531	20.655	23.045	25.733
12	15.026	15.917	16.870	17.888	18.977	20.141	21.384	24.133	27.271	30.850
13	16.627	17.713	18.882	20.141	21.495	22.953	24.523	28.029	32.089	36.786
14	18.292	19.599	21.015	22.550	24.215	26.019	27.975	32.393	37.581	43.672
15	20.024	21.579	23.276	25.129	27.152	29.361	31.772	37.280	43.842	51.660
16	21.825	23.657	25.673	27.888	30.324	33.003	35.950	42.753	50.980	60.925
17	23.698	25.840	28.213	30.840	33.750	36.974	40.545	48.884	59.118	71.673
18	25.645	28.132	30.906	33.999	37.450	41.301	45.599	55.750	68.394	84.141
19	27.671	30.539	33.760	37.379	41.446	46.018	51.159	63.440	78.969	98.603
20	29.778	33.066	36.786	40.995	45.762	51.160	57.275	72.052	91.025	115.380

Future Value of Annuity of $1

EXHIBIT 15A-4
Future Value of Annuity of $1

same time line. Suppose an investment promises to pay you $5,000 at the *end* of one year. How much would you pay *now* to acquire this investment? You would be willing to pay the present value of the $5,000 future amount.

Present value also depends on three factors: (1) the amount of payment (or receipt), (2) the length of time between investment and future receipt (or payment), and (3) the interest rate. The process of computing a present value is called *discounting* because the present value is *less* than the future value.

In our investment example, the future receipt is $5,000. The investment period is one year. Assume that you demand an annual interest rate of 10% on your investment. With all three factors specified, you can compute the present value of $5,000 at 10% for one year:

$$\frac{\text{Future value}}{(1 + \text{Interest rate})} = \frac{\$5,000}{1.10} = \$4,545$$

By turning the data around into a future-value problem, we verify the present-value computation:

Amount invested (present value)...	$4,545
Expected earnings ($4,545 × 0.10)...	455
Amount to be received one year from now (future value).........	$5,000

This example illustrates that present value and future value are based on the same equation:

$$\text{Present value} \times (1 + \text{Interest rate}) = \text{Future value}$$

$$\frac{\text{Future value}}{(1 + \text{Interest rate})} = \text{Present value}$$

If the $5,000 is to be received two years from now, you will pay only $4,132 for the investment, as shown in Exhibit 15A-5. By turning the data around, we verify that $4,132 accumulates to $5,000 at 10% for two years:

EXHIBIT 15A-5
Two-Year Investment

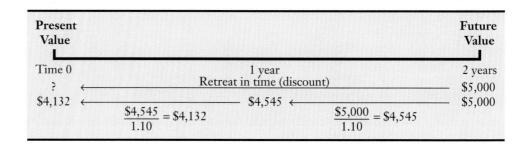

Amount invested (present value)	$4,132
Expected earnings for first year ($4,132 × 0.10)	413
Value of investment after one year	4,545
Expected earnings for second year ($4,545 × 0.10)....................	455
Amount to be received two years from now (future value).........	$5,000

You would pay $4,132—the present value of $5,000—to receive the $5,000 future amount at the end of two years at 10% per year. The $868 difference between the amount invested ($4,132) and the amount to be received ($5,000) is the return on the investment, the sum of the two interest receipts: $413 + $455 = $868.

Present-Value Tables

We have shown the simple formula for computing present value. However, figuring present value "by hand" for investments spanning many years becomes drawn out. The "number crunching" presents too many opportunities for arithmetical errors. Present-value tables ease our work. Let's reexamine our examples of present value by using Exhibit 15A-6, Present Value of $1.

For the 10% investment for one year, we find the junction in the 10% column and across from 1 in the Periods column. The figure 0.909 is computed as follows: $1/1.10 = 0.909$. This work has been done for us, and only the present values are given in the table. The heading in Exhibit 15A-6 states $1. To figure present value for $5,000, we multiply $5,000 by 0.909. The result is $4,545, which matches the result we obtained by hand.

EXHIBIT 15A-6
Present Value of $1

				Present Value of $1					
Period	**4%**	**5%**	**6%**	**7%**	**8%**	**10%**	**12%**	**14%**	**16%**
1	0.962	0.952	0.943	0.935	0.926	0.909	0.893	0.877	0.862
2	0.925	0.907	0.890	0.873	0.857	0.826	0.797	0.769	0.743
3	0.889	0.864	0.840	0.816	0.794	0.751	0.712	0.675	0.641
4	0.855	0.823	0.792	0.763	0.735	0.683	0.636	0.592	0.552
5	0.822	0.784	0.747	0.713	0.681	0.621	0.567	0.519	0.476
6	0.790	0.746	0.705	0.666	0.630	0.564	0.507	0.456	0.410
7	0.760	0.711	0.665	0.623	0.583	0.513	0.452	0.400	0.354
8	0.731	0.677	0.627	0.582	0.540	0.467	0.404	0.351	0.305
9	0.703	0.645	0.592	0.544	0.500	0.424	0.361	0.308	0.263
10	0.676	0.614	0.558	0.508	0.463	0.386	0.322	0.270	0.227
11	0.650	0.585	0.527	0.475	0.429	0.350	0.287	0.237	0.195
12	0.625	0.557	0.497	0.444	0.397	0.319	0.257	0.208	0.168
13	0.601	0.530	0.469	0.415	0.368	0.290	0.229	0.182	0.145
14	0.577	0.505	0.442	0.388	0.340	0.263	0.205	0.160	0.125
15	0.555	0.481	0.417	0.362	0.315	0.239	0.183	0.140	0.108
16	0.534	0.458	0.394	0.339	0.292	0.218	0.163	0.123	0.093
17	0.513	0.436	0.371	0.317	0.270	0.198	0.146	0.108	0.080
18	0.494	0.416	0.350	0.296	0.250	0.180	0.130	0.095	0.069
19	0.475	0.396	0.331	0.277	0.232	0.164	0.116	0.083	0.060
20	0.456	0.377	0.312	0.258	0.215	0.149	0.104	0.073	0.051

For the two-year investment, we read down the 10% column and across the Period 2 row. We multiply 0.826 (computed as 0.909/1.10 = 0.826) by $5,000 and get $4,130, which confirms our earlier computation of $4,132 (the difference is due to rounding in the present-value table). Using the table, we can compute the present value of any single future amount.

Present Value of an Annuity

Let's return to the investment example beginning near the bottom of page 668. That investment provided the investor with only a single future receipt ($5,000 at the end of two years). Annuity investments provide multiple receipts of an equal amount at fixed intervals over the investment's duration.

Consider an investment that promises *annual* cash receipts of $10,000 to be received at the end of each of three years. Assume that you demand a 12% return on your investment. What is the investment's present value? What would you pay today to acquire the investment? The investment spans three periods, and you would pay the sum of three present values. The computation is as follows:

Year	Annual Cash Receipt	×	Present Value of $1 at 12% (Exhibit 15A-6)	=	Present Value of Annual Cash Receipt
1	$10,000	×	0.893	=	$8,930
2	10,000	×	0.797	=	7,970
3	10,000	×	0.712	=	7,120
			Total present value of investment		$24,020

The present value of this annuity is $24,020. By paying this amount today, you will receive $10,000 at the end of each of the three years while earning 12% on your investment.

The example illustrates repetitive computations of the three future amounts, a time-consuming process. One way to ease the computational burden is to add the three present values of $1 (0.893 + 0.797 + 0.712) and multiply their sum (2.402) by the annual cash receipt ($10,000) to obtain the present value of the annuity ($10,000 × 2.402 = $24,020).

An easier approach is to use a present value of an annuity table. Exhibit 15A-7 shows the present value of $1 to be received at the end of each period for a given number of periods. The present value of a three-period annuity at 12% is 2.402 (the junction of the Period 3 row and the 12% column). Thus $10,000 received annually at the end of each of three years, discounted at 12%, is $24,020 ($10,000 × 2.402), which is the present value.

Present Value of Bonds Payable

The present value of a bond—its market price—is the present value of the future principal amount at maturity plus the present value of the future contract interest payments. The principal is a single amount to be paid at maturity. The interest is an annuity because it occurs periodically.

Let's compute the present value of the 9%, five-year bonds of Bethlehem Steel. The face value of the bonds is $100,000, and they pay 4 1/2% contract (cash) interest semiannually. At issuance, the market interest rate is expressed as 10%, but it is computed at 5% semiannually. Therefore, the effective interest rate for each of the ten semiannual periods is 5 percent. We use 5% in computing the present value (PV) of the maturity and of the interest. The market price of these bonds is $96,149, as follows:

	Effective annual interest rate ÷ 2	Number of semiannual interest payments	
PV of principal:			
$100,000 × PV of single amount at 5%		for 10 periods	
($100,000 × 0.614—Exhibit 15A-6)			$61,400
PV of interest:			
($100,000 × 0.045) × PV of annuity at 5%		for 10 periods	
($4,500 × 7.722—Exhibit 15A-7)			34,749
PV (market price) of bonds			$96,149

Period	4%	5%	6%	7%	8%	10%	12%	14%	16%
				Present Value of Annuity of $1					
1	0.962	0.952	0.943	0.935	0.926	0.909	0.893	0.877	0.862
2	1.886	1.859	1.833	1.808	1.783	1.736	1.690	1.647	1.605
3	2.775	2.723	2.673	2.624	2.577	2.487	2.402	2.322	2.246
4	3.630	3.546	3.465	3.387	3.312	3.170	3.037	2.914	2.798
5	4.452	4.329	4.212	4.100	3.993	3.791	3.605	3.433	3.274
6	5.242	5.076	4.917	4.767	4.623	4.355	4.111	3.889	3.685
7	6.002	5.786	5.582	5.389	5.206	4.868	4.564	4.288	4.039
8	6.733	6.463	6.210	5.971	5.747	5.335	4.968	4.639	4.344
9	7.435	7.108	6.802	6.515	6.247	5.759	5.328	4.946	4.607
10	8.111	7.722	7.360	7.024	6.710	6.145	5.650	5.216	4.833
11	8.760	8.306	7.887	7.499	7.139	6.495	5.938	5.453	5.029
12	9.385	8.863	8.384	7.943	7.536	6.814	6.194	5.660	5.197
13	9.986	9.394	8.853	8.358	7.904	7.103	6.424	5.842	5.342
14	10.563	9.899	9.295	8.745	8.244	7.367	6.628	6.002	5.468
15	11.118	10.380	9.712	9.108	8.559	7.606	6.811	6.142	5.575
16	11.652	10.838	10.106	9.447	8.851	7.824	6.974	6.265	5.669
17	12.166	11.274	10.477	9.763	9.122	8.022	7.120	6.373	5.749
18	12.659	11.690	10.828	10.059	9.372	8.201	7.250	6.467	5.818
19	13.134	12.085	11.158	10.336	9.604	8.365	7.366	6.550	5.877
20	13.590	12.462	11.470	10.594	9.818	8.514	7.469	6.623	5.929

EXHIBIT 15A-7
Present Value of Annuity of $1

The market price of the Bethlehem Steel bonds show a discount because the contract interest rate on the bonds (9%) is less than the market interest rate (10%). We discuss these bonds in more detail on pages 637–638.

Let's consider a premium price for the Bethlehem Steel bonds. Assume that the market interest rate is 8% at issuance. The effective interest rate is 4% for each of the ten semiannual periods:

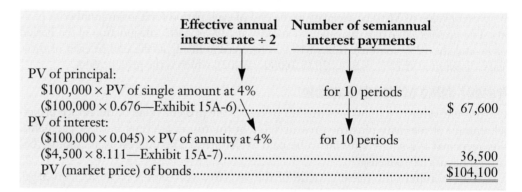

	Effective annual interest rate ÷ 2	Number of semiannual interest payments	
PV of principal:			
$100,000 × PV of single amount at 4%			
($100,000 × 0.676—Exhibit 15A-6)		for 10 periods	$ 67,600
PV of interest:			
($100,000 × 0.045) × PV of annuity at 4%			
($4,500 × 8.111—Exhibit 15A-7)		for 10 periods	36,500
PV (market price) of bonds			$104,100

We discuss accounting for these bonds on pages 639 and 640.

Capital Leases

Objective A3

Determine the cost of an asset acquired through a capital lease

How does a lessee compute the cost of an asset acquired through a capital lease? Consider that the lessee gets the use of the asset but does *not* pay for the leased asset in full at the beginning of the lease. A capital lease is therefore similar to an installment purchase of the leased asset. The lessee must record the leased asset at the present value of the lease liability. The time value of money must be weighed.

The cost of the asset to the lessee is the sum of any payment made at the beginning of the lease period plus the present value of the future lease payments. The lease payments are equal amounts occurring at regular intervals—that is, they are annuity payments.

Consider the 20-year building lease of Safeway. The lease requires 20 annual payments of $10,000 each, with the first payment due immediately. The interest rate in the lease is 10%, and the present value of the 19 future payments at the end of each period is

$83,650 ($10,000 × PV of annuity at 10% for 19 periods, or 8.365 from Exhibit 15A-7). Safeway's cost of the storage building is $93,650 (the sum of the initial payment, $10,000, plus the present value of the future payments, $83,650). The entries for a capital lease are illustrated on page 646.

Appendix Problems

P15A-1 For each situation, compute the required amount.

Computing the future value of an investment
(Obj. A1)

1. Summit Enterprises is budgeting for the acquisition of land over the next several years. Summit can invest $400,000 today at 9 percent. How much cash will Summit have for land acquisitions at the end of five years? At the end of six years?

2. Alston Associates is planning to invest $5,000 each year for five years. The company's investment adviser believes that Alston can earn 6% interest without taking on too much risk. What will be the value of Alston's investment on the date of the last deposit if Alston can earn 6 percent? If Alston can earn 8 percent?

P15A-2 For each situation, compute the required amount.

Relating the future and present values of an investment
(Obj. A1, A2)

1. The U.S. operations of Fuji Film's operations are generating excess cash that will be invested in a special fund. During 19X2, Fuji invests $5,643,400 in the fund for a planned advertising campaign for a new product to be released six years later, in 19X8. If Fuji's investments can earn 10% each year, how much cash will the company have for the advertising campaign in 19X8?

2. Fuji will need $10 million to advertise a new type of photo film in 19X8. How much must Fuji invest in 19X2 to have the cash available for the advertising campaign? Fuji's investments can earn 10% annually.

3. Explain the relationship between your answers to (1) and (2).

P15A-3 Determine the present value of the following notes and bonds:

Computing the present values of various notes and bonds
(Obj. A2)

a. A $50,000, five-year note payable with contract interest rate of 9%, paid annually. The market interest rate at issuance is 10 percent.

b. Ten-year bonds payable with maturity value of $100,000 and contract interest rate of 12%, paid semiannually. The market rate of interest is 10% at issuance.

c. Same bonds payable as in b, but the market interest rate is 8 percent.

d. Same bonds payable as in b, but the market interest rate is 12 percent.

P15A-4 On December 31, 19X1, when the market interest rate is 8%, Fairview Land Co. issues $300,000 of 7.25%, ten-year bonds payable. The bonds pay interest semiannually.

Computing a bond's present value, recording its issuance at a discount and interest payments
(Obj. A2)

1. Determine the present value of the bonds at issuance.

2. Assume that the bonds are issued at the price computed in requirement 1. Prepare an effective-interest method amortization table for the first two semiannual interest periods.

REQUIRED

3. Using the amortization table prepared in requirement 2, journalize issuance of the bonds and the first two interest payments.

P15A-5 Osaka Children's Choir needs a fleet of vans to transport the children to singing engagements throughout Japan. Nissan offers the vehicles for a single payment of 6,300,000 yen due at the end of four years. Toyota prices a similar fleet of vans for four annual payments of 1,500,000 yen each. The children's home could borrow the funds at 6%, so this is the appropriate interest rate. Which company should get the business, Nissan or Toyota? Base your decision on present value, and give your reason.

Deciding between two payment plans
(Obj. A2)

P15A-6 Rykoff, Inc., acquired equipment under a capital lease that requires six annual lease payments of $10,000. The first payment is due when the lease begins, on January 1, 19X6. Future payments are due on January 1 of each year of the lease term. The interest rate in the lease is 16 percent.

Computing the cost of equipment acquired under a capital lease and recording the lease transactions
(Obj. A3)

1. Compute Rykoff's cost of the equipment.

REQUIRED

2. Journalize the (a) acquisition of the equipment, (b) depreciation for 19X6, (c) accrued interest at December 31, 19X6, and (d) second lease payment on January 1, 19X7.

CHAPTER 16

Accounting for Investments and International Operations

After studying this chapter, you should be able to

1. Account for trading investments

2. Account for available-for-sale investments

3. Use the equity method for investments

4. Understand consolidated financial statements

5. Account for long-term investments in bonds

6. Account for transactions stated in a foreign currency

7. Report investing transactions on the statement of cash flows

> **" Over a third of General Motors' assets are employed outside the United States, and the company earns more than half its profits outside the United States. "**
>
> —GENERAL MOTORS ANNUAL REPORT, 1996

General Motors Corporation (GM) is the world's largest business entity. The GM organization includes hundreds of investments in other companies. Some of those companies' financial statements are combined and reported under the General Motors name. For example, Libbey-Owens-Ford makes the glass for GM cars, Fisher Body makes the auto chassis, and Delco makes the batteries. GM's financial statements are called *consolidated* financial statements because they combine the reports of various GM companies. This chapter shows how a company accounts for investments.

Many of the companies that GM owns are located in foreign countries. In fact, over a third of GM's assets are employed outside the United States, and the company earns more than half its profits in other countries. The chapter also shows how to account for international operations.

hroughout this course, you have become increasingly familiar with the financial statements of companies such as NIKE, Intel, and IHOP. This chapter, which discusses long-term investments and international operations, continues your education in the financial statements and how to prepare and use them.

Accounting for Investments

Investments come in all sizes and shapes—from the purchase of a few shares of a company's stock, to an investment in bonds, to the acquisition of an entire company. In earlier chapters, we discussed stocks and bonds from the perspective of the company that issued the securities. In this chapter, we examine stocks and bonds from the perspective of the investor who bought them as an investment.

Different accounting methods apply to different types of investments. We begin with stock investments and then move to investments in bonds and notes.

Stock Investments: A Review

Stock Prices

Investors buy more stock in transactions among themselves than from the issuing company. Each share of stock is issued only once, but it may be traded among investors many times thereafter. Individuals and businesses buy and sell stocks from each other in markets, such as the New York Stock Exchange and the American Stock Exchange. Brokers such as Merrill Lynch and Prudential Securities, Inc. handle stock transactions for a commission.

A broker may "quote a stock price," which means to state the current market price per share. The financial community quotes stock prices in dollars and one-eighth fractions. A stock selling at 32 1/8 costs $32.125 per share. A stock listed at 55 3/4 sells at $55.75. Financial publications and many newspapers carry daily information on the stock issues of thousands of corporations. These one-line summaries carry information as of the close of trading on the previous day.

■ Daily Exercise 16-1

Exhibit 16-1 presents information for the common stock of The Boeing Company, the aircraft manufacturer, just as this information appeared in newspaper listings. During the previous 52 weeks, Boeing common stock reached a high price of $114.50 and a low price of $74.125 per share. The annual cash dividend is $1.12 per share. During the previous day, 1,059,800 (10,598 × 100) shares of Boeing common stock were traded. The prices of these transactions ranged from a high of $109.875 to a low of $108.75 per share. The day's closing price of $109.125 was $0.50 lower than the closing price of the preceding day.

Investors and Investees

To move further into our discussion of investments in stock, we need to define two key terms. The person or company that owns stock in a corporation is the *investor*. The corporation that issued the stock is the *investee*. If you own shares of Boeing common stock, you are an investor and Boeing is the investee.

A corporation may purchase another corporation's stock simply to put extra cash to work in the hope of earning dividends and gains on the sale of the stock. Such investments are rare, however. Most companies prefer to invest in inventory, employees, and plant assets in their own line of business. However, corporations do buy the stock of other corporations to gain a degree of control over the investee's operation. An investor holding 25% of the investee's outstanding stock owns one-fourth of the business. This one-quarter voice in electing the directors of the corporation is likely to give the investor a lot of say in how the

EXHIBIT 16-1
Stock Price Information for
The Boeing Company

52 weeks								
High	**Low**	**Stock**	**Dividend**	**Sales 100s**	**High**	**Low**	**Close**	**Net Change**
114 1/2	74 1/8	Boeing	1.12	10598	109 7/8	108 3/4	109 1/8	−1/2

EXHIBIT 16-2
Reporting Investments on the
Balance Sheet

ASSETS		
Current Assets		
Cash		$X
Short-term investments		X
Accounts receivable		X
Inventories		X
Prepaid expenses		X
Total current assets		$X
Long-term investments [or simply Investments]		X
Property, plant, and equipment		X
Intangible assets		X
Other assets		X

investee conducts its business. An investor holding more than 50% of the outstanding shares controls the investee.

Classifying Investments

Investments in stock are assets to the investor. The investments may be short-term or long-term. **Short-term investments**—sometimes called **marketable securities**—are current assets. To be listed on the balance sheet as short-term, investments must be liquid (readily convertible to cash). Also, the investor must intend either to convert the investments to cash within one year or to use them to pay a current liability.

Investments not meeting the two requirements of short-term investments are classified on the balance sheet as **long-term investments**, a category of noncurrent assets. Long-term investments include stocks and bonds that the investor expects to hold longer than one year or that are not readily marketable—for instance, real estate not used in the operations of the business. Exhibit 16-2 shows the positions of short-term and long-term investments on the balance sheet.

We report assets in the order of their liquidity, starting with cash and the other current assets. Long-term investments are less liquid than current assets but more liquid than property, plant, and equipment. However, many companies report their long-term investments after property, plant, and equipment.

Stock Investments

We begin our discussion of stock investments with those situations in which the investor holds less than a 20% interest in the investee company. These investments in stock are classified as either trading securities or as available-for-sale securities. **Trading securities** are investments that are to be sold in the very near future—days, weeks, or only a few months—with the intent of generating profits on price changes. Trading securities are therefore recorded as short-term investments and reported on the balance sheet under *current assets*, as shown in Exhibit 16-2.

Available-for-sale securities are all investments other than trading securities in which the investor cannot exercise significant influence over the investee. They are classified as current assets if the business expects to sell the investments within the next year or within the business's normal operating cycle if longer than a year. All other available-for-sale securities are classified as long-term investments (Exhibit 16-2).

After classifying an investment as a trading security or as an available-for-sale security, the investor accounts for the two categories separately. We begin by illustrating the accounting for a trading investment. Then we show how to account for a long-term available-for-sale investment.

Accounting for Short-Term Investments

The **market-value method** is used to account for all trading investments because they will be sold in the near future at their current market value. Cost is used only as the initial amount to record trading investments. Assume Intel Corporation has excess cash for short-term investing. Suppose Intel buys 500 shares of Ford Motor Company stock for $50 per share on October 23, 19X5. Assume further that Intel's management hopes to sell

Short-Term Investment. A current asset; an investment that is readily convertible to cash and that the investor intends either to convert to cash within one year or to use to pay a current liability. Also called a **marketable security.**

Long-Term Investment. A noncurrent asset, a separate asset category reported on the balance sheet between current assets and plant assets.

Trading Securities. Investments that are to be sold in the very near future with the intent of generating profits on price changes.

Available-for-Sale Securities. Stock investments other than trading securities in which the investor cannot exercise significant influence over the investee.

■ **Daily Exercise 16-2**
■ **Daily Exercise 16-3**

Objective 1

Account for trading investments

Market-Value Method for Investments. Used to account for all trading investments. These investments are reported at their current market value.

this stock within three months, so the investment is a trading security. Intel's entry to record purchase of the investment is

Short-Term Investment

25,000	

```
19X5
Oct. 23   Short-Term Investment (500 × $50)..........   25,000
                 Cash....................................................         25,000
                 To purchase investment.
```

Ford stock pays a cash dividend of $1.40 per share, so Intel would receive a dividend on the investment. Intel's entry to record receipt of a cash dividend is

```
19X5
Nov. 14   Cash (500 × $1.40)...................   700
                 Dividend Revenue ...........         700
                 To receive cash dividend.
```

Reporting Trading Investments at Current Market Value

Trading investments are reported on the balance sheet at current market value, not at their cost. This rule requires a year-end adjustment of the trading investments from their last carrying amount to current market value. Assume that the Ford stock has decreased in value, and at December 31, 19X5, Intel's investment in Ford stock is worth $20,000 (which is $5,000 less than the purchase price). At year end, Intel would make the following adjustment:

Short-Term Investment

25,000	5,000

```
19X5
Dec. 31   Unrealized Loss on Trading
                 Investment ($25,000 – $20,000)..............................   5,000
                       Short-Term Investment....................................         5,000
                 To adjust trading investment to market value.
```

The T-account shows the $20,000 ($25,000 – $5,000) balance of Short-Term Investment. Intel would report its trading investment on the balance sheet at December 31, 19X5, and the unrealized loss on trading investment on the 19X5 income statement, as follows:

■ **Daily Exercise 16-4**

Balance Sheet (partial):		Income Statement (partial):	
ASSETS		Other gains and losses:	
Current assets:		Unrealized gain (loss) on	
Short-term investments, at		trading investment	$(5,000)
market value............................	$20,000		

An *unrealized* gain (or loss) is one that is not the result of a sale transaction. If the investment's market value had increased above $25,000, Intel would have debited Short-Term Investment and credited Unrealized Gain on Trading Investment.

Selling a Trading Investment

When a company sells a trading investment, the gain or loss on the sale is the difference between

- The sale proceeds and
- The last carrying amount of the investment

For example, suppose Intel sells the Ford stock for $18,000 on January 19, 19X6. Intel would record the sale as follows:

Short-Term Investment

25,000	5,000
	20,000

```
19X6
Jan. 19   Cash .............................................   18,000
          Loss on Sale of Investment ...........    2,000
                 Short-Term Investment........                   20,000
                 To sell investment.
```

Observe that this loss results from the sale of the investment. For reporting on the income statement, Intel could combine all gains and losses on short-term investments and report a single net amount under "Other gains and losses."

■ Daily Exercise 16-5
■ Daily Exercise 16-6
■ Daily Exercise 16-7

Accounting for Long-Term Available-for-Sale Investments

Objective 2

Account for available-for-sale investments

The *market-value method* is used to account for all available-for-sale investments in stock because the company expects to resell the stock at its market value. Available-for-sale investments are therefore reported on the balance sheet at their *current market value*.

Suppose that Dade, Inc., purchases 1,000 shares of Hewlett-Packard Company common stock at the market price of 35 3/4. Dade intends to hold this investment for longer than a year and therefore classifies it as a long-term available-for-sale investment. Dade's entry to record the investment is

19X1
Feb. 23 Long-Term Available-for-Sale Investment
         (1,000 × $35.75)... 35,750
           Cash 35,750
         To purchase investment.

Dade receives a $0.22 per share cash dividend on the Hewlett-Packard stock. Dade's entry to record receipt of the dividend is

19X1
July 14 Cash (1,000 × $0.22)................ 220
           Dividend Revenue 220
         To receive cash dividend.

Receipt of a *stock* dividend is different from receipt of a cash dividend. ◀▬ For a stock dividend, the investor records no dividend revenue. Instead, the investor makes a memorandum entry in the accounting records to show the new number of shares of stock held as an investment. Because the number of investment shares has increased, the investor's cost per share of the stock decreases. For example, suppose Dade, Inc., receives a 5% stock dividend from Hewlett-Packard Company. Dade would receive 50 shares (5% of 1,000 shares previously held) and make this memorandum entry in its accounting records:

◀▮◀▮◀▮ For a review of stock dividends, see Chapter 14, page 585.

MEMORANDUM—Receipt of stock dividend: Received 50 shares of Hewlett-Packard common stock in 5% stock dividend. New cost per share is $34.05 (cost of $35,750 ÷ 1,050 shares).

■ Daily Exercise 16-8

In all future transactions affecting its Hewlett-Packard investment, Dade will use the new cost per share of $34.05.

Reporting Available-for-Sale Investments at Current Market Value

Because of the relevance of market values for decision making, available-for-sale investments in stock are reported on the balance sheet at their market value. This reporting requires an adjustment of the investments from their last carrying amount to current market value. Assume that the market value of Dade's investment in Hewlett-Packard's common stock is $36,400 on December 31, 19X1. In this case, Dade, Inc., makes the following adjustment:

19X1
Dec. 31 Allowance to Adjust Investment to Market
         ($36,400 − $35,750) 650
           Unrealized Gain on Available-for-Sale
           Investment... 650
         To adjust investment to market value.

Allowance to Adjust Investment to Market is a companion account that is used in conjunction with the Long-Term Investment account to bring the investment's carrying amount to current market value. In this case, the investment's cost ($35,750) plus the Allowance ($650) equals the investment carrying amount ($36,400).

Long-Term Available-for-Sale Investment	Allowance to Adjust Investment to Market
35,750	650

Investment carrying amount = Market value of $36,400

Here the Allowance has a debit balance because the market value of the investment increased. If the investment's market value declines, the Allowance is credited, and the investment carrying amount is its cost minus the Allowance. If the Allowance account has a credit balance, the Allowance becomes a contra account. ◀ The other side of the December 31 adjustment entry is a credit to Unrealized Gain on Investment.

If the market value of the investment declines, the company debits Unrealized Loss on Investment. Recall that an *unrealized* gain or loss results from a change in the investment's market value, not from the sale of the investment. For available-for-sale investments, the Unrealized Gain account or the Unrealized Loss account is reported on the balance sheet as part of stockholders' equity, as shown here.

◀|||◀|||◀||| For a review of other contra accounts, see Chapter 3, page 100, for Accumulated Depreciation, and Chapter 8, page 339, for Allowance for Uncollectible Accounts.

Balance Sheet (partial)

ASSETS		STOCKHOLDERS' EQUITY	
Total current assets	$ XXX	Common stock	$ XXX
Long-term available-for-sale investments—at market value ($35,750 + $650)	36,400	Retained earnings	XXX
		Unrealized gain on available-for-sale investments	650
Property, plant, and equipment, net	XXX		

Selling an Available-for-Sale Investment

The sale of an available-for-sale investment can result in a *realized* gain or loss. For available-for-sale investments, realized gains and losses measure the difference between the amount received from the sale of the investment and the cost of the investment.

Suppose Dade, Inc., sells its investment in Hewlett-Packard stock for $34,000 during 19X2. Dade would record the sale as follows:

19X2			
May 19	Cash	34,000	
	Loss on Sale of Investment	1,750	
	Long-Term Available-for-Sale Investment (cost)		35,750
	To sell investment.		

■ Daily Exercise 16-9
■ Daily Exercise 16-10

Dade would report the Loss on Sale of Investments as an "Other gain or loss" on the income statement. ◀

◀|||◀|||◀||| We show how to report Other gains and losses on the income statement near the middle of page 676.

Working It Out Suppose Xenon Corporation holds the following available-for-sale securities as long-term investments at December 31, 19X8:

Stock	Cost	Current Market Value
The Coca-Cola Company	$ 85,000	$ 71,000
Eastman Kodak Company	16,000	12,000
Scott Paper Company	122,000	136,000
	$223,000	$219,000

Show how Xenon Corporation will report long-term investments and the unrealized loss on its December 31, 19X8, balance sheet.

Answer

ASSETS
Long-term available-for-sale investments, at market value.................................. $219,000

STOCKHOLDERS' EQUITY
Unrealized loss on available-for-sale investments ($223,000 – $219,000)......... $ (4,000)

Accounting for Equity-Method Investments

Objective 3

Use the equity method for investments

An investor who holds less than 20% of the investee's voting stock usually plays no important role in the investee's operations. However, an investor with a larger stock holding—between 20 and 50% of the investee's voting stock—may *significantly influence* how the investee operates the business. Such an investor can likely affect the investee's decisions on dividend policy, product lines, sources of supply, and other important matters.

For this reason, investments in the range of 20–50% of another company's stock are common. For example, General Motors owns nearly 40% of Isuzu Motors Overseas Distribution Corporation. Chrysler Corporation owns 50% of a partnership with Renault of France. Because the investor has a voice in shaping business policy and operations, accountants believe that some measure of the investee's success and failure should be included in accounting for the investment. We use the **equity method** to account for investments in which the investor owns 20–50% of the investee's stock and thus can significantly influence the investee's decisions. A recent survey of 600 companies by *Accounting Trends & Techniques* indicated that 253 (42%) of the corporations held investments that they accounted for by the equity method. These investee companies are often referred to as *affiliates*.

Equity Method for Investments. The method used to account for investments in which the investor has 20–50% of the investee's voting stock and can significantly influence the decisions of the investee. The investment account is debited for ownership in the investee's net income and credited for ownership in the investee's dividends.

RECORDING THE INITIAL INVESTMENT Investments accounted for by the equity method are recorded initially at cost. Suppose Phillips Petroleum Company pays $400,000 for 30% of the common stock of White Rock Corporation. Phillips may refer to White Rock Corporation as an *affiliated company*. Phillips's entry to record the purchase of this investment is as follows:

Jan. 6	Long-Term Equity-Method Investment.........	400,000	
	Cash		400,000
	To purchase equity-method investment.		

ADJUSTING THE INVESTMENT ACCOUNT FOR INVESTEE NET INCOME Under the equity method, Phillips, as the investor, applies its percentage of ownership (30%) to record its share of the investee's net income and dividends. If White Rock reports net income of $250,000 for the year, Phillips records 30% of this amount as an increase in the investment account and as equity-method investment revenue, as follows:

Dec. 31	Long-Term Equity-Method Investment ($250,000 × 0.30)...	75,000	
	Equity-Method Investment Revenue.........		75,000
	To record investment revenue.		

The Investment Revenue account carries the Equity-Method label to identify its source. This labeling is similar to distinguishing Sales Revenue from Service Revenue.

The investor increases the Investment account and records Investment Revenue when the investee reports income because of the close relationship between the two companies. As the investee's (affiliate's) owners' equity increases, so does the Investment account on the investor's books.

Thinking It Over Suppose White Rock reported a $200,000 net loss for the year. What journal entry would Phillips make in this case?

Answer

Dec. 31	Equity-Method Investment Loss.................................	60,000	
	Long-Term Equity-Method Investment		
	($200,000 × 0.30)		60,000
	To record investment loss.		

RECORDING RECEIPT OF DIVIDENDS ON AN EQUITY-METHOD INVESTMENT

Phillips records its proportionate part of cash dividends received from White Rock. Assuming that White Rock declares and pays a cash dividend of $100,000, Phillips receives 30% of this dividend, and makes this journal entry:

19X2

Jan. 17	Cash ($100,000 × 0.30)...	30,000	
	Long-Term Equity-Method Investment.........		30,000
	To receive cash dividend on equity-method investment.		

The Investment account is credited for the receipt of a dividend on an equity-method investment. Why? Because the dividend decreases the investee's owners' equity, and so it also reduces the investor's investment. The investor received cash for this portion of the investment and reduced the investor's claim against the investee.

After the preceding entries are posted, Phillips's Investment account reflects Phillips's equity in the net assets of White Rock:

■ **Daily Exercise 16-11**

Long-Term Equity-Method Investment

19X1				19X2		
Jan.	6	Purchase	400,000	Jan. 17 Dividends received		30,000
Dec.	31	Net income	75,000			
19X2						
Jan. 17		Balance	445,000			

Phillips would report the long-term investment on the balance sheet and the equity-method investment revenue on the income statement as follows:

Balance sheet (partial):
ASSETS

Total current assets	$ XXX
Long-term equity-method investments	445,000
Property, plant, and equipment, net................	XXX

Income statement (partial):

Income from operations	$ XXX
Other revenue:	
Equity-method investment revenue	75,000
Net income	$ XXX

RECORDING THE SALE OF AN EQUITY-METHOD INVESTMENT

Gain or loss on the sale of an equity-method investment is measured as the difference between the sale proceeds and the carrying amount of the investment. For example, sale of one-tenth of the White Rock common stock for $41,000 would be recorded as follows:

■ **Daily Exercise 16-12**

Feb. 13	Cash	41,000	
	Loss on Sale of Investment......................................	3,500	
	Long-Term Equity-Method Investment		
	($445,000 × 1/10)...		44,500
	Sold one-tenth of investment.		

Learning Tip: The T-account illustrates how to account for equity-method investments:

Long-Term Equity-Method Investments	
Cost	Share of losses
Share of income	Share of dividends

Joint Ventures—Accounted for by the Equity Method

A *joint venture* is a separate entity or project owned and operated by a small group of businesses. Joint ventures are common in risky endeavors such as oil exploration in the petroleum industry and the construction of nuclear power plants. For example, Aramco, which stands for Arabian American Oil Company, is a joint venture half owned by Saudi Arabia. Several multinational oil companies (Exxon, Chevron, and others) own the remaining 50 percent.

A participant in a joint venture, such as Exxon, accounts for its investment in a joint venture by the equity method even when the investor owns less than 20% of the venture. The equity method is used for accounting purposes because a joint venturer is presumed to have a significant influence on the investee company.

Accounting for Consolidated Subsidiaries

Most large corporations own controlling interests in other corporations. A **controlling** (or **majority**) **interest** is the ownership of more than 50% of the investee's voting stock. Such an investment enables the investor to elect a majority of the investee's board of directors and so control the investee. The corporation that controls the other company is called the **parent company,** and the company that is controlled by another corporation is called the **subsidiary.** For example, Saturn Corporation is a subsidiary of General Motors, the parent, so the stockholders of GM control Saturn, as diagrammed in Exhibit 16-3.

". . . Saturn Corporation is a subsidiary of General Motors, the parent, so the stockholders of GM control Saturn. . ."

Why have subsidiaries? Why not have the corporation take the form of a single legal entity? Subsidiaries may enable the parent to save on income taxes, limit the parent's liabilities in a risky venture, and ease expansion into foreign countries. For example, IBM finds it more feasible to operate in France through a French-based subsidiary company than through the U.S. parent company. Exhibit 16-4 shows some of the subsidiaries of the "Big Three" U.S. automakers.

Consolidation Method for Majority-Owned Subsidiaries

Consolidation accounting is a method of combining the financial statements of two or more companies that are controlled by the same owners. This method implements the entity

Controlling Interest. Ownership of more than 50% of an investee company's voting stock. Also called **majority interest.**

Parent Company. An investor company that owns more than 50% of the voting stock of a subsidiary company.

Subsidiary Company. A company in which a parent company owns more than 50% of the voting stock.

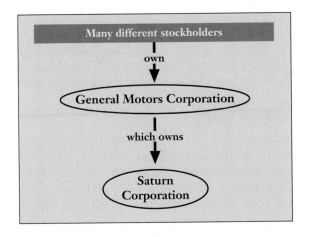

EXHIBIT 16-3
Ownership Structure of General Motors Corporation and Saturn Corporation

Parent Company	Selected Subsidiaries
General Motors Corporation Total assets: $222 billion	Saturn Corporation Hughes Aircraft Company
Ford Motor Company Total assets: $263 billion	Ford Aerospace Corporation Jaguar, Ltd.
Chrysler Corporation Total assets: $56 billion	Jeep/Eagle Corporation Thrifty Rent-a-Car System, Inc.

Objective 4

Understand consolidated financial statements

Consolidated Statements. Financial statements of the parent company plus those of majority-owned subsidiaries as if the combination were a single legal entity.

Concept Highlight

EXHIBIT 16-5
Accounting Methods for Stock Investment by Percentage of Ownership

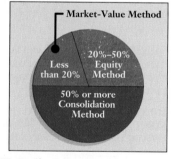

■ **Daily Exercise 16-13**

Minority Interest. A subsidiary company's equity that is held by stockholders other than the parent company.

■ **Daily Exercise 16-14**

concept by reporting a single set of financial statements for the consolidated entity, which carries the name of the parent company.

Most published financial reports include consolidated statements. To understand the statements you are likely to encounter, you need to know the basic concepts underlying consolidation accounting. **Consolidated statements** combine the balance sheets, income statements, and cash-flow statements of the parent company with those of its majority-owned subsidiaries into an overall set of statements as if the parent and its subsidiaries were a single entity. The goal is to provide a better perspective on total operations than could be obtained by examining the separate reports of each individual company.

In consolidation accounting, the assets, liabilities, revenues, and expenses of each subsidiary are added to the parent's accounts. The consolidated financial statements report the combined account balances. For example, the balance in the Cash account of Saturn Corporation is added to the balance in the General Motors Cash account, and the sum of the two amounts is presented as a single cash amount in the consolidated balance sheet of General Motors Corporation. The consolidated financial statements bear the name of the parent company only.

Exhibit 16-5 illustrates the accounting method that should be used for stock investments according to the percentage of the investor's ownership in the investee company.

Goodwill and Minority Interest

GOODWILL Goodwill is an intangible asset account that arises in the purchase of another company. As we saw in Chapter 10, *goodwill* is the excess of the cost to acquire another company over the sum of the market value of its net assets (assets minus liabilities). Accountants identify goodwill in the process of preparing consolidated financial statements. Only the parent company reports the goodwill. Goodwill appears among the intangible assets on the consolidated balance sheet.

MINORITY INTEREST A parent company may purchase less than 100% of the stock of a subsidiary company. For example, Atlantic Richfield, the giant oil company, owns 82% of Vastar Resources. The remaining 18% of Vastar is called the minority interest in Vastar. **Minority interest** is the portion (less than 50%) of a subsidiary's stock that is owned by stockholders other than the parent company. Atlantic Richfield Company, the parent company, therefore reports on its consolidated balance sheet an account titled Minority Interest. Most companies list Minority Interest among their liabilities.

Preparing consolidated financial statements is illustrated in the chapter appendix. Advanced accounting courses cover consolidation accounting in more detail.

Income of a Consolidated Entity

The income of a consolidated entity is the net income of the parent plus the parent's proportion of the subsidiaries' net income. Suppose Parent Company owns all the stock of Subsidiary S-1 and 60% of the stock of Subsidiary S-2. During 19X8, Parent earned net income of $330,000, S-1 earned $150,000, and S-2 had a net loss of $100,000. Parent Company would report consolidated net income of $420,000, computed as follows:

	Net Income (Net Loss)	×	Parent Stockholders' Ownership	=	Parent's Consolidated Net Income (Net Loss)
Parent Company......................	$ 330,000	×	100%	=	$330,000
Subsidiary S-1	150,000	×	100%	=	150,000
Subsidiary S-2	(100,000)	×	60%	=	(60,000)
Consolidated net income..........					$420,000

Thinking It Over Answer these questions about consolidated financial statements:

1. Whose name appears on the consolidated statements—the parent company, the subsidiary company, or both?

2. Company A owns 90% of Company B. What is the remaining 10% of Company B's stock called, and where does it appear, if at all, in Company A's financial statements?

3. Company C paid $1 million to acquire Company D, whose stockholders' equity (same as net assets) totaled $700,000. What is the $300,000 excess called? Which company reports the excess? Where in the financial statements is the excess reported?

Answers

1. Parent Company only.

2. Minority Interest—reported on (Parent) Company A's balance sheet among the liabilities.

3. Goodwill—reported on (Parent) Company C's balance sheet as an intangible asset.

Computers and Consolidations

Consider diversified companies such as W. R. Grace & Co., the world's largest specialty chemicals company. Grace includes nearly 30 subsidiary firms, with more than 100 different product lines—from food packaging to construction materials to health-care products. A company such as Grace can prepare its consolidated financial statements automatically with a fully integrated accounting information system.

Long-Term Investments in Bonds and Notes

Industrial and commercial companies invest far more in stocks than they invest in bonds. The major investors in bonds are financial institutions, such as pension plans, bank trust departments, mutual funds, and insurance companies. The relationship between the issuing corporation and the investor (bondholder) may be diagrammed as follows:

Objective 5

Account for long-term investments in bonds

Issuing Corporation	Investor (Bondholder)
Bonds payable ⟷	Investment in bonds
Interest expense ⟷	Interest revenue

The dollar amount of a bond transaction is the same for issuer and investor, but the accounts debited and credited differ. For example, the issuing corporation's interest expense is the investor's interest revenue. Chapter 15 covered the accounting for bonds payable.

An investment in bonds is classified either as short-term (a current asset) or as long-term. Short-term investments in bonds are rare. Here, we focus on long-term investments in bonds and notes that the investor intends to hold until the bonds mature. These are called **held-to-maturity investments.**

Held-to-Maturity Securities. Investment in bonds, notes, and other debt securities that the investor expects to hold until their maturity date.

Accounting for Held-to-Maturity Investments—The Amortized Cost Method

Bond investments are recorded at cost. At maturity, the investor will receive the bonds' face value. For held-to-maturity investments, discount or premium is amortized to account more precisely for interest revenue over the period the bonds will be held. The amortization of discount or premium on a bond investment affects both Interest Revenue for the investor and the carrying amount of the bonds for the company that issued the bonds. Held-to-maturity investments in bonds are reported at their *amortized cost*, which determines the carrying amount.

Suppose an investor purchases $10,000 of 6% CBS bonds at a price of 95.2 on April 1, 19X2. The investor intends to hold the bonds as a long-term investment until their maturity. Interest dates are April 1 and October 1. These bonds mature on April 1, 19X6, so they will be outstanding for 48 months. Assume amortization of the discount by the straight-line method. ⬸▮▮▮ The following are the entries for this long-term investment:

<table>
<tr><td>Apr. 1</td><td>Long-Term Investment in Bonds ($10,000 × 0.952)...........</td><td>9,520</td><td></td></tr>
<tr><td></td><td>Cash..</td><td></td><td>9,520</td></tr>
<tr><td></td><td>To purchase bond investment.</td><td></td><td></td></tr>
<tr><td>Oct. 1</td><td>Cash ($10,000 × 0.06 × 6/12)...</td><td>300</td><td></td></tr>
<tr><td></td><td>Interest Revenue...</td><td></td><td>300</td></tr>
<tr><td></td><td>To receive semiannual interest.</td><td></td><td></td></tr>
<tr><td>Oct. 1</td><td>Long-Term Investment in Bonds
[($10,000 − $9,520)/48] × 6....................................</td><td>60</td><td></td></tr>
<tr><td></td><td>Interest Revenue...</td><td></td><td>60</td></tr>
<tr><td></td><td>To amortize discount on bond investment.</td><td></td><td></td></tr>
</table>

At December 31, the year-end adjustments are

<table>
<tr><td>Dec. 31</td><td>Interest Receivable ($10,000 × 0.06 × 3/12).......................</td><td>150</td><td></td></tr>
<tr><td></td><td>Interest Revenue...</td><td></td><td>150</td></tr>
<tr><td></td><td>To accrue interest revenue.</td><td></td><td></td></tr>
<tr><td>Dec. 31</td><td>Long-Term Investment in Bonds
[($10,000 − $9,520)/48] × 3....................................</td><td>30</td><td></td></tr>
<tr><td></td><td>Interest Revenue...</td><td></td><td>30</td></tr>
<tr><td></td><td>To amortize discount on bond investment.</td><td></td><td></td></tr>
</table>

This amortization entry has two effects: (1) It increases the Long-Term Investment account on its march toward maturity value, and (2) it records the related interest revenue that the investor has earned as a result of the increase in the carrying amount of the investment.

The financial statements at December 31, 19X2, report the following effects of this investment in bonds:

Balance sheet at December 31, 19X2:
Current assets:

Interest receivable..	$ 150
Total current assets	X,XXX
Long-term investments in bonds ($9,520 + $60 + $30)—Note 6...........	9,610
Property, plant, and equipment..	X,XXX

Note 6: Long-term investments:
Bond investments that will be held-to-maturity are reported at *amortized cost*. At December 31, 19X2, the market value of long-term investments in bonds was $10,200 (assumed).

Income statement (multiple-step) for the year ended December 31, 19X2:
Other revenues:

Interest revenue ($300 + $60 + $150 + $30).................................	$ 540

Summary of Accounting Methods

This chapter has illustrated how to account for various types of investments. The Decision Guidelines feature shows which accounting method to use for each type of investment.

(margin notes)

⬸▮▮▮ ⬸▮▮▮ ⬸▮▮▮   Straight-line amortization of premium or discount on a bond investment is calculated the same way as it is calculated for bonds payable (see Chapter 15, pages 631–633).

▪ **Daily Exercise 16-15**
▪ **Daily Exercise 16-16**

▪ **Daily Exercise 16-17**

SUMMARY PROBLEM FOR YOUR REVIEW MID-CHAPTER

1. Identify the appropriate accounting method for each of the following situations:
   a. Investment in 25% of investee company's stock.
   b. Available-for-sale investment in stock.
   c. Investment in more than 50% of investee company's stock.

2. At what amount should the following available-for-sale investment portfolio be reported on the December 31 balance sheet? All the investments are less than 5% of the investee's stock.

Stock	Investment Cost	Current Market Value
DuPont	$ 5,000	$ 5,500
Exxon	61,200	53,000
Procter & Gamble	3,680	6,230

Journalize any adjusting entry required by these data.

3. Investor paid $67,900 to acquire a 40% equity-method investment in the common stock of Investee. At the end of the first year, Investee's net income was $80,000, and Investee declared and paid cash dividends of $55,000. Journalize Investor's (a) purchase of the investment, (b) share of Investee's net income, (c) receipt of dividends from Investee, and (d) sale of Investee stock for $80,100.

▪ SOLUTION

1. (a) Equity   (b) Market value   (c) Consolidation
2. Report the investments at market value, $64,730.

Stock	Investment Cost	Current Market Value
DuPont	$ 5,000	$ 5,500
Exxon	61,200	53,000
Procter & Gamble	3,680	6,230
Totals	$69,880	$64,730

Adjusting entry:

Unrealized Loss on Investments ($69,880 − $64,730)..................	5,150	
Allowance to Adjust Investment to Market...........................		5,150
To adjust investments to current market value.		

3. a. Long-Term Equity-Method Investment....................................... 67,900

Cash..		67,900
To purchase equity-method investment.		

b. Long-Term Equity-Method Investment ($80,000 × 0.40)......... 32,000
        Equity-Method Investment Revenue 32,000
    To record investment revenue.

c. Cash ($55,000 × 0.40)... 22,000
        Long-Term Equity-Method Investment............................ 22,000
    To record receipt of cash dividend on equity-method investment.

d. Cash 80,100
        Long-Term Equity-Method Investment
            ($67,900 + $32,000 − $22,000) 77,900
        Gain on Sale of Investment 2,200
    Sold investment.

Accounting for International Operations

Did you know that Exxon and Bank of America earn most of their revenue outside the United States? It is common for U.S. companies to do a large part of their business abroad. Coca-Cola, IBM, and Johnson & Johnson are also very active in other countries. Exhibit 16-6 shows the percentages of international sales and operating income for these companies.

Accounting for business activities across national boundaries makes up the field of *international accounting*. As communications and transportation improve and trade barriers fall, global integration makes international accounting more important. This section starts with economic structures and their impact on international accounting and then shows several applications to specific areas.

Economic Structures and Their Impact on International Accounting

The business environment varies widely across the globe. New York reflects the diversity of the market-driven economy of the United States. Japan's economy is similar to that of the United States, although Japanese business activity focuses more on imports and exports. The central government controls the economy of China, so private business decisions are only beginning to take root there. In Brazil, high rates of inflation have made historical-cost amounts meaningless, so accounting amounts are altered periodically to measure changes in the purchasing power of the cruzeiro, Brazil's monetary unit. International accounting deals with such differences in economic structures.

Foreign Currencies and Foreign-Currency Exchange Rates

Each country uses its own national currency. If Boeing, a U.S.–owned company, sells a 747 jet to Air France, will Boeing receive U.S. dollars or French francs? If the transaction takes place in dollars, Air France must exchange its francs for dollars to pay Boeing in U.S. currency. If the transaction takes place in francs, Boeing will receive francs, which it must exchange for dollars. In either case, a step has been added to the transaction: One company must convert domestic currency into foreign currency, or the other company must convert foreign currency into domestic currency.

EXHIBIT 16-6
Extent of International
Business

Company	Sales	Percent of International Operating Income or Net Income
Coca-Cola	71%	82%
IBM	60	86
Johnson & Johnson	51	48

Country	Monetary Unit	U.S. Dollar Value	Country	Monetary Unit	U.S. Dollar Value
Canada	Dollar	$0.70	Great Britain	Pound	$1.6748
European Common Market	European currency unit	1.11	Italy	Lira	0.0006
France	Franc	0.17	Japan	Yen	0.0076
Germany	Mark	0.56	Mexico	Peso	0.1182

Source: The Wall Street Journal, April 22, 1998, p. C17.

EXHIBIT 16-7
Foreign-Currency Exchange Rates

The price of one nation's currency may be stated in terms of another country's monetary unit. This measure of one currency against another currency is called the **foreign-currency exchange rate.** In Exhibit 16-7, the U.S. dollar value of a French franc is $0.17. This means that one French franc can be bought for 17 cents. Other currencies, such as the pound and the yen (also listed in Exhibit 16-7), are similarly bought and sold.

Foreign-Currency Exchange Rate. The measure of one currency against another currency.

We use the exchange rate to convert the cost of an item given in one currency to its cost in a second currency. We call this conversion a *translation.* Suppose an item costs 200 French francs. To compute its cost in dollars, we multiply the amount in francs by the conversion rate: 200 French francs × $0.17 = $34.

Strong Currency. A currency that is rising relative to other nations' currencies.

Currencies are often described as "strong" or "weak." The exchange rate of a **strong currency** is rising relative to other nations' currencies. The exchange rate of a **weak currency** is falling relative to other currencies.

Weak Currency. A currency that is falling relative to other nations' currencies.

Objective 6

Account for transactions stated in a foreign currency

Managing Cash in International Transactions

As international transactions become common, more companies manage their cash transactions conducted in foreign currencies. D. E. Shipp Belting, a small family-owned company in Waco, Texas, provides an example. Shipp makes conveyor belts that are used in a variety of industries. For example, M&M Mars, which makes Snickers candy bars in Waco, is an important customer of Shipp Belting. Farmers in the Rio Grande Valley along the Texas-Mexico border use Shipp conveyor belts to process vegetables. Some of these customers are on the Mexican side of the border, so Shipp Belting conducts some of its business in pesos, the Mexican monetary unit.

"... M&M Mars, which makes Snickers candy bars in Waco, is an important customer of Shipp Belting."

CASH RECEIPTS IN A FOREIGN CURRENCY Consider Shipp Belting's sale of conveyor belts to Artes de Mexico, a vegetable grower in Matamoros, Mexico. The sale can be conducted either in dollars or in pesos. If Artes de Mexico agrees to pay in dollars, Shipp avoids the complication of dealing in a foreign currency, and the transaction is the same as selling to M&M Mars across town. But suppose that Artes de Mexico orders 1 million pesos (approximately $130,000) worth of conveyor belts from Shipp. This large sale would be very important to Shipp Belting. Further suppose that Artes demands to pay in pesos and that Shipp reluctantly agrees to receive pesos instead of dollars.

Shipp will need to convert the pesos to dollars, so the transaction poses a challenge. What if the peso loses value—weakens as it takes more pesos to obtain each dollar—before Shipp collects from Artes? In this case, Shipp will not earn as much as expected on the sale. The following example shows how to account for international transactions that result in the receipt of a foreign currency. It also shows how to measure the effects of such transactions on a company's cash position and profits.

Shipp Belting sells goods to Artes de Mexico for a price of 1 million pesos on June 2. On that date, a peso was worth $0.1316. One month later, on July 2, the peso has weakened against the dollar and a peso is worth only $0.1266. Shipp receives 1 million pesos from Artes on July 2, but the dollar value of Shipp's cash receipt is $5,000 less than expected, so Shipp ends up earning less than hoped for on the transaction.

The following journal entries show how Shipp Belting would account for these transactions:

June 2	Accounts Receivable—Artes		
	(1,000,000 pesos × $0.1316)	131,600	
	Sales Revenue		131,600
	Sale on account.		
July 2	Cash (1,000,000 pesos × $0.1266)	126,600	
	Foreign-Currency Transaction Loss	5,000	
	Accounts Receivable—Artes		131,600
	Collection on account.		

■ Daily Exercise 16-18

If Shipp had required Artes to pay at the time of the sale, Shipp would have received pesos worth $131,600. But by waiting the normal 30-day collection period to receive cash, Shipp exposed itself to *foreign-currency exchange risk*, the risk of loss in an international transaction. In this case, Shipp experienced a $5,000 foreign-currency transaction loss and received $5,000 less cash than expected, as shown in the collection entry.

CASH DISBURSEMENTS IN A FOREIGN CURRENCY   Purchasing from a foreign company may also expose a company to foreign-currency exchange risk. To illustrate, assume Shipp Belting buys inventory from Gesellschaft Ltd., a Swiss company. After lengthy negotiations, the two companies decide on a price of 20,000 Swiss francs. On August 10, when Shipp receives the goods, the Swiss franc is quoted in international currency markets at $0.7999. When Shipp pays two weeks later, on August 24, the Swiss franc has weakened against the dollar—decreased in value to $0.7810. Shipp would record the purchase and payment as follows:

Aug. 10	Inventory (20,000 Swiss francs × $0.7999)	15,998	
	Accounts Payable—Gesellschaft Ltd		15,998
	Purchase on account.		
Aug. 24	Accounts Payable—Gesellschaft Ltd.	15,998	
	Foreign-Currency Transaction Gain		378
	Cash (20,000 Swiss francs × $0.7810)		15,620
	Payment on account.		

■ Daily Exercise 16-19

In this case, the Swiss franc weakened against the dollar, which caused Shipp to have a foreign-currency transaction gain. A company with a payable denominated in a foreign currency hopes that the dollar gets stronger. When the payment date arrives, the company can use fewer dollars to purchase the foreign currency and thereby reduce its cost.

REPORTING FOREIGN-CURRENCY TRANSACTION GAINS AND LOSSES ON THE INCOME STATEMENT   The Foreign-Currency Transaction Gain account is the record of the gains on transactions settled in a currency other than the dollar. Likewise, the Foreign-Currency Transaction Loss account shows the amount of the losses on transactions conducted in foreign currencies. The company reports the *net amount* of these two accounts on the income statement as Other gains (losses), as the case may be. For example, Shipp Belting would combine the $5,000 foreign-currency loss and the $378 gain and report the net loss of $4,622 on the income statement as follows:

Other gains (losses):	
Foreign-currency transaction loss, net ($5,000 – $378)	$(4,622)

These gains and losses fall into the "Other" category because they arise from buying and selling foreign currencies, not from the main line of the company's business (in the case of D. E. Shipp Belting, selling conveyor belts).

Managers examine these gains and losses to see how well the company is faring in foreign-currency transactions. The gains and losses may offset each other, and the net gain or loss may be small. But if losses exceed gains and the net loss reaches a critical level, managers may take action to shield themselves against the risk of further loss. One such action is hedging, which we discuss next.

HEDGING—A STRATEGY TO AVOID FOREIGN-CURRENCY TRANSACTION LOSSES

One way for U.S. companies to avoid foreign-currency transaction losses is to insist that international transactions be settled in dollars. This requirement puts the burden of currency translation on the foreign party. However, such a strategy may alienate customers and decrease sales, or it may cause customers to demand unreasonable credit terms. Another way for a company to protect itself from the effects of fluctuating foreign-currency exchange rates is by hedging.

Hedging means to protect oneself from losing money in one transaction by engaging in a counterbalancing transaction. A U.S. company selling goods to be collected in Mexican pesos expects to receive a fixed number of pesos in the future. If the peso is losing value, the U.S. company would expect the pesos to be worth fewer dollars than the amount of the receivable—an expected loss situation, as we saw for Shipp Belting.

The U.S. company may have accumulated payables stated in a foreign currency in the normal course of its business, such as the amount payable by Shipp to the Swiss company. Losses on the receipt of pesos may be approximately offset by gains on the payment of Swiss francs to Gesellschaft Ltd. Most companies do not have equal amounts of receivables and payables in foreign currency, so offsetting receivables and payables is imprecise. To obtain a more precise hedge, some companies buy *futures contracts*, which are contracts for foreign currencies to be received in the future. Futures contracts can effectively create a payable to exactly offset a receivable, and vice versa. Many companies that do business internationally use hedging techniques.

Hedging. Protecting oneself from losing money in one transaction by engaging in a counterbalancing transaction.

Consolidation of Foreign Subsidiaries

A U.S. company with a foreign subsidiary must consolidate the subsidiary's financial statements into its own statements for reporting to the public. The consolidation of a foreign subsidiary poses two special challenges. Many countries outside the United States specify accounting treatments that differ from American accounting principles. For the purpose of reporting to the American public, accountants for the parent company must first bring the subsidiary's statements into conformity with American GAAP.

The second accounting challenge arises when the subsidiary statements are expressed in a foreign currency. A preliminary step in the consolidation process is to translate the subsidiary statements into dollars. Then the dollar-value statements of the subsidiary can be combined with the parent's statements in the usual manner, as illustrated in the first part of this chapter.

The process of translating a foreign subsidiary's financial statements into dollars usually creates a *foreign-currency translation adjustment*. This item appears in the financial statements of most multinational companies and is reported as a separate item in stockholders' equity on the consolidated balance sheet. A translation adjustment arises due to changes in the foreign exchange rate over time. A positive translation adjustment can be viewed as an unrealized gain, similar to an unrealized gain on available-for-sale investments. A negative translation adjustment can be viewed as an unrealized loss, similar to an unrealized loss on available-for-sale investments.

International Accounting Standards

In this text, we focus on the principles of accounting that are generally accepted in the United States. Most of the methods of accounting are consistent throughout the world. Double-entry accounting, the accrual system, and the basic financial statements are used worldwide. Differences, however, do exist among countries, as shown in Exhibit 16-8.

In discussing depreciation (Chapter 10), we emphasized that in the United States the methods used for reporting to tax authorities differ from the methods used for reporting to shareholders. However, tax reporting and shareholder reporting are identical in many countries. For example, France has a "Plan Compatible" that specifies that a National Uniform Chart of Accounts be used for both tax returns and reporting to shareholders. German financial reporting is also determined primarily by tax laws. In Japan, certain principles are allowed for tax purposes only if they are also used for shareholder reporting.

Country	Inventories	Goodwill	Research and Development Costs
United States	Specific unit cost, FIFO, LIFO, weighted-average.	Amortized over period not to exceed 40 years.	Expensed as incurred.
Germany	LIFO is unacceptable for tax purposes and is not widely used.	Amortized over 5 years.	Expensed as incurred.
Japan	Similar to U.S.	Amortized over 5 years.	May be capitalized and amortized over 5 years.
United Kingdom (Great Britain)	LIFO is unacceptable for tax purposes and is not widely used.	Amortized over useful life or not amortized if life is indefinite.*	Expense research costs. Some development costs may be capitalized.

*Proposal being considered.

EXHIBIT 16-8
Some International Accounting Differences

For inventory, goodwill, and research and development costs, German accounting practices are more similar to those of the United States than to those of other countries. Despite the common heritage of the United States and the United Kingdom, U.S. and British accounting practices vary widely.

A company that sells its stock through a foreign stock exchange must follow the accounting principles of the foreign country. For example, British Petroleum (BP) stock is available through the New York Stock Exchange, so BP financial statements issued in the United States follow American GAAP.

A significant difference among countries is the extent to which the financial statements account for inflation. The FASB has experimented with requiring supplementary disclosure of inflation-adjusted numbers, but there is no requirement for such supplementary disclosure in the United States. In contrast, some countries have full or partial adjustments for inflation as part of their reporting to both investors and tax authorities. For example, Argentina and Brazil, which have experienced very high inflation rates, require all statements to be adjusted for changes in the general price level.

■ **Daily Exercise 16-20**

The globalization of business enterprises and capital markets is creating much interest in establishing common, worldwide accounting standards. There are probably too many cultural, social, and political differences to expect complete worldwide standardization of financial reporting in the near future. However, the number of differences is decreasing.

Several organizations are working to achieve worldwide harmony of accounting standards. Chief among these is the *International Accounting Standards Committee (IASC)*. Headquartered in London, the IASC operates much as the Financial Accounting Standards Board in the United States. It has the support of the accounting professions in the United States, most of the British Commonwealth countries, Japan, France, Germany, the Netherlands, and Mexico. However, the IASC has no authority to require compliance with its accounting standards. It must rely on cooperation by the various national accounting professions. The IASC tries to narrow the differences in international accounting standards.

Reporting Comprehensive Income

We introduced the reporting of comprehensive income in Chapter 14 (page 602) as required by *FASB Statement 130*. This chapter's coverage of accounting for available-for-sale investments and international operations completes the discussion of comprehensive income. Recall that *other comprehensive income* is a new category that can be reported below net income on the income statement. Two of the main elements of other comprehensive income are

- Unrealized gains and losses on available-for-sale investments
- Foreign-currency translation adjustments

EXHIBIT 16-9
Comprehensive Income

PANEL A—Reporting Comprehensive Income

NATIONAL EXPRESS COMPANY
Income Statement
December 31, 19X1

Revenues..		$10,000
Expenses (summarized)..		6,000
Net income...		4,000
Other comprehensive income:		
Unrealized loss on available-for-sale investments..............	$(1,000)	
Foreign-currency translation adjustment—a gain..............	2,000	1,000
Comprehensive income		$ 5,000

PANEL B—Reporting Unrealized Gains and Losses on Available-for-Sale Investments and Foreign-Currency Translation Adjustments on the Balance Sheet

NATIONAL EXPRESS COMPANY
Balance Sheet (partial)
December 31, 19X1

Stockholders' Equity

Common stock		$3,000
Retained earnings...		7,000
Accumulated other comprehensive income:		
Unrealized loss on available-for-sale investments..............		(1,000)
Foreign-currency translation adjustment—a gain..............		2,000
Total stockholders' equity..		$11,000

Both of these items are reported in two places in the financial statements:

1. The income statement—other comprehensive income
2. The balance sheet—within stockholders' equity

Exhibit 16-9 illustrates how to report these items, using assumed amounts for the first year of the company.

Reporting Investing Activities on the Statement of Cash Flows

Objective 7

Report investing transactions on the statement of cash flows

Investing activities include many types of transactions. In Chapter 10, we covered investing transactions in which companies purchase and sell long-term assets such as plant and equipment. Because the purchase of equipment is a type of long-term investment, it follows that the sale of equipment is also an investing activity. This chapter illustrates another type of investing activity that actually carries the name *investment*. The purchase and sale of investments in the stocks and bonds of other companies are also investing activities that are reported on the cash-flow statement.

Investing activities are reported on the statement of cash flows as the second category, after operating activities and before financing activities. This ordering is by design. Many business people view investing activities as the second most important thing a company does—less important than operating activities but more important than financing activities. Here is the logic:

1. What a company does with its cash (operating activities) is the major factor in business success or failure.
2. The assets in which a company invests (investing activities) shape the direction of the company's operations.

CAMPBELL SOUP COMPANY		
Consolidated Statement of Cash Flows (partial, adapted)		
(In millions)		1996
Cash Flows from Operating Activities:		
1	Net cash provided by operating activities..........	$X,XXX
	Cash Flows from Investing Activities:	
2	Purchases of plant assets	$ (416)
3	Sales of plant assets..	33
4	Businesses acquired (investments in stock)............	(186)
5	Sales of businesses (sales of investments)...............	80
6	Other	(120)
7	Net cash used in investing activities..................	(609)
	Cash Flows from Financing Activities:	
8	Net cash provided by financing activities	$ XXX

3. How a company finances its operations and its investments (financing activities) is less important than what the business buys and how it operates.

■ **Daily Exercise 16-21**

These are not hard-and-fast rules, and there are exceptions. Nevertheless, a company's investing transactions are vital to its ability to earn profits and provide jobs for its work force. Exhibit 16-10 provides excerpts from Campbell Soup Company's statement of cash flows. During 1996, Campbell Soup spent $186 million to acquire other companies (line 4). Campbell Soup sold other companies for a total of $80 million (line 5). In terms of its investing activities, Campbell Soup Company is definitely growing.

The Decision Guidelines feature summarizes the second half of the chapter. Study it before working the Summary Problem for Review.

"During 1996, Campbell Soup spent $186 million to acquire other companies (line 4). Campbell Soup sold other companies for a total of $80 million (line 5). In terms of its investing activities, Campbell Soup Company is definitely growing."

DECISION GUIDELINES	Foreign-Currency, Comprehensive Income, and Statement of Cash Flows
DECISION	**GUIDELINES**
When to record a • Foreign-currency transaction gain?	• When you receive foreign currency worth *more* in U.S. dollars than the amount of the receivable recorded earlier. • When you pay foreign currency that costs *less* in U.S. dollars than the amount of the payable recorded earlier.
• Foreign-currency transaction loss?	• When you receive foreign currency worth *less* in U.S. dollars than the amount of the receivable recorded earlier. • When you pay foreign currency that costs *more* in U.S. dollars than the amount of the payable recorded earlier.

What are the elements of comprehensive income?	• Net income, plus other comprehensive income:
	    Unrealized gains and losses on available-for-sale investments
	    Foreign-currency translation adjustments

What investment-related transactions are reported on the statement of cash flows?	• Purchases of investments (cash payments) • Sales of investments (cash receipts)

1. Journalize the following transactions of American Corp. Explanations are not required.

> **19X5**
> Nov. 16 Purchased equipment on account for 40,000 Swiss francs when the exchange rate was $0.63 per Swiss franc.
> 27 Sold merchandise on account to a Belgian company for 700,000 Belgian francs. Each franc is worth $0.0305.
> Dec. 22 Paid the Swiss company when the franc's exchange rate was $0.625.
> 31 Adjusted for the change in the exchange rate of the Belgian franc. Its current exchange rate is $0.0301.
> **19X6**
> Jan. 4 Collected from the Belgian company. The exchange rate is $0.0307.

2. In the 19X5 transactions, identify each of the following currencies as strong or weak:
   a. Swiss franc   **b.** Belgian franc   **c.** U.S. dollar

   Which currency strengthened during 19X6? Which currency weakened during 19X6?

■ SOLUTION

1. Entries for transactions stated in foreign currencies:

19X5				
Nov. 16	Equipment (40,000 × $0.63)		25,200	
	Accounts Payable			25,200
27	Accounts Receivable (700,000 × $0.0305)		21,350	
	Sales Revenue			21,350
Dec. 22	Accounts Payable		25,200	
	Cash (40,000 × $0.625)			25,000
	Foreign-Currency Transaction Gain			200
31	Foreign-Currency Transaction Loss			
	[700,000 × ($0.0305 − $0.0301)]		280	
	Accounts Receivable			280
19X6				
Jan. 4	Cash (700,000 × $0.0307)		21,490	
	Accounts Receivable ($21,350 − $280)			21,070
	Foreign-Currency Transaction Gain			420

2. During 19X5:
   a. Swiss franc—weak   **b.** Belgian franc—weak   **c.** U.S. dollar—strong

   During 19X6, the Belgian franc strengthened and the U.S. dollar weakened.

Summary of Learning Objectives

1. Account for trading investments. *Trading investments* are those the investor expects to sell within a few months. Therefore, trading investments are reported as short-term investments among the current assets. They are reported at their current market value.

2. Account for available-for-sale investments. *Available-for-sale securities* are all stock investments other than trading securities. They are classified as current assets if the business expects to sell them within a year or during the business's normal operating cycle if longer than a year. All other available-for-sale securities are classified as long-term investments. The *market-value* method is used to account for available-for-sale investments.

3. Use the equity method for investments. The *equity method* is used when an investor owns 20–50% of the stock of an investee. The investor applies its percentage of ownership in recording its share of the investee's net income and dividends. Equity-method investment revenue is reported under Other revenues on the income statement.

4. Understand consolidated financial statements. Ownership of more than 50% of a company's voting stock creates a *parent-subsidiary* relationship, and the parent company must use the *consolidation method* to account for its subsidiaries. Because the parent has control over the subsidiary, the subsidiary's financial statements are included in the parent's consolidated financial statements.

5. Account for long-term investments in bonds. *Held-to-maturity investments* are bonds and notes that the investor intends to hold until maturity. The *amortized-cost method* is used to account for held-to-maturity investments. An important part of this method is accruing interest receivable and amortizing any bond discount or premium over the life of the bond. Long-term bonds are presented on the balance sheet after current assets; interest revenue from bond investments appears on the income statement under Other revenues.

6. Account for transactions stated in a foreign currency. When two or more currencies are involved in a transaction, each company may incur a gain or loss on foreign-currency exchanges. These gains and losses are reported on the income statement under the category Other gains (losses). To protect themselves against foreign-currency transaction losses, some companies engage in *hedging*—they protect themselves from losing money on one transaction by engaging in a counterbalancing transaction.

7. Report investing transactions on the statement of cash flows. Investing activities are the second major category of transactions reported on the statement of cash flows (after operating activities and before financing activities). The cash-flow statement provides vital information regarding a company's sources and uses of cash for investing activities.

Accounting Vocabulary

available-for-sale securities (p. 675)
consolidated statements (p. 682)
controlling interest (p. 681)
equity method for investments (p. 679)

foreign-currency exchange rate (p. 687)
hedging (p. 689)
held-to-maturity securities (p. 683)
long-term investment (p. 675)
majority interest (p. 681)

marketable security (p. 675)
market-value method for investments (p. 675)
minority interest (p. 682)
parent company (p. 681)
short-term investment (p. 675)

strong currency (p. 687)
subsidiary company (p. 681)
trading securities (p. 675)
weak currency (p. 687)

Questions

1. How are stock prices quoted in the securities market? What is the investor's cost of 1,000 shares of Ford Motor Company stock at 55 3/4?
2. Show the positions of short-term investments and long-term investments on the balance sheet.
3. Outline the accounting methods for the different types of investments.
4. How does an investor record the receipt of a cash dividend on an available-for-sale investment? How does this investor record receipt of a stock dividend?
5. An investor paid $11,000 for 1,000 shares of stock—a trading investment—and later received a 10% stock dividend. At December 31, the investment's market value is $11,800. Compute the unrealized gain or loss on the investment.
6. When is an investment accounted for by the equity method? Outline how to apply the equity method. Mention how to record the purchase of the investment, the investor's proportion of the investee's net income, and receipt of a cash dividend from the investee.
7. Identify three transactions that cause increases or decreases to an equity-method investment acount.
8. Name the account that expresses the excess of the cost of an investment over the market value of the subsidiary's owners' equity. What type of account is this, and where in the financial statements is it reported?
9. When a parent company buys more than 50% but less than 100% of a subsidiary's stock, a new category of owners' equity

must appear on the balance sheet. What is this category called, and under what heading do most companies report it?
10. How would you measure the net income of a parent company with three subsidiaries? Assume that two subsidiaries are wholly (100%) owned and that the parent owns 60% of the third subsidiary.
11. An investor purchases Texaco bonds as a long-term investment. Suppose the face amount of the bonds is $100,000 and the purchase price is 101.3. The bonds pay interest at the stated annual rate of 8 percent. How much did the investor pay for the bonds? How much principal will the investor collect at maturity?
12. The purchase date of the bond investment in the preceding question was August 1, 19X2. The bonds pay semiannual interest on January 31 and July 31. How much cash interest will the investor receive during the year ended December 31, 19X2?
13. McVey, Inc., purchased inventory from a French company, agreeing to pay 100,000 francs. On the purchase date, the franc was quoted at $0.17. When McVey paid the debt, the price of a franc was $0.18. What account does McVey debit for the $1,000 difference between the cost of the inventory and the amount of cash paid?
14. Which country does not allow the use of the LIFO method for inventories?
15. On which financial statement should a company report cash payments to purchase the stock of another company? On what section of this financial statement?

Daily Exercises

Computing the cost of a stock investment
(Obj. 1, 2)

DE16-1 Compute the cost of each investment. Carry figures to the nearest cent.

a. 100 shares of Intel stock at 85 3/8.
b. 500 shares of IBM stock at 99 7/8. IBM pays a cash dividend of $3.20 per year.
c. 10,000 shares of Reebok stock at 46 1/2.
d. 50 shares of Sears stock at 52 3/4.

DE16-2 ◀▥ Link Back to Chapter 4 (Current Assets). Answer these questions about investments.

Classifying investments as current or long-term
(Obj. 1, 2)

1. Why is a trading investment always a current asset? Explain.
2. Is an available-for-sale investment a current asset or a long-term asset? What is the deciding factor?

DE16-3 Prentiss Corp. reports its annual financial statements on June 30 each year. Prentiss purchased 100 shares of stock in each of three companies:

Classifying investments as trading or available-for-sale
(Obj. 1, 2)

a. Investment to be sold within the next 9–12 months.
b. Investment to be sold within the next two years.
c. Investment to be sold within the next 90 days.

Classify each investment as (1) a current asset or a long-term asset, and (2) a trading investment or an available-for-sale investment.

DE16-4 Return to page 675, the example of Intel Corporation's short-term trading investment in Ford Motor Company stock.

Accounting for a trading investment
(Obj. 1)

1. How much did Intel pay for the short-term investment in Ford stock? Stated differently, what was Intel's cost of the Ford stock?
2. At December 31, 19X5, what was the current market value of Intel's short-term investment in Ford stock?
3. Suppose the Ford stock had increased in value to $29,000 on December 31, 19X5. Give Intel's adjusting entry at December 31, and show how Intel would report the short-term investment on its balance sheet.

DE16-5 Northland Food Stores completed the following investment transactions during 19X8 and 19X9:

Accounting for an investment; unrealized loss
(Obj. 1)

19X8
Dec. 6   Purchased 1,000 shares of Xerox stock at a price of $92 1/4 per share, intending to sell the investment next month.
    23   Received a cash dividend of $1.12 per share on the Xerox stock.
    31   Adjusted the investment to its market value of $91 per share.
19X9
Jan. 27   Sold the Xerox stock for $89 3/8 per share.

1. Classify Northland's investment as trading or available-for-sale.
2. Journalize Northland's investment transactions. Explanations are not required.

DE16-6 Southland Food Stores completed the following investment transactions during 19X6 and 19X7:

Accounting for an investment; unrealized gain
(Obj. 1)

19X6
Dec. 12   Purchased 500 shares of MCI stock at a price of $41 1/8 per share, intending to sell the investment next month.
    21   Received a cash dividend of $.23 per share on the MCI stock.
    31   Adjusted the investment to its market value of $43 1/8 per share.
19X7
Jan. 16   Sold the MCI stock for $45 3/8 per share.

1. Classify Southland's investment as trading or available-for-sale.
2. Journalize Southland's investment transactions. Explanations are not required. Round all amounts to the nearest dollar.

DE16-7 Newscorp of America holds a significant portfolio of short-term investments. On November 19, 19X6, Newscorp purchased a trading investment for $85,000. At December 31, 19X6, the market value of the trading investment was $84,000. Newscorp sold the investment for $88,000 on January 6, 19X7.

Measuring realized and unrealized gains and losses on a trading investment
(Obj. 1)

Compute Newscorp's gains and losses for 19X6 and 19X7. Identify each gain or loss as unrealized or as a gain or loss on sale of the investment.

DE16-8 An investor buys 500 shares of Exxon stock, paying $64 per share. Suppose Exxon distributes a 10% stock dividend. Later, the investor sells the Exxon stock for $60 per share.

Measuring gain or loss on the sale of an investment after receiving a stock dividend
(Obj. 2)

1. Compute the investor's new cost per share after receiving the stock dividend.
2. Compute the investor's gain or loss on the sale of this available-for-sale investment.

DE16-9 TFC Financial, Inc., completed these long-term available-for-sale investment transactions during 19X7.

19X7
Jan. 14 Purchased 300 shares of Sysco stock, paying $19 3/4 per share. TFC intends to hold the investment for the indefinite future.
Aug. 22 Received a cash dividend of $1.25 per share on the Sysco stock.
Dec. 31 Adjusted the Sysco investment to its current market value of $5,663.

1. Journalize TFC's investment transactions. Explanations are not required.
2. Show how to report the investment and any unrealized gain or loss on TFC's balance sheet at December 31, 19X7.

DE16-10 Use the data given in Daily Exercise 16-9. On August 4, 19X8, TFC Financial, Inc., sold its investment in Sysco stock for $21.50 per share.

1. Journalize the sale. No explanation is required.
2. How does the gain or loss that you recorded differ from the gain or loss that was recorded at December 31, 19X7?

DE16-11 Suppose on January 6, 19X8, General Motors paid $100 million for its 40% investment in Isuzu Motors. Assume Isuzu earned net income of $12.5 million and paid cash dividends of $10 million during 19X8.

1. What method should General Motors use to account for the investment in Isuzu? Give your reason.
2. Journalize these three transactions on the books of General Motors. Show all amounts in millions of dollars and include an explanation for each entry.
3. Post to the Long-Term Equity-Method Investment T-account. What is its balance after all the transactions are posted?

DE16-12 Use the data given in Daily Exercise 16-11. Assume that early in January 19X9, General Motors sold half its investment in Isuzu to Toyota. The sale price was $62 million. Compute General Motors' gain or loss on the sale.

DE16-13 Answer these questions about consolidation accounting:

1. Define a parent company. Define a subsidiary company.
2. How do consolidated financial statements differ from the financial statements of a single company?
3. Which company's name appears on the consolidated financial statements? How much of the subsidiary's stock must the parent own before reporting consolidated statements?

DE16-14 Two accounts that arise from consolidation accounting are goodwill and minority interest.

1. What is goodwill, and how does it arise? Which company reports goodwill, the parent or the subsidiary? Where is goodwill reported?
2. What is minority interest, and which company reports it, the parent or the subsidiary? Where is minority interest reported?

DE16-15 Prudential Securities owns vast amounts of corporate bonds. Suppose Prudential buys $1,000,000 of Eastman Kodak bonds at a price of 96. The Eastman Kodak bonds pay cash interest at the annual rate of 7% and mature within five years.

1. How much did Prudential pay to purchase the bond investment? How much will Prudential collect when the bond investment matures?
2. How much cash interest will Prudential Securities receive each year from Eastman Kodak?
3. Will Prudential Securities' annual interest revenue on the bond investment be more or less than the amount of cash interest received each year? Give your reason.
4. Compute Prudential Securities' annual interest revenue on this bond investment. Use the straight-line method to amortize the discount on the investment.

DE16-16 Return to Daily Exercise 16-15, the Prudential Securities investment in Eastman Kodak bonds. Journalize on Prudential's books:

a. Purchase of the bond investment on January 2, 19X1. Prudential expects to hold the investment to maturity.

b. Receipt of annual cash interest on December 31, 19X1.

c. Amortization of discount on December 31, 19X1.

d. Collection of the investment's face value at the maturity date on January 2, 19X6. (Assume the receipt of 19X5 interest and amortization of discount for 19X5 have already been recorded, so you may ignore these entries.)

DE16-17   Return to the bond investment situation on page 684. Assume the investor purchased the CBS bond investment on June 1, 19X2. Also assume that CBS pays cash interest on June 1 and December 1 each year. The bonds mature on June 1, 19X6.

Recording interest revenue on a bond investment
(Obj. 5)

1. Journalize the investor's accrual of cash interest and amortization of discount on the investment at December 31, 19X2. Use the straight-line amortization method.
2. What is the carrying amount of the bond investment at December 31, 19X2?

DE16-18   Suppose Coca-Cola Company sells soft-drink syrup to a Russian company on March 14. Coca-Cola agrees to accept 20,000,000 Russian rubles. On the date of sale, the ruble is quoted at $0.00017. Coca-Cola collects half the receivable on April 19, when the ruble is worth $0.00016. Then, on May 10, when the foreign-exchange rate of the ruble is $0.00019, Coca-Cola collects the final amount.
 Journalize these three transactions for Coca-Cola.

Accounting for transactions stated in a foreign currency
(Obj. 6)

DE16-19   Page 688 includes a sequence of Shipp Belting journal entries for transactions denominated in Mexican pesos. Suppose the foreign-exchange rate for a peso is $0.1370 on July 2. Record Shipp Belting's collection of cash on July 2.
 On page 688, Shipp Belting buys inventory for which Shipp must pay Swiss francs. Suppose a Swiss franc costs $0.8221 on August 24. Record Shipp Belting's payment of cash on August 24.

Accounting for transactions stated in a foreign currency
(Obj. 6)

DE16-20   Exhibit 16-8, page 690, outlines some differences between accounting in the United States and accounting in other countries. American companies transact more business with British companies than with any other. Interestingly, however, there are several important differences between American and British accounting. In your own words, describe those differences for inventories, goodwill, and research and development.

International accounting differences
(Obj. 6)

DE16-21   Companies divide their cash flows into three categories for reporting on the statement of cash flows.

Reporting cash flows
(Obj. 7)

1. List the three categories of cash flows in their order of importance, from most important to least important. Which category of cash flows is most closely related to the subject of this chapter?
2. Identify two types of transactions that companies report as cash flows from investing activities.

Exercises

E16-1   Curtiss-Wright Corporation developed the Wankel engine that thrust Mazda automobiles into prominence. Suppose Curtiss-Wright completed the following investment transactions:

Accounting for a trading investment
(Obj. 1)

19X8
Nov. 6   Purchased 1,000 shares of Titan Corporation stock for $69,000. Curtiss-Wright plans to sell the stock at a profit in the near future.
     30   Received a quarterly cash dividend of $0.85 per share on the Titan stock.
Dec. 31   Adjusted the investment in Titan stock. Current market value is $67,000, but Curtiss-Wright still plans to sell the stock early in 19X9.
19X9
Jan. 14   Sold the Titan stock for $70,000.

1. Make the entries to record Curtiss-Wright's investment transactions. Explanations are not required.

REQUIRED

2. Show how Curtiss-Wright would report its investment in the Titan stock on the balance sheet at December 31, 19X8.

E16-2   Journalize the following long-term available-for-sale investment transactions of McDermott, Inc.:

Journalizing transactions for an available-for-sale investment
(Obj. 2)

a. Purchased 400 shares (8%) of Vehicle Safety Corporation common stock at $44 per share, with the intent of holding the stock for the indefinite future.

b. Received cash dividend of $1 per share on the Vehicle Safety investment.

c. At year end, adjusted the investment account to current market value of $45 per share.

d. Sold the Vehicle Safety stock for the market price of $49 per share.

Journalizing transactions for an available-for-sale investment
(Obj. 2)

E16-3 Journalize the following investment transactions of Chateau Rose, Inc.:

Aug. 1   Purchased 300 shares (2%) of Madison Corporation common stock as a long-term available-for-sale investment, paying $44 per share.

Sep. 12   Received cash dividend of $1 per share on the Madison investment.

Nov. 23   Received 150 shares of Madison common stock in a 50% stock dividend. Round new cost per share to three decimal places.

Dec. 4   Unexpectedly sold the Madison stock for $29 per share.

Accounting for long-term investment transactions
(Obj. 2)

E16-4 Late in the current year, Travel Consumer Corporation bought 3,000 shares of Boeing common stock at $37.375, 600 shares of Anheuser-Busch stock at $46.75, and 1,400 shares of Hitachi stock at $79—all as available-for-sale investments. At December 31, *The Wall Street Journal* reports Boeing stock at $39.125, Anheuser-Busch at $48.50, and Hitachi at $68.25.

REQUIRED

1. Determine the cost and the market value of the long-term investment portfolio at December 31.

2. Record any adjusting entry needed at December 31.

3. What two items would Travel Consumer Corporation report on its balance sheet for the information given? Make the necessary disclosures.

Accounting for transactions under the equity method
(Obj. 3)

E16-5 Sears, Roebuck & Co. owns equity-method investments in several companies. Suppose Sears paid $2 million to acquire a 25% investment in Thai Imports Company. Assume that Thai Imports Company reported net income of $640,000 for the first year and declared and paid cash dividends of $420,000. Record the following in Sears' journal: (a) purchase of the investment, (b) its proportion of Thai Imports' net income, and (c) receipt of the cash dividends.

Measuring gain or loss on the sale of an equity-method investment
(Obj. 3)

E16-6 Without making journal entries, record the transactions of Exercise 16-5 directly in the Sears account, Long-Term Equity-Method Investment in Thai Imports. Assume that after all the noted transactions took place, Sears sold its entire investment in Thai Imports for cash of $2,400,000. How much is Sears's gain or loss on the sale of the investment?

Applying the appropriate accounting method for investments
(Obj. 3)

E16-7 Analog Measurement Corporation paid $160,000 for a 40% investment in the common stock of Kahn, Inc. For the first year, Kahn reported net income of $84,000 and at year end declared and paid cash dividends of $16,000. On the balance sheet date, the market value of Analog's investment in Kahn stock was $134,000.

REQUIRED

1. Which method is appropriate for Analog to use in accounting for its investment in Kahn? Why?

2. Show everything that Analog would report for the investment and any investment revenue in its year-end financial statements.

3. What role does the market value of the investment play in this situation?

Recording bond investment transactions
(Obj. 5)

E16-8 On March 31, 19X3, Crusader Corporation paid 92 1/4 for 7% bonds of Mattson Financial Services as a long-term held-to-maturity investment. The maturity value of the bonds will be $20,000 on September 30, 19X7. The bonds pay interest on March 31 and September 30. At December 31, the bonds' market value is 93.

REQUIRED

1. What method should Crusader Corporation use to account for its investment in the Mattson bonds?

2. Using the straight-line method of amortizing the discount, journalize all of Crusader Corporation's transactions on the bonds for 19X3.

3. Show how Crusader would report the bond investment on its balance sheet at December 31, 19X3.

Managing and accounting for foreign-currency transactions
(Obj. 6)

E16-9 Journalize the following foreign-currency transactions. Explanations are not required.

Nov. 17   Purchased inventory on account from a Japanese company. The price was 200,000 yen, and the exchange rate of the yen was $0.0090.

Dec. 16   Paid the Japanese supplier when the exchange rate was $0.0091.

19   Sold merchandise on account to a French company at a price of 60,000 French francs. The exchange rate of the franc was $0.16.

30   Collected from the French company when the exchange rate was $0.17.

On November 18, immediately after your purchase, and on December 20, immediately after your sale, which currencies did you want to strengthen? Which currencies did in fact strengthen? Explain your reasoning in detail.

E16-10 During fiscal year 19X5, The Home Depot, which operates over 400 home improvement centers throughout the United States, reported net income of $604 million and paid $162 million to acquire other businesses. Home Depot paid $1,103 million to open new stores and sold property, plant, and equipment for $50 million. The company purchased long-term investments in stocks and bonds at a cost of $94 million and sold other long-term investments for $454 million. During the year, the company also cashed in other investments for $96 million.

Preparing the statement of cash flows **(Obj. 7)**

Prepare the investing activities section of The Home Depot's statement of cash flows. Based on The Home Depot's investing activities, does it appear that the company is growing or shrinking? How can you tell?

REQUIRED

CHALLENGE EXERCISES

E16-11 AMP Incorporated, a world leader in the manufacture of electronic connection devices, reported the following stockholders' equity on its balance sheet at December 31:

Analyzing available-for-sale investments **(Obj. 2)**

AMP INCORPORATED Balance Sheet (partial, adapted)	
	(In thousands) 19X4
Shareholders' Equity:	
Common stock...	$ 12,480
Other capital...	214,090
Net unrealized gains on available-for-sale investments..........	21,585
Retained earnings	2,329,691
Treasury stock, at cost	(243,431)
Total shareholders' equity	$2,334,415

1. AMP's balance sheet also reports available-for-sale investments at $287,898,000 ($287,898 thousand). What was AMP's cost of the investments? What was the market value of the investments on December 31, 19X4?

2. Suppose AMP sold its available-for-sale investments in 19X5 for $259,000,000 ($259,000 thousand). Determine the gain or loss on sale of the investments.

REQUIRED

E16-12 Whirlpool Corporation is a leading manufacturer of household appliances. In Brazil and Mexico, Whirlpool operates through affiliated companies, whose stock Whirlpool owns in various percentages between 20 and 50 percent. Whirlpool's financial statements reported these items (adapted):

Analyzing equity-method investments **(Obj. 3)**

	(In millions)	
	19X8	19X7
Balance Sheet (adapted)		
Equity-method investments....................................	$286	$296
Statement of Cash Flows		
Increase in equity-method investments.................	12	2
Income Statement		
Equity-method investment revenue (losses)..........	(13)	4

Whirlpool's financial statements reported no sales of equity-method investments during 19X8 or 19X7.

Prepare a T-account for Equity-Method Investments to determine the amount of dividends Whirlpool Corporation received from investee companies during 19X8. Show your work.

REQUIRED

Beyond the Numbers

BN16-1 Prudyat Sen inherited some investments, and he has received the annual reports of the companies in which the funds are invested. The financial statements of the companies are puzzling to Sen, and he asks you the following questions:

Understanding the consolidation method for investments **(Obj. 4)**

1. The companies label their financial statements as *consolidated* balance sheet, *consolidated* income statement, and so on. What are consolidated financial statements?

2. The consolidated balance sheet lists the asset Goodwill. What is goodwill? Does the presence of goodwill mean that the company's stock has increased in value?

Write a memo to respond to each of Sen's questions.

ETHICAL ISSUE

Citizen Utilities owns 18% of the voting stock of Mohawk Electric Power Company. The remainder of the Mohawk stock is held by numerous investors with small holdings. Monica Kurtz, president of Citizen Utilities and a member of Mohawk's board of directors, heavily influences Mohawk Electric Power Company's policies.

Under the market-value method of accounting for investments, Citizen's net income increases as it receives dividend revenue from Mohawk Power. Citizen Utilities pays President Kurtz a bonus computed as a percentage of Citizen's net income. Therefore, Kurtz can control her personal bonus to a certain extent by influencing Mohawk's dividends.

A recession occurs in 19X0, and Citizen Utilities' income is low. Kurtz uses her power to have Mohawk Electric Power pay a large cash dividend. The action requires Mohawk to borrow in order to pay the dividend.

REQUIRED

1. In getting Mohawk to pay the large cash dividend, is Kurtz acting within her authority as a member of the Mohawk board of directors? Are Kurtz's actions ethical? Whom can her actions harm?

2. Discuss how using the equity method of accounting for investments would decrease Kurtz's potential for manipulating her bonus.

Problems (GROUP A)

Accounting for trading investments
(Obj. 1)

P16-1A During the second half of 19X6, operations of Four Seasons, Inc., generated excess cash, which the company invested in securities, as follows:

July	3	Purchased 5,000 shares of common stock as a trading investment, paying $9.25 per share.
Aug.	14	Received semiannual cash dividend of $0.32 per share on the trading investment.
Sep.	15	Sold the trading investment for $10.50 per share.
Nov.	24	Purchased trading investments for $226,000.
Dec.	31	Adjusted the trading securities to their market value of $219,000.

REQUIRED

1. Record the transactions in the journal of Four Seasons. Explanations are not required.

2. Post to the Short-Term Investment account. Then show how to report the short-term investment on the Four Seasons balance sheet at December 31.

Accounting for available-for-sale and equity-method investments
(Obj. 2, 3)

P16-2A The beginning balance sheet of Nation Online Incorporated included the following:

Long–Term Equity-Method Investments.......... $344,000

The company completed the following investment transactions during the year:

Mar.	2	Purchased 2,000 shares of ATI, Inc., common stock as a long-term available-for-sale investment, paying $12 1/4 per share.
	5	Purchased new long-term equity-method investment at cost of $540,000.
Apr.	21	Received cash dividend of $0.75 per share on the ATI investment.
May	17	Received cash dividend of $47,000 from the equity-method investment.
Oct.	8	Purchased long-term available-for-sale investment in Bell Corp. stock for $136,000.
	17	Received cash dividend of $49,000 from the equity-method investment.
Dec.	31	Received annual reports from the equity-method investee companies. Their total net income for the year was $550,000. Of this amount, Nation Online's proportion is 22 percent.
	31	Adjusted the available-for-sale investments to market value. The market values of Nation Online's investments are ATI, $29,800; Bell, $132,400; Equity-Method Investments, $800,000.

REQUIRED

1. Record the transactions in the journal of Nation Online Incorporated.

2. Post entries to the Long-Term Equity-Method Investments T-account, and determine its balance at December 31. Do likewise for the Long-Term Available-for-Sale Investments T-account and the Allowance to Adjust Investments to Market T-account.

3. Show how to report the Long-Term Available-for-Sale Investments and the Long-Term Equity-Method Investments accounts on Nation Online's balance sheet at December 31.

P16-3A Manhattan Company owns numerous investments in the stock of other companies. Assume that Manhattan completed the following long-term investment transactions:

Reporting investments on the balance sheet and the related revenue on the income statement
(Obj. 2, 3)

19X2

Feb.	12	Purchased 20,000 shares, which exceeds 20%, of the common stock of Agribusiness, Inc., at total cost of $715,000.
July	1	Purchased 8,000 additional shares of Agribusiness common stock at cost of $300,000.
Aug.	9	Received annual cash dividend of $0.90 per share on the Agribusiness investment.
Oct.	16	Purchased 800 shares of Apex Company common stock as an available-for-sale investment, paying $41 1/2 per share.
Nov.	30	Received semiannual cash dividend of $0.60 per share on the Apex investment.
Dec.	31	Received annual report from Agribusiness, Inc. Net income for the year was $510,000. Of this amount, Manhattan's proportion is 35 percent.

The current market value of the Apex stock is $34,100. The market value of the Agribusiness stock is $967,000.

REQUIRED

1. For which investment is current market value used in the accounting? Why is market value used for one investment and not the other?

2. Show what Manhattan Company would report on its year-end balance sheet for these investments. It is helpful to use a T-account for the investment in Agribusiness stock.

P16-4A Financial institutions such as insurance companies hold large quantities of bond investments. Suppose Ostway Insurance Co. purchases $600,000 of 9% bonds of Royal Corporation for 103 on March 1, 19X1. These bonds pay interest on March 1 and September 1 each year. They mature on March 1, 19X8. At December 31, 19X1, the market price of the bonds is 103 1/2.

Accounting for a bond investment; straight line amortization of premium
(Obj. 5)

REQUIRED

1. Journalize Ostway's purchase of the bonds as a long-term investment on March 1, 19X1 (to be held to maturity). Then record Ostway's receipt of cash interest and amortization of premium at September 1, 19X1, and the amortization of premium and accrual of interest revenue at December 31, 19X1. The straight-line method is appropriate for amortizing premium.

2. Show how to report this long-term bond investment on Ostway Insurance Co.'s balance sheet at December 31, 19X1.

P16-5A ◄▥ *Link Back to Chapter 15 (Effective-Interest Amortization of Discount).* On December 31, 19X1, when the market interest is 8%, an investor purchases $500,000 of Bali Corp., 7.4%, six-year bonds at issuance. The cost of this long-term bond investment is $486,123, and the investor expects to hold the investment to maturity.

Accounting for a bond investment; effective-interest amortization of discount
(Obj. 5)

REQUIRED

Journalize the purchase on December 31, 19X1, the first semiannual interest receipt on June 30, 19X2, and the year-end interest receipt on December 31, 19X2. The investor uses the effective-interest amortization method. Prepare a schedule for amortizing the discount on bond investment through December 31, 19X2. Use Exhibit 15-4, page 637, as a guide.

P16-6A Suppose United Rubber Corporation completed the following transactions:

Recording foreign-currency transactions and reporting the transaction gain or loss
(Obj. 6)

May	1	Sold inventory on account to Pirelli Tire Company for $19,000. The exchange rate of the Italian lira is $0.0007, and Pirelli agrees to pay in dollars.
	10	Purchased supplies on account from a Canadian company at a price of Canadian $50,000. The exchange rate of the Canadian dollar is $0.80, and payment will be in Canadian dollars.
	17	Sold inventory on account to an English firm for 100,000 British pounds. Payment will be in pounds, and the exchange rate of the pound is $1.50.
	22	Collected from Pirelli.
June	18	Paid the Canadian company. The exchange rate of the Canadian dollar is $0.77.
	24	Collected from the English firm. The exchange rate of the British pound is $1.47.

REQUIRED

1. Record these transactions in United's journal, and show how to report the transaction gain or loss on the income statement.

2. How will what you learned in this problem help you structure international transactions?

P16-7A Excerpts from Intel Corporation's statement of cash flows, as adapted, appear as follows:

(In millions)	19X5	19X4	19X3
INTEL CORPORATION			
Consolidated Statement of Cash Flows (partial, adapted)			
Three Years Ended December 31			
Cash flows provided by (used for) investing activities:			
Additions to property, plant, and equipment	$(3,550)	$(2,441)	$(1,933)
Purchases of long-term, available-for-sale investments	(129)	(975)	(1,165)
Sales of long-term, available-for-sale investments	114	10	5
Maturities [sales of] available-for-sale investments................	878	503	(244)
Net cash (used for) investing activities....................................	**$(2,687)**	**$(2,903)**	**$(3,337)**

REQUIRED

As the chief executive officer of Intel Corporation, your duty is to write the management letter to your stockholders to explain Intel's investing activities during 19X5. Compare the company's overall level of investment with preceding years.

Problems (GROUP B)

Accounting for trading investments
(Obj. 1)

P16-1B During the second half of 19X8, the operations of Picadilly, Inc., generated excess cash, which the company invested in securities, as follows:

July   2   Purchased 2,000 shares of common stock as a trading investment, paying $12.75 per share.
Aug. 21   Received semiannual cash dividend of $0.45 per share on the trading investment.
Sep. 16   Sold the trading investment for $13.50 per share.
Oct.   8   Purchased trading investments in stock for $136,000.
Dec. 31   Adjusted the trading securities to their market value of $132,000.

REQUIRED

1. Record the transactions in the journal of Picadilly, Inc. Explanations are not required.
2. Post to the Short-Term Investments account, and show how to report the short-term investments on Picadilly's balance sheet at December 31.

Accounting for available-for-sale and
equity-method investments
(Obj. 2, 3)

P16-2B The beginning balance sheet of Lions, Inc., included the following:

Long-Term Equity-Method Investments.......... $657,000

The company completed the following investment transactions during the year:

Mar. 3   Purchased 5,000 shares of BCM Software common stock as a long-term available-for-sale investment, paying $9 1⁄4 per share.
        4   Purchased new long-term equity-method investment at cost of $408,000.
May 14   Received cash dividend of $0.82 per share on the BCM investment.
June 15   Received cash dividend of $27,000 from equity-method investment.
Oct. 24   Purchased long-term available-for-sale investment in Northern Communication stock for $226,000.
Dec. 15   Received cash dividend of $29,000 from equity-method investment.
        31   Received annual reports from equity-method investee companies. Their total net income for the year was $620,000. Of this amount, Lions' proportion is 30 percent.
        31   Adjust the available-for-sale investments to market value. The market values of Lions' investments are BCM, $48,100; Northern, $219,000; Affiliated companies, $947,000.

REQUIRED

1. Record the transactions in the journal of Lions, Inc.
2. Post entries to the Long-Term Equity-Method Investments T-account, and determine its balance at December 31. Do likewise for the Long-Term Available-for-Sale Investments T-account and the Allowance to Adjust Investments to Market T-account.
3. Show how to report the Long-Term Available-for-Sale Investments and the Long-Term Equity-Method Investments on the Lions balance sheet at December 31.

P16-3B Sterling Chemical Company owns stock in numerous other companies. Assume that Sterling completed the following long-term investment transactions:

Reporting investments on the balance sheet and the related revenue on the income statement
(Obj. 2, 3)

19X4

May 1	Purchased 8,000 shares, which exceeds 20%, of the common stock of MIC Company at total cost of $720,000.
July 1	Purchased 1,600 additional shares of MIC Company common stock at cost of $140,000.
Sep. 15	Received semiannual cash dividend of $1.40 per share on the MIC investment.
Oct. 12	Purchased 1,000 shares of JAX Corporation common stock as an available-for-sale investment paying $22 1/2 per share.
Dec. 14	Received semiannual cash dividend of $0.75 per share on the JAX investment.
Dec. 31	Received annual report from MIC Company. Net income for the year was $350,000. Of this amount, Sterling's proportion is 21.25 percent.

The current market value of the JAX stock is $20,700. The market value of the MIC stock is $865,000.

REQUIRED

1. For which investment is current market value used in the accounting? Why is market value used for one investment and not the other?

2. Show what Sterling Chemical Company would report on its year-end balance sheet for these investments. (It is helpful to use a T-account for the investment in MIC stock.)

P16-4B Financial institutions such as insurance companies and pension plans hold large quantities of bond investments. Suppose Prudential Bache, Inc., purchases $500,000 of 8% bonds of General Motors Corporation for 92 on January 31, 19X0. These bonds pay interest on January 31 and July 31 each year. They mature on July 31, 19X8. At December 31, 19X0, the market price of the bonds is 93.

Accounting for a bond investment; amortizing discount by the straight-line method
(Obj. 5)

REQUIRED

1. Journalize Prudential Bache's purchase of the bonds as a long-term investment on January 31, 19X0 (to be held to maturity), receipt of cash interest and amortization of discount on July 31, 19X0, and accrual of interest revenue and amortization of discount at December 31, 19X0. The straight-line method is appropriate for amortizing discount.

2. Show how to report this long-term bond investment on Prudential Bache's balance sheet at December 31, 19X0.

P16-5B ◄▥ *Link Back to Chapter 15 (Effective-Interest Amortization of Discount)*. On December 31, 19X1, when the market interest rate is 10%, an investor purchases $400,000 of Tepotzlan, Inc., 9.5%, ten-year bonds at issuance. The cost of this bond investment was $387,578 and the investor expects to hold the investment to maturity.

Accounting for a bond investment; amortizing discount by the effective-interest method
(Obj. 5)

REQUIRED

Journalize the purchase on December 31, 19X1, the first semiannual interest receipt on June 30, 19X2, and the year-end interest receipt on December 31, 19X2. The investor uses the effective-interest amortization method. Prepare a schedule for amortizing the discount on the bond investment through December 31, 19X2. Use Exhibit 15-4, page 637, as a guide.

P16-6B Suppose PepsiCo, Inc., completed the following transactions:

Recording foreign-currency transactions and reporting the transaction gain or loss
(Obj. 6)

May 4	Sold soft-drink syrup on account to a Mexican company for $71,000. The exchange rate of the Mexican peso is $0.141, and the customer agrees to pay in dollars.
13	Purchased inventory on account from a Canadian company at a price of Canadian $100,000. The exchange rate of the Canadian dollar is $0.75, and payment will be in Canadian dollars.
20	Sold goods on account to an English firm for 70,000 British pounds. Payment will be in pounds, and the exchange rate of the pound is $1.50.
27	Collected from the Mexican company.
June 21	Paid the Canadian company. The exchange rate of the Canadian dollar is $0.72.
July 17	Collected from the English firm. The exchange rate of the British pound is $1.47.

REQUIRED

1. Record these transactions in PepsiCo's journal, and show how to report the transaction gain or loss on the income statement.

2. How will what you learned in this problem help you structure international transactions?

P16-7B   Excerpts from The Coca-Cola Company's statement of cash flows, as adapted, appear as follows:

| THE COCA-COLA COMPANY AND SUBSIDIARIES | |
Consolidated Statements of Cash Flows (partial, adapted)	
(In millions)	**Year Ended December 31,** 19X5
Investing Activities	
Acquisitions and investments, principally bottling companies	$(338)
Purchases of investment securities	(190)
Proceeds from disposals of investments	580
Purchases of property, plant, and equipment	(937)
Proceeds from disposals of property, plant, and equipment	44
Other investing activities	(172)
Net cash used in investing activities	$(1,013)

REQUIRED

As the chief executive officer of The Coca-Cola Company, your duty is to write the management letter to your stockholders explaining Coca-Cola's individual investing activities during 19X5.

Applying Your Knowledge

DECISION CASE

Explaining the market value and equity methods of accounting for investments
(Obj. 1, 2)

Sarah Ringo is the manager of Avanti Corp., whose year end is December 31. The company made two investments during the first week of January 19X7. Both investments are to be held for the indefinite future. Information about the investments follows:

a.   Avanti purchased 30% of the common stock of Rotary Motor Co. for its book value of $200,000. During the year ended December 31, 19X7, Rotary earned $106,000 and paid a total dividend of $53,000. At year end, the market value of the Rotary investment is $261,000.

b.   One thousand shares of the common stock of Oxford Medical Corporation were purchased as an available-for-sale investment for $95,000. During the year ended December 31, 19X7, Oxford paid Avanti a dividend of $3,000. Oxford earned a profit of $317,000 for that period, and at year end, the market value of Avanti's investment in Oxford stock was $107,000.

Ringo has come to you to ask how to account for the investments. Avanti has never had such investments before. Explain the proper accounting to her by indicating that different accounting methods apply to different situations.

REQUIRED

Help Ringo understand by writing a memo to

1.   Describe the methods of accounting applicable to these investments.
2.   Identify which method should be used to account for the investments in Rotary Motor Co. and Oxford Medical Corporation. Also indicate the dollar amount to report for each investment on the year-end balance sheet.

FINANCIAL STATEMENT CASE

Investments in stock
(Obj. 3, 4)

Obtain the annual report of a company of your choosing. Answer the following questions about the company. Concentrate on the current year in the annual report you select.

REQUIRED

1.   Many companies refer to other companies in which they own equity-method investments as *affiliated companies.* This signifies the close relationship between the two entities even though the investor does not own a controlling interest.
     Does the company have equity-method investments? Cite the evidence. If present, what were the balances in the investment account at the beginning and the end of the current year? If the company had no equity-method investments, skip the next question.
2.   Scan the income statement. If equity-method investments are present, what amount of revenue (or income) did the company earn on the investments during the current year? Scan the statement of cash flows. What amount of dividends did the company receive during the current year from companies in which it held equity-method investments? *Note:* The

amount of dividends received may not be disclosed. If not, you can still compute the amount of dividends received, from the following T-account:

Investments, at Equity

Beg. bal. (from balance sheet)	W		
Equity-method revenue (from income statement)	X	Dividends received (unknown; must compute)	Y
End. bal. (from balance sheet)	Z		

3. The company probably owns some consolidated subsidiaries. You can tell whether the parent company owns 100% or less of the subsidiaries. Examine the income statement and the balance sheet to determine whether there are any minority interests. If so, what does that fact indicate?

4. The stockholders' equity section of most balance sheets lists Foreign Currency Translation Adjustment or a similar account title. A positive amount signifies a gain, and a negative amount indicates a loss. The change in this account balance from the beginning of the year to the end of the year signals whether the U.S. dollar was strong or weak during the year in comparison to the foreign currencies. For the company you are analyzing, was the dollar strong or weak during the current year?

Team Project

Pick a stock from *The Wall Street Journal* or other database or publication. Assume that your group purchases 1,000 shares of the stock as a short-term trading investment and that your 1,000 shares are less than 20% of the company's outstanding stock. Research the stock in *Value Line, Moody's Investor Record*, or other source to determine whether the company pays cash dividends and, if so, how much and at what intervals.

1. Track the stock for a period assigned by your professor. Over the specified period, keep a daily record of the price of the stock to see how well your investment has performed. Each day, search the Corporate Dividend News in *The Wall Street Journal* to keep a record of any dividends you've received. End the period of your analysis with a month end, such as September 30 or December 31.

REQUIRED

2. Journalize all transactions that you have experienced, including the investment purchase, dividends received (both cash dividends and stock dividends), and any year-end adjustment required by the accounting method that is appropriate for your investment. Assume you will prepare financial statements on the ending date of your study.

3. Show what you will report on your company's balance sheet, income statement, and statement of cash flows as a result of your investment transactions.

Internet Exercise

General Motors is a truly global company. Some of its automobiles are, in part, designed in Australia, assembled in Mexico using raw materials from South Africa, and ultimately sold in the United States. One of the largest companies in the world, General Motors employs hundreds of thousands of people across 50 countries and must manage its operations with a worldwide perspective.

GM's financial statements reflect this international orientation. The company's results are subdivided by geographic sales regions or by subsidiaries. This organization provides investors with a strong understanding of the sources behind GM's success.

PHLIP

1. Go to **http://www.gm.com**. From the home page click on **About Our Company**. Using the pull-down menu for *Investor Information*, select *Annual Reports* and click on **Go**. The sections titled *Financial Highlights, Sector Reviews*, and *Management's Discussion and Analysis* will be used to answer the following questions.

2. Refer to the **Sector Reviews**. Information for how many sectors is reported?

REQUIRED

3. Select the **North American Operations Review** (GM-NAO). Scroll down to review the Financial Highlights and Vehicle Unit Deliveries. For the most recent year, record the amount of *Net sales and revenues, Net income*, and the number of vehicle *Wholesale Sales* for GM-NAO.

4. Go back and select the **International Operations Review** (GMIO). Scroll down to review the Financial Highlights and Vehicle Unit Deliveries. For the most recent year, record the amount of *Net sales and revenues, Net income*, and the number of vehicle *Wholesale Sales* for GMIO.

5. Refer to the **Financial Highlights** section. For the most recent year, record the amount of *Net sales and revenues from manufactured products, Net income*, and *Worldwide whole salesales* (in units). Are these amounts reported on consolidated financial statements? Explain. Compare the amounts reported for *Net sales and revenues from manufactured products, Net income*, and *Worldwide wholesale sales* (in units) to the amounts reported earlier for GM-NAO and GMIO. Using only the information reported above, calculate the amount of *Net sales and revenues from manufactured products, Net income*, and *Worldwide wholesale sales* (in units) contributed by the other sectors. Comment on the results of your calculations.

Preparing Consolidated Financial Statements

The preparation of consolidated financial statements includes summing the statement amounts (cash, receivables, inventory, and so on) of the parent company and its majority-owned subsidiaries. This appendix shows how the consolidation method works for the balance sheet. We illustrate two cases:

- Parent Company owns all of Subsidiary's Stock (called a wholly-owned subsidiary)
- Parent Company owns less than 100% of Subsidiary's Stock

Consolidated Balance Sheet—Parent Corporation Owns All of Subsidiary's Stock

Suppose that Parent Corporation has purchased all the outstanding common stock of Subsidiary Corporation at its book value of $150,000. In addition, Parent Corporation loaned Subsidiary Corporation $80,000. To record these transactions, Parent Corporation and Subsidiary Corporation would make the following entries:

Parent Corporation Books[1]			Subsidiary Corporation Books		
Investment in Subsidiary					
Corporation............................	150,000		No entry		
Cash.................................		150,000			
Note Receivable from			Cash	80,000	
Subsidiary	80,000		Note Payable to Parent...........		80,000
Cash		80,000			

Each legal entity has its individual set of books. The consolidated entity does not keep a separate set of books. Instead, a work sheet is used to prepare the consolidated statements. (We will see two of these work sheets shortly.) A major concern in consolidation accounting is this:

> Do not double-count—that is, do not count the same item twice in a set of consolidated financial statements.

EXPLANATION OF ELIMINATION ENTRY (A)   Exhibit 16-A1 on page 707 shows the work sheet for consolidating the balance sheet. Consider the elimination entry for the parent-subsidiary ownership accounts. Entry (a) credits the parent Investment account to eliminate its debit balance. It also eliminates the subsidiary stockholder's equity accounts by debiting Common Stock for $100,000 and Retained Earnings for $50,000. Because these accounts represent the same thing—Subsidiary's equity—they must be eliminated from the consolidated totals. If they weren't, the same item would be counted twice.

The resulting consolidated balance sheet reports no Investment in Subsidiary account, and the consolidated totals for Common Stock and Retained Earnings are those of Parent Corporation only. The consolidated amounts appear in the final column of the consolidation work sheet.

EXPLANATION OF ELIMINATION ENTRY (B)   Parent Corporation loaned $80,000 to Subsidiary Corporation, and Subsidiary signed a note payable to Parent. Therefore, Parent's balance sheet includes an $80,000 note receivable, and Subsidiary's balance sheet reports a note payable for the same amount. The parent's receivable and the subsidiary's payable represent the same resources (all entirely within the consolidated entity) and so

---

[1]The parent company may use either the cost method or the equity method for entries to the Investment account. Regardless of the method used, the consolidated statements are the same. Advanced accounting courses deal with this topic.

Assets	Parent Corporation	Subsidiary Corporation	Eliminations Debit	Eliminations Credit	Consolidated Amounts
Cash	12,000	18,000			30,000
Note receivable from Subsidiary	80,000	—		(b) 80,000	—
Inventory	104,000	91,000			195,000
Investment in Subsidiary..........	150,000	—		(a) 150,000	—
Other assets	218,000	138,000			356,000
Total............................	564,000	247,000			581,000
Liabilities and Stockholders' Equity					
Accounts payable	43,000	17,000			60,000
Notes payable	190,000	80,000	(b) 80,000		190,000
Common stock	176,000	100,000	(a) 100,000		176,000
Retained earnings	155,000	50,000	(a) 50,000		155,000
Total............................	564,000	247,000	230,000	230,000	581,000

EXHIBIT 16-A1
Work Sheet for Consolidated Balance Sheet—Parent Corporation Owns All of Subsidiary's Stock

must be eliminated. Entry (b) accomplishes this. After this work sheet entry, the consolidated amount for notes receivable is zero. The $190,000 balance of Notes Payable is the amount that the Consolidated entity owes outsiders.

Consolidated Balance Sheet—Parent Company Owns Less than 100% of Subsidiary's Stock

When a parent company owns more than 50% (a majority) of the subsidiary's stock but less than 100% of it, a new category of owners' equity, called *minority interest*, must appear on the consolidated balance sheet. Suppose Parent Company buys 75% of Subsidiary's common stock. *Minority interest* is the subsidiary's equity that is held by stockholders other than the parent company. Thus minority interest in this example is the remaining 25% of Subsidiary's equity. Most companies report minority interest as a liability. Exhibit 16-A2 is the consolidation work sheet. Again, focus on the Eliminations columns and the Consolidated Amounts.

Entry (a) in Exhibit 16-A2 eliminates P Company's Investment balance of $120,000 against the $160,000 owners' equity (common stock plus retained earnings) of S Company. All of S's equity is eliminated even though P holds only 75% of S's stock. The outside 25%

EXHIBIT 16-A2
Work Sheet for Consolidated Balance Sheet—Parent Company Owns Less than 100% of Subsidiary's Stock (There will be a minority interest.)

Assets	P Company	S Company	Eliminations Debit	Eliminations Credit	Consolidated Amounts
Cash...........................	33,000	18,000			51,000
Note receivable from P............	—	50,000		(b) 50,000	—
Accounts receivable, net...........	54,000	39,000			93,000
Inventory......................	92,000	66,000			158,000
Investment in S	120,000	—		(a) 120,000	—
Plant and equipment, net..........	230,000	123,000			353,000
Total...........................	529,000	296,000			655,000
Liabilities and Stockholders' Equity					
Accounts payable................	141,000	94,000			235,000
Notes payable...................	50,000	42,000	(b) 50,000		42,000
Minority interest................	—	—		(a) 40,000	40,000
Common stock...................	170,000	100,000	(a) 100,000		170,000
Retained earnings................	168,000	60,000	(a) 60,000		168,000
Total...........................	529,000	296,000	210,000	210,000	655,000

EXHIBIT 16-A3
Consolidated Balance Sheet of
P Company

P COMPANY AND CONSOLIDATED SUBSIDIARY
Consolidated Balance Sheet
December 31, 19XX

Assets

Cash	$ 51,000
Accounts receivable, net	93,000
Inventory	158,000
Plant and equipment, net	353,000
Total assets	$655,000

Liabilities and Stockholders' Equity

Accounts payable	$235,000
Notes payable	42,000
Minority interest	40,000
Common stock	170,000
Retained earnings	168,000
Total liabilities and stockholders' equity	$655,000

interest in S's equity is credited to Minority Interest ($160,000 × 0.25 = $40,000). Thus entry (a) reclassifies 25% of S Company's equity as minority interest. Entry (b) in Exhibit 16-A2 eliminates S Company's $50,000 note receivable against P's note payable of the same amount. The consolidated amount of notes payable ($42,000) is the amount that S Company owes to outsiders.

The consolidated balance sheet of P Company in Exhibit 16-A3 is based on the work sheet of Exhibit 16-A2. The consolidated balance sheet reveals that ownership of P Company and its consolidated subsidiary is divided between P's stockholders (common stock and retained earnings totaling $338,000) and the minority interest of S Company ($40,000).

Learning Tip: The elimination entries that we illustrate require, at most, four steps:

1. Eliminate intercompany receivables and payables.
2. Eliminate the stockholders' equity accounts of the subsidiary.
3. Eliminate the Investment in Subsidiary account.
4. Record any minority interest.

Appendix Problems

P16-A1 ◀▥ *Link Back to Chapter 4 (Debt Ratio)*. This problem demonstrates the dramatic effect that consolidation accounting can have on a company's ratios. Ford Motor Company (Ford) owns 100% of Ford Motor Credit Corporation (FMCC), its financing subsidiary. Ford's main operations consist of manufacturing automotive products. FMCC mainly helps people finance the purchase of automobiles from Ford and its dealers. The two companies' individual balance sheets are adapted and summarized as follows (amounts in billions):

Analyzing consolidated financial statements

	Ford (Parent)	FMCC (Subsidiary)
Total assets................................	$89.6	$170.5
Total liabilities..........................	$65.1	$156.9
Total stockholders' equity.........	24.5	13.6
Total liabilities and equity.........	$89.6	$170.5

Assume that FMCC's liabilities include $3.2 billion owed to Ford, the parent company.

1. Compute the debt ratio of Ford Motor Company considered alone.
2. Determine the consolidated total assets, total liabilities, and stockholders' equity of Ford Motor Company after consolidating the financial statements of FMCC into the totals of Ford, the parent company. Remember to eliminate the subsidiary's stockholders' equity.
3. Recompute the debt ratio of the consolidated entity. Explain why it took an FASB statement to get companies to consolidate their financing subsidiaries into their own financial statements.

REQUIRED

P16-A2 Ben Silver Corp. paid $266,000 to acquire all the common stock of Massada, Inc., and Massada owes Ben Silver $81,000 on a note payable. Immediately after the purchase on June 30, 19X3, the two companies' balance sheets were as follows:

Consolidating a wholly-owned subsidiary

	Ben Silver Corp.	Massada, Inc.
Assets		
Cash...	$ 24,000	$ 20,000
Accounts receivable, net....................................	91,000	42,000
Note receivable from Massada........................	81,000	—
Inventory	145,000	214,000
Investment in Massada................................	266,000	—
Plant assets, net	178,000	219,000
Total..	$785,000	$495,000
Liabilities and Stockholders' Equity		
Accounts payable....................................	$ 57,000	$ 49,000
Notes payable.......................................	177,000	149,000
Other liabilities..	129,000	31,000
Common stock...	274,000	118,000
Retained earnings.....................................	148,000	148,000
Total..	$785,000	$495,000

1. Prepare the consolidated balance sheet for Ben Silver Corp. (It is sufficient to complete a consolidation work sheet.)
2. Why aren't total assets of the consolidated entity equal to the sum of total assets for both companies combined? Why isn't consolidated equity equal to the sum of the two companies' stockholders' equity amounts?

REQUIRED

P16-A3 ◀▥ *Link Back to Chapter 13 (Return on Stockholders' Equity).* On March 22, 19X4, Viking Travel Corp. paid $280,000 to purchase 80% of the common stock of Seaboard Cruise Line, and Seaboard owes Viking $67,000 on a note payable. Immediately after the purchase, the two companies' individual balance sheets were as follows:

	Viking Travel Corp.	Seaboard Cruise Line
Assets		
Cash	$ 41,000	$ 43,000
Accounts receivable, net	86,000	75,000
Note receivable from Seaboard	67,000	—
Inventory	128,000	36,000
Investment in Seaboard	280,000	—
Plant assets, net	277,000	338,000
Total	$879,000	$492,000
Liabilities and Stockholders' Equity		
Accounts payable	$ 72,000	$ 65,000
Notes payable	301,000	67,000
Other liabilities	11,000	10,000
Minority interest	—	—
Common stock	141,000	160,000
Retained earnings	354,000	190,000
Total	$879,000	$492,000

1. Prepare Viking Travel's consolidated balance sheet. (It is sufficient to complete a consolidation work sheet.)

2. Answer these questions about Viking Travel Corp.:
   a. How much in total assets does Viking Travel control?
   b. During the most recent year, Viking earned net income of $86,000, and Seaboard's net income was $41,000. Compute Viking's consolidated net income.
   c. Suppose you are an investor considering the purchase of Viking stock. What was Viking's consolidated rate of return on stockholders' equity for the year? Assume stockholders' equity changed very little during the year. Did Viking reach its goal of a 20% return on equity?

Comprehensive Problem for Part Three

Gateway International's corporate charter authorizes the company to issue 1 million shares of $1 par value common stock and 200,000 shares of 5%, $10 par-value preferred stock. During the first quarter of operations, Gateway completed the following selected transactions:

Oct. 1 Issued 75,000 shares of common stock for cash of $6 per share.

2 Signed a capital lease for equipment. The lease requires a down payment of $50,000, plus 20 quarterly lease payments of $10,000. Present value of the future lease payments is $135,900 at an annual interest rate of 16 percent.

5 Issued 2,000 shares of preferred stock, receiving cash of $22,000.

22 Received land from the county as an incentive for locating in Augusta. Fair market value of the land was $260,000.

30 Purchased 5,000 shares (20%) of the outstanding common stock of Newbold Corp. as a long-term equity-method investment, $85,000.

Nov. 1 Issued $200,000 of 9%, ten-year bonds payable at 94.

14 Purchased long-term available-for-sale investments in the common stocks of PepsiCo, $22,000, and Data General, $31,000.

19 Experienced an extraordinary flood loss of inventory that cost $21,000. Cash received from the insurance company was $8,000.

30 Purchased 10,000 shares of Gateway common stock for the treasury at $5 per share.

Dec. 1 Received cash dividends of $1,100 on the PepsiCo investment.

1 Sold 1,000 shares of the treasury stock for cash of $6.25 per share.

29 Received a report from Newbold Corp. indicating that net income for November and December was $70,000.

30 Sold merchandise on account, $716,000. Cost of the goods was $439,000. Operating expenses totaled $174,000, with $166,000 of this amount paid in cash. Gateway uses a perpetual inventory system.

31 Accrued interest and amortized discount (straight-line method) on the bonds payable.

31 Accrued interest on the capital lease liability.

31 Depreciated the equipment acquired by the capital lease. The company uses the double-declining-balance depreciation method.

31 Adjusted the available-for-sale investments to current market value. Market values of the available-for-sale investments: PepsiCo stock, $24,000, and the Data General stock, $30,000.

31 Accrued income tax expense of $136,000.

31 Closed all revenues, expenses, and losses to Retained Earnings in a single closing entry.

31 Declared a quarterly cash dividend of $0.125 per share on the preferred stock. Record date is January 11, with payment scheduled for January 19.

REQUIRED

1. Record these transactions in the general journal. Explanations are not required.

2. Prepare a single-step income statement, including earnings per share, for the quarter ended December 31. Income tax expense of $136,000 should be reported as follows: Income tax expense of $141,000 applies to income before extraordinary items. The tax effect of the extraordinary loss is an income tax saving of $5,000.

3. Report the liabilities and the stockholders' equity as they would appear on Gateway's balance sheet at December 31.

Preparing and Using the Statement of Cash Flows

W. T. GRANT COMPANY
Statement of Cash Flows (Adapted)
Year Ended January 31, 19X3

		In millions
Cash flows from *operating* activities:		
1	Cash receipts from customers	$ 1,579
2	Cash receipts from other revenues	10
3	Cash payments to suppliers and employees	(1,684)
4	Cash payments for interest	(21)
5	Cash payments for taxes	(8)
6	Other, net	10
7	Net cash inflow (outflow) from operating activities	(114)
Cash flows from *investing* activities:		
8	Acquisition of property, plant, and equipment	$ (26)
9	Investments in securities	(2)
10	Other, net	2
11	Net cash inflow (outflow) from investing activities	(26)
Cash flows from *financing* activities:		
12	New borrowing—issuing notes payable	$ 152
13	Issuance of common stock	3
14	Retirement of notes payable	(2)
15	Payment of dividends	(21)
16	Purchase of treasury stock	(11)
17	Net cash inflow (outflow) from financing activities	121
18	Increase (decrease) in cash	$ (19)
19	Cash balance, beginning of year	50
20	Cash balance, end of year	$ 31

LEARNING OBJECTIVES

After studying this chapter, you should be able to

1. Identify the purposes of the statement of cash flows

2. Distinguish among operating, investing, and financing activities

3. Prepare a statement of cash flows by the direct method

4. Use the financial statements to compute the cash effects of a wide variety of business transactions

5. Prepare a statement of cash flows by the indirect method

APPENDIX LEARNING OBJECTIVES

A1. Prepare a work sheet for the statement of cash flows—direct method

A2. Prepare a work sheet for the statement of cash flows—indirect method

W. T. Grant was once one of the leading retailers in the United States, a serious rival to Kmart, Target, and other discount chains. Grant's income statement reported rising profits as the company slid into bankruptcy. What went wrong? Despite the company's profitability, Grant's operations simply did not generate enough cash to pay the bills. If anyone had analyzed Grant's cash flows, the cash shortage would have been crystal clear.

Examine the company's statement of cash flows on page 712. Notice that operating activities generated a net cash *outflow* of $114 million (line 7). Cash receipts from customers (line 1) were not even as high as cash payments to suppliers and employees (line 3). Grant's situation was like a lemonade stand losing money on every glass of lemonade and hoping to make up the difference with high sales volume. The cash-flow statement shows that W. T. Grant's sales were draining cash, little by little. The only thing keeping the company afloat was borrowing (see cash flows from financing activities, line 12). Borrowing large amounts can continue only so long. Sooner or later, the company would go bankrupt, and it did.

Prior to W. T. Grant's bankruptcy, companies were not required to include a statement of cash flows in the annual report. Grant's failure rippled through the business community, with the result that cash-flow analysis has taken on new importance. Investors, creditors, and the accounting profession realized that net income is not the only measure of success in business. After all, a company does *not* pay the bills with net income—it pays bills with cash. And now, as we've seen throughout this text, the statement of cash flows is a basic financial statement on a par with the income statement and the balance sheet.

In preceding chapters, we have included cash-flow analysis as it related to the topics covered: receivables, inventory, plant assets, long-term debt, and so on. But we have not yet discussed the statement of cash flows in its entirety. We do so in this chapter. Our goals are to round out your introduction to cash-flow analysis and to show how to prepare the statement of cash flows. We begin by explaining the statement format preferred by the Financial Accounting Standards Board. It is very clear and is thus called the *direct approach*. We end the chapter with the more common format of the statement of cash flows, the *indirect approach*. By the time you have worked through this chapter, you will feel more confident in your ability to analyze the cash flows of any company you might encounter.

◀▥ ◀▥ ◀▥   We learned in Chapter 1 (Exhibit 1-8) that the statement of cash flows is a required financial statement.

The statement of cash flows, a required financial statement, reports where cash came from and how it was spent. ◀▥ Like the other two major financial reports—the income statement and the balance sheet—the statement of cash flows enables investors and creditors to make informed decisions about a company. The income statement of W. T. Grant Company presented one picture of the company: relatively high net income. The cash-flow statement gave a different view: not enough cash. This example underscores the challenge of financial analysis—that a company's signals may point in different directions. Astute investors and creditors know what to look for; increasingly, they are focusing on cash flows.

Purpose of the Statement of Cash Flows: Basic Concepts

The balance sheet reports the company's cash balance at the end of the period. By examining balance sheets from two consecutive periods, you can tell whether cash increased or decreased during the period. However, the balance sheet does not indicate *why* the cash balance changed. The income statement reports revenues, expenses, and net income—clues about the sources and uses of cash—but it does not tell *why* cash increased or decreased.

Statement of Cash Flows. Reports cash receipts and cash disbursements classified according to the entity's major activities: operating, investing, and financing.

Cash Flows. Cash receipts and cash payments (disbursements).

The **statement of cash flows** reports the entity's **cash flows** (cash receipts and cash payments) during the period—where cash came from and how it was spent. It explains the *causes* of the change in the cash balance. This information cannot be learned solely from other financial statements. The statement of cash flows covers a span of time and therefore is dated "For the Year Ended XXX" or "For the Month Ended XXX." Exhibit 17-1 illustrates the timing of the statements.

EXHIBIT 17-1
Timing of the Financial Statements

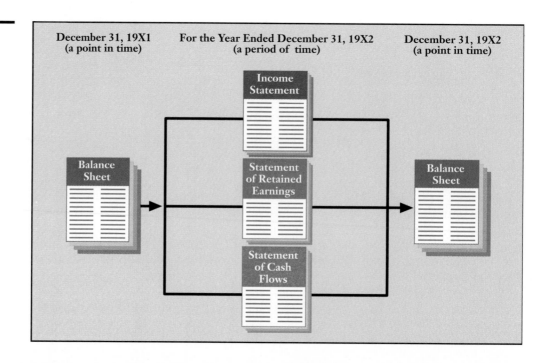

| December 31, 19X1 (a point in time) | For the Year Ended December 31, 19X2 (a period of time) | December 31, 19X2 (a point in time) |

Overview of the Statement of Cash Flows

The statement of cash flows is designed to fulfill the following purposes:

Objective 1

Identify the purposes of the statement of cash flows

1. *To predict future cash flows.* Cash, not reported accounting income, pays the bills. The experience of W. T. Grant Company illustrates this fact. In many cases, past cash receipts and disbursements are a reasonably good predictor of future cash receipts and disbursements.

2. *To evaluate management decisions.* If managers make wise investment decisions, their business prospers. If they make unwise investments, the business suffers financially. The statement of cash flows reports the company's investment in plant assets and thus gives investors and creditors cash-flow information for evaluating managers' decisions. W. T. Grant's statement of cash flows (page 712) shows that the company was investing much less in new facilities (line 8, $26 million) than it was borrowing (line 12, $152 million).

3. *To determine the company's ability to pay dividends to stockholders and interest and principal to creditors.* Stockholders are interested in receiving dividends on their investments. Creditors want to receive their interest and principal amounts on time. The statement of cash flows reports where the business's cash comes from and how it is being spent. This information helps investors and creditors predict whether the business can make dividend and debt payments.

4. *To show the relationship of net income to changes in the business's cash.* Usually, cash and net income move together. High levels of income tend to lead to increases in cash, and vice versa. However, a company's cash balance can decrease when net income is high, and cash can increase when income is low. The failures of companies such as W. T. Grant, which was earning net income but had insufficient cash, have pointed to the need for cash-flow information.

■ **Daily Exercise 17-1**

Cash and Cash Equivalents

On a statement of cash flows, *Cash* has a broader meaning than just cash on hand and cash in the bank. It includes **cash equivalents,** which are highly liquid short-term investments that can be converted into cash with little delay. Because their liquidity is one reason for holding these investments, they are treated as cash. Examples of cash equivalents are money-market investments and investments in U.S. Government Treasury bills. Businesses invest their extra cash in these types of liquid assets rather than let cash remain idle. Throughout this chapter, the term *cash* refers to cash and cash equivalents.

Cash Equivalents. Highly liquid short-term investments that can be converted into cash with little delay.

Operating, Investing, and Financing Activities

A business may be evaluated in terms of three types of business activities. After the business is up and running, *operations* are the most important activity, followed by *investing activities* and *financing activities.* Investing activities are generally more important than financing activities because *what* a company invests in is usually more important than *how* the company finances the acquisition.

Objective 2

Distinguish among operating, investing, and financing activities

The statement of cash flows in Exhibit 17-2 on page 716 shows how cash receipts and disbursements are divided into operating activities, investing activities, and financing activities for Anchor Corporation, a small manufacturer of glass products. As Exhibit 17-2 illustrates, each set of activities includes both cash inflows (receipts) and cash outflows (payments). Outflows are shown in parentheses to indicate that payments must be subtracted. Each section of the statement reports a net cash inflow or a net cash outflow.

Operating activities create revenues and expenses. The statement of cash flows reports the impacts of the revenues and expenses on cash. The largest cash inflow from operations is the collection of cash from customers. Smaller inflows are receipts of interest on loans and dividends on stock investments. The operating cash outflows include payments to suppliers and to employees and payments for interest and taxes. Exhibit 17-2 shows that Anchor's net cash inflow from operating activities is $68,000. A large positive operating cash flow is a good sign. *In the long run, operations must be the main source of a business's cash.*

Operating Activity. Activity that creates revenue or expense in the entity's major line of business; a section of the statement of cash flows. Operating activities affect the income statement.

ANCHOR CORPORATION
Statement of Cash Flows
Year Ended December 31, 19X2

		(In thousands)
Cash flows from operating activities:		
Receipts:		
Collections from customers...	$ 271	
Interest received on notes receivable.............................	10	
Dividends received on investments in stock...................	9	
Total cash receipts...		$ 290
Payments:		
To suppliers...	$(133)	
To employees	(58)	
For interest..	(16)	
For income tax	(15)	
Total cash payments..		(222)
Net cash inflow from operating activities		68
Cash flows from investing activities:		
Acquisition of plant assets..	$(306)	
Loan to another company	(11)	
Proceeds from sale of plant assets	62	
Net cash outflow from investing activities.....................		(255)
Cash flows from financing activities:		
Proceeds from issuance of common stock.........................	$ 101	
Proceeds from issuance of long-term notes payable..........	94	
Payment of long-term notes payable................................	(11)	
Payment of dividends..	(17)	
Net cash inflow from financing activities......................		167
Net (decrease) in cash..		**$ (20)**
Cash balance, December 31, 19X1		42
Cash balance, December 31, 19X2		$ 22

Operating activities are related to the
transactions that make up net income.[1]

Cash flows from operating activities require analysis of each revenue and expense on the
income statement, along with the related current asset or current liability from the balance sheet.

Investing Activity. Activity that
increases and decreases the long-term
assets available to the business; a section of the statement of cash flows.

Investing activities increase and decrease the long-term assets available to the
business. A purchase or sale of a plant asset such as land, a building, or equipment is an
investing activity, as is the purchase or sale of an investment in the stock or bonds of another company. Investing activities on the statement of cash flows include more than the
buying and selling of assets that are classified as investments on the balance sheet. Making a loan is an investing activity because the loan creates a receivable for the lender, and
collecting on the loan is also reported as an investing activity on the statement of cash
flows. The acquisition of plant assets dominates Anchor Corporation's investing activities, which produce a net cash outflow of $255,000.

Investing activities require analysis
of the long-term asset accounts.

Investments in plant assets lay the foundation for future operations. A company that invests in plant and equipment appears stronger than one that is selling off its plant assets.
Why? The latter company may be selling income-producing assets to pay the bills. Its
outlook is bleak.

Financing Activity. Activity that
obtains the funds from investors and
creditors needed to launch and sustain
the business; a section of the statement of cash flows.

Financing activities obtain the cash needed to launch and sustain the business. Financing activities include issuing stock, borrowing money by issuing notes and bonds
payable, buying or selling treasury stock, and paying dividends to the stockholders.

[1]The authors thank Alfonso Oddo for suggesting this display.

Payments to the creditors include *principal* payments only. The payment of *interest* is an operating activity. Financing activities of Anchor Corporation brought in net cash receipts of $167,000. One thing to watch among financing activities is whether the business is borrowing heavily. Excessive borrowing has been the downfall of many companies.

> Financing activities require analysis of the long-term liability accounts and the owners' equity accounts.

Overall, Anchor's cash decreased by $20,000 during 19X2. The company began the year with cash of $42,000 and ended with $22,000. Each of these categories of activities includes both cash receipts and cash disbursements, as shown in Exhibit 17-3 below. The exhibit lists the more common cash receipts and cash disbursements that appear on the statement of cash flows.

■ Daily Exercise 17-2
■ Daily Exercise 17-3
■ Daily Exercise 17-4
■ Daily Exercise 17-5

 Thinking It Over Examine W. T. Grant's statement of cash flows on page 712, and reread the chapter opening story. Which of the following statements explains why W. T. Grant's cash outflow from operations occurred? Give your reason.

a. W. T. Grant's cash drain resulted from investing too heavily in new properties.
b. Payments to suppliers and employees exceeded cash receipts from customers.
c. W. T. Grant did not borrow enough money to finance operations during the year.
d. Net income was too low.

Answer: The statement of cash flows reports that cash payments to suppliers and employees exceeded cash receipts from customers, so the answer is b.

Interest and Dividends

You may be puzzled by the listing of receipts of interest and dividends as operating activities. After all, these cash receipts result from investing activities. Interest comes from investments in loans, and dividends come from investments in stock. Equally puzzling is listing the payment of interest as part of operations. Interest expense results from borrowing money—a financing activity. After much debate, the FASB decided to include all these items as part of operations. Why? Mainly because they affect the computation of net income. Interest revenue and dividend revenue increase net income, and interest

Concept Highlight

EXHIBIT 17-3
Cash Receipts and Disbursements on the Statement of Cash Flows

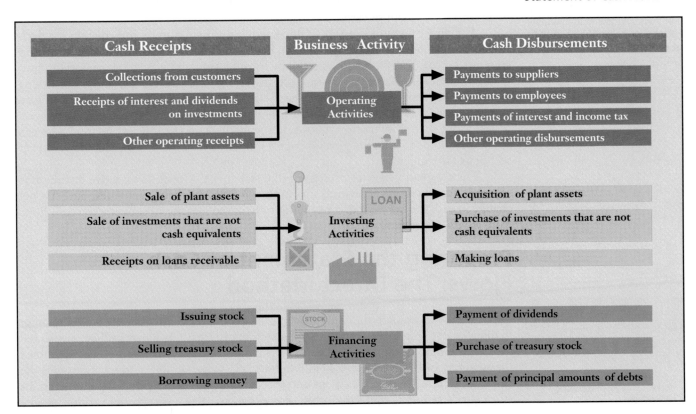

EXHIBIT 17-4
Converting from the Accrual
Basis to the Cash Basis for the
Statement of Cash Flows

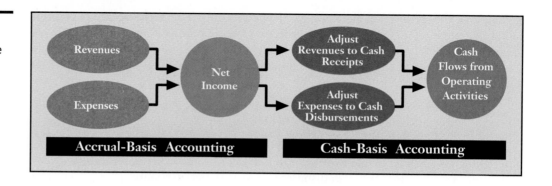

expense decreases income. Therefore, cash receipts of interest and dividends and cash payments of interest are reported as operating activities on the cash-flow statement.

In contrast, dividend payments are not listed among the operating activities of Exhibit 17-3. Why? Because they do not enter the computation of income. Dividend payments are reported in the financing activities section of the cash-flow statement because they go to the entity's owners, who finance the business by holding its stock.

Format of the Statement of Cash Flows

In *FASB Statement No. 95*, the FASB approved two formats for reporting cash flows from operating activities. The **direct method,** illustrated in Exhibit 17-2, lists cash receipts from specific operating activities and cash payments for each major operating activity. *FASB Statement No. 95* expresses a clear preference for the direct method because it reports where cash came from and how it was spent on operating activities. The direct method is required for some insurance companies, and most governmental entities use the direct method.

In keeping with GAAP, companies' accounting systems are designed for accrual, rather than cash-basis, accounting. These systems make it easy for companies to compute cash flows from operating activities by a shortcut method. The **indirect method** starts with net income and reconciles to cash flows from operating activities. Exhibit 17-4 gives an overview of the process of converting from accrual-basis income to the cash basis for the statement of cash flows.

The direct method is easier to understand, it provides more information for decision making, and the FASB prefers it. By learning how to compute the cash-flow amounts for the direct method, you will be learning something far more important: how to determine the cash effects of business transactions. This is a critical skill for analyzing financial statements because accrual-basis accounting often hides cash effects. Then, after you have a firm foundation in cash-flow analysis, it is easier to learn the indirect method. But if your instructor chooses to focus solely on the indirect method, you can study that method, which begins on page 733, with a minimum of references to earlier sections of this chapter.

The two basic ways of presenting the statement of cash flows arrive at the same subtotals for operating activities, investing activities, financing activities, and the net change in cash for the period. They differ only in the manner of showing the cash flows from *operating activities.*

Preparing the Statement of Cash Flows: The Direct Method

Let's see how to prepare the statement of cash flows by the direct method illustrated in Exhibit 17-2. (This is the format of the statement of cash flows that we have presented for W. T. Grant Company on page 712.) Suppose Anchor Corporation has assembled the summary of 19X2 transactions in Exhibit 17-5. These summary transactions give the data for both the income statement and the statement of cash flows. Some transactions affect one statement, some the other. For example, sales are reported on the income

EXHIBIT 17-5
Summary of Anchor
Corporation's 19X2
Transactions

Operating Activities:
1. Sales on credit, $284,000
*2. Collections from customers, $271,000
3. Interest revenue on notes receivable, $12,000
*4. Collection of interest receivable, $10,000
*5. Cash receipt of dividend revenue on investments in stock, $9,000
6. Cost of goods sold, $150,000
7. Purchases of inventory on credit, $147,000
*8. Payments to suppliers, $133,000
9. Salary and wage expense, $56,000
*10. Payments of salary and wages, $58,000
11. Depreciation expense, $18,000
12. Other operating expense, $17,000
*13. Interest expense and payments, $16,000
*14. Income tax expense and payments, $15,000

Investing Activities:
*15. Cash payments to acquire plant assets, $306,000
*16. Loan to another company, $11,000
*17. Proceeds from sale of plant assets, $62,000, including $8,000 gain

Financing Activities:
*18. Proceeds from issuance of common stock, $101,000
*19. Proceeds from issuance of long-term note payable, $94,000
*20. Payment of long-term note payable, $11,000
*21. Declaration and payment of cash dividends, $17,000

*Indicates a cash-flow transaction to be reported on the statement of cash flows.

statement, but cash collections appear on the cash-flow statement. Other transactions, such as the cash receipt of dividend revenue, affect both. *The statement of cash flows reports only those transactions with cash effects* (those with an asterisk in Exhibit 17-5).

To prepare the statement of cash flows, follow these steps: (1) Identify the activities that increased cash or decreased cash—those items with asterisks in Exhibit 17-5; (2) classify each cash increase and each cash decrease as an operating activity, an investing activity, or a financing activity; and (3) identify the cash effect of each transaction.

Cash Flows from Operating Activities

Operating cash flows are listed first because they are the largest and most important source of cash for most businesses. The failure of a company's operations to generate the bulk of its cash inflows for an extended period may signal trouble. Exhibit 17-2 shows that Anchor is sound; its operating activities were the largest source of cash receipts, $290,000.

CASH COLLECTIONS FROM CUSTOMERS   Cash sales bring in cash immediately. However, credit sales increase Accounts Receivable but not Cash. Receipts of cash on account are a separate transaction, and only cash receipts are reported on the statement of cash flows. "Collections from customers" in Exhibit 17-2 include both cash sales and collections of accounts receivable from credit sales—$271,000.

CASH RECEIPTS OF INTEREST   Interest revenue is earned on notes receivable. The income statement reports interest revenue. As the clock ticks, interest accrues, but cash interest is received only on specific dates. Only the cash receipts of interest appear on the statement of cash flows—$10,000 in Exhibit 17-2.

CASH RECEIPTS OF DIVIDENDS   Dividends are earned on investments in stock. Dividend revenue is ordinarily recorded as an income statement item when cash is received. This cash receipt is reported on the statement of cash flows—$9,000 in Exhibit 17-2. (Dividends *received* are part of operating activities, but dividends *paid* are a financing activity.)

PAYMENTS TO SUPPLIERS   Payments to suppliers include all cash disbursements for inventory and operating expenses except employee compensation, interest, and income taxes. *Suppliers* are those entities that provide the business with its inventory and essential services. For example, a clothing store's payments to Levi Strauss, Liz Claiborne, and Reebok are listed as payments to suppliers. A grocery store makes payments to suppliers such as Nabisco, Campbell's Soup, and Coca-Cola. Other suppliers provide advertising, utility, and other services that are classified as operating expenses. The payments to suppliers category *excludes* payments to employees, payments for interest, and payments for income taxes because these are separate categories of operating cash payments. In Exhibit 17-2, Anchor Corporation reports payments to suppliers of $133,000.

PAYMENTS TO EMPLOYEES This category includes disbursements for salaries, wages, commissions, and other forms of employee compensation. Accrued amounts are excluded because they have not yet been paid. The income statement reports the expense, including accrued amounts. The statement of cash flows in Exhibit 17-2 reports only the cash payments ($58,000).

PAYMENTS FOR INTEREST EXPENSE AND INCOME TAX EXPENSE These cash payments are reported separately from the other expenses. Interest payments show the cash cost of borrowing money. Excessive borrowing can lead to a large amount of interest payments that could result in financial trouble. Macy's and Trump Hotels & Casino Resorts, Inc. are examples of businesses that have faced problems because of too much borrowing. Income tax payments are also important because of their significant amount. In the Anchor Corporation example, interest and income tax expenses equal the cash payments. Therefore, the same amount appears on the income statement and the statement of cash flows. In practice, this is rarely the case. Year-end accruals and other transactions usually cause the expense and cash payment amounts to differ. The cash-flow statement reports the cash payments for interest ($16,000) and income tax ($15,000).

"Macy's and Trump Hotels & Casino Resorts, Inc. are examples of businesses that have faced problems because of too much borrowing."

■ **Daily Exercise 17-6**

DEPRECIATION, DEPLETION, AND AMORTIZATION EXPENSE These expenses are *not* listed on the statement of cash flows in Exhibit 17-2 because they do not affect cash. For example, depreciation is recorded by debiting the expense and crediting Accumulated Depreciation. No debit or credit to the Cash account occurs.

Cash Flows from Investing Activities

Many analysts regard investing as a critical activity because a company's investments determine its future course. Large purchases of plant assets signal expansion, which is usually a good sign. Low levels of investing activities over a lengthy period indicate that the business is not replenishing its capital assets. Knowing these cash flows helps investors and creditors evaluate the direction that managers are charting for the business.

CASH PAYMENTS TO ACQUIRE PLANT ASSETS AND INVESTMENTS, AND LOANS TO OTHER COMPANIES These cash payments are similar because they acquire a noncash asset. The first investing activity reported by Anchor Corporation on its statement of cash flows in Exhibit 17-2 is the purchase of plant assets, such as land, buildings, and equipment ($306,000). In the second transaction, Anchor makes an $11,000 loan and obtains a note receivable. These are investing activities because the company is investing in assets for use in the business rather than for resale. These transactions have no effect on revenues or expenses and thus are not reported on the income statement. Another transaction in this category—not shown in Exhibit 17-2—is a purchase of an investment in the stocks or bonds of another company.

PROCEEDS FROM THE SALE OF PLANT ASSETS AND INVESTMENTS, AND THE COLLECTIONS OF LOANS These transactions are the opposites of acquisitions of plant assets and investments, and making loans. They are cash receipts from investment transactions.

The sale of the plant assets needs explanation. The statement of cash flows in Exhibit 17-2 reports that Anchor Corporation received $62,000 cash on the sale of plant assets. The income statement shows an $8,000 gain on this transaction. What is the appropriate amount to show on the cash-flow statement? It is $62,000, the cash proceeds from the sale. If we assume that Anchor sold equipment that cost $64,000 and had accumulated depreciation of $10,000, the following journal entry would record the sale:

Cash	62,000	
Accumulated Depreciation	10,000	
Equipment		64,000
Gain on Sale of Plant Assets (from income statement)		8,000

The analysis indicates that the book value of the equipment was $54,000 ($64,000 – $10,000). However, the book value of the asset sold is not reported on the statement of cash flows. Only the cash proceeds of $62,000 are reported on the statement. For the income statement, only the gain is reported. Because a gain occurred, you may wonder why this cash receipt is not reported as part of operations. Operations consist of buying and selling merchandise or rendering services to earn revenue. Investing activities are the acquisition and disposition of assets used in operations. Therefore, the FASB views the sale of plant assets and the sale of investments as cash inflows from investing activities.

Working It Out Suppose Scott Paper Company sold timber land at a $35 million gain. The land cost Scott Paper $9 million when it was purchased in 1979. What amount will Scott Paper Company report as an investing activity on the statement of cash flows?

Answer: Cash receipt of $44 million (cost of $9 million plus the gain of $35 million).

Investors and creditors are often critical of a company that sells large amounts of its plant assets. Such sales may signal an emergency. Because of budget cuts in the defense industry, the defense contractor Grumman Corp. recently shed almost one-third of its facilities worldwide. The closing of Grumman's aircraft manufacturing plant on Long Island, and of laboratories and other facilities—plus massive employee layoffs—promised to save the company $600 million in operating expenses. Despite the downsizing, Grumman could no longer compete and was taken over by Martin Marietta.

> "Because of budget cuts in the defense industry, the defense contractor Grumman Corp. recently shed almost one-third of its facilities worldwide."

In other situations, selling off fixed assets may be good news about the company if it is getting rid of an unprofitable division. Whether sales of plant assets are good news or bad news should be evaluated in light of a company's operating and financing characteristics.

■ **Daily Exercise 17-7**

Cash Flows from Financing Activities

Cash flows from financing activities include the following.

PROCEEDS FROM ISSUANCE OF STOCK AND NOTES PAYABLE Readers of financial statements want to know how the entity obtains its financing. Issuing stock (preferred and common) and notes payable are two common ways to finance operations. In Exhibit 17-2, Anchor Corporation reports that it issued common stock for cash of $101,000 and long-term notes payable for $94,000.

PAYMENT OF NOTES PAYABLE AND PURCHASES OF THE COMPANY'S OWN STOCK
The payment of notes payable decreases Cash, which is the opposite effect of borrowing money. Anchor Corporation paid $11,000 on its long-term notes payable. Other transactions in this category are purchases of treasury stock and payments to retire the company's stock.

PAYMENT OF CASH DIVIDENDS The payment of cash dividends decreases Cash and is therefore reported as a cash payment, as illustrated by Anchor's $17,000 payment in Exhibit 17-2. A dividend in another form—a stock dividend, for example—has no effect on Cash and is *not* reported on the cash-flow statement.

When the statement of cash flows became a required financial statement, computerized accounting systems were programmed to generate this statement as easily as they

■ Daily Exercise 17-8
■ Daily Exercise 17-9
■ Daily Exercise 17-10

do the balance sheet and the income statement. Consider the direct method for preparing the statement of cash flows. The amounts for the operating section can be obtained by drawing cash inflows and outflows from the posted accounts. Specifically, the cash receipts postings to Accounts Receivable provide the information necessary to show Cash Collections from Customers. The computer adds the monthly postings to reach the yearly total. All other cash flows for operating activities, as well as cash flows for financing and investing activities, are handled similarly.

SUMMARY PROBLEM FOR YOUR REVIEW   MID-CHAPTER

Drexel Corporation's accounting records include the following information for the year ended June 30, 19X8:

a. Salary expense, $104,000.
b. Interest revenue, $8,000.
c. Proceeds from issuance of common stock, $31,000.
d. Declaration and payment of cash dividends, $22,000.
e. Collection of interest receivable, $7,000.
f. Payments of salaries, $110,000.
g. Credit sales, $358,000.
h. Loan to another company, $42,000.
i. Proceeds from sale of plant assets, $18,000, including $1,000 loss.
j. Collections from customers, $369,000.
k. Cash receipt of dividend revenue on stock investments, $3,000.
l. Payments to suppliers, $319,000.
m. Cash sales, $92,000.
n. Depreciation expense, $32,000.

o. Proceeds from issuance of short-term notes payable, $38,000.
p. Payments of long-term notes payable, $57,000.
q. Interest expense and payments, $11,000.
r. Loan collections, $51,000.
s. Proceeds from sale of investments, $22,000, including $13,000 gain.
t. Amortization expense, $5,000.
u. Purchases of inventory on credit, $297,000.
v. Income tax expense and payments, $16,000.
w. Cash payments to acquire plant assets, $83,000.
x. Cost of goods sold, $284,000.
y. Cash balance: June 30, 19X7—$83,000
          June 30, 19X8—$54,000

REQUIRED

Prepare Drexel Corporation's income statement and statement of cash flows for the year ended June 30, 19X8. Follow the cash-flow statement format of Exhibit 17-2 and the single-step format for the income statement (grouping all revenues together and all expenses together, as shown in Exhibit 17-5).

■ **SOLUTION**

DREXEL CORPORATION
Income Statement
Year Ended June 30, 19X8

Item (Reference Letter)		(In thousands)	
	Revenue and gains:		
(g, m)	Sales revenue ($358 + $92)	$450	
(s)	Gain on sale of investments..........	13	
(b)	Interest revenue	8	
(k)	Dividend revenue............................	3	
	Total revenues and gains...........		$474
	Expenses and losses:		
(x)	Cost of goods sold........................	$284	
(a)	Salary expense	104	
(n)	Depreciation expense.....................	32	
(v)	Income tax expense	16	
(q)	Interest expense..............................	11	
(t)	Amortization expense	5	
(i)	Loss on sale of plant assets...........	1	
	Total expenses		453
	Net income		$ 21

DREXEL CORPORATION
Statement of Cash Flows
Year Ended June 30, 19X8

Item (Reference Letter)		(In thousands)	
	Cash flows from operating activities:		
	Receipts:		
(j, m)	Collections from customers ($369 + $92)	$ 461	
(e)	Interest received on notes receivable	7	
(k)	Dividends received on investments in stock	3	
	Total cash receipts		$ 471
	Payments:		
(l)	To suppliers	$(319)	
(f)	To employees	(110)	
(q)	For interest	(11)	
(v)	For income tax	(16)	
	Total cash payments		(456)
	Net cash inflow from operating activities		15
	Cash flows from investing activities:		
(w)	Acquisition of plant assets	$ (83)	
(h)	Loan to another company	(42)	
(s)	Proceeds from sale of investments	22	
(i)	Proceeds from sale of plant assets	18	
(r)	Collection of loans	51	
	Net cash outflow from investing activities		(34)
	Cash flows from financing activities:		
(o)	Proceeds from issuance of short-term notes payable	$ 38	
(c)	Proceeds from issuance of common stock	31	
(p)	Payments of long-term notes payable	(57)	
(d)	Dividends declared and paid	(22)	
	Net cash outflow from financing activities		(10)
	Net (decrease) in cash		$ (29)
(y)	Cash balance, June 30, 19X7		83
(y)	Cash balance, June 30, 19X8		$ 54

Computing Individual Amounts for the Statement of Cash Flows

How do accountants compute the amounts for the statement of cash flows? Many accountants prepare the statement of cash flows from the income statement amounts and from *changes* in the related balance sheet accounts. For the *operating* cash-flow amounts, the adjustment process follows this basic approach:

> **Revenue or expense from the income statement** $\pm$ **Adjustment for the change in the related balance sheet account(s)** $=$ **Amount for the statement of cash flows**

Objective 4

Use the financial statements to compute the cash effects of a wide variety of business transactions

Accountants call this the T-account approach.[2] Learning to analyze T-accounts in this manner is one of the most useful accounting skills you will acquire. It will enable you to identify the cash effects of a wide variety of transactions. It will also strengthen your grasp of accrual-basis accounting.

The following discussions use Anchor Corporation's income statement in Exhibit 17-6 and comparative balance sheet in Exhibit 17-7, as well as the cash-flow statement in Exhibit 17-2. For continuity, trace the ending and beginning cash balances of $22,000 and $42,000, respectively, from the balance sheet in Exhibit 17-7 to the bottom part of the cash-flow statement in Exhibit 17-2.

---

[2]The chapter appendix covers the work sheet approach to preparing the statement of cash flows.

EXHIBIT 17-6
Income Statement

ANCHOR CORPORATION Income Statement Year Ended December 31, 19X2		
		(In thousands)
Revenues and gains:		
Sales revenue	$284	
Interest revenue	12	
Dividend revenue	9	
Gain on sale of plant assets	8	
Total revenues and gains		$313
Expenses:		
Cost of goods sold	$150	
Salary and wage expense	56	
Depreciation expense	18	
Other operating expense	17	
Interest expense	16	
Income tax expense	15	
Total expenses		272
Net income		$ 41

Computing the Cash Amounts of Operating Activities

COMPUTING CASH COLLECTIONS FROM CUSTOMERS   Collections can be computed by converting sales revenue (an accrual-basis amount) to the cash basis. Anchor Corporation's income statement (Exhibit 17-6) reports sales of $284,000. Exhibit 17-7 shows that Accounts Receivable increased from $80,000 at the beginning of the year to $93,000 at year end, a $13,000 increase. Based on those amounts, Cash Collections equal $271,000, as shown in the Accounts Receivable T-account:

Accounts Receivable			
Beginning balance	80,000		
Sales	284,000	Collections	271,000
Ending balance	93,000		

Accounts Receivable

$$\text{Beginning balance} + \text{Sales} - \text{Collections} = \text{Ending balance}$$

$$\$80,000 + \$284,000 - X = \$93,000$$
$$-X = \$93,000 - \$80,000 - \$284,000$$
$$X = \$271,000$$

Another explanation: Because Accounts Receivable increased by $13,000, we can say that Anchor Corporation received $13,000 less cash than sales revenue for the period. A decrease in Accounts Receivable would mean that the company received more cash than the amount of sales revenue. This computation is summarized as the first item in Exhibit 17-8.

All collections of receivables are computed in the same way. In our example, Anchor Corporation's income statement, Exhibit 17-6, reports interest revenue of $12,000. Interest Receivable's balance in Exhibit 17-7 increased $2,000. Cash receipts of interest must be $10,000 (Interest Revenue of $12,000 minus the $2,000 increase in Interest Receivable). Exhibit 17-8 summarizes this computation.

COMPUTING PAYMENTS TO SUPPLIERS   This computation includes two parts, payments for inventory and payments for expenses other than interest and income tax.

Payments for inventory are computed by converting cost of goods sold to the cash basis. We accomplish this by analyzing the Inventory and Accounts Payable accounts. Many companies also purchase inventory on short-term notes payable. In that case, we would analyze Short-Term Notes Payable in the same manner as Accounts Payable. The

EXHIBIT 17-7
Comparative Balance Sheet

ANCHOR CORPORATION Comparative Balance Sheet December 31, 19X2 and 19X1			
(In thousands)	19X2	19X1	Increase (Decrease)
Assets			
Current:			
Cash	$ 22	$ 42	$ (20)
Accounts receivable	93	80	13
Interest receivable	3	1	2
Inventory	135	138	(3)
Prepaid expenses	8	7	1
Long-term receivable from			
another company	11	—	11
Plant assets, net of depreciation	453	219	234
Total	$725	$487	$238
Liabilities			
Current:			
Accounts payable	$ 91	$ 57	$ 34
Salary and wage payable	4	6	(2)
Accrued liabilities	1	3	(2)
Long-term notes payable	160	77	83
Stockholders' Equity			
Common stock	359	258	101
Retained earnings	110	86	24
Total	$725	$487	$238

Changes in current assets—**Operating**

Changes in noncurrent assets—**Investing**

Changes in current liabilities—**Operating**

Changes in long-term liabilities and paid-in capital accounts—**Financing**

Change due to net income—**Operating** and change due to dividends—**Financing**

computation of Anchor Corporation's cash payments for inventory is given by this analysis of the T-accounts (again, we are using Exhibits 17-6 and 17-7 for our numbers):

Inventory					Accounts Payable		
Beg. inventory	138,000	Cost of goods sold	150,000	Payments for inventory	113,000	Beg. bal.	57,000
Purchases	147,000					Purchases	147,000
End. inventory	135,000					End. bal.	91,000

Inventory

$$\frac{\text{Beginning}}{\text{inventory}} + \text{Purchases} - \frac{\text{Cost of}}{\text{goods sold}} = \frac{\text{Ending}}{\text{inventory}}$$

$$\$138,000 + X - \$150,000 = \$135,000$$
$$X = \$135,000 - \$138,000 + \$150,000$$
$$X = \$147,000$$

Now we can insert the figure for purchases into Accounts Payable to determine the amount of cash paid for inventory, as follows:

Accounts Payable

$$\frac{\text{Beginning}}{\text{balance}} + \text{Purchases} - \frac{\text{Payments}}{\text{for inventory}} = \frac{\text{Ending}}{\text{balance}}$$

$$\$57,000 + \$147,000 - X = \$91,000$$
$$-X = \$91,000 - \$57,000 - \$147,000$$
$$X = \$113,000$$

Beginning and ending inventory amounts are taken from the balance sheet, and Cost of Goods Sold from the income statement. We must solve for purchases, which affect both Inventory and Accounts Payable. *Payments for inventory* show up as a debit to Accounts Payable.

EXHIBIT 17-8
Direct Method of Determining
Cash Flows from Operating
Activities

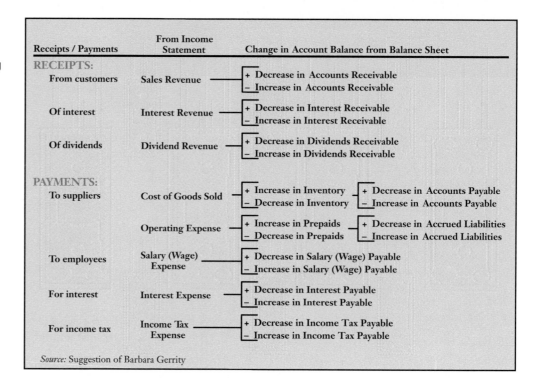

Receipts / Payments	From Income Statement	Change in Account Balance from Balance Sheet
RECEIPTS:		
From customers	Sales Revenue	+ Decrease in Accounts Receivable – Increase in Accounts Receivable
Of interest	Interest Revenue	+ Decrease in Interest Receivable – Increase in Interest Receivable
Of dividends	Dividend Revenue	+ Decrease in Dividends Receivable – Increase in Dividends Receivable
PAYMENTS:		
To suppliers	Cost of Goods Sold	+ Increase in Inventory + Decrease in Accounts Payable – Decrease in Inventory – Increase in Accounts Payable
	Operating Expense	+ Increase in Prepaids + Decrease in Accrued Liabilities – Decrease in Prepaids – Increase in Accrued Liabilities
To employees	Salary (Wage) Expense	+ Decrease in Salary (Wage) Payable – Increase in Salary (Wage) Payable
For interest	Interest Expense	+ Decrease in Interest Payable – Increase in Interest Payable
For income tax	Income Tax Expense	+ Decrease in Income Tax Payable – Increase in Income Tax Payable

Source: Suggestion of Barbara Gerrity

■ **Daily Exercise 17-11**

By another explanation, payments for inventory appear in the Accounts Payable account. But we must first work through the Inventory account, as summarized in Exhibit 17-8 under Payments to Suppliers.

Payments to suppliers ($133,000 in Exhibit 17-2) equal the sum of payments for inventory ($113,000) plus payments for operating expenses ($20,000), as explained next.

COMPUTING PAYMENTS FOR OPERATING EXPENSES   Payments for operating expenses other than interest and income tax can be computed as plug figures by analyzing Prepaid Expenses and Accrued Liabilities, as follows for Anchor Corporation (again, all numbers are taken from Exhibits 17-6 and 17-7):

Prepaid Expenses		
Beg. bal.	7,000	Expiration of
Payments	8,000	prepaid
		expense 7,000
End. bal.	8,000	

Accrued Liabilities			
Payment	3,000	Beg. bal.	3,000
		Accrual of expense at year end	1,000
		End. bal.	1,000

Operating Expenses (other than Salaries, Wages, and Depreciation)

Accrual of expense at year end	1,000	
Expiration of prepaid expense	7,000	
Payments	9,000	
End. bal.	17,000	

Prepaid Expenses

$$\underset{\text{balance}}{\text{Beginning}} + \text{Payments} - \underset{\text{prepaid expense}}{\text{Expiration of}} = \underset{\text{balance}}{\text{Ending}}$$

$$\$7{,}000 \quad + \quad X \quad - \quad \$7{,}000 \quad = \$8{,}000$$
$$X \qquad\qquad\qquad\qquad = \$8{,}000 - \$7{,}000 + \$7{,}000$$
$$X \qquad\qquad\qquad\qquad = \$8{,}000$$

Accrued Liabilities

$$\underset{\text{balance}}{\text{Beginning}} + \underset{\text{at year end}}{\text{Accrual of expense}} - \text{Payments} = \underset{\text{balance}}{\text{Ending}}$$

$$\$3{,}000 \quad + \quad \$1{,}000 \quad - \quad X \quad = \$1{,}000$$
$$-X \quad = \$1{,}000 - \$3{,}000 - \$1{,}000$$
$$X \quad = \$3{,}000$$

Operating Expenses

Accrual of expense at year end +	Expiration of prepaid expense	+ Payments =	Ending balance
$1,000 +	7,000	+ X	= $17,000
		X	= $17,000 − $1,000 − $7,000
		X	= $9,000

Total payments for operating expenses = $20,000
$8,000 + $3,000 + $9,000 = $20,000

By another explanation: Increases in prepaid expenses require cash payments, and decreases indicate that payments were less than expenses. Decreases in accrued liabilities can occur only from cash payments, and increases mean that cash was *not* paid. Exhibit 17-8 shows a streamlined version of this computation.

COMPUTING PAYMENTS TO EMPLOYEES   The company may have separate accounts for salaries, wages, and other forms of cash compensation to employees. Payments to employees can be computed conveniently by combining them into one account. Anchor's calculation adjusts Salary and Wage Expense for the change in Salary and Wage Payable, as shown in the Salary and Wage Payable T-account:

Salary and Wage Payable

		Beginning balance	6,000
Payments to employees	58,000	Salary and wage expense	56,000
		Ending balance	4,000

Salary and Wage Payable

Beginning balance +	Salary and wage expense	− Payments =	Ending balance
$6,000 +	$56,000	− X	= $4,000
		−X	= $4,000 − $6,000 − $56,000
		X	= $58,000

Exhibit 17-8 summarizes this computation under Payments to Employees.

■ **Daily Exercise 17-12**

COMPUTING PAYMENTS OF INTEREST AND INCOME TAXES   In our example, the expense and payment amounts are the same for each expense. Therefore, no analysis is required to determine the payment amount. If the expense and the payment differ, the payment can be computed by analyzing the related liability account. The payment computation follows the pattern illustrated for payments to employees; Exhibit 17-8 summarizes the procedure.

Computing the Cash Amounts of Investing Activities

Investing activities affect asset accounts, such as Plant Assets, Investments, and Notes Receivable. The cash amounts of investing activities can be identified by analyzing those accounts. Most data for the computations are taken directly from the income statement and the beginning and ending balance sheets. Other amounts come from analysis of accounts in the ledger.

COMPUTING ACQUISITIONS AND SALES OF PLANT ASSETS   Most companies have separate accounts for Land, Buildings, Equipment, and other plant assets. It is helpful to combine these accounts into a single summary for computing the cash flows from acquisitions and sales of these assets. Also, we subtract accumulated depreciation from the assets' cost and get a net figure for plant assets. This approach allows us to work with a single plant asset account as opposed to a large number of plant asset and related accumulated depreciation accounts.

To illustrate, observe that Anchor Corporation's balance sheet (Exhibit 17-7) reports beginning plant assets, net of depreciation, of $219,000 and an ending net amount of $453,000. The income statement (Exhibit 17-6) shows depreciation expense of

$18,000 and an $8,000 gain on sale of plant assets. Further, the acquisitions of plant assets total $306,000 (see Exhibit 17-2). How much are the proceeds from the sale of plant assets? First, we must determine the book value of plant assets sold from the Plant Assets T-account, as follows:

Plant Assets, Net			
Beginning balance	219,000	Depreciation	18,000
Acquisitions	306,000	Book value of assets sold	54,000
Ending balance	453,000		

Plant Assets, Net

$$\underset{\text{balance}}{\text{Beginning}} + \text{Acquisitions} - \text{Depreciation} - \underset{\text{assets sold}}{\text{Book value of}} = \underset{\text{balance}}{\text{Ending}}$$

$$
\begin{aligned}
\$219{,}000 + \$306{,}000 - \$18{,}000 - \ \ X \ \ &= \$453{,}000 \\
-X &= \$453{,}000 - \$219{,}000 - \$306{,}000 + \$18{,}000 \\
X &= \$54{,}000
\end{aligned}
$$

Now we can compute the sale proceeds as follows:

$$\underset{\text{assets sold}}{\text{Book value of}} + \text{Gain} - \text{Loss} = \text{Sale proceeds}$$

$$\$54{,}000 \ \ + \$8{,}000 - \ \$0 \ = \ \ \$62{,}000$$

Trace the sale proceeds of $62,000 to the statement of cash flows in Exhibit 17-2. If the sale resulted in a loss of $3,000, the sale proceeds would be $51,000 ($54,000 − $3,000), and the statement would report $51,000 as a cash receipt from this investing activity.

> **Learning Tip:** Proceeds from the sale of an asset need not equal the asset's book value. Remember:
>
> **Book value + Gain = Proceeds**
> **Book value − Loss = Proceeds**
>
> The book-value information comes from the balance sheet; the gain or loss comes from the income statement.

COMPUTING ACQUISITIONS AND SALES OF ASSETS CLASSIFIED AS INVESTMENTS, AND LOANS AND THEIR COLLECTIONS   Accountants use a separate category of assets for investments in stocks, bonds, and other types of assets. The cash amounts of transactions involving these assets can be computed in the manner illustrated for plant assets. Investments are easier to analyze, however, because there is no depreciation to account for, as shown in the following T-account:

Investments			
Beginning balance*	XXX		
Purchases**	XXX	Book value of investments sold	XXX
Ending balance*	XXX		

*From the balance sheet.
**From the statement of cash flows.

Investments (amounts assumed for illustration only)

■ **Daily Exercise 17-13**

$$\underset{\text{balance}}{\text{Beginning}} + \text{Purchases} - \underset{\text{sold}}{\overset{\text{Book value of}}{\text{investments}}} = \underset{\text{balance}}{\text{Ending}}$$

$$
\begin{aligned}
\$100{,}000 + \$50{,}000 - \ \ X \ \ &= \$140{,}000 \\
-X &= \$140{,}000 - \$100{,}000 - \$50{,}000 \\
X &= \$10{,}000
\end{aligned}
$$

Loan transactions follow the pattern described on page 724 for collections from customers. New loans cause a debit to a receivable and an outflow of cash. Collections increase cash and cause a credit to the receivable:

Loans and Notes Receivable

Beginning balance*	XXX		
New loans made**	XXX	Collections	XXX
Ending balance*	XXX		

*From the balance sheet.
**From the statement of cash flows.

Loans and Notes Receivable (amounts assumed for illustration only)

$$\underset{\text{balance}}{\text{Beginning}} + \underset{\text{made}}{\text{New loans}} - \text{Collections} = \underset{\text{balance}}{\text{Ending}}$$

$$\$90{,}000 \;+\; \$10{,}000 \;-\; X \;= \$30{,}000$$
$$-X \;= \$30{,}000 - \$90{,}000 - \$10{,}000$$
$$X \;= \$70{,}000$$

Exhibit 17-9 summarizes the computation of cash flows from investing activities. We must solve for the dollar amount of each item highlighted in color. For example, to determine the amount of cash received from the sale of plant assets, we must first solve for the book value of the assets sold. Then, the book value of the assets sold, plus a gain or minus a loss on the sale, equals the amount of cash received from the sale of the assets.

Computing the Cash Amounts of Financing Activities

Financing activities affect liability and stockholders' equity accounts, such as Notes Payable, Bonds Payable, Long-Term Debt, Common Stock, Paid-in Capital in Excess of Par, and Retained Earnings. The cash amounts of financing activities can be computed by analyzing these accounts.

COMPUTING ISSUANCES AND PAYMENTS OF LONG-TERM NOTES PAYABLE The beginning and ending balances of Long-Term Debt, Notes Payable, or Bonds Payable are taken from the balance sheet. If either the amount of new issuances or the amount of the payments is known, the other amount can be computed. New issuances of notes payable total $94,000 (see Exhibit 17-2). The computation of payments of notes payable

Concept Highlight

EXHIBIT 17-9
Computation of Cash Flows from Investing Activities

RECEIPTS

From sale of plant assets

$$\underset{\text{assets (net)}}{\text{Beginning plant}} + \text{Acquisition cost} - \text{Depreciation} - \underset{\text{assets sold}}{\text{Book value of}} = \underset{\text{assets (net)}}{\text{Ending plant}}$$

$$\text{Cash received} = \underset{\text{assets sold}}{\text{Book value of}} + \underset{\text{or} - \text{Loss on sale}}{\text{Gain on sale}}$$

From sale of investments

$$\underset{\text{investments}}{\text{Beginning}} + \underset{\text{of investments}}{\text{Purchase cost}} - \underset{\text{investments sold}}{\text{Book value of}} = \underset{\text{investments}}{\text{Ending}}$$

$$\text{Cash received} = \underset{\text{investments sold}}{\text{Book value of}} + \underset{\text{or} - \text{Loss on sale}}{\text{Gain on sale}}$$

From collection of loans and notes receivable

$$\underset{\text{notes receivable}}{\text{Beginning loans or}} + \text{New loans made} - \text{Collections} = \underset{\text{notes receivable}}{\text{Ending loans or}}$$

PAYMENTS

For acquisition of plant assets

$$\underset{\text{assets (net)}}{\text{Beginning plant}} + \text{Acquisition cost} - \text{Depreciation} - \underset{\text{assets sold}}{\text{Book value of}} = \underset{\text{assets (net)}}{\text{Ending plant}}$$

For purchase of investments

$$\underset{\text{investments}}{\text{Beginning}} + \underset{\text{of investments}}{\text{Purchase cost}} - \underset{\text{investments sold}}{\text{Book value of}} = \underset{\text{investments}}{\text{Ending}}$$

For new loans made

$$\underset{\text{notes receivable}}{\text{Beginning loans or}} + \text{New loans made} - \text{Collections} = \underset{\text{notes receivable}}{\text{Ending loans or}}$$

follows from analysis of the Long-Term Notes Payable T-account, using amounts from Anchor Corporation's balance sheet, Exhibit 17-7:

Long-Term Notes Payable

		Beginning balance	77,000
Payments	11,000	Issuance of new debt	94,000
		Ending balance	160,000

Long-Term Notes Payable

$$\underset{\text{balance}}{\text{Beginning}} + \underset{\text{of new debt}}{\text{Issuance}} - \underset{\text{of debt}}{\text{Payments}} = \underset{\text{balance}}{\text{Ending}}$$

$$\$77,000 + \$94,000 - X = \$160,000$$
$$-X = \$160,000 - \$77,000 - \$94,000$$
$$X = \$11,000$$

COMPUTING ISSUANCES AND RETIREMENTS OF STOCK AND PURCHASES AND SALES OF TREASURY STOCK   The cash effects of these financing activities can be determined by analyzing the various stock accounts. For example, the amount of a new issuance of common stock is determined by combining the Common Stock and any related Capital in Excess of Par account. It is convenient to work with a single summary account for stock as we do for plant assets. Using data from Exhibits 17-2 and 17-7, we have

Common Stock

		Beginning balance	258,000
Retirements of stock	0	Issuance of new stock	101,000
		Ending balance	359,000

Common Stock

$$\underset{\text{balance}}{\text{Beginning}} + \underset{\text{of new stock}}{\text{Issuance}} - \underset{\text{of stock}}{\text{Retirements}} = \underset{\text{balance}}{\text{Ending}}$$

$$\$258,000 + \$101,000 - X = \$359,000$$
$$-X = \$359,000 - \$258,000 - \$101,000$$
$$X = 0$$

Cash flows affecting Treasury Stock, a debit-balance account, can be analyzed by using the Treasury Stock T-account:

Treasury Stock

Beginning balance	XXX		
Purchases of treasury stock	XXX	Cost of treasury stock sold	XXX
Ending balance	XXX		

Treasury Stock (amounts assumed for illustration only)

$$\underset{\text{balance}}{\text{Beginning}} + \underset{\text{treasury stock}}{\text{Purchase of}} - \underset{\text{sold}}{\underset{\text{treasury stock}}{\text{Cost of}}} = \underset{\text{balance}}{\text{Ending}}$$

$$\$16,000 + \$3,000 - X = \$5,000$$
$$-X = \$5,000 - \$16,000 - \$3,000$$
$$X = \$14,000$$

If either the purchase amount or the cost of treasury stock sold is known, the other amount can be computed. For a sale of treasury stock, the amount to report on the cash-flow statement is the sale proceeds. Suppose a sale brought in cash that was $2,000 less than the $14,000 cost of the treasury stock sold. In this case, the statement of cash flows would report a cash receipt of $12,000 ($14,000 – $2,000).

COMPUTING DIVIDEND PAYMENTS   If the amount of the dividends is not given elsewhere (for example, in a statement of retained earnings), it can be computed as follows:

Retained Earnings					Dividends Payable		
Dividend declarations	17,000	Beg. bal.	86,000			Beg. bal. (assumed)	0
		Net income	41,000	Dividend payments	17,000	Dividend declarations	17,000
		End. bal.	110,000			End. bal. (assumed)	0

First, we compute dividend declarations by analyzing the Retained Earnings T-account. Then we solve for dividend payments with the Dividends Payable T-account. Anchor Corporation has no Dividends Payable account, so dividend payments are the same as declarations. The following computations show how to determine the amount of Anchor Corporation's dividend payments.

Retained Earnings

$$\text{Beginning balance} + \text{Net income} - \text{Dividend declarations} = \text{Ending balance}$$

$$\$86,000 + \$41,000 - X = \$110,000$$
$$-X = \$110,000 - \$86,000 - \$41,000$$
$$X = \$17,000$$

Dividends Payable

$$\text{Beginning balance} + \text{Dividend declarations} - \text{Dividend payments} = \text{Ending balance}$$

$$\$0 + \$17,000 - X = \$0$$
$$-X = \$0 - \$17,000 - \$0$$
$$X = \$17,000$$

■ **Daily Exercise 17-14**

Exhibit 17-10 summarizes the computation of cash flows from financing activities. The color highlights indicate amounts that must be computed. For example, cash receipts from issuance of long-term debt can be computed from the equation given.

EXHIBIT 17-10
Computation of Cash Flows from Financing Activities

RECEIPTS

From issuance of long-term debt (notes payable)	Beginning long-term notes payable	+	Cash received from issuance of long-term notes payable	−	Payment of notes payable	=	Ending long-term notes payable
From issuance of stock	Beginning stock	+	Cash received from issuance of new stock	−	Payments to retire stock	=	Ending stock
From sale of treasury stock	Beginning treasury stock	+	Purchase cost of treasury stock	−	Cost of treasury stock sold	=	Ending treasury stock
	Cash received =		Cost of treasury stock sold	+	Extra amount of sale above cost or − amount of cost in excess of sale amount		

PAYMENTS

Of long-term debt (notes payable)	Beginning long-term notes payable	+	Cash received from issuance of long-term notes payable	−	Payment of notes payable	=	Ending long-term notes payable
To retire stock	Beginning stock	+	Cash received from issuance of new stock	−	Payments to retire stock	=	Ending stock
To purchase treasury stock	Beginning treasury stock	+	Purchase cost of treasury stock	−	Cost of treasury stock sold	=	Ending treasury stock
For dividends	Beginning retained earnings	+	Net income −		Dividend declarations	=	Ending retained earnings
	Beginning dividends payable	+	Dividend declarations −		Dividend payments	=	Ending dividends payable

Noncash investing and financing activities:	
Acquisition of building by issuing common stock	$320
Acquisition of land by issuing note payable	72
Payment of long-term debt by transferring investments to the creditor	104
Acquisition of equipment by issuing short-term note payable	37
Total noncash investing and financing activities	$533

Noncash Investing and Financing Activities

Companies make investments that do not require cash. They also obtain financing other than cash. Our examples thus far have included none of these transactions. Now suppose that Anchor Corporation issued no-par common stock valued at $320,000 to acquire a warehouse. Anchor would journalize this transaction as follows:

Warehouse Building	320,000	
Common Stock		320,000

This transaction would not be reported on the cash-flow statement because Anchor paid no cash. But the importance of the investment in the warehouse and the financing aspect of issuing stock require that the transaction be reported. Noncash investing and financing activities like this transaction are reported in a separate schedule that accompanies the statement of cash flows. Exhibit 17-11 illustrates how to report noncash investing and financing activities (all amounts are assumed). This information is required in a schedule immediately after any cash-flow statement or in a note.

■ **Daily Exercise 17-15**

Reconciling Net Income to Net Cash Flow from Operating Activities

The FASB requires companies that format operating activities by the direct method to report a reconciliation from net income to net cash inflow (or outflow) from operating activities. The reconciliation shows how the company's net income is related to net cash flow from operating activities. Exhibit 17-12 shows the reconciliation for Anchor Corporation.

ANCHOR CORPORATION
Reconciliation of Net Income to Net Cash Inflow from Operating Activities

	(In thousands)	
Net income		$41
Add (subtract) items that affect net income and cash flows differently:		
Depreciation	$ 18	
Gain on sale of plant assets	(8)	
Increase in accounts receivable	(13)	
Increase in interest receivable	(2)	
Decrease in inventory	3	
Increase in prepaid expenses	(1)	
Increase in accounts payable	34	
Decrease in salary and wage payable	(2)	
Decrease in accrued liabilities	(2)	27
Net cash inflow from operating activities		$68

The end result—net cash inflow from operating activities of $68,000—is the same as the result we derived earlier under the *direct* method (see Exhibit 17-2). The reconciliation is also the same as the *indirect* method of computing operating cash flows. We now turn to the indirect method.

Preparing the Statement of Cash Flows: The Indirect Method

Objective 5

Prepare a statement of cash flows by the indirect method

An alternative to the direct method of computing cash flows from *operating* activities is the *indirect method,* or the **reconciliation method,** as shown in Exhibit 17-12. This method starts with net income, which is taken directly from the income statement, and shows the reconciliation from net income to operating cash flows. For example, the consolidated cash-flow statement of the Washington Post Company lists first "Net income" and then "Adjustments to reconcile net income to net cash provided by operating activities." The indirect method shows the link between net income and cash flow from operations better than the direct method. In fact, 585 companies (97.5%) of a 600-firm survey (*Accounting Trends and Techniques, 1996)* use the indirect method even though the FASB recommends the direct method. The main drawback of the indirect method is that it does not report the detailed operating cash flows—collections from customers and other cash receipts, payments to suppliers, payments to employees, and payments for interest and taxes.

Reconciliation Method. Another name for the indirect method.

These two methods (direct and indirect) of preparing the cash-flow statement affect only the operating activities section of the statement. No difference exists in the reporting of investing activities or financing activities.

Exhibit 17-13 is Anchor Corporation's cash-flow statement prepared by the indirect method. Only the operating section of the statement differs from the direct-method

EXHIBIT 17-13
Statement of Cash Flows
(Indirect Method for Operating Activities)

	ANCHOR CORPORATION Statement of Cash Flows Year Ended December 31, 19X2		
		(In thousands)	
Cash flows from operating activities:			
Net income			$ 41
Add (subtract) items that affect net income and cash flows differently:			
(A) Depreciation		$ 18	
(B) Gain on sale of plant assets		(8)	
Increase in accounts receivable		(13)	
Increase in interest receivable		(2)	
Decrease in inventory		3	
(C) Increase in prepaid expenses		(1)	
Increase in accounts payable		34	
Decrease in salary and wage payable		(2)	
Decrease in accrued liabilities		(2)	27
Net cash inflow from operating activities			$ 68
Cash flows from investing activities:			
Acquisition of plant assets		$(306)	
Loan to another company		(11)	
Proceeds from sale of plant assets		62	
Net cash outflow from investing activities			$(255)
Cash flows from financing activities:			
Proceeds from issuance of common stock		$ 101	
Proceeds from issuance of long-term notes payable		94	
Payment of long-term notes payable		(11)	
Payment of dividends		(17)	
Net cash inflow from financing activities			167
Net (decrease) in cash			$ (20)
Cash balance, December 31, 19X1			42
Cash balance, December 31, 19X2			$ 22

From Exhibit 17-2

■ **Daily Exercise 17-16**

EXHIBIT 17-14
Income Statement
(Repeated from Exhibit 17-6)

ANCHOR CORPORATION
Income Statement
Year Ended December 31, 19X2

	(In thousands)	
Revenues and gains:		
Sales revenue	$284	
Interest revenue	12	
Dividend revenue	9	
Gain on sale of plant assets	8	
Total revenues and gains		$313
Expenses:		
Cost of goods sold	$150	
Salary and wage expense	56	
Depreciation expense	18	
Other operating expense	17	
Interest expense	16	
Income tax expense	15	
Total expenses		272
Net income		$ 41

EXHIBIT 17-15
Comparative Balance Sheet
(Repeated from Exhibit 17-7)

ANCHOR CORPORATION
Comparative Balance Sheet
December 31, 19X2 and 19X1

(In thousands)	19X2	19X1	Increase (Decrease)
Assets			
Current:			
Cash	$ 22	$ 42	$ (20)
Accounts receivable	93	80	13
Interest receivable	3	1	2
Inventory	135	138	(3)
Prepaid expenses	8	7	1
Long-term receivable from another company	11	—	11
Plant assets, net of depreciation	453	219	234
Total	$725	$487	$238
Liabilities			
Current:			
Accounts payable	$ 91	$ 57	$34
Salary and wage payable	4	6	(2)
Accrued liabilities	1	3	(2)
Long-term notes payable	160	77	83
Stockholders' Equity			
Common stock	359	258	101
Retained earnings	110	86	24
Total	$725	$487	$238

format in Exhibit 17-2. The new items are keyed to their explanations, which are discussed in the following section. One reason companies prefer the indirect method is its ease of preparation from the income statement and the beginning and ending balance sheets. For ease of reference, we repeat Anchor Corporation's income statement and balance sheet here as Exhibits 17-14 and 17-15.

Logic behind the Indirect Method

The operating section of the cash-flow statement begins with net income, taken from the income statement. Additions and subtractions follow. These are labeled "Add (subtract) items that affect net income and cash flows differently." We discuss these items in the following sections.

DEPRECIATION, DEPLETION, AND AMORTIZATION EXPENSES   These expenses are added back to net income when we go from net income to cash flow from operations. Let's see why.

Depreciation(A) is recorded as follows:

Depreciation Expense	18,000	
Accumulated Depreciation		18,000

This entry contains no debit or credit to Cash, so depreciation expense has no cash effect. However, depreciation expense is deducted from revenues in the computation of income. Therefore, in going from net income to cash flows from operations, we add depreciation back to net income. The addback cancels the earlier deduction. The following example should help clarify this practice: Suppose a company had only two transactions during the period, a $1,000 cash sale and depreciation expense of $300. Net income is $700 ($1,000 – $300). Cash flow from operations is $1,000. To show how net income ($700) is related to cash flow ($1,000), we must add back the depreciation amount of $300.

> All expenses with no cash effects are added back
> to net income on the cash-flow statement.

Depletion and amortization are also added back.

> Likewise, revenues that do not provide cash are subtracted from net income.

An example is equity-method investment revenue.

GAINS AND LOSSES ON THE SALE OF ASSETS(B)   Sales of plant assets are investing activities on the cash-flow statement. A gain or loss on the sale is an adjustment to income. Exhibit 17-13 includes an adjustment for a gain. Recall that Anchor sold equipment with a book value of $54,000 for $62,000, producing a gain of $8,000.

The $8,000 gain is reported on the income statement and is therefore included in net income. However, the cash receipt from the sale is $62,000, which includes the gain. To avoid counting the gain twice, we need to remove its effect from income and report the cash receipt of $62,000 in the investing activities section of the statement. Starting with net income, we subtract the gain. This deduction removes the gain's earlier effect on income. The sale of plant assets is reported as a $62,000 cash receipt from an investing activity, as shown in Exhibits 17-2 and 17-13.

A loss on the sale of plant assets is also an adjustment to net income on the statement of cash flows. However, a loss is *added back* to income to compute cash flow from operations. The proceeds from selling the plant assets are reported under investing activities.

CHANGES IN THE CURRENT ASSET AND CURRENT LIABILITY ACCOUNTS(C)   Most current assets and current liabilities result from operating activities. Changes in the current accounts are reported as adjustments to net income on the cash-flow statement. The following rules apply:

1.   **An *increase* in a current asset other than cash is subtracted from net income to compute cash flow from operations.** Suppose a company makes a sale. Income is increased by the sale amount. However, collection of less than the full amount increases Accounts Receivable. For example, Exhibit 17-15 reports that Anchor Corporation's Accounts Receivable increased by $13,000 during 19X2. To compute the impact of revenue on Anchor's cash-flow amount, we must subtract the $13,000 increase in Accounts Receivable from net income in the cash-flow statement (see Exhibit 17-13). The reason is this: We have *not* collected this $13,000 in cash. The same logic applies to the other current assets. If they increase during the period, subtract the increase from net income.

2.   **A *decrease* in a current asset other than cash is added to net income.** Suppose Anchor's Accounts Receivable balance decreased by $4,000 during the period. Cash receipts cause the Accounts Receivable balance to decrease and cash to increase, so decreases in Accounts Receivable and the other current assets are *added* to net income.

EXHIBIT 17-16
Indirect Method of
Determining Cash Flows from
Operating Activities

Net Income

Add (subtract) items
that affect net income
and cash flow differently

+ Depreciation
+ Depletion
+ Amortization
+ Loss on disposal or exchange of long-term asset or early
   extinguishment of note payable or bond payable
− Gain on disposal of long-term asset or early
   extinguishment of note payable or bond payable
+ Decrease in current asset other than cash
− Increase in current asset other than cash
+ Increase in current liability*
− Decrease in current liability*

Net cash inflow (or outflow) from operating activities

*Short-term notes payable for general borrowing, and current portion of long-term notes payable, are related to *financing* activities, not to operating activities.

Source: We thank Barbara Gerrity and Jean Marie Hudson for suggesting this exhibit.

3.   A *decrease* in a current liability is subtracted from net income. The payment of a current liability causes both cash and the current liability to decrease, so decreases in current liabilities are subtracted from net income. For example, in Exhibit 17-13, the $2,000 decrease in Accrued Liabilities is *subtracted* from net income to compute net cash inflow from operating activities.

4.   An *increase* in a current liability is added to net income. Anchor's Accounts Payable increased during the year. This increase can occur only if cash is not spent to pay this liability, which means that cash payments are less than the related expense and we have more cash on hand. Thus, increases in current liabilities are *added* to net income.

Computing net cash inflow or net cash outflow from *operating* activities by the indirect method takes a path that is very different from the direct-method computation. However, both methods arrive at the same amount of net cash flow from operating activities, as shown in Exhibits 17-2 and 17-13, both of which report a net cash inflow of $68,000.

Exhibit 17-16 summarizes the adjustments needed to convert net income to net cash inflow (or net cash outflow) from operating activities by the indirect method.

If you are studying *only* the indirect method for operating cash flows, please turn to page 727 for coverage of investing and financing activities.

■ **Daily Exercise 17-17**
■ **Daily Exercise 17-18**

NIKE's Statement of Cash Flows for Operating Activities—An Application of the Indirect Method

". . . NIKE uses the indirect method to report cash flows from operating activities."

NIKE, Inc., is a well-known maker of athletic shoes and clothing. As Exhibit 17-17 shows, NIKE uses the indirect method to report cash flows from operating activities. We've discussed most of the items in NIKE's statement of cash flows earlier, but three need clarification. First, "additions to long-term debt" means to borrow money by signing a long-term note payable. Second, "reductions of long-term debt" means to pay long-term notes payable. Third, changes in exchange rates show the cash effect of fluctuations in foreign currencies.

EVALUATION OF NIKE's 19X7 CASH-FLOW RESULTS   NIKE's cash flows for 19X7 look very strong. Cash increased from $18 million to almost $127 million. Most importantly, virtually all the cash increase came from operations—a sign of strength. During 19X7, NIKE invested in new plant and equipment ($11.9 million) and paid off more than $29 million ($10.7 million + $18.5 million) of debt. The company issued only $30 million of new debt.

EXHIBIT 17-17
NIKE, Inc.
Statement of Cash Flows
(Indirect Method)

NIKE, INC. Statement of Cash Flows (Adapted) (Indirect Method for Operating Activities) Year Ended May 31, 19X7	
	(In thousands)
Cash provided (used) by operations:	
Net income	$ 35,879
Income charges (credits) not affecting cash:	
Depreciation	12,078
Other non-cash expenses..	10,980
Changes in [current accounts]:	
Decrease in inventory...	59,542
Decrease in accounts receivable	1,174
Decrease in other current assets...	4,331
Increase in accounts payable, accrued liabilities,	
and income taxes payable..	8,462
Cash provided by operations...	132,446
Cash provided (used) by investing activities:	
Additions to property, plant, and equipment...................................	(11,874)
Disposals of property, plant, and equipment	1,728
Additions to other assets...	(930)
Cash used by investing activities	(11,076)
Cash provided (used) by financing activities:	
Additions to long-term debt (notes payable)	30,332
Reductions in long-term debt (notes payable) including current portion	(10,678)
Decrease in notes payable to banks..	(18,489)
Proceeds from issuance of common stock	1,911
Dividends—common and preferred	(15,188)
Cash used by financing activities..	(12,112)
Effect of foreign-currency exchange-rate changes on cash............................	(529)
Net increase (decrease) in cash	108,729
Cash and equivalents, beginning of year	18,138
Cash and equivalents, end of year...	$126,867

■ Daily Exercise 17-19

Thinking It Over Examine Anchor Corporation's statement of cash flows, Exhibit 17-13.

1. Does Anchor Corporation appear to be growing or shrinking? How can you tell?

2. Where did Anchor's cash for expansion come from?

3. Suppose Accounts Receivable increased by $40,000 (instead of $13,000) during the current year. What would this increase signal about the company?

Answers

1. This is an *INVESTING* question. Anchor appears to be growing. The company acquired more plant assets ($306,000) than it sold during the year.

2. This is a *FINANCING* question. The cash for expansion came from the issuance of common stock ($101,000) and from borrowing ($94,000).

3. This an *OPERATING* question. If accounts receivable had increased by $40,000, Anchor Corporation would have $27,000 less cash ($40,000 minus $13,000). A large increase in accounts receivable may signal difficulty in collecting cash from customers or a sharp increase in sales. A manager, stockholder, or creditor of Anchor Corporation should compare current-year sales with sales revenue for the preceding year. If sales are up, higher accounts receivable are good news. If sales are down, higher receivables may signal a cash shortage.

Computers and the Indirect Method of Generating the Statement of Cash Flows

The computer can easily generate the statement of cash flows by the indirect method. After the income statement is prepared, the computer picks up net income, depreciation, and the other noncash expenses. Changes in the current assets and the current liabilities and the data for the investing and financing activities are obtained from the specific account balances in the general ledger.

The statement of cash flows created from a computer's general ledger files is not automatically correct from a GAAP point of view. For example, noncash financing and investing activities of a large corporation, such as Abbott Laboratories (a manufacturer of pharmaceuticals), might be incorrectly combined with the company's cash flows. The computerized system must be sophisticated enough to distinguish among the various categories of cash activities. Most important, accountants must analyze the information fed into the computer and check that its output adheres to generally accepted accounting principles. Revisions to a company's computer accounting system are common.

Using Cash-Flow Information in Investment and Credit Analysis

The chapter opening story of W. T. Grant Company's bankruptcy makes it very clear that cash flows are important to a company's survival. A cash shortage is usually the most pressing problem of a struggling organization. Abundant cash allows a company to expand, invest in research and development, and hire the best employees. How, then, do investors (and their representatives, financial analysts) and creditors use cash-flow information to aid in decision making?

Neither cash-flow data, net-income information, balance sheet figures, nor the financial statement notes tell investors all they need to know about a company. Investor decision making is much more complex than plugging a few amounts into simple formulas. Investors analyze the financial statements, articles in the financial press, data about the company's industry, and predictions about the world economy to decide whether to invest in a company's stock. To evaluate a loan request, a bank loan officer will interview a company's top management to decide whether they are trustworthy. Both investors and creditors are interested mainly in where a company is headed. They want to make predictions about a company's net income and future cash flows.

It has been said that cash-flow data help to spot losers better than they help to spot winners. This is often true. When a company's business is booming, profits are high, and the financial position is usually improving. As the case of W. T. Grant Company vividly illustrates, a negative cash flow from operations warrants investigation. A cash downturn in a single year is not necessarily a danger signal. But negative cash flows for two consecutive years may hurt a company. This is especially true if operating activities generate negative cash flows for two or more years. Without cash coming in from basic operations, a business simply cannot survive.

You may ask, "Can't the business raise money by issuing stock or by borrowing?" The answer is no, because if operations cannot generate enough cash, then stockholders will not find the company's stock very attractive. Bankers will not lend money to an organization whose operations do not provide enough cash; lenders are well aware that companies need cash to pay off their loans. Over the long run, if a company cannot generate cash from operations, it is doomed. The Decision Guidelines feature provides investors and creditors with a few suggestions on how to use cash-flow information for their decision making.

DECISION GUIDELINES	Investors' and Creditors' Use of Cash-Flow and Related Information	
INVESTORS		
Question	Financial Statement	What to Look For
Where is most of the company's cash coming from?	Statement of cash flows	Operating activities ⟶ Good sign Investing activities ⟶ Bad sign Financing activities ⟶ Okay sign *(continued)*

DECISION GUIDELINES (continued)

Question	Financial Statement	What to Look For
If sales and profits are high, does that translate into more cash?	Statement of cash flows	Cash flows from *operating* activities must be the main source of cash for long-term success.
If sales and profits are low, how is the company generating cash?	Statement of cash flows	If *investing* activities are generating the cash, the business may be in trouble because it is selling off its long-term assets. If *financing* activities are generating the cash, that cannot go on forever. Sooner or later, investors will demand cash flow from operating activities.
Is the cash balance large enough to provide for expansion?	Balance sheet	The cash balance should be growing over time. If not, the company may be stagnant or in trouble.

CREDITORS

Question	Financial Statement	What to Look For
Can the business pay its debts?	Income statement Statement of cash flows Balance sheet	Increasing trend of net income. Cash flows from operating activities should be the main source of cash. Current ratio, debt ratio

SUMMARY PROBLEM FOR YOUR REVIEW

Prepare the 19X3 statement of cash flows for Robins Corporation, using the indirect method to report cash flows from operating activities. In a separate schedule, report Robin's noncash investing and financing activities.

	December 31,	
	19X3	19X2
Current Assets:		
Cash and cash equivalents	$19,000	$ 3,000
Accounts receivable	22,000	23,000
Inventories	34,000	31,000
Prepaid expenses	1,000	3,000
Current Liabilities:		
Notes payable (for inventory purchases)	$11,000	$ 7,000
Accounts payable	24,000	19,000
Accrued liabilities	7,000	9,000
Income tax payable	10,000	10,000

Transaction Data for 19X3:

Purchase of equipment	$98,000	Depreciation expense	$ 7,000
Payment of cash dividends	18,000	Issuance of long-term note	
Net income	26,000	payable to borrow cash	7,000
Issuance of common stock to		Issuance of common stock	
retire bonds payable	13,000	for cash	19,000
Purchase of long-term		Sale of building	74,000
investment	8,000	Amortization expense	3,000
Issuance of long-term note		Purchase of treasury stock	5,000
payable to purchase patent	37,000	Loss on sale of building	2,000

■ SOLUTION

ROBINS CORPORATION Statement of Cash Flows Year Ended December 31, 19X3		
Cash flows from operating activities:		
Net income		$26,000
Add (subtract) items that affect net income and cash flows differently:		
Depreciation	$ 7,000	
Amortization	3,000	
Loss on sale of building	2,000	
Decrease in accounts receivable	1,000	
Increase in inventories	(3,000)	
Decrease in prepaid expenses	2,000	
Increase in notes payable, short-term	4,000	
Increase in accounts payable.......................	5,000	
Decrease in accrued liabilities	(2,000)	19,000
Net cash inflow from operating activities.................		45,000
Cash flows from investing activities:		
Purchase of equipment.................................	$(98,000)	
Sale of building	74,000	
Purchase of long-term investment	(8,000)	
Net cash outflow from investing activities		(32,000)
Cash flows from financing activities:		
Issuance of common stock.............................	$ 19,000	
Payment of cash dividends...........................	(18,000)	
Issuance of long-term note payable..............	7,000	
Purchase of treasury stock	(5,000)	
Net cash inflow from financing activities..............		3,000
Net increase in cash and cash equivalents...........................		$16,000
Noncash investing and financing activities:		
Issuance of long-term note payable to purchase patent..		$37,000
Issuance of common stock to retire bonds payable.........		13,000
Total noncash investing and financing activities		$50,000

Summary of Learning Objectives

1. Identify the purposes of the statement of cash flows. The *statement of cash flows* reports a business's cash receipts, cash disbursements, and net change in cash for the accounting period. It shows *why* cash increased or decreased during the period. A required financial statement, it gives a different view of the business from that given by accrual-basis statements. The cash-flow statement helps financial statement users predict the future cash flows of the entity. It also allows investors to evaluate management decisions, determine the company's ability to pay dividends to stockholders and interest and principal to creditors, and ascertain the relationship of net income to changes in the business's cash. Cash includes cash on hand, cash in the bank, and *cash equivalents* such as liquid short-term investments.

2. Distinguish among operating, investing, and financing activities. The cash-flow statement is divided into *operating activities, investing activities,* and *financing activities.* Operating activities create revenues and expenses in the entity's major line of business. Investing activities increase and decrease the long-term assets available to the business. Financing activities obtain from investors and creditors the cash needed to launch and sustain the business. Each section of the statement includes cash receipts and cash payments and concludes with a net cash increase or decrease. In addi-

tion, *noncash investing and financing activities* are reported in an accompanying schedule.

3. Prepare a statement of cash flows by the direct method. Two formats can be used to report *operating* activities—the direct method and the indirect method. The *direct method* lists the major categories of operating cash receipts (collections from customers and receipts of interest and dividends) and cash disbursements (payments to suppliers, payments to employees, and payments for interest and income taxes). Investing cash flows and financing cash flows are unaffected by the method used to report operating activities.

4. Use the financial statements to compute the cash effects of a wide variety of business transactions. The analysis of T-accounts aids the computation of the cash effects of business transactions. Much of the information needed to compute these amounts comes from the balance sheet, the income statement, and the related accounts.

5. Prepare a statement of cash flows by the indirect method. The *indirect method* starts with net income and reconciles to cash flow from operations. Although the FASB permits both the indirect and the direct methods, it prefers the direct method. However, the indirect method is more widely used.

Accounting Vocabulary

cash equivalents *(p. 715)*   financing activity *(p. 716)*   operating activity *(p. 715)*   statement of cash flows
cash flows *(p. 714)*   indirect method *(p. 718)*   reconciliation method   *(p. 714)*
direct method *(p. 718)*   investing activity *(p. 716)*   *(p. 718)*

Questions

1. What information does the statement of cash flows report that is not shown on the balance sheet, the income statement, or the statement of retained earnings?
2. Identify four purposes of the statement of cash flows.
3. Identify and briefly describe the three types of activities that are reported on the statement of cash flows.
4. How is the statement of cash flows dated, and why?
5. What is the check figure for the statement of cash flows? (In other words, which figure do you check to make sure you've done your work correctly?) Where is it obtained, and how is it used?
6. What is the most important source of cash for most successful companies?
7. How can cash decrease during a year when income is high? How can cash increase during a year when income is low? How can investors and creditors learn these facts about the company?
8. DeBerg, Inc., prepares its statement of cash flows by the *direct* method for operating activities. Identify the section of De-Berg's statement of cash flows where each of the following transactions will appear. If the transaction does not appear on the cash-flow statement, give the reason.

   a. Cash 14,000
      Note Payable,
      Long-Term..................... 14,000
   b. Salary Expense...................... 7,300
      Cash................................ 7,300
   c. Cash 28,400
      Sales Revenue................ 28,400
   d. Amortization Expense 6,500
      Goodwill 6,500
   e. Accounts Payable................. 1,400
      Cash................................ 1,400

9. Why are depreciation, depletion, and amortization expenses *not* reported on a cash-flow statement that reports operating activities by the direct method? Why and how are these expenses reported on a statement prepared by the indirect method?
10. Mainline Distributing Company collected cash of $92,000 from customers and $6,000 interest on notes receivable. Cash payments included $24,000 to employees, $13,000 to suppliers, $6,000 as dividends to stockholders, and $5,000 as a loan to another company. How much was Mainline's net cash inflow from operating activities?
11. Summarize the major cash receipts and cash disbursements in the three categories of activities that appear on the cash-flow statement.
12. Kirchner, Inc., recorded salary expense of $51,000 during a year when the balance of Salary Payable decreased from $10,000 to $2,000. How much cash did Kirchner pay to employees during the year? Where on the statement of cash flows should Kirchner report this item?
13. Marshall Corp.'s beginning plant asset balance, net of accumulated depreciation, was $193,000, and the ending amount was $176,000. Marshall recorded depreciation of $37,000 and sold plant assets with a book value of $9,000. How much cash did Marshall pay to purchase plant assets during the period? Where on the statement of cash flows should Marshall report this item?
14. How should issuance of a note payable to purchase land be reported in the financial statements? Identify three other transactions that fall in this same category.
15. Which format of the cash-flow statement gives a clearer description of the individual cash flows from operating activities? Which format better shows the relationship between net income and operating cash flow?
16. An investment that cost $65,000 was sold for $80,000, resulting in a $15,000 gain. Show how to report this transaction on a statement of cash flows prepared by the indirect method.
17. Identify the cash effects of increases and decreases in current assets other than cash. What are the cash effects of increases and decreases in current liabilities?
18. Milano Corporation earned net income of $38,000 and had depreciation expense of $22,000. Also, noncash current assets decreased $13,000, and current liabilities decreased $9,000. What was Milano's net cash flow from operating activities?
19. What is the difference between the direct and indirect methods of reporting investing activities and financing activities?
20. Milgrom Company reports operating activities by the direct method. Does this method show the relationship between net income and cash flow from operations? If so, state how. If not, how can Milgrom satisfy this purpose of the cash-flow statement?

Daily Exercises

DE17-1 How does the statement of cash flows help investors and creditors:

1. Predict future cash flows?
2. Evaluate management decisions?
3. Predict the company's ability to pay dividends and interest?

Purposes of the statement of cash flows
(Obj. 1)

DE17-2 Describe operating activities, investing activities, and financing activities. For each category, give an example of (a) a cash receipt and (b) a cash payment.

Distinguishing operating, investing, and financing activities
(Obj. 2)

DE17-3 ◀▥ *Link Back to Chapter 2 (Journal Entries)*. Return to Daily Exercise 17-2. For each cash receipt and each cash payment that you identified, give the journal entry, using made-up figures.

Journal entries for operating, investing, and financing activities
(Obj. 2)

Using an actual statement of cash flows
(Obj. 1)

DE17-4 Examine the statement of cash flows of W. T. Grant Company on page 712. What is the main danger signal about the company's cash flows?

Using an actual statement of cash flows
(Obj. 1)

DE17-5 Return to the W. T. Grant Company cash-flow statement on page 712. Suppose Grant experiences two more years (19X4 and 19X5) exactly like 19X3. What will the company's cash balance be at the end of 19X5? What is likely to happen to the company?

Identifying operating cash flows
(Obj. 2, 3)

DE17-6 (Daily Exercise 17-9 is an alternative exercise.) Mid-America Resources, Inc., accountants have assembled the following data for the year ended June 30, 19X9:

Payment of dividends	$ 6,000	Cost of goods sold	$100,000
Proceeds from issuance		Payments to suppliers	80,000
of common stock	20,000	Purchase of equipment	40,000
Sales revenue	210,000	Payments to employees	70,000
Collections from customers	190,000	Payment of note payable	30,000
Payment of income tax	10,000	Proceeds from sale of land	60,000
Purchase of treasury stock	5,000	Depreciation expense	15,000

Prepare the *operating* activities section of Mid-America's statement of cash flows for the year ended June 30, 19X9. Mid-America uses the direct method for operating cash flows.

Identifying investing cash flows
(Obj. 2, 3)

DE17-7 (Daily Exercise 17-9 is an alternative exercise.) Use the data in Daily Exercise 17-6 to prepare the *investing* activities section of Mid-America's statement of cash flows for the year ended June 30, 19X9.

Identifying financing cash flows
(Obj. 2, 3)

DE17-8 (Daily Exercise 17-9 is an alternative exercise.) Use the data in Daily Exercise 17-6 to prepare the *financing* activities section of Mid-America's statement of cash flows for the year ended June 30, 19X9.

Preparing a statement of cash flows—direct method
(Obj. 3)

DE17-9 Mid-America Resources, Inc., accountants have assembled the following data for the year ended June 30, 19X9:

Payment of dividends	$ 6,000	Cost of goods sold	$100,000
Proceeds from issuance		Payments to suppliers	80,000
of common stock	20,000	Purchase of equipment	40,000
Sales revenue	210,000	Payments to employees	70,000
Collections from customers	190,000	Payment of note payable	30,000
Payment of income tax	10,000	Proceeds from sale of land	60,000
Purchase of treasury stock	5,000	Depreciation expense	15,000

Prepare Mid-America's statement of cash flows for the year ended June 30, 19X9. Mid-America uses the *direct* method for operating activities. Use Exhibit 17-2, page 716, as a guide.

Preparing a statement of cash flows—direct method
(Obj. 3)

DE17-10 Wellness Health Laboratories began 19X7 with cash of $104,000. During the year, Wellness earned service revenue of $600,000 and collected $590,000 from customers. Expenses for the year totaled $420,000, of which Wellness paid $410,000 in cash to suppliers and employees. Wellness also paid $140,000 to purchase equipment and a cash dividend of $50,000 to its stockholders during 19X7.

1. Compute net income for the year.
2. Determine the cash balance at the end of the year.
3. Prepare the company's statement of cash flows for the year. Format operating activities by the direct method, and show the beginning and ending balances of cash.

Computing cash-flow amounts
(Obj. 4)

DE17-11 Grace Chemical Company reported the following financial statements for 19X8:

GRACE CHEMICAL COMPANY
Income Statement
Year Ended December 31, 19X8

(In thousands)

Sales revenue	$710
Cost of goods sold	$340
Depreciation expense	60
Salary expense	50
Other expenses	150
Total expenses	600
Net income	$110

GRACE CHEMICAL COMPANY						
Comparative Balance Sheet						
December 31, 19X8 and 19X7						

(In thousands)

ASSETS	19X8	19X7	LIABILITIES	19X8	19X7
Current:			Current:		
Cash	$ 19	$ 16	Accounts payable....................	$ 47	$ 42
Accounts receivable	54	48	Salary payable.........................	23	21
Inventory..............................	80	84	Accrued liabilities..................	8	11
Prepaid expenses.................	3	2	Long-term notes payable..........	66	68
Long-term investments..........	75	90			
Plant assets, net......................	225	185	**STOCKHOLDERS' EQUITY**		
			Common stock..........................	40	37
			Retained earnings.....................	272	246
Total......................................	$456	$425	Total..	$456	$425

Compute the following operating cash flows:

a. Collections from customers.

b. Payments for inventory.

DE17-12 Use the Grace Chemical Company data in Daily Exercise 17-11 to compute

Computing cash-flow amounts (Obj. 4)

a. Payments of other expenses. (Use the computational approach for Operating Expense outlined in Exhibit 17-8, page 726.)

b. Payments to employees.

DE17-13 Use the Grace Chemical Company data in Daily Exercise 17-11 to compute

Computing investing cash flows (Obj. 4)

a. Proceeds from the sale of long-term investments. (Study Grace's income statement to see whether there was a gain or loss on the sale. Grace purchased no investments during the year.)

b. Acquisitions of plant assets (all acquisitions were for cash). Grace sold no plant assets during the year.

DE17-14 Use the Grace Chemical Company data in Daily Exercise 17-11 to compute

Computing financing cash flows (Obj. 4)

a. New borrowing or payment of long-term notes payable. Grace had only one long-term note payable transaction during the year.

b. Issuance of common stock or retirement of common stock. Grace had only one common stock transaction during the year.

c. Payment of cash dividends (same as amount of dividends declared).

DE17-15 Return to the Anchor Corporation income statement (Exhibit 17-6, page 724) and comparative balance sheet (Exhibit 17-7, page 725). Assume that Anchor sold no plant assets during 19X2.

Noncash investing and financing transactions (Obj. 4)

1. Compute the cost of Anchor's plant asset acquisition during the year.

2. Anchor financed the plant asset by signing a long-term note payable for $83,000 and paying the remainder in cash. Journalize this transaction.

3. Show how to report Anchor's acquisition of the plant assets on the statement of cash flows.

DE17-16 Post Corporation is preparing its statement of cash flows for the year ended September 30, 19X9. Post reports cash flows from operating activities by the *indirect* method. The company's head bookkeeper has provided the following list of items for you to consider in preparing the company's statement of cash flows. Identify each item as an operating activity—addition to net income (O+) or subtraction from net income (O–); an investing activity (I); a financing activity (F); or an activity that is not used to prepare the cash-flow statement by the indirect method (N). Answer by placing the appropriate symbol in the blank space.

Identifying items for reporting cash flows from operations—indirect method (Obj. 5)

____	a. Loss on sale of land		____	e. Decrease in accounts receivable
____	b. Depreciation expense		____	f. Purchase of equipment
____	c. Increase in inventory		____	g. Collection of cash from customers
____	d. Decrease in prepaid expense		____	h. Increase in accounts payable

_____ **i.** Sales revenue   _____ **l.** Issuance of common stock

_____ **j.** Payment of dividends   _____ **m.** Gain on sale of building

_____ **k.** Decrease in accrued liabilities   _____ **n.** Retained earnings

Reporting cash flows from operating activities, indirect method
(Obj. 5)

DE17-17 Grisham Publishing Company began 19X8 with accounts receivable, inventory, and prepaid expenses totaling $65,000. At the end of the year, the company had a total of $78,000 for these current assets. At the beginning of 19X8, Grisham owed current liabilities of $42,000, and at year end current liabilities totaled $40,000.

    Net income for the year was $81,000, after including all revenues and gains and after subtracting all expenses and losses. Included in the computation of net income were a $4,000 gain on the sale of land and depreciation expense of $9,000.

    Show how Grisham should report cash flows from operating activities for 19X8. Grisham uses the *indirect* method. Use Exhibit 17-13, page 733, as a guide.

Preparing a statement of cash flows, indirect method
(Obj. 5)

DE17-18 Grace Chemical Company reported the following financial statements for 19X8:

GRACE CHEMICAL COMPANY
Income Statement
Year Ended December 31, 19X8

(In thousands)

Sales revenue	$710
Cost of goods sold	$340
Depreciation expense	60
Salary expense	50
Other expenses, including income taxes	150
Total expenses	600
Net income	$110

GRACE CHEMICAL COMPANY
Comparative Balance Sheet
December 31, 19X8 and 19X7

(In thousands)

ASSETS	19X8	19X7	LIABILITIES	19X8	19X7
Current:			Current:		
Cash	$ 19	$ 16	Accounts payable	$ 47	$ 42
Accounts receivable	54	48	Salary payable	23	21
Inventory	80	84	Accrued liabilities	8	11
Prepaid expenses	3	2	Long-term notes payable	66	68
Long-term investments	75	90			
Plant assets, net	225	185	**STOCKHOLDERS' EQUITY**		
			Common stock	40	37
			Retained earnings	272	246
Total	$456	$425	Total	$456	$425

Additional data during 19X8:

a. Grace purchased no investments.

b. Grace sold no plant assets.

c. Grace had only one long-term note payable transaction.

d. Grace had only one common stock transaction.

Prepare Grace's statement of cash flows for the year ended December 31, 19X8. Grace uses the *indirect* method for operating activities. Use Exhibit 17-13, page 733, as a guide.

Using an actual company's statement of cash flows
(Obj. 5)

DE17-19 ◀▥ *Link Back to Chapter Opening Story*. A friend is a stockholder in NIKE, Inc., and has received the company's statement of cash flows, which is reproduced in Exhibit 17-17, page 737. Answer the following questions to help your friend understand this financial statement and its purpose.

1. What does the statement of cash flows reveal that you cannot learn from the income statement and the balance sheet? Use the W. T. Grant Company case to explain why cash flows are important.

2. NIKE's statement indicates that the company uses the indirect method to report cash flows from operating activities. When you see other cash-flow statements, how can you tell that the company uses the indirect method?

3. Do NIKE's cash flows for 19X7 look strong or weak? Give your reason. What are two things you should look for in evaluating a company's cash flows?

Exercises

E17-1 James River Realty, a real-estate partnership in Virginia, has experienced an unbroken string of ten years of growth in net income. Nevertheless, the business is facing bankruptcy! Creditors are calling all of James River's outstanding loans for immediate payment, and the cash is simply not available. Attempts to explain where James River Realty went wrong make it clear that managers placed undue emphasis on net income and gave too little attention to cash flows.

Identifying the purposes of the statement of cash flows
(Obj. 1)

REQUIRED

Write a brief memo, in your own words, to explain to the managers of James River Realty the purposes of the statement of cash flows.

E17-2 Identify each of the following transactions as an operating activity (O), an investing activity (I), a financing activity (F), a noncash investing and financing activity (NIF), or a transaction that is not reported on the statement of cash flows (N). Assume that the direct method is used to report cash flows from operating activities.

Identifying activities for the statement of cash flows
(Obj. 2)

____ a. Purchase of long-term investment	____ k. Payment of account payable
____ b. Payment of wages to employees	____ l. Issuance of preferred stock for
____ c. Collection of cash interest	cash
____ d. Cash sale of land	____ m. Payment of cash dividend
____ e. Distribution of stock dividend	____ n. Sale of long-term investment
____ f. Acquisition of equipment by	____ o. Amortization of bond discount
issuance of note payable	____ p. Collection of account receivable
____ g. Payment of long-term debt	____ q. Issuance of long-term note payable
____ h. Acquisition of building by issuance	to borrow cash
of common stock	____ r. Depreciation of equipment
____ i. Accrual of salary expense	____ s. Purchase of treasury stock
____ j. Issuance of common stock for cash	

E17-3 Indicate where, if at all, each of the following transactions would be reported on a statement of cash flows prepared by the *direct* method and the accompanying schedule of noncash investing and financing activities.

Classifying transactions for the statement of cash flows
(Obj. 2)

a.	Accounts Payable..........	8,300	i.	Salary Expense..............	4,300
	Cash	8,300		Cash	4,300
b.	Cash	81,000	j.	Equipment...................	18,000
	Common Stock.....	12,000		Cash	18,000
	Paid-in Capital		k.	Cash	7,200
	in Excess of			Long-Term	
	Par—Common...	69,000		Investment	7,200
c.	Treasury Stock..............	13,000	l.	Bonds Payable	45,000
	Cash	13,000		Cash	45,000
d.	Retained Earnings........	36,000	m.	Building	164,000
	Common Stock.....	36,000		Note Payable,	
e.	Cash	2,000		Long-Term	164,000
	Interest Revenue...	2,000	n.	Cash	1,400
f.	Land.............................	87,700		Accounts	
	Cash	87,700		Receivable	1,400
g.	Dividends Payable	16,500			
	Cash	16,500			
h.	Furniture and				
	Fixtures.........................	22,100			
	Note Payable,				
	Short-Term	22,100			

E17-4 Analysis of the accounting records of Kirchner Corporation reveals the following:

Collection of accounts receivable	$93,000		Increase in current assets other than cash	$17,000
Payment of salaries and wages	34,000		Payment of dividends	7,000
Depreciation	12,000		Cash sales	9,000
Decrease in current liabilities	23,000		Loss on sale of land	5,000
Collection of dividend revenue	1,000		Acquisition of land	37,000
Payment of interest	16,000		Payment of accounts payable	48,000
			Net income	21,000
			Payment of income tax	13,000

REQUIRED

Compute cash flows from operating activities by the direct method. Use the format of the operating section of Exhibit 17-2. Evaluate the operating cash flow of Kirchner Corporation. Give the reason for your evaluation.

E17-5 Selected accounts of CMI, Inc., show the following:

Accounts Receivable

Beginning balance	9,000	Cash receipts from customers	118,000
Sales revenue	120,000		
Ending balance	11,000		

Investment in Land

Beginning balance	90,000	Cost of investments sold	109,000
Acquisitions	127,000		
Ending balance	108,000		

Long-Term Debt

Payments	69,000	Beginning balance	273,000
		Issuance of debt for cash	83,000
		Ending balance	287,000

REQUIRED

For each account, identify the item or items that should appear on a statement of cash flows prepared by the direct method. State where to report the item.

E17-6 The income statement and additional data of Boyce Computing Company follow.

BOYCE COMPUTING COMPANY
Income Statement
Year Ended September 30, 19X2

Revenues:		
Sales revenue		$237,000
Expenses:		
Cost of goods sold	$103,000	
Salary expense	45,000	
Depreciation expense	29,000	
Rent expense	11,000	
Interest expense	2,000	
Income tax expense	9,000	199,000
Net income		$ 38,000

Additional data during fiscal year 19X2:

a. Collections from customers were $7,000 more than sales.

b. Payments to suppliers were $5,000 less than the sum of cost of goods sold plus rent expense.

c. Payments to employees were $1,000 more than salary expense.

d. Interest expense and income tax expense equal their cash amounts.

e. Acquisition of equipment is $116,000. Of this amount, $101,000 was paid in cash, $15,000 by signing a long-term note payable. Boyce sold no equipment during fiscal year 19X2.

f. Proceeds from sale of land, $14,000.

g. Proceeds from issuance of common stock, $35,000.

h. Payment of long-term note payable, $20,000.

i. Payment of dividends, $10,000.

j. Decrease in cash balance, $4,000.

1. Prepare Boyce Computing Company's statement of cash flows and accompanying schedule of noncash investing and financing activities. Report operating activities by the *direct* method.

2. Evaluate Boyce Computing Company's cash flows for the year. In your evaluation, mention all three categories of cash flows, and give the reason for your evaluation.

E17-7 Compute the following items for the statement of cash flows,

Computing amounts for the statement of cash flows
(Obj. 3, 4)

a. Beginning and ending Accounts Receivable are $22,000 and $26,000, respectively. Credit sales for the period total $81,000. How much are cash collections?

b. Cost of goods sold is $82,000. Beginning Inventory balance is $25,000, and ending Inventory balance is $21,000. Beginning and ending Accounts Payable are $11,000 and $8,000, respectively. How much are cash payments for inventory?

E17-8 Compute the following items for the statement of cash flows:

Computing investing and financing amounts for the statement of cash flows
(Obj. 4)

a. Beginning and ending Retained Earnings are $45,000 and $73,000, respectively. Net income for the period is $62,000, and stock dividends are $22,000. How much are cash dividend payments?

b. Beginning and ending Plant Assets, net, are $103,000 and $107,000, respectively. Depreciation for the period is $16,000, and acquisitions of new plant assets are $27,000. Plant assets were sold at a $1,000 gain. What were the cash proceeds of the sale?

E17-9 The accounting records of Steitz Corporation reveal the following:

Computing cash flows from operating activities—indirect method
(Obj. 5)

Payment of accounts payable............	$48,000	Cash sales	$ 9,000
Net income	21,000	Loss on sale of land	5,000
Payment of income tax	13,000	Acquisition of land	37,000
Collection of accounts		Collection of dividend revenue........	7,000
receivable......................................	93,000	Payment of interest	16,000
Payment of salaries and wages.........	34,000	Increase in current assets	
Depreciation	12,000	other than cash	17,000
Decrease in current liabilities..........	29,000	Payment of dividends......................	7,000

Compute cash flows from operating activities by the indirect method. Use the format of the operating section of Exhibit 17-13. Then evaluate Steitz's operating cash flows as strong or weak.

E17-10 Two transactions of Colgate Baking Co. are recorded as follows:

Classifying transactions for the statement of cash flows
(Obj. 3, 5)

a. Cash... 16,000
   Accumulated Depreciation 83,000
      Equipment... 92,000
      Gain on Sale of Equipment.............. 7,000

b. Land 290,000
      Cash 130,000
      Note Payable 160,000

1. Indicate where, how, and in what amount to report these transactions on the statement of cash flows and accompanying schedule of noncash investing and financing activities. Colgate reports cash flows from operating activities by the *direct* method.

2. Repeat requirement 1, assuming that Colgate reports cash flows from operating activities by the *indirect* method.

E17-11 Use the income statement of Boyce Computing Company in Exercise 17-6, plus these additional data during fiscal year 19X2:

Preparing the statement of cash flows by the indirect method
(Obj. 5)

a. Acquisition of equipment was $116,000. Of this amount, $101,000 was paid in cash, $15,000 by signing a long-term note payable. Boyce sold no equipment during fiscal year 19X2.

b. Proceeds from sale of land, $14,000.

c. Proceeds from issuance of common stock, $35,000.

d. Payment of long-term note payable, $20,000.

e. Payment of dividends, $10,000.

f. Change in cash balance, $?

g. The comparative balance sheet:

BOYCE COMPUTING COMPANY Comparative Balance Sheet September 30, 19X2 and 19X1				
		19X2		**19X1**
Current assets:				
Cash..		$ 14,000		$ 18,000
Accounts receivable......................................		65,000		72,000
Inventory..		59,000		53,000
Prepaid expenses..		6,000		5,000
Total current assets.......................................		144,000		148,000
Property, plant and equipment:				
Land...		-0-		14,000
Equipment..	$207,000		$91,000	
Less Accumulated depreciation	(70,000)	137,000	(41,000)	50,000
Total assets...		$281,000		$212,000
Current liabilities:				
Accounts payable		$ 41,000		$ 28,000
Accrued liabilities..		19,000		21,000
Total current liabilities		60,000		49,000
Long-term notes payable		85,000		90,000
Stockholders' equity:				
Common stock, no-par		71,000		36,000
Retained earnings..		65,000		37,000
Total liabilities and stockholders' equity		$281,000		$212,000

REQUIRED

1. Prepare Boyce Computing Company's statement of cash flows for the year ended September 30, 19X2, using the indirect method.
2. Evaluate Boyce Computing Company's cash flows for the year. In your evaluation, mention all three categories of cash flows, and give the reason for your evaluation.

Computing cash flows from operating activities—indirect method (Obj. 5)

E17-12 The accounting records of Sunbury Printing Company include these selected accounts:

Cash			
Mar. 1	5,000		
Receipts	447,000	Payments	448,000
Mar. 31	4,000		

Accounts Receivable			
Mar. 1	18,000		
Sales	443,000	Collections	447,000
Mar. 31	14,000		

Inventory			
Mar. 1	19,000		
Purchases	337,000	Cost of sales	335,000
Mar. 31	21,000		

Equipment		
Mar. 1	93,000	
Acquisition	6,000	
Mar. 31	99,000	

Accumulated Depreciation—Equipment		
	Mar. 1	52,000
	Depreciation	6,000
	Mar. 31	58,000

Accounts Payable		
	Mar. 1	14,000
Payments	332,000	Purchases	337,000
	Mar. 31	19,000

Accrued Liabilities		
	Mar. 1	9,000
Payments	14,000	Expenses	11,000
	Mar. 31	6,000

Retained Earnings		
	Mar. 1	64,000
Quarterly dividend	18,000	Net income	19,000
	Mar. 31	65,000

Compute Sunbury's net cash inflow or outflow from operating activities during March. Use the indirect method. Does Sunbury have trouble collecting receivables or selling inventory? How can you tell?

E17-13   Consider three independent cases for the cash-flow data of Cape Town Banking Company:

Interpreting a cash-flow statement—indirect method
(Obj. 5)

	Case A	Case B	Case C
Cash flows from operating activities:			
Net income	$ 30,000	$ 30,000	$ 30,000
Depreciation and amortization	11,000	11,000	11,000
Increase in current assets......................	(1,000)	(19,000)	(7,000)
Decrease in current liabilities...............	-0-	(6,000)	(8,000)
	$ 40,000	$ 16,000	$ 26,000
Cash flows from investing activities:			
Acquisition of plant assets	$(91,000)	$(91,000)	$(91,000)
Sales of plant assets..............................	8,000	97,000	4,000
	$(83,000)	$ 6,000	$(87,000)
Cash flows from financing activities:			
New borrowing......................................	$ 50,000	$ 16,000	$104,000
Payment of debt....................................	(9,000)	(21,000)	(29,000)
	$ 41,000	$ (5,000)	$ 75,000
Net increase (decrease) in cash	$ (2,000)	$ 17,000	$ 14,000

For each case, identify from the cash-flow statement how Cape Town Banking Company generated the cash to acquire new plant assets.

CHALLENGE EXERCISE

E17-14   PepsiCo's statement of cash flows, as adapted, for 19X2 is reproduced on page 750.

Analyzing an actual company's statement of cash flows
(Obj. 5)

REQUIRED

1. Which format does PepsiCo use for reporting cash flows from operating activities?
2. What was PepsiCo's largest source of cash during 19X2? During 19X1? Give each amount.
3. What was PepsiCo's largest use of cash during 19X2? During 19X1? Give each amount.
4. The operating activities section of the statement lists (in millions):

> Accounts and notes receivable.......... ($45.7)
> Accounts payable.............................. ($102.0)

Did these accounts' balances increase or decrease during 19X2? How can you tell?

5. During 19X2, PepsiCo sold property, plant, and equipment. The gain or loss on this transaction is included in "Other noncash charges and credits, net" of $263.6 million. Assume that the book value of the plant assets that PepsiCo sold during 19X2 was $104.3 million. Journalize the sale of the property, plant, and equipment.

(In millions)	19X2	19X1
Cash Flows—Continuing Operations:		
Income from continuing operations	$ 1,301.7	$ 1,080.2
Adjustments to reconcile income from continuing operations to net cash provided by continuing operations:		
Depreciation and amortization	1,214.9	1,034.5
Other noncash charges and credits, net	263.6	325.2
Changes in [current accounts]:		
Accounts and notes receivable	(45.7)	(55.9)
Inventories	(11.8)	(54.8)
Prepaid expenses, taxes and other current assets	(27.4)	(75.6)
Accounts payable	(102.0)	57.8
Other current liabilities	118.3	118.9
Net change in operating working capital	(68.6)	(9.6)
Net Cash Provided by Continuing Operations	2,711.6	2,430.3
Cash Flows—Investing Activities:		
Acquisitions and investments in affiliates	(1,209.7)	(640.9)
Purchases of property, plant, and equipment	(1,549.6)	(1,457.8)
Proceeds from sales of property, plant, and equipment	89.0	69.6
Other, net	(83.2)	(246.7)
Net Cash Used for Investing Activities	(2,753.5)	(2,275.8)
Cash Flows—Financing Activities:		
Proceeds from issuances of long-term debt	1,092.7	2,799.6
Payments of long-term debt	(616.3)	(1,348.5)
Net payments of short-term borrowings	(76.1)	(1,012.6)
Cash dividends paid	(395.5)	(343.2)
Purchases of treasury stock	(32.0)	(195.2)
Proceeds from issuance of stock	82.8	15.8
Other, net	(30.9)	(47.0)
Net Cash Provided by (Used for) Financing Activities	24.7	(131.1)
Effect of Exchange Rate Changes on Cash and Cash Equivalents	0.4	(7.5)
Net Increase (Decrease) in Cash and Cash Equivalents	(16.8)	15.9
Cash and Cash Equivalents—Beginning of Year	186.7	170.8
Cash and Cash Equivalents—End of Year	$ 169.9	$ 186.7

PEPSICO, INC.
Statement of Cash Flows (Adapted)
Years Ended December 31, 19X2 and 19X1

Beyond the Numbers

Using cash-flow data to evaluate an investment
(Obj. 1, 2)

BN17-1 Magna Corp. and Altex, Inc., are asking you to recommend their stock to your clients. Magna and Altex earn about the same net income and have similar financial positions, so your decision depends on their cash-flow statements, summarized as follows:

	Magna Corp.		Altex, Inc.	
Net cash inflows from operating activities		$ 70,000		$ 30,000
Net cash inflows (outflows) from investing activities:				
Purchase of plant assets	$(100,000)		$(20,000)	
Sale of plant assets	10,000	(90,000)	40,000	20,000
Net cash inflows (outflows) from financing activities:				
Issuance of common stock		30,000		—
Paying off long-term debt		—		(40,000)
Net increase in cash		$ 10,000		$ 10,000

Based on their cash flows, which company looks better? Give your reasons.

ETHICAL ISSUE

Jarvis Travel Agency is having a bad year. Net income is only $65,000. Also, two important clients are falling behind in their payments to Jarvis, and the agency's accounts receivable are ballooning. The company desperately needs a loan. The Jarvis board of directors is considering ways to put the best face on the company's financial statements. The agency's bank closely examines cash flow from operations. Gwen Morris, Jarvis's controller, suggests reclassifying as long-term the receivables from the slow-paying clients. She explains to the board that removing the $30,000 rise in accounts receivable will increase net cash inflow from operations. This approach will increase the company's cash balance and may help Jarvis get the loan.

REQUIRED

1. Using only the amounts given, compute net cash inflow from operations both with and without the reclassification of the receivables. Which reporting makes Jarvis look better?

2. Where else in the agency's cash-flow statement will the reclassification of the receivable be reported? What cash-flow effect will this item report? What effect would the reclassification have on *overall* cash flow from all activities?

3. Under what condition would the reclassification of the receivables be ethical? Unethical?

Problems (GROUP A)

P17-1A Top managers of Drexel Stationery, Inc., are reviewing company performance for 19X7. The income statement reports a 20% increase in net income over 19X6. However, most of the increase resulted from an extraordinary gain on insurance proceeds from storm damage to a building. The balance sheet shows a large increase in receivables. The cash-flow statement, in summarized form, reports the following:

Using cash-flow information to evaluate performance
(Obj. 1)

Net cash outflow from operating activities..........	$(80,000)
Net cash inflow from investing activities.............	40,000
Net cash inflow from financing activities.............	50,000
Increase in cash during 19X7	$ 10,000

Write a memo giving Drexel managers your assessment of 19X7 operations and your outlook for the future. Focus on the information content of the cash-flow data.

REQUIRED

P17-2A Accountants for Humana Hospital Supply, Inc., have developed the following data from the company's accounting records for the year ended April 30, 19X5:

Preparing the statement of cash flows—direct method
(Obj. 2, 3)

a. Credit sales, $583,900.

b. Loan to another company, $12,500.

c. Cash payments to acquire plant assets, $59,400.

d. Cost of goods sold, $382,600.

e. Proceeds from issuance of common stock, $8,000.

f. Payment of cash dividends, $48,400.

g. Collection of interest, $4,400.

h. Acquisition of equipment by issuing short-term note payable, $16,400.

i. Payments of salaries, $93,600.

j. Proceeds from sale of plant assets, $22,400, including a $6,800 loss.

k. Collections on accounts receivable, $462,600.

l. Interest revenue, $3,800.

m. Cash receipt of dividend revenue on stock investments, $4,100.

n. Payments to suppliers, $368,500.

o. Cash sales, $171,900.

p. Depreciation expense, $59,900.

q. Proceeds from issuance of short-term debt, $19,600.

r. Payments of long-term debt, $50,000.

s. Interest expense and payments, $13,300.

t. Salary expense, $95,300.

u. Loan collections, $12,800.

v. Proceeds from sale of investments, $9,100, including a $2,000 gain.

w. Payment of short-term note payable by issuing long-term note payable, $63,000.

x. Amortization expense, $2,900.

y. Income tax expense and payments, $37,900.

z. Cash balance: April 30, 19X4—$39,300
April 30, 19X5—$?

REQUIRED

1. Prepare Humana's statement of cash flows for the year ended April 30, 19X5. Follow the format of Exhibit 17-2, but do *not* show amounts in thousands. Include an accompanying schedule of noncash investing and financing activities.

2. Evaluate 19X5 from a cash-flow standpoint. Give your reasons.

P17-3A The 19X5 comparative balance sheet and income statement of MultiFood Corp. follow.

MULTIFOOD CORP. Comparative Balance Sheet			
	December 31,		Increase
	19X5	19X4	(Decrease)
Current assets:			
Cash and cash equivalents	$ 7,200	$ 5,300	$ 1,900
Accounts receivable	28,600	26,900	1,700
Interest receivable	1,900	700	1,200
Inventories	83,600	87,200	(3,600)
Prepaid expenses	2,500	1,900	600
Plant assets:			
Land	89,000	60,000	29,000
Equipment, net	53,500	49,400	4,100
Total assets	$266,300	$231,400	$34,900
Current liabilities:			
Accounts payable	$ 31,400	$ 28,800	$ 2,600
Interest payable	4,400	4,900	(500)
Salary payable	3,100	6,600	(3,500)
Other accrued liabilities	13,700	16,000	(2,300)
Income tax payable	8,900	7,700	1,200
Long-term liabilities:			
Notes payable	75,000	100,000	(25,000)
Stockholders' equity:			
Common stock, no-par	88,300	64,700	23,600
Retained earnings	41,500	2,700	38,800
Total liabilities and stockholders' equity	$266,300	$231,400	$34,900

MULTIFOOD CORP. Income Statement for 19X5		
Revenues:		
Sales revenue		$213,000
Interest revenue		8,600
Total revenues		221,600
Expenses:		
Cost of goods sold	$70,600	
Salary expense	27,800	
Depreciation expense	4,000	
Other operating expense	10,500	
Interest expense	11,600	
Income tax expense	29,100	
Total expenses		153,600
Net income		$ 68,000

MultiFood had no noncash investing and financing transactions during 19X5. During the year, there were no sales of land or equipment, no issuances of notes payable, no retirements of stock, and no treasury stock transactions.

1. Prepare the 19X5 statement of cash flows, formating operating activities by the direct method.
2. How will what you learned in this problem help you evaluate an investment?

P17-4A Use the MultiFood Corp. data from Problem 17-3A.

1. Prepare the 19X5 statement of cash flows by the indirect method. If your instructor also assigned Problem 17-3A, prepare only the operating activities section of the statement.
2. How will what you learned in this problem help you evaluate an investment?

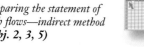

P17-5A Villanova Corporation accountants have assembled the following data for the year ended December 31, 19X7:

	December 31,	
	19X7	19X6
Current Accounts (All Result from Operations)		
Current assets:		
Cash and cash equivalents	$55,700	$22,700
Accounts receivable	69,700	64,200
Inventories	88,600	83,000
Prepaid expenses	5,300	4,100
Current liabilities:		
Notes payable (for inventory purchases)	$22,600	$18,300
Accounts payable	52,900	55,800
Income tax payable	18,600	16,700
Accrued liabilities	15,500	27,200

Transaction Data for 19X7:

Acquisition of land by issuing long-term note payable	$107,000	Purchase of treasury stock	$14,300
Stock dividends	31,800	Loss on sale of equipment	11,700
Collection of loan	8,700	Payment of cash dividends	18,300
Depreciation expense	26,800	Issuance of long-term note payable to borrow cash	34,400
Acquisition of building	125,300	Net income	57,100
Retirement of bonds payable by issuing common stock	65,000	Issuance of common stock for cash	41,200
		Sale of equipment	58,000
Acquisition of long-term investment	31,600	Amortization expense	5,300

Prepare Villanova Corporation's statement of cash flows, using the *indirect* method to report operating activities. Include an accompanying schedule of noncash investing and financing activities.

REQUIRED

P17-6A The comparative balance sheet of Vaughn-Johnson Company at March 31, 19X7, reported the following:

	March 31,	
	19X7	19X6
Current Assets:		
Cash and cash equivalents	$13,600	$ 4,000
Accounts receivable	14,900	21,700
Inventories	63,200	60,600
Prepaid expenses	1,900	1,700
Current Liabilities:		
Notes payable (for inventory purchases)	$ 4,000	$ 4,000
Accounts payable	30,300	27,600
Accrued liabilities	10,700	11,100
Income tax payable	8,000	4,700

Vaughn-Johnson's transactions during the year ended March 31, 19X7, included the following:

Acquisition of land by issuing note payable	$76,000	Sale of long-term investment	$13,700
Amortization expense	2,000	Depreciation expense	9,000
Payment of cash dividend	30,000	Cash acquisition of building	47,000
Cash acquisition of equipment	78,700	Net income	70,000
Issuance of long-term note payable to borrow cash	50,000	Issuance of common stock for cash	11,000
		Stock dividend	18,000

1. Prepare Vaughn-Johnson's statement of cash flows for the year ended March 31, 19X7, using the *indirect* method to report cash flows from operating activities. Report noncash investing and financing activities in an accompanying schedule.

2. Evaluate Vaughn-Johnson's cash flows for the year. Mention all three categories of cash flows, and give the reason for your evaluation.

REQUIRED

P17-7A To prepare the statement of cash flows, accountants for Columbia, Inc., have summarized 19X3 activity in two accounts as follows:

Cash			
Beginning balance	53,600	Payments on accounts payable	399,100
Collection of loan	13,000		
Sale of investment	8,200	Payments of dividends	27,200
Receipts of interest	12,600	Payments of salaries and wages	143,800
Collections from customers	678,700	Payments of interest	26,900
		Purchase of equipment	31,400
Issuance of common stock	47,300	Payments of operating expenses	34,300
Receipts of dividends	4,500	Payment of long-term debt	41,300
		Purchase of treasury stock	26,400
		Payment of income tax	18,900
Ending balance	68,600		

Common Stock			
		Beginning balance	84,400
		Issuance for cash	47,300
		Issuance to acquire land	80,100
		Issuance to retire long-term debt	19,000
		Ending balance	230,800

REQUIRED

1. Prepare the statement of cash flows of Columbia, Inc., for the year ended December 31, 19X3, using the *direct* method to report operating activities. Also prepare the accompanying schedule of noncash investing and financing activities.

2. Use the following data from Columbia's 19X3 income statement and (selected) balance sheet to prepare a supplementary schedule showing cash flows from operating activities by the *indirect* method. All activity in the current accounts results from operations.

COLUMBIA, INC.
Income Statement
Year Ended December 31, 19X3

Revenues:		
Sales revenue		$706,300
Interest revenue		12,600
Dividend revenue		4,500
Total revenues		723,400
Expenses and losses:		
Cost of goods sold	$402,600	
Salary and wage expense	150,800	
Depreciation expense	24,300	
Other operating expense	44,100	
Interest expense	28,800	
Income tax expense	16,200	
Loss on sale of investments	1,100	
Total expenses		667,900
Net income		$ 55,500

COLUMBIA, INC.
Balance Sheet Data
December 31, 19X3

	Increase (Decrease)
Current assets:	
Cash and cash equivalents	$?
Accounts receivable	27,600
Inventories	(11,800)
Prepaid expenses	600
Loan receivable	(13,000)
Long-term investments	(9,300)
Equipment, net	7,100
Land	80,100
Current liabilities:	
Accounts payable	$ (8,300)
Interest payable	1,900
Salary payable	7,000
Other accrued liabilities	10,400
Income tax payable	(2,700)
Long-term debt	(60,300)
Common stock, no-par	146,400
Retained earnings	28,300
Treasury stock	26,400

P17-8A The comparative balance sheet of Hartford Hotel Co. at June 30, 19X7, included the following balances:

Preparing the statement of cash flows—indirect and direct methods (Obj. 3, 4, 5)

HARTFORD HOTEL CO. Balance Sheet June 30, 19X7 and 19X6			
	19X7	**19X6**	**Increase (Decrease)**
Current assets:			
Cash..	$ 16,500	$ 8,600	$ 7,900
Accounts receivable....................	45,900	48,300	(2,400)
Interest receivable	2,900	3,600	(700)
Inventories..................................	68,600	60,200	8,400
Prepaid expenses	3,700	2,800	900
Long-term investment..................	10,100	5,200	4,900
Equipment, net	82,500	73,600	8,900
Land	42,400	96,000	(53,600)
	$272,600	$298,300	$(25,700)
Current liabilities:			
Notes payable, short-term			
(for general borrowing)..........	$ 13,400	$ 18,100	$ (4,700)
Accounts payable........................	42,400	40,300	2,100
Income tax payable.....................	13,800	14,500	(700)
Accrued liabilities.......................	8,200	9,700	(1,500)
Interest payable	3,700	2,900	800
Salary payable.............................	900	2,600	(1,700)
Long-term notes payable..............	47,400	94,100	(46,700)
Common stock.............................	59,800	51,200	8,600
Retained earnings........................	83,000	64,900	18,100
	$272,600	$298,300	$(25,700)

Transaction data for the year ended June 30, 19X7:

a. Net income, $56,200.
b. Depreciation expense on equipment, $5,400.
c. Purchased long-term investment, $4,900.
d. Sold land for $46,900, including a $6,700 loss.
e. Acquired equipment by issuing long-term note payable, $14,300.
f. Paid long-term note payable, $61,000.
g. Received cash for issuance of common stock, $3,900.
h. Paid cash dividends, $38,100.
i. Paid short-term note payable by issuing common stock, $4,700.

1. Prepare the statement of cash flows of Hartford Hotel Co. for the year ended June 30, 19X7, using the *indirect* method to report operating activities. Also prepare the accompanying schedule of noncash investing and financing activities. All current accounts except short-term notes payable result from operating transactions.

2. Prepare a supplementary schedule showing cash flows from operations by the *direct* method. The income statement reports the following: sales, $237,300; interest revenue, $10,600; cost of goods sold, $82,800; salary expense, $38,800; other operating expenses, $42,000; depreciation expense, $5,400; income tax expense, $9,900; loss on sale of land, $6,700; interest expense, $6,100.

REQUIRED

Problems (GROUP B)

P17-1B Top managers of Miller Communication, Inc., are reviewing company performance for 19X4. The income statement reports a 15% increase in net income, the fifth consecutive year with an income increase above 10 percent. The income statement includes a nonrecurring loss without which net income would have increased by 16 percent. The balance sheet shows modest increases in assets, liabilities, and stockholders' equity. The assets posting the largest increases are plant and equipment because the company is halfway through a five-year expansion program. No other assets and no liabilities are increasing dramatically. A summarized version of the cash-flow statement reports the following:

Using cash-flow information to evaluate performance (Obj. 1)

Net cash inflow from operating activities..............	$ 310,000
Net cash outflow from investing activities	(290,000)
Net cash inflow from financing activities	70,000
Increase in cash during 19X4...............................	$ 90,000

Write a memo giving top managers of Miller Communication your assessment of 19X4 and your outlook for the future. Focus on the information content of the cash-flow data.

Preparing the statement of cash flows—direct method
(Obj. 2, 3)

P17-2B Thermal Electronics Corporation accountants have developed the following data from the company's accounting records for the year ended July 31, 19X9:

a. Salary expense, $105,300.
b. Cash payments to purchase plant assets, $181,000.
c. Proceeds from issuance of short-term debt, $44,100.
d. Payments of long-term debt, $18,800.
e. Proceeds from sale of plant assets, $59,700, including a $10,600 gain.
f. Interest revenue, $12,100.
g. Cash receipt of dividend revenue on stock investments, $2,700.
h. Payments to suppliers, $673,300.
i. Interest expense and payments, $37,800.
j. Cost of goods sold, $481,100.
k. Collection of interest revenue, $11,700.
l. Acquisition of equipment by issuing short-term note payable, $35,500.
m. Payments of salaries, $104,000.
n. Credit sales, $608,100.

o. Loan to another company, $35,000.
p. Income tax expense and payments, $56,400.
q. Depreciation expense, $27,700.
r. Collections on accounts receivable, $673,100.
s. Loan collections, $74,400.
t. Proceeds from sale of investments, $34,700, including a $3,800 loss.
u. Payment of long-term debt by issuing preferred stock, $107,300.
v. Amortization expense, $23,900.
w. Cash sales, $146,000.
x. Proceeds from issuance of common stock, $116,900.
y. Payment of cash dividends, $50,500.
z. Cash balance: July 31, 19X8—$53,800
      July 31, 19X9—$?

REQUIRED

1. Prepare Thermal's statement of cash flows for the year ended July 31, 19X9. Follow the format of Exhibit 17-2, but do *not* show amounts in thousands. Include an accompanying schedule of noncash investing and financing activities.
2. Evaluate 19X9 in terms of cash flow. Give your reasons.

Preparing the statement of cash flows—direct method
(Obj. 2, 3, 4)

P17-3B The 19X3 income statement and comparative balance sheet of Alden Group, Inc., are given below and at the top of the next page.

ALDEN GROUP, INC.		
Income Statement for 19X3		
Revenues:		
Sales revenue............................		$438,000
Interest revenue		11,700
Total revenues		449,700
Expenses:		
Cost of goods sold....................	$205,200	
Salary expense	76,400	
Depreciation expense...............	15,300	
Other operating expense...........	49,700	
Interest expense........................	24,600	
Income tax expense	16,900	
Total expenses		388,100
Net income		$ 61,600

Alden had no noncash investing and financing transactions during 19X3. During the year, there were no sales of land or equipment, no issuances of notes payable, no retirements of stock, and no treasury stock transactions.

REQUIRED

1. Prepare the 19X3 statement of cash flows, formating operating activities by the direct method.
2. How will what you learned in this problem help you evaluate an investment?

ALDEN GROUP, INC.
Comparatiave Balance Sheet

	December 31, 19X3	December 31, 19X2	Increase (Decrease)
Current assets:			
Cash and cash equivalents	$ 13,700	$ 15,600	$ (1,900)
Accounts receivable	41,500	43,100	(1,600)
Interest receivable..	600	900	(300)
Inventories...	94,300	89,900	4,400
Prepaid expenses..	1,700	2,200	(500)
Plant assets:			
Land...	35,100	10,000	25,100
Equipment, net...	100,900	93,700	7,200
Total assets..	$287,800	$255,400	$ 32,400
Current liabilities:			
Accounts payable	$ 16,400	$ 17,900	$ (1,500)
Interest payable..	6,300	6,700	(400)
Salary payable	2,100	1,400	700
Other accrued liabilities	18,100	18,700	(600)
Income tax payable	6,300	3,800	2,500
Long-term liabilities:			
Notes payable	55,000	65,000	(10,000)
Stockholders' equity:			
Common stock, no-par	131,100	122,300	8,800
Retained earnings	52,500	19,600	32,900
Total liabilities and stockholders' equity..........	$287,800	$255,400	$ 32,400

Preparing the statement of cash flows—indirect method
(Obj. 2, 3, 5)

REQUIRED

P17-4B Use the Alden Group data from Problem 17-3B.

1. Prepare the 19X3 statement of cash flows by the indirect method. If your instructor also assigned Problem 17-3B, prepare only the operating activities section.
2. How will what you learned in this problem help you evaluate an investment?

P17-5B Accountants for Forbes Candy Company have assembled the following data for the year ended December 31, 19X4:

Preparing the statement of cash flows—indirect method
(Obj. 2, 5)

	December 31, 19X4	December 31, 19X3
Current Accounts (All Result from Operations)		
Current assets:		
Cash and cash equivalents.................................	$38,600	$34,800
Accounts receivable...	70,100	73,700
Inventories	90,600	96,500
Prepaid expenses...	3,200	2,100
Current liabilities:		
Notes payable (for inventory purchases)..........	$36,300	$36,800
Accounts payable..	72,100	67,500
Income tax payable...	5,900	6,800
Accrued liabilities...	28,300	23,200

Transaction Data for 19X4:

Stock dividends..............................	$ 12,600	Payment of cash dividends	$48,300
Collection of loan...........................	10,300	Issuance of long-term debt	
Depreciation expense	19,200	to borrow cash.............................	71,000
Acquisition of equipment..............	69,000	Net income	50,500
Payment of long-term debt		Issuance of preferred stock	
by issuing common stock	89,400	for cash	36,200
Acquisition of long-term		Sale of long-term investment..........	12,200
investment	44,800	Amortization expense	1,100
Acquisition of building by issu-		Payment of long-term debt.............	47,800
ing long-term note payable........	118,000	Gain on sale of investment..............	3,500

Prepare Forbes Candy Company's statement of cash flows, using the *indirect* method to report operating activities. Include an accompanying schedule of noncash investing and financing activities.

REQUIRED

P17-6B The comparative balance sheet of Tech DataBase, Inc., at December 31, 19X5, reported the following:

	December 31,	
	19X5	**19X4**
Current Assets:		
Cash and cash equivalents..................................	$10,600	$12,500
Accounts receivable...	28,600	29,300
Inventories	51,600	53,000
Prepaid expenses...	4,200	3,700
Current Liabilities:		
Notes payable (for inventory purchases)..........	$ 9,200	$ -0-
Accounts payable...	21,900	28,000
Accrued liabilities..	14,300	16,800
Income tax payable..	11,000	14,300

Tech's transactions during 19X5 included the following:

Amortization expense................	**$ 5,000**	**Cash acquisition of building....**	**$124,000**
Payment of cash dividends	**17,000**	**Net income**	**31,600**
Cash acquisition of equipment..	**55,000**	**Issuance of common stock**	
Issuance of long-term note		**for cash**.................................	**105,600**
payable to borrow cash	**32,000**	**Stock dividend**	**13,000**
Retirement of bonds payable		**Sale of long-term investment..**	**6,000**
by issuing common stock.......	**55,000**	**Depreciation expense**..............	**15,000**

REQUIRED

1. Prepare the statement of cash flows of Tech DataBase for the year ended December 31, 19X5. Use the *indirect* method to report cash flows from operating activities. Report non-cash investing and financing activities in an accompanying schedule.
2. Evaluate Tech DataBase's cash flows for the year. Mention all three categories of cash flows, and give the reason for your evaluation.

P17-7B To prepare the statement of cash flows, accountants for Ohio Valley Corp. have summarized 19X8 activity in two accounts as follows:

Cash			
Beginning balance	87,100	Payments of operating expenses	46,100
Issuance of common stock	34,600	Payment of long-term debt	78,900
Receipts of dividends	1,900	Purchase of treasury stock	10,400
Collection of loan	18,500	Payment of income tax	8,000
Sale of investments	9,900	Payments on accounts payable	101,600
Receipts of interest	12,200	Payment of dividends	1,800
Collections from customers	298,100	Payments of salaries and wages	67,500
Sale of treasury stock	26,200	Payments of interest	21,800
		Purchase of equipment	79,900
Ending balance	72,500		

Common Stock	
Beginning balance	103,500
Issuance for cash	34,600
Issuance to acquire land	62,100
Issuance to retire long-term debt	21,100
Ending balance	221,300

REQUIRED

1. Prepare Ohio Valley's statement of cash flows for the year ended December 31, 19X8, using the *direct* method to report operating activities. Also prepare the accompanying schedule of noncash investing and financing activities. Ohio Valley's 19X8 income statement and selected balance sheet data follow.

2. Use these data to prepare a supplementary schedule showing cash flows from operating activities by the *indirect* method. All activity in the current accounts results from operations.

OHIO VALLEY CORP.
Income Statement
Year Ended December 31, 19X8

Revenues and gains:		
Sales revenue..............................		$281,800
Interest revenue		12,200
Dividend revenue.........................		1,900
Gain on sale of investments..........		700
Total revenues and gains...........		296,600
Expenses:		
Cost of goods sold	$103,600	
Salary and wage expense..............	66,800	
Depreciation expense	10,900	
Other operating expense	44,700	
Interest expense	24,100	
Income tax expense.......................	2,600	
Total expenses		252,700
Net income		$ 43,900

OHIO VALLEY CORP.
Balance Sheet Data

	19X8 Increase (Decrease)
Current assets:	
Cash and cash equivalents..........	$?
Accounts receivable....................	(16,300)
Inventories..................................	5,700
Prepaid expenses	(1,900)
Loan receivable	(18,500)
Investments	(9,200)
Equipment, net	69,000
Land	62,100
Current liabilities:	
Accounts payable........................	$ 7,700
Interest payable	2,300
Salary payable.............................	(700)
Other accrued liabilities.............	(3,300)
Income tax payable.....................	(5,400)
Long-term debt............................	(100,000)
Common stock.............................	117,800
Retained earnings.........................	42,100
Treasury stock	(15,800)

P17-8B Toledo Company's comparative balance sheet at September 30, 19X4, included the following balances:

Preparing the statement of cash flows—
indirect and direct methods
(Obj. 3, 4, 5)

TOLEDO COMPANY
Balance Sheet
September 30, 19X4 and 19X3

	19X4	19X3	Increase (Decrease)
Current assets:			
Cash...	$ 48,700	$ 17,600	$ 31,100
Accounts receivable	41,900	44,000	(2,100)
Interest receivable......................	4,100	2,800	1,300
Inventories	121,700	116,900	4,800
Prepaid expenses........................	8,600	9,300	(700)
Long-term investments................	51,100	13,800	37,300
Equipment, net............................	131,900	92,100	39,800
Land	47,100	74,300	(27,200)
	$455,100	$370,800	$ 84,300
Current liabilities:			
Notes payable, short-term..........	$ 22,000	$ -0-	$ 22,000
Accounts payable	61,800	70,300	(8,500)
Income tax payable	21,800	24,600	(2,800)
Accrued liabilities......................	17,900	29,100	(11,200)
Interest payable..........................	4,500	3,200	1,300
Salary payable	1,500	1,100	400
Long-term note payable................	123,000	121,400	1,600
Common stock.............................	113,900	62,000	51,900
Retained earnings	88,700	59,100	29,600
	$455,100	$370,800	$ 84,300

Transaction data for the year ended September 30, 19X4:

a. Net income, $93,900.
b. Depreciation expense on equipment, $8,500.
c. Acquired long-term investments, $37,300.
d. Sold land for $38,100, including a $10,900 gain.
e. Acquired equipment by issuing long-term note payable, $26,300.
f. Paid long-term note payable, $24,700.
g. Received cash of $51,900 for issuance of common stock.
h. Paid cash dividends, $64,300.
i. Acquired equipment by issuing short-term note payable, $22,000.

REQUIRED

1. Prepare Toledo's statement of cash flows for the year ended September 30, 19X4, using the *indirect* method to report operating activities. Also prepare the accompanying schedule of noncash investing and financing activities. All current accounts except short-term notes payable result from operating transactions.

2. Prepare a supplementary schedule showing cash flows from operations by the *direct* method. The income statement reports the following: sales, $370,600; gain on sale of land, $10,900; interest revenue, $7,300; cost of goods sold, $161,500; salary expense, $63,400; other operating expenses, $29,600; income tax expense, $18,400; interest expense, $13,500; depreciation expense, $8,500.

Applying Your Knowledge

DECISION CASE

Preparing and using the statement of cash flows to evaluate operations (Obj. 4, 5)

CASE 1. The 19X6 comparative income statement and the 19X6 comparative balance sheet of Biovan Industries, have just been distributed at a meeting of the company's board of directors. The members of the board of directors raise a fundamental question: Why is the cash balance so low? This question is especially troublesome to the board members because 19X6 showed record profits. As the controller of the company, you must answer the question.

REQUIRED

1. Prepare a statement of cash flows for 19X6 in the format that best shows the relationship between net income and operating cash flow. The company sold no plant assets or long-term investments and issued no notes payable during 19X6. The changes in all current accounts except short-term notes payable arose from operations. There were *no* noncash investing and financing transactions during the year. Show all amounts in thousands.

2. Answer the board members' question: Why is the cash balance so low? In explaining the business's cash flows, identify two significant cash receipts that occurred during 19X5 but not in 19X6. Also point out the two largest cash disbursements during 19X6.

3. Considering net income and the company's cash flows during 19X6, was it a good year or a bad year? Give your reasons.

BIOVAN INDUSTRIES Comparative Income Statement Years Ended December 31, 19X6 and 19X5		
(In thousands)	19X6	19X5
Revenues and gains:		
Sales revenue..	$444	$310
Gain on sale of of equipment (sale price, $33)..........	—	18
Total revenues and gains.......................................	$444	$328
Expenses and losses:		
Cost of goods sold...	$221	$162
Salary expense	48	28
Depreciation expense...	46	22
Interest expense	13	20
Amortization expense on patent...............................	11	11
Loss on sale of land (sale price, $61)	—	35
Total expenses and losses	339	278
Net income	$105	$ 50

BIOVAN INDUSTRIES		
Comparative Balance Statement		
December 31, 19X6 and 19X5		
(In thousands)	19X6	19X5
Assets		
Cash	$ 33	$ 63
Accounts receivable, net	72	61
Inventories	194	181
Long-term investments	31	-0-
Property, plant, and equipment..........	361	259
Accumulated depreciation	(244)	(198)
Patents..	177	188
Totals	$624	$554
Liabilities and Owners' Equity		
Notes payable, short-term		
(for general borrowing)	$ 32	$101
Accounts payable	63	56
Accrued liabilities.............................	12	17
Notes payable, long-term...................	147	163
Common stock, no-par......................	149	61
Retained earnings	221	156
Totals	$624	$554

FINANCIAL STATEMENT CASES

Using the statement of cash flows
(Obj. 2, 4)

CASE 1. Use the NIKE, Inc., statement of cash flows along with the company's other financial statements, all in Appendix A, to answer the following questions.

REQUIRED

1. Which method does NIKE use to report net cash flows from *operating* activities? How can you tell?
2. Suppose NIKE reported net cash flows from operating activities by the direct method. Compute these amounts for the year ended May 31, 1997:
   a. Collections from customers
   b. Payments for inventory
   c. Payments for operating expenses (Use Selling and Administrative Expense, Prepaid Expenses, and Accrued Liabilities.)
3. Evaluate the year ended May 31, 1997, in terms of net income, cash flows, balance sheet position, and overall results. Be specific.

Computing cash-flow amounts and
using cash-flow data for analysis
(Obj. 2, 4)

CASE 2. Obtain the annual report of a company of your choosing. Answer the following questions about the company. Concentrate on the current year in the annual report you select.

REQUIRED

1. By which method does the company report net cash flows from *operating activities?* How can you tell?
2. Suppose the company reported net cash flows from operating activities by the direct method. Compute these amounts for the current year.
   a. Collections from customers
   b. Payments for inventory
   c. Payments for operating expenses (Use Selling, General, and Administrative Expenses or expense of similar title, Prepaid Expenses, and Accrued Liabilities.)
3. Evaluate the current year in terms of net income (or net loss), cash flows, balance sheet position, and overall results. Be specific.

Team Projects

PROJECT 1. Select a company and obtain its annual report, including all the financial statements. Focus on the statement of cash flows and the cash flows from operating activities in particular. Identify whether the company uses the direct method or the indirect method to report operating cash flows. Use the other financial statements (income statement, balance sheet, and statement of stockholders' equity) and the notes, if necessary, to prepare the company's cash flows from operating activities by the *other* method.

PROJECT 2. Each member of the group should obtain the annual report of a different company. Select companies in different industries. Evaluate each company's trend of cash flows for the most recent two years. In your evaluation of the companies' cash flows, you may use any other information that is publicly available—for example, the other financial statements (income statement, balance sheet, statement of stockholders' equity, and the related notes) and news stories from magazines and newspapers. Rank the companies' cash flows from best to worst, and write a two-page report on your findings.

Internet Exercise   NETSCAPE CORP.

Netscape, the popular Internet browser, was developed on the University of Illinois campus by a graduate student, Marc Andreesen, to help scientists more easily navigate the cumbersome Internet. Today, Netscape is the leading provider of Internet browsers.

1. Go to **www.netscape.com/**, the home page for Netscape.
2. At the very bottom of the home page click on **Company Information.** Under *Investor Relations* click on **business operations.** In **Financial Statments** click on the *most recent annual report* (Form 10-K). This takes you to the annual report filed with the SEC. Scroll down more than half way through the report, and then start looking for numbers. Refer to the **Statement of Cash flows** to answer the following questions.

REQUIRED

  a. For the most recent year, list the amount of net cash inflow or outflow for each of the three major types of activities reported on the statement of Cash Flows. Which activity is providing the primary source of cash? Is this considered favorable or unfavorable?
  b. For the most recent year, what amount is reported for *Net Income/Loss* and *Net Cash provided by Operating Activities*? What accounts for the difference between these two numbers?
  c. For the most recent year, did Nescape purchase or sell more property, plant and equipment (capital expenditures)? Is this considered favorable or unfavorable? How much was the net amount purchased/sold? Which activity section contained this information?
  d. For the most recent year, was the primary source of financing debt or equity? Is this considered favorable or unfavorable? What was the net amount of financing from the major source? Which activity section contained this information?

Internet Exercise   COMPAQ

This innovative company started operations at the beginning of the personal computer revolution in 1982. During the first year Compaq had net sales of $111 million—a new first year record. Now it is a Fortune 100 company and the number one supplier of PCs in the world with sales exceeding $20 billion annually.

  The computer industry is highly competitive, especially for PC manufacturers. Numerous PC manufacturers have come and gone, but Compaq has strengthened its leadership position year after year. The statement of Cash Flows demonstrates the company's financial strength.

1. Go to **www.compaq.com**.
2. Click on **Inside Compaq, Investor Relations,** and then continue clicking until you find the financial statments for the most recent year. Refer to the **consolidated statement of cash flows** to answer the following questions.

REQUIRED

  a. For the most recent year, list the amount of net cash inflow or outflow for each of the three major types of activities reported on the Statement of Cash Flows. Which activity is providing the primary source of cash? Is this considered favorable or unfavorable?
  b. For the most recent year, what amount is reported for *Net income/Loss* and *Net Cash provided by Operating Activities*? What accounts for the difference between these two numbers? Is the direct or indirect method of formatting used? How can you tell?
  c. For the most recent year, did Compaq purchase or sell more property, plant and equipment? Is this considered favorable or unfavorable? How much was the net amount purchased/sold? Which activity section contained this information?
  d. For the most recent year, did Compaq borrow or repay more long-term debt? Is this considered favorable or unfavorable? How much was the net amount borrowed/repaid? Which activity section contained this information?

A P P E N D I X to Chapter 17

The Work Sheet Approach to Preparing the Statement of Cash Flows

The body of this chapter discusses the uses of the statement of cash flows in decision making and shows how to prepare the statement by using T-accounts. The T-account approach works well as a learning device. In practice, however, most companies face complex situations. In these cases, a work sheet can help accountants prepare the statement of cash flows. This appendix shows how to prepare that statement using a specially designed work sheet.

The work sheet starts with the beginning balance sheet and concludes with the ending balance sheet. Two middle columns—one for debit amounts and the other for credit amounts—complete the work sheet. These columns, labeled Transaction Analysis, contain the data for the statement of cash flows. Exhibit 17A-1 presents the work sheet. Accountants can prepare the statement directly from the lower part of the work sheet (Panel B in Exhibit 17A-1). All the exhibits in this appendix are based on the Anchor Corporation data presented earlier in the chapter.

Preparing the Work Sheet— Direct Method for Operating Activities

The direct method separates operating activities into cash receipts and cash payments. The work sheet can be prepared by following these steps:

Objective A1

Prepare a work sheet for the statement of cash flows—direct method

Step 1: Panel A gives the beginning and ending balances for Cash and all other balance sheet accounts through Retained Earnings. The amounts are taken directly from the beginning and ending balance sheets in Exhibit 17-7.

Step 2: Panel B lays out the framework of the statement of cash flows—that is, the headings for cash flows from operating, investing, and financing activities. Exhibit 17A-1 is based on the direct method and splits operating activities into Receipts and Payments.

Step 3: The bottom of the work sheet shows Net Increase in Cash or Net Decrease in Cash, as the case may be. This final amount on the work sheet is the difference between ending cash and beginning cash, from the balance sheet. The statement of cash flows explains why this change in cash occurred during the period.

Step 4: Analyze the period's transactions in the middle columns of the work sheet. The remainder of this appendix explains this crucial step.

Step 5: Prepare the statement of cash flows directly from Panel B of the work sheet.

Transaction Analysis on the Work Sheet—Direct Method

For your convenience, we repeat the Anchor Corporation transaction data from Exhibit 17-5. These data are given at the top of page 765.

The transaction analysis on the work sheet appears in the form of journal entries. Only balance sheet accounts appear on the work sheet. There are no income statement accounts. Therefore, revenue transactions are entered on the work sheet as credits to Retained Earnings. For example, in transaction (a), sales on account are entered on the work sheet by debiting Accounts Receivable and crediting Retained Earnings. Cash is neither debited nor credited because credit sales do not affect cash. But all transactions should be entered on the work sheet to identify all the cash effects of the period's transactions. In transaction (c), the earning of interest revenue is entered by debiting Interest Receivable and crediting Retained Earnings. The revenue transactions that generate cash are also recorded by crediting Retained Earnings.

Expense transactions are entered on the work sheet as debits to Retained Earnings. In transaction (f), cost of goods sold is entered by debiting Retained Earnings and crediting

ANCHOR CORPORATION
Work Sheet for Statement of Cash Flows (Direct Method)
Year Ended December 31, 19X2

	Balances	Transaction Analysis				Balances
		(In thousands)				
	Dec. 31, 19X1	Debit		Credit		Dec. 31, 19X2
PANEL A—Account Titles						
Cash	42			(v)	20	22
Accounts receivable	80	(a)	284	(b)	271	93
Interest receivable	1	(c)	12	(d)	10	3
Inventory	138	(g)	147	(f)	150	135
Prepaid expenses	7	(h3)	1			8
Long-term receivable from another company	—	(p)	11			11
Plant assets, net	219	(o)	306	(k)	18	
				(q)	54	453
Totals	487					725
Accounts payable	57	(h1)	113	(g)	147	91
Salary and wage payable	6	(j)	58	(i)	56	4
Accrued liabilities	3	(h2)	19	(l)	17	1
Long-term notes payable	77	(t)	11	(s)	94	160
Common stock	258			(r)	101	359
Retained earnings	86	(f)	150	(a)	284	110
		(l)	17	(c)	12	
		(i)	56	(e)	9	
		(k)	18	(q)	8	
		(m)	16			
		(n)	15			
		(u)	17			
Totals	487		1,251		1,251	725
PANEL B—Statement of Cash Flows						
Cash flows from operating activities:						
Receipts:						
Collections from customers		(b)	271			
Interest received		(d)	10			
Dividends received		(e)	9			
Payments:						
To suppliers				(h1)	113	
				(h2)	19	
				(h3)	1	
To employees				(j)	58	
For interest				(m)	16	
For income tax				(n)	15	
Cash flows from investing activities:						
Acquisition of plant assets				(o)	306	
Proceeds from sale of plant		(q)	62			
Loan to another company				(p)	11	
Cash flows from financing activities:						
Proceeds from issuance of common stock		(r)	101			
Proceeds from issuance of long-term debt		(s)	94			
Payment of long-term debt				(t)	11	
Payment of dividends				(u)	17	
			547		567	
Net decrease in cash		(v)	20			
Totals			567		567	

EXHIBIT 17A-1
Work Sheet for Statement of
Cash Flows—Direct Method

Operating Activities:

1. Sales on credit, $284,000
*2. Collections from customers, $271,000
3. Interest revenue on notes receivable, $12,000
*4. Collection of interest receivable, $10,000
*5. Cash receipt of dividend revenue on investments in stock, $9,000
6. Cost of goods sold, $150,000
7. Purchases of inventory on credit, $147,000
*8. Payments to suppliers, $133,000
9. Salary and wage expense, $56,000
*10. Payments of salary and wages, $58,000
11. Depreciation expense, $18,000
12. Other operating expense, $17,000
*13. Interest expense and payments, $16,000
*14. Income tax expense and payments, $15,000

Investing Activities:

*15. Cash payments to acquire plant assets, $306,000
*16. Loan to another company, $11,000
*17. Proceeds from sale of plant assets, $62,000, including $8,000 gain

Financing Activities:

*18. Proceeds from issuance of common stock, $101,000
*19. Proceeds from issuance of long-term note payable, $94,000
*20. Payment of long-term note payable, $11,000
*21. Declaration and payment of cash dividends, $17,000

*Indicates a cash-flow transaction to be reported on the statement of cash flows.

Inventory. Transaction (m) is a cash payment of interest expense. The work sheet entry debits Retained Earnings and credits Payments for Interest under operating activities. The remaining expense transactions follow a similar pattern.

NET INCREASE (DECREASE) IN CASH   The net increase or net decrease in cash for the period is the balancing amount needed to equate the total debits and total credits ($567,000) on the statement of cash flows. In Exhibit 17A-1, Anchor Corporation experienced a $20,000 decrease in cash. This amount is entered as a credit to Cash, transaction (v), at the top of the work sheet and a debit to Net Decrease in Cash at the bottom. Totaling the columns completes the work sheet.

Preparing the Statement of Cash Flows from the Work Sheet

To prepare the statement of cash flows, Exhibit 17-2 in the text, the accountant can rewrite Panel B of the work sheet and add subtotals for the three categories of activities.

Preparing the Work Sheet— Indirect Method for Operating Activities

The indirect method shows the reconciliation from net income to net cash inflow (or net cash outflow) from operating activities. Exhibit 17A-2 on page 766 is the work sheet for preparing the statement of cash flows by the indirect method.

The steps in completing the work sheet by the indirect method are the same as those taken in the direct method. The analysis of investing activities and financing activities uses the information presented in Exhibit 17-5 and given at the top of this page. As mentioned previously, there is no difference for investing activities or financing activities between the direct- and indirect-method work sheets. Therefore, the analysis that follows focuses on cash flows from operating activities. The Anchor Corporation data come from the income statement (Exhibit 17-6, p. 724) and the comparative balance sheet (Exhibit 17-7, p. 725).

Objective A2

Prepare a work sheet for the statement of cash flows—indirect method

ANCHOR CORPORATION
Work Sheet for Statement of Cash Flows (Indirect Method)
Year Ended December 31, 19X2

(In thousands)

	Balances Dec. 31, 19X1	Transaction Analysis Debit		Transaction Analysis Credit		Balances Dec. 31, 19X2
PANEL A—Account Titles						
Cash	42			(q)	20	22
Accounts receivable	80	(d)	13			93
Interest receivable	1	(e)	2			3
Inventory	138			(f)	3	135
Prepaid expenses	7	(g)	1			8
Long-term receivable from another company	—	(l)	11			11
Plant assets, net	219	(k)	306	(b)	18	
				(c)	54	453
Totals	487					725
Accounts payable	57			(h)	34	91
Salary and wage payable	6	(i)	2			4
Accrued liabilities	3	(j)	2			1
Long-term notes payable	77	(o)	11	(n)	94	160
Common stock	258			(m)	101	359
Retained earnings	86	(p)	17	(a)	41	110
Totals	487		365		365	725
PANEL B—Statement of Cash Flows						
Cash flows from operating activities:						
Net income		(a)	41			
Add (subtract) items that affect net income and cash flow differently:						
Depreciation		(b)	18			
Gain on sale of plant assets				(c)	8	
Increase in accounts receivable				(d)	13	
Increase in interest receivable				(e)	2	
Decrease in inventory		(f)	3			
Increase in prepaid expenses				(g)	1	
Increase in accounts payable		(h)	34			
Decrease in salary and wage payable				(i)	2	
Decrease in accrued liabilities				(j)	2	
Cash flows from investing activities:						
Acquisition of plant assets				(k)	306	
Proceeds from sale of plant assets		(c)	62			
Loan to another company				(l)	11	
Cash flows from financing activities:						
Proceeds from issuance of common stock		(m)	101			
Proceeds from issuance of long-term debt		(n)	94			
Payment of long-term debt				(o)	11	
Payment of dividends				(p)	17	
			353		373	
Net decrease in cash		(q)	20			
Totals			373		373	

EXHIBIT 17A-2
Work Sheet for Statement of
Cash Flows—Indirect Method

Transaction Analysis on the Work Sheet—Indirect Method

Net income, transaction (a), is the first operating cash inflow.* Net income is entered on the work sheet as a debit to Net Income under cash flows from operating activities and a credit to Retained Earnings. Next come the additions to, and subtractions from, net income, starting with depreciation—transaction (b)—which is debited to Depreciation on the work sheet and credited to Plant Assets, Net. Transaction (c) is the sale of plant assets. The $8,000 gain on the sale is entered as a credit to Gain on Sale of Plant Assets under operating cash flows—a subtraction from net income. This credit removes the $8,000 gain in cash flow from operations because the cash proceeds from the sale were not $8,000. The cash proceeds were $62,000, so this amount is entered on the work sheet as a debit under investing activities. Entry (c) is completed by crediting the plant assets' book value of $54,000 ($62,000 – $8,000) to the Plant Assets, Net account.

Entries (d) through (j) reconcile net income to cash flows from operations for increases and decreases in the current assets other than Cash and for increases and decreases in the current liabilities. Entry (d) debits Accounts Receivable for its $13,000 increase during the year. This decrease in cash flows is credited to Increase in Accounts Receivable under operating cash flows. Entries (e) and (g) are similar for Interest Receivable and Prepaid Expenses.

The final item in Exhibit 17A-2 is the Net Decrease in Cash—transaction (q) on the work sheet—a credit to Cash and a debit to Net Decrease in Cash, exactly as in Exhibit 17A-1. To prepare the statement of cash flows, the accountant merely rewrites Panel B of the work sheet, adding subtotals for the three categories of activities.

NONCASH INVESTING AND FINANCING ACTIVITIES ON THE WORK SHEET Noncash investing and financing activities can also be analyzed on the work sheet. Because these types of transaction include both an investing activity and a financing activity, they require two work sheet entries. For example, suppose Anchor Corporation purchased a building by issuing common stock of $320,000. Exhibit 17A-3 illustrates the transaction analysis of this noncash investing and financing activity. Cash is unaffected.

Work sheet entry (t1) records the purchase of the building, and entry (t2) records the issuance of the stock. The order of these entries is unimportant.

EXHIBIT 17A-3
Noncash Investing and Financing Activities on the Work Sheet

ANCHOR CORPORATION Work Sheet for Statement of Cash Flows Year Ended December 31, 19X2	Balances	Transaction Analysis		Balances
	Dec. 31, 19X1	Debit	Credit	Dec. 31, 19X2
PANEL A—Account Titles				
Cash				
Building	650,000	(t1) 320,000		970,000
Common stock	890,000		(t2) 320,000	1,210,000
PANEL B—Statement of Cash Flows				
Noncash investing and financing transactions:				
Purchase of building by issuing common stock..........		(t2) 320,000	(t1) 320,000	

*Note that we are now using the *indirect* method. The transactions we analyze here are *not* the same as those listed on page 763–765.

Chapter 17 Preparing and **767**
Using the Statement of Cash Flows

Appendix Problems

Preparing the work sheet for the statement of cash flows—direct method (Obj. A1)

P17A-1 The 19X3 comparative balance sheet and income statement of Alden Group, Inc., follow. Alden had no noncash investing and financing transactions during 19X3.

ALDEN GROUP, INC. Comparative Balance Sheet	December 31, 19X3	December 31, 19X2	Increase (Decrease)
Current assets:			
Cash and cash equivalents	$ 13,700	$ 15,600	$ (1,900)
Accounts receivable	41,500	43,100	(1,600)
Interest receivable	600	900	(300)
Inventories	94,300	89,900	4,400
Prepaid expenses	1,700	2,200	(500)
Plant assets:			
Land	35,100	10,000	25,100
Equipment, net	100,900	93,700	7,200
Total assets	$287,800	$255,400	$ 32,400
Current liabilities:			
Accounts payable	$ 16,400	$ 17,900	$ (1,500)
Interest payable	6,300	6,700	(400)
Salary payable	2,100	1,400	700
Other accrued liabilities	18,100	18,700	(600)
Income tax payable	6,300	3,800	2,500
Long-term liabilities:			
Notes payable	55,000	65,000	(10,000)
Stockholders' equity:			
Common stock, no-par	131,100	122,300	8,800
Retained earnings	52,500	19,600	32,900
Total liabilities and stockholders' equity	$287,800	$255,400	$ 32,400

ALDEN GROUP, INC. Income Statement for 19X3		
Revenues:		
Sales revenue		$438,000
Interest revenue		11,700
Total revenues		449,700
Expenses:		
Cost of goods sold	$205,200	
Salary expense	76,400	
Depreciation expense	15,300	
Other operating expense	49,700	
Interest expense	24,600	
Income tax expense	16,900	
Total expenses		388,100
Net income		$ 61,600

REQUIRED

Prepare the work sheet for the 19X3 statement of cash flows. Format cash flows from operating activities by the *direct* method.

Preparing the work sheet for the statement of cash flows—indirect method (Obj. A2)

P17A-2 Using the Alden Group, Inc., data from Problem 17A-1, prepare the work sheet for Alden's 19X3 statement of cash flows. Format cash flows from operating activities by the *indirect* method.

P17A-3 Toledo Company's comparative balance sheet at September 30, 19X4, follows.

TOLEDO COMPANY
Balance Sheet
September 30, 19X4 and 19X3

	19X4	19X3	Increase (Decrease)
Current assets:			
Cash	$ 48,700	$ 17,600	$ 31,100
Accounts receivable	41,900	44,000	(2,100)
Interest receivable	4,100	2,800	1,300
Inventories	121,700	116,900	4,800
Prepaid expenses	8,600	9,300	(700)
Long-term investments	55,400	18,100	37,300
Plant assets:			
Land	65,800	93,000	(27,200)
Equipment, net	89,500	49,700	39,800
Total assets	$435,700	$351,400	$ 84,300
Current liabilities:			
Notes payable, short-term	$ 22,000	$ -0-	$ 22,000
Accounts payable	61,800	70,300	(8,500)
Income tax payable	21,800	24,600	(2,800)
Accrued liabilities	17,900	29,100	(11,200)
Interest payable	4,500	3,200	1,300
Salary payable	1,500	1,100	400
Notes payable, long-term	62,900	61,300	1,600
Stockholders' equity:			
Common stock	142,100	90,200	51,900
Retained earnings	101,200	71,600	29,600
Total liability and stockholders' equity	$435,700	$351,400	$ 84,300

Transaction data for the year ended September 30, 19X4, are as follows:

a. Net income, $93,900.
b. Depreciation expense on equipment, $8,500.
c. Acquired long-term investments, $37,300.
d. Sold land for $38,100, including $10,900 gain.
e. Acquired equipment by issuing long-term note payable, $26,300.
f. Paid long-term note payable, $24,700.
g. Received cash of $51,900 for issuance of common stock.
h. Paid cash dividends, $64,300.
i. Acquired equipment by issuing short-term note payable, $22,000.

REQUIRED

Prepare Toledo's work sheet for the statement of cash flows for the year ended September 30, 19X4, using the *indirect* method to report operating activities. Include on the work sheet the non-cash investing and financing activities.

P17A-4 Refer to the data of Problem 17A-3.

REQUIRED

Prepare Toledo's work sheet for the statement of cash flows for the year ended September 30, 19X4, using the *direct* method for operating activities. The income statement reports the following: sales, $370,600; gain on sale of land, $10,900; interest revenue, $7,300; cost of goods sold, $161,500; salary expense, $63,400; other operating expenses, $29,600; income tax expense, $18,400; interest expense, $13,500; depreciation expense, $8,500. Include on the work sheet the noncash investing and financing activities.

CHAPTER 18

Financial Statement Analysis

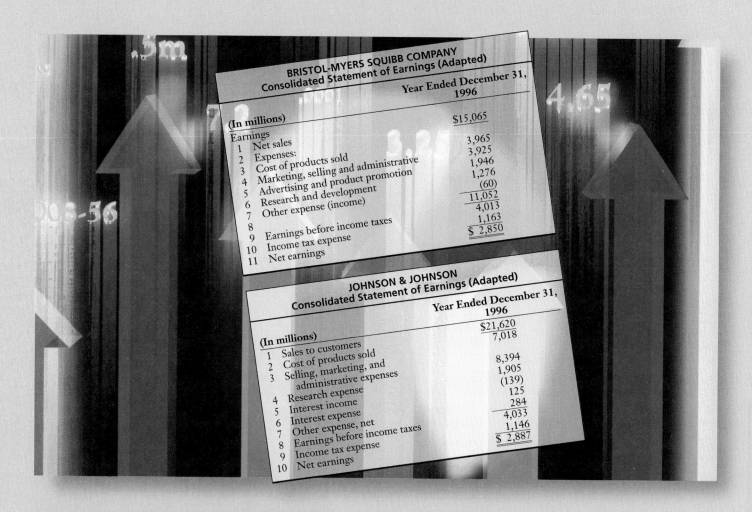

BRISTOL-MYERS SQUIBB COMPANY
Consolidated Statement of Earnings (Adapted)

(In millions)	Year Ended December 31, 1996
Earnings	
1 Net sales	$15,065
2 Expenses:	
3 Cost of products sold	3,965
4 Marketing, selling and administrative	3,925
5 Advertising and product promotion	1,946
6 Research and development	1,276
7 Other expense (income)	(60)
	11,052
8 Earnings before income taxes	4,013
9 Income tax expense	1,163
10 Net earnings	$ 2,850

JOHNSON & JOHNSON
Consolidated Statement of Earnings (Adapted)

(In millions)	Year Ended December 31, 1996
1 Sales to customers	$21,620
2 Cost of products sold	7,018
3 Selling, marketing, and administrative expenses	8,394
4 Research expense	1,905
5 Interest income	(139)
6 Interest expense	125
7 Other expense, net	284
	4,033
8 Earnings before income taxes	1,146
9 Income tax expense	$ 2,887
10 Net earnings	

LEARNING OBJECTIVES

After studying this chapter, you should be able to

1. Perform a horizontal analysis of comparative financial statements

2. Perform a vertical analysis of a company's financial statements

3. Prepare common-size financial statements for benchmarking against the industry average and key competitors

4. Compute the standard financial ratios used for decision making

5. Use ratios in decision making

6. Measure economic value added by a company's operations

> **❝** *To compare the operating results of two companies like Bristol-Myers Squibb and Johnson & Johnson, we need to use standard measures. Financial ratio analysis plays an important part in the recommendations we make to our clients regarding which companies' stock to buy.* **❞**
>
> —ANGELA LANE, SENIOR ANALYST, BAER & FOSTER

Analysts at Baer & Foster, an investment banking firm, have identified health-care and consumer products as growth areas and will be recommending these companies' stocks to their clients. Angela Lane heads a team of analysts who are focusing on two companies: Bristol-Myers Squibb and Johnson & Johnson. Bristol-Myers is best known for Clairol hair products, Ban deodorant, and Excedrin pain medicine. Some of Johnson & Johnson's key products are baby and skin care items, Neutrogena soap and cream, and Tylenol pain medicine.

Lane and her team wish to compare the performance of Bristol-Myers and Johnson & Johnson. However, the two companies differ in size. Johnson & Johnson has sales of $22 billion, compared to $15 billion for Bristol-Myers Squibb. Johnson & Johnson's total assets of $20 billion exceed Bristol-Myers' assets of $15 billion. How can Lane's team compare two companies of different size?

Investors and creditors face similar challenges every day. The way to compare companies of different size is to use *standard* measures. Throughout this book, we have discussed financial ratios, such as the current ratio, the debt ratio, inventory turnover, and return on stockholders' equity. These ratios are standard measures that enable investors to compare companies of different size or companies that operate in different industries. Managers use the ratios to monitor operations and help make business decisions. In this chapter, we discuss most of the basic ratios and related measures that managers use to run a company and that investors and lenders use to search for good investments and loan prospects. The informational value of these ratios is one reason accounting is called the "language of business."

Financial Statement Analysis

Financial statement analysis focuses on the techniques used by internal managers and by analysts external to the organization. A major source of their information is the annual report. In addition to the financial statements (income statement, balance sheet, and statement of cash flows), annual reports usually contain the following:

1. Notes to the financial statements
2. A summary of the accounting methods used
3. Management's discussion and analysis of the financial results
4. The auditor's report
5. Comparative financial data for a series of years

Management's discussion and analysis (MD&A) of financial results is especially important because top management is in the best position to know how well or how poorly the company is performing. The SEC requires the MD&A from public corporations. For example, the 1996 annual report of Bristol-Myers Squibb Company includes six pages of MD&A. The report's Financial Review begins as follows:

> *"Nineteen ninety-six marked another year of record growth for Bristol-Myers Squibb. Worldwide sales were $15.1 billion, a 9% increase over 1995. Domestic sales increased 10% to $8.5 billion, while international sales increased 9% to $6.6 billion."*

Nineteen ninety-six marked another year of record growth for Bristol-Myers Squibb. Worldwide sales were $15.1 billion, a 9% increase over 1995. Domestic sales increased 10% to $8.5 billion, while international sales increased 9% to $6.6 billion.

Bristol-Myers Squibb management also discusses its sales and profits in various industry segments—pharmaceuticals, medical devices, and beauty aids. The MD&A includes graphical data, such as the graphs in Exhibit 18-1.

The Objectives of Financial Statement Analysis

Investors who purchase a company's stock expect to receive dividends and hope the stock's value will increase. Creditors make loans to receive interest and principal. Both groups bear the risk that they will not receive their expected returns. They use financial statement analysis to (1) predict the amount of expected returns, and (2) assess the risks associated with those returns.

Creditors generally expect to receive specific fixed amounts and have the first claim on a company's assets, so they are most concerned with assessing short-term liquidity and long-term solvency. **Short-term liquidity** is an organization's ability to meet current payments as they come due. **Long-term solvency** is the ability to generate enough cash to pay long-term debts as they mature.

In contrast, *investors* are more concerned with profitability, dividends, and future stock prices. Why? Because dividends and stock-price increases depend on profitable operations. Creditors also assess profitability because profitable operations are the company's main source of cash to repay loans.

The tools and techniques that the business community uses in evaluating financial statement information can be divided into three broad categories: horizontal analysis, vertical analysis, and ratio analysis.

Short-Term Liquidity. Ability to meet current payments as they come due.

Long-term Solvency. Ability to generate enough cash to pay long-term debts as they mature.

Horizontal Analysis

Many managerial decisions hinge on whether the numbers—in sales, income, expenses, and so on—are increasing or decreasing over time. Has the sales figure risen from last year? From two years ago? By how much? We may find that the net sales figure has risen by $200,000. This fact may be interesting, but considered alone it is not very useful for decision making. An analysis of the *percentage change* in the net sales figure over time improves our ability to make decisions. It is more useful to know that sales have increased by 20% than to know that the increase in sales is $200,000.

The study of percentage changes in comparative statements is called **horizontal analysis.** Computing a percentage change in comparative statements requires two steps:

1. Compute the dollar amount of the change from the base (earlier) period to the later period.

2. Divide the dollar amount of change by the base-period amount.

Horizontal analysis is illustrated for Bristol-Myers Squibb as follows (dollar amounts in millions):

> **Objective 1**
>
> **Perform a horizontal analysis of comparative financial statements**

Horizontal Analysis. Study of percentage changes in comparative financial statements.

	1996	1995	Increase (Decrease) Amount	Increase (Decrease) Percent
Sales	$15,065	$13,767	$1,298	9.4%
Net income	2,850	1,812	1,038	57.3%

The percentage change in Bristol-Myers Squibb's sales during 1996 is computed as follows:

Step 1. Compute the dollar amount of change in sales from 1995 to 1996:

$$\underset{\$15,065}{\overset{1996}{}} - \underset{\$13,767}{\overset{1995}{}} = \underset{\$1,298}{\overset{Increase}{}}$$

Step 2. Divide the dollar amount of change by the base-period amount to compute the percentage change during the later period:

$$\text{Percentage change} = \frac{\text{Dollar amount of change}}{\text{Base-year amount}}$$

$$= \frac{\$1,298}{\$13,767} = 9.4\%$$

During 1996, Bristol-Myers Squibb's sales increased by 9.4 percent.

Detailed horizontal analyses of comparative income statements and comparative balance sheets are shown in the two right-hand columns of Exhibits 18-2 and 18-3, the financial statements of Bristol-Myers Squibb Company. The income statements (statements of earnings) reveal that net sales increased by 9.4% during 1996. Cost of goods sold and the largest operating expense grew less. Also, the company had no special charge or restructuring expense in 1996. As a result, net income increased by 57.3 percent.

The comparative balance sheet in Exhibit 18-3 shows that 1996 was a year of expansion for Bristol-Myers Squibb. Total assets increased by $756 million, or 5.4 percent. Total liabilities increased by only $8 million, and total stockholders' equity grew by 748 million, or 12.8 percent.

 Thinking It Over Identify the item on Bristol-Myers Squibb's 1996 income statement that experienced the largest percentage *increase* from 1995. Considering all other changes on the 1996 income statement, is this a good sign or a bad sign about the company?

Answer: Income tax expense increased by 97.1 percent. This is a good sign about the company because earnings before tax and net income also increased by high percentages.

Trend Percentages

Trend percentages are a form of horizontal analysis. Trends are important indicators of the direction a business is heading. How have sales changed over a five-year period? What trend does gross profit show? These questions can be answered by an analysis of trend percentages over a representative period, such as the most recent five or ten years.

Trend percentages are computed by selecting a base year whose amounts are set equal to 100 percent. The amounts of each following year are expressed as a percentage

EXHIBIT 18-2
Comparative Income
Statement—Horizontal
Analysis

■ **Daily Exercise 18-1**

			Increase (Decrease)	
BRISTOL-MYERS SQUIBB COMPANY Statement of Earnings (Adapted) Years Ended December 31, 1996 and 1995				
(Dollar amounts in millions)	1996	1995	Amount	Percent
Net sales	$15,065	$13,767	$1,298	9.4%
Cost of products sold	3,965	3,637	328	9.0
Gross profit	11,100	10,130	970	9.6
Operating expenses:				
Marketing, selling, and administrative	3,925	3,670	255	6.9
Advertising and product promotion	1,946	1,646	300	18.2
Research and development	1,276	1,199	77	6.4
Special charge (expense)		950	(950)	(100.0)*
Restructuring expense		310	(310)	(100.0)*
Other	(60)	(47)	(13)	(27.7)
Earnings before income taxes	4,013	2,402	1,611	67.1
Income tax expense	1,163	590	573	97.1
Net earnings	$ 2,850	$ 1,812	$1,038	57.3

*Note: A decrease from any number to zero is a decrease of 100 percent. An increase from zero to any positive number is treated as an increase of 100 percent.

BRISTOL-MYERS SQUIBB COMPANY
Balance Sheet (Adapted)
December 31, 1996 and 1995

(Dollar amounts in millions)	1996	1995	Increase (Decrease) Amount	Increase (Decrease) Percent
Assets				
Current Assets:				
Cash and cash equivalents	$ 1,681	$ 1,645	$ 36	2.2%
Short-term investments	504	533	(29)	(5.4)
Receivables, net of allowances	2,651	2,356	295	12.5
Inventories	1,669	1,451	218	15.0
Prepaid expenses	1,023	1,033	(10)	(1.0)
Total Current Assets	7,528	7,018	510	7.3
Property, Plant, and Equipment—net	3,964	3,760	204	5.4
Insurance Recoverable	853	959	(106)	(11.1)
Other Assets	832	973	(141)	(14.5)
Excess of cost over net tangible assets received in business acquisitions [Goodwill]	1,508	1,219	289	23.7
Total Assets	$14,685	$13,929	$ 756	5.4%
Liabilities				
Current Liabilities:				
Short-term borrowings (notes payable)	$ 513	$ 575	$ (62)	(10.8)%
Accounts payable	1,064	848	216	25.5
Accrued expenses [payable]	1,962	1,939	23	1.2
U.S. and foreign income taxes payable	711	744	(33)	(4.4)
Product liability*	800	700	100	14.3
Total Current Liabilities	5,050	4,806	244	5.1
Product Liability [Long-term]	1,031	1,645	(614)	(37.3)
Other Liabilities	1,068	1,021	47	4.6
Long-Term Debt (notes payable)	966	635	331	52.1
Total Liabilities	8,115	8,107	8	0.1
Stockholders' Equity				
Common stock	108	54	54	100.0
Capital in excess of par value of stock	382	375	7	1.9
Cumulative translation adjustments	(361)	(327)	(34)	(10.4)
Retained earnings	9,260	7,917	$1,343	17.0
Less cost of treasury stock	(2,819)	(2,197)	(622)	(28.3)
Total Stockholders' Equity	6,570	5,822	748	12.8
Total Liabilities and Stockholders' Equity	$14,685	$13,929	$ 756	5.4%

*Warranties, guarantees, and the like.

■ Daily
Exercise 18-2

EXHIBIT 18-3
Comparative Balance
Sheet—Horizontal Analysis

of the base amount. To compute trend percentages, divide each item for following years by the corresponding amount during the base year:

$$\text{Trend \%} = \frac{\text{Any year \$}}{\text{Base year \$}}$$

Bristol-Myers Squibb Company showed sales, cost of goods sold, and gross profit for the past six years as follows:

(In millions)	1996	1995	1994	1993	1992	1991
Net sales	$15,065	$13,767	$11,984	$11,413	$11,156	$10,571
Cost of products sold	3,965	3,637	3,122	3,029	2,857	2,717
Gross profit	11,100	10,130	8,862	8,384	8,299	7,854

We want trend percentages for a five-year period starting with 1992. We use 1991 as the base year. Trend percentages for net sales are computed by dividing each net sales amount by the 1991 amount of $10,571 million. Trend percentages for Cost of products sold are calculated by dividing each Cost of products sold amount by $2,717 (the base-year amount), and trend percentages for Gross profit are calculated by dividing each gross profit amount by $7,854 (the base-year amount). The resulting trend percentages are as follows (1991, the base year = 100%):

	1996	1995	1994	1993	1992	1991
Net sales..............................	143%	130%	113%	108%	106%	100%
Cost of products sold.........	146	134	115	111	105	100
Gross profit........................	141	129	113	107	106	100

■ Daily Exercise 18-3

Bristol-Myers Squibb's sales and cost of goods sold have trended upward. Gross profit has increased steadily, with the most dramatic growth during 1995 and 1996. This information suggests that gross profit is increasing steadily.

Vertical Analysis

Objective 2

Perform a vertical analysis of a company's financial statements

Vertical Analysis. Analysis of a financial statement that reveals the relationship of each statement item to the total, which is 100 percent.

Horizontal analysis highlights changes in an item over time. However, no single financial analysis technique provides a complete picture of a business. Another method of analyzing a company is vertical analysis.

Vertical analysis of a financial statement reveals the relationship of each statement item to a specified base, which is the 100% figure. Every item on the financial statement is then reported as a percentage of that base. When an income statement is subjected to vertical analysis, net sales is usually the base. Suppose under normal conditions a company's gross profit is 70% of net sales. A drop in gross profit to 60% of net sales may cause the company to report a net loss on the income statement. Management, investors, and creditors view a large decline in gross profit with alarm. Exhibit 18-4 shows the vertical analysis of Bristol-Myers Squibb's income statement as a percentage of net sales. In this case,

$$\text{Vertical analysis \%} = \frac{\text{Each income statement item}}{\text{Net sales}}$$

So, for example, the vertical analysis percentage for Cost of products sold for 1996 equals 26.3% ($3,965/$15,065 = 0.263). Exhibit 18-5 shows the vertical analysis of the balance sheet amounts as a percentage of total assets.

EXHIBIT 18-4
Comparative Income
Statement—Vertical Analysis

BRISTOL-MYERS SQUIBB COMPANY Statement of Earnings (Adapted) Years Ended December 31, 1996 and 1995				
	1996		**1995**	
(Dollar amounts in millions)	**Amount**	**Percent**	**Amount**	**Percent**
Net sales	$15,065	100.0%	$13,767	100.0%
Cost of products sold..	3,965	26.3	3,637	26.4
Gross profit...	11,100	73.7	10,130	73.6
Operating expenses:				
Marketing, selling, and administrative..........	3,925	26.1	3,670	26.7
Advertising and product promotion..............	1,946	12.9	1,646	12.0
Research and development............................	1,276	8.5	1,199	8.7
Special charge (expense)...............................	—	—	950	6.9
Restructuring expense	—	—	310	2.2
Other expense (income)................................	(60)	(0.4)	(47)	(0.3)
Earnings before income taxes	4,013	26.6	2,402	17.4
Provision for income taxes	1,163	(7.7)	590	4.2
Net earnings...	$ 2,850	18.9%	$ 1,812	13.2%

■ Daily Exercise 18-4

BRISTOL-MYERS SQUIBB COMPANY
Balance Sheet (Adapted)
December 31, 1996 and 1995

(Dollar amounts in millions)	1996 Amount	1996 Percent	1995 Amount	1995 Percent
Assets				
Current Assets:				
Cash and cash equivalents	$ 1,681	11.4%	$ 1,645	11.8%
Short-term investments	504	3.4	533	3.8
Receivables, net of allowances	2,651	18.1	2,356	16.9
Inventories	1,669	11.4	1,451	10.4
Prepaid expenses	1,023	7.0	1,033	7.4
Total Current Assets	7,528	51.3	7,018	50.3
Property, Plant, and Equipment—net	3,964	27.0	3,760	27.0
Insurance Recoverable	853	5.8	959	6.9
Other Assets	832	5.6	973	7.0
Excess of cost over net tangible assets received in business acquisitions [Goodwill]	1,508	10.3	1,219	8.8
Total Assets	$14,685	100.0%	$13,929	100.0%
Liabilities				
Current Liabilities:				
Short-term borrowings (notes payable)	$ 513	3.5%	$ 575	4.1%
Accounts payable	1,064	7.3	848	6.1
Accrued expenses [payable]	1,962	13.4	1,939	13.9
U.S. and foreign income taxes payable	711	4.8	744	5.4
Product liability	800	5.4	700	5.0
Total Current Liabilities	5,050	34.4	4,806	34.5
Product Liability [Long-term]	1,031	7.0	1,645	11.8
Other [Long-term] Liabilities	1,068	7.3	1,021	7.3
Long-Term Debt (notes payable)	966	6.6	635	4.6
Total Liabilities	8,115	55.3	8,107	58.2
Stockholders' Equity				
Common stock	108	0.7	54	0.4
Capital in excess of par value of stock	382	2.6	375	2.7
Cumulative translation adjustments	(361)	(2.5)	(327)	(2.3)
Retained earnings	9,260	63.1	7,917	56.8
Less cost of treasury stock	(2,819)	(19.2)	(2,197)	(15.8)
Total Stockholders' Equity	6,570	44.7	5,822	41.8
Total Liabilities and Stockholders' Equity	$14,685	100.0%	$13,929	100.0%

■ Daily Exercise 18-5

■ Daily Exercise 18-6

EXHIBIT 18-5
Comparative Balance Sheet—Vertical Analysis

The vertical analysis of Bristol-Myers Squibb's income statement (Exhibit 18-4) shows no unusual relationships. The gross profit percentage was essentially the same as in 1995. Net income's percentage of sales increased in 1996 because there was no special charge or restructuring expense.

The vertical analysis of Bristol-Myers Squibb's balance sheet (Exhibit 18-5) also yields few surprises. Current assets' percentage of total assets increased a little in 1996, while current liabilities' percentage was unchanged. The best news on the balance sheet is the decrease in long-term product liability.

The company's financial position remains strong. For example, the current ratio is 1.49 ($7,528 million/$5,050 million). ◀▥▥ The company has very little long-term debt, and retained earnings (accumulated profit from operations) is the largest single source of financing.

◀▥▥ ◀▥▥ ◀▥▥ Recall from Chapter 4 (page 153) that the current ratio is equal to total current assets divided by total current liabilities.

Common-Size Statements

Objective 3

Prepare common-size financial statements for benchmarking against the industry average and key competitors

The percentages in Exhibits 18-4 and 18-5 can be presented as a separate statement that reports only percentages (no dollar amounts). Such a statement is called a **common-size statement**.

-Size Statement. A fi-
.atement that reports only
..ages (no dollar amounts); a
..e of vertical analysis.

On a common-size income statement, each item is expressed as a percentage of the net sales amount. Net sales is the *common size* to which we relate the statement's other amounts. In the balance sheet, the common size is total assets *or* the sum of total liabilities and stockholders' equity. A common-size statement eases the comparison of different companies because their amounts are stated in percentages.

Common-size statements may identify the need for corrective action. Exhibit 18-6 is the common-size analysis of current assets taken from Exhibit 18-5. Exhibit 18-6 shows cash as a relatively high percentage of total assets at the end of each year. Receivables are a growing percentage of total assets. What could have caused the increase in receivables? Bristol-Myers Squibb may have been lax in collecting accounts receivable, a policy that could lead to a cash shortage. The company may need to pursue collection more vigorously. Or, the company may have sold to less-creditworthy customers. In any event, the company should monitor its cash position and collection of receivables to avoid a cash shortage. Common-size statements provide information useful for this purpose.

Working it Out Calculate the common-size percentages for the following income statement:

Net sales	$150,000
Cost of goods sold	60,000
Gross margin	90,000
Operating expense	40,000
Operating income	50,000
Income tax expense	15,000
Net income	$ 35,000

EXHIBIT 18-6
Common-Size Analysis of
Current Assets

BRISTOL-MYERS SQUIBB COMPANY
Analysis of Current Assets
December 31, 1996 and 1995

	Percent of Total Assets	
	1996	1995
Current Assets:		
Cash and cash equivalents	11.4%	11.8%
Short-term investments	3.4	3.8
Receivables, net of allowances	18.1	16.9
Inventories	11.4	10.4
Prepaid expenses	7.0	7.4
Total Current Assets	51.3	50.3
Long-Term Assets	48.7	49.7
Total Assets	100.0%	100.0%

Percent of Total Assets

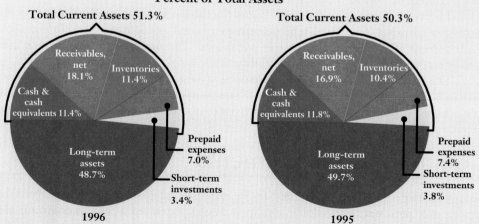

Net sales.............................	100%	(= $150,000 ÷ $150,000)
Cost of goods sold	40	(= $ 60,000 ÷ $150,000)
Gross margin	60	(= $ 90,000 ÷ $150,000)
Operating expense	27	(= $ 40,000 ÷ $150,000)
Operating income.............	33	(= $ 50,000 ÷ $150,000)
Income tax expense...........	10	(= $ 15,000 ÷ $150,000)
Net income	23%	(= $ 35,000 ÷ $150,000)

Benchmarking

Benchmarking is the practice of comparing a company to a standard set by other companies, with a view toward improvement.

Benchmarking Against the Industry Average

We study a company's records to help us understand past results and predict future performance. Still, the knowledge that we can develop from a company's records is limited to that one company. We may learn that gross profit has decreased and that net income has increased steadily for the last ten years. This information is helpful, but it does not consider how businesses in the same industry have fared over the same time period. Have other companies in the same line of business increased their sales? Is there an industrywide decline in gross profit? Managers, investors, creditors, and other interested parties need to know how one company compares with other companies in the same line of business. For example, Apple Computer's gross margin has steadily declined in relation to its competitors'.

Exhibit 18-7 gives the common-size income statement of Bristol-Myers Squibb Company compared with the average for the pharmaceuticals (health-care) industry. This

Benchmarking. The practice of comparing a company to a standard set by other companies, with a view toward improvement.

EXHIBIT 18-7
Common-Size Income Statement Compared with the Industry Average

BRISTOL-MYERS SQUIBB COMPANY Common-Size Income Statement for Comparison with Industry Average Year Ended December 31, 1996		
	Bristol-Myers Squibb	**Industry Average**
Net sales...	100.0%	100.0%
Cost of products sold..	26.3	55.3
Gross profit	73.7	44.7
Operating expenses..	47.1	37.7
Earnings from continuing operations before income tax..............	26.6	7.0
Income tax expense..	7.7	1.7
Earnings from continuing operations	18.9	5.3
Special items (discontinued operations, extraordinary gains and losses, and effects of accounting changes)..	—	1.1
Net earnings...	18.9%	4.2%

Percent of Net Sales

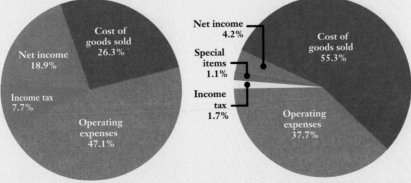

Bristol-Myers Squibb Company	**Industry Average**

analysis compares Bristol-Myers Squibb with all other companies in its line of business. The industry averages were adapted from Robert Morris Associates' *Annual Statement Studies*. Analysts at Merrill Lynch and other companies specialize in a particular industry and make such comparisons in deciding which companies' stocks to buy or sell. For example, financial-service companies such as Merrill Lynch have health-care industry specialists, airline-industry specialists, and so on. Exhibit 18-7 shows that Bristol-Myers Squibb compares favorably with competing companies in its industry. Its gross profit percentage is much higher than the industry average. The company does a good job of controlling total expenses, and as a result, its percentage of income from continuing operations and net income percentage are significantly higher than the industry average.

Benchmarking Against a Key Competitor

Common-size statements are also used to compare the company to another specific company. Suppose you are a member of Angela Lane's team at Baer & Foster. You are considering an investment in the stock of a manufacturer of health-care and other consumer products, and you are choosing between Bristol-Myers Squibb and Johnson & Johnson. A direct comparison of their financial statements in dollar amounts is not meaningful because the amounts are so different (see the income statements on page 770). However, you can convert the two companies' income statements to common size and compare the percentages.

Exhibit 18-8 presents the common-size income statements of Bristol-Myers Squibb and Johnson & Johnson. Johnson & Johnson serves as an excellent benchmark because most of its products are market leaders. In this comparison, Bristol-Myers Squibb has higher percentages of gross profit, earnings from continuing operations, and net earnings.

■ Daily Exercise 18-7
■ Daily Exercise 18-8

EXHIBIT 18-8
Common-Size Income
Statement Compared with a
Key Competitor

BRISTOL-MYERS SQUIBB COMPANY
Common-Size Income Statement (Adapted) for Comparison with Key Competitor
Year Ended December 31, 1996

	Bristol-Myers Squibb	Johnson & Johnson
Net sales	100.0%	100.0%
Cost of products sold	26.3	32.4
Gross profit	73.7	67.6
Operating expenses	47.1	48.9
Earnings from continuing operations, before income tax	26.6	18.7
Income tax expense	7.7	5.3
Net earnings	18.9%	13.4%

Percent of Net Sales

Bristol-Myers
Squibb Company

Johnson & Johnson

Perform a horizontal analysis and a vertical analysis of the comparative income statement of TRE Corporation, which makes metal detectors. State whether 19X3 was a good year or a bad year, and give your reasons.

TRE CORPORATION
Comparative Income Statement
Months Ended December 31, 19X3 and 19X2

	19X3	19X2
Total revenues	$275,000	$225,000
Expenses:		
Cost of products sold	$194,000	$165,000
Engineering, selling, and administrative expenses	54,000	48,000
Interest expense	5,000	5,000
Income tax expense	9,000	3,000
Other expense (income)	1,000	(1,000)
Total expenses	263,000	220,000
Net earnings	$ 12,000	$ 5,000

■ **SOLUTION**

TRE CORPORATION
Horizontal Analysis of Comparative Income Statement
Months Ended December 31, 19X3 and 19X2

	19X3	19X2	Increase (Decrease) Amount	Increase (Decrease) Percent
Total revenues	$275,000	$225,000	$50,000	22.2%
Expenses:				
Cost of products sold	$194,000	$165,000	$29,000	17.6
Engineering, selling, and administrative expenses	54,000	48,000	6,000	12.5
Interest expense	5,000	5,000	—	—
Income tax expense	9,000	3,000	6,000	200.0
Other expense (income)	1,000	(1,000)	2,000	—*
Total expenses	263,000	220,000	43,000	19.5
Net earnings	$ 12,000	$ 5,000	$ 7,000	140.0%

*Percentage changes are typically not computed for shifts from a negative amount to a positive amount, and vice versa.

TRE CORPORATION
Vertical Analysis of Comparative Income Statement
Months Ended December 31, 19X3 and 19X2

	19X3 Amount	19X3 Percent	19X2 Amount	19X2 Percent
Total revenues	$275,000	100.0%	$225,000	100.0%
Expenses:				
Cost of products sold	$194,000	70.5	$165,000	73.3
Engineering, selling, and administrative expenses	54,000	19.6	48,000	21.3
Interest expense	5,000	1.8	5,000	2.2
Income tax expense	9,000	3.3	3,000	1.4*
Other expense (income)	1,000	0.4	(1,000)	(0.4)
Total expenses	263,000	95.6	220,000	97.8
Net earnings	$ 12,000	4.4%	$ 5,000	2.2%

*Number rounded up.

The horizontal analysis shows that total revenues increased 22.2 percent. This percentage increase was greater than the 19.5% increase in total expenses, resulting in a 140% increase in net earnings.

The vertical analysis shows decreases in the percentages of net sales consumed by the cost of products sold (from 73.3% to 70.5%) and by the engineering, selling, and administrative expenses (from 21.3% to 19.6%). These two items are TRE's largest dollar expenses, so their percentage decreases are quite important. The relative reduction in expenses raised December 19X3 net earnings to 4.4% of sales, compared with 2.2% the preceding December. The overall analysis indicates that December 19X3 was significantly better than December 19X2.

Using Ratios to Make Business Decisions

Objective 4

Compute the standard financial ratios used for decision making

An important part of financial analysis is the calculation and interpretation of ratios. A ratio expresses the relationship of one number to another number. For example, if the balance sheet shows current assets of $100,000 and current liabilities of $25,000, the ratio of current assets to current liabilities is $100,000 to $25,000. We simplify this numerical expression to the ratio of 4 to 1, which may also be written 4:1 and 4/1. Other acceptable ways of expressing this ratio include (1) "current assets are 400% of current liabilities," (2) "the business has four dollars in current assets for every one dollar in current liabilities," or simply, (3) "the current ratio is 4.0."

We often reduce the ratio fraction by writing the ratio as one figure over the other—for example, 4/1—and then dividing the numerator by the denominator. In this way, the ratio 4/1 may be expressed simply as 4. The 1 that represents the denominator of the fraction is understood, not written. Consider the ratio $175,000:$165,000. After dividing the first figure by the second, we come to 1.06:1, which we state as 1.06. The second part of the ratio, the 1, again is understood. Ratios provide a convenient and useful way of expressing a relationship between numbers.

"*Rubbermaid Incorporated—the well-known manufacturer of plastic products for the home and garden, office, and industry—displays ratio data in the consolidated financial summary section of its annual report.*"

A manager, lender, or financial analyst may use any ratio that is relevant to a particular decision. Many companies include ratios in a special section of their annual financial reports. Rubbermaid Incorporated—the well-known manufacturer of plastic products for the home and garden, office, and industry—displays ratio data in the consolidated financial summary section of its annual report. Exhibit 18-9 shows an excerpt from that summary section. Investment services—Moody's, Standard & Poor's, Robert Morris Associates, and others—report these ratios for companies and industries.

The Decision Guidelines feature on pages 784–785 summarizes the widely used ratios that we will discuss in this chapter. The ratios may be classified as follows:

1. Ratios that measure the company's ability to pay current liabilities
2. Ratios that measure the company's ability to sell inventory and collect receivables

EXHIBIT 18-9

Consolidated Financial Summary of Rubbermaid, Incorporated (Dollar Amounts in Thousands except Per-Share Amounts)

Years Ended December 31,	19X3	19X2	19X1	19X0
Operating Results				
Net earnings	$211,413	$164,095	$162,650	$143,520
Per common share	$1.32	$1.02	$1.02	$0.90
Percent of sales	10.8%	9.1%	9.8%	9.4%
Return on average shareholders' equity	20.0%	17.5%	19.7%	20.2%
Financial Position				
Current assets	$829,744	$699,650	$663,999	$602,697
Current liabilities	$259,314	$223,246	$245,500	$235,300
Working capital	$570,430	$476,404	$418,499	$367,397
Current ratio	3.20	3.13	2.70	2.56

3. Ratios that measure the company's ability to pay short-term and long-term debt
4. Ratios that measure the company's profitability
5. Ratios used to analyze the company's stock as an investment

How much can a computer help in analyzing financial statements for investment purposes? Time yourself as you perform one of the financial-ratio problems in this chapter. Multiply your efforts by, say, 100 companies that you are comparing by means of this ratio. Now consider ranking these 100 companies on the basis of four or five additional ratios.

Online financial databases, such as Lexis/Nexis and the Dow Jones News Retrieval Service, offer quarterly financial figures for thousands of public corporations going back as far as ten years. Assume that you want to compare companies' recent earnings histories. You might have the computer compare hundreds of companies on the basis of price/earnings ratio and rates of return on stockholders' equity and total assets. The computer could then give you the names of the 20 (or however many) companies that appear most favorable in terms of these ratios.

> **Learning Tip:** Take some time and make sure you really understand the relationships among the numbers on a financial statement. Horizontal and vertical analyses are one way to study the relationships. Ratios are another way. We compare financial statement amounts to other items to assess what the ratio indicates about the company. How do we assess a ratio? We consider prior years, industry averages, budgeted ratios, and so on. These comparisons give a ratio added meaning.

Measuring a Company's Ability to Pay Current Liabilities

Working capital is defined as follows:

$$\text{Working capital} = \text{Current assets} - \text{Current Liabilities}$$

Working capital is widely used to measure a business's ability to meet its short-term obligations with its current assets. In general, the larger the working capital, the better able the business is to pay its debt. Recall that capital, or owners' equity, is total assets minus total liabilities. Working capital is like a "current" version of total capital. The working capital amount considered alone does not give a complete picture of the entity's working capital position, however. Consider two companies with equal working capital:

Working Capital. Current assets minus current liabilities; measures a business's ability to meet its short-term obligations with its current assets.

	Company A	Company B
Current assets......................	$100,000	$200,000
Less: Current liabilities.........	(50,000)	(150,000)
Working capital....................	$ 50,000	$ 50,000

Both companies have working capital of $50,000, but Company A's working capital is as large as its current liabilities. Company B's working capital is only one-third as large as its current liabilities. Which business has a better working-capital position? Company A, because its working capital is a higher percentage of current assets and current liabilities. To use working-capital data in decision making, it is helpful to develop ratios. Two decision-making tools based on working-capital data are the *current ratio* and the *acid-test ratio*.

Current Ratio. Total current assets divided by total current liabilities. Measures the ability to pay current liabilities from current assets.

CURRENT RATIO The most common ratio using current-asset and current-liability data is the **current ratio,** which is total current assets divided by total current liabilities. ◀▥▥ Recall the makeup of current assets and current liabilities. Current assets consist of cash, short-term investments, net receivables, inventory, and prepaid expenses. Current liabilities include accounts payable, short-term notes payable, unearned revenues, and all types of accrued liabilities. The current ratio measures the company's ability to pay current liabilities with current assets.

◀▥▥ ◀▥▥ ◀▥▥ We introduced the current ratio in Chapter 4 (page 153).

Exhibits 18-10 and 18-11 give the comparative income statement and balance sheet of Palisades Furniture, Inc., respectively. The current ratios of Palisades Furniture, Inc., at December 31, 19X7 and 19X6, follow, along with the average for the retail furniture industry, a benchmark for evaluating Palisades Furniture's ratios.

| | | Palisades' Current Ratio | | |
Formula		19X7	19X6	Industry Average
Current ratio = $\dfrac{\text{Total current assets}}{\text{Total current liabilities}}$		$\dfrac{\$262,000}{\$142,000} = 1.85$	$\dfrac{\$236,000}{\$126,000} = 1.87$	1.80

■ **Daily Exercise 18-9**

The current ratio decreased slightly during 19X7. In general, a higher current ratio indicates a stronger financial position. A higher current ratio suggests that the business has sufficient liquid assets to maintain normal business operations. Compare Palisades Furniture's current ratio of 1.85 with the industry average of 1.80 and with the current ratios of some well-known companies:

Company	Current Ratio
Chesebrough-Pond's, Inc.	2.50
Wal-Mart Stores, Inc.	1.51
The Superior Oil Company	1.46
General Mills, Inc.	1.05

What is an acceptable current ratio? The answer depends on the nature of the industry. The norm for companies in most industries is between 1.60 and 1.90, as reported by Robert Morris Associates. Palisades Furniture's current ratio of 1.85 is within the range of those values. In most industries, a current ratio of 2.0 is considered good.

◀▥▥ ◀▥▥ ◀▥▥ We saw in Chapter 8 (pages 353–354) that the higher the acid-test ratio, the better able the business is to pay its current liabilities.

Acid-Test Ratio. Ratio of the sum of cash plus short-term investments plus net current receivables to current liabilities. Tells whether the entity could pay all its current liabilities if they came due immediately. Also called the **quick ratio.**

ACID-TEST RATIO The **acid-test** (or **quick**) **ratio** tells us whether the entity could pay all its current liabilities if they came due immediately. ◀▥ That is, could the company pass this *acid test?* To do so, the company would have to convert its most liquid assets to cash.

To compute the acid-test ratio, we add cash, short-term investments, and net current receivables (accounts and notes receivable, net of allowances) and divide by total current liabilities. Inventory and prepaid expenses are the two current assets *not* included in the acid-test computations because they are the least liquid of the current assets. A business may not be able to convert inventory and prepaid expense to cash immediately to pay current liabilities. The acid-test ratio uses a narrower asset base to measure liquidity than the current ratio does.

EXHIBIT 18-10
Comparative Financial Statements

PALISADES FURNITURE, INC. Comparative Income Statement Years Ended December 31, 19X7 and 19X6		
	19X7	19X6
Net sales...	$858,000	$803,000
Cost of goods sold	513,000	509,000
Gross profit....................................	345,000	294,000
Operating expenses:		
Selling expenses	126,000	114,000
General expenses	118,000	123,000
Total operating expenses	244,000	237,000
Income from operations...............	101,000	57,000
Interest revenue............................	4,000	—
Interest expense	(24,000)	(14,000)
Income before income taxes..........	81,000	43,000
Income tax expense.......................	33,000	17,000
Net income	$ 48,000	$ 26,000

EXHIBIT 18-11
Comparative Financial
Statements

PALISADES FURNITURE, INC. Comparative Balance Sheet December 31, 19X7 and 19X6		
	19X7	**19X6**
Assets		
Current assets:		
Cash	$ 29,000	$ 32,000
Accounts receivable, net	114,000	85,000
Inventories	113,000	111,000
Prepaid expenses..	6,000	8,000
Total current assets	262,000	236,000
Long-term investments	18,000	9,000
Property, plant, and equipment, net	507,000	399,000
Total assets	$787,000	$644,000
Liabilities		
Current liabilities:		
Notes payable	$ 42,000	$ 27,000
Accounts payable	73,000	68,000
Accrued liabilities...	27,000	31,000
Total current liabilities......................................	142,000	126,000
Long-term debt	289,000	198,000
Total liabilities..	431,000	324,000
Stockholders' Equity		
Common stock, no par...	186,000	186,000
Retained earnings	170,000	134,000
Total stockholders' equity.................................	356,000	320,000
Total liabilities and stockholders' equity	$787,000	$644,000

Palisades Furniture's acid-test ratios for 19X7 and 19X6 are as follows:

		Palisades' Current Ratio		
	Formula	**19X7**	**19X6**	**Industry Average**
Acid-test ratio	=	Cash + Short-term investments + Net current receivables / Total current liabilities	$\dfrac{\$29{,}000 + \$0 + \$114{,}000}{\$142{,}000} = 1.01$	$\dfrac{\$32{,}000 + \$0 + \$85{,}000}{\$126{,}000} = 0.93$	0.60

The company's acid-test ratio improved considerably during 19X7 and is significantly better than the industry average. Compare Palisades' 1.01 acid-test ratio with the acid-test values of some well-known companies:

■ **Daily Exercise 18-10**

Company	Acid-Test Ratio
Chesebrough-Pond's, Inc.	1.25
General Motors, Inc.	0.91
Wal-Mart Stores, Inc.	0.08

How can a leading company such as Wal-Mart function with so low an acid-test ratio? Wal-Mart has almost no receivables. Its inventory is priced low to turn over very quickly. The norm ranges from 0.20 for shoe retailers to 1.00 for manufacturers of paperboard containers and certain other equipment, as reported by Robert Morris Associates. An acid-test ratio of 0.90 to 1.00 is acceptable in most industries.

Thinking It Over Palisades Furniture's current ratio is 1.85, which looks strong, while the company's acid-test ratio is 1.01, also strong. Suppose Palisades' acid-test ratio were dangerously low, say 0.48. What would be the most likely reason for the discrepancy between a high current ratio and a weak acid-test ratio?

RATIO	COMPUTATION	INFORMATION PROVIDED
Measuring the company's ability to pay current liabilities:		
1. Current ratio	$$\frac{\text{Total current assets}}{\text{Total current liabilities}}$$	Measures ability to pay current liabilities with current assets.
2. Acid-test (quick) ratio	$$\frac{\text{Cash} + \frac{\text{Short-term}}{\text{investments}} + \frac{\text{Net current}}{\text{receivables}}}{\text{Total current liabilities}}$$	Shows ability to pay all current liabilities if they come due immediately.
Measuring the company's ability to sell inventory and collect receivables:		
3. Inventory turnover	$$\frac{\text{Cost of goods sold}}{\text{Average inventory}}$$	Indicates saleability of inventory—the number of times a company sells its average inventory level during a year.
4. Accounts receivable turnover	$$\frac{\text{Net credit sales}}{\text{Average net accounts receivable}}$$	Measures ability to collect cash from credit customers.
5. Days' sales in receivables	$$\frac{\text{Average net accounts receivable}}{\text{One day's sales}}$$	Shows how many days' sales remain in Accounts Receivable—how many days it takes to collect the average level of receivables.
Measuring the company's ability to pay short-term and long-term debt:		
6. Debt ratio	$$\frac{\text{Total liabilities}}{\text{Total assets}}$$	Indicates percentage of assets financed with debt.
7. Times-interest-earned ratio	$$\frac{\text{Income from operations}}{\text{Interest expense}}$$	Measures the number of times operating income can cover interest expense.

Answer: It would appear that the company is having trouble selling its inventory. The level of inventory must be relatively high, and the inventory is propping up the current ratio. The rate of inventory turnover may be low. This leads us into the next topic.

Measuring a Company's Ability to Sell Inventory and Collect Receivables

The ability to sell inventory and collect receivables is fundamental to business success. Recall the operating cycle of a merchandiser: cash to inventory to receivables and back to cash. ◄▦ In this section, we discuss three ratios that measure the company's ability to sell inventory and collect receivables.

◄▦◄▦◄▦ If you need to, refer to the discussion of the operating cycle in Chapter 5, page 183.

◄▦◄▦◄▦ We introduced inventory turnover in Chapter 5, pages 201–202. Average inventory is computed as follows: (Beginning inventory + Ending inventory)/2.

Inventory Turnover. Ratio of cost of goods sold to average inventory. Measures the number of times a company sells its average level of inventory during a year.

INVENTORY TURNOVER **Inventory turnover** is a measure of the number of times a company sells its average level of inventory during a year. ◄▦ In general, companies prefer a high rate of inventory turnover. A value of 6 means that the company's average level of inventory has been sold six times during the year. This is generally better than a turnover of 3 or 4. However, a high value can mean that the business is not keeping enough inventory on hand, and inadequate inventory can result in lost sales if the company cannot fill a customer's order. Therefore, a business strives for the *most profitable* rate of inventory turnover, not necessarily the *highest* rate.

To compute the inventory turnover ratio, we divide cost of goods sold by the average inventory for the period. We use the cost of goods sold—not sales—in the computation because both cost of goods sold and inventory are stated *at cost*. Sales is stated at the sales value of inventory and therefore is not comparable with inventory cost.

Palisades Furniture's inventory turnover for 19X7 is

RATIO	COMPUTATION	INFORMATION PROVIDED
Measuring the company's profitability:		
8. Rate of return on net sales	$$\frac{\text{Net income}}{\text{Net sales}}$$	Shows the percentage of each sales dollar earned as net income.
9. Rate of return on total assets	$$\frac{\text{Net income} + \text{Interest expense}}{\text{Average total assets}}$$	Measures how profitably a company uses its assets.
10. Rate of return on common stockholders' equity	$$\frac{\text{Net income} - \text{Preferred dividends}}{\text{Average common stockholders' equity}}$$	Gauges how much income is earned with the money invested by common shareholders.
11. Earnings per share of common stock	$$\frac{\text{Net income} - \text{Preferred dividends}}{\text{Number of shares of common stock outstanding}}$$	Gives the amount of net income per one share of the company's common stock.
Analyzing the company's stock as an investment:		
12. Price/earnings ratio	$$\frac{\text{Market price per share of common stock}}{\text{Earnings per share}}$$	Indicates the market price of $1 of earnings.
13. Dividend yield	$$\frac{\text{Dividends per share of common (or preferred) stock}}{\text{Market price per share of common (or preferred) stock}}$$	Shows the percentage of a stock's market value returned to stockholders as dividends each period.
14. Book value per share of common stock	$$\frac{\text{Total stockholders' equity} - \text{Preferred equity}}{\text{Number of shares of common stock outstanding}}$$	Indicates the recorded accounting amount for each share of common stock outstanding.

Formula	Palisades' Inventory Turnover	Industry Average
Inventory turnover = $\dfrac{\text{Cost of goods sold}}{\text{Average inventory}}$	$\dfrac{\$513,000}{\$112,000} = 4.58$	2.70

Cost of goods sold appears in the income statement (Exhibit 18-10). Average inventory is figured by averaging the beginning inventory ($111,000) and ending inventory ($113,000). (See the balance sheet, Exhibit 18-11.) If inventory levels vary greatly from month to month, compute the average by adding the 12 monthly balances and dividing the sum by 12.

Inventory turnover varies widely with the nature of the business. For example, companies that remove natural gas from the ground hold their inventory for a very short period of time and have an average turnover of 30. Palisades Furniture's turnover of 4.58 times a year is high for the retail furniture industry, which has an average turnover of 2.70. Palisades' high inventory turnover results from its policy of keeping little inventory on hand. The company takes customer orders and has its suppliers ship directly to some customers.

Inventory turnover rates can vary greatly within a company. At Toys "Я" Us, diapers and formula turn over more than 12 times a year, while seasonal toys turn over less than three times a year. The entire Toys "Я" Us inventory turns over an average of three times a year. The company's inventory is at its lowest point around January 31 and at its highest point around October 31.

To evaluate fully a company's inventory turnover, we must compare the ratio over time. A sudden sharp decline or a steady decline over a long period suggests the need for corrective action.

Receivable Turnover.
credit sales to average net
receivable. Measures ability
collect cash from credit customers.

ACCOUNTS RECEIVABLE TURNOVER

Accounts receivable turnover measures a company's ability to collect cash from credit customers. In general, the higher the ratio, the more successfully the business collects cash, and the better off its operations are. However, a receivable turnover that is too high may indicate that credit is too tight, causing the loss of sales to good customers. To compute the accounts receivable turnover, we divide net credit sales by average net accounts receivable. The resulting ratio indicates how many times during the year the average level of receivables was turned into cash.

Palisades Furniture's accounts receivable turnover ratio for 19X7 is computed as follows:

Formula	Palisades' Accounts Receivable Turnover	Industry Average
$\text{Accounts receivable turnover} = \dfrac{\text{Net credit sales}}{\text{Average net accounts receivable}}$	$\dfrac{\$858,000}{\$99,500} = 8.62$ times	22.2 times

The net credit sales figure comes from the income statement. Palisades Furniture makes all sales on credit. If the company makes both cash and credit sales, this ratio is best computed by using only net *credit* sales. Average net accounts receivable is figured by adding the beginning accounts receivable balance ($85,000) and the ending balance ($114,000), then dividing by 2. If the accounts receivable balances exhibit a seasonal pattern, compute the average by using the 12 monthly balances.

Palisades' receivable turnover of 8.62 is much lower than the industry average. The explanation is simple: The company is a home-town store that sells to local people who tend to pay their bills over a lengthy period of time. Many larger furniture stores sell their receivables to other companies called *factors*, a practice that keeps receivables low and receivable turnover high. But companies that factor (sell) their receivables receive less than face value of the receivables. Palisades Furniture follows a different strategy.

Days' Sales in Receivables.
Ratio of average net accounts receivable to one day's sales. Tells how many days' sales remain in Accounts Receivable awaiting collection.

DAY'S SALES IN RECEIVABLES

Businesses must convert accounts receivable to cash. All else equal, the lower the Accounts Receivable balance, the more successful the business has been in converting receivables into cash, and the better off the business is.

The **days'-sales-in-receivables** ratio tells us how many days' sales remain in Accounts Receivable. To compute the ratio, we follow a two-step process. First, divide net sales by 365 days to figure the average sales amount for one day. Second, divide this average day's sales amount into the average net accounts receivable.

The data to compute this ratio for Palisades Furniture, Inc., for 19X7 are taken from the income statement and the balance sheet (Exhibits 18-10 and 18-11):

Recall from Chapter 8 (page 354) that days' sales in receivables indicates how many days it takes to collect the average level of receivables.

Formula	Palisades' Days' Sales in Accounts Receivables	Industry Average
Days' Sales in Accounts Receivable:		
1. One day's sales $= \dfrac{\text{Net sales}}{365 \text{ days}}$	$\dfrac{\$858,000}{365 \text{ days}} = \$2,351$	
2. $\dfrac{\text{Days' sales in accounts receivable}}{} = \dfrac{\text{Average net accounts receivable}}{\text{One day's sales}}$	$\dfrac{\$99,500}{\$2,351} = 42$ days	16 days

■ **Daily Exercise 18-11**

Days' sales in receivables can also be computed in a single step: $\$99,500/(\$858,000/365 \text{ days}) = 42$ days.

Palisades' ratio tells us that 42 days' sales remained in average accounts receivable during the year. The company will increase its cash inflow if it can decrease this ratio. The days' sales in receivables for Palisades is higher (worse) than the industry average because the company collects its own receivables. Many other furniture stores sell their receivables and carry fewer days' sales in receivables. Palisades Furniture remains competitive because of its personal relationship with its customers. Without their good paying habits, the company's cash flow would suffer.

Measuring a Company's Ability to Pay Short-Term and Long-Term Debt

The ratios discussed so far give us insight into current assets and current liabilities. Most businesses also have long-term liabilities. Two measures of a business's ability to pay both short-term and long-term liabilities are the *debt ratio* and the *times-interest-earned ratio.*

DEBT RATIO The ratio of total liabilities to total assets—called the **debt ratio**—tells us the proportion of the company's assets that it has financed with debt. ◄▥ If the debt ratio is 1, then debt has been used to finance all the assets. A debt ratio of 0.50 means that the company has financed half its assets with debt and half with owners' equity. The higher the debt ratio, the higher the strain of paying interest each year and the principal amount at maturity. The lower the ratio, the lower the business's future obligations. Creditors view a high debt ratio with caution. If a business seeking financing already has large liabilities, then additional debt payments may be too much for the business to handle. To help protect themselves, creditors generally charge higher interest rates on new borrowing to companies with an already-high debt ratio.

Palisades Furniture's debt ratios at the end of 19X7 and 19X6 are as follows:

◄▥◄▥◄▥ We introduced the debt ratio in Chapter 4, page 154.

Debt Ratio. Ratio of total liabilities to total assets. Tells the proportion of a company's assets that it has financed with debt.

	Palisades' Debt Ratio		
Formula	19X7	19X6	Industry Average
Debt ratio = $\dfrac{\text{Total liabilities}}{\text{Total assets}}$	$\dfrac{\$431{,}000}{\$787{,}000} = 0.55$	$\dfrac{\$324{,}000}{\$644{,}000} = 0.50$	0.61

Palisades Furniture expanded operations during 19X7 by financing the purchase of property, plant, and equipment through borrowing, which is common. This expansion explains the firm's increased debt ratio. Even after the increase in 19X7, the company's debt is not very high. Robert Morris Associates reports that the average debt ratio for most companies ranges around 0.57–0.67, with relatively little variation from company to company. Palisades' 0.55 debt ratio indicates a fairly low-risk debt position compared to the retail furniture industry average of 0.61.

TIMES-INTEREST-EARNED RATIO The debt ratio measures the effect of debt on the company's *financial position* (balance sheet). However, the debt ratio says nothing about the ability to pay interest expense. Analysts use a second ratio—the **times-interest-earned ratio**—to relate income to interest expense. To compute this ratio, we divide income from operations by interest expense. This ratio measures the number of times that operating income can *cover* interest expense. For this reason, the ratio is also called the **interest-coverage ratio.** A high times-interest-earned ratio indicates ease in paying interest expense; a low value suggests difficulty.

Calculation of Palisades' times-interest-earned ratios follows:

		Palisades' Times-Interest-Earned Ratio		Industry Average
Formula		19X7	19X6	
Times-interest-earned ratio = $\dfrac{\text{Income from operations*}}{\text{Interest expense}}$		$\dfrac{\$101{,}000}{\$24{,}000} = 4.21$ times	$\dfrac{\$57{,}000}{\$14{,}000} = 4.07$ times	2.00 times

*A company's income statement may not report income from operations. To estimate income from operations, you can add interest expense to income before income tax.

The company's times-interest-earned ratio increased in 19X7. This is a favorable sign, especially since the company's short-term notes payable and long-term debt rose substantially during the year. Palisades Furniture's new plant assets, we conclude, have earned more in operating income than they have cost the business in interest expense. The company's times-interest-earned ratio of around 4.00 is significantly better than the 2.00 average for furniture retailers. The norm for U.S. business, as reported by Robert Morris Associates, falls in the range of 2.0 to 3.0 for most companies.

On the basis of its debt ratio and its times-interest-earned ratio, Palisades Furniture appears to have little difficulty *servicing its debt*—that is, paying its liabilities.

Times-Interest-Earned Ratio. Ratio of income from operations to interest expense. Measures the number of times that operating income can cover interest expense. Also called the **interest-coverage ratio.**

■ **Daily Exercise 18-12**

Measuring a Company's Profitability

The fundamental goal of business is to earn a profit. Ratios that measure profitability play a large role in decision making. These ratios are reported in the business press, by investment services, and in companies' annual financial reports.

Rate of Return on Net Sales. Ratio of net income to net sales. A measure of profitability. Also called **return on sales.**

RATE OF RETURN ON NET SALES In business, the term *return* is used broadly and loosely as an evaluation of profitability. Consider a ratio called the **rate of return on net sales,** or simply **return on sales.** (The word *net* is usually omitted for convenience, even though the net sales figure is used to compute the ratio.) This ratio shows the percentage of each sales dollar earned as net income. The rate-of-return-on-sales ratios for Palisades Furniture are calculated as follows:

Formula	Palisades' Rate of Return on Sales		Industry Average
	19X7	19X6	
Rate of return on sales = $\dfrac{\text{Net income}}{\text{Net sales}}$	$\dfrac{\$48,000}{\$858,000} = 0.056$	$\dfrac{\$26,000}{\$803,000} = 0.032$	0.008

Companies strive for a high rate of return. The higher the rate of return, the more that sales are providing income to the business and the less of sales that are absorbed by expenses. The increase in Palisades Furniture's return on sales is significant and identifies the company as more successful than the average furniture store. Compare Palisades' rate of return on sales to the rates of some other companies:

Company	Rate of Return on Sales
Chesebrough-Pond's, Inc.	0.076
General Motors	0.054
Wal-Mart Stores, Inc.	0.036

As these numbers indicate, the rate of return on sales varies widely from industry to industry.

A return measure can be computed on any revenue and sales amount. Return on net sales, as we have seen, is net income divided by net sales. *Return on total revenues* is net income divided by total revenues. A company can compute a return on other specific portions of revenue as its information needs dictate.

RATE OF RETURN ON TOTAL ASSETS The **rate of return on total assets,** or **return on assets (ROA),** measures a company's success in using its assets to earn a profit. ◀▥
Creditors have loaned money to the company, and the interest they receive is the return on their investment. Shareholders have invested in the company's stock, and net income is their return. The sum of interest expense and net income is thus the return to the two groups that have financed the company's operations, and this amount is the numerator of the return-on-assets ratio. Average total assets is the denominator. Palisades Furniture's return on total assets is computed as follows:

◀▥ ◀▥ ◀▥ We first discussed the rate of return on total assets in Chapter 13, page 562.

Rate of Return on Total Assets. The sum of net income plus interest expense divided by average total assets. This ratio measures the success a company has in using its assets to earn income for the persons who finance the business. Also called **return on assets.**

Formula	Palisades' 19X7 Rate of Return on Total Assets	Industry Average
Rate of return on assets = $\dfrac{\text{Net income} + \text{Interest expense}}{\text{Average total assets}}$	$\dfrac{\$48,000 + \$24,000}{\$715,500} = 0.101$	0.049

Net income and interest expense are taken from the income statement (Exhibit 18-10). To compute average total assets, we take the average of beginning and ending total assets from the comparative balance sheet (Exhibit 18-11). Compare Palisades Furniture's rate of return on assets to the rates of some other companies:

Company	Rate of Return on Assets
The Gap, Inc.	0.170
Wal-Mart Stores, Inc.	0.129
General Mills, Inc.	0.124

As you can see, the rate of return on assets varies widely from industry to industry.

RATE OF RETURN ON COMMON STOCKHOLDERS' EQUITY   A popular measure of profitability is **rate of return on common stockholders' equity,** which is often shortened to **return on stockholders' equity,** or simply **return on equity (ROE).**

◀▥ This ratio shows the relationship between net income and common stockholders' investment in the company—how much income is earned for every $1 invested by the common shareholders. To compute this ratio, we first subtract preferred dividends from net income. This remainder is net income available to the common stockholders. We then divide net income available to common stockholders by the average stockholders' equity during the year. The 19X7 rate of return on common stockholders' equity for Palisades Furniture is calculated as follows:

	Formula	Palisades' 19X7 Rate of Return on Common Stockholders' Equity	Industry Average
Rate of return on common stockholders' equity =	$\dfrac{\text{Net income} - \text{Preferred dividends}}{\text{Average common stockholders' equity}}$	$\dfrac{\$48,000 - \$0}{\$338,000} = 0.142$	0.093

We compute average equity by using the beginning and ending balances [($356,000 + $320,000)/2 = $338,000]. Common stockholders' equity is total equity minus preferred equity.

Observe that Palisades' return on equity (14.2%) is higher than its return on assets (10.1%). This difference results from borrowing at one rate—say, 8%—and investing the funds to earn a higher rate, such as the firm's 14.2% return on stockholders' equity. This practice is called **trading on the equity,** or using **leverage.**

It is critically important that a company's return on equity exceed its return on assets. Why? For two reasons:

- The stockholders take more risk and therefore demand a higher return on equity than the company's lenders, who take less risk.
- If return on assets exceeds return on equity, that means the company's lenders are getting a better return from the interest they receive than the company's stockholders are getting from net income. This cannot continue forever. At some point the stockholders will cease to finance the company's operations.

Fortunately, Palisades Furniture's return on equity (14.2%) exceeds its return on assets (10.1%). Let's compare Palisades Furniture's rate of return on common stockholders' equity with the rates of some leading companies:

Company	Rate of Return on Common Equity
Wal-Mart Stores, Inc.	0.25
Chesebrough-Pond's, Inc.	0.20
General Motors	0.20

Palisades Furniture is not as profitable as these leading companies—perhaps because Wal-Mart and General Motors must satisfy millions of stockholders worldwide. Palisades Furniture, on the other hand, is a much smaller company with stockholders who do not demand so high a return on their equity.

EARNINGS PER SHARE OF COMMON STOCK   *Earnings per share of common stock,* or simply **earnings per share (EPS),** is perhaps the most widely quoted of all financial statistics. ◀▥ EPS is the only ratio that must appear on the face of the income statement. EPS is the amount of net income per share of the company's outstanding *common* stock. Earnings per share is computed by dividing net income available to common stockholders

Rate of Return on Common Stockholders' Equity. Net income minus preferred dividends, divided by average common stockholders' equity. A measure of profitability. Also called **return on stockholders' equity.**

◀▥ ◀▥ ◀▥   We examined this ratio in detail in Chapter 13. For a review, see page 562.

■ **Daily Exercise 18-13**

Trading on the Equity. Earning more income on borrowed money than the related expense, thereby increasing the earnings for the owners of the business. Also called **leverage.**

Earnings Per Share (EPS). Amount of a company's income per share of its outstanding common stock.

◀▥ ◀▥ ◀▥   Recall from Chapter 14, pages 600–601, that GAAP requires corporations to disclose EPS figures on the income statement.

by the number of common shares outstanding during the year. Preferred dividends are subtracted from net income because the preferred stockholders have a prior claim to their dividends. Palisades Furniture, Inc., has no preferred stock outstanding and thus has no preferred dividends. Computation of the firm's EPS for 19X7 and 19X6 follows (the company had 10,000 shares of common stock outstanding throughout 19X6 and 19X7):

	Formula	Palisades' Earnings per Share	
		19X7	19X6
Earnings per share of common stock	$= \dfrac{\text{Net income} - \text{Preferred dividends}}{\text{Number of shares of common stock outstanding}}$	$\dfrac{\$48{,}000 - \$0}{10{,}000} = \$4.80$	$\dfrac{\$26{,}000 - \$0}{10{,}000} = \$2.60$

Palisades Furniture's EPS increased 85 percent. Its stockholders should not expect such a significant boost in EPS every year. Most companies strive to increase EPS by 10–15% annually, and the more successful companies do so. But even the most successful companies have an occasional bad year.

Analyzing a Company's Stock as an Investment

Investors purchase stock to earn a return on their investment. This return consists of two parts: (1) gains (or losses) from selling the stock at a price that differs from the investors' purchase price, and (2) dividends, the periodic distributions to stockholders. The ratios we examine in this section help analysts evaluate stock in terms of market price or dividend payments.

Price/Earnings Ratio. Ratio of the market price of a share of common stock to the company's earnings per share. Measures the value that the stock market places on $1 of a company's earnings.

PRICE/EARNINGS RATIO The **price/earnings ratio** is the ratio of the market price of a share of common stock to the company's earnings per share. This ratio, abbreviated P/E, appears in *The Wall Street Journal* stock listings. P/E ratios play an important part in decisions to buy, hold, and sell stocks. They indicate the market price of $1 of earnings.

Calculations for the P/E ratios of Palisades Furniture, Inc., follow. The market price of its common stock was $58 at the end of 19X7 and $35 at the end of 19X6. These prices can be obtained from a financial publication, a stockbroker, or some other source outside the accounting records.

	Formula	Palisades' Price/Earnings Ratio	
		19X7	19X6
P/E ratio $=$	$\dfrac{\text{Market price per share of common stock}}{\text{Earnings per share}}$	$\dfrac{\$58.00}{\$4.80} = 12.1$	$\dfrac{\$35.00}{\$2.60} = 13.5$

Given Palisades Furniture's 19X7 P/E ratio of 12.1, we would say that the company's stock is selling at 12.1 times earnings. The decline from the 19X6 P/E ratio of 13.5 is not a cause for alarm because the market price of the stock is not under Palisades Furniture's control. Net income is more controllable, and it increased during 19X7. Like most other ratios, P/E ratios vary from industry to industry. P/E ratios range from 8 to 10 for electric utilities (Pennsylvania Power and Light, for example) to 40 or more for "glamor stocks" such as CIBER Systems and Oracle Systems, which develop computer software.

The higher a stock's P/E ratio the higher its *downside risk*—the risk that the stock's market price will fall. Many investors interpret a sharp increase in a stock's P/E ratio as a signal to sell the stock.

■ **Daily Exercise 18-14**
■ **Daily Exercise 18-15**

Dividend Yield. Ratio of dividends per share of stock to the stock's market price per share. Tells the percentage of a stock's market value that the company pays to stockholders as dividends.

DIVIDEND YIELD **Dividend yield** is the ratio of dividends per share of stock to the stock's market price per share. This ratio measures the percentage of a stock's market value that is returned annually as dividends, an important concern of stockholders. *Preferred* stockholders, who invest primarily to receive dividends, pay special attention to this ratio.

Palisades Furniture paid annual cash dividends of $1.20 per share of common stock in 19X7 and $1.00 in 19X6, and market prices of the company's common stock were $58 in 19X7 and $35 in 19X6. Calculation of the firm's dividend yields on common stock is as follows:

| Formula | | Dividend Yield on Palisades' Common Stock | |
		19X7	19X6
Dividend yield on common stock[1] $=$	$\dfrac{\text{Dividend per share of common stock}}{\text{Market price per share of common stock}}$	$\dfrac{\$1.20}{\$58.00} = 0.021$	$\dfrac{\$1.00}{\$35.00} = \$0.029$

An investor who buys Palisades Furniture common stock for $58 can expect to receive almost 2.1% of the investment annually in the form of cash dividends. Dividend yields vary widely, from 5% to 8% for older, established firms (such as Procter & Gamble and General Motors) down to the range of 0–3% for young, growth-oriented companies. Palisades Furniture's dividend yield places the company in the second group.

BOOK VALUE PER SHARE OF COMMON STOCK   Book value per share of common **stock** is simply common stockholders' equity divided by the number of shares of common stock outstanding. Common shareholders' equity equals total stockholders' equity less preferred equity. Palisades Furniture has no preferred stock outstanding. Calculations of its book value follows. Recall that 10,000 shares of common stock were outstanding at the end of years 19X7 and 19X6.

Book Value Per Share of Common Stock. Common stockholders' equity divided by the number of shares of common stock outstanding.

| Formula | | Book Value per Share of Palisades' Common Stock | |
		19X7	19X6
Book value per share of common stock $=$	$\dfrac{\text{Total stockholders' equity} - \text{Preferred equity}}{\text{Number of shares of common stock outstanding}}$	$\dfrac{\$356,000 - \$0}{10,000} = \$35.60$	$\dfrac{\$320,000 - \$0}{10,000} = \$32.00$

Book value indicates the recorded accounting amount for each share of common stock outstanding. Many experts argue that book value is not useful for investment analysis. ◄▬ It bears no relationship to market value and provides little information beyond stockholders' equity reported on the balance sheet. But some investors base their investment decisions on book value. For example, some investors rank stocks on the basis of the ratio of market price to book value. To these investors, the lower the ratio, the more attractive the stock. These investors are called "value" investors, as contrasted with "growth" investors, who focus more on trends in a company's net income.

◄▬◄▬◄▬ Recall from Chapter 13, pages 561–562, that book value depends on historical costs, while market value depends on investors' outlook for dividends and an increase in the stock's value.

■ Daily Exercise 18-16
■ Daily Exercise 18-17
■ Daily Exercise 18-18

Limitations of Financial Analysis: The Complexity of Business Decisions

Objective 5

Use ratios in decision making

Business decisions are made in a world of uncertainty. As useful as ratios are, they have limitations. We may liken their use in decision making to a physician's use of a thermometer. A reading of 101.6° Fahrenheit indicates that something is wrong with the patient, but the temperature alone does not indicate what the problem is or how to cure it.

In financial analysis, a sudden drop in a company's current ratio signals that *something* is wrong, but this change does not identify the problem or show how to correct it. The business manager must analyze the figures that go into the ratio to determine whether current assets have decreased, current liabilities have increased, or both. If current

---

[1]Dividend yields may also be calculated for preferred stock.

assets have dropped, is the problem a cash shortage? Are accounts receivable down? Are inventories too low? Only by analyzing the individual items that make up the ratio can the manager determine how to solve the problem. The manager must evaluate data on all ratios in the light of other information about the company and about its particular line of business, such as increased competition or a slowdown in the economy.

Legislation, international affairs, competition, scandals, and many other factors can turn profits into losses, and vice versa. To be most useful, ratios should be analyzed over a period of years to take into account a representative group of these factors. Any one year, or even any two years, may not be representative of the company's performance over the long term.

Economic Value Added (EVA®)—A New Measure of Performance

Economic Value Added (EVA®). Combines the concepts of accounting income and corporate finance to measure whether the company's operations have increased stockholder wealth.

Cost of Capital. A weighted average of the returns demanded by a company's stockholders and lenders.

Capital Charge. The amount that stockholders and lenders charge a company for the use of their money.

The top managers of Coca-Cola, Quaker Oats, AT&T, and other leading companies use **economic value added (EVA®)** to evaluate a company's operating performance. EVA® combines the concepts of accounting income and corporate finance to measure whether the company's operations have increased stockholder wealth. EVA® can be computed as follows:

$$\text{EVA}^\circledR = \text{Net income} + \text{Interest expense} - \text{Capital charge}$$

where

$$\text{Capital charge} = \left(\frac{\text{Notes}}{\text{payable}} + \frac{\text{Loans}}{\text{payable}} + \frac{\text{Long-term}}{\text{debt}} + \frac{\text{Stockholders'}}{\text{equity}} \right) \times \frac{\text{Cost of}}{\text{capital}}$$

All amounts for the EVA® computation, except the cost of capital, are taken from the financial statements. The **cost of capital** is a weighted average of the returns demanded by the company's stockholders and lenders. The cost of capital varies with the company's level of risk. For example, stockholders would demand a higher return from a start-up computer software company than from AT&T because the new company is untested and therefore more risky. Lenders would also charge the new company a higher interest rate because of this greater risk. Thus the new company has a higher cost of capital than AT&T. The cost of capital is a major topic in finance classes. In the following discussions, we merely assume a value for the cost of capital (such as 10%, 12%, or 15%) to illustrate the computation of EVA® and its use in decision making.

The idea behind EVA® is that the returns to the company's stockholders (net income) and to its creditors (interest expense) should exceed the company's capital charge. The **capital charge** is the amount that stockholders and lenders *charge* a company for the use of their money. A positive EVA® amount indicates an increase in stockholder wealth, and the company's stock should remain attractive to investors. If the EVA® measure is negative, the stockholders will probably be unhappy with the company's progress and sell its stock, resulting in a decrease in the stock's price. Different companies tailor the EVA® computation to meet their own needs.

The Coca-Cola Company is a leading user of EVA®. Coca-Cola's EVA® for 1995 can be computed as follows, assuming a 12% cost of capital for the company (dollar amounts in millions):

$$\text{Coca-Cola's EVA}^\circledR = \frac{\text{Net}}{\text{income}} + \frac{\text{Interest}}{\text{expense}} - \left[\left(\frac{\text{Loans and}}{\text{notes payable}} + \frac{\text{Long-term}}{\text{debt}} + \frac{\text{Stockholders'}}{\text{equity}} \right) \times \frac{\text{Cost of}}{\text{capital}} \right]$$

$$= \underbrace{\$2,986 + \$272}_{} - \underbrace{[(\$2,371 + \$1,141 + \$5,392)}_{} \times 0.12]$$

$$= \underbrace{\$3,258}_{} - \underbrace{\$8,904}_{} \times 0.12$$

$$= \underbrace{\$3,258 - \underbrace{\$1,068}_{}}_{}$$

$$= \$2,190$$

■ **Daily Exercise**

18-19

By this measure, Coca-Cola's operations during 1995 added $2.19 billion ($2,190 million) of value to its stockholders' wealth after meeting the company's capital charge. This performance is outstanding. Coca-Cola's positive EVA® measures explain why the company's stock price increased an average of 29% per year over the ten-year period from 1985 to 1995. A $100 investment in Coca-Cola stock in 1985 had grown to a value of $1,287 in 1995.

Efficient Markets, Management Action, and Investor Decisions

An **efficient capital market** is one in which market prices fully reflect all information available to the public. Stocks are priced in full recognition of all publicly accessible data, so it can be argued that the stock market is efficient. Market efficiency has implications for management action and for investor decisions. It means that managers cannot fool the market with accounting gimmicks. If the information is available, the market as a whole can translate accounting data into a "fair" price for the company's stock.

Efficient Capital Market. A capital market in which market prices fully reflect all information available to the public.

Suppose you are the president of Anacomp Company. Reported earnings per share are $4, and the stock price is $40—so the P/E ratio is 10. You believe the corporation's stock is underpriced in comparison with other companies in the same industry. To correct this situation, you are considering changing your depreciation method from accelerated to straight-line. The accounting change will increase earnings per share to $5. Will the stock price then rise to $50? Probably not. The company's stock price will probably remain at $40 because the market can understand the accounting change. After all, the company merely changed its method of computing depreciation. There is no effect on the company's cash flows, and its economic position is unchanged.

In an efficient market, the search for "underpriced" stock is fruitless unless the investor has relevant private information. Moreover, it is unlawful to invest on the basis of *inside* information. For outside investors, an appropriate strategy seeks to manage risk, diversify, and minimize transaction costs. The role of financial statement analysis consists mainly of identifying the risks of various stocks to manage the risk of the overall investment portfolio.

SUMMARY PROBLEM FOR YOUR REVIEW

The following financial data are adapted from the annual report of The Gap, Inc., which operates The Gap, Banana Republic, and Old Navy clothing stores.

THE GAP, INC. Five-Year Selected Financial Data					
Operating Results*	**19X5**	**19X4**	**19X3**	**19X2**	**19X1**
Net sales	$2,960	$2,519	$1,934	$1,587	$1,252
Cost of goods sold and occupancy expenses, excluding depreciation and amortization	1,856	1,496	1,188	1,007	814
Interest expense (net)	4	4	1	3	3
Income from operations	340	371	237	163	126
Income taxes	129	141	92	65	52
Net earnings	211	230	145	98	74
Cash dividends	44	41	30	23	18
Financial Position					
Merchandise inventory	366	314	247	243	193
Total assets	1,379	1,147	777	579	481
Working capital	355	236	579	129	434
Current ratio	2.06:1	1.71:1	1.39:1	1.69:1	1.70:1
Stockholders' equity	888	678	466	338	276
Average number of shares of common stock outstanding (in thousands)	144	142	142	141	145

*(Dollar amounts in thousands)

Compute the following ratios for 19X5 through 19X2, and evaluate The Gap's operating results. Are operating results strong or weak? Did they improve or deteriorate during the four-year period?

a. Gross profit percentage
b. Net income as a percentage of sales
c. Earnings per share

d. Inventory turnover
e. Times-interest-earned ratio
f. Rate of return on stockholders' equity

■ SOLUTION

Requirement	19X5	19X4	19X3	19X2
a. Gross profit percentage	$\dfrac{\$2{,}960 - \$1{,}856}{\$2{,}960}$	$\dfrac{\$2{,}519 - \$1{,}496}{\$2{,}519}$	$\dfrac{\$1{,}934 - \$1{,}188}{\$1{,}934}$	$\dfrac{\$1{,}587 - \$1{,}007}{\$1{,}587}$
	= 37.3%	= 40.6%	= 38.6%	= 36.5%
b. Net income as a percentage of sales	$\dfrac{\$211}{\$2{,}960} = 7.1\%$	$\dfrac{\$230}{\$2{,}519} = 9.1\%$	$\dfrac{\$145}{\$1{,}934} = 7.5\%$	$\dfrac{\$98}{\$1{,}587} = 6.2\%$
c. Earnings per share	$\dfrac{\$211}{144} = \$1.47$	$\dfrac{\$230}{142} = \$1.62$	$\dfrac{\$145}{142} = \$1.02$	$\dfrac{\$98}{141} = \$0.70$
d. Inventory turnover	$\dfrac{\$1{,}856}{(\$366 + \$314)/2}$	$\dfrac{\$1{,}496}{(\$314 + \$247)/2}$	$\dfrac{\$1{,}188}{(\$247 + \$243)/2}$	$\dfrac{\$1{,}007}{(\$243 + \$193)/2}$
	= 5.5 times	= 5.3 times	= 4.8 times	= 4.6 times
e. Times-interest-earned ratio	$\dfrac{\$340}{\$4} = 85$ times	$\dfrac{\$371}{\$4} = 93$ times	$\dfrac{\$237}{\$1} = 237$ times	$\dfrac{\$163}{\$3} = 54$ times
f. Rate of return on stockholders' equity	$\dfrac{\$211}{(\$888 + \$678)/2}$	$\dfrac{\$230}{(\$678 + \$466)/2}$	$\dfrac{\$145}{(\$466 + \$338)/2}$	$\dfrac{\$98}{(\$338 + \$276)/2}$
	= 26.9%	= 40.2%	= 36.1%	= 31.9%

Evaluation: During this four-year period, The Gap's operating results were outstanding. Operating results improved, with all ratio values but return on stockholders' equity higher in 19X5 than in 19X2. Moreover, all the performance measures indicate high levels of income and return to investors.

Summary of Learning Objectives

1. *Perform a horizontal analysis of comparative financial statements.* Banks loan money, investors buy stocks, and managers make decisions on the basis of accounting information. *Horizontal analysis* is the study of percentage changes in financial statement items from one period to the next. To compute these percentage changes, (1) calculate the dollar amount of the change from the base (earlier) period to the later period, and (2) divide the dollar amount of change by the base-period amount. *Trend percentages* are a form of horizontal analysis.

2. *Perform a vertical analysis of a company's financial statements.* *Vertical analysis* of a financial statement reveals the relationship of each statement item to a specified base, which is the 100% figure. In an income statement, net sales is usually the base. On a balance sheet, total assets is usually the base.

3. *Prepare common-size financial statements for benchmarking against the industry average and key competitors.* A form of vertical analysis, *common-size statements* report only percentages, no dollar amounts. Common-size statements ease the comparison of different companies and may signal the need for corrective action. *Benchmarking* is the practice of comparing a company to a standard set by other companies, with a view toward improvement.

4. *Compute the standard financial ratios used for decision making.* An important part of financial analysis is the calculation

and interpretation of financial ratios. A ratio expresses the relationship of one item to another. The most important financial ratios measure a company's ability to pay current liabilities (current ratio, acid-test ratio); its ability to sell inventory and collect receivables (inventory turnover, accounts receivable turnover, days' sales in receivables); its ability to pay long-term debt (debt ratio, times-interest-earned ratio); its profitability (rate of return on net sales, rate of return on total assets, rate of return on common stockholders' equity, earnings per share of common stock); and its value as an investment (price/earnings ratio, dividend yield, book value per share of common stock).

5. *Use ratios in decision making.* Analysis of financial ratios over time is an important way to track a company's progress. A change in one of the ratios over time may signal the existence of a problem. It is up to the company's managers to find the source of this problem and take actions to correct it.

6. *Measure economic value added by a company's operations.* *Economic value added (EVA®)* measures whether a company's operations have increased its stockholders' wealth. EVA® can be defined as the excess of net income and interest expense over the company's capital charge, which is the amount that the company's stockholders and lenders charge for the use of their money. A positive amount of EVA® indicates an increase in stockholder wealth; a negative amount indicates a decrease.

Accounting Vocabulary

accounts receivable turnover
  (p. 788)
acid-test ratio (p. 784)
benchmarking (p. 779)
book value per share of common stock (p. 793)
capital charge (p. 794)
common-size statement
  (p. 778)
cost of capital (p. 794)
current ratio (p. 783)
days' sales in receivables
  (p. 788)
debt ratio (p. 789)

dividend yield (p. 792)
earnings per share (EPS)
  (p. 791)
economic value added (EVA®)
  (p. 794)
efficient capital market
  (p. 795)
horizontal analysis
  (p. 773)
interest-coverage ratio
  (p. 789)
inventory turnover
  (p. 786)
leverage (p. 791)

long-term solvency (p. 772)
price/earnings ratio
  (p. 792)
quick ratio (p. 784)
rate of return on common
  stockholders' equity
  (p. 791)
rate of return on net sales
  (p. 790)
rate of return on total assets
  (p. 790)
return on assets (p. 790)
return on stockholders' equity (p. 791)

return on sales (p. 790)
short-term liquidity
  (p. 772)
times-interest-earned ratio
  (p. 789)
trading on the equity
  (p. 791)
vertical analysis (p. 776)
working capital (p. 783)

Questions

1. Identify two groups of users of accounting information and the decisions they base on accounting data.
2. Name the three broad categories of analytical tools that are based on accounting information.
3. Briefly describe horizontal analysis. How do decision makers use this analytical tool?
4. What is vertical analysis, and what is its purpose?
5. What is the purpose of common-size statements?
6. Why are ratios an important tool of financial analysis? Give an example of an important financial ratio.
7. Identify two ratios used to measure a company's ability to pay current liabilities. Show how they are computed.
8. Why is the acid-test ratio given that name?
9. What does the inventory turnover ratio measure?
10. Suppose the days'-sales-in-receivables ratio of Gomez, Inc., increased from 36 at January 1 to 43 at December 31. Is this a good sign or a bad sign? What might Gomez management do in response to this change?
11. Company A's debt ratio has increased from 0.50 to 0.70. Identify a decision maker to whom this increase is important, and state how the increase affects this party's decisions about the company.
12. Which ratio measures the *effect of debt* on (a) financial position (the balance sheet), and (b) the company's ability to pay interest expense (the income statement)?
13. Company A is a chain of grocery stores, and Company B is a computer manufacturer. Which company is likely to have the higher (a) current ratio, (b) inventory turnover, and (c) rate of return on sales? Give your reasons.

14. Identify four ratios used to measure a company's profitability. Show how to compute these ratios and state what information each ratio provides.
15. The price/earnings ratio of General Motors was 6, and the price/earnings ratio of American Express was 45. Which company did the stock market favor? Explain.
16. McDonald's Corporation paid cash dividends of $0.78⅔ (78 and ⅔ cents) per share when the market price of the company's stock was $58. What was the dividend yield on McDonald's stock? What does dividend yield measure?
17. Hold all other factors constant and indicate whether each of the following situations generally signals good or bad news about a company:
  a. Increase in current ratio
  b. Decrease in inventory turnover
  c. Increase in debt ratio
  d. Decrease in interest-coverage ratio
  e. Increase in return on sales
  f. Decrease in earnings per share
  g. Increase in price/earnings ratio
  h. Increase in book value per share
18. Explain how an investor might use book value per share of stock in making an investment decision.
19. Describe how decision makers use ratio data. What are the limitations of ratios?
20. What is EVA®, and how is it used in financial analysis?

Daily Exercises

DE18-1 NIKE, Inc., reported the following amounts on its 1996 comparative income statement:

Horizontal analysis of revenues and gross profit
(Obj. 1)

(In millions)	1996	1995	1994
Revenues...............	$6,471	$4,761	$3,790
Cost of sales..........	3,907	2,865	2,301

Perform a horizontal analysis of revenues and gross profit—both in dollar amounts and in percentages—for 1996 and 1995.

DE18-2 Study Exhibit 18-3 (page 775), the horizontal analysis of Bristol-Myers Squibb's balance sheet at December 31, 1996. Focus on the 12.5% increase in receivables and the 15.0% increase in

Using horizontal analysis for decision making
(Obj. 1)

inventories during 1996. Assume that Bristol-Myers Squibb's income statement reported a decrease in sales during 1996.

Would the large percentage increases in receivables and inventories convey good news or bad news about the company? Explain your reasoning.

Trend analysis of revenues and net income
(Obj. 1)

DE18-3   NIKE, Inc., reported the following revenues and net income amounts:

(In millions)	1996	1995	1994	1993	1992	1991
Revenues.............	$6,471	$4,761	$3,790	$3,930	$3,405	$3,004
Net income..........	553	400	299	365	329	287

1. Show NIKE's trend percentages for revenues and net income. Start with 1991, and use 1991 as the base year.
2. Which trend looks better—revenues or net income?

Vertical analysis of the income statement
(Obj. 2)

DE18-4   T-Shaft Sporting Goods has recently introduced a new titanium shaft for golf clubs. Demand for the product has been high, and T-Shaft is shipping goods to many new golf shops. T-Shaft's comparative income statement reports these figures for 19X8 and 19X7:

	19X8	19X7
Net sales	$193,000	$151,000
Cost of goods sold..........	61,000	50,000
Selling expenses..............	45,000	36,000
General expenses............	18,000	17,000
Net income....................	$ 69,000	$ 48,000

Perform a vertical analysis of T-Shaft's income statements for 19X8 and 19X7. Does the analysis reflect favorably or poorly on the company? Cite specifics in your answer.

Vertical analysis to correct a cash shortage
(Obj. 2)

DE18-5   T-Shaft Sporting Goods reported the following amounts on its balance sheets at December 31, 19X8, 19X7, and 19X6:

	19X8	19X7	19X6
Cash	$ 6,000	$ 6,000	$ 5,000
Receivables, net	46,000	32,000	19,000
Inventory	32,000	26,000	24,000
Prepaid expenses..............	2,000	2,000	1,000
Property, plant, and equipment, net.............	96,000	88,000	87,000
Total assets......................	$182,000	$154,000	$136,000

1. Sales and profits are high. Nevertheless, the company is experiencing a cash shortage. Perform a vertical analysis of T-Shaft's assets at the end of each year 19X8, 19X7, and 19X6. Use the analysis to explain the reason for the cash shortage.
2. Suggest a way for T-Shaft to generate more cash.

Using vertical analysis for decision making
(Obj. 2)

DE18-6   Return to Exhibit 18-5 (page 777), the vertical analysis of Bristol-Myers Squibb's balance sheets at December 31, 1996 and 1995. Consider that Bristol-Myers Squibb's sales and profits reached all-time highs during 1996. Focus on receivables and inventories.

1. Did receivables and inventories make up more or less of total assets in 1996 than in 1995? Give the percentages for each year.
2. Do the increases in receivables and inventories worry you? Explain your reasoning.

Common-size income statements of two leading companies
(Obj. 3)

DE18-7   NIKE, Inc., and The Home Depot are leaders in their respective industries. Compare the two companies by converting their income statements (adapted) to common size.

(In millions)	NIKE	Home Depot
Net sales	$6,471	$19,536
Cost of goods sold	3,907	14,101
Selling and administrative expenses	1,589	3,846
Interest expense	39	16
Other expense	37	38
Income tax expense	346	597
Net income	$ 553	$ 938

Which company earns more net income? Which company's net income is a higher percentage of net sales? Which company is more profitable? Explain your answer.

DE18-8   Prepare a common-size analysis to compare NIKE, Inc., and The Home Depot on the makeup of their assets (amounts in millions).

Common-size analysis of assets
(Obj. 3)

Assets	NIKE	Home Depot
Current assets:		
Cash and equivalents	$ 262	$ 146
Short-term investments	—	413
Accounts receivable, net	1,346	388
Inventories	931	2,708
Other current assets	188	54
Total current assets	2,727	3,709
Property, plant, and equipment, net	644	5,437
Goodwill and other intangibles	475	87
Other assets	106	109
Total assets	$3,952	$9,342

To which company are *current assets* more important? Which company places more emphasis on its *plant assets?*

DE18-9   Examine the actual financial data of Rubbermaid Incorporated in Exhibit 18-9, page 782. Show how to compute Rubbermaid's current ratio for each year 19X0 through 19X3. Is the company's ability to pay its current liabilities improving or deteriorating?

Evaluating the trend in a company's current ratio
(Obj. 4, 5)

DE18-10   Use the Bristol-Myers Squibb balance sheet data in Exhibit 18-3, page 775.

Evaluating a company's acid-test ratio
(Obj. 4, 5)

1. Compute the company's acid-test ratio at December 31, 1996 and 1995.
2. Compare Bristol-Myers Squibb's ratio values to those of Chesebrough-Pond's, General Motors, and Wal-Mart on page 785. Is Bristol-Myers Squibb's acid-test ratio strong or weak? Explain.

DE18-11   Use the Bristol-Myers Squibb 1996 income statement (page 774) and year-end balance sheet (page 775) to compute

Computing inventory turnover and days' sales in receivables
(Obj. 4)

a. Inventory turnover for 1996.
b. Days' sales in receivables during 1996. All sales are made on account. (Round dollar amounts to one decimal place.)

DE18-12   Use the actual financial statements of Bristol-Myers Squibb Company (pages 776 and 777).

Measuring ability to pay long-term debt
(Obj. 4, 5)

1. Compute the company's debt ratio at December 31, 1996.
2. Compute the company's times-interest-earned ratio for 1996. For income from operations, use the sum of earnings before income taxes plus interest expense. Interest expense is not reported in the financial statements. Assume interest expense for 1996 was 7% of the sum of Short-term borrowings and Long-term debt at December 31, 1995. Round interest expense to the nearest million dollars.
3. Is Bristol-Myers Squibb's ability to pay its liabilities and interest expense strong or weak? Comment on the value of each ratio computed for requirements 1 and 2.

Measuring profitability
(Obj. 4, 5)

DE18-13   Use the financial statements of Bristol-Myers Squibb Company (pages 776 and 777) to determine or, if necessary, to compute these profitability measures for 1996:

a.   Rate of return on net sales.

b.   Rate of return on total assets. Assume interest expense for 1996 was 7% of the sum of Short-term debt and Long-term borrowings at December 31, 1995. Round interest expense to the nearest $1 million.

c.   Rate of return on common stockholders' equity.

Are these rates of return strong or weak? Explain.

Computing EPS and the price/earnings ratio
(Obj. 4)

DE18-14   The annual report of The Home Depot for the year ended January 31, 1997, included the following items:

Market price per share of common stock	$48
Preferred stock outstanding	$0
Net earnings (net income)..	$937,739,000
Number of shares of common stock outstanding..........	487,752,000

1.   Compute earnings per share (EPS) and the price/earnings ratio for The Home Depot's stock. Round to the nearest cent.

2.   How much does the stock market say that $1 of The Home Depot's net income is worth?

Working with earnings per share
(Obj. 4)

DE18-15   During 1996, Bristol-Myers Squibb had earnings per share of common stock (EPS) of $2.84. The company had no preferred stock outstanding, so there were no preferred dividends. Use the income statement (Exhibit 18-4, page 776) and the formula for EPS (page 792) to compute the number of shares of common stock that Bristol-Myers Squibb had outstanding during 1996. Keep in mind that net income (net earnings) is in millions of dollars. Therefore, you will need to multiply the reported net earnings figures by 1,000,000.

Computing book value per share of common stock
(Obj. 4)

DE18-16   Use Bristol-Myers Squibb's balance sheet (Exhibit 18-3, page 775) to compute the book value per share of the company's common stock at December 31, 1996 and at December 31, 1995. The par value of Bristol-Myers Squibb's common stock is $0.10 per share. You will notice a significant decrease in book value per share from 1995 to 1996. The reason for the decrease: Bristol-Myers Squibb issued a large stock dividend during 1996.

Using ratio data to reconstruct an income statement
(Obj. 4)

DE18-17   A skeleton of Campbell Soup's income statement (as adapted) for the year ended July 31, 19X5 appears as follows (amounts in millions):

Income Statement	
Net sales	$7,278
Cost of goods sold..................	(a)
Selling expenses.......................	1,390
Administrative expenses..........	326
Interest expense.......................	(b)
Other expenses........................	151
Income before taxes	1,042
Income tax expense	(c)
Net income...............................	$ (d)

Use the following ratio data to complete Campbell Soup's income statement. Round all dollar amounts to the nearest million.

a.   Inventory turnover was 5.53 (beginning inventory was $787; ending inventory was $755).

b.   Rate of return on sales is 0.0959.

Using ratio data to reconstruct a balance sheet
(Obj. 4)

DE18-18   A skeleton of Campbell Soup Company's balance sheet at June 30, 19X5 (as adapted) appears as follows (amounts in millions):

Balance Sheet			
Cash	$ 53	Total current liabilities	$2,164
Receivables..................................	(a)	Long-term debt..........................	(e)
Inventories..................................	755	Other long-term liabilities	826
Prepaid expenses........................	(b)		
Total current assets	(c)	Common stock	185
Plant assets, net..........................	(d)	Retained earnings.......................	2,755
Other assets	2,150	Other stockholders' equity..........	(472)
Total assets..................................	$6,315	Total liabilities and equity	$ (f)

Use the following ratio data to complete Campbell Soup's balance sheet:

a. Debt ratio is 0.6092.
b. Current ratio is 0.7306.
c. Acid-test ratio is 0.3161.

DE18-19 Use the financial statements of Bristol-Myers Squibb (pages 776 and 777).

Computing economic values added
(Obj. 6)

1. Compute economic value added (EVA®) by the company's operations during 1996. Use beginning-of-year amounts to compute the capital charge. Assume the company's cost of capital is 12% and that interest expense for 1996 was $85 million. Round all amounts to the nearest million dollars.

2. Should the company's stockholders be happy with the EVA® for 1996?

Exercises

E18-1 What were the amount of change and the percentage change in Alamo Leasing Corporation's working capital during 19X6 and 19X7? Is this trend favorable or unfavorable?

Computing year-to-year changes in working capital
(Obj. 1)

	19X7	19X6	19X5
Total current assets	$312,000	$290,000	$280,000
Total current liabilities	150,000	117,000	140,000

E18-2 Prepare a horizontal analysis of the following comparative income statement of Dynasty International. Round percentage changes to the nearest one-tenth percent (three decimal places):

Horizontal analysis of an income statement
(Obj. 1)

DYNASTY INTERNATIONAL Comparative Income Statement Years Ended December 31, 19X9 and 19X8		
	19X9	**19X8**
Total revenue.....................................	$410,000	$373,000
Expenses:		
Cost of goods sold	$202,000	$188,000
Selling and general expenses..........	98,000	93,000
Interest expense..............................	7,000	4,000
Income tax expense.........................	42,000	37,000
Total expenses.................................	349,000	322,000
Net income.......................................	$ 61,000	$ 51,000

Why did net income increase by a higher percentage than total revenues during 19X9?

E18-3 Compute trend percentages for Maxim Corporation's net sales and net income for the following five-year period, using year 1 as the base year. Round to the nearest full percent.

Computing trend percentages
(Obj. 1)

(In thousands)	Year 5	Year 4	Year 3	Year 2	Year 1
Net sales	$1,410	$1,187	$1,106	$1,009	$1,043
Net income...............	117	114	83	71	85

Which grew faster during the period, net sales or net income?

E18-4 Pirelli, Incorporated, has requested that you perform a vertical analysis of its balance sheet to determine the component percentages of its assets, liabilities, and stockholders' equity.

PIRELLI, INCORPORATED
Balance Sheet
December 31, 19X3

Assets

Total current assets	$ 72,000
Long-term investments	35,000
Property, plant, and equipment, net	217,000
Total assets	$324,000

Liabilities

Total current liabilities	$ 58,000
Long-term debt	118,000
Total liabilities	176,000

Stockholders' Equity

Total stockholders' equity	148,000
Total liabilities and stockholders' equity	$324,000

Preparing a common-size income statement
(Obj. 3)

E18-5 Prepare a comparative common-size income statement for Dynasty International, using the 19X9 and 19X8 data of Exercise 18-2 and rounding percentages to one-tenth percent (three decimal places).

Computing five ratios
(Obj. 4)

E18-6 The financial statements of TGI Holdings, Inc., include the following items:

	Current Year	Preceding Year
Balance sheet		
Cash	$ 17,000	$ 22,000
Short-term investments	11,000	26,000
Net receivables	64,000	73,000
Inventory	87,000	71,000
Prepaid expenses	6,000	8,000
Total current assets	185,000	200,000
Total current liabilities	121,000	91,000
Income statement		
Net credit sales	$454,000	
Cost of goods sold	257,000	

REQUIRED

Compute the following ratios for the current year: (a) current ratio, (b) acid-test ratio, (c) inventory turnover, (d) accounts receivable turnover, and (e) days' sales in average receivables.

Analyzing the ability to pay current liabilities
(Obj. 4, 5)

E18-7 Liberty Financial Products has asked you to determine whether the company's ability to pay its current liabilities and long-term debts has improved or deteriorated during 19X2. To answer this question, compute the following ratios for 19X2 and 19X1: (a) current ratio, (b) acid-test ratio, (c) debt ratio, and (d) times-interest-earned ratio. Summarize the results of your analysis in a written report.

	19X2	19X1
Cash	$ 21,000	$ 47,000
Short-term investments	28,000	—
Net receivables	102,000	116,000
Inventory	226,000	263,000
Prepaid expenses	11,000	9,000
Total assets	503,000	489,000
Total current liabilities	205,000	241,000
Total liabilities	261,000	273,000
Income from operations	165,000	158,000
Interest expense	36,000	39,000

E18-8 Compute four ratios that measure ability to earn profits for Falcon Fuel Supply, Inc., whose comparative income statement follows.

Analyzing profitability
(Obj. 4, 5)

FALCON FUEL SUPPLY, INC. Comparative Income Statement Years Ended December 31, 19X6 and 19X5		
	19X6	**19X5**
Net sales	$174,000	$158,000
Cost of goods sold	93,000	86,000
Gross profit	81,000	72,000
Selling and general expenses	48,000	41,000
Income from operations	33,000	31,000
Interest expense	21,000	10,000
Income before income tax	12,000	21,000
Income tax expense	4,000	8,000
Net income	$ 8,000	$ 13,000

Additional data:

	19X6	**19X5**
Average total assets	$204,000	$191,000
Average common stockholders' equity	$ 96,000	$ 89,000
Preferred dividends	$ 3,000	$ 3,000
Shares of common stock outstanding	20,000	20,000

Did the company's operating performance improve or deteriorate during 19X6?

E18-9 Evaluate the common stock of ARKTEX, Inc., as an investment. Specifically, use the three stock ratios to determine whether the stock has increased or decreased in attractiveness during the past year.

Evaluating a stock as an investment
(Obj. 4, 5)

	19X8	**19X7**
Net income	$ 58,000	$ 55,000
Dividends (half on preferred stock)	28,000	28,000
Common stockholders' equity at year end (80,000 shares)	530,000	500,000
Preferred stockholders' equity at year end	200,000	200,000
Market price per share of common stock at year end	$ 10.12	$ 7.75

E18-10 Two companies with very different economic-value-added (EVA®) profiles are IHOP, the restaurant chain, and Texaco, the giant oil company. Adapted versions of the two companies' 1995 financial statements are presented here (in millions):

Using economic value added to measure corporate performance
(Obj. 6)

	IHOP	**Texaco**
Balance sheet data		
Total assets	$252	$24,937
Interest-bearing debt	$ 35	$ 4,240
All other liabilities	109	11,178
Stockholders' equity	108	9,519
Total liabilities and equity	$252	$24,937
Income statement data		
Total revenue	$164	$36,787
Interest expense	9	483
All other expenses	139	35,697
Net income	$ 16	$ 607

1. Before performing any calculations, which company do you think would represent the better investment? Give your reason.

2. Compute the EVA® for each company, and then decide which company's stock you would rather hold as an investment. Assume each company's cost of capital is 12 percent.

CHALLENGE EXERCISES

Using ratio data to reconstruct a company's income statement
(Obj. 2, 3, 4)

E18-11 The following data (dollar amounts in millions) are from the financial statements of McDonald's Corporation, which operates more than 13,000 restaurants in 65 countries.

Average stockholders' equity	$3,605
Interest expense	$ 413
Preferred stock	-0-
Operating income as a percent of sales	24.04%
Rate of return on sales	11.13%
Rate of return on stockholders' equity	20.50%
Income tax rate	37.53%

Complete the following condensed income statement. Report amounts to the nearest million dollars.

Sales	$?
Operating expenses	?
Operating income	?
Interest expense	?
Income before tax	?
Income tax expense	?
Net income	$?

Using ratio data to reconstruct a company's balance sheet
(Obj. 2, 3, 4)

E18-12 The following data (dollar amounts in millions) are from the financial statements of Wal-Mart Stores, Inc., the largest retailer in the world:

Total liabilities	$11,806
Preferred stock	$ -0-
Total current assets	$10,196
Accumulated depreciation	$ 448
Debt ratio	57.408%
Current ratio	1.51

Complete the following condensed balance sheet. Report amounts to the nearest million dollars.

Current assets		$?
Property, plant, and equipment	$?	
Less Accumulated depreciation	?	?
Total assets		$?
Current liabilities		$?
Long-term liabilities		?
Stockholders' equity		?
Total liabilities and stockholders' equity		$?

Beyond the Numbers

Understanding the components of accounting ratios
(Obj. 4, 5)

BN18-1 Consider the following business situations.

1. Lance Alton has asked you about the stock of a particular company. He finds it attractive because it has a high dividend yield relative to another stock he is also considering. Explain to him the meaning of the ratio and the danger of making a decision based on it alone.

2. Edison Publishing's owners are concerned because the number of days' sales in receivables has increased over the previous two years. Explain why the ratio might have increased.

Taking unethical action to improve the ratios
(Obj. 4)

BN18-2 John Metz is the controller of ANOVA Sales, whose year end is December 31. Metz prepares checks for suppliers in December and posts them to the appropriate accounts in that month. However, he holds on to the checks and mails them to the suppliers in January. What financial ratio(s) are most affected by the action? What is Metz's purpose in undertaking the activity?

ETHICAL ISSUE

DuPont Power Co.'s long-term debt agreements make certain demands on the business. DuPont may not purchase treasury stock in excess of the balance of Retained Earnings. Also, Long-Term Debt may not exceed Stockholders' Equity, and the current ratio may not fall below 1.50. If DuPont fails to meet these requirements, the company's lenders have the authority to take over management of the corporation.

Changes in consumer demand have made it hard for DuPont to attract customers. Current liabilities have mounted faster than current assets, causing the current ratio to fall to 1.47. Before releasing financial statements, DuPont management is scrambling to improve the current ratio. The controller points out that an investment can be classified as either long-term or short-term, depending on management's intention. By deciding to convert an investment to cash within one year, DuPont can classify the investment as short-term—a current asset. On the controller's recommendation, DuPont's board of directors votes to reclassify long-term investments as short-term.

1. What effect will reclassifying the investments have on the current ratio? Is DuPont's financial position stronger as a result of reclassifying the investments?

2. Shortly after the financial statements are released, sales improve and so, then, does the current ratio. As a result, DuPont management decides not to sell the investments it had reclassified as short-term. Accordingly, the company reclassifies the investments as long-term. Has management behaved unethically? Give your reason.

REQUIRED

Problems (GROUP A)

P18-1A Net sales, net income, and total assets for Born Corporation for a six-year period follow:

Trend percentages, return on sales, and comparison with the industry (Obj. 1, 4, 5)

(In thousands)	19X6	19X5	19X4	19X3	19X2	19X1
Net sales	$347	$313	$266	$281	$245	$241
Net income..............	27	21	11	18	14	13
Total assets................	296	254	209	197	181	166

1. Compute trend percentages for each item for 19X2 through 19X6. Use 19X1 as the base year. Round to the nearest percent.

2. Compute the rate of return on net sales for 19X2 through 19X6, rounding to three decimal places. In this industry, rates above 5% are considered good, and rates above 7% are outstanding.

3. How does Born's return on net sales compare with that of the industry?

REQUIRED

P18-2A Top managers of Ing Steel Company have asked your help in comparing the company's profit performance and financial position with the average for the specialty steel industry. The accountant has given you the company's income statement and balance sheet and also the following data for the specialty steel industry.

Common-size statements, analysis of profitability, and comparison with the industry (Obj. 2, 3, 4, 5)

ING STEEL COMPANY
Income Statement
Compared with Industry Average
Year Ended December 31, 19X3

	Ing	Industry Average
Net sales.................................	$957,000	100.0%
Cost of goods sold	653,000	65.9
Gross profit..........................	304,000	34.1
Operating expenses..............	257,000	28.1
Operating income................	47,000	6.0
Other expenses.....................	2,000	0.4
Net income	$ 45,000	5.6%

ING STEEL COMPANY
Balance Sheet
Compared with Industry Average
December 31, 19X3

	Ing	Industry Average
Current assets........................	$448,000	74.4%
Plant assets, net....................	127,000	20.0
Intangible assets, net............	42,000	0.6
Other assets..........................	13,000	5.0
Total	$630,000	100.0%
Current liabilities.................	$246,000	35.6%
Long-term liabilities............	144,000	19.0
Stockholders' equity.............	240,000	45.4
Total	$630,000	100.0%

1. Prepare a two-column common-size income statement and balance sheet for Ing Steel Company. The first column of each statement should present Ing's common-size statement, and the second column should show the industry averages.

2. For the profitability analysis, compute Ing's (a) ratio of gross profit to net sales, (b) ratio of operating income (loss) to net sales, and (c) ratio of net income (loss) to net sales. Compare these figures with the industry averages. Is Ing's profit performance better or worse than the average for the industry?

3. For the analysis of financial position, compute Ing's (a) ratio of current assets to total assets, and (b) ratio of stockholders' equity to total assets. Compare these ratios with the industry averages. Is Ing's financial position better or worse than average for the industry?

Effects of business transactions on selected ratios
(Obj. 4, 5)

P18-3A Financial statement data on AutoMasters include the following items:

Cash	$ 47,000	Accounts payable	$ 96,000
Short-term investments	21,000	Accrued liabilities	50,000
Accounts receivable, net	102,000	Long-term notes payable	146,000
Inventories	274,000	Other long-term liabilities	78,000
Prepaid expenses	15,000	Net income	119,000
Total assets	933,000	Number of common	
Short-term notes payable	72,000	shares outstanding	22,000

1. Compute AutoMasters' current ratio, debt ratio, and earnings per share.

2. Compute each of the three ratios after evaluating the effect of each transaction that follows. Consider each transaction *separately*.
   a. Borrowed $76,000 on a long-term note payable.
   b. Sold short-term investments for $44,000 (cost, $66,000); assume no tax effect of the loss.
   c. Issued 14,000 shares of common stock, receiving cash of $168,000.
   d. Received cash on account, $6,000.
   e. Paid short-term notes payable, $51,000.
   f. Purchased merchandise costing $48,000 on account, debiting Inventory.
   g. Paid off long-term liabilities, $78,000.
   h. Declared, but did not pay, a $51,000 cash dividend on the common stock.

Use the following format for your answer:

REQUIREMENT 1

	Current Ratio	Debt Ratio	Earnings per Share

REQUIREMENT 2

Transaction (letter)	Current Ratio	Debt Ratio	Earnings per Share

Using ratios to evaluate a stock investment
(Obj. 4, 5)

P18-4A Comparative financial statement data of Waldorf, Inc., follow.

WALDORF, INC. Comparative Income Statement Years Ended December 31, 19X6 and 19X5		
	19X6	**19X5**
Net sales	$667,000	$599,000
Cost of goods sold	378,000	283,000
Gross profit	289,000	316,000
Operating expenses	129,000	147,000
Income from operations	160,000	169,000
Interest expense	57,000	41,000
Income before income tax	103,000	128,000
Income tax expense	34,000	53,000
Net income	$ 69,000	$ 75,000

	19X6	19X5	19X4

	19X6	19X5	19X4
Current assets:			
Cash	$ 37,000	$ 40,000	
Current receivables, net	208,000	151,000	$138,000
Inventories..	352,000	286,000	184,000
Prepaid expenses...	5,000	20,000	
Total current assets	602,000	497,000	
Property, plant, and equipment, net	287,000	276,000	
Total assets..	$889,000	$773,000	707,000
Total current liabilities	$286,000	$267,000	
Long-term liabilities	245,000	235,000	
Total liabilities	531,000	502,000	
Preferred stockholders' equity, 4%, $20 par	50,000	50,000	
Common stockholders' equity, no-par	308,000	221,000	148,000
Total liabilities and stockholders' equity	$889,000	$773,000	

Other information:

a. Market price of Waldorf's common stock: $30.75 at December 31, 19X6, and $40.25 at December 31, 19X5.

b. Common shares outstanding: 15,000 during 19X6 and 14,000 during 19X5.

c. All sales on credit.

1. Compute the following ratios for 19X6 and 19X5:
   a. Current ratio
   b. Inventory turnover
   c. Accounts receivable turnover
   d. Times-interest-earned ratio
   e. Return on assets
   f. Return on common stockholders' equity
   g. Earnings per share of common stock
   h. Price/earnings ratio
   i. Book value per share of common stock

2. Decide whether (a) Waldorf's financial position improved or deteriorated during 19X6, and (b) the investment attractiveness of its common stock appears to have increased or decreased.

3. How will what you learned in this problem help you evaluate an investment?

REQUIRED

P18-5A ◄▥ *Link Back to Chapter 17 (Statement of Cash Flows).* Incomplete and adapted versions of the financial statements of The Coca-Cola Company follow (amounts in millions).

Using ratio data to complete a set of financial statements
(Obj. 4)

Income Statement
Year Ended December 31, 19X6

Net sales...	$18,018
Cost of goods sold	(a)
Gross margin	(b)
Selling and general expenses..........	6,986
Other expense (income)	(236)
Income before income tax...............	(c)
Income tax expense (31%)..............	(d)
Net income	$ (e)

Comparative Balance Sheet December 31, 19X6 and 19X5		
ASSETS	**19X6**	**19X5**
Current:		
Cash...	$ (f)	$ 1,386
Short-term investments	148	145
Receivables, net..	1,750	1,525
Inventories...	1,117	1,047
Prepaid expenses	(g)	1,102
Total current assets	(h)	5,205
Long-term assets...	9,591	8,668
Total assets	$ (i)	$13,873
LIABILITIES		
Current liabilities..	$ 7,348	$ 6,177
Long-term liabilities....................................	(j)	2,461
Total liabilities..	(k)	8,638
STOCKHOLDERS' EQUITY		
Common stockholders' equity......................	(l)	5,235
Total liabilities and equity............................	$ (m)	$13,873

Statement of Cash Flows Year Ended December 31, 19X6	
Net cash inflow from operating activities	$3,115
Net cash outflow from investing activities.............	(1,013)
Net cash outflow from financing activities.............	(2,321)
Net increase (decrease) in cash during 19X6	$ (n)

Ratio data:

a. Current ratio at December 31, 19X6 is 0.7417.

b. Inventory turnover for 19X6 was 6.414.

c. Debt ratio at December 31, 19X6 is 0.6415.

REQUIRED

Complete the financial statements. Start with the income statement. Then go to the statement of cash flows. Complete the balance sheet last.

Using ratios to decide between two stock investments; measuring economic value added
(Obj. 4, 5, 6)

P18-6A   Assume that you are considering purchasing stock in a company in the hospital supply industry. You have narrowed the choice to Providence, Inc., and Medical Technology, Inc., and have assembled the following data.

Selected income statement data for current year:

	Providence, Inc.	Medical Technology, Inc.
Net sales (all on credit)	$519,000	$603,000
Cost of goods sold..	387,000	454,000
Income from operations	72,000	93,000
Interest expense..	8,000	—
Net income	38,000	56,000

Selected balance sheet and market price data at end of current year:

	Providence, Inc.	Medical Technology, Inc.
Current assets:		
Cash...	$ 39,000	$ 25,000
Short-term investments	13,000	6,000
Current receivables, net..............................	164,000	189,000
Inventories...	183,000	211,000
Prepaid expenses	15,000	19,000
Total current assets..................................	414,000	450,000
Total assets	938,000	974,000
Total current liabilities...............................	338,000	366,000
Total liabilities...	691,000*	667,000*
Preferred stock, 4%, $100 par	25,000	
Common stock, $1 par (150,000 shares)		150,000
$5 par (20,000 shares)	100,000	
Total stockholders' equity............................	247,000	307,000
Market price per share of common stock..........	$47.50	$9

*Notes and bonds payable: Providence, Inc., $303,000
Medical Technology, Inc., $4,000

Selected balance sheet data at beginning of current year:

	Providence, Inc.	Medical Technology, Inc.
Current receivables, net....................................	$193,000	$142,000
Inventories	197,000	209,000
Total assets	909,000	842,000
Preferred stock, 4%, $100 par	25,000	
Common stock, $1 par (150,000 shares)		150,000
$5 par (20,000 shares)	100,000	
Total stockholders' equity.................................	215,000	263,000

Your investment strategy is to purchase the stocks of companies that have low price/earnings ratios but appear to be in good shape financially. Assume that you have analyzed all other factors, and your decision depends on the results of the ratio analysis to be performed.

1. Compute the following ratios for both companies for the current year and decide which company's stock better fits your investment strategy.

REQUIRED

   a. Current ratio
   b. Acid-test ratio
   c. Inventory turnover
   d. Days' sales in average receivables
   e. Debt ratio
   f. Times-interest-earned ratio

   g. Return on net sales
   h. Return on total assets
   i. Return on common stockholders' equity
   j. Earnings per share of common stock
   k. Book value per share of common stock
   l. Price/earnings ratio

2. Compute each company's economic-value-added (EVA®) measure, and determine whether their EVA®s confirm or alter your investment decision. Each company's cost of capital is 10 percent. Round all amounts to the nearest $1,000.

Problems (GROUP B)

P18-1B Net sales, net income, and common stockholders' equity for Vance Paper Company for a six-year period follow.

Trend percentages, return on common equity, and comparison with the industry
(Obj. 1, 4, 5)

(In thousands)	19X7	19X6	19X5	19X4	19X3	19X2
Net sales...............................	$761	$714	$641	$662	$642	$634
Net income	61	45	32	48	41	40
Ending common stockholders' equity	386	354	330	296	272	252

1. Compute trend percentages for each item for 19X3 through 19X7. Use 19X2 as the base year. Round to the nearest percent.

2. Compute the rate of return on average common stockholders' equity for 19X3 through 19X7, rounding to three decimal places. In this industry, rates of 13% are average, rates above 16% are good, and rates above 20% are outstanding.

3. How does Vance's return on common stockholders' equity compare with the industry?

Common-size statements, analysis of profitability, and comparison with the industry
(Obj. 2, 3, 4, 5)

P18-2B DSC Vacuum Cleaners has asked your help in comparing the company's profit performance and financial position with the average for the vacuum cleaner industry. The general manager has given you the company's income statement and balance sheet and also the industry average data for vacuum cleaner companies.

DSC VACUUM CLEANERS Income Statement Compared with Industry Average Year Ended December 31, 19X6		
	DSC	**Industry Average**
Net sales..........................	$781,000	100.0%
Cost of goods sold	497,000	65.8
Gross profit......................	284,000	34.2
Operating expenses..........	163,000	19.7
Operating income............	121,000	14.5
Other expenses.................	5,000	0.4
Net income	$116,000	14.1%

DSC VACUUM CLEANERS Balance Sheet Compared with Industry Average December 31, 19X6		
	DSC	**Industry Average**
Current assets	$350,000	70.9%
Plant assets, net..................	74,000	23.6
Intangible assets, net..........	4,000	0.8
Other assets........................	22,000	4.7
Total	$450,000	100.0%
Current liabilities...............	$207,000	48.1%
Long-term liabilities..........	62,000	16.6
Stockholders' equity	181,000	35.3
Total	$450,000	100.0%

1. Prepare a two-column common-size income statement and balance sheet for DSC. The first column of each statement should present DSC's common-size statement, and the second column should show the industry averages.

2. For the profitability analysis, compute DSC's (a) ratio of gross profit to net sales, (b) ratio of operating income to net sales, and (c) ratio of net income to net sales. Compare these figures with the industry averages. Is DSC's profit performance better or worse than the industry average?

3. For the analysis of financial position, compute DSC's (a) ratio of current assets to total assets, and (b) ratio of stockholders' equity to total assets. Compare these ratios with the industry averages. Is DSC's financial position better or worse than the industry averages?

Effects of business transactions on selected ratios
(Obj. 4, 5)

P18-3B Financial statement data of Kaplan Sales, Inc., include the following items:

Cash	$ 22,000	Accounts payable....................	$103,000
Short-term investments.........	19,000	Accrued liabilities..................	38,000
Accounts receivable, net	83,000	Long-term notes payable.......	160,000
Inventories.............................	141,000	Other long-term liabilities	31,000
Prepaid expenses....................	8,000	Net income.............................	71,000
Total assets.............................	657,000	Number of common shares	
Short-term notes payable	49,000	outstanding......................	40,000

1. Compute Kaplan's current ratio, debt ratio, and earnings per share.
2. Compute each of the three ratios after evaluating the effect of each transaction that follows. Consider each transaction *separately*.
   a. Purchased merchandise costing $26,000 on account, debiting Inventory.
   b. Paid off long-term liabilities, $31,000.
   c. Declared, but did not pay, a $22,000 cash dividend on common stock.
   d. Borrowed $85,000 on a long-term note payable.
   e. Sold short-term investments for $18,000 (cost, $11,000); assume no income tax on the gain.
   f. Issued 5,000 shares of common stock, receiving cash of $120,000.
   g. Received cash on account, $19,000.
   h. Paid short-term notes payable, $32,000.

Use the following format for your answer:

	Current Ratio	Debt Ratio	Earnings per Share
Transaction (letter)	Current Ratio	Debt Ratio	Earnings per Share

P18-4B Comparative financial statement data of DimeBox Foods, Inc., follow.

Using ratios to evaluate a stock investment
(Obj. 4, 5)

DIMEBOX FOODS, INC.
Comparative Income Statement
Years Ended December 31, 19X4 and 19X3

	19X4	19X3
Net sales	$462,000	$427,000
Cost of goods sold	229,000	218,000
Gross profit	233,000	209,000
Operating expenses	136,000	134,000
Income from operations	97,000	75,000
Interest expense	11,000	12,000
Income before income tax	86,000	63,000
Income tax expense	30,000	27,000
Net income	$ 56,000	$ 36,000

DIMEBOX FOODS, INC.
Comparative Balance Sheet
December 31, 19X4 and 19X3
(selected 19X2 amounts given for computation of ratios)

	19X4	19X3	19X2
Current assets:			
Cash	$ 96,000	$ 97,000	
Current receivables, net	112,000	116,000	$103,000
Inventories	172,000	162,000	207,000
Prepaid expenses	16,000	7,000	
Total current assets	396,000	382,000	
Property, plant, and equipment, net	189,000	178,000	
Total assets	$585,000	$560,000	598,000
Total current liabilities	$206,000	$223,000	
Long-term liabilities	119,000	117,000	
Total liabilities	325,000	340,000	
Preferred stockholders' equity, 6%, $100 par	100,000	100,000	
Common stockholders' equity, no par	160,000	120,000	90,000
Total liabilities and stockholders' equity	$585,000	$560,000	

Other information:

a. Market price of DimeBox's common stock: $49 at December 31, 19X4, and $32.50 at December 31, 19X3.

b. Common shares outstanding: 10,000 during 19X4 and 9,000 during 19X3.

c. All sales on credit.

REQUIRED

1. Compute the following ratios for 19X4 and 19X3:
   a. Current ratio
   b. Inventory turnover
   c. Accounts receivable turnover
   d. Times-interest-earned ratio
   e. Return on assets
   f. Return on common stockholders' equity
   g. Earnings per share of common stock
   h. Price/earnings ratio
   i. Book value per share of common stock

2. Decide (a) whether DimeBox's financial position improved or deteriorated during 19X4, and (b) whether the investment attractiveness of its common stock appears to have increased or decreased.

3. How will what you learned in this problem help you evaluate an investment?

Using ratio data to complete a set of financial statements
(Obj. 4)

P18-5B ◀▥ *Link Back to Chapter 17 (Statement of Cash Flows).* Incomplete and adapted versions of the financial statements of PepsiCo, Inc., follow (amounts in millions).

Income Statement
Year Ended May31, 19X6

Net sales	$28,472
Cost of goods sold	(a)
Gross margin	(b)
Selling and general expenses	11,244
Other expense (income)	881
Income before income tax	(c)
Income tax expense (33.43%)	(d)
Net income	$ (e)

Comparative Balance Sheet
May31, 19X6 and 19X5

ASSETS	19X6	19X5
Current:		
Cash	$ (f)	$ 227
Short-term investments	1,157	1,574
Receivables, net	2,051	1,883
Inventories	970	925
Prepaid expenses	(g)	500
Total current assets	(h)	5,109
Long-term assets	19,720	18,597
Total assets	$ (i)	$23,706
LIABILITIES		
Current liabilities	$ 5,270	$ 6,575
Long-term liabilities	(j)	10,792
Total liabilities	(k)	17,367
STOCKHOLDERS' EQUITY		
Common stockholders' equity	(l)	6,339
Total liabilities and equity	$ (m)	$23,706

Statement of Cash flows
Year Ended May 31, 19X6

Net cash inflow from operating activities	$ 3,716
Net cash outflow from investing activities	(2,361)
Net cash outflow from financing activities	(1,251)
Net increase (decrease) in cash during 19X6	$ (n)

Ratio data:

a. Current ratio at May 31, 19X6 is 0.9624.

b. Inventory turnover for year ended May 31, 19X6, was 14.475.

c. Debt ratio at May 31, 19X6 is 0.72346.

Complete the financial statements. Start with the income statement. Then go to the statement of cash flows. Complete the balance sheet last.

REQUIRED

P18-6B Assume that you are purchasing an investment and have decided to invest in a company in the air-conditioning and heating business. You have narrowed the choice to Dover, Inc., and Cigna Corp. and have assembled the following data.

Using ratios to decide between two stock investments; measuring economic value added

(Obj. 4, 5, 6)

Selected income statement data for current year:

	Dover, Inc.	Cigna Corp.
Net sales (all on credit)	$497,000	$371,000
Cost of goods sold	258,000	209,000
Income from operations	138,000	79,000
Interest expense	19,000	—
Net income	72,000	48,000

Selected balance sheet and market price data at end of current year:

	Dover, Inc.	Cigna Corp.
Current assets:		
Cash..	$ 19,000	$ 22,000
Short-term investments	18,000	20,000
Current receivables, net..............................	46,000	42,000
Inventories...	100,000	87,000
Prepaid expenses	3,000	2,000
Total current assets...................................	186,000	173,000
Total assets	328,000	265,000
Total current liabilities................................	98,000	108,000
Total liabilities...	131,000*	108,000*
Preferred stock: 5%, $100 par	20,000	
Common stock, $1 par (10,000 shares)		10,000
$2.50 par (5,000 shares)..........	12,500	
Total stockholders' equity............................	197,000	157,000
Market price per share of common stock..........	$ 112	$ 51

*Notes payable: Dover, $86,000
Cigna, $ 1,000

Selected balance sheet data at beginning of current year:

	Dover, Inc.	Cigna Corp.
Current receivables, net......................................	$ 48,000	$ 40,000
Inventories	88,000	93,000
Total assets	270,000	259,000
Preferred stock, 5%, $100 par	20,000	—
Common stock, $1 par (10,000 shares)		10,000
$2.50 par (5,000 shares)..........	12,500	
Total stockholders' equity..................................	126,000	118,000

Your investment strategy is to purchase the stocks of companies that have low price/earnings ratios but appear to be in good shape financially. Assume that you have analyzed all other factors and your decision depends on the results of the ratio analysis to be performed.

1. Compute the following ratios for both companies for the current year, and decide which company's stock better fits your investment strategy.
   - **a.** Current ratio
   - **b.** Acid-test ratio
   - **c.** Inventory turnover
   - **d.** Days' sales in average receivables
   - **e.** Debt ratio
   - **f.** Times-interest-earned ratio
   - **g.** Return on net sales
   - **h.** Return on total assets
   - **i.** Return on common stockholders' equity
   - **j.** Earnings per share of common stock
   - **k.** Book value per share of common stock
   - **l.** Price/earnings ratio

2. Compute each company's economic-value-added (EVA®) measure, and determine whether their EVA®s confirm or alter your investment decision. Each company's cost of capital is 12 percent. Round all amounts to the nearest $1,000.

Applying Your Knowledge

DECISION CASE

Identifying action to cut losses and establish profitability
(Obj. 2, 4, 5)

Suppose you manage Dollar or Less, a variety store that lost money during the past year. Before you can set the business on a successful course, you must analyze the company and industry data for the current year to learn what is wrong. The company's data follow.

Dollar or Less Balance Sheet Data		
	Dollar or Less	**Industry Average**
Cash and short-term investments	3.0%	6.8%
Inventory	79.4	71.5
Prepaid expenses	1.0	0.0
Total current assets	83.4	78.3
Plant assets, net	12.6	15.2
Other assets	4.0	6.5
Total assets	100.0%	100.0%
Notes payable, short-term, 12%	24.1%	14.0%
Accounts payable	14.1	25.1
Accrued liabilities	7.8	7.9
Total current liabilities	46.0	47.0
Long-term debt, 11%	19.7	16.4
Total liabilities	65.7	63.4
Common stockholders' equity	34.3	36.6
Total liabilities and stockholders' equity	100.0%	100.0%

Dollar or Less Income Statement Data		
	Dollar or Less	**Industry Average**
Net sales	100.0%	100.0%
Cost of sales	(68.2)	(64.8)
Gross profit	31.8	35.2
Operating expense	(37.1)	(32.3)
Operating income (loss)	(5.3)	2.9
Interest expense	(5.8)	(1.3)
Other revenue	1.1	0.3
Income (loss) before income tax	(10.0)	1.9
Income tax (expense) saving	4.4	(0.8)
Net income (loss)	(5.6)%	1.1%

On the basis of your analysis of these figures, suggest three courses of action Dollar or Less might take to reduce its losses and establish profitable operations. Give your reasons for each suggestion.

FINANCIAL STATEMENT CASES

Measuring profitability and analyzing stock as an investment
(Obj. 1)

CASE 1. Use the Financial History that appears at the beginning of the NIKE, Inc., financial statements (Appendix A) to answer the following questions.

1. From the Financial History, perform a nine-year trend analysis of
   a. Revenues
   b. Net income
   c. Earnings per share of common stock

   Start with 1989, and end with 1997. Use 1988 as the base year.

2. Evaluate NIKE's profitability trend during this nine-year period.

Measuring profitability and analyzing stock as an investment
(Obj. 4, 5)

REQUIRED

CASE 2. Obtain the annual report of a company of your choosing.

1. Use the financial statements and the multi-year summary data to chart the company's progress during the three most recent years, including the current year. Compute the following ratios that measure profitability and are used to analyze stock as an investment:

Profitability Measures

   a. Rate of return on net sales
   b. Rate of return on common stockholders' equity
   c. Rate of return on total assets

Stock Analysis Measure

   d. Price/earnings ratio (If given, use the average of the "high" and "low" stock prices for each year.)

2. Is the trend in the profitability measures consistent with the trend in the stock analysis measure? Evaluate the company's overall outlook for the future.

Team Projects

PROJECT 1. Select an industry in which you are interested, and use the leading company in that industry as the benchmark. Then select two other companies in the same industry. For each category of ratios in the Decision Guidelines feature on pages 784–785, compute at least two ratios for all three companies. Write a two-page report that compares the two companies with the benchmark company.

PROJECT 2. Select a company and obtain its financial statements. Convert the income statement and the balance sheet to common-size, and compare the company you selected to the industry average. Robert Morris Associates' *Annual Statement Studies*, Dun & Bradstreet's *Industry Norms & Key Business Ratios*, and Prentice Hall's *Almanac of Business and Industrial Financial Ratios*, by Leo Troy, all publish common-size statements for most industries.

Internet Exercises   BRISTOL-MYERS SQUIBB AND JOHNSON & JOHNSON

Visit the Web sites of Bristol-Myers Squibb (**www.bms.com**) and Johnson & Johnson (**www.jnj.com**), both manufacturers of health care products.

Computing ratios for two well-known companies
(Obj. 4)

1. For each company, access the most recent annual report and obtain the amounts reported for Net Sales and Net Earnings for the three most recent years.

2. Using the earliest year as the base year, compute the trend percentages for both sales and earnings. For each company, comment on whether sales or earnings increased at a greater ratio.

3. For each company, compute the Return on Sales (ROS) ratio for the three most recent years. Comment on which company has the stronger ratio.

4. Describe how different companies within the same industry can best be compared.

Comprehensive Problem For Part Four

ANALYZING A COMPANY FOR ITS INVESTMENT POTENTIAL

In its 1997 annual report, NIKE, Inc., includes a Financial History that covers ten years. Analyze the company's Financial History for the fiscal years 1993–1997 to decide whether to invest or not to invest in the common stock of NIKE. Include the following sections in your analysis, and fully explain your final decision.

- Trend analysis (use 1993 as the base year)
- Profitability analysis
- Measuring ability to sell inventory
- Cash-flow analysis (net cash inflow or outflow from operating activities)
- Measuring ability to pay debts

CHAPTER 19

Introduction to Management Accounting

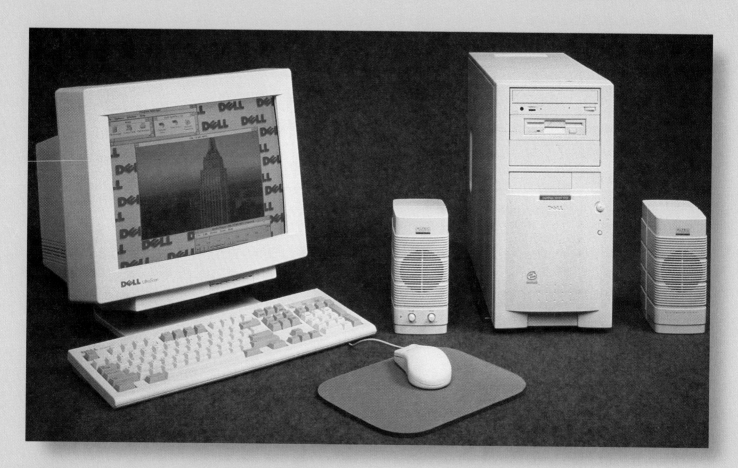

LEARNING OBJECTIVES

After studying this chapter, you should be able to

1. Distinguish between financial accounting and management accounting, and use management accounting information for decision making

2. Describe the value chain and classify costs by value-chain function

3. Distinguish direct costs from indirect costs

4. Distinguish among full product costs, inventoriable product costs, and period costs

5. Prepare the financial statements of a manufacturing company

6. Identify major trends in the business environment, and use cost-benefit analysis to make business decisions

7. Use reasonable standards to make ethical judgments

Dell Computer Corporation—the well-known direct-order computer-assembly firm—saw its first quarter 1997 net income soar to $198 million, more than double its net income in the first quarter of 1996. "Business is very good," said chief executive Michael Dell, in a dramatic understatement. Dell's outlook hasn't always been so rosy, however. Just a few years earlier, the company posted its first-ever net loss—$36 million—after suffering a major product recall and a shareholder lawsuit.

How did Michael Dell turn his company around? What decisions did he make, and what information helped Dell make wise choices?

Dell knew that cost control should drive his computer business, because most customers prefer a good price over a specific brand name. Dell executives also had to decide how to market and distribute the computers. Should the company sell via telephone and eliminate middleman costs? Or should it sell computers through discount chains like Sam's Club and Best Buy? Should Dell continue to focus on the U.S. market, or should the company expand into Europe or the Pacific? Decisions! Decisions!

Accounting information helps executives like Michael Dell make these and other decisions. For ex-

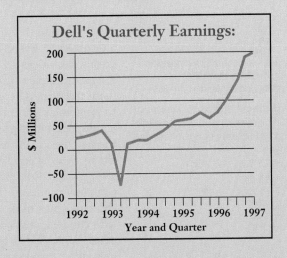

Dell's Quarterly Earnings:

ample, the accounting system provides managers with cost and profit information broken down by

1. Type of product, such as desktop and laptop models
2. Marketing strategy, such as direct-telephone sales versus sales to retailers like Best Buy
3. Geographic units, such as U.S., European, or Pacific operations

This kind of information helps Michael Dell steer Dell Computer in the right direction. *Source:* Adapted from Louise Lee, "Dell Computer Profit Soars, Tops Forecasts," *The Wall Street Journal*, May 21, 1997, p. A3; Toni Mack, "Michael Dell's New Religion," *Forbes*, June 6, 1994, pp. 45–46.

Thus far, our study of accounting has focused on reporting information for decision makers *outside* the organization: investors, creditors, and government authorities. Accounting that reports to parties outside the business is called *financial accounting*. In Chapters 1–18, we analyzed financial accounting reports—the income statement, the balance sheet, and the statement of cash flows. These statements report the *past* performance and financial position of a business.

We now shift our focus to how accounting information helps shape the business's *future*. We examine accounting through the eyes of the people who run the business. Decision makers *inside* a company are called managers, and accounting designed to meet their information needs is called *management accounting*. ◀▥

The Functions of Management

Business managers perform two broad functions: planning and controlling (Exhibit 19-1). **Planning** means choosing goals and deciding how to achieve them. For example, one goal of ice cream maker Baskin Robbins may be to increase operating income. The company's managers may decide to

1. Increase sale price of ice cream,
2. Increase advertising to generate more sales, or
3. Develop a new recipe that uses less fruit and more low-cost flavorings

Suppose that management planning leads Baskin Robbins executives to decide on alternative 3. Based on the new ice cream recipe, the managers budget the costs of ice cream, considering both costs per gallon and expected production quantities. A **budget** is a quantitative expression of a plan of action that helps managers coordinate and implement the plan. After the budget is created, controlling begins. **Controlling** means acting to implement planning decisions and then evaluating the performance of operations and employees, comparing the results to the plan. Baskin Robbins managers communicate the new ice cream recipes to both the purchasing officer who buys the ingredients, and the workers, who mix ingredients in the plant.

Baskin Robbins' accounting system records how many gallons of ice cream the company produces. The system also records the purchase prices and quantities of fruits and flavorings used. After production is completed, managers compare the actual costs with the budgeted costs in order to evaluate performance. If actual costs fall below budgeted costs, that is good news. But if actual costs exceed budgeted amounts, managers may need to take corrective action. The operating costs provide feedback that helps managers decide whether their decision to change recipes was a good decision that increased profits or a bad decision that decreased profits.

The chapter opening story illustrates both the short- and long-term aspects of planning and controlling. In the short term, Dell must decide whether direct telephone sales that reduce the number of middlemen will significantly cut costs and thus increase profits.

◀▥◀▥◀▥ We introduced the distinction between financial and management accounting in Chapter 1, page 7.

Planning. Choosing goals and deciding how to achieve them.

Budget. Quantitative expression of a plan of action that helps managers coordinate and implement the plan.

Controlling. Acting to implement planning decisions and then evaluating the performance of operations and employees.

EXHIBIT 19-1
The Functions of Management

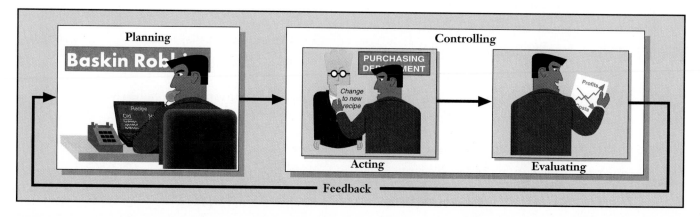

Dell's executives must also plan far into the future when they decide whether to expand into the Pacific. Building a new plant in Malaysia will tie up cash for years to come.

Management Accounting and Financial Accounting

Objective 1

Distinguish between financial accounting and management accounting, and use management accounting information for decision making.

Exhibit 19-2 summarizes the distinctions between management accounting and financial accounting. Consider points 1 and 2 of the exhibit. The decision whether to build a new production plant in Malaysia is related to Dell's future, and the decision makers are Dell managers. Dell will budget (predict) the future income and cash flows generated by the plant. Managers will then compare the benefits and costs of operating the plant with the benefits and costs of alternative investments. For example, the money required for the Malaysian plant could be used to develop a new laptop model instead. Dell executives will choose the investment with the greatest expected net benefit to the company.

■ **Daily Exercise 19-1**

Now consider point 3 of Exhibit 19-2—accounting reports used by decision makers. Companies must adhere to GAAP for external accounting purposes. In contrast, there are no GAAP-type standards for preparing the information managers use to plan and control a company's operations. Managers have complete freedom to tailor the company's management accounting system to provide information that will help them make better decisions. Managers weigh

- The *benefits* of the system—helping managers make better decisions that increase profit, against
- The *cost* of the system—including costs of training managers and other users, as well as the cost to develop and run the system

The weighing of costs against benefits to aid decision-making is called **cost-benefit analysis.** Cost-benefit analysis occurs in many areas of accounting and business. Because the costs and benefits of any particular management accounting system differ from one company to the next, it is not surprising that different companies create different management accounting systems. For example, different companies figure the manufacturing cost of a product differently, as we shall see in Chapters 20 and 21. For external reporting, though, all businesses must follow GAAP and use the accrual basis of accounting.

Cost-Benefit Analysis. The weighing of costs against benefits to aid decision making.

Point 3 of Exhibit 19-2 highlights another difference between management accounting and financial accounting—the scope of the information provided. Management accounting often generates detailed reports on parts of the company (products,

Concept Highlight

EXHIBIT 19-2
Differences between Management Accounting and Financial Accounting

	Management Accounting	**Financial Accounting**
1. Primary users	Internal—managers of the business	External—investors, creditors, and government authorities such as the IRS and SEC
2. Focus	Relevance and focus on the future—example: 1999 budget prepared in 1998	Reliability, objectivity, and focus on the past—example: 1998 actual performance reported in 1999
3. Reports and scope of information	Not restricted by GAAP—determined by cost-benefit analysis; detailed reports on parts of the company (products, departments, territories, often on a daily, weekly, or monthly basis)	Restricted by GAAP; summary reports primarily on the company as a whole, usually on a quarterly or annual basis
4. Behavioral implications	Concern about how reports will affect employee behavior	Concern about adequacy of disclosure; behavioral implications are secondary

departments, or territories), often on a daily, weekly, or monthly basis. In contrast, financial accounting more often generates summary reports that provide information on the company as a whole, typically on a quarterly or annual basis.

Point 4 of Exhibit 19-2 highlights another major difference between management accounting and financial accounting: The behavioral implications of management accounting reports deserve the front-and-center attention of managers and accountants. Managers' actions are heavily influenced by how their performance is measured, and the accounting system is used to measure performance. For example, the manager of a Baskin Robbins store will care about cleanliness and cheerful service if her performance evaluation is based on the store's profit. Excellent customer service leads to higher sales, which increase profit. The manager will be less concerned about customer service if she is evaluated only on her ability to control costs. In that case, she may save money by cleaning the store less often. Top executives create performance evaluation plans very carefully. They understand that "you get what you measure," and these plans do affect employee behavior.

Management's Use of Accounting Information

Investors and creditors do not need the same kind of information that managers need to make decisions. For example, a manager might need to evaluate the cost of long-distance calls; investors and creditors do not. Managers use accounting information for three broad purposes:

Purpose 1. To determine the cost of products and services. A company must know the cost of each product it produces and each service it provides. Companies need this information for planning and controlling business operations (purpose 2), and for external financial reporting (purpose 3).

Purpose 2. To plan and control business operations. This includes evaluating the performance of people and activities.

Purpose 3. To report to external parties the company's financial position and results of operations.

Service, Merchandising, and Manufacturing Companies

Service Company. A company that provides intangible services, rather than tangible products.

Merchandising Company. A company that buys ready-made inventory for resale to customers.

Manufacturing Company. A company that uses labor, plant, and equipment to convert raw materials into new finished products.

"Like other merchandisers, Footlocker buys ready-made inventory for resale to customers."

◄▥ ◄▥ ◄▥   See Chapter 5, pages 184–192, for a review of inventory in merchandising firms.

Previous chapters focused on service and merchandising firms. **Service companies** do not sell tangible products. Rather, they provide intangible services such as house painting, hair styling, and legal advice. Labor is typically their most significant cost—often as high as 70% of total costs. Well-known service businesses include H&R Block (tax return preparation), Randstad (temporary personnel services), and Saatchi & Saatchi (advertising agency).

In contrast, merchandisers and manufacturers sell tangible products. **Merchandising companies** resell products previously bought from suppliers. Wal-Mart, 7-Eleven, and Footlocker are merchandising companies. Consider Footlocker, which sells athletic shoes. Like other merchandisers, Footlocker buys ready-made inventory for resale to customers. Determining Footlocker's cost of the shoes is relatively easy. Cost is the price that the merchandiser pays for the shoes plus the freight-in costs and any applicable customs duties. ◄▥ Because merchandise inventory consists only of goods ready for sale, a merchandiser's balance sheet typically reports a single category of inventory.

In contrast to merchandisers, **manufacturing companies** use labor, plant, and equipment to convert raw materials into new finished products. For example, companies

	Service Companies	**Merchandising Companies**	**Manufacturing Companies**
Examples	Advertising agencies HBO H&R Block Law firms Merrill Lynch	Wal-Mart Kroger Lands' End May Department Stores Wholesalers	Bethlehem Steel Dell Computer General Mills Mead Paper RJR Nabisco
Primary Output	Intangible services (for example, advice or entertainment)	Tangible products purchased from suppliers	New tangible products made as work- ers and equipment convert raw mate- rials (purchased from suppliers) into new finished products
Type(s) of Inventory	None	Inventory	Materials inventory Work in process inventory Finished goods inventory

Concept Highlight

EXHIBIT 19-3
Service, Merchandising, and
Manufacturing Companies

that supply athletic shoes to stores such as Footlocker—Reebok and NIKE—begin their manufacturing processes with materials (cloth, rubber, plastics, and so on). These materials are cut, glued, stitched, and formed into athletic shoes. Converting raw materials into finished products makes it more difficult to measure NIKE's inventory cost than to measure Footlocker's cost of inventory.

Manufacturers have three kinds of inventory:

1. *Materials inventory consists of raw materials for use in the manufacturing process.* For example, a shoe manufacturer's materials include leather, glue, plastic, cloth, and thread. Raw materials for Bethlehem Steel include iron ore, coal, and chemicals.

2. *Work in process inventory consists of goods that are partway through the manufacturing process, but not yet complete.* At Dell Computer, partially completed computers make up work in process inventory. At Texaco, work in process inventory is half-processed crude oil that is being refined into gasoline. Work in process is also called *work in progress* or *goods in process.*

3. *Finished goods inventory consists of completed goods that have not yet been sold.* Finished goods are what the manufacturer sells to a merchandising business. For example, Proctor & Gamble (P&G) manufactures Tide laundry soap and Crest toothpaste, which are finished goods that P&G sells to Safeway and Kmart. P&G's finished goods inventory then becomes the inventory of Safeway and Kmart.

Exhibit 19-3 summarizes the differences among service, merchandising, and manufacturing companies.

Materials Inventory. Raw materials for use in the manufacturing process.

Work in Process Inventory. Goods that are partway through the manufacturing process but not yet complete.

Finished Goods Inventory. Completed goods that have not yet been sold.

The Value Chain

Objective 2

Describe the value chain and classify costs by value-chain function

Many people describe Dell (or IBM or Hewlett-Packard) as a manufacturing company. Dell may be described more accurately as a company that does manufacturing. Why? Because manufacturing or production is only one of its major business functions.

Companies that do manufacturing also do many other things. For example, Dell also conducts research and development to determine what kinds of new computers to introduce into the market. It uses that information to design new computers, which it then produces, markets, and distributes. These business functions collectively are called the **value chain**—the sequence of activities that adds value to a firm's products or services (Exhibit 19-4).

- **Research and development (R&D)**—the process of researching and developing new or improved products or services, or the processes for producing them. For example, market research may identify a need for a lighter laptop computer, or the company's scientists may develop a breakthrough technology that drastically reduces the size or weight of the motherboard.

Value Chain. Sequence of activities that adds value to a firm's products or services. Includes R&D, design, production or purchases, marketing, distribution, and customer service.

Research and Development (R&D). The process of researching and developing new or improved products or services, or the processes for producing them.

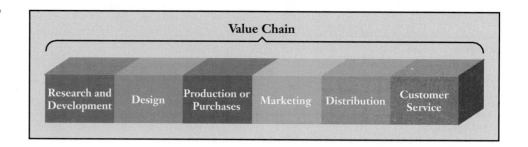

Design. Detailed engineering of products and services, or processes for producing them.

Production or Purchases. Resources used to produce a product or service, or the purchase of finished merchandise.

Marketing. Promotion of products or services.

Distribution. Delivery of products or services to customers.

Customer Service. Support provided for customers after the sale.

- **Design**—detailed engineering of products and services, or the processes for producing them. Example: redesigning the laptop's case and reengineering the manufacturing process to accommodate the new case.
- **Production or purchases**—Resources used to produce a product or service, or the purchase of finished merchandise. Examples: (1) For a manufacturer such as Dell, the actual production of products—for example, the materials, labor, and equipment used to manufacture the new laptop. (2) For a merchandiser such as Best Buy, the purchase of merchandise inventory (such as laptop computers) to resell to customers.
- **Marketing**—promotion of products or services. Example: an ad campaign for the new laptop.
- **Distribution**—delivery of products or services to customers. Example: delivery of the new laptop via truck to Best Buy and Circuit City.
- **Customer service**—support provided for customers after the sale. Example: a hotline for owners of the new laptop.

Managers do not necessarily proceed step by step in this exact order through the value chain. Indeed, managers may form a laptop project team to work on R&D, design, production, marketing, and customer service simultaneously.

The value chain applies equally to service, merchandising, and manufacturing firms. For example, an advertising agency such as Saatchi & Saatchi incurs

- *Marketing* costs to obtain a new client
- *Research and development* and *design* costs to develop the new client's ad campaign
- *Customer service* costs to address the new client's concerns
- *Distribution* costs to get the ads to the media

Managers are concerned about the value chain taken as a whole. They want to control the total costs of the entire chain. For example, Dell may deliberately decide to spend more in product design to improve the quality of its computers and thereby reduce production costs and the customer service costs of honoring product warranties. Even though product design costs are higher, the total cost of the computer—as measured by the entire value chain—may be lower.

Cost Objects, Direct Costs, and Indirect Costs

Cost Object. Anything for which a separate measurement of costs is desired.

Managers need cost data on all aspects of the business to make wise decisions. A **cost object** is anything for which a separate measurement of costs is desired. For example, Dell Computer's cost objects may include

- Individual products (laptop computers or desktop models)
- Alternative marketing strategies (direct telephone sales versus sales to retailers like Best Buy and Circuit City)
- Geographical segments of the business (United States, European, or Pacific)
- Departments (personnel, accounting, or information systems)

Direct Cost. A cost that can be specifically traced to a cost object.

Indirect Cost. A cost that cannot be specifically traced to a cost object.

Costs that can be specifically traced to the cost object are **direct costs.** Costs that cannot be specifically traced to the cost object are **indirect costs.**

Suppose a Dell Computer plant assembles laptop and desktop models. Assume the plant manager wants to know the cost of producing a specific laptop. The cost of the chip in the laptop is a *direct* cost of that computer because the chip can be specifically traced to the particular laptop. In contrast, the plant manager's salary cannot be specifically traced to any one computer, so the plant manager's salary is an *indirect* cost of the laptop.

Consider another example. Suppose Dell headquarters asks for the costs incurred by its production plant. The plant now becomes the cost object. The plant manager's salary becomes a direct cost because it can be specifically traced to the plant.

Now let's focus on the most common cost object: products.

Product Costs

Objective 4

Distinguish among full product costs, inventoriable product costs, and period costs

Accountants use the term *product costs* for the costs of producing (or purchasing) tangible products intended for sale. There are two types of product costs:

- *Full product costs* include the costs of all resources that are used throughout the value chain. They are used for internal decisions such as setting selling prices and deciding which products to emphasize. Full product costs do not conform to GAAP.
- *Inventoriable product costs* do not include costs from all elements of the value chain, so they are narrower in scope than full product costs. They include only those costs of a product that are regarded as an asset for external financial reporting. Inventoriable product costs must conform to GAAP.

Full Product Costs

For some planning, controlling, and other decisions, managers need to know full product costs. **Full product costs** are the costs of all resources that are used throughout the value chain for a product. The profit that Reebok earns on a particular shoe model is the difference between its sales revenue and the total cost that Reebok incurs to research, design, manufacture, market, and distribute the model, as well as to service the customers who buy it. Before launching a new model, managers must predict all these costs. Also, Reebok must decide which of its many products to emphasize. If Reebok managers determine that the profit (revenue minus full product costs) of a children's sneaker is much less than the profit on a jogging suit, they may drop the sneaker in order to produce more jogging suits. The more accurately costs are assigned to individual products, the more likely managers will make profitable decisions.

Full Product Costs. The costs of all resources that are used throughout the value chain for a product.

External Reporting: Inventoriable Product Costs versus Period Costs

Product costs affect the financial statements. For merchandising and manufacturing companies, product costs are used to compute the amount for Inventory on the balance sheet, and Cost of Goods Sold for the income statement. GAAP requires a very specific definition of product cost for the financial statements. Product costs that are used for external reporting are called **inventoriable product costs,** and they include only a *portion* of full product costs. Inventoriable product costs include all costs of a product that are regarded as an asset for external financial reporting.

What costs are inventoriable under GAAP? The answer depends on whether the company is a merchandiser or a manufacturer.

Inventoriable Product Costs. All costs of a product that are regarded as an asset for external financial reporting. Must conform to GAAP.

MERCHANDISING COMPANIES' INVENTORIABLE PRODUCT COSTS As we saw in Chapter 5, inventoriable costs for merchandising companies include *only* the cost of purchasing the inventory from suppliers (for example, the price Footlocker pays Reebok for shoes), plus freight-in. Footlocker's inventoriable cost (purchase price plus freight-in) of shoes represents an asset—Inventory—in Footlocker's accounting records. This inventoriable cost remains an asset (Inventory) until the shoes are *sold*. Then it becomes an expense—Cost of Goods Sold.

For external reporting, merchandisers' inventoriable product costs include only costs that are incurred in the purchase of goods for resale. These costs are included only in the third element of the value chain in Exhibit 19–4. Costs incurred in other elements of the value chain—such as Footlocker's employees' salaries, commissions paid to its sales staff, and distribution costs—are not inventoriable product costs. Instead, these are **period costs,** operating costs that are always expensed in the period in which they are

Period Costs. Operating costs that are expensed in the period in which they are incurred.

incurred. They are never part of the Inventory asset account. Notice that this contrasts with inventoriable product costs that are first considered inventory (an asset) and are not expensed (as cost of goods sold) until later when the products are sold.

Thinking It Over What would be the inventoriable costs for a service firm such as H&R Block?

Answer: Service firms like H&R Block have no tangible inventory of products intended for sale. Services cannot be produced today and stored up to sell later. For example, H&R Block cannot work ahead to produce an inventory of completed tax returns, ready to sell to customers as they walk in! Because service firms have no inventory, they have no inventoriable costs. Instead, they have only period costs that are expensed as incurred.

MANUFACTURING COMPANIES' INVENTORIABLE PRODUCT COSTS Manufacturing firms' product cost computations are more complex than those for merchandising firms. For manufacturing firms, inventoriable costs include the cost of raw materials plus all other costs incurred in the manufacturing/production process. Let's take a closer look at manufacturing firms' inventoriable product costs.

Exhibit 19-5 illustrates the major categories of inventoriable product costs for a manufacturer such as Reebok:

- **Direct materials** must meet two requirements: (1) They must become a physical part of the finished product, and (2) their costs (invoice cost plus freight-in) must be separately and conveniently traceable through the manufacturing process to the finished product. Again consider Reebok. The leather uppers, the rubber and plastic soles, and the shoelaces are direct materials. They become part of the finished shoe. Also, we can trace the costs directly to the shoe as it moves through the production process and is finally completed.
- **Direct labor** is the compensation of employees who physically convert materials into the company's products. For Reebok, direct labor includes the wages of machine operators and persons who assemble the shoes. For Dell, direct labor is the pay of employees who work on the computer-assembly lines. The effort of these persons can be traced *directly* to the finished products.
- **Manufacturing overhead** includes all manufacturing costs other than direct materials and direct labor. Examples include indirect materials, indirect labor, plant utilities, plant repairs, plant maintenance, plant rent, insurance on the plant, plant property taxes, and depreciation on plant buildings and equipment. Manufacturing overhead also is called **factory overhead** or **indirect manufacturing cost.**

This is the key point: manufacturing overhead includes only indirect manufacturing costs— that is, indirect costs related to the manufacturing plant. For example, depreciation on the plant's building and equipment is an indirect manufacturing cost, so it is part of manufacturing overhead. Likewise, insurance on the plant's building and equipment is part of manufacturing overhead. In contrast, depreciation on delivery trucks is not a

■ **Daily Exercise 19-4**

Direct Materials. Materials that become a physical part of a finished product and whose costs are separately and conveniently traceable through the manufacturing process to a finished product.

Direct Labor. The compensation of employees who physically convert materials into the company's products; labor costs that are directly traceable to finished products.

Manufacturing Overhead. All manufacturing costs other than direct materials and direct labor. Also called **factory overhead** or **indirect manufacturing cost.**

EXHIBIT 19-5
Inventoriable Product Costs for a Manufacturer

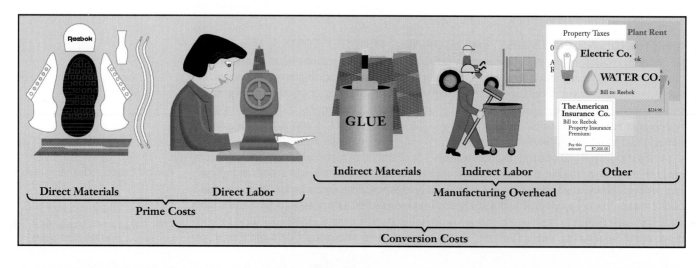

Direct Materials	Direct Labor	Indirect Materials	Indirect Labor	Other
Prime Costs		Manufacturing Overhead		
	Conversion Costs			

manufacturing cost. Delivery is part of the distribution element of the value chain, not the production (or manufacturing) element. Depreciation on delivery trucks is therefore part of distribution expense (a period expense), not part of manufacturing overhead. Similarly, auto insurance for the sales force is not a manufacturing cost. Costs incurred to support the sales force are part of the marketing element of the value chain, not the production element. Therefore, insurance related to the sales force is part of marketing expense (a period expense), not part of manufacturing overhead.

Let's take a closer look at two major components of manufacturing overhead: indirect materials and indirect labor. First consider **indirect materials.** The glue and thread used in athletic shoes become physical parts of the finished product. But, compared with the cost of the leather uppers and rubber soles, the costs of glue and thread are minor. It is hard to measure the costs of those low-priced materials for a single pair of shoes. How would a supervisor figure the cost of a brushful of glue? How useful would such detailed information be? These kinds of materials, whose costs cannot conveniently be directly traced to particular finished products, are called indirect materials. Indirect materials are accounted for as part of manufacturing overhead cost.

Indirect Materials. Materials whose costs cannot conveniently be directly traced to particular finished products.

Some manufacturing labor costs are classified as **indirect labor.** Like indirect materials, indirect labor is difficult to trace to specific products. Examples include the pay of forklift operators, janitors, and plant managers. Indirect labor, like indirect materials, is part of manufacturing overhead.

Indirect Labor. Labor costs that are difficult to trace to specific products.

Learning Tip: For a manufacturing company,

> Direct materials
> + Direct labor
> + Manufacturing overhead
> = Inventoriable product costs

Managers of manufacturing companies often refer to prime costs and conversion costs.

- **Prime costs** are the direct costs of the manufacturing process, usually direct materials plus direct labor.
- **Conversion costs** are the costs of converting direct materials into finished products, usually direct labor plus manufacturing overhead. Notice that direct labor is included in both prime costs and conversion costs, as illustrated in Exhibit 19-5.

Prime Costs. Direct costs of the manufacturing process, usually direct materials plus direct labor.

Conversion Costs. Costs of converting direct materials into finished products, usually direct labor plus manufacturing overhead.

The balance sheet of Reebok, a manufacturing company, will report the inventoriable cost of the finished shoes on hand at the end of the period (direct materials, direct labor, and manufacturing overhead) as an asset—Finished Goods Inventory. Reebok's income statement will report as Cost of Goods Sold the inventoriable costs of the shoes the company sold.

Note that Reebok's inventoriable product costs include *only* the manufacturing costs. Remember that *the inventoriable costs are incurred only in the third element of the value chain in Exhibit 19-4.* Costs incurred in other elements of the value chain—such as Reebok's cost to research and develop a new style of shoe, and to advertise and deliver shoes to customers—are *not* inventoriable product costs for external reporting. Instead, these are period costs that are expensed in the income statement in the period incurred. Period costs are never part of the inventory asset account.

■ **Daily Exercise 19-5**

Exhibit 19-6 summarizes the differences between inventoriable and period costs for service, merchandising, and manufacturing companies. Study this exhibit carefully. When are costs like depreciation, insurance, utilities, and property taxes treated as inventoriable product costs? Only when those costs are related to the manufacturing plant. A manufacturer treats depreciation, insurance, utilities, and property taxes as inventoriable product costs *only* when these costs are related to manufacturing. Otherwise—when those costs are related to nonmanufacturing activities like R&D or marketing—they are treated as period costs. Service companies and merchandisers do no manufacturing, so they always treat depreciation, insurance, utilities, and property taxes as period costs. The difference between inventoriable product costs and period costs is important because these two kinds of cost are treated differently in the financial statements. The next section takes a closer look at how the financial statements of service companies, merchandisers, and manufacturers differ.

	Inventoriable Product Costs	Period Costs
	Initially an asset (inventory), and not expensed (Cost of Goods Sold) until inventory is sold	Expensed in period incurred; never considered an asset
Service Companies	None	Salaries, depreciation expense, utilities, insurance, property taxes, advertising
Merchandising Companies	Purchases plus freight-in	Salaries, depreciation expense, utilities, insurance, property taxes, advertising, freight-out
Manufacturing Companies	Direct materials, plus direct labor, plus manufacturing overhead (including indirect materials; indirect labor; depreciation on plant and equipment; plant insurance, plant utilities and property taxes on plant)	R&D; freight-out; depreciation expense, utilities, insurance, and property taxes on executive headquarters (separate from plant); advertising; CEO's salary

Concept Highlight

EXHIBIT 19-6
Examples of Inventoriable Product Costs and Period Costs for Service, Merchandising, and Manufacturing Companies

■ Daily Exercise 19-6

Objective 5

Prepare the financial statements of a manufacturing company

◄▌▌◄▌▌◄▌▌ Chapter 1, page 19, introduced income statements for service companies.

Financial Statements for Service, Merchandising, and Manufacturing Companies

How do inventoriable product costs and period costs affect companies' financial statements? We begin with a short review to help you see how a manufacturer's financial statements differ from those of service and merchandising companies.

Service Companies

We begin with service companies because they have the simplest accounting. Exhibit 19-7 shows the income statement of Bailey, Banks, & Hancock (BBH), a group of landscape architects. ◄▌▌ As you would imagine, the firm carries no inventory and thus has no inventoriable costs. Consequently, BBH's income statement in Exhibit 19-7 includes no Cost of Goods Sold. The income statement groups all expenses (period costs) together. As for most service companies, BBH's largest expense is for the salaries of employees who perform the services.

Merchandising Companies

Exhibit 19-8, Panel A, presents a bird's-eye view of how inventoriable costs and period costs affect the financial statements of merchandising companies. Consider Apex Showrooms, a merchandiser of lighting fixtures. Apex buys goods such as chandeliers and track lights, which are ready for sale. Apex's *only* inventoriable costs are for the purchase of these goods, plus freight-in.

EXHIBIT 19-7
Service Company Income Statement

BAILEY, BANKS, & HANCOCK Income Statement Month Ended December 31, 19X8		
Revenues		$160,000
Expenses:		
Salary expense	$104,000	
Office rent expense	18,000	
Depreciation expense—furniture and equipment	3,500	
Marketing expense	2,500	
Other expenses	2,000	(130,000)
Operating income		$ 30,000

PANEL A—Inventoriable Costs and Period Costs in Merchandising Companies

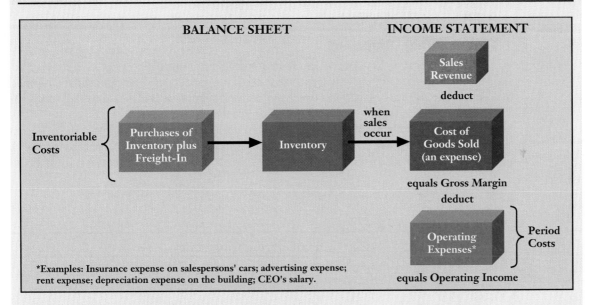

BALANCE SHEET   INCOME STATEMENT

Inventoriable Costs { Purchases of Inventory plus Freight-In → Inventory → when sales occur → Cost of Goods Sold (an expense)

Sales Revenue — deduct

equals Gross Margin
deduct

Operating Expenses* } Period Costs

equals Operating Income

*Examples: Insurance expense on salespersons' cars; advertising expense; rent expense; depreciation expense on the building; CEO's salary.

PANEL B—Merchandising Company Income Statement

APEX SHOWROOMS
Income Statement
Month Ended December 31, 19X8

Sales revenue		$150,000
Cost of goods sold:		
Beginning inventory	$ 9,500	
Purchases and freight-in	110,000	
Cost of goods available for sale	119,500	
Ending inventory	(13,000)	
Cost of goods sold		106,500
Gross margin		43,500
Operating expenses:		
Showroom rent expense	5,000	
Sales salary expense	2,500	
Administrative expense	1,500	9,000
Operating income		$ 34,500

EXHIBIT 19-8
Merchandising Company: Inventoriable Costs, Period Costs, and the Income Statement

◀ ◀ ◀ Panel B of Exhibit 9-3, page 381, shows a merchandiser's cost-of-goods-sold computation.

Panel B of Exhibit 19-8 shows Apex's income statement.[1] ◀ In contrast to the service company (Exhibit 19-7), the merchandiser's income statement features the Cost of Goods Sold as the major expense. Merchandisers like Apex can compute cost of goods sold as follows:

Beginning inventory	$ 9,500	What Apex had at the beginning of the period
+ Purchases and freight-in	110,000	What Apex bought during the period
= Cost of goods available for sale	119,500	Total available for sale during the period
− Ending inventory	13,000	What Apex had left at the end of the period
= Cost of goods sold	$106,500	What Apex sold

[1]To highlight the roles of beginning inventory, purchases, freight-in, and ending inventory, we assume that Apex uses a periodic inventory system. However, the concepts in this chapter apply equally to companies that use perpetual inventory systems.

■ Daily Exercise 19-7
■ Daily Exercise 19-8

On the income statement, Cost of goods sold is deducted from Sales revenue to obtain Gross margin. Apex's operating expenses (period costs) are deducted from gross margin to measure operating income. ◄▦

Manufacturing Companies

Exhibit 19-9, Panel A, shows that manufacturing firms have the most complicated accounting with three kinds of inventory: materials, work in process, and finished goods. Direct labor and manufacturing overhead convert raw materials into finished goods. As shown in Panel A, these are all inventoriable costs.

Consider Top-Flight, a manufacturer of golf equipment and athletic shoes. Compare its income statement in Panel B of Exhibit 19-9 with the merchandiser's income statement in Panel B of Exhibit 19-8. Both Apex and Top-Flight subtract cost of goods

◄▦ ◄▦ ◄▦   For further review of the cost of goods sold computation, see Chapter 5, page 182.

■ **Daily Exercise 19-9**

EXHIBIT 19-9

Manufacturing Company: Inventoriable Costs, Period Costs, and the Income Statement

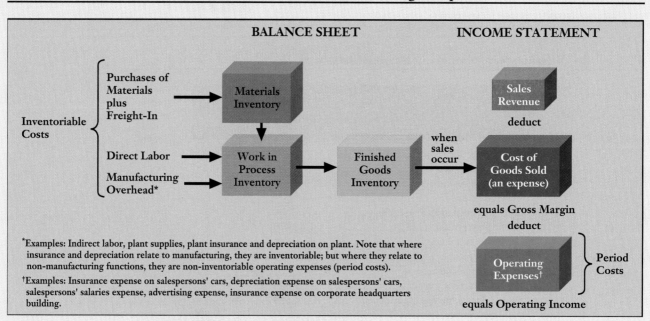

PANEL A—Inventoriable Costs and Period Costs in Manufacturing Companies

*Examples: Indirect labor, plant supplies, plant insurance and depreciation on plant. Note that where insurance and depreciation relate to manufacturing, they are inventoriable; but where they relate to non-manufacturing functions, they are non-inventoriable operating expenses (period costs).

†Examples: Insurance expense on salespersons' cars, depreciation expense on salespersons' cars, salespersons' salaries expense, advertising expense, insurance expense on corporate headquarters building.

PANEL B—Manufacturing Company Income Statement

TOP-FLIGHT		
Income Statement		
Year Ended December 31, 19X8		
Sales revenue..		$65,000
Cost of goods sold:		
Beginning finished goods inventory..........	$ 6,000	
Cost of goods manufactured*....................	42,000	
Cost of goods available for sale.................	48,000	
Ending finished goods inventory...............	(8,000)	
Cost of goods sold..		40,000
Gross margin		25,000
Operating expenses:		
Sales salary expense.....................................	3,000	
Delivery expense	5,000	
Administrative expense	2,000	10,000
Operating income..		$15,000

*From Cost-of-goods-manufactured schedule in Exhibit 19-10.

sold from sales revenue to obtain gross margin. Both companies subtract operating expenses from gross margin to get operating income. *The only difference between the two statements is that the merchandiser (Apex) uses purchases in computing cost of goods sold, while the manufacturer (Top-Flight) uses the cost of goods manufactured in computing cost of goods sold. Otherwise, the format of a manufacturer's income statement is identical to the format of a merchandiser's income statement.*

Now let's see how to compute cost of goods manufactured.

COST OF GOODS MANUFACTURED   The **cost of goods manufactured** is the (manufacturing) cost of the goods that were *finished*—that is, the cost of the units that completed the production process this period. This is the manufacturer's counterpart to the merchandiser's purchases because it is the cost that is added to beginning inventory of finished goods during the period.

The cost of goods manufactured computation is more complex than the merchandiser's simple tally of purchases. Panel A of Exhibit 19-10 shows how Top-Flight computes cost of goods manufactured during 19X8. The computation begins with the Work

Cost of Goods Manufactured. The (manufacturing) cost of the goods that were *finished*—that is, the cost of the units that completed the production process this period. This is the manufacturer's counterpart to the merchandiser's purchases.

PANEL A—Manufacturing Company Schedule of Cost of Goods Manufactured

EXHIBIT 19-10
Schedule of Cost of Goods Manufactured

- Daily Exercise 19-10
- Daily Exercise 19-11
- Daily Exercise 19-12
- Daily Exercise 19-13

TOP-FLIGHT
Schedule of Cost of Goods Manufactured
Year Ended December 31, 19X8

Beginning work in process inventory			$ 2,000
Add: Direct materials used:			
Beginning materials inventory	$ 9,000		
Purchases of direct materials	27,000		
Available for use	36,000		
Ending materials inventory	(22,000)		
Direct materials used		$14,000	
Direct labor		19,000	
Manufacturing overhead:			
Indirect materials	$ 1,500		
Indirect labor	3,500		
Depreciation—plant building	2,000		
Depreciation—plant equipment	1,000		
Plant utilities	2,500		
Plant insurance	1,000		
Property taxes on plant and equipment	500	12,000	
Total manufacturing costs incurred during year			45,000
Total manufacturing costs to account for			47,000
Less: Ending work in process inventory			(5,000)
Cost of goods manufactured			$42,000

PANEL B—Flow of Costs through a Manufacturer's Inventory Accounts

Direct Materials Inventory	Work in Process Inventory	Finished Goods Inventory

Beginning inventory
+ Purchases and
    freight-in
	Beginning inventory
	+ Direct materials used
	+ Direct labor
	+ Manufacturing overhead
		Beginning inventory
		+ Cost of goods
		    manufactured

= Direct materials
    available for use
− Ending inventory
	= Total manufacturing costs
	    to account for
	− Ending inventory
		= Cost of goods
		    available for sale
		− Ending inventory

= Direct materials
    used
	= Cost of goods
	    manufactured
		= Cost of goods sold

Source: The authors are indebted to Judith Cassidy for this presentation.

in Process Inventory balance at the beginning of the year ($2,000). To this amount, we add the three components of total manufacturing cost incurred during the year: direct materials used ($14,000), direct labor ($19,000), and manufacturing overhead ($12,000). Adding the sum of these costs ($45,000) to the beginning Work in Process Inventory balance of $2,000 gives the total cost assigned to goods worked on during the year—$47,000. Some of these goods were completed and sent into Finished Goods Inventory during the year; the others are still in process at the end of the year. Thus we subtract the cost of goods in process at the end of the year on December 31 ($5,000) to arrive at the cost of goods manufactured total of $42,000.

Panel B of Exhibit 19-10 diagrams the flow of costs through a manufacturer's inventory accounts. It reveals a similar computational format at all three stages—direct materials, work in process, and finished goods. For example, the cost of direct materials used is the beginning inventory plus purchases minus the ending inventory. The final amount at each stage flows into the next stage. This flow of costs through the inventory accounts can be seen in the income statement in Panel B of Exhibit 19-9 and the schedule of cost of goods manufactured in Exhibit 19-10.

Learning Tip: Cost of Goods Manufactured is not the same as Manufacturing Costs.

Manufacturing Costs:	**Cost of Goods Manufactured:**
Direct Materials Used	Beginning Work in Process Inventory
+ Direct Labor	+ Manufacturing Costs
+ Manufacturing Overhead	− Ending Work in Process Inventory
= Manufacturing Costs	= Cost of Goods Manufactured

The Cost of Goods Manufactured includes costs from the previous period (beginning work in process inventory) and current period manufacturing costs, but does not include costs for goods started but not yet finished (ending work in process inventory). The Cost of Goods Manufactured refers to the cost of goods that were *finished* during the period.

Working It Out Goods worked on during a production period may be classified according to when they are begun and when they are completed. Suppose that at Top-Flight some of the goods worked on in 19X8 were begun in 19X7 and completed in 19X8. Other goods worked on in 19X8 were both begun and completed during the year. Still others were begun late in 19X8 but not completed until 19X9. Refer to Exhibit 19-10. Assume that $3,000 of the total manufacturing cost incurred during the year was incurred to complete the beginning work in process inventory (which was begun in 19X7). What is the total cost of the goods that were both begun and completed in 19X8?

Answer: The total manufacturing cost incurred during the year was $45,000 (Exhibit 19-10). The flow of costs through production can be viewed as follows:

Start	Production Process	End

1. Complete beginning work in process inventory (given above) — $3,000
2. Start *and* complete goods in 19X8 — ?
3. Start ending work in process inventory (from Exhibit 19-10) — $5,000

Total 19X8 manufacturing costs = $45,000

Total 19X8 manufacturing costs	$45,000
− Cost to complete beginning work in process inventory	(3,000)
− Cost to start ending work in process inventory	(5,000)
= Cost of goods both started *and* completed in 19X8	$37,000

Bailey, Banks, & Hancock (Service Company)		Apex Showrooms (Merchandising Company)		Top-Flight (Manufacturing Company)	
Cash	$ 4,000	Cash	$ 4,000	Cash	$ 4,000
Accounts Receivable	5,000	Accounts Receivable	5,000	Accounts Receivable	5,000
		Inventory (from Exhibit 19-8)	13,000	Materials inventory (from Exhibit 19-10)	22,000
				Work in process inventory (from Exhibit 19-10)	5,000
				Finished goods inventory (from Exhibit 19-9)	8,000
Prepaid expenses	1,000	Prepaid expenses	1,000	Prepaid expenses	1,000
Total current assets	$10,000	Total current assets	$23,000	Total current assets	$45,000

EXHIBIT 19-11
Current Asset Sections of Balance Sheets

Effects on the Balance Sheet

The only difference in the balance sheets of service, merchandising, and manufacturing companies is related to inventories. Exhibit 19-11 shows how the current asset sections of Bailey, Banks, & Hancock (service company), Apex Showrooms (merchandising company), and Top-Flight (manufacturing company) might differ at the end of 19X8. Notice that Bailey, Banks, & Hancock has no inventory at all, Apex has a single category of inventory, and Top-Flight has three categories of inventory (materials, work in process, and finished goods).

■ **Daily Exercise 19-14**

We have now

1. Learned the differences between financial and management accounting
2. Considered the six business functions that comprise the value chain
3. Distinguished direct costs from indirect costs
4. Distinguished among full product costs, inventoriable product costs, and period costs
5. Seen the differences among service, merchandising, and manufacturing companies' financial statements

We will use these concepts many times throughout our discussion of management accounting. It is important that you take time now to review the following Decision Guidelines. Make sure you have a solid understanding of all these concepts before you read any further.

DECISION GUIDELINES	Building Blocks of Management Accounting
DECISION	**GUIDELINES**
What information should management accountants provide? What is the primary focus of management accounting?	Management accounting provides information that helps managers make better decisions. It has a: • *Future* orientation • Focus on *relevance* to business decisions *(continued)*

DECISION GUIDELINES *(continued)*

How do you determine a company's management accounting system, which is not restricted by GAAP?	Cost-benefit analysis: Design management accounting system so that benefits (from helping managers make wiser decisions) outweigh the cost of the system (including costs of management time and education).

How do you distinguish among service, merchandising, and manufacturing companies? How do their balance sheets differ?

Service companies:

- Provide customers with intangible services
- Have no inventories on the balance sheet

Merchandising companies:

- Resell tangible products they purchased ready-made from suppliers
- Have only one category of inventory on the balance sheet

Manufacturing companies:

- Apply labor, plant, and equipment to transform raw materials into new finished products
- Have three categories of inventory on the balance sheet:
  - Materials inventory
  - Work in process inventory
  - Finished goods inventory

How do you compute cost of goods sold?

- *Service companies:* No cost of goods sold, because they don't sell tangible goods

- *Merchandising companies:*

> Beginning inventory
> + Purchases and freight-in
> − Ending inventory
> = Cost of goods sold

- *Manufacturing companies:*

> Beginning finished goods inventory
> + Cost of goods manufactured
> − Ending finished goods inventory
> = Cost of goods sold

How do you compute the cost of goods manufactured for a manufacturer?

> Beginning work in process inventory
> + Current period manufacturing costs (Direct materials used + direct labor + manufacturing overhead)
> − Ending work in process inventory
> = Cost of goods manufactured

Which costs are initially treated as assets for external reporting? When are these costs expensed?

For external reporting, *inventoriable product costs* are initially treated as assets (Inventory). These costs are not expensed (as Cost of goods sold) until the products are sold.

What costs are inventoriable under GAAP?

- *Service companies:* No inventoriable product costs because they do not sell tangible products
- *Merchandising companies:* Purchases and freight-in
- *Manufacturing companies:* Direct materials used, direct labor, and manufacturing overhead

---

SUMMARY PROBLEM FOR YOUR REVIEW   MID-CHAPTER

1. Show how to compute cost of goods manufactured. Use the following amounts: direct materials used ($24,000); direct labor ($9,000); manufacturing overhead ($17,000); and work in process, beginning ($5,000) and ending ($4,000).

2. Assume a manufacturing company is evaluating its costs.
Identify the following as either an inventoriable product cost or a period cost:
a. Depreciation on plant equipment   c. Insurance on plant building
b. Depreciation on salespersons' automobiles   d. Marketing manager's salary

■ **SOLUTION**

1. Cost of goods manufactured:

Beginning work in process inventory		$ 5,000
Add: Direct materials used	$24,000	
Direct labor	9,000	
Manufacturing overhead	17,000	
Total manufacturing costs incurred during the period		50,000
Total manufacturing costs to account for		55,000
Less: Ending work in process inventory		(4,000)
Cost of goods manufactured		$51,000

2. **a.** Inventoriable product cost; **b.** Period cost; **c.** Inventoriable product cost; **d.** Period cost

The Modern Business Environment

The rest of this textbook describes management accounting tools and techniques designed to help managers make wise business decisions that in turn lead to profits. Before we turn to these specific accounting tools, let's first consider recent trends in business that affect managers' decisions and the management accounting systems that support these decisions. These trends include: the shift toward a service economy, the rise of the global marketplace, the just-in-time management philosophy, and total quality management.

> **Objective 6**
>
> Identify major trends in the business environment, and use cost-benefit analysis to make business decisions

Shift toward a Service Economy

Service companies provide health care, insurance, transportation, banking, and other important benefits to society. The last century has seen our economy shift from manufacturing to service. Service companies now make up the largest sector of the U.S. economy, with 55% of the work force employed in service companies. The U.S. Bureau of the Census expects this number to increase to 60% by 2005. Even companies that do manufacturing, such as General Electric (GE), are shifting their focus away from manufacturing products toward selling services. It's easy to see why. In GE's jet engine business, services contribute only 30% of the revenues, but generate two-thirds of the profit.

Managers of service companies need information to make decisions. For example, banks must include the cost of servicing checking and savings accounts in the fees they charge customers. Hospitals need to know the cost of performing appendectomies to justify reimbursement from insurance companies and from Medicare. Our discussions will consider how service companies, as well as merchandising and manufacturing firms, use management accounting information.

Competing in the Global Marketplace

The costs of international trade have plummeted over the last decade, largely due to

- Improved worldwide transportation, such as UPS's worldwide overnight delivery services ("We deliver anywhere")
- Reduced barriers to free trade, including the European Union free-trade zone (which includes more than a dozen European countries) and the North American Free Trade Agreement trading bloc (composed of the United States, Canada, and Mexico)
- Improved telecommunications, including video conferencing and the Internet

These changes have made it easier for foreign companies to compete with local firms, and firms that are not world-class competitors will not survive in the global marketplace. For example, RCA stereos have largely been replaced by Yamaha, Sony, and JVC models. However, global markets do provide highly competitive companies with tremendous potential. For instance, GE's revenue is growing three times faster in foreign countries than in the United States, and foreign operations account for over 40% of GE's

revenues. McDonald's is expanding in Russia and China, two countries with billions of consumers.

Manufacturers often move production operations to other countries where labor is less expensive. Suppose that Top-Flight, a golf equipment and athletic shoe company, is considering whether to build a new manufacturing plant just across the border in Mexico. Top-Flight's managers will compare the costs with the benefits of building the plant in Mexico. They will decide to build the plant if the benefits (less expensive labor) outweigh the costs of building the new plant.

Globalization has several implications for management accounting:

1. Stiffer competition means that managers need more accurate information to make wise decisions. For example, if Sony overestimates the cost of its new cordless phone model, it may set too high a selling price and lose business to competitors.

2. Companies must decide whether to expand sales and/or production into foreign countries. To make good decisions, managers need estimates of the costs and benefits of international expansion.

3. Globalization fosters the transfer of management philosophy across international borders. For example, many U.S. companies follow the just-in-time philosophy that was developed in Japan.

The Just-in-Time Management Philosophy

Just-in-Time (JIT). A system in which a company schedules production just in time to satisfy needs. Materials are purchased and finished goods are completed only as needed to satisfy customer demand.

Toyota is generally credited with pioneering the **just-in-time (JIT)** management philosophy. As the name suggests, a company with a JIT philosophy schedules production *just in time* to satisfy needs. Materials are purchased and finished goods are completed only as needed to satisfy customer demand. Ideally, materials necessary for today's production are delivered in (small) batches of exactly the right quantities *just in time* to begin production, and finished units are completed *just in time* for delivery to customers.

Firms adopting JIT report sharp reductions in inventory, often averaging about 50 percent. The reduction in inventory and speeding up of the production process reduces **throughput time,** the time between buying raw materials and selling the finished products. For example, Dell Computer recently cut its throughput time from 31 days to 12 days. The rapid obsolescence of computer parts makes it especially important for companies like Dell to minimize their materials, work in process, and finished goods inventories.

Throughput Time. The time between buying raw materials and selling the finished products.

■ Daily Exercise 19-15
■ Daily Exercise 19-16

Manufacturers who adopt JIT depend on their suppliers to make on-time deliveries of perfect-quality raw materials. Thus JIT requires close communication with suppliers. To develop closer relations, companies rely on fewer suppliers.

Another hallmark of JIT is the focus on perfect quality. When a defect occurs, the production line stops until the problem is fixed. To avoid disrupting production, defects must be rare.

Managers considering JIT want to know its costs and benefits. Suppose New-Tell, a computer chip manufacturer, is considering JIT. If New-Tell adopts JIT, the company will incur costs, including employee training, searching for the most reliable suppliers, and lost sales due to initial slowing of production as it makes the transition to JIT. New-Tell estimates that these costs will total $2 million. The benefits of adopting JIT include savings on inventory and storage space. JIT also reduces inventory obsolescence and yields higher sales because of better-quality products. New-Tell estimates that these benefits will save an average of $650,000 a year for ten years.

To make a decision, New-Tell must compare the benefits of adopting JIT with the $2 million cost. The cost of adopting JIT comes immediately, but the benefits occur later. New-Tell must determine the present value today of the future benefits of adopting JIT. In business, we refer to this as *discounting* the future amounts to their *present values.* ◄▥ Let's assume that New-Tell's benefits of adopting JIT have a present value of $3,141,450.[2]

◄▥◄▥◄▥ The Appendix to Chapter 15, pages 664–671, discusses present-value computations, and we will cover this subject in more detail in Chapter 26.

---

[2]JIT will reduce New-Tell's costs by $650,000 per year for ten years. Using a 16% discount rate, the present value of $650,000 per year for ten years is $3,141,450 ($650,000 × 4.833 from Exhibit 15A-7 on page 670 of the appendix to Chapter 15).

The costs of adopting JIT are incurred now, so the cost data are already stated at their present values. With all amounts stated at present values, we can compare New-Tell's costs and benefits of adopting a JIT system. New-Tell's decision follows this rule:

- Present value of JIT's benefits exceed the cost of adopting JIT → Adopt JIT
- Cost of adopting JIT exceeds the present value of JIT's benefits → Do not adopt JIT

The analysis is as follows:

Present value of benefits	$3,141,450
Present value of costs	(2,000,000)
Excess of benefits over costs	$1,141,450
Decision: Invest in JIT system	

Quality

The quality of goods and services is critical for remaining competitive. Businesses that deliver the best-quality products gain market share. Hewlett-Packard and Ford in the United States, British Telecom in the United Kingdom, and Toyota in Japan view **total quality management (TQM)** as one of the keys to success in a global economy. The goal of total quality management is to delight customers by providing them with superior products and services. Companies achieve this goal by improving quality and by eliminating defects and waste throughout the value chain. Each business function examines its own activities and works to improve by setting higher and higher goals.

Total Quality Management (TQM). A philosophy of delighting customers by providing them with superior products and services. Involves improving quality and eliminating defects and waste throughout the value chain.

TQM emphasizes educating, training, and cross-training employees to do multiple tasks. Motorola's purchasing department is an example. Motorola wanted to reduce the time taken to issue a purchase order. Before starting the project, a departmental team took a two-day company course called High-Commitment, High-Performance Team Training. Team members then reduced the number of steps in handling a purchase order from 17 to 6, slashing average processing time from 30 minutes to 3. The department now processes 45% more purchase orders with no added employees.

Like the adoption of JIT, quality improvement programs cost money today. The benefits usually do not occur until later. Because no one can foresee the future, the amount of the future benefits is not known exactly. Accountants often adjust for this uncertainty.

Consider GE. In 1996, the company started nearly 3,000 quality-related projects at a cost of more than $200 million. The first-year cost savings from these projects totaled only $170 million. Does this mean that GE made a bad decision? Not necessarily. GE expects these quality projects to continue yielding benefits in the future.

Suppose GE managers predict these projects will be either moderately successful or extremely successful. Assume that if the projects are moderately successful, they will yield additional benefits (cost savings) with a present value of $20 million. If the projects are extremely successful, they will yield extra benefits with a present value of $100 million. GE managers think the projects are more likely to be extremely successful than moderately successful, but they do not know for sure. Suppose they estimate a 60% chance that the projects will be extremely successful, and a 40% chance that they will be moderately successful.

■ **Daily Exercise 19-17**

In an uncertain environment such as GE's, managers make decisions based on expected values. We compute expected values by multiplying the dollar value of each possible outcome by the probability of that outcome, and then adding the results:

Outcome:	Benefit × Probability	Expected Value (of = Additional Benefit)
Extremely successful:	$100 million × 60% chance =	$60 million
Moderately successful:	20 million × 40% chance =	8 million
Total expected value of benefits		$68 million

What does this $68 million mean? If GE faced this exact situation ten times, it would expect to get $100 million in extra benefits six times, and only $20 million of additional benefits four times. The *average* extra benefits across the ten situations is $68 million, calculated as [(6 × $100) + (4 × $20)]/10 = $68. In effect, GE's best guess of the additional benefit is the expected value of $68 million.

The following summary shows that the total benefits expected from GE's quality projects ($238 million) exceeds the $200 million cost of the projects, suggesting that GE's quality project was worthwhile:

	Total Benefits	Total Costs
Initial benefits and costs................	$170 million	$200 million
Additional expected benefits.........	$ 68 million	
Total	$238 million	$200 million

Continuous Improvement. A philosophy requiring employees to continually look for ways to improve performance.

Even after adopting quality programs, companies cannot rest on their laurels. TQM requires that companies (and individual employees) continually look for ways to improve performance. This is the **continuous improvement** philosophy.

How do companies improve? Many businesses find that investments in higher quality earlier in the value-chain (R&D and design) generate savings in later stages (production, marketing, and customer service). Successful companies design and build quality into the product or service rather than doubling back to inspect quality and make repairs later. Carefully designed products and better employee training reduce costs of inspections, rework, and warranty claims, all of which eat into profits.

Professional Ethics for Management Accountants

A key indicator of quality is ethical behavior. Global competition pressures managers to compete and to meet continuous improvement goals. Such pressure can tempt managers to cheat. This is especially true for companies that operate in countries without established legal systems. Because bribes are common in some countries, Congress passed the Foreign Corrupt Practices Act to prohibit U.S. companies from paying bribes abroad.

As we've seen throughout this text, ethical behavior is necessary for the orderly functioning of society and business. How would you feel if parents, teachers, employers, friends, and co-workers constantly lied to you? Relationships necessary for everyday life would break down. Business would become much more difficult to conduct, and the range and quality of goods and services would decline. Because ethical behavior is so important, society enacts laws that require social responsibility. For example, it is illegal for companies to sell products that are clearly defective, such as automobiles that do not meet government safety standards.

Unfortunately, the ethical path is not always clear. You may want to act ethically and do the right thing, but the consequences involved can make it difficult to decide what to do. Consider the following examples:

- Sarah Baker is examining the expense reports of her staff accountants, who counted inventory at Top-Flight's warehouses in Arizona. She discovers that Mike Flinders has not included hotel receipts for over $1,000 of accommodation expenses. Each of the other staff members who also claimed $1,000 did attach hotel receipts. When asked about the receipt, Mike admits that he had stayed with an old friend, not in the hotel. His wife is expecting their first child, and he believes that he deserves the money he saved. After all, the company would have paid his hotel bill.
- As the accountant of Entreé Computer Co., you are aware of your company's weak financial condition. Entreé is close to signing a lucrative contract that should ensure its future. To do so, the controller states that the company *must* report a profit this year (ending December 31). He makes the following suggestion. "Two customers have placed orders that are really not supposed to be shipped until early January. Ask production to fill and ship those orders on December 31, so we can record them in this year's sales."

Concept Highlight

EXHIBIT 19-12
IMA Standards of Ethical
Conduct for Management
Accountants (excerpt)

■ **Daily Exercise 19-18**
■ **Daily Exercise 19-19**

Management accountants have an obligation to the organizations they serve, their profession, the public, and themselves to maintain the highest standards of ethical conduct including:

Competence

- Maintain an appropriate level of professional competence by ongoing development of their knowledge and skills.
- Perform their professional duties in accordance with relevant laws, regulations, and technical standards.

Confidentiality

- Refrain from disclosing confidential information acquired in the course of their work except when authorized, unless legally obligated to do so.

Integrity

- Avoid actual or apparent conflicts of interest and advise all appropriate parties of any potential conflict.
- Refuse any gift, favor, or hospitality that would influence or would appear to influence their actions.
- Communicate unfavorable as well as favorable information and professional judgments or opinions.

Objectivity

- Communicate information fairly and objectively.

Source: Adapted from Institute of Management Accountants, *Standards of Ethical Conduct for Management Accountants* (Montvale, N.J.).

The Institute of Management Accountants (IMA) has developed standards to help management accountants deal with these kinds of situations. An excerpt from the *Standards of Ethical Conduct for Management Accountants* appears in Exhibit 19-12. These standards require management accountants to

- Maintain their professional competence
- Preserve the confidentiality of the information they handle
- Act with integrity and objectivity

To resolve ethical dilemmas, the IMA also suggests discussing ethical situations with your immediate supervisor, or with an objective adviser.

Let's return to the two preceding ethical dilemmas. By asking to be reimbursed for hotel expenses he did not incur, Mike Flinders clearly violated the IMA's integrity standards (conflict of interest in which he tried to enrich himself at company expense). Because Sarah Baker discovered the inflated expense report, she would not be fulfilling her ethical responsibilities (integrity and objectivity) if she allowed the reimbursement and did not take disciplinary action.

The second dilemma, in which the controller asked you to accelerate the shipments, is less clear-cut. You should discuss the available alternatives and their consequences with others. Many people believe that following the controller's suggestion to manipulate the company's income would violate the standards of competence, integrity, and objectivity. Others would argue that because Entreé Computer already had the customer order, Entreé could behave ethically by shipping the goods and recording the sale in December. If you refused to ship the goods in December and you simply resigned without attempting to find an alternative solution, you might only hurt yourself and your family.

There are fairly clear-cut solutions to many situations, but not to true ethical dilemmas. The IMA's *Standards of Ethical Conduct* serve as a reminder that society expects professional accountants to uphold the highest level of ethical behavior.

You have now seen cost-benefit analysis applied to several different business decisions. The general approach of weighing costs versus benefits to make the best decision comes up again and again in management accounting. Study the "Cost-Benefit Analysis" Decision Guidelines to make sure you understand this important concept.

DECISION GUIDELINES — Cost-Benefit Analysis

DECISION	GUIDELINES
How to decide whether to undertake new projects like international expansion, JIT, and TQM?	Cost-benefit analysis: Compute the benefits of the project, and compare with the costs. Undertake the project if benefits exceed costs. Abandon the project if costs exceed benefits.
How to adjust the cost-benefit analysis if the exact amount of the benefit (or cost) is not known?	Compute the *expected value* of the benefits (or costs) of each outcome as follows:

$$\text{Estimated amount} \times \text{Probability of occurrence} = \text{Expected Value}$$

	Then add up the expected values across all possible outcomes.
How to resolve an ethical dilemma?	Weigh the costs and benefits of alternative courses of action. Consult the IMA's *Standards of Ethical Conduct for Management Accountants* (Exhibit 19-12). Also consult the Framework for Ethical Judgments in Chapter 7.

SUMMARY PROBLEM FOR YOUR REVIEW

Cost-benefit analysis applies to many decisions. This chapter showed how managers can use cost-benefit analysis to decide whether to adopt JIT or TQM. Managers can also use cost-benefit analysis for more specific decisions. This summary review problem shows how you can apply cost-benefit analysis to a more specific decision about international expansion.

EZ-Rider Motorcycles is considering whether to expand into Germany, where reunification has increased market size. Public concern over air pollution may cause the government to raise gasoline taxes. If gas prices increase, EZ-Rider expects more interest in fuel-efficient transportation such as motorcycles. Thus EZ-Rider is considering setting up a motorcycle-assembly plant in the outskirts of Berlin.

EZ-Rider estimates that it will cost $850,000 to convert an existing building to motorcycle production. The workers will need training for specific jobs, at a total cost to the company of $65,000. The CEO of EZ-Rider, Dennis Popper, would have to spend a month in Berlin to organize the business and to establish relationships. He estimates the cost of this travel at $43,000. All these costs would be incurred in the next six months.

Popper sees a 60% chance that the price of gasoline in Germany will increase significantly. If this increase occurs, he believes EZ-Rider can sell enough motorcycles over the next eight years to earn profits (before considering the costs in the prior paragraph) with a present value of $1,624,000. However, if gas prices remain stable, Popper would expect to earn profits of only about $812,000. He believes that there is a 40% chance that gas prices will remain stable.

REQUIRED

1. What are the total costs of EZ-Rider's proposed expansion into Germany?
2. Compute the *expected value* of the benefits Dennis Popper expects EZ-Rider to receive if EZ-Rider expands into Germany.
3. Do the benefits outweigh the costs of expanding into Germany?

■ **SOLUTION**

REQUIREMENT 1

The total costs are as follows:

Conversion of manufacturing plant	$850,000
Work force training	65,000
Popper's trip to Berlin	43,000
Total costs	$958,000

REQUIREMENT 2

Expected value of the benefits is computed as follows:

Benefit	×	Probability	=	Expected Value
$1,624,000	×	0.60	=	$ 974,400
812,000	×	0.40	=	324,800
				$1,299,200

The *expected value* of the benefits, or profits, is $1,299,200. This means that if EZ-Rider were to be in this exact situation many times, its average benefits in the form of profits across all the situations would be $1,299,200.

Yes, the total expected benefits outweigh the costs of the expansion:

REQUIREMENT 3

Total expected benefits of expansion (from requirement 2) $1,299,200
Total costs of expansion (from requirement 1) 958,000
Net benefits of expansion .... $ 341,200

Summary of Learning Objectives

1. Distinguish between financial accounting and management accounting, and use management accounting information for decision making. Financial accounting information is used primarily by external groups such as investors, creditors, and government authorities; it focuses on past performance; and it is restricted by GAAP. Financial accounting deals primarily with the company as a whole, usually on a quarterly or annual basis. In contrast, management accounting information is used primarily by internal managers of the business. It focuses on the future, is restricted only by the cost of generating the information versus the benefits of that information, often reports on parts of the company, and is often produced on a daily, weekly, or monthly basis. Management accounting is concerned with how reports will affect employee behavior. Management accounting information is used to determine the cost of products and services, to plan and control business operations, and to value inventory and cost of goods sold for financial statements.

2. Describe the value chain and classify costs by value-chain function. The *value chain* is the sequence of activities that adds value to a firm's products or services. Value-chain functions are research and development, design, production or purchases, marketing, distribution, and customer service. Managers want to control total costs throughout the value chain as a whole. They may incur more costs in one function to reduce costs in other parts of the value chain.

3. Distinguish direct costs from indirect costs. Managers need cost data on many aspects of a business to make wise decisions. A *cost object* is anything for which a separate measurement of costs is desired. Costs that can be specifically traced to the cost object are *direct costs*. Costs that cannot be specifically traced to the cost object are *indirect costs*.

4. Distinguish among full product costs, inventoriable product costs, and period costs. *Product costs* are costs of producing (or purchasing) tangible products intended for sale. *Full product*

costs include the costs of all resources used throughout the value chain. These costs are used for internal decisions such as setting prices and do not conform to GAAP. *Inventoriable product costs* include only costs of the *production or purchases* element of the value chain, and must conform to GAAP because they are used for external financial reporting. These costs are first considered inventory (an asset), and are not expensed (as cost of goods sold) until the products are sold. *Period costs* are operating costs that are always expensed in the period in which they are incurred, and are never part of the Inventory asset account.

5. Prepare the financial statements of a manufacturing company. Manufacturers use three inventory accounts. *Materials Inventory* is the cost of materials on hand for use in production. *Work in Process Inventory* is the cost of goods that are in the manufacturing process but are not yet complete. *Finished Goods Inventory* is the cost of completed goods that have not yet been sold. Manufacturers compute cost of goods sold by adding the *cost of goods manufactured* to beginning finished goods inventory, and subtracting ending finished goods inventory.

6. Identify major trends in the business environment, and use cost-benefit analysis to make business decisions. Major trends in the business environment influencing management accounting are the shift toward a service economy, the rise of the global marketplace, the just-in-time management philosophy, and total quality management. In making business decisions, managers compare the present value of expected future costs and benefits of alternative courses of action.

7. Use reasonable standards to make ethical judgments. Ethical behavior is necessary for the orderly functioning of society and business. The Institute of Management Accountants (IMA) has developed standards to help management accountants make ethical choices. These standards require management accountants to maintain their professional competence, preserve the confidentiality of the information they handle, and act with integrity and objectivity.

Accounting Vocabulary

budget *(p. 818)*
continuous improvement
  (p. 836)
controlling *(p. 818)*
conversion costs *(p. 825)*
cost-benefit analysis
  (p. 819)
cost object *(p. 822)*
cost of goods manufactured
  (p. 829)
customer service *(p. 822)*
design *(p. 822)*
direct cost *(p. 822)*
direct labor *(p. 824)*

direct materials *(p. 824)*
distribution *(p. 822)*
factory overhead *(p. 824)*
finished goods inventory
  (p. 821)
full product costs *(p. 823)*
indirect cost *(p. 822)*
indirect labor *(p. 825)*
indirect manufacturing cost
  (p. 824)
indirect materials *(p. 825)*
inventoriable product costs
  (p. 823)
just-in-time (JIT) *(p. 834)*

manufacturing company
  (p. 820)
manufacturing overhead
  (p. 824)
marketing *(p. 822)*
materials inventory
  (p. 821)
merchandising company
  (p. 820)
period costs *(p. 823)*
planning *(p. 818)*
prime costs *(p. 825)*
production or purchases
  (p. 822)

research and development
  (R&D) *(p. 821)*
service company *(p. 820)*
throughput time *(p. 834)*
total quality management
  (TQM) *(p. 835)*
value chain *(p. 821)*
work in process inventory
  (p. 821)

Questions

1. Explain the difference between planning and control, and give an example of each.
2. Explain three distinctions between management accounting and financial accounting.
3. What are the purposes of management accounting information?
4. How do manufacturing companies differ from service firms and merchandisers? What inventory accounts does each type of company use?
5. Identify the six business functions in the value chain of a manufacturing company. To which function(s) is management accounting relevant?
6. Give three examples of cost objects and explain why managers might want information about these cost objects.
7. What is the manufacturer's counterpart to the merchandiser's purchases?
8. Give examples of direct materials and indirect materials for a home builder.
9. Identify at least six examples of manufacturing overhead costs.
10. Outline the flow of inventory costs through a manufacturing company's accounting system.
11. Distinguish between inventoriable product costs and period costs. Which is initially an asset, and which is never an asset, only an expense?
12. What costs should managers consider in deciding on the long-term sale price of a product: inventoriable product costs or full product costs? Give your reason.
13. What is the main difference between a service company's income statement and the income statements of merchandising and manufacturing companies?
14. What is the primary difference between a merchandiser's and a manufacturer's income statement?
15. Summarize the computation of cost of goods manufactured. Use any dollar amounts.
16. List and briefly explain four recent changes in the business environment.
17. Explain two ways globalization affects management accounting.
18. Once a company decides to adopt a just-in-time philosophy, what kinds of costs and benefits should it expect?
19. Why do management accountants need a code of ethics?
20. The Institute of Management Accountants' *Standards of Ethical Conduct for Management Accountants* lists four broad requirements. In your own words, list and briefly explain three.

Daily Exercises

Distinguishing financial from management accounting
(Obj. 1)

DE19-1 Do the following phrases better describe financial or management accounting?

a. Provides information mostly for decision makers inside the company
b. Much of the information has to do with the future
c. Is more concerned with proper disclosure than with how the numbers will affect users' behavior
d. Is primarily determined by an analysis of benefits and costs of the system
e. Is more concerned with objectivity and reliability than relevance
f. Focuses on providing detailed information about individual parts of the company

Classifying costs by value chain function
(Obj. 2)

DE19-2 List the six business functions in the value chain (Exhibit 19-4, page 822). Give an example of costs that Coca-Cola might incur in each function.

Classifying costs by value chain function
(Obj. 2)

DE19-3 Give an example of costs that H&R Block (tax return preparers) might incur in each of the six business functions in the value-chain. Provide another example that shows how H&R Block might deliberately decide to spend more money on one of the six business functions, in order to reduce the costs in other business functions.

Distinguishing between direct and indirect costs
(Obj. 3)

DE19-4 Consider General Motors' Saturn car manufacturing plant. Give two examples of

a. Direct materials
b. Direct labor
c. Indirect materials
d. Indirect labor
e. Other manufacturing overhead

Direct versus indirect, full versus inventoriable costs
(Obj. 3, 4)

DE19-5 Listed below are several terms relating to various cost definitions. Complete the following statements with one of these terms. You may use a term more than once, and some terms may not be used at all.

Conversion cost	Full product cost	Merchandising company
Cost object	Indirect cost	Period cost
Direct cost	Inventoriable product cost	Prime cost
Direct materials	Manufacturing company	Service company
Direct labor	Manufacturing overhead	

a. The product cost used for external reporting is called _____.
b. _____ plus _____ equals prime cost.

c. The sum of direct materials, direct labor, and manufacturing overhead is _____ for a manufacturing company.

d. _____ is included in both prime cost and conversion cost.

e. _____ includes all the elements of the value-chain and is used for internal decisions such as setting long-run average selling prices.

f. _____ is initially considered an asset, and is not expensed until the related products are sold.

DE19-6 Consider Coca-Cola, Uniglobe Travel Agency, and Wal-Mart. For each company, answer the following questions.

1. Is this a service company, a merchandiser, or a manufacturer?
2. What is the primary output the company sells to customers?
3. What inventory accounts would this company have on its balance sheet?
4. Does this company have any inventoriable product costs? If so, how would you compute these costs?

Inventoriable costs; balance sheets of service, merchandising and manufacturing companies
(Obj. 4, 5)

DE19-7 ◄▬ *Link Back to Chapter 5.* Refer to Exhibit 19-8 on page 827. What would be Apex's beginning inventory if revenues, purchases and freight-in, and ending inventory are all the same as in Exhibit 19-8, but gross margin is $50,000 rather than $43,500?

Preparing the cost of goods sold section of a merchandiser's income statement
(Obj. 5)

DE19-8 ◄▬ *Link Back to Chapter 5.* Given the following information for Pym's, a discount retailer of menswear, compute the cost of goods sold.

Prepare the cost of goods sold section of a merchandiser's income statement
(Obj. 5)

Sales salaries......................	$1,000	Delivery expenses..............	$ 500
Freight-in	2,500	Purchases...........................	30,000
Ending inventory..............	5,000	Revenues	60,000
Marketing expenses	6,000	Beginning inventory..........	3,000

DE19-9 Look at Exhibit 19-9 (page 828). What would be Top-Flight's cost of goods sold and operating income if the cost of goods manufactured were $50,000 rather than $42,000? (Other costs and revenues remain the same as in Exhibit 19-9.)

Income statement for a manufacturing company
(Obj. 5)

DE19-10 Turn to Exhibit 19-10 (page 829). If direct material purchases were $30,000 rather than $27,000, what would be the cost of direct materials used and the cost of goods manufactured? (Other costs remain the same as in Exhibit 19-10.)

Computing the cost of goods manufactured
(Obj. 5)

DE19-11 Jell's manufactures women's plastic sandals. Suppose the company's March records include the following items. What is Jell's total manufacturing overhead cost in March?

Computing manufacturing overhead
(Obj. 5)

Ink for printing shoe boxes	$ 100	Company president's salary	$15,000
Depreciation expense on company		Plant foreman's salary	2,000
cars used by sales force	3,000	Plant janitor's salary	1,000
Plant depreciation expense...................	10,000	Oil for manufacturing equipment.........	25
Interest expense...................................	1,500	Plastic for shoes	50,000

DE19-12 You are a new accounting intern at Mom's Spaghetti Sauce, Inc. Your boss gives you the following information and asks you to compute direct materials used.

Computing direct materials used
(Obj. 5)

Purchases of direct materials	$23,000
Freight-in..	200
Freight-out	1,000
Ending inventory of direct materials	1,500
Beginning inventory of direct materials	4,000

DE19-13 Use Exhibit 19-10 (page 829) and the Learning Tip on page 830 to explain the differences between *manufacturing costs* and the *cost of goods manufactured.* How much are the *manufacturing costs?* How much is the *cost of goods manufactured?* Explain the difference between these two amounts.

Explaining the cost of goods manufactured schedule
(Obj. 5)

DE19-14 The current asset sections of three companies' balance sheets follow. Which company is a service company? Which is a merchandiser? Which is a manufacturer? How can you tell?

Apco		Bibco		Cotco	
Cash	$ 2,000	Cash	$3,000	Cash	$ 2,500
Accounts receivable	5,000	Accounts receivable	6,000	Accounts receivable	5,500
Materials inventory	1,000	Prepaid expenses	500	Inventory	8,000
Work in process	800	Total	$9,500	Prepaid expenses	300
Finished goods	4,000			Total	$16,300
Total	$12,800				

DE19-15 Becky Barth is an accounting intern at Zip-Z's Zippers, a manufacturing company that has just adopted JIT. Becky says, "Firms that adopt JIT must make sure they get on-time deliveries of raw materials. They can't afford to wait for a supplier that's late. Shouldn't we line up even more suppliers than we have now, just to make sure that we can always get raw materials when we need them?" Reply to Becky Barth.

DE19-16 Would JIT be more appropriate for Lay-Dee's, a manufacturer of trendy womenswear, or Mouton-Rothschild, a French winemaker specializing in fine red wines? Explain.

DE19-17 Consider the cost-benefit analysis for the GE quality program discussed on page 835. Suppose that GE's managers now estimate a 90% chance that the projects will yield an extra $20 million in benefits, and only a 10% chance that the projects will yield an extra $100 million. What is the expected value of the additional benefits *now?* Assuming total costs remain $200 million, does this change your mind about whether the quality program is a worthwhile investment?

DE19-18 Explain the necessity for each of the four broad ethical standards in the Institute of Management Accountants' *Standards of Ethical Conduct for Management Accountants* (Exhibit 19-12, page 837).

DE19-19 The Institute of Management Accountants' *Standards of Ethical Conduct for Management Accountants* (Exhibit 19-12, page 837) require management accountants to meet standards regarding

- Competence   • Confidentiality   • Integrity   • Objectivity

Consider each of the following situations. Which guidelines are violated in each situation?

a. You see that others take home office stationery and supplies for personal use. As a new employee you do the same thing, assuming that this is a "perk" of your new job.

b. You are very appreciative that one of your company's key suppliers is a sponsor of your son's baseball team. To show your gratitude, you provide another parent who works for the supplier with details of a contract that your firm is soon going to put out for bid.

c. You failed to read the detailed specifications of a new payroll accounting package that you asked your company to purchase. After it is installed, you are surprised to find out that it is incompatible with some of the older accounting software on which your firm still relies.

d. You do not provide top management with the detailed job descriptions they requested, because you fear that management may use this information to cut a position from your department.

e. While attending a conference on the latest management accounting software, you decide to skip the afternoon session and spend the time by the hotel pool.

Exercises

E19-1 Listed below are several terms relating to the functions of managers and the differences between financial and management accounting. Complete the following statements with one of these terms. You may use a term more than once, and some terms may not be used at all.

Budget	Creditors	Managers	Planning
Controlling	Financial accounting	Management accounting	Shareholders

a. _____ are decision makers inside a company.

b. _____ provides information on a company's past performance.

c. When managers evaluate the company's performance compared to the plan, they are performing the _____ role of management.

d. Companies must follow GAAP in their _____ systems.

e. _____ systems are not restricted by GAAP, but are determined by comparing the costs versus the benefits of the system.

f. A quantitative expression of a plan (often in dollar terms) is called a _____.

g. Choosing goals and the means to achieve them is the _____ function of management.

Value chain, direct and indirect costs, inventoriable costs
(Obj. 2, 3, 4)

E19-2 Suppose Dell Computer provides the following information for its costs last month (all numbers in hundreds of thousands):

Hard drives	$35	Salaries of telephone salespeople....	$ 4
Rearrange production process		Depreciation on manufacturing	
to accommodate new robot	2	plant and equipment	52
Assembly-line workers' wages	10	Exterior case for computer	6
Technical support hotline for		Salaries of scientists who developed	
customer support after purchase...	3	new lightweight laptop model.....	12
1-800 (toll-free) line for telephoned		Delivery expense via Airborne	
customer orders	1	air freight	7

REQUIRED

1. Use the following format to classify each of these costs according to its place in the value chain. (*Hint:* You should have at least one cost in each value chain function.)

Design of Products, Services, or R&D	Production			Marketing	Distribution	Customer Service
	Direct Materials	Direct Labor	Manufacturing Overhead			

2. Compute the total costs for each value-chain category.

3. How much are the total inventoriable product costs?

Value chain, inventoriable costs
(Obj. 2, 4)

E19-3 Suppose Dayton-Hudson, a department store with branches nationwide, incurred the following costs at its Charleston, South Carolina, store.

Rearranging store layout	$ 1,500	Salespersons' salaries	$ 8,000
Newspaper advertisements	10,000	Customer complaint	
Depreciation expense on		department	800
delivery trucks	2,000	Research to determine whether	
Payment to consultant for advice		store should add a new travel	
on location of new store	2,500	agency service	500
Freight-in	3,000	Purchases of merchandise........	40,000

REQUIRED

1. Use the following format to classify each of these costs according to its place in the value chain.

Design of Products, Services, or R&D	Purchases of Merchandise Inventory	Marketing	Distribution	Customer Service

2. Compute the total costs for each value-chain category.

3. How much are the total inventoriable product costs?

Service, merchandising, and manufacturing companies and their inventories
(Obj. 5)

E19-4 Listed below are several terms relating to service, merchandising, and manufacturing firms and their inventories. Complete the following statements with one of these terms. You may use a term more than once, and some terms may not be used at all.

Finished goods inventory	Inventory (merchandise)	Service companies
Manufacturing companies	Merchandising companies	Work in process inventory
Materials inventory		

a. _____ resell products they previously purchased ready-made from suppliers.

b. _____ produce their own inventory.

c. _____ typically have a single category of inventory.

d. _____ use their work force and equipment to transform raw materials into new finished products.

e. Broyhill, a company based in North Carolina, makes furniture. Partially completed sofas would be _____. Completed sofas that remain unsold in their warehouse would be _____. Fabric and wood would be _____.

f. _____ do not have tangible products intended for sale.

g. For Post Cereals Co., corn, cardboard boxes, and waxed paper liners would be _____.

Reporting current assets
(Obj. 5)

E19-5 Consider the following selected amounts and account balances of Jax Fax:

Cost of goods sold	$101,000	Prepaid expenses	$ 6,000
Direct labor	47,000	Marketing expense	39,000
Direct materials	25,000	Work in process inventory	42,000
Accounts receivable	75,000	Manufacturing overhead	26,000
Cash	19,000	Finished goods inventory	72,000
Cost of goods manufactured	94,000	Materials inventory	17,000

Show how Jax Fax would report current assets on the balance sheet. Not all data are used. Is Jax Fax a service company, a merchandiser, or a manufacturer? How do you know?

Computing cost of goods manufactured
and cost of goods sold
(Obj. 4, 5)

E19-6 Compute cost of goods manufactured and cost of goods sold from the following amounts:

	Beginning of Year	End of Year		Beginning of Year	End of Year
Materials inventory	$22,000	$28,000	Depreciation—plant building		
Work in process inventory	38,000	30,000	and equipment		$16,000
Finished goods inventory	18,000	25,000	Repairs and maintenance—plant		4,000
Purchases of raw materials		78,000	Marketing expenses		77,000
Direct labor		82,000	General and administrative expenses		29,000
Indirect labor		15,000	Income tax expense		30,000
Insurance on plant		9,000			

Preparing a manufacturer's income
statement (Obj. 5)

E19-7 Prepare an income statement for the company in Exercise 19-6. Assume that it sold 27,000 units of its product at a price of $14 during the current year.

Computing gross margin for a manu-
facturer
(Obj. 5)

E19-8 Supply the missing amounts from the following computation of gross margin:

Sales revenue			$437,000
Cost of goods sold:			
Beginning finished goods inventory		$ 91,000	
Cost of goods manufactured:			
Beginning work in process inventory		$ 52,000	
Direct materials used	$64,000		
Direct labor	X		
Manufacturing overhead	51,000		
Total manufacturing costs incurred during the period		226,000	
Total manufacturing costs to account for		X	
Ending work in process inventory		(40,000)	
Cost of goods manufactured		X	
Cost of goods available for sale		X	
Ending finished goods inventory		(107,000)	
Cost of goods sold			X
Gross margin			$ X

Understanding the modern business
environment
(Obj. 6)

E19-9 Listed below are several terms relating to the modern business environment. Complete the following statements with one of these terms. You may use a term more than once, and some terms may not be used at all.

Expected value	JIT	Present value
Future	North American Free Trade	Shift to service economy
Future value	Agreement (NAFTA)	Throughput time
Globalization	Present	TQM

a. Because we cannot foresee the future, the amounts of costs and benefits to be incurred in the future are not known exactly. To account for this uncertainty, we compute the _____ by multiplying the probability of each outcome by the dollar value of that outcome.

b. Firms adopting _____ report sharp reductions in inventory.

c. To make a cost-benefit decision today, we must find the _____ of the costs and benefits that are incurred in the future.

d. The goal of _____ is to delight customers. The path to delighting customers is providing them with superior products and services by eliminating defects and waste throughout the value chain.

e. Most of the costs of adopting JIT, expanding into a foreign market, or improving quality are incurred in the _____, but most of the benefits occur in the _____.

f. _____ is the time between buying raw materials and selling the finished products.

g. The main purpose of _____ is to loosen trade restrictions and promote trade among the United States, Canada, and Mexico.

E19-10 Jazzy DJ's manufactures casual menswear. Kevin Jeffries, the CEO, is trying to decide whether he should ask the plant to adopt a just-in-time (JIT) philosophy. He expects that in present-value terms, adopting JIT would save $113,000 in warehousing expenses, and $67,800 in spoilage costs.

Costs and benefits of adopting JIT
(Obj. 6)

Kevin also expects that adopting JIT will require several one-time up-front expenditures: (1) $27,000 for an employee training program, (2) $54,000 to streamline the plant's production process, and (3) $8,000 to identify suppliers that will guarantee zero defects and on-time delivery.

REQUIRED

1. What are the total costs of adopting the JIT approach?
2. What are the total benefits of adopting JIT?
3. Should Jazzy DJ's adopt JIT? Why or why not?

E19-11 For a little over a year, Susan Cheon has been the assistant controller for Caltronics, a manufacturer of high-end stereo equipment. Ted Branson, the senior bookkeeper, called in sick this week. Susan temporarily took over Ted's duties, which include maintaining the petty cash fund. She found a shortage and confronted Ted when he returned to work. Ted admitted that he occasionally took advantage of his access to petty cash in order to pay for his lunch and other small expenses. Susan estimated that the amounts have added up to over $2,000. Susan had earlier wondered about Ted's control over the petty cash fund. However, she had not followed up on her concern because Ted was well liked and she regarded him as hard working and loyal.

Ethics in management accounting
(Obj. 7)

REQUIRED

1. What should Susan do?
2. Would you change your answer to the previous question in each of the following situations?
   a. Ted has worked for Caltronics for ten years, and is now only six months from retirement. If Susan reports the theft, Ted will probably be fired and lose his pension.
   b. Ted has worked at Caltronics for only eight months.

CHALLENGE EXERCISE

E19-12 Nantucket Breezes manufactures and sells a new line of sun-protection clothing. Unfortunately, Nantucket suffered serious hurricane damage in October. The hurricane partially destroyed—and completely jumbled—the accounting records for the month of October. Nantucket Breezes has hired you to help figure out the missing pieces of the accounting puzzle.

Flow of costs through manufacturing companies
(Obj. 4, 5)

Accounts payable, October 1	$ 3,000	Work in process inventory, October 31	$ 1,000
Direct materials used in October	8,000	Finished goods inventory, October 1	4,000
Accounts payable, October 31	4,800	Direct labor in October	3,000
Accounts receivable, October 31	6,000	Purchases of direct materials in	
Direct materials inventory,		October	9,000
October 31	2,000	Work in process inventory, October 1	0
Manufacturing overhead in		Revenues in October	27,000
October	7,000	Accounts receivable, October 1	2,000
Gross margin in October	9,300		

Find the following amounts:

REQUIRED

a. Cost of goods sold in October

b. Beginning direct materials inventory

c. Ending finished goods inventory

(*Hint:* You may find Panel B of Exhibit 19-10 helpful.)

Beyond the Numbers

Inventoriable costs
(Obj. 3)

BN19-1 Utilities and property taxes on Coca-Cola's executive headquarters in Atlanta are not directly traceable to individual containers of Coca-Cola syrup produced by a plant in Ohio. Are these property taxes part of manufacturing overhead? Is depreciation on the automobiles used by the sales force part of manufacturing overhead? How about interest expense on long-term debt issued primarily to finance the construction of a new plant?

Ethics
(Obj. 7)

BN19-2 Edward Michaels is the management accountant for PromptCare, Inc., which operates emergency medical clinics in several states. Based largely on Michaels' proposal, PromptCare is developing an intranet communication system to improve the accounting and inventory control at each location. (An *intranet* system is an internal network that uses Internet technology to link company workers.)

Michaels is responsible for researching and selecting an intranet software provider. One provider, Network Specialists, has offered Michaels two tickets and hotel accommodations for the Master's Golf Tournament in Augusta. Network Specialists is hosting a reception one evening for its top salespersons and customers. Network Specialists suggests that if Michaels attends the reception, he will learn more about the company and get valuable feedback from current customers. However, Michaels is concerned that Network Specialists may try to obtain information about PromptCare that could give Network Specialists an edge in preparing its bid for developing the PromptCare system.

Consider the alternatives open to Michaels. Use the IMA standards in Exhibit 19-12 to evaluate the consequences of each alternative. What would you do? Can you think of a compromise?

ETHICAL ISSUE

Ethics
(Obj. 7)

◀▥▥ *Link Back to Chapter* 7. Ricardo Valencia recently resigned his position as controller for Tom White Automotive, a small, struggling foreign car dealer in Austin, Texas. Ricardo has just started a new job as controller for Mueller Imports, a much larger dealer for the same car manufacturer. Demand for this particular make of car is exploding, and the manufacturer cannot produce enough to satisfy demand. The manufacturer's regional sales managers are each given a certain number of cars. Each sales manager then decides how to divide the cars among the independently owned dealerships in the region. Since most dealerships can sell every car they receive, the key is getting a large number of cars from the manufacturer's regional sales manager.

Ricardo's former employer, White Automotive, received only about 25 cars a month. Consequently, the dealership was not very profitable.

Ricardo is surprised to learn that his new employer, Mueller Imports, receives over 200 cars a month. Ricardo soon gets another surprise. Every couple of months, a local jeweler bills the dealer $5,000 for "miscellaneous services." Franz Mueller, the owner of the dealership, personally approves payment of these invoices, noting that each invoice is a "selling expense." From casual conversations with a salesperson, Ricardo learns that Mueller frequently gives Rolex watches to the manufacturer's regional sales manager and other sales executives. Before talking to anyone about this, Ricardo decides to work through his ethical dilemma using the following framework from Chapter 7.

1. List the facts.
2. Identify the ethical issues.
3. Specify the alternatives.
4. Identify the people involved.
5. Assess the possible consequences.
6. Make a decision.

Put yourself in Ricardo's place and complete the framework.

Problems (GROUP A)

*Value chain, direct and indirect costs,
inventoriable costs
(Obj. 2, 3, 4)*

P19-1A Reynolda Foods produces canned chicken à la king—chicken, mushrooms, and bell peppers in a cream sauce. The production process starts with raw chicken that workers debone. Cream sauce is prepared, the chicken is cooked, and the two are combined with the vegetables. Because chickens naturally vary in salt content, the amount of salt added varies from batch to batch.

Reynolda incurs the following costs (in thousands):

Mushrooms and peppers	$ 500	Plant utilities..	$ 900
Production costs of "cents-off" store		Depreciation on plant and equipment	2,500
coupons for customers...............................	600	Payment to chef for developing new	
Delivery truck drivers' wages	250	low-fat recipe..	1,200
Cream...	1,300	Salt..	20
Sales commissions......................................	400	Replace products with expired dates	
Plant janitors' wages	1,000	upon customer complaint	50
Wages of workers who debone chicken	10,000	Rearranging plant layout to smooth	
Customer hotline for recipes and problems ...	200	production flow	1,100
Depreciation on delivery truck.......................	150	Chicken	18,000
Freight-in	1,500	Total	$39,670

REQUIRED

1. Use the following format to classify each of these costs according to its place in the value chain. (*Hint:* You should have at least one cost in each value chain function.)

Design of Products or R&D	Processes	Production			Marketing	Distribution	Customer Service
		Direct Materials	Direct Labor	Manufacturing Overhead			

2. Compute the total costs for each value chain category.
3. How much are the total inventoriable product costs?
4. How much are the prime costs?
5. How much are the conversion costs?

P19-2A *Part One:* In 19X7, Kathleen Bisset opened Neon Nails Boutique, a small retail boutique dedicated solely to selling nail polish and other nail care accessories. On December 31, 19X8, her accounting records show the following:

Preparing financial statements for merchandising and manufacturing companies (Obj. 4, 5)

Inventory on December 31, 19X8	$ 9,850
Inventory on January 1, 19X8................	10,700
Sales revenue	47,000
Utilities for boutique.............................	2,450
Rent for boutique	4,000
Sales commissions	1,500
Purchases of merchandise.....................	27,000

Prepare an income statement for Neon Nails Boutique, a merchandiser.

REQUIRED

Part Two: Neon Nails Boutique became so successful that Kathleen Bisset decided to manufacture her own brand of nail polish—Nite-Glo Neon Nails. At the end of December 19X9, her accounting records show

Sales salaries	$ 4,500	Work in process inventory,	
Plant janitorial services	1,250	December 31, 19X9..............	$ 350
Direct labor	17,500	Finished goods inventory,	
Direct material purchases........	30,000	December 31, 19X8..............	0
Rent on manufacturing plant...	9,000	Finished goods inventory,	
Direct materials inventory,		December 31, 19X9..............	5,700
December 31, 19X8..............	12,000	Sales revenue	97,450
Direct materials inventory,		Customer service hotline.........	1,000
December 31, 19X9..............	8,750	Utilities for plant......................	3,400
Work in process inventory,		Delivery expense	1,500
December 31, 19X8..............	0		

1. Prepare a schedule of cost of goods manufactured for Nite-Glo Neon Nails Manufacturing.
2. Prepare an income statement for Nite-Glo Neon Nails Manufacturing.

REQUIRED

3. How does the format of the income statement for Nite-Glo Neon Nails Manufacturing differ from the income statement of Neon Nails Boutique?

Part Three: Show the ending inventories that would appear on the balance sheet of

1. Neon Nails Boutique at December 31, 19X8.
2. Nite-Glo Neon Nails Manufacturing at December 31, 19X9.

Preparing financial statements for a manufacturer
(Obj. 5)

P19-3A Certain item descriptions and amounts are missing from the monthly schedule of cost of goods manufactured and income statement of Yazumaki Manufacturing Company. Fill in the missing items.

_____ MANUFACTURING COMPANY		
_____		
_____ June 30, 19X9		
Beginning _____		$ 18,000
Direct _____ :		
Beginning inventory of materials	$ X	
Purchases of materials	62,000	
_____	82,000	
Ending materials inventory	(23,000)	
Direct _____		$ X
Direct _____		X
Manufacturing overhead		40,000
Total _____ costs _____		166,000
Total _____ costs _____		X
Ending _____		(30,000)
_____		$ X

_____ MANUFACTURING COMPANY		
_____		
_____ June 30, 19X9		
Sales revenue		$ X
Cost of goods sold:		
Beginning _____	$101,000	
_____	X	
Cost of goods _____	X	
Ending _____	X	
Cost of goods sold		197,000
Gross Margin		230,000
_____ expenses:		
Marketing expense	99,000	
Administrative expense	X	154,000
_____ income		$ X

TQM, cost-benefit analysis, expected value
(Obj. 6)

P19-4A Eastclox manufactures fine watches. The company is having trouble with one of its watches. If the parts are not engineered to exact specifications, the watch will not operate. Even a speck of dust under the crystal causes the watch to stop. About half the time, Eastclox employees find the defects while the watch is still on the production line. These watches are immediately reworked in the plant. When a defect escapes detection until the customer complains, Eastclox repairs the watch.

Eastclox CEO Rajiv Nanda has just returned from a seminar on total quality management (TQM). He forms a team to attack this quality problem. The team includes the plant engineer, the production foreman, the plant's watch repair specialist, the marketing director, and the management accountant.

Three months later, the team proposes a major project to *prevent* these quality problems. Eastclox accountant Joy Reeve reports that implementing the team's proposal will require Eastclox to spend the following over the next six months:

a. $45,000 to redesign the watch so it still operates even with small deviations from specified part sizes

b. $80,000 for Eastclox scientists to develop a completely new watch mechanism that is tolerant of dust particles

The project team is unsure whether this investment will pay off. If the effort fixes the problem, Reeve expects the following to occur:

a. The plant will have no defective watches to rework. The present value of this savings is $44,380.

b. Fewer watches will fail after customer use. The present value of the savings from fewer warranty repairs is $101,440.

c. A reputation for higher quality will increase sales, which in turn will increase the present value of profits by $126,800.

However, if this project is not successful, there will be no cost savings and no additional sales. The team predicts that there is a 60% chance that the project will succeed, and a 40% chance that it will fail.

REQUIRED

1. If the quality improvement project succeeds, what is the dollar amount of the benefits?
2. Should Eastclox undertake this project? Why or why not? Show supporting calculations.

P19-5A   Problem 19-4A provided both quantitative and qualitative information about Eastclox's quality project, and asked you to perform a *quantitative* analysis to help Eastclox managers decide whether to embark on the quality project. Now consider some *qualitative* factors in Eastclox's quality improvement project.

Value chain, TQM
(Obj. 2, 6)

REQUIRED

1. Why did Rajiv Nanda create a team to attack this quality problem, rather than assigning the task to one person? Consider each piece of cost/benefit information reported by management accountant Joy Reeve. Which person on the team is most likely to have contributed each item? (*Hint:* Which team member is likely to have the most information about each cost or benefit?)
2. Classify the following costs into one of the six value chain business functions:
   a. $45,000 cost to redesign the watch so it still operates even with small deviations from specified part sizes
   b. $80,000 cost to develop a completely new watch mechanism that is more tolerant of dust particles
   c. $44,380 to rework watches identified as defective while still in the factory
   d. $101,440 to make warranty repairs on the watches that customers have returned as defective
3. The Eastclox problem illustrates how managers make trade-offs across different business functions in the value chain. Which of the six value chain functions are involved in the trade-offs proposed by the quality improvement team? What specific trade-offs do they propose? In what other situations are these trade-offs likely to be effective?

P19-6A   Cost-benefit analysis applies to many kinds of decisions. This problem applies cost-benefit analysis to a decision about international expansion, similar to the chapter summary review problem on page 838.

Globalization, cost-benefit analysis
(Obj. 6)

Mr. Greenjeans, a manufacturer of designer-label jeans, is trying to decide whether to expand production and sales into Russia. CEO Ralph Green has contacted Denis Pankratov in Moscow to estimate the costs and benefits of the proposed expansion. Pankratov's market research indicates that Russian consumers love American products, especially jeans. Excluding the one-time up-front costs outlined below, Pankratov estimates that Mr. Greenjeans could sell enough jeans to earn profit with a present value of $811,125 (in U.S. dollars).

Pankratov believes that within two months an existing plant could be converted at a cost of $320,000. Mr. Greenjeans will have to advertise at an estimated cost of $55,000. To cut through the Russian red tape, Ralph Green will have to go to Moscow for two months to acquire the license to operate and to oversee renovation of the plant and hiring of employees. Pankratov estimates Green's expenses for these two months will amount to $73,000. Finally, if Mr. Greenjeans expands into Russia, Ralph Green will retain Denis Pankratov's consulting service for a fee of $20,000.

REQUIRED

1. Would you recommend that Mr. Greenjeans expand into Russia? Give your reason, showing supporting calculations.
2. What other factors should Ralph Green consider when making this decision?

P19-7A   Consider Mr. Greenjeans' proposed expansion into Russia in Problem 19-6A. Denis Pankratov revises his estimate of the profits Mr. Greenjeans is likely to earn. Specifically, Pankratov now sees only a 30% chance that Mr. Greenjeans will sell enough jeans to earn the $811,125 profit. He now thinks there is a 70% chance that Mr. Greenjeans will make only $162,225 in profit.

Globalization, cost-benefit analysis, expected value
(Obj. 6)

1. Compute the expected value of the benefits, or profits of expanding into Russia.
2. Would you recommend that Mr. Greenjeans expand into Russia? Why or why not? Show your calculations.

Ethics
(Obj. 7)

P19-8A Christine Gatewood is the new controller for Cannon Software, Inc., which develops and sells computer games. Shortly before the December 31 fiscal year end, Bert Ryder, the company president, asks Gatewood how things look for the year-end numbers. He is not happy to learn that earnings growth may be below 20% for the first time in the company's five-year history. Ryder explains that financial analysts have again predicted a 20% earnings growth for the company and that he does not intend to disappoint them. He suggests that Gatewood talk to the assistant controller, who could explain how the previous controller dealt with this situation. The assistant controller suggests the following strategies:

a. Delay the year-end closing a few days into January of the next year, so that some of next year's sales are included as this year's sales.
b. Reduce the allowance for bad debts (and bad debts expense), given the company's continued strong performance.
c. Record as sales certain goods awaiting sale that are held in a public warehouse.
d. Postpone routine monthly maintenance expenditures from December to January.
e. Persuade suppliers to postpone billing us until January 1.

Which of these suggested strategies are inconsistent with IMA standards? What should Gatewood do if Ryder insists that she follow all of these suggestions?

Problems (GROUP B)

Value chain, direct versus indirect costs,
inventoriable costs
(Obj. 2, 3, 4)

P19-1B Dairybell, Inc. produces small batches of super-premium ice cream. The ice cream base is prepared, special ingredients such as nuts and fruit are added, and the mixture is frozen. Because milk and cream naturally vary in salt content, the amount of salt added varies from batch to batch. Dairybell incurs the following costs:

Customer hotline for quality problems	$ 350	Depreciation on delivery van	$ 250
Redesign the production process to keep nuts in bigger chunks	750	Milk	5,000
		Wages of production-line workers	10,000
Replacements for products past expiration date (upon customer complaint)	75	Wages of plant maintenance workers	900
		Sales force salaries	400
Salt	10	Cream	8,000
Payment to food scientist for developing new recipe with much longer shelf-life	1,500	Cost of advertisements	350
		Delivery drivers' wages	450
Depreciation expense on plant and equipment	1,800	Nuts and fruits	3,500
Insurance on plant	800	Total	$35,735
Freight-in	1,600		

1. Use the following format to classify each of these costs according to its place in the value chain. (*Hint:* You should have at least one cost in each value chain function.)

	Design of Products or Processes	Production					
R&D		Direct Materials	Direct Labor	Manufacturing Overhead	Marketing	Distribution	Customer Service

2. Compute the total costs for each category.
3. How much are the total inventoriable product costs?
4. How much are the prime costs?
5. How much are the conversion costs?

Preparing financial statements for
merchandising and manufacturing
companies
(Obj. 4, 5)

P19-2B *Part One:* On January 1, 19X4, Jarrod Beaudrot opened Beaudrot's Auto Care Products, a small retail store dedicated solely to selling car polish, bug cleaner, chamois, and other auto care accessories. On December 31, 19X4, his accounting records show the following:

Store rent......................	$ 4,500	Sales revenue	$74,000
Sales salaries	3,500	Store utilities	1,950
Freight-in.........................	750	Purchases of merchandise........	42,000
Inventory on December		Inventory on January 1, 19X4 ...	12,700
31, 19X4	8,750	Advertising expense..................	2,300

REQUIRED

Prepare an income statement for Beaudrot's Auto Care Products, a merchandiser.

Part Two: Beaudrot's Auto Care Products became so successful that Jarrod Beaudrot decided to manufacture his own special brand of bug cleaner—Bugz-B-Gone. At the end of December 19X9, his accounting records show

Finished goods inventory,		Rent on manufacturing plant...	$ 9,000
December 31, 19X9............	$ 4,000	Finished goods inventory,	
Work in process inventory,		December 31, 19X8............	0
December 31, 19X9............	2,750	Depreciation expense on	
Direct materials inventory,		delivery trucks	2,500
December 31, 19X9............	7,750	Depreciation expense on	
R&D for plastic squirt		manufacturing equipment...	4,700
container............................	3,700	Work in process inventory,	
Sales commissions..................	6,500	December 31, 19X8............	0
Utilities for plant....................	2,900	Sales revenue..........................	126,450
Plant janitorial services	1,750	Customer warranty refunds...	1,500
Direct labor	23,500	Direct materials inventory,	
Direct material purchases......	37,000	December 31, 19X8............	15,000

REQUIRED

1. Prepare a schedule of cost of goods manufactured for Bugz-B-Gone Manufacturing.
2. Prepare an income statement for Bugz-B-Gone Manufacturing.
3. How does the format of the income statement for Bugz-B-Gone Manufacturing differ from the income statement of Beaudrot's Auto Care Products?

Part Three: Show the ending inventories that would appear on the Balance Sheet of
1. Beaudrot's Auto Care Products at December 31, 19X4.
2. Bugz-B-Gone Manufacturing at December 31, 19X9.

P19-3B Certain item descriptions and amounts are missing from the monthly schedule of cost of goods manufactured and income statement of Eastpoint Manufacturing Company. Fill in the missing items. (This problem is continued on the next page.)

Preparing financial statements for a manufacturer
(Obj. 5)

MANUFACTURING COMPANY		
April 30, 19X8		
_____ work in process inventory		$ 15,000
Direct materials used:		
_____ materials _____	$ X	
_____ of materials	62,000	
_____	75,000	
_____ materials _____	(23,000)	
Direct _____	$ X	
Direct _____	68,000	
Manufacturing overhead	X	
Total _____ costs _____		X
Total _____ costs _____		175,000
_____ work in process inventory		X
_____		$143,000

_____ MANUFACTURING COMPANY		
_____		
_____ April 30, 19X8		
_____ revenue		$445,000
_____:		
Beginning _____	$ X	
	X	
_____		
Cost of goods _____	X	
Ending _____	(67,000)	
Cost of goods sold		$ X
_____		248,000
_____ expenses:		
Marketing expenses	X	
Administrative expenses	$64,000	X
_____		$ 81,000

P19-4B Tower, Inc., manufactures computer disk drives. It sells these disk drives to other manufacturers, which use them in assembling computers. Tower is having trouble with its new DVD drive. If the parts are not engineered to exact specifications, the drive will not operate. About half the time, Tower employees find these defects while the disk drive is still on the production line. These drives are immediately reworked in the plant. Otherwise, Tower's customers do not identify the problem until they are installing the disk drives they've purchased from Tower. Customers return defective disk drives for replacement under warranty, and they have also complained that after they install the disk drive, the drive's connector (which plugs into the computer system board) often shakes loose while the computer is assembled. The customer must then reassemble the computer after fixing the loose connection.

Tower CEO Bill Dram has just returned from a seminar on total quality management (TQM). He forms a team to attack these quality problems. The team includes the plant engineer, the production foreman, a customer service representative, the marketing director, and the management accountant.

Three months later, the team proposes a major project to *prevent* these quality problems. Tower's accountant Holly Adams reports that implementing the team's proposal will require Tower to spend the following over the next three months:

a. $180,000 for Tower research scientists to develop a completely new disk drive that still operates even with small deviations from specified part sizes

b. $70,000 for company engineers to redesign the connector so that it is more tolerant to rough treatment

The project team is unsure whether this investment will pay off. If the effort fixes the problem, Adams expects

a. A reputation for higher quality will increase sales, which in turn will increase the present value of profits by $200,442.

b. Fewer disk drives will fail after customer use. The present value of the savings from fewer warranty repairs is $163,998.

c. The plant will have fewer defective disk drives to rework. The present value of this savings is $100,221.

However, if this project is not successful, there will be no cost savings and no additional sales. The team predicts a 70% chance that the project will succeed, and a 30% chance it will fail.

1. If the quality improvement project succeeds, what is the dollar amount of the benefits?

2. Should Tower undertake this project? Why or why not? Show supporting calculations.

P19-5B Problem 19-4B provided both quantitative and qualitative information about Tower's quality project, and asked you to perform a *quantitative* analysis to help Tower's managers decide whether to embark on the quality project. Now consider some *qualitative* factors in Tower's quality improvement project.

1. Why did Bill Dram create a team to attack this quality problem, rather than assigning the task to one person? Consider each piece of cost/benefit information reported by management accountant Holly Adams. Which person on the team is most likely to have contributed each item? (*Hint:* Which team member is likely to have the most information about each cost or benefit?)

2. Classify the following amounts into one of the six value-chain business functions.
   a. $180,000 cost to develop the completely new disk drive that still operates even with small deviations from specified part sizes
   b. $70,000 cost to redesign the connector so that it is more tolerant of rough treatment
   c. $163,998 for warranty repairs on disk drives that customers have returned as defective
   d. $100,221 to rework disk drives identified as defective while still in the factory

3. This problem illustrates how Tower can make trade-offs across different business functions in the value chain. Which of the six value-chain functions are involved in the trade-offs proposed by the quality improvement team? What specific trade-offs do they propose? In what other situations are these trade-offs likely to be effective?

P19-6B Cost-benefit analysis applies to many kinds of decisions. This problem applies cost-benefit analysis to a decision about international expansion, similar to the chapter summary review problem on page 838.

Globalization, cost-benefit analysis (Obj. 6)

Chocolate D'Lites is a new chain that sells chocolate chunk cookies baked fresh in the store. CEO Debbie Fielding is trying to decide whether to expand into Europe. She has contacted Arabella Grimaldi in Brussels to estimate the costs and benefits of an initial store in Brussels. Grimaldi's market research indicates that European consumers love chocolate. Her initial taste tests show they very much enjoyed Chocolate D'Lites' products.

Excluding the one-time up-front costs outlined below, Grimaldi estimates that Chocolate D'Lites could sell enough cookies to earn profit with a present value of $255,145 (in U.S. dollars). Grimaldi believes that within two months a store could be ready in Brussels, at a cost of $120,000. Fielding would have to go to Brussels for two months to acquire the license to operate, and to oversee renovation of the store and hiring of the employees. Grimaldi estimates that Fielding's expenses for these two months will amount to $36,000. Chocolate D'Lites will also have to advertise at an estimated total cost of $93,000. Finally, if Chocolate D'Lites expands into Belgium, Fielding will retain Arabella Grimaldi's consulting service, for a fee of $12,000.

Would you recommend that Chocolate D'Lites expand into Europe? Give your reason, showing supporting calculations.

REQUIRED

P19-7B Consider Chocolate D'Lites' proposed expansion into Europe in Problem 19-6B. Arabella Grimaldi revises her estimates of the profits Chocolate D'Lites is likely to earn. Specifically, Grimaldi sees a 40% chance that Chocolate D'Lites will earn $255,145 in profit. She now thinks there is a 60% chance that Chocolate D'Lites will earn $463,900 in profit.

Globalization, cost-benefit analysis, expected value (Obj. 6)

1. Compute the expected value of the benefits (profits) from the proposed expansion.
2. Would you recommend that Chocolate D'Lites expand into Europe? Why or why not? Show your calculations.
3. What other factors should Debbie Fielding consider when making this decision?

REQUIRED

P19-8B Sally Evans is the new controller for Kromeware, a designer and manufacturer of trendy women's swimwear. Shortly before the December 31 fiscal year end, Wynona Krome (the company president) asks Sally how things look for the year-end numbers. Wynona is not happy to learn that earnings growth may be below 10% for the first time in the company's five-year history. Wynona explains that financial analysts have again predicted a 20% earnings growth for the company and that she does not intend to disappoint them. She suggests that Sally talk to the assistant controller, who could explain how the previous controller dealt with this situation. The assistant controller suggests the following strategies:

Ethics (Obj. 7)

a. Change the dates on January's shipping documents to December so that they can be recorded in this year's sales.

b. Reduce the allowance for bad debts, given the company's continued strong performance.

c. Kromeware has very limited warehouse space. It regularly ships finished goods to public warehouses across the country for temporary storage, until Kromeware receives firm orders from customers. As Kromeware receives orders, it directs the warehouse to ship the goods to the nearby customer. The assistant controller suggests recording goods sent to the public warehouses as sales.

d. Postpone planned advertising expenditures from December to January.

e. Persuade retail customers to accelerate January orders to December.

Which of these suggested strategies are inconsistent with IMA standards? What should Sally Evans do if Wynona Krome insists that she follow all of these suggestions?

Applying Your Knowledge

DECISION CASE

Effects of adopting JIT
(Obj. 6)

◀▦ *Link Back to Chapter 18 (Current Ratio).* Roberto Lopez of Lopez Lures (a manufacturer of fly-fishing lures) has attended a seminar on the just-in-time (JIT) management philosophy. Roberto returned to his plant in Tallahassee full of enthusiasm for making the switch to JIT. Linda Lopez, the plant controller, is not as enthusiastic as her brother Roberto. Linda is concerned that adopting JIT might reduce inventory so much that the company may violate its loan covenants. In exchange for loaning the company $20,000, the long-term note payable agreement with TrustSun Bank lists several requirements, or covenants. One requirement is that Lopez Lures maintain a current ratio of at least 2.0. Both the company (Lopez Lures) and the Lopez family have had a long-standing relationship with the bank—particularly with their loan officer, Michael Simms.

Linda Lopez prepares two separate projected balance sheets for the end of the 19X9 fiscal year, under the assumptions that

- Lopez Lures does not adopt JIT
- Lopez Lures does adopt JIT

These two highly summarized balance sheets collapse the materials inventory, work in process inventory, and finished goods inventory under the single "Inventory" heading:

LOPEZ LURES
Projected Balance Sheet If Lopez Does Not Adopt JIT
December 31, 19X9

Assets		Liabilities	
Current assets:		Current liabilities:	
Cash	$ 10,000	Accounts payable	$ 19,500
Accounts receivable	17,000	Long-term liabilities:	
Inventories	15,000	Note payable	20,000
Total current assets	42,000	Total liabilities	39,500
Property, plant, and equipment	97,000	**Stockholders' Equity**	
Total assets	$139,000	Common stock	64,000
		Retained earnings	35,500
		Total stockholders' equity	99,500
		Total liabilities and	
		stockholders' equity	$139,000

LOPEZ LURES
Projected Balance Sheet If Lopez Does Adopt JIT
December 31, 19X9

Assets		Liabilities	
Current assets:		Current liabilities:	
Cash	$ 10,000	Accounts payable	$ 14,300
Accounts receivable	17,000	Long-term liabilities:	
Inventories	1,000	Note payable	20,000
Total current assets	28,000	Total liabilities	34,300
Property, plant, and equipment	97,000	**Stockholders' Equity**	
Total assets	$125,000	Common stock	64,000
		Retained earnings*	26,700
		Total stockholders' equity	90,700
		Total liabilities and	
		stockholders' equity	$125,000

*Retained earnings are expected to temporarily decline in the year Lopez adopts JIT, because of up-front costs that will reduce income in the transition year. However, a cost-benefit analysis (not shown) indicates that adopting JIT should lead to future benefits that far outweigh JIT's up-front transition costs.

1. Compute Lopez Lures' current ratio if
   a. The company does not adopt JIT
   b. The company adopts JIT

(Chapter 18 covers the current ratio.) If Lopez adopts JIT, will the company violate the loan covenant?

2. As a consultant to Lopez Lures, would you recommend that the company adopt JIT?
   a. If you recommend against adopting JIT, take the role of Linda Lopez and write a memo to CEO Roberto Lopez explaining why Lopez Lures should *not* adopt JIT this year. Your memo should take the following form:

Date: _____
To: Roberto Lopez, CEO, Lopez Lures
From: Linda Lopez, Controller
Subject: Adopting JIT

   b. If you recommend that Lopez adopt JIT, write Linda Lopez's memo to Michael Simms of TrustSun Bank explaining the situation. Regardless of whether you expect Lopez to violate the loan covenant this year, adopting JIT will increase the likelihood that Lopez Lures will violate the covenant in the future. Write a memo asking Michael Simms to work with Lopez Lures to reduce the likelihood that the company will violate its loan covenant in the future because of Lopez's switch to JIT. Your memo should explain why reducing the minimum required current ratio is in everyone's interests. Your memo should take the form shown in part a, with the appropriate changes.

Team Project

Arrange an interview with a management accountant, a controller, or other accounting/finance officer of a nearby company. Before you conduct the interview, answer the following questions:

Management accounting in the real world
(Obj. 1, 2, 3, 4, 5, 6, 7)

1. Is this a service, merchandising, or manufacturing company?
2. What is the company's primary product or service?
3. Would the company incur costs in each element of the value chain? Give examples of the costs the company might incur in the different value-chain elements.
4. Describe and provide examples of the company's inventoriable product costs (if any) and its period costs.
5. For what kinds of decisions do you think the company's managers would use management accounting information?

At the interview, begin by clarifying your answers to questions 1–5, and ask the following additional questions:

6. Is management accounting information more or less important to the company than it was five to ten years ago? Why?
7. Is the company's management accounting information system more or less complex than it was five to ten years ago? Explain.
8. Has the company adopted JIT, TQM, or expanded operations internationally? If so, how have these changes affected the management accounting system?
9. Does the company have a code of ethics? If so, ask for a copy. After the interview, compare it to the ethical standards in the Institute of Management Accountants's *Standards of Ethical Conduct for Management Accountants* (Exhibit 19-12).

Prepare a report describing the results of your interview.

The Difference Between Financial and Management Accounting

In your Internet tour at the end of Chapter 1, you explored the world of financial accounting. Financial accounting information is strictly regulated: It must be presented to the public in standardized form at specific intervals. The public nature of the Internet makes it an ideal vehicle for delivering financial information.

In contrast, management accounting information is internal to the firm. Budgets and cost information do not have to be made public. Such information often is considered proprietary—a competitive edge that can be exploited. Thus, while a richness of financial accounting information is available on the Internet, management accounting information is relatively scarce. Nevertheless, here are some resources to get you started.

Institute of Management Accountants

The IMA puts cases from management accounting practice on the Internet at

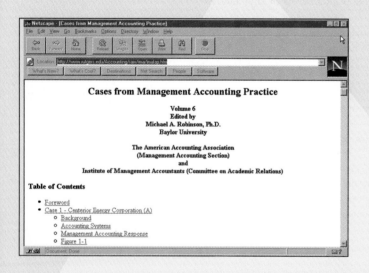

http://www.rutgers.edu/accounting/raw/ima/imafap.htm

Note that you can access these cases through the RAW. While you cannot use the Internet to call up specific firms' cost data, the cases give you a good introduction to issues and problems that companies actually face.

Ethics

The Institute of Management Accountants also publishes ethical guidelines. These can be accessed at

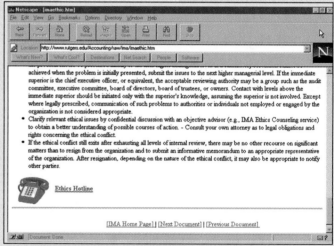

http://www.rutgers.edu/Accounting/raw/ima/ima.htm

Click on the site map icon. Under **About the IMA,** click on **Ethical Guidance.** Note that you can access an ethics hotline. With growing concern that accountants make ethical decisions and behave in an ethical manner, it is good to know that you are not alone out there — help is on the way.

Careers in Accounting

Now the most important thing about the Internet—can you use it to get a job? Let's look at two key ways you can use the Internet to help you establish a career in accounting.

First, let's go to the RAW's home page and click on **Accounting Resources,** and then click on the icon for the big accounting firms. Doing so brings up links to each of the largest accounting firms. Notice that besides providing a wide range of information, the page also lets you go to recruiting. This is a quick and convenient way to learn about job opportunities in the top accounting firms.

There are many more jobs out there. One good source is **accountants on call,** an accounting placement agency found at

http://www.aocnet.com/aoc/

Click on **Quick Search.** One can search through the database of job entries by geographical location.

Job hunting is serious business. Let's end this tour with some fun. When the job search becomes exhausting, or when costing and budgeting start to appear in your dreams, you might want to escape to

http://www.execpc.com/~thorsten/ JOKE.HTML

This will take you to the accountant's joke page. The quality of the jokes varies, but one never knows what will be there. And you thought accountants did not have a sense of humor. ∎

CHAPTER 20

Job Costing

LEARNING OBJECTIVES

After studying this chapter, you should be able to

1. Distinguish between job costing and process costing

2. Account for materials and labor in a manufacturer's job costing system

3. Account for manufacturing overhead, including underallocated and overallocated overhead, in a manufacturer's job costing system

4. Account for noninventoriable costs in job costing

66 *In a competitive industry like the personal computer industry, understanding your costs . . . is all-important. Being able to drive cost reductions, to pass those cost reductions on to the customer, and to grow market share are keys to success.* 99

–KEN HASHMAN, CONTROLLER FOR NORTH AMERICAN OPERATIONS, DELL COMPUTER

How did Michael Dell turn Dell Computer around from losses in 1993 to record profits in 1997? The answer is simple. Dell got manufacturing costs under control. In 1994, manufacturing costs ate up 85% of sales revenue, leaving only a 15% gross margin to cover operating expenses and provide a profit. By 1997, Dell's gross margin percentage had rocketed to 22%.

Most companies increase gross margin by increasing selling prices or reducing costs. Computer prices were falling throughout the industry, so Dell knew he could not increase selling prices. He had no choice—Dell had to reduce manufacturing costs.

Management accounting information helped Dell and his managers find cost-cutting opportunities. Their target: costs that were too high. But which costs could be cut? The first step was to figure out how much it cost the company to produce a computer.

To determine the manufacturing cost of its products, Dell uses a *job costing* system. Each computer is built to a specific customer order, which is called a *job*. Dell's job costing system traces direct materials (such as CD-ROMs and hard drives) and direct labor (such as assembly-line labor) to each job. Then Dell allocates indirect manufacturing overhead costs (such as depreciation on the plant) to each job. The sum of the job's direct materials, direct labor, and manufacturing overhead is its total cost.

Dell needs to know how much a product—for example, a particular computer model—costs for two main reasons:

1. *To help managers plan and control business operations; so they can*
   - Control costs
   - Identify the most profitable products
   - Develop financial plans
   - Set selling prices for products
2. *To help managers gather information for external reporting:*
   - Cost of goods manufactured and cost of goods sold for the income statement
   - Inventory for the balance sheet

I n this chapter, we will explain in detail how Dell Computer and other companies use a job cost system to measure the cost of producing a product or a service.

As you read this chapter, keep in mind that *products* are not the only cost objects (segments of the company for which managers want cost information). ◄◄◄ For example, knowing the costs of serving different *customers* allows managers to identify their most profitable (valuable) customers. Knowing the costs of doing business in different *geographic regions*—for example, North America versus Europe—can help managers decide which regions are more profitable and thus better candidates for expansion. Managers also use costs of *manufacturing processes* to identify inefficiencies and to cut costs.

Nevertheless, because products are the most common cost objects, this chapter and the next focus on assigning costs to products.

Two Approaches to Product Costing: Process Costing and Job Costing

◄◄◄ For a review of cost objects, see Chapter 19, page 822.

Objective 1

Distinguish between job costing and process costing

◄◄◄ We discussed direct and indirect costs in Chapter 19, page 822.

It is hard for companies like Dell to figure out how much it costs to manufacture a particular computer. Dell can trace the cost of direct materials like hard drives to the individual computers in which they are installed. In contrast, indirect costs such as depreciation on the manufacturing plant cannot be traced directly to an individual product because Dell cannot determine exactly how much depreciation a particular computer "caused." ◄◄◄ Also, Dell makes many different computer models, and each requires different resources. How can Dell accurately measure product costs?

Unfortunately, in the real world it is impossible to determine the precise costs of producing a specific individual product like a particular computer. Instead, companies use a product costing system that *averages* costs across products.

There are two broad types of product costing systems:

■ Daily Exercise 20-1

- Process costing
- Job costing

In *process costing*, costs are accumulated for each production process. In *job costing*, costs are accumulated for each individual job. Process costing and job costing also differ in the extent to which they average costs.

Process Costing

Process Costing. System for assigning costs to large numbers of identical units that usually proceed in a continuous fashion through a series of uniform production steps or processes.

Process costing is used by companies that produce large numbers of identical units in a continuous fashion through a series of uniform production steps or processes. Consider Pace Foods, the producer of picante sauce. Production of picante sauce requires two major processes: (1) chopping vegetables, and (2) mixing and bottling the picante sauce. Pace separately accumulates the costs for each of the two production processes. Next, the company averages the costs of the chopping process over all the units passing through the process. Then it averages the costs of the mixing and bottling process over all the units passing through that process. For example, if Pace spent $30,000 to mix and bottle 100,000 pints of picante sauce, the mixing and bottling cost per pint would be

$$\text{Cost per pint of mixing and bottling picante sauce} = \frac{\$30,000}{100,000 \text{ pints}} = \$0.30$$

To get the total cost of a pint of picante sauce, Pace would add the $0.30 per pint of mixing and bottling cost to the cost per pint of vegetables and the chopping process. Each pint of picante sauce is identical to every other pint, so each pint bears the same average cost of the mixing and bottling process. In process costing, the cost assigned to each unit (pint) is a broad average, because the costs of the production process are spread evenly over the thousands of units (pints) passing through the production process.

Process costing systems are common in companies that produce large numbers of similar products that proceed through several production processes in a continuous flow. Some examples:

■ Daily Exercise 20-2
■ Daily Exercise 20-3

- Oil refining—Texaco produces billions of gallons of unleaded gasoline.
- Food and beverage—Kellogg's produces thousands of pounds of cornflakes.
- Pharmaceuticals—Bayer produces millions of aspirin tablets.

Exhibit 20-1 shows that process costing is not confined to manufacturers. Service companies like banks use process costing to determine the cost of processing customer transactions. Merchandisers, such as granaries, use process costing to determine the storage cost for each bushel of grain. We consider process costing in detail in Chapter 21.

Job Costing

This chapter focuses on **job costing,** which assigns costs to a specific unit or to a small batch of products or services that proceeds through production steps as a distinct identifiable job lot. Different jobs can vary considerably in terms of materials, labor, and overhead costs, so job costing accumulates costs separately for each individual job. The job may be a customer order for a mail-order catalogue company like L.L. Bean, a production order for specialized machinery for a metal fabricator, or a project such as the construction of the new Olympic Stadium in Sydney, Australia. Job costing is common in industries that produce goods to customer specifications, such as

- Aircraft—in Seattle, Boeing produces five new 767 airplanes to complete an order from Delta.
- Furniture—in High Point, North Carolina, Swaim Furniture produces eight dining room chairs for a customer in Baltimore.
- Construction—in Atlanta, John Wieland Homes constructs a new home for a linebacker on the Atlanta Falcons football team.

Boeing, Swaim, and John Wieland Homes produce individual products or small batches of products. Similarly, Dell Computer assembles computers to specific customer orders. In each company, different jobs can vary widely in the resources and time required, and in the complexity of the production process. Because the jobs are so different, they are not assigned equal costs.

To assign job costs accurately, accountants try to determine the *drivers* of the costs. A **cost driver** is the primary factor that caused costs. When a cost driver changes, the job's total cost changes. For example, direct labor *hours* drive direct labor *costs*. If Dell Computer uses an extra half hour of direct labor to complete an order of three computers, Dell's total direct labor cost of the three computers also increases. Because Dell is in a competitive industry where selling prices are declining, cost control is the key to earning a profit on each job. If costs are too high, profits are reduced or eliminated. Managers can monitor each job to make sure that costs stay within reasonable limits.

A job may consist of one unit, like the custom home built by John Wieland. Or a job may consist of a group of similar units in a distinct batch, like the eight dining room chairs ordered by Swaim's customer. When a single job includes more than one unit, the manufacturer determines the average cost of each unit in that job. Suppose Swaim's total cost for the eight chairs is $800. Then Swaim's average cost per chair is

$$\text{Average cost per chair} = \frac{\$800}{8 \text{ chairs}} = \$100$$

Job Costing. System for assigning costs to a specific unit or to a small batch of products or services that (1) proceeds through production steps as a distinct identifiable job lot, and (2) can vary considerably in terms of materials, labor, and overhead costs.

Cost Driver. The primary factor that causes costs.

	Service	Merchandising	Manufacturing
Job Costing	Law firms (cases) Health care (diagnoses, procedures, or patients) Public relations (campaigns)	Mail-order catalogue company such as Lands' End or L.L. Bean	Commercial building construction Custom furniture
Process Costing	Banks and other financial institutions (processing customer deposit transactions)	Granaries (redistribute tons of identical grains)	Paper mills Steel mills Textile mills

EXHIBIT 20-1
Job and Process Costing in Service, Merchandising, and Manufacturing Companies

EXHIBIT 20-2
Differences between Job and Process Costing

	Job Costing	Process Costing
Cost object	Job	Process
Outputs	Single units or small batches, with large differences between jobs	Large quantities of identical units
Extent of averaging	Less averaging—costs are averaged over the small number of units in a batch (often 1 unit)	More averaging—costs are averaged over the many identical units in the large batch

The cost per individual unit (chair) in job costing may require averaging, just as in process costing. However, the number of units over which costs are averaged is typically much smaller in job costing than in process costing. And because each job is distinct, there is less averaging of costs *across* jobs. Exhibit 20-2 summarizes key differences between job costing and process costing.

Job costing is not confined to manufacturers. Exhibit 20-1 shows that service organizations such as hospitals and physicians also use job costing. A hospital might consider each medical procedure a different job, while a doctor considers each individual patient a job. Professional service providers such as architects, accountants, and attorneys use job costing to determine the costs of jobs for individual clients. Merchandisers like Lands' End can use job costing to determine the cost of meeting each customer order (job).

Job costing is most complex for manufacturers, so this chapter focuses on job costing in a manufacturing setting. The last section of the chapter applies the same job costing principles to nonmanufacturing companies.

Job Cost Record. Document used to accumulate the costs of an individual job.

JOB COST RECORD   Let's consider how a manufacturer, E-Z-Boy Furniture Company, could use job costing. For E-Z-Boy, each individual customer order can be treated as a different job. **Job cost records** are documents used to accumulate the costs of individual jobs. Exhibit 20-3 shows a completed job cost record for the Macy's New York City order of ten recliner chairs from E-Z-Boy, Job 293. The job cost record has separate sections for the costs of direct materials, direct labor, and manufacturing overhead allocated to Job 293. The total cost of the job is $1,220. The average cost of each of the ten recliners is $122 ($1,220 ÷ 10).

EXHIBIT 20-3
Job Cost Record

Job Cost Record

E-Z-Boy

Job No.   293
Customer Name and Address   Macy's New York City
Job Description   10 recliner chairs

Date Promised	7-31	Date Started	7-24	Date Completed	7-29

Date	Direct Materials		Direct Labor		Manufacturing Overhead Allocated		
	Requisition Numbers	Amount	Time Ticket Numbers	Amount	Date	Rate	Amount
19X8 7-24 25 28	334 338 347	$ 90 180 230	236, 251, 258 264, 269, 273, 291 305	$150 200 50	7-29	80% of direct labor cost	$320
					Overall Cost Summary		
					Direct materials . . . . $ 500		
					Direct labor 400		
					Manufacturing overhead allocated 320		
Totals		$500		$400	**Total Job Cost** $1,220		

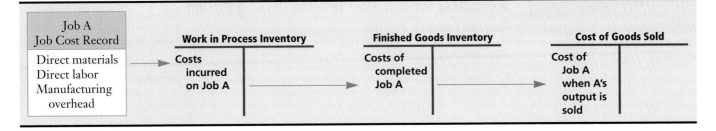

Managers use job cost data to plan and control manufacturing operations. Suppose managers planned to spend $450 on direct materials for Job 293. Then the $500 actual cost exceeds the plan by more than 10 percent. Production managers may investigate this cost overrun to help them reduce costs in the future.

The job cost record is the basic record for product costing. The company starts a job cost record when it begins working on a job. Records of jobs in process (started but not yet completed) form a subsidiary ledger for the general ledger account Work in Process Inventory. ◄▥▥ As costs are incurred, they are added to the job cost record. When the job is completed, its costs are totaled and transferred to Finished Goods Inventory. When the job's output is sold, its costs are moved to Cost of Goods Sold. Exhibit 20-4 summarizes this process.

We now illustrate accounting procedures for a job costing system. There are two major goals:

1. *Accumulating* the total direct material costs, direct labor costs, and manufacturing overhead costs incurred during the period for all jobs, and

2. *Assigning* appropriate amounts of these costs to individual jobs

Our illustration will show you how E-Z-Boy's management accountants accumulate total direct materials, direct labor, and manufacturing overhead costs during the year, and how they assign these costs to individual jobs such as Job 293.

EXHIBIT 20-4
Job Costing—Flow of Costs through the Accounts

■ **Daily Exercise 20-4**

◄▥▥◄▥▥◄▥▥ For a review of ledgers and subsidiary ledgers, see Chapter 6, page 255.

Job Costing Illustrated

Suppose that on December 31, 19X7, E-Z-Boy reports the following inventories:

Materials inventory (many kinds)	$20,000
Work in process inventory (5 jobs)	29,000
Finished goods inventory (unsold units from 2 completed jobs)	12,000

The following data summarize transactions for the year 19X8:

1. Materials purchased on account	$320,000
2. Direct materials used for manufacturing	285,000
Indirect materials used for manufacturing	40,000
3. Manufacturing wages incurred	335,000
4. Direct labor on jobs	250,000
Indirect labor to support manufacturing	85,000
5. Manufacturing overhead (depreciation on plant and equipment)	50,000
6. Manufacturing overhead (plant utilities)	20,000
7. Manufacturing overhead (plant insurance)	5,000
8. Manufacturing overhead (property taxes—plant)	10,000
9. Manufacturing overhead allocated to jobs	200,000
10. Cost of goods manufactured	740,000
11. Sales on account	996,000
Cost of goods sold	734,000

We will explain the accounting for these transactions, step by step.

Accounting for Materials in a Job Costing System

Suppose that E-Z-Boy Furniture Company receives an order for ten recliner chairs. In practice, general ledger entries are usually made monthly. To offer an overview of the big picture of job costing, we use a summary entry for the entire year 19X8. Our first entry is for purchases of materials—in this case, lumber (data from page 863):

(1) Materials Inventory 320,000
      Accounts Payable.........   320,000

"E-Z Boy's materials are logged in by receiving report number . . ."

E-Z-Boy receives the lumber and stores it. Control over materials is established with a subsidiary *materials ledger.* This ledger holds perpetual inventory records that list the quantity and cost of all manufacturing materials on hand. Exhibit 20-5 shows a subsidiary materials ledger record for the lumber that goes into the recliner chairs.

E-Z-Boy's materials are logged in by receiving report number (abbreviated as *Rec. Report No.* in Exhibit 20-5). Here we see that E-Z-Boy received 20 units of lumber, at a cost of $9 each, on July 23, 19X8. Materials used in the product are recorded by materials requisition number *(Mat. Req. No.).* From Exhibit 20-5, we can see that E-Z-Boy used ten units of lumber on July 24. Management can use these records to trace materials into the production process and thereby control operations.

The general ledger has a Materials Inventory account. This account is supported by a subsidiary ledger—the materials ledger—that includes a separate record for each type of raw material. Exhibit 20-6 illustrates the Materials Inventory account and the subsidiary ledger for the materials E-Z-Boy uses. The balance of Materials Inventory in the general ledger ($1,170) equals the sum of the balances in the subsidiary materials ledger.

Managers need a great deal of information to plan manufacturing operations and to control costs. A company may have a materials ledger with thousands of accounts. No wonder most manufacturers have computerized their accounting systems!

Materials Requisition. Request for materials, prepared by manufacturing personnel.

After materials are purchased, the manufacturing process begins with a document called a **materials requisition.** This is a request for materials, prepared by manufacturing personnel. In effect, they ask that the lumber be moved from storage to the manufacturing plant so work can begin. Exhibit 20-7 illustrates a materials requisition for the lumber needed to manufacture the ten recliner chairs that make up E-Z-Boy's Job 293. (See the "Used" section in Exhibit 20-5.)

The "Direct Materials" section in the job cost record (Exhibit 20-3) shows how the details of the materials requisitions are posted to the individual job cost records. Be sure to follow the $90 cost of the lumber from materials requisition 334 (Exhibit 20-7) to the

---

EXHIBIT 20-5
Materials Ledger Record

■ Daily Exercise 20-5

Materials Ledger Record

E-Z-Boy

Item No.   B-220   Description   Lumber/Recliner chairs

Date	Received				Used				Balance		
	Rec. Report No.	Units	Cost	Total Cost	Mat. Req. No.	Units	Cost	Total Cost	Units	Cost	Total Cost
19X8 7-20									30	$9.00	$270
7-23	678	20	$9.00	$180					50	9.00	450
7-24					334	10	$9.00	$90	40	9.00	360

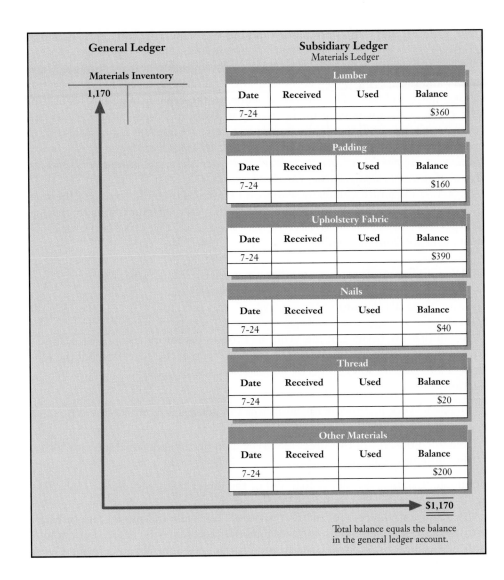

EXHIBIT 20-6
Materials Inventory Accounts

■ **Daily Exercise 20-6**

materials ledger record (Exhibit 20-5) to the job cost record (Exhibit 20-3). Similar requisitions are used for nails, thread, and other indirect materials.

■ **Learning Tip:** All the dollar amounts in Exhibits 20-3 through 20-13 show E-Z-Boy's *costs*—not the prices at which E-Z-Boy *sells* its products.

Computerized accounting systems simplify the collection of data, including direct material costs. Many companies, such as Dell Computer, use electronic bar codes to track material costs. Dell can record its usage of direct materials in producing individual computers by scanning bar codes on the component parts as they are installed.

DIRECT AND INDIRECT MATERIALS Materials Inventory is debited for the costs of all materials purchased—both direct materials and indirect materials. Note that the Materials Inventory account in Exhibit 20-6 includes the costs of both direct materials

EXHIBIT 20-7
Materials Requisition

Materials Requisition No. 334

E-Z-Boy

Date 7-24-X8   Job No. 293

Item No.	Item	Quantity	Unit Cost	Amount
B-220	Lumber/Recliner chairs	10	$9.00	$90

(lumber, padding, and upholstery fabric) and indirect materials (nails, thread, and other materials).

When either direct or indirect materials are requisitioned from storage, Materials Inventory and the accompanying account in the subsidiary materials ledger are credited. What account is debited? The answer depends on the type of materials requisitioned. For direct materials, the debit is made directly to Work in Process Inventory. When indirect materials are used, the debit is made to a separate account called Manufacturing Overhead. ◀▥▥ Keep this distinction in mind: *Indirect manufacturing costs, such as indirect materials used, are not debited directly to Work in Process Inventory. Instead, they are accumulated in the (separate) Manufacturing Overhead account.*

◀▥▥ ◀▥▥ ◀▥▥ Recall from Chapter 19, page 824, that manufacturing overhead includes all manufacturing costs other than direct materials and direct labor.

■ **Daily Exercise 20-7**

E-Z-Boy Furniture Company works on many jobs over the course of the year. At regular intervals, accountants collect the data from materials requisitions to make a single journal entry for all the materials that have been used. The 19X8 entry for E-Z-Boy is (again, data are from page 863):

(2) Work in Process Inventory (for direct materials)	285,000	
Manufacturing Overhead (for indirect materials).........	40,000	
Materials Inventory		325,000

Recall that the balance of the Work in Process Inventory account equals the total cost of all the jobs currently in process. This is the sum of the costs from all the job cost records of jobs that are still in process. For each job, the E-Z-Boy accountants have taken two actions:

1. Debited Work in Process Inventory (in the general ledger) for the cost of direct materials used, *and*
2. Recorded the cost of the direct materials used on the individual job cost record (in the subsidiary ledger)

For example, Exhibit 20-7 shows that $90 of the direct materials relate to Job 293. Exhibit 20-8 includes this $90 on Job 293's job cost record.

By definition, the costs of indirect materials like nails and thread cannot be traced directly to individual jobs. Thus, indirect material costs *cannot* be entered in the job cost records of specific jobs. Indirect costs are simply debited to the Manufacturing Overhead account in the general ledger.

■ **Daily Exercise 20-8**

The flow of materials costs through the T-accounts is as follows:

◀▥▥ ◀▥▥ ◀▥▥ Chapter 11, pages 481–483, defined the payroll register as a special journal that lists each employee and the data to record payroll amounts.

Labor Time Ticket. Document that identifies the employee, the amount of time spent on a particular job, and the labor cost charged to the job; a source document that manufacturing firms commonly use to trace direct labor time to specific job cost records.

Accounting for Labor in a Job Costing System

Control over labor costs in a job costing system is established through payroll registers and time tickets. ◀▥▥ A **labor time ticket** identifies the employee, the amount of time spent on a particular job, and the labor cost charged to the job. Time tickets are accumulated for each job to determine its total direct labor cost. Exhibit 20-9 shows a labor time ticket used in a job costing system like E-Z-Boy's.

A computerized accounting system can simplify collection of direct labor cost data. Computer terminals may be set up on a company's production floor. At various stages in the manufacturing process of Saturn automobiles, for example, employees insert their identification cards into the terminals. The system thus captures direct labor time and cost without detailed labor documents.

EXHIBIT 20-8
Job Cost Record Entry for
Direct Materials

Job Cost Record

E-Z-Boy

Job No. ___293___

Customer Name and Address ___Macy's New York City___

Job Description ___10 recliner chairs___

Date Promised	7-31	Date Started	7-24	Date Completed		
	Direct Materials		**Direct Labor**		**Manufacturing Overhead Allocated**	
Date	Requisition Numbers	Amount	Time Ticket Numbers	Amount	Date	Rate	Amount
19X8							
7-24	334	$90					
					Overall Cost Summary		
					Direct materials . . . . $		
					Direct labor		
					Manufacturing overhead		
					allocated		
Totals					**Total Job Cost** . . . . $		

E-Z-Boy's entry for 19X8 for all manufacturing wages incurred for all jobs is (data from page 863) as follows:

(3) Manufacturing Wages   335,000

         Wages Payable   335,000

This entry records the actual labor costs incurred. Direct labor and indirect labor are then accounted for separately. The separation, similar to that for direct materials and indirect materials, is shown in the following T-accounts (data from page 863):

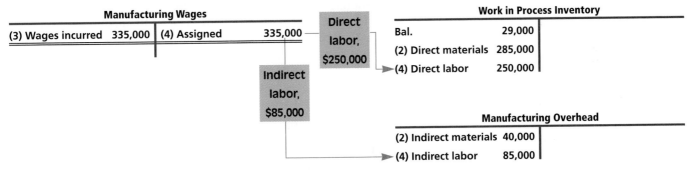

DIRECT AND INDIRECT LABOR As the preceding T-accounts indicate, direct labor is debited directly to Work in Process Inventory. Indirect labor is added to the Manufacturing

■ **Daily Exercise 20-9**

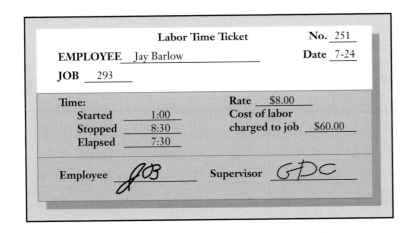

EXHIBIT 20-9
Labor Time Ticket

EXHIBIT 20-10
Job Cost Record Entry for
Direct Labor

Job Cost Record

E-Z-Boy

Job No. 293

Customer Name and Address   Macy's New York City

Job Description   10 recliner chairs

Date Promised	7-31	Date Started	7-24	Date Completed	

Date	Direct Materials		Direct Labor		Manufacturing Overhead Allocated		
	Requisition Numbers	Amount	Time Ticket Numbers	Amount	Date	Rate	Amount
19X8 7-24	334	$90	236, 251, 258	$150			

Overall Cost Summary

Direct materials . . . . $
Direct labor . . . .
Manufacturing overhead
   allocated . . . .

| Totals | | | | | Total Job Cost . . . . $ | | |

Overhead account. The assignment of labor cost to production results in a credit to Manu-facturing Wages.

(4)	Work in Process Inventory (for direct labor)	250,000	
	Manufacturing Overhead (for indirect labor)	85,000	
	Manufacturing Wages		335,000

This entry brings the balance in Manufacturing Wages to zero, its transferred balance now divided between Work in Process Inventory (direct labor) and Manufacturing Over-head (indirect labor).

Assume that $150 of one day's direct labor cost is for Job 293. E-Z-Boy Furniture enters Job 293's direct labor on the job cost record. The $150 amount in the Direct Labor section of Exhibit 20-10 includes Jay Barlow's wages of $60 (from time ticket 251, Exhibit 20-9) and the labor costs entered on time tickets 236 and 258 (not shown).

The Work in Process Inventory account now contains the costs of direct materials and direct labor charged to Job 293—and the costs of many other jobs as well. Work in Process Inventory serves as a control account, with the job cost records giving the sup-porting details for each job. To see why, keep in mind that the total direct labor debits to Work in Process Inventory equal the total direct labor costs assigned to all the individual jobs worked on during the period (and recorded on the individual job cost records). Sim-ilarly, the total direct material debits to Work in Process Inventory equal the total costs of direct materials used on all the jobs worked on during the period (and recorded on their job cost records). The job cost records thus serve as a subsidiary ledger for the gen-eral ledger balance in Work in Process Inventory.

Exhibit 20-11 summarizes the accounting for materials and labor. It shows that ac-counting data are most condensed in the general ledger and most detailed in the source documents.

Work in process inventory	=	General ledger (usually monthly totals only)
↑		↑
Job cost records	=	Subsidiary ledger (perhaps daily summaries)
↑		↑
Materials requisitions and labor time tickets	=	Source documents (minute-to-minute, hour-to-hour records)

We have now discussed several documents used in a job costing system, including job cost records. In a computerized job costing system, physical job cost records may not exist. To record the cost of direct materials used on a job, an employee simply calls up the online job cost record and records the cost. Direct labor costs are added electronically as work is performed. The computer tallies materials and labor costs and automatically posts to the appropriate general ledger accounts.

SUMMARY PROBLEM FOR YOUR REVIEW   MID-CHAPTER

Ecosphere Associates, Ltd. in Tucson, Arizona, produces ecospheres—self-sustaining enclosed glass spheres that include water, algae, tiny shrimp, and snails. Suppose Ecosphere has the following transactions:

a. Purchased raw materials on account, $35,000.
b. Materials costing $30,000 were requisitioned for production. Of this total, $3,000 were indirect materials.
c. Labor time tickets for the month show direct labor of $22,000, and indirect labor of $4,000.

Prepare journal entries for each transaction.   **REQUIRED**

■ SOLUTION

a. Materials Inventory...................... 35,000
     Accounts Payable......................   35,000

When materials are purchased on account:

- Debit (increase) the Materials Inventory asset for the *cost* of the materials, and
- Credit (increase) Accounts Payable to record the liability for the cost of the materials.

b. Work in Process Inventory 27,000
   Manufacturing Overhead............. 3,000
     Materials Inventory..................   30,000

When materials are requisitioned (used) in production, we record the movement of materials out of materials inventory and into production:

- Debit (increase) Work in Process Inventory for the cost of the *direct* materials (in this case, $27,000—the $30,000 total materials requisitioned less the $3,000 indirect materials),
- Debit (increase) Manufacturing Overhead for the cost of the *indirect* materials, and
- Credit (decrease) Materials Inventory for the cost of both direct and indirect materials moved out of the materials storage area and into production

c. Manufacturing Wages.................. 26,000
     Wages Payable..........................   26,000

To record total labor costs actually incurred ($22,000 + $4,000):

- Debit (increase) Manufacturing Wages, and
- Credit (increase) Wages Payable to record the liability for wages incurred, but not paid

Work in Process Inventory 22,000
Manufacturing Overhead............. 4,000
     Manufacturing Wages   26,000

To assign the labor costs:

- Debit (increase) Work in Process Inventory for the cost of the *direct* labor,
- Debit (increase) Manufacturing Overhead for the cost of the *indirect* labor, and
- Credit (decrease) Manufacturing Wages for the cost of both direct and indirect labor

Objective 3

Account for manufacturing overhead, including underallocated and overallocated overhead, in a manufacturer's job costing system

Accounting for Manufacturing Overhead in a Job Costing System

As our indirect materials and indirect labor examples showed, all overhead costs are debited to a single general ledger account—Manufacturing Overhead. Entries 5 through 8 below complete the recording of the manufacturing overhead costs E-Z-Boy Furniture actually incurred, as given on page 863. The account titles in parentheses indicate the specific records that are debited in an overhead subsidiary ledger. Planning for these individual overhead costs and then analyzing the differences between planned and actual amounts helps managers control overhead costs.

(5)	Manufacturing Overhead (Depreciation—Plant and Equipment)	50,000	
	Accumulated Depreciation—Plant and Equipment		50,000
(6)	Manufacturing Overhead (Plant Utilities)	20,000	
	Cash		20,000
(7)	Manufacturing Overhead (Plant Insurance)	5,000	
	Prepaid Insurance—Plant		5,000
(8)	Manufacturing Overhead (Property Taxes—Plant)	10,000	
	Property Taxes Payable		10,000

The actual manufacturing overhead costs (such as indirect materials, indirect labor, and depreciation, utilities, insurance and property taxes related to the plant) are debited to the Manufacturing Overhead account as they occur throughout the year. By the end of the year, the Manufacturing Overhead account contains all the actual overhead costs as debits:

■ Daily Exercise 20-10

Manufacturing Overhead

(2) Indirect materials	40,000
(4) Indirect labor	85,000
(5) Depreciation—plant and equipment	50,000
(6) Plant utilities	20,000
(7) Plant insurance	5,000
(8) Property taxes—plant	10,000
Total overhead cost	210,000

How are overhead costs assigned to individual jobs? Materials requisitions and labor time tickets make it easy to trace direct materials and direct labor costs to specific jobs. But manufacturing overhead includes a variety of costs that cannot be traced to individual jobs. For example, it is virtually impossible to say that a specific amount of the cost incurred to cool the factory is related to Job 293. Yet manufacturing overhead costs are as essential as direct materials and direct labor in producing goods. We now see how accountants assign overhead costs to jobs.

Allocating Overhead Costs to Jobs

Managers want to know the costs incurred in each job, including both direct and indirect costs. Accountants use **cost tracing** to assign direct costs (such as direct materials and direct labor) to cost objects such as jobs. They use **cost allocation** to distribute manufacturing overhead and other indirect costs among cost objects. The general term **cost assignment** refers to the process of tracing direct costs and allocating indirect costs to cost objects (jobs, in a job costing system). In summary,

Cost Tracing. Assigning direct costs (such as direct materials and direct labor) to cost objects (such as jobs or production processes).

Cost Allocation. Distribution of indirect costs (such as manufacturing overhead) to cost objects (such as jobs or production processes).

Cost Assignment. Process of tracing direct costs to cost objects and allocating indirect costs to cost objects.

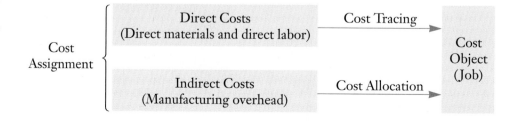

Direct material and direct labor costs are traced directly to each job, as we've seen. But managers also want to know the *total* manufacturing costs incurred on each job, including manufacturing overhead costs. Somehow, the company must allocate to each individual job its share of the wide variety of indirect manufacturing costs like depreciation and insurance on the plant and equipment, indirect materials, and indirect labor.

The most accurate allocation cannot be made until the total amount of the manufacturing overhead costs is known, at the end of the year. But that would be much too late. Managers making decisions today cannot wait until the end of the year for product cost information. To solve this timing problem, accountants develop an estimated manufacturing overhead allocation rate at the beginning of the year. This **predetermined manufacturing overhead rate** (sometimes called the **budgeted manufacturing overhead rate**) is computed as follows:

Predetermined Manufacturing Overhead Rate. Estimated manufacturing overhead rate computed at the beginning of the year, calculated as the total estimated manufacturing overhead costs divided by the total estimated quantity of the manufacturing overhead allocation base. Also called the **budgeted manufacturing overhead rate.**

$$\text{Predetermined manufacturing overhead rate} = \frac{\text{Total estimated manufacturing overhead costs}}{\text{Total estimated quantity of the manufacturing overhead allocation base}}$$

Both the numerator and the denominator of the predetermined manufacturing overhead rate are based on *estimated* amounts. These are estimated *before* the year begins. They cannot be actual amounts because actual overhead costs and the actual quantity of the allocation base are not known until after the end of the period.

■ **Daily Exercise 20-11**

The manufacturing overhead **allocation base** is a common denominator that links indirect manufacturing overhead costs to the cost objects—jobs, in the case of job costing. Ideally, the allocation base is the primary cost driver of manufacturing overhead costs. For example, in many companies, manufacturing overhead costs rise and fall with direct labor costs. In this case, accountants can use either direct labor costs or direct labor hours as the manufacturing overhead allocation base. The more direct labor a job uses, the more manufacturing overhead cost the job is allocated. This is a wise choice if direct labor is a driver of manufacturing overhead costs.

Allocation Base. A common denominator that links indirect costs to cost objects. Ideally, the allocation base is the primary cost driver that causes the indirect cost to be incurred.

Direct labor is not always the best allocation base. Labor is less important in companies that have highly automated production processes, like Saturn. Saturn's manufacturing overhead costs are primarily machine-related rather than labor-driven. Depreciation, maintenance, and utilities are likely to fluctuate with the number of machine hours used. Companies with automated operations often use machine hours as the manufacturing overhead allocation base. The important point here is that the cost allocation base should accurately represent the primary cost driver of the manufacturing overhead costs.

A company generally follows six steps to develop its predetermined manufacturing overhead rate and then to allocate its manufacturing overhead cost to jobs:

1. Select the manufacturing overhead (cost) allocation base. As the Manufacturing Overhead section of Exhibit 20-3 shows, E-Z-Boy's accountants selected direct labor cost.
2. Estimate the total overhead cost for the planning period, which is ordinarily a year. Assume that late in 19X7, E-Z-Boy predicted overhead costs for 19X8 of $220,000.
3. Estimate the total quantity of the overhead allocation base. E-Z-Boy production managers expect to incur $275,000 of direct labor cost during 19X8.
4. Compute the predetermined manufacturing overhead rate as follows:

$$\text{Predetermined manufacturing overhead rate} = \frac{\text{Total estimated manufacturing overhead costs}}{\text{Total estimated quantity of the manufacturing overhead allocation base}}$$

$$= \frac{\text{Total estimated manufacturing overhead costs}}{\text{Total estimated direct labor cost}}$$

$$= \frac{\$220,000}{\$275,000} = 0.80 \text{ or } 80\%$$

Thus the predetermined manufacturing overhead rate is computed as the total *estimated* manufacturing overhead cost (estimated *before* the year starts) divided by the total *estimated* quantity of the allocation base (also estimated *before* the year starts). Because the numerator and the denominator are both based on amounts that are *estimated before* the year starts, this overhead rate is *predetermined.*

Job Cost Record

E-Z-Boy

Job No. 293

Customer Name and Address   Macy's New York City

Job Description   10 recliner chairs

| Date Promised | 7-31 | Date Started | 7-24 | Date Completed | 7-29 |

Date	Direct Materials		Direct Labor		Manufacturing Overhead Allocated		
	Requisition Numbers	Amount	Time Ticket Numbers	Amount	Date	Rate	Amount
19X8							
7-24	334	$ 90	236, 251, 258	$150	7-29	80% of direct labor cost	$320
25	338	180	264, 269, 273, 291	200			
28	347	230	305	50			

Overall Cost Summary

Direct materials . . . . $ 500
Direct labor   400
Manufacturing overhead
allocated   320

| Totals | | $500 | | $400 | Total Job Cost . . . . $1,220 |

5. Obtain *actual* quantities of the overhead allocation base used by individual jobs, as the year unfolds. The total actual direct labor cost of Job 293 is $400, as Exhibits 20-3 and 20-12 show.

6. Allocate manufacturing overhead to jobs by multiplying the *predetermined* manufacturing overhead rate (computed in step 4) by the *actual* quantity of the allocation base used by each job (from step 5). The same predetermined rate is used to allocate manufacturing overhead to all jobs worked on throughout the year. After the direct material and direct labor costs have been traced to a job, the manufacturing overhead is allocated, as shown in the job cost record for Job 293 (Exhibit 20-12). Recall that the total direct labor cost for Job 293 is $400. Because the predetermined overhead allocation rate is 80% of direct labor cost, the manufacturing overhead allocated to Job 293 is $320 ($400 × 0.80).

The job cost record of Job 293 now is complete. It provides the details that support the $1,220 total cost and the $122 ($1,220 ÷ 10) unit cost of the Macy's order.

 Working It Out The Jarvis Company allocates manufacturing overhead based on direct labor cost. The company records the following actual costs for the year:

Indirect labor	$40,000	Rent on plant	$16,000
Plant supplies	20,000	Plant utilities	10,000
Machinery repair	14,000	Sales commissions	30,000
Advertising	6,000	Direct labor	64,000

Jarvis had budgeted $60,000 of direct labor cost and $90,000 of manufacturing overhead costs for the year.

Questions

1. Compute the predetermined manufacturing overhead rate.
2. How much is actual manufacturing overhead?
3. Compute the allocated manufacturing overhead.

Answers

1. Predetermined manufacturing overhead rate based on budgeted direct labor cost = $90,000 ÷ $60,000 = 150% of direct labor cost.

2. Actual manufacturing overhead = $100,000 ($40,000 + $20,000 + $14,000 + $16,000 + $10,000).

3. Allocated manufacturing overhead equals the *actual* quantity of the allocation base (direct labor cost) multiplied by the *predetermined* overhead rate:

$$\text{Allocated manufacturing overhead} = \$64,000 \times 150\%$$
$$= \$96,000$$

Of course, there have been similar allocations of manufacturing overhead for each of the other jobs E-Z-Boy worked on during 19X8. The total overhead allocated to all jobs is 80% of the total $250,000 direct labor cost, or $200,000 (data from page 863). The journal entry to allocate manufacturing overhead costs to Work in Process Inventory is

(9) Work in Process Inventory 200,000
      Manufacturing Overhead   200,000

E-Z-Boy's allocation of manufacturing overhead may be diagrammed through the T-accounts in this way:

Manufacturing Overhead					Work in Process Inventory	
(2)	40,000	(9) Allocated	200,000	Bal.	29,000	
(4)	85,000			(2)	285,000	
(5)	50,000		Manufacturing	(4)	250,000	
(6)	20,000		Overhead	(9)	200,000	
(7)	5,000		Allocated			
(8)	10,000					
Actual costs	210,000					
Bal.	10,000					

Note that after allocation, there is still a $10,000 debit balance in the Manufacturing Overhead account. This means that E-Z-Boy's actual overhead costs exceed the amount of overhead allocated to Work in Process Inventory. We say that E-Z-Boy's Manufacturing Overhead is *underallocated*. We'll discuss how accountants correct this problem on page 875, but first we must explain the accounting for finished goods and the sale of finished goods inventory.

Accounting for Finished Goods, Sales, and Cost of Goods Sold

As each job is completed, its total cost is transferred out of Work in Process Inventory into Finished Goods Inventory. Sales of finished goods are recorded as they occur.

The $740,000 cost of goods manufactured (from the data on page 863) is the cost of the jobs that E-Z-Boy finished this year. E-Z-Boy credits Work in Process Inventory as the jobs leave the plant floor. The corresponding debit is to Finished Goods Inventory because the completed products are moving into the finished goods storage area. A summary entry for E-Z-Boy Furniture's goods completed in 19X8 is as follows:

(10) Finished Goods Inventory 740,000
      Work in Process Inventory.........   740,000

In turn, the usual entries are made for sales and cost of goods sold (data from page 863):

(11) Accounts Receivable........................... 996,000
      Sales Revenue   996,000
    Cost of Goods Sold 734,000
      Finished Goods Inventory   734,000

The key T-accounts for E-Z-Boy's manufacturing costs now show

Work in Process Inventory		Finished Goods Inventory		Cost of Goods Sold
Bal. 29,000	(10) 740,000	Bal. 12,000	(11) 734,000 ⟶	(11) 734,000
(2) 285,000		(10) 740,000		
(4) 250,000		Bal. 18,000		
(9) 200,000				
Bal. 24,000				

The Work in Process Inventory T-account summarizes what happens on the manufacturing plant floor. We start the period with beginning inventory of partially completed jobs ($29,000). During the period, the plant uses direct materials ($285,000) and direct labor ($250,000), and manufacturing overhead is allocated to the jobs passing through the plant floor ($200,000). Some jobs are completed, and their costs are transferred out to Finished Goods ($740,000). We end the period with other jobs still in process ($24,000).

Notice also that the Work in Process T-account summarizes the Schedule of Cost of Goods Manufactured. For E-Z-Boy, the Work in Process T-account shows

Beginning Work in Process Inventory		$ 29,000
Current manufacturing costs:		
Direct materials used......................................	$285,000	
Direct labor...	250,000	
Manufacturing overhead allocated...............	200,000	735,000
Total manufacturing costs to account for		764,000
Ending Work in Process Inventory		24,000
Cost of Goods Manufactured		$740,000

 Working It Out Use these T-accounts to answer the following questions. (All beginning balances are zero.)

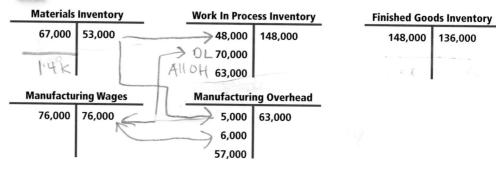

What is

1. The cost of direct materials used?
2. The cost of indirect materials used?
3. The cost of direct labor assigned to production?
4. The cost of indirect labor?
5. The cost of goods manufactured?

6. The actual manufacturing overhead?
7. The allocated manufacturing overhead?
8. The cost of goods sold?
9. The budgeted manufacturing overhead rate, as a percentage of direct labor cost?

Answers

1. $48,000
2. $5,000
3. $70,000
4. $6,000
5. $148,000

6. $68,000 ($5,000 + $6,000 + $57,000)
7. $63,000
8. $136,000
9. 90% ($63,000 ÷ $70,000)

Disposing of Underallocated or Overallocated Manufacturing Overhead

During the year, E-Z-Boy's accountants debit Manufacturing Overhead for the overhead costs the company actually incurred, and credit Manufacturing Overhead for amounts allocated to Work in Process Inventory. The total debits rarely equal the total credits. Why? Because overhead is allocated to jobs using a *predetermined* allocation rate that represents the *expected* relation between overhead costs and the allocation base. In our example, the $10,000 debit balance of Manufacturing Overhead shown on page 873 is called **underallocated manufacturing overhead** (or simply **underallocated overhead**) because the amount of manufacturing overhead allocated to Work in Process Inventory is *less* than the amount of manufacturing overhead costs actually incurred. (**Overallocated manufacturing overhead** is just the opposite.)

Accountants usually ignore underallocated overhead and overallocated overhead during the year, and dispose of it at year end, when the Manufacturing Overhead account is closed. When overhead is underallocated, as in our example, a credit to Manufacturing Overhead brings the account balance to zero. What accounts are debited?

To see the answer, you need to understand why $10,000 of manufacturing overhead was underallocated. In our example, E-Z-Boy's accountants expected to incur 19X8 manufacturing overhead at the predetermined rate of

$$\frac{\$220,000 \text{ } \textit{expected} \text{ manufacturing overhead costs}}{\$275,000 \text{ } \textit{expected} \text{ direct labor cost}} = 80\%$$

The accountants computed this 80% manufacturing overhead rate at the beginning of the year before they knew the *actual* manufacturing overhead cost and the *actual* quantity of the allocation base (direct labor cost, in this example).

Without a crystal ball to foretell the future, it would be surprising indeed if *actual* manufacturing overhead costs and *actual* quantities of the allocation base—which are not known until the end of the year—exactly match the expected amounts. At the end of 19X8, E-Z-Boy's actual manufacturing overhead rate turns out to be

$$\frac{\$210,000 \text{ } \textit{actual} \text{ manufacturing overhead costs}}{\$250,000 \text{ } \textit{actual} \text{ direct labor cost}} = 84\%$$

If E-Z-Boy's accountants had a crystal ball at the beginning of the year, they would have predicted a manufacturing overhead rate of 84 percent. But they did not. They *underestimated* the manufacturing overhead rate, expecting it to be only 80 percent.

Because the predetermined manufacturing overhead rate that E-Z-Boy used to allocate overhead to each job was *less* than the actual manufacturing overhead rate, the company allocated *too little* manufacturing overhead to every job. In other words, every job worked on in 19X8 was *undercosted*. To correct this error, the cost of these jobs should be *increased*.

Ideally, E-Z-Boy would go back and increase the cost of each individual job. Some companies have computer programs that automatically correct each job at the end of the year. However, even without such a program, accountants can make an approximate correction. Accountants make this adjustment using **proration** to distribute underallocated or overallocated manufacturing overhead among ending inventories and cost of goods sold. To prorate, accountants need to answer the following questions:

1. *Which accounts should be corrected?*
   Answer: Because all the jobs E-Z-Boy worked on during the year were undercosted, there are undercosted jobs in ending Work in Process Inventory, ending Finished Goods Inventory, and Cost of Goods Sold. These accounts need to be corrected.

2. *To correct these accounts, should they be increased or decreased?*
   Answer: Because the jobs are *undercosted*, the correction should increase (debit) these accounts.

3. *How much of the correction should go to each account?*
   Answer: The correction is prorated in proportion to the amount of the ending account balances. For E-Z-Boy, the total $10,000 underallocated manufacturing overhead (from closing out the Manufacturing Overhead account) is prorated as follows:

Underallocated (Manufacturing) Overhead. The amount of manufacturing overhead allocated to Work in Process Inventory is *less* than the amount of manufacturing overhead costs actually incurred.

Overallocated (Manufacturing) Overhead. The amount of manufacturing overhead allocated to Work in Process Inventory is *more* than the amount of manufacturing overhead costs actually incurred.

Proration. Distributing underallocated or overallocated manufacturing overhead among ending inventories and cost of goods sold.

Unadjusted Ending Balances (see T-accounts on page 874)		Proration	
Work in Process Inventory	$24,000	$\dfrac{24}{776} \times \$10,000 = \$$	309
Finished Goods Inventory	18,000	$\dfrac{18}{776} \times \$10,000 =$	232
Cost of Goods Sold	734,000	$\dfrac{734}{776} \times \$10,000 =$	9,459
Total	$776,000		$10,000

The resulting journal entry would be

■ Daily Exercise 20-16
■ Daily Exercise 20-17
■ Daily Exercise 20-18

Work in Process Inventory	309	
Finished Goods Inventory	232	
Cost of Goods Sold	9,459	
Manufacturing Overhead.........		10,000

This December 31 adjusting entry increases the inventory and expense (Cost of Goods Sold) balances to approximately what they would have been if the 84% actual overhead rate had been used throughout the year.

Notice that the dollar amount of the adjustments to Work in Process Inventory and Finished Goods Inventory ($309 + 232 = $541) is small in relation to the total manufacturing overhead ($210,000). When accountants believe that the amount of the correction to Work in Process and Finished Goods inventories would be insignificant, they typically do not bother with proration. Instead, they close the balance in the Manufacturing Overhead account directly to the current year's Cost of Goods Sold, as shown in the following journal entry:

(12) Cost of Goods Sold	10,000	
Manufacturing Overhead		10,000

With or without proration, the entry to close Manufacturing Overhead ensures that the total actual overhead cost incurred—$210,000 in this case—will be expensed as part of Cost of Goods Sold either in the current period, or in future periods when the inventory is sold.

The Manufacturing Overhead balance now is zero. Assuming the underallocated overhead was closed directly to Cost of Goods Sold, the T-accounts would show:

Manufacturing Overhead				Cost of Goods Sold	
Actual	210,000	Allocated	200,000	734,000	
		Closed	10,000 →	10,000	

Learning Tip: A simple T-account helps in working with overhead:

Manufacturing Overhead	
Actual	Allocated

A debit balance at the end of the period means actual was greater than allocated and is called underallocated overhead. A credit balance means allocated was greater than actual and is called overallocated overhead.

Working It Out Suppose E-Z-Boy's actual manufacturing overhead costs had been $180,000 rather than $210,000.

Questions

1. What would the actual overhead rate have been?
2. Would manufacturing overhead have been underallocated or overallocated?
3. What journal entry would you make to close the Manufacturing Overhead account?

Answers

1. The actual manufacturing overhead rate would have been

$$\frac{\$180{,}000 \; \textit{actual} \text{ manufacturing overhead costs}}{\$250{,}000 \; \textit{actual} \text{ direct labor cost}} = 72\%$$

2. The predetermined manufacturing overhead rate (80%) is *higher* than the actual manufacturing overhead rate (72%). In this case, E-Z-Boy would have allocated *too much* manufacturing overhead to every job. Each job would be *overcosted*. And Manufacturing Overhead would be *overallocated* by $20,000, as shown in this T-account:

Manufacturing Overhead

Actual	Allocated
$180,000	$200,000

3. To prorate the $20,000 of overallocated manufacturing overhead, E-Z-Boy would answer the three questions outlined in the text:

   - *Which accounts should be corrected?*
     Answer: Because all jobs worked on during the year were overcosted, there are overcosted jobs in ending Work in Process Inventory, ending Finished Goods Inventory, and Cost of Goods Sold. These are the accounts that need to be corrected.
   - *To correct these accounts, should they be increased or decreased?*
     Answer: Because the jobs are *overcosted*, the correction should decrease (credit) these accounts.
   - *How much of the correction should go to each account?*
     Answer: The total $20,000 overallocated manufacturing overhead (from closing out the Manufacturing Overhead account) is prorated as follows:

Unadjusted Ending Balances **(see T-accounts on page 874)**		**Proration**	
Work in Process Inventory	$ 24,000	$\frac{24}{776} \times \$20{,}000 = \$$	618
Finished Goods Inventory	18,000	$\frac{18}{776} \times \$20{,}000 =$	464
Cost of Goods Sold	734,000	$\frac{734}{776} \times \$20{,}000 =$	18,918
Total	$776,000		$20,000

The adjusting journal entry would be

Manufacturing Overhead	20,000	
Work in Process Inventory		618
Finished Goods Inventory		464
Cost of Goods Sold		18,918

However, because the amount of the correction to Work in Process and Finished Goods is not very large, the E-Z-Boy accountants might choose not to bother with proration. Instead, they could close the Manufacturing Overhead account balance directly to Cost of Goods Sold with the following entry:

Manufacturing Overhead	20,000	
Cost of Goods Sold		20,000

Overview of Job Costing in a Manufacturing Company

Exhibit 20-13 provides an overview of the E-Z-Boy Furniture Company's job costing illustration. Each entry is keyed to one of the 12 transactions described on pages 863–876 (amounts in thousands). Take your time to study this exhibit carefully.

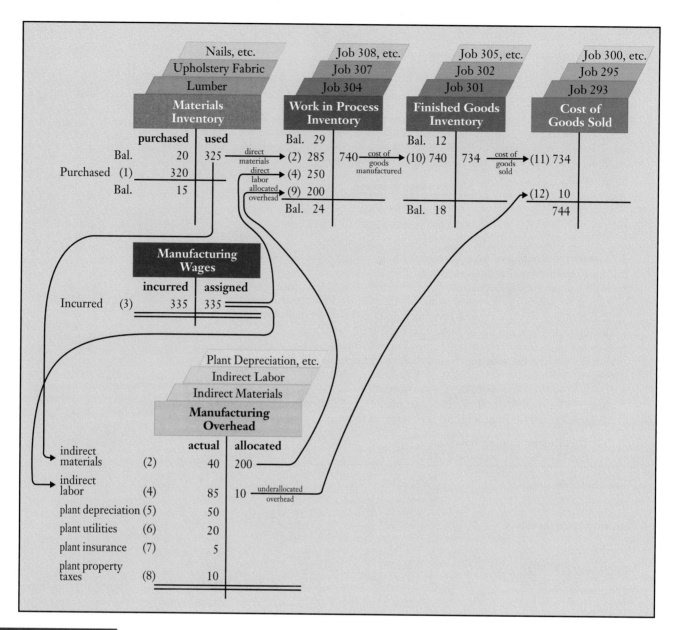

EXHIBIT 20-13
E-Z-Boy Furniture Company Job
Costing Illustration—Flow of
Costs through Accounts
(amounts in thousands)

Review the flow of costs through the general ledger accounts:

- Material and labor costs are split between directs costs (traced directly to specific jobs in Work in Process Inventory) and indirect costs (added to Manufacturing Overhead).
- The Work in Process Inventory account summarizes the transactions that occurred on the floor of the manufacturing plant.
- The $740,000 credit to Work in Process (debit to Finished Goods) is the cost of goods manufactured—the manufacturer's counterpart to merchandise purchases.

Study the Manufacturing Overhead account. Actual overhead items are recorded as debits as they occur throughout the period. Credits to the Manufacturing Overhead account represent allocated overhead. Exhibit 20-13 assumes that E-Z-Boy considered the $10,000 underallocated overhead insignificant and therefore closed the Manufacturing Overhead account directly to Cost of Goods Sold.

The T-accounts shown in Exhibit 20-13 are general ledger control accounts. ◄▦▦ Be-hind each general ledger account appear three examples of subsidiary accounts that would underlie each general ledger control account.

◄▦▦ ◄▦▦ ◄▦▦ We discussed control accounts in Chapter 6, page 256.

Inventoriable Costs, Noninventoriable Costs, and Job Costing

Job costing can be complex for manufacturers, because manufacturers have

Objective 4

Account for noninventoriable costs in job costing

1. The most complex business operations—they use labor and overhead to transform raw materials into different finished goods
2. Three different kinds of inventory—materials, work in process, and finished goods

Job costing in manufacturing companies has traditionally focused on assigning *manufacturing* costs (*inventoriable* costs) to jobs. This is why the E-Z-Boy illustration in this chapter focuses on assigning only manufacturing costs to jobs. We have not considered costs incurred in other elements of the value chain, such as R&D or marketing.

The focus on manufacturing costs stems from external reporting requirements. GAAP requires that the accounting records treat only inventoriable costs (manufacturing costs, for a manufacturer) as assets. Costs incurred in other elements of the value chain are treated as expenses for financial accounting. For this reason, the general ledger entries in this chapter have been limited to manufacturing costs.

Managers often want to know the total costs of a product (or a job), not just the inventoriable costs. The same principles of tracing direct costs and allocating indirect costs (using predetermined allocation rates) apply to costs incurred in other elements of the value chain. However, these noninventoriable costs are assigned to products (or jobs) *only for internal decision making*. No journal entries assign noninventoriable costs to individual jobs, because noninventoriable costs are not assigned to products for external reporting.

Management accounting is becoming increasingly important to service firms. Recall that a service firm has no inventoriable costs because it has no inventory. Service firms incur only noninventoriable costs. Nevertheless, managers of service companies still need to know the (noninventoriable) costs of different jobs to make decisions such as setting selling prices, or fees. Thus we shift our focus to illustrate the assignment of noninventoriable costs to jobs in a service firm. However, a manufacturer such as E-Z-Boy or a merchandiser such as L.L. Bean could use the same approach to assign noninventoriable costs to individual jobs.

Job Costing in a Nonmanufacturing Company

We now illustrate how companies that are not manufacturers can use job costing. Barnett Legal Associates specializes in employment law. Each client is considered a separate job.

As with most service firms, Barnett's most significant cost is direct labor—the cost of attorney time spent on the clients' cases. How is direct labor traced to individual jobs? As in many professional service firms, attorneys at Barnett fill out a computerized weekly **time record.** The software tallies the weekly total attorney time spent on each client. For example, attorney Teresa Fox's time record appears in Exhibit 20-14. Fox's time record shows that she devoted 14 hours to client 367 during the week of June 10, 19X9.

Fox's salary and benefits total $100,000 per year. Assuming a 40-hour workweek and 50 workweeks in each year, Fox has 2,000 available workhours per year (50 weeks × 40 hours per week). Barnett Legal Associates' hourly (cost) rate of employing Teresa Fox is

Time Record. Source document used primarily by employees in service activities, to trace direct labor to specific jobs.

■ **Daily Exercise 20-19**

$$\text{Hourly cost rate to the employer} = \frac{\$100,000 \text{ per year}}{2,000 \text{ hours per year}} = \$50 \text{ per hour}$$

Fox is the only attorney who served client 367, so the direct labor cost traced to the client is 14 hours × $50 per hour = $700.

Founding partner John Barnett wants to know the total costs of serving clients, not just the direct labor cost. Consequently, Barnett Legal Associates also allocates indirect

EXHIBIT 20-14
Time Record

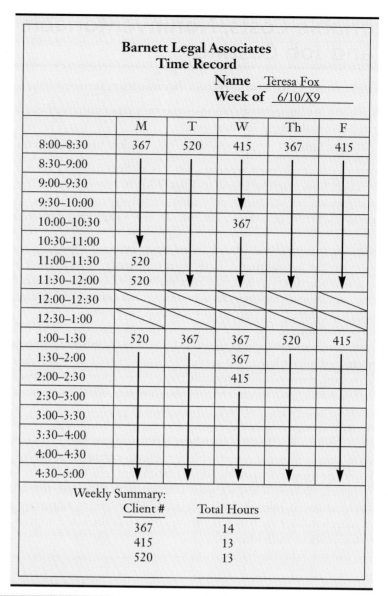

Barnett Legal Associates
Time Record

Name   Teresa Fox
Week of   6/10/X9

	M	T	W	Th	F
8:00–8:30	367	520	415	367	415
8:30–9:00					
9:00–9:30					
9:30–10:00					
10:00–10:30			367		
10:30–11:00					
11:00–11:30	520				
11:30–12:00	520				
12:00–12:30					
12:30–1:00					
1:00–1:30	520	367	367	520	415
1:30–2:00			367		
2:00–2:30			415		
2:30–3:00					
3:00–3:30					
3:30–4:00					
4:00–4:30					
4:30–5:00					

Weekly Summary:

Client #	Total Hours
367	14
415	13
520	13

"[Barnett Legal Associates] wants to know the total costs of serving clients, not just the direct labor cost . . . [so it] also allocates indirect costs to individual jobs (clients)."

costs to individual jobs (clients). The law firm develops a predetermined indirect cost allocation rate, following the same six-step approach that E-Z-Boy (page 871) used to develop its indirect manufacturing (overhead) cost rate:

1.   *Select a cost allocation base.*
Barnett uses direct labor hours as the allocation base, because the number of hours that attorneys work on clients' cases is the main driver of indirect costs.

2.   *Estimate the total indirect costs.*
In December 19X8, Barnett estimates that the following indirect costs will be incurred in 19X9:

Maintaining and updating law library for case research.........	$ 25,000
Advertisements in the yellow pages	2,000
Sponsorship of the symphony	3,000
Office rent	200,000
Office support staff...	70,000
Total indirect costs	$300,000

3.   *Estimate the total quantity of the indirect cost allocation base.*
Barnett estimates that its attorneys will work 10,000 direct labor hours in 19X9.

4. *Compute the predetermined indirect cost allocation rate. (Divide step 2 by step 3.)*

$$\text{Predetermined indirect} \atop \text{cost allocation rate} = \frac{\$300,000 \text{ expected indirect costs}}{10,000 \text{ expected direct labor hours}} = \frac{\$30 \text{ per direct}}{\text{labor hour}}$$

■ **Daily Exercise 20-20**

5. *Obtain the actual quantity of the indirect cost allocation base used by individual jobs, as the year unfolds.*
Exhibit 20-14 shows that client 367 required 14 direct labor hours.

6. *Allocate indirect costs to jobs by multiplying the predetermined indirect cost rate (step 4) by the actual quantity of the allocation base used by each job (step 5).*
Client 367 is allocated indirect costs as follows:

14 direct labor hours × $30/hour = $420

To summarize, the total costs assigned to client 367 are

Direct labor: 14 hours × $50/hour	= $ 700
Indirect costs: 14 hours × $30/hour	= 420
Total costs	$1,120

Thinking It Over Would John Barnett want to know the total cost of each job for each of the following purposes? Why or why not?

    a. Inventory valuation
b. External financial reporting
c. To determine fees charged to clients

Answers

a. No. Service firms like Barnett Legal Associates have no inventories.
b. No. Costs need not be assigned to individual clients to prepare Barnett's financial statements.
c. Yes. Fees charged to clients must be high enough to cover indirect costs (and profits) as well as direct labor costs.

In summary: Noninventoriable costs are assigned to jobs only for internal decision making, not for external financial reporting.

You have now learned how to use a job cost system to assign costs to jobs. Review the Job Costing Decision Guidelines to solidify your understanding.

DECISION GUIDELINES — Job Costing

DECISION	GUIDELINES
Should I use job costing or process costing? How to record:	• *Job costing* for unique products produced in small batches • *Process costing* for identical products produced in large batches, often in a continuous flow

• Purchase and use of materials?	*Purchase:*
	Materials Inventory XX
	    Accounts Payable (or Cash) XX
	Use:
	Work in Process (direct materials) XX
	Manufacturing Overhead (indirect materials) XX
	    Materials Inventory.. XX

• Incurrence and assignment of labor?	*Incurred:*
	Manufacturing Wages XX
	    Wages Payable (or Cash) XX
	Assigned:
	Work in Process (direct labor)........................... XX
	Manufacturing Overhead (indirect labor) XX
	    Manufacturing Wages..................................... XX

(continued)

DECISION GUIDELINES *(continued)*

How to determine whether utilities, insurance, property taxes, depreciation, and so on are

• Manufacturing overhead?	Utilities, insurance, property taxes, and depreciation expense are part of manufacturing overhead *only* if they are incurred in the manufacturing plant.
• Operating expenses?	If not related to manufacturing, such expenses are operating expenses. For example, if related to a sales office or store, such expenses are marketing expenses. If related to executive headquarters, they are administrative expenses. If related to delivery vehicles or distribution centers, they are distribution expenses. These are all operating expenses, not manufacturing overhead.

How to record *actual* manufacturing overhead costs?

Manufacturing Overhead XXX
    Accumulated Depreciation—Plant and
        Equipment XX
    Prepaid Insurance—Plant and Equipment ... XX
    Utilities Payable (or Cash)............................ XX
    and so on.. XX

How to compute a predetermined manufacturing overhead rate?

$$\frac{\text{Total estimated manufacturing overhead cost}}{\text{Total estimated quantity of allocation base}}$$

How to allocate manufacturing overhead?

Work in Process Inventory XX
    Manufacturing Overhead............................. XX

What is the *amount* of the allocated manufacturing overhead?

$$\begin{array}{c} \text{Actual quantity} \\ \text{of the manufacturing} \\ \text{overhead allocation base} \end{array} \times \begin{array}{c} \text{Predetermined} \\ \text{manufacturing} \\ \text{overhead rate} \end{array}$$

How to close Manufacturing Overhead at the end of the period?

- If balance is significant—prorate to Work in Process, Finished Goods, Cost of Goods Sold.
- If balance is insignificant—close directly to Cost of Goods Sold.

Which T-account summarizes the schedule of cost of goods manufactured?

Work in Process Inventory

How do service companies trace direct labor to individual jobs?

Time record—employees record the time spent on each client.

Why do companies allocate noninventoriable costs to jobs?

Because they need total product costs for internal decisions (such as setting selling prices). For external reporting, companies assign only inventoriable costs to jobs.

SUMMARY PROBLEM FOR YOUR REVIEW

Hillis Incorporated had the following inventories at the end of 19X8:

Materials Inventory......................	$20,000
Work in Process Inventory	17,000
Finished Goods Inventory	11,000

During January 19X9, Hillis completed the following transactions:

a. Purchased materials on account, $31,000.
b. Requisitioned (placed into production) direct materials, $39,000.
c. Manufacturing labor cost incurred was $40,000.
d. Manufacturing labor was: 90% direct labor; 10% indirect labor.
e. Requisitioned indirect materials, $3,000.
f. Incurred other manufacturing overhead, $13,000 (credit Accounts Payable).
g. Allocated manufacturing overhead to production at 50% of direct labor cost.
h. Completed production, $99,000.
i. Sold goods on account, $172,000; cost of goods sold, $91,400.

1. Record the transactions in the general journal.
2. Post the transactions and inventory balances to the following accounts:

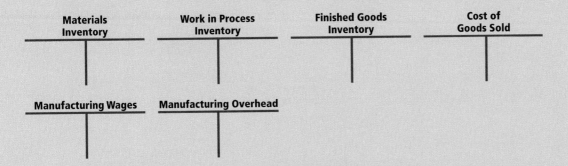

Materials Inventory	Work in Process Inventory	Finished Goods Inventory	Cost of Goods Sold

Manufacturing Wages	Manufacturing Overhead

3. Record the journal entry to close the ending balance of Manufacturing Overhead directly to Cost of Goods Sold. Post your entry to the T-accounts.
4. What are the ending balances in the three inventory accounts and Cost of Goods Sold?

■ Solution

Journal entries:

REQUIREMENT 1

a.	Materials Inventory	31,000	
	Accounts Payable		31,000
b.	Work in Process Inventory	39,000	
	Materials Inventory		39,000
c.	Manufacturing Wages	40,000	
	Wages Payable		40,000
d.	Work in Process Inventory ($40,000 × 0.90)	36,000	
	Manufacturing Overhead ($40,000 × 0.10)	4,000	
	Manufacturing Wages		40,000
e.	Manufacturing Overhead	3,000	
	Materials Inventory		3,000
f.	Manufacturing Overhead	13,000	
	Accounts Payable		13,000
g.	Work in Process Inventory ($36,000 × 0.50)	18,000	
	Manufacturing Overhead		18,000
h.	Finished Goods Inventory	99,000	
	Work in Process Inventory		99,000
i.	Accounts Receivable	172,000	
	Sales Revenue		172,000
	Cost of Goods Sold	91,400	
	Finished Goods Inventory		91,400

Post the transactions:

REQUIREMENT 2

Materials Inventory

Bal.	20,000	(b)	39,000
(a)	31,000	(e)	3,000
Bal.	9,000		

Work In Process Inventory

Bal.	17,000	(h)	99,000
(b)	39,000		
(d)	36,000		
(g)	18,000		
Bal.	11,000		

Finished Goods Inventory

Bal.	11,000	(i)	91,400
(h)	99,000		
Bal.	18,600		

Cost of Goods Sold

(i)	91,400	

Manufacturing Wages

(c)	40,000	(d)	40,000

Manufacturing Overhead

(d)	4,000	(g)	18,000
(e)	3,000		
(f)	13,000		
Bal.	2,000		

REQUIREMENT 3

Close Manufacturing Overhead:

Cost of Goods Sold........................... 2,000
Manufacturing Overhead.......... 2,000

Manufacturing Overhead				Cost of Goods Sold	
(d)	4,000	(g)	18,000	(i)	91,400
(e)	3,000		2,000		2,000
(f)	13,000			Bal.	93,400

REQUIREMENT 4

Ending Balances:

Materials Inventory (from requirement 2)..................... $ 9,000
Work in Process Inventory (from requirement 2).......... 11,000
Finished Goods Inventory (from requirement 2)........... 18,600
Cost of Goods Sold (from requirement 3)..................... 93,400

Summary of Learning Objectives

1. Distinguish between job costing and process costing.
Process costing is used by companies that produce large numbers of identical products, often in a continuous fashion, using a series of uniform production steps. Costs are accumulated for each production process, and then averaged over the many (identical) units passing through that process.

In contrast, companies that use job costing usually produce individual products or small batches of products that proceed through production steps as a distinct, identifiable job lot. Jobs can differ greatly from one another in terms of materials, labor, and overhead. Costs are accumulated for each individual job. For external reporting, only inventoriable costs are assigned to jobs. This is why a manufacturing *job cost record* includes only direct materials, direct labor, and manufacturing overhead costs of producing the job. Management uses the individual job cost records to accumulate and control costs, and to make other internal decisions.

2. Account for materials and labor in a manufacturer's job costing system. *Direct materials* are the important materials used to make a product. The costs of direct materials are traced to individual jobs using *materials requisitions*. Direct material costs are added (debited) to Work in Process Inventory. *Indirect materials* cannot be easily traced to specific jobs, so their costs are added (debited) to the Manufacturing Overhead account. *Direct labor* is the compensation of employees who physically convert materials into the company's products. Direct labor costs are traced to jobs by labor time tickets, and direct labor is added (debited) to Work in Process Inventory. *Indirect labor* is the cost of labor that is difficult to trace to individual jobs, such as maintenance and janitorial labor. Indirect labor costs are added (debited) to Manufacturing Overhead.

3. Account for manufacturing overhead, including under-allocated and overallocated overhead, in a manufacturer's job costing system. *Manufacturing overhead* is all manufacturing costs besides direct materials and direct labor. Actual manufacturing overhead costs are accumulated as debits in the Manufacturing Overhead account. Manufacturing Overhead is allocated to jobs using a predetermined rate per unit of a *cost allocation base*. Ideally, the allocation base is the driver of the manufacturing overhead costs. Allocating manufacturing overhead requires a debit to Work in Process and a credit to Manufacturing Overhead. At the end of the period, any underallocated or overallocated manufacturing overhead is closed. If the amount of this leftover balance is insignificant, it may be closed directly to Cost of Goods Sold. Otherwise, the balance is prorated to Work in Process Inventory, Finished Goods Inventory, and Cost of Goods Sold.

4. Account for noninventoriable costs in job costing. Because companies can allocate noninventoriable costs to jobs for internal decision making, even companies that are not manufacturers can also use job costing. For a service company, direct labor is traced to individual jobs (clients) using time records. Indirect costs such as marketing, office rent, and support staff salaries are allocated to jobs using predetermined indirect cost allocation rates. Service companies have no inventoriable costs, so they use job costing only for internal decisions, such as setting fees.

Accounting Vocabulary

allocation base *(p. 871)*
budgeted manufacturing
   overhead rate *(p. 871)*
cost allocation *(p. 870)*
cost assignment *(p. 870)*
cost driver *(p. 861)*

cost tracing *(p. 870)*
job cost record *(p. 862)*
job costing *(p. 861)*
labor time ticket *(p. 866)*
materials requisition
   (p. 864)

overallocated (manufacturing) overhead *(p. 875)*
predetermined manufactur-
   ing overhead rate
   (p. 871)
process costing *(p. 860)*

proration *(p. 875)*
time record *(p. 879)*
underallocated (manufacturing) overhead *(p. 875)*

Questions

1. Explain the basic difference between job costing and process costing.

2. Give three examples of companies that would use job costing rather than process costing, and explain why.

3. How can computers simplify the tracing of direct materials and direct labor to specific jobs?

4. What source document requests that raw materials be brought to the production floor? What journal entry does this source document support?

5. Distinguish direct materials from indirect materials and direct labor from indirect labor. Direct materials and direct labor are debited directly to what account when placed in production? To what account are indirect materials and indirect labor debited?

6. Give examples of direct materials and indirect materials for a caterer.

7. Is Manufacturing Overhead a temporary or permanent account? Explain how the account operates. What do the debits represent? What do the credits represent?

8. What document is used to trace direct manufacturing labor cost to specific jobs? Briefly describe how the document is used.

9. Is manufacturing overhead cost allocated to jobs by a precise identification of the overhead cost of each job or by an estimation? Explain.

10. What source document is the subsidiary ledger for the Work in Process control account?

11. Explain the distinctions among cost tracing, cost allocation, and cost assignment.

12. Transactions in what account summarize the cost of goods manufactured? Show the T-account and label the transactions.

13. Would a heavily automated manufacturing plant be more likely to use machine hours or direct labor hours as the manufacturing overhead allocation base? Explain.

14. Why do companies use predetermined rather than actual manufacturing overhead rates?

15. When is manufacturing overhead underallocated? When is it overallocated?

16. Insignificant amounts of over- or underallocated overhead are closed to what account? Significant amounts are prorated to what three accounts?

17. Which of the following accounts have their balances brought to zero at the end of the period, and which keep their ending balances to start the next period? Materials Inventory, Manufacturing Overhead, Finished Goods Inventory, Manufacturing Wages.

18. Summarize the computation of cost of goods manufactured. Use any dollar amounts.

19. Why would an international professional services firm like Arthur Andersen use job costing?

20. How do professional service firms such as law firms and management consulting firms trace direct labor to individual jobs?

Daily Exercises

DE20-1 Job costing and process costing differ in (a) the cost object, and (b) the number of units over which costs are averaged. Explain these two differences.

Distinguishing between job and process costing
(Obj. 1)

DE20-2 Would the following companies use job costing or process costing?

a. A manufacturer of paper
b. A local catering business
c. A builder of defense aircraft
d. A manufacturer of glass
e. A boat repair shop

Distinguishing between job and process costing
(Obj. 1)

DE20-3 Suppose a Shell Oil refining plant incurs $45,000 to refine 150,000 gallons of unleaded gasoline. What is the cost per gallon? Would Shell Oil use job costing or process costing? Why?

Distinguishing between job and process costing
(Obj. 1)

DE20-4 For a manufacturer that uses job costing, diagram the flow of costs through the accounts. Label each transaction. Include the following accounts in your diagram: Manufacturing Overhead, Finished Goods Inventory, Materials Inventory, Cost of Goods Sold, Work in Process Inventory, Manufacturing Wages.

Flow of costs in job costing
(Obj. 2, 3)

DE20-5 ◀▥ Link Back to Chapter 9 (Inventory). Refer to E-Z-Boy's Material Ledger Record in Exhibit 20-5. Suppose material requisition #334 indicated that on July 24, 15 units of lumber (rather than ten), had been used in Job 293. What is the ending balance of item B-220—Lumber/Recliner Chairs?

Accounting for materials
(Obj. 2)

DE20-6 Turn to E-Z-Boy's Materials subsidiary ledger in Exhibit 20-6. Suppose that on July 24, the balance of the Nails account was $75 rather than $40. What would be the total Materials Inventory balance?

Accounting for materials
(Obj. 2)

DE20-7 Jasper Jax Tux manufactures men's formal wear. Its plant records the following materials-related transactions:

Accounting for materials
(Obj. 2)

Purchases of cloth (on account)	$50,000
Purchases of thread (on account)	500
Material requisitions:	
Cloth	45,000
Thread	200

What journal entries record these transactions? Post these transactions to the Materials Inventory account. If the company had $20,400 of Materials Inventory at the beginning of the period, what is the ending balance of Materials Inventory?

Accounting for materials
(Obj. 2)

DE20-8 Use the following T-accounts to determine direct materials used and indirect materials used.

Materials Inventory			
Bal.	10		
Purchases	200	X	
Bal.	15		

Work in Process Inventory			
Bal.	20		
Direct materials	Y		
Direct labor	150	Cost of goods	
Manufacturing overhead	125	manufactured	465
Bal.	5		

Accounting for labor
(Obj. 2)

DE20-9 Candy Carpenter Cosmetics reports the following labor-related transactions at its plant in Bar Harbor, Florida.

Assembly-line workers' wages	$60,000
Plant janitors' wages.........................	300
Maintenance workers' wages	450

Record the journal entries for the incurrence and assignment of these wages.

Accounting for overhead
(Obj. 3)

DE20-10 ◀▥ *Link Back to Chapter 19*. L&B Recordings reports the following costs in 19X9. What is the balance in the Manufacturing Overhead account?

Depreciation expense on salespersons' autos.......................	$20,000
Indirect materials..	40,000
Depreciation on delivery trucks..	12,000
Depreciation on manufacturing plant and equipment	50,000
Indirect manufacturing labor	85,000
Customer service hotline	17,000
Property taxes on the plant	13,000

Computing a predetermined manufacturing overhead rate
(Obj. 3)

DE20-11 Super-Tex Products produces specialized textile weaving equipment. The company uses a predetermined manufacturing overhead rate to allocate overhead based on the machine hours each job requires. Super-Tex reports the following data for 19X9:

	Expected	Actual
Manufacturing overhead	$550,000	$600,000
Direct labor hours	10,000	9,375
Direct labor costs	$100,000	$103,125
Machine hours	11,000	10,000

Compute Super-Tex's predetermined manufacturing overhead rate.

Accounting for overhead
(Obj. 3)

DE20-12 Refer to Daily Exercise 20-11. Super Tex's Job 744 required

a. 20 direct labor hours, at a total cost of $4,096
b. $2,000 of direct materials
c. 15 machine hours

Answer the following questions:

1. Record the journal entry to allocate the manufacturing overhead to Job 744.
2. Compute the total cost of Job 744.

Accounting for overhead
(Obj. 3)

DE20-13 In the E-Z-Boy job cost record (Exhibit 20-12), how much manufacturing overhead cost would be allocated to Job 293 if the predetermined manufacturing overhead allocation rate is 60% of direct labor cost rather than 80 percent? What would be the total cost assigned to Job 293?

Accounting for materials, labor, and overhead
(Obj. 2, 3)

DE20-14 Quark Entertainment Enterprises produces laser-tag equipment. The company reports the following information at December 31, 19X9. Quark began operations on January 30, 19X9.

Materials Inventory		Manufacturing Wages		Work in Process Inventory		Finished Goods Inventory		Manufacturing Overhead	
52,000	44,000	70,000	70,000	40,000	136,000	136,000	122,000	4,000	48,000
				60,000				10,000	
				48,000				37,000	

Answer the following questions.

1. What is the cost of direct materials used? The cost of indirect materials used?
2. What is the cost of direct labor? The cost of indirect labor?
3. What is the cost of goods manufactured?
4. What is actual manufacturing overhead? Allocated manufacturing overhead?
5. What is cost of goods sold?
6. What is the predetermined manufacturing overhead rate, as a percentage of direct labor cost?
7. Is manufacturing overhead underallocated or overallocated? By how much?

DE20-15   Turn to the E-Z-Boy illustration on pages 863–874. Suppose direct material requisitions had totaled $270,000 rather than $285,000. Use T-accounts to show the new ending balances of Materials Inventory and Work in Process Inventory (before disposing of underallocated or overallocated manufacturing overhead).

Accounting for materials, labor, and work in process inventory
(Obj. 2, 3)

DE20-16   Supp-Cal Supplements produces small batches of specially designed dietary supplements for herbalists. The company had $10,000 of underallocated manufacturing overhead in 19X9. Before closing out the Manufacturing Overhead account, Supp-Cal reports the following unadjusted ending account balances:

Prorating underallocated overhead
(Obj. 3)

Materials Inventory......................	$100,000
Work in Process Inventory	25,000
Finished Goods Inventory	75,000
Cost of Goods Sold	400,000

Give the journal entry for prorating the $10,000 underallocated overhead.

DE20-17   In the E-Z-Boy illustration on pages 873–876, actual manufacturing overhead was $210,000. Suppose instead that the actual manufacturing overhead was $187,500.

Under/overallocated overhead
(Obj. 3)

1. What would be the actual manufacturing overhead rate?
2. Is manufacturing overhead underallocated or overallocated? By how much?
3. Are Work in Process Inventory, Finished Goods Inventory, and Cost of Goods Sold too high or too low?

DE20-18   Refer to Daily Exercise 20-17. Make the journal entry to close out E-Z-Boy's Manufacturing Overhead account if

Prorating under/overallocated overhead
(Obj. 3)

a.   The balance is closed directly to Cost of Goods Sold
b.   The balance is prorated

DE20-19   In the Barnett Legal Associates example on page 879, suppose Teresa Fox's annual salary is $80,000 rather than $100,000.

Job costing in a service company
(Obj. 4)

1. What would be the hourly (cost) rate to Barnett Legal Associates of employing Fox?
2. What direct labor cost would be traced to client 367?

DE20-20   Return to the original data in the Barnett Legal Associates example on pages 879–881. Suppose the Barnett attorneys expected to work a total of 15,000 direct labor hours rather than 10,000 direct labor hours.

Job costing in a service company
(Obj. 4)

1. What is the indirect cost allocation rate?
2. What indirect costs will be allocated to client 367?

Exercises

Distinguishing job and process costing
(Obj. 1)

E20-1   Listed below are several terms. Complete the following statements with one of these terms. You may use a term more than once, and some terms may not be used at all.

Cost allocation	Cost driver	Job costing	Process costing
Cost tracing	Job cost record	Materials requisition	

a. A _____ is any factor that affects costs.

b. Georgia Pacific pulverizes wood into pulp to manufacture cardboard. The company would use a _____ system.

c. To record costs of maintaining thousands of identical mortgage files, financial institutions like Fleet Mortgage would use a _____ system.

d. _____ is assigning direct costs to cost objects.

e. A _____ accumulates the costs of an individual job.

f. Companies that produce large numbers of identical products use _____ systems for product costing.

g. The computer repair service that visits your home and repairs your computer would use a _____ system.

h. A _____ is manufacturing personnel's request that materials be moved to the production floor.

i. _____ is assigning indirect costs to cost objects.

j. _____ is used by companies that produce small quantities of many different products.

Accounting for job costs
(Obj. 2, 3)

E20-2   Pritchard's Publishing job cost records yielded the following information:

Job No.	Date			Total Cost of Job at March 31
	Started	Finished	Sold	
1	February 19	March 14	March 15	$ 1,700
2	February 29	March 21	March 26	17,000
3	March 3	April 11	April 13	5,700
4	March 7	March 29	April 1	6,200
5	March 9	March 30	April 2	2,600
6	March 22	April 11	April 13	1,300
7	March 23	March 27	March 29	5,400

REQUIRED

Compute Pritchard's cost of (a) work in process inventory at March 31, (b) finished goods inventory at March 31, and (c) cost of goods sold for March.

Job costing journal entries
(Obj. 2, 3)

E20-3   Record the following transactions in the general journal.

a. Incurred and paid marketing expenses, $4,000.

b. Incurred and paid manufacturing wages, $16,500.

c. Purchased materials on account, $11,100.

d. Used in production: direct materials, $9,000; indirect materials, $2,000.

e. Assigned $16,000 of manufacturing labor to jobs, 80% of which was direct labor and 20% of which was indirect labor.

f. Recorded manufacturing overhead: depreciation on plant, $13,000; plant insurance, $1,700; plant property tax, $4,200 (credit Property Tax Payable).

g. Allocated manufacturing overhead to jobs, 200% of direct labor cost.

h. Completed production, $27,000.

i. Sold inventory on account, $22,000; cost of goods sold, $14,000.

Identifying job costing journal entries
(Obj. 2, 3)

E20-4   Describe the lettered transactions in the following manufacturing accounts:

Materials Inventory			Work in Process Inventory			Finished Goods Inventory	
(a)	(b)		(b)	(h)		(h)	(i)
	(e)		(d)			(j)	
			(g)				
			(j)				

Manufacturing Wages			Manufacturing Overhead			Cost of Goods Sold	
(c)	(d)		(d)	(g)		(i)	
			(e)	(j)		(j)	
			(f)				

E20-5 August production generated the following activity in the Work in Process Inventory account of Zumikazi Manufacturing Company:

Using the Work in Process Inventory account
(Obj. 2, 3)

Work in Process Inventory

August 1 Bal.	10,000
Direct materials used	28,000
Direct labor assigned to jobs	31,000
Manufacturing overhead allocated to jobs	11,000

Completed production, not yet recorded, consists of Jobs B-78, G-65, and Y-11, with total costs of $16,000, $27,000, and $33,000, respectively.

1. Compute the cost of work in process at August 31.
2. Prepare the journal entry for production completed in August.
3. Prepare the journal entry to record the sale (on credit) of Job G-65 for $41,000. Also make the cost-of-goods-sold entry.
4. What is the gross margin on Job G-65? What other costs does this gross margin have to cover?

REQUIRED

E20-6 Selected cost data for Sverge Co. are as follows:

Accounting for manufacturing overhead
(Obj. 3)

Expected manufacturing overhead cost for the year	$105,000
Expected direct labor cost for the year	43,750
Actual manufacturing overhead cost for the year..............	96,600
Actual direct labor cost for the year...................................	40,500

1. Compute the predetermined manufacturing overhead rate per direct labor dollar.
2. Prepare the journal entry to allocate overhead cost for the year.
3. By what amount is manufacturing overhead overallocated or underallocated? Is this amount significant or insignificant?
4. On the basis of your answer to requirement 3, journalize disposition of the overhead balance.

REQUIRED

E20-7 The Aadvantage Luggage Company in St. Louis, Missouri, uses a predetermined manufacturing overhead rate to allocate overhead to individual jobs, based on the direct labor hours required. At the beginning of 19X9, the company expected to incur the following:

Accounting for manufacturing overhead
(Obj. 3)

Manufacturing overhead costs	$ 400,000
Direct labor cost...............................	$1,000,000
Machine hours..................................	50,000 hours
Direct labor hours	100,000 hours

At the end of 19X9, the company had actually incurred:

Direct labor cost..	$1,210,000
Depreciation on manufacturing property, plant, and equipment	350,000
Property taxes on plant	20,000
Sales salaries...	25,000
Delivery drivers' wages	15,000
Plant janitors' wages	10,000
Machine hours..	45,000 hours
Direct labor hours..	110,000 hours

1. Compute Aadvantage's predetermined manufacturing overhead rate.
2. Record the summary journal entry for *allocating* manufacturing overhead.
3. Post the manufacturing overhead transactions to the Manufacturing Overhead T-account. Is manufacturing overhead underallocated or overallocated? By how much? Is cost of goods sold understated or overstated?
4. Close the Manufacturing Overhead account to Cost of Goods Sold. Does your entry increase or decrease cost of goods sold?

Prorating underallocated or over-allocated manufacturing overhead
(Obj. 3)

E20-8 Refer to the data in Exercise 20-7. The Aadvantage accountant found an error in her 19X9 expense records. Depreciation on manufacturing property, plant, and equipment was actually $500,000, not the $350,000 she had originally reported. Unadjusted balances at the end of 19X9 include

Materials Inventory......................	$200,000
Work in Process Inventory	70,000
Finished Goods Inventory	130,000
Cost of Goods Sold	600,000

REQUIRED

1. Is manufacturing overhead underallocated or overallocated? By how much?
2. Record the entry to prorate the underallocated or overallocated manufacturing overhead.
3. What are the adjusted ending balances of Materials Inventory, Work in Process Inventory, Finished Goods Inventory, and Cost of Goods Sold?

Job costing in a service company
(Obj. 4)

E20-9 Sierra Green, an environmental consulting firm, specializes in advising electric utilities on compliance with recent environmental regulations. Sierra uses a job cost system with a predetermined indirect cost allocation rate, computed as a percentage of expected direct labor costs.

At the beginning of 19X8, managing partner Mark Green prepared the following plan, or budget, for 19X8:

Direct labor hours (professionals)	16,000 hours
Direct labor costs (professionals)	$1,120,000
Office rent	250,000
Support staff salaries	556,000
Utilities	146,000

Southwest Light & Gas is inviting several consultants to bid for their work. Mark Green estimates that this job will require about 220 direct labor hours.

REQUIRED

1. Compute Sierra Green's (a) hourly direct labor cost rate, and (b) indirect cost allocation rate.
2. Compute the predicted cost of the Southwest Light & Gas job.
3. If Green wants to earn a profit that equals 20% of the job's cost, how much should he bid for the Southwest Light & Gas job?

CHALLENGE EXERCISE

Prorating manufacturing overhead
(Obj. 3)

E20-10 At the end of the 19X9 fiscal year, Barton Creek Golf Products' manufacturing records show the following unadjusted ending account balances:

	Work in Process Inventory	Finished Goods Inventory	Cost of Goods Sold
Direct materials	$100,000	$170,000	$ 360,000
Direct labor	80,000	250,000	600,000
Manufacturing overhead	60,000	300,000	540,000
Total	$240,000	$720,000	$1,500,000

Barton Creek's accountants allocated overhead during the year using a predetermined rate of $50 per machine hour. At year end, they computed the actual rate of $55 per machine hour. The beginning balances of both Work in Process Inventory and Finished Goods Inventory were zero.

REQUIRED

1. How many machine hours did Barton Creek work in 19X9?
2. Was manufacturing overhead over- or underallocated for the year? By how much?
3. Record the entry to prorate the over- or underallocated overhead to the three accounts above. What are their balances after proration?

Beyond the Numbers

Accounting for manufacturing overhead
(Obj. 3)

BN20-1 The predetermined rate used to allocate manufacturing overhead usually turns out to be inaccurate (different from the actual overhead rate). As a result, accountants have to make adjusting entries at the end of the year to correct this error in allocating the manufacturing overhead. Because this predetermined overhead rate usually turns out to be "wrong," aren't these allocated costs misleading? Why don't accountants just use the actual manufacturing overhead rate?

Accounting for manufacturing overhead
(Obj. 3)

BN20-2 Jazwell Preserves is a small manufacturer of fruit preserves. The plant operates 50 weeks a year, and closes for the holidays during the last two weeks of December. Jazwell's manufacturing overhead cost is mostly straight-line depreciation on the manufacturing plant and equipment. This cost is constant from month to month. The company allocates manufacturing overhead to products based on direct labor hours.

If Jazwell uses a predetermined manufacturing overhead rate calculated on a monthly basis, will the December rate be higher or lower than in the other months? Why?

Now suppose that air-conditioning costs are a significant component of manufacturing overhead. Jazwell expects to incur much higher air-conditioning costs in July than in other months. If Jazwell uses predetermined overhead rates calculated on a monthly basis, will the July manufacturing overhead rate be higher or lower than the rate in other months?

Should Jazwell compute its predetermined manufacturing overhead rate on an annual basis or a monthly basis? Explain.

ETHICAL ISSUE

Ariel Sound designs, builds, and installs sound systems for theaters and stadiums. To develop a bid price (selling price) for new business, Ariel estimates its total cost from all elements of the value chain, and then adds a profit margin. To improve the quality of its installations, it has recently changed from using wired speakers to a new wireless speaker technology. This change increased Ariel's direct material costs.

Ariel controller Sandra Muñoz is going over the final contract numbers for a bid that was recently accepted by Turner Stadiums. Muñoz discovers that by mistake, the old direct cost numbers had been used to price the bid. Muñoz is concerned that if she revises the price now to reflect the higher current direct costs, Ariel might lose the contract. This would hurt her reputation in the company. The company president, whose bonus is based on sales, has already made it clear that he is looking forward to his bonus from the Turner contract. Muñoz is not sure what to do.

Identify the parties involved in Sandra Muñoz's ethical dilemma. What are her alternatives? How would each party be affected by each alternative?

Problems (GROUP A)

Analyzing job cost data
(Obj. 2, 3)

P20-1A Craftstar Conversion Van's job cost records yield the following information. The company uses a perpetual inventory system.

Job No.	Started	Finished	Sold	Total Cost of Job at March 31	Total Manufacturing Cost Added in April
1	2/26	3/7	3/9	$2,200	
2	2/3	3/12	3/13	1,600	
3	3/29	3/31	4/3	300	
4	3/31	4/1	4/1	500	$ 400
5	3/17	4/24	4/27	1,500	2,500
6	4/8	4/12	4/14		700
7	4/23	5/6	5/9		1,200
8	4/30	5/22	5/26		600

REQUIRED

1. Compute Craftstar's cost of (a) work in process inventory at March 31 and April 30, (b) finished goods inventory at March 31 and April 30, and (c) cost of goods sold for March and April.

2. Make summary journal entries to record the transfer of completed units from work in process to finished goods for March and April.

3. Record the sale of Job 5 for $6,000.

4. Compute the gross margin for Job 5. What costs must the gross margin cover?

*Computing manufacturing cost
amounts for the financial statements
(Obj. 2, 3)*

P20-2A Assume that Wrangler's accounting records include the following cost information on jobs for the manufacture of a line of jeans. For the year ended December 31, 19X8, Wrangler incurred a total manufacturing cost of $170.2 million for materials, labor, and manufacturing overhead, of which $26.2 million was the cost of direct materials used. Beginning balances for the year were Materials Inventory, $3.4 million; Work in Process Inventory, $3.8 million; and Finished Goods Inventory, $9.4 million. The company allocates overhead on the basis of the relationship between overhead and direct labor costs. At year end, the inventory accounts showed these balances (in millions):

	Materials	Direct Labor	Manufacturing Overhead
Materials inventory....................	$0.9	$–0–	$–0–
Work in process inventory..........	1.5	2.0	2.5
Finished goods inventory............	2.4	3.2	4.0

REQUIRED

1. Prepare Wrangler's schedule of cost of goods manufactured for the line of jeans. (*Hint:* First determine the *sum* of direct labor incurred plus manufacturing overhead-allocated. Then use the relation between direct labor and manufacturing overhead-allocated (apparent from the above inventory accounts) to determine the amount of direct labor incurred.)
2. Compute the cost of goods sold. (See Exhibit 19-9 if you need a review.)
3. Record the transfer from Work in Process Inventory to Finished Goods Inventory and the transfer from Finished Goods Inventory to Cost of Goods Sold during the year.

P20-3A Lakefront Homes builds prefabricated houses in a factory near Toronto, Canada. The company uses a perpetual inventory system and a job cost system in which each house is a job. The following transactions and events occurred during May:

a. Purchased materials on account, $221,000.
b. Incurred manufacturing wages of $132,800. Requisitioned direct materials and used direct labor in manufacturing:

	Direct Materials	Direct Labor
House 613	$26,100	$11,600
House 614	41,700	22,500
House 615	51,000	15,000
House 616	54,000	23,800
House 617	43,900	20,700
House 618	32,800	17,600

c. Depreciation of manufacturing equipment used on different houses, $14,300.
d. Other overhead costs incurred on houses 613–618:

Indirect labor...	$21,600
Equipment rentals paid in cash	8,000
Liability insurance expired	3,900

e. Allocated overhead to jobs at the predetermined rate of 30% of direct labor cost.
f. Houses completed: 613, 615, 616.
g. Houses sold: 615 for $79,000; 616 for $103,900.

REQUIRED

1. Record the preceding transactions and events in the general journal.
2. Open T-accounts for Work in Process Inventory and Finished Goods Inventory. Post the appropriate entries to these accounts, identifying each entry by letter. Determine the ending account balances, assuming that the beginning balances were zero.
3. Add the costs of unfinished houses, and show that this total amount equals the ending balance in the Work in Process Inventory account.
4. Add the costs of completed houses that have not yet been sold, and show that this total amount equals the ending balance in the Finished Goods Inventory account.
5. Compute the gross margin on each house that was sold. What costs must the gross margin cover for Lakefront Homes?

P20-4A   E. Dan Smith Company produces conveyor belts that other companies use in their manufacturing processes. Smith uses job costing and has a perpetual inventory system.

On September 22, Smith received an order for 50 industrial-grade belts from Guiterrez Corporation at a price of $56 each. The job, assigned number 449, was promised for October 10. After purchasing the materials, Smith began production on September 30 and incurred the following costs in completing the order:

Date	Materials Requisition No.	Description	Amount
9/30	593	20 lb. rubber @ $9	$180
10/2	598	30 meters polyester fabric @ $9	270
10/3	622	12 meters steel cord @ $12	144

Date	Time Ticket No.	Description	Amount
9/30	1754	10 hours @ $9	$ 90
10/3	1805	40 hours @ $8	320

Smith allocates manufacturing overhead to jobs on the basis of the relationship between expected overhead ($375,000) and direct labor ($250,000). Job 449 was completed on October 3 and shipped to Guiterrez on October 5.

1. Prepare a job cost record similar to Exhibit 20-3 for Job 449.
2. Journalize in summary form the requisition of direct materials and the assignment of direct labor and manufacturing overhead to Job 449.
3. Journalize completion of the job and sale of the goods.

P20-5A   ◄▥ *Link Back to Chapters 2 and 19.* Pacific Electric manufactures specialized parts used in the generation of power. Initially, the company manufactured the parts for its own use, but it gradually began selling them to other public utilities as well. The trial balance of Pacific Electric's manufacturing operation on January 1 is as follows:

PACIFIC ELECTRIC—MANUFACTURING OPERATIONS
Trial Balance
January 1, 19XX

Cash	$ 33,000	
Accounts receivable	65,860	
Inventories:		
Materials	14,180	
Work in process	43,350	
Finished goods	78,550	
Plant assets	342,860	
Accumulated depreciation		$145,960
Accounts payable		83,920
Wages payable		5,700
Common stock		200,000
Retained earnings		142,220
Sales revenue		—
Cost of goods sold	—	
Manufacturing wages	—	
Manufacturing overhead	—	
Marketing and general expenses	—	—
	$577,800	$577,800

January 1 balances in the subsidiary ledgers were

- Materials ledger: petrochemicals, $5,280; electronic parts, $7,800; indirect materials, $1,100.
- Work in process ledger: Job 86, $43,350.
- Finished goods ledger: transformers, $35,770; transmission lines, $21,910; switches, $20,870.

January transactions are summarized as follows:

a. Payments on account, $79,330.

b. Marketing and general expenses incurred and paid, $21,660.

c. Collections on account, $187,880.

d. Materials purchased on credit: petrochemicals, $19,570; electronic parts, $28,360; indirect materials, $6,130.

e. Materials used in production (requisitioned):
   - Job 86: petrochemicals, $3,800.
   - Job 87: petrochemicals, $9,870; electronic parts, $5,690.
   - Job 88: petrochemicals, $7,680; electronic parts, $29,920.
   - Indirect materials, $5,760.

f. Manufacturing wages incurred during January, $52,080, of which $49,560 was paid. Wages payable at December 31 were paid during January, $5,700.

g. Labor time tickets for the month: Job 86, $4,000; Job 87, $20,880; Job 88, $16,560; indirect labor, $10,640.

h. Other actual miscellaneous manufacturing overhead costs incurred on account, $27,660.

i. Depreciation on manufacturing plant and equipment (not included in item h above), $6,710.

j. Manufacturing overhead was allocated at the predetermined rate of 120% of direct labor cost.

k. Jobs completed during the month: Job 86, one transformer at total cost of $55,950; Job 87, 400 switches at total cost of $61,496.

l. Credit sales on account: All of Job 86 for $91,490 (cost $55,950); Job 87, 300 switches for $88,030 (cost, $46,122).

m. Close Manufacturing Overhead account to Cost of Goods Sold.

REQUIRED

1. Open T-accounts for the general ledger, the materials ledger, the work in process ledger, and the finished goods ledger. Insert each account balance as given, and use the reference *Bal.*

2. Record the January transactions directly in the accounts, using the letters as references. Pacific Electric uses a perpetual inventory system.

3. Prepare a trial balance at January 31.

4. Use the work in process T-account to prepare a schedule of cost of goods manufactured for the month of January.

5. Prepare an income statement for the month of January. To calculate cost of goods sold, you may want to review Exhibit 19-9. (*Hint:* In transaction **m** you closed any under/overallocated manufacturing overhead to Cost of Goods Sold. In the income statement, show this correction as an adjustment to Cost of Goods Sold. If manufacturing overhead is underallocated, the adjustment will increase Cost of Goods Sold. If overhead is overallocated, the adjustment will reduce Cost of Goods Sold.)

Job costing in a service company
(Obj. 4)

P20-6A Michael Steadman Associates is an advertising agency. The firm uses a job cost system in which each client is a different "job." Steadman traces direct labor, fax costs, and travel costs directly to each job (client). The company allocates indirect costs to jobs based on a predetermined indirect cost allocation rate, computed as a percentage of direct labor costs.

At the beginning of 19X8, managing partner Michael Steadman prepared the following plan, or budget:

Direct labor hours (professional)	**20,000 hours**
Direct labor costs (professional)	**$1,500,000**
Support staff salaries............................	**440,000**
Utilities..	**124,000**
Art supplies	**16,000**
Office rent..	**320,000**

In January 19X8, Steadman served several clients. Records for two clients appear here:

	Port Armor Tennis and Golf Resort	**Ying's Cuisine**
Direct labor hours	325 hours	25 hours
Fax costs	$ 250	$15
Travel costs	$6,000	—

1. Compute Steadman's predetermined indirect cost allocation rate for 19X8.
2. Compute the total cost of each job.
3. If Steadman wants to earn profits equal to 20% of sales revenue, how much (what total fee) should he charge each of these two clients?
4. Why does Steadman assign costs to jobs?

Problems (GROUP B)

P20-1B Castlebury Manufacturing Company job cost records yield the following information. The company uses a perpetual inventory system.

Analyzing job cost data (Obj. 2, 3)

Job No.	Date Started	Date Finished	Sold	Total Cost of Job at November 30	Total Manufacturing Costs Added in December
1	10/26	11/7	11/9	$ 700	
2	11/3	11/12	11/13	1,400	
3	11/3	11/30	12/1	2,800	
4	11/17	12/24	12/27	200	$ 600
5	11/29	12/29	1/3	400	1,600
6	12/8	12/12	12/14		750
7	12/23	1/6	1/9		500
8	12/30	1/22	1/26		2,900

1. Compute Castlebury's cost of (a) work in process inventory at November 30 and December 31, (b) finished goods inventory at November 30 and December 31, and (c) cost of goods sold for November and December.
2. Record summary journal entries for the transfer of completed units from work in process to finished goods for November and December.
3. Record the sale of Job 4 for $900.
4. What is the gross margin for Job 4? What other costs must this gross margin cover?

P20-2B Bass Shoe Company makes the Weejun loafer. Assume that Bass's accounting records include the following cost information on jobs for the manufacture of the basic brown leather Weejun during 19X9.

Computing manufacturing cost amounts for the financial statements (Obj. 2, 3)

During the year, Bass incurred manufacturing costs of $26.3 million for materials, labor, and manufacturing overhead, of which $5.4 million was allocated overhead. Beginning balances for the year were Materials Inventory, $700,000; Work in Process Inventory, $900,000; and Finished Goods Inventory, $600,000. The company allocates overhead on the basis of the relationship between overhead and direct labor costs. At year end, the inventory accounts showed these balances:

	Materials	Direct Labor	Manufacturing Overhead
Materials Inventory	$600,000	$ –0–	$ –0–
Work in Process Inventory	400,000	450,000	150,000
Finished Goods Inventory	100,000	150,000	50,000

1. Prepare Bass's schedule of cost of goods manufactured for the brown leather Weejun. (*Hint:* Use the relation between direct labor and manufacturing overhead—allocated apparent from the above inventory accounts to determine the amount of direct labor incurred.)
2. Compute the cost of goods sold. (See Exhibit 19-9 if you need a review.)
3. Use the Materials Inventory T-account to compute the cost of materials purchased during the year.

P20-3B John Walter Homes, Inc., is a home builder in Atlanta, Georgia. Walter uses a perpetual inventory system and a job cost system in which each house is a job. Because it constructs houses, the company uses accounts titled Construction Wages, Construction Overhead, and Supervisory Salaries (for indirect labor). The following transactions and events occurred during August:

a. Purchased materials on account, $395,600.
b. Incurred construction wages of $149,200. Requisitioned direct materials and used direct labor in construction:

	Direct Materials	Direct Labor
House 302	$36,800	$19,100
House 303	49,100	17,400
House 304	45,600	20,500
House 305	27,400	12,000
House 306	63,900	33,700
House 307	52,800	27,500

c. Depreciation of construction equipment, $5,800.
d. Other overhead costs incurred on houses 302–307:

Indirect labor	$19,000
Equipment rentals paid in cash	17,300
Liability insurance expired	5,100

e. Allocated overhead to jobs at the predetermined overhead rate of 35% of direct labor cost.
f. Houses completed: 302, 304, 305, 307.
g. Houses sold: 305 for $51,500; 307 for $115,000.

1. Record the transactions and events in the general journal.
2. Open T-accounts for Work in Process Inventory and Finished Goods Inventory. Post the appropriate entries to these accounts, identifying each entry by letter. Determine the ending account balances, assuming that the beginning balances were zero.
3. Add the costs of unfinished houses, and show that this total amount equals the ending balance in the Work in Process Inventory account.
4. Add the costs of completed houses that have not yet been sold, and show that this total amount equals the ending balance in the Finished Goods Inventory account.
5. Compute the gross margin on each house that was sold. What costs must the gross margin cover for John Walter Homes?

P20-4B Sounds Alive! manufactures tapes for use in reproducing sound. Sounds Alive! uses job costing and has a perpetual inventory system.

On November 2, Sounds Alive! began production of 10,000 tapes, Job 378, to be sold to music stores for $1.20 each. The company incurred the following costs:

Date	Materials Requisition No.	Description	Amount
11-2	36	31 lb. polypropylene @ $8	$248
11-2	37	10,525 plastic cases @ $0.08	842
11-3	42	7 lb. bucylic acid @ $48	336

Date	Time Ticket No.	Description	Amount
11-2	556	12 hours @ $10	$120
11-3	557	25 hours @ $8	200

Sounds Alive! allocates overhead to jobs on the basis of the relationship between expected overhead ($537,600) and expected direct labor ($448,000). Job 378 was completed on November 3 and shipped to music stores when ordered.

1. Prepare a job cost record similar to Exhibit 20-3 for Job 378.
2. Journalize in summary form the requisition of direct materials and the assignment of direct labor and manufacturing overhead to Job 378.
3. Journalize completion of the job and the sale of 1,000 of the 10,000 tapes.

P20-5B ◀ⅢⅢ *Link Back to Chapters 2 and 19.* Stack Screw Machine Products manufactures specialized parts used in its business. Initially, the company manufactured the parts for its own use, but it gradually began selling them to other companies as well.

Comprehensive accounting for manufacturing transactions (Obj. 2, 3)

April 1 balances in the subsidiary ledgers were

- Materials ledger: steel, $1,580; electronic parts, $1,960; indirect materials, $430.
- Work in process ledger: Job 145, $35,880.
- Finished goods ledger: transformers, $5,310; relays, $4,780; switches, $8,870.

Stack's trial balance on April 1 follows.

STACK SCREW MACHINE PRODUCTS
Trial Balance
April 1, 19XX

Cash	$ 19,160	
Accounts receivable	74,290	
Inventories:		
Materials	3,970	
Work in process	35,880	
Finished goods	18,960	
Plant assets	244,570	
Accumulated depreciation		$103,680
Accounts payable		23,960
Wages payable		3,670
Common stock		120,000
Retained earnings		145,520
Sales revenues		—
Cost of goods sold	—	
Manufacturing wages	—	
Manufacturing overhead	—	
Marketing and general expenses	—	—
	$396,830	$396,830

April transactions are summarized as follows:

a. Collections on account, $137,470.
b. Marketing and general expenses incurred and paid, $27,470.
c. Payments on account, $36,040.
d. Materials purchased on credit: steel, $6,540; electronic parts, $15,830; indirect materials, $3,590.
e. Materials used in production (requisitioned):
   - Job 145: steel, $340.
   - Job 146: steel, $3,570; electronic parts, $4,980.
   - Job 147: steel, $1,970; electronic parts, $3,730.
   - Indirect materials, $2,580.
f. Manufacturing wages incurred during April, $32,430, of which $30,520 was paid. Wages payable at March 31 were paid during April, $3,670.
g. Labor time tickets for the month: Job 145, $3,500; Job 146, $11,050; Job 147, $9,940; indirect labor, $7,940.
h. Other actual miscellaneous manufacturing overhead costs incurred on account, $4,630.
i. Depreciation on plant and equipment (not included in item h above), $3,450.
j. Manufacturing overhead was allocated at the predetermined rate of 70% of direct labor cost.
k. Jobs completed during the month: Job 145, two transformers at total cost of $42,170; Job 146, 200 switches at total cost of $27,335.

l. Credit sales on account: all of Job 145 for $97,640 (cost $42,170); Job 146, 120 switches for $35,100 (cost, $16,401).

m. Closed the Manufacturing Overhead account to Cost of Goods Sold.

REQUIRED

1. Open T-accounts for the general ledger, the materials ledger, the work in process ledger, and the finished goods ledger. Insert each account balance as given, and use the reference *Bal.*

2. Record the April transactions directly in the accounts, using the letters as references. Stack uses a perpetual inventory system.

3. Prepare a trial balance at April 30.

4. Use the work in process T-account to prepare a schedule of cost of goods manufactured for the month of April.

5. Prepare an income statement for the month of April. (*Hint:* In transaction **m** you closed any under/overallocated manufacturing overhead to Cost of Goods Sold. In the income statement, show this correction as an adjustment to Cost of Goods Sold. If manufacturing overhead is underallocated, the adjustment will increase Cost of Goods Sold. If overhead is overallocated, the adjustment will reduce Cost of Goods Sold.)

Job costing in a service company
(Obj. 4)

P20-6B Katherine Bell Associates is an advertising agency. The firm uses a job cost system, where each client is a different "job." Bell traces direct labor, fax costs, and travel costs directly to each job (client). It allocates indirect costs to jobs based on a predetermined indirect cost allocation rate, computed as a percentage of direct labor costs.

At the beginning of 19X9, managing partner Katherine Bell prepared the following plan, or budget:

Direct labor hours (professional)	**4,000 hours**
Direct labor costs (professional)	**$400,000**
Support staff salaries...........................	**40,000**
Utilities..	**24,000**
Office supplies	**1,000**
Office rent..	**35,000**

In November 19X9, Bell served several clients. Records for two clients appear here:

	ELQ Enterprises	Deception Fragrances
Direct labor hours	675 hours	18 hours
Fax costs	$ 325	$25
Travel costs	$10,500	—

REQUIRED

1. Compute Bell's predetermined indirect cost allocation rate for 19X9.
2. Compute the total cost of each job.
3. If Bell wants to earn profits equal to 30% of sales revenue, how much (what total fee) should she charge each of these two clients?
4. Why does Bell assign costs to jobs?

Applying Your Knowledge

DECISION CASES

Costing and pricing identical products
(Obj. 2, 3)

CASE 1. Mellencamp Chocolate Ltd. is located in Indianapolis. The company prepares gift boxes of chocolates for private parties and corporate promotions. Each order contains a selection of chocolates determined by the customer, and the box is designed to the customer's specifications. Accordingly, Mellencamp uses a job cost system, and allocates manufacturing overhead based on direct labor cost.

One of Mellencamp's largest customers is the Bailey and Choi law firm. This organization sends chocolates to its clients each Christmas and also provides them to employees at the firm's gatherings. The law firm's managing partner, Peter Bailey, placed the client gift order in September for 500 boxes of cream-filled dark chocolates. But Bailey and Choi did not place its December staff-party order until the last week of November. This order was for an additional 100 boxes of chocolates identical to the ones to be distributed to clients.

The cost per box for the original 500-box order was budgeted as follows:

Chocolate, filling, wrappers, box...............................	$14.00
Employee time to fill and wrap the box (10 min.)	2.00
Manufacturing overhead	1.00
Total manufacturing cost	$17.00

Joan Mellencamp, the president of Mellencamp Chocolate Ltd., priced the order at $20 per box.

In the past few months, Mellencamp Chocolate Ltd. has experienced price increases for both dark chocolate and direct labor. *All other costs have remained the same.* The cost per box for the second order was budgeted as:

Chocolate, filling, wrappers, box...............................	$15.00
Employee time to fill and wrap the box (10 min.)	2.20
Manufacturing overhead	1.10
Total manufacturing cost	$18.30

REQUIRED

1. Do you agree with the cost analysis for the second order? Explain your answer.
2. Should the two orders be accounted for as one job or two in Mellencamp's system?
3. What sale price per box should Joan Mellencamp set for the second order? What are the advantages and disadvantages of this price?

CASE 2. Defense Electronics (DE) is a government contractor that specializes in electronics systems for military applications. The company's job cost system has two direct cost categories: direct materials and direct labor. DE uses direct labor hours as its manufacturing overhead cost allocation base. For the current fiscal year, expected total manufacturing overhead cost was $2,500,000. Expected direct labor hours for all production totaled 100,000.

Costing jobs and using job cost information to bid on contracts
(Obj. 2, 3)

DE bids on government contracts (jobs) by adding 80% to the predicted total manufacturing cost of the contract. The 80% markup covers the nonmanufacturing costs of the contract and provides the company's profit.

DE is preparing to bid on two new contracts. If the bids are accepted, the contracts will be produced as Job A and Job B. Budget data relating to the contracts are as follows:

	Job A	Job B
Direct materials cost	$30,000	$210,000
Direct labor cost	$10,000	$180,000
Total direct labor hours	500	9,000
Number of output units	100	1,000

REQUIRED

1. Compute DE's manufacturing overhead cost allocation rate.
2. Compute the predicted total manufacturing cost and the cost per unit of Job A and of Job B.
3. Determine the amount per output unit that DE should bid on each contract.
4. Suppose that the government awards both contracts to DE. What factors will determine the actual profit that DE will earn?

Team Project

Martin Lockheed produces aircraft for both commercial and military use. This year the company delivered on a major sale to the Air Force. This single job constituted 75% of Martin Lockheed's Cost of Goods Sold this year. At the end of the year, Martin Lockheed has no other jobs for the military in progress or under contract.

Prorating underallocated manufacturing overhead
(Obj. 3)

Martin Lockheed's nonmilitary business is based on fixed price contracts (the customer agrees to pay a set amount for an aircraft). In contrast, Martin Lockheed's contract with the Air

Force was on a cost-plus basis. This means that the Air Force paid Martin Lockheed for the cost of producing the aircraft, plus a flat profit.

At the end of the year, Martin Lockheed's records show the following (unadjusted) ending balances (in millions):

Materials Inventory	$100
Work in Process	280
Finished Goods	20
Cost of Goods Sold	500
Manufacturing Overhead	50 underallocated

Martin Lockheed's controller, Jay Chen, then closed the Manufacturing Overhead account directly to Cost of Goods Sold, which resulted in an adjusted Cost of Goods Sold of $550 million.

To ensure that Martin Lockheed is correctly assigning costs to the Air Force contract, Air Force Lieutenant Pam Hungerbuhler is auditing Martin Lockheed's accounting records. She finds that the $50 million underallocated manufacturing overhead was closed to Cost of Goods Sold, and she heads into Jay Chen's office to discuss the issue.

If Jay and Pam cannot decide how to deal with the underallocated overhead, the dispute will be settled in court.

REQUIRED

Form groups of three students for a role-play.

- The first person assumes the role of Martin Lockheed's controller, Jay Chen. Before your meeting, prepare a written report that determines the method of closing the Manufacturing Overhead account that is "best" for your employer, Martin Lockheed. Also, prepare arguments supporting your position.
- The second person assumes the role of Air Force lieutenant Pam Hungerbuhler. Before your meeting, prepare a written report determining which method of closing the Manufacturing Overhead account is "best" for your employer, the Air Force. Also, prepare arguments supporting your position.
- The third person assumes the role of the judge settling the dispute. Before your meeting, prepare a written report that determines which method of closing the Manufacturing Overhead account is fairest, and provide an explanation for your decision.

During the meeting, Jay and Pam should try to come to an agreement themselves. If they cannot come to an agreement, then the judge will have to settle the dispute. Jay and Pam should present their arguments to the judge, who will then render a decision based on his or her own analysis, along with the arguments presented by Jay and Pam.

Internet Exercise DELL COMPUTER

Michael Dell, the founder of Dell Computer, has amassed a personal fortune greater than Microsoft's Bill Gates had by the same age. One factor in Dell's success is the innovative build-to-order, flexible manufacturing process that has revolutionized the PC manufacturing environment. Rather than build a computer that the customer may want, Dell waits until the customer orders the computer and then builds and ships the machine, usually within 48 hours after order placement.

Through job costing, Dell Computer is able to identify and control the costs of the manufacturing process. As a result, Dell can carry less inventory including both materials and finished goods. In the high-tech world of computers where obsolescence occurs rapidly, maintaining low inventories is an important competitive advantage.

REQUIRED

1. Go to **http://www.dell.com.** This is Dell Computer's home page. Because Dell has significant internet sales, the Web site is set up for selling its products.
2. In the *Corporate* section of the home page, click on **About Dell.** This section is designed to provide you with an understanding of Dell's business strategy and financial information.
3. Click on **Investor Relations** followed by **Annual Reports,** and then click on the most recent annual report. At the top of the page, click on the **Financial Report** drop-down menu. Review **Management's Discussion and Analysis** and the information presented for each of the financial statements and their notes to answer the following questions about Dell's manufacturing and inventory levels.

a. Refer to **Management's Discussion and Analysis** and record Dell's *gross margin percentages* for each of the past three years. How does Dell's management explain the differences in the gross margin percentage?

b. Refer to **Management's Discussion and Analysis** and record the *days of supply in inventory* Dell reported for each of the past three years. Compare Dell's *days of supply in inventory* for each of the past three years. In general, is this trend favorable or unfavorable? Explain why. Explain the likely reasons for the trend.

c. Refer to the appropriate financial statement and record Dell's inventory balances at the end of each of the past two fiscal years. Is the trend upward or downward? Explain the likely reasons for the trend.

d. Refer to the **Consolidated Statement of Financial Position.** Scroll to the bottom of the page and click on **Notes.** Find the note reporting ending balances for each type of inventory account. (*Hint:* In the 1998 Annual Report, note #12, Supplemental Consolidated Financial Information, reports detailed inventory account information.) Record the inventory balances at fiscal year end for both *Production materials* inventory and *Work-in-process and finished goods* inventory for each of the past two years. Which type of inventory has the greatest dollar value? Explain the reason for the different amounts of these two types of inventory.

e. Explain how job costing helps Dell Computer manage its *gross margin percentage* and *days of supply in inventory.*

Process Costing

LEARNING OBJECTIVES

After studying this chapter, you should be able to

1. Distinguish between the flow of costs in process costing and job costing

2. Record process costing transactions

3. Compute equivalent units

4. Assign costs to units completed and to units in ending work in process inventory

5. Account for a second processing department by the FIFO method

6. Account for a second processing department by the weighted-average method

" *Analysis, improvement, and management of the activities within our manufacturing processes allow Pace Foods to continue to provide high quality, low cost, and on-schedule products for our consumers. Timely, internal reporting of product-specific manufacturing costs, by activity, is essential to accomplish our continuous improvement goals and to fulfill our mission to remain the world's best marketer and manufacturer of Mexican food sauces.* **"**

KATHLEEN K. MAXFIELD, CONTROLLER OF PACE FOODS, LTD.

Pace Foods, a division of Campbell Soup Co., is the market leader in the dynamic "Mexican sauces" food category, which has surpassed ketchup in supermarket sales in the United States. The San Antonio, Texas, company mass-produces several-ton batches of mild, medium, and hot sauces in both regular and thick-and-chunky styles. In a typical year, Pace Foods produces more than 150 million pounds of picante sauce and salsa.

Making picante sauce at Pace is a two-process operation. In the first process, jalapeño peppers, onions, and other fresh vegetables are chopped into small pieces shortly after they are received from suppliers. The chopped vegetables are then transferred to another facility for further processing. In the second process, the vegetables are mixed with tomato products and spices, and the ingredients are cooked, bottled, and boxed for shipping. Each batch is continually inspected to ensure purity and consistency in texture and flavor.

Despite intense competition from major international food companies, Pace Foods has achieved steady double-digit growth. The company's managers have invested heavily in state-of-the-art manufacturing processes as well as in employee training. Through effective communications, Pace's self-directed work teams carry out management's strategy of continuous improvement in quality and productivity. At Pace, managers and employees work together to maintain their coveted market leadership position.

H ow much does it cost Pace Foods to make a batch of hot picante sauce? What is the value of the inventory of fresh vegetables in the chopping process? How efficient was the cooking and bottling process last week? Like their counterparts in other manufacturing companies, managers at Pace Foods use accounting information to answer these questions.

Process Costing: An Overview

◄▥ ◄▥ ◄▥ Chapter 20 covers job costing.

The two basic types of product costing systems are *job costing* and *process costing*. We saw in Chapter 20 that job costing is a system for costing custom goods. ◄▥ It uses job cost records to accumulate the costs of individual jobs. Process costing, in contrast, is a system for assigning costs to goods that are mass-produced in a continuous sequence of steps, called processes. Process industries produce large numbers of identical units, such as steel rods, boxes of cereal, gallons of paint, and cases of picante sauce. Many companies in the petroleum, food and beverage, pharmaceutical, and chemical industries use process costing.

". . . to produce Total Corn Flakes, General Mills has one department for forming and toasting the flakes and a second department for packaging."

Companies in mass-production industries typically divide their operations into departments—one for each manufacturing process. The flow of goods through the departments is continuous and repetitive. For example, to produce Total Corn Flakes, General Mills has one department for forming and toasting the flakes and a second department for packaging. The company does not use job cost records to keep track of costs. Instead, it accumulates costs in each department for each production period. Unit cost is computed by dividing the cost incurred in a department by the number of units produced in that department. For example, if the forming and toasting department incurs $350,000 of costs to produce 1,000,000 pounds of corn flakes, the unit cost of the forming and toasting department is $0.35 ($350,000/1,000,000). If the packaging department then incurs $50,000 to package 1,000,000 pounds of corn flakes, the packaging department's unit cost is $0.05 ($50,000/1,000,000). The *total* cost per pound of formed, toasted, and packaged corn flakes is then $0.40 ($0.35 + $0.05).

Thinking It Over Why are job cost records used in job costing systems but not in process costing systems?

Answer: Job cost records keep track of the costs of custom goods because the unit costs of the goods differ. For example, a 2,000-square-foot house built by a contractor for one customer does not cost the same as a 2,000-square-foot house built for another customer. The contractor uses job cost records to keep track of the costs of each house. But companies in process industries sell identical goods—with identical unit costs—to different customers. General Mills may sell 300,000 boxes of corn flakes to Kroger and 100,000 boxes to Safeway. Job cost records are not needed to determine the costs of the two orders. The company's accountants simply multiply the order quantities by the $0.40 unit cost computed previously.

Objective 1

Distinguish between the flow of costs in process costing and job costing

Exhibit 21-1 compares the flow of costs in

- A job costing system for Blue Ridge Fabrication, a manufacturer of custom-built machinery, and
- A process costing system for Pace Foods, the manufacturer of picante sauce in the chapter opening story

Panel A shows that in Blue Ridge Fabrication's job costing system, there is a single Work in Process Inventory control account, supported by individual subsidiary job cost records for each job in process. Direct materials, direct labor, and manufacturing overhead are assigned to individual jobs, as explained in Chapter 20. When the job is finished, the job's costs flow directly into Finished Goods Inventory. *In job costing, costs of completed jobs flow directly into Finished Goods Inventory. They do not flow from one Work in Process Inventory account into another.*

EXHIBIT 21-1
Comparison of Process Costing and Job Costing

■ Daily Exercise 21-1

Job Costing:
PANEL A: Blue Ridge Fabrication, custom-built machinery

Direct Materials / Direct Labor / Manufacturing Overhead → Job 100, Job 101, Job 102 → Finished Goods → Cost of Goods Sold

Materials Inventory — xx
Manufacturing Wages — xx
Manufacturing Overhead — xx

Work in Process: xx xx xx / xx → Finished Goods: xx xx → Cost of Goods Sold: xx

Process Costing:
PANEL B: Pace Picante Sauce

Direct Materials / Direct Labor / Manufacturing Overhead → Chopping Process → Mixing & Bottling Process → Finished Goods → Cost of Goods Sold

Materials Inventory — xx xx
Manufacturing Wages — xx xx xx
Manufacturing Overhead — xx xx

Work in Process— Chopping: xx xx xx / xxx → Work in Process— Mixing & Bottling: xx xxx xx xx / xxx → Finished Goods: xxx xxx → Cost of Goods Sold: xxx

EXHIBIT 21-2
Flow of Costs in Production of Picante Sauce

■ Daily Exercise 21-2

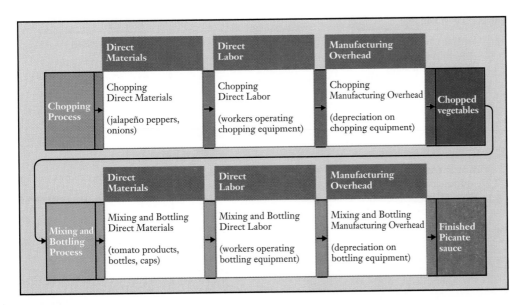

	Direct Materials	Direct Labor	Manufacturing Overhead	
Chopping Process	Chopping Direct Materials (jalapeño peppers, onions)	Chopping Direct Labor (workers operating chopping equipment)	Chopping Manufacturing Overhead (depreciation on chopping equipment)	Chopped vegetables
Mixing and Bottling Process	Mixing and Bottling Direct Materials (tomato products, bottles, caps)	Mixing and Bottling Direct Labor (workers operating bottling equipment)	Mixing and Bottling Manufacturing Overhead (depreciation on bottling equipment)	Finished Picante sauce

In contrast to Blue Ridge Fabrication's individual jobs, Pace Foods uses a series of *manufacturing processes* to produce large quantities of picante sauce. Pace has two manufacturing departments: (1) Chopping, and (2) Mixing & Bottling. The manufacturing process is shown in Exhibit 21-2. In the chopping process, Pace uses labor and equipment to chop jalapeño peppers and onions into small pieces. Then the chopped vegetables are transferred into the Mixing & Bottling Department. In this second process, Pace uses labor and equipment first to add tomato products, and then to mix and bottle the sauce. Companies, like Pace, that use a series of manufacturing processes to produce large quantities of similar products typically use process costing systems.

Notice four aspects of the process costing system illustrated in Panel B of Exhibit 21-1:

1. Each manufacturing process has its own separate Work in Process Inventory account.

2. Direct materials, direct labor, and manufacturing overhead are assigned to *each manufacturing process*. For example

	Work in Process Inventory—Chopping	Work in Process Inventory— Mixing & Bottling
Direct materials	Peppers, onions	Tomato products, bottles, caps
Direct labor	Wages of workers operating chopping equipment	Wages of workers operating bottling equipment
Manufacturing overhead	Depreciation on chopping equipment	Depreciation on bottling equipment

■ **Daily Exercise 21-3**

3. When the chopping process is complete, the chopped vegetables are transferred out of the chopping process and into the mixing and bottling process. The cost of the chopped vegetables is likewise transferred out of Work in Process Inventory—Chopping, and into Work in Process Inventory—Mixing & Bottling.

4. When the mixing and bottling process is complete, the finished picante sauce goes to the finished goods storage area. The costs (including costs from the Chopping Department as well as the Mixing & Bottling Department) flow into Finished Goods Inventory. Notice that costs flow into Finished Goods Inventory only from the Work in Process Inventory of the *last* manufacturing process.

Exhibit 21-3 summarizes the flow of costs through this process costing system (all amounts are in thousands and are assumed).

EXHIBIT 21-3
Flow of Costs through a
Process Costing System
(Amounts in Thousands)

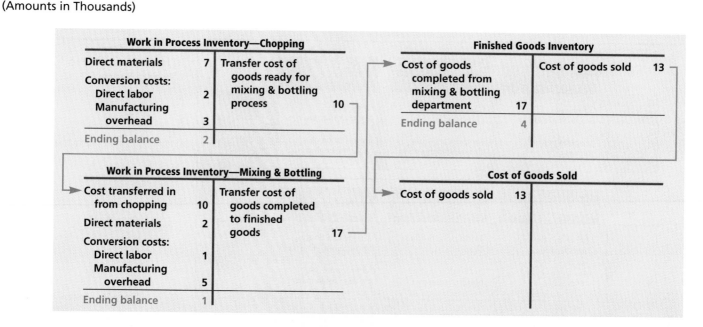

Recording Costs

The journal entries for a process cost accounting system are similar to those for a job costing system. As in job costing, accountants first accumulate the costs of direct materials purchased, and direct labor and actual manufacturing overhead incurred during the period (for all processes). These journal entries are identical to those made in job costing. For example, to record the purchase of materials ($11,000), and the incurrence of manufacturing labor ($4,000) and actual manufacturing overhead ($10,000), Pace would make the following journal entries (amounts in thousands):

Objective 2

Record process costing transactions

Materials Inventory	11	
Accounts Payable		11
Manufacturing Wages	4	
Wages Payable		4
Manufacturing Overhead	10	
Accumulated Depreciation—Plant		2
Property Tax Payable—Plant		2
Accounts Payable, and so on		6

To purchase materials and incur direct labor and actual manufacturing overhead.

The main difference between job costing and process costing is in assigning the costs of direct materials, direct labor, and manufacturing overhead. ◀▥ Job costing assigns costs to individual *jobs* that are transferred from Work in Process Inventory directly to Finished Goods Inventory. In contrast, process costing assigns costs to *processes*. There is a separate Work in Process Inventory account for each process. As products move from one process to the next, their costs flow from one Work in Process Inventory account to the next.

The following entries detail the flow of costs through the process costing system in Exhibit 21-3.

◀▥ ◀▥ ◀▥   Chapter 20, page 863, distinguishes between *accumulating* actual costs and *assigning* costs to jobs and processes.

■ Daily Exercise 21-4

Work in Process Inventory—Chopping	7	
Materials Inventory		7
Work in Process Inventory—Chopping	2	
Manufacturing Wages		2
Work in Process Inventory—Chopping	3	
Manufacturing Overhead		3

To requisition direct materials, assign direct labor cost, and allocate manufacturing overhead to the Chopping Department.

Work in Process Inventory—Mixing & Bottling	10	
Work in Process Inventory—Chopping		10

To transfer cost out of the Chopping Department and into the Mixing & Bottling Department.

Work in Process Inventory—Mixing & Bottling	2	
Materials Inventory		2
Work in Process Inventory—Mixing & Bottling	1	
Manufacturing Wages		1
Work in Process Inventory—Mixing & Bottling	5	
Manufacturing Overhead		5

To record the additional direct materials, direct labor, and overhead allocated to the Mixing & Bottling Department.

Finished Goods Inventory	17	
Work in Process Inventory—Mixing & Bottling		17

To transfer the cost of goods completed out of the Mixing & Bottling Department and into Finished Goods Inventory.

```
Cost of Goods Sold............................    13
        Finished Goods Inventory .........         13
    To account for the cost of goods sold.
```

Notice that in process costing

- Direct materials, direct labor, and manufacturing overhead costs are assigned to separate Work in Process Inventory accounts *for each process*.
- Costs are transferred, along with the units, from one Work in Process Inventory account to the next. Costs are not transferred to Finished Goods Inventory *until the last process is completed*.

■ Daily Exercise 21-5
■ Daily Exercise 21-6

Conversion Costs

◀◁ ◀◁ ◀◁ See Chapter 19, page 824.

Chapter 19 introduced a threefold classification of manufacturing costs: direct materials, direct labor, and indirect manufacturing costs (manufacturing overhead). ◀◁ Many companies that use process costing and automation find that direct labor costs have become less and less important in relation to total manufacturing costs. Such companies often use only two categories:

Conversion Costs. Direct labor plus manufacturing overhead.

- Direct materials
- **Conversion costs** (direct labor plus manufacturing overhead)

This twofold cost classification reduces accounting expense by eliminating the elaborate tracking of labor cost.

> **Learning Tip:** Conversion cost is merely a grouping of direct labor and manufacturing overhead into a single category. Conversion cost is the cost of converting direct materials into finished products.

Tracking the Flow of Costs

In process costing, the accounting task is to track the flow of costs through the production process. This task has two parts:

1. Account for the cost of goods that have been completed in one department and transferred out to the next department.
2. Account for the cost of incomplete units that remain as a department's ending work in process inventory.

Let's examine SeaView, a sporting goods company that manufactures swim masks. Suppose the company's Shaping Department shapes the body of the swim masks. The shaping process begins with direct materials (including plastic) that labor and equipment transform into shaped masks. Thus, the direct materials are added at the beginning of the process, but conversion costs (direct labor and manufacturing overhead) are incurred evenly throughout the shaping process. After shaping, the partially completed masks move to the Finishing Department, where the mask bodies are finished and the clear faceplates are inserted and sealed in place.

During October, the Shaping Department incurs the following costs in processing 50,000 masks:

Direct materials............................		**$140,000**
Conversion costs:		
Direct labor............................	$21,250	
Manufacturing overhead	46,750	68,000
Costs to account for..................		**$208,000**

If the shaping process is complete for all 50,000 masks, the costs transferred to Work in Process Inventory—Finishing are the full $208,000. The unit cost is $4.16

($208,000/50,000 masks). But suppose that shaping is complete for only 40,000 units. At October 31, the Shaping Department still has 10,000 masks that are only one-quarter of the way through the shaping process. How do we compute unit cost when the total cost applies to finished units *and* unfinished units? Accountants answer this question using *equivalent units*.

Equivalent Units

Objective 3

Compute equivalent units

Equivalent units, also called **equivalent units of production,** is a measure of the amount of work done during a period, expressed in terms of fully complete units of output. For example, assume a department's ending work in process inventory consists of 5,000 units that are each 80% complete. If costs are incurred evenly throughout the production process, then getting 5,000 units each 80% of the way through the production process takes about the same amount of work as getting 4,000 units (5,000 × 80%) all the way through the process. Thus we say the ending work in process inventory has 4,000 equivalent units.

Equivalent Units. A measure of the amount of work done during a period, expressed in terms of fully complete units of output. Also called **equivalent units of production.**

Number of partially complete units	×	Percentage of process completed	=	Number of equivalent units
5,000	×	80%	=	4,000

(The next section shows how to compute equivalent units when costs are *not* incurred evenly throughout the production process.)

The idea of equivalent units is not confined to manufacturing. It is a basic common denominator for measuring activities, output, and workload. For example, colleges and universities measure student enrollments in "full-time equivalents." Suppose a full-time class load is 12 hours per term. Assume that 1,000 students are taking a full load and that 1,000 other students are taking an average of six hours in classes. The school has a full-time equivalent enrollment of 1,500 students [1,000 + (1,000 × 6/12)].

■ **Daily Exercise 21-7**

Steps in Process Cost Accounting

Using the SeaView swim mask data, we outline the five steps of process costing for each production department. We begin with the Shaping Department.

Step 1: Summarize the Flow of Production in Physical Units

Exhibit 21-4 tracks the movement of swim masks into and out of the Shaping Department. We assume for simplicity that work began October 1, so the Work in Process Inventory account had a zero balance at September 30. Of the 50,000 masks started in October, 40,000 were completely shaped and transferred out to the Finishing Department, and the remaining 10,000 partially shaped masks are the Shaping Department's ending work in process inventory on October 31.

Step 2: Compute Output in Terms of Equivalent Units

Management accountants compute equivalent units separately for direct materials and conversion costs. Why? Because work may progress differently for materials and for conversion, as shown by the Shaping Department time line in Exhibit 21-5. This time line shows that all direct materials are added at the beginning of the shaping process. In contrast, conversion costs are incurred evenly throughout the process. As Exhibit 21-5 shows, the 40,000 completely shaped masks are complete as to both materials and conversion costs. These completed masks have incurred 40,000 equivalent units of direct materials, and 40,000 equivalent units of conversion costs.

The Shaping Department has another 10,000 masks that are only 25% of the way through the shaping process on October 31. Direct materials are added at the beginning of the process, so the time line shows that all the direct materials have been added to these 10,000 masks, even though the masks are only 25% of the way through the shaping

■ **Daily Exercise 21-8**
■ **Daily Exercise 21-9**

SEAVIEW
SHAPING DEPARTMENT
Month Ended October 31, 19XX

Flow of Production	Step 1 Flow of Physical Units	Step 2 Equivalent Units Direct Materials	Conversion Costs
Units to account for:			
Beginning work in process, September 30.....	—		
Started in production during October...........	50,000		
Total physical units to account for	50,000		
Units accounted for:			
Completed and transferred out			
during October..	40,000	40,000	40,000
Ending work in process, October 31	10,000	10,000	2,500*
Total physical units accounted for.................	50,000		
Equivalent units		50,000	42,500

*10,000 units each 25% complete = 2,500 equivalent units

process. Thus the total equivalent units of direct materials include the 40,000 finished masks plus the 10,000 masks in ending (work in process) inventory that are complete as to direct materials, as shown in step 2 of Exhibit 21-4.

Shaping Department conversion costs are incurred evenly throughout the process. The time line shows that for each of the 10,000 partially completed masks, 25% of the conversion costs have been incurred by October 31. The equivalent units of conversion costs are

$$10,000 \times 25\% = 2,500 \text{ equivalent units of conversion costs}$$

■ **Daily Exercise 21-10**

Concept Highlight

EXHIBIT 21-5
Shaping Department Process
Time Line

The total equivalent units of conversion costs include the 40,000 finished masks plus the 2,500 equivalent units of conversion costs from the masks in ending work in process inventory that are only partially completed on October 31, as shown in step 2 of Exhibit 21-4.

Exhibit 21-4 combines the data for steps 1 and 2. Note that the number of equivalent units for direct materials and conversion costs are different. This often is the case.

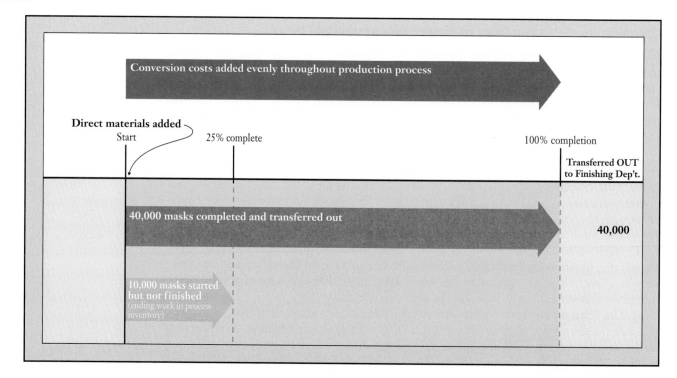

Working It Out Suppose that direct materials were added at the *end* of SeaView's shaping process rather than at the beginning of the process.

1. Draw a new time line similar to Exhibit 21-5.
2. Use the time line to determine the number of equivalent units of direct materials in the Shaping Department.

Answers

1.
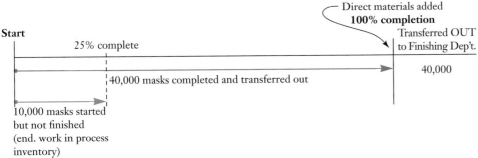

2. The time line above shows that the direct materials are not added until the *end* of the process. The time line shows that the ending work in process inventory has not passed the point in the shaping process where the materials are added. Since *no* direct materials have been added to the ending work in process inventory, materials have been added *only* to the 40,000 masks completed and transferred out, as shown in the time line. Thus there are 40,000 equivalent units of direct materials.

Sometimes direct materials are added evenly throughout the production process, rather than all at once at a specific point in the production process. In this case, the number of equivalent units of direct materials in the ending work in process inventory is computed as

$$\frac{\text{Number of}}{\text{partially complete units}} \times \frac{\text{Percentage of}}{\text{process completed}} = \frac{\text{Number of}}{\text{equivalent units}}$$

For example, if the 10,000 masks in the ending work in process inventory of SeaView's Shaping Department were 40% complete with regard to direct materials, the number of direct material equivalent units in ending inventory would be

$$10,000 \times 40\% = 4,000$$

Step 3: Summarize Total Costs to Account For

Exhibit 21-6 summarizes the total costs to account for in the Shaping Department (cost data are from page 908). These costs are the total debits in Work in Process Inventory—

EXHIBIT 21-6
Step 3: Summarize Total Costs
to Account For

SHAPING DEPARTMENT					
Month Ended October 31, 19XX					
Work in Process Inventory—Shaping					
	Physical Units	*Dollars*		*Physical Units*	*Dollars*
Beginning inventory, September 30	–0–	$ –0–	Transferred out	40,000	$?
Production started:	50,000				
Direct materials		140,000			
Conversion costs:					
Direct labor		21,250			
Manufacturing overhead		46,750			
Total to account for	50,000	$208,000			
Ending inventory, October 31	10,000	$?			

Shaping, including any beginning balance. The Shaping Department has 50,000 units and $208,000 of costs to account for. Our task is to split these costs between the 40,000 masks completely shaped and transferred out to the Finishing Department, and the 10,000 masks that remain in the Shaping Department's ending work in process inventory.

Step 4: Compute the Cost per Equivalent Unit

In step 2, we computed the total number of equivalent units for direct materials (50,000) and conversion costs (42,500). Because the equivalent units differ, we must compute a separate cost per unit for each category. Exhibit 21-6 provides the cost data. The direct materials cost is $140,000. Conversion cost is $68,000, which is the sum of direct labor ($21,250) and manufacturing overhead ($46,750).

To compute the direct material cost per equivalent unit, remember that the word *per* means "divided by." So the direct material cost *per* equivalent unit is the direct material cost *divided by* the number of direct material equivalent units:

$$\frac{\$140{,}000 \text{ total direct material cost}}{50{,}000 \text{ total direct material equivalent units}} = \$2.80 \text{ direct material cost per equivalent unit}$$

We compute the conversion cost per equivalent unit similarly:

$$\frac{\$68{,}000 \text{ total conversion cost}}{42{,}500 \text{ total conversion cost equivalent units}} = \$1.60 \text{ conversion cost per equivalent unit}$$

■ Daily Exercise 21-11
■ Daily Exercise 21-12

Exhibit 21-7 summarizes the computation of equivalent-unit costs.

Step 5: Assign Costs to Units Completed and to Units in Ending Work in Process Inventory

Objective 4

Assign costs to units completed and to units in ending work in process inventory

Exhibit 21-8 shows how the equivalent-unit costs computed in step 4 are assigned to the equivalent units computed in step 2 (Exhibit 21-4). The goal of Exhibit 21-8 is to determine how much of the $208,000 total costs incurred by the Shaping Department should be assigned to (1) the 40,000 completely shaped masks that have been transferred out to the Finishing Department, and (2) the 10,000 partially shaped masks remaining in Shaping's ending work in process inventory.

EXHIBIT 21-7
Step 4: Compute the Cost per Equivalent Unit

SHAPING DEPARTMENT
Month Ended October 31, 19XX

	Direct Materials	Conversion Costs
Beginning work in process, September 30..........	$ –0–	$ –0–
Costs added during October..............................	$140,000	$68,000
Divide by equivalent units..................................	÷50,000	÷42,500
Cost per equivalent unit......................................	$ 2.80	$ 1.60

EXHIBIT 21-8
Step 5: Assign Costs to Units Completed and to Units in Ending Work in Process Inventory

SHAPING DEPARTMENT
Month Ended October 31, 19XX

	Direct Materials	Conversion Costs		Total
Units completed and transferred out (40,000)	[40,000 × ($2.80 + $1.60)]		=	$176,000
Units in ending work in process inventory (10,000):				
Direct materials...	[10,000 × $2.80]		=	$ 28,000
Conversion costs...		[2,500 × $1.60]	=	4,000
Total cost of ending work in process inventory..............				$ 32,000
Total cost accounted for...				$208,000

First consider the 40,000 masks completed and transferred out (that is, transferred into the Finishing Department). Exhibit 21-4 reveals 40,000 equivalent units of work for both direct materials and conversion costs. Thus the total cost of these completed masks is (40,000 × $2.80) + (40,000 × $1.60), or simply 40,000 × $4.40 = $176,000.

Next consider the 10,000 masks still being shaped at the end of the month. These masks have 10,000 equivalent units of direct materials (at $2.80 per unit), so the direct material cost is 10,000 × $2.80 = $28,000. The 2,500 equivalent units of conversion work in the ending inventory at $1.60 per equivalent unit yields conversion costs of $4,000 (2,500 × $1.60). As Exhibit 21-8 shows, the total cost of the 10,000 partially completed masks in Shaping's ending (work in process) inventory is the sum of these direct material and conversion costs: $28,000 + $4,000 = $32,000.

Exhibit 21-8 has accomplished our goal of splitting the $208,000 total cost identified in step 3 (Exhibit 21-6) between

The 40,000 masks completed and transferred out to the Finishing Department	$176,000
The 10,000 masks remaining in the Shaping Department's ending work in process inventory	32,000
Total costs of the Shaping Department	$208,000

Journal entries to record October production in the Shaping Department follow (data from Exhibit 21-6):

Work in Process Inventory—Shaping......................	140,000	
Materials Inventory..		140,000
Work in Process Inventory—Shaping......................	21,250	
Manufacturing Wages.......................................		21,250
Work in Process Inventory—Shaping......................	46,750	
Manufacturing Overhead................................		46,750
To requisition materials and assign labor and overhead cost to the Shaping Department.		

The entry to transfer the cost of the 40,000 completed masks out of the Shaping Department and into the Finishing Department is as follows:

Work in Process Inventory—Finishing	176,000	
Work in Process Inventory—Shaping.........		176,000

After these entries are posted, the Work in Process Inventory—Shaping account appears as follows:

Work in Process Inventory—Shaping

Balance, September 30	—	Transferred to Finishing	176,000
Direct materials	140,000		
Direct labor	21,250		
Manufacturing overhead	46,750		
Balance, October 31	32,000		

■ **Daily Exercise 21-13**

 Working It Out What is the shaping cost per mask for each of the 40,000 masks completed and transferred out of the Shaping Department and into the Finishing Department? Why might SeaView's managers be interested in this information?

Answer: Shaping's cost per mask is the $176,000 total Shaping department cost assigned to the masks completed and transferred out (from Exhibit 21-8), divided by the total number of masks completed and transferred out of Shaping and into Finishing (40,000):

$$\text{Shaping Department cost per mask} = \frac{\$176,000}{40,000 \text{ masks}}$$
$$= \$4.40 \text{ per mask}$$

SeaView's managers could use the cost per mask of the shaping process to evaluate the efficiency of the Shaping Department's operations.

EXHIBIT 21-9
The Five Steps of Process
Costing

5. Assign costs to
units completed
and to units in
ending work
in process
inventory

4. Compute cost
per equivalent
unit

3. Summarize
total costs to
account for

2. Compute
output in terms
of equivalent
units

1. Summarize
the flow of
production in
physical units

Exhibit 21-9 summarizes the five steps of process costing. Before continuing, re-view the Process Costing Decision Guidelines to make sure you understand equivalent units and the flow of costs in process costing.

DECISION GUIDELINES	Process Costing—First Process (No Beginning Inventory)
DECISION	**GUIDELINES**
How do costs flow from Work in Process Inventory to Finished Goods Inventory?	Job costing → Costs flow from Work in Process Inventory directly to Finished Goods Inventory. Process costing → Costs flow from one Work in Process Inventory account to the next, until the last process. Costs flow from Work in Process Inventory of the last process into Finished Goods Inventory.
How many Work in Process Inventory accounts in a process costing system?	There is one Work in Process Inventory account for each separate manufacturing process.
How to account for partially complete goods?	Use equivalent units: $$\text{Equivalent units} = \begin{array}{c}\text{Number of} \\ \text{partially} \\ \text{complete} \\ \text{units}\end{array} \times \begin{array}{c}\text{Percentage} \\ \text{of} \\ \text{process} \\ \text{completed}\end{array}$$
Which costs require separate equivalent-unit computations?	Perform separate equivalent-unit computations for each input added at a different point in the production process. Often this requires separate equivalent-unit computations for (1) direct materials, and (2) conversion costs.

(continued)

SUMMARY PROBLEM FOR YOUR REVIEW   MID-CHAPTER

Use the five steps of process costing to identify the missing amounts X and Y in the following production cost report prepared by Florida Tile Industries for May.

TILE-FORMING DEPARTMENT
Production Cost Report
Month Ended May 31, 19XX

	Physical Units	Total Costs
Beginning work in process, April 30	—	$ —
Started in production during May	20,000	43,200*
Total to account for	20,000	$43,200
Completed and transferred to Finishing Department during May	16,000	$ X
Ending work in process, May 31 (25% complete as to direct materials, 55% complete as to conversion cost)	4,000	Y
Total accounted for	20,000	$43,200

*Includes direct materials of $6,800 and conversion costs of $36,400.

■ SOLUTION

Step 1: Summarize the flow of production in physical units.
Step 2: Compute output in terms of equivalent units.

TILE-FORMING DEPARTMENT
Month Ended May 31, 19XX

	Step 1	Step 2 Equivalent Units	
Flow of Production	**Flow of Physical Units**	**Direct Materials**	**Conversion Costs**
Units to account for:			
Beginning work in process, April 30	—		
Started in production during May	20,000		
Total physical units to account for	20,000		
Units accounted for:			
Completed and transferred out in May	16,000	16,000	16,000
Ending work in process, May 31	4,000	1,000*	2,200*
Total physical units accounted for	20,000		
Equivalent units		17,000	18,200

*Direct materials: 4,000 units each 25% complete = 1,000 equivalent units
 Conversion costs: 4,000 units each 55% complete = 2,200 equivalent units

Step 3: Summarize total costs to account for.

TILE-FORMING DEPARTMENT
Month Ended May 31, 19XX

	Direct Materials	Conversion Costs	Total
Beginning work in process, April 30..........	$ –0–	$ –0–	$ –0–
Costs added during May*.........................	6,800	36,400	43,200
Total cost to account for............................			$43,200

*From information in the Production Cost Report on page 915.

Step 4: Compute the cost per equivalent unit.

TILE-FORMING DEPARTMENT
Month Ended May 31, 19XX

	Direct Materials	Conversion Costs
Beginning work in process, April 30	$ –0–	$ –0–
Costs added during May..	$ 6,800	$36,400
Divide by equivalent units...	÷17,000	÷18,200
Cost per equivalent unit	$ 0.40	$ 2.00

Step 5: Assign costs to units completed and to units in ending work in process inventory.

TILE-FORMING DEPARTMENT
Month Ended May 31, 19XX

	Direct Materials	Conversion Costs		Total
X: Units completed and transferred out (16,000).................	[16,000 × ($0.40 + $2.00)]		=	$38,400
Units in ending work in process inventory (4,000):				
Direct materials..	[1,000 × $0.40]		=	400
Conversion costs		[2,200 × $2.00]	=	4,400
Y: Total cost of ending work in process inventory				4,800
Total cost accounted for...				$43,200

Process Costing for a Second Department—FIFO Method

Objective 5

Account for a second processing department by the FIFO method

Most manufacturing systems have a series of processing steps. In this section, we introduce a second department—the Finishing Department of SeaView—to complete the picture of process costing. We also introduce beginning inventories of work in process, a complicating factor that was not present in our examples thus far.

As in many areas of accounting, there are alternative methods of accounting for process costs. We discuss two: the first-in, first-out (FIFO) method and the weighted-average method. (A third method, standard costing, is covered in cost accounting texts.)

FIFO and weighted-average differ in their treatment of beginning work in process inventory. When there is no beginning inventory, the two methods are identical. They use the same five steps that we applied earlier to SeaView's Shaping Department.

The **first-in, first out (FIFO) method** of process costing assigns to each period's equivalent units of production that period's costs per equivalent unit. ◀▮▮▮ Consider a batch of swim masks that were transferred out of the Shaping Department and into the Finishing Department at the end of September. These masks did not make it completely through the Finishing Department during September, so the masks are in Finishing's ending (work in process) inventory at the end of September. The masks are not completed until October. Under the FIFO method, when these masks are completed in October, the total Finishing Department cost of these masks is the sum of

◀▮▮▮ ◀▮▮▮ ◀▮▮▮ In Chapter 9, page 386, we saw that in the FIFO method of inventory costing, the first costs into inventory are the first costs out to Cost of Goods Sold.

- September's equivalent units of Finishing's work on these masks, costed at September's cost per equivalent unit, *plus*
- October's equivalent units of Finishing's work on these masks, costed at October's cost per equivalent unit

First-In, First-Out (FIFO) Process Costing Method. A process costing method that assigns to each period's equivalent units of production that period's costs per equivalent unit.

Now let's take a closer look at the Finishing Department's manufacturing process. The Finishing Department receives the shaped masks, then smoothes and polishes them before inserting the faceplates. Thus

- Shaped masks are transferred in from Shaping at the beginning of Finishing's process.
- Finishing's conversion costs are added evenly throughout the process.
- Finishing's direct materials (faceplates) are not added until the end of the finishing process.

Keep in mind that the label *direct materials* in the Finishing Department refers to the faceplates added *in that department* and not to the materials (the plastic) added in the previous department, Shaping. Likewise, *conversion cost* in the Finishing Department refers to all manufacturing costs (other than direct materials) incurred in Finishing—not in Shaping.

Steps 1 and 2: Summarize the Flow of Production in Physical Units and Compute Output in Terms of Equivalent Units

Exhibit 21-10 lists October information for SeaView's Finishing Department. Exhibit 21-11 diagrams these data on a time line to help you see what equivalent units of work the Finishing Department performed *during October*. This is important because under FIFO, the focus is on the current period—October in this example. The FIFO method determines October equivalent units of work and costs those units with October unit costs. This is a major advantage of the FIFO method: Managers can use these current amounts to measure the efficiency of production during the month of October.

■ **Daily Exercise 21-14**

EXHIBIT 21-10
Finishing Department Data for October

Units:		
Beginning work in process, September 30 (0% complete as to direct materials, 60% complete as to conversion work)		5,000 units
Transferred in from Shaping Department during October		40,000 units
Completed and transferred out to Finished Goods Inventory during October		38,000 units
Ending work in process, October 31 (0% complete as to direct materials, 30% complete as to conversion work)		7,000 units
Costs:		
Beginning work in process, September 30 (transferred-in cost $22,900; conversion costs, $1,100)		$ 24,000
Transferred in from Shaping Department during October		176,000
Direct materials added during October in Finishing Department		19,000
Conversion costs added during October in Finishing Department:		
Direct labor	$ 3,710	
Manufacturing overhead	11,130	14,840

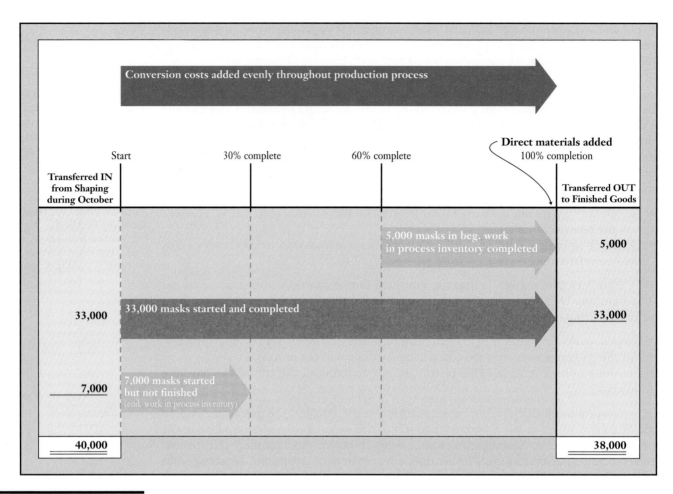

EXHIBIT 21-11
Finishing Department Process
Time Line (FIFO)

Exhibits 21-11 and 21-12 summarize the flow of physical units (step 1). The Finishing Department time line in Exhibit 21-11 is more complex than Shaping's time line in Exhibit 21-5. The reason is that Finishing has beginning work in process inventory (left over from September), while Shaping did not. Thus the 38,000 total masks that were completed and transferred out of the Finishing Department and into Finished Goods Inventory include

- 5,000 masks that were the Finishing Department's beginning work in process inventory. These masks were *completed* (but not started) in October.
- 33,000 masks that Finishing both *started* and *completed* during October. This number is computed as

    38,000 masks completed and transferred out of the Finishing Department in October
    <u>(5,000)</u> masks completed from Finishing's beginning inventory
    <u>33,000</u> masks *started and completed during October*

The time line also shows that the 40,000 masks *transferred into* Finishing from Shaping during October (see Exhibits 21-4 and 21-5) also fall into two categories:

- 33,000 masks *started and completed* in the Finishing Department during October, plus
- 7,000   masks *started* in Finishing, but not completed in October

Again, the Finishing Department did all the work on the 33,000 masks started and completed during October, but it only *started* the 7,000 masks in its ending work in process inventory. These 7,000 masks will not be completed until November.

Exhibit 21-12 uses the flow of physical units from step 1 and the time line diagram in Exhibit 21-11 to perform step 2—tabulating Finishing's equivalent units of work performed in October. The Finishing Department has three categories of equivalent units. In addition to equivalent units for direct materials (faceplates) and conversion costs added in the Finishing Department, SeaView must also compute equivalent units for the

FINISHING DEPARTMENT
Month Ended October 31, 19XX

Flow of Production	Step 1 Flow of Physical Units	Step 2 Equivalent Units Transferred In	Direct Materials	Conversion Costs
Units to account for:				
Beginning work in process, September 30	5,000			
Transferred in during October	40,000			
Total physical units to account for	45,000			
Units accounted for:				
Completed and transferred out during October:				
From beginning work in process inventory	5,000	—	5,000*	2,000*
Started and completed during October				
(38,000 − 5,000)	33,000	33,000	33,000	33,000
Ending work in process, October 31	7,000	7,000	— †	2,100†
Total physical units accounted for	45,000			
Equivalent units		40,000	38,000	37,100

During October in the Finishing Department:
*Finish beginning inventory
  Direct materials: 5,000 units each 100% completed = 5,000 equivalent units
  Conversion costs: 5,000 units each 40% completed = 2,000 equivalent units
†Start ending inventory
  Direct materials: 7,000 units each   0% completed =   0 equivalent units
  Conversion costs: 7,000 units each 30% completed = 2,100 equivalent units

shaped swim masks that are *transferred in* from Shaping. All second and later departments in a production sequence have units (and costs) transferred in from preceding departments.

For each of the three categories of equivalent units (transferred in, direct materials, and conversion costs), SeaView must figure out how many equivalent units of work the Finishing Department performed *during October.* Exhibit 21-11 shows that during October, Finishing first *completed* the 5,000 masks in beginning inventory that had been started in September. Finishing then did *all* of the work on the 33,000 masks that were both *started and completed* during October. Finally, Finishing started (but did not complete) the 7,000 masks that make up the department's work in process inventory at the end of October.

To find the number of equivalent units of work performed in October, SeaView adds up the number of equivalent units of work performed to

- *Complete* the beginning inventory,
- *Start and complete* some additional units, and
- *Start* the ending inventory

SeaView repeats these computations for each of the three categories of costs.

Let's begin with the Transferred In column of Exhibit 21-12. Keep in mind that our goal is to figure the number of equivalent units of work performed *during October.*

After the Shaping Department completes its work on the masks and transfers them out, the Finishing Department receives those units (and their accumulated costs) for final processing. The time line in Exhibit 21-11 shows that the 5,000 units in Finishing's beginning inventory were *not* transferred in from Shaping *this* month. (Instead, these 5,000 units were transferred in from Shaping *last month.*) Consequently, beginning inventory has no transferred-in equivalent units *during October.* Look at the time line again—it shows that the 33,000 masks the Finishing Department started and completed during October, and the 7,000 masks in Finishing's ending inventory, *were* transferred in from Shaping during October. Exhibit 21-12 summarizes this equivalent-unit tabulation, showing that the total transferred in equivalent-units during October is 40,000 (33,000 + 7,000).

    Learning Tip: Transferred-in costs "act like" direct materials added at the very beginning of the production process.

EXHIBIT 21-12
FIFO Method,
Step 1: Summarize the Flow of Production in Physical Units;
Step 2: Compute Output in Terms of Equivalent Units

■ **Daily Exercise 21-15**
■ **Daily Exercise 21-16**

Now let's turn to the direct materials added in the Finishing Department (faceplates). Direct materials are not added until the end of the finishing process, as shown in Exhibit 21-11. Exhibit 21-11 shows that during October, the 5,000 units in beginning inventory were completed, so they reached the point in the production process where the faceplates are added. The 33,000 units started and completed also reached the point where the faceplates are added. However, the time line shows that the ending inventory has not yet made it to the end of the process where the faceplates are added. The ending inventory does not yet have faceplates, so it has not incurred Finishing Department direct materials during October. Thus Finishing added 5,000 + 33,000 = 38,000 equivalent units of materials (faceplates) during October, as shown in Exhibit 21-12.

Finally, consider conversion costs. According to the time line, beginning inventory was 60% complete at the beginning of October. This means that during October, these 5,000 masks went through the final 40% of the Finishing Department's process. This yields 5,000 × 0.40 = 2,000 equivalent units of conversion work during October. The 33,000 masks started and completed during October went through the entire Finishing Department process during October, so these units incurred 33,000 units of conversion work. Finally, the time line shows that the 7,000 masks in ending inventory that were *started* in Finishing during October made it 30% of the way through the process by October 31. The Finishing Department performed 7,000 × 0.30 = 2,100 equivalent units of conversion work on this ending inventory during October. Thus the total conversion work performed in Finishing during October includes

> 2,000 units to *complete* the beginning inventory
> 33,000 units from masks started *and* completed during October
> <u>2,100</u> units to *start* the ending inventory
> <u>37,100</u> total equivalent units of conversion costs during October

The conversion cost column of step 2 in Exhibit 21-12 summarizes this calculation.

Steps 3 and 4: Summarize Total Costs to Account for and Compute the Cost per Equivalent Unit

The October costs of the Finishing Department are accumulated as shown in Exhibit 21-13. The exhibit shows how to compute the cost per equivalent unit. The $24,000 beginning balance of work in process is kept separate from the costs incurred during the current period. That is, the $24,000 is not included in computing the cost per equivalent unit for work done in October because this $24,000 was incurred in *September* to start the 5,000 physical units still in process on October 1. Under FIFO, each *October* cost per equivalent unit is computed by dividing October costs by the number of equivalent units of work performed in October.

Exhibit 21-13 shows that the Finishing Department has transferred-in costs as well as direct material costs and conversion costs. **Transferred-in costs** are incurred in a previous process (the Shaping Department, in the SeaView example), and are carried forward as part of the product's cost when it moves to the next process. All second (and later) processes have transferred-in costs from previous processes.

Transferred-In Costs. Costs incurred in a previous process that are carried forward as part of the product's cost when it moves to the next process.

EXHIBIT 21-13
FIFO Method, Steps 3 and 4: Summarize Total Costs to Account for and Compute the Cost per Equivalent Unit

	Transferred In	Direct Materials	Conversion Costs	Total
FINISHING DEPARTMENT **Month Ended October 31, 19XX**				
Beginning work in process, September 30 (from Exhibit 21-10)				$ 24,000
Costs added during October (from Exhibit 21-10)	$176,000	$19,000	$14,840	209,840
Divide by equivalent units (from Exhibit 21-12)	÷ 40,000	÷38,000	÷37,100	
Cost per equivalent unit	$ 4.40	$ 0.50	$ 0.40	
Total cost to account for				$233,840

Step 5: Assign Costs to Units Completed and to Units in Ending Work in Process Inventory

Exhibit 21-14 shows how to assign the costs of SeaView's Finishing Department to

- Units completed and transferred out to Finished Goods Inventory, and
- Units still in process in the Finishing Department's ending work in process inventory

The method illustrated in Exhibit 21-14 is identical to the approach used for the Shaping Department in Exhibit 21-8: Multiply the number of equivalent units from step 2 (Exhibit 21-12) by the cost per equivalent unit from step 4 (Exhibit 21-13).

The difference from the Shaping Department arises because the Finishing Department has beginning work in process inventory, while the Shaping Department did not. Exhibit 21-14 shows that when computing the cost of masks completed and transferred out of Finishing, we must remember to include the costs of the beginning inventory:

- $24,000 of Finishing Department beginning inventory costs (incurred in September), and
- $3,300 of costs to complete that beginning inventory in October [(5,000 equivalent units of materials added × $0.50) + (2,000 equivalent units of conversion costs added × $0.40)]

Working It Out

1. What is the average total cost per mask of the masks completed and transferred out of the Finishing Department into Finished Goods Inventory?

2. For what decisions would SeaView's managers use this cost per mask information?

Answers

1. The total costs of the masks completed and transferred out to Finished Goods Inventory is $202,200 (from Exhibit 21-14). Exhibit 21-11 shows that 38,000 masks were completed and transferred out. Thus the average total cost per mask of the masks completed and transferred out to Finished Goods Inventory is

$$\frac{\text{Total cost}}{\text{per mask}} = \frac{\$202,200}{38,000 \text{ masks}}$$

$$= \$5.3211 \text{ (rounded)}$$

2. SeaView's managers would use the $5.3211 cost per mask in
   - Setting the masks' sale price
   - Profitability analysis aimed at deciding which products to emphasize
   - Controlling costs and evaluating the efficiency of the production process
   - Assigning costs to Finished Goods Inventory for financial reporting

■ **Daily Exercise 21-17**

EXHIBIT 21-14
FIFO Method, Step 5: Assign Costs to Units Completed and to Units in Ending Work in Process Inventory

	Transferred In	Direct Materials	Conversion Costs	Total
FINISHING DEPARTMENT				
Month Ended October 31, 19XX				
Units completed and transferred out to Finished Goods Inventory:				
From beginning work in process, September 30				$ 24,000
Costs added during October:				
Direct materials..		[5,000 × $0.50]		2,500
Conversion costs			[2,000 × $0.40]	800
Total completed from beginning inventory				27,300
Units started and completed during October	[33,000 × ($4.40 + $0.50 + $0.40)]			174,900
Total cost transferred out...				202,200
Ending work in process, October 31:				
Transferred-in costs	[7,000 × $4.40]			30,800
Direct materials..		—		—
Conversion costs...			[2,100 × $0.40]	840
Total ending work in process, October 31				31,640
Total cost accounted for...				$233,840

The journal entries for the Finishing Department are also similar to those for the Shaping Department. First, recall the entry SeaView previously made to transfer the cost of shaped swim masks into the Finishing Department (page 913):

Work in Process Inventory—Finishing	176,000	
Work in Process Inventory—Shaping		176,000

The following entries record other Finishing Department activity during October (data from Exhibit 21-10):

Work in Process Inventory—Finishing	19,000	
Materials Inventory		19,000
Work in Process Inventory—Finishing	3,710	
Manufacturing Wages		3,710
Work in Process Inventory—Finishing	11,130	
Manufacturing Overhead		11,130

To requisition materials and assign conversion costs to the Finishing Department.

The entry to transfer the cost of completed units out of the Finishing Department and into Finished Goods Inventory is based on the dollar amount in Exhibit 21-14:

■ **Daily Exercise 21-18**

Finished Goods Inventory	202,200	
Work in Process Inventory—Finishing		202,200

After posting, the key accounts appear as follows. Observe the accumulation of costs as debits to Work in Process Inventory and the transfer of costs from one account to the next.

Work in Process Inventory—Shaping

(Exhibit 21-6)		(Exhibit 21-8)	
Balance, September 30	—	Transferred to Finishing	176,000
Direct materials	140,000		
Direct labor	21,250		
Manufacturing overhead	46,750		
Balance, October 31	32,000		

Work in Process Inventory—Finishing

(Exhibit 21-10)		(Exhibit 21-14)	
Balance, September 30	24,000	Transferred to Finished Goods Inventory	202,200
Transferred in from Shaping	176,000		
Direct materials	19,000		
Direct labor	3,710		
Manufacturing overhead	11,130		
Balance, October 31	31,640		

Finished Goods Inventory

Balance, September 30	—
Transferred in from Finishing	202,200

Production Cost Report. Summarizes the operations of a processing department for a period.

Production Cost Report

A **production cost report** summarizes the operations of a processing department for the period. Exhibit 21-15 is a FIFO production cost report for SeaView's Finishing Department for

	Transferred In	Direct Materials	Conversion Costs	Total
FINISHING DEPARTMENT				
Production Cost Report (FIFO Method)				
Month Ended October 31, 19XX				
Beginning work in process, September 30				$ 24,000
Costs added during October	$176,000	$19,000	$14,840	209,840
Total cost to account for				$233,840
Equivalent units	÷ 40,000	÷38,000	÷37,100	
Cost per equivalent unit	$ 4.40	$ 0.50	$ 0.40	
Assignment of total costs:				
Units completed during October:				
From beginning work in process, September 30....				$ 24,000
Costs added during October	—	[5,000 × $0.50]	[2,000 × $0.40]	
		= $2,500	= $800	3,300
Total completed from beginning inventory				27,300
Units started and completed during October	[33,000 × ($4.40 + $0.50 + $0.40)]			174,900
Total completed and transferred out				202,200
Ending work in process, October 31:				
Transferred-in costs	[7,000 × $4.40]			30,800
Direct materials		—		—
Conversion costs			[2,100 × $0.40]	840
Total ending work in process, October 31				31,640
Total cost accounted for				$233,840

October. It shows the department's beginning inventory, the cost transferred in during the month, and the costs added in the Finishing Department during the month. The report also shows the costs transferred out of the department, and the ending work in process inventory.

How is the production cost report used for decision making? SeaView managers compare actual direct materials and conversion costs—particularly the unit costs in Exhibit 21-15—with expected amounts for the department. If these costs are too high, corrective action may be taken. If costs are less than expected, the employees responsible may receive incentive awards.

Concept Highlight

EXHIBIT 21-15
FIFO Method Production Cost Report

"*SeaView managers compare actual direct materials and conversion costs . . . with expected amounts for the department.*"

Process Costing for a Second Department— Weighted-Average Method

Objective 6

Account for a second processing department by the weighted-average method

We now rework SeaView's Finishing Department example to demonstrate the second process costing method, weighted-average.

We learned that the FIFO method makes a separate computation of the cost per equivalent unit for each different month. The work performed in a particular month is then costed by that specific month's cost per equivalent unit. In contrast, the **weighted-average method** costs all equivalent units of work with a weighted average of that period's and the previous period's costs per equivalent unit. Exhibits 21-16 through 21-20 are the weighted-average equivalents of Exhibits 21-11 through 21-15. We apply the weighted-average method using the same five steps that we used with FIFO.

Chapter 9, page 385 introduced the weighted-average method of inventory costing.

Weighted-Average Process Costing Method. A process costing method that costs all equivalent units of work with a weighted average of that period's and the previous period's costs per equivalent unit.

Steps 1 and 2: Summarize the Flow of Production in Physical Units and Compute Output in Terms of Equivalent Units

The weighted-average method does not require SeaView to separate the work and costs for beginning inventory versus units started and completed this period. Instead, all the units completed and transferred out—whether from beginning inventory or units started

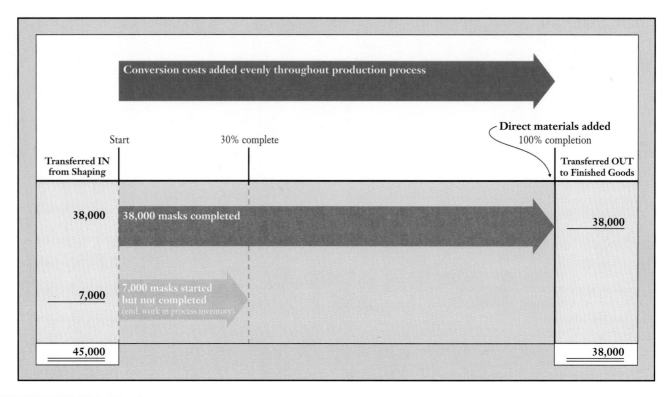

EXHIBIT 21-16
Finishing Department Process
Time Line (Weighted-Average)

and completed this period—are treated identically and are assigned the same total cost per unit. Thus the weighted-average method is simpler than the FIFO method.

Unlike the FIFO method, which creates a separate "layer" for beginning inventory costs (and work) from last period, the weighted-average method computes an average cost per equivalent unit, using

- All costs incurred for the physical units in process this period, whether those costs were incurred this period or last period, and
- All work performed on the physical units in process this period, whether that work was performed this period or last.

Exhibit 21-16 shows the time line for SeaView's Finishing Department, using the weighted-average method. The weighted-average time line is simpler than the FIFO time line. The weighted-average method combines all 38,000 units that are completed during October—whether those units are from the beginning work in process inventory, or are both started and completed in October.

Exhibits 21-10, 21-16, and 21-17 show that 38,000 masks were completed and transferred out of the Finishing Department in October (5,000 masks from beginning inventory are completed, plus 33,000 masks are started and completed). The weighted-average method computes the equivalent units of all the work ever done on these units completed and transferred out—not just the work done this period. Because these 38,000 masks have been transferred to Finished Goods Inventory, they are complete with respect to transferred-in costs, direct materials, and conversion costs. Consequently, the masks have incurred 38,000 equivalent units of transferred-in costs, direct materials costs, and conversion costs, as shown in Exhibit 21-17.

The equivalent units for ending work in process inventory are the same under the weighted-average method as with FIFO. These 7,000 units

- have been transferred in from Shaping, so they have incurred 7,000 equivalent units of transferred-in costs
- have not reached the end of Finishing's process where faceplates are inserted; thus they have no equivalent units of Finishing Department direct materials
- are 30% of the way through Finishing's process, so they have incurred $7,000 \times 0.30 = 2,100$ equivalent units of conversion costs

FINISHING DEPARTMENT
Month Ended October 31, 19XX

Flow of Production	Step 1 Flow of Physical Units	Step 2 Equivalent Units		
		Transferred In	Direct Materials	Conversion Costs
Units to account for:				
Beginning work in process, September 30	5,000			
Transferred in during October	40,000			
Total physical units to account for................................	45,000			
Units accounted for:				
Completed and transferred out during October	38,000	38,000	38,000*	38,000*
Ending work in process, October 31	7,000	7,000	— †	2,100†
Total physical units accounted for	45,000			
Equivalent units		45,000	38,000	40,100

In the Finishing Department:
*Units completed and transferred out
  Direct materials: 38,000 units each 100% completed = 38,000 equivalent units
  Conversion costs: 38,000 units each 100% completed = 38,000 equivalent units
†Start ending inventory
  Direct materials: 7,000 units each   0% completed =   0 equivalent units
  Conversion costs: 7,000 units each 30% completed = 2,100 equivalent units

Step 3: Summarize Total Costs to Account for

The total cost to account for (Exhibit 21-18) is the sum of work in process beginning inventory cost ($24,000) and the costs added to the Work in Process—Finishing account during October ($209,840). (Data are taken from Exhibit 21-10.) The total is $233,840.

Step 4: Compute the Cost per Equivalent Unit

In the weighted-average method, step 2 computes the equivalent units of all the work ever done on the units in process this period, including work done last period to start the beginning inventory. To find the weighted-average cost per equivalent unit, we match these units with all the costs ever incurred for the units in process this period. This includes costs incurred last period to start the beginning work in process inventory, as well as costs incurred in the current period (October).

Exhibit 21-18 shows the weighted-average cost per equivalent unit for SeaView's Finishing Department. Consider conversion costs first. The Finishing Department incurred $1,100 of conversion costs in September to get the 5,000 masks in beginning inventory 60% of the way through the production process by the end of September. This $1,100 is added to the $14,840 total Finishing Department conversion cost incurred in October. We divide the sum, $15,940, by the total number of (weighted-average) equivalent units, 40,100, to obtain a weighted-average conversion cost per equivalent unit of $0.3975. The transferred-in cost per equivalent unit and the direct materials cost per equivalent unit are computed in the same way.

EXHIBIT 21-17
Weighted-Average Method, Step 1: Summarize the Flow of Production in Physical Units; Step 2: Compute Output in Terms of Equivalent Units

■ **Daily Exercise 21-19**

EXHIBIT 21-18
Weighted-Average Method, Step 3: Summarize Total Costs to Account For; Step 4: Compute the Cost per Equivalent Unit

FINISHING DEPARTMENT
Month Ended October 31, 19XX

	Transferred In	Direct Materials	Conversion Costs	Total
Beginning work in process, September 30 (from Exhibit 21-10)...	$ 22,900	$ —	$ 1,100	$ 24,000
Costs added during October (from Exhibit 21-10)	176,000	19,000	14,840	209,840
Total cost	$198,900	$19,000	$15,940	
Divide by equivalent units (from Exhibit 21-17)..............	÷ 45,000	÷38,000	÷40,100	
Cost per equivalent unit...	$ 4.42	$ 0.50	$0.3975	
Total cost to account for..				$233,840

FINISHING DEPARTMENT
Month Ended October 31, 19XX

	Transferred In	Direct Materials	Conversion Costs	Total
Units completed and transferred out to Finished Goods Inventory:	[38,000 × ($4.42 + $0.50 + $0.3975)]			$202,065
Ending work in process, October 31:				
Transferred-in costs	[7,000 × $4.42]			30,940
Direct materials		—		—
Conversion costs			[2,100 × $0.3975]	835
Total ending work in process, October 31				31,775
Total cost accounted for				$233,840

EXHIBIT 21-19
Weighted-Average Method, Step 5: Assign Total Cost to Units Completed and to Units in Ending Work in Process Inventory

■ Daily Exercise 21-20
■ Daily Exercise 21-21

■ Daily Exercise 21-22

◀▥ ◀▥ ◀▥   Chapter 9 covered FIFO and weighted-average cost flows.

Concept Highlight

EXHIBIT 21-20
Weighted-Average Method Production Cost Report

Step 5: Assign Total Cost to Units Completed and to Units in Ending Work in Process Inventory

With the weighted-average method, the 38,000 physical units completed and transferred out of SeaView's Finishing Department are costed in one step. The 38,000 equivalent units are multiplied by the full equivalent-unit cost of $5.3175 ($4.42 + $0.50 + $0.3975). The result is $202,065 (Exhibit 21-19). Equivalent units in the October 31 ending work in process inventory also are costed at the appropriate unit amounts.

The weighted-average production cost report in Exhibit 21-20 is similar to its FIFO counterpart, Exhibit 21-15. The weighted-average report may signal the need for action if actual unit costs or production quantities differ materially from planned amounts. But weighted-average costs per equivalent unit are not as useful for evaluating the efficiency of October production because they are affected by costs incurred in September. Even so, managers may use the weighted-average method because (1) the computations are simpler than those of the FIFO method, and (2) the difference between FIFO and weighted-average results is often insignificant.

Thinking It Over When will the FIFO and weighted-average methods give significantly different results? ◀▥

Answer: FIFO and weighted-average methods give different results when

- There is beginning inventory. If there is no beginning inventory, FIFO and weighted-average yield identical results.

FINISHING DEPARTMENT
Production Cost Report (Weighted-Average Method)
Month Ended October 31, 19XX

	Transferred In	Direct Materials	Conversion Costs	Total
Beginning work in process, September 30	$ 22,900	$ —	$ 1,100	$ 24,000
Costs added during October	176,000	19,000	14,840	209,840
Total cost to account for	$198,900	$19,000	$15,940	$233,840
Equivalent units	÷ 45,000	÷38,000	÷40,100	
Cost per equivalent unit	$ 4.42	$ 0.50	$0.3975	
Assignment of total costs:				
Units completed during October	[38,000 × ($4.42 + $0.50 + $0.3975)]			$202,065
Ending work in process, October 31:				
Transferred-in costs	[7,000 × $4.42]			30,940
Direct materials		—		—
Conversion costs			[2,100 × $0.3975]	835
Total ending work in process, October 31				31,775
Total cost accounted for				$233,840

- The cost per unit changes from one period to the next. If the cost per unit in the current period is the same as in the prior period, then FIFO and weighted-average yield identical results.

FIFO and weighted-average yield significantly different results only when there are large beginning inventories *and* costs change dramatically from one period to the next. This could happen, for example, in the wine-making industry, where there are significant work in process inventories, and where the cost of grapes fluctuates depending on weather and other crop conditions.

The following Decision Guidelines review key issues arising in process costing systems with multiple processes and beginning work in process inventories.

DECISION GUIDELINES	Process Costing—Second Process (with Beginning Inventory)
DECISION	**GUIDELINES**
At what point in a second process are transferred-in costs incurred?	Transferred in costs are typically incurred at the *beginning* of the second (or subsequent) process.
When do FIFO and weighted-average methods of process costing yield different results?	When there is beginning work in process inventory *and* cost per unit changes from one period to the next.
Which periods' costs are included in the cost per equivalent unit computation?	• *FIFO* → Only costs incurred in current period • *Weighted average* → Cost of work done in prior period to start the beginning inventory, plus all costs incurred in the current period
How to compute equivalent units using	
• FIFO method?	*FIFO* equivalent units of work done in current period equals work done to • *Complete* beginning inventory, plus • *Start and complete* additional units, plus • *Start* ending inventory
• Weighted-average method?	*Weighted-average* equivalent units of all work done on units in process equals • All work ever done on units completed and transferred out this period (whether work was done this period or last period), plus • Work done to *start* the ending inventory

SUMMARY PROBLEM FOR YOUR REVIEW

This problem extends the mid-chapter review problem on page 915 to a second processing department. During May, Florida Tile Industries has the following activity in its Finishing Department:

Finishing Department Data for May

Units:

Beginning work in process, April 30 (20% complete as to direct materials, 70% complete as to conversion work)	4,000 units
Transferred in from Tile-Forming Department during May	16,000 units
Completed and transferred out to Finished Goods Inventory during May	15,000 units
Ending work in process, May 31 (36% complete as to direct materials, 80% complete as to conversion work)	5,000 units

Costs:

Work in process, April 30 (Transferred-in costs, $11,982; direct materials costs, $488; conversion costs, $5,530)	$18,000
Transferred in from Tile-Forming Department during May (from page 916)	38,400
Direct materials added during May	6,400
Conversion costs added during May	24,300

Assign total cost to units completed and to units in ending work in process inventory for the Finishing Department in May, using

1. The FIFO method
2. The weighted-average method

■ SOLUTION

1. The FIFO method

Step 1: Summarize the flow of production in physical units.
Step 2: Compute output in terms of equivalent units.

FINISHING DEPARTMENT
Month Ended May 31, 19XX

Flow of Production	Step 1 Flow of Physical Units	Transferred In	Direct Materials	Conversion Costs
			Step 2 Equivalent Units	
Units to account for:				
Beginning work in process, April 30	4,000			
Transferred in from Tile-Forming during May..................	16,000			
Total physical units to account for.......................................	20,000			
Units accounted for:				
Completed and transferred out during May:				
From beginning inventory...	4,000	—	3,200*	1,200*
Started and completed during May (15,000 – 4,000)..........	11,000	11,000	11,000	11,000
Ending work in process, May 31	5,000	5,000	1,800†	4,000†
Total physical units accounted for	20,000			
Equivalent units		16,000	16,000	16,200

During May in the Finishing Department
*Finish beginning inventory
Direct materials: 4,000 units each 80% completed = 3,200 equivalent units
(Work entered the period 20% complete, so the final 80% took place in May.)
Conversion costs: 4,000 units each 30% completed = 1,200 equivalent units
(Work entered the period 70% complete, so the final 30% took place in May.)
(See data in the finishing department facts for May, page 927.)
†Start ending inventory
Direct materials: 5,000 units each 36% completed = 1,800 equivalent units
Conversion costs: 5,000 units each 80% completed = 4,000 equivalent units
(See data in the finishing department facts for May, page 927.)

Step 3: Summarize total costs to account for.
Step 4: Compute the cost per equivalent unit.

FINISHING DEPARTMENT
Month Ended May 31, 19XX

	Transferred In	Direct Materials	Conversion Costs	Total
Beginning work in process, April 30..........				$18,000
Costs added during May	$38,400	$ 6,400	$24,300	69,100
Divide by equivalent units.........................	÷16,000	÷16,000	÷16,200	
Cost per equivalent unit............................	$ 2.40	$ 0.40	$ 1.50	
Total cost to account for............................				$87,100

Step 5: Assign costs to units completed and to units in ending work in process inventory.

FINISHING DEPARTMENT
Month Ended May 31, 19XX

	Transferred In	Direct Materials	Conversion Costs	Total
Units completed and transferred out to Finished Goods Inventory:				
From beginning work in process, April 30.............				$18,000
Costs added during May:				
Direct materials..................................		[3,200 × $0.40]		1,280
Conversion costs			[1,200 × $1.50]	1,800
Total completed from beginning inventory				21,080
Units started and completed during May.................		[11,000 × ($2.40 + $0.40 + $1.50)]		47,300
Total cost transferred out...........................				68,380
Ending work in process, May 31:				
Transferred-in costs.................................	[5,000 × $2.40]			12,000
Direct materials		[1,800 × $0.40]		720
Conversion costs.......................................			[4,000 × $1.50]	6,000
Total ending work in process, May 31......................				18,720
Total cost accounted for				$87,100

2. The weighted-average method

REQUIREMENT 2

Step 1: Summarize the flow of production in physical units.
Step 2: Compute output in terms of equivalent units.

FINISHING DEPARTMENT
Month Ended May 31, 19XX

	Step 1	Step 2 Equivalent Units		
Flow of Production	Flow of Physical Units	Transferred In	Direct Materials	Conversion Costs
Units to account for:				
Beginning work in process, April 30......................	4,000			
Transferred in from Tile-Forming during May	16,000			
Total physical units to account for	20,000			
Units accounted for:				
Completed and transferred out during May..........	15,000	15,000	15,000	15,000
Ending work in process, May 31............................	5,000	5,000	1,800*	4,000*
Total physical units accounted for........................	20,000			
Equivalent units..		20,000	16,800	19,000

*Finish beginning inventory
Direct materials: 5,000 units each 36% completed = 1,800 equivalent units
Conversion costs: 5,000 units each 80% completed = 4,000 equivalent units

Step 3: Summarize total costs to account for.
Step 4: Compute the cost per equivalent unit.

FINISHING DEPARTMENT
Month Ended May 31, 19XX

	Transferred In	Direct Materials	Conversion Costs	Total
Beginning work in process, April 30..........	$11,982	$ 488	$ 5,530	$18,000
Costs added during May	38,400	6,400	24,300	69,100
Total cost..	$50,382	$ 6,888	$29,830	
Divide by equivalent units.........................	÷20,000	÷16,800	÷19,000	
Cost per equivalent unit............................	$2.5191	$ 0.41	$ 1.57	
Total cost to account for............................				$87,100

Step 5: Assign costs to units completed and to units in ending work in process inventory.

FINISHING DEPARTMENT
Month Ended May 31, 19XX

	Transferred In	Direct Materials	Conversion Costs	Total
Units completed and transferred out to Finished Goods Inventory		$[15,000 \times (\$2.5191 + \$0.41 + \$1.57)]$		$\underline{\$67,486}$
Ending work in process, May 31:				
Transferred-in costs	$[5,000 \times \$2.5191]$			12,596
Direct materials		$[1,800 \times \$0.41]$		738
Conversion costs			$[4,000 \times \$1.57]$	6,280
Total ending work in process, May 31				$\underline{19,614}$
Total cost accounted for				$\underline{\underline{\$87,100}}$

Summary of Learning Objectives

1. *Distinguish between the flow of costs in process costing and job costing.* *Process costing* is a system for assigning costs to goods that are produced in a continuous sequence of steps, or processes. Process costing is used by companies that mass-produce identical goods in large quantities. Job costing is for companies that produce custom goods in relatively small quantities. In process costing systems, costs are accumulated by processing departments and flow from one department to the next until the product is completed. In contrast, job cost systems accumulate costs for each individual job using job cost records.

2. *Record process costing transactions.* Journal entries in a process costing system are like those in a job cost system, with one key exception: A job cost system typically uses one Work in Process Inventory account, but a process costing system uses one such account for each processing department. Direct materials and conversion (direct labor and overhead) costs are debited to the Work in Process Inventory accounts of the individual processing departments where the costs are incurred. As goods move from one department to the next, the Work in Process Inventory account of the receiving department is debited and the account of the transferring department is credited. After processing is completed, the cost of the goods moves with them into Finished Goods Inventory and Cost of Goods Sold.

3. *Compute equivalent units.* The main accounting task in process costing is to determine, for each department, the costs assigned to (1) units of product completed and transferred out (either into the next process or into Finished Goods Inventory), and (2) ending inventory of work in process. A complication arises because goods in process may be in various stages of completion. To assign costs to the two categories of output units, accountants compute *equivalent units*—the amount of work expressed in terms of fully completed units of output. Equivalent units are computed for each input that is added at a different point in the production process.

4. *Assign costs to units completed and to units in ending work in process inventory.* Accounting for a department's costs is a five-step procedure. First, the flow of production in physical (output) units is determined. Second, equivalent units are computed for units completed and transferred out and for ending work in process inventory. Third, the total cost to account for is determined by adding the beginning balance of work in process to costs incurred during the current period. Fourth, costs per equivalent unit are computed for each input that is added at a different point in the production process. And fifth, physical units are costed by multiplying equivalent units from step 2 by equivalent-unit costs from step 4.

5. *Account for a second processing department by the FIFO method.* FIFO focuses on current-period work. FIFO matches equivalent units of work done in the current period with costs incurred in the current period. This yields a cost per equivalent unit based solely on current period data. Equivalent units of work performed in the current month are costed at current-month unit costs. The operations of processing departments are summarized in monthly *production cost reports.* Managers compare the actual costs in the reports with planned costs to evaluate processing performance.

6. *Account for a second processing department by the weighted-average method.* The *weighted-average method* costs all work to account for each month—work in process at the beginning of the month and the current month's work—with unit costs that are a weighted average of current- and prior-month costs. In contrast to FIFO, the weighted-average method computes the equivalent units of all work ever performed on units in process—whether this work was done in the current period or the prior period. These equivalent units are matched with all costs ever incurred for those units, to obtain a weighted-average cost per equivalent unit.

Accounting Vocabulary

conversion costs   *(p. 908)*
equivalent units (of production)   *(p. 909)*

first-in, first-out (FIFO) process costing method *(p. 917)*

production cost report *(p. 922)*
transferred-in costs   *(p. 920)*

weighted-average process costing method   *(p. 923)*

Questions

1. Distinguish a process costing system from a job cost system.
2. Give the type of costing system—job or process—that is better suited to account for the following products: (a) chemicals, (b) textbook publisher, (c) lumber, (d) specialty machinery, (e) custom lampshades.
3. Why does a process costing system use multiple Work in Process Inventory accounts but a job costing system uses only one such account?
4. Give the entries (accounts only) to record the following: (a) purchase of materials on account; (b) incurrence of labor; (c) incurrence of manufacturing overhead cost; (d) requisition of materials and assignment of labor and overhead to Work in Process Inventory—Department 1 (combine in one entry); (e) transfer of cost of work in process inventory from Department 1 to Department 2; (f) transfer of cost of completed units to finished goods; (g) cost of goods sold.
5. What is an equivalent unit? Give an example of equivalent units.
6. Georgia-Pacific completed and transferred 35,000 units of its product to a second department during the period. At the end of the period, another 10,000 units were in the first department's work in process inventory, 20% complete. How many equivalent units did the first department produce during the period?
7. Outline the five steps of process cost accounting.
8. How are equivalent units used in Exhibits 21-7 and 21-8?
9. Why might a company have different numbers of equivalent units for direct materials and conversion costs?
10. What information does a production cost report give?
11. What is the major accounting challenge in a process costing system that has more than one processing department? Why is this such a challenge?
12. Using the FIFO method, compute the equivalent units for Department 2 during July:

Work in process, June 30	
(10% complete as to direct materials, 40% complete as to conversion costs)	1,000 units
Transferred in from Department 1 during July	25,000 units
Completed during July..................................	22,000 units
Work in process, July 31	
(20% complete as to direct materials, 70% complete as to conversion costs)	4,000 units

13. Repeat Question 12, using the weighted-average method.
14. Under what conditions are FIFO equivalent-unit costs equal to weighted-average equivalent-unit costs?
15. "Unit costs in process costing are averages, but this is not true in job costing." Do you agree or disagree? Explain.

Daily Exercises

DE21-1 Use Exhibit 21-1 to help you describe, in your own words, the major difference in the flow of costs between a job costing system and a process costing system.

Distinguishing between the flow of costs in job costing and process costing (Obj. 1)

DE21-2 Consider the SeaView example on pages 908–926. Diagram the flow of costs for the Shaping and Finishing Departments' production of swim masks, similar to Exhibit 21-2.

Flow of costs in process costing (Obj. 1)

DE21-3 In Exhibit 21-3 (page 906), suppose direct materials added in the chopping process were $12 rather than $7 (keep all amounts in thousands as in the exhibit). Assume that direct labor and manufacturing overhead amounts remain the same, as do each of the ending inventory balances.

Flow of costs in process costing (Obj. 1)

1. Show the revised flow of costs through the Work in Process Inventory—Chopping; Work in Process Inventory—Mixing & Bottling; Finished Goods Inventory; and Cost of Goods Sold T-accounts.
2. How much are the following?
   a. Cost of goods completed and transferred out of the Chopping Department and into the Mixing & Bottling Department
   b. Cost of goods completed and transferred out of the Mixing & Bottling Department and into Finished Goods Inventory
   c. Cost of goods sold

DE21-4 Refer to your answer to Daily Exercise 21-3. Record the journal entries for the following:

Process costing journal entries (Obj. 2)

1. The use of $12 rather than $7 of direct materials in the chopping process
2. Cost of goods completed and transferred out of the Chopping Department and into the Mixing & Bottling Department
3. Cost of goods completed and transferred out of the Mixing & Bottling Department and into Finished Goods Inventory
4. Cost of goods sold

DE21-5 Enesco produces ceramic figurines. Suppose that Enesco uses two manufacturing processes:

Flow of costs in process costing, cost per equivalent unit (Obj. 1, 3)

- Mixing and injection, where workers mix liquid ceramic and inject the ceramic into molds
- Finishing, where workers polish and package the molded figurines

During February, assume that Enesco incurs the following costs in processing 100,000 figurines in the Mixing and Injection process:

Wages of workers operating the mixing vats	$ 5,550
Manufacturing overhead allocated to Mixing & Injection...........	12,025
Clay...	50,000
Wages of workers operating injection equipment........................	6,425

Enesco has no beginning inventories.

1. Compute the February conversion costs in the Mixing & Injection Department.
2. If the Mixing & Injection Department completely processed 100,000 figurines, what is the *total* Mixing & Injection cost per figurine?
3. Assume now that 80,000 of the figurines are completely mixed and injected, while the remaining 20,000 are only part way through the mixing and injection process at the end of February. Is the cost per completely mixed and injected figurine higher, lower, or the same as in requirement 2? Why?

Process costing journal entries
(Obj. 2)

DE21-6 Record the journal entries for the *use* of direct materials and direct labor, and for the allocation of manufacturing overhead to Enesco's mixing and injection process, described in Daily Exercise 21-5.

Computing equivalent units
(Obj. 3)

DE21-7 Colleges and universities use the equivalent-unit concept in describing the number of faculty as well as the number of students. The University of Georgia has about 1,900 full-time faculty and 270 part-time faculty. Assume the following:

- A full-time faculty member teaches six courses per year
- 120 part-time faculty teach three courses per year
- 150 part-time faculty teach two courses per year

What is the number of "full-time equivalent" faculty—the number of equivalent units of faculty?

Drawing a time line, computing equivalent units
(Obj. 3)

DE21-8 Refer to Daily Exercise 21-5. At Enesco, clay is added at the beginning of the mixing and injection process. Conversion costs are added evenly throughout the process, and 80,000 figurines have been completed and transferred out of the Mixing & Injection Department, and into the Finishing Department. The 20,000 units remaining in Mixing & Injection's ending work in process inventory are 80% of the way through the mixing and injection process. Recall that Enesco has no beginning inventories.

1. Draw a time line for the mixing and injection process, similar to the one in Exhibit 21-5.
2. Compute the equivalent units of direct materials and conversion costs for the Mixing & Injection Department. (Refer to Exhibit 21-4 if necessary.)

Computing equivalent units
(Obj. 3)

DE21-9 Look at SeaView Shaping Department's equivalent-unit computation in Exhibit 21-4. Suppose the ending work in process inventory is 80% of the way through the shaping process, rather than 25% of the way through. Compute the equivalent units of direct materials and conversion costs.

Drawing a time line, computing equivalent units
(Obj. 3)

DE21-10 Consider the original SeaView Shaping Department equivalent-unit computations in Exhibit 21-4. Suppose that plastic and chemicals are added at the beginning of the shaping process, and that another direct material—a hardening agent—is added at the end of the shaping process. SeaView needs to compute the equivalent units separately for each input that is added at a different point in the production process. This means that SeaView needs a separate computation of equivalent units for the hardening agent.

1. Draw a time line of the Shaping Department process, similar to the one in Exhibit 21-5.
2. How many equivalent units of the hardening agent are incurred in the Shaping Department during October?

Computing the cost per equivalent unit
(Obj. 4)

DE21-11 Return to the original SeaView example on pages 908–913. Suppose that direct labor had been $29,750 rather than $21,250. What would the conversion cost per equivalent unit have been? (Use Exhibit 21-7 to format your answer.)

Computing the cost per equivalent unit
(Obj. 4)

DE21-12 Return to Enesco's Mixing & Injection Department described in Daily Exercise 21-5 and Daily Exercise 21-8. Using your answers to those exercises, compute the cost per equivalent unit for direct materials and for conversion costs in the Mixing & Injection Department. (Recall that there were no beginning inventories.)

DE21-13 Return to Enesco's Mixing & Injection Department. Use the information in Daily Exercises 21-5, 21-8, and 21-12 to fulfill the following requirements:

Assigning costs to units completed and ending inventory; journal entry; T-account
(Obj. 2, 4)

1. What is the cost of the 80,000 figurines completed and transferred out of Enesco's Mixing & Injection Department?
2. What is the cost of the 20,000 figurines remaining in Mixing & Injection's ending work in process inventory?
3. Record the journal entry to transfer the cost of the 80,000 figurines completed and transferred out of Mixing & Injection and into the Finishing Department.
4. Record all the transactions in the Work in Process Inventory—Mixing & Injection T-account. (*Hint:* Use SeaView's Work in Process Inventory—Shaping T-account on page 913 as a guide.)

DE21-14 Look at the SeaView Finishing Department example on page 917. Suppose 45,000 masks had been transferred in rather than 40,000 masks. Beginning inventory remains at 5,000 units and ending inventory remains at 7,000 units. How many units did the Finishing Department start and complete during October?

Physical flow of units in second department, FIFO method
(Obj. 5)

DE21-15 Turn to the original SeaView Finishing Department illustration in Exhibits 21-10 and 21-11. Suppose the beginning work in process inventory was 20% of the way through the finishing process at the beginning of October, and the ending work in process inventory was 70% of the way through the finishing process at the end of October.

Drawing a time line, equivalent units; second department, FIFO method
(Obj. 5)

1. Draw a time line similar to the one in Exhibit 21-11, using the FIFO method.
2. Use the time line to help you compute equivalent units of transferred in, direct materials, and conversion costs, using the FIFO method.

DE21-16 Enesco produces ceramic figurines. Prior daily exercises considered Enesco's first process—mixing and injection. We now consider Enesco's second process—finishing. In the Finishing Department, workers polish the figurines and pack them into cushioned boxes. Conversion costs are incurred evenly throughout the process, but packaging materials are not added until the end of the finishing process.

Drawing a time line, equivalent units; second department, FIFO method
(Obj. 5)

February data from Enesco's Finishing Department are as follows:

Figurines

Beginning work in process inventory	
(40% of the way through the process)	4,000 figurines
Transferred in from Mixing & Injectionª	80,000 figurines
Completed and transferred out to	
Finished Goods Inventory in February	77,000 figurines
Ending work in process inventory	
(70% of the way through the finishing process)	7,000 figurines

Costs in beginning work in process inventory:		Costs added during February:	
Transferred in	$480	Transferred inª	$ 60,000
Direct materials	0	Direct materials	15,400
Direct labor	250	Direct labor	16,863
Manufacturing overhead	150	Manufacturing overhead	11,242
Total beginning work in process inventory as of		Total costs added during February	
February 1	$880		$103,505

ªDaily Exercise 21-13 showed that Enesco's Mixing & Injection Department completed and transferred out 80,000 figurines at a total cost of $60,000.

1. Draw a time line for Enesco's Finishing Department, similar to the one in Exhibit 21-11, assuming that Enesco uses FIFO.
2. Use the time line to help you compute the Finishing Department's equivalent units, using the FIFO method.

DE21-17 Consider Enesco's Finishing Department, as described in Daily Exercise 21-16.

Cost per equivalent unit, assigning costs to goods completed and in ending inventory; FIFO; second department
(Obj. 5)

1. Compute the cost per equivalent unit, using FIFO.
2. Assign the costs to units completed and transferred out, and to ending inventory, using FIFO.

Journal entry; T-account; second department; FIFO
(Obj. 1, 2, 5)

DE21-18 Refer to Enesco's Finishing Department and the computations you made in Daily Exercises 21-16 and 21-17.

1. Prepare the journal entry to record the cost of units completed and transferred out, using FIFO.
2. Post all transactions from Daily Exercises 21-16 and 21-17 to the Work in Process Inventory—Finishing Department T-account. What is the ending balance?

Drawing a time line; computing equivalent units; second department; weighted-average method
(Obj. 1, 6)

DE21-19 Using the data from Enesco's Finishing Department from Daily Exercise 21-16:

1. Draw a time line similar to the one in Exhibit 21-16, using the weighted-average method.
2. Use the time line to help you compute the Finishing Department equivalent units, using the weighted-average method.

Cost per equivalent unit; assigning costs to units completed and ending inventory; second department; weighted-average method
(Obj. 6)

DE21-20 Using data from Enesco's Finishing Department in Daily Exercise 21-16 and the equivalent units computed in Daily Exercise 21-19:

1. Compute the cost per equivalent unit, using the weighted-average method.
2. Assign the costs to units completed and transferred out, and to ending inventory, using the weighted-average method. (*Hint:* The conversion cost per unit does not work out to an even number. Carry your computation to at least three decimal places. Should you have a "rounding error" of less than $10 in your "Total costs accounted for," assign the rounding error to the cost of units completed and transferred out.)

Journal entry, T-account; second department, weighted-average method
(Obj. 1, 2, 6)

DE21-21 Using data from Enesco's Finishing Department in Daily Exercise 21-16 and the cost assignments in Daily Exercise 21-20:

1. Prepare the journal entry to record the cost of units completed and transferred out under the weighted-average method.
2. Post all transactions from Daily Exercises 21-16 and 21-20 to the Work in Process Inventory—Finishing Department T-account. What is the ending balance?

Comparing FIFO and weighted-average results; second department
(Obj. 5, 6)

DE21-22 ◀▥ *Link Back to Chapter 9; (difference between FIFO and weighted average).* For Enesco's Finishing Department, use your answers to Daily Exercise 21-17 and Daily Exercise 21-20 to compare the cost of the units completed and transferred out under FIFO to that under weighted-average. Compare the costs of the Finishing Department's ending work in process inventory under FIFO to that under weighted-average. Did the Finishing Department cost per unit increase or decrease in February? How do you know?

Exercises

Diagramming flows through a process costing system
(Obj. 1)

E21-1 Heritage Outdoor Furniture produces wood picnic tables in a three-stage process that includes milling, assembling, and finishing, in that order. Direct materials are added in the Milling and Finishing Departments. Direct labor and overhead are incurred in all three departments. The company's general ledger includes the following accounts:

Work in Process Inventory—Finishing	Cost of Goods Sold
Materials Inventory	Manufacturing Wages
Finished Goods Inventory	Work in Process Inventory—Milling
Manufacturing Overhead	Work in Process Inventory—Assembling

Outline the flow of costs through the company's accounts. Include a T-account for each account title given.

Journalizing process costing transactions
(Obj. 2)

E21-2 Record the following process costing transactions in the general journal:

a. Purchase of raw materials on account, $7,600.
b. Requisition of direct materials to
  Assembly Department, $3,800
  Finishing Department, $1,400
c. Incurrence and payment of manufacturing labor, $10,800.
d. Incurrence of manufacturing overhead costs:
  Property taxes—plant, $1,900
  Utilities—plant, $2,700
  Insurance—plant, $800
  Depreciation—plant, $3,400

e. Assignment of conversion costs to the Assembly Department:
   Direct labor, $4,700
   Manufacturing overhead, $2,900

f. Assignment of conversion costs to the Finishing Department:
   Direct labor, $6,100
   Manufacturing overhead, $5,800

g. Cost of goods completed and transferred out of Assembly and into Finishing, $10,250.

h. Cost of goods completed and transferred out of the Finishing Department into Finished Goods Inventory, $20,750.

E21-3 A small dairy in Wisconsin, Cable Dairy, pasteurizes and packages fluid milk products. Cable has two departments: (1) Pasteurization and (2) Packaging. Direct materials are added at the beginning of the pasteurization process (raw milk) and at the end of the packaging process (cartons). Conversion costs are added evenly throughout each process. Data from the month of May for the Pasteurization Department are as follows:

Drawing a time line; computing equivalent units and assigning cost to completed units and ending work in process; no beginning inventory or cost transferred in
(Obj. 3, 4)

Gallons	
Beginning work in process inventory...	0
Started production..	5,000 gallons
Completed and transferred out to Packaging in May..............	4,500 gallons
Ending work in process inventory	
(10% of the way through the pasteurization process)...........	500 gallons

Costs	
Beginning work in process inventory..	$ 0
Costs added during May:	
Direct materials (raw milk)	2,750
Direct labor...	300
Manufacturing overhead...	610
Total costs added during May..	$3,660

REQUIRED

1. Draw a time line for the Pasteurization Department, similar to Exhibit 21-5.
2. Use the time line to help you compute the equivalent units for direct materials and for conversion costs.
3. Compute the total costs of the units (gallons)
   a. Completed and transferred out to the Packaging Department
   b. In the Pasteurization Department ending work in process inventory

E21-4 Return to the Pasteurization Department for Cable Dairy in Exercise 21-3.

Journal entries, work in process T-account
(Obj. 1, 2, 4)

REQUIRED

1. Present the journal entries to record the use of direct materials and direct labor, and the allocation of manufacturing overhead to the Pasteurization Department. Also, give the journal entry to record the costs of the gallons completed and transferred out to the Packaging Department.
2. Post the journal entries to the Work in Process Inventory—Pasteurization T-account. What is the ending balance?
3. What is the average cost per gallon transferred out of Pasteurization and into Packaging? Why would Cable Dairy's managers want to know this cost?

E21-5 The Mixing Department of Eastman Chemicals began February with no work in process inventory. During the month, production that cost $36,550 (direct materials, $8,550, and conversion costs, $28,000) was started on 21,000 units. A total of 17,000 units were completed and transferred to the Heating Department. The ending work in process inventory was 50% complete as to direct materials and 75% complete as to conversion work.

Computing equivalent units; assigning costs to goods completed and ending work in process inventory; first department, no beginning inventory
(Obj. 2, 3, 4)

REQUIRED

1. Compute the equivalent units for direct materials and conversion costs.
2. Compute the cost per equivalent unit.
3. Assign the costs to units completed and transferred out and ending work in process inventory.
4. Record the journal entry for the costs transferred out of Mixing and into Heating.
5. Post all the transactions in the Work in Process Inventory—Mixing Department T-account. What is the ending balance?

Drawing a time line; computing equivalent units; assigning cost to completed units and ending work in process; no beginning inventory or cost transferred in
(Obj. 3, 4)

E21-6 TerrapinAle is a microbrewery in College Park, Maryland. TerrapinAle has two departments—Fermenting and Packaging. Direct materials are added at the beginning of the fermenting process (barley, malt, hops) and at the end of the packaging process (bottles). Conversion costs are added evenly throughout each process. Data from the month of March for the Fermenting Department are as follows:

Gallons	
Beginning work in process inventory..	0
Started production	6,000 gallons
Completed and transferred out to Packaging in March..........	5,250 gallons
Ending work in process inventory	
(70% of the way through the fermenting process)...............	750 gallons
Costs	
Beginning work in process inventory..	$ 0
Costs added during March:	
Direct materials...	8,100
Direct labor..	1,540
Manufacturing overhead	3,080
Total costs added during March	$12,720

REQUIRED

1. Draw a time line for the Fermenting Department, similar to Exhibit 21-5.
2. Use the time line to help you compute the equivalent units for direct materials and for conversion costs.
3. Compute the total costs of the units (gallons)
    a. Completed and transferred out to the Packaging Department
    b. In the Fermenting Department ending work in process inventory

Journal entries, work in process T-account
(Obj. 1, 2, 4)

E21-7 Return to the Fermenting Department for TerrapinAle in Exercise 21-6.

REQUIRED

1. Present the journal entries to record the use of direct materials and direct labor, and the allocation of manufacturing overhead to the Fermenting Department. Also give the journal entry to record the costs of the gallons completed and transferred out to the Packaging Department.
2. Post the journal entries to the Work in Process Inventory—Fermenting T-account. What is the ending balance?
3. What is the average cost per gallon transferred out of Fermenting and into Packaging? Why would TerrapinAle's managers want to know this cost?

Computing equivalent units; assigning cost to goods completed and ending work in process inventory; first department, no beginning inventory
(Obj. 2, 3, 4)

E21-8 The following information was taken from the ledger of Lancaster Glass. Ending inventory is 70% complete as to direct materials but 30% complete as to conversion work.

	Work in Process—Forming				
	Physical Units	**Dollars**		**Physical Units**	**Dollars**
Beginning inventory, November 30	-0-	$ -0-	Transferred to Finishing	72,000	$?
Production started:	80,000				
Direct materials		271,600			
Conversion costs		238,080			
Ending inventory	8,000	?			

Journalize the transfer of cost to the Finishing Department. (*Hint:* First compute the number of equivalent units and the cost per equivalent unit.)

Computing equivalent units in a single department that has beginning inventory, FIFO
(Obj. 5)

E21-9 Assume that Squibb-Meyers, a manufacturer of pharmaceuticals, reports the following data from its FIFO process costing system. Insert the missing values.

Flow of Production	Flow of Physical Units	Equivalent Units	
		Direct Materials	Conversion Costs
Units to account for:			
Beginning work in process, November 30	14,000		
Started in production during December.............	X		
Total physical units to account for......................	67,000		
Units accounted for:			
Completed and transferred out during December:			
From beginning inventory..............................	14,000	X*	X*
Started and completed during December	47,000	X	X
Ending work in process, December 31	X	X†	X†
Total physical units accounted for	67,000		
Equivalent units		X	X

*Finished beginning inventory
  Direct materials: 40% completed during December
  Conversion costs: 60% completed during December
†Started ending inventory
  Direct materials: 10% completed during December
  Conversion costs: 30% completed during December

E21-10   Selected production and cost data of Harmon's Hardwood Flooring, follow for May 19X9.

Computing equivalent units, 2 departments, FIFO method (Obj. 5)

Flow of Production	Flow of Physical Units	
	Sanding Department	Finishing Department
Units to account for:		
Beginning work in process, April 30	20,000	6,000
Transferred in during May	70,000	80,000
Total physical units to account for	90,000	86,000
Units accounted for:		
Completed and transferred out during May:		
From beginning inventory	20,000	6,000
Started and completed during May....................	60,000	75,000
Work in process, May 31...	10,000	5,000
Total physical units accounted for...........................	90,000	86,000

Harmon's uses FIFO process costing.

1. Fill in the blanks:
    a. On April 30, the Sanding Department beginning work in process inventory was 80% complete as to materials and 90% complete as to conversion costs. This means that for the beginning inventory, _____% of the materials and _____% of the conversion costs were added during May.
    b. On May 31, the Sanding Department ending work in process inventory was 60% complete as to materials and 40% complete as to conversion costs. This means that for the ending inventory _____% of the materials and _____% of the conversion costs were added during May.
    c. On April 30, the Finishing Department beginning work in process inventory was 33⅓% complete as to materials and 60% complete as to conversion costs. This means that for the beginning inventory _____% of the materials and _____% of the conversion costs were added during May.
    d. On May 31, the Finishing Department ending work in process inventory was 70% complete as to materials and 60% complete as to conversion costs. This means that for the ending inventory, _____% of the materials and _____% of the conversion costs were added during May.

2. Use the information in the Flow of Production chart and the information in Requirement 1 to compute the equivalent units for transferred-in costs (if necessary), direct materials, and conversion costs for both the Sanding Department and the Finishing Department.

E21-11   Repeat Requirement 2 of Exercise 21-10 for the Finishing Department, using the weighted-average method.

Computing equivalent units in a second department, weighted-average method (Obj. 6)

Computing equivalent units and assigning costs to completed units and to ending work in process inventory; second department, FIFO
(Obj. 5)

E21-12 Papermaid Industries, Inc., experienced the following activity in its Heating Department during December. Materials are added at the beginning of the heating process.

Units	
Work in process, November 30 (80% of the way through the process)	8,000 units
Transferred in from the Grinding Department during December	31,000 units
Completed during December	26,000 units
Work in process, December 31 (70% of the way through the process)	13,000 units

Costs	
Work in process, November 30	$ 67,146
Transferred in from the Grinding Department during December	102,300
Direct materials added during December	77,500
Conversion costs added during December	97,580

REQUIRED

1. Draw a time line for the Heating Department using the FIFO method. (See Exhibit 21-11.)
2. Use the time line to help you compute the number of equivalent units of work performed by the Heating Department during December. Use the FIFO method.
3. Compute the costs per equivalent unit, and assign total cost to (a) units completed and transferred to Finished Goods Inventory, and (b) units in December 31 work in process inventory.

Computing equivalent units and assigning costs to completed units and to ending work in process inventory; second department, weighted average
(Obj. 6)

E21-13 Repeat Exercise 21-12, using the weighted-average method. (See Exhibit 21-16 for a weighted-average time line.) The November 30 balance of Work in Process Inventory—Heating Department ($67,146) is composed of the following amounts: transferred-in costs, $26,010; direct materials costs, $20,780; and conversion costs, $20,356.

CHALLENGE EXERCISE

Using equivalent units to determine the physical flow of production
(Obj. 5, 6)

E21-14 The following data pertain to the Packaging Department of Chemex, Inc., for the month of April 19X9:

	Equivalent Units		
Method	Transferred In	Direct Materials	Conversion Costs
Weighted-average	420,000	420,000	417,500
FIFO	400,000	420,000	412,500

Direct materials are added when the units are halfway through the packaging process. During April, 410,000 physical units were completed and transferred out.

REQUIRED

1. How many physical units were transferred in to the Packaging Department in April?
2. How many physical units were in the beginning work in process inventory?
3. How many physical units were both transferred in (started) and completed in April?
4. How many physical units were in the ending work in process inventory?
5. What percentage of the total required conversion work had been done on the beginning work in process inventory during March? That is, at what percentage of completion were the beginning inventory units on April 1?

Beyond the Numbers

FIFO versus weighted-average costs; first department
(Obj. 1, 5, 6)

BN21-1 The first part of this chapter considers SeaView's first department—the Shaping Department. In that discussion, we did not worry about whether SeaView used the FIFO or weighted-average method. Why? Would the choice of FIFO versus weighted average ever matter in a first department? If so, under what circumstances?

FIFO versus weighted-average costs; second department
(Obj. 5, 6)

BN21-2 ◄▥ *Link Back to Chapter 9 (difference between FIFO and weighted average).* Compare SeaView's Finishing Department's cost per equivalent unit under the FIFO versus weighted-average method (Exhibits 21-13 and 21-18). Consider transferred-in costs, direct materials, and conversion costs separately. Did the cost per equivalent unit increase or decrease during October? How do you know?

ETHICAL ISSUE

Effect of percentage completion of ending inventory on financial results (Obj. 1, 3, 4)

You recently accepted a job as controller for Jackson Brothers Quarries. The company uses process costing to account for mining and crushing limestone rock for the construction industry. The rock passes through a large crusher several times until it has a sufficiently fine consistency for shipment. Once crushing is completed, the limestone is immediately shipped to customers. At the request of Jackson Quarries' president Rolfe Jackson, you prepare a rough draft of the year-end financial results. The president, however, is dissatisfied with your numbers. He asks you to treat the ending Work in Process Inventory as 70% complete. You believe that the 30% completion figure you originally used is more accurate.

1. If you follow the president's request, how would the change affect this year's
    a. Ending work in process inventory?
    b. Total assets?
    c. Gross margin?
    d. Net income?

2. The president's contract specifies that his annual bonus is based on net income. What effect is this contract likely to have on his request? Explain.

3. Suppose you increase your estimate of the percentage completion of this year's ending work in process inventory to 70 percent. How would this change affect next year's financial results? How would the change affect the president's bonus next year?

4. ◀━━ *Link Back to Chapter 7*. Apply the ethical framework from Chapter 7 (page 313) in considering how you should respond to the president's suggestion.

Problems (GROUP A)

P21-1A Unicomp, Inc., produces components for hand-held calculators. One part, a diode generator, is manufactured in a single processing department. No diode generators were in process on May 31, and Unicomp started production on 12,000 units during June. Direct materials are added at the beginning of the process, but conversion costs are incurred evenly throughout the process. Completed production for June totaled 9,900 units. The June 30 work in process was 30% of the way through the production process. Direct materials costing $6,600 were placed in production during June, and direct labor of $5,100 and manufacturing overhead of $2,271 were assigned to the process.

Computing equivalent units and assigning cost to completed units and ending work in process; no beginning inventory or cost transferred in (Obj. 1, 3, 4)

REQUIRED

1. Draw a time line for Unicomp, similar to Exhibit 21-5.
2. Use the time line to help you compute the number of equivalent units and the cost per equivalent unit for June.
3. Assign total cost to (a) units completed and transferred to finished goods, and (b) units still in process at June 30.
4. Prepare a T-account for Work in Process Inventory to show activity during June, including the June 30 balance.

P21-2A The Guernsey Wool Company produces wool fabric in a three-stage process: cleaning, spinning, and weaving. Costs incurred in the Cleaning Department during September are summarized as follows:

Computing equivalent units; assigning cost to completed units and ending work in process; journalizing transactions; no beginning inventory or cost transferred in (Obj. 2, 3, 4)

Work in Process Inventory—Cleaning	
Sept. 1 balance	0
Direct materials	66,500
Direct labor	2,580
Manufacturing overhead	7,430

Direct materials (raw wool) are added at the beginning of the cleaning process, while conversion costs are incurred evenly throughout the process. September activity in the Cleaning Department included cleansing of 17,000 pounds of wool, which were transferred to the Spinning Department. Also, work began on 2,000 pounds of wool, which on September 30 were 60% of the way through the cleaning process.

REQUIRED

1. Compute the number of equivalent units and the cost per equivalent unit in the Cleaning Department for September.
2. Show that the sum of (a) cost of goods transferred out of the Cleaning Department, and (b) ending Work in Process Inventory—Cleaning equals the total cost accumulated in the department during September.
3. Journalize all transactions affecting the company's cleaning process during September, including those already posted.

Computing equivalent units and assigning costs to completed units and ending work in process; materials added at different points in the production process; no beginning inventory or costs transferred in
(Obj. 1, 2, 3, 4)

P21-3A Chick'n Quick produces canned chicken à la king. The chicken à la king passes through three departments—(1) Mixing, (2) Retort (sterilization), and (3) Packing. In the Mixing Department, chicken and cream are added at the beginning of the process, the mixture is partly cooked, and then chopped green peppers and mushrooms are added at the end of the mixing process. Conversion costs are added evenly throughout the mixing process. April data from the Mixing Department are as follows:

Gallons		Costs	
Beginning work in		Beginning work in	
process inventory.....	0 gallons	process inventory..............	$ 0
Started production.......	10,000 gallons	Costs added during April:	
Completed and		Chicken................................	12,500
transferred out to		Cream..................................	4,500
Retort in April	9,300 gallons	Green peppers and	
Ending work in		mushrooms.......................	6,045
process inventory		Direct labor	7,776
(60% of the way		Manufacturing	
through the		overhead...........................	2,916
mixing process).........	700 gallons	Total costs	$33,737

REQUIRED

1. Draw a time line for the Mixing Department, similar to Exhibit 21-5.
2. Use the time line to help you compute the equivalent units. (*Hint:* Each direct material added at a different point in the production process requires its own equivalent-unit computation.)
3. Compute the total costs of the units (gallons)
    a. Completed and transferred out to the Retort Department
    b. In the Mixing Department's ending work in process inventory
4. Prepare the journal entry to record the cost of the gallons completed and transferred out to the Retort Department.
5. Post the transactions to the Work in Process Inventory—Mixing T-account. What is the ending balance?
6. What is the primary purpose of the work required in steps 1–3?

Computing equivalent units for a second department with beginning inventory; assigning cost to completed units and ending work in process; FIFO method
(Obj. 3, 4, 5)

P21-4A Bumperworks, Inc., manufactures auto bumpers in a two-stage process that includes shaping and plating. Steel alloy is the basic raw material of the shaping process. The steel is molded according to the design specifications of automobile manufacturers (Ford and General Motors). The Plating Department then adds a chrome finish.

At March 31, before recording the transfer of cost from the Plating Department to Finished Goods Inventory, the Bumperworks general ledger included the following account:

Work in Process Inventory—Plating

Feb. 28 balance	24,600
Transferred in from Shaping	36,000
Direct materials	24,200
Direct labor	17,100
Manufacturing overhead	38,760

The direct materials (chrome) are added at the end of the plating process. Conversion costs are incurred evenly throughout the process. Work in process of the Plating Department on February 28 consisted of 600 bumpers that were 40% of the way through the production process. During March, 3,000 bumpers were transferred in from the Shaping Department. The Plating Department transferred 2,200 bumpers to Finished Goods Inventory in March, and 1,400 bumpers were still in process on March 31. This ending inventory was 70% of the way through the plating process. Bumperworks uses FIFO process costing.

REQUIRED

1. Draw a time line for the Plating Department, similar to Exhibit 21-11.
2. Use the time line to help you compute the equivalent units, cost per equivalent unit, and total costs to account for in the Plating Department for March.
3. Assign total Plating Department cost to (a) goods transferred out of the Plating Department, and (b) Work in Process Inventory—Plating on March 31.

P21-5A Refer to Problem 21–4A.

1. Prepare the March production cost report for the Plating Department.
2. Journalize all transactions affecting the Plating Department during March, including the entries that have already been posted.

Preparing a production cost report and recording transactions on the basis of the report's information
(Obj. 3, 4, 5)

P21-6A Sidchrome Corporation uses three departments to produce screwdrivers with plastic handles. Forming the handles requires mixing the raw materials, molding, and drying.

Sidchrome's Drying Department requires no direct materials. Other process costing information follows:

Computing equivalent units for a second department with beginning inventory; assigning cost to completed units and ending work in process; FIFO method
(Obj. 3, 4, 5)

Units	
Beginning work in process (30% complete as to conversion work)..........	**7,000 units**
Transferred in from the Molding Department during the period.............	**32,000 units**
Completed during the period	**16,000 units**
Ending work in process (20% complete as to conversion work)	**23,000 units**

Costs	
Beginning work in process...	**$ 845**
Transferred in from the Molding Department during the period	**3,840**
Conversion costs added during the period	**1,665**

After the drying process, production of the screwdrivers is completed by assembling the handles and shanks and packaging for shipment to retail outlets. The cost transferred in to the assembling phase is the cost of the plastic handles transferred out of the Drying Department. Assembling-operation direct materials are the metal shanks, which cost $1,444 for the period. Automated assembling occurs at the rate of 4,000 units per hour and packaging at 2,000 units per hour. Conversion cost is allocated to the assembling operation at the predetermined rate of $25.00 per machine hour and to packaging at the rate of $30 per machine hour. Sidchrome uses FIFO process costing.

1. Draw a time line of the Drying Department's process, similar to the one in Exhibit 21-11.

REQUIRED

2. Use the time line to compute the number of equivalent units of work performed by the Drying Department during the period, the cost per equivalent unit, and the total costs to account for.
3. Assign total cost to (a) units completed and transferred to the assembly operation, and (b) units in the Drying Department's ending work in process inventory.
4. Compute the total manufacturing cost of the 16,000 screwdrivers completed and transferred to Finished Goods Inventory. Also compute the unit cost of each complete screwdriver. (*Hint*: Remember that the total cost of the screwdrivers transferred into Finished Goods Inventory includes direct materials and conversion costs of the assembly and packaging that occur after the drying process is complete.)

P21-7A Repeat Problem 21-6A, using the weighted-average method. The $845 beginning balance of Work in Process—Drying includes $450 of transferred-in cost and $395 of conversion cost. For requirement 1, use the time line in Exhibit 21-16 as a guide.

Computing equivalent units for a second department with beginning inventory; assigning cost to completed units and ending work in process; weighted-average method
(Obj. 3, 4, 6)

Problems (GROUP B)

P21-1B Meditext, Inc., engraves and prints medical textbooks. Production occurs in three processes: engraving, printing, and binding. The Engraving Department had no work in process on May 31. In mid-June, Meditext started production on 65,000 books. Of this number, 52,600 books were engraved during June. Direct materials are added at the beginning of the engraving process. Conversion costs are incurred evenly throughout the process. The June 30 work in process in the Engraving Department was 60% of the way through the engraving process. Direct materials costing $162,500 were placed in production in Engraving during June, and direct labor of $43,140 and manufacturing overhead of $82,944 were assigned to that department.

Computing equivalent units and assigning cost to completed units and ending work in process; no beginning inventory or cost transferred in
(Obj. 1, 3, 4)

1. Draw a time line for the Engraving Department, similar to Exhibit 21-5.

REQUIRED

2. Use the time line to help you compute the number of equivalent units and the cost per equivalent unit in the Engraving Department for June.
3. Assign total cost in the Engraving Department to (a) units completed and transferred to Printing during June, and (b) units still in process at June 30.
4. Prepare a T-account for Work in Process Inventory—Engraving to show its activity during June, including the June 30 balance.

P21-2B DSI Newsprint, Inc., manufactures the paper on which newspapers are printed. Newsprint's four-stage process includes mixing, cooking, rolling, and cutting. In the Mixing Department, wood pulp and chemicals are blended. The resulting mix is heated in the Cooking Department in much the same way food is prepared. Then the cooked mix is rolled to produce sheets. The final process, cutting, divides the sheets into large rolled units.

The Mixing Department incurred the following costs during August:

Work in Process Inventory—Mixing	
Aug. 1 balance	0
Direct materials	26,000
Direct labor	7,400
Manufacturing overhead	18,340

During August, the Mixing Department started and completed mixing for 2,500 rolls of newsprint. The department started but did not finish the mixing for an additional 300 rolls, which were one-third complete with respect to both direct materials and conversion work at the end of August.

REQUIRED

1. Compute the number of equivalent units and the cost per equivalent unit in the Mixing Department for August.
2. Show that the sum of (a) cost of goods transferred out of the Mixing Department, and (b) ending Work in Process Inventory—Mixing equals the total cost accumulated in the department during August.
3. Journalize all transactions affecting the company's mixing process during August, including those already posted.

P21-3B Georgia-Pacific produces particle board. The Preparation Department begins with wood, which is chopped into small bits. At the end of the process, an adhesive mixture is added. Then the wood/adhesive mixture goes on to the Compression Department, where the wood is compressed into particle board. Assume conversion costs are added evenly throughout the Preparation Department. Suppose that November data for the Preparation Department are as follows (in millions):

Sheets		Costs	
Beginning work in process inventory.........	0 sheets	Beginning work in process inventory..................................	$ 0
Started production...........	1,000 sheets	Costs added during November:	
Completed and transferred out to Compression in November	950 sheets	Wood.................................	1,050
		Adhesives...........................	380
		Direct labor.......................	194
Ending work in process inventory (40% of the way through the preparation process)....	50 sheets	Manufacturing overhead...	291
		Total costs	$1,915

REQUIRED

1. Draw a time line for the Preparation Department, similar to Exhibit 21-5.
2. Use the time line to help you compute the equivalent units for direct materials and for conversion costs. (*Hint:* Each direct material added at a different point in the production process requires its own equivalent-unit computation.)
3. Compute the total costs of the units (sheets)
   a. Completed and transferred out to the Compression Department
   b. In the Preparation Department's ending work in process inventory
4. Prepare the journal entry to record the cost of the sheets completed and transferred out to the Compression Department.
5. Post the journal entries to the Work in Process Inventory—Preparation T-account. What is the ending balance?

P21-4B Pierpont Mills manufactures broadloom carpet in seven processes: spinning, dyeing, plying, spooling, tufting, latexing, and shearing. First, fluff nylon purchased from a company such as DuPont or Monsanto is spun into yarn that is dyed the desired color. Then threads of the yarn are joined together, or plied, for added strength. The plied yarn is spooled for carpet making. Tufting is the process by which yarn is added to burlap backing. After the backing is latexed to hold it together and make it skid-resistant, the carpet is sheared to give it an even appearance and feel.

Computing equivalent units for a second department with beginning inventory; assigning cost to completed units and ending work in process; FIFO method (Obj. 3, 4, 5)

At March 31, before recording the transfer of costs out of the Dyeing Department, the Pierpont Mills general ledger included the following account for one of its lines of carpet:

Work in Process Inventory—Dyeing	
Feb. 28 Balance	10,900
Transferred in from Spinning	22,400
Direct materials	11,760
Direct labor	7,207
Manufacturing overhead	42,900

In the Dyeing Department, direct materials (dye) are added at the beginning of the process. Conversion costs are incurred evenly throughout the process. Work in process inventory of the Dyeing Department on February 28 consisted of 75 rolls that were 60% of the way through the production process. During March, 560 rolls were transferred in from the Spinning Department. The Dyeing Department completed and transferred to the Plying Department 500 rolls in March, and 135 rolls were still in process on March 31. The ending inventory was 80% of the way through the Dyeing process. Pierpont Mills uses FIFO process costing.

1. Prepare a time line for the Dyeing Department, similar to Exhibit 21-11.
2. Use the time line to help you compute the equivalent units, cost per equivalent unit, and total costs to account for in the Dyeing Department for March.
3. Assign total Dyeing Department cost to (a) goods transferred from Dyeing to Plying, and (b) Work in Process Inventory—Dyeing on March 31.

REQUIRED

P21-5B Refer to Problem 21-4B.

Preparing a production cost report and recording transactions on the basis of the report's information (Obj. 3, 4, 5)

1. Prepare the March production cost report for the Dyeing Department.
2. Journalize all transactions affecting the Dyeing Department during March, including the entries that have already been posted.

P21-6B Cadet Power Equipment Co., uses three processes to manufacture lawn mowers: forming the blade housing from steel, assembling the parts of the mower, and testing the completed mowers. The mowers are transferred to finished goods before shipment to Sears, Montgomery Ward, and Wal-Mart.

Computing equivalent units for a second department with beginning inventory; assigning cost to completed units and ending work in process; FIFO method (Obj. 3, 4, 5)

Cadet's Testing Department requires no direct materials. Other process costing information follows:

Units	
Beginning work in process (60% complete as to conversion work)	2,000 units
Transferred in from the Assembling Department during the period	9,000 units
Completed during the period	6,000 units
Ending work in process (30% complete as to conversion work)	5,000 units
Costs	
Beginning work in process	$137,600
Transferred in from the Assembling Department during the period	675,000
Conversion costs added during the period	50,400

The cost transferred into Finished Goods Inventory is the cost of the mowers transferred out of the Testing Department plus the cost of boxing the mowers. Boxing requires both labor and equipment, but takes only one minute of machine time and direct labor per mower. The boxes cost $1 each. Conversion costs are $30 per machine hour and $24 per labor hour for boxing. Cadet uses FIFO process costing.

1. Draw a time line for the Testing Department, similar to the one in Exhibit 21-11.

2. Use the time line to compute the number of equivalent units of work performed by the Testing Department during the period, the cost per equivalent unit, and total costs to account for.

3. Assign total cost to (a) units completed and transferred out of Testing, and (b) units in Testing's ending work in process inventory.

4. Compute the total manufacturing cost of the 6,000 mowers completed and transferred to finished goods. Also compute the unit cost of each complete mower. (*Hint:* Remember that the total cost of the mowers transferred into Finished Goods Inventory includes direct materials and conversion costs of the boxing that occurs after the testing process is complete.)

Computing equivalent units for a second department with beginning inventory; assigning cost to completed units and ending work in process; weighted-average method
(Obj. 3, 4, 6)

P21-7B Repeat Problem 21-6B, using the weighted-average method. The $137,600 beginning balance of Work in Process—Testing includes $128,000 of transferred-in cost and $9,600 of conversion cost. (For requirement 1, use the time line in Exhibit 21-16 as a guide.)

Applying Your Knowledge

Using FIFO process cost information to evaluate production performance
(Obj. 5)

DECISION CASES

CASE 1. Crane Auto Parts makes automobile parts. Kevin Campbell, foreman of Crane's Finishing Department, receives the following data for his department's October operations:

			Equivalent Units	
Flow of Production	Flow of Physical Units	Transferred In	Direct Materials	Conversion Costs
Units to account for:				
Beginning work in process inventory......................	12,000			
Transferred in during October..............................	28,000			
Total units to account for.......................................	40,000			
Units accounted for:				
Completed and transferred out to Finished Goods Inventory during October:				
From beginning inventory.............................	12,000	—	7,200	6,000
Started and completed during October..........	24,000	24,000	24,000	24,000
Ending work in process, October 31....................	4,000	4,000	800	1,200
Total physical units accounted for.........................	40,000			
Equivalent units..		28,000	32,000	31,200

	Transferred In	Direct Materials	Conversion Costs	Total
Unit costs:				
Beginning work in process, September 30...				$ 59,000
Costs added during October..	$64,400	$35,200	$49,920	149,520
Divide by equivalent units	÷28,000	÷32,000	÷31,200	
Cost per equivalent unit..	$ 2.30	$ 1.10	$ 1.60	
Total cost to account for				$208,520
Assignment of total cost:				
Units completed and transferred out to Finished Goods Inventory:				
From beginning work in process, September 30				$ 59,000
Costs added during October:				
Direct materials...		[7,200 × $1.10]		7,920
Conversion costs..			[6,000 × $1.60]	9,600
Total completed from beginning inventory....................................				76,520
Units transferred in from Molding and				
completed during October..		[24,000 × ($2.30 + $1.10 + $1.60)]		120,000
Total cost transferred out...				196,520
Ending work in process, October 31:				
Transferred-in costs	[4,000 × $2.30]			9,200
Direct materials..		[800 × $1.10]		880
Conversion costs			[1,200 × $1.60]	1,920
Total ending work in process, October 31				12,000
Total cost accounted for..				$208,520

The transferred-in cost per unit has remained stable at $2.30 for several months.

1. Compute the cost per unit for
   a. October production
   b. Units completed and transferred out to finished goods.
2. Has Campbell done a better or poorer job of controlling Finishing Department costs in October than in September? How do you know?
3. Earlier in the fall, Campbell set a goal of holding the cost per completed unit to $5.05. Has Campbell met his goal? Explain.
4. To evaluate Campbell's ability to control costs in the Finishing Department, what other information would you like to have?

CASE 2. Refer to the data for Decision Case 1. Crane Auto Parts is approached by another manufacturer, Voluparts, that offers to finish Crane's products for $2.50 per unit. If Crane accepts this offer to "outsource" the finishing operation, it will shut down its Finishing Department.

Using process cost information to make an outsourcing decision
(Obj. 5)

REQUIRED

1. What process costing information is useful in deciding whether to make or buy the finishing operations?
2. Considering only cost information, should Crane accept or reject Volupart's offer?
3. What factors other than cost should Crane's managers consider before accepting or rejecting Volupart's offer?

Team Project

Chick'n Quick produces a variety of chicken-based prepared foods: chicken broth, chicken à la king, and chicken and noodles. The chicken à la king and chicken and noodles require cooked and shredded chicken. In its first manufacturing operation, Chick'n Quick cooks and shreds the chicken. Then the shredded chicken is used to produce chicken à la king and chicken and noodles. Direct materials are added at the beginning of each process, and conversion costs are incurred evenly throughout each process. Chick'n Quick uses the FIFO method of process costing.

The U.S. Navy offers Chick'n Quick $2.80 per gallon for a large order of chicken and noodles. Charlie Whitehorse, who manages the chicken and noodle production process, has been asked whether Chick'n Quick should accept the Navy's offer. Whitehorse gathers the following information from March's chicken and noodle operations:

Computing allowable cost per unit; computing cost per equivalent unit; second process; FIFO
(Obj. 3, 5)

Gallons	
Beginning work in process inventory (40% of the way through the process)	2,000 gallons
Gallons started during March	29,000 gallons
Gallons completed and transferred out during March	30,000 gallons
Ending work in process inventory (30% of the way through the process)	1,000 gallons

Costs	
Costs incurred to start the 2,000 gallons of beginning work in process inventory in February	$ 3,400
Costs added during March:	
Direct materials	43,500
Conversion costs	22,125

LaKeisha Thompson manages the chicken cooking and shredding process. She has received the following data for her department's March operations:

	Pounds
Beginning work in process inventory (40% of the way through the process)	2,500 pounds
Pounds started during March	30,000 pounds
Pounds completed and transferred out during March	29,500 pounds
Ending work in process inventory (60% of the way through the process)	3,000 pounds

	Costs
Costs incurred to start the 2,500 pounds of beginning work in process inventory in February	$ 2,000
Costs added during March:	
Direct materials	18,900
Conversion costs	18,180

Each gallon of chicken and noodles requires 1/2 pound of cooked and shredded chicken, in addition to the direct materials information already provided to Charlie Whitehorse. Assume that if Chick'n Quick accepts the Navy's offer, the extra cost per equivalent unit that Chick'n Quick will incur equals the March cost per equivalent unit.

Split your team into two groups. Each group should meet separately *before* a meeting of the entire team.

REQUIRED

1. The first group takes the role of Charlie Whitehorse, manager of the chicken and noodle production process. Before meeting with the entire team, determine the maximum transferred-in cost *per pound* the chicken and noodle operation can incur from the chicken cooking and shredding process, if Chick'n Quick is to make a profit on the Navy's order. (*Hint:* You may find it helpful to prepare a time line and to use Exhibits 21-11 through 21-14 as a guide to your analysis.)

2. The second group takes the role of LaKeisha Thompson, manager of the chicken cooking and shredding process. Before meeting with the entire team, determine the cost per pound of the chicken cooking and shredding process. (*Hint:* You may find it helpful to prepare a time line, and to use Exhibits 21-11 through 21-14 as a guide to your analysis.)

3. After each group meets, the entire team should meet to decide whether Chick'n Quick should accept or reject the Navy's offer.

Internet Exercise   CARLSBERG BEER

The process of brewing beer is over 6,000 years old. The earliest records from Mesopotamia indicate that the Sumerians inadvertently discovered the fermentation process. Because beer is a vitamin-rich porridge, it is reported to have increased health and longevity, and reduced disease and malnutrition.

Today, beer brewing can be found all across the world—from the largest corporations to microbreweries to do-it-yourself types. However, the process of making beer is similar in all instances. Carlsberg Beer, a Scandinavian company, illustrates the brewing process on its Web site.

REQUIRED

1. Go to **http://www.carlsberg.com.** This is Carlsberg's home page. Here you can see Carlsberg's latest advertisements, review its history, and view the locations throughout the world where Carlsberg is sold.

2. Click on the **Brewery** button. Review Carlsberg's brewing process to answer the following questions.
   a. Identify the five major stages in the beer-making process.
   b. Should Carlsberg use job costing or process costing? Why?
   c. How many raw material inventory accounts should Carlsberg maintain for its beer process? (*Hint:* Identify the raw materials needed for each stage of brewing.)

d. How many work in process accounts should Carlsberg maintain for its beer processing? (*Hint:* Review each stage of the brewing process. If a stage can be completed within one day, it is unlikely to require a separate work in process account.)

e. Assume the entire beer-making process takes 40 days: 9 days for malting, 1 day for brewing, 29 days for fermentation and storing, and 1 day for filtration and bottling. Also assume that the computation for equivalent units is based on the percentage of completion of the beer-making process. Compute the equivalent units for 200,000 liters of beer that have completed the brewing stage, but have not yet started fermentation.

f. At what point in the brewing process would costs be transferred to finished goods?

CHAPTER 22

Cost-Volume-Profit Analysis and the Contribution Margin Approach to Decision Making

LEARNING OBJECTIVES

After studying this chapter, you should be able to

1. Identify different cost behavior patterns

2. Use a contribution margin income statement to make business decisions

3. Compute break-even sales

4. Compute the sales level needed to earn a target operating income

5. Graph a set of cost-volume-profit relationships

6. Compute a margin of safety

7. Use the sales mix in CVP analysis

8. Compute income using variable costing and absorption costing

"All aboard!" shouts the conductor of the Grand Canyon Railway as the train departs from the Williams, Arizona, depot. The restored turn-of-the-century train features musicians in period costumes. Passengers can have breakfast on the morning trip to the canyon and appetizers on the afternoon trip back to Williams. The railway offers three classes of service: (1) Coach, in restored 1923 cars; (2) Club, with a mahogany bar; and (3) Chief, with an open-air rear platform.

Restoration of the railway cost $20 million for the tracks, locomotive, and cars. Few of the railway's costs vary with the number of passengers because most costs are *fixed*. Track maintenance, insurance, the costs to operate the depot's railway museum, and depreciation on the locomotive and cars stay the same whether 1 or 1,000 passengers travel the scenic 65-mile route. But food and beverage costs are *variable*. They rise and fall with the number of passengers on board.

The railway's managers have to find a delicate balance. They must set ticket prices high enough to cover their costs and earn a profit, but low enough to fill the seats. Because most of the railway's costs are fixed, the extra costs to serve each additional passenger are low. Once fixed costs are covered, most of the revenue from an extra guest goes toward providing a profit.

Cost-Volume-Profit (CVP) Analysis. Expresses the relationships among costs, volume, and profit or loss.

H ow do the railway's managers ensure that revenues will cover costs and provide profits? How do the managers decide on the number of seats to offer in each class? How many seats must the railway fill to cover its costs? As we shall see in this chapter, managers like controller Ken Cash perform cost-volume-profit analysis to answer these important questions.

Cost-volume-proft (CVP) analysis expresses the relationships among costs, volume, and profit or loss. It is a key tool for short-term business decisions. In the first half of this chapter, we explain how to compute *profit* in a way that is tailor-made for CVP analysis. But first we need to discuss the different types of *costs*.

Variable, Fixed, and Mixed Costs

Objective 1

Identify different cost behavior patterns

In Chapter 20, we defined a *cost driver* as any factor that affects costs. A common cost driver is *volume*—often expressed as physical *units* produced or sold, or as sales *dollars*. For example, the more T-shirts Hanes produces—that is, the greater its production volume—the more costs the company incurs. Nonvolume factors can also drive costs. For example, weight drives freight costs. However, to emphasize basic concepts in this chapter, we focus on volume as the cost driver. **Cost behavior** describes how costs change—if they change at all—as the cost driver changes. We examine three basic types of costs: variable, fixed, and mixed.

Cost Behavior. Describes how costs change as a cost driver changes.

Variable Costs

Variable Costs. Costs that change in total in direct proportion to changes in volume of activity.

Variable costs change in total in direct proportion to changes in the volume of activity. Sales commissions are one example of variable costs. Suppose an auto salesman earns a $200 commission for each auto he sells. If he sells 20% more cars this month, his total sales commission will increase by 20 percent. Similarly, if he sells 10% fewer cars, his total sales commission will decline by 10 percent. The total amount of the sales commission fluctuates with the number of units (cars) sold, but the per-unit amount of the sales commission remains constant at $200 per car. The key point is: *total variable costs fluctuate with the volume of activity, but the variable cost per unit remains constant.* Other variable costs include direct material costs, delivery costs, and hourly labor costs.

Consider Grand Canyon Railway from the chapter opening story. On the morning trip from Williams, Arizona, to Grand Canyon National Park, passengers receive a continental breakfast including pastries, orange juice, and coffee. Assume this breakfast costs the railway $3 per person. On the afternoon return trip, passengers enjoy appetizers, champagne, and soft drinks. Suppose this afternoon snack costs Grand Canyon Railway $10 per person. Exhibit 22-1 graphs these two variable costs. Notice that total variable costs are plotted on the vertical axis, and total volume is on the horizontal axis.

Exhibit 22-1(a) presents total variable costs for breakfast service. If there are no passengers, Grand Canyon incurs no breakfast costs. Therefore, the total variable cost line begins at the bottom left corner. This point is called the *origin*. It is the point at which the cost and volume axes intersect, and represents zero volume and zero cost. The *slope* of the total variable cost line is the change in total variable cost (on the vertical axis) divided by the change in the total volume (on the horizontal axis). This equals the variable cost per unit. In Exhibit 22-1(a), the slope of Grand Canyon Railway's breakfast service total variable cost line is the $3 variable cost per passenger. This means that the railway spends an additional $3 on breakfast for each additional passenger. If the railroad carries 2,000 passengers, it will spend a total of $6,000 (2,000 passengers × $3 each) for breakfast service. Follow this total variable cost line to the right to see that doubling the number of passengers to 4,000 likewise doubles the total variable cost for breakfast service to $12,000 (4,000 × $3 = $12,000).

Exhibit 22-1(b) shows total variable costs for afternoon snacks and beverages. The slope of the total variable cost line for the afternoon snack service is the $10 variable cost of providing the afternoon refreshments for each passenger. This line is much steeper than the total variable cost line for breakfast service, which costs only $3 per person.

The higher the variable cost per unit, the steeper the slope of the line in the total variable cost graph.

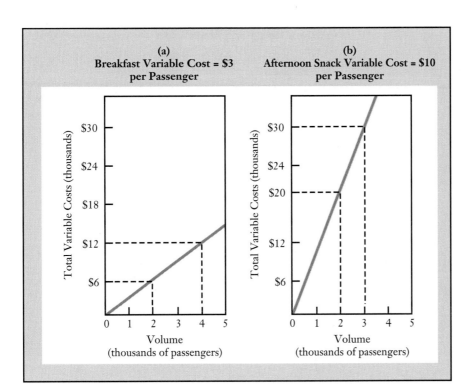

EXHIBIT 22-1
Variable Costs

(a)
**Breakfast Variable Cost = $3
per Passenger**

(b)
**Afternoon Snack Variable Cost = $10
per Passenger**

Study Exhibit 22-1(b) to confirm that the total cost of afternoon snacks for 2,000 passengers is $20,000 (2,000 × $10). This is much higher than the breakfast cost for 2,000 passengers ($6,000), so the slope of the snack's total variable cost line is much steeper than that for breakfast. Exhibit 22-1(b) also shows that if the number of passengers increases to 3,000 (a 50% increase), then the total variable cost of providing snack service also increases by 50%—from $20,000 to $30,000 (3,000 × $10).

Exhibit 22-1 shows that the total variable cost line begins at the origin, where the cost and the volume axes intersect. Why? Because at zero volume, the variable cost is zero. If there are no passengers, Grand Canyon Railway incurs no costs for breakfast or afternoon snacks. As volume increases, total variable cost increases in a straight line that leads out from the origin. The line's steepness depends on the variable cost per unit. The Grand Canyon Railway example shows that the afternoon snack service's higher variable cost per passenger results in a steeper total variable cost line. The line representing the lower total variable cost of breakfast service is flatter.

Fixed Costs

A **fixed cost** does not change in total despite wide changes in volume. Most of Grand Canyon Railway's costs are fixed. The train makes one round-trip each day, regardless of the number of passengers on the train. Many costs remain the same, whether the number of passengers rises, falls, or stays the same. These fixed costs include

Fixed Cost. Cost that does not change in total despite wide changes in volume.

■ **Daily Exercise 22-1**
■ **Daily Exercise 22-2**

- Depreciation and maintenance on the track, the locomotive, and the Williams Depot museum
- Entertainment costs (salaries of the strolling musicians)
- Administrative expenses (for example, salaries of accountants and general managers)

Suppose Grand Canyon Railway has $200,000 of fixed costs per month, as shown in Exhibit 22-2. Like all graphs of fixed costs, Exhibit 22-2 shows a flat line that intersects the cost axis at the level of the total fixed cost. This graph shows that the $200,000 monthly total fixed cost is the same for any volume of passengers. However, the *fixed cost per passenger* depends on the number of passengers carried. If the railway carries 2,000 passengers, the fixed cost per passenger is $100 ($200,000 ÷ 2,000 passengers). If the number of passengers doubles to 4,000, the fixed cost per passenger is cut in half to $50 ($200,000 ÷ 4,000 passengers). Thus the fixed cost per passenger is *inversely* proportional to the number of passengers. The key point is: *total fixed costs remain constant, but fixed cost per unit is inversely proportional to the volume of activity.*

EXHIBIT 22-2
Fixed Costs

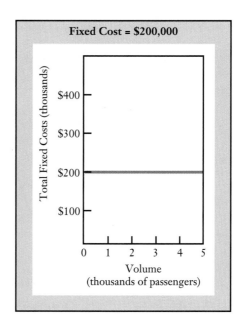

Learning Tip: Generally, sale prices and variable costs are expressed in per-unit amounts, and fixed costs are expressed in total amounts.

Mixed Costs

Mixed Cost. Cost that is part variable and part fixed.

A **mixed cost** is part variable and part fixed. Suppose you start a business finding information on the Internet. MCI offers you a plan that charges $50 per month for several password accounts plus $0.05 per minute for connect time. In this plan you will pay a fixed cost of $600 per year ($50 per month × 12 months), plus $3 per hour ($0.05 per minute × 60 minutes) for connect time. Exhibit 22-3 shows the *total* (variable plus fixed) yearly costs at different volume (connect-time) levels.

■ Daily Exercise 22-3

In graphs of mixed costs like Exhibit 22-3, total cost is the sum of the fixed cost plus the variable cost. If you use 250 hours of connect time, your total annual cost is $1,350 [fixed cost of $600 plus variable cost of $750 (250 hours × $3 per hour)]. If you double your connect time to 500 hours, you will pay $2,100 [fixed cost of $600 plus variable cost of $1,500 (500 hours × $3 per hour)]. Even if you use no connect time, you will still pay the $600 fixed cost. Thus graphs of mixed costs start at total fixed costs—not at zero as with variable costs. The slope of the total mixed cost line is the variable cost per unit.

EXHIBIT 22-3
Mixed Costs

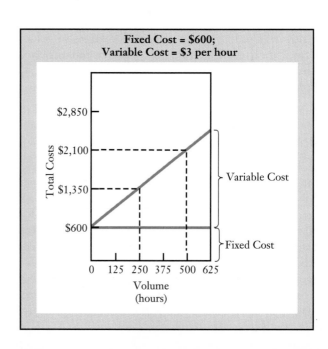

Accountants frequently treat the fixed and variable components of mixed costs as two separate costs. They add the fixed component to other fixed costs to determine the total cost that does not vary with the volume of goods and services produced or sold. Similarly, they combine the variable component with other variable costs to compute the costs that increase in direct proportion to volume.

 Working It Out In the Internet example of mixed costs (Exhibit 22-3), if you double your connect time from 250 hours to 500 hours, does your cost double? Explain.

Answer: No, your total cost increases, but by less than double [($2,100 − $1,350) ÷ $1,350 = 55.6% increase]. Your variable costs double (from $750 to $1,500) when you double connect time, but the $600 fixed portion of the cost remains unchanged.

Relevant Range

A **relevant range** is a band of volume in which a specific relationship exists between cost and volume. Outside the relevant range, the cost either increases or decreases. A fixed cost is fixed only within a given relevant range of volume (usually large) and a given time span (often a month or a year). Exhibit 22-4 shows a fixed cost of $50,000 for the volume range of 0 to 10,000 units. Between 10,000 and 20,000 units, fixed costs increase to $80,000, and they increase to $120,000 for volumes above 20,000 units.

Companies use the relevant range concept in planning costs. Suppose a Footlocker store in Exhibit 22-4 expects to sell 12,000 pairs of shoes next year. For this period, the relevant range is between 10,000 and 20,000 pairs of shoes, so managers budget fixed expenses of $80,000. If actual sales for the year exceed 20,000 pairs, Footlocker will consider expanding the store, which will increase rent expense. Exhibit 22-4 shows how fixed costs increase as the relevant range shifts to a higher band of volume.

Conversely, if Footlocker expects to sell only 8,000 pairs of shoes next year, the store will budget fixed costs of $50,000. Its managers may have to cut back operating hours, lay off employees, or take other actions to reduce costs.

The relevant range concept also applies to variable costs. Some variable costs behave differently at different levels of volume. For example, utility costs for water and electricity often decrease per unit as usage increases. Also, a company may pay higher sales commission rates for higher levels of sales to encourage extra selling effort. Therefore,

Relevant Range. A band of volume in which a specific relationship exists between cost and volume.

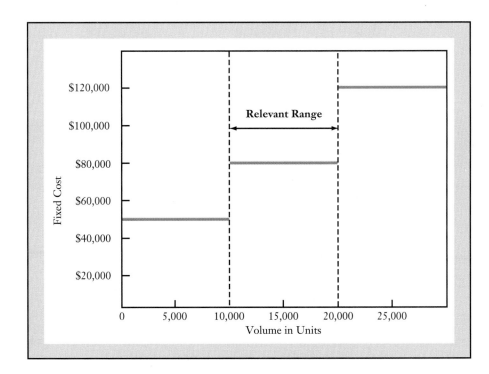

EXHIBIT 22-4
Relevant Range

businesses should consider how fixed and variable costs change over the full range of sales volumes that are likely to occur.

Accountants and managers analyze cost behavior to predict how different business decisions will affect costs and therefore profits. For example, Grand Canyon Railway managers may decide between (1) setting a higher ticket price and selling fewer seats, and (2) setting a lower price and selling more seats. To determine which alternative is likely to lead to higher profits, managers must predict total costs at both volume levels. Variable costs throughout the value chain will be higher at the higher volume level. Fixed costs may or may not be higher, depending on their relevant ranges. Thus managers must understand how costs vary with volume to predict profits from the two actions.

Objective 2

Use a contribution margin income statement to make business decisions

◀▪▪▪◀▪▪▪◀▪▪▪ Recall from Chapter 19, page 822, that managers are concerned with *all* costs related to a product: the costs of the entire value chain, from R&D through manufacturing, distribution, and customer service.

◀▪▪▪◀▪▪▪◀▪▪▪ See Chapter 5, page 198, for a discussion of operating income.

Contribution Margin Income Statement. Income statement that groups variable and fixed expenses separately, and highlights the contribution margin.

Contribution Margin. The excess of sales revenue over variable expenses.

Concept Highlight

EXHIBIT 22-5
Alternative Income Statement Formats

The Contribution Margin Income Statement

Earlier chapters presented the conventional income statement. That format, illustrated for Martin Manufacturing Company in Panel A of Exhibit 22-5, classifies expenses by value-chain function. ◀▪▪▪ Manufacturing costs of units sold are expensed as cost of goods sold. Sales revenue minus cost of goods sold equals gross margin. Most other costs (for example, marketing and distribution costs) are grouped as "operating expenses." As explained in Chapter 5, gross margin minus operating expenses equals operating income. ◀▪▪▪

Cost of goods sold on a conventional income statement includes both variable and fixed manufacturing costs. Variable costs include direct materials, direct labor, and the cost of electricity used by production equipment. In contrast, manufacturing costs like depreciation, factory rent, and property taxes are fixed. As Panel A shows, conventional income statements do not distinguish between variable and fixed expenses.

Companies use conventional income statements to report the results of operations to external parties. But for decision making, many managers prefer a different income statement format. To see why, let's suppose that executives want to predict the operating income that Martin Manufacturing Company will earn if sales volume increases by 10 percent.

The conventional income statement does not help Martin's managers predict how the change in volume will affect income. This is because the conventional income statement does not separate variable costs from fixed costs. To solve this problem, the **contribution margin income statement** in Panel B of Exhibit 22-5 groups variable and fixed expenses separately. It highlights the **contribution margin,** which is the excess of sales revenue over variable expenses.

PANEL A—Conventional Format

MARTIN MANUFACTURING COMPANY Conventional Income Statement Year Ended December 31, 19X9		
Sales revenue..........................		$2,100,000
Cost of goods sold		1,320,000
Gross margin		780,000
Operating expenses:		
Marketing expense.............	$310,000	
Distribution expense..........	290,000	600,000
Operating income.................		$ 180,000

PANEL B—Contribution Margin Format

MARTIN MANUFACTURING COMPANY Contribution Margin Income Statement Year Ended December 31, 19X9		
Sales revenue.......................................		$2,100,000
Variable expenses:		
Variable manufacturing cost of goods sold	$840,000	
Variable marketing expense	150,000	
Variable distribution expense..........	210,000	1,200,000
Contribution margin..........................		900,000
Fixed expenses:		
Fixed manufacturing expense	480,000	
Fixed marketing expense................	160,000	
Fixed distribution expense..............	80,000	720,000
Operating income		$ 180,000

The contribution margin is so named because the excess of revenues over variable expenses is the amount that contributes to "covering" fixed expenses and to providing operating income. Think about fixed expenses. Many fixed costs are incurred before any production or sales take place. For instance, machines must be purchased before goods can be produced. The cost of these machines becomes depreciation expense. As goods are produced and sold, the contribution margin grows and covers this depreciation expense. In effect, the company recovers its machine investment. After all fixed costs are recovered by the contribution margin, the contribution from additional sales provide operating income.

Compare the conventional income statement in Exhibit 22-5, Panel A, with the contribution margin income statement in Panel B. The conventional income statement subtracts cost of goods sold (including both variable and fixed manufacturing costs) from sales to obtain gross margin. In contrast, the contribution margin income statement subtracts all variable costs (both manufacturing and nonmanufacturing) to obtain contribution margin. The following chart highlights the differences between gross margin and contribution margin:

■ **Daily Exercise 22-4**
■ **Daily Exercise 22-5**
■ **Daily Exercise 22-6**

Conventional Income Statement	Contribution Margin Income Statement
Sales revenue	**Sales revenue**
deduct Cost of Goods Sold:	**deduct Variable Expenses:**
Variable manufacturing cost of goods sold	Variable manufacturing cost of goods sold
Fixed manufacturing cost of goods sold	Variable marketing expenses
= Gross margin	Other variable expenses
	= Contribution margin

The two major differences are

- Fixed manufacturing cost of goods sold is subtracted from sales to compute gross margin, but not to compute contribution margin.
- Variable marketing expenses and other variable nonmanufacturing expenses are subtracted from sales to calculate contribution margin, but not to compute gross margin.

Managers use the contribution margin for planning and decision making, because the contribution margin distinguishes between variable and fixed costs. As an example, let's examine how Martin Manufacturing's managers can use the contribution margin income statement to predict the company's operating income if sales volume increases by 10 percent. If sales volume increases by 10%, then variable costs (expenses) should also increase by 10 percent. Fixed costs (expenses), however, should remain the same, assuming Martin remains in the same relevant range:

■ **Daily Exercise 22-7**

Increase in sales (10% × $2,100,000)	$ 210,000
Increase in variable expenses (10% × $1,200,000)	(120,000)
Increase in contribution margin	90,000
Increase in fixed expenses	0
Increase in operating income...	$ 90,000

Now suppose that Martin could achieve the same 10% increase in sales only by spending an additional $20,000 on a new advertising campaign. Should Martin undertake the advertising campaign?

Increase in contribution margin (from above)	$ 90,000
Increase in marketing expenses..............................	(20,000)
Increase in operating income.................................	$ 70,000

The increased profits from higher sales outweigh the increased costs of the new advertising campaign, so Martin should undertake the campaign.

This analysis cannot be performed using the conventional income statement, because that statement's format does not show which expenses are variable and which are fixed.

 Working It Out Refer to Exhibit 22-5. Suppose that Martin Manufacturing Company sold 6,000 units during the year.

1. How much did each unit contribute to cover fixed expenses and provide operating income?
2. What would have been the company's operating income (loss) if no units had been sold?

Answers

1. The total contribution margin is $900,000, so each unit contributed $150 ($900,000 ÷ 6,000 units).
2. With no sales, the operating loss would have been $720,000 (the amount of the total fixed expenses), unless some of the fixed expenses could have been saved by moving to the lowest range of activity.

SUMMARY PROBLEM FOR YOUR REVIEW   MID-CHAPTER

The 19X8 contribution margin income statement of the Country Gentleman Shirt Company follows. The average price of Country Gentleman's shirts is $45.

COUNTRY GENTLEMAN SHIRT COMPANY
Contribution Margin Income Statement
Year Ended December 31, 19X8

Sales revenue		$900,000
Variable expenses:		
Variable manufacturing cost of goods sold	$280,000	
Variable operating expenses	120,000	400,000
Contribution margin...		500,000
Fixed expenses:		
Fixed manufacturing expenses	225,000	
Fixed operating expenses	75,000	300,000
Operating income		$200,000

REQUIRED

1. How many shirts did Country Gentleman sell in 19X8?
2. What operating income will the company earn in 19X9 if sales volume increases by 20% and all sale prices, unit variable costs, and total fixed costs do not change? Also, there are no beginning or ending inventories.
3. Recast the 19X8 income statement in the conventional format.

■ SOLUTION

REQUIREMENT 1

Country Gentleman sold 20,000 shirts in 19X8:

$$\text{Sales revenue} = \left(\begin{array}{c}\text{Sale price}\\\text{per shirt}\end{array}\right) \times \left(\begin{array}{c}\text{Number of}\\\text{shirts sold}\end{array}\right)$$

$$\$900,000 = \$45 \times (\text{Number of shirts sold})$$

$$\frac{\$900,000}{\$45} = \text{Number of shirts sold}$$

$$20,000 = \text{Number of shirts sold}$$

Increase in sales revenue (20% × $900,000)	$180,000
Increase in variable expenses (20% × 400,000).........	80,000
Increase in contribution margin................................	100,000
Increase in fixed expenses.......................................	0
Increase in operating income	100,000
19X8 operating income	200,000
19X9 operating income	$300,000

REQUIREMENT 2

REQUIREMENT 3

COUNTRY GENTLEMAN SHIRT COMPANY
Conventional Income Statement
Year Ended December 31, 19X8

Sales revenue..	$900,000
Cost of goods sold*..	505,000
Gross margin	395,000
Operating expenses[†]	195,000
Operating income..	$200,000

*$280,000 variable manufacturing cost of goods sold + $225,000 fixed manufacturing cost from contribution margin statement.
[†]$120,000 variable operating expense + $75,000 fixed operating expense.

Cost-Volume-Profit (CVP) Analysis

The Martin Manufacturing Company example illustrated how changes in volume affect costs and profit—this is one type of cost-volume-profit (CVP) analysis. The example also showed that CVP analysis is closely tied to the format of the contribution margin income statement.

The easiest way to learn more about CVP analysis is with an example. Suppose Kay Pak is thinking of renting a booth at a trade fair for travel agents. She plans to sell international travel posters for $3.50 each. Pak can purchase the posters for $2.10 each and can return any unsold posters for a full refund. The booth rents for $700. Using this information, let's answer six questions about Pak's business.

QUESTION 1: What is Pak's Break-Even Sales Level?
The **break-even point** is the sales level at which operating income is zero: Total revenues equal total expenses. Sales below the break-even point result in a loss. Sales above break-even provide a profit.

Break-even analysis is only one component of CVP analysis. The break-even point often is only incidental to managers of ongoing operations because their focus is on the sales level needed to earn a target profit. However, when demand for an old product is declining, or when managers are evaluating a new product or market opportunity, the break-even point becomes important. Many managers view the break-even point as a useful place to start the analysis of a new product's sales potential.

Let's use two different methods to determine the break-even point.

The Income Statement Equation Approach

To determine the break-even point, we start by separating total expenses into variable expenses and fixed expenses. For Kay Pak, the variable cost is her cost to purchase the posters. Her total variable expense equals the number of posters sold multiplied by her $2.10 cost per poster. Her total fixed cost is the rent expense, $700. Large companies have many more variable expenses and fixed expenses. Such businesses combine all variable expenses into a single total and compute a single total for fixed expenses.

Our next step is to express income in equation form:

Sales revenue − Variable expenses − Fixed expenses = Operating income

Objective 3

Compute break-even sales

Break-Even Point. The sales level at which operating income is zero: Total revenues equal total expenses.

At the break-even point, operating income is zero, so sales revenue equals expenses. Sales revenue equals the unit sale price multiplied by the number of units sold. Variable expenses equals variable cost per unit times the number of units sold. We substitute these terms into the equation and enter the dollar amounts:

Sales revenue	−	Variable expenses	− Fixed expenses = Operating income
$\left(\dfrac{\text{Sale price}}{\text{per unit}} \times \text{Units sold}\right)$ −		$\left(\dfrac{\text{Variable cost}}{\text{per unit}} \times \text{Units sold}\right)$	− Fixed expenses = Operating income

($3.50 × Units sold) −	($2.10 | × Units sold) −	$700	=	$0
($3.50 − | $2.10)	× Units sold −	$700	=	$0
	$1.40	× Units sold		=	$700
		Units sold		=	$700/$1.40
		Break-even sales in units		=	500 posters

Kay Pak must sell 500 posters to break even. Her break-even sales level in dollars is $1,750 (500 units × $3.50).

It is wise to check your calculations by "proving" the break-even point with a contribution margin income statement:

Sales revenue (500 × $3.50)...................		$1,750
less:		
Variable expenses (500 × $2.10).........	$1,050	
Fixed expenses....................................	700	(1,750)
Operating income.................................		$ 0

The Contribution Margin CVP Formula: A Shortcut Method

Contribution Margin per Unit.
Excess of the sales revenue per unit (sale price) over the variable expense per unit.

There is a shortcut method for CVP analysis. To use the shortcut, we first need to understand more about Pak's contribution margin. Each unit sold has a **contribution margin per unit,** which is the excess of the sales revenue per unit (sale price) over the variable expense per unit.

$$\text{Contribution margin} = \text{Sales revenue} - \text{Variable expense}$$

Contribution margin can be expressed on a per-unit basis or as a ratio computed as the percentage of sales revenue. For Kay Pak's business:

	Per Unit	Percent	Ratio
Sales revenue	$3.50	100%	1.00
Deduct: variable expense..........	(2.10)	(60)%	(0.60)
Contribution margin	$1.40	40%	0.40

Contribution Margin Ratio.
The ratio of contribution margin to sales revenue.

Contribution margin ratio is the ratio of contribution margin to sales revenue:

$$\text{Contribution margin ratio} = \frac{\text{Contribution margin}}{\text{Sales revenue}}$$

For Kay Pak's poster business, the contribution margin ratio is 40% ($1.40/$3.50). The contribution margin ratio tells how much a dollar of sales revenue contributes to contribution margin. Kay Pak's 40% contribution margin ratio means that each dollar of sales revenue contributes $0.40 toward fixed costs and profit, as shown in Exhibit 22-6.

COMPUTING THE BREAK-EVEN POINT IN NUMBER OF UNITS SOLD We now rearrange the income statement equation and use the contribution margin to develop a shortcut method of finding the break-even point. Our goal is to find the number of posters that Pak must sell to break even. Consequently, we solve the equation for the number of units sold:

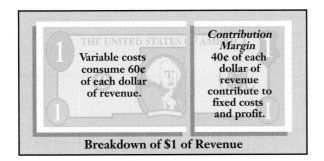

EXHIBIT 22-6
Breakdown of $1 of Revenue
into Variable Costs and
Contribution Margin

Breakdown of $1 of Revenue

$$\text{Sales revenue} \quad - \quad \text{Variable expenses} \quad - \text{Fixed expenses} = \text{Operating income}$$

$$\left(\begin{array}{c}\text{Sale price}\\\text{per unit}\end{array} \times \text{Units sold}\right) - \left(\begin{array}{c}\text{Variable cost}\\\text{per unit}\end{array} \times \text{Units sold}\right) - \text{Fixed expenses} = \text{Operating income}$$

$$\underbrace{\left(\begin{array}{c}\text{Sale price}\\\text{per unit}\end{array} - \begin{array}{c}\text{Variable cost}\\\text{per unit}\end{array}\right) \times \text{Units sold}}_{\text{Contribution margin per unit}} \qquad = \begin{array}{c}\text{Fixed}\\\text{expenses}\end{array} + \begin{array}{c}\text{Operating}\\\text{income}\end{array}$$

The sale price per unit minus the variable cost per unit equals the contribution margin per unit, so

■ **Daily Exercise 22-8**
■ **Daily Exercise 22-12**

Contribution margin per unit × Units sold = Fixed expenses + Operating income

Dividing both sides of the equation by contribution margin per unit yields

$$\text{Units sold} = \frac{\text{Fixed expenses} + \text{Operating income}}{\text{Contribution margin per unit}}$$

Kay Pak can use this contribution margin CVP formula to find her break-even point. The contribution margin per poster is $1.40 ($3.50 sale price − $2.10 variable cost). Operating income is zero at the break-even point. Pak's break-even computation is

$$\text{Units sold} = \frac{\text{Fixed expenses} + \text{Operating income}}{\text{Contribution margin per unit}}$$

$$= \frac{\$700 + \$0}{\$1.40}$$

$$= 500 \text{ posters}$$

The contribution margin CVP formula is derived from the income statement equation, so the two approaches are mathematically equivalent. Both approaches always give the same answer (500 posters, in Pak's case).

Why does this shortcut method work? The formula shows that each poster Pak sells provides $1.40 of contribution margin. To break even, Pak must generate enough contribution margin to cover her $700 of fixed expenses. At the rate of $1.40 per poster, Pak will have to sell 500 posters ($700/$1.40) to cover her $700 of fixed expenses.

COMPUTING THE BREAK-EVEN POINT IN SALES DOLLARS USING THE CONTRIBU-TION MARGIN RATIO It is easy to compute the break-even point for a simple business, like Kay Pak's, that has only one product. The sale price per poster and the variable cost per poster are readily available. But what about companies that have hundreds of products, like Sony and Procter & Gamble?

Large companies often use the contribution margin ratio to compute break-even points in terms of *sales dollars*, without detailed information on individual products. The contribution margin ratio approach differs from the contribution margin CVP formula we've just seen in only one way—fixed expenses plus operating income are divided by the *contribution margin ratio* to yield sales in *dollars*:

$$\text{Sales in dollars} = \frac{\text{Fixed expenses} + \text{Operating income}}{\text{Contribution margin ratio}}$$

Using this formula, Kay Pak's break-even point in sales dollars is

$$\text{Sales in dollars} = \frac{\$700 + 0}{0.40}$$

$$= \$1,750$$

This is the same break-even sales revenue as shown in the proof on page 958.

Why does the contribution margin ratio formula work? Each dollar of Kay Pak's sales contributes $0.40 to fixed expenses and profit. To break even, she must generate enough contribution margin at the rate of $0.40 per sales dollar to cover the $700 fixed expenses ($700 ÷ 0.40 = $1,750).

Large companies find it easier to compute break-even points in sales dollars using the contribution margin ratio approach because it does not require detailed information on individual products. The only information required is total fixed expenses and the contribution margin ratio. Suppose Sony's total fixed expenses are $10 billion and its contribution margin ratio is 40 percent. Then the break-even point in sales dollars would be

$$\text{Break-even sales in dollars} = \frac{\$10 \text{ billion}}{0.40}$$

$$= \$25 \text{ billion}$$

QUESTION 2.   If the Sale Price Per Unit Is Changed, What Will the New Break-Even Sales Be?

Now suppose that the sale price per poster is $3.85 rather than $3.50. Variable expense per poster remains at $2.10, and fixed expenses stay at $700. What is the revised break-even point in units and in dollars? The unit contribution margin becomes $1.75 ($3.85 − $2.10), and the new contribution margin ratio is 0.4545 ($1.75 ÷ $3.85).

Using the contribution margin CVP formula:

$$\textbf{Sales in units} = \frac{\textbf{Fixed expenses} + \textbf{Operating income}}{\textbf{Contribution margin per unit}}$$

$$= \frac{\$700 + 0}{\$1.75}$$

$$= 400 \text{ posters}$$

Observe that

- Sale price per unit increased, so
- Contribution margin per unit increased, and as a result,
- Fewer posters had to be sold to break even

Proof:

Sales revenue ($3.85 × 400)..................		$1,540
Deduct:		
Variable expenses (400 × $2.10).........	$840	
Fixed expenses.................................	700	(1,540)
Operating income................................		$ 0

The proof shows that Pak needs sales revenue of $1,540 to break even with a $3.85 sales price. Alternatively, we could directly compute the break-even sales in dollars using the contribution margin ratio form of the CVP formula:

$$\text{Sales in dollars} = \frac{\text{Fixed expenses} + \text{Operating income}}{\text{Contribution margin ratio}}$$

$$= \frac{\$700 + 0}{0.4545}$$

$$= \$1,540$$

This example shows that an increase in sale price reduces break-even sales, both in units and in dollars. With a higher sale price, each poster contributes more toward fixed expenses, so Pak can break even with fewer sales. Conversely, cutting the sale price would decrease the contribution margin. Then Kay Pak would have to increase the number of units sold just to break even.

 Working It Out Kay Pak believes she could dominate the travel poster business if she cut the sale price to $2.00. Would this be a good idea?

Answer: No. The variable cost per poster is $2.10. If Pak sold posters for $2.00 each, she would lose $0.10 on each poster. There can be no profit if sale price does not even cover variable expenses.

QUESTION 3. If Variable Costs Change, What Will Break-Even Sales Be?

Suppose Pak's variable expense per poster is $2.38 instead of $2.10. The sale price per poster remains $3.50, and fixed expenses stay at $700. What is the break-even point in units and in dollars?

The new contribution margin per unit drops to $1.12 ($3.50 – $2.38), and the new contribution margin ratio declines to 0.32 ($1.12/$3.50). Break-even sales are

$$\text{Sales in units} = \frac{\text{Fixed expenses} + \text{Operating income}}{\text{Contribution margin per unit}}$$

$$= \frac{\$700 + 0}{\$1.12}$$

$$= 625 \text{ posters}$$

$$\text{Sales in dollars} = \frac{\text{Fixed expenses} + \text{Operating income}}{\text{Contribution margin ratio}}$$

$$= \frac{\$700 + 0}{0.32}$$

$$= \$2,187.50$$

As these numbers make clear, an increase in variable expense per unit

- Reduces the contribution margin, and as a result,
- More posters must be sold to break even

Pak must increase sales in units and in dollars just to break even. Conversely, a decrease in variable cost per unit would lower the break-even point.

QUESTION 4. If Fixed Costs Change, What Will Break-Even Sales Be?

Suppose the booth rental costs $1,050 instead of the original $700. Variable expense per poster remains at $2.10, and sale price stays at $3.50. What is Kay Pak's break-even point in units and in dollars?

Using the contribution margin CVP formula:

$$\text{Sales in units} = \frac{\text{Fixed expenses} + \text{Operating income}}{\text{Contribution margin per unit}}$$

$$= \frac{\$1,050 + 0}{\$1.40}$$

$$= 750 \text{ posters}$$

$$\text{Sales in dollars} = \frac{\text{Fixed expenses} + \text{Operating income}}{\text{Contribution margin ratio}}$$

$$= \frac{\$1,050 + 0}{0.40}$$

$$= \$2,625$$

The $1,050 in fixed expenses is an increase of $350, or 50%, over the original fixed cost of $700. Note that

- Fixed expenses increased by 50%, and
- Break-even sales also increased by 50% [(750 – 500) ÷ 500]

Pak must sell more posters to cover the higher fixed costs. However, if fixed expenses had declined, she could have sold fewer posters and still covered these (lower) costs.

In general, managers prefer a lower break-even point to a higher one. But don't overemphasize this one aspect of CVP analysis. Managers are more interested in profits than in break-even sales levels. In our example, Kay Pak may be willing to pay an extra $350 ($1,050 – $700) for a better location if the expected increase in sales volume provides enough contribution margin to cover the extra rent expense and to provide extra operating income.

Objective 4

Compute the sales level needed to earn a target operating income

QUESTION 5. How Many Units Must Be Sold to Earn a Target Operating Income?

Suppose Pak hopes to earn operating income of $490. Assuming fixed expenses of $700, variable expenses of $2.10 per poster, and a $3.50 per poster sale price, how many posters must she sell to earn a profit of $490?

Until now, we have concentrated on break-even sales, the point at which operating income is zero. How should we consider a target operating income greater than zero? The contribution margin must be high enough to cover the fixed expenses *and* provide the profit. We can still use the contribution margin CVP formula. The only difference is that target operating income is $490, compared to zero when we computed break-even sales.

■ **Daily Exercise 22-13**
■ **Daily Exercise 22-14**

With a $1.40 contribution margin per unit and a 0.40 contribution margin ratio:

$$\text{Sales in units} = \frac{\text{Fixed expenses} + \text{Operating income}}{\text{Contribution margin per unit}}$$

$$= \frac{\$700 + \$490}{\$1.40} = \frac{\$1,190}{\$1.40} = 850 \text{ units}$$

Proof:

Sales revenue (850 × $3.50)		$2,975
less:		
Variable expenses (850 × $2.10)	$1,785	
Fixed expenses	700	(2,485)
Target operating income		$ 490

This proof shows that Pak needs sales revenues of $2,975 to earn profit of $490. Alternatively, we could directly compute the dollar sales necessary to earn a $490 profit, using the contribution margin ratio form of the CVP formula:

$$\text{Sales in dollars} = \frac{\text{Fixed expenses} + \text{Operating income}}{\text{Contribution margin ratio}}$$

$$= \frac{\$700 + \$490}{0.40} = \frac{\$1,190}{0.40} = \$2,975$$

Objective 5

Graph a set of cost-volume-profit relationships

QUESTION 6. What Operating Income Is Expected at Various Sales Levels?

A convenient way to determine expected operating income at various sales levels is to graph the cost-volume-profit relationships, as shown in Exhibit 22-7. As in the cost behavior graphs earlier in this chapter (Exhibits 22-1 through 22-4), we place units on the horizontal axis and dollars on the vertical axis. We use Kay Pak's data (as originally given on page 957) and follow five steps:

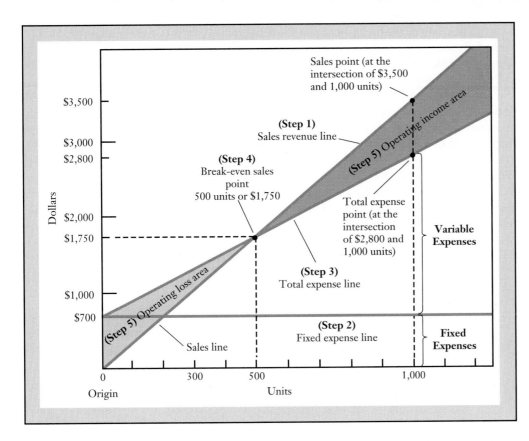

Step 1. Choose a sales volume, such as 1,000 units. Plot the point for total sales revenue at that volume: 1,000 units × $3.50 per unit = sales of $3,500. Draw the *sales revenue line* from the origin through the $3,500 point. Why does the sales revenue line start at the origin? If no posters are sold, there is no sales revenue.

Step 2. Draw the *fixed expense line*, a horizontal line that intersects the dollars axis at $700. Why is the fixed expense line flat? Because fixed expenses are the same ($700) no matter how many posters Kay Pak sells.

Step 3. Draw the *total expense* line. Total expense is the sum of variable expense plus fixed expense. Compute variable expense at the chosen sales volume: 1,000 units × $2.10 per unit = variable expense of $2,100. Add variable expense to fixed expense: $2,100 + $700 = $2,800. Plot the total expense point ($2,800) for 1,000 units. Then draw a line through this point from the $700 fixed expense intercept on the dollars axis. This is the *total expense line*. Why does the total expense line start at the fixed expense line? If Pak sells no posters, she still incurs the $700 fixed cost for the booth rental, but she incurs no variable costs.

Step 4. Identify the *break-even point*. The break-even point is the spot where the sales revenue line intersects the total expense line. This is the point where sales revenue exactly equals total expenses. The equations we used earlier told us that Pak's break-even point is 500 units, or $1,750 in sales. The graph shows us the same information visually.

Step 5. Mark the *operating income* and the *operating loss* areas on the graph. To the left of the break-even point, the total expense line lies above the sales revenue line. Expenses exceed sales revenue, leading to an operating loss. For example, Exhibit 22-7 shows that if Pak sells only 300 posters, she will incur an operating loss. The amount of the loss is the vertical distance between the total expense line and the sales revenue line:

Sales revenue (300 × $3.50).....................		$1,050
Deduct:		
Variable expenses (300 × $2.10).........	$630	
Fixed expenses....................................	700	(1,330)
Operating loss..		$ (280)

To the right of the break-even point in Exhibit 22-7, Pak's business earns a profit. The vertical distance between the sales revenue line and the total expense line equals the amount of operating income. For example, the graph shows that if Kay Pak sells 1,000 posters, she will earn operating income of $700 ($3,500 sales revenue – $2,800 total expenses).

Why bother with a graph like Exhibit 22-7? Why don't managers just use the equation approach or the contribution margin CVP formula? Graphs like Exhibit 22-7 help managers quickly estimate the profit or loss earned at different levels of sales. In contrast, the equation or formula approaches only indicate income or loss for a single sales amount.

Computer spreadsheets are ideally suited for cost-volume-profit analysis. Managers can use these spreadsheets to answer what-if questions such as, What will variable expenses be if sales rise by $1,000? By 200 units? If we cut fixed expenses by $20,000, how many units must we sell to earn a profit of $100,000? Spreadsheets allow managers to analyze the results of any one change or the results of several changes in the business's operations. Most software also displays graphs of CVP relationships, similar to the one in Exhibit 22-7.

Learning Tip: Remember these features of a CVP graph:

1. The sales revenue line always passes through the origin—when no units are sold, there is no revenue.
2. The fixed expense line is flat because fixed expenses do not change with changes in units (assuming there is no change in the relevant range).
3. The total expense line and the fixed expense line intersect the vertical axis in the same place (the amount of total fixed expenses).
4. The point where the total expense line crosses the sales revenue line is the break-even point.

Margin of Safety

Margin of Safety. Excess of expected sales over break-even sales. Drop in sales a company can absorb before incurring an operating loss.

■ Daily Exercise 22-17
■ Daily Exercise 22-18

The **margin of safety** is the excess of expected sales over break-even sales. In other words, the margin of safety is the drop in sales that the company can absorb before incurring an operating loss. A high margin of safety serves as a cushion. A low margin of safety is a warning. Managers use the margin of safety to evaluate current operations or to measure the risk of a new business plan. The lower the margin, the higher the risk. The higher the margin, the lower the risk.

Pak's break-even point in our original data is 500 posters. Suppose she expects to sell 950 posters during the period. Her margin of safety is computed as follows:

Margin of safety in units	= Expected sales in units – Break-even sales in units		
=	950	– 500	= 450 units

Margin of safety in dollars	= Margin of safety in units × Sale price per unit		
=	450	× $3.50	= $1,575

Sales can drop by 450 posters, or $1,575, before Pak incurs a loss.

For any level of sales, managers can compute the margin of safety as a percentage. Simply divide the margin of safety by sales. We obtain the same percentage whether we perform this computation in terms of units or dollars.

In units:

$$\text{Margin of safety as a percentage} = \frac{\text{Margin of safety in units}}{\text{Expected sales in units}}$$

$$= \frac{450 \text{ units}}{950 \text{ units}}$$

$$= 47.4\%$$

In dollars:

$$\text{Margin of safety as a percentage} = \frac{\text{Margin of safety in dollars}}{\text{Expected sales in dollars}}$$

$$= \frac{450 \text{ units} \times \$3.50}{950 \text{ units} \times \$3.50}$$

$$= \frac{\$1,575}{\$3,325}$$

$$= 47.4\%$$

Assumptions Underlying CVP Analysis

Cost-volume-profit analysis is based on the following assumptions:

1. Expenses can be classified as either variable or fixed.
2. Cost-volume-profit relationships are linear over a wide range of production and sales. Linear relationships can be graphed as straight lines (as in Exhibit 22-7).
3. Sale prices, unit variable costs, and total fixed expenses will not change during the period.
4. Volume is the only cost driver. The influences of other possible cost drivers (such as weight or size) are held constant or are insignificant.
5. The relevant range of volume is specified.
6. Inventory levels will not change.
7. The sales mix of products will not change during the period. **Sales mix** is the combination of products that make up total sales. For example, the sales mix of a Furniture Warehouse store may be 70% household furniture and 30% office furniture. We discuss sales mix in the next section.

Sales Mix. Combination of products that make up total sales.

When these conditions are met, CVP analysis is accurate. But most actual business conditions do not perfectly correspond to these assumptions. That is why managers regard the answers to our CVP questions as approximations rather than precise amounts.

Sales Mix

Our example thus far has focused on a single product, travel posters. Companies that sell more than one product must consider sales mix in figuring CVP relationships. Sales mix has an important effect on profits. A company earns more income by selling high-margin products than by selling an equal number of low-margin items.

For example, Continental Airlines has focused on attracting more business fliers. Business travelers generally pay more for the same flight than leisure travelers. By increasing the proportion of higher-paying business fliers, Continental boosted its sales revenue per available seat-mile (available seats × miles flown) from $0.074 in 1994 to $0.09 in 1996. Improving sales mix by selling a greater proportion of high margin tickets reduced Continental's break-even point. Before the change, Continental had to fill 63% of its seats to break even. After attracting more business travelers, Continental only had to fill 61% of its seats to break even.

In contrast to Continental's more favorable sales mix, the annual report of Deere and Company, manufacturer of John Deere farm equipment, stated that profits decreased because of "a less favorable mix of products sold." What is a *less favorable mix* of products? It is a mix with a higher percentage of items that have below-average contribution margins.

Objective 7

Use the sales mix in CVP analysis

"... the annual report of Deere and Company, manufacturer of John Deere farm equipment, stated that profits decreased because of 'a less favorable mix of products sold.'"

We can perform CVP analysis for a company that sells more than one product by using the same equations that we used for a company with a single product. But first, we must compute the *weighted-average contribution margin* of all products. The sales mix provides the weights. ◀▥

◀▥ ◀▥ ◀▥ We saw another weighted-average procedure—for inventory costing—in Chapter 9.

Suppose that Kay Pak plans to sell two types of posters instead of one. Recall that the regular poster costs $2.10 and sells for $3.50. Its contribution margin is $1.40 ($3.50 − $2.10). The second, larger poster costs $4.00 and sells for $7.00. Its contribution margin is $3.00 ($7.00 − $4.00).

An established business estimates its sales mix based on experience. Kay Pak, however, is starting a new venture. Suppose she estimates that she will sell 500 regular posters and 300 large posters. This is a 5:3 sales mix. For every 5 regular posters, Pak expects to sell 3 large posters. In other words, she expects 5/8 of the posters sold to be regular posters and 3/8 to be large posters. To compute break-even sales in units, Pak arranges the data as follows:

	Regular Posters	Large Posters	Total
Sale price per unit	$3.50	$7.00	
Deduct: Variable expense per unit	(2.10)	(4.00)	
Contribution margin per unit	$1.40	$3.00	
Sales mix in units	× 5	× 3	8
Contribution margin	$7.00	$9.00	$ 16
Weighted-average contribution margin per unit ($16/8)			$2.00

$$\frac{\text{Sales in}}{\text{total units}} = \frac{\text{Fixed expenses + Operating income}}{\text{Weighted-average contribution margin per unit}}$$

$$= \frac{\$700 + 0}{\$2.00} = 350 \text{ units}$$

■ Daily Exercise 22-19
■ Daily Exercise 22-20

Break-even sales of regular posters (350 × 5/8) .... 219 regular posters
Break-even sales of large posters (350 × 3/8) .... 131 large posters

The overall break-even point in sales dollars is $1,684 (amounts round to the nearest dollar):

219 regular posters at $3.50 each......... $ 767
131 large posters at $7.00 each 917
Total revenues $1,684

We can check these amounts by preparing a contribution margin income statement (amounts rounded to the nearest dollar):

	Regular	Large	Total
Sales revenue:			
Regular (219 × $3.50)	$767		
Large (131 × $7.00)		$917	$1,684
Variable expenses:			
Regular (219 × $2.10)	460		
Large (131 × $4.00)		524	984
Contribution margin	$307	$393	$ 700
Fixed expenses			(700)
Operating income			$ 0

Let's review our approach:

- First, compute the weighted-average contribution margin per unit. This figure expresses both types of posters in terms of a single hypothetical product that has a contribution margin of $2.00. From here on, the contribution margin approach follows the usual pattern.
- Second, divide fixed expenses (plus operating income) by the weighted-average contribution margin per unit to determine the required sales in total units.
- Third, separate total units (350) into regular posters (219) and large posters (131).

The break-even proof shows that Pak's break-even sales are $1,684. Kay Pak could use an alternative approach to estimating break-even sales in dollars—the contribution margin ratio formula. But first, Pak must estimate her contribution margin ratio:

Total expected contribution margin:

Regular posters (500 × $1.40)	$ 700	
Large posters (300 × $3.00).................	900	$1,600

Divided by total expected sales:

Regular posters (500 × $3.50)	$1,750	
Large posters (300 × $7.00).................	2,100	÷ 3,850
Contribution margin ratio		41.56%

Second, Pak uses the contribution margin ratio form of the CVP formula to estimate break-even sales in dollars:

$$\textbf{Sales in dollars} = \frac{\textbf{Fixed expenses + Operating income}}{\textbf{Contribution margin ratio}}$$

$$= \frac{\$700 + 0}{0.4156}$$

$$= \underline{\$1,684}$$

If Pak's actual sales mix is not 5 regular posters to 3 large posters, her actual operating income will differ from the planned amount, even if she sells exactly 800 total posters. For each total number of units sold, there are as many different operating incomes as there are unique sales mixes. Similarly, there are as many different break-even points—in total units and in sales dollars—as there are sales mixes. Therefore, the sales-mix factor greatly complicates planning.

Thinking It Over Suppose that Kay Pak plans to sell 800 total posters in the 5:3 sales mix (5 regular posters sold for every 3 large posters). She *actually* sells 800 posters—375 regular and 425 large. The unit sale prices and variable expenses are exactly as predicted, and the fixed expense is the budgeted $700. Can you tell, without computations, whether Pak's actual operating income is greater than, less than, or equal to her expected income?

Answer: Pak sold more of the higher-margin large posters. This favorable change in the sales mix increased her operating income.

Companies can use CVP analysis to motivate their sales force. Salespeople who know the contribution margin of each product they sell can generate more profit by emphasizing high-margin products. To motivate the sales force, many companies base all or part of their sales commissions on the contribution margins produced by sales rather than on sales revenue alone.

The next section uses building blocks of CVP analysis (contribution margin, the distinction between variable and fixed costs) to explain a costing approach that many managers find useful for internal decision making. Before continuing, stop and review the CVP Analysis Decision Guidelines to make sure you understand these basic concepts.

DECISION GUIDELINES	Cost-Volume-Profit Analysis
DECISION	**GUIDELINE**
How do changes in the number of units affect	
• total costs?	Total fixed costs ⟶ no change
	Total variable costs ⟶ change in proportion to changes in volume
• cost per unit?	Variable cost per unit ⟶ no change
	Fixed cost per unit:
	Increases when volume decreases
	(Divide fixed costs by a lower volume)
	Decreases when volume increases
	(Divide fixed costs by a higher volume)
	(continued)

What is the difference between gross margin and contribution margin?

Gross margin = Sales – Cost of goods sold
Contribution margin = Sales – Total variable expenses

How to compute sales needed to break even or earn a target operating income

• in units?

$$\frac{\text{Fixed expense} + \text{Operating income}}{\text{Contribution margin per unit}}$$

• in dollars?

$$\frac{\text{Fixed expense} + \text{Operating income}}{\text{Contribution margin ratio}}$$

How to use CVP analysis to measure risk?

Margin of safety = Expected sales – Break-even sales

Variable Costing and Absorption Costing

Objective 8

Compute income using variable costing and absorption costing

Absorption Costing. The costing method that assigns both variable and fixed manufacturing costs to products.

Variable Costing. The costing method that assigns only variable manufacturing costs to products.

Thus far, we have assigned both variable and fixed manufacturing costs to products. This approach is called **absorption costing** because products *absorb* fixed manufacturing costs as well as variable manufacturing costs. Supporters of absorption costing argue that products cannot be produced without fixed manufacturing costs, so these costs are an important part of product costs.

For planning and decision making, many managers prefer a different costing approach. **Variable costing** assigns only variable manufacturing costs to products. Under variable costing, fixed manufacturing costs are considered period costs, and are expensed in the period when they are incurred. Supporters of variable costing argue that fixed manufacturing costs (such as depreciation on the plant) provide the capacity to produce during a period. These fixed expenses are incurred whether or not the company produces any products or services. Thus they argue, these fixed manufacturing expenses are period costs, not product costs. However, GAAP requires that inventory be costed at the full cost to manufacture (or purchase) the goods. Consequently, published financial statements are based on absorption costing. While variable costing often provides a more useful basis for management decisions, companies can only use variable costing for internal reports. Exhibit 22-8 clarifies the difference between variable costing and absorption costing.

Concept Highlight

EXHIBIT 22-8
Differences Between
Absorption Costing and
Variable Costing

		Absorption Costing	Variable Costing
Product Costs		Direct materials	Direct materials
		Direct labor	Direct labor
		Variable manufacturing overhead	Variable manufacturing overhead
		Fixed manufacturing overhead	
Period Costs			Fixed manufacturing overhead
		Variable non-manufacturing costs	Variable non-manufacturing costs
		Fixed non-manufacturing costs	Fixed non-manufacturing costs
Focus		External reporting— required by GAAP	Internal reporting only
Typical Income Statement Format		Conventional income statement as in Chapters 1–19	Contribution margin income statement

The only difference between absorption costing and variable costing is that absorption costing considers fixed manufacturing costs as inventoriable product costs, while variable costing considers fixed manufacturing costs as period costs (expenses). All other costs are treated the same way under both absorption and variable costing:

- Variable manufacturing costs are inventoriable products costs.
- All nonmanufacturing costs are period costs.

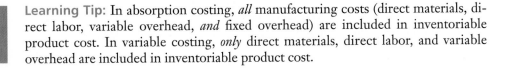 **Learning Tip:** In absorption costing, *all* manufacturing costs (direct materials, direct labor, variable overhead, *and* fixed overhead) are included in inventoriable product cost. In variable costing, *only* direct materials, direct labor, and variable overhead are included in inventoriable product cost.

To see the difference between absorption costing and variable costing, let's consider the following example. Sportade manufactures a sports beverage in both liquid and powdered form. Sportade incurs the following costs for its powdered mix in March 19X9:

Direct material cost per case	$ 6.00
Direct labor cost per case	3.00
Variable manufacturing overhead cost per case	2.00
Sales commission per case	2.50
Total fixed manufacturing overhead expenses	50,000
Total fixed marketing and administrative expenses	25,000

Sportade produced 10,000 cases of powdered mix as planned, but sold only 8,000 cases, at a price of $30 per case. There were no beginning inventories, so Sportade has 2,000 cases of powdered mix in ending finished goods inventory (10,000 case produced – 8,000 cases sold).

What is Sportade's inventoriable product cost per case under absorption costing and variable costing?

	Absorption Costing	Variable Costing
Direct materials	$ 6.00	$ 6.00
Direct labor	3.00	3.00
Variable manufacturing overhead	2.00	2.00
Fixed manufacturing overhead	5.00*	
Total cost per unit	$16.00	$11.00

$$\frac{*\$50,000 \text{ fixed manufacturing overhead}}{10,000 \text{ cases}} = \$5 \text{ per case}$$

The only difference between absorption costing and variable costing is that fixed manufacturing overhead is a product cost under absorption costing, but a period cost under variable costing. This is why the cost per case is $5 higher under absorption costing (total cost of $16) than under variable costing ($11).

Exhibit 22-9, Panel A, shows that absorption costing income statements are typically presented using the conventional format from Chapters 1–19. As usual, cost of goods sold is deducted from sales to obtain gross margin. Chapter 19 showed that manufacturers compute cost of goods sold by starting with beginning finished goods inventory (zero, in Sportade's case), and adding the cost of goods *manufactured*. The cost of goods *manufactured* is computed by multiplying the number of units *produced* by the absorption costing product cost per unit.

PANEL A—Conventional Income Statement (Absorption Costing)

SPORTADE		
Income Statement (Absorption Costing)		
Month Ended March 31, 19X9		
Sales revenue (8,000 × $30)		$240,000
Deduct: Cost of goods sold:		
Beginning finished goods inventory	$ 0	
Cost of goods manufactured (10,000 × $16)	160,000	
Cost of goods available for sale	160,000	
Ending finished goods inventory (2,000 × $16)	(32,000)	
Cost of goods sold		(128,000)
Gross Margin		112,000
Deduct: Operating expenses [(8,000 × $2.50) + $25,000)]		(45,000)
Operating income		$ 67,000

PANEL B—Contribution Margin Income Statement (Variable Costing)

SPORTADE		
Income Statement (Variable Costing)		
Month Ended March 31, 19X9		
Sales revenue (8,000 × $30)		$240,000
Deduct: Variable expenses:		
Variable cost of goods sold:		
Beginning finished goods inventory	$ 0	
Variable cost of goods manufactured (10,000 × $11)	110,000	
Variable cost of goods available for sale	110,000	
Ending finished goods inventory (2,000 × $11)	(22,000)	
Variable cost of goods sold	88,000	
Sales commission expense (8,000 × $2.50)	20,000	(108,000)
Contribution margin		132,000
Deduct: Fixed expenses:		
Fixed manufacturing overhead	50,000	
Fixed marketing and administrative expenses	25,000	(75,000)
Operating income		$ 57,000

Sportade produced 10,000 cases at an absorption cost per case of $16, so the cost of goods manufactured is $160,000 (10,000 cases × $16 per case). This cost of goods manufactured plus beginning inventory of finished goods is the cost of goods available for sale. We then subtract the ending finished goods inventory—the number of units multiplied by the absorption cost per unit (2,000 cases × $16 per case in our example)—to obtain the cost of goods sold.

From gross margin we subtract operating expenses (nonmanufacturing expenses) to find absorption costing operating income. The data on page 969 indicate that Sportade paid $2.50 per case sales commission for each case *sold*, so the total sales commission is $20,000 (8,000 cases sold × $2.50 per case). Fixed marketing and administrative costs are $25,000, so marketing and administrative expenses total $45,000 ($20,000 + $25,000).

> **Learning Tip:** The total cost of goods manufactured is the number of cases *produced* multiplied by the total manufacturing cost per case. In contrast, total variable marketing expenses (for example, sales commissions) equal the variable cost per case multiplied by the number of cases *sold*.

Exhibit 22-9, Panel B shows that variable costing income statements are presented using the contribution margin income statement format illustrated earlier in Exhibit 22-5 (Panel B). All the variable expenses are deducted from sales to get contribution margin. First, notice that the details of the (variable) cost of goods sold computation parallel those in the absorption costing income statement, *except we use the $11 variable costing product cost per case rather than the $16 absorption cost per case.* To the beginning finished goods inventory, we add the variable cost of goods manufactured (10,000 cases produced × $11 variable costing product cost per case). This yields the variable cost of goods available for sale, from which we subtract ending finished goods inventory (2,000 cases × $11 variable costing product cost per case) to obtain variable cost of goods sold.

To get the contribution margin, we subtract from sales both the variable cost of goods sold and variable operating expenses like the sales commission (8,000 cases sold × $2.50 sales commission per case). Finally, to obtain variable costing operating income, we subtract all the fixed expenses ($50,000 fixed manufacturing overhead + $25,000 fixed marketing and administrative expenses) from contribution margin.

Panel A of Exhibit 22-9 shows that Sportade's absorption costing operating income is $67,000. However, Panel B shows that variable costing yields only $57,000 of operating income. Why is operating income $10,000 lower under variable costing? To answer this question, we need to understand what happened to the $160,000 ($110,000 variable + $50,000 fixed) total manufacturing costs under each costing method.

The total manufacturing costs incurred in March are either

- Expensed in March, or else
- Held back in inventory (an asset)

Exhibit 22-10 shows that of the $160,000 manufacturing costs incurred during March, absorption costing holds back $32,000 (2,000 × $16) as inventory. This $32,000 assigned to inventory is not expensed until next month, when the units are sold. Thus only $160,000 − $32,000 = $128,000 of the manufacturing costs are expensed as cost of goods sold during March.

Variable costing holds back in ending inventory only $22,000 (2,000 × $11) of the total manufacturing costs. This is $10,000 *less* ($22,000 − $32,000) than absorption costing holds back in inventory. The difference arises because absorption costing assigns the $5 per case fixed manufacturing overhead costs to the 2,000 cases in ending inventory, while variable costing does not—it expenses all the fixed manufacturing overhead in the current month.

Costs that are not held back in inventory are expensed in the current period, so variable costing expenses $138,000 ($160,000 − $22,000) of manufacturing costs in March. (This $138,000 also equals the $88,000 variable cost of goods sold plus the $50,000 fixed manufacturing overhead.) This is $10,000 *more* than absorption costing expenses during March. *Variable costing has $10,000 more expense in March, so its income is $10,000 lower than absorption costing income.*

The Sportade example shows that when the quantity of inventory on hand increases, absorption costing reports higher operating income than variable costing. This is because absorption costing holds back some of the fixed manufacturing overhead in inventory (an asset), whereas variable costing expenses all the fixed manufacturing cost immediately. Because absorption costing expenses less fixed manufacturing overhead, it has higher income in the current period.

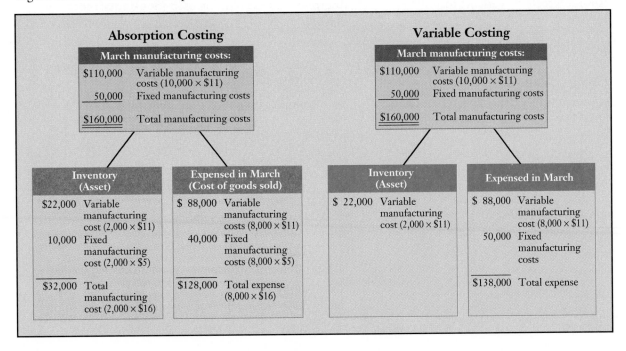

Thinking It Over Suppose Sportade has no inventory at the end of the next month—April. Will absorption costing report higher or lower operating income than variable costing for the month of April?

Answer: Absorption costing will report *less* income than variable costing during April. Ending inventory in March becomes the beginning inventory of April. Absorption costing assigns a higher value to beginning inventory in April. The higher beginning inventory costs increase absorption costing's cost of goods sold for April, which in turn reduces its income.

■ **Daily Exercise 22-22**

The general rule is this: When inventories increase (more units are produced than sold), absorption costing income is higher than variable costing income. When inventories decline (when fewer units are produced than sold), absorption costing income is lower than variable costing income. Managers can use this relation to their own advantage. Suppose the Sportade manager receives a bonus based on absorption costing income. Will the manager want to increase or decrease production?

The manager knows that absorption costing assigns each case of Sportade $5 of fixed manufacturing overhead.

- For every case that is produced but not sold, absorption costing "hides" $5 of fixed overhead in ending inventory (an asset).
- The more cases added to inventory, the more fixed overhead is "hidden" in ending inventory at the end of the month.
- The more fixed overhead in ending inventory, the smaller the cost of goods sold, and the higher the operating income.

To maximize the bonus under absorption costing, the manager will want to increase production to build up inventory.

◀▥ ◀▥ ◀▥ The just-in-time philosophy was introduced in Chapter 19.

This incentive directly conflicts with the just-in-time philosophy, which emphasizes minimal inventory levels. ◀▥ Companies that have adopted just-in-time should either (1) evaluate their managers based on variable costing income, or (2) implement strict controls to prevent inventory build-up.

Before continuing, take time to study the Absorption and Variable Costing Decision Guidelines to make sure you understand the differences between absorption and variable costing.

DECISION GUIDELINES	**Absorption and Variable Costing**	
DECISION	**GUIDELINE**	
When to use absorption costing? Variable costing?	Absorption costing must be used for external reporting. Variable costing is used only for internal reporting.	
What is the difference between absorption and variable costing?	Fixed manufacturing costs are treated as • inventoriable product costs under absorption costing • period costs under variable costing	
How to compute product costs under absorption costing and variable costing?	**Absorption Costing**	**Variable Costing**
	Direct materials + Direct labor + Variable overhead + Fixed overhead = Total product cost	Direct materials + Direct labor + Variable overhead — = Total product cost
How to determine whether absorption costing income is higher, lower, or the same as variable costing income?	If units produced > units sold: Absorption costing income > Variable costing income	
	If units produced < units sold: Absorption costing income < Variable costing income	
	If units produced = units sold: Absorption costing income = Variable costing income	

PROBLEM 1

Bronson Company buys jogging shorts for $6 and sells them for $10. Management budgets monthly fixed costs of $10,000 for sales volumes between 0 and 12,000 pairs of shorts.

1. Use both the income statement equation approach and the shortcut contribution margin CVP formula to compute the company's monthly break-even sales in units.

2. Use the contribution margin ratio approach to compute the break-even point in sales dollars.

3. Compute the monthly sales level (in units) required to earn a target operating income of $14,000. Use either the income statement equation approach or the contribution margin approach.

4. Prepare a graph of Bronson's CVP relationships, similar to Exhibit 22-7. Draw the sales revenue line, the fixed expense line, and the total expense line. Label the axes, the break-even point, the operating income area, and the operating loss area.

REQUIRED

PROBLEM 2

Suppose that Bronson sells a second product—sweatpants. Each pair costs $7 and sells for $15. Fixed costs remain $10,000 a month.

1. If Bronson sells 2 pairs of jogging shorts for every 3 pairs of sweatpants, what is the company's break-even sales in units? (Use the contribution margin method.)

2. If expected sales total 11,000 units, what is Bronson's margin of safety in units?

3. In a sales mix of 2:3 (2 pairs of jogging shorts sold for every 3 pairs of sweatpants), what operating income will Bronson Company earn if it sells a total of 11,000 items? Use the contribution margin approach.

REQUIRED

■ SOLUTION

PROBLEM 1

Income statement equation approach:

REQUIREMENT 1

$$\text{Sales} - \text{Variable expenses} - \text{Fixed expenses} = \text{Operating income}$$

$$\left(\begin{array}{c}\text{Sale price} \\ \text{per unit}\end{array} \times \begin{array}{c}\text{Sales in} \\ \text{units}\end{array}\right) - \left(\begin{array}{c}\text{Variable cost} \\ \text{per unit}\end{array} \times \begin{array}{c}\text{Sales in} \\ \text{units}\end{array}\right) - \text{Fixed expenses} = \begin{array}{c}\text{Operating} \\ \text{income}\end{array}$$

($10 × Sales in units)	− ($6 × Sales in units)	− $10,000	= $0
($10	− $6) × Sales in units		= $10,000
	$4 × Sales in units		= $10,000
	Sales in units		= $10,000 ÷ $4
	Break-even sales in units		= 2,500 units

Contribution margin approach:

$$\text{Sales in units} = \frac{\text{Fixed expenses} + \text{Operating income}}{\text{Contribution margin per unit}}$$

$$\text{Break-even sales in units} = \frac{\$10,000 + 0}{(\$10 - \$6)} = \frac{\$10,000}{\$4} = 2,500 \text{ units}$$

$$\text{Break-even sales in dollars} = \frac{\text{Fixed expenses} + \text{Operating income}}{\text{Contribution margin ratio}} = \frac{\$10,000 + 0}{0.40^*} = \$25,000$$

REQUIREMENT 2

$$^*\text{Contribution margin ratio} = \frac{\text{Contribution margin per unit}}{\text{Sale price per unit}} = \frac{\$4}{\$10} = 0.40$$

Income statement equation approach:

REQUIREMENT 3

$$\text{Sales} - \text{Variable expenses} - \text{Fixed expenses} = \begin{array}{c}\text{Operating} \\ \text{income}\end{array}$$

$$\left(\begin{array}{c}\text{Sale price} \\ \text{per unit}\end{array} \times \begin{array}{c}\text{Sales in} \\ \text{units}\end{array}\right) - \left(\begin{array}{c}\text{Variable cost} \\ \text{per unit}\end{array} \times \begin{array}{c}\text{Sales in} \\ \text{units}\end{array}\right) - \text{Fixed expenses} = \begin{array}{c}\text{Operating} \\ \text{income}\end{array}$$

($10 × Sales in units)	− ($6 × Sales in units)	− $10,000	= $14,000
($10	− $6) × Sales in units		= $10,000 + $14,000
	$4 × Sales in units		= $24,000
	Sales in units		= $24,000 ÷ $4
	Sales in units		= 6,000 units

Contribution margin approach:

$$\text{Sales in units} = \frac{\text{Fixed expenses} + \text{Operating income}}{\text{Contribution margin per unit}}$$

$$= \frac{\$10,000 + \$14,000}{(\$10 - \$6)} = \frac{\$24,000}{\$4}$$

Sales in units = 6,000 units

REQUIREMENT 4

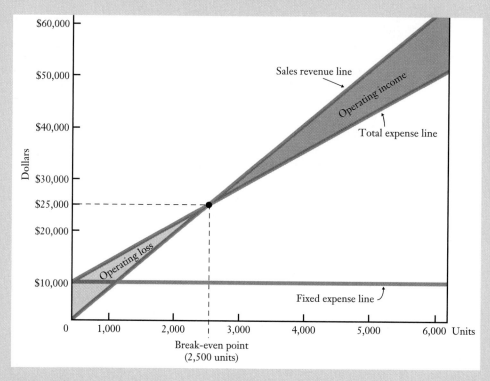

Break-even point
(2,500 units)

PROBLEM 2

REQUIREMENT 1

	Jogging Shorts	Sweatpants	Total
Sale price per unit	$10	$15	
Deduct: Variable expense per unit	6	7	
Contribution margin per unit	$ 4	$ 8	
Sales mix in units....................................	× 2	× 3	5
Contribution margin...............................	$ 8	$24	$ 32
Weighted-average contribution margin per unit ($32 ÷ 5 units)			$6.40

$$\text{Break-even sales in units} = \frac{\text{Fixed expenses} + \text{Operating income}}{\text{Weighted-average contribution margin per unit}}$$

$$= \frac{\$10,000 + 0}{\$6.40} = 1,563 \text{ units}$$

Break-even sales of jogging shorts (1,563 × 2/5) .... 625 jogging shorts
Break-even sales of sweatpants (1,563 × 3/5) .... 938 sweatpants

REQUIREMENT 2

Margin of safety in units = Expected sales in units − Break-even sales
= 11,000 − 1,563 = 9,437 units

REQUIREMENT 3

$$\text{Sales in units} = \frac{\text{Fixed expenses} + \text{Operating income}}{\text{Weighted-average contribution margin per unit}}$$

$$11,000 = \frac{\$10,000 + \text{Operating income}}{\$6.40}$$

$$\$70,400 = \$10,000 + \text{Operating income}$$

Operating income = $60,400

Summary of Learning Objectives

1. Identify different cost behavior patterns. Cost-volume-profit (CVP) analysis expresses the relationships among a company's costs, volume of activity, and profit. These relationships depend on *cost behavior*. We classify costs as *variable, fixed,* or *mixed.*

2. Use a contribution margin income statement to make business decisions. A *contribution margin income statement* reports variable expenses and fixed expenses separately. It features the total *contribution margin,* the excess of sales revenues over variable expenses. This format helps managers predict the operating income that will result from various decisions.

3. Compute break-even sales. Two popular ways to perform CVP analysis are the income statement equation approach and the contribution margin approach. Both approaches use an equation or formula derived from the contribution margin income statement. The contribution margin approach uses the product's contribution margin per unit or its *contribution margin ratio,* which give the increase in operating income for each additional unit sold or for each dollar of sales revenue, respectively. Either approach to CVP analysis can be used to compute a company's *break-even point*—the sales level at which operating income is zero.

4. Compute the sales level needed to earn a target operating income. CVP analysis also can be used to compute how many units must be sold to earn a target operating income. The target operating income is added to the total fixed expense to determine the total contribution margin required to earn the income. That amount is divided by the unit contribution margin to give the number of units that must be sold.

5. Graph a set of cost-volume-profit relationships. Graphic displays of CVP relationships present information over a *relevant range* of sales levels. CVP graphs show the break-even point and the ranges of sales volume that yield operating incomes and operating losses.

6. Compute a margin of safety. The *margin of safety* is the excess of expected sales over break-even sales. The larger the margin, the lower the risk of a given plan.

7. Use the sales mix in CVP analysis. CVP analysis has several limitations. For example, it assumes that volume is the only cost driver and that all cost-volume-profit relationships are linear over the relevant range of activity. Also, CVP analysis assumes that the sales mix of products will not change during the period. *Sales mix* is the combination of products that make up total sales.

8. Compute income using variable costing and absorption costing. Variable and absorption costing differ only in the way they treat fixed manufacturing costs. Variable costing considers fixed manufacturing costs as providing capacity to produce during the period. In this view, fixed manufacturing costs are period costs that are expensed in the period incurred. In contrast, absorption costing considers fixed manufacturing costs necessary to produce the product or service. As a result, absorption costing treats fixed manufacturing costs as inventoriable product costs. Variable and absorption costing yield different income figures when the number of units in inventory changes. This is because absorption costing assigns some of the current period's fixed manufacturing costs to ending inventory, so this portion of current period fixed manufacturing cost is not expensed until future periods when the units are sold. In contrast, variable costing always expenses all fixed manufacturing costs in the current period. GAAP requires companies to use absorption costing for external reporting. However, many managers prefer variable costing income statements for internal use because the separation of variable and fixed costs is helpful in making business decisions.

Accounting Vocabulary

absorption costing *(p. 968)*
break-even point *(p. 957)*
contribution margin *(p. 954)*
contribution margin income statement *(p. 954)*

contribution margin per unit *(p. 958)*
contribution margin ratio *(p. 958)*
cost behavior *(p. 950)*

cost-volume-profit (CVP) analysis *(p. 950)*
fixed cost *(p. 951)*
margin of safety *(p. 964)*
mixed cost *(p. 952)*

relevant range *(p. 953)*
sales mix *(p. 965)*
variable costs *(p. 950)*
variable costing *(p. 968)*

Questions

1. How is cost-volume-profit analysis used in planning?
2. Define the three types of cost behavior patterns.
3. Draw graphs of the three types of costs.
4. What are three questions cost-volume-profit analysis can answer?
5. How does a contribution margin income statement differ from a conventional income statement? Which is more useful for predicting the income effect of a change in sales? Why?
6. Why is the relevant range important in cost-volume-profit analysis?
7. Draw a graph of fixed expenses from 0 to 50,000 units. The relevant range lies between 20,000 and 35,000 units, where fixed expenses are $300,000. Below the relevant range, fixed expenses are $200,000. Above the relevant range, fixed expenses are $400,000.
8. What is the break-even point? What is its significance to a business?

9. Give the contribution margin cost-volume-profit formulas for break-even sales in units and in dollars.
10. How does an increase in fixed expenses affect the break-even point? How does a decrease in fixed expenses affect break-even sales? Give the reason for each answer.
11. How does an increase in variable expenses affect the break-even point? How does a decrease in variable expenses affect break-even sales? Give the reason for each answer.
12. How does an increase in sale price affect the break-even point? How does a decrease in sale price affect break-even sales? Give the reason for each answer.
13. Briefly outline two ways to compute the sales in dollars needed to earn a target operating income.
14. Give the contribution margin cost-volume-profit formula for sales in units needed to earn a target operating income. Do the same for sales in dollars.
15. Identify the steps in the preparation of a CVP graph.

16. What advantages does a CVP graph have over the equation approach and the contribution margin approach?

17. How does the margin of safety serve as a measure of risk?

18. Give the assumptions underlying CVP analysis.

19. Briefly describe how to perform CVP analysis when a company sells more than one product.

20. How is fixed manufacturing overhead cost expensed under absorption costing? Under variable costing?

Daily Exercises

Variable and fixed costs
(Obj. 1)

DE22-1 TreeScapes makes preserved palm trees for indoor landscaping. The company soaks palm leaves in the preserving solution for several days. Workers attach the preserved fronds to artificial trunks made from steel and fiberglass. Identify the following costs as variable or fixed:

a. Patent on the preserving solution

b. Chemicals used to mix the preserving solution

c. Palm fronds

d. Fiberglass and steel

e. Straight-line depreciation on the soaking vats

f. Glue

g. CEO Dennis Gabrick's salary

Variable and fixed costs
(Obj. 1)

DE22-2 Fill in the blanks using one of the following:

• Increases   • Decreases   • Stays the same

a. As the number of units increases, the variable cost per unit _____.

b. As the number of units decreases, the variable cost per unit _____.

c. As the number of units increases, the total variable cost _____.

d. As the number of units decreases, the total variable cost _____.

e. As the number of units increases, the fixed cost per unit _____.

f. As the number of units decreases, the fixed cost per unit _____.

g. As the number of units increases, the total fixed cost _____.

h. As the number of units decreases, the total fixed cost _____.

Mixed costs
(Obj. 1)

DE22-3 Suppose AT&T offers an international calling plan that charges $3.00 per month plus $0.45 per minute for calls to Australia.

1. Under this plan, what is your monthly international long-distance cost if you call Australia for:
   a. 10 minutes?   b. 60 minutes?   c. 100 minutes?

2. Draw a graph illustrating your total cost under this plan. Label the axes, and show your costs at 10, 60, and 100 minutes.

Gross margin and contribution margin
(Obj. 2)

DE22-4 You were recently hired as an accounting intern at WestCoast Cableco. Your boss, Senyo Tse, hands you the following information from September's operations and asks you to compute gross margin and contribution margin.

Variable manufacturing cost of goods sold	$50,000
Fixed marketing expense	12,000
Research and development (fixed)	3,000
Sales commissions	2,500
Fixed manufacturing cost of goods sold...............	20,000
Sales revenue	100,000
Delivery expense (variable).................................	5,000

Gross margin and contribution margin
(Obj. 2)

DE22-5 Your boss at WestCoast Cableco (Daily Exercise 22-4) is puzzled by the difference between gross margin and contribution margin. Write a short memo explaining the primary difference between gross margin and contribution margin. Your memo should use the following format:

Date: _____

To: _____

From: _____

Subject: _____

Cost of goods sold
(Obj. 2)

DE22-6 Consider the Martin Manufacturing Company income statements in Exhibit 22-5, page 954. How much of the total cost of goods sold consists of fixed manufacturing costs?

DE22-7   Flex-Med, Inc., produces medical tubing. The company incurs $100,000 of fixed expenses per month. It sells the tubing for $20 per yard, and it incurs variable expenses at the rate of $9 per yard.

Using the contribution margin income statement to make a decision
(Obj. 2)

1. Prepare a contribution margin income statement, assuming that Flex-Med sells 15,000 yards of tubing in July.
2. CEO John Hand thinks Flex-Med could increase its sales to 25,000 yards of tubing in August if the company paid its sales force a commission of $1 per yard. What would be Flex-Med's operating income if it adopted the sales commission plan? Should Flex-Med adopt the sales commission plan? Why or why not?

DE22-8   Consider the Grand Canyon Railway example from the chapter opening story. Suppose the Railway decides to offer only one class of service, Coach class, at an all-inclusive round-trip ticket price of $52 per passenger. Assume variable expenses of $12 per passenger. If Grand Canyon has $200,000 of fixed expenses per month, compute the number of round-trip tickets it must sell to break even

Computing break-even point in units
(Obj. 3)

a.   Using the income statement equation approach
b.   Using the shortcut contribution margin CVP formula.

Perform a numerical proof to ensure that your answer is correct.

DE22-9   Refer to the information given in Daily Exercise 22-8.

Computing break-even point in sales dollars
(Obj. 3)

1. Compute Grand Canyon Railway's contribution margin ratio. Carry your computation to five decimal places.
2. Use the contribution margin ratio form of the contribution margin CVP formula to determine the sales revenue Grand Canyon needs to break-even.

DE22-10   Refer to the information given in Daily Exercise 22-8.

Effect of changing sale price and variable expense on break-even point
(Obj. 3)

1. Suppose Grand Canyon Railway decreases its round-trip ticket price from $52 to $44, in order to increase the number of passengers. Compute the new break-even point in units (passenger round-trips) and in sales dollars.
2. Return to the original information in Daily Exercise 22-8. Grand Canyon Railway could reduce its variable costs by eliminating champagne from the afternoon beverages. Suppose this would reduce the variable expense from $12 to $10 per passenger. Compute the new break-even point in units (passenger round-trips) and in dollars.

DE22-11   Consider the Grand Canyon Railway information in Daily Exercise 22-8. Suppose Grand Canyon embarks on a cost reduction drive, and slashes fixed expenses from $200,000 per month to $150,000 per month.

Effect of changing fixed cost on break-even point
(Obj. 3)

1. Compute the new break-even point in units (passenger round-trips) and in sales dollars.
2. Is the break-even point higher or lower than in Daily Exercise 22-8? Explain.

DE22-12   Chrysler Corporation is considering building a new luxury car, the LX. By designing the car around an existing body "platform," Chrysler could hold fixed costs to $300 million. It has been estimated that Chrysler could break even on the new luxury car by selling 30,000 autos per year. Given these estimates, what is the contribution margin per car on the LX model?

Break-even point in units
(Obj. 3)

DE22-13   If Grand Canyon Railway has a target operating income of $30,000 per month, how many round-trip tickets must the company sell? Use the original data given in Daily Exercise 22-8.

Sales needed to earn target income
(Obj. 4)

DE22-14   Suppose that Mir-A-Mar, a resort in upper Wisconsin, has determined that selling 2,000 room-nights per month will yield its target operating income of $50,000. The resort's fixed costs are $100,000 per month, and its variable costs are $10 per room-night. What is Mir-A-Mar's average sale price for a room for one night? (*Hint:* Use the contribution margin CVP formula.)

Sales needed to earn target income
(Obj. 4)

DE22-15   Using the original information in Daily Exercise 22-8, draw a graph of Grand Canyon Railway's cost-volume-profit relationships. Include the sales revenue line, the fixed expense line, and the total expense line. Label the axes, the break-even point, the income area, and the loss area.

Graphing cost-volume-profit relationships
(Obj. 5)

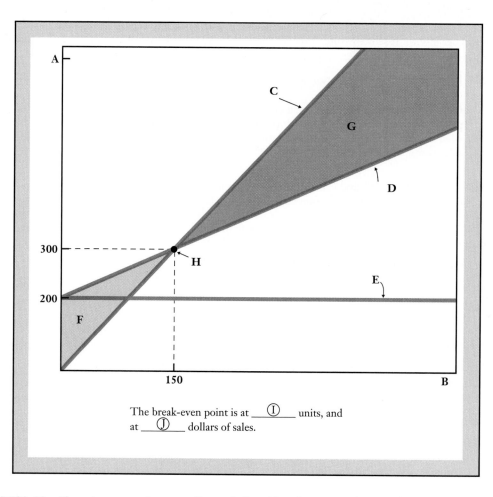

The break-even point is at ___⟨I⟩___ units, and at ___⟨J⟩___ dollars of sales.

Interpreting a CVP graph
(Obj. 5)

DE22-16 Above is a cost-volume-profit graph. Provide a description for each letter.

Computing margin of safety
(Obj. 6)

DE22-17 Consider the original Grand Canyon Railway information in Daily Exercise 22-8. If Grand Canyon expects to sell 6,000 round-trip tickets, compute the margin of safety

a. In units (round-trip tickets)
b. In sales dollars
c. As a percentage of expected sales

Computing margin of safety
(Obj. 6)

DE22-18 Consider Kay Pak's travel poster business described on pages 957–965. Suppose Pak expects to sell 1,200 posters. Using the original data on pages 957–958 compute her margin of safety

a. In units (posters)
b. In sales dollars
c. As a percentage of expected sales

Break-even point and sales mix
(Obj. 7)

DE22-19 Kay Pak's travel poster business incurs $700 of fixed expenses and has the following sales and variable expenses per poster:

	Regular Posters	Large Posters
Sale price per unit	$3.50	$7.00
Variable expense per unit	2.10	4.00

Suppose Pak estimates she will sell 10 regular posters for every 2 large posters. Compute

a. The weighted-average contribution margin per unit. Carry your computations to five decimal places.
b. The total number of posters Pak must sell to break even.
c. The number of regular posters and the number of large posters she must sell to break even.
d. Compare your answer to the break-even point calculated on page 966. Does the 10:2 sales mix increase or decrease the break-even point? Why?

DE22-20 Consider the Grand Canyon Railway example from the chapter opening story. Suppose Grand Canyon decides to offer two classes of service: Coach class and Chief class. Assume Grand Canyon incurs $200,000 of fixed expenses per month and that it has the following ticket prices and variable expenses:

Break-even point and sales mix
(Obj. 7)

	Coach Class	Chief Class
Sale price per ticket............................	$52.00	$114.00
Variable expense per passenger..........	12.00	14.00

If Grand Canyon Railway expects to sell five tickets in Coach class for every three tickets in Chief class, compute

a. The weighted-average contribution margin per unit (round-trip ticket).
b. The total number of tickets Grand Canyon must sell to break even.
c. The number of Coach class tickets and the number of Chief class tickets the company must sell to break even.

DE22-21 Consider the Sportade example on pages 969–972. Suppose that during April, the company produces 10,000 cases of powdered drink mix, and sells 12,000 cases. Sale price, variable cost per case, and total fixed expenses remain the same as in March.

Computing absorption costing and variable costing income
(Obj. 8)

1. Prepare April income statements using absorption costing, and then variable costing.
2. Is absorption costing income higher or lower than variable costing income? Explain why.

DE22-22 For a service company like Grand Canyon Railway, will absorption and variable costing give different operating income figures? Explain.

Absorption and variable costing
(Obj. 8)

Exercises

E22-1 Graph each of the following cost behavior patterns over a relevant range from 0 to 10,000 units:

Graphing cost behavior
(Obj. 1)

a. Variable expenses of $8 per unit
b. Mixed expenses made up of fixed costs of $10,000 and variable costs of $3 per unit
c. Fixed expenses of $35,000

E22-2 Saville Row Shirtmakers' April income statement follows:

Preparing a contribution margin income statement
(Obj. 2)

SAVILLE ROW SHIRTMAKERS Income Statement For the Month of April 19XX		
Sales revenue		$640,000
Cost of goods sold		448,000
Gross margin		192,000
Operating expenses:		
Marketing expense.....................................	$72,000	
General and administrative expense..........	42,000	114,000
Operating income..		$ 78,000

Saville Row's cost of goods sold is a variable expense. Marketing expense is 20% fixed and 80% variable. General and administrative expense is 60% fixed and 40% variable. Prepare Saville Row's contribution margin income statement for April. Compute the expected increase in operating income to the nearest $1,000 if sales increase by $50,000.

E22-3 For its top managers, Prudhoe Bay Refining Corp. formats its income statement as follows:

Using a contribution margin income statement and computing break-even sales
(Obj. 2, 3)

PRUDHOE BAY REFINING CORP.	
Contribution Margin Income Statement	
Three Months Ended March 31, 200X	
Sales revenue..................................	$385,000
Variable expenses	154,000
Contribution margin	231,000
Fixed expenses..............................	210,000
Operating income........................	$ 21,000

Prudhoe Bay's relevant range is between sales of $310,000 and $430,000. Prepare contribution margin income statements at those volume levels. Also, compute break-even sales in dollars.

Computing break-even sales by the contribution margin approach
(Obj. 3)

E22-4 Coyote Cuisine of Santa Fe produces family-sized packages of frozen enchiladas. The company has fixed expenses of $75,000, and variable expenses of $4.50 per package. Each package sells for $6.00.

REQUIRED

1. Compute the company's contribution margin per package and its contribution margin ratio.
2. Determine the break-even point in units and in dollars, using the contribution margin approach.

Computing a change in break-even sales
(Obj. 3)

E22-5 For several years, Gotham Diner has offered a lunch special for $5.00. Monthly fixed expenses have been $4,500. The variable cost of a meal has been $2.00. Rebecca Klein, the owner, believes that by remodeling the diner and upgrading the food services, she can increase the price of the lunch special to $5.25. Monthly fixed expenses would increase to $6,600 and the variable expenses would increase to $2.10 per meal. Use the contribution margin ratio approach to compute Klein's monthly break-even sales in dollars before and after remodeling.

Computing break-even sales and operating income or loss under different conditions
(Obj. 3, 4)

E22-6 Great Plains Motor Freight delivers freight throughout Iowa, Nebraska, and Kansas. The company has monthly fixed expenses of $490,000 and a contribution margin of 80% of revenues.

REQUIRED

1. Compute Great Plains' monthly break-even sales in dollars. Use the contribution margin ratio approach.
2. Compute Great Plains' monthly operating income or operating loss if revenues are $500,000 and if they are $800,000.

Analyzing a cost-volume-profit graph
(Obj. 5)

E22-7 The top managers of Hines-Robinson, Inc., are planning for the year 20XX. The accountant who prepared the following CVP graph forgot to label the lines.

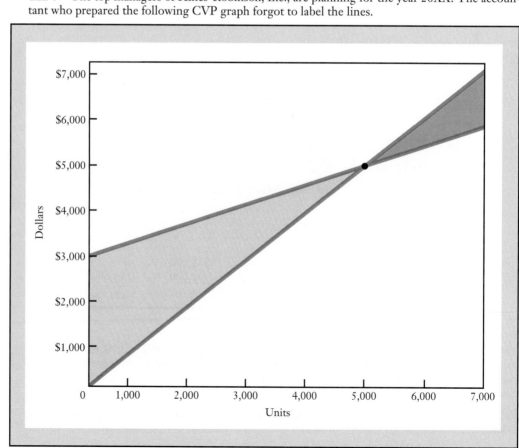

1. What do the lines mean?
2. What will be operating income (or operating loss) if sales are 3,400 units?
3. What are break-even sales in units and in dollars?
4. Where is the operating income area? The operating loss area?

REQUIRED

E22-8 Suppose that Dodger Stadium, the home of the Los Angeles Dodgers, earns total revenue that averages $18 for every ticket sold. Assume that annual fixed expenses are $16 million, and variable expenses are $2 per ticket. Prepare the ballpark's CVP graph under these assumptions. Show the break-even point in dollars and in tickets. Label the axes, sales revenue line, fixed expense line, variable expense line, the operating loss area, and the operating income area on the graph.

Graphing cost-volume-profit relationships
(Obj. 5)

E22-9 Kwick-Mart convenience store has a monthly operating income target of $6,000. Variable expenses are 70% of sales, and monthly fixed expenses are $9,000. Compute the monthly margin of safety in dollars if the store achieves its income goal. Express Kwick-Mart's margin of safety as a percentage of target sales.

Computing a margin of safety
(Obj. 6)

E22-10 Three college friends open an off-campus shop named Joe Cotton. They plan to sell a standard T-shirt for $6 and a fancier version for $7.50. The $6 shirt costs them $4, and the $7.50 shirt costs them $4.50. The friends expect to sell two fancy T-shirts for every three standard T-shirts. Their monthly fixed expenses are $2,400. How many of each type of T-shirt must they sell monthly to break even? To earn $1,200?

Cost-volume-profit analysis with a sales mix
(Obj. 7)

E22-11 The 19X9 data that follow pertain to Cedardine, a manufacturer of solid cedar picnic tables. (Cedardine has no beginning inventories in January 19X9.)

Preparing absorption costing and variable costing income statements; business decision
(Obj. 2, 8)

Sale price	$125	Fixed manufacturing overhead	$500,000
Variable manufacturing expense per table	$ 95	Fixed operating expense	$250,000
Variable operating expense per table	$ 15	Number of tables produced..............	100,000
		Number of tables sold......................	90,000

1. Prepare both conventional (absorption costing) and contribution margin (variable costing) income statements for Cedardine.
2. Which statement shows the higher operating income? Why?
3. Cedardine's marketing vice president believes a new sales promotion that costs $85,000 would increase sales to 100,000 tables. Should the company go ahead with the promotion? Give your reason.

REQUIRED

CHALLENGE EXERCISE

E22-12 Himalaya's, Inc., manufactures two styles of climbing shoe—the Mountaineer and the Pro Mountaineer. The following data pertain to the Mountaineer:

Computing contribution margin for one of two products
(Obj. 7)

Sale price	$80
Variable manufacturing cost	35
Variable operating cost	10

Himalaya's monthly fixed expenses total $70,000. When Mountaineers and Pro Mountaineers are sold in the mix of 7:3, respectively, the sale of 2,000 total pair results in an operating income of $30,000. Compute the contribution margin per pair for the Pro Mountaineers.

Beyond the Numbers

BN22-1 Your best friend, who is majoring in marketing, has just opened a small business selling T-shirts with your school's logo. Variable expenses include buying and printing the T-shirts, and sales commissions. Fixed expenses include rent for space at the student union.

Your friend has excellent sales skills, but he knows little about accounting. He is surprised that even though he is selling 200 T-shirts per month, he seems to be losing money. After studying this chapter, you realize that part of his problem is that his break-even point is too high. What steps can your friend take to reduce the break-even point?

Break-even point
(Obj. 3)

BN22-2 ◀▥ *Link Back to Chapter 19 (just-in-time philosophy).* You serve on the board of directors of Jasper, Inc., a medium-size manufacturing company that has recently adopted a just-in-time production philosophy. Part of your responsibility is to develop a compensation contract for Lisa Lopez, the Vice President of Manufacturing Operations. To give her the incentive to make

Absorption and variable costing incentives
(Obj. 8)

decisions that will increase the company's profits, the Board decides to give Lopez a year-end bonus if Jasper meets a target operating income.

Write a memo to the Chairman of the Board, Hans Theil, explaining your view on whether the bonus contract should be based on absorption costing or variable costing. Use the memo format outlined in Daily Exercise 22-5.

ETHICAL ISSUE

Effect of error on cost-volume-profit analysis
(Obj. 3, 4)

You have just begun your summer internship at MedEx. The company supplies sterilized surgical instruments for physicians. To expand sales, MedEx is considering paying a commission to its sales force. The controller, Jane Loftus, asks you to compute (1) the new break-even sales figure, and (2) the operating profit if sales increase 15% under the new sales commission plan. She thinks you can handle this task because you learned CVP analysis in your accounting class.

You spend the next day collecting information from the accounting records, performing the analysis, and writing a memo to explain the results. The company president is pleased with your memo. You report that the new sales commission plan will lead to a significant increase in operating income and only a small increase in break-even sales.

The following week, you realize that you made an error in the CVP analysis. You overlooked the sales personnel's $2,500 monthly salaries and you did not include this fixed marketing expense in your computations. You are not sure what to do. If you tell Jane Loftus of your mistake, she will have to tell the president. In this case, you are afraid MedEx might not offer you permanent employment after your internship.

1. How would your error affect break-even sales and operating income under the proposed sales commission plan? Could this cause the president to reject the sales commission proposal?
2. Consider your ethical responsibilities. Is there a difference between (a) initially making an error, and (b) subsequently failing to inform the controller?
3. Suppose you tell Jane Loftus of the error in your analysis. Why might the consequences not be as bad as you fear? Should Loftus take any responsibility for your error? What could Loftus have done differently?
4. After considering all the factors, should you inform Jane Loftus or simply keep quiet?

Problems (GROUP A)

Explaining the effects of different cost behavior patterns on the break-even point and on likely profits
(Obj. 1)

P22-1A Amequip Restaurant Supply is opening early next year. Julie Constanza, the owner, is considering two plans for obtaining the plant assets and employee labor needed for operations. Plan 1 calls for purchasing all equipment and paying employees straight salaries. Under plan 2, Amequip would lease equipment month by month and pay employees low salaries but give them a big part of their pay in commissions on sales. Discuss the effects of the two plans on variable expenses, fixed expenses, break-even sales, and likely profits for a new business in the start-up stage. Indicate which plan you favor for Amequip.

Computing contribution margins and break-even points
(Obj. 2, 3)

P22-2A The budgets of four companies yield the following information:

	L	M	N	O
Target sales...............................	$250,000	$600,000	$280,000	$
Variable expenses	100,000			130,000
Fixed expenses		312,000	130,000	
Operating income (loss)..............	$ 15,000	$	$	$160,000
Units sold		112,000	11,000	8,000
Unit contribution margin...........	$5		$12	$40
Contribution margin ratio..........		0.30		

Fill in the blanks for each company. Which company has the lowest break-even point in sales dollars? What causes the low break-even point?

Computing break-even sales and the sales needed to earn a target operating income; preparing a contribution margin income statement
(Obj. 2, 3, 4)

P22-3A Bali Hai Cruises sails a schooner from Sanur, Bali. The average cruise has 80 tourists on board. Each person pays $75 for a day's sail in the Pacific. The ship sails 100 days each year. The schooner has a crew of 12. Each crew member earns an average of $85 per cruise. The crew is paid only when the ship sails. Other variable expenses are for refreshments, which average $14 per passenger per cruise. Annual fixed expenses total $154,400.

1. Compute revenue and variable expenses for each cruise.

2. Use the equation approach to compute the number of cruises needed annually to break even.

3. Use the contribution margin approach to compute the number of cruises needed annually to earn $193,000. Is this profit goal realistic? Give your reason.

4. Prepare Bali Hai's contribution margin income statement for 100 cruises each year. Report only two categories of expenses: variable and fixed.

P22-4A Digicolor Express imprints calendars with company names. The company has fixed expenses of $420,000 each month plus variable expenses of $2 per carton of calendars. Digicolor sells each carton of calendars for $3.20.

Analyzing CVP relationships (Obj. 2, 3, 4)

1. Use the income statement equation approach to compute the number of cartons of calendars Digicolor must sell each month to break even.

REQUIRED

2. Use the contribution margin ratio CVP formula to compute the dollar amount of monthly sales Digicolor needs to earn $60,000 in operating income.

3. Prepare Digicolor's contribution margin income statement for June for sales of 450,000 cartons of calendars. Cost of goods sold is 70% of variable expenses. Operating expenses make up the rest of the variable expenses and all of the fixed expenses.

4. The company is considering an expansion that will increase fixed expenses by 40% and variable expenses by 10 percent. Compute the new break-even point in units and in dollars. Use either the income statement equation approach or the contribution margin approach.

5. How would this expansion affect Digicolor's risk?

P22-5A All Seasons Travel is opening an office in Philadelphia. Fixed monthly expenses are office rent ($3,400), depreciation of office furniture ($190), utilities ($140), a special telephone line ($390), a connection with the airlines' computerized reservation service ($480), and the salary of a travel agent ($1,800). Variable expenses include commissions for the travel agent (6% of sales), advertising (6% of sales), supplies and postage (1% of sales), and usage fees for the telephone line and computerized reservation service (7% of sales).

Computing break-even sales and sales needed to earn a target operating income; graphing CVP relationships (Obj. 1, 3, 4, 5)

1. Use the contribution margin ratio CVP formula to compute the travel agency's break-even sales in dollars. If the average sale is an $800 plane ticket, how many tickets must be sold to break even?

REQUIRED

2. Use the income statement equation approach to compute dollar sales needed to earn monthly operating income of $3,500.

3. Graph the travel agency's CVP relationships. Assume that an average sale is an $800 plane ticket. Show the break-even point, sales revenue line, fixed expense line, variable expense line, operating loss area, operating income area, and the sales in units (tickets) and dollars when monthly operating income of $3,500 is earned. The graph should range from 0 to 20 units (plane tickets).

4. Assume that the average sale price decreases to $500 per ticket. Use the contribution margin approach to compute the new break-even point in units (tickets). How does the lower sale price affect the break-even point?

P22-6A The November 19X9 contribution margin income statement of International Male menswear store follows:

Using a contribution margin income statement for break-even analysis; sales mix, margin of safety, and changes in CVP relationships (Obj. 2, 3, 6 ,7)

INTERNATIONAL MALE Contribution Margin Income Statement For the Month of November 19X9		
Sales revenue		$60,000
Variable expenses:		
Cost of goods sold	$22,000	
Marketing expenses	13,000	
General and administrative expenses	7,000	42,000
Contribution margin		18,000
Fixed expenses:		
Marketing expenses	11,000	
General and administrative expenses	3,000	14,000
Operating income		$ 4,000

International Male sells two ties for every belt. The ties sell for $30, with a variable expense of $12 each. The belts sell for $49, with a variable cost of $35 each.

1. Determine International Male's monthly break-even point in the numbers of ties and belts. Prove your answer by preparing a summary contribution margin income statement at the break-even level of sales. Show only two categories of expenses: variable and fixed.

REQUIRED

2. Compute International Male's margin of safety in dollars.

3. Suppose International Male increases monthly sales volume by 15%. Compute operating income.

Preparing absorption and variable costing income statements and explaining the difference in income
(Obj. 8)

P22-7A ◀▥ *Link Back to Chapter 19 (manufacturing company income statement) and Chapter 20 (manufacturing overhead).* Recycall Corporation manufactures plastic recycling bins, which it sells for $6 each. The company uses the FIFO inventory costing method, and it computes a new monthly fixed manufacturing overhead rate based on the actual number of bins produced that month. All costs and production levels are exactly as planned. The following data are from Recycall's first two months in business:

	January 19X9	February 19X9
Sales	1,000 bins	1,200 bins
Production	1,400 bins	1,000 bins
Variable manufacturing expense per bin	$2	$2
Variable marketing and administrative expenses per bin	$1	$1
Total fixed manufacturing overhead	$700	$700
Total fixed marketing and administrative expenses	$400	$400

REQUIRED

1. Compute the product cost per bin produced under absorption costing and under variable costing. Do this first for January and then for February.

2. Prepare separate monthly income statements for January and February, using
   a. Absorption costing
   b. Variable costing

3. Is operating income higher under absorption costing or variable costing in January? In February? Explain the pattern of differences in operating income based on absorption costing versus variable costing.

Problems (GROUP B)

Explaining the contribution margin approach and the margin of safety
(Obj. 2, 6)

P22-1B Huntington Clothiers is managed as traditionally as the button-down shirts that have made it famous. Arch Huntington founded the business in 1952 and has directed operations "by the seat of his pants" ever since. Approaching retirement, he must turn the business over to his son, Ralph. Recently Arch and Ralph had this conversation:

Ralph:	Dad, I am convinced that we can increase sales by advertising. I think we can spend $700 monthly on advertising and increase monthly sales by $7,000. With our 60% contribution margin, operating income should increase by $3,500.
Arch:	You know how I feel about advertising. We've never needed it in the past. Why now?
Ralph:	Two new shops have opened near us this year, and those guys are getting lots of business. Our profit margin is slipping. Our margin of safety is at its lowest point ever.
Arch:	Profit margin I understand, but what is this contribution margin that you mentioned? And what is this "margin of safety"?

REQUIRED

Explain to Arch Huntington the contribution margin approach to decision making. Show how Ralph Huntington computed the $3,500 increase in operating income. (Advertising is a fixed cost.) Also, describe what Ralph means by margin of safety, and explain why the business's situation is critical.

P22-2B The budgets of four companies yield the following information:

	A	B	C	D
Target sales.....................................	$290,000	$	$500,000	$
Variable expenses	120,000	104,000		100,000
Fixed expenses	138,000			82,000
Operating income (loss).................	$	$ 35,000	$ 60,000	$
Units sold			100,000	5,000
Unit contribution margin	$ 100	$ 12	$ 2	
Contribution margin ratio.............		0.60		0.20

Fill in the blanks for each company. Which company has the lowest break-even point in sales dollars? What causes the low break-even point?

P22-3B The Arctic Explorer is a schooner that sails in Glacier Bay, Alaska, during the summer. The average cruise has 45 tourists on board, and each person pays $50 for a day's sail. The ship sails 80 days each year.

　　The Arctic Explorer has a crew of eight. Each crew member earns an average of $100 per cruise. The crew is paid only when the ship sails. The other variable expense is for refreshments, which average $10 per passenger per cruise. Annual fixed expenses total $57,000.

1. Compute revenue and variable expenses for each cruise.
2. Use the income statement equation approach to compute the number of cruises the Arctic Explorer must make each year to break even.
3. Use the contribution margin approach to compute the number of cruises needed each year to earn $70,000. Is this profit goal realistic? Give your reason.
4. Prepare the Arctic Explorer's contribution margin income statement for 80 cruises for the year. Report only two categories of expenses: variable and fixed.

P22-4B Flo-Rite Ballpoints imprints ballpoint pens with company logos. Flo-Rite has fixed expenses of $300,000 per year plus variable expenses of $1.80 per box of pens. Each box of pens sells for $3.00.

1. Use the income statement equation approach to compute the number of boxes of pens Flo-Rite must sell each year to break even.

2. Use the contribution margin ratio CVP formula to compute the dollar sales Flo-Rite needs to earn $25,500 in operating income.
3. Prepare Flo-Rite's contribution margin income statement for 19X9 for sales of 240,000 boxes of pens. Cost of goods sold is 80% of variable expenses. Operating expenses make up the rest of variable expenses and all of fixed expenses.
4. The company is considering an expansion that will increase fixed expenses by 30% and variable expenses by 20 cents per box of pens. Compute the new break-even point in units and in dollars. Use either the income statement equation approach or the contribution margin approach.
5. Should Flo-Rite undertake the expansion? Give your reason.

P22-5B Latin Adventure Travel is opening an office in Tucson. Fixed monthly expenses are office rent ($3,000), depreciation on office furniture ($200), utilities ($110), a special telephone line ($520), a connection with the airlines' computerized reservation service ($380), and the salary of a travel agent ($1,400). Variable expenses include commissions for the travel agent (5% of sales), advertising (6% of sales), supplies and postage (1% of sales), and usage fees for the telephone line and computerized reservation service (3% of sales).

1. Use the contribution margin ratio CVP formula to compute Latin Adventure's break-even sales in dollars. If the average sale is a $600 plane ticket, how many tickets must be sold to break even?

2. Use the income statement equation approach to compute the dollar sales needed to earn a target monthly operating income of $6,290.
3. Graph the travel agency's CVP relationships. Assume that an average sale is a $600 plane ticket. Show the break-even point, sales revenue line, fixed expense line, variable expense line, operating loss area, operating income area, and the sales in units (tickets) and dollars when monthly operating income of $6,290 is earned. The graph should range from 0 to 25 units (plane tickets).
4. Assume that the average sale price decreases to $440 per ticket. Use the contribution margin approach to compute the new break-even point in tickets sold. How does the lower sale price affect the break-even point?

P22-6B The contribution margin income statement of Pricci's Trattoria for February 19XX follows:

PRICCI'S TRATTORIA Contribution Margin Income Statement For the Month of February 19XX		
Sales revenue...		$160,000
Variable expenses:		
Cost of goods sold..................................	$32,000	
Marketing expense	25,000	
General and administrative expense..........	3,000	60,000
Contribution margin		100,000
Fixed expenses:		
Marketing expense	20,750	
General and administrative expense..........	10,500	31,250
Operating income......................................		$ 68,750

Pricci's sells three small pizzas for every large pizza. A small pizza sells for $10, with a variable expense of $4.25. A large pizza sells for $20, with a variable expense of $6.

1. Determine Pricci's monthly break-even point in the numbers of small pizzas and large pizzas. Prove your answer by preparing a summary contribution margin income statement at the break-even level of sales. Show only two categories of expenses: variable and fixed.
2. Compute Pricci's margin of safety in dollars.
3. If Pricci's can increase monthly sales volume by 15%, what will operating income be?

P22-7B ◄▦ *Link Back to Chapter 19 (manufacturing company income statement) and Chapter 20 (manufacturing overhead).* Precision Optics manufactures kaleidoscopes, which it sells for $50 each. The company uses the FIFO inventory costing method, and it computes a new monthly fixed manufacturing overhead rate based on the actual number of kaleidoscopes produced that month. All costs and production levels are exactly as planned. The following data are from Precision Optics's first two months in business during 19X9:

	October	November
Sales	2,000 units	2,200 units
Production..	2,500 units	2,000 units
Variable manufacturing expense per kaleidoscope	$20	$20
Variable marketing and administrative expenses per kaleidoscope............................	$8	$8
Total fixed manufacturing overhead	$10,000	$10,000
Total fixed marketing and administrative expenses..............	$ 5,000	$ 5,000

1. Compute the product cost per kaleidoscope produced under absorption costing and under variable costing. Do this first for October and then for November.
2. Prepare separate monthly income statements for October and November, using
   a. Absorption costing
   b. Variable costing
3. Is operating income higher under absorption costing or variable costing in October? In November? Explain the pattern of differences in operating income based on absorption costing versus variable costing.

Applying Your Knowledge

DECISION CASES

CASE 1. Promoter Jerry Breece represents boxer Freddie Stone. In the match with Bruce Paul, Stone received a $15 million paycheck, and Paul received $5 million. Breece incurred $7 million in expenses to promote the fight, and $3 million in other fixed administrative expenses.

The fight was televised on a pay-per-view basis. Each location tuning in the fight paid $50. The cable broadcaster kept 70% of the pay-per-view revenues, with the remaining 30% going to promoter Jerry Breece.

Given the preceding data, answer the following questions:

REQUIRED

1. Promoter Jerry Breece pays both fighters as well as his marketing and administrative expenses. What is Breece's total fixed expense?
2. What is Jerry Breece's break-even point? (How many pay-per-view televisions must tune in the fight?) If prior boxing matches have attracted 1 to 2 million pay-per-view homes, would you advise Breece to promote the Stone-Paul match?
3. Breece was also able to sell closed-circuit and overseas broadcasting rights. After deducting expenses incurred in these negotiations, he was able to earn an additional $12 million.
   a. Given this additional earnings, what is Breece's break-even point? (How many pay-per-view televisions must tune in the fight if Breece is to break even?) How would you advise Breece about promoting the fight?
   b. Breece earned $5 million profit from this match. Assuming he received $12 million from the closed-circuit and overseas broadcasting rights, how many pay-per-view televisions had to be tuned in for Breece to earn a $5 million profit?

CASE 2. Richard and Poornsiri Sen live in Bloomington, Indiana. Two years ago, they visited Thailand. Poornsiri, a professional chef, was impressed with the cooking methods and the spices used in the Thai food. Bloomington does not have a Thai restaurant, and the Sens are contemplating opening one. Poornsiri would supervise the cooking, and Richard would leave his current job to be the maitre'd. The restaurant would serve dinner Tuesday through Saturday.

Using CVP analysis to make business decisions
(Obj. 1, 3, 4)

Richard has noticed a restaurant for lease. The restaurant has seven tables, each of which can seat four. Tables can be moved together for a large party. Poornsiri is planning two seatings per evening and the restaurant will be open 50 weeks per year.

The Sens have drawn up the following estimates:

Average revenue, including beverages and dessert	$40 per meal
Average cost of the food	$12 per meal
Chef's and dishwasher's salaries	$50,400 per *year*
Rent (premises, equipment)	$4,000 per month
Cleaning (linen and premises)	$800 per month
Replacement of dishes, cutlery, glasses	$300 per month
Utilities, advertising, telephone	$1,900 per month

Compute *annual* break-even sales revenue for the restaurant. Also compute the amount of sales revenue needed to earn operating income of $75,600 for the year. How many meals must the Sens serve each night to earn their target income of $75,600? Should the couple open the restaurant?

REQUIRED

Team Projects

PROJECT 1. The members of your team are the top executives of Leatherworks, a manufacturer of leather belts. Your team is trying to decide whether to close the Phoenix plant and move operations to Hermosillo, Mexico. The primary reason is labor cost. The 50 unionized workers in the Phoenix plant receive guaranteed wages of $1,000 per month, regardless of the plant's level of production. In contrast, workers in Mexico would be paid 6 pesos per belt. (Assume that $1 U.S. is equivalent to 8 Mexican pesos.) Information on other expected costs under each of the two alternatives follows:

Identifying variable and fixed costs; computing break-even points; and profits at different sales levels; trade-offs of variable and fixed costs; international issues
(Obj. 1, 2, 3, 4, 5)

	Phoenix	**Hermosillo**
Leather	$8.00 per belt	$8.00 per belt
Distribution	$0.75 per belt	$2.25 per belt
Other variable marketing and administrative expenses	$1.75 per belt	$1.75 per belt
Fixed manufacturing overhead costs	$20,000 per month	$20,000 per month
Fixed marketing and administrative expenses	$14,100 per month	$14,300 per month

Each belt sells for $25. The cost and sale price information is valid for Leatherwork's relevant range from 0 to 30,000 belts.

Before your meeting, each team member should answer requirement 1. At the team meeting, compare your responses to requirement 1 and reconcile any differences before proceeding further. Then split your team into two groups. The first group should respond to requirement 2, and the second group should respond to requirements 3 and 4. (The group that finishes first can help the other group.) Share the results of your responses to requirements 2–4. Based on this information, everyone should participate in answering requirement 5.

REQUIRED

1. **a.** If manufacturing is moved to Hermosillo, compute the wage rate per belt in U.S. dollars.
   b. Compute the variable cost per belt and the contribution margin per belt in each plant, and the total fixed costs in each plant.
   c. Compute the break-even point for the Phoenix plant and the Hermosillo plant.
   d. Based only on the financial information, which plant would minimize the risk of incurring a loss?

2. **a.** Prepare a CVP graph similar to Exhibit 22-7 for the Phoenix plant, and one for the Hermosillo plant. Your graphs should cover the range from 1 to 30,000 belts. (Also, the graphs should show increments of $100,000 on the "Dollars" axis and 10,000 belts on the "Belts" axis.)
   b. If Leatherworks plans to produce at the upper end of its relevant range, should it move its operations to Hermosillo? What if the company plans to produce at the lower end of its relevant range? Give your reason.

3. Use the information you developed in requirement 1b to determine Leatherworks' operating income if it produces (and sells) 10,000 belts with
   a. The Phoenix plant
   b. The Hermosillo plant

4. Use the information you developed in requirement 1b to determine Leatherworks' operating income if it produces (and sells) 30,000 belts with
   a. The Phoenix plant
   b. The Hermosillo plant

5. Are your answers to requirements 3 and 4 consistent with your answer to requirement 2b? Why or why not?

Combining financial and nonfinancial data to make decisions; ethics; international issues
(Obj. 2, 3)

PROJECT 2. (Continuation of Project 1)   Many people will be affected by Leatherworks' decision on moving its manufacturing operations to Hermosillo. The groups of people affected by a business decision are called stakeholders. For example, stockholders are one group of stakeholders, and customers are another group of stakeholders.

Before meeting as a team, each team member should sketch out a response to requirements 1–3. At the team meeting, use these notes as a basis for discussion and team response to each requirement.

REQUIRED

1. Identify Leatherworks' stakeholders who will be affected by the decision whether to close the Phoenix plant and move manufacturing operations to Hermosillo.

2. Consider how each stakeholder group would be affected if you decide to close the Phoenix plant and move manufacturing to Hermosillo.

3. Considering all the financial and nonfinancial factors, decide whether Leatherworks should close the Phoenix plant and move manufacturing operations to Hermosillo.

Sitting down in a dark theater with a box of popcorn and a soft drink to watch the latest block-buster is one of America's favorite pastimes. The theater works hard to ensure that going to the movies is a fun experience. Movie theaters have become more than a "movie house." They are big and bright, offering more screens and expanded concessions as well as arcades.

Managing a theater chain requires a thorough understanding of cost-volume-profit analysis. Each movie presented requires management to conduct a careful CVP analysis. Consider Regal Cinemas, a small chain of theaters that operates mostly in the southern United States. Identified by *Forbes Magazine* as one of the best 200 small companies in America for three straight years, Regal Cinemas has one of the highest profit margins in the industry.

REQUIRED

1. Go to **http://www.regalcinemas.com.** The Regal Cinemas home page is where you can find what movies are playing at what time, and at what location. The corporate side of the home page takes you to the business side of the company.

2. Click on **Corporate Lobby** to learn more about Regal Cinemas. The company's financial statements, history, press releases, and other information appear here.

3. Click on the **Financials** button. Review *Management's Discussion* and the *Statements of Income* to respond to the following requirements.

    a. Refer to *Management's Discussion.* List the accounts considered to be "direct theater costs." For the remainder of this exercise, assume the "direct theater costs" are the only variable costs for Regal Cinemas.

    b. Refer to the *Statements of Income.* For the most recent year, calculate the contribution margin for Regal Cinemas. (*Hint:* Remember to use the information from *a.*)

    c. Assume the average ticket price is $5. For the most recent year, compute the estimated number of tickets sold by Regal Cinemas.

    d. For the most recent year, compute the average amount spent on concessions by each ticket holder. (*Hint:* Use your answer from *c* in responding to this requirement.)

    e. For this requirement, ignore the effects of *other operating revenues* and *theater operating expenses.* For the most recent year, compute the contribution margin for ticket sales (admissions) and for concession sales. Compare the contribution margins. For the most recent year, compute the contribution margin ratio for ticket sales (admissions) and for concessions. Compare the contribution margin ratios. Comment on how this information should affect the management of a Regal Cinema.

    f. Suppose Regal Cinemas is considering playing the movie, *The Accounting Professor's Mysterious Death.* The cost of film rental is $100,000 plus 50% of ticket sales. Regal's managers estimate that 70,000 people (mostly college students) will watch the movie in Regal Cinemas nationwide. If Regal decides to show this movie, calculate the estimated effect on revenues. (Remember to consider both admissions and concessions revenues.) Calculate the effect of showing this movie on expenses—film rental costs, concessions costs, and theater operating costs. If Regal decides to show the movie, what will be the effect on contribution margin? Should Regal show this movie? Explain. (*Hint:* Use information obtained in *a* through *e* to answer this requirement.)

CHAPTER 23

The Master Budget and Responsibility Accounting

After studying this chapter, you should be able to

1. Identify the benefits of budgeting

2. Prepare an operating budget for a company

3. Prepare the components of a financial budget

4. Use sensitivity analysis in budgeting

5. Distinguish among different types of responsibility centers

6. Prepare a performance report for management by exception

7. Allocate indirect costs to departments

Ritz-Carlton. The name signals luxury. Ritz-Carlton operates more than 30 hotels with 11,000 rooms in the United States and seven other countries. A single hotel can cater both to individual travelers and to large groups of 1,000 or more. With such large and complex operations, how does Ritz-Carlton plan and control its business?

Budgets are the key. Budgets provide the road map for each hotel. The budget is a financial plan that spells out how each hotel expects to achieve its target profit. Each hotel sends its budget to company headquarters in Atlanta. Headquarters uses these individual hotel budgets to prepare the companywide budget—the financial plan to achieve the company's profit goals.

Each hotel's budget begins with a sales forecast of room occupancy, group events, and banquets. Then the hotel controller estimates the costs. For example, budgeted room occupancy is multiplied by the hotel's cost per room (including housekeeping, supplies, and cable TV service) to help managers predict their costs. The budgeted sales and cost data help managers plan the hotel's target profit (revenues minus expenses).

Ritz-Carlton managers also use the budget to control operations. Reports compare actual revenues to budgeted revenues and actual expenses to budgeted expenses.

Managers can then investigate differences between actual and budgeted figures. For the most important items—revenues, labor costs, and quality indicators—managers identify and investigate differences *each day*. Once a month, each hotel receives a detailed report from the Atlanta headquarters that helps managers evaluate their hotel's actual performance relative to the budget, relative to last year, and relative to other Ritz-Carlton hotels.

The chapter opening story shows that managers of companies like Ritz-Carlton play three key roles. First, they develop strategies—overall business goals. Second, they plan and take specific actions to achieve the goals. Third, they evaluate operations by comparing actual results with their plans. This performance evaluation provides feedback that helps managers monitor current operations and fine-tune their plans. Exhibit 23-1 shows how managers use budgets to plan and control business operations. The process is continuous: plan, act, evaluate, and plan again.

In Chapter 19, we defined a *budget* as a quantitative expression of a plan of action that helps managers coordinate and implement the plan. Budgets can focus on either the short-term or the long-term. To plan actions that will affect the company over several years, managers must predict the goods and services their customers will demand. For example, in deciding whether to add a hotel property in Cancun, Mexico, Ritz-Carlton would use a long-range budget based on their predicted demand for luxury hotel accommodations in Cancun.

Other budgets have a short-term focus. Many companies budget their cash flows monthly, weekly, and daily to ensure that they have enough cash to meet their needs. They also budget revenues and expenses—and thus operating income—for months, quarters, and years. This chapter focuses on shorter-term budgets of a year or less. Chapter 26 focuses on budgets for large capital expenditures (for property, plant, and equipment, for example) that naturally have a longer-term focus.

Budgeting for a Service Company

Let's begin by considering a budget for a small service company. Ram Dharan started a small business—an on-line service that provides travel itineraries for leisure travelers. Dharan wants to earn $275 per month to help cover his college expenses. He develops a budget to determine whether he can expect to meet this goal.

Dharan expects to sell 100 itineraries per month at a price of $3 each. Over the last six months, he paid his Internet service provider an average of $18 per month, and he spent an additional $20 per month on travel-related reference materials. He expects these monthly costs to remain about the same. Finally, he spends 5% of his sales revenues advertising on the Internet.

To prepare the budget, Dharan computes his total budgeted revenues and subtracts his total budgeted expenses:

RAM DHARAN TRAVEL ITINERARIES Budget for May 19X9		
Budgeted sales revenue ($3 × 100)............		$300
Less Budgeted expenses:		
Internet access expense.........................	$18	
Reference materials expense	20	
Advertising expense (5% × $300)..........	15	53
Budgeted operating income		$247

The budget shows that if business goes according to plan, Ram Dharan will not meet his $275 per month operating income goal. Dharan will have to increase revenue (by using word-of-mouth advertising) or cut expenses (by finding a less expensive Internet access provider) to meet his income goal.

The Budget Unit

Ram Dharan is the sole proprietor of a simple business, so his budget covers the entire company's operations. While managers of large companies also prepare budgets for the organization as a whole, individual subunits prepare their own budgets, as well. For example, each individual Ritz-Carlton hotel prepares a budget. Company headquarters in Atlanta then uses the individual hotel budgets to prepare the companywide budget.

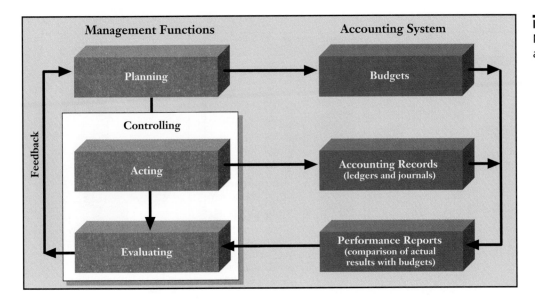

EXHIBIT 23-1
Management's Use of Budgets
and Performance Reports

In the first part of this chapter, we examine a company's master (comprehensive) budget for a fiscal year. More than 90% of large industrial companies prepare these budgets. We then consider how top management can use budgets to evaluate the performance of subunits—such as the Phoenix Ritz-Carlton hotel—for which individual managers are responsible.

Benefits of Budgeting

Budgets are key management tools that help large companies like Ritz-Carlton just as much as sole proprietors like Ram Dharan. Consider this comment by a former chief executive officer of Wells Fargo Bank:

> I say our budget is the most important thing we do. I like to have all the debates over with when it is adopted. I'm not too sympathetic about hearing a lot of excuses after the fact. If budget planning is done well, there is no room for infighting and personality conflicts.

As summarized in Exhibit 23-2, budgeting offers several benefits:

1. *Budgeting requires planning.* After preparing his budget, Ram Dharan discovered that his expected income fell short of his target. The sooner he learns of the expected shortfall, the more time he has to plan how to increase revenues or cut expenses. The better his plan and the more time he has to execute the plan, the more likely he will meet his income target.

This example shows that budgeting helps managers set realistic goals by requiring them to plan specific actions to meet their goals. Budgeting also helps managers prepare for a range of conditions. It leads them to ask what-if questions and to plan for contingencies. Suppose that Honda assigns a plant with 3 million units of capacity to production of Accord cars. What if actual demand turns out to be 3.2 million? To satisfy all demand, Honda must add 200,000 units of capacity. If, in the budgeting process, Honda considered the possibility of such a high demand, the adjustments probably will be smoother and less costly than if Honda is forced to "manage by crisis."

2. *Budgeting promotes coordination and communication.* The master budget coordinates the company's activities. It forces managers to consider relationships among operations across the entire value chain. Consider Cincinnati Milacron, Inc., a manufacturer of machine tools and accessories. The sales managers of Cincinnati Milacron are evaluated on the basis of sales volume, so they prefer to accept all special orders for unique machinery. But some special orders cost the company more than the customer is willing to pay. The budget promotes coordination by encouraging sales managers to accept orders only for machines that Cincinnati Milacron can manufacture at a profit.

Objective 1

Identify the benefits of budgeting

■ **Daily Exercise 23-2**

1. Budgets require managers to plan.

2. Budgets promote coordination and communication.

3. Budgets help managers evaluate performance.

4. Budgets motivate employees to help achieve the company's goals.

Concept Highlight

EXHIBIT 23-2
Benefits of Budgeting

Coordination requires effective communication. Suppose Mazda's engineers plan to redesign the Miata's brake system. By participating in the budgeting process alongside engineers, the manufacturing vice president can see the need to change the production process. He explains the plan to plant managers so they can make the changes in an orderly way. Budgets can communicate a consistent set of plans throughout the company.

3. *Budgeting provides a benchmark that helps managers evaluate performance.* Managers can evaluate a department or activity by comparing its actual results with either its budget or its past performance. In general, the budget is a better benchmark. One problem with comparisons with past results is that the company's operations or its markets may have changed since last year. Comparing this year's results with last year's may be like comparing apples with oranges. In contrast, the budget is based on the company's current status. It considers all changes from past conditions.

Suppose that Coldwell Banker's real-estate agents sell 10% more houses in the third quarter of 2000 than in the third quarter of 1999. Is this good performance? Not necessarily. If nationwide sales are up 20% for the quarter, Coldwell Banker's results may be disappointing. But if the overall market has declined, the 10% increase may be excellent.

Another problem with past results is that they may represent inefficient performance. An average production cost of $42.50 for a telephone answering machine may have been incurred when the manufacturer had problems with materials quality. An average cost of $40 the following year is better, but still may not be praiseworthy if the budgeted cost per machine is $36.

4. *A budget motivates employees.* Budgets affect behavior. The budgeting process prompts managers to look into the future. This helps them foresee and avoid problems. For example, Ram Dharan's discovery of an expected shortfall in operating income may prompt him to cut expenses. Budgets also motivate employees to achieve the business's goals. Motivation is especially strong when employees believe the budget is fair. For this reason, companies often ask employees to help prepare budgets that will be used to judge their performance.

Unrealistic budgets can hurt employee morale. Suppose Coldwell Banker's management imposed a budgeted increase of 15% in house sales for each territory. That budget may be acceptable to agents in areas with strong economies. They may work hard to achieve the increase. In contrast, agents in depressed areas may believe it is impossible to meet the budget. They may become resentful and simply give up if they believe it is not possible to meet the budget. Allowing agents in each territory a voice in the budget will result in budgets tailored to local conditions.

	Actual	Budget	Variance (Actual − Budget)
Sales revenue	$550,000	$600,000	$(50,000)
Total expenses..........	510,000	520,000	10,000
Net income..............	$ 40,000	$ 80,000	$(40,000)

EXHIBIT 23-3
Summary Income Statement
Performance Report

The Performance Report

We have seen how budgets can help managers plan and foresee obstacles. However, budgets are just as useful for controlling as for planning. To control operations, managers prepare performance reports that compare actual results to the budget. These reports help managers

- Evaluate operations
- Decide on corrective action
- Prepare next period's budget

Suppose that Cincinnati Milacron has the performance report in Exhibit 23-3. Actual sales in Exhibit 23-3 are $550,000, which is $50,000 less than budgeted sales. The actual net income is half the budgeted amount. Top managers will ask what went wrong. The vice president of sales will have to explain why sales revenue was so far below the budgeted amount. The vice president, in turn, will meet with the sales staff to learn why they failed to meet the budget. There are three possible explanations:

- The budget was unrealistic.
- The sales force did a poor job of selling during the period.
- Uncontrollable factors (such as a sluggish economy) reduced sales.

Of course, all three factors may have contributed to the poor results.

Managers use performance reports like the one in Exhibit 23-3 to decide on corrective action. If the sales department did not perform well, managers must decide what to do. Perhaps sales staff compensation should be tied more closely to sales revenue to increase the incentive to sell. Or the company may need a new advertising campaign. Managers must decide whether to reduce budgeted sales for the next period—a decision that directly affects next period's budgeted net income. This example shows how managers use a budget to plan and control operations to achieve their goals.

 Thinking It Over The performance report in Exhibit 23-3 shows that actual sales revenue is 8.33% less than budgeted sales revenue ($50,000 ÷ $600,000). However, actual expenses are only 1.9% less than budgeted expenses ($10,000 ÷ $520,000). Why is the percentage shortfall in expenses so much lower than the percentage shortfall in revenue?

Answer: One reason why expenses did not fall as far short of the budget is that some expenses do not increase or decrease with revenue (sales volume). For example, the vice president of sales may receive a salary of $90,000 regardless of sales revenue. Expenses such as depreciation, rent, and insurance are *fixed* and do not vary with the amount of revenue. When revenue and variable expenses decline, fixed expenses remain the same. Thus total expense does not decline as rapidly as revenue.

Components of the Master Budget

The **master budget** is the set of budgeted financial statements and supporting schedules for the entire organization. This comprehensive budget includes (1) the operating budget, (2) the capital expenditures budget, and (3) the financial budget. The **operating budget** sets the expected revenues and expenses—and thus operating income—for the period. The **capital expenditures budget** presents the company's plan for purchases of property, plant, equipment, and other long-term assets. The **financial budget** projects cash inflows and outflows, the period-ending balance sheet, and the statement of cash flows. This chapter focuses on components of the operating budget and the financial budget. While

Master Budget. The set of budgeted financial statements and supporting schedules for the entire organization. This comprehensive budget includes the operating budget, the capital expenditures budget, and the financial budget.

Operating Budget. Sets the expected revenues and expenses—and thus operating income—for the period.

Capital Expenditures Budget. A company's plan for purchases of property, plant, equipment, and other long-term assets.

Financial Budget. Projects cash inflows and outflows, the period-ending balance sheet, and the statement of cash flows.

EXHIBIT 23-4
Master Budget for a
Merchandising Company

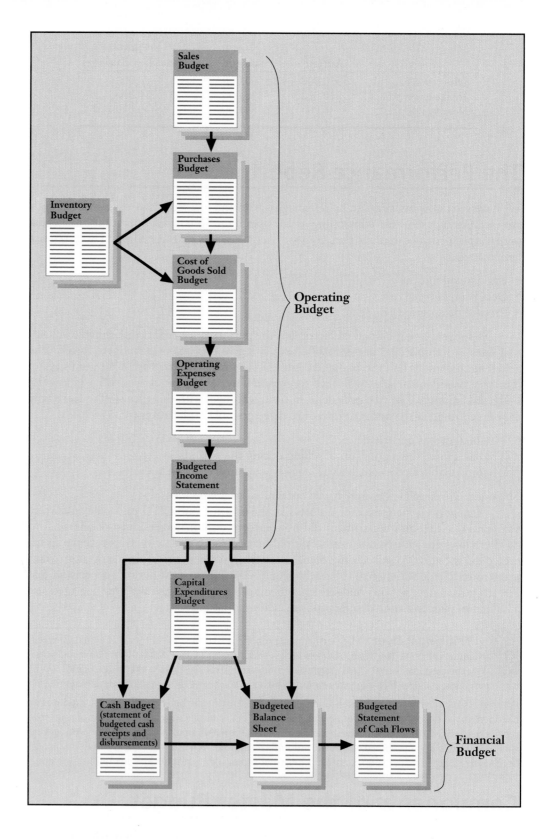

you learned about the cash budget in Chapter 7, we will show more details behind the figures in the cash budget. Chapter 26 covers budgeting for capital expenditures.

The components of the master budget include:

1. Operating budget
   a. Sales budget
   b. Purchases, inventory, and cost of goods sold budgets
   c. Operating expenses budget
   d. Budgeted income statement

2. Capital expenditures budget
3. Financial budget
   a. Cash budget: statement of budgeted cash receipts and disbursements
   b. Budgeted balance sheet
   c. Budgeted statement of cash flows

The end result of the *operating* budget is the budgeted income statement, which shows expected revenues, expenses, and operating income for the period. The *financial* budget results in the budgeted statement of cash flows, which shows budgeted cash flows for operating, investing, and financing activities. The budgeted financial statements look exactly like ordinary statements. The only difference is that they list budgeted rather than actual figures. Exhibit 23-4 diagrams the various sections of the master budget for a merchandising company such as Safeway or J.C. Penney.

■ **Daily Exercise 23-3**

The sales budget is the cornerstone of the master budget, because sales affect most of the other components of the master budget. After sales and expenses are projected, the budgeted income statement can be prepared. The income statement, the capital expenditures budget, and plans for raising cash and paying debts provide information for the cash budget, which feeds into the budgeted balance sheet. The budgeted statement of cash flows is usually the last step in the process.

Preparing the Master Budget

To learn about the budgeting process, you should prepare a master budget.

Data for Whitewater Sporting Goods Master Budget

1. *You manage Whitewater Sporting Goods Store No. 18, which carries a complete line of outdoor recreation gear.* You are to prepare the master budget for your store for April, May, June, and July, the main selling season. The division manager and the assistant controller (head of the Accounting Department) of the company will arrive from headquarters next week to review the budget with you.

2. *Cash collections follow sales because the company sells on account.* When the company needs extra cash, it borrows on six-month installment notes payable.

3. *Your store's balance sheet at March 31, 19X9, the beginning of the budget period, appears in Exhibit 23-5.* ◄▪▪

4. *Sales in March were $40,000.* The sales force estimates future monthly sales:

◄▪▪ ◄▪▪ ◄▪▪ We examined the balance sheet in Chapter 5, page 197–198.

April..........	$50,000
May..........	80,000
June..........	60,000
July..........	50,000

WHITEWATER SPORTING GOODS STORE NO. 18
Balance Sheet
March 31, 19X9

Assets		Liabilities	
Current assets:		Current liabilities:	
Cash	$ 15,000	Accounts payable..................	$ 16,800
Accounts receivable	16,000	Salary and commissions	
Inventory	48,000	payable..............................	4,250
Prepaid insurance	1,800	Total liabilities..........................	21,050
Total current assets.................	80,800		
Plant assets:		**Owners' Equity**	
Equipment and fixtures	32,000	Owners' equity........................	78,950
Accumulated depreciation.......	(12,800)		
Total plant assets.....................	19,200	Total liabilities	
Total assets..............................	$100,000	and owners' equity	$100,000

EXHIBIT 23-5
Balance Sheet

Sales are 60% cash and 40% on credit. All credit sales are collected in the month following the sale. The $16,000 of accounts receivable at March 31 arose from credit sales made in March (40% of $40,000). Uncollectible accounts are insignificant.

5. *Whitewater maintains inventory equal to $20,000 plus 80% of the budgeted cost of goods sold for the following month.* Target ending inventory on July 31 is $42,400. Cost of goods sold averages 70% of sales. (These percentages are based on the business's past experience.) These data explain why inventory on March 31 is $48,000:

$$\text{March 31 inventory} = \$20,000 + 0.80 \times (0.70 \times \text{April sales of } \$50,000)$$
$$= \$20,000 + (0.80 \times \$35,000)$$
$$= \$20,000 + \$28,000 = \$48,000$$

Whitewater pays for inventory as follows: 50% during the month of purchase and 50% during the next month. Accounts payable consists of inventory purchases only. March purchases were $33,600, so accounts payable at the end of March total $16,800 ($33,600 × 0.50).

6. *Monthly payroll has two parts: a salary of $2,500 plus sales commissions equal to 15% of sales.* The company pays half this amount during the month and half early in the following month. Therefore, at the end of each month Whitewater reports salary and commissions payable equal to half the month's payroll. The $4,250 liability on the March 31 balance sheet is half the March payroll of $8,500:

$$\text{March payroll} = \text{Salary of } \$2,500 + \text{Sales commissions of } \$6,000 \ (0.15 \times \$40,000)$$
$$= \$8,500$$
$$\text{March 31 salary and commissions payable} = 0.50 \times \$8,500 = \$4,250$$

7. *Other monthly expenses are as follows:*

Rent expense	$2,000, paid as incurred
Depreciation expense, including truck	500
Insurance expense	200 expiration of prepaid amount
Miscellaneous expenses.................................	5% of sales, paid as incurred

8. *Whitewater plans to purchase a used delivery truck in April for $3,000 cash.*

9. *Whitewater requires each store to maintain a minimum cash balance of $10,000 at the end of each month.* The store can borrow money on 6-month notes payable of $1,000 each at an annual interest rate of 12 percent. Management borrows no more than the amount needed to maintain the $10,000 minimum. Notes payable require six equal monthly payments of principal, plus monthly interest on the entire unpaid principal. Borrowing and all principal and interest payments occur at the end of the month.

10. *Income taxes are the responsibility of corporate headquarters, so you can ignore tax for budgeting purposes.*

You have studied the company guidelines on how to prepare a budget. The directions instruct you to prepare the following detailed schedules:

Schedule	Title
A	Sales budget
B	Purchases, cost of goods sold, and inventory budget
C	Operating expenses budget
D	Budgeted cash collections from customers
E	Budgeted cash disbursements for purchases
F	Budgeted cash disbursements for operating expenses

After compiling these schedules, you can prepare the following statements:

- Budgeted income statement for the four months ending July 31, 19X9 (see Exhibit 23-6)
- Cash budget for the four months ending July 31, 19X9 (see Exhibit 23-13)
- Budgeted balance sheet at July 31, 19X9 (see Exhibit 23-14)
- Budgeted statement of cash flows for the four months ending July 31, 19X9 (see Exhibit 23-15).

EXHIBIT 23-6
Budgeted Income Statement

WHITEWATER SPORTING GOODS STORE NO. 18		
Budgeted Income Statement		
Four Months Ending July 31, 19X9		

	Amount		Source
Sales revenue		$240,000	Schedule A (Exhibit 23-7)
Cost of goods sold		168,000	Schedule B (Exhibit 23-8)
Gross margin		72,000	
Operating expenses:			
Salary and commissions	$46,000		Schedule C (Exhibit 23-9)
Rent expense	8,000		Schedule C (Exhibit 23-9)
Depreciation expense	2,000		Schedule C (Exhibit 23-9)
Insurance expense	800		Schedule C (Exhibit 23-9)
Miscellaneous expenses	12,000	68,800	Schedule C (Exhibit 23-9)
Operating income		3,200	
Interest expense		225*	Cash Budget (Exhibit 23-13)
Net income		$ 2,975	

*$90 + $75 + $60

Preparing the Operating Budget

As you prepare the master budget, remember that you are developing the company's operating and financial plan for the next four months. The steps in this process may seem mechanical, but remember that budgeting stimulates ideas about pricing, product lines, job assignments, needs for additional equipment, and negotiations with banks. Preparation of the budget leads to decisions that affect the future course of Whitewater—or of any business. The operating budget—consisting of the sales budget; the purchases, cost of goods sold, and inventory budgets; and the operating expenses budgets—results in the budgeted income statement.

"Preparation of the budget leads to decisions that affect the future course of Whitewater—or of any business."

PREPARING THE BUDGETED INCOME STATEMENT There are four steps to preparing the budgeted income statement shown in Exhibit 23-6.

Step 1. **The sales budget** (Schedule A). Sales is the key business activity. Budgeted total sales for each product is the sale price multiplied by the expected number of units sold. The overall sales budget in Exhibit 23-7 is the sum of the budgets for the individual products. Trace the April through July total sales ($240,000) to the budgeted income statement in Exhibit 23-6.

Step 2. **Purchases, cost of goods sold, and inventory budget** (Schedule B). This schedule determines cost of goods sold for the budgeted income statement, ending inventory for the budgeted balance sheet, and purchases for the cash budget. The relationship among these items is given by the familiar cost-of-goods-sold computation:

Beginning inventory + Purchases − Ending inventory = Cost of goods sold

| WHITEWATER SPORTING GOODS STORE NO. 18 | | | | | |
Schedule A—Sales Budget (item 4, pages 997–998)					
	April	May	June	July	April–July Total
Cash sales, 60%	$30,000	$48,000	$36,000	$30,000	
Credit sales, 40%	20,000	32,000	24,000	20,000	
Total sales, 100%	$50,000	$80,000	$60,000	$50,000	$240,000

WHITEWATER SPORTING GOODS STORE NO. 18
Schedule B—Purchases, Cost of Goods Sold,
and Inventory Budget (item 5, page 998)

	April	May	June	July	April–July Total
Cost of goods sold (0.70 × sales, from Schedule A in Exhibit 23-7)..........	$ 35,000	$ 56,000	$ 42,000	$ 35,000	$168,000
+ Desired ending inventory ($20,000 + 0.80 × Cost of goods sold for the next month)..............	64,800*	53,600	48,000	42,400‡	
= Total inventory required........................	99,800	109,600	90,000	77,400	
– Beginning inventory	(48,000)†	(64,800)	(53,600)	(48,000)	
= Purchases..	$ 51,800	$ 44,800	$ 36,400	$ 29,400	

*$20,000 + (0.80 × $56,000) = $64,800.
† Balance at March 31 (Exhibit 23-5).
‡Given in item 5 on page 998.

EXHIBIT 23-8
Purchases, Cost of Goods Sold,
and Inventory Budget,
Schedule B

■ Daily Exercise 23-5
■ Daily Exercise 23-6
■ Daily Exercise 23-8

Beginning inventory is known, budgeted cost of goods sold is a fixed percentage of sales, and budgeted ending inventory is a computed amount. You must solve for the budgeted purchases figure. To do this, take the cost-of-goods-sold computation and then move beginning inventory and ending inventory to the right side of the equation, isolating purchases on the left side:

Beginning inventory + Purchases − Ending inventory = Cost of goods sold

Purchases = Cost of goods sold + Ending inventory − Beginning inventory

This second equation also makes sense. How much does Whitewater have to purchase? Enough to cover sales and desired ending inventory, less the amount of beginning inventory already on hand at the start of the period. Exhibit 23-8 shows Whitewater's purchases, cost of goods sold, and ending inventory budget.

To see how this information fits into the operating budget, trace the total budgeted cost of goods sold from Exhibit 23-8 ($168,000) to the budgeted income statement in Exhibit 23-6. We will be using the budgeted inventory and purchases amounts later.

Step 3. **Operating expenses budget** (Schedule C). Some budgeted operating expenses, such as sales commissions and delivery expenses, fluctuate with sales. Other expenses, such as rent and insurance, are the same each month (fixed).

Trace the April through July totals from the operating expenses budget in Exhibit 23-9 (salary and commissions of $46,000, rent expense of $8,000, and so on) to the budgeted income statement in Exhibit 23-6.

EXHIBIT 23-9
Operating Expenses Budget,
Schedule C

WHITEWATER SPORTING GOODS STORE NO. 18
Schedule C—Operating Expenses Budget (items 6 and 7, page 998)

	April	May	June	July	April–July Total
Salary, fixed amount (item 6, page 998)......................	$ 2,500	$ 2,500	$ 2,500	$ 2,500	
Commission, 15% of sales from Schedule A (Item 6, page 998 and Exhibit 23-7)	7,500	12,000	9,000	7,500	
Total salary and commissions..................................	10,000	14,500	11,500	10,000	$46,000
Rent expense, fixed amount (item 7, page 998)........................	2,000	2,000	2,000	2,000	8,000
Depreciation expense, fixed amount (item 7, page 998)	500	500	500	500	2,000
Insurance expense, fixed amount (item 7, page 998)................	200	200	200	200	800
Miscellaneous expenses, 5% of sales from Schedule A (item 7, page 998 and Exhibit 23-7)	2,500	4,000	3,000	2,500	12,000
Total operating expenses..	$15,200	$21,200	$17,200	$15,200	$68,800

WHITEWATER SPORTING GOODS STORE NO. 18
Schedule D—Budgeted Cash Collections from Customers

	April	May	June	July	April–July Total
Cash sales from Schedule A (Exhibit 23-7)..........	$30,000	$48,000	$36,000	$30,000	
Collections of last month's credit sales, from Schedule A (Exhibit 23-7).......................	16,000*	20,000	32,000	24,000	
Total collections...	$46,000	$68,000	$68,000	$54,000	$236,000

*March 31 accounts receivable, Exhibit 23-5.

Step 4. **Budgeted income statement.** Use steps 1 through 3 to prepare the budgeted income statement in Exhibit 23-6. We explain the computation of interest expense as part of the cash budget in the next section.

Preparing the Financial Budget

The second major section of the master budget that we will discuss is the financial budget. This includes the cash budget, the budgeted balance sheet and the budgeted statement of cash flows. The **cash budget,** or **statement of budgeted cash receipts and disbursements,** details how the business expects to go from the beginning cash balance to the desired ending balance. ◄▦ Cash receipts and disbursements depend on revenues and expenses, which appear in the budgeted income statement. This is why the cash budget is not prepared until after the budgeted income statement.

PREPARING THE CASH BUDGET   The cash budget has four major parts:

- Cash collections from customers (Schedule D, Exhibit 23-10)
- Cash disbursements for purchases of inventory (Schedule E, Exhibit 23-11)
- Cash disbursements for operating expenses (Schedule F, Exhibit 23-12)
- Capital expenditures (for example, the $3,000 capital expenditure to acquire the delivery truck)

Carefully study Exhibits 23-10, 23-11, and 23-12. Exhibit 23-10 shows how to compute cash collections using data on cash and credit sales from the sales budget (Exhibit 23-7). Trace the monthly total cash collections to the cash budget in Exhibit 23-13.

Exhibit 23-11 uses the purchases budget (Exhibit 23-8) and payment information from item 5 on page 998 to compute total cash disbursements for purchases. Trace the monthly cash outlays for purchases to the cash budget in Exhibit 23-13. See how cash disbursements for operating expenses in Exhibit 23-12 are computed using information in items 6 and 7 on page 998 and data from the operating expenses budget (Exhibit 23-9). (Depreciation expense and insurance expense are *not* current period cash outlays, so they are *not* included in the budgeted cash disbursements for operating expenses.) Follow the total monthly cash disbursements for operating expenses from Exhibit 23-12 to the cash budget in Exhibit 23-13.

EXHIBIT 23-10
Budgeted Cash Collections,
Schedule D

■ Daily Exercise 23-9
■ Daily Exercise 23-11

Objective 3

Prepare the components of a financial budget

◄▦◄▦◄▦   We introduced the cash budget in Chapter 7, page 309.

Cash Budget. Details how the business expects to go from the beginning cash balance to the desired ending balance. Also called the **statement of budgeted cash receipts and disbursements.**

■ Daily Exercise 23-10

EXHIBIT 23-11
Budgeted Cash Disbursements
for Purchases, *Schedule E*

WHITEWATER SPORTING GOODS STORE NO. 18
Schedule E—Budgeted Cash Disbursements for Purchases of Inventory

	April	May	June	July	April–July Total
50% of last month's purchases from Schedule B (Exhibit 23-8)..........	$16,800*	$25,900	$22,400	$18,200	
50% of this month's purchases from Schedule B (Exhibit 23-8)..........	25,900	22,400	18,200	14,700	
Total disbursements for purchases	$42,700	$48,300	$40,600	$32,900	$164,500

*March 31 accounts payable, Exhibit 23-5.

WHITEWATER SPORTING GOODS STORE NO. 18
Schedule F—Budgeted Cash Disbursements for Operating Expenses

	April	May	June	July	April–July Total
Expense amounts, from Schedule C (Exhibit 23-9)					
Salary and commissions:					
50% of last month's expenses, from Schedule C (Exhibit 23-9)	$ 4,250*	$ 5,000	$ 7,250	$ 5,750	
50% of this month's expenses, from Schedule C (Exhibit 23-9)	5,000	7,250	5,750	5,000	
Total salary and commissions	9,250	12,250	13,000	10,750	
Rent expense, from Schedule C (Exhibit 23-9)	2,000	2,000	2,000	2,000	
Miscellaneous expenses, from Schedule C (Exhibit 23-9)	2,500	4,000	3,000	2,500	
Total disbursements for operating expenses	$13,750	$18,250	$18,000	$15,250	$65,250

*March 31 salary and commissions payable, Exhibit 23-5.

EXHIBIT 23-12
Budgeted Cash Disbursements
for Operating Expenses,
Schedule F

EXHIBIT 23-13
Cash Budget

WHITEWATER SPORTING GOODS STORE NO. 18
Cash Budget
Four Months Ending July 31, 19X9

	April	May	June	July
Beginning cash balance	$15,000*	$10,550	$10,410	$18,235
Cash collections from customers (Schedule D, Exhibit 23-10)	46,000	68,000	68,000	54,000
Cash available	$61,000	$78,550	$78,410	$72,235
Cash disbursements:				
Purchases of inventory (Schedule E, Exhibit 23-11)	$42,700	$48,300	$40,600	$32,900
Operating expenses (Schedule F, Exhibit 23-12)	13,750	18,250	18,000	15,250
Purchase of delivery truck (Item 8, page 998)	3,000	—	—	—
Total cash disbursements	59,450	66,550	58,600	48,150
(1) Ending cash balance before financing	1,550	12,000	19,810	24,085
Minimum cash balance desired	10,000	10,000	10,000	10,000
Cash excess (deficiency)	$ (8,450)	$ 2,000	$ 9,810	$14,085
Financing of cash deficiency (see notes a–c):				
Borrowing (at end of month)	$ 9,000			
Principal payments (at end of month)		$ (1,500)	$(1,500)	$ (1,500)
Interest expense (at 12% annually)		(90)	(75)	(60)
(2) Total effects of financing	9,000	(1,590)	(1,575)	(1,560)
Ending cash balance (1) + (2)	$10,550	$10,410	$18,235	$22,525

*March 31 cash balance, Exhibit 23-5.
Notes
a. Borrowing occurs in multiples of $1,000 and only for the amount needed to maintain a minimum cash balance of $10,000.
b. Monthly principal payments: $9,000 ÷ 6 = $1,500.
c. Interest expense:
   May: $9,000 × (0.12 × 1/12) = $90
   June: ($9,000 − $1,500) × (0.12 × 1/12) = $75
   July: ($9,000 − $1,500 − $1,500) × (0.12 × 1/12) = $60

In preparing the cash budget (Exhibit 23-13), first determine the cash available (beginning cash balance plus cash collections). Then subtract total cash disbursements to find the ending cash balance before financing. For April, Exhibit 23-13 shows that this is

Cash available	$61,000
Total cash disbursements............................	(59,450)
Ending cash balance before financing.........	$ 1,550

Item 9 on page 998 states that Whitewater requires a minimum cash balance of $10,000. The $1,550 budgeted cash balance before financing falls $8,450 short of the minimum required balance ($10,000 – $1,550). Because Whitewater borrows in $1,000 notes, the company will have to borrow $9,000 to cover April's expected shortfall. The budgeted ending cash balance equals the "ending cash balance before financing," adjusted for the total effects of the financing (a $9,000 inflow in April). Exhibit 23-13 shows that Whitewater expects to end April with $10,550 of cash ($1,550 + $9,000). The exhibit also shows the cash balance at the end of May, June, and July.

Item 9 on page 998 states that Whitewater must repay the notes in six equal installments. Thus May through July show principal repayments of $1,500 ($9,000 ÷ 6) per month. Whitewater also pays interest expense on the outstanding notes payable, at 12% per year. For example, the June interest expense is $75 [($9,000 principal – $1,500 repayment at the end of May) × 12% × 1/12]. Interest expense for the four months totals $225 ($90 + $75 + $60). This interest expense appears on the budgeted income statement in Exhibit 23-6.

Also, notice that the cash balance at the end of July is $22,525. This becomes the cash balance in the July 31 budgeted balance sheet in Exhibit 23-14.

PREPARING THE BUDGETED BALANCE SHEET   The next step in preparing the master budget is to complete the balance sheet. You project each asset, liability, and owners' equity account based on the plans outlined in the previous exhibits. Exhibit 23-14 presents the budgeted balance sheet. Study Exhibit 23-14 carefully to make certain you understand the computation of each figure on the budgeted balance sheet.

EXHIBIT 23-14
Budgeted Balance Sheet

WHITEWATER SPORTING GOODS STORE NO. 18		
Budgeted Balance Sheet		
July 31, 19X9		
Assets		
Current assets:		
Cash (Exhibit 23-13)..	$ 22,525	
Accounts receivable (Schedule A, Exhibit 23-7).........................	20,000	
Inventory (Schedule B, Exhibit 23-8)...	42,400	
Prepaid insurance (beginning balance of $1,800 – $800		
for four months' expiration; Schedule C, Exhibit 23-9)...........	1,000	$ 85,925
Plant assets:		
Equipment and fixtures (beginning balance of $32,000 +		
$3,000 truck acquisition; item 8, page 998)	$ 35,000	
Accumulated depreciation (beginning balance of $12,800 +		
$2,000 for four months' depreciation; Schedule C,		
Exhibit 23-9)	(14,800)	20,200
Total assets...		$106,125
Liabilities		
Current liabilities:		
Accounts payable (0.50 × July purchases of $29,400;		
Schedule B, Exhibit 23-8)	$14,700	
Short-term note payable ($9,000 – $4,500 paid back;		
Exhibit 23-13)...	4,500	
Salary and commissions payable (0.50 × July expenses of		
$10,000; Schedule C, Exhibit 23-9)......................................	5,000	
Total liabilities...		$ 24,200
Owners' Equity		
Owners' equity (beginning balance of $78,950 + $2,975		
net income; Exhibit 23-6)		81,925
Total liabilities and owners' equity		$106,125

PREPARING THE BUDGETED STATEMENT OF CASH FLOWS   The final step in preparing the master budget is completing the budgeted statement of cash flows. Use the information from the schedules of cash collections and disbursements, the cash budget, and the beginning balance of cash to project cash flows from operating, investing, and financing activities. Take your time to study Exhibit 23-15, and make sure you understand the origin of each figure on the budgeted statement of cash flows.

Now the *master budget* is complete. It consists of the budgeted financial statements and all supporting schedules.

Summary of Budgeting Procedures

The most important budget documents are the budgeted income statement (Exhibit 23-6), the cash budget (Exhibit 23-13), and the budgeted balance sheet (Exhibit 23-14). Top management analyzes these statements to ensure that all the budgeted figures are consistent with company goals. As the business strives to reach those goals, management controls operations by comparing actual results with the budget, as shown in performance reports like Exhibit 23-3.

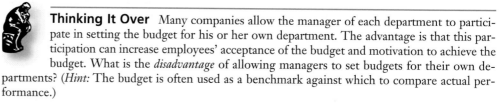

Thinking It Over   Many companies allow the manager of each department to participate in setting the budget for his or her own department. The advantage is that this participation can increase employees' acceptance of the budget and motivation to achieve the budget. What is the *disadvantage* of allowing managers to set budgets for their own departments? (*Hint:* The budget is often used as a benchmark against which to compare actual performance.)

Answer: Managers who are evaluated by comparing their department's actual results to the budget have incentives to build *slack* into their budgets. For example, the manager might budget sales to be less than she really expected, and budget purchases costs higher than really expected. This increases the chance that her department's actual performance will be better than the budget, and that the manager will receive a favorable performance evaluation. Consequently, higher-level managers usually negotiate with lower-level managers to remove at least part of the slack lower-level managers add to the budget.

EXHIBIT 23-15
Budgeted Statement of Cash Flows

WHITEWATER SPORTING GOODS STORE NO. 18 Budgeted Statement of Cash Flows Four Months Ending July 31, 19X9		
Cash flows from operating activities:		
Receipts:		
Collections from customers (Schedule D, Exhibit 23-10)	$ 236,000	
Total cash receipts		$236,000
Disbursements:		
Purchases of inventory (Schedule E, Exhibit 23-11).............	$(164,500)	
Operating expenses, excluding interest expense		
(Schedule F, Exhibit 23-12)...................................	(65,250)	
Payment of interest expense (Exhibits 23-13 and 23-6).........	(225)	
Total cash disbursements		(229,975)
Net cash inflow from operating activities..................................		6,025
Cash flows from investing activities:		
Acquisition of delivery truck (item 8, page 998)	$ (3,000)	
Net cash outflow from investing activities		(3,000)
Cash flows from financing activities:		
Proceeds from issuance of notes payable (Exhibit 23-13).........	$ 9,000	
Payment of notes payable (Exhibit 23-13)	(4,500)	
Net cash inflow from financing activities................................		4,500
Net increase in cash		$ 7,525
Cash balance, April 1, 19X9 (Exhibit 23-5)		15,000
Cash balance, July 31, 19X9 (Exhibits 23-13 and 23-14).............		$ 22,525

Budgeting and Sensitivity Analysis

Objective 4

Use sensitivity analysis in budgeting

The master budget is a model of the organization's *planned* activities. But actual results often deviate from plans. This is why managers conduct sensitivity analyses to plan for various possibilities. **Sensitivity analysis** is a what-if technique that asks *what* a result will be *if* a predicted amount is not achieved or *if* an underlying assumption changes. *What* operating income will Ritz-Carlton earn *if* room occupancy is 10% less than predicted? Will Ritz-Carlton have to postpone an equipment purchase? *What* will be Whitewater Store No. 18's cash balance on July 31 *if* the period's sales are 45% cash, not 60% cash? Will Whitewater need to borrow more cash?

Sensitivity Analysis. A what-if technique that asks what a result will be if a predicted amount is not achieved or if an underlying assumption changes.

■ **Daily Exercise 23-14**

Sensitivity analyses may affect very specific plans. For example, suppose that Ford Motor Company executives examine different levels of car sales for May. Their analysis may lead to changes in Ford's materials purchasing plan and projected cash payments to individual suppliers, not just for May but also for June and July.

Many companies use computer spreadsheet programs to prepare master budget schedules and statements. In fact, one of the earliest spreadsheet programs was developed by graduate business students specifically to perform master budget sensitivity analyses. The students realized that computers could take the drudgery out of hand-computed master budget sensitivity analyses. Managers and accountants could answer what-if questions simply by changing a number. At the press of a key, the computer prepares a revised budget that includes all the effects of the change. The computer's ability to provide a nearly instant display of changes makes sensitivity analysis a powerful planning tool.

Thinking It Over Consider two budget situations: (1) Whitewater Sporting Goods' marketing analysts produce a near-certain forecast for four-month sales of $4,500,000 for the company's 20 stores. (2) Much uncertainty exists about the period's sales. The most likely amount is $4,500,000, but marketing considers any amount between $3,900,000 and $5,100,000 to be possible. How will the budgeting process differ in these two circumstances?

Answer: Whitewater will prepare a master budget for the expected sales level of $4,500,000 in either case. Because of the uncertainty about sales in situation 2, the company's executives will want a set of budgets covering the entire range of volume rather than a single level. Whitewater's managers may use a spreadsheet program to prepare budgets based on sales of, say, $3,900,000, $4,200,000, $4,500,000, $4,800,000, and $5,100,000. These budgets help managers plan actions for sales levels throughout the forecasted range.

SUMMARY PROBLEM FOR YOUR REVIEW   MID-CHAPTER

Review the Whitewater Sporting Goods example in this chapter. You now think July sales might be $40,000 instead of the projected $50,000 in Exhibit 23-7, page 999. You want to perform a sensitivity analysis to see how this change in sales affects the budget.

1. Revise the sales budget (Schedule A in Exhibit 23-7), the purchases, cost of goods sold, and inventory budget (Schedule B in Exhibit 23-8), and the operating expenses budget (Schedule C in Exhibit 23-9). Prepare a revised budgeted income statement for the four months ended July 31, 19X9.

2. Revise the schedule of budgeted cash collections (Schedule D in Exhibit 23-10), the schedule of budgeted cash disbursements for purchases (Schedule E in Exhibit 23-11), and the schedule of budgeted cash disbursements for operating expenses (Schedule F in Exhibit 23-12). Prepare a revised cash budget, a revised budgeted balance sheet at July 31, 19X9, and a revised budgeted statement of cash flows for the four months ended July 31, 19X9.

REQUIRED

Note: You need not repeat the parts of the revised schedules that do not change.

■ **SOLUTION**

Although not required, this solution repeats the budgeted amounts for April, May, and June. Revised figures appear in boldface type for emphasis.

WHITEWATER SPORTING GOODS STORE NO. 18
REVISED SCHEDULE A—Sales Budget

	April	May	June	July	Total
Cash sales, 60%	$30,000	$48,000	$36,000	**$24,000**	
Credit sales, 40%	20,000	32,000	24,000	**16,000**	
Total sales, 100%	$50,000	$80,000	$60,000	**$40,000**	$230,000

WHITEWATER SPORTING GOODS STORE NO. 18
REVISED SCHEDULE B—Purchases, Cost of Goods Sold, and Inventory Budget

	April	May	June	July	Total
Cost of goods sold ($0.70 \times$ sales, from Revised Schedule A)	$35,000	$ 56,000	$ 42,000	**$28,000**	$161,000
+ Desired ending inventory ($20,000 + 0.80 \times$ cost of goods sold for next month)	64,800	53,600	**42,400**	42,400[†]	
= Total inventory required	99,800	109,600	**84,400**	70,400	
− Beginning inventory	(48,000)*	(64,800)	(53,600)	(42,400)	
= Purchases	$51,800	$ 44,800	$30,800	$28,000	

*Balance at March 31, Exhibit 23-5.
[†]Given in item 5 on page 998.

WHITEWATER SPORTING GOODS STORE NO. 18
REVISED SCHEDULE C—Operating Expenses Budget

	April	May	June	July	Total
Salary, fixed amount	$ 2,500	$ 2,500	$ 2,500	$ 2,500	
Commission, 15% of sales from Revised Schedule A	7,500	12,000	9,000	**6,000**	
Total salary and commissions	10,000	14,500	11,500	**8,500**	$44,500
Rent expense, fixed amount	2,000	2,000	2,000	2,000	8,000
Depreciation expense, fixed amount	500	500	500	500	2,000
Insurance expense, fixed amount	200	200	200	200	800
Miscellaneous expenses, 5% of sales from Revised Schedule A	2,500	4,000	3,000	**2,000**	11,500
Total operating expenses	$15,200	$21,200	$17,200	$13,200	$66,800

WHITEWATER SPORTING GOODS STORE NO. 18
Revised Budgeted Income Statement
Four Months Ending July 31, 19X9

	Amount		Source
Sales		$230,000	Revised Schedule A
Cost of goods sold		161,000	Revised Schedule B
Gross margin		69,000	
Operating expenses:			
Salary and commissions	$44,500		Revised Schedule C
Rent expense	8,000		Revised Schedule C
Depreciation expense	2,000		Revised Schedule C
Insurance expense	800		Revised Schedule C
Miscellaneous expenses	11,500	66,800	Revised Schedule C
Operating income		2,200	
Interest expense		225	Revised Cash Budget
Net income		$ 1,975	

WHITEWATER SPORTING GOODS STORE NO. 18
REVISED SCHEDULE D—Budgeted Cash Collections from Customers

	April	May	June	July	Total
Cash sales, from Revised Schedule A..............	$30,000	$48,000	$36,000	**$24,000**	
Collections of last month's credit sales, from Revised Schedule A	16,000*	20,000	32,000	24,000	
Total collections	$46,000	$68,000	$68,000	**$48,000**	**$230,000**

*March 31 accounts receivable, Exhibit 23-5.

WHITEWATER SPORTING GOODS STORE NO. 18
REVISED SCHEDULE E—Budgeted Cash Disbursements for Purchases of Inventory

	April	May	June	July	Total
50% of last month's purchases, from Revised Schedule B...................................	$16,800*	$25,900	$ 22,400	**$15,400**	
50% of this month's purchases, from Revised Schedule B...................................	25,900	22,400	**15,400**	**14,000**	
Total disbursements for purchases	$42,700	$48,300	**$37,800**	**$29,400**	**$158,200**

*March 31 accounts payable, Exhibit 23-5.

WHITEWATER SPORTING GOODS STORE NO. 18
REVISED SCHEDULE F—Budgeted Cash Disbursements for Operating Expenses

	April	May	June	July	Total
Expense amounts, from Revised Schedule C:					
Salary and commissions:					
50% of last month's expenses, from Revised Schedule C	$ 4,250*	$ 5,000	$ 7,250	$ 5,750	
50% of this month's expenses, from Revised Schedule C	5,000	7,250	5,750	**4,250**	
Total salary and commissions	9,250	12,250	13,000	**10,000**	
Rent expense, from Revised Schedule C	2,000	2,000	2,000	2,000	
Miscellaneous expenses, from Revised Schedule C..........	2,500	4,000	3,000	**2,000**	
Total disbursements for operating expenses	$13,750	$18,250	$18,000	**$14,000**	**$64,000**

*March 31 salary and commissions payable, Exhibit 23-5.

WHITEWATER SPORTING GOODS STORE NO. 18
Revised Cash Budget
Four Months Ending July 31, 19X9

	April	May	June	July
Beginning cash balance	$15,000*	$10,550	$ 10,410	**$21,035**
Cash collections from customers (Revised Schedule D)	46,000	68,000	68,000	**48,000**
Cash available	$61,000	$78,550	$ 78,410	**$69,035**
Cash disbursements:				
Purchases of inventory (Revised Schedule E)	$42,700	$48,300	**$37,800**	**$29,400**
Operating expenses (Revised Schedule F)	13,750	18,250	18,000	**14,000**
Purchase of delivery truck (Item 8, page 998)	3,000	—	—	—
Total cash disbursements	59,450	66,550	**55,800**	**43,400**
(1) Ending cash balance before financing	1,550	12,000	**22,610**	**25,635**
Minimum cash balance desired	10,000	10,000	10,000	10,000
Cash excess (deficiency)	$ (8,450)	$ 2,000	**$12,610**	**$15,635**
Financing of cash deficiency (see notes a–c):				
Borrowing (at end of month)	$ 9,000			
Principal payments (at end of month)		$ (1,500)	$ (1,500)	$ (1,500)
Interest expense (at 12% annually)		(90)	(75)	(60)
(2) Total effects of financing	9,000	(1,590)	(1,575)	(1,560)
Ending cash balance (1) + (2)	$10,550	$10,410	**$21,035**	**$24,075**

*March 31 cash balance, Exhibit 23-5.

Notes

a. Borrowing occurs in multiples of $1,000 and only for the amount needed to maintain a minimum cash balance of $10,000.

b. Monthly principal payments: $9,000 ÷ 6 = $1,500

c. Interest expense:

  May: $9,000 × (0.12 × 1/12) = $90

  June: ($9,000 − $1,500) × (0.12 × 1/12) = $75

  July: ($9,000 − $1,500 − $1,500)× (0.12 × 1/12) = $60

WHITEWATER SPORTING GOODS STORE NO. 18
Revised Budgeted Balance Sheet
July 31, 19X9

Assets

Current assets:		
Cash (Revised Cash budget)	$24,075	
Accounts receivable (Revised Schedule A)	**16,000**	
Inventory	42,400	
Prepaid insurance	1,000	$ 83,475
Plant assets:		
Equipment and fixtures	$ 35,000	
Accumulated depreciation	(14,800)	20,200
Total assets		$103,675

Liabilities

Current liabilities:		
Accounts payable (0.50 × July purchases of **$28,000**;		
Revised Schedule B)	$14,000	
Short-term note payable	4,500	
Salary and commissions payable (0.50 × July		
expenses of **$8,500**; Revised Schedule C)	4,250	
Total liabilities		$ 22,750

Owners' Equity

Owners' equity (beginning balance of $78,950 + **$1,975**		
net income, Revised Budgeted Income Statement)		80,925
Total liabilities and owners' equity		$103,675

WHITEWATER SPORTING GOODS STORE NO. 18 Revised Budgeted Statement of Cash Flows Four Months Ending July 31, 19X9		
Cash flows from operating activities:		
Receipts:		
Collections from customers (Revised Schedule D)	$ 230,000	
Total cash receipts		$230,000
Disbursements:		
Purchases of inventory (Revised Schedule E)	(158,200)	
Operating expenses, excluding interest expense (Revised Schedule F)	(64,000)	
Payment of interest expense	(225)	
Total cash disbursements		(222,425)
Net cash inflow from operating activities		7,575
Cash flows from investing activities:		
Acquisition of delivery truck	$ (3,000)	
Net cash outflow from investing activities		(3,000)
Cash flows from financing activities:		
Proceeds from issuance of notes payable	$ 9,000	
Payment of notes payable	(4,500)	
Net cash inflow from financing activities		4,500
Net increase in cash		$ 9,075
Cash balance, April 1, 19X9 (Exhibit 23-5)		15,000
Cash balance, July 31, 19X9 (Revised Cash Budget)		$ 24,075

Responsibility Accounting

Objective 5

Distinguish among different types of responsibility centers

■ **Daily Exercise 23-15**

To achieve the goals of the master budget, a company must coordinate the actions of all its employees, from hourly wage earners to the chief executive officer. Each manager is responsible for planning and controlling some portion of the firm's activities. At lower levels, a manager's responsibility may be defined by value-chain function. For example, one manager is responsible for *design* of Ford Explorer engines; another manager for *production* of Explorers at Ford's Louisville, Kentucky, plant; and a third for *distribution* of Explorers to dealerships.

Managers at higher levels are responsible for product lines. Ford's vice president, Truck Vehicle Center, is ultimately responsible for the entire engineering cycle of the Explorer line. Lower-level managers are accountable to the vice president for meeting their budget goals, just as that executive is accountable to the president of Ford Motor Company, Automotive Operations.

"Ford's vice president, Truck Vehicle Center, is ultimately responsible for the entire engineering cycle of the Explorer line."

How does a business evaluate the performance of managers and the activities they supervise? By comparing plans (budgets) with actions (actual results) for each responsibility center. A **responsibility center** is a part or subunit of an organization whose manager is accountable for specific activities. In the chapter opening story, the individual Ritz-Carlton hotels are responsibility centers. **Responsibility accounting** is a system for evaluating the performance of each responsibility center and its manager. Exhibit 23-16 illustrates four common types of responsibility centers: cost centers, revenue centers, profit centers, and investment centers.

Responsibility Center. A part or subunit of an organization whose manager is accountable for specific activities.

Responsibility Accounting. A system for evaluating the performance of each responsibility center and its manager.

1. *Cost center: A responsibility center where managers are accountable for costs (expenses) only.* Examples include a Ritz-Carlton hotel's Housekeeping Department or Personnel Department. It is important for these departments to control costs; but they are not responsible for generating revenues. Consequently, only costs are reported for their

(a) A **cost center**, such as a personnel department—where managers are responsible for costs

(b) A **revenue center**, such as Ford's Midwest sales region—where managers are responsible for generating sales revenue

(c) A **profit center**, such as a Sears appliance department—where managers are responsible for generating income

(d) An **investment center**, such as General Motors' Saturn car division—where managers are responsible for income and invested capital

activities. The Housekeeping Department manager is evaluated, for example, on the cost of cleaning a certain number of hotel rooms.

2. *Revenue center: A responsibility center where managers are primarily accountable for revenues.* Examples include the Midwest and Southeast sales regions of companies like Ford and Reebok. Managers of revenue centers are primarily responsible for generating sales revenue, although they may also be held responsible for costs of their own sales operations. Revenue center performance reports include revenues and, perhaps, the costs incurred by the revenue center itself.

3. *Profit center: A responsibility center where managers are accountable for revenues and costs (expenses).* Examples are a Bennigan's restaurant and the appliance department of a Sears store. Managers of these profit centers are responsible for generating income (revenues minus expenses). Both revenues and expenses are reported to show the income of a profit center.

4. *Investment center: A responsibility center where managers are accountable for investments, revenues, and costs (expenses).* Examples are the Nevada region of Safeway Stores, the Nutrasweet Company which is owned by Monsanto, and the Saturn division of General Motors. Investment in the business is reported in addition to revenues and expenses so that return on investment (income divided by investment) can be computed. ◀▥ Top managers, like investors, evaluate these responsibility centers by comparing their returns with required investments.

◀▥ ◀▥ ◀▥   Chapter 18 introduced a common return on investment measure—the rate of return on total assets.

Example of Responsibility Accounting

The simplified organization chart in Exhibit 23-17 shows how a company may assign responsibility in the fast-food industry. At the top level of O'Toole Restaurant Corporation, the Northern California district manager oversees the branch managers, who supervise the managers of the individual restaurants (called stores).

Store managers have limited freedom to make operating decisions. They may decide the quantities of food to order, the number of employees and their schedules, and store hours. Branch managers oversee several stores, evaluate store managers' performance, and set store managers' compensation levels. In turn, district managers oversee several branches, evaluate branch managers' performance and compensation, set food prices, and approve sales promotions. District managers are accountable to regional managers, who answer to home-office vice presidents.

 Thinking It Over O'Toole's store managers do not have authority to set sale prices or control advertising. Both factors affect store revenues. But the corporation nevertheless evaluates each store as a profit center instead of as a cost center. Why?

Answer: O'Toole's top management could have designated each store as a cost center. But then each store manager would be motivated to cut costs to keep actual costs below the budget. Excessive cost cutting can hurt quality and service. By evaluating each store as a profit center, executives give store managers the incentive to keep stores clean and to ensure that employees provide fast and friendly service. Store managers thus are more likely to work hard to increase customer satisfaction, the foundation of long-run profitability.

Exhibit 23-18 provides a more detailed view of how managers can use responsibility accounting performance reports to evaluate profit centers. At each level, the reports compare actual results with the budget. Examine the lowest level and move to the top. Follow how the reports are related through the three levels of responsibility.

Trace the $54,000 operating income from the Beale store manager's report to the San Francisco branch manager's report. The branch manager's report summarizes the results of the stores under his supervision. In addition, charges incurred by the branch manager's office are included in this report.

Now trace the $465,000 total from the San Francisco branch manager's report to the Northern California district manager's report. The report of the district manager includes data for her own district office plus a summary of each branch's operating performance.

Management by Exception

Exhibit 23-18 stresses variances from budget. This reporting format aids **management by exception**, which directs executives' attention to important differences between

Management by Exception. Directs management's attention to important differences between actual and budgeted amounts.

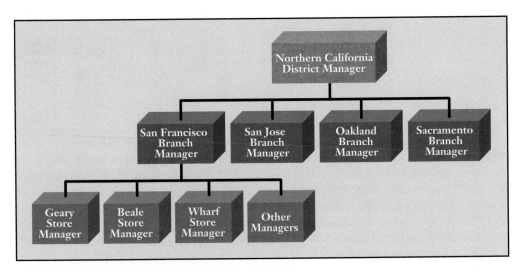

EXHIBIT 23-17
O'Toole Restaurant Corporation Partial Organization Chart

O'TOOLE RESTAURANT CORPORATION
Responsibility Accounting at Various Levels
(In Thousands of Dollars)

NORTHERN CALIFORNIA DISTRICT MANAGER—
Monthly Responsibility Report

Operating Income of Branches and District Manager Office Expense	Budget		Actual		Variance Favorable/(Unfavorable)	
	This Month	Year to Date	This Month	Year to Date	This Month	Year to Date
District manager office expense	$ (150)	$ (600)	$ (154)	$ (620)	$ (4)	$(20)
San Francisco branch	465	1,730	460	1,780	(5)	50
San Jose branch	500	1,800	560	1,994	60	194
Oakland branch	390	1,540	475	1,855	85	315
Sacramento branch	520	2,240	468	2,061	(52)	(179)
Operating income	$1,725	$6,710	$1,809	$7,070	$84	$360

SAN FRANCISCO BRANCH MANAGER—
Monthly Responsibility Report

Operating Income of Stores and Branch Manager Office Expense	Budget		Actual		Variance Favorable/(Unfavorable)	
	This Month	Year to Date	This Month	Year to Date	This Month	Year to Date
Branch manager office expense	$ (20)	$ (306)	$ (25)	$ (302)	$(5)	$ 4
Geary store	48	148	40	136	(8)	(12)
Beale store	54	228	61	244	7	16
Wharf store	38	160	42	170	4	10
Others	345	1,500	342	1,532	(3)	32
Operating income	$465	$1,730	$460	$1,780	$(5)	$50

BEALE STORE MANAGER—
Monthly Responsibility Report

Revenues and Expenses	Budget		Actual		Variance Favorable/(Unfavorable)	
	This Month	Year to Date	This Month	Year to Date	This Month	Year to Date
Revenues	$170	$690	$178	$702	$8	$12
Food expense	50	198	45	184	5	14
Paper expense	15	62	18	64	(3)	(2)
Wages expense	24	98	28	103	(4)	(5)
Repairs expense	5	19	4	20	1	(1)
General expense	12	45	12	47	—	(2)
Depreciation expense	10	40	10	40	—	—
Total expenses	116	462	117	458	(1)	4
Operating income	$ 54	$228	$ 61	$244	$7	$16

EXHIBIT 23-18
Responsibility Accounting
Performance Report

■ Daily Exercise 23-16
■ Daily Exercise 23-17
■ Daily Exercise 23-18

actual and budgeted amounts. Look at the district manager's report, and consider the San Francisco branch. Its actual operating income of $460,000 is very close to its budget for the current month ($465,000). Under management by exception, the district manager will not waste time investigating such a small variance. In contrast, both the San Jose and Oakland branches substantially exceeded budgeted performance. The district manager will want to determine the causes of these large favorable variances. For example, suppose that the Oakland manager believes that a local sales promotion was especially effective. That promotion may be repeated and may also be used in other cities.

Learning Tip: Managers investigate large favorable variances as well as large unfavorable variances. A large favorable variance could reflect good performance. But a large favorable variance for costs such as food or repairs could indicate that the store manager is skimping on the food served or postponing maintenance and repairs.

The Northern California district manager will concentrate her efforts on improving the Sacramento branch. Its actual income of $468,000 is 10% ($52,000 ÷ $520,000) lower than its budget. The district manager may ask to see the Sacramento branch manager's monthly responsibility report. That report reveals whether the income shortfall is due to excessively high office expenses, below-budget operating income from individual stores, or both. The two managers will work together to identify and correct any problems.

Exhibit 23-18 also shows that highly summarized data may hide problems. Although the San Francisco branch as a whole performed well, the Geary store did not. Its actual income of $40,000 is 16.7% ($8,000 ÷ $48,000) below its budgeted amount. This shortfall is offset by excellent performances by the Beale and Wharf stores. If the district manager receives only the condensed report at the top of the exhibit, she must rely on branch managers to spot and correct problems with individual stores. Some upper-level executives prefer the more-detailed middle-level reports so they can keep tighter control over their responsibility centers (districts, in this example).

The performance report format in Exhibit 23-18 can be expanded to provide more information about variances. The first line of the Beale store manager's report might be extended as follows:

	Budget		Actual		Variance: Favorable/(Unfavorable)		Variance: Percent of Budgeted Amount	
	This Month	Year to Date	This Month	Year to Date	This Month	Year to Date	This Month	Year to Date
Revenues	$170	$690	$178	$702	$8	$12	4.7%	1.7%

What caused the Beale store's $8,000 favorable revenue variance? Perhaps it sold more meals than expected. Or perhaps the average sale price per meal was higher than budgeted. Similarly, the revenue variance of a Ritz-Carlton hotel can be divided by cause: the difference between the budgeted and actual (1) number of rooms rented, and (2) average room rental rate. Chapter 24 considers such variances in more detail.

No single reporting format appeals to all managers—some prefer more detail, others less. The choice is a matter of personal preference.

Not a Question of Blame

Responsibility accounting is a management tool. It helps top executives delegate decisions. Responsibility accounting assigns lower-level managers responsibility for their unit's actions and provides a way to evaluate the manager's and unit's performance. By allowing top managers to delegate decisions, responsibility accounting and management by exception free top managers to concentrate on strategic issues that affect the entire business.

Responsibility accounting systems should not be misused to find fault or to place blame. The question is not, Who should be blamed for an unfavorable variance? Instead, the question is, Who is in the best position to explain why a specific variance occurred? Consider again the performance of the Sacramento branch in Exhibit 23-18. Suppose that a month of unusually nasty weather resulted in a 15% drop in restaurant volume. It may be that only efficient operations by the branch's stores kept the income variance as low as $52,000 (only 10% below the budget). Therefore, the Sacramento branch manager may have done a good job despite the unfavorable variance.

Departmental Accounting

Responsibility centers are often called *departments*. Consider a department store such as Macy's, Lazarus, or Nordstrom. Top managers of a department store want more information than just the net income of the store as a whole. At a minimum, they want to know each department's gross margin (sales minus cost of goods sold). They also usually want to know each department's operating income. These data can help identify the most profitable departments, so managers can decide whether to expand some departments and phase out others.

It is easy to measure gross margin for each department because the department keeps records for sales and cost of goods sold. However, it is more difficult to measure a department's operating income (gross margin minus operating expenses). Why? Many operating expenses are indirect costs that are not directly traceable to the department.

As we discussed in Chapter 19, *direct costs* are traceable to a particular department or product. Consider Macy's Shoe Department. Clerks' wages, the cost of ads for shoes, and depreciation on display racks are all directly traceable to the Shoe Department. *Indirect costs*—all expenses other than direct costs—are not traceable to a single department. For example, Macy's Receiving Department and Stockroom serve all departments. How should Macy's allocate the cost of its Receiving Department and its Stockroom?

Allocation of Indirect Costs

Chapters 20 and 21 explained how indirect costs are allocated to *products*. Indirect costs are allocated to *departments* or responsibility centers using a similar process.

- Choose an allocation base for the indirect cost
- Compute an indirect cost allocation rate:

> Divide the total indirect costs by the total quantity of the allocation base

- Allocate the indirect cost:

> Multiply the quantity of the allocation base used by the
> department times the indirect cost allocation rate

As we discussed in Chapter 20, the ideal cost allocation base is also a cost driver. Because different costs have different cost drivers, a company can use several different allocation bases to allocate different indirect costs to the various departments. Exhibit 23-19 lists common allocation bases for different indirect costs.

Consider Macy's receiving costs. Suppose Macy's decides that these costs are driven by the number of orders placed to purchase inventory. If 15% of the orders are for the Shoe Department and 20% are for the Menswear Department, then Macy's will allocate 15% of the Receiving Department costs to the Shoe Department and 20% to the Menswear Department. (The remaining Receiving Department costs will be allocated to other departments in proportion to the number of orders each issued.)

There is no single "correct" allocation base for each indirect cost. Managers use their experience and judgment to choose these bases. If managers help identify cost allocation bases, they will be more confident that the indirect cost allocations are reasonable.

■ **Daily Exercise 23-19**

EXHIBIT 23-19
Bases for Allocating Costs to Departments

Cost or Expense	Base for Allocating Cost to Departments
Direct materials	Separately traced
Merchandise inventory purchases	Separately traced
Direct labor	Separately traced
Other labor	Time spent in each department
Supervision	Time spent, or number of employees, in each department
Equipment depreciation	Separately traced, or hours used by each department
Building depreciation, property taxes	Square feet of space
Heat, light, and air conditioning	Square feet or cubic feet of space
Janitorial services	Square feet of space
Advertising	Separately traced if possible; otherwise, in proportion to sales
Materials Handling Department	Number or weight of items handled for each department
Payroll Department	Number of employees in each department
Personnel Department	Number of employees in each department
Purchasing Department	Number of purchase orders placed for each department

An Illustration

Exhibit 23-20 shows a departmental income statement for WorldPC, a retail computer store. We focus on the allocation of indirect operating expenses to the store's two departments: Hardware and Software.

SALARIES AND WAGES Salespersons' salaries and department managers' salaries are directly traced to each department.

RENT WorldPC allocates the $600,000 rent expense based on the square feet occupied by each department. The Hardware and Software Departments occupy 20,000 square feet and 5,000 square feet, respectively. Rent is allocated as follows:

■ **Daily Exercise 23-20**

Rent for entire store	$600,000
Total square feet (20,000 + 5,000)	÷ 25,000
Rent per square foot	$ 24

Hardware Department: 20,000 square feet × $24 per square foot = $480,000
Software Department: 5,000 square feet × $24 per square foot = 120,000
Total rent expense = $600,000

PURCHASING DEPARTMENT WorldPC found that it takes just as long to complete a purchase order for inexpensive modems as for expensive "loaded" notebook computers. Consequently, the company allocates the $48,000 costs of the Purchasing Department based on the number of purchase orders processed. Hardware had 300 purchase orders, while Software had 100 purchase orders.

Purchasing Department costs	$48,000
Total number of purchase orders (300 + 100).........	÷ 400
Cost per purchase order	$ 120

Hardware Department: 300 purchase orders × $120 per purchase order = $36,000
Software Department: 100 purchase orders × $120 per purchase order = 12,000
Total Purchase Department cost = $48,000

WorldPC's top executives can use the departmental income statements in Exhibit 23-20 to evaluate how well each department and its manager performed in 19X9. The Hardware Department was more profitable than the Software Department. Hardware's profit margin (income divided by sales) was $1,324 ÷ $7,000 = 18.9%, while Software's profit margin was only $128 ÷ $3,000 = 4.3%. However, it is usually better to compare a department's actual results to its budget, rather than to another department's results. For example, if WorldPC just added the Software Department, performance may have exceeded expectations.

	Total	Department Hardware	Software
WORLD PC Departmental Income Statement Year Ended December 31, 19X9 (In Thousands)			
Sales revenue	$10,000	$7,000	$3,000
Cost of goods sold...................................	6,500	4,500	2,000
Gross margin	3,500	2,500	1,000
Operating expenses:			
Salaries and wages expense..................	1,400	660	740
Rent expense.......................................	600	480	120
Purchasing department expense..........	48	36	12
Total operating expenses	2,048	1,176	872
Operating income...................................	$ 1,452	$1,324	$ 128

EXHIBIT 23-20
Departmental Income Statement

The following Decision Guidelines feature reviews budgets and how they are used in responsibility accounting. Take a moment to study these guidelines before working the summary review problem.

DECISION GUIDELINES — The Master Budget and Responsibility Accounting

DECISION	GUIDELINES
Why should a company develop a budget?	• Requires managers to plan • Promotes organization and communication • Helps managers evaluate performance by providing a benchmark • Motivates employees
In what order should you prepare the components of the master budget?	Begin with the *operating budget.* • Start with the *sales budget,* which feeds into all other budgets. • The sales and *ending inventory budgets* determine the *purchases* and *cost of goods sold budgets.* • The sales, cost of goods sold, and *operating expense budgets* determine the *budgeted income statement.* Next, prepare the *capital expenditures budget.* Finally, prepare the *financial budget.* • Start with the *cash budget.* • The cash budget provides the ending cash balance for the *budgeted balance sheet,* and the details for the *budgeted statement of cash flows.*
What if the sales forecast is uncertain?	Prepare a *sensitivity analysis* and project budgeted results at different sales levels.
How to compute budgeted purchases?	$$\text{Beginning inventory} + \text{Purchases} - \text{Ending inventory} = \text{Cost of goods sold}$$ so $$\text{Purchases} = \text{Cost of goods sold} + \text{Ending inventory} - \text{Beginning inventory}$$
What kind of a responsibility center does a given manager supervise?	Cost center: Manager is responsible for costs. Revenue center: Manager is responsible for revenues. Profit center: Manager is responsible for both revenues and costs. Investment center: Manager is responsible for revenues, costs, and the amount of the investment required to earn these revenues.
How to evaluate managers?	Compare actual performance with the budget for the manager's responsibility center. *Management by exception* focuses only on large differences between budgeted and actual results.
How to identify the most profitable departments or product lines?	Departmental or product line income statements
How to allocate indirect costs to departments or product lines?	1. Choose an allocation base for each indirect cost. 2. Compute an indirect cost allocation rate: $$\frac{\text{Total indirect cost (\$)}}{\text{Total quantity of allocation base}}$$ 3. Allocate the indirect cost: Multiply the quantity of the allocation base used by the department or product line by the indirect cost allocation rate.

The Ritz-Carlton Club, an exclusive "hotel within a hotel," provides an even more luxurious atmosphere than the hotel's regular accommodations. Access is limited to guests residing on the hotel's top floors. The Club's private lounge serves complimentary continental breakfast, afternoon snacks, and evening cocktails and chocolates. The Club has its own concierge staff that provides personal service to Club guests. Guests staying in regular accommodations do not receive complimentary snacks and beverages, nor do they have a private concierge.

Ritz-Carlton Club floors are considered one department, and regular accommodations are considered a separate department.

Suppose the general manager of the new Ritz-Carlton hotel in St. Thomas, an island in the West Indies, wants to know the costs of her hotel's Club Accommodations Department and Regular Accommodations Department. Housekeeping costs are allocated based on the number of occupied room-nights, utilities are allocated based on the number of cubic feet, and building depreciation is allocated based on the number of square feet. Assume each department reports the following information for March:

	Club Accommodations	Regular Accommodations
Number of occupied room-nights	540	7,560
Cubic feet	192,000	1,440,000
Square feet...	16,000	144,000

1. Given the following (assumed) total costs, what are the costs assigned to the Club Accommodations and the Regular Accommodations Departments?

REQUIRED

Food and beverage expense	$ 12,000
Housekeeping expense......................	194,400
Utilities expense.................................	97,920
Building depreciation expense..........	480,000
Concierge staff salaries	15,000
Total	$799,320

2. What is the cost per occupied room in Club Accommodations? In Regular Accommodations?

■ Daily Exercise 23-21

■ SOLUTION

Cost assignment

REQUIREMENT 1

	Club Accommodations	Regular Accommodations	Total
Food and beverage expense[a]	$12,000	$ —	$ 12,000
Housekeeping expense[b]......................	12,960	181,440	194,400
Utilities expense[c]	11,520	86,400	97,920
Building depreciation expense[d]..........	48,000	432,000	480,000
Concierge staff salaries[a]....................	15,000	—	15,000
Total...	$99,480	$699,840	$799,320

[a]Food and beverage expenses and concierge staff salaries are directly traced to the Club Accommodations Department.

[b]Housekeeping expense

$$\text{Cost per occupied room} = \frac{\$194,400}{540 + 7,560}$$

$$= \$24/\text{room}$$

Club Accommodations: 540 rooms × $24/room = $ 12,960
Regular Accommodations: 7,560 rooms × $24/room = 181,440
Total housekeeping expense.................................. = $194,400

[c]Utilities expense

$$\text{Cost per cubic foot} = \frac{\$97,920}{192,000 + 1,440,000}$$

$$= \$0.06/\text{cubic foot}$$

Club Accommodations: 192,000 cu. ft. × $0.06/cu. ft. = $11,520
Regular Accommodations: 1,440,000 cu. ft. × $0.06/cu. ft. = 86,400
Total utilities expense.. = $97,920

[d]Building depreciation expense

$$\text{Cost per square foot} = \frac{\$480,000}{16,000 + 144,000}$$

$$= \$3/\text{square foot}$$

Club Accommodations: 16,000 sq. ft. × $3/sq. ft. = $ 48,000
Regular Accommodations: 144,000 sq. ft. × $3/sq. ft. = 432,000
Total building depreciation expense .... = $480,000

Cost per occupied room

	Club Accommodations	Regular Accommodations
Total costs	$99,480	$699,840
÷ Occupied rooms	÷ 540	÷ 7,560
= Cost per occupied room.................	$184.22	$ 92.57

Summary of Learning Objectives

1. *Identify the benefits of budgeting.* A budget is a quantitative expression of a plan of action that helps managers coordinate and implement the plan. Budgets require managers to plan, coordinate activities, and communicate plans throughout the company. Budgets also help managers evaluate performance, and motivate employees to achieve goals. Most companies prepare a master budget for each fiscal year. The *master budget* consists of the operating budget, the capital expenditures budget, and the financial budget.

2. *Prepare an operating budget for a company.* The *operating budget* sets the target revenues and expenses—and thus operating income—for the period. To budget income, accountants must budget sales, inventory, purchases, cost of goods sold, and operating expenses. Sales revenue is budgeted first because other income statement elements—and some assets and liabilities—depend on sales volume.

3. *Prepare the components of a financial budget.* A capital expenditures budget presents plans for purchasing long-term capital assets. This budget and the budgeted income statement provide data for the cash budget. All three are used to prepare the budgeted balance sheet and the budgeted statement of cash flows.

4. *Use sensitivity analysis in budgeting.* Managers should make contingency plans in case actual results differ from predictions. *Sensitivity analysis* is a what-if technique for assessing the effects of changes on a company's operations and financial position.

Many managers use spreadsheets to study a broad range of budget possibilities.

5. *Distinguish among different types of responsibility centers.* Most companies are organized by *responsibility centers* to establish authority for planning and controlling business operations. *Responsibility accounting* is a system for evaluating the performance of responsibility centers and their managers. Four types of responsibility centers are: cost centers, revenue centers, profit centers, and investment centers.

6. *Prepare a performance report for management by exception.* Performance reports show differences between budgeted and actual amounts. By focusing on important variances, managers can direct attention to areas that need improvement. This is called *management by exception.*

7. *Allocate indirect costs to departments.* Indirect costs are allocated to responsibility centers called departments. The process is similar to the allocation of indirect costs to products, as explained in Chapter 20. The first step is to choose an allocation base, which ideally should be a cost driver. The second step is to calculate an indirect cost allocation rate: Divide the total amount of the indirect costs by the total quantity of the allocation base. Third, use this indirect cost allocation rate to allocate indirect costs to departments: Multiply the quantity of the allocation base used by the department times the indirect cost allocation rate.

Accounting Vocabulary

capital expenditures budget *(p. 995)*
cash budget *(p. 1001)*
financial budget *(p. 995)*
management by exception *(p. 1011)*

master budget *(p. 995)*
operating budget *(p. 995)*
responsibility accounting *(p. 1009)*

responsibility center *(p. 1009)*
sensitivity analysis *(p. 1005)*

statement of budgeted cash receipts and disbursements *(p. 1001)*

Questions

1. What are four benefits of budgeting?
2. How does a manager use a performance report?
3. List the components of a master budget.
4. A Ford dealer sets a goal of selling more Ford automobiles than any other dealer in the city. Is this goal a budget? Give your reason.
5. Taft Corporation installs a budgeting system in which the president sets all the goals for the company. The vice president checks up on all 90 employees to ensure that they are meeting the president's budget goals. What is the weakness in this budgeting system? How can the system be improved?
6. Why should the capital expenditures budget be prepared before the cash budget, the budgeted balance sheet, and the budgeted statement of cash flows?
7. How does a company budget inventory purchases? In your answer, show the relationships among purchases, cost of goods sold, and inventory.

8. Outline the four steps in preparing an operating budget.
9. Is sales forecasting important only to a profit-seeking business, or is it used by nonprofit organizations such as colleges and hospitals? Give your reason.
10. Why are computer spreadsheets well suited for budgeting?
11. What three amounts are included in the "financing" section of the cash budget?
12. Which manager will control expenses better: Grant, whose performance is measured by his department's sales, or Bruns, whose performance is gauged by her department's income? Why?
13. Identify four types of responsibility centers, and give examples of each. State the information they report.
14. A company owns 50 Burger King restaurants in Philadelphia, Pittsburgh, and Harrisburg. In each city, a local manager oversees operations. Starting at the individual store level, describe the likely flow of information in a responsibility accounting system. What data are reported?

15. What is the objective of management by exception?
16. What question about unfavorable variances is a responsibility accounting system designed to answer? How can managers abuse such a system?
17. Distinguish between direct expenses and indirect expenses of a department in a department store. Give examples of each type.
18. Identify a reasonable allocation base for the following indirect expenses: heating expense, depreciation of manufacturing equipment used by three departments, and advertising expense.
19. Suppose that supplies expense is allocated to departments at the end of each period on the basis of the period's sales. In a recent month, departments X, Y, and Z had sales of $5,000, $12,000, and $8,000, respectively. How much of the month's $900 supplies expense was allocated to each department?
20. Why do managers allocate indirect costs to departments?

Daily Exercises

DE23-1 What are three key roles managers play in running their business operations? How do budgets help managers with each role?

Managers' use of budgets
(Obj. 1)

DE23-2 Consider Ram Dharan's budget for his travel itinerary business (page 992). Explain how Dharan benefits from preparing the budget

Identifying benefits of budgeting
(Obj. 1)

DE23-3 In what order should you prepare the following components of the master budget?

Ordering components of the master budget
(Obj. 2, 3)

Operating expense budget	Budgeted income statement	Capital expenditures budget
Purchases, cost of goods sold, and inventory budgets	Budgeted statement of cash flows	Cash budget
Sales budget	Budgeted balance sheet	

Which are components of the operating budget? Which are components of the financial budget?

DE23-4 In a series of Daily Exercises, we are going to prepare parts of the master budget for Coleman Enterprises, a major West Coast wholesaler of heavy-duty rubber rafts used in whitewater rafting. We will concentrate on Coleman's budget for January and February.

Coleman expects to sell 3,000 rafts for $135 each in January, and 4,500 rafts for $137.50 each in February. All sales are cash only. Prepare the sales budget for January and February.

Preparing a sales budget
(Obj. 2)

DE23-5 Your roommate has recently been hired by A. L. Vickers, an office supplies wholesaler. After seeing Vickers' master budget, your roommate says:

Purchases, cost of goods sold, and inventory budget
(Obj. 2)

> One thing I didn't understand is why there is a *budget* for ending inventory. I thought ending inventory was just what is left over at the end of the period. Why do we need a budget for that? Don't we already know total goods available for sale (beginning inventory plus purchases), so ending inventory is just what's left unsold at the end of the period?
>
> But the master budget seems backwards! In the master budget, it looks like purchases, not ending inventory, is the component that is the "leftover" amount. Can you explain this to me in words so I'll understand what's going on at work tomorrow?

DE23-6 In Daily Exercise 23-4, Coleman's expects cost of goods sold to average 65% of sales revenue, and the company expects to sell 4,300 rafts in March for $137.50 each. Coleman's target ending inventory is $10,000 plus 50% of the next month's cost of goods sold. Use this information and the sales budget from Daily Exercise 23-4 to prepare Coleman's purchases, cost of goods sold, and inventory budget for January and February.

Preparing a purchases, cost of goods sold, and inventory budget
(Obj. 2)

DE23-7 Turn to the Whitewater Sporting Goods example on pages 997–1004. Suppose June sales are expected to be $90,000 rather than $60,000. Revise Whitewater's sales budget (Schedule A).

What other components of Whitewater's master budget would be affected by this change in the sales budget?

Preparing a sales budget
(Obj. 2, 4)

DE23-8 Refer to the original Whitewater Sporting Goods example on pages 997–1004. Suppose cost of goods sold averages 60% of sales rather than 70 percent. Revise Whitewater's purchases, cost of goods sold, and inventory budget (Schedule B) for April and May.

What other components of Whitewater's master budget would be affected by the change in the budgeted cost of goods sold?

Preparing a purchases, cost of goods sold, and inventory budget
(Obj. 2, 4)

DE23-9 Turn to the original Whitewater Sporting Goods example on pages 997–1004. Suppose 70% of sales are cash and only 30% are credit. Revise Whitewater's sales budget (Schedule A) and budgeted cash collections from customers (Schedule D) for April and May.

Preparing a sales budget and cash collections budget
(Obj. 2, 3, 4)

DE23-10 Refer to the original Whitewater Sporting Goods example on pages 997–1004. Suppose Whitewater pays for 60% of inventory purchases in the month of the purchase and 40% during the next month. Revise Whitewater's budgeted cash disbursements for purchases of inventory (Schedule E) for April and May. (*Hint:* Assume these new percentages also apply to March purchases of $33,600.)

Preparing a cash disbursements for purchases budget
(Obj. 3, 4)

DE23-11 You prepared Coleman's sales budget in Daily Exercise 23-4. Now assume that Coleman Enterprise's sales are 25% cash and 75% on credit. Coleman's collection history indicates that credit sales are collected as follows:

- 30% in the month of the sale
- 60% in the month after the sale
- 8% two months after the sale
- 2% are never collected

November sales totaled $391,500 and December sales were $398,250. Prepare a schedule for the budgeted cash collections for January and February.

DE23-12 Refer to Daily Exercise 23-11. Coleman Enterprises has $8,300 cash on hand on January 1. The company requires a minimum cash balance of $7,500. January cash collections are $395,077.50 (as you calculated in Daily Exercise 23-11). Total cash disbursements for January are $483,200. Prepare a cash budget for January. Will Coleman need to borrow cash by the end of January?

DE23-13 Return to the original Whitewater Sporting Goods example on pages 997–1004. Suppose Whitewater can borrow only in notes payable of $2,000 each, at an annual interest rate of 18 percent. The notes payable require eight equal monthly payments of the principal. Whitewater must also pay interest on the unpaid principal. Borrowing and all principal and interest payments occur at the end of the month. Answer the following questions.

1. How much will Whitewater have to borrow in April?
2. How much principal will Whitewater repay each month?
3. How much interest expense will Whitewater pay in May, June, and July?

DE23-14 Personal computer capabilities have increased dramatically. Today employees have more computational power in their desktop computers than entire businesses had in their mainframes only a decade ago. How has this increased computing power affected sensitivity analysis in budgeting?

DE23-15 Fill in the blanks with the phrase that best completes the sentence.

- A cost center
- An investment center
- A profit center
- A responsibility center
- A revenue center
- Higher
- Lower

a. The Menswear Department at Macy's, which is responsible for buying and selling merchandise, is _____.
b. A production line at a Dell computer plant is _____.
c. _____ is any segment of the business whose manager is accountable for specific activities.
d. Gatorade, a division of Quaker Oats, is _____.
e. The sales manager in charge of NIKE's northwest sales territory oversees _____.
f. The Maintenance Department at the Ritz-Carlton hotel in Phoenix is _____.
g. The concession stand at an AMC Theater is _____.
h. Managers of cost and revenue centers are at _____ levels of the organization than are managers of profit and investment centers.

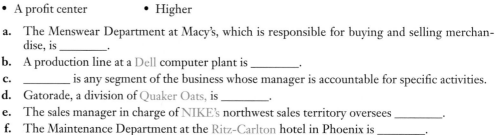

DE23-16 In Exhibit 23-18, the first line of the district manager's report and the first line of the branch manager's report consist entirely of expenses. Describe the kinds of expenses that would be included in these categories. Explain why the store manager's report at the bottom of Exhibit 23-18 does not have a similar expense line item.

DE23-17 Examine the performance report in Exhibit 23-18. On which variances should the Beale store manager focus his efforts next month, according to the management by exception principle? For these variances, compute the variance as a percent of the budgeted amount, and suggest some questions that the Beale store manager may want to investigate.

DE23-18 Exhibit 23-18 shows that the Beale store had unfavorable paper and wage expense variances. Explain how each of these two unfavorable variances could occur even if the Beale store manager was doing an excellent job. In other words, give an explanation how these variances could be due to factors beyond the Beale store manager's control.

DE23-19 Listed below are several cost drivers:

Number of customer complaints

Number of inches

Number of machine hours

Number of pages

Number of square feet

Number of employees

Number of loads of materials moved

Number of purchase orders

Number of shipments received

Which of these is most likely the driver for the following costs?

a. Receiving Department costs
b. Customer Service Department costs
c. Purchasing Department costs
d. Material handling costs
e. Maintenance Department costs
f. Personnel Department costs
g. Building rent and utilities
h. Newspaper advertising costs
i. Photocopying Department costs

DE23-20 Consider the WorldPC example on page 1015. Suppose the Hardware Department occupies 20,000 square feet and the Software Department occupies 10,000 square feet. How would the $600,000 rent expense be allocated?

Allocating indirect costs to departments (Obj. 7)

DE23-21 ◄▥▥ *Link Back to Chapter 20 (uses of product cost information).* Study the summary review problem on pages 1017–1018. Why might the general manager of the new Ritz-Carlton hotel in St. Thomas want to know the cost per occupied room for the Club Accommodations and the Regular Accommodations?

Using departmental costs (Obj. 7)

Exercises

E23-1 Ralph Greenberg owns a store that sells athletic shoes. Last year, his sales staff sold 8,000 pairs of shoes at an average sale price of $65. Variable expenses were 70% of sales revenue, and the total fixed expense was $100,000. This year the store sold more expensive product lines. Sales were 7,000 pairs at an average price of $80. The variable expense percentage and the total fixed expense were the same both years. Greenberg evaluates the store manager by comparing this year's income with last year's income.

    Prepare a performance report for this year, similar to Exhibit 23-3. How would you improve Greenberg's performance evaluation system to better analyze this year's results?

Budgeting and performance evaluation (Obj. 1)

E23-2 Edina Systems' sales budget for the nine months ended September 30 follows:

Budgeting purchases, cost of goods sold, and inventory (Obj. 2)

| | Quarter Ended | | | |
	March 31	June 30	Sep. 30	Nine-Month Total
Cash sales, 30%	$ 30,000	$ 45,000	$ 33,000	$108,000
Credit sales, 70%	70,000	105,000	77,000	252,000
Total sales, 100%	$100,000	$150,000	$110,000	$360,000

In the past, cost of goods sold has been 70% of total sales. The director of marketing and the financial vice president agree that each quarter's ending inventory should not be below $20,000 plus 10% of cost of goods sold for the following quarter. Edina expects sales of $100,000 during the fourth quarter. The January 1 inventory was $22,000.

    Prepare a purchases, cost of goods sold, and inventory budget for each of the first three quarters of the year. Compute cost of goods sold for the entire nine-month period. (Use Exhibit 23-8 as a model.)

E23-3 Remax is a nationwide real-estate firm. Suppose that its Seattle office projects that 19X9 quarterly sales will increase by 3% in quarter 1, by 3% in quarter 2, by 5% in quarter 3, and by 5% in quarter 4. Management expects operating expenses to be 85% of revenues during each of the first two quarters, 86% of revenues during the third quarter, and 81% during the fourth. The office manager expects to borrow $100,000 on July 1, with quarterly principal payments of $10,000 beginning on September 30 and interest paid at an annual rate of 18 percent. Assume that fourth quarter 19X8 sales were $2,000,000.

    Prepare a budgeted income statement for each of the four quarters of 19X9 and for the entire year. Present the 19X9 budget as follows:

Budgeting quarterly income for a year (Obj. 2)

Quarter 1	Quarter 2	Quarter 3	Quarter 4	Full Year

E23-4 Remedy Ltd. is a distributor of herbal supplements. For each of items a through d, compute the amount of cash receipts or disbursements Remedy will budget for December. The solution to one item may depend on the answer to an earlier item.

Computing cash receipts and disbursements (Obj. 3)

a. Management expects to sell equipment that cost $14,100 at a gain of $2,000. Accumulated depreciation on this equipment is $8,000.

b. Management expects to sell 8,000 bottles in November and 8,400 in December. Each bottle sells for $6. Cash sales average 30% of total sales, and credit sales make up the rest. Two-thirds of credit sales are collected in the month of sale, with the balance collected the following month.

c. The company pays rent and property taxes of $4,000 each month. Commissions and other selling expenses average 20% of sales. Remedy pays two-thirds of commissions and other selling expenses in the month incurred, with the balance paid in the following month.

d. Management has budgeted inventory purchases of $30,000 for November and $25,000 for December (before any discounts). Remedy pays for 50% of its inventory at the time of purchase in order to get a 2% discount. The business pays the balance the following month, with no discount.

Preparing a cash budget; sensitivity analysis
(Obj. 3, 4)

E23-5 Flack's Interiors, a family-owned furniture store, began October with $7,500 cash. Management forecasts that collections from credit customers will be $9,500 in October and $12,200 in November. The store is scheduled to receive $6,000 cash on a business note receivable in November. Projected cash disbursements include inventory purchases ($10,200 in October and $12,100 in November) and operating expenses ($3,000 each month).

Flack's bank requires a $7,500 minimum balance in the store's checking account. At the end of any month when the account balance dips below $7,500, the bank automatically extends credit to the store in multiples of $1,000. Flack's borrows as little as possible and pays back these loans in quarterly installments of $3,000, plus 4.5% interest on the entire unpaid principal. The first payment occurs three months after the loan.

REQUIRED

1. Prepare the store's cash budget for October and November.
2. How much cash will Flack's borrow in November if collections from customers that month total $7,200 instead of $12,200?

Preparing a budgeted balance sheet
(Obj. 3)

E23-6 Use the following information to prepare a budgeted balance sheet for Off-Campus Book Store at March 31, 19X9. Show computations for the cash and owners' equity amounts.

a. March 31 inventory balance, $16,000.

b. March payments for inventory, $5,900.

c. March payments of accounts payable and accrued liabilities, $6,100.

d. March 31 accounts payable balance, $4,900.

e. February 28 furniture and fixtures balance, $34,800; accumulated depreciation balance, $27,700.

f. February 28 owner's equity, $25,700.

g. March depreciation expense, $300.

h. Cost of goods sold, 50% of sales.

i. Other March expenses, including income tax, total $5,000; paid in cash.

j. February 28 cash balance, $10,300.

k. March budgeted sales, $12,400.

l. March 31 accounts receivable balance, one-fourth of March sales.

m. March cash receipts, $12,300.

Identifying different types of responsibility centers
(Obj. 5)

E23-7 Identify each responsibility center as a cost center, a revenue center, a profit center, or an investment center.

a. The manager of a BP service station is evaluated based on the station's revenues and expenses.

b. The hospital cardiac unit reports both revenues and expenses.

c. The Personnel Department of an insurance company prepares its budget and subsequent performance report on the basis of its expected expenses for the year.

d. A charter airline records revenues and expenses for each airplane each month. The airplane's performance report shows its ratio of operating income to average book value.

e. Accountants compile the cost of radiology supplies for evaluating the Purchasing Department of a hospital.

f. A division manager's performance is judged by the ratio of the division's operating income to the corporation's investment in the division.

g. The manager of the southwest sales territory is evaluated based on a comparison of current period sales against budgeted sales.

Using responsibility accounting to evaluate profit centers
(Obj. 6)

E23-8 Flotex Industries is a Texas-based company that produces life preservers. Flotex has managers for its Houston, Dallas, and Austin operations. These managers report to an East Texas manager, who reports to Paquita Davis, the manager of Texas operations. Davis received the following data for November operations.

	East Texas		
	Houston	**Dallas and Austin**	**West Texas**
Revenues, budget..........	$102,000	$600,000	$1,100,000
Expenses, budget	70,000	390,000	750,000
Revenues, actual	110,000	620,000	1,000,000
Expenses, actual...........	62,000	400,000	710,000

Arrange the data in a performance report similar to Exhibit 23-18. Show November results, in thousands of dollars, for Houston, East Texas, and Texas as a whole. Should Davis investigate the performance of Houston's operations?

E23-9 Pittsburgh Fabricating incurred the following indirect costs in January:

Allocating indirect expenses to departments
(Obj. 7)

Indirect labor expense	$14,000
Equipment depreciation expense	22,500
Marketing expense................................	24,000

Data for cost allocations:

	Department		
	Priming	Welding	Custom Orders
Sales revenue	$60,000	$50,000	$90,000
Indirect labor hours...........	400	500	100
Machine hours...................	300	450	150
Building square feet...........	9,000	3,000	1,500
Marketing expense-allocated to departments in proportion to sales.			

REQUIRED

1. Allocate Pittsburgh Fabricating's January indirect expenses to the three departments.
2. Compute total indirect expenses for each department.

E23-10 Portland Gear has two departments, Electronics and Industrial. The company's income statement for 19X9 appears as follows:

Preparing a departmental income statement
(Obj. 7)

Sales revenue.................................	$350,000
Cost of goods sold	116,000
Gross margin.................................	234,000
Operating expenses:	
Salaries expense.........................	$ 75,000
Depreciation expense...............	15,000
Advertising expense	6,000
Other expenses.........................	10,000
Total operating expenses	106,000
Operating income	$128,000

Sales are Electronics, $136,000; Industrial, $214,000. Cost of goods sold is distributed $42,000 to Electronics and $74,000 to Industrial. Salaries are traced directly to departments: Electronics, $33,000; Industrial, $42,000. Electronics accounts for 80% of advertising. Depreciation is allocated on the basis of square footage: Electronics has 20,000 square feet; Industrial has 40,000 square feet. Other expenses are allocated based on the number of employees. An equal number of employees work in each of the two departments.

REQUIRED

1. Prepare departmental income statements that show revenues, expenses, and operating income for each of the two departments.
2. Which of the expenses in the departmental performance report are the most important for evaluating Portland Gear's department managers? Give your reason.

CHALLENGE EXERCISE

E23-11 You recently began a job as an accounting intern at Cablevision Ltd. Your first task was to help prepare the cash budget for May and June. Unfortunately, the computer with the budget file crashed, and you did not have a backup or even a hard copy. You ran a program to salvage bits of data from the budget file. After entering the following data in the budget, you may have just enough information to reconstruct the budget.

Preparing a cash budget
(Obj. 3)

Cablevision eliminates any cash deficiency by borrowing the exact amount needed from First State Bank, where the current interest rate is 12 percent. Cablevision repays all borrowed amounts at the end of the month, as cash becomes available.

Complete the following cash budget.

CABLEVISION, LTD. Cash Budget May and June		
	May	**June**
Beginning cash balance....................................	$10,900	$?
Cash collections from customers.......................	?	74,800
Cash from sale of plant assets	0	900
Cash available	88,800	?
Cash disbursements:		
Purchases of inventory................................	$?	$41,400
Operating expenses....................................	31,900	?
Total disbursements	84,300	?
(1) Ending cash balance before financing	?	14,100
Minimum cash balance desired	10,000	10,000
Cash excess (deficiency)................................	?	?
Financing of cash deficiency:		
Borrowing (at end of month)......................	$?	$?
Principal repayments (at end of month)........	?	?
Interest expense.......................................	?	?
(2) Total effects of financing............................	?	?
Ending cash balance (1) + (2)...........................	$?	$?

Beyond the Numbers

Using a budgeted income statement
(Obj. 1)

BN23-1 Kate Fawcett is the accountant for Paperie, a Miami retailer of handmade paper products. Paperie president Carrie Pronai asked Fawcett to prepare a budgeted income statement for 19X9. Fawcett's budget follows:

PAPERIE Budgeted Income Statement For the Year Ending July 31, 19X9		
Sales revenue..		$240,000
Cost of goods sold		172,000
Gross margin		68,000
Operating expenses:		
Salary and commission expense..........	$46,000	
Rent expense	8,000	
Depreciation expense.......................	2,000	
Insurance expense	800	
Miscellaneous expenses....................	12,000	68,800
Operating loss		(800)
Interest expense		225
Net loss		$ (1,025)

Kate Fawcett does not want to give Pronai this budget without making constructive suggestions for steps Paperie could take to improve expected performance. Write a memo to Pronai outlining your suggestions. Your memo should take the following form:

Date:	_____
To:	Ms. Carrie Pronai, President
From:	Kate Fawcett
Subject:	Paperie's 19X9 budgeted income statement

Responsibility accounting
(Obj. 5, 6)

BN23-2 Asko Machine Tool Company has not been performing well. Production has fallen to a ten-year low. The company has several skilled machinists who would be difficult to replace if demand picks up. To avoid laying-off these skilled workers, three have been temporarily transferred to the Janitorial Services Department. The machinists continue to earn their regular wages of $20

per hour, which were charged to the Janitorial Services Department. Supervisor of janitorial services Jill Clayton is dismayed to receive the following performance report:

	Actual Results	Budget	Variance
Wages expense	$10,080	$4,032	$6,048 Unfavorable

Clayton confronts the controller, "This unfavorable wage expense variance is not my fault. Asko laid off my regular workers who earned $8 per hour, and transferred these highly paid machinists into my department. Instead of charging my department $20 per hour for these workers, you should charge us $8."

Who is responsible for the unfavorable wage expense variance? As the controller, how would you respond to Clayton's request?

ETHICAL ISSUE

Budget slack
(Obj. 2, 6)

◀▥ *Link Back to Chapter 7, (page 313, for Ethics Guidelines).* VIP-Tel operates a regional motel chain. Each motel is operated by a manager and an assistant manager/controller. Many of the staff who run the front desk, clean the rooms and prepare the breakfast buffet work part-time or have a second job, so turnover is high.

An accounting student recently accepted the bookkeeper's position at the local VIP-Tel. Assistant manager/controller May Johnson asked the new bookkeeper to help prepare the motel's master budget. The master budget is prepared once a year and submitted to company headquarters for approval. Once approved, the master budget is used to evaluate the motel's performance. These performance evaluations affect motel managers' bonuses and they also affect company decisions on which motels deserve extra funds for capital improvements.

When the budget was almost complete, Johnson asked the bookkeeper to increase amounts budgeted for labor and supplies by 20 percent. When asked why, Johnson responded that motel manager John Hetter told her to do this when she began working at the motel. Hetter explained that this budgetary cushion gave him flexibility in running the motel. For example, since company headquarters tightly controls capital improvement funds, Hetter can use the extra money budgeted for labor and supplies to replace broken televisions or pay "bonuses" to keep valued employees. Johnson accepted this explanation because she had observed similar behavior at the motel where she worked previously.

Put yourself in Johnson's position. Use the ethical judgment decision guidelines in Chapter 7 (page 313) to decide how Johnson should deal with the situation.

Problems (GROUP A)

P23-1A The budget committee of Voltex has assembled the following data. As the business manager, you must prepare the budgeted income statements for May and June 19X9.

Budgeting income for two months
(Obj. 2)

a. Sales in April were $31,300. You forecast that monthly sales will increase 1.3% in May and 1.3% in June.

b. Voltex maintains inventory of $8,000 plus 25% of sales budgeted for the following month. Monthly purchases average 55% of sales. Actual inventory on April 30 is $12,000. Sales budgeted for July are $32,700.

c. Monthly salaries amount to $4,000. Sales commissions equal 5% of sales. Combine salaries and commissions into a single figure.

d. Other monthly expenses are

Rent expense........................	$2,700, paid as incurred
Depreciation expense	$ 500
Insurance expense	$ 100, expiration of prepaid amount
Income tax	20% of operating income

Prepare Voltex's budgeted income statements for May and June. Show cost of goods sold computations. Round *all* amounts to the nearest $100. For example, budgeted May sales are $31,700 ($31,300 × 1.013), and June sales are $32,100 ($31,700 × 1.013).

P23-2A Refer to Problem 23-1A. Voltex's sales are 60% cash and 40% credit. Credit sales are collected in the month after sale. Inventory purchases are paid 70% in the month of purchase and 30% the following month. Salaries and sales commissions are paid half in the month earned and half the next month. Income tax is paid at the end of the year.

The April 30, 19X9 balance sheet showed the following balances:

Cash	$10,000
Accounts payable	5,100
Salary and commissions payable	2,800

REQUIRED

1. Prepare schedules of (a) budgeted cash collections from customers, (b) budgeted cash disbursements for purchases, and (c) budgeted cash disbursements for operating expenses. Show amounts for each month and totals for May and June. Carry your computations to the nearest dollar.

2. Prepare a cash budget similar to Exhibit 23-13. If no financing activity took place, what is the budgeted cash balance on June 30, 19X9?

Preparing a budgeted balance sheet and budgeted statement of cash flows
(Obj. 3)

P23-3A City Motors of Charlotte, North Carolina has applied for a loan. Nation's Bank has requested a budgeted balance sheet at April 30, 19X8 and a budgeted statement of cash flows for April. As the controller (chief accounting officer) of City Motors, you have assembled the following information:

a. March 31 equipment balance, $35,200; accumulated depreciation, $22,800.

b. April capital expenditures of $41,700 budgeted for cash purchase of equipment.

c. April depreciation expense, $700.

d. Cost of goods sold, 60% of sales.

e. Other April operating expenses, including income tax, total $13,600, 25% of which will be paid in cash and the remainder accrued at April 30.

f. March 31 owners' equity, $84,900.

g. March 31 cash balance, $36,200.

h. April budgeted sales, $80,000, 60% of which is for cash. Of the remaining 40%, half will be collected in April and half in May.

i. April cash collections on March sales, $31,200.

j. April cash payments of March 31 liabilities incurred for March purchases of inventory, $17,300.

k. March 31 inventory balance, $22,400.

l. April purchases of inventory, $9,000 for cash and $40,600 on credit. Half of the credit purchases will be paid in April and half in May.

REQUIRED

1. Prepare the budgeted balance sheet for City Motors at April 30, 19X8. Show separate computations for cash, inventory, and owners' equity balances.

2. Prepare the budgeted statement of cash flows for April.

3. Suppose that City Motors has become aware of more efficient (and more expensive) equipment than it budgeted for purchase in April. What is the total amount of cash available for equipment purchases in April, before financing, if the minimum desired ending cash balance is $18,000? (For this requirement, disregard the $41,700 initially budgeted for equipment purchases.)

Preparing a budgeted balance sheet; sensitivity analysis
(Obj. 3, 4)

P23-4A Refer to Problem 23-3A. Before granting a loan to City Motors, Nation's Bank asks for a sensitivity analysis assuming April sales are only $60,000 rather than the $80,000 originally budgeted. (While the cost of goods sold will change, assume that purchases, depreciation, and the other operating expenses will remain the same as in Problem 23-3A.)

REQUIRED

1. Prepare a revised budgeted balance sheet for City Motors, showing separate computations for cash, inventory, and owners' equity balances.

2. Suppose City Motors has a minimum desired cash balance of $21,000. Will the company need to borrow cash in April?

3. In this sensitivity analysis, sales declined by 25% ($20,000 ÷ $80,000). Is the decline in expenses and income more or less than 25 percent? Explain why.

Identifying different types of responsibility centers
(Obj. 5)

P23-5A Is each of the following most likely a cost center, a revenue center, a profit center, or an investment center?

a. Accounting Department of Quaker Oats

b. Disneyland

c. Music director of a church or synagogue

d. Catering operation of a restaurant

e. Executive director of a United Way agency
f. Men's Clothing Department in Bloomingdale's department store
g. Proposed new office of Coldwell Banker, a real-estate firm
h. Work crews of a painting contractor
i. The Empire State Building in New York City
j. Branch warehouse of Dalton Carpets
k. American subsidiary of a Japanese manufacturer
l. Service Department of Audio Forest stereo shop
m. Eastern district of a salesperson's territory
n. Assembly-line supervisors at Dell Computer
o. Accounts payable section of the Accounting Department at Home Depot
p. Surgery unit of a privately owned hospital
q. Personnel Department of Goodyear Tire and Rubber Company
r. Different product lines of a gift shop
s. Typesetting Department of Northend Press, a printing company
t. Investments Department of Citibank
u. Order-Taking Department at L.L. Bean

P23-6A EZ-Lube Company is organized with store managers reporting to a statewide manager, who in turn reports to the vice president of marketing. Suppose the *actual* income statements of the Concord store, all stores in New Hampshire (including the Concord store), and the company as a whole (including New Hampshire stores) are summarized as follows for July 19X9:

Preparing a profit-center performance report for management by exception; benefits of budgeting
(Obj. 1, 6)

	Concord	New Hampshire	Companywide
Sales revenue	$139,800	$1,647,000	$4,200,000
Expenses:			
State manager/vice president's office	$ —	$ 59,000	$ 116,000
Cost of goods sold	57,000	671,900	1,507,000
Salary expense	38,100	415,500	1,119,000
Depreciation expense	7,200	91,000	435,000
Utilities expense	4,200	46,200	260,000
Rent expense	2,400	34,700	178,000
Total expenses	108,900	1,318,300	3,615,000
Operating income	$ 30,900	$ 328,700	$ 585,000

Budgeted amounts for July were as follows:

	Concord	New Hampshire	Companywide
Sales revenue	$151,300	$1,769,700	$4,400,000
Expenses:			
State manager/vice president's office	$ —	$ 65,600	$ 118,000
Cost of goods sold	61,500	763,400	1,672,000
Salary expense	38,800	442,000	1,095,000
Depreciation expense	7,200	87,800	449,000
Utilities expense	4,700	54,400	271,000
Rent expense	2,800	32,300	174,000
Total expenses	115,000	1,445,500	3,779,000
Operating income	$ 36,300	$ 324,200	$ 621,000

REQUIRED

1. Prepare a report for July 19X9 that shows the performance of the Concord store, all the stores in New Hampshire, and the company as a whole. Follow the format of Exhibit 23-18.
2. As New Hampshire manager, would you investigate the Concord store on the basis of this report? Why or why not?
3. Briefly discuss the benefits of budgeting. Base your discussion on EZ-Lube's performance report.

P23-7A Aladdin Travel has a Custom Travel Department and a Group Discount Travel Department. At August 31, the end of Aladdin's fiscal year, the bookkeeper prepared the following adjusted trial balance:

Cash	$ 1,300	
Receivables	24,600	
Prepaid expenses	1,700	
Building and office furniture	108,600	
Accumulated depreciation—building and furniture		$ 28,200
Other assets	5,300	
Accounts payable		11,400
Accrued liabilities		6,900
Unearned service revenue		5,800
Owners' equity		19,200
Custom travel service revenue		80,000
Group discount travel service revenue		120,000
Salary expense—travel agents	37,500	
Commission expense—travel agents	26,000	
Salary expense—office manager	25,000	
Salary expense—bookkeeper	16,800	
Computerized reservation system expense	15,000	
Property tax expense	2,200	
Depreciation expense—building and furniture	4,600	
Insurance expense	1,700	
Advertising expense	1,200	
	$271,500	$271,500

Last September, Aladdin hired a specialist in group discount travel, at an annual salary of $25,000. Remaining agent salaries of $12,500 are for part-time agents who handle custom travel plans. The office manager spends 70% of her time on group discount plans and 30% on custom travel planning. The bookkeeper spends approximately two-thirds of his time on accounting for custom travel and the remainder on group discount plans. Aladdin uses a computerized reservation system. About 80% of the time spent on the system is for custom travel, and the remaining 20% is for group discount packages. Insurance expense is evenly divided between the two departments. The company allocates commissions and all other expenses based on relative service revenue.

REQUIRED

1. Prepare departmental income statements.
2. Which department is more profitable? Was the decision to hire the group specialist wise? Give your reason.

Problems (GROUP B)

P23-1B Representatives of the various departments of Star Athletics have assembled the following data. As the business manager, you must prepare the budgeted income statements for August and September 19X9.

a. Sales in July were $184,000. You forecast that monthly sales will increase 2% in August and 2% in September.

b. Star Athletics tries to maintain inventory of $50,000 plus 20% of sales budgeted for the following month. Monthly purchases average 65% of sales. Actual inventory on July 31 is $80,000. Sales budgeted for October are $198,000.

c. Monthly salaries amount to $12,000. Sales commissions equal 6% of sales. Combine salaries and commissions into a single figure.

d. Other monthly expenses are:

Rent expense	$14,000, paid as incurred
Depreciation expense	$ 3,000
Insurance expense	$ 1,000, expiration of prepaid amount
Income tax	30% of operating income

Prepare Star Athletics' budgeted income statements for August and September. Show cost of goods sold computations. Round *all* amounts to the nearest $1,000. For example, budgeted August sales are $188,000 ($184,000 × 1.02) and September sales are $192,000 ($188,000 × 1.02).

P23-2B Refer to Problem 23-1B. Star Athletics' sales are 50% cash and 50% credit. Credit sales are collected in the month after sale. Inventory purchases are paid 60% in the month of purchase and 40% the following month. Salaries and sales commissions are paid half in the month earned and half the next month. Income tax is paid at the end of the year.

Budgeting cash receipts and disbursements
(Obj. 3)

The July 31, 19X9 balance sheet showed the following balances:

Cash..	$20,000
Accounts payable	48,000
Salaries and commissions payable	11,500

REQUIRED

1. Prepare schedules of (a) budgeted cash collections from customers, (b) budgeted cash disbursements for purchases, and (c) budgeted cash disbursements for operating expenses. Show amounts for each month and totals for August and September. Carry your computations to the nearest dollar.

2. Prepare a cash budget similar to Exhibit 23-13. If no financing activity took place, what is the budgeted cash balance on September 30, 19X9?

P23-3B Pager Depot has applied for a loan. First Nations Bank has requested a budgeted balance sheet at June 30, 19X9, and a budgeted statement of cash flows for June. As the controller (chief accounting officer) of Pager Depot, you have assembled the following information:

Preparing a budgeted balance sheet and budgeted statement of cash flows
(Obj. 3)

a. May 31 equipment balance, $60,600; accumulated depreciation, $11,700.

b. June capital expenditures of $15,800 budgeted for cash purchase of equipment.

c. June depreciation expense, $400.

d. Cost of goods sold, 45% of sales.

e. Other June operating expenses, including income tax, total $38,800, 75% of which will be paid in cash and the remainder accrued at June 30.

f. May 31 owners' equity, $104,400.

g. May 31 cash balance, $40,900.

h. June budgeted sales, $70,000, 40% of which is for cash. Of the remaining 60%, half will be collected in June and half in July.

i. June cash collections on May sales, $14,900.

j. June cash payments of liabilities for May inventory purchases on credit, $10,700.

k. May 31 inventory balance, $10,400.

l. June purchases of inventory, $11,000 for cash and $27,400 on credit. Half the credit purchases will be paid in June and half in July.

REQUIRED

1. Prepare the budgeted balance sheet for Pager Depot at June 30, 19X9. Show separate computations for cash, inventory, and owners' equity balances.

2. Prepare the budgeted statement of cash flows for June.

3. On the basis of this data, if you were a First Nations Bank loan officer, would you grant Pager Depot a loan? Give your reason.

P23-4B Refer to Problem 23-3B. Before granting a loan to Pager Depot, First Nations Bank asks for a sensitivity analysis assuming that June sales are only $50,000 rather than the $70,000 originally budgeted. (While cost of goods sold will change, assume that purchases, depreciation, and the other operating expenses will remain the same as in Problem 23-3B.)

Preparing a budgeted balance sheet; sensitivity analysis
(Obj. 3, 4)

REQUIRED

1. Prepare a revised budgeted balance sheet for Pager Depot, showing separate computations for cash, inventory, and owners' equity balances.

2. Suppose Pager Depot has a minimum desired cash balance of $15,000. Will the company borrow cash in June?

3. How would this sensitivity analysis affect First Nations' loan decision?

P23-5B Is each of the following most likely a cost center, a revenue center, a profit center, or an investment center?

Identifying different types of responsibility centers
(Obj. 5)

a. Quality Control Department of Litchfield Dairies

b. Different product lines of Broyhill, a furniture manufacturer

c. European subsidiary of Coca-Cola

d. Proposed new office of Andersen Consulting

e. Lighting Department in a Sears store

f. Children's nursery in a church or synagogue

g. McDonald's restaurants under the supervision of a regional manager

h. A small clothing boutique

i. Personnel Department of PepsiCo.

j. Consumer Complaint Department of Procter & Gamble Co.

k. Service Department of an automobile dealership
l. Southwest region of Pizza Inns, Inc.
m. Payroll Department of the University of Maryland
n. Order-Taking Department at Lands' End mail order company
o. Editorial Department of *The Wall Street Journal*
p. Delta Air Lines, Inc.
q. Police Department of Boston
r. Century 21 Real Estate Co.
s. Job superintendents of a home builder
t. Northeast sales territory for Boise-Cascade

Preparing a profit-center performance report for management by exception; benefits of budgeting
(Obj. 1, 6)

P23-6B Opti-Lens is a chain of optical shops. Each store has a manager who answers to a city manager, who in turn reports to a statewide manager. The actual income statements of Store No. 8, all stores in the Chicago area (including Store No. 8), and all stores in the state of Illinois (including all Chicago stores) are summarized as follows for April:

	Store No. 8	Chicago	State of Illinois
Sales revenue	$39,900	$486,000	$3,264,500
Expenses:			
City/state manager's office expenses	$ —	$ 16,000	$ 44,000
Cost of goods sold	13,000	171,300	1,256,800
Salary expense	5,000	37,500	409,700
Depreciation expense	3,000	26,100	320,000
Utilities expense	2,700	19,300	245,600
Rent expense	1,600	16,400	186,000
Total expenses	25,300	286,600	2,462,100
Operating income	$14,600	$199,400	$ 802,400

Budgeted amounts for April were as follows:

	Store No. 8	Chicago	State of Illinois
Sales revenue	$42,000	$468,000	$3,143,000
Expenses:			
City/state manager's office expenses	$ —	$ 17,000	$ 43,000
Cost of goods sold	14,200	172,800	1,209,000
Salary expense	5,600	37,900	412,000
Depreciation expense	3,500	25,400	320,000
Utilities expense	2,100	17,000	240,000
Rent expense	1,600	15,700	181,000
Total expenses	27,000	285,800	2,405,000
Operating income	$15,000	$182,200	$ 738,000

REQUIRED

1. Prepare a report for April that shows the performance of Store No. 8, all the stores in the Chicago area, and all the stores in the state of Illinois. Follow the format of Exhibit 23-18.
2. As the city manager of Chicago, would you investigate Store No. 8 on the basis of this report? Why or why not?
3. Briefly discuss the benefits of budgeting. Base your discussion on Opti-Lens's performance report.

Allocating indirect costs; departmental income statements
(Obj. 7)

P23-7B Insti-Print has both a Printing and a Copy Services Department. At May 31, the end of Insti-Print's fiscal year, the bookkeeper prepared the adjusted trial balance on the following page.

Insti-Print owns its printing equipment and leases a high-speed copier from Xerox. Insti-Print performs print jobs on a credit basis for established customers, but copy services are cash only. The store manager spends 60% of her time on Printing Services and 40% on Copy Services. The bookkeeper spends approximately two-thirds of his time on accounts receivable and other Printing Department transactions, and the remainder on Copy Services transactions. Insurance expense is evenly divided between the two departments. The company allocates all other expenses based on relative service revenue.

Cash	$ 2,400	
Accounts receivable...	3,600	
Prepaid expenses..	1,100	
Building and office furniture	84,900	
Accumulated depreciation—building and furniture		$ 25,800
Other assets..	4,700	
Accounts payable...		3,200
Unearned service revenue...		2,200
Owners' equity		24,800
Printing service revenue		68,750
Copy service revenue		56,250
Salary expense—machine operators	23,600	
Salary expense—store manager	22,900	
Salary expense—bookkeeper	18,300	
Lease expense—copy equipment..............................	12,000	
Property tax expense...	2,800	
Depreciation expense—building................................	1,500	
Depreciation expense—printing equipment	1,300	
Insurance expense..	1,600	
Bad debt expense...	300	
	$181,000	$181,000

REQUIRED

1. Prepare departmental income statements.
2. Which department is more profitable? What factor contributes most to the profit differences between the two departments?

Applying Your Knowledge

DECISION CASES

Budgeting cash flows and financial statements to analyze alternatives (Obj. 2, 3)

CASE 1.   Each autumn, as a hobby, Suzanne De Angelo weaves cotton placemats to sell through a local craft shop. The mats sell for $20 per set of four. The shop charges a 10% commission and remits the net proceeds to De Angelo at the end of December. De Angelo has woven and sold 25 sets each of the last two years. She has enough cotton in inventory to make another 25 sets. She paid $7 per set for the cotton. De Angelo uses a four-harness loom that she purchased for cash exactly two years ago. It is depreciated at the rate of $10 per month. The accounts payable relate to the cotton inventory and are payable by September 30.

De Angelo is considering buying an eight-harness loom so that she can weave more intricate patterns in linen. The new loom costs $1,000; it would be depreciated at $20 per month. Her bank has agreed to lend her $1,000 at 18% interest, with $200 principal plus accrued interest payable each December 31. De Angelo believes that she can weave 15 linen placemat sets in time for the Christmas rush if she does not weave any cotton mats. She predicts that each linen set will sell for $50. Linen costs $18 per set. De Angelo's supplier will sell her linen on credit, payable December 31.

De Angelo plans to keep her old loom whether or not she buys the new loom. The balance sheet for her weaving business at August 31, 19X9, is as follows:

SUZANNE DE ANGELO, WEAVER
Balance Sheet
August 31, 19X9

Current assets:		Current liabilities:	
Cash	$ 25		
Inventory of cotton	175	Accounts payable	$ 74
	200		
Fixed assets:			
Loom	500	Owner's equity.................................	386
Accumulated depreciation............	(240)		
	260	Total liabilities	
Total assets..	$460	and owner's equity........................	$460

REQUIRED

1. Prepare a cash budget for the four months ending December 31, 19X9, for two alternatives: weaving the placemats in cotton and weaving the placemats in linen. For each alternative, prepare a budgeted income statement for the four months ending December 31, 19X9, and a budgeted balance sheet at December 31, 19X9.
2. On the basis of financial considerations only, what should De Angelo do? Give your reason.
3. What nonfinancial factors might De Angelo consider in her decision?

CASE 2. X-Sports designs, manufactures, and sells wakeboards through water-sports specialty stores and sports superstores. In 19X9, X-Sports incurred the following costs that are directly traceable to its Airadical product line:

Production—Molding (direct materials and direct labor)...........	$338,000
Production—Graphics (direct materials and direct labor)..........	430,000
Advertising for Airadical...	140,000

In addition to these direct costs, X-Sports also incurred other costs that cannot be traced directly to individual product lines. These indirect costs are allocated to the different product lines. For 19X9, X-Sports reports the following information about its indirect costs:

	Total Indirect Costs	Allocation Base for Indirect Costs	Total Quantity of Allocation Base
Product design	$ 240,000	New designs	6 new designs
Production—Molding	1,200,000	Machine hours	6,000 machine hours
Production—Graphics	1,800,000	Labor hours	18,000 labor hours
Distribution	300,000	Shipments	1,000 shipments

During 19X9, the whole Airadical product line required a total of one new product design, 1,000 machine hours, 3,500 labor hours, and 140 shipments. There were no beginning inventories of any kind.

1. Compute an indirect cost allocation rate for each of the four indirect costs.
2. Use the indirect cost allocation rates from requirement 1 to compute the *total costs* for the Airadical wakeboard product line, including all direct and indirect costs. Assuming X-Sports produced 7,000 Airadical wakeboards, what is the total cost per wakeboard?
3. At the end of 19X9, X-Sports' ending inventory consists solely of 600 Airadical wakeboards. What inventory value would appear on X-Sports' December 31, 19X9 balance sheet? ◄▮▮ (*Hint:* Round your inventoriable cost per unit to the nearest penny.)

◄▮▮ ◄▮▮ ◄▮▮ To review *inventoriable product costs*, see Chapter 19, page 823.

4. A snow ski manufacturer has asked X-Sports to produce snowboards, which the ski manufacturer would sell under its own name. Suppose X-Sports decides to produce the snowboards for the snow ski manufacturer on a cost-plus-fixed-fee basis. (That is, the sale price is X-Sports' cost to make the snowboards plus a fixed fee of $50,000.) The rest of X-Sports' business is at fixed sale prices—for example, $300 for Airadical wakeboards. What cost allocation incentives would this give X-Sports' managers? When there are difficult allocation decisions, will X-Sports be tempted to allocate a bigger or smaller share of indirect costs to the snowboards? Why?
5. X-Sports' top management knows that the sale price of Airadical wakeboards may change over the product's life. But management wishes to identify a target sale price they should receive on average, over the life of the product. Which of X-Sports' costs are relevant in setting the long-run average sale price for Airadical wakeboards? Give your reason.

Team Project

(Adapted from a description by Harold Bierman, Jr.) The city of Greensboro hired Gwen Martin as its first city manager four years ago. She set up many profit responsibility centers, including the Sanitation Department, the Utility Department, and the Repair Shop.

For several months, Sanitation Department manager Andrew Wexler had been complaining to Utility manager Joe Sanchez that electrical wires were too low at the corner of Broad and High Streets. There was barely clearance for large sanitation trucks. Wexler asked the repair shop to tighten the wires. Repair Shop manager Pauline Fong asked, "Should I charge the Sanitation or Utility Department for the $3,000 to make the repair?" Both departments refused to accept the charge, so the Repair Department refused to do the work.

Late one day, the top of a sanitation truck caught the wires and ripped them down. The Repair Department made an emergency repair at a cost of $3,800. The city lost $8,000 of utility income because of the disruption of service.

An investigation showed that the sanitation truck had failed to clamp down its top properly. The extra three inches of height caught the wires.

Wexler and Sanchez argued about who should bear the $3,800 cost. Sanchez also demanded that the Sanitation Department reimburse the Utility Department for the $8,000 of lost utility income.

Form groups of four students. Each person will play one of the four roles: City Manager Gwen Martin, Utility Manager Joe Sanchez, Sanitation Manager Andrew Wexler, and Repair Shop Manager Pauline Fong.

Before your group meeting, each person should prepare recommendations for allocating the $3,800 expense, for assigning the $8,000 lost utility income, and for a new policy designed to avoid this problem in the future.

At your group meeting, decide how to allocate the $3,800 expense, what to do about the $8,000 lost utility income, and develop a policy to eliminate this problem in the future. Write a memo to City Council outlining your proposed policy. Your memo should take the following form:

Date:	_____
To:	City Council Members
From:	Gwen Martin, City Manager
	Andrew Wexler, Sanitation Department Manager
	Joe Sanchez, Utility Department Manager
	Pauline Fong, Repair Shop Manager
Subject:	Proposed utility line clearance policy

Internet Exercise K-MART

The 1990's saw a dramatic shift in consumer retailing—the advent of Wal-Mart. With its super-store concept and unique distribution system, Wal-Mart swept the country with stores that provide a broad choice of well-known products at very competitive prices. This boon to consumers proved disastrous for the nation's other retailers, both large and small.

Kmart, the world's largest discount retailer in 1990, suffered badly from Wal-Mart's success as customers fled Kmart aisles. One survey showed that 49% of Wal-Mart shoppers drove past a Kmart to get to a Wal-Mart. Placed on many bankruptcy watch lists, investors and creditors feared that Kmart would soon be gone. To turn itself around, in 1995 Kmart hired Mr. Floyd Hall—the former turnaround CEO of Target Stores and Grand Union retail food stores as well as the founder of The Museum Co., a successful chain store selling reproductions of museum merchandise.

Kmart has made significant improvement over the past several years, but it has a long way to go to return to the top. Mr. Hall has implemented a number of initiatives, including slashing costs, dropping various merchandise lines, converting to the Super Kmart stores concept, and adding celebrities like Martha Stewart, Kathy Ireland, U2, Rosie O'Donnell, and Penny Marshall.

The master budget is a key element in controlling the firm. This management tool helps the company coordinate its activities within the firm, facilitates communications between managers and employees, and provides a benchmark against which to measure future performance.

1. Go to **http://www.kmart.com,** the home page for Kmart. At the Kmart Web site, you can view the latest TV commercials, see what is on sale this week, browse the food aisles of a Super Kmart store, and find a store close to you.

2. Click on **About Kmart.** This button takes you to the corporate information section where you can find Kmart financial statements and much more. Click on **The Kmart Story** and review *The Kmart Story* and *Kmart Fun Facts* to better understand Kmart's corporate profile.

3. Click on **Kmart Fact Book.** Review the sections on the *Discount Department Store Industry* and the *Consolidated Financial Information* to answer the following questions.
   a. Refer to the **Discount Department Store Industry** section. What is Kmart's percentage market share of the Discount Retail Industry?
   b. What is the annual projected growth for this sector over the next several years?
   c. For the most recent year, what is Kmart's average for *sales per selling square foot?* Compute expected sales for an average Kmart store with 70,000 square feet of selling space.
   d. How does Kmart's *sales per selling square foot* compare to other discount stores? Why is the sales per selling square foot a key operating statistic in the retail industry?
   e. Refer to the **Consolidated Financial Information** section. For the most recent year, what is Kmart's gross margin percentage?
   f. For the most recent year, operating expenses (selling, general and administrative) are what percentage of net sales?
   g. Prepare a budget for next year assuming you are the manager of an average Kmart store with 70,000 square feet of selling space. Sales growth of 8% is expected. Percentage of net sales for gross margin and operating expenses are expected to remain the same as the most recent year. For the next year compute budgeted sales, budgeted gross margin, budgeted operating expenses, and budgeted income from operations. You will use your answers to requirements *c, e,* and *f.*

4. What is the appropriate type of responsibility center for a Kmart store?

CHAPTER 24

Flexible Budgets and Standard Costs

LEARNING OBJECTIVES

After studying this chapter, you should be able to

1. Prepare a flexible budget for the income statement

2. Prepare an income statement performance report

3. Identify the benefits of standard costs

4. Compute standard cost variances for direct materials and direct labor

5. Analyze manufacturing overhead in a standard cost system

6. Record transactions at standard cost

7. Prepare a standard cost income statement for management

How does McDonald's ensure that its 24,800 restaurants deliver quality, service, cleanliness, and value to over 35 million customers worldwide daily? How do McDonald's managers use management accounting to earn a profit?

The answers are budgets, standards, and variances. McDonald's managers budget sales for each hour. The manager schedules just enough workers to handle the budgeted level of sales. During the day, the manager computes variances for sales (for example, actual sales minus budgeted sales) and for direct labor. These variances are computed *hourly*. If actual sales fall short of the budget, the manager quickly sees an unfavorable sales variance. If sales are less than budgeted, the manager can send employees home early. This helps control direct labor cost.

McDonald's also sets budgets and standards for direct materials. From Beijing to Miami, the standards for a regular McDonald's hamburger are the same: 1 bun, 1 hamburger patty, 1 pickle slice, 1/8 teaspoon dehydrated onion, 1/8 teaspoon mustard, and 1/3 fluid ounce of ketchup. To control direct materials costs, the manager compares the number of, say, hamburger patties actually used with the number of patties that should have been used.

McDonald's uses budgets, standards, and variances to control costs so prices remains low enough that customers believe McDonald's provides good *value*. McDonald's also uses standards and variances to motivate employees to focus on *quality*, *service*, and *cleanliness:*

- Quality—sandwiches unsold within 10 minutes are thrown away.
- Service—customers should receive food within 90 seconds of beginning to order.
- Cleanliness—visiting inspectors score restaurants on cleanliness.

In Chapter 23, we discussed how managers use budgets to quantify their plans. We learned that executives compare actual revenues and expenses with budgeted amounts to evaluate the performance of responsibility centers and their managers. This chapter explores budgeting in greater depth. The first half of the chapter shows how flexible budgets and variances help managers learn *why* actual results differed from planned performance. Understanding the causes of variances helps managers plan and control operations. The second half of the chapter discusses standard costs, which many companies use to build flexible budgets.

Static versus Flexible Budgets

Objective 1

Prepare a flexible budget for the income statement

Static Budget. The budget prepared for only one level of volume. Also called the **master budget.**

Variance. The difference between an actual amount and the corresponding budgeted amount. A variance is labeled as favorable if it increases operating income and unfavorable if it decreases operating income.

Flexible Budget. A summarized budget that can easily be computed for several different volume levels. Flexible budgets separate variable costs from fixed costs; it is the variable costs that put the "flex" in the flexible budget.

■ **Daily Exercise 24-1**

The master budget in Chapter 23 is a **static budget**—it is prepared for one level of volume. That volume is the company's goal. The static budget is not changed after it is developed, regardless of changes in volume, sale prices, or costs.

Consider Kool-Time Pools, a company that installs residential swimming pools. Kool-Time buys direct materials—gunite (a concrete derivative). It then uses labor and equipment to convert the gunite into finished outputs—installed pools. Kool-Time's static master budget forecasts that the company will install eight pools in June. However, due to an early heat wave, Kool-Time actually installed ten pools.

The comparison of June's actual results with the static budget in Exhibit 24-1 shows that Kool-Time's actual operating income is $3,000 higher than originally expected. This is a $3,000 favorable difference, or variance, in Kool-Time's June operating income. A **variance** is the difference between an actual amount and the corresponding budgeted amount. The variances in the third column of Exhibit 24-1 are favorable (F) if a higher actual amount increases operating income, and unfavorable (U) if a higher actual amount decreases operating income. The variance for the number of pools installed is favorable because higher volume (ten rather than eight pools) tends to increase income.

The report in Exhibit 24-1 is hard to analyze because the static budget is based on eight pools, but actual results are for ten pools. Why did the $21,000 unfavorable expense variance occur? Were direct materials wasted? Did the cost of gunite suddenly increase? How much of the additional expense arose because Kool-Time built ten rather than eight pools? Exhibit 24-1's simple comparison of actual results with the static budget does not provide enough information to answer these questions.

Managers often use flexible budgets to help answer such questions. Exhibit 24-2 illustrates the difference between static and flexible budgets. A static master budget—like the Whitewater Sporting Goods Store budget developed in Chapter 23—is computed for only a single level of sales volume. In contrast, **flexible budgets** are summarized budgets that can easily be computed for several different volume levels. Flexible budgets separate variable costs from fixed costs. Exhibit 24-3 uses flexible budgets to show how Kool-Time's revenues and costs are expected to vary as sales volume increases from five pools, to eight pools, to eleven pools.

Managers prepare flexible budgets like those in Exhibit 24-3 either

- *Before* the period, or
- At the *end* of the period

EXHIBIT 24-1

Comparison of Actual Results with Static Budget

	KOOL-TIME POOLS		
	Comparison of Actual Results with Static Budget		
	Month Ended June 30, 19X9		
	Actual Results	**Static Budget**	**Variance**
Output units (pools installed)..........	10	8	2 F
Sales revenue.....................................	$120,000	$96,000	$24,000 F
Expenses...	(105,000)	(84,000)	21,000 U
Operating income..............................	$ 15,000	$12,000	$ 3,000 F

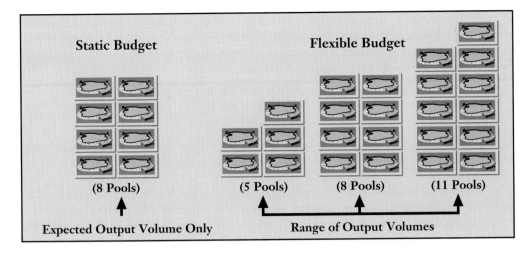

EXHIBIT 24-2
Static versus Flexible Budgets

Flexible budgets prepared *before* the period are useful for *planning*. Flexible budgets prepared at the *end* of the period help managers *control* operations. We focus on the planning aspect first.

Managers prepare flexible budgets before the period to

- Estimate revenues, costs and profits
- Analyze cost-volume-profit relations over the entire range of likely activity
- Plan for uncertainties such as alternative levels of sales

Managers can easily develop flexible budgets like Exhibit 24-3 using a simple spreadsheet on a personal computer.

Exhibit 24-3 shows condensed flexible budgets for Kool-Time. The budgeted sale price per pool is $12,000, and the budgeted variable cost per pool is $8,000. Exhibit 24-3 also shows that Kool-Time's total monthly fixed expenses are $20,000 throughout the range of five to eleven pools. ◄▦ A more detailed budget would separately identify individual expenses, such as direct materials, direct labor, and depreciation on equipment.

◄▦ ◄▦ ◄▦ See Chapter 22, page 950, to review the distinction between variable costs and fixed costs.

■ **Daily Exercise 24-2**

Kool-Time's flexible budgets are based on the *flexible budget formula for total costs:*

$$\text{Flexible budget total cost} = \text{Total fixed cost} + \left(\begin{array}{c} \text{Variable cost} \\ \text{per output unit} \end{array} \times \begin{array}{c} \text{Number} \\ \text{of output units} \end{array} \right)$$

Notice that the budgeted total fixed costs (such as administrative salaries and depreciation on equipment) remain constant at $20,000. In contrast, the budgeted total variable costs (such as the cost of gunite and labor) increase at the rate of $8,000 per pool installed. Thus it is the variable costs that put the "flex" in the flexible budget.

". . . (For Kool-Time) the budgeted total variable costs (such as the cost of gunite and labor) increase at the rate of $8,000 per pool installed."

EXHIBIT 24-3
Flexible Budget

		Output Units (Pools Installed)		
	Flexible Budget per Output Unit	**5**	**8**	**11**
Sales revenue..............	$12,000	$60,000	$96,000	$132,000
Variable expenses..........	8,000	40,000	64,000	88,000
Fixed expenses*.............		20,000	20,000	20,000
Total expenses...............		60,000	84,000	108,000
Operating income.........		$ 0	$12,000	$ 24,000

KOOL-TIME POOLS
Flexible Budget
Month Ended June 30, 19X9

Fixed expenses are given as a total amount rather than as a cost per unit.

In preparing the flexible budgets shown in Exhibit 24-3, Kool-Time used the flexible budget formula to compute total budgeted costs for 5 pools and for 11 pools, as well as for the static master budget sales forecast of 8 pools. For example, Kool-Time Pool's flexible budget for installing 11 pools is $108,000:

$$\text{Flexible budget total cost} = \$20,000 + (\$8,000 \text{ per pool} \times 11 \text{ pools})$$
$$= \$20,000 + \$88,000$$
$$= \$108,000$$

■ Daily Exercise 24-3

Kool-Time's flexible budget could include additional columns for seven, nine, or any other number of pools for which management wants to know budgeted sales revenues, costs, and profits.

The flexible budget total cost formula applies only to a specific relevant range. Why? Because total monthly fixed costs and the variable cost per pool will change outside this range. Kool-Time's relevant range is 0–11 pools. If the company installs 12 pools, they will have to rent additional equipment, so the fixed cost portion of the flexible budget formula will be more than $20,000. Kool-Time will also have to pay workers an overtime premium, so the variable cost per pool will be more than $8,000.

Graphing the Flexible Budget

The flexible budget projects total costs at different output levels, or volumes. Managers often use a graph to forecast total cost at various output levels. Exhibit 24-4 shows budgeted total costs for the entire relevant range of 0–11 pools.  The flexible budget total cost line in Exhibit 24-4 intersects the vertical axis at the amount of the total fixed cost ($20,000) Kool-Time will incur whether it installs 0 pools or 11 pools. The flexible budget's total cost line slopes upward at the rate of $8,000 per pool, which is Kool-Time's variable cost per pool.

 The flexible budget cost line in Exhibit 24-4 follows the same principles as the cost-volume-profit graph's total cost line in Exhibit 22-7, page 963.

We assume throughout that Kool-Time's managers initially expected to install eight pools per month. Hence, the graph highlights the static budget costs for eight pools ($84,000). Notice that the graph also shows the flexible budget costs for 5 pools ($60,000) and 11 pools ($108,000).

At the end of the period, managers use the flexible budget to help control costs. They plot actual costs on the flexible budget graph as shown in Exhibit 24-5. Consider the month of June during which Kool-Time actually installed ten pools. The flexible budget graphs in Exhibit 24-4 and 24-5 show that *budgeted* total costs for ten pools are

Variable (10 × $8,000)	$ 80,000
Fixed	20,000
Total	$100,000

EXHIBIT 24-4
Kool-Time Pools Graph of Monthly Flexible Budget

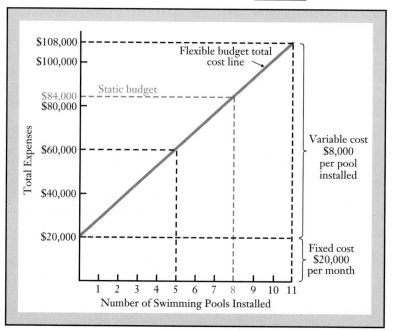

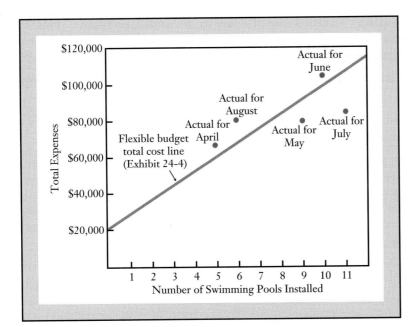

EXHIBIT 24-5
Kool-Time Pools Graph of
Actual and Budgeted Monthly
Costs

■ **Daily Exercise 24-4**
■ **Daily Exercise 24-5**

June's *actual* costs, or expenses, were $105,000 (Exhibit 24-1). Consequently, Exhibit 24-5 shows that June's actual costs for ten pools ($105,000) exceed the budget for ten pools ($100,000). Using graphs of actual versus budgeted costs, managers can see at a glance whether actual costs are

- Higher than budgeted for the actual level of output, as in April, June, and August, or
- Lower than budgeted for the actual level of output, as in May and July

Working It Out Use the graph in Exhibit 24-5 and Kool-Time's flexible budget formula (page 1037) to answer the following questions:

1. How many pools did Kool-Time install in July?
2. How much were Kool-Time's actual costs in July?
3. Using Kool-Time's flexible budget formula, what is the flexible budget total cost for the month of July?
4. Is Kool-Time's variance for total costs favorable or unfavorable in July?

Answers

1. Exhibit 24-5 shows that Kool-Time installed 11 pools in July.
2. Exhibit 24-5 shows that Kool-Time's actual costs in July were about $82,000.
3. Using Kool-Time's flexible budget total cost formula:

Variable costs (11 × $8,000)	$ 88,000
Fixed costs	20,000
Total costs.....................................	$108,000

4. Kool-Time's July variance for total costs is $26,000 ($82,000 – $108,000) favorable, since actual costs are less than the budget.

The Flexible Budget and Variance Analysis

Managers also use flexible budgets at the *end* of the period to help control business operations. Flexible budgets developed at the *end* of the period can help explain why actual results differ from budgeted results.

Let's step back for a moment and consider managers' key activities. Successful managers continuously cycle through four major planning and controlling activities:

1. Quantify the company's goals in a static master budget.
2. Take actions to achieve the goals.

Objective 2

Prepare an income statement performance report

3. Analyze the variance between actual results and static budget amounts (the static budget variance).

4. Change actions (or plans) so that future results conform to the plan.

The flexible budget is an important tool in step 3. To analyze the variance (step 3), managers begin by asking

- How many units did we actually sell?
- How much *should* this number of output units have cost us?

The *flexible budget for the number of units that were actually sold* helps answer the second question. Of course, the number of units actually sold is not known until the end of the period. But why calculate a budget for a period that is already over? Because *the flexible budget for the number of units actually sold shows how much the company should have spent to obtain that level of output.* This allows managers to divide the static budget variance into two broad categories:

Sales Volume Variance. The difference arising only because the number of units actually sold differs from the number of units expected to be sold according to the static budget. This is computed as the difference between a flexible budget amount and a static budget amount.

Flexible Budget Variance. The difference between what the company actually spent at the actual level of output and what it should have spent to obtain the actual level of output. This is computed as the difference between the actual amount and a flexible budget amount.

- **Sales volume variance**—the difference arising only because the number of units actually sold differs from the number of units expected to be sold according to the static budget.
- **Flexible budget variance**—the difference between what the company actually spent at the actual level of output and what it should have spent to obtain the actual level of output.

As shown in Exhibit 24-6, the sales volume variance is the difference between

1. the *static* (master) budget—for the number of units *expected* to be sold (8 pools, for Kool-Time), and

2. the *flexible* budget—for the number of units that were *actually* sold (10 pools in June).

Consider Kool-Time Pool's performance report in Exhibit 24-7. The static budget amounts in column 5 are based on the static budget sales forecast developed at the *beginning* of the period—the eight pools Kool-Time *expected* to install. For these eight pools, Kool-Time's

- Budgeted sales revenue is $96,000 (8 × $12,000).
- Budgeted variable expenses (costs) are $64,000 (8 × $8,000).
- Budgeted fixed expenses (costs) are $20,000.

In contrast to the static budget, which is developed *before* the period, the flexible budget used in the performance report is not developed until the *end* of the period.

EXHIBIT 24-6
The Static Budget Variance, the Sales Volume Variance, and the Flexible Budget Variance

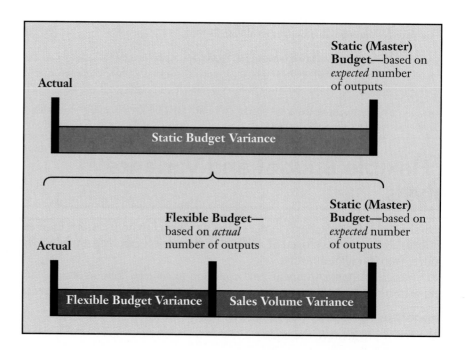

KOOL-TIME POOLS
Income Statement Performance Report
Month Ended June 30, 19X9

	(1) Actual Results at Actual Prices	(2) (1) – (3) Flexible Budget Variance	(3) Flexible Budget for Actual Number of Output Units*	(4) (3) – (5) Sales Volume Variance	(5) Static (Master) Budget*
Output units (pools installed)	10	–0–	10	2 F	8
Sales revenue	$120,000	$ –0–	$120,000	$24,000 F	$96,000
Variable expenses	83,000	3,000 U	80,000	16,000 U	64,000
Fixed expenses	22,000	2,000 U	20,000	–0–	20,000
Total expenses	105,000	5,000 U	100,000	16,000 U	84,000
Operating income	$ 15,000	$5,000 U	$ 20,000	$ 8,000 F	$12,000

Flexible budget variance, $5,000 U

Sales volume variance, $8,000 F

Static budget variance, $3,000 F

*Budgeted sale price is $12,000 per pool, budgeted variable expense is $8,000 per pool, and budgeted total monthly fixed expenses are $20,000.

EXHIBIT 24-7
Income Statement Performance Report

■ Daily Exercise 24-6
■ Daily Exercise 24-7

Why? Because *flexible budgets used in performance reports are based on the actual number of outputs, which is not known until the end of the period.* For Kool-Time, the flexible budget used in the performance report (column 3 of Exhibit 24-7) is based on the ten pools actually installed. For these ten pools actually installed, Kool-Time's

- Budgeted sales revenue is $120,000 (10 × $12,000).
- Budgeted variable expenses are $80,000 (10 × $8,000).
- Budgeted fixed expenses are $20,000.

The only difference between the static budget and the flexible budget used in the performance report is the number of outputs on which the budget is based (eight pools versus ten pools in the Kool-Time example). Both budgets use the same

- Budgeted sale price per unit ($12,000 per pool)
- Budgeted variable cost per unit ($8,000 per pool)
- Budgeted total fixed costs ($20,000 per month)

Holding selling price per unit, variable cost per unit, and total fixed costs constant at their budgeted amounts highlights the effects of differences in sales volume—the sales volume variance in column 4. Exhibit 24-7 shows that by installing two more pools than initially expected, Kool-Time's

- Sales revenue should increase from $96,000 (8 × $12,000) to $120,000 (10 × $12,000)—a $24,000 favorable sales volume variance.
- Variable costs should increase from $64,000 (8 × $8,000) to $80,000 (10 × $8,000)—a $16,000 unfavorable sales volume variance.

Budgeted total fixed expenses are unaffected because eight pools and ten pools are within the relevant range where fixed expenses total $20,000 (0–11 pools). Consequently, the net effect of installing two more pools is an expected increase in operating income of $8,000 ($24,000 F – $16,000 U).

The sales volume variance in column 4 of Exhibit 24-7 shows the changes in revenues, expenses, and profits arising simply because the number of units actually sold differs from the budget. This variance captures the effects of differences in the number of units sold, which is typically the responsibility of the marketing staff.

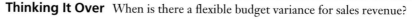

Thinking It Over When is there a sales volume variance for fixed expenses?

Answer: Only when the number of units actually sold falls within a different relevant range from the number of units expected to be sold (per the static budget). When actual and expected number of units sold fall within the same relevant range, there is no sales volume variance for fixed expenses.

Exhibit 24-6 shows that the second piece of the static budget variance is the flexible budget variance—the difference between

• Actual amounts and
• Flexible budget amounts *for the actual number of output units*

The flexible budget variance (column 2 in Exhibit 24-7) highlights the difference between actual amounts (column 1) and flexible budget amounts that should have been incurred for the actual number of units (column 3).

Exhibit 24-7 shows that Kool-Time actually incurred $83,000 of variable costs to install the ten pools. This is $3,000 more than the $80,000 (10 pools × $8,000 per pool) budgeted variable cost for ten pools. The company also spent $2,000 more than budgeted on fixed expenses ($22,000 − $20,000). Consequently, the flexible budget variance for total expenses is $5,000 unfavorable ($3,000 U + $2,000 U). The $5,000 unfavorable flexible budget variance offsets much of the $8,000 favorable sales volume variance, resulting in a $3,000 favorable static budget variance (Exhibits 24-1 and 24-7).

Thinking It Over When is there a flexible budget variance for sales revenue?

Answer: When the actual sale price differs from the budgeted sale price, the difference is a flexible budget variance for sales revenue. In the Kool-Time Pools illustration, suppose the actual sale price was $13,000 rather than $12,000 per pool. Actual sales revenue would have been $130,000 (10 × $13,000) and there would have been a $10,000 favorable flexible budget variance for sales revenue ($130,000 − $120,000).

We have seen that a simple comparison of the *static budget* with *actual results* (like Exhibit 24-1) does not explain much. This is because the *actual* number of units sold may differ from the *expected* sales used to prepare the static budget. The flexible budget provides the information needed to understand why actual revenues, expenses, and income differ from budgeted amounts. Specifically, Exhibit 24-7 shows how the flexible budget splits the static budget variance into the sales volume variance and the flexible budget variance.

How would Kool-Time's managers use these variances? Variance information can direct a manager to areas of the business deserving praise or needing improvement. The sales volume variance reveals that strong sales caused actual income to exceed the budget by $8,000. However, the company failed to control expenses as well as expected, resulting in an unfavorable flexible budget variance of $5,000.

Kool-Time's managers may reward their sales staff, and management would certainly want to determine why expenses were too high. The performance report (Exhibit 24-7) shows the unfavorable $5,000 flexible budget total cost variance, but it does not identify the specific reasons why expenses exceeded the budget. For example, Kool-Time's higher-than-expected expenses might have resulted from an uncontrollable increase in the cost of gunite. Or higher costs might have resulted from more controllable factors such as employees wasting materials or working inefficiently. If so, managers can take action to reduce waste or inefficiency. The second half of this chapter explains how Kool-Time's managers can further analyze flexible budget variances to identify the reason for the cost overrun.

> **Learning Tip:** Managers prepare flexible budgets at two different times:
> • At the *beginning* of the period, managers prepare flexible budgets for *different output levels* to help *plan* operations, as in Exhibit 24-3.
> • At the *end* of the period, managers prepare flexible budgets for a *single output level*—the number of actual outputs—to help *control* costs and revenues, as in column 3 of Exhibit 24-7.

Before proceeding, take some time to test your understanding of the flexible budget, static budget, and variances by reviewing the Decision Guidelines and then working the mid-chapter review problem.

DECISION	GUIDELINES
How to estimate sales revenues, costs, and profits over the range of likely output levels?	Prepare a set of flexible budgets for different output levels.
How to prepare a flexible budget for total costs?	$$\begin{aligned} \text{Flexible budget} \atop \text{total cost} = {\text{Fixed} \atop \text{cost}} + \left(\begin{array}{c} \text{Variable} \\ \text{cost per} \\ \text{output} \\ \text{unit} \end{array} \times \begin{array}{c} \text{Number} \\ \text{of} \\ \text{output} \\ \text{units} \end{array} \right) \end{aligned}$$
How to use budgets to help control costs?	• Graph actual costs versus flexible budget costs, as in Exhibit 24-5. • Prepare an income statement performance report, as in Exhibit 24-7.
On which output level is the budget based?	Static (master) budget—*expected* number of outputs, estimated before the period Flexible budget (made at the end of the period)—*actual* number of outputs, not known until the end of the period
Why does actual income differ from budgeted income?	Prepare income statement performance report comparing actual results, flexible budget for actual number of outputs, and static (master) budget.
How much of the difference occurs because the actual number of output units sold does not equal budgeted sales?	Compute the sales volume variance by comparing the flexible budget with the static budget.

How much of the difference occurs because actual revenues and costs are not what they should have been for the actual number of outputs?	Compute the flexible budget variance (FBV) by comparing actual results with the flexible budget.
	
	• Favorable FBV—Income effect if
	    Actual sales revenue > Flexible budget sales revenue
	    Actual expenses < Flexible budget expenses
	• Unfavorable FBV—Income effect if
	    Actual sales revenue < Flexible budget sales revenue
	    Actual expenses > Flexible budget expenses

SUMMARY PROBLEM FOR YOUR REVIEW   MID-CHAPTER

Exhibit 24-7 indicates that Kool-Time Pools installed ten swimming pools during June. Now assume that Kool-Time installed seven pools (instead of ten), and that the actual sale price averaged $12,500 per pool instead of $12,000. Actual variable expenses were $57,400, and actual fixed expenses were $19,000.

REQUIRED

1. Prepare a revised income statement performance report using Exhibit 24-7 as a guide.
2. Show that the sum of the flexible budget variance and the sales volume variance for operating income equals the static budget variance for operating income.
3. As the company owner, which employees would you praise or criticize after you analyze this performance report?

■ **SOLUTION**

	KOOL-TIME POOLS Income Statement Performance Report—Revised Month Ended June 30, 19X9				
	(1) Actual Results at Actual Prices	(2) (1) – (3) Flexible Budget Variance	(3) Flexible Budget for Actual Number of Output Units	(4) (3) – (5) Sales Volume Variance	(5) Static (Master) Budget
Output units.................	7	–0–	7	1 U	8
Sales revenue.................	$87,500	$3,500 F	$84,000	$12,000 U	$96,000
Variable expenses...........	57,400	1,400 U	56,000	8,000 F	64,000
Fixed expenses	19,000	1,000 F	20,000	—	20,000
Total expenses...............	76,400	400 U	76,000	8,000 F	84,000
Operating income..........	$11,100	$3,100 F	$ 8,000	$ 4,000 U	$12,000

Flexible budget variance, $3,100 F

Sales volume variance, $4,000 U

Static budget variance, $900 U

As the company owner, you should refrain from praise or criticism until you determine the *causes* of the variances. Those causes may or may not be controllable by managers. For example, the unfavorable sales volume variance may be due to employee absenteeism that slowed work. Managers are responsible for having enough workers at each job each day. On the other hand, the variance may be due to a long period of heavy rain that brought work to a standstill. Also, an employee may have saved Kool-Time $1,000 (the flexible budget variance for fixed expenses) by finding a lower-cost source of rented equipment. Or the savings may have come from delaying a needed overhaul of equipment that could increase the company's costs in the long run. The key point is that variances raise questions and direct attention. They do not fix blame or praise.

Standard Costing

We have learned that to budget a variable cost, accountants multiply a number of output units by a budgeted cost per unit. They use the *expected* or *budgeted* number of output units in the static budget and the *actual* number of output units in the after-the-fact flexible budget. Let's continue our Kool-Time Pools example. We will show that the $8,000 budgeted variable cost of an installed pool is made up of *inputs*, including direct materials, direct labor, and variable overhead costs.

Standard Cost. A carefully predetermined cost that usually is expressed on a per-unit basis.

Many companies—especially those that routinely produce similar or identical products—use standard costs for budgeting and control. A **standard cost** is a carefully predetermined cost that usually is expressed on a per-unit basis. In contrast, the term *budgeted cost* usually refers to a total amount. For example, suppose the budgeted variable costs in Exhibit 24-3 include direct materials costs as follows:

	Flexible Budget per Output Unit	Output Units (Pools Installed)		
		5	8	11
Direct materials	$2,000	$10,000	$16,000	$22,000

The standard cost of direct materials is $2,000 *per pool*. Budgeted cost is the expected total cost of all pools sold during the month. As volume increases from five to eleven pools, the budgeted direct materials cost increases from $10,000 to $22,000. But the standard direct materials cost is $2,000 per pool at all three flexible budget output levels. Think of a standard cost as *a budget for a single unit of output*.

In a standard cost system, each resource used to make a product has both a quantity standard and a price standard. Thompson Consumer Electronics, which produces the RCA brand, has a standard for the time required to solder the chassis of a VCR and for the wage rate of workers who operate the robots that do the soldering. McDonald's has a standard for the amount of beef per hamburger and for the price paid per pound of beef. Likewise, Kool-Time Pools has a standard for the cubic feet of gunite per pool and for the price per cubic foot of gunite.

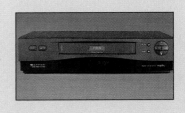

"Thompson Consumer Electronics, which produces the RCA brand, has a standard for the time required to solder the chassis of a VCR and for the wage rate of workers who operate the robots that do the soldering."

Setting Standards

Accountants help managers set price standards. For direct materials, accountants consider quantity discounts, early-payment discounts, and freight and receiving costs in addition to base purchase prices. For direct labor, they take into account payroll taxes and fringe benefits as well as hourly wage rates. And for overhead, accountants help identify the overhead allocation bases and then compute the allocation rates used in budgeting and product costing.

Accountants are less involved in setting quantity standards than in setting price standards. Standards for direct materials and direct labor are frequently set by engineers and production managers. Boeing engineers may perform a time-and-motion study to analyze every movement in the wiring of a 747's instrument panel. Their aims are to (1) eliminate unnecessary work, (2) reduce the time and effort required for necessary work, and (3) set a standard time for the wiring activity.

Another approach to setting standards is to base them on continuous improvement goals. Suppose that in 19X7 Frito Lay required four pounds of potatoes to produce one pound of potato chips. If management believes employees can reduce waste and spoilage (of potatoes) by 4% per year, then the standard for 19X8 will be set at 3.84 pounds (4 pounds × 0.96), and the standard for 19X9 at 96% of 19X8's actual result. By budgeting an annual 4% reduction in the quantity of potatoes used, Frito Lay's management signals to employees the importance of continually finding ways to cut costs.

Companies also work with their suppliers to set continuous improvement standards for direct materials prices. For example, Toyota sent its own engineers to the plant of one of its bumper suppliers to help the supplier cut costs. Much of these cost savings were passed on to Toyota through lower prices for the bumpers.

Whether managers use engineering studies, continuous improvement goals, or some other approach, they usually set currently attainable standards that allow normal amounts of waste and spoilage. This represents very good performance that can be achieved, but with difficulty. However, an increasing number of companies are using standards based on the "best practice" level of performance. This is often called **benchmarking**. *Best practice* may be an internal benchmark from inside the company, or an external benchmark from other companies. Internal benchmarks are easy to obtain, but how does a manager obtain external benchmark data?

Companies can purchase external benchmark data from consulting firms. Consider a consulting firm that develops reports comparing the costs of treating specific diagnoses (say an appendectomy) across hospitals. Riverside Hospital in Columbus, Ohio, can compare its cost of an appendectomy with the "best practice" cost as identified from the report. However, cost is only one factor in evaluating hospital performance. More important factors include the patient outcomes and the quality of patient care.

Benchmarking. Using standards based on the "best practice" level of performance. Best practice may be an internal benchmark from inside the company, or an external benchmark from other companies.

Benefits of Standard Costs

Objective 3

Identify the benefits of standard costs

◀▥ ◀▥ ◀▥ Chapter 23, page 1011, introduced the management by exception principle.

■ **Daily Exercise 24-10**

When standard costs are set carefully and used wisely, they yield several benefits to an organization (Exhibit 24-8):

1. They help managers plan by providing the unit amounts—the building blocks—for budgeting.
2. They help managers control business operations by setting target levels of operating performance. *Management by exception* suggests that managers focus attention where actual results differ significantly from standards. ◀▥
3. They help motivate employees by serving as benchmarks against which their performance is measured.
4. They provide unit costs that are useful in setting the sale prices of products or services.
5. They help simplify record keeping and so reduce clerical costs.

Standard cost systems might appear to be expensive. Indeed, the company must make a start-up investment to develop the standards. But *using* standards can save data-processing costs. For example, it is more economical to value all inventories at standard costs rather than at actual costs. By using standard costs, accountants avoid the expense of tracking down actual unit costs and of making LIFO, FIFO, or average-cost computations.

Given these benefits, it is not surprising that standard costing is popular worldwide. U.S. surveys have shown that over 80% of responding companies use standard costing. International surveys suggest that over half the responding companies in Ireland, the United Kingdom, Sweden, and Japan use standard costing, primarily because it helps managers control costs.

Objective 4

Compute standard cost variances for direct materials and direct labor

An Example of Standard Costing

Let's return to our Kool-Time Pools example. Recall that Kool-Time installed ten swimming pools during June. Exhibit 24-9 provides cost data for this actual level of output. To focus on the main aspects of standard costing, we assume that Kool-Time's standard costing system pertains to direct materials (gunite), direct labor, and manufacturing overhead but not to design, marketing, or administrative expenses. We assume also that the quantity of direct materials purchased equals the quantity used.

Concept Highlight

EXHIBIT 24-8
The Benefits of Standard Costs

Exhibit 24-9 shows Kool-Time's flexible budget variances for direct materials ($3,100 U) and direct labor ($200 F). Accountants separate these variances into two components: a price variance and an efficiency variance.

Price and Efficiency Variances

A **price variance** measures how well the business keeps unit prices of material and labor inputs within standards. As the name suggests, the price variance is the *difference in prices* (actual unit price − standard unit price) of an input, multiplied by the *actual quantity* of the input:

Price Variance. Measures how well the business keeps unit prices of material and labor inputs within standards. This is computed as the difference in prices (actual unit price minus standard unit price) of an input, multiplied by the actual quantity of the input.

$$\text{Price variance} = \begin{pmatrix} \text{Difference between} \\ \text{actual and standard} \\ \text{unit prices of inputs} \end{pmatrix} \times \begin{pmatrix} \text{Actual quantity} \\ \text{of input} \end{pmatrix}$$

$$\text{Price variance} = \begin{pmatrix} \text{Actual} \\ \text{unit price} \\ \text{of input} \end{pmatrix} - \begin{pmatrix} \text{Standard} \\ \text{unit price} \\ \text{of input} \end{pmatrix} \times \begin{pmatrix} \text{Actual quantity} \\ \text{of input} \end{pmatrix}$$

EXHIBIT 24-9
Data for Standard Costing Example

KOOL-TIME POOLS
Data for Standard Costing Example
Month of June, 19X9

PANEL A—Comparison of Actual Results with Flexible Budget for 10 Swimming Pools

	Actual Results at Actual Prices	Flexible Budget for 10 Pools	Flexible Budget Variance
Variable expenses:			
Direct materials...	$ 23,100*	$ 20,000‡	$3,100 U
Direct labor...	41,800†	42,000‡	200 F
Variable overhead..	9,000	8,000§	1,000 U
Marketing and administrative expenses..........	9,100	10,000	900 F
Total variable expenses.............................	83,000	80,000	3,000 U
Fixed expenses:			
Fixed overhead...	12,300	12,000‖	300 U
Marketing and administrative expenses..........	9,700	8,000	1,700 U
Total fixed expenses.................................	22,000	20,000	2,000 U
Total expenses	$105,000	$100,000	$5,000 U

*$23,100 = 11,969 cubic feet of gunite actually used at actual price of $1.93 per cubic foot.
†$41,800 = 3,800 direct labor hours actually used at actual price of $11.00 per hour.
‡See Panel B.
§Variable overhead was budgeted at $2.00 per direct labor hour, so total budgeted variable overhead is:
 $8,000 = (10 pools × 400 direct labor hours) × $2.00 per direct labor hour.
‖Fixed overhead was budgeted at $12,000 per month.

PANEL B—Computation of Flexible Budget for Direct Materials and Direct Labor for 10 Swimming Pools

	(1) Standard Quantity of Inputs Allowed for 10 Pools	(2) Standard Price per Unit of Input	(1) × (2) Flexible Budget for 10 Pools
Direct materials........................	1,000 cubic feet per pool × 10 pools = 10,000 cubic feet	$ 2.00	$20,000
Direct labor	400 hours per pool × 10 pools = 4,000 hours	10.50	42,000

Efficiency Variance. Measures whether the quantity of materials or labor used to make the actual number of outputs is within the standard allowed for that number of outputs. This is computed as the difference in quantities (actual quantity of input used minus standard quantity of input allowed for the actual number of outputs), multiplied by the standard unit price of the input.

The standard price is often referred to as the *price that should have been paid per unit* of the input (per cubic foot of gunite or per direct labor hour). If the company actually pays less than the standard price, then the price variance is favorable. Conversely, if the company actually pays more than the standard price, then the price variance is unfavorable.

An **efficiency variance** measures whether the quantity of materials or labor actually used to make the *actual number of outputs* is within the standard allowed for that number of outputs. The efficiency variance is the *difference in quantities* (actual quantity of input used − standard quantity of input allowed for the actual number of outputs), multiplied by the *standard unit price* of the input.

$$\text{Efficiency variance} = \begin{pmatrix} \text{Difference between actual quantity of} \\ \text{inputs used and the standard quantity} \\ \text{of inputs that should have been used} \\ \text{for the actual number of outputs} \end{pmatrix} \times \begin{pmatrix} \text{Standard unit} \\ \text{price of input} \end{pmatrix}$$

$$\text{Efficiency variance} = \begin{pmatrix} \text{Actual} & & \text{Standard} \\ \text{quantity} & - & \text{quantity} \\ \text{of input} & & \text{of input} \end{pmatrix} \times \begin{pmatrix} \text{Standard unit price} \\ \text{of input} \end{pmatrix}$$

The standard quantity of inputs is often referred to as the *quantity that should have been used*, or the standard quantity of inputs *allowed*, for the actual output. If the company actually uses less than the standard quantity of inputs allowed to produce the output, then the efficiency variance is favorable. Conversely, if the company uses more than the standard quantity, then the efficiency variance is unfavorable.

Price variances show how changes in prices of raw materials and labor affect the company's profit. But price variances that reflect changes in the market prices of materials and labor are largely beyond the company's control. Because managers generally cannot control changes in prices, *efficiency* variances are computed by multiplying the difference in quantity by the *standard* unit price. Efficiency variances thus capture the controllable aspect of how the company's *use* of materials and labor affects profits.

We now compute Kool-Time Pool's standard cost variances for direct materials and direct labor.

Direct Materials Variances

We begin our analysis of direct materials variances by compiling the relevant data from Exhibit 24-9, as follows:

■ Daily Exercise 24-12
■ Daily Exercise 24-13

Direct Materials	Actual	Flexible Budget	Flexible Budget Variance
Cubic feet	11,969	10,000	
Unit price	× $1.93	× $2.00	
Total..................	$23,100	$20,000	$3,100 U

We use these data to compute the price and efficiency variances:

$$\text{Price variance} = \begin{pmatrix} \text{Actual} & & \text{Standard} \\ \text{unit price} & - & \text{unit price} \\ \text{of input} & & \text{of input} \end{pmatrix} \times \begin{matrix} \text{Actual} \\ \text{quantity} \\ \text{of input} \end{matrix}$$

$$= \begin{pmatrix} \$1.93 \text{ per} \\ \text{cubic foot} \end{pmatrix} - \begin{pmatrix} \$2.00 \text{ per} \\ \text{cubic foot} \end{pmatrix} \times 11,969 \text{ cubic feet} = \$838 \text{ F}$$

$$\text{Efficiency variance} = \begin{pmatrix} \text{Actual} & & \text{Standard} \\ \text{quantity} & - & \text{quantity} \\ \text{of input} & & \text{of input} \end{pmatrix} \times \begin{matrix} \text{Standard} \\ \text{unit price} \\ \text{of input} \end{matrix}$$

$$= \begin{pmatrix} 11,969 \\ \text{cubic feet} \end{pmatrix} - \begin{pmatrix} 10,000 \\ \text{cubic feet} \end{pmatrix} \times \begin{matrix} \$2.00 \text{ per} \\ \text{cubic foot} \end{matrix} = \$3,938 \text{ U}$$

The price variance indicates that Kool-Time's operating income will be $838 higher because the company paid less than the standard price for gunite in June. The efficiency variance indicates that Kool-Time's operating income will be $3,938 lower because workers used more gunite than the standard allowance for ten pools.

Exhibit 24-10 summarizes the direct materials variance computations. Variance analysis begins with a total variance to be explained—in this example, the $3,100 unfavorable flexible budget variance for direct materials.

The $3,100 unfavorable variance is the sum of the price and efficiency variances:

Direct materials price variance........................	**$ 838 F**
Direct materials efficiency variance................	**3,938 U**
Direct materials flexible budget variance........	**$3,100 U**

Splitting the $3,100 unfavorable direct materials flexible budget variance into price and efficiency variances explains why Kool-Time actually spent $3,100 more than it should have spent for gunite:

- A good price for the gunite increased profits by $838, but
- Inefficient use of the gunite reduced profits by $3,938

Who is most likely responsible for the direct materials price variance? For the direct materials efficiency variance?

- Purchasing personnel are typically responsible for the direct materials price variance, because they should know why the actual price differs from the standard price. Purchasing personnel may have negotiated a good price for gunite, thus obtaining the favorable variance. Similarly, should the gunite supplier raise prices, purchasing personnel will know why the unfavorable price variance occurred.
- Production personnel are generally responsible for the direct materials efficiency variance. Perhaps their equipment malfunctioned, causing them to use more than the standard quantity of gunite. This would explain the unfavorable material efficiency variance.

> **Learning Tip:** As the braces in Exhibit 24-10 show, the price variance and the efficiency variance are components of the flexible budget variance—the difference between actual amounts and flexible budget amounts. The $838 F + $3,938 U = $3,100 U direct materials flexible budget variance is part of the $3,000 U flexible budget variance for variable expenses shown in column 2 of Exhibit 24-7. (The rest of the variable cost flexible budget variance is comprised of flexible budget variances for other variable expenses, as shown in Exhibit 24-9.) Notice in particular that the static budget in column 5 of Exhibit 24-7 has nothing to do with the computation of the flexible budget variance or how it is split into the price and efficiency variances as shown in Exhibit 24-10. Exhibit 24-7 shows that the static budget is used *only* in computing the sales volume variance—not in computing the flexible budget variance (or its component price and efficiency variances).

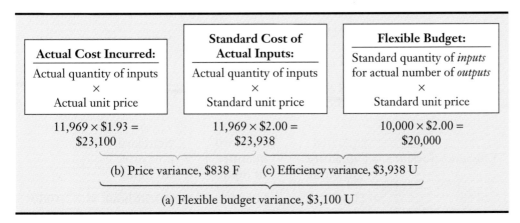

EXHIBIT 24-10
Kool-Time Pools Direct
Materials Variances

Actual Cost Incurred:	Standard Cost of Actual Inputs:	Flexible Budget:
Actual quantity of inputs × Actual unit price	Actual quantity of inputs × Standard unit price	Standard quantity of *inputs* for actual number of *outputs* × Standard unit price
11,969 × $1.93 = $23,100	11,969 × $2.00 = $23,938	10,000 × $2.00 = $20,000

(b) Price variance, $838 F   (c) Efficiency variance, $3,938 U

(a) Flexible budget variance, $3,100 U

Avoiding Common Pitfalls in Computing Price and Efficiency Variance

Make sure you avoid three common pitfalls in computing price and efficiency variances:

1. The price and efficiency variances are components of the *flexible budget variance.* Thus the static budget plays no role in computing price and efficiency variances.

2. In the efficiency variance, the standard quantity is the *standard quantity of inputs allowed for the actual number of outputs*—the basis for the flexible budget. To compute the standard quantity of inputs allowed, first determine the actual number of outputs. For Kool-Time Pools, the actual number of outputs is ten pools. Next, compute how many inputs should have been used to produce the actual number of outputs (10 pools). Each pool should use 1,000 cubic feet of gunite, so the standard quantity of gunite allowed for ten pools is $10 \times 1,000$ cubic feet = 10,000 cubic feet.

   Notice that the standard quantity of inputs is *not* based on the budgeted number of outputs (8 pools). That number is the basis for the static budget, which is not used to compute price and efficiency variances.

3. In the direct materials price variance, the difference in prices is multiplied by the *actual quantity* of materials. In the direct materials efficiency variance, the difference in quantities is multiplied by the *standard price* of the materials. The following explanation can help you remember this difference.
   - The materials price variance is usually the responsibility of purchasing personnel; they purchase the actual quantity used, not just the amount of materials that should have been used (the standard quantity). So the price variance is the difference in prices multiplied by the *actual quantity* of materials.
   - The materials efficiency variance is usually the responsibility of production personnel; they have no influence over the actual price. So the efficiency variance is computed as the difference in quantities multiplied by the *standard* price (the price that should have been paid).

Direct Labor Variances

We begin our analysis of direct labor variances by compiling the relevant data from Exhibit 24-9, as follows:

Direct Labor	Actual	Flexible Budget	Flexible Budget Variance
Hours..........................	3,800	4,000	
Hourly rate	× $11.00	× $10.50	
Total..........................	$41,800	$42,000	$200 F

We then use these data to compute the direct labor price and efficiency variances in the same manner as we computed the direct materials variances:

■ Daily Exercise 24-14

$$\text{Price variance} = \left(\begin{array}{c} \text{Actual} \\ \text{unit price} \\ \text{of input} \end{array} - \begin{array}{c} \text{Standard} \\ \text{unit price} \\ \text{of input} \end{array} \right) \times \begin{array}{c} \text{Actual quantity} \\ \text{of input} \end{array}$$

$$= \left(\begin{array}{c} \$11.00 \text{ per} \\ \text{hour} \end{array} - \begin{array}{c} \$10.50 \\ \text{per hour} \end{array} \right) \times 3,800 \text{ hours} = \$1,900 \text{ U}$$

$$\text{Efficiency variance} = \left(\begin{array}{c} \text{Actual} \\ \text{quantity} \\ \text{of input} \end{array} - \begin{array}{c} \text{Standard} \\ \text{quantity} \\ \text{of input} \end{array} \right) \times \begin{array}{c} \text{Standard} \\ \text{unit price} \\ \text{of input} \end{array}$$

$$= (3,800 \text{ hours} - 4,000 \text{ hours}) \times \$10.50/\text{hour} = \$2,100 \text{ F}$$

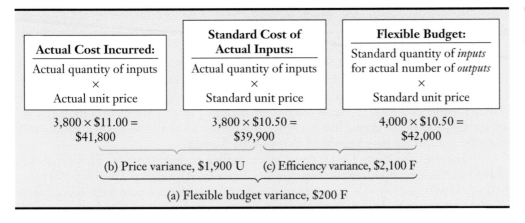

EXHIBIT 24-11
Kool-Time Pools Direct Labor
Variances

Actual Cost Incurred:	Standard Cost of Actual Inputs:	Flexible Budget:
Actual quantity of inputs × Actual unit price	Actual quantity of inputs × Standard unit price	Standard quantity of *inputs* for actual number of *outputs* × Standard unit price
3,800 × $11.00 = $41,800	3,800 × $10.50 = $39,900	4,000 × $10.50 = $42,000

(b) Price variance, $1,900 U   (c) Efficiency variance, $2,100 F

(a) Flexible budget variance, $200 F

Kool-Time's operating income will be $1,900 lower because the company paid its employees an average of $11.00 per hour in June instead of the standard rate of $10.50. But operating income will be $2,100 higher because the ten pools were installed in 3,800 hours instead of the budgeted quantity of 4,000 hours. As with direct materials, the price and efficiency variances sum to the flexible budget variance:

Direct labor price variance	**$1,900 U**
Direct labor efficiency variance	**2,100 F**
Direct labor flexible budget variance	**$ 200 F**

Exhibit 24-11 summarizes the direct labor variance computations.

Using Variance Information

Variances by themselves do not identify problems or opportunities. But large variances raise questions that deserve attention. Significant unfavorable variances may indicate problems that are preventing the company from accomplishing its budget goals. Significant favorable variances may indicate opportunities for continuing cost reductions. Managers usually regard small variances as normal and do not investigate them.

How often should variances be computed? If significant efficiency variances are likely, the company may monitor direct materials quantities and direct labor hours on a day-to-day or even hour-to-hour basis. Bar coding and computerized data-entry make such monitoring economically feasible. In contrast, if a long-term contract with a supplier or a labor union makes a large price variance unlikely, monthly comparisons of actual and standard prices may be enough. That is the case for the camera manufacturer Nikon, Inc.

When is a variance "large" or "significant"? The answer is a matter of managerial judgment. One manager may believe that variances of less than 8% do not warrant investigation. Another may believe that a 5% variance from a $1 million budget deserves attention while a 20% variance from a $10,000 budget does not. Rules of thumb, such as "investigate all variances greater than $10,000" and "investigate all variances equal to 8% or more of the standard cost" are common in practice. Nikon, for example, looks into any operating expense variance that is greater than 10% of the budget.

In June, Kool-Time Pools bought gunite for $1.93 per cubic foot (less than the standard price of $2.00). Kool-Time's 3.5% [($1.93 − $2.00)/$2.00] favorable direct materials price variance could arise because the purchasing officer did a good job negotiating prices with suppliers, or because the officer purchased lower-quality gunite. However, many managers consider a 3.5% variance insignificant and not worth investigating.

Favorable direct materials price variances can also arise when purchasing personnel buy materials in larger lot sizes to get a greater quantity discount. Because Kool-Time purchased only the quantity of gunite needed for June, there was no buildup of inventory. But a manager who is evaluated on price variance may place large orders to receive larger discounts. Purchasing more materials than currently needed is inconsistent with the just-in-time philosophy introduced in Chapter 19. Purchasing too large a quantity of

■ **Daily Exercise 24-15**

materials increases inventory, which increases inventory carrying costs, obsolescence, theft, and damage costs. Thus, we must interpret variances carefully—even a "favorable" variance can hurt the company's long-run profits.

Kool-Time's 19.7% [(11,969 − 10,000)/10,000] unfavorable direct materials efficiency variance may indicate that the gunite used was of low quality. Poor quality materials spoil, break, or crack more often, requiring replacement. Or perhaps an uncontrollable event led to excess usage. For example, earth tremors may have cracked several pools after the gunite had hardened but before all work was completed. Some of the extra gunite may have been used to repair the damage.

Now consider Kool-Time's direct labor flexible budget variance. This variance is only $200. Dividing it into its two components, however, is revealing. The 4.8% [($11.00 − $10.50)/$10.50] unfavorable price variance indicates that the company used more expensive labor than was budgeted. But those workers were more efficient. The average number of hours worked per pool (3,800 hours ÷ 10 pools = 380) was 5% less than the standard of 400 hours per pool. Kool-Time's managers may have decided to hire more-experienced workers and trade off an unfavorable price variance for a favorable efficiency variance. If so, the strategy was successful—the overall effect of their decision was favorable.

The preceding examples lead to two conclusions:

1. *Executives should be careful in using standard cost variances to evaluate performance.* Some variances are caused by factors that managers cannot control. Also, price and efficiency variances are often linked. For example, purchasing personnel may decide to buy higher quality (but more expensive) direct materials to reduce materials waste and spoilage. In this case, an unfavorable price variance may be more than offset by a favorable efficiency variance.

2. *Executives should consider using several measures to evaluate managers' performance.* Evaluations based on only one variance sometimes inadvertently encourage managers to take actions that make the variance look good, but hurt the company in the long-run. For example, Kool-Time's managers could
   - Buy more gunite than needed when the price is below standard to get a favorable price variance
   - Purchase low-quality gunite or hire less-experienced labor to get favorable price variances
   - Use less gunite or less labor (resulting in lower-quality installed pools) to get favorable efficiency variances

How can upper management discourage such actions? One approach is to base performance evaluation on *nonfinancial* measures as well—for example,

- The difference between the quantities of materials purchased and materials used, and
- Quality indicators such as:
  variances in the grade of gunite or labor used
  variances in the thickness or smoothness of the pool walls

McDonald's faces similar challenges (see the chapter opening story). McDonald's discourages skimping on labor by evaluating nonfinancial measures such as the difference betwen actual and standard time to serve drive-through customers. If the McDonald's shift manager sends too many workers home, McDonald's drive-through customers may have to wait too long to get their French fries. They may take their business to Wendy's or Burger King. Nonfinancial performance measures often prevent such abuses and enable managers to detect problem areas.

Manufacturing Overhead Variances

Ideally, manufacturing overhead cost variances should be computed and monitored for individual overhead costs like plant-related property taxes, utilities, and insurance. However, many companies compute variances on total overhead costs. These companies often split the variances on total manufacturing overhead cost into two parts: a *flexible budget variance* and a *production volume variance*.

The *flexible budget variance* for manufacturing overhead shows whether managers are keeping total overhead cost within the budgeted amount, given the actual number of outputs during the period. The *production volume variance* arises when the actual number of outputs differs from the expected number of outputs used in the static (master) budget. The two variances combine to explain the difference between actual overhead cost and the standard overhead cost that has been allocated to production (under- or overallocated overhead). Before discussing the computation of overhead variances, let's review how manufacturing overhead is allocated to production.

Allocating Manufacturing Overhead to Production

■ Daily Exercise 24-16

Kool-Time allocates manufacturing overhead to production based on standard direct labor hours for the actual number of outputs. Exhibit 24-12 shows Kool-Time's standard direct labor hours and budgeted manufacturing overhead costs for

- The flexible budget for actual output, which is based on actual output of 10 pools (not known until the end of the period)
- The static budget, which is based on expected output of 8 pools (known at the beginning of the period)

Notice that the $12,000 budgeted *fixed* manufacturing overhead is the same in both the static budget for 8 pools and the flexible budget for 10 pools. In contrast, the budgeted *variable* manufacturing overhead is higher in the flexible budget for 10 pools than in the static budget for 8 pools.

In a standard cost system, manufacturing overhead is allocated to production based on a *predetermined* overhead rate. We use a predetermined rate because managers cannot wait until the end of the year to determine the manufacturing overhead cost of products. As explained in Chapter 20, the predetermined overhead rate is the budgeted manufacturing overhead cost, divided by the budgeted quantity of the allocation base. ◀▥ But which budget? Keep in mind that the *predetermined* overhead rate must use data that are available at the *beginning* of the year. Consequently, most companies base their predetermined overhead rates on amounts from the static (master) budget, which is known at the beginning of the year. (The predetermined manufacturing overhead rate cannot be based on the flexible budget for actual production, because the actual number of outputs is not known until the end of the year.)

◀▥ ◀▥ ◀▥ To review the computation of the predetermined overhead rate, see Chapter 20, page 871.

Exhibit 24-12 shows that Kool-Time's standard manufacturing overhead rates are

- Variable—$2.00 per direct labor hour ($6,400 static budget variable manufacturing overhead divided by 3,200 static budget standard direct labor hours),
- Fixed—$3.75 per direct labor hour ($12,000 static budget fixed manufacturing overhead divided by 3,200 static budget standard direct labor hours),
- Total—$5.75 per direct labor hour ($2.00 + $3.75). This is the rate used to allocate manufacturing overhead to products.

EXHIBIT 24-12
Budgeted Manufacturing Overhead Costs and Allocation Rates

KOOL-TIME POOLS Budget Data for the Month Ended June 30, 19X9		
	Flexible Budget for Actual Output	**Static Budget for Expected Output**
Output units (pools installed)	10	8
Standard direct labor hours (400 hours per pool)	4,000	3,200
Budgeted manufacturing overhead cost:		
Variable	$ 8,000	$ 6,400
Fixed	12,000	12,000
Total	$20,000	$18,400
Standard variable manufacturing overhead rate per direct labor hour		$ 6,400 ÷ 3,200 = $2.00
Standard fixed manufacturing overhead rate per direct labor hour		$12,000 ÷ 3,200 = $3.75
Standard total manufacturing overhead rate per direct labor hour		$18,400 ÷ 3,200 = $5.75

To review under- and overallocated overhead, see Chapter 20, pages 875–877.

The total manufacturing overhead variance is the amount of under- or overallocated manufacturing overhead. This is the difference between actual and allocated manufacturing overhead, as explained in Chapter 20. Exhibit 24-13 shows that actual manufacturing overhead is $21,300. In a standard costing system, the amount of manufacturing overhead allocated to production is

Manufacturing overhead allocated to production	=	Standard predetermined manufacturing overhead rate	×	Standard quantity of the allocation base allowed for the *actual* number of outputs

For Kool-Time, this is

$$\text{Manufacturing overhead allocated to production} = \$5.75 \text{ per hour} \times 4,000 \text{ hours}$$
$$= \$23,000$$

It is important to remember that allocated manufacturing overhead is computed as: the standard predetermined manufacturing overhead rate × the standard quantity of the allocation base allowed *for the actual number of outputs*. Kool-Time allocates manufacturing overhead based on direct labor hours, so the allocation is based on the 4,000 direct labor hours allowed for the actual output of 10 pools. Notice that the 4,000 direct labor hours is the standard number of direct labor hours for the flexible budget at the actual output of 10 pools.

Given $21,300 of actual manufacturing overhead and $23,000 of allocated manufacturing overhead, Kool-Time has *overallocated* overhead of $1,700. Overallocated overhead is considered a favorable variance because actual overhead costs are less than allocated overhead costs. We now will see how this total $1,700 favorable manufacturing overhead variance is split into the overhead flexible budget variance and the production volume variance.

Overhead Flexible Budget Variance

The **overhead flexible budget variance** is the difference between the actual overhead cost and the flexible budget overhead for the actual number of outputs. Kool-Time's overhead flexible budget variance for June is computed as follows (data from Exhibit 24-13):

Actual overhead cost...	$21,300
Flexible budget overhead for actual outputs	20,000
Overhead flexible budget variance.......................	$ 1,300 U

Overhead Flexible Budget Variance. The difference between the actual overhead cost and the flexible budget overhead for the actual number of outputs.

■ **Daily Exercise 24-17**

EXHIBIT 24-13
Data for Computing Manufacturing Overhead Variances

KOOL-TIME POOLS			
Data for Computing Manufacturing Overhead Variances			
	Actual Overhead Cost (Exhibit 24-9)	Flexible Budget Overhead for Actual Number of Outputs (Exhibits 24-9 and 24-12)	Standard Overhead Allocated to Production (Rates from Exhibit 24-12)
Variable overhead	$ 9,000	$ 8,000	$2.00 × 4,000 direct labor hours = $ 8,000
Fixed overhead..............	12,300	12,000	$3.75 × 4,000 direct labor hours = 15,000
Total overhead	$21,300	$20,000	$5.75 × 4,000 direct labor hours = $23,000

Overhead flexible budget variance, $1,300 U

Production volume variance, $3,000 F

Total manufacturing overhead cost variance $1,700 F

Total June overhead was actually $21,300, compared with the flexible budget amount of $20,000. The unfavorable variance raises questions regarding managers' control of costs.

Production Volume Variance

The **production volume variance** is the difference between the manufacturing overhead cost in the flexible budget for actual outputs and the standard overhead allocated to production (data from Exhibit 24-13):

Production Volume Variance. The difference between the manufacturing overhead cost in the flexible budget for actual outputs and the standard overhead allocated to production.

Flexible budget overhead for actual outputs...................	$20,000
Standard overhead allocated to (actual) production........	23,000
Production volume variance	$ 3,000 F

The production volume variance is favorable whenever actual output (ten pools, for Kool-Time) exceeds expected output—(eight pools, Exhibit 24-12). The idea is that by installing ten pools instead of eight, Kool-Time used its production capacity more fully than originally planned. If Kool-Time had installed seven or fewer pools, the production volume variance would have been unfavorable because the company would have used less production capacity than expected.

Exhibit 24-13 reveals that the *variable* overhead cost in the flexible budget for actual outputs is always the same as the standard variable overhead allocated (standard predetermined variable overhead rate × the standard quantity of the allocation base allowed for the actual number of outputs). Thus the production volume variance is due only to fixed overhead.

The production volume variance is simply the portion of the total overhead variance that is not accounted for by the overhead flexible budget variance. Most companies use the term "production volume variance" because this variance arises only when actual production is not equal to expected (static budget) production. However, the term "production volume variance" can be somewhat misleading because it does *not* tell you how changes in production volume affect profits. To see how changes in production affect profits, use the contribution margin income statement approach from Chapter 22. For example, installing two more pools than expected should increase Kool-Time's profits by $8,000:

Increase in sales revenue (2 × $12,000).............	$24,000
Increase in variable expenses (2 × $8,000)	16,000
Increase in contribution margin.........................	8,000
Increase in fixed expenses...................................	–0–
Increase in operating income	$ 8,000

Standard Costs in the Accounts

Objective 6

Record transactions at standard cost

Recall that manufacturing companies have three inventory accounts: Materials Inventory, Work in Process Inventory, and Finished Goods Inventory. Firms with standard cost accounting systems assign costs to these accounts in various ways, but most companies record individual variances in separate accounts.

We use Kool-Time Pools' June transactions to demonstrate standard costing in a job costing context. Our entries are based on an important assumption: Kool-Time recognizes variances from standards as soon as possible. This means that direct materials price variances are recorded when materials are purchased. It also means that Work in Process Inventory is debited (swimming pools are costed) at standard input quantities and prices. June's entries follow.

■ Daily Exercise 24-18

1.	Materials Inventory (11,969 × $2.00)	23,938	
	Direct Materials Price Variance................................		838
	Accounts Payable (11,969 × $1.93)		23,100
	To record purchases of direct materials.		

By maintaining Materials Inventory at the *standard* price for gunite ($2.00), Kool-Time accountants can record the direct materials price variance at time of purchase. Recall that Kool-Time's direct materials price variance was $838 favorable (page 1048). A favorable variance has a credit balance in the accounts, and is a contra expense, or a reduction in expense. Consequently, the $838 favorable direct materials price variance is a contra expense that increases Kool-Time's June profits.

2.	Work in Process Inventory (10,000 × $2.00).....................	20,000	
	Direct Materials Efficiency Variance...............................	3,938	
	Materials Inventory (11,969 × $2.00).........................		23,938
	To record use of direct materials.		

Kool-Time's direct materials efficiency variance was $3,938 unfavorable (page 1048). An unfavorable variance has a debit balance, which increases expense. Consequently, Kool-Time's $3,938 unfavorable direct materials efficiency variance is an expense that decreases June profits. Notice also that Work in Process is debited for the standard price × standard quantity of direct materials that should have been used for the actual output of ten pools.

3.	Manufacturing Wages (3,800 × $10.50)	39,900	
	Direct Labor Price Variance...	1,900	
	Wages Payable (3,800 × $11.00)		41,800
	To record direct labor costs incurred.		

By maintaining Manufacturing Wages at the *standard* price for direct labor ($10.50), Kool-Time records the direct labor price variance at the time work is performed.

4.	Work in Process Inventory (4,000 × $10.50).....................	42,000	
	Direct Labor Efficiency Variance		2,100
	Manufacturing Wages (3,800 × $10.50)....................		39,900
	To assign direct labor costs.		

Work in Process is debited for the standard price × standard quantity of direct labor that should have been used for ten pools, similar to the (earlier) direct materials entry #2.

5.	Manufacturing Overhead	21,300	
	Accounts Payable, Accumulated Depreciation,		
	and so on...		21,300
	To record actual overhead costs incurred.		
	(See Exhibit 24-13.)		

6.	Work in Process Inventory (4,000 × $5.75).....................	23,000	
	Manufacturing Overhead...		23,000
	To allocate overhead. (See Exhibit 24-13.)		

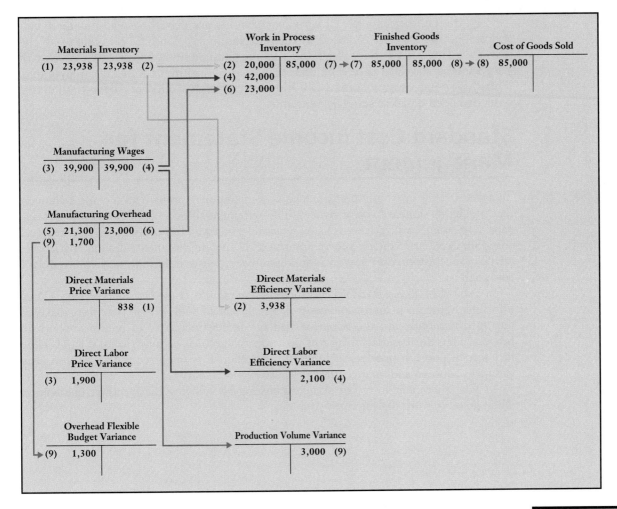

EXHIBIT 24-14
Kool-Time Pools Flow of Costs in Standard Costing System

In standard costing, the overhead allocated to Work in Process Inventory is computed as: the standard predetermined overhead rate × standard quantity of the allocation base that should have been used for the actual output (ten pools, in this case).

7.	Finished Goods Inventory............................	85,000	
	Work in Process Inventory...................		85,000
	To record completion of 10 pools ($20,000 + $42,000 + $23,000).		

8.	Cost of Goods Sold.......................................	85,000	
	Finished Goods Inventory....................		85,000
	To record the cost of sales of 10 pools.		

9.	Manufacturing Overhead..............................	1,700	
	Overhead Flexible Budget Variance	1,300	
	Production Volume Variance		3,000
	To record overhead variances and close the Manufacturing Overhead account. (See Exhibit 24-13.)		

■ Daily Exercise 24-19
■ Daily Exercise 24-20

Entry 9 closes Manufacturing Overhead. Many companies wait until the end of the fiscal year to close the account. This keeps a running total of underallocated (debit balance) or overallocated (credit balance) overhead during the year.

    Exhibit 24-14 shows selected Kool-Time accounts, after posting the preceding journal entries.

At the end of the year, all variance accounts are closed to zero-out their balances. The net amount is closed to Income Summary. Exhibit 24-15 shows all the manufacturing cost variances on the Income Statement as adjustments to cost of goods sold at standard cost. The net effect of the adjustment is $1,200 unfavorable. Thus June's operating income is $1,200 lower than it would have been if all actual costs had been equal to standard amounts.

Standard Cost Income Statement for Management

Objective 7

Prepare a standard cost income statement for management

To assess overall operating performance, a company may prepare an income statement that highlights standard cost variances. The statement shows cost of goods sold at standard cost. Then, each variance is listed separately, followed by cost of goods sold at actual cost. Similar detail can be shown for research and development, design, marketing, distribution, customer service, and administrative expenses if they are subject to standard cost analysis.

Exhibit 24-15 is a standard cost income statement that the managers of Kool-Time Pools might use for planning and control. Recall that all pools sold in June were installed during that month and the company had no ending inventory of gunite or work in process. Thus the manufacturing cost variances relate solely to June's sales. If Kool-Time had several pools in process on June 30, its accountants might consider prorating the variances between ending inventory and cost of goods sold.

Take a moment to review standard costing by studying the Decision Guidelines. Then go on to work the summary problem.

EXHIBIT 24-15
Standard Cost Income Statement

■ Daily Exercise 24-21

KOOL-TIME POOLS Standard Cost Income Statement Month Ended June 30, 19X9		
Sales revenue (10 × $12,000)		$120,000
Cost of goods sold at standard cost		85,000
Manufacturing cost variances:		
Direct materials price variance	$ (838)	
Direct materials efficiency variance	3,938	
Direct labor price variance	1,900	
Direct labor efficiency variance	(2,100)	
Manufacturing overhead flexible budget variance	1,300	
Production volume variance	(3,000)	
Total manufacturing variances		1,200
Cost of goods sold at actual cost		86,200
Gross margin		33,800
Marketing and administrative expenses*		18,800
Operating income		$ 15,000

*$9,100 + $9,700 from Exhibit 24-9.

DECISION GUIDELINES — Standard Costs

DECISION	GUIDELINES
How to set standards?	Historical performance data Engineering analysis Continuous improvement standards Benchmarking
How to compute a price variance for materials or labor?	$\text{Price variance} = \begin{pmatrix} \text{Actual unit price of input} - \text{Standard unit price of input} \end{pmatrix} \times \text{Actual quantity of input}$
How to compute an efficiency variance for materials or labor?	$\text{Efficiency variance} = \begin{pmatrix} \text{Actual quantity of input} - \text{Standard quantity of input for actual number of outputs} \end{pmatrix} \times \text{Standard unit price of input}$

Who is most likely responsible for
  Sales volume variance?
  Sales revenue flexible budget variance?
  Direct material price variance?
  Direct material efficiency variance?
  Direct labor price variance?
  Direct labor efficiency variance?
	Marketing Department
	Marketing Department
	Purchasing Department
	Production Departments
	Personnel Department or Production Department
	Production Department

How to analyze over- or underallocated manufacturing overhead?	Split over- or underallocated overhead into $\text{Flexible budget variance} = \text{Actual overhead} - \text{Flexible budget overhead}$ $\text{Production volume variance} = \text{Flexible budget overhead} - \text{Standard overhead allocated to actual outputs}$
How to allocate manufacturing overhead to production in a standard costing system?	$\text{Manufacturing overhead allocated} = \begin{pmatrix} \text{Standard predetermined manufacturing overhead rate} \end{pmatrix} \times \begin{pmatrix} \text{Standard quantity of allocation base allowed for actual outputs} \end{pmatrix}$
How to record standard costs in the accounts?	Materials Inventory: Actual quantity at standard price Work in Process Inventory (and Finished Goods Inventory and Cost of Goods Sold): Standard quantity of inputs allowed for actual outputs, at standard price of inputs

SUMMARY PROBLEM FOR YOUR REVIEW

Exhibit 24-9 indicates that Kool-Time Pools installed ten swimming pools in June. Suppose Kool-Time had installed seven pools instead of ten and that actual expenses were:

Direct materials (gunite)..........	7,400 cubic feet @ $2.00 per cubic foot
Direct labor..............................	2,740 hours @ $10.00 per hour
Variable overhead	$ 5,400
Fixed overhead	$11,900

REQUIRED

1. Given these new data, prepare two exhibits similar to Exhibits 24-9 and 24-12. Ignore marketing and administrative expenses in your first exhibit.

2. Compute price and efficiency variances for direct materials and direct labor.

3. Compute the total variance, the flexible budget variance, and the production volume variance for manufacturing overhead.

4. Prepare a June income statement through operating income for the president of Kool-Time Pools. Report all standard cost variances; assume that actual marketing and administrative expenses for the month were $17,700.

■ **SOLUTION**

KOOL-TIME POOLS
Revised Data for Standard Costing Example
Month of June, 19X9

PANEL A—Comparison of Actual Results with Flexible Budget for 7 Swimming Pools

	Actual Results at Actual Prices	Flexible Budget for 7 Pools	Flexible Budget Variance
Variable expenses:			
Direct materials................................	$14,800*	$14,000‡	$ 800 U
Direct labor..	27,400†	29,400‡	2,000 F
Variable overhead.............................	5,400	5,600§	200 F
Total variable expenses..................	47,600	49,000	1,400 F
Fixed expenses:			
Fixed overhead	11,900	12,000‖	100 F
Total expenses	$59,500	$61,000	$1,500 F

*$14,800 = 7,400 cubic feet of gunite actually used at actual price of $2.00 per cubic foot.
†$27,400 = 2,740 direct labor hours actually used at actual price of $10.00 per hour.
‡See Panel B.
§Variable overhead was budgeted at $2.00 per direct labor-hour, so total budgeted variable overhead is:
  $5,600 = (7 pools × 400 direct labor-hours per pool) × $2.00 per direct labor hour.
‖Fixed overhead was budgeted at $12,000 per month.

PANEL B—Computation of Flexible Budget for Direct Materials and Direct Labor for 7 Swimming Pools

	(1) Standard Quantity of Inputs Allowed for 7 Pools	(2) Standard Price per Unit of Input	(1) × (2) Flexible Budget for 7 Pools
Direct materials..........	1,000 cubic feet × 7 = 7,000 cubic feet	$ 2.00	$14,000
Direct labor	400 hours × 7 = 2,800 hours	10.50	29,400

KOOL-TIME POOLS
Revised Budget Data for Month Ended June 30, 19X9

	Flexible Budget for Actual Outputs	Static Budget for Expected Outputs
Output units (pools installed)	7	8
Standard direct labor hours (400 hours per pool)	2,800	3,200
Budgeted manufacturing overhead cost:		
Variable...	$ 5,600*	$ 6,400
Fixed	12,000†	12,000
Total..	$17,600	$18,400
Standard variable manufacturing overhead rate per direct labor hour		$ 6,400 ÷ 3,200 = $2.00
Standard fixed manufacturing overhead rate per direct labor hour		$12,000 ÷ 3,200 = 3.75
Standard total manufacturing overhead rate per direct labor hour		$18,400 ÷ 3,200 = $5.75

*Flexible budget variable overhead is computed as the standard quantity of the allocation base allowed for actual outputs (2,800 direct labor hours = 7 pools × 400 direct labor hours per pool) multiplied by the $2.00 standard variable manufacturing overhead rate per direct labor hour: 2,800 hours × $2.00 per hour = $5,600.

†Budgeted fixed overhead is *fixed* within the relevant range, so flexible budget fixed overhead is $12,000, the same as static budget fixed overhead.

$$\text{Price variance} = \begin{pmatrix} \text{Actual} \\ \text{unit price} \\ \text{of input} \end{pmatrix} - \begin{matrix} \text{Standard} \\ \text{unit price} \\ \text{of input} \end{matrix} \times \begin{matrix} \text{Actual} \\ \text{quantity} \\ \text{of input} \end{matrix}$$

Direct materials:

Price variance = ($2.00 – $2.00) × 7,400 cubic feet = $ –0–

Direct labor:

Price variance = ($10.00 – $10.50) × 2,740 hours = **$1,370 F**

$$\text{Efficiency variance} = \begin{pmatrix} \text{Actual} \\ \text{quantity} \\ \text{of input} \end{pmatrix} - \begin{matrix} \text{Standard} \\ \text{quantity} \\ \text{of input} \end{matrix} \times \begin{matrix} \text{Standard} \\ \text{unit price} \\ \text{of input} \end{matrix}$$

Direct materials:

Efficiency variance = $\left(\dfrac{7,400}{\text{cubic feet}} - \dfrac{7,000}{\text{cubic feet}}\right)$ × $\dfrac{\$2.00 \text{ per}}{\text{cubic foot}}$ = **$800 U**

Direct labor:

Efficiency variance = $\left(\dfrac{2,740}{\text{hours}} - \dfrac{2,800}{\text{hours}}\right)$ × $\dfrac{\$10.50}{\text{per hour}}$ = **$630 F**

Total overhead variance:

Actual overhead cost (variable, $5,400 + fixed, $11,900)	$17,300
Standard overhead allocated to production	
(2,800 standard direct labor hours × $5.75)....................................	16,100
Total overhead variance	$ 1,200 U

Overhead flexible budget variance:

Actual overhead cost ($5,400 + $11,900)	$17,300
Flexible budget overhead for actual outputs ($5,600 + $12,000)	17,600
Overhead flexible budget variance	$ 300 F

Production volume variance:

Flexible budget overhead for actual outputs ($5,600 + $12,000)	$17,600
Standard overhead allocated to (actual) production	
(2,800 standard direct labor hours × $5.75)	16,100
Production volume variance...	$ 1,500 U

KOOL-TIME POOLS
Revised Standard Cost Income Statement
Month Ended June 30, 19X9

Sales revenue (7 × $12,000).............................		$84,000
Cost of goods sold at standard cost*...............		59,500
Manufacturing cost variances:		
Direct materials price variance	$ 0	
Direct materials efficiency variance............	800	
Direct labor price variance..........................	(1,370)	
Direct labor efficiency variance	(630)	
Overhead flexible budget variance..............	(300)	
Production volume variance	1,500	
Total manufacturing variances....................		0
Cost of goods sold at actual cost....................		59,500
Gross margin..		24,500
Marketing and administrative expenses..........		17,700
Operating income		$ 6,800

*Cost of goods sold at standard cost:

Direct materials (7,000 cubic feet × $2.00 per cubic foot)	$14,000
Direct labor (2,800 direct labor hours × $10.50 per direct labor hour)..........	29,400
Standard overhead allocated (2,800 direct labor hours ×	
$5.75 per direct labor hour)	16,100
Cost of goods sold at standard cost..	$59,500

Summary of Learning Objectives

1. Prepare a flexible budget for the income statement. A *static budget* is prepared for only one level of output, which usually is the expected sales level for a period. A *flexible budget* is a summarized budget that can easily be computed for several different volume levels. Flexible budgets separate variable costs from fixed costs, and it is the variable costs that put the "flex" in the flexible budget. These budgets show how revenues and costs vary—if at all—as the number of outputs varies within the budget range. An after-the-fact flexible budget is prepared for the actual number of outputs.

2. Prepare an income statement performance report. Static budget variances are differences between actual amounts and corresponding amounts (revenues and expenses) in the static budget. At the end of the period, accountants prepare an after-the-fact flexible budget for the actual number of outputs. Accountants use this flexible budget to divide static budget variances into two broad categories. *Sales volume variances* are differences between flexible budget amounts and static budget amounts. *Flexible budget variances* are differences between actual amounts and flexible budget amounts.

3. Identify the benefits of standard costs. *Standard costs* are carefully predetermined costs that usually are expressed on a per-unit basis. Standards represent either very good performance or "best practice" performance. When used wisely, standards help managers plan and control, motivate employees, provide unit costs, and simplify record keeping.

4. Compute standard cost variances for direct materials and direct labor. Companies divide flexible budget variances for direct materials and direct labor into price and efficiency (quantity) variances. A *price variance* reveals the effect on total cost—and thus the effect on operating income—of paying more or less for an input than the standard allows. An *efficiency variance* reveals the effect on total cost of using more or less input than allowed by the flexible budget for the actual number of outputs. Managers often have to make trade-offs between price and efficiency variances.

5. Analyze manufacturing overhead in a standard cost system. Many companies compute a total variance between actual manufacturing overhead cost incurred and standard overhead cost allocated to production. This variance has two components: the *overhead flexible budget variance* and the *production volume variance*. The overhead flexible budget variance is the difference between the actual overhead and the flexible budget overhead that should have been incurred given the actual number of outputs. The production volume variance is the difference between the flexible budget overhead for actual outputs and the standard overhead allocated to production.

6. Record transactions at standard cost. Many companies record standard costs in their inventory and expense accounts. They also record standard cost variances. At year's end, all variance accounts are closed out. A net favorable (unfavorable) variance increases (decreases) operating income.

7. Prepare a standard cost income statement for management. Some companies prepare an income statement for management that highlights standard cost variances. The statement shows cost of goods sold at standard cost, lists all variances, and then shows the adjusted cost of goods sold—at actual cost. Operating expenses are treated similarly if they are part of the company's standard cost system.

Accounting Vocabulary

benchmarking (p. 1045)
efficiency variance (p. 1048)
flexible budget (p. 1036)
flexible budget variance
  (p. 1040)

master budget (p. 1036)
overhead flexible budget
  variance (p. 1054)
price variance (p. 1047)

production volume variance
  (p. 1055)
sales volume variance
  (p. 1040)

standard cost (p. 1044)
static budget (p. 1036)
variance (p. 1036)

Questions

1. What is the relevant range, and why must it be considered in preparing a flexible budget?
2. How does a static budget differ from a flexible budget?
3. Explain how managers use variance information from an income statement performance report.
4. McLaren, Inc., prepared its static (master) budget for a sales level of 35,000 for the month. Actual sales totaled 46,000. Describe the problem of using the static budget to evaluate company performance for the month. Propose a better way to evaluate McLaren's performance.
5. What advantage does a flexible budget graph offer over a columnar flexible budget with four levels of volume?
6. What do the sales volume variance and the flexible budget variance for operating income measure?
7. Describe the benefits of a standard cost system.
8. What two general categories of prime cost variances do most standard cost systems provide?
9. Identify the similarities and differences between a standard cost and a budgeted cost.
10. Your company is installing a standard cost system. What sort of standard cost is most popular? For employees, what purpose does a standard cost fulfill?

11. What does a price variance measure? How is it computed?
12. What does an efficiency variance measure? How is it computed?
13. How are the price variance and the efficiency variance related to the flexible budget variance for direct materials and direct labor?
14. Describe how managers can trade off direct materials price and efficiency variances.
15. Describe a trade-off a manager might make for labor cost.
16. When should a cost variance be investigated?
17. What causes an overhead flexible budget variance? What information does this variance provide?
18. What information is provided by the production volume variance? How is this variance computed?
19. Scott & White, Inc., uses standard costing. The standard cost of the actual quantity of direct materials used to manufacture inventory was $21,600. The direct materials efficiency variance was $1,400 favorable. Make the journal entry to record the use of materials in production.
20. How does a standard cost income statement for management differ from an income statement reported to the public?

Daily Exercises

DE24-1 Fill in the blank with the phrase that best completes the sentence.

- Flexible budget
- Flexible budget variance
- Sales volume variance
- Static budget
- Static budget variance

a. The master budget is a _____.

b. A _____ can be prepared at either the beginning or the end of the period.

c. The difference between actual amounts and flexible budget amounts is the _____.

d. The _____ is usually the responsibility of the Marketing Department.

e. A _____ can easily be computed for several different volume levels.

f. The difference between the flexible budget and the static budget is the _____.

g. A _____ is prepared for only one level of sales volume.

DE24-2 Consider the Kool-Time Pools example on page 1037.

1. Using the data from Exhibit 24-3 (page 1037), develop flexible budgets for four- and nine-pool levels of output.

2. Would Kool-Time's managers use the flexible budgets you developed in requirement 1 for planning or for controlling? What specific insights can Kool-Time's managers gain from the flexible budgets you prepared in requirement 1?

DE24-3 In a series of Daily Exercises, we are going to prepare budgets and variance analyses for Homeguard, Inc., a firm that installs home security systems. For each installation, Homeguard has budgeted direct materials costs of $500 and budgeted direct labor costs of $400. The company has budgeted fixed expenses at $8,000 per month, for 0–50 installations per month. Homeguard's budgeted sale price is $1,700 per installation.

1. Write out Homeguard's flexible budget total cost formula.

2. Using Exhibit 24-3 (page 1037) as a guide, prepare flexible budgets for Homeguard for
    a. 20 installations per month
    b. 30 installations per month

DE24-4 Refer to Kool-Time Pools' graph of actual and budgeted monthly costs in Exhibit 24-5 on page 1039.

1. How many pools did Kool-Time install in August?

2. How much were Kool-Time's actual expenses in August?

3. Using Kool-Time's flexible budget formula, what is the flexible budget total cost for the month of August?

4. Is Kool-Time's flexible budget variance for total costs favorable or unfavorable in August?

DE24-5 ◀━ *Link Back to Chapter 22, Exhibit 22-7 (page 963).* Refer to Daily Exercise 24-3. Homeguard reports the following actual results for January and February:

	January	February
Expected number of installations, per the static budget	20	30
Actual number of installations	25	20
Actual sale price per installation	$1,700	$1,800
Actual direct materials cost per installation............................	$ 450	$ 560
Actual direct labor cost per installation	$ 380	$ 400
Actual fixed monthly expenses	$7,000	$9,000

1. Prepare a graph of Homeguard's monthly flexible budget total cost formula using data from Daily Exercise 24-3. Use Exhibit 24-4 on page 1038 as a guide.

2. Plot January's and February's actual costs on the flexible budget graph from requirement 1.

3. Compute January and February flexible budget variances. Has Homeguard done a better-than-expected job or a worse-than-expected job of controlling costs in January? In February? Explain.

DE24-6 Use your results from Daily Exercise 24-4 to prepare an income statement performance report for Kool-Time Pools for August. Use Exhibit 24-7 (page 1041) as a guide. Assume that the actual sale price per pool remains $12,000, actual variable expenses total $59,000, and actual fixed expenses are $21,000 in August. The static budget number of pools remains eight.

Explain to Kool-Time's management why August operating income differs from the static budget operating income.

DE24-7 Use the data in Daily Exercises 24-3 and 24-5 to prepare an income statement performance report for Homeguard for January. Use Exhibit 24-7 (page 1041) as a guide. Interpret the variances for Homeguard's management.

DE24-8 Consider the Kool-Time Pools example on pages 1036–1042.

1. What is the relevant range for the flexible budget total cost formula?
2. Explain whether Kool-Time would have a sales volume variance for fixed expenses in Exhibit 24-7 (page 1041) if
   a. Kool-Time installs 10 pools per month.
   b. Kool-Time installs 15 pools per month.

DE24-9 Fill in the blank with the phrase that best completes the sentence.

Beginning of the period   Actual number of outputs   Static budget variance
End of the period   Expected number of outputs
Flexible budget variance   Sales volume variance

a. The master budget is based on the _____.
b. The flexible budget used in a performance report is developed at the _____.
c. The difference between actual costs and the costs that should have been incurred for the actual number of outputs is the _____.
d. The static budget is developed at the _____.
e. The flexible budget used in a performance report is based on the _____.

DE24-10 Denby is a British manufacturer of ceramic dinnerware. The raw materials are mixed to form clay, which is shaped into bowls, plates, and so on. The pieces are then glazed and fired at high temperatures.

Explain how the five benefits of standard costs (page 1046) apply to Denby. Be as specific as possible.

DE24-11 As explained in the chapter opening story, each McDonald's uses historical data to budget sales for each hour, and the restaurant computes hourly sales variances. If actual sales are less than budgeted, the manager can send employees home.

1. What sales variance does McDonald's compute hourly?
2. What variance does McDonald's control by sending employees home early if actual sales fall short of the budget? Explain.

DE24-12 In a series of Daily Exercises, we will compute variances and record journal entries for GardenArts, a manufacturer of small ceramic garden figurines. The company has the following standards:

Direct materials (clay).....................	1 pound per figurine, at a cost of $0.25 per pound
Direct labor	1/5 hour per figurine, at a cost of $13 per hour
Static budget variable overhead......	$60,000
Static budget fixed overhead...........	$20,000
Static budget direct labor hours	10,000 hours

GardenArts allocates manufacturing overhead to production based on standard direct labor hours. Last month, GardenArts reported the following actual results for the production of 60,000 figurines:

Direct materials...........................	1.1 pound per figurine, at a cost of $0.30 per pound
Direct labor	1/4 hour per figurine, at a cost of $12 per hour
Actual variable overhead.............	$84,000
Actual fixed overhead..................	$18,000

Compute GardenArts' variances for materials.

DE24-13 As explained in the chapter opening story, the standard direct materials for a regular McDonald's hamburger are

1 bun	1/8 teaspoon dehydrated onion
1 hamburger patty	1/4 teaspoon mustard
1 pickle slice	1/2 ounce ketchup

Assume that the Greensboro, Georgia, McDonald's sold 500 hamburgers yesterday, and they actully used the following materials:

510 buns	70 teaspoons dehydrated onion
520 hamburger patties	120 teaspoons mustard
490 pickle slices	300 ounces ketchup

Compute the direct material efficiency variances for each material, using the following standard material prices (all amounts assumed):

Buns............................	$0.09 each	Dehydrated onion	$0.04 per teaspoon
Hamburger patties.....	0.12 each	Mustard	0.02 per teaspoon
Pickle slices	0.01 per slice	Ketchup....................	0.04 per ounce

DE24-14 Refer to the GardenArts data in Daily Exercise 24-12. Compute the direct labor variances.

Computing direct labor variances (Obj. 4)

DE24-15 Refer to Daily Exercises 24-12 and 24-14. For each variance, who in GardenArts' organization is most likely responsible? Interpret the direct materials and direct labor variances for GardenArts' management.

Interpreting materials and labor variances (Obj. 4)

DE24-16 Examine Exhibit 24-6. Show where the following variances would fall:

a. Direct materials price variance
b. Direct materials efficiency variance
c. Direct labor price variance
d. Direct labor efficiency variance.
e. Flexible budget overhead variance

Relations among variances (Obj. 4, 5)

DE24-17 Refer to the GardenArts data in Daily Exercise 24-12.

1. Compute the standard predetermined variable manufacturing overhead rate and the standard predetermined fixed manufacturing overhead rate.
2. Compute the overhead variances. (Use Exhibit 24-13 as a guide.)
3. Is manufacturing overhead under- or overallocated? By how much?

Computing overhead variances (Obj. 5)

DE24-18 Refer to the information in Daily Exercises 24-12 and 24-14. Record GardenArts' direct materials and direct labor journal entries.

Recording materials and labor journal entries in a standard cost system (Obj. 6)

DE24-19 Refer to the information in Daily Exercises 24-12 and 24-17. Record GardenArts' journal entries for Manufacturing Overhead, including the entry to record the overhead variances and to close the Manufacturing Overhead account.

Recording overhead journal entries in a standard cost system (Obj. 6)

DE24-20 Refer to the information in Daily Exercises 24-12, 24-14, and 24-17 through 24-19. GardenArts sold on account each of the 60,000 figurines at a sale price of $7.25 each. There were no beginning or ending inventories of any kind.
    Record the journal entries for the completion and sale of the 60,000 figurines.

Recording journal entries for goods completed and sold in a standard cost system (Obj. 6)

DE24-21 Use the information from Daily Exercises 24-12, 24-14, and 24-17 through 24-20 to prepare a standard cost income statement for GardenArts' management, using Exhibit 24-15 as a guide. Actual marketing and administrative expenses were $88,500.

Preparing a standard cost income statement for management (Obj. 7)

Exercises

E24-1 Kandlestix Company sells its main product, an elaborate candle, for $7.50 each. Its variable cost is $2 per candle. Fixed expenses are $200,000 per month for volumes up to 60,000 candles. Above 60,000 candles, monthly fixed expenses are $240,000.
    Prepare a monthly flexible budget for the product, showing sales, variable expenses, fixed expenses, and operating income or loss for volume levels of 40,000, 50,000, and 70,000 candles.

Preparing a flexible budget for the income statement (Obj. 1)

E24-2 ◄▥ *Link Back to Chapter 22, Exhibit 22-7 (page 963).* Graph the flexible budget total cost line for Kandlestix Company in Exercise 24-1. Show total costs for volume levels of 40,000, 50,000, and 70,000 candles.

Graphing cost behavior (Obj. 1)

E24-3 Custom Canvas Products managers received the following incomplete performance report:

	Actual Results at Actual Prices	Flexible Budget Variance	Flexible Budget for Actual Number of Output Units	Sales Volume Variance	Static (Master) Budget
CUSTOM CANVAS PRODUCTS **Income Statement Performance Report** **Year Ended July 31, 19X9**					
Output units.................	24,000	_____	24,000	4,000 F	_____
Sales revenue...............	$192,000	_____	$192,000	$32,000 F	_____
Variable expenses	85,000	_____	72,000	12,000 U	_____
Fixed expenses..............	104,000	_____	100,000	–0–	_____
Total expenses	189,000	_____	172,000	12,000 U	_____
Operating income	$ 3,000	_____	$ 20,000	$20,000 F	_____

Complete the performance report. Identify the employee group that may deserve praise and the group that may be subject to criticism. Give your reasons.

E24-4 Top managers of Vasquez Industries predicted 19X9 sales of 145,000 units of its product at a unit price of $6. Actual sales for the year were 140,000 units at $7 each. Variable expenses were budgeted at $2.20 per unit, and actual variable expenses were $2.25 per unit. Actual fixed expenses of $420,000 exceeded budgeted fixed expenses by $5,000. Prepare Vasquez's income statement performance report in a format similar to Exercise 24-3. What variance contributed most to the year's favorable results? What caused this variance?

Computing price and efficiency
variances for direct materials
(Obj. 4)

E24-5 The following direct materials variance computations are incomplete:

$$\text{Price variance} = (\$? - \$14) \times 14{,}500 \text{ pounds} = \$5{,}075 \text{ U}$$
$$\text{Efficiency variance} = (? - 14{,}700 \text{ pounds}) \times ? = ? \text{ F}$$
$$\text{Flexible budget variance} = \$?$$

Fill in the missing values, and identify the flexible budget variance as favorable or unfavorable.

Computing price and efficiency
variances for materials and labor
(Obj. 4)

E24-6 Cumberland Framing, which uses a standard cost accounting system, manufactured 400,000 picture frames during the year, using 1,350,000 board feet of lumber purchased at $1.55 per foot. Production required 9,500 direct labor hours that cost $10.50 per hour. The materials standard was 3 board feet of lumber per frame, at a standard cost of $1.60 per foot. The labor standard was 0.025 direct labor hour per frame, at a standard cost of $10.00 per hour. Compute the price and efficiency variances for direct materials and direct labor.

E24-7 Make the journal entries to record the purchase and use of direct materials and direct labor in Exercise 24-6.

E24-8 The managers of Mai-Fu, Inc., are seeking explanations for the variances in the report below. Explain the meaning of each of Mai-Fu's materials, labor, and overhead variances.

MAI-FU, INC.
Standard Costing Income Statement
Year Ended December 31, 19X9

Sales revenue...		$1,200,000
Cost of goods sold—standard		700,000
Manufacturing cost variances:		
Materials: price	$ 8,000 F	
efficiency......................................	12,000 U	
Labor: price	24,000 U	
efficiency......................................	10,000 F	
Overhead: flexible budget...........................	28,000 U	
production volume	16,000 F	
Total manufacturing variances......................		30,000
Cost of goods sold—actual.............................		730,000
Gross margin		470,000
Marketing and administrative expenses		418,000
Operating income..		$ 52,000

E24-9 Synmar manufactures cultured marble. The company charges the following standard unit costs to production on the basis of static budget volume of 30,000 linear feet of cultured marble per month:

Computing overhead variances
(Obj. 5)

Direct materials	$4.50
Direct labor..................................	2.00
Manufacturing overhead..............	1.50
Standard unit cost	$8.00

Synmar uses the following monthly flexible budget overhead:

	Number of Outputs (linear feet)		
	27,000	30,000	33,000
Standard machine hours...................................	2,700	3,000	3,300
Budgeted manufacturing overhead cost:			
Variable	$13,500	$15,000	$16,500
Fixed..	30,000	30,000	30,000

Actual values: monthly production, 33,000 linear feet; variable overhead, $15,700; fixed overhead, $30,500; machine hours worked, 3,250. Compute the total overhead variance, the overhead flexible budget variance, and the production volume variance.

E24-10 Cavalier International Co. revenue and expense information for the month of November follows.

Preparing a standard cost income statement for management
(Obj. 7)

Sales revenue	$440,000
Cost of goods sold (standard)	242,000
Direct materials price variance	2,000 U
Direct materials efficiency variance................	4,000 F
Direct labor price variance..............................	1,000 U
Direct labor efficiency variance.......................	2,000 F
Overhead flexible budget variance..................	2,500 U
Production volume variance.............................	5,000 U

Prepare a standard cost income statement for management through gross margin. Report all standard cost variances for management's use.

CHALLENGE EXERCISE

E24-11 Trio TV repairs televisions. The company measures "production output" in terms of the number of televisions repaired. The company allocates overhead at the rate of $80 per television repaired:

Overhead variances
(Obj. 5)

	Overhead Rate per Unit
Variable	$30
Fixed	50

In April, 19X9, Trio TV "produced" 5,200 repaired televisions. Its production volume variance was $5,000 favorable. Compute Trio's budgeted fixed overhead cost per month. What monthly capacity level did Trio use to compute the fixed overhead rate of $50 per unit?

Beyond the Numbers

BN24-1 You recently accepted a management trainee position with Creative Barriers, a company that installs residential fencing. At the end of your first month on the job, July 19X9, your boss asks

Explaining benefits of flexible budgets
(Obj. 1, 2)

you to prepare a flexible budget for July's actual output of 228,000 yards of fencing. You are delighted to be assigned a task that uses your management accounting knowledge. Upon returning home that evening, you tell your roommate about your new task. Your roommate, a health sciences major, replies:

> Making a budget for a period that is already over reminds me of the round-the-world hot-air ballooner who lost track of his location. He landed in a meadow in a remote wilderness. Just as he was landing a hiker happened by:
>
> | | |
> |---|---|
> | Ballooner: | Can you tell me where I am? |
> | Hiker: | Standing in a hot-air balloon basket in a meadow. |
> | Ballooner: | You must be an accountant. |
> | Hiker: | Yes! How in the world did you know that? |
> | Ballooner: | Because what you told me was precisely correct and utterly useless! |
>
> Why are you wasting time preparing an accurate budget for *last* month? Wouldn't it be more useful to develop a budget for *next* month?

Explain to your roommate how managers can use a budget for a period that has already finished.

Explaining benefits of standard costing
(Obj. 3)

BN24-2 One of your fellow classmates who is frustrated by the details of variance analysis complains:

> Our textbook says that standard costing is easier than actual costing. But if it's so much easier, why does the book need an extra half chapter just to explain it? I don't get it . . .

Use the Kool-Time Pools example to explain why standard costing can simplify record-keeping in real companies.

Explaining materials and labor variances
(Obj. 4)

BN24-3 You have a summer internship at Kellogg's plant in Battle Creek, Michigan. Part of your job is to help the plant manager interpret accounting reports. One day the manager says:

> I can see that the direct materials price variance is based on the difference in prices. And I can see that the direct materials efficiency variance is based on the difference in quantities. What I've never understood is why we
>
> - Multiply the difference in prices by the *actual* quantity for the price variance, but
> - Multiply the difference in quantities by the *standard* price for the efficiency variance

Respond to the plant manager.

ETHICAL ISSUE

Setting standards
(Obj. 4)

Joel Gregory is the accountant for Outdoor Living, a manufacturer of outdoor furniture that is sold through nurseries and mail-order catalogue companies. Annually, Gregory is responsible for reviewing the standard costs for the following year. While reviewing the standard costs for the coming year, two ethical issues arise. Use the IMA's ethical guidelines, page 837, to identify the ethical dilemma in each situation. Identify the relevant factors in each situation and suggest what Gregory should recommend to the controller.

ISSUE 1 Gregory has been approached by Elizabeth Hayes, a former colleague who worked with Gregory when they were both employed by a public accounting firm. Hayes has recently started her own firm, Hayes Benchmarking Associates, which collects and sells data on industry benchmarks. She offers to provide Gregory with benchmarks for the outdoor furniture industry free of charge, if he will provide her with the last three years of Outdoor Living's standard and actual costs. Hayes explains that this is how she obtains most of her firm's benchmarking data. Gregory always has a difficult time with the standard-setting process and believes that the benchmark data would be very useful.

ISSUE 2 Outdoor Living's management is starting a continuous improvement policy that requires a 15% reduction in standard costs each year for the next three years. Dan Jones, manufacturing foreman of the Heritage wood furniture line, asks Gregory to set loose standard costs this year before the continuous improvement policy is implemented. Jones argues that there is no other way to meet the tightening standards while maintaining the high quality of the Heritage line.

Problems (GROUP A)

P24-1A ◀ *Link Back to Chapter 22, Exhibit 22-7 (page 963).* Bioseptic, Inc., produces and sells prepackaged kits for testing water purity. The company's static budget income statement for August 19X8 follows. It is based on expected sales volume of 55,000 test kits.

Preparing a flexible budget income statement and graphing cost behavior (Obj. 1)

BIOSEPTIC, INC. Static Budget Income Statement August 19X8	
Sales revenue............................	$220,000
Variable expenses:	
Cost of goods sold..................	60,500
Sales commissions.................	16,500
Utilities expense....................	5,500
Fixed expenses:	
Salary expense	36,500
Depreciation expense............	24,000
Rent expense	11,500
Utilities expense....................	6,200
Total expenses...........................	160,700
Operating income.....................	$ 59,300

Bioseptic's plant capacity is 62,500 kits. If actual volume exceeds 62,500 kits, the company must expand the plant. In that case, salaries will increase by 10%, depreciation by 20%, and rent by $5,500. Fixed utilities will be unchanged by any volume increase.

REQUIRED

1. Prepare flexible budget income statements for the company, showing output levels of 55,000, 60,000, and 65,000 test kits.
2. Graph the behavior of the company's total costs.

P24-2A Refer to Bioseptic, Inc., of Problem 24-1A. The company sold 60,000 test kits during August 19X8, and its actual operating income was as follows:

Preparing an income statement performance report (Obj. 2)

BIOSEPTIC, INC. Income Statement August 19X8	
Sales revenue	$243,500
Variable expenses:	
Cost of goods sold...............	$ 66,500
Sales commissions	19,500
Utilities expense	6,000
Fixed expenses:	
Salary expense.......................	38,000
Depreciation expense	24,000
Rent expense.........................	9,500
Utilities expense	6,200
Total expenses..........................	169,700
Operating income	$ 73,800

REQUIRED

1. Prepare an income statement performance report for August 19X8.
2. What accounts for most of the difference between actual operating income and static budget operating income?
3. What is Bioseptic's static budget variance? Explain why the income statement performance report provides more useful information than the simple static budget variance. What insights can Bioseptic's managers draw from this performance report?

Preparing a flexible budget and
computing standard cost variances
(Obj. 1, 3, 4, 5)

P24-3A Accuview, Inc., assembles VCRs and uses flexible budgeting and a standard cost system. Accuview allocates overhead based on the number of direct materials parts. The company's performance report includes the following selected data:

	Static Budget (20,000 VCRs)	Actual Results (22,000 VCRs)
Sales (20,000 VCRs × $200)	$4,000,000	
(22,000 VCRs × $210)		$4,620,000
Variable manufacturing expenses:		
Direct materials (200,000 parts @ $8.00)	1,600,000	
(214,200 parts @ $7.90)		1,692,180
Direct labor (40,000 hours @ $10.00)	400,000	
(42,500 hours @ $10.25)		435,625
Variable overhead (200,000 parts @ $2.00)	400,000	
(214,200 parts @ $2.10)		449,820
Fixed manufacturing expenses:		
Fixed overhead	600,000	610,000
Total cost of goods sold	3,000,000	3,187,625
Gross margin	$1,000,000	$1,432,375

REQUIRED

1. Prepare a flexible budget based on the actual number of VCRs sold.
2. Compute the price variance and the efficiency variance for direct materials and for direct labor. For manufacturing overhead, compute the total variance, the flexible budget variance, and the production volume variance.

3. What is the total flexible budget variance for Accuview's manufacturing costs? Show how the total flexible budget variance is divided into materials, labor, and overhead variances.
4. Describe how Accuview's managers can benefit from the standard costing system.

Using incomplete cost and variance
information to determine the number of
direct labor hours worked
(Obj. 4)

P24-4A The City of Columbus has a shop that manufactures lampposts. The manager of the shop uses standard costs to judge performance. Recently, a clerk mistakenly threw away some of the records, and the manager has only partial data for October. The manager knows that the direct labor flexible budget variance for the month was $349 F and that the standard labor price was $6.70 per hour. A recent pay cut caused a favorable labor price variance of $0.30 per hour. The standard direct labor hours for actual October output were 2,870.

REQUIRED

1. Find the actual number of direct labor hours worked during October. First, find the actual direct labor price per hour. Then, determine the actual number of direct labor hours worked by setting up the computation of the direct labor flexible budget variance of $349 F.
2. Compute the direct labor price and efficiency variances.

P24-5A K-2 Products manufactures hiking boots. The company prepares flexible budgets and uses a standard cost system to control manufacturing costs. The following standard unit cost of a pair of boots is based on the static budget volume of 14,000 pairs per month:

Direct materials (2.8 sq. ft @ $2.00 per sq. ft)		**$ 5.60**
Direct labor (2 hours @ $9.50 per hour)		**19.00**
Manufacturing overhead:		
Variable (2 hours @ $0.65 per hour)	**$1.30**	
Fixed (2 hours @ $2.20 per hour)	**4.40**	**5.70**
Total cost per pair		**$30.30**

Data for November of the current year include the following:

a. Actual production was 13,600 pair.
b. Actual direct materials usage was 2.70 square feet per pair of boots at an actual cost of $2.20 per square foot.
c. Actual direct labor usage of 24,480 hours cost $235,008.
d. Total actual overhead cost was $78,500.

REQUIRED

1. Compute the price and efficiency variances for direct materials and direct labor.
2. Journalize the usage of direct materials and the assignment of direct labor, including the related variances.

3. For manufacturing overhead, compute the total variance, the flexible budget variance, and the production volume variance.
4. K-2's management intentionally purchased superior materials for November production. How did this decision affect the other cost variances? Overall, was the decision wise?

P24-6A Plasco Manufacturing produces industrial plastics. During October, the company produced and sold 42,000 sheets of plastic and recorded the following cost data:

Computing standard cost variances and reporting to management (Obj. 4, 5, 7)

	Standard Unit Cost	Actual Total Cost
Direct materials:		
Standard (3 lb @ $1.25 per lb)	$3.75	
Actual (134,400 lb @ $1.18 per lb)		$158,592
Direct labor:		
Standard (0.1 hr @ $7.00 per hr)	0.70	
Actual (4,400 hr @ $6.80 per hr)		29,920
Manufacturing overhead:		
Standard:		
Variable (0.2 machine hr @ $6.00 per hr)............ $1.20		
Fixed ($64,000 for static budget volume of		
40,000 units and 8,000 machine hours)............ 1.60	2.80	
Actual		118,900
Total manufacturing costs...	$7.25	$307,412

1. Compute the price and efficiency variances for direct materials and direct labor.
2. For manufacturing overhead, compute the total variance, the flexible budget variance, and the production volume variance.
3. Prepare a standard cost income statement through gross margin to report all variances to management. Sale price of the plastic was $10.50 per sheet.
4. Plasco intentionally purchased cheaper materials during October. Was the decision wise? Discuss the trade-off between the two materials variances.

Problems (GROUP B)

P24-1B ◀▥ *Link Back to Chapter 22, Exhibit 22-7 (page 963).* Audex Components Company manufactures capacitors for stereo equipment. The company's static budget income statement for October 19X9 follows. It is based on expected sales volume of 9,000 units.

Preparing a flexible budget income statement and graphing cost behavior (Obj. 1)

Audex's plant capacity is 9,500 units. If actual volume exceeds 9,500 units, Audex must rent additional space. In that case, salaries will increase by 10%, rent will double, and insurance expense will increase by $500. Depreciation will be unaffected.

AUDEX COMPONENTS COMPANY
Static Budget Income Statement
October 19X9

Sales revenue...............................	$189,000
Variable expenses:	
Cost of goods sold.................	72,000
Sales commissions..................	9,450
Shipping expense	4,500
Fixed expenses:	
Salary expense	27,500
Depreciation expense............	13,250
Rent expense	11,250
Insurance expense	2,750
Total expenses	140,700
Operating income.......................	$ 48,300

1. Prepare flexible budget income statements for 7,500, 9,000, and 11,000 units.
2. Graph the behavior of the company's total costs.

Preparing an income statement performance report
(Obj. 2)

P24-2B Refer to Audex Components Company, Problem 24-1B. The company sold 11,000 units during October 19X9, and its actual operating income was as follows.

AUDEX COMPONENTS COMPANY Income Statement October 19X9	
Sales revenue.............................	$232,000
Variable expenses:	
Cost of goods sold................	90,250
Sales commissions................	11,250
Shipping expense	6,750
Fixed expenses:	
Salary expense	31,750
Depreciation expense............	13,250
Rent expense	22,000
Insurance expense	3,500
Total expenses.........................	178,750
Operating income.....................	$ 53,250

REQUIRED

1. Prepare an income statement performance report for October.
2. What was the effect on Audex's operating income of selling 2,000 units more than the static budget level of sales?
3. What is Audex's static budget variance? Explain why the income statement performance report provides more useful information to Audex's managers than the simple static budget variance. What insights can Audex's managers draw from this performance report?

Preparing a flexible budget and computing standard cost variances
(Obj. 1, 3, 4, 5)

P24-3B Bijoux Ltd. manufactures ladies jackets and uses flexible budgeting and a standard cost system. Bijoux allocates overhead based on yards of direct materials. The company's performance report includes the following selected data:

	Static Budget (1,000 jackets)	Actual Results (975 jackets)
Sales (1,000 jackets × $200)	$200,000	
(975 jackets × $192)		$187,200
Variable manufacturing expenses:		
Direct materials (4,000 yd. × $8.00).............	32,000	
(4,100 yd. × $7.80).............		31,980
Direct labor (5,000 hr × $6.00).....................	30,000	
(4,825 hr × $6.03).....................		29,095
Variable overhead (4,000 yd. × $5.00)..........	20,000	
(4,100 yd. × $6.40)..........		26,240
Fixed manufacturing expenses:		
Fixed overhead...	28,000	28,500
Gross margin	$ 90,000	$ 71,385

REQUIRED

1. Prepare a flexible budget based on the actual number of jackets sold.
2. Compute the price variance and the efficiency variance for direct materials and for direct labor. For manufacturing overhead, compute the total variance, the flexible budget variance, and the production volume variance.
3. What is the total flexible budget variance for Bijoux's manufacturing costs? Show how the total flexible budget variance is divided into materials, labor, and overhead variances.
4. Describe how Bijoux's managers can benefit from the standard costing system.

Using incomplete cost and variance information to determine the number of direct labor hours worked
(Obj. 4)

P24-4B The State of Texas has a shop that manufactures road signs used throughout the state. The manager of the shop uses standard costs to judge performance. Recently a clerk mistakenly threw away some of the records, and the manager has only partial data for July. The manager knows that the direct labor flexible budget variance for the month was $250 U and that the standard labor price was $6 per hour. The shop experienced an unfavorable labor price variance of $0.25 per hour. The standard direct labor hours for actual July output were 3,500.

1. Find the actual number of direct labor hours worked during July. First, find the actual direct labor price per hour. Then, determine the actual direct labor hours by setting up the computation of the direct labor flexible budget variance of $250 U.
2. Compute the direct labor price and efficiency variances.

P24-5B Pinpoint Mills manufactures T-shirts that it sells to other companies for customizing with their own logos. Pinpoint prepares flexible budgets and uses a standard cost system to control manufacturing costs. The standard unit cost of a basic white T-shirt is based on static budget volume of 40,000 T-shirts per month. The unit cost is computed as follows:

Computing and journalizing standard cost variances (Obj. 4, 5, 6)

Direct materials (2 sq. yd. @ $0.15 per sq. yd.)		$0.30
Direct labor (3 minutes @ $0.12 per minute)....................		0.36
Manufacturing overhead:		
Variable (3 minutes @ $0.08 per minute).......................	$0.24	
Fixed (3 minutes @ $0.14 per minute)	0.42	0.66
Total cost per T-shirt..		$1.32

Transactions during May of the current year included the following:

a. Actual production and sales were 42,700 T-shirts.
b. Actual direct materials usage was 1.80 square yards per T-shirt at an actual cost of $0.13 per square yard.
c. Actual direct labor usage of 130,000 minutes cost $18,850.
d. Actual overhead cost was $27,800.

1. Compute the price and efficiency variances for direct materials and direct labor.
2. Journalize the usage of direct materials and the assignment of direct labor, including the related variances.
3. For manufacturing overhead, compute the total variance, the flexible budget variance, and the production volume variance.

P24-6B Cascade Office Supply manufactures ring binders. During August, the company produced and sold 104,000 binders and recorded the following cost data:

Computing standard cost variances and reporting to management (Obj. 4, 5, 7)

	Standard Unit Cost		Actual Total Cost
Direct materials:			
Standard (2 parts @ $0.14 per part)		$0.28	
Actual (209,500 parts @ $0.16 per part)			$33,520
Direct labor:			
Standard (0.02 hr @ $5.00 per hr)		0.10	
Actual (1,560 hr @ $5.25 per hr).........................			8,190
Manufacturing overhead:			
Standard:			
Variable (0.03 machine hr @ $6.00 per hr).......	$0.18		
Fixed ($24,000 for static budget volume of			
100,000 units and 3,000 machine hours)	0.24	0.42	
Actual..			45,500
Total manufacturing costs.................................		$0.80	$87,210

1. Compute the price and efficiency variances for direct materials and direct labor.
2. For manufacturing overhead, compute the total variance, the flexible budget variance, and the production volume variance.
3. Prepare a standard cost income statement through gross margin to report all variances to management. Sale price of the binders to college bookstores was $1.25 each.
4. Cascade's management used more-experienced workers during August. Discuss the trade-off between the two direct labor variances.

Applying Your Knowledge

DECISION CASES

Preparing a performance report and using it to evaluate performance; nonprofit organization
(Obj. 1, 2)

CASE 1. St. Margaret's Church is a small congregation in Altamont, Oregon. At the end of 1998, the church membership was 87 families. Each family donated an average of $400 per year to the church's operating fund and $100 per year to the mission and service fund.

At the beginning of 1999, the Church's Finance Committee estimated that, due to a new factory built ten miles outside Altamont, the church membership would grow by 11 families. In addition, the committee planned a campaign for 1999 aimed at increasing average donations to $450 for the operating fund and $125 for mission and service.

During 1999, seven new families became members at St. Margaret's, and no families left the congregation. The 1999 receipts amounted to $43,768 for operations and $12,029 for mission and service.

REQUIRED

1. As Chair of St. Margaret's 1999 Finance Committee, prepare an analysis of the congregation's 1999 donations.
2. The pastor has asked the Finance Committee if a sermon on giving is in order. Write a one-paragraph memo to the pastor in reply to his question.

Preparing a performance report and using it to evaluate performance
(Obj. 1, 2)

CASE 2. The board of directors of Leaderboard Golf, Inc., a distributor of golf clubs, is meeting to evaluate the company's performance for the year just ended. The accompanying performance report has been prepared for the meeting.

The directors are disappointed by the operating income results. Further, they are puzzled by the presence of so many favorable variances. After all, actual operating income for the year is only 48% of the static budget amount.

In response to the directors' initial questions, Leaderboard Golf's controller revealed that the actual sale price of $120 per club was equal to the budgeted sale price. Also, there were no changes in inventories for the year.

LEADERBOARD GOLF, INC.
Income Statement Performance Report
Year Ended March 31, 19X9

	Actual Results	Static Budget	Variance
Sales revenue	$1,992,000	$2,490,000	$498,000 U
Variable expenses:			
Cost of goods sold	891,750	1,162,000	270,250 F
Sales commissions	87,675	124,500	36,825 F
Shipping expense	48,000	62,250	14,250 F
Fixed expenses:			
Salary expense	331,200	320,250	10,950 U
Depreciation expense	229,500	234,750	5,250 F
Rent expense	128,250	128,250	–0–
Advertising expense	95,100	82,500	12,600 U
Total expenses	1,811,475	2,114,500	303,025 F
Operating income	$ 180,525	$ 375,500	$194,975 U

REQUIRED

1. Prepare a more informative performance report. Be sure to include a flexible budget for the actual quantity of golf clubs purchased and sold.
2. A downturn in the economy was responsible for the company's inability to sell more golf clubs. In light of this information, how would you rate the company's performance? As a member of Leaderboard Golf's top management, which variances would you want investigated? Why?

Team Project

Setting standards
(Obj. 4)

Pella Corporation is the world's second largest manufacturer of wood windows and doors. In 1992, Pella entered the national retail market with its ProLine windows and doors, manufactured in Carroll, Iowa. The company has recently expanded its product lines to include the Designer Series and the Architect Series, both of which are produced in the 1.5 million square foot plant in Pella, Iowa.

Suppose Pella has been using a standard cost system that bases price and quantity standards on Pella's historical long-run average performance. Assume Pella's controller has engaged your team of management consultants to advise him whether Pella should use some basis other than historical performance for setting standards.

1. List the types of variances you recommend that Pella compute (for example, direct materials price variance for glass). For each variance, what specific standards would Pella need to develop? In addition to cost standards, do you recommend that Pella develop any nonfinancial standards?

2. There are many approaches to setting standards other than simply using long-run average historical prices and quantities.
   a. List three alternative approaches that Pella could use to set standards, and explain how Pella could implement each alternative.
   b. Evaluate each alternative method of setting standards, including the pros and cons of each method.
   c. Write a memo to Pella's controller detailing your recommendations. First, should Pella retain its historical-data-based standard cost approach? If not, which of the alternative approaches should it adopt? Use the following format for your memo:

Date:	_____
To:	Controller, Pella Corporation
From:	_____, Management Consultants
Subject:	Standard Costs

Activity-Based Costing and Other Tools for Cost Management

After studying this chapter you should be able to

1. Describe and develop activity-based costs (ABC)

2. Use ABC to make business decisions

3. Decide when ABC is most likely to pass the cost-benefit test

4. Compare a traditional production system to a just-in-time (JIT) production system

5. Record manufacturing costs for a just-in-time costing system

6. Contrast the four types of quality costs and use these costs to make decisions

7. Relate a life-cycle budget for a product to target costing and value engineering

Dell Computer pioneered in custom-building microcomputers for individual orders on a just-in-time basis. But when the company reported its first-ever quarterly loss in 1993, CEO Michael Dell had to act quickly to turn the company around.

Dell decided to focus on the company's most profitable products. But which were the most profitable? The accounting system traced direct materials and direct labor to individual product lines, but did not do a good job matching indirect costs with the specific products that caused those costs.

Dell needed a more finely tuned cost accounting system. The answer was *activity-based costing (ABC)*. Employee teams identified the ten most important indirect activities from all elements of the value chain—for example, purchases of raw materials, indirect assembly labor, and warranty service. Then, *for each activity*, the teams developed a separate indirect cost allocation rate. The goal was to assign the cost of each activity to the product lines that caused that activity's cost. For example,

- Purchasing costs are assigned based on the number of different "part numbers" in a product.
- Indirect assembly labor is assigned based on the number of times the product is "touched."
- Warranty costs are assigned based on the number of service calls (failure rate) for the product line.

ABC assigns the indirect costs of each activity to the products that *cause* those costs. ABC costing is more accurate than traditional cost systems that combine the indirect costs of many activities into a single cost pool and then allocate these indirect costs using a single allocation base, often direct labor or machine hours. Such traditional cost systems can result in a crude assignment of indirect costs to products. Where can this lead? To a hit-or-miss pricing structure.

Has ABC worked for Dell? By 1997, Dell was earning record profits. John Jonez, Vice President and Controller of Dell Americas Operations, says: "Activity-based costing has really allowed Dell to go to the next level of understanding of its profitability for each of the products it sells." Given the rapidly changing costs in the computer industry, Dell uses ABC costs for pricing its computers every day. Then monthly, Dell analyzes the profitability of each product line. ABC also helps Dell's managers find ways to cut costs, especially by highlighting non-value-added activities such as inventory storage.

To thrive in a globally competitive market, Dell Computer must provide customers with goods or services at an attractive price, while managing costs so the company still earns a profit. This is called delivering value to the customer. This chapter will show you several methods managers use to control costs so the company can deliver value to the customer at a profit:

- Activity-based costing
- Just-in-time systems
- Costs of quality
- Life-cycle budgeting
- Target costing and value engineering

These methods, largely unheard of 15 years ago, are now routinely used by companies like Dell, General Motors, and Toyota.

Activity-Based Costing

Objective 1

Describe and develop activity-based costs (ABC)

To control operations, managers divide companywide functions (such as production) into different departments (for example, different production lines for various products, or different processes like machining, assembly, and finishing). Managers then use budgets to plan and control operations in each department.

Consider this: If dividing companywide functions into departments helps managers control operations, wouldn't splitting departments into various activities further sharpen managers' focus? The answer is, Yes. Exhibit 25-1, Panel A, lists the value-chain functions for a manufacturer like Dell Computer. Panel B shows how the production function is divided into departments, and Panel C lists common activities in the Desktop Product Line production department.

Managers need to know the costs of many cost objects, including

- Business functions—such as Dell Computer's production function

Concept Highlight

EXHIBIT 25-1
Overview of Business Functions, Departments, and Activities

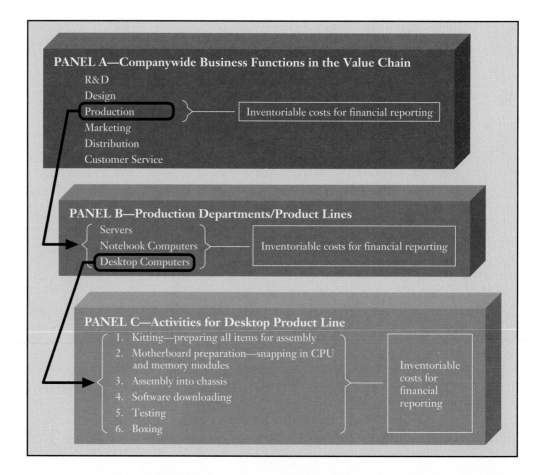

- Departments—such as Dell Computer's desktop product line
- Activities—such as Dell Computer's assembly or software downloading

To support this sharpening focus from

business functions → departments within those functions → activities within the departments

companies are updating their cost accounting systems. For example, many manufacturing companies have refined their accounting for manufacturing overhead as follows:

From a single plantwide manufacturing overhead rate

↓

To separate manufacturing overhead rates for each different department (such as the desktop product line for Dell)

↓

To narrower manufacturing overhead rates for each activity within a department (such as motherboard preparation for Dell), where each overhead rate is based on a different cost driver.

This third type of system is called activity-based costing.

Activity-based costing (ABC) focuses on *activities* as the fundamental cost objects. The costs of those activities are then used as building blocks for compiling costs. That is, ABC links costs to the activities that cause those costs. Activity-based costing can be used with job costing or process costing, and it is used by many banks and hospitals as well as by manufacturers such as Dell, General Motors, and Hewlett-Packard.

In ABC systems, direct costs such as direct materials and direct labor are traced to cost objects as described in Chapter 20. ◀▥ The only difference is the allocation of indirect costs. While direct materials and direct labor are easy to trace, it is more difficult to allocate *indirect* costs—such as manufacturing overhead—to the products that caused these costs. Many companies start out using a cost system with a single indirect cost allocation base, like those in Chapter 20. These simple systems combine all the indirect costs into a single cost pool, and then allocate those costs using a single allocation base—often direct labor. However, inaccurate product costs can result if

1. *The allocation base is not a cost driver.* Recall that a *cost driver* is any factor whose change causes a change in a related total cost. For example, if the production process is highly automated, most overhead costs are not related to direct labor, so direct labor is not the main driver of overhead costs.

2. *One allocation base is insufficient.* In most companies, no *single* factor drives all manufacturing overhead costs, much less all (indirect) costs in the value chain.

In either case, using allocation bases that are not cost drivers leads to inaccurate product costs.

Activity-based costing reduces these problems by separately estimating the indirect costs of each activity, and then allocating the costs of each activity based on what caused those costs. This means that each activity's indirect cost has its own (usually unique) cost allocation base, or cost driver. For example, Dell's ABC system allocates indirect assembly labor costs based on the number of times an individual computer is touched as it moves through the assembly process. A computer that requires more touches is allocated more of the indirect assembly labor activity cost than a different model that requires fewer touches.

The manufacturing cost of each computer is built up from the direct costs plus the indirect costs of the specific activities required to produce it. This buildup of *manufacturing costs* determines the inventoriable product cost used for *financial reporting* purposes. However, for internal decisions such as pricing and product profitability analysis, Dell also assigns the costs of nonmanufacturing activities to products. For example, Dell assigns the costs of the warranty service activity to product lines based on the number of service calls.

Activity-Based Costing (ABC). A system that focuses on activities as the fundamental cost objects and uses the costs of those activities as building blocks for compiling costs.

◀▥ ◀▥ ◀▥ See Chapter 20, pages 864–868, to review how direct materials and direct labor are traced to cost objects.

■ **Daily Exercise 25-1**

Learning Tip: Exhibit 25-1 shows that *only* production (manufacturing) costs are assigned to products for financial reporting. However, companies need to know the full costs (from all elements of the value chain) to set a sale price that covers all their costs, and to determine the profitability of different products. Many companies began developing ABC systems in the production/manufacturing function, but others like Dell Computer also use ABC to assign costs from activities throughout the value chain, for internal decision-making purposes.

Exhibit 25-2 lists common activities and related cost drivers. By using cost drivers that capture causal relationships, ABC systems yield more accurate product costs than systems that use a single allocation base. Hence, managers can make wiser decisions about what sale price to charge customers, and which products to push.

Accountants have long known that product costs would be more accurate if companies allocated indirect costs using several cost drivers rather than a single allocation base. Until recently, however, it was too expensive to develop multiple-cost-driver costing systems. This is why most companies started out using direct labor as their only allocation base. However, computers have made ABC feasible. For example, optical scanning and bar coding have reduced the cost of collecting and processing activity costs and cost driver information required by ABC. Companies can buy commercial ABC software packages or develop their own ABC software. For example, Dell Computer developed its ABC system using Excel spreadsheets.

Steps in Developing an Activity-Based Costing System

In many ways, ABC systems are similar to traditional systems. The main difference is that ABC systems have separate indirect cost allocation rates for each activity. This means ABC systems have (1) more indirect cost pools, and (2) more indirect cost allocation bases. The greater detail makes ABC systems more accurate, but more expensive than traditional costing systems.

ABC requires seven steps. Managers must

- Daily Exercise 25-2
- Daily Exercise 25-3

1. Identify the activities.
2. Estimate the total indirect costs of each activity.
3. Identify the allocation base for each activity's indirect costs—this is the primary cost driver.
4. Estimate the total quantity of each allocation base.
5. Compute the cost allocation rate for each activity:

$$\text{Cost allocation rate for activity} = \frac{\text{Estimated total indirect costs of activity}}{\text{Estimated total quantity of cost allocation base}}$$

6. Obtain the actual quantity of each allocation base used by the cost object (for example, the quantity of each allocation base used by a particular product).
7. Allocate the costs to the cost object:

$$\text{Allocated activity cost} = \text{Cost allocation rate for activity} \times \text{Actual quantity of cost allocation base used by the cost object}$$

The first step in developing an activity-based costing system is identifying the activities. Analyzing all the activities required to make a product forces managers to think about how each activity might be improved—or whether the activity is necessary at all. It also helps executives manage operations more efficiently.

EXHIBIT 25-2
Activities and Cost Drivers

Activity	Cost Driver
Materials purchasing	Number of purchase orders
Materials handling	Number of parts
Production scheduling	Number of batches
Quality inspections	Number of inspections
Photocopying	Number of pages copied
Warranty services	Number of service calls
Shipping	Number of pounds

Steps 2 through 7 are the same approach used to allocate manufacturing overhead, as explained in Chapter 20. The only difference is

- ABC systems repeat steps 2–7 for each activity, but
- Single-allocation-base systems perform steps 2–7 only once for the lump sum of all the indirect costs

Traditional versus Activity-Based Costing Systems

We use a streamlined example to emphasize the basic distinctions between activity-based costing systems and traditional costing systems. Our example necessarily simplifies the process that would occur in a real company like Dell, which identifies as many as 40 different activities.

Our example uses the Chemical Manufacturing Department of Chemtech, a company that produces hundreds of different chemicals. Chemtech has focused on producing mass quantities of "commodity" chemicals for many large customers. But it also manufactures small quantities of specialty chemicals for individual customers.

Last updated in 1988, the Chemical Manufacturing Department's cost system uses a single indirect cost pool and allocates manufacturing overhead at 200% of direct labor cost. Chemtech's controller, Martha Wise, gathered data for two of the department's many products:

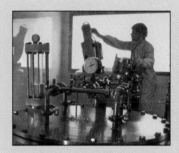

"Chemtech has focused on producing mass quantities of 'commodity' chemicals for many large customers. But it also manufactures small quantities of specialty chemicals for individual customers."

- Aldehyde—a commodity chemical used in producing plastics
- Phenylephrine Hydrochloride (PH)—a specialty chemical (A single customer uses PH in manufacturing blood-pressure medications.)

	Aldehyde	Phenylephrine Hydrochloride (PH)
Number of pounds per year	7,000 lb.	5 lb.
Direct materials cost per pound	$ 5	$20
Direct labor cost per pound	$ 1	$10
Sale price per pound	$10	$70

Wise used this information to compute each product's gross margin, as shown in Exhibit 25-3.

The gross margin for the PH (phenylephrine hydrochloride) specialty chemical is $20 per pound—ten times as high as the gross margin for the aldehyde commodity chemical ($2). Chemtech CEO Randy Smith is surprised that PH appears so much more profitable (per pound) than aldehyde, so he asks Wise to check 50 of the department's other products. After doing so, Wise confirms that the gross margin per pound is ten times as high for specialty chemicals as it is for commodity chemicals. As a result, Smith wonders whether Chemtech should switch its focus to manufacturing specialty chemicals.

	Aldehyde	PH
Sale price per pound	$10.00	$70.00
Less manufacturing cost per pound:		
Direct materials	5.00	20.00
Direct labor	1.00	10.00
Manufacturing overhead (at 200% of direct labor cost)	2.00	20.00
Total manufacturing cost per pound	8.00	50.00
Gross margin per pound	$ 2.00	$20.00

EXHIBIT 25-3
Chemtech's Traditional Cost System—Product Cost and Gross Margin

■ **Daily Exercise 25-4**

Working It Out

1. What is the *total* direct labor cost assigned to
   a. Aldehyde?
   b. PH (phenylephrine hydrochloride)?
2. What is the *total* manufacturing overhead allocated to
   a. Aldehyde?
   b. PH?

Answers

1. Total direct labor cost assigned to aldehyde is 7,000 pounds × $1 per pound = $7,000. Total direct labor cost assigned to PH is 5 pounds × $10 per pound = $50. Thus Chemtech assigns to aldehyde 140 times as much total direct labor cost as it does to PH ($7,000 ÷ $50 = 140).

2. **Key Point:** Because Chemtech uses direct labor cost as its single allocation base, Chemtech also allocates 140 times as much total overhead to aldehyde as to PH. Total overhead allocated to aldehyde is 7,000 pounds × $2 per pound = $14,000. Total overhead allocated to PH is 5 pounds × $20 per pound = $100. Thus the original single-allocation-base (direct labor) system allocates 140 times as much total overhead to aldehyde as to PH ($14,000 ÷ $100). This traditional costing procedure is accurate only if aldehyde really does cause 140 times as much overhead as PH. That is, the existing system assumes that direct labor really is the primary overhead cost driver and that total manufacturing overhead really does change in direct proportion to direct labor.

Based on Martha Wise's accounting report, Chemtech CEO Randy Smith is considering switching the Chemical Manufacturing Department's focus to specialty chemicals. Before making a decision, Smith calls a meeting with the department's foreman Steve Pronai and controller Martha Wise.

Smith is perplexed that the accounting numbers show that specialty chemicals like PH are more profitable (on a per-pound basis) than commodity chemicals like aldehyde. He expected the opposite. Smith thought the department would be more efficient producing a few different commodity chemicals (in a few very large batches) than producing a wide variety of specialty chemicals (in many small batches). Foreman Pronai echoes Smith's concern. For example, Pronai says it takes just as long to mix a small batch of specialty chemicals as a large batch of commodity chemicals. Finally, Smith is puzzled because other commodity chemical manufacturers seem to be earning good profits, even though these competitors usually undercut Chemtech's sale prices on commodity chemicals.

After listening to this discussion, Wise fears that the problem could be Chemtech's cost accounting system. For years she had tried to get Smith to update the costing system, but Smith ignored accounting and invested in new equipment and in marketing. Now Wise has Smith's attention. Wise suggests that foreman Pronai and the plant engineer work with her to develop a pilot ABC system for part of the Chemical Manufacturing Department's operations. Exhibit 25-4 compares the original direct-labor-single-allocation-base system (Panel A) with the new ABC system (Panel B).

In developing their new ABC system, Chemtech's ABC team followed the seven steps:

Step 1. *Identify the activities.*

Wise and her team identify three activities in the Chemical Manufacturing Department: mixing, processing, and testing.

Step 2. *Estimate the total indirect costs of each activity.*

Pronai estimates that total mixing costs for all products will be $600,000. Estimated costs for each activity appear in Exhibit 25-5, column 2.

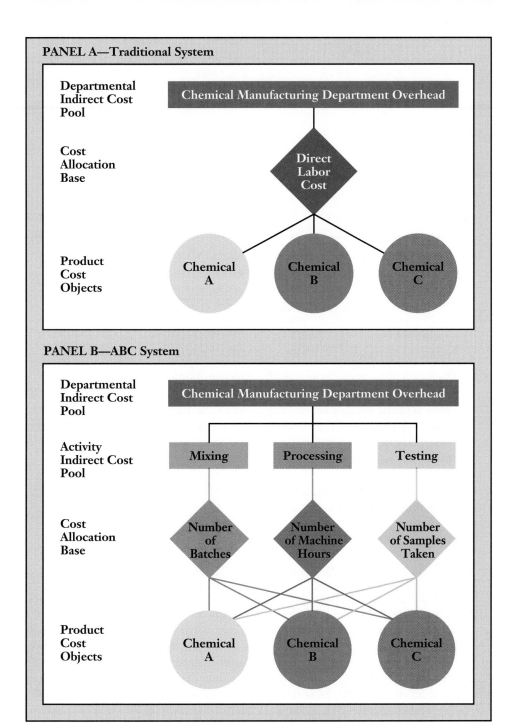

EXHIBIT 25-4
Chemtech's Traditional and
ABC Systems

PANEL A—Traditional System

Departmental
Indirect Cost
Pool

Chemical Manufacturing Department Overhead

Cost
Allocation
Base

Direct
Labor
Cost

Product
Cost
Objects

Chemical
A

Chemical
B

Chemical
C

PANEL B—ABC System

Departmental
Indirect Cost
Pool

Chemical Manufacturing Department Overhead

Activity
Indirect Cost
Pool

Mixing

Processing

Testing

Cost
Allocation
Base

Number
of
Batches

Number
of Machine
Hours

Number
of Samples
Taken

Product
Cost
Objects

Chemical
A

Chemical
B

Chemical
C

Step 3. *Identify the allocation base for each activity's indirect costs—the primary cost driver.*
Workers mix ingredients separately for each batch of chemicals, so the number
of batches drives mixing costs. Exhibit 25-5, column 3, lists the allocation base
(cost driver) for each activity.

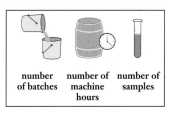

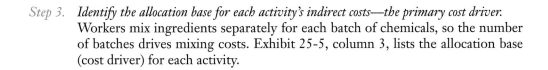

number   number of   number of
of batches   machine   samples
hours

Step 4. *Estimate the total quantity of each allocation base.*
Wise and Pronai estimate that the department will produce a total of 4,000
batches of chemicals. Estimated quantities of the cost driver allocation bases appear in column 4 of Exhibit 25-5.

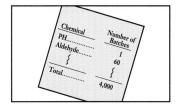

Chemical	Number of Batches
PH.........	
Aldehyde.........	1
{	60
Total..........	4,000

EXHIBIT 25-5
Chemtech's Activity-Based
Costing System

(1)	(2)	(3)	(4)
Activity	Estimated Costs	Cost Allocation Base	Estimated Quantity of Cost Allocation Base
Mixing	$ 600,000	# Batches	4,000 batches
Processing	$3,000,000	# Machine hours (MH)	50,000 MH
Testing	$ 600,000	# Samples	3,000 samples

Step 5. *Compute the cost allocation rate for each activity.*
Wise computes the allocation rate for mixing costs, as follows:

$$\text{Cost allocation rate for mixing} = \frac{\$600,000}{4,000 \text{ batches}}$$

$$= \$150 \text{ per batch}$$

Column 5 of Exhibit 25-5 shows the cost allocation rate for each activity.

Step 6. *Obtain the actual quantity of each allocation base used by each product.*
During the year, Chemtech produces 60 batches of aldehyde and 1 batch of PH. (This total of 61 batches is only a small fraction of the 4,000 total batches Chemtech produces. The remaining batches consist of Chemtech's other chemicals.) Exhibit 25-5, column 6, shows the actual quantities of each activity's allocation base used by aldehyde and PH.

Step 7. *Allocate the costs to each product.*
Wise allocates mixing costs as follows:

Aldehyde:	60 batches × $150 per batch =	$9,000
PH:	1 batch × $150 per batch =	$ 150

Column 7 of Exhibit 25-5 shows the cost allocation for all three activities.

Wise then recomputes manufacturing overhead costs (Panel A) and gross margins (Panel B), as shown in Exhibit 25-6. For each product, Wise adds the total costs of the three activities to obtain the total manufacturing overhead allocated to each product. Panel A shows that the total ABC overhead is $13,630 for aldehyde and $470 for PH. As in the original direct-labor-single-allocation-base system, this multiple-allocation-base ABC system allocates more *total* overhead to aldehyde, because Chemtech produces much more aldehyde than PH. However, there is a big difference in the *ratio* of overhead allocated to aldehyde versus PH. The ABC system allocates only 29 times as much overhead to aldehyde as to PH ($13,630 ÷ $470 = 29). This is much less than in the original direct-labor-based system, which allocated 140 times as much overhead to aldehyde as to PH (see Working It Out on page 1082).

After totaling the manufacturing overhead costs for each product, Wise computes the overhead cost per pound, as shown in Exhibit 25-6, Panel A. For aldehyde, Wise divides the $13,630 total manufacturing overhead by the 7,000 pounds of aldehyde produced, to get an overhead cost per pound of $1.95 (rounded). For PH, the ABC overhead cost per pound is $94.00 ($470 ÷ 5 pounds).

Now, let's compare the overhead cost per pound under the original direct-labor-based system with the ABC costs:

■ **Daily Exercise 25-5**

Overhead Cost per Pound	Traditional Direct Labor System (Exhibit 25-3)	ABC System (Exhibit 25-6)
Aldehyde	$ 2.00	$ 1.95
PH	20.00	94.00

	(5)		(6) Actual Quantity of Cost Allocation Base Used by:		(7) Allocated Activity Cost	
	Cost Allocation Rate		Aldehyde	PH	Aldehyde	PH
	$\dfrac{\$600,000}{4,000} = \$150\text{/batch}$		60 batches	1 batch	$\$150 \times 60 = \$9,000$	$\$150 \times 1 = \$150$
	$\dfrac{\$3,000,000}{50,000} = \$60\text{/MH}$		30½ MH	2 MH	$\$60 \times 30½ = \$1,830$	$\$60 \times 2 = \$120$
	$\dfrac{\$600,000}{3,000} = \$200\text{/sample}$		14 samples	1 sample	$\$200 \times 14 = \$2,800$	$\$200 \times 1 = \$200$

EXHIBIT 25-5 (cont.)

Which cost approach is more accurate? *ABC costs are more accurate because ABC represents the resources (mixing costs, machine time, and testing) that each product actually uses.* The old direct-labor-single-allocation-base system allocated too much overhead to the product that uses more total direct labor (aldehyde) and too little overhead to the product that uses less total direct labor (PH). (The Working It Out on page 1082 shows that aldehyde uses a total of $7,000 of direct labor cost, while PH uses a total of only $50 of direct labor.) We would say that the traditional system *overcosted* aldehyde and *undercosted* PH.

With more precise allocations, ABC shifts costs out of aldehyde and into PH where the costs belong. Why? Exhibit 25-5 shows that aldehyde used more of each activity than PH but *not* 140 times as much. Column 6 shows that aldehyde used 60 times as much mixing, about 15 times as many machine hours (processing costs), and 14 times as much testing as PH. Even though aldehyde did *not* use 140 times as much of these resources as PH, the original direct-labor-based system allocated 140 times as much overhead cost to aldehyde as to PH.

Although Chemtech made only five pounds of PH, this product still required

- Workers to mix a batch, at a mixing cost of $150
- 2 machine hours at $60 per hour
- One sample tested at a cost of $200

Spreading these costs over the five pounds of PH yields an overhead cost of $94 per pound, as shown in Exhibit 25-6, Panel A.

EXHIBIT 25-6
Chemtech's Activity-Based Costing System

■ **Daily Exercise 25-6**
■ **Daily Exercise 25-7**

PANEL A—Manufacturing Overhead per Pound

	Aldehyde	PH
Mixing (from Exhibit 25-5)	$ 9,000	$150
Processing (from Exhibit 25-5)	1,830	120
Testing (from Exhibit 25-5)	2,800	200
Total manufacturing overhead	$13,630	$470
Divide by number of pounds	÷ 7,000 lb	÷ 5 lb
Manufacturing overhead per pound	$ 1.95/lb	$ 94/lb

PANEL B—Gross Margin per Pound

	Aldehyde	PH
Sale price	$10.00	$ 70.00
Less manufacturing costs:		
Direct materials	$ 5.00	$ 20.00
Direct labor	1.00	10.00
Manufacturing overhead (from Panel A)	1.95	94.00
Total manufacturing cost	7.95	124.00
Gross margin (Loss)	$ 2.05	$ (54.00)

Allocating overhead based on actual *usage* of the resources increases the costs of low-volume products like PH that are produced in small batches. Why? Because costs like mixing and testing a batch are spread over the small number of units in that batch. On the other hand, mixing and testing costs are spread over the larger number of pounds for high-volume products that are produced in large batches, like aldehyde.

Controller Martha Wise is now ready to recompute product costs and gross margins using the ABC data. Exhibit 25-6, Panel B, shows that the cost per pound of aldehyde is $7.95 under the ABC system. Contrast this with the $8.00 cost per pound under Chemtech's original system (Exhibit 25-3). More important, the ABC data in Exhibit 25-6 show that specialty chemical PH costs $124 per pound, rather than $50 per pound as indicated by the old direct-labor-single-allocation-base system (Exhibit 25-3). Panel B shows that by selling PH for $70 per pound, Chemtech has been losing $54 on each pound. Wise finds that most of Chemtech's other specialty chemicals have similar increases in cost under the ABC system.

The Chemtech example shows that ABC can dramatically affect product costs. Hewlett-Packard reported similar changes after switching to an ABC system. For example, the cost of one model circuit board increased from $5 to $25, while the cost of another model declined from $123 to $45.

Companies that have developed ABC systems often discover that their previous cost systems

- Undercosted low-volume products like Chemtech's specialty chemicals, and
- Overcosted higher-volume products like Chemtech's commodity chemicals

In many cases, ABC systems show that companies lose money on their low-volume products, such as Chemtech's PH. One business consultant says: "20% of a company's products usually produce 80% of its profits." ABC spurs many companies to cut their money-losing products.

■ Daily Exercise 25-8
■ Daily Exercise 25-11
■ Daily Exercise 25-12
■ Daily Exercise 25-13

Objective 2

Use ABC to make business decisions

Using Activity-Based Costing Information in Business Decisions

Two main benefits of ABC are

1. More accurate product cost information
2. More detailed information on costs of activities and the drivers of those costs

These benefits help managers make better decisions about cost control, the sale prices to charge for their products, and which products to emphasize.

The ABC system shows that Chemtech's manufacturing cost for PH is $124 (Panel B of Exhibit 25-6), rather than the $50 reported by the old system (Exhibit 25-3). Chemtech was losing $54 on every pound ($70 – $124) of PH—and this is before considering nonmanufacturing costs such as research and development (R&D), marketing, and distribution. Chemtech has three alternatives:

- Cut the cost of PH
- Increase the sale price of PH
- Drop the PH product

The ABC system suggests several ways that Chemtech might *cut costs:*

- Use fewer units of the cost driver to produce PH. For example, process PH in one machine hour rather than two.
- Reduce the department's overhead costs. For example, find a way to mix ingredients more efficiently, and thereby reduce total mixing cost.
- Reduce mixing and testing costs per pound by producing (and selling) a larger batch of PH.

If these steps do not cut costs enough for Chemtech to earn a profit, then Chemtech should consider *increasing the sale price* of PH. If customers will not pay a higher price, then Chemtech should consider *dropping the PH product* and using its facilities to produce other, more profitable products.

When Is Activity-Based Costing Most Likely to Pass the Cost-Benefit Test?

The ABC concept is deceptively simple: Products cause activities, and activities consume resources. However, it is not easy for a company to develop an ABC system. In the Chemtech example shown in Exhibit 25-4, ABC triples the number of allocation bases—from the single allocation base (direct labor) in the original system, to three allocation bases (for mixing, processing, and testing) under ABC. ABC systems are even more complex in real-world companies that have many more activities and cost drivers. Thus, companies find it expensive to

Objective 3

Decide when ABC is most likely to pass the cost-benefit test

- Assign teams of managers to conduct ABC studies
- Identify activities and their related indirect costs
- Choose an allocation base for each activity and collect information on those allocation bases
- Purchase or develop ABC software
- Train managers to use ABC information
- Continuously update ABC systems

■ **Daily Exercise 25-9**
■ **Daily Exercise 25-10**

As you can see, ABC is not a "quick fix." Companies that jump into ABC without counting the costs may be disappointed. The business press has reported several failed ABC implementations. Most companies perform hundreds of activities, so a common problem is starting out with too many activities. This happened at Dell Computer—the ABC team initially identified too many activities, and the system was becoming too complex. To get the ABC system started, controller Ken Hashman stepped in and asked the ABC team to focus on the ten most important activities. Over time, Dell continues to update and refine its system, which now identifies 40 different activities.

Like all other management tools, ABC must pass the cost-benefit test. The system should be refined enough to provide accurate product costs, but simple enough for managers to understand. It is especially important that ABC has the wholehearted support of operating managers, not just accountants. For example, Dell's ABC team included representatives from all areas affected by ABC—from product engineering, to manufacturing, to customer service. Such cross-functional teams increase the chance that ABC will succeed. The ABC system will be more accurate because it incorporates a wider variety of perspectives, and managers of different functions are more likely to understand and believe costs from the ABC system they helped build.

Activity-based costing passes the cost-benefit test when the benefits of adopting ABC exceed the costs. Benefits of adopting ABC are higher for companies in competitive markets because

- Accurate product cost information is essential for setting competitive sale prices that still allow the company to earn a profit.
- ABC can pinpoint opportunities for cost savings, which increase the company's profit, or are passed on to customers in lower sale prices.

ABC's benefits are higher when ABC gives managers new insights by reporting different product costs than the old system. This is likely to happen when

- The company produces many different products that use different amounts of resources. (If all products use similar amounts of resources, then a simple single-allocation-base system works fine.)
- The company has high indirect costs. (If indirect costs are immaterial, it does not matter how they are allocated.)

- The company produces high volumes of some products, and low volumes of other products. (Traditional single-allocation-base systems tend to overcost high-volume products and undercost low-volume products.)

   The costs of adopting ABC are lower when the company has

- Accounting and information system expertise to develop the system
- Information technology like bar coding and optical scanning to record cost driver data

   Contrast General Motors with Burrito Brothers (a burrito take-out in Gainesville, Florida).

General Motors	Burrito Brothers
Wide variety of different automotive products	Limited variety of similar burritos
High indirect costs	Low indirect costs
Employs experts in accounting and information systems	No accounting or information systems experts
Advanced information technology	Limited information technology

These differences help explain why General Motors was an early adopter of ABC, while Burrito Brothers has not adopted ABC.

Warning Signs that the Cost System May Be Broken

Broken cars or computers simply stop running. But unlike cars and computers, product cost systems continue to report "product costs," even if those systems are broken or badly outdated. Without flashing lights or ringing bells, how can you tell whether a company's cost system needs repair?

   Robin Cooper and others have identified such signs. A company's product cost system may need repair when

- Managers cannot explain changes in profits.
- In bidding for jobs, managers lose bids they expected to win, and win bids they expected to lose.
- Competitors with products similar to our high-volume products price their products below our costs, but still earn good profits.
- Employees do not believe the cost numbers reported by the accounting system.
- The company uses a single-allocation-base system that was developed long ago.
- The company has reengineered its production process, but has not changed its accounting system.

 Thinking It Over Review the Chemtech example on pages 1081–1086. List the symptoms that Chemtech's original cost system may be broken.

Answer

1. The Chemical Manufacturing Department uses a single allocation base (direct labor cost) in a cost system that was developed over ten years ago.
2. Competitors that focused on high-volume commodity chemicals earned good profits, despite undercutting Chemtech's sale prices. This was puzzling because Chemtech should be especially efficient at producing large batches of commodity chemicals.
3. Cost numbers reported by the accounting system were inconsistent with employees' intuition.

At this point, you should make sure you understand activity-based costing. Take a few minutes to study the Decision Guidelines feature before working the mid-chapter review problem.

DECISION GUIDELINES · Activity-Based Costing

DECISION	GUIDELINES
How to develop an ABC system?	1. Identify the activities.
	2. Estimate total indirect costs of each activity.
	3. Identify the allocation base (primary cost driver) for each activity's indirect costs.
	4. Estimate the total quantity of each allocation base.
	5. Compute the cost allocation rate for each activity.
	6. Obtain the actual quantity of each allocation base used by cost object.
	7. Allocate costs to cost object.
How to compute a cost allocation rate for an activity?	$$\frac{\text{Estimated total indirect cost of activity}}{\text{Estimated total quantity of allocation base}}$$
How to allocate an activity's cost to the cost object?	$$\begin{array}{c}\text{Cost allocation} \\ \text{rate for activity}\end{array} \times \begin{array}{c}\text{Actual quantity of allocation} \\ \text{base used by cost object}\end{array}$$
What are the main benefits of ABC?	• More accurate product cost information • More detailed information on costs of activities and drivers of those costs helps managers control costs
When is ABC most likely to pass the cost-benefit test?	• Company is in competitive environment and needs accurate product costs. • Company makes different products that use different amounts of resources. • Company has high indirect costs. • Company produces high volumes of some products and lower volumes of other products. • Company has accounting and information system expertise to implement system. • Old cost system appears "broken."
How to tell when a cost system needs revision?	• Managers cannot explain changes in profit. • Managers lose bids they expected to win and win bids they expected to lose. • Competitors earn profits despite pricing high-volume products below our costs. • Employees do not believe cost numbers. • Company uses a single-allocation-base system developed long ago. • Company has reengineered the production process but not the accounting system.

SUMMARY PROBLEM FOR YOUR REVIEW · MID-CHAPTER

Indianapolis Auto Parts (IAP) has a Seat Manufacturing Department that uses activity-based costing. IAP's system has the following features:

Activity	Allocation Base	Cost Allocation Rate
Purchasing	Number of purchase orders	$60.00 per purchase order
Assembling	Number of parts	0.50 per part
Packaging	Number of finished seats	0.90 per finished seat

Each seat has 20 parts; direct materials cost per seat is $11. Suppose Ford has asked for a bid on 50,000 built-in baby seats that would be installed as an option on some Ford vans. IAP will use a total of 200 purchase orders if Ford accepts IAP's bid.

REQUIRED

1. Compute the total cost that IAP will incur to purchase the needed parts and then assemble and package 50,000 baby seats. Also compute the average cost per seat.

2. For bidding, IAP adds a 30% markup to total cost. What price will the company bid for the Ford order?

3. Suppose that instead of an ABC system, IAP has a traditional product costing system that allocates all costs other than direct materials at the rate of $65 per direct labor hour. The baby-seat order will require 10,000 direct labor hours. What price will IAP bid using this system's total cost?

4. Use your answers to requirements 2 and 3 to explain how ABC can help IAP make a better decision about the bid price it will offer Ford.

■ SOLUTION

REQUIREMENT 1

Total Cost of Order and Average Cost Per Seat:

Direct materials, 50,000 × $11.00	$ 550,000
Activity costs:	
Purchasing, 200 × $60.00......................	12,000
Assembling, 50,000 × 20 × $0.50..........	500,000
Packaging, 50,000 × $0.90	45,000
Total cost of order....................................	$1,107,000
Divide by number of seats	÷ 50,000
Average cost per seat................................	$22.14

REQUIREMENT 2

Bid Price (ABC System):

$$\$1,107,000 \times 130\% = \underline{\$1,439,100}$$

REQUIREMENT 3

Bid Price (Traditional System):

Direct materials, 50,000 × $11.00	$ 550,000
Other product costs, 10,000 × $65	650,000
Total cost of order................................	$1,200,000
Bid price ($1,200,000 × 130%)...................	$1,560,000

REQUIREMENT 4

IAP's bid would be $120,900 higher using the direct-labor-single-allocation-base system than using ABC ($1,560,000 − $1,439,100). Assuming the ABC system more accurately captures the costs caused by the order, the traditional direct labor system overcosts the order. This leads to a higher bid price that in turn reduces IAP's chance of winning the bid. The ABC system shows that IAP can increase its chance of winning the bid by bidding a lower price and still make a profit.

Traditional versus Just-in-Time Production Systems

We now turn our attention to a second strategy for managing costs and delivering customer value—just-in-time (JIT) production. We expand on Chapter 19's introduction to just-in-time by contrasting just-in-time production systems with traditional production systems. We begin with traditional systems.

Traditional Production Systems

Traditional production systems often waste time and money. This waste is especially apparent in inventories and manufacturing processes.

INVENTORIES Many businesses keep large inventories of raw materials, work in process, and finished goods. Why? First, to protect against poor quality. Poor quality raw materials leads companies to buy more than they need strictly for production. Also, machine breakdowns and poor-quality production *within* departments prompt managers to keep extra work in process *between* departments. Consider Exhibit 25-7, which describes

EXHIBIT 25-7
Sequence of Operations for Drill-Bit Production

the production of drill bits from bar stock (the raw material). Work in process inventory between the grinding and smoothing operations allows smoothing work to continue even if grinding machines break down.

A second reason for large inventories is long setup times on production equipment. Manufacturing operations can require setup times ranging from several hours to several days, with correspondingly high setup costs. Such companies often make products in large batches to spread setup costs over many units.

A third reason for stocking large inventories is uncertainty in both deliveries from suppliers and demand from customers. Large amounts of raw materials protect against delayed deliveries, because the company still has materials to use in production. Large inventories of finished goods protect against lost sales if customer demand is higher than expected.

Why are large inventories a problem? First, inventories tie up cash. Companies either incur interest expense or forgo interest revenue on that cash. Second, inventories hide problems. Quality problems, production bottlenecks, and obsolescence are often hidden by inventories.

MANUFACTURING PROCESSES   Traditionally, manufacturers grouped machines according to function. Shaping machines might be located in one area of a plant, grinding machines in another area, and smoothing machines in yet another area. Raw materials and parts can travel several *miles* back and forth through a factory—often detouring to storage areas along the way—before they become finished goods. This wastes time and increases the chance that an order will be lost or damaged, leading to delayed shipments and angry customers.

Managers of traditional production processes try to keep machines busy to maximize output. They "push" materials through the manufacturing process. For example, the grinding-machine operator pushes bits to the smoothing-machine operator whether or not the smoothing machines are ready for them. Too often, the bits are pushed forward whether or not they meet quality standards. The desire to keep busy is another reason for high work in process inventory levels.

The time between receipt of raw materials and completion of finished products is called **throughput time.** Throughput time is computed as follows:

> **Throughput time = Processing time + Waiting time + Moving time + Inspection time + Reworking time**

Processing adds value to the products. The rest of throughput time is spent on **non-value-added activities,** which do not increase customer value. In many manufacturing systems, processing time is less than 10% of throughput time. The rest is waste.

Just-in-Time Production Systems

As Chapter 19 explained, the just-in-time (JIT) philosophy that is so popular in the U.S. originated in Japan. Toyota is generally credited with pioneering this philosophy. As the name suggests, companies with JIT systems buy materials and complete finished goods *just in time* for delivery to customers. This reduces waste. Indeed, many managers regard JIT as a *general philosophy of waste elimination* rather than a particular type of manufacturing system. Companies that follow JIT have several common characteristics:

  1. *Arrangement of production activities.* Companies following JIT arrange their equipment differently than traditional manufacturers. A traditional drill-bit manufacturer would group all the shaping machines in one area, all the grinding machines in another area, and all the smoothing machines in a third area, as illustrated in Exhibit 25-8. After switching to JIT, the company would rearrange the machines by grouping them in self-contained production cells, or production lines, as in Panel B of Exhibit 25-8. Equipment for cutting bar stock is immediately followed by a shaping machine, which in turn is followed by a grinding machine. The smoothing machine immediately follows the grinding machine. Machines performing sequential steps may even be physically joined. The goal is continuous production without interruptions or work in process inventories.

Throughput Time. The time between receipt of raw materials and completion of finished products.

■ **Daily Exercise 25-14**

Non-Value-Added Activities. Activities that do not increase customer value.

■ **Daily Exercise 25-15**

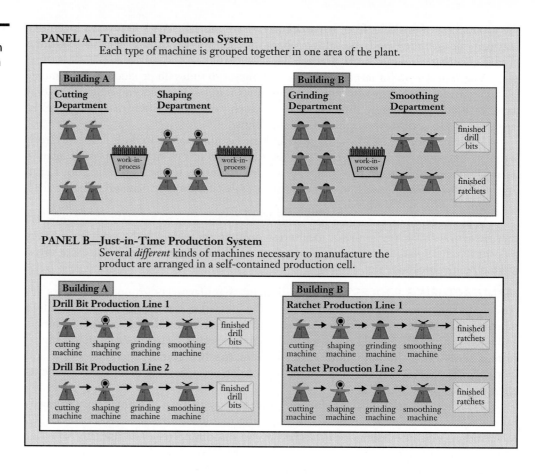

PANEL A—Traditional Production System
Each type of machine is grouped together in one area of the plant.

PANEL B—Just-in-Time Production System
Several *different* kinds of machines necessary to manufacture the product are arranged in a self-contained production cell.

Arranging machines in sequential production cells slashes throughput time. For example, within six years after adopting JIT, Harley-Davidson had reduced the time to produce a motorcycle by 77 percent.

2. *Setup times.* JIT companies reduce setup times on machines used for more than one product. Employee training and technology helped Toyota cut setup times from several hours to a few minutes. This increases flexibility in scheduling production to meet customer orders, which in turn increases customer satisfaction and company profits.

3. *Production scheduling.* JIT businesses schedule production in small batches *just in time* to satisfy needs. Manufacturing starts from a customer order. The final operation in the production sequence (smoothing, in our drill-bit example) "pulls" parts from the preceding operation (grinding). The grinding-machine operator pulls shaped parts from shaping, and so on. This "demand-pull" system extends back to suppliers of materials. Suppliers make frequent deliveries of defect-free materials *just in time* for production.

JIT requires coordination with suppliers. After adopting JIT, most companies only use suppliers that make on-time deliveries of defect-free materials. Reducing the number of suppliers saves costs of negotiating and contracting with suppliers.

Purchasing and producing only what customers demand reduces inventory quantities. As inventory declines, problems formerly hidden by inventory are exposed. Any problems can be corrected before the company produces a large number of defective units. This saves rework and scrap costs. Also, floor space is freed up for more productive use. When Hewlett-Packard adopted JIT, the company reduced its work in process inventory by 82% and production floor space was cut by 40 percent.

4. *Employee roles.* Employees in JIT systems do more than operate a single machine. They also conduct maintenance, perform setups, and operate other machines. This cross-training boosts employee morale and decreases costs.

Exhibit 25-9 compares traditional production systems with JIT production systems. The next section shows how JIT can simplify cost accounting.

Just-in-Time Costing

Just-in-time costing, sometimes called **backflush costing,** is a standard costing system that starts with output completed and then assigns manufacturing costs to units sold and to inventories. Businesses that use JIT costing typically (1) assign standard costs to each product, and (2) have either low inventories or constant levels of work in process.

Just-in-time costing differs from the more common standard costing system described in Chapter 24. The latter is a sequential tracking system—it traces costs through each step of the production process, from direct materials, to work in process, to finished goods, and to cost of goods sold. The simpler JIT method does not track direct materials or labor to individual processes or products and thus is less costly than traditional standard costing.

Just-In-Time (JIT) Costing. A standard costing system that starts with output completed and then assigns manufacturing costs to units sold and to inventories. Also called **backflush costing.**

EXAMPLE OF JUST-IN-TIME COSTING   The following example shows that JIT systems do not use a separate Work in Process Inventory account. Mintel Company, which converts silicon wafers into integrated circuits for computers, uses only two inventory accounts:

- Raw and In Process (RIP) Inventory, which is a combination of direct materials and work in process
- Finished Goods Inventory, which is the usual Finished Goods account

Mintel has only one direct manufacturing product cost: silicon wafers, which are labeled "raw." All other manufacturing costs, including labor and various chemicals, are indirect costs of converting the "raw" silicon wafers into the finished integrated circuits. These indirect costs are collected in an account called "Conversion Costs," which works just like the Manufacturing Overhead account introduced in Chapter 20. In JIT costing, no cost, whether direct or indirect, is separately tracked to work in process.

The Mintel JIT system has two **trigger points,** which prompt entries in the accounting records. The trigger points are (1) the purchase of direct materials, and (2) the transfer of completed units to finished goods.

Trigger Points. Points in operations that prompt entries in the accounting records in just-in-time costing.

Mintel has $100,000 of Raw and In Process (RIP) Inventory and $900,000 of Finished Goods Inventory at July 31. In August, the company's accountants:

1.   Record direct materials purchases of $3,020,000.

RIP Inventory	3,020,000	
Accounts Payable		3,020,000

2.   Record the actual conversion costs incurred.

Conversion Costs	18,540,000	
Various Accounts (such as payables and accumulated depreciation)............................		18,540,000

3.   Determine the number of units completed. Mintel produced 3,000,000 integrated circuits in August.

4.   Calculate the standard cost per finished unit. The company develops a standard conversion cost for each operation in the production process. Standard costs are "built up" for each circuit, depending on the operations required. In August, Mintel produced only one type of circuit. Its standard cost is $7 ($1 direct materials + $6 conversion cost).

Traditional Production Systems	Just-in-Time Production Systems
Arrange machines by function.	Arrange machines in sequence of operations.
High machine setup costs are acceptable.	Work to reduce machine setup costs.
Schedule production in large batches.	Schedule production in small batches.
Production workers operate a single machine.	Cross-trained workers perform many tasks.

5. Record the standard cost of goods completed during the month; 3,000,000 circuits × $7 per circuit = $21,000,000.

Finished Goods Inventory..	21,000,000	
RIP Inventory (3,000,000 × $1).....................		3,000,000
Conversion Costs (3,000,000 × $6)................		18,000,000

This is the second trigger point and the essence of JIT costing. Notice that the costs were not tracked as the circuits moved through manufacturing operations. Instead, *completion* of the circuits triggered the accounting system to go back and pull costs from RIP inventory.

6. Record cost of goods sold in the usual manner. Mintel sold 2,930,000 circuits (2,930,000 circuits × $7 per circuit = $20,510,000).

Cost of Goods Sold	20,510,000	
Finished Goods Inventory.............................		20,510,000

The August 31 inventory balances are

RIP inventory ($100,000 + $3,020,000 − $3,000,000)	$ 120,000
Finished goods inventory ($900,000 + $21,000,000 − $20,510,000)	1,390,000
Total inventory	$1,510,000

Exhibit 25-10 shows Mintel's major accounts. Not using a Work in Process Inventory account eliminates detail. Although Mintel tracks the number of physical units in process, the company does not use material requisitions or time records to assign *costs* to circuits as they flow through the production process. Costs are not assigned to physical products until the second trigger point, when the goods are completed.

Exhibit 25-10 shows that conversion costs are underallocated by $540,000 ($18,540,000 − $18,000,000). Under- and overallocated conversion costs are treated just like under- and overallocated manufacturing overhead. Companies that use JIT costing typically have low inventory levels, so they write off under- or overallocated conversion costs to Cost of Goods Sold. The entry to close Mintel's Conversion Costs account is

 See Chapter 20, page 875, for a review of under- and overallocated manufacturing overhead.

Cost of Goods Sold	540,000	
Conversion Costs.........		540,000

Mintel uses a two-trigger point system where the completion of goods is the second trigger point. This is the most popular version of JIT costing, but some companies use other trigger points. For example, Toyota's cost accounting system for its Kentucky plant uses the sale of units—not completion—as the second trigger point.

 Thinking It Over Activity-based costing is a more detailed and complex costing method that provides more accurate product costs. Just-in-time costing is simplified and does not track costs through the sequence of manufacturing operations. Are these two costing systems incompatible? Or can they be used together?

Answer: ABC and JIT costing can be compatible. The standard conversion costs used in JIT costing could be provided by an ABC system.

EXHIBIT 25-10
Mintel's Major JIT Costing Accounts

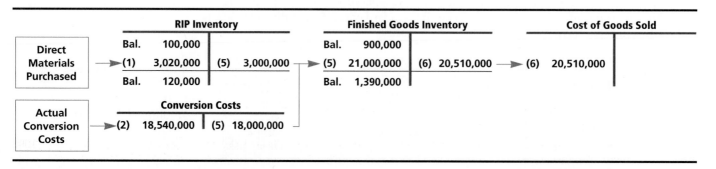

	RIP Inventory		Finished Goods Inventory		Cost of Goods Sold
Direct Materials Purchased	Bal. 100,000		Bal. 900,000		
	(1) 3,020,000	(5) 3,000,000	(5) 21,000,000	(6) 20,510,000	(6) 20,510,000
	Bal. 120,000		Bal. 1,390,000		
Actual Conversion Costs	Conversion Costs				
	(2) 18,540,000	(5) 18,000,000			

Continuous Improvement and the Management of Quality

Companies with a just-in-time philosophy strive for high-quality production. Because goods are produced only as needed, there are no inventories to hide inefficiencies. Therefore, poor quality materials or defective manufacturing processes shut down production.

Today's competitive marketplace demands ever-higher quality. Managers know that if they fail to satisfy customers' demand for high-quality goods, their competitors will. As explained in Chapter 19, many companies have adopted *total quality management* to meet this challenge. Recall that the goal of total quality management is to provide customers with superior products and services. Companies achieve this goal by improving quality and by eliminating defects and waste throughout the value chain. Each business function examines its own activities and sets higher and higher goals.

Many managers decide to invest in the front end of the value chain (R&D and design) to generate savings in the back end (production, marketing, and customer service). They strive to *design* and *build* quality into the product rather than having to *inspect* and *repair* it later. Carefully designed products reduce inspections, rework, and warranty claims. The theme of total quality management is that superior work benefits the whole organization. We now consider several types of quality costs.

Objective 6

Contrast the four types of quality costs and use these costs to make decisions

Types of Quality Costs

Business analysts have identified four types of quality-related costs: prevention costs, appraisal costs, internal failure costs, and external failure costs.

Prevention Costs. Costs incurred to avoid poor-quality goods or services.

Appraisal Costs. Costs incurred to detect poor-quality goods or services.

1. *Prevention costs are incurred to* avoid *poor-quality goods or services.* For example, Arthur Andersen LLP and other accounting firms invest heavily to train personnel in auditing and consulting procedures. Highly trained accountants are more likely to follow company policies and to make fewer errors.

2. *Appraisal costs are incurred to detect poor-quality goods or services.* For example, Intel, a manufacturer of integrated circuits, incurs appraisal costs when it tests its products. One procedure, called burn-in, heats circuits to a high temperature. A circuit that fails the burn-in test is also likely to fail when used by a customer.

". . . Intel, a manufacturer of integrated circuits, incurs appraisal costs when it tests its products."

3. *Internal failure costs occur when the company detects and corrects poor-quality goods or services* before *delivery to customers.* An example is the labor of a BMW mechanic who reworks a faulty brake job after inspection by a supervisor. It's better to detect and fix the problem in-house than to inconvenience the customer.

4. *External failure costs occur when poor-quality goods or services are not detected until* after *delivery to customers.* If an auto-repair shop does faulty work, the customer will discover the flawed brakes. Then the shop may have to repair the body of the car as well as the brakes. External failures can ruin a company's reputation.

Internal Failure Costs. Costs incurred when the company detects and corrects poor-quality goods or services before delivery to customers.

External Failure Costs. Costs incurred when poor-quality goods or services are not detected until after delivery to customers.

■ **Daily Exercise 25-18**

Exhibit 25-11 shows some examples of the four quality costs. Study these examples closely and you will see that most prevention costs occur in the R&D and design stages of the value chain. In contrast, most of the appraisal and internal failure costs occur in the production element of the value chain. External failure costs either occur in the customer service stage, or are opportunity costs of lost sales. As mentioned earlier, companies make trade-offs among these costs, often spending more on prevention and appraisal to cut internal and external failure costs.

Let's revisit Chemtech, the chemical processing company. Suppose Chemtech is considering spending the following amounts on a new quality program:

Prevention Costs	Appraisal Costs
Training of personnel	Inspection of incoming materials
Evaluating potential suppliers	Inspection at various stages of production
Improved materials	Inspection of final products or services
Preventive maintenance	Product testing
Improved equipment and processes	

Internal Failure Costs	External Failure Costs
Production loss caused by downtime	Lost profits from lost customers
Rework	Warranty costs
Scrap	Service costs at customer sites
Rejected product units	Sales returns and allowances due to quality problems
Disposal of rejected units	Product liability claims

Inspect raw materials	$100,000
Reengineer the production process to improve product quality	750,000
Inspect finished goods	150,000
Supplier screening and evaluation	25,000
Preventative maintenance of plant and equipment	75,000

Chemtech expects this quality program to reduce the following costs:

Avoid lost profits from lost sales due to disappointed customers	$800,000
Process fewer sales returns	50,000
Avoid lost profits from lost production time due to rework	250,000
Reduced warranty costs	125,000

Chemtech's CEO Randy Smith asks controller Martha Wise to

1. Classify each of these costs into one of the four categories (prevention, appraisal, internal failure, external failure) and total the estimated costs in each category.

2. Recommend whether Chemtech should undertake the quality program.

Exhibit 25-12 classifies each cost and totals the estimated costs in each of the four categories. Wise uses these results to analyze Chemtech's two alternatives:

- Incur the prevention and appraisal costs to undertake the quality program, or
- Do not undertake the quality program and incur the internal and external failure costs

Undertake the Quality Program		Do Not Undertake the Quality Program	
Prevention costs	$ 850,000	Internal failure costs	$ 250,000
Appraisal costs	250,000	External failure costs	975,000
Total costs	$1,100,000	Total costs	$1,225,000
See Exhibit 25-12		See Exhibit 25-12	

■ Daily Exercise 25-19

These estimates suggest that Chemtech would save $125,000 ($1,225,000 – $1,100,000) by undertaking the quality program.

These quality costs can be hard to measure. For example, design engineers may spend only part of their time on quality projects. Allocating their salaries to various activities is subjective. It is especially hard to measure external failure costs. The biggest external failure cost—profits lost because unhappy customers never return ($800,000)—is not recorded in the accounts at all. Consequently, total quality management programs also emphasize nonfinancial measures such as number of customer complaints.

Nonfinancial Quality Measures

Nonfinancial quality measures include number of customer complaints, percentage of defective units, and first-time inspection pass rates. Companies use benchmarking to evaluate their performance on these dimensions. As explained in Chapter 24, *benchmarking* means comparing current performance to the "best practice" level of

EXHIBIT 25-12
Chemtech's Quality Costs

Prevention

Reengineer the production process to improve product quality	$750,000
Supplier screening and evaluation	25,000
Preventative maintenance of plant and equipment	75,000
Total prevention costs	$850,000

Appraisal

Inspect raw materials	$100,000
Inspect finished goods	150,000
Total appraisal costs	$250,000

Internal Failure

Lost profits from lost production time due to rework	$250,000
Total internal failure costs	$250,000

External Failure

Lost profits from lost sales due to disappointed customers	$800,000
Sales return processing	50,000
Warranty costs	125,000
Total external failure costs	$975,000

performance. ◀▥ Best practice may be an internal benchmark from inside the company, or an external benchmark from other companies.

◀▥ ◀▥ ◀▥ For more on benchmarking, see Chapter 24, page 1045.

Cummins Engine Company uses the nonfinancial quality measures listed in Exhibit 25-13. This list shows how businesses are broadening their performance measures. Companies no longer concentrate solely on financial measures such as operating income or return on investment. Instead, managers' compensation also depends on product quality, speed to market, and customer satisfaction.

Product Life-Cycle Costs, Target Costing, and Value Engineering

To manage costs and deliver customer value, companies strive for continuous improvement by finding ways to increase quality and reduce costs. We have just considered the quality side. But quality alone is not enough. Successful companies must also reduce costs at every stage of their products' life cycles. A **product life cycle** extends from research and development through the product's sales and on to the end of customer service. Some high-tech goods, such as disposable cameras, have life cycles of less than one year. Other products, such as automobiles and refrigerators, have longer life cycles.

Objective 7

Relate a life-cycle budget for a product to target costing and value engineering

Product Life Cycle. The time from research and development through the product's sales and on to the end of customer service.

This section shows how managers use continuous improvement in planning new products. We use a Toyota example, because Toyota and other Japanese automobile companies pioneered the continuous improvement philosophy.

Learning Tip: The key point of continuous improvement is that a business should always try to improve. The adage "If it isn't broken, don't fix it" does not apply.

Initial Planning

In Japan—and increasingly in the United States—a proposal to develop a new automobile often is made by a product line's chief engineer. The initial focus is on the

- Percentage of engines passing test first time
- Incoming supplier quality—percentage of suppliers with acceptance rate of 98% or better
- Average machine downtime
- Number of machine breakdowns
- Number of product failures in the field
- Percentage of engines delivered on time
- Average supplier delivery in percentage of parts on time
- Training hours as percentage of total hours worked

marketplace. What product, with what features, will appeal to customers? At what price? How many cars will customers demand at that price?

Suppose Toyota predicts that it could sell 400,000 units of a proposed Lexus model to retail dealers at an average price of $36,000. The company expects the model's life cycle to be eight years: three years in product development and five years in the market-place.

After predicting sale price and production volume, a planning team that includes design, engineering, manufacturing, marketing, and accounting personnel calculates desired profit and allowable cost over the model's life cycle. Suppose the desired profit is 30% of target sales. Allowable cost is the cost that will result in, or "allow," the desired profit. This includes all costs in the value chain. Thus our measure of profit for evaluating the proposal is *life-cycle operating contribution*—sales less costs directly traceable to the product. The allowable average cost over the Lexus model's life cycle is computed as follows:

Life-cycle average sale price...	$36,000
Desired life-cycle operating contribution (30%).........	10,800
Allowable average cost over the life cycle	$25,200

Life-Cycle Budget

Life-Cycle Budget. A budget that predicts a product's revenues and costs over its entire life cycle.

The next step in product development is preparing the initial life-cycle budget. A **life-cycle budget** predicts a product's revenues and costs over its entire life cycle. The life-cycle budget shows the costs of all activities in the value chain that can be directly linked to the product. The *initial* life-cycle budget is based on current technology and methods, before any cost reduction efforts. The budget for our proposed Lexus model appears in Exhibit 25-14 (all numbers assumed).

After preparing the initial life-cycle budget, the planning team decides whether the project is worth pursuing. The budgeted average cost of the Lexus is $27,000 [($6,000,000,000 + $970,000,000 + $1,670,000,000 + $2,160,000,000)/400,000]. This average cost is $1,800 ($27,000 − $25,200) more than the allowable cost. Nonetheless, top management may approve the model. Why? Because cost reduction efforts, especially in the design stage, may reduce the $27,000 budgeted cost to the allowable cost of $25,200.

■ Daily Exercise 25-20
■ Daily Exercise 25-21

EXHIBIT 25-14
Initial Life-Cycle Budget

	In Millions	
Sales revenue (400,000 units × $36,000).....................................	$14,400	(100%)
Direct materials and purchased parts (400,000 × $15,000)..........	6,000	
Materials contribution margin..	8,400	
Other costs direct to product:		
Variable conversion costs:		
Indirect materials (400,000 × $400) .... $ 160		
Direct labor (400,000 × $1,500)... 600		
Indirect labor (400,000 × $300) 120		
Utilities (400,000 × $225)... 90	970	
Product contribution margin	7,430	
Fixed conversion costs:		
Indirect labor.. $ 200		
Depreciation on equipment 1,270		
Maintenance 200	1,670	
Life-cycle manufacturing contribution	5,760	(40%)
Other fixed costs:		
Design and engineering .... $ 760		
Marketing.. 900		
Customer service.. 500	2,160	
Life-cycle operating contribution..	$ 3,600	(25%)

Target Costing and Value Engineering

To achieve allowable product costs, Japanese automakers reduce costs continuously by improving manufacturing, marketing, and customer service. However, they usually focus their cost reduction efforts on the design stage. This is because design improvements provide larger and faster cost savings than improvements in the production stage. **Target costing** helps managers set goals for cost savings through product design.

Suppose the product planning team believes that gradual continuous improvement *after* production begins will trim $300 from the life-cycle average cost of each car. The target unit cost at the beginning of production is therefore $25,500 ($25,200 allowable average cost + $300). Designers, engineers, and management accountants work together to develop a Lexus whose cost at the *beginning* of production does not exceed the target cost of $25,500.

In the target costing process, the planning team budgets a currently attainable cost for each element of the proposed car. Then, cost planners use their experience to establish cost reduction goals. At that point, value engineering begins. **Value engineering** means designing products that achieve cost targets and meet specified quality and performance standards. Engineers study the company's processes and individual activities, rethinking their methods. They may redesign a painting process or the shape of a part. They may specify new materials, or substitute parts that are common to several product lines for parts designed for one product only. For example, *The Wall Street Journal* reported this comment by a Nissan engineer: "If we use fewer different screws, plant workers can save time changing the heads on their power tools. We can save 50 seconds per car. And one second equals one yen."

> **Thinking It Over** In what other way does reducing the number of different screws—or the number of unique parts in general—cut costs?
>
> *Answer:* Each part has its own part number in a company's database, so the number of parts becomes a cost driver for many manufacturing companies. Each part must be planned, negotiated with suppliers, scheduled for use, ordered, received, stored, retrieved, and paid for. These activities are costly. Indeed, Tektronix, Inc.—a producer of electronic test instruments—reports that over half of its materials-related overhead cost is related to the number of unique parts.

Through value engineering (VE), design teams reduce the budgeted costs of automobile elements to meet target costs. Target costing proceeds as follows (amounts assumed):

Product Element	Budgeted Cost	− VE Cost Reduction	= Target Cost
Engine	$ 3,000	$ 300	$ 2,700
Body	6,000	500	5,500
Drive train	2,000	150	1,850
⁓	⁓	⁓	⁓
Distribution	1,000	75	925
Customer service	500	25	475
Total	$27,000	$1,500	$25,500

Management accountants play an important role in value engineering. Accountants help engineers identify expensive activities whose costs can be reduced. Accountants also calculate the cost effects of design changes. For example, accountants at Chrysler used activity-based costs to evaluate dashboard-wiring alternatives for a new minivan. Target costing requires teamwork. Design engineers, production personnel, marketing managers, and accountants work together to design, produce, and sell high-quality products at a competitive price that still provides a good profit.

Target Costing. A cost management technique that helps managers set goals for cost savings through product design.

■ **Daily Exercise 25-22**

Value Engineering (VE). Designing products that achieve cost targets and meet specified quality and performance standards.

The Decision Guidelines feature summarizes key points about just-in-time, quality costs, life-cycle budgeting, and target costing. Study these guidelines before working through the summary review problems.

DECISION GUIDELINES	Just-in-Time, Quality Costs, Life-Cycle Budgeting, and Target Costing

DECISION	GUIDELINES
How to distinguish between just-in-time and traditional production systems?	**JIT** / **Traditional** (see below)

	JIT	**Traditional**
	Production cells	Like machines grouped together
	Short setup times	Longer setup times
	Smaller batches	Larger batches
	"Pull" system	"Push" system
	Lower inventories	Higher inventories
	An individual does wider range of tasks	An individual does fewer tasks

How does JIT costing differ from traditional costing?

In JIT costing,

1. Raw materials and work in process are combined into a single RIP Inventory account.
2. Summary journal entries are not made until units are completed—costs are not separately tracked as units move through production.

How to make trade-offs among the four types of quality costs?

Investment in prevention costs and appraisal costs reduces later internal failure costs and external failure costs.

How to set target cost at the time production begins?

$$
\begin{array}{l}
\text{Life-cycle average sale price} \\
-\ \text{Desired life-cycle operating contribution} \\
\hline
=\ \text{Allowable average life-cycle cost} \\
\\
+\ \text{Continuous improvement cost savings} \\
\quad\ \text{after production begins} \\
\hline
=\ \text{Target cost at beginning of production}
\end{array}
$$

SUMMARY PROBLEMS FOR YOUR REVIEW

PROBLEM 1. The Flores Company manufactures telephones. Flores uses a JIT costing system with two trigger points: (1) when direct materials are purchased, and (2) when completed telephones are transferred to finished goods inventory. The standard unit cost is $37: $24 direct materials and $13 conversion costs. Direct materials purchased during June totaled $2,540,000. Actual conversion costs totaled $1,295,000.

Flores completed 102,000 telephones in June, and sold 98,000.

REQUIRED

1. Prepare the June journal entries for these transactions.
2. Make the entry to close the under- or overallocated conversion costs to Cost of Goods Sold.

PROBLEM 2. The Ishikawa Motorcycle Company is considering a new product line with a budgeted average sale price of $8,000. The desired life-cycle operating contribution is $3,000 per motorcycle.

REQUIRED

1. Compute the allowable average life-cycle cost per motorcycle.
2. Gradual continuous improvement after production begins is expected to cut $250 per motorcycle. The value-engineering cost reduction goal has been set at $900 per unit. Compute the target cost at the beginning of production and the initial budgeted unit cost in the initial life-cycle budget.
3. Some of Ishikawa Company's costs are
   a. Product recall repairs
   b. Training of supplier personnel
   c. Inspection costs of incoming materials
   d. Rework

   Classify each cost in one of the four categories of quality costs: prevention, appraisal, internal failure, or external failure.

SOLUTIONS

PROBLEM 1

RIP Inventory	2,540,000	
Accounts Payable		2,540,000
Conversion Costs......................................	1,295,000	
Various Accounts (such as payables)		1,295,000
Finished Goods Inventory................................	3,774,000	
RIP Inventory (102,000 × $24)		2,448,000
Conversion Costs (102,000 × $13)............		1,326,000
Cost of Goods Sold (98,000 × $37)	3,626,000	
Finished Goods Inventory		3,626,000

Conversion Costs	31,000	
Cost of Goods Sold.................................		31,000

PROBLEM 2

1. Allowable average life-cycle cost is $8,000 − $3,000 = $5,000.
2. Target cost is $5,000 + $250 = $5,250. Initial budgeted cost in initial life-cycle budget was $5,250 + $900 = $6,150.
3. **a.** External failure   **c.** Appraisal
      b. Prevention   **d.** Internal failure

Summary of Learning Objectives

1. Describe and develop activity-based costs (ABC). *Activity-based costing* focuses on activities as the fundamental cost objects. It uses the costs of activities as building blocks for compiling the costs of products and other cost objects. ABC uses multiple cost allocation bases to allocate activity costs.

2. Use ABC to make business decisions. ABC systems give better information for decision making than single-allocation-base systems. ABC's more precise relationships between costs and cost allocation bases produce more accurate product costs and help managers set sale prices. Management also uses information on costs of different activities and cost allocation bases to help control costs.

3. Decide when ABC is most likely to pass the cost-benefit test. ABC passes the cost-benefit test when the benefits (more accurate product cost information, better information for cost control) outweigh the costs of implementing the system. Companies (1) in competitive markets with (2) high indirect costs that (3) produce a wide variety of different products that make different demands on resources, and that (4) have accounting and information technology to collect the data and implement the system are most likely to pass the cost-benefit test, especially if the company produces (5) high volumes of some products but low volumes of other products.

4. Compare a traditional production system to a just-in-time (JIT) production system. Traditional production systems often produce enormous waste in both inventories and manufacturing processes. They have functionally arranged clusters of machines, "push" production, large inventories, long setup times, and relatively inflexible employees. *Just-in-time production systems* are designed to eliminate waste. They have sequentially arranged production activities, "demand-pull" production scheduling, minimal inventories, quick setup times, and cross-trained employees. JIT systems rely on dependable suppliers to deliver perfect quality materials just in time for production.

5. Record manufacturing costs for a just-in-time costing system. *Just-in-time costing* is a standard costing system that begins with output completed and then assigns manufacturing cost to units sold and to inventories. This differs from traditional sequential tracking standard costing that moves forward, step by step, from direct materials inventory, to work in process inventory, to finished goods inventory, to cost of goods sold. Because JIT costing does not use a Work in Process Inventory account, it simplifies record keeping.

6. Contrast the four types of quality costs and use these costs to make decisions. The goal of total quality management is to delight customers by providing superior products and services. Companies achieve this goal by improving quality and eliminating defects and waste throughout the value chain. Four types of quality costs are *prevention*, *appraisal*, *internal failure*, and *external failure*. Managers make trade-offs among these costs, often investing more in prevention and appraisal to reduce internal and external failure costs. Because quality costs are hard to measure, many companies use nonfinancial measures to evaluate quality management.

7. Relate a life-cycle budget for a product to target costing and value engineering. Successful companies strive to reduce costs at every stage of their products' life cycles. A *life-cycle budget* compiles predicted revenues and costs of a product over its entire life. Managers compare budgeted costs with allowable life-cycle costs to estimate the cost reductions required to meet profitability goals. *Target costing* helps managers set goals for cost reductions through product design. *Value engineering* refers to design activities that reduce the cost of a product without reducing its ability to satisfy the customer via high quality and performance. Life-cycle budgeting, target costing, and value engineering are continuous improvement in action.

Accounting Vocabulary

activity-based costing (ABC)
  (p. 1079)
appraisal costs (p. 1095)
backflush costing (p. 1093)
external failure costs
  (p. 1095)

internal failure costs
  (p. 1095)
just-in-time (JIT) costing
  (p. 1093)
life-cycle budget (p. 1098)

non-value-added activities
  (p. 1091)
prevention costs (p. 1095)
product life cycle (p. 1097)
target costing (p. 1099)

throughput time (p. 1091)
trigger points (p. 1093)
value engineering (VE)
  (p. 1099)

Questions

1. List four management accounting techniques that managers use to achieve their strategic goal of delivering value to customers.
2. Give two reasons why allocating manufacturing overhead based on direct labor can yield inaccurate product costs.
3. "For costing-system alternatives, accountants have activity-based costing, job costing, and process costing." True or false? Explain.
4. In what way do activity-based costing systems place more emphasis on nonfinancial measures than do traditional single-allocation-base systems?
5. Give three examples of technology that have made gathering activity-based accounting information less expensive.
6. What are the two major benefits of activity-based costing?
7. "Activity-based costing systems provide more accurate information than traditional systems that use a single allocation rate. Every company should adopt ABC." Do you agree? Why or why not?
8. Contrast the traditional and JIT approaches to managing machine setups.

9. Describe "demand-pull" production scheduling.
10. Companies that implement JIT production systems usually reduce the number of suppliers they use. Give two benefits of doing so.
11. The just-in-time costing account RIP Inventory represents two accounts in a sequential-tracking system. What are they?
12. "Prevention costs are the most important quality costs." Explain.
13. Why is target costing important in achieving allowable life-cycle cost?
14. A new car's target cost at the beginning of production is $25,000 per unit. Gradual continuous improvement after production begins is expected to reduce its life-cycle average cost by $500. The car's life-cycle average sale price is budgeted at $43,500. If management expects the model to achieve its allowable average cost, what is the desired life-cycle operating contribution percentage (operating contribution/sale price)?
15. "Financial performance measures are used almost exclusively in evaluating quality management efforts." Do you agree? Why or why not?

Daily Exercises

Distinctive features of activity-based costing
(Obj. 1)

DE25-1 Fill in each blank with a term. You may use a term more than once. Some terms may not be used at all.

Activity-based costing	Direct labor	Life-cycle budgeting
A cost allocation base	Direct material	Overcost
A cost driver	Indirect	Target costing
Correctly cost	Job costing	Undercost

a. Traditional costing systems that use a single overhead allocation base usually _____ high-volume products that are produced in large batches.
b. _____ is any factor whose change causes a change in the related total cost.
c. _____ uses the costs of activities as building blocks for compiling product costs.
d. Traditional cost systems that allocate manufacturing overhead based on direct labor hours or direct labor costs usually _____ direct-labor-intensive products.
e. ABC systems differ from traditional cost systems in the treatment of _____ costs.

Distinctive features of activity-based costing
(Obj. 1)

DE25-2 List the seven steps in developing an ABC system. For each step, decide whether primary responsibility for the step should be assigned to

- The company accountant
- Production personnel (for example, the production foreman), or
- Shared equally between the accountant and production personnel

(*Hint:* Think about who would likely have the most information about each step.)

Activity-based costing
(Obj. 1)

DE25-3 While studying this chapter, your roommate becomes frustrated and exclaims, "I'm a management major, not an accountant! I'm going to concentrate in production operations. I don't need to know anything about this activity-based costing stuff. It's just an accounting exercise, and I want to leave that to the accountants." Use your answer to Daily Exercise 25-2 as a basis for responding to your roommate.

DE25-4 Consider Chemtech's original cost system on pages 1081–1082. Suppose Chemtech allocates manufacturing overhead at 250% of direct labor cost, instead of 200% of direct labor cost.

Allocating manufacturing overhead **(Obj. 1)**

1. Compute the gross margin per pound for aldehyde and for PH.
2. Compute the *total overhead* assigned to all the aldehyde and to all the PH.
3. Did the new manufacturing overhead rate change the ratio of total overhead allocated to aldehyde versus PH?

DE25-5 Suppose Chemtech's activity-based costing team identifies a fourth activity—machine setup. The foreman estimates that the total setup cost will be $225,000, and that production will require 3,000 setups. (This is less than the 4,000 total batches in Exhibit 25-5 on pages 1084–1085. Chemtech often eliminates a setup by running two batches of the same chemical in a row.) Aldehyde will require 40 setups, and PH will require 1 setup.

Developing an activity cost allocation rate **(Obj. 1)**

1. Compute the cost allocation rate for machine setups.
2. Compute the total machine setup costs allocated to aldehyde and to PH.
3. Did Chemtech's original allocation base (200% of direct labor cost) allocate setup costs appropriately? Give your reason.

DE25-6 Consider the Chemtech example on pages 1081–1086 and your analysis in Daily Exercise 25-5.

Computing activity costs and explaining changes **(Obj. 1)**

1. Compute the machine setup cost per pound for aldehyde and for PH.
2. Use your answer to requirement 1 to explain why switching from a traditional single-allocation-base system to an ABC system usually shifts costs away from high-volume products, toward low-volume products.

DE25-7 Use the results of Daily Exercise 25-6 and the information in Exhibit 25-6 on page 1085 to revise the

Using activity-based costing to allocate indirect costs **(Obj. 1)**

1. Manufacturing overhead cost per pound for aldehyde and for PH
2. Gross margin per pound for aldehyde and for PH

DE25-8 Daily Exercises 25-8 through 25-13 center on Meyer and Associates, a law firm in Portland, Oregon. Managing partner Erin Meyer's ear is ringing after an unpleasant call from client Roland Barron. Barron was irate after opening his bill for Meyers' legal services for his divorce. Barron said that Meyer's major competitor, Shepherd & Tomlinson, had charged much more reasonable fees to his friend who went through a similar divorce about three months ago.

Allocating indirect costs and computing income **(Obj. 1)**

Meyer is puzzled for two reasons. First, she is confident that she knows divorce law as well as any of her competitors. Before opening her practice in Portland, she spent ten years with a large Los Angeles law firm primarily handling divorce cases. She cannot see how Shepherd & Tomlinson can undercut her rates and still make a profit. But Shepherd & Tomlinson is reputed to be one of the most profitable practices in town, and Meyer is confident that they do not lose money on divorce cases. Second, just yesterday Meyer received a call from client Bob Megginson. Megginson was happy with the excellent service and reasonable fees that Meyer charged him for handling some international real-estate transactions. Meyer was surprised by Megginson's compliments, as she had felt a little uneasy accepting an engagement so far afield from her expertise.

Like most professional service firms, Meyer traces direct labor to individual engagements (jobs) using time sheets. She allocates indirect costs to jobs using a budgeted rate based on direct labor hours. She is happy with this system, which she has used for 15 years since opening her practice in Portland.

Meyer expects to incur $45,000 of indirect costs this year, and she expects her firm to work 3,000 direct labor hours. Meyer and the other attorneys each earn $50 per hour. Clients are billed at 150% of the direct labor cost. Last month Meyer's attorneys spent 90 hours on Barron's engagement, and they also spent 90 hours on Megginson's engagement.

REQUIRED

1. Compute Meyer and Associates' indirect cost allocation rate.
2. Compute the total costs assigned to the Barron engagement and to the Megginson engagement.
3. Compute the operating income from the Barron engagement and from the Megginson engagement.

DE25-9 Review Meyer and Associates' situation in Daily Exercise 25-8. List all the signals or clues that Meyer's cost system may be "broken."

Identifying signals of a broken cost system **(Obj. 3)**

DE25-10 Erin Meyer has employed your management consulting firm to help her decide whether to develop an activity-based costing system. After reviewing the information in Daily Exercises 25-8 and 25-9, draft a memo to Meyer. Make a recommendation whether her firm should develop an ABC system. Be sure to include an explanation of the costs and benefits Meyer could expect from adopting ABC. Use the format at the top of the next page for your memo.

Deciding whether ABC will pass cost-benefit test **(Obj. 2, 3)**

Computing ABC allocation rates
(Obj. 1)

DE25-11 Erin Meyer from Daily Exercise 25-8 suspects that her allocation of indirect costs could be giving misleading results, so she decides to develop an ABC system. She identifies three activities: word processing, photocopying, and training. Meyer figures that word processing costs are driven by the number of pages typed, photocopying costs are driven by the number of copies made, and training costs are most closely associated with the number of direct labor hours worked. Estimates of the costs and quantities of the allocation bases follow:

Activity	Estimated Cost	Allocation Base	Estimated Quantity of Cost Driver
Word processing	$25,000	Pages typed	3,125 pages
Photocopying	14,000	Pages copied	140,000 pages
Training	6,000	Direct labor hours	3,000 hours
Total indirect costs	$45,000		

Compute the cost allocation rate for each activity.

Using ABC to allocate costs and
compute profit
(Obj. 1)

DE25-12 Refer to the Meyer and Associates example in Daily Exercises 25-8 and 25-11. The Barron and Megginson engagements used the following resources last month:

Cost Driver	Barron	Megginson
Direct labor hours	90	90
Pages typed	50	300
Pages copied	100	750

REQUIRED

1. Compute the cost assigned to the Barron engagement and to the Megginson engagement, using the ABC system.
2. Compute the operating income from the Barron engagement and from the Megginson engagement.

Explaining results of ABC analysis
(Obj. 2)

DE25-13 Write a memo to Erin Meyer comparing the costs of the Barron and Megginson jobs using the original direct labor–single-allocation-base system (Daily Exercise 25-8) and the ABC system (Daily Exercise 25-12). Be sure to explain

• How have the costs changed under the ABC system?
• Why have the costs changed in the direction they changed, rather than in the opposite direction?
• Do the ABC results solve Meyer's puzzle from Daily Exercise 25-8?

Your memo should follow the format outlined in Daily Exercise 25-10.

Computing throughput time in
traditional and JIT production systems
(Obj. 4)

DE25-14 Bumperworks manufactures chrome bumpers for pickup trucks and vans. Under the traditional manufacturing system, the sequence of manufacturing operations is as follows:

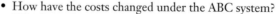

Stamping	3 days	Chrome plating	10 days	Assembly	2 days	Inspection
5 minutes	$\Rightarrow$	2 hours	$\Rightarrow$	15 minutes	$\Rightarrow$	3 minutes

Bumperworks does not rework any bumpers.

1. Compute throughput time for Bumperworks' manufacturing process.
2. How much of the throughput time is spent on value-added activities? How much of the time is spent on non-value-added activities?
3. If Bumperworks implements JIT production, which component of throughput time would you expect to change the most? Give your reason.

DE25-15   Indicate whether each of the following is characteristic of a JIT production system or a traditional production system.

Comparing JIT and traditional production systems
(Obj. 4)

a. Products produced in large batches.

b. Large stocks of finished goods protect against lost sales if customer demand is higher than expected.

c. Processing time is less than 10% of throughput time.

d. Faster throughput time.

e. Suppliers make frequent deliveries of small quantities of raw materials.

f. Long setup times.

g. Employees are cross-trained to do a variety of jobs, including maintenance and setups as well as operating machines.

h. Machines are grouped into self-contained production cells or production lines.

i. Machines are grouped together according to function. For example, all cutting machines are located in one area.

j. Workers "push" materials through the manufacturing process.

k. The final operation in the production sequence "pulls" parts from the preceding operation.

l. Each employee is responsible for inspecting his or her own work.

DE25-16   Look at the Mintel Company example on pages 1093–1094. Suppose Mintel's standard cost per circuit had been $1.02 for materials and $6.20 for conversion costs, and that Mintel actually sold 2,950,000 circuits. How would this change Mintel's journal entries, including the entry to close the Conversion Cost account? Prepare new journal entries as necessary.

Recording JIT costing journal entries
(Obj. 5)

DE25-17   Jerome Jordan uses a JIT system to manufacture trading pins for the 2002 Olympic Games in Salt Lake City. The standard cost per pin is $2 for raw materials and $1 for conversion costs. Last month Jordan recorded the following data:

Recording JIT costing journal entries
(Obj. 5)

Number of pins completed	4,000 pins	Raw material purchases.....................	$8,800
Number of pins sold......................	3,500 pins	Conversion costs	$4,220

Use JIT costing to prepare journal entries for the month, including the entry to close the Conversion Cost account.

DE25-18   Swaim Inc. in High Point, North Carolina, manufactures upholstered furniture. Give examples of costs Swaim might incur in each of the four categories of quality costs:

Giving examples of four types of quality costs
(Obj. 6)

- Prevention costs
- Appraisal costs
- Internal failure costs
- External failure costs

Be as specific as possible.

DE25-19   Bombardier, Inc., manufactures SeaDoo personal watercraft (jet-skis). Suppose Bombardier is considering spending the following amounts on a new quality program:

Classifying quality costs and using in decision-making
(Obj. 6)

Additional 20 minutes of in-water testing for each SeaDoo	$ 50,000
Negotiating with and training suppliers to obtain higher quality materials and on-time delivery	20,000
Redesigning a popular model to make it easier to manufacture.............	120,000

Bombardier expects this quality program to save costs:

Reduced warranty repair costs	$15,000
Avoid inspection of raw materials	40,000
Rework avoided because there are fewer defective units........................	55,000

They also expect this program to avoid lost profits from:

Lost sales due to disappointed customers	$80,000
Lost production time due to rework	25,000

1. Classify each of these costs into one of the four categories of quality costs (prevention, appraisal, internal failure, external failure).

2. Should Bombardier implement the quality program? Give your reasons.

DE25-20   Phoenix Brands is trying to decide whether to develop and market a nutritional supplement for athletes called "Go!" The life-cycle average sale price is $100 per case, and Phoenix's target life-cycle operating contribution is 25 percent of sales. Phoenix expects to sell 100,000 cases over the product's life.

Given current technology, Phoenix expects to incur the following costs over the life of Go!

Variable costs per case:	
Direct materials..	$30.00
Direct labor	9.00
Indirect labor..	1.25
Utilities...	0.15
Other variable manufacturing overhead..........	2.35
Fixed costs over product's life:	
Research and development	$ 800,000
Indirect labor..	200,000
Marketing...	1,500,000
Equipment depreciation	850,000

Prepare an initial life-cycle budget for Go! using Exhibit 25-14 as a guide.

DE25-21   Refer to Phoenix Brand's proposal to develop Go! in Daily Exercise 25-20.

1. Compute the *allowable* life-cycle average cost per case.
2. Compute the initial *budgeted* life-cycle cost per case.
3. Compare the initial budgeted life-cycle cost per case with the allowable life-cycle cost per case. Decide whether Phoenix should approve development of Go! Give your reason.

DE25-22   Refer to Phoenix Brand's proposed development of Go! in Daily Exercises 25-20 and 25-21. Suppose Phoenix managers believe that gradual continuous improvement after production begins will trim $0.50 per case from the average life-cycle cost of each case.

1. Compute the new target cost per case at the beginning of production.
2. If Phoenix is to develop Go!, *value engineering* must cut the cost per case by at least how much?
3. Give three specific examples of how Phoenix might achieve the value engineering cost reduction goal.

Exercises

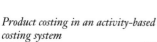

E25-1   Chromium Ltd. uses activity-based costing to account for its chrome wheel manufacturing process. Company managers have identified four manufacturing activities: materials handling, machine setup, insertion of parts, and finishing. The budgeted activity costs for 19X8 and their allocation bases are as follows:

Activity	Total Budgeted Cost	Allocation Base
Materials handling	$12,000	Number of parts
Machine setup	2,400	Number of setups
Insertion of parts	24,000	Number of parts
Finishing	60,000	Finishing direct labor hours
Total	$98,400	

Chromium expects to produce 2,000 chrome wheels during the year. The wheels are expected to use 12,000 parts, require 6 setups, and consume 1,000 hours of finishing time.

REQUIRED

1. Compute the cost allocation rate for each activity.
2. Compute the indirect manufacturing cost of each wheel.

E25-2   Several years after reengineering its production process, Chromex hired a new controller, Rebecca Steinberg. She developed an ABC system very similar to the one used by Chromex's chief rival, Chromium, Ltd. of Exercise 25-1. Part of the reason Steinberg developed the ABC system was that Chromex's profits had been declining, even though the company had shifted its product mix toward the product that had appeared most profitable under the old system. Before adopting the new ABC system, Chromex had used a direct labor hour single-allocation-base system that was developed 20 years ago.

For 19X8, Chromex's budgeted ABC allocation rates are

Activity	Allocation Base	Cost Allocation Rate
Materials handling	Number of parts	$ 1.25 per part
Machine setup	Number of setups	300.00 per setup
Insertion of parts	Number of parts	3.00 per part
Finishing	Finishing direct labor hours	70.00 per hour

The number of parts is now a feasible allocation base because Chromex recently purchased bar coding technology. Chromex produces two wheel models: standard and deluxe. Budgeted data for 19X8 are as follows:

	Standard	Deluxe
Parts per wheel	5.0	7.0
Setups per 1,000 wheels	3.0	3.0
Finishing direct labor hours per wheel	0.2	1.0
Total direct labor hours per wheel	2.0	3.0

The company's managers expect to produce 1,000 units of each model during the year.

1. Compute the total budgeted indirect manufacturing cost for 19X8.
2. Compute the ABC indirect manufacturing cost per unit of each model.
3. Using Chromex's old direct labor hour single-allocation-base system, compute the (single) allocation rate based on direct labor hours. Use this rate to determine the cost per wheel for each model under the old single-allocation-base method.

REQUIRED

E25-3 Refer to Exercise 25-2. For 19X9, Chromex's managers have decided to use the same indirect manufacturing costs per wheel that they computed in 19X8. In addition to the unit indirect manufacturing costs, the following data are budgeted for the company's standard and deluxe models for 19X9:

Using activity-based costing to make decisions
(Obj. 2)

	Standard	Deluxe
Sale price	$110.00	$155.00
Direct materials	15.00	25.00

Because of limited machine hour capacity, Chromex can produce either 2,000 standard wheels or 2,000 deluxe wheels.

1. If the managers rely on the ABC unit cost data computed in Exercise 25-2, which model will they produce? (All nonmanufacturing costs are the same for both models.)
2. If the managers rely on the single-allocation-base cost data, which model will they produce?
3. Which course of action will yield more income for Chromex?

REQUIRED

E25-4 Refer to Exercise 25-2. Why might controller Rebecca Steinberg have expected ABC to pass the cost-benefit test? Were there any warning signs that Chromex's old direct-labor-based allocation system was "broken"?

Explaining why ABC passes the cost-benefit test
(Obj. 3)

E25-5 Electromag Engineering produces electronic components. Electromag uses a JIT costing system with two trigger points: the purchase of direct materials and the transfer of completed units to finished goods. One of the company's products has a standard direct materials cost of $4 per unit and a standard conversion cost of $20 per unit.

Recording manufacturing costs in a JIT costing system
(Obj. 5)

During 19X9, Electromag produced 500,000 units of the component and sold 480,000. It purchased $2,100,000 of direct materials and incurred actual conversion costs totaling $10,950,000.

1. Prepare summary journal entries for 19X9.
2. The January 1, 19X9, balance of the RIP Inventory account was $80,000. What is the December 31, 19X9, balance?
3. Is conversion cost over- or underallocated for the year? By how much? Give the journal entry to close the Conversion Cost account.

REQUIRED

E25-6 Sony produces cordless telephones. Suppose that Sony's standard cost per phone is $26 for materials and $30 for conversion costs. The following data apply to July production:

Materials purchased..................................	$5,300,000
Conversion costs incurred......................	$6,080,000
Number of telephones completed..........	200,000 telephones
Number of telephones sold....................	192,000 telephones

Assume that Sony uses JIT costing with trigger points at the purchase of materials and at the completion of finished telephones.

REQUIRED

1. Prepare summary journal entries for July, including the entry to close the Conversion Costs account.
2. The beginning balance of Finished Goods Inventory was $100,000. What is the ending balance of Finished Goods Inventory?

E25-7 Smithfield, Inc., makes electronic components for microwave ovens. Ron Smithfield, the president, recently instructed vice president Roy Yamaguchi to develop a total quality control program. "If we don't at least match the quality improvements our competitors are making," he told Yamaguchi, "we'll soon be out of business."

Yamaguchi began by listing various "costs of quality" that Smithfield incurs. The first six items that came to mind were

a. Costs incurred by Smithfield customer representatives in traveling to customer sites to repair defective products.
b. Costs of electronic components returned by customers.
c. Costs of inspecting components in one of Smithfield's production processes.
d. Lost profits from lost sales due to reputation for less than perfect quality products.
e. Salaries of engineers who are designing components to withstand electrical overloads.
f. Costs of reworking defective components after discovery by company inspectors.

REQUIRED

Classify each item as a prevention cost, an appraisal cost, an internal failure cost, or an external failure cost.

E25-8 Anchor Hocking, in Lancaster, Ohio, manufactures kitchen glassware. Suppose Anchor Hocking is considering spending the following amounts on a new total quality management (TQM) program:

Strength-testing one item from each batch of glassware...................................	**$50,000**
Training employees in TQM	**35,000**
Training suppliers in TQM..	**45,000**
Identifying preferred suppliers who commit to on-time delivery of perfect quality materials..	**60,000**

Anchor Hocking expects the new program would save costs through the following:

Avoid lost profits from lost sales due to disappointed customers....................	**$75,000**
Avoid rework and spoilage..	**30,000**
Avoid inspection of raw materials...	**40,000**
Avoid warranty costs	**15,000**

REQUIRED

1. Classify each item as a prevention cost, an appraisal cost, an internal failure cost, or an external failure cost.
2. Should Anchor Hocking implement the new quality program? Give your reason.

E25-9 R2D2 produces robots for computer-controlled manufacturing systems. Kate Floyd, the engineering vice president, is developing a proposal for a new line of robots with an expected life cycle of five years. The sales staff predicts that a total of 10,000 robots can be sold at an average sale price of $15,000. Floyd believes that with today's technology and methods, R2D2 can manufacture the robots at the following product-line costs.

Variable costs per robot:		
Direct materials cost per robot............	$	4,500
Variable conversion cost per robot		1,400
Fixed costs for robot product line:		
Fixed conversion costs..........................		$34,000,000
Research and development		5,000,000
Marketing		8,000,000
Customer service.................................		3,000,000

REQUIRED

1. Prepare an initial life-cycle budget.
2. At the predicted volume level of 10,000 robots, what is the original budgeted life-cycle cost per robot?
3. What percentage of sales revenue is the initial life-cycle operating contribution?

E25-10   The sales staff of R2D2 of Exercise 25-9 is less sure of their sales volume prediction than they would like to be. They would not be surprised if life-cycle sales volume is as low as 8,000 units or as high as 12,000. Vice president Kate Floyd is uneasy about this uncertainty.

Using target costing and value engineering to achieve cost reductions (Obj. 7)

Top management of R2D2 expects each product line to earn a life-cycle operating contribution of 35% of sales revenue. Continuous improvement efforts after production begins should reduce the life-cycle average cost of the robots by $200.

REQUIRED

1. Compute the allowable life-cycle average cost per robot.
2. Compute the target cost per robot at the beginning of production.
3. Determine the value engineering cost reduction per robot that is required to achieve the target cost if the life-cycle sales volume is (a) 10,000 units, (b) 8,000 units, and (c) 12,000 units.

CHALLENGE EXERCISE

E25-11   Archco completed two jobs in June 19X9. Archco recorded the following costs assigned to the jobs by the company's activity-based costing system:

Using activity-based costing (Obj. 1, 2)

		Allocated Cost	
Activity	**Allocation Base**	**Job 103**	**Job 407**
Materials handling	Number of parts	$ 400	$ 800
Lathe work	Number of turns	4,000	12,000
Milling	Number of machine hours	3,000	21,000
Grinding	Number of parts	400	1,200
Testing	Number of output units	150	3,000

Job 407 required 2,000 parts; 60,000 lathe turns; and 1,050 machine hours. All 200 of the job's output units were tested, and all units of the Job 103 were tested.

REQUIRED

1. How do you know that at least one of the costs recorded for the two jobs is inaccurate?
2. Disregard materials-handling costs. How many parts were used for Job 103? How many lathe turns did Job 103 require? How many machine hours? How many units were produced in Job 103?
3. A nearby company has offered to test all product units for $13 each. On the basis of ABC data, should Archco accept or reject the offer? Give your reason.

Beyond the Numbers

BN25-1   Write a memo to Erin Meyer (Daily Exercises 25-8 through 25-13) explaining how she can use the ABC information to make decisions about her law practice. Consider how she could use ABC information in

Using ABC information to make decisions (Obj. 2)

- Setting fees (prices)
- Responding to client concerns about fees
- Controlling costs

Your memo should follow the format outlined in Daily Exercise 25-10.

BN25-2   JIT costing is typically used by businesses that

- Assign standard costs to each product
- Have low inventories

Explain why each of these conditions make JIT costing more feasible.

ETHICAL ISSUE

ABC and ethical decisions
(Obj. 1, 2)

Marilyn Hicks is assistant controller at Industrial Packaging, Inc., a manufacturer of cardboard boxes and other packaging materials. Hicks has just returned from a packaging industry conference on activity-based costing. She realizes that ABC may help Industrial Packaging meet its goal of reducing costs by 5% over each of the next three years.

Industrial Packaging's Order Department is a likely candidate for ABC. While orders are entered into a computer that updates the accounting records, clerks manually check customers' credit history and hand-deliver orders to shipping. This process occurs whether the sales order is for a dozen specialty boxes worth $60, or 10,000 basic boxes worth $8,500.

Hicks believes that identifying the cost of processing a sales order would justify (1) further computerization of the order process, and (2) changing the way the company processes small orders. However, the significant cost savings would arise from elimination of two positions in the Order Department. The company's sales order clerks have been with the company many years. Hicks is uncomfortable with the prospect of proposing a change that will likely result in terminating these employees.

REQUIRED

Use the IMA's ethical standards (Exhibit 19-12) to consider Hick's responsibility when cost savings come at the expense of jobs.

Problems (GROUP A)

Product costing in an ABC system
(Obj. 1)

P25-1A   Nova Computer's Desktop PC Department, which assembles and tests printed circuit (PC) boards, reports the following data regarding PC Board XR1:

Direct materials cost......................	$45.00
Activity costs allocated..................	?
Manufacturing product cost..........	?

The activities required to build the PC boards are as follows:

Activity	Allocation Base	Cost Allocated to Each Board
Start station	Number of raw PC boards	$1 \times \$\ 0.90 = \$0.90$
Dip insertion	Number of dip insertions	$20 \times\ 0.25\ =\ ?$
Manual insertion	Number of manual insertions	$6 \times\ ?\ =\ 3.60$
Wave solder	Number of boards soldered	$1 \times\ 3.50\ =\ 3.50$
Backload	Number of backload insertions	$? \times\ 0.70\ =\ 2.80$
Test	Standard time each board is in test activity	$0.25 \times\ 80.00\ =\ ?$
Defect analysis	Standard time for defect analysis and repair	$0.16 \times\ ?\ =\ 8.00$
Total		$\$\ ?$

REQUIRED

1. Fill in the blanks in both the opening schedule and the list of activities.
2. How is labor cost assigned to products under this product costing system?
3. Why might managers favor this ABC system instead of the older system, which allocated all conversion costs on the basis of direct labor?

Product costing in an ABC system
(Obj. 1, 2)

P25-2A   Timberlake Company's Chair Department manufactures rustic dining room chairs in its Asheville, North Carolina, plant. The company uses activity-based costing. Its activities and related data follow.

Activity	Budgeted Cost of Activity	Allocation Base	Cost Allocation Rate
Materials handling	$ 300,000	Number of parts	$ 0.50
Assembling	3,000,000	Direct labor hours	15.00
Painting	170,000	Number of painted chairs	4.00

Two styles of chairs were produced in March—the standard chair and an unpainted chair, which has fewer parts and requires no painting. The totals for quantities, direct materials costs, and other data are as follows:

Product	Units Produced	Direct Materials Costs	Number of Parts	Assembling Direct Labor Hours
Standard chair	5,000	$90,000	100,000	7,500
Unpainted chair	1,000	15,000	15,000	1,200

REQUIRED

1. Compute the per-unit manufacturing product cost of standard chairs and unpainted chairs.
2. "Upstream" activities, such as product design, were assigned to the standard chairs at $5 each and to the unpainted chairs at $2 each. Similar analyses were conducted of "downstream" activities such as distribution, marketing, and customer service. The downstream costs were $21 per standard chair and $18 per unpainted chair. Compute the full product costs per chair.
3. Which product costs are reported in the external financial statements? Which costs are used for management decision making? Explain the difference.
4. What price should Timberlake's managers set for standard chairs to earn a $21.50 profit per chair?

P25-3A The Software Department of Netware, Inc., develops software for Internet applications. The software market is very competitive, and Netware's competitors continue to introduce new products at low prices. Netware offers a wide variety of different software—from simple programs that enable new users to create personal Web pages, to complex commercial search engines. Like most software companies, Netware's raw material costs are insignificant.

Comparing costs from ABC versus single-rate systems; clues that ABC passes cost-benefit test (Obj. 1, 3)

Netware has just hired Jamie Hernandez, a recent graduate of State University's accounting program. Hernandez asks Software Department manager Sue Yang to join him in a pilot activity-based costing study. Hernandez and Yang identify the following activities, related costs, and cost allocation bases.

Activity	Estimated Indirect Activity Costs	Allocation Base	Estimated Quantity of Allocation Base
Applications development	$3,000,000	# New applications	6 new applications
Content production	4,800,000	# Lines of code	12 million lines
Testing	315,000	# Testing hours	1,800 testing hours
Total indirect costs	$8,115,000		

Netware has recently developed two new applications:

- EZPage—for developing personal Web pages
- Eureka!—a commercial search engine

EZPage required 500,000 lines of code and 100 hours of testing, while Eureka! required 5 million lines of code and 600 hours of testing. Netware expects to produce and sell 35,000 units of EZPage and 5 units of Eureka!

REQUIRED

1. Compute the cost allocation rate for each activity.
2. Use the activity-based cost allocation rates to compute the indirect costs of EZPage and Eureka! (*Hint:* First compute the total indirect costs allocated to each product line, and then compute the cost per unit.)
3. Netware's original single-allocation-base cost system allocated indirect costs to products at $100 per programmer hour. EZPage required 10,000 programmer hours, while Eureka! required 20,000 programmer hours. Compute the total indirect costs allocated to EZPage and Eureka! under the original system. Then compute the indirect cost per unit for each product.
4. Compare the activity-based costs per unit to the costs from the original system. How have the unit costs changed? Explain why the costs changed as they did.
5. What are the clues that Netware's ABC system is likely to pass the cost-benefit test?

Recording manufacturing costs for a
JIT costing system
(Obj. 4, 5)

P25-4A   CellTech produces cellular phones. The company has a JIT production system and uses JIT costing. Its cost system has two trigger points: the purchase of raw materials and the completion of the phones.

CellTech has two inventory accounts, RIP Inventory and Finished Goods Inventory. On August 1, 19X9, the account balances were RIP Inventory, $1,000; Finished Goods Inventory, $2,500.

CellTech's standard cost per phone is $45—$30 direct materials plus $15 conversion costs. The following data pertain to August manufacturing and sales:

Number of phones completed....	10,000 phones	Raw materials purchased	$301,000
Number of phones sold	9,900 phones	Conversion costs incurred.....	$142,000

1.   What are the major features of a JIT production system such as CellTech's?
2.   Prepare summary journal entries for August. Under- and overallocated conversion costs are closed to Cost of Goods Sold at the end of each month.
3.   What is the August 31, 19X9, balance of RIP Inventory?

Recording just-in-time costs, second
trigger point is sale
(Obj. 5)

P25-5A   (Continues P25-4A.) CellTech of Problem 25-4A has two trigger points in its JIT costing system, but now suppose the second trigger point is the sale, not the completion, of cellular phones. The company has only one inventory account, labeled simply "Inventory." Only direct materials costs are assigned to Inventory; the account balance is the sum of the costs of materials in the storeroom (if any), in process, and in finished units that have not been sold.

Conversion costs are not inventoried. They are assigned to units sold. Under- and overallocated conversion costs are closed to Cost of Goods Sold at the end of the month.

1.   Use the data in Problem 25-4A to prepare summary journal entries for August.
2.   How much of the $142,000 actual conversion cost was (eventually) expensed in August?
3.   Why might a company use the point of sale as the second trigger point instead of the point of completion?

P25-6A   Java Pro is using a costs-of-quality approach to evaluate design engineering efforts for a new electric coffeemaker. The company's senior managers expect the engineering work to reduce appraisal, internal failure, and external failure activities. The predicted reductions in activities over the two-year life cycle of the coffeemaker follow. Also shown are the cost allocation rates for each activity.

Activity	Predicted Reduction in Activity Units	Activity Cost Allocation Rate per Unit
Inspection of incoming materials	200	$20
Inspection of finished goods	200	25
Number of defective units discovered in-house	3,000	15
Number of defective units discovered by customers	800	30
Lost sales to dissatisfied customers	200	55

1.   Calculate the predicted quality cost savings from the design engineering work.
2.   Java Pro spent $55,000 on design engineering for the new coffeemaker. What is the net benefit of this "preventive" quality activity?
3.   What major difficulty would Java Pro's managers have had in implementing this costs-of-quality approach? What alternative approach could they use to measure quality improvement?

P25-7A   Suppose that Samsung's *final* life-cycle budget for a new line of personal computers takes into account both expected value engineering cost reductions and expected continuous improvement cost reductions from the company's new total quality management initiative (in millions):

Final Life-Cycle Budget, Proposed Computer Product Line		
Sales revenue...		$250
Direct materials		68
Materials contribution margin		182
Variable conversion costs		22
Product-line contribution margin..................		160
Fixed conversion costs...................................		60
Life-cycle manufacturing contribution.........		100
Other fixed costs:		
Design and engineering..........................	$15	
Marketing	5	
Customer service....................................	10	30
Life-cycle operating contribution		$ 70

In this budget, the new product line exactly achieves management's desired life-cycle operating contribution.

REQUIRED

1. Assume that the final life-cycle budget is based on an expected life-cycle sales volume of 100,000 units. Compute the life-cycle average sale price. Then compute the allowable life-cycle average operating cost.

2. Repeat requirement 1 for a sales volume of 200,000 units.

3. Again assume that the budget is based on 100,000 units. Suppose Samsung's managers expect continuous improvement efforts to reduce variable conversion costs by $50 per unit and fixed conversion costs by a total of $7 million over the product line's life cycle. Calculate the target cost at the beginning of production.

4. Continuing from requirement 3, if Samsung's engineers predict a value engineering cost reduction of $350 per unit, what is the original budgeted cost per computer?

Problems (GROUP B)

P25-1B The Electronics Manufacturing Department of Stereophile, Inc., in Phoenix, Arizona, assembles and tests electronic components used in high-end stereo equipment. Consider the following data regarding component J47:

Product costing in an ABC system (Obj. 1)

Direct materials cost	$71.00
Activity costs allocated	?
Manufacturing product cost	?

The activities required to build the component follow.

Activity	Allocation Base	Cost Allocated to Each Unit
Start station	Number of raw component chassis	1 × $ 1.30 = $1.30
Dip insertion	Number of dip insertions	? × 0.60 = 9.00
Manual insertion	Number of manual insertions	11 × 0.80 = ?
Wave solder	Number of components soldered	1 × 1.50 = 1.50
Backload	Number of backload insertions	6 × ? = 4.20
Test	Standard time each component is in test activity	0.30 × 90.00 = ?
Defect analysis	Standard time for defect analysis and repair	0.10 × ? = 7.00
Total		$?

REQUIRED

1. Fill in the blanks in both the opening schedule and the list of activities.
2. How is labor cost assigned to products under this product costing system?
3. Why might managers favor this ABC system instead of the older system, which allocated all conversion costs on the basis of direct labor?

P25-2B Emerson, Inc., manufactures CD racks and uses an activity-based costing system. Emerson's activity areas and related data follow.

Product costing in an ABC system (Obj. 1, 2)

Activity	Budgeted Cost of Activity	Allocation Base	Cost Allocation Rate
Materials handling	$ 200,000	Number of parts	$ 0.20
Assembling	3,000,000	Direct labor hours	18.00
Finishing	160,000	Number of finished units	5.00

Two styles of CD racks were produced in April—the standard rack and an unfinished rack, which has fewer parts and requires no finishing. The totals for quantities, direct materials costs, and other data follow.

Product	Units Produced	Direct Materials Costs	Number of Parts	Assembling Direct Labor Hours
Standard CD rack	2,000	$24,000	30,000	3,000
Unfinished CD rack	3,000	27,000	36,000	2,800

1. Compute the manufacturing product cost per unit of each type of CD rack.
2. Suppose that upstream activities, such as product design, were assigned to the standard CD racks at $4 each and to the unfinished racks at $3 each. Similar analyses were conducted of downstream activities such as distribution, marketing, and customer service. The downstream costs were $18 per standard rack and $13 per unfinished rack. Compute the full product costs per unit.
3. Which product costs are reported in the external financial statements? Which costs are used for management decision making? Explain the difference.
4. What price should Emerson's managers set for unfinished racks to earn a unit profit of $15?

Comparing costs from ABC versus single-rate systems; clues that ABC passes cost-benefit test
(Obj. 1, 3)

P25-3B LaCroix Pharmaceuticals in Montreal, Canada, manufactures an over-the-counter pain medication called Relieve. LaCroix is trying to win market share from Bayer and Tylenol. LaCroix has developed several different Relieve products tailored to specific markets. For example, the company sells large commercial containers of 1,000 capsules to health-care facilities and travel packs of ten capsules to sundry shops in airports, train stations, and hotels.

LaCroix's controller Yvette Chandon has just returned from a conference on activity-based costing. She asks Roland Turnot, foreman of the Relieve product line, to help her develop an activity-based costing system. Chandon and Turnot identify the following activities, related costs, and cost allocation bases:

Activity	Estimated Indirect Activity Costs	Allocation Base	Estimated Quantity of Allocation Base
Materials handling	$180,000	# Kilos	18,000 kilos
Packaging	300,000	# Machine hours	2,000 hours
Quality assurance	112,500	# Samples	1,500 samples
Total indirect costs	$592,500		

The commercial container Relieve product line had a total weight of 6,000 kilos, used 1,000 machine hours, and required 200 samples. The travel pack line had a total weight of 4,000 kilos, used 250 machine hours, and required 300 samples. LaCroix produced 2,500 commercial containers of Relieve and 50,000 travel packs.

1. Compute the cost allocation rate for each activity.
2. Use the activity-based cost allocation rates to compute the indirect costs of the commercial containers and the travel packs. (*Hint:* First compute the total indirect costs allocated to each product line, and then compute the cost per unit.)
3. LaCroix's original single-allocation base cost system allocated indirect costs to products at $250 per machine hour. Compute the total indirect costs allocated to the commercial containers and to the travel packs under the original system. Then compute the indirect cost per unit for each product.
4. Compare the activity-based costs per unit to the costs from the original system. How have the unit costs changed? Explain why the costs changed as they did.
5. What are the clues that LaCroix's ABC system is likely to pass the cost-benefit test?

Recording manufacturing costs for a JIT costing system
(Obj. 4, 5)

P25-4B Backcountry Outfitters produces backpacks. The company uses JIT costing for its JIT production system. Its costing system has two trigger points: the purchase of direct materials and the completion of the backpacks.

Backcountry has two inventory accounts: RIP Inventory and Finished Goods Inventory. On December 1, 19X9, the account balances were RIP Inventory, $3,000; Finished Goods Inventory, $5,000.

The standard cost of a backpack is $45—$15 direct materials plus $30 conversion costs. Data for December's activity follow.

Number of backpacks completed............................	15,000 backpacks	Direct materials purchased	$227,000
Number of backpacks sold	14,800 backpacks	Conversion costs incurred	467,000

1. What are the major features of a JIT production system such as Backcountry Outfitters'?
2. Prepare summary journal entries for December. Under- or overallocated conversion costs are closed to Cost of Goods Sold monthly.
3. What is the December 31, 19X9, balance of RIP Inventory?

P25-5B (Continues P25-4B) Backcountry Outfitters of Problem 25-4B has two trigger points in its JIT costing system, but now suppose that the second trigger point is the sale, not the completion, of backpacks. The company has only one inventory account, labeled simply "Inventory." Only direct materials costs are assigned to Inventory; the account balance is the sum of the costs of materials in the storeroom (if any), in process, and in finished units not yet sold.

Recording just-in-time costs, second trigger point is sale **(Obj. 5)**

Conversion costs are not inventoried. They are assigned to units sold. The Conversion Costs account is closed to Cost of Goods Sold monthly.

1. Use the data in Problem 25-4B to prepare summary journal entries for December.
2. How much of the $467,000 actual conversion cost was (eventually) expensed in December?
3. Why might a company use the point of sale as the second trigger point instead of the point of completion?

REQUIRED

P25-6B Lazer, Inc., is using a costs-of-quality approach to evaluate design engineering efforts for a new laser tag set. Lazer's senior managers expect the engineering work to reduce appraisal, internal failure, and external failure activities. The predicted reductions in activities over the two-year life cycle of the laser tag sets follow. Also shown are the cost allocation rates for each activity.

Analyzing costs of quality **(Obj. 6)**

Activity	Predicted Reduction in Activity Units	Activity Cost Allocation Rate per Unit
Inspection of incoming materials	300	$ 40
Inspection of work in process	300	20
Number of defective units discovered in-house	1,000	45
Number of defective units discovered by customers	500	70
Lost sales to dissatisfied customers	150	110

1. Calculate the predicted quality cost savings from the design engineering work.
2. Lazer spent $110,000 on design engineering for the new laser tag set. What is the net benefit of this "preventive" quality activity?
3. What major difficulty would Laser's managers have in implementing this costs-of-quality approach? What alternative approach could they use to measure quality improvement?

REQUIRED

P25-7B Sony produces cordless telephones. Suppose the company's *final* life-cycle budget for a new product line takes into account both expected value engineering cost reductions and expected continuous improvement cost reductions from the company's new total quality management initiative (in millions):

Life-cycle budgeting, target costing, and value engineering **(Obj. 7)**

Final Life-Cycle Budget, Proposed Telephone Product Line		
Sales revenue		$95
Direct materials		26
Materials contribution margin		69
Variable conversion costs		10
Product-line contribution margin		59
Fixed conversion costs		14
Life-cycle manufacturing contribution		45
Other fixed costs:		
Design and engineering	$3	
Marketing	5	
Customer service	1	9
Life-cycle operating contribution		$36

In this budget, assume that the new product line achieves management's desired life-cycle operating contribution exactly.

1. Assume that the final life-cycle budget is based on an expected life-cycle sales volume of 1 million telephones. Compute the life-cycle average sale price. Then compute the allowable life-cycle average operating cost.
2. Repeat requirement 1 for a sales volume of 2 million telephones.
3. Again assume the budget is based on 1 million telephones. Suppose Sony's managers expect continuous improvement efforts to reduce average variable conversion costs by $4 per unit and fixed conversion costs by a total of $3 million over the product line's life cycle. Calculate the target cost at the beginning of production.
4. Continuing from requirement 3, Sony's engineers predict a value engineering cost reduction of $15 per unit. What is the original budgeted cost per telephone?

REQUIRED

Applying Your Knowledge

DECISION CASES

Comparing costs from ABC versus single-rate systems; using these costs to make decisions
(Obj. 1, 2)

CASE 1. Nastar Systems specializes in electronics systems used in space exploration. The company's original job cost system has two direct cost categories—direct materials and direct labor. Overhead is allocated to jobs at the single rate of $23 per direct labor hour.

A task force headed by Nastar's senior management accountant recently designed an ABC system with five activities. The ABC system retains the current system's two direct cost categories. Thus it budgets only overhead costs for each activity. Pertinent data follow.

Activity	Allocation Base	Cost Allocation Rate
Materials handling	Number of parts	$ 0.75
Machine setup	Number of setups	500.00
Machining	Machining hours	32.00
Assembling	Assembling hours	18.00
Shipping	Number of shipments	1,500.00

Nastar has been awarded two new government contracts, which will be produced as Job A and Job B. Budget data relating to the contracts follow.

	Job A	Job B
Number of parts	15,000	2,000
Number of setups	6	4
Number of machining hours	3,000	700
Number of assembling hours	1,500	200
Number of shipments	1	1
Total direct labor hours	8,000	600
Number of output units	100	10
Direct materials cost	$210,000	$30,000
Direct labor cost	$160,000	$12,000

REQUIRED

1. Compute the manufacturing product cost per unit for each job, using the original costing system (with two direct cost categories and a single overhead allocation rate).
2. Suppose Nastar adopts the ABC system. Compute the manufacturing product cost per unit for each job using ABC.
3. Which costing system more accurately assigns to jobs the costs of the resources consumed to produce them? Explain.
4. A dependable company has offered to produce both jobs for Nastar for $6,000 per output unit. Nastar may outsource (buy from the outside company) either Job A only, Job B only, or both jobs. Which course of action will Nastar's managers take if they base their decision on (a) the original system? (b) ABC system costs? Which course of action will yield more income? Explain.

Using life-cycle budgeting and target costing to make a production decision
(Obj. 7)

CASE 2. Suppose that Ford Motor Company is using life-cycle budgeting and target costing in the development stage of a new sport utility vehicle. Assume that the predicted average sale price of the car is $30,000, and that Ford's senior managers desire a life-cycle operating contribution of 30% of sales revenue. Company engineers predict that continuous improvement efforts will reduce the average cost of the vehicles over the product life cycle by $300.

If the original budgeted cost of the vehicle is $23,100, should Ford proceed with production if the value engineering cost reduction is (a) $1,000? (b) $3,000? Explain.

Team Projects

Developing an ABC system; explaining how ABC changes costs; signs of a broken cost system
(Obj. 1, 2, 3)

PROJECT 1. Mauna Loa Shrimp Farms in Hilo, Hawaii, has a Processing Department that processes raw shrimp into two products:

- Headless shrimp
- Peeled and deveined shrimp

Mauna Loa recently submitted bids for two orders: (1) headless shrimp for a cruise line, and (2) peeled and deveined shrimp for a large urban hospital. Mauna Loa won the first bid, but lost the second. The production and sales managers are upset. They believe that Mauna Loa's state-of-the-art equipment should have given the company an edge in the peeled and deveined market. Consequently, production managers are starting to keep their own sets of product cost records.

Mauna Loa is reexamining both its production process and its cost system. The company is considering changing its cost accounting system, which has been in place since 1989. The existing system allocates all indirect costs based on direct labor hours. Mauna Loa is considering adopting activity-based costing. Controller Jodie Braselton and a team of production managers performed a preliminary study. The team identified six activities, with the following (department-wide) estimated indirect costs and cost drivers:

Activity	Total Estimated Cost of Activity	Allocation Base
Redesign of production process (costs of changing process and equipment)	$ 5,000	Number of design changes
Production scheduling (production scheduler's salary)	$ 6,000	Number of batches
Chilling (depreciation on refrigerators)	$ 1,500	Weight (in pounds)
Processing (utilities and depreciation on equipment)	$21,000	Number of cuts
Packaging (indirect labor and depreciation on equipment)	$ 1,425	Cubic feet of surface exposed
Order filling (order-takers' and shipping clerks' wages)	$ 7,000	Number of orders
Total indirect costs for the entire department	$41,925	

The raw shrimp are chilled and then cut. For headless shrimp, employees remove the heads, then rinse the shrimp. For peeled and deveined shrimp, the headless shrimp are further processed—the shells are removed and the backs are slit for deveining. Both headless shrimp and peeled and deveined shrimp are packaged in foam trays and covered with shrink wrap. The Order-Filling Department assembles orders of headless shrimp as well as peeled and deveined shrimp.

Braselton estimates that Mauna Loa will produce 10,000 packages of headless shrimp, and 50,000 packages of peeled and deveined shrimp. The two products incur the following costs per package:

	Costs Per Package	
	Headless Shrimp	Peeled and Deveined Shrimp
Shrimp	$3.50	$4.50
Foam trays	$0.05	$0.05
Shrink wrap	$0.05	$0.02
Number of cuts	12 cuts	48 cuts
Cubic feet of exposed surface	1 cubic foot	0.75 cubic foot
Weight (in pounds)	2 1/2 pounds	1 pound
Direct labor hours	0.01 hour	0.05 hour

Mauna Loa pays direct laborers $20 per hour. Braselton estimates that each product line will also require the following *total* resources:

	Headless Shrimp		Peeled and Deveined Shrimp	
Design changes	1 change	for all	4 changes	for all
Batches	40 batches	10,000	20 batches	50,000
Sales orders	90 orders	packages	110 orders	packages

Form groups of four students. All group members should work together to develop the group's answers to the four requirements. However, the first two students have primary responsibility for writing up the final responses to requirements 1 and 4, while the other two students have primary responsibility for writing up the responses to requirements 2 and 3.
(Carry all computations at least four decimal places.)

1. List the clues that Mauna Loa's original cost system may be broken.

2. Using the original cost system with the single indirect cost allocation base (direct labor hours), compute the *total budgeted cost per package* for the headless shrimp and then for the peeled and deveined shrimp. (*Hint:* First compute the indirect cost allocation rate—that is, the predetermined overhead rate. Then compute the total budgeted cost per package for each product.)

3. Use activity-based costing to recompute the *total budgeted cost per package* for the headless shrimp and then for the peeled and deveined shrimp. (*Hint:* First, calculate the budgeted cost allocation rate for each activity. Then calculate the total indirect costs of (a) the entire headless shrimp product line, and (b) the entire peeled and deveined shrimp product line. Next compute the indirect cost per package of each product. Finally, calculate the total cost per package of each product.)

4. Write a memo to Mauna Loa CEO George Onapuko, explaining the results of the ABC study. Compare the costs reported by the ABC system with the costs reported by the original system. Point out whether the ABC system shifted costs toward headless shrimp, or toward peeled and deveined shrimp, and explain why. Finally, explain whether Onapuko should feel more comfortable making decisions using cost data from the original system, or from the new ABC system. Use the memo format outlined in Daily Exercise 25-10.

Interviewing a company about its ABC system
(Obj. 1, 2, 3)

PROJECT 2. Form groups of four to six students. Identify a local company that has developed an activity-based costing system, and interview the accounting staff. Before the interview, learn

- The name of your company contact
- What the company produces
- Who are the company's major customers

As part of your advance preparation, decide who will ask which questions during the interview.

The purpose of your interview is to learn how the company developed its ABC system. Be sure to cover the following questions. By listening carefully in the interview, you will likely think of other questions to add to this list.

1. How did the company perform each of the seven steps in developing an ABC system (see pages 1082–1084)? Who was involved in each step? Which step was most difficult? Why?

2. How many separate activities, indirect activity cost pools, and allocation bases does the company's ABC system use? Are there plans to increase or decrease the number of activities, cost pools, and allocation bases in the future?

3. Are the ABC product costs used in the general ledger, or is ABC a separate stand-alone system used primarily for management decisions? If the latter, are there plans to integrate ABC into the general ledger?

4. What spurred the company to develop an ABC system?

5. What benefits has ABC provided? Has the ABC system lived up to expectations?

6. What problems arose in developing the ABC system? How did the company solve these problems?

7. Have the benefits of the ABC system outweighed its costs?

As directed by your instructor, report the results of your interview in

- A 3–5 page typed paper, or
- A 5–8 minute oral class presentation

Start with the background information (name of the company, contact person, company's major products and customers). Then discuss the company's ABC system, using the seven questions as a guide. If you don't have space in the paper (or time in the oral report) to cover everything, focus on the insights you found most interesting. (*Hint:* Make sure everyone in your group has a chance to critique the report. Use their suggestions to improve the report before you turn in the written report or make the oral presentation.)

Internet Exercise KELLOGG'S

As you stroll down the cereal aisle of a grocery store, you see an amazing display of different brands. Hundreds of choices are available. You want all your vitamins and minerals in a bowl of flakes? It's there. Hunting for a sugar rush? It's there. Looking for a snack in the afternoon? It's there. New cereals have arrived since your last shopping trip! How do they do it?

Kellogg's, the largest ready-to-eat cereal producer, reveals its secrets at its Internet site. Kellogg's makes some of the most popular cereals, such as Rice Krispies™, Frosted Flakes™, Fruit Loops™, and the venerable Corn Flakes™. However, they each share a common manufacturing process. Controlling the process and the resulting costs to meet consumer demand presents quite a challenge for Kellogg's management.

1. Go to **http://www.kelloggs.com.** This is the welcome page for Kellogg's. Click on **Cereal City Headquarters U.S.A.** to move to Kellogg's home page. Cereal City is a fun location with a lot of activities and games. Kellogg's web site has won several awards for its creativity.

2. Click on **Kellogg's Factory** followed by **FAQs.** That's cyberspeak for frequently asked questions.

3. Click on **How Cereal Is Made** and review Kellogg's manufacturing process to answer the following questions. Kellogg's makes more than 45 different cereals, yet the manufacturing process is similar for each cereal.
   a. List the seven steps in Kellogg's cereal manufacturing process.
   b. Does the cereal manufacturing process lend itself to activity-based costing? Explain.
   c. Identify the primary cost drivers for any three of the manufacturing steps listed in (a).
   d. How would Kellogg's allocate the indirect costs of each activity to the various cereal products?
   e. Would Kellogg's need to maintain a JIT inventory management system?
   f. Quality is very important to Kellogg's. Consider the four types of quality costs. Would you expect Kellogg's to make tradeoffs among these four types of quality costs, intentionally spending more on one type to reduce another type of quality cost? Explain.

ABC, JIT, and quality costs
(Obj. 1, 4, 6)

REQUIRED

CHAPTER 26

Special Business Decisions and Capital Budgeting

LEARNING OBJECTIVES

After studying this chapter, you should be able to

1. Identify the relevant information for a special business decision

2. Make six types of short-term special business decisions

3. Explain the difference between correct and incorrect analysis of a particular business decision

4. Use opportunity costs in decision making

5. Use four capital budgeting models to make longer-term investment decisions

6. Compare and contrast popular capital budgeting methods

On the slopes of Deer Valley ski resort in Park Valley, Utah—site of the 2002 Winter Olympics slalom competition—management accounting seems a world away. But the counter where you rent your skis, the chairlift that whisks you up the mountain, and the restaurant that serves you dinner are all part of the resort's recent expansion. How did Deer Valley's developers decide to spend $13 million to expand the Snow Park Lodge?

Director of Finance Jim Madsen explains that the answer is *capital budgeting*. Deer Valley has a long-term strategic expansion plan. When the resort reaches a target number of skiers per day and target level of profit, the owners expand.

Each expansion project must meet two requirements. First, the project must be profitable. Second, Deer Valley must expect to "get its money back" on the investment in a relatively short time. To figure out which projects meet these requirements, Deer Valley's accountants compare

• The amount of the investment needed to expand the resort, with

• The additional revenues expected from expansion.

How do the accountants make this comparison? They use two management accounting techniques:

• Net present value—to predict whether the investment will be profitable

• Payback period—to predict how long it will take to "get the money back"

We'll see how companies like Deer Valley use net present value, payback period, and other capital budgeting techniques to decide which long-term capital investments to make.

T his chapter explains how companies make *long-term* and *short-term* special decisions. Deer Valley's capital expansion project is a *long-term* special decision because it will tie up the company's resources for years to come. We'll tackle these long-term special decisions in the second half of this chapter. But first we need to consider special decisions of a *shorter-term* nature.

Relevant Information for Decision Making

Objective 1

Identify the relevant information for a special business decision

Strategy. A set of business goals and the tactics to achieve them.

Business managers develop and implement strategies. A **strategy** is a set of business goals and the tactics to achieve them. The main financial goals in business are to earn profits and to build a strong financial position. But managers must make many decisions about how to achieve those goals. The first half of this chapter explains how managers make short-term special decisions while the second half of the chapter explains how managers make long-term special decisions (like Deer Valley's expansion project).

Decision making means choosing among alternative courses of action. To choose, managers

- Identify the alternative courses of action
- Gather information relevant (useful) for making the decision
- Analyze the information to compare alternatives
- Choose the best alternative to achieve the strategic goal

Exhibit 26-1 illustrates the decision-making process. Computers are ideally suited for decision analysis. Managers use spreadsheets to quickly compute expected results of different actions.

Relevant Information. Expected future data that differ among alternative courses of action.

Managers often select the course of action that maximizes expected operating income. To do this, they analyze relevant information. **Relevant information** has two distinguishing characteristics. It is

- expected *future data* that also
- *differs among alternatives*

■ **Daily Exercise 26-1**

Suppose you are deciding whether to buy your first car, a Toyota or a Ford. The cost of the car you want to buy, the insurance premium on this car, and the cost to maintain the car are all relevant because these costs

- will be incurred in the *future* (after you decide to buy the car), and
- will *differ between alternatives* (Each car has a different cost, and the maintenance and insurance costs will also differ.)

The cost of the car, the insurance, and the maintenance are *relevant* because they can affect your decision of which car to purchase.

In contrast, costs that were incurred in the past and costs that do not differ between alternatives are *irrelevant* because they do not affect your decision. For example, a campus parking sticker will cost the same whether you buy the Toyota or the Ford, so that cost is irrelevant to your decision. It will not differ between the two alternatives.

The same distinction applies to all situations—*only relevant data affect decisions*. Let's consider another application of this general principle.

Concept Highlight

EXHIBIT 26-1
How Businesses Make Special Decisions

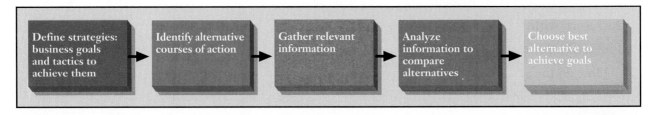

Suppose Pendleton Woolen Mills is deciding whether to use pure wool or a wool blend in a new line of sweaters. Assume Pendleton predicts the following costs under the two alternatives:

	Expected Materials and Labor Cost Per Sweater		
	Wool	Wool Blend	Cost Difference
Direct materials...	$10	$6	$4
Direct labor	2	2	0
Total cost of direct materials and direct labor	$12	$8	$4

The cost of direct materials is relevant because this cost differs between alternatives (the wool costs $4 more than the wool blend). The labor cost is irrelevant because that cost is the same for both alternatives.

The following point is worth emphasizing:

> Relevant information is expected *future* data that differ among
> alternative courses of action.

Managers should base their decisions on expected future data rather than on historical data. Historical data supplied by the accounting system are useful guides for predictions. However, historical data by themselves are irrelevant. They are useful only to the extent that managers can use them to predict future data.

 Thinking It Over You are considering replacing your Pentium computer with the latest model. Is the $1,500 you spent (in 1997) on the Pentium relevant to your decision about buying the new model?

Answer: The $1,500 cost of your Pentium is irrelevant. The $1,500 is a *past* (sunk) cost that has already been incurred, so it is the same whether or not you buy the new computer.

Our approach to making decisions is called the *relevant information approach*, or the *incremental analysis approach*. This approach applies to a wide variety of special business decisions. We now consider six shorter-term special decisions:

- Special sales orders
- Dropping products, departments, and territories
- Product mix
- Make or buy
- Best use of facilities
- Selling as is or processing further

As you study these decisions, keep in mind that two keys in analyzing shorter-term special business decisions are

1. Focus on *relevant* revenues, costs, and profits.
2. Use a *contribution margin* approach that separates variable costs from fixed costs. ◀▥

◀▥ ◀▥ ◀▥ Chapter 22, page 954, explains that contribution margin equals revenues minus all variable expenses.

Special Sales Order

Suppose that ACDelco, a manufacturer of automobile parts, ordinarily sells oil filters for $3.20 each. Assume that a mail-order company has offered ACDelco $35,000 for 20,000 oil filters, or $1.75 per filter ($35,000 ÷ 20,000 = $1.75). This sale will not affect regular business in any way. Furthermore, the special sales order

- Will not change fixed costs
- Will not require any additional variable marketing and administrative expenses
- Will put to use idle manufacturing capacity

Assume that ACDelco's manufacturing product cost is $2 per oil filter.

Objective 2

Make six types of short-term special business decisions

INCOME STATEMENT
Year Ended December 31, 19X9

Conventional Format		Contribution Margin Format		
Sales revenue	$800,000	Sales revenue		$800,000
Less manufacturing		Less variable expenses:		
cost of goods sold	500,000	Manufacturing	$300,000	
Gross margin	300,000	Marketing and		
Less marketing and		administrative	75,000	375,000
administrative		Contribution margin		425,000
expenses	200,000	Less fixed expenses:		
		Manufacturing	$200,000	
		Marketing and		
		administrative	125,000	325,000
Operating income	$100,000	Operating income		$100,000

Should ACDelco accept the special order at a sale price of $1.75? At first glance, the answer appears to be No, because each oil filter costs $2 to make. But first appearances can be deceiving.

To set the stage for the analysis, let's examine ACDelco's income statement. Exhibit 26-2 presents the income statement in both conventional format and the more helpful contribution margin format.

Contribution margin income statements separate variable expenses from fixed expenses. ◀▥ This format is more useful for decision analysis because it shows how sales volume affects costs and income.

◀▥ ◀▥ ◀▥ Chapter 22, page 954, compares conventional and contribution margin income statements.

Suppose that ACDelco made and sold 250,000 oil filters before considering the special order. Under absorption costing, the manufacturing cost per unit is $2 ($500,000 ÷ 250,000). But the contribution margin approach shows that the *variable* manufacturing cost per unit is only $1.20 ($300,000 ÷ 250,000). We can now answer the key question facing ACDelco: How would the special sale affect the company's operating income?

Correct Analysis: Contribution Margin Approach

The correct analysis shown in Exhibit 26-3 is an incremental approach that follows the two key guidelines for special business decisions:

1. Focus on relevant revenues, costs, and profits, and
2. Use a contribution margin approach.

Exhibit 26-3 shows that this special sale increases revenues by $35,000 (20,000 × $1.75). The only cost that will differ between the alternatives is the variable manufacturing cost, which is expected to increase by $24,000 (20,000 × $1.20). The other costs do not enter the analysis because they are irrelevant. Variable marketing and administrative expenses will be the same whether ACDelco accepts the special order or not, because no special efforts were made to get this sale. Fixed expenses are unchanged because ACDelco has enough idle capacity to produce 20,000 extra oil filters without requiring additional facilities.

To decide whether to accept the special order, ACDelco should compare the additional (incremental) revenues with the additional (incremental) expenses of producing the goods. As long as the increase in revenues exceeds the increase in expenses, the sale contributes to profits. ACDelco management predicts that the special sales order will increase operating income by $11,000, as shown in Exhibit 26-3.

■ Daily Exercise 26-2
■ Daily Exercise 26-3
■ Daily Exercise 26-4

EXHIBIT 26-3
Incremental Analysis of Special
Sales Order

Expected increase in revenues—	
sale of 20,000 oil filters × $1.75 each	$35,000
Expected increase in expenses—variable manufacturing costs:	
20,000 oil filters × $1.20 each	(24,000)
Expected increase in operating income	$11,000

INCOME STATEMENT
Year Ended December 31, 19X9

	(1) Without Special Order (250,000 units)	(2) With Special Order (270,000 units)	(3) Difference (20,000 units) Total	Per Unit
Sales revenue	$800,000	$835,000	$35,000	$1.75
Variable expenses:				
Manufacturing..............	$300,000	$324,000	$24,000	$1.20
Marketing and				
administrative	75,000	75,000	—	—
Total variable				
expenses	375,000	399,000	24,000	1.20
Contribution margin........	425,000	436,000	11,000	0.55
Fixed expenses:				
Manufacturing..............	200,000	200,000	—	—
Marketing and				
administrative	125,000	125,000	—	—
Total fixed expenses......	325,000	325,000	—	—
Operating income	$100,000	$111,000	$11,000	$0.55

Exhibit 26-4 gives ACDelco's contribution margin income statements both without the special sales order (column 1) and with it (column 2). Column 3 shows the differences from accepting the special order, an $11,000 increase in operating income.

We have shown two correct ways of deciding whether to accept or reject a special sales order at a sale price less than the total cost per unit:

- An incremental analysis that quickly summarizes the differences (Exhibit 26-3)
- An analysis of total revenues, expenses, and operating income under both courses of action (Exhibit 26-4)

Should you use the incremental (summary) analysis like Exhibit 26-3, or the total analysis like Exhibit 26-4? The answer depends on your question. The *incremental* analysis answers the question: What will be the *difference* in revenues, expenses, and operating income if the business accepts the special order? The *total* analysis shows the summary of differences and answers an additional question: What will be the *total* revenues, expenses, and operating income under each course of action? Managers can use either analysis to decide whether to accept or reject the special sales order.

Incorrect Analysis: Ignoring the Nature of Fixed Costs

Now consider an incorrect analysis of the ACDelco special sales order decision. The conventional approach, using only the left-hand side of Exhibit 26-2, leads to an incorrect prediction of the change in expenses resulting from the sale.

Total manufacturing costs	$ 500,000
Units produced...	÷250,000
Manufacturing product cost per unit ($500,000 ÷ 250,000)	$ 2.00
Expected increase in revenues—sale of 20,000 oil filters × $1.75 each........	$ 35,000
Expected increase in expenses—*total* manufacturing expenses:	
20,000 oil filters × $2.00 each	(40,000)
Expected decrease in operating income	$ (5,000)

■ Daily Exercise 26-5

A manager who follows this incorrect approach reasons that it costs $2 to make an oil filter, so it is unprofitable to sell the product for less than $2. *The flaw in this analysis* *arises from treating a fixed cost as though it changes in total like a variable cost does. Manufacturing one additional oil filter will only cost $1.20—the variable manufacturing cost. Fixed expenses are irrelevant to the decision because ACDelco will incur the fixed expenses whether or not the company accepts the special sales order.* Producing 20,000 more oil filters will not increase *total* fixed expenses. As volume increases, manufacturing costs increase at the rate of $1.20 per unit, not $2.00 per unit. In the correct (contribution margin) analysis, the variable expenses are relevant, and the fixed expenses are irrelevant.

> **Learning Tip:** To make special sales order decisions, we analyzed changes in revenues and costs among the different alternatives. We will use this same approach of analyzing differences in revenues and costs for the remaining short-term special decisions.

Short-Term versus Long-Term: Other Factors to Consider

Our special sales order analysis focused on the short-term expected effect on operating income. We must also consider long-term factors. How will the special order affect ACDelco's regular customers? Will acceptance of the order at $1.75 per unit hurt ACDelco's ability to sell the oil filter at the regular price of $3.20? Will regular customers find out about the special price and balk at paying more? And how will competitors react? Will this sale start a price war?

Accepting the order increases operating income by $11,000. Will potential disadvantages offset this income? The sales manager may think so and reject the order. In turning away the business, the manager would say that the company is better off passing up $11,000 now to protect its long-term market position and customer relations. Rejecting the special sales order may be an $11,000 "investment" in the company's long-term future.

Now let's turn to another short-term special decision.

Dropping Products, Departments, Territories—Fixed Costs Unchanged

■ **Daily Exercise 26-6**
■ **Daily Exercise 26-7**

To decide whether a company should drop a product line, a department, or a territory, let's modify our ACDelco example. We will assume that ACDelco already is operating at the 270,000-unit level, as shown in column 2 of Exhibit 26-4. Suppose the company is now considering dropping the air cleaner product line with $35,000 (20,000 units) in sales and total variable costs per unit of $1.20. A contribution margin income statement that is divided by product line follows:

| | | Product Line | |
	Total (270,000 units)	Oil Filters (250,000 units)	Air Cleaners (20,000 units)
Sales revenue	$835,000	$800,000	$ 35,000
Variable expenses	399,000	375,000	24,000
Contribution margin	436,000	425,000	11,000
Fixed expenses:			
Manufacturing	200,000	185,185*	14,815*
Marketing and administrative	125,000	115,741†	9,259†
Total fixed expenses	325,000	300,926	24,074
Operating income (loss)	$111,000	$124,074	$(13,074)

*$200,000 ÷ 270,000 units = $0.74074 per unit; 250,000 units × $0.74074 = $185,185;
  20,000 units × $0.74074 = $14,815
†$125,000 ÷ 270,000 units = $0.462963 per unit; 250,000 units × $0.462963 = $115,741;
  20,000 units × $0.462963 = $9,259

Suppose that to measure product-line operating income, ACDelco allocates fixed expenses in proportion to the number of units sold. Dividing the fixed manufacturing expense of $200,000 by 270,000 total units yields a fixed manufacturing cost of $0.74074 per unit. Allocating this unit cost to the 250,000 units of the oil filter product line results

EXHIBIT 26-5
Dropping a Product—Fixed
Costs Unchanged

Expected decrease in revenues:	
Sale of 20,000 air cleaners × $1.75 each..........	$35,000
Expected decrease in expenses:	
Variable manufacturing expenses—	
20,000 air cleaners × $1.20 each..................	24,000
Expected decrease in operating income..............	$11,000

in a fixed manufacturing cost of $185,185 for this product. The same procedure allocates $14,815 to air cleaners. Fixed marketing and administrative expenses are allocated in the same manner. This allocation method results in an operating loss of $13,074 for air cleaners. Should ACDelco drop the air cleaner product line?

This situation is similar to the special sales order example. We follow the two key guidelines for special business decisions: (1) focus on relevant data items, and (2) use a contribution margin approach. The relevant items are still the changes in revenues and expenses, but now we are considering a decrease in volume rather than an increase. If ACDelco's fixed costs will in fact remain the same whether or not the air cleaner product line is dropped, the fixed costs are not relevant to the decision. Only the revenues and variable expenses are relevant. The preceding table shows that the air cleaner product line has a positive contribution margin of $11,000. If this product line is dropped, the company will forego this $11,000 contribution. Exhibit 26-5 further verifies this amount—expected revenue would decrease by $35,000, and expected variable expenses would decrease by $24,000, a net $11,000 decrease in operating income (since fixed costs are unaffected). This analysis suggests that ACDelco should *not* drop air cleaners.

Dropping Products, Departments, Territories—Fixed Costs Changed

In our previous examples, total fixed expenses did not change. But don't jump to the conclusion that fixed costs never change and are always irrelevant. Suppose ACDelco had employed a foreman to oversee the air cleaner product line. The foreman's $18,000 salary can be avoided if the company stops producing air cleaners. Exhibit 26-6 shows how this additional savings affects the analysis.

In this situation, operating income will increase by $7,000 if ACDelco drops air cleaners. Here, a "fixed" cost *is* relevant, so the change in the cost must be considered. Special decisions should take into account all costs affected by the choice of action. Managers must ask, What costs—variable *and* fixed—will change?

■ **Daily Exercise 26-8**

Thinking It Over The ACDelco example considers the $18,000 paid to the foreman a fixed cost. But how can this be a "fixed" cost if it is eliminated by dropping the air cleaner product line?

Answer: Some fixed costs are directly traceable to a particular product line. ACDelco's foreman is employed specifically to oversee the air cleaner product line. Dropping air cleaners eliminates the need for the foreman, so ACDelco can save the $18,000 it would otherwise pay the foreman. Recall that fixed costs are fixed *only* within the relevant range of production. ACDelco usually produces 20,000 air cleaners. Complete elimination of the air cleaner line is outside ACDelco's normal (relevant) range of production, so "fixed" costs can change.

EXHIBIT 26-6
Dropping a Product—Fixed
Costs Changed

Expected decrease in revenues:		
Sale of air cleaners (20,000 × $1.75).....................................		$35,000
Expected decrease in expenses:		
Variable manufacturing expenses (20,000 × $1.20)..............	$24,000	
Fixed expenses—foreman's salary...	18,000	
Expected decrease in total expenses		42,000
Expected increase in operating income...................................		$ 7,000

Product Mix—Which Product to Emphasize?

■ Daily Exercise 26-9
■ Daily Exercise 26-10

Companies do not have unlimited resources. They must decide which products to emphasize and which to deemphasize. This decision affects profits. If salespersons push products with low profit margins at the expense of products with higher profit margins, the company's operating income may decrease. How should a manager decide which product to emphasize?

Consider Esprit, a clothing manufacturer that produces shirts and slacks. The following (assumed) data suggest that shirts are more profitable than slacks:

	Per Unit	
	Shirts	**Slacks**
Sale price	$30	$60
Variable expenses	12	48
Contribution margin	$18	$12
Contribution margin ratio:		
Shirts—$18 ÷ $30	60%	
Slacks—$12 ÷ $60		20%

Constraint. A factor that restricts production or sale of a product.

However, an important piece of information is missing—the time it takes to manufacture each product. This factor, called the **constraint**, restricts production or sale of a product. In some companies, the constraint is production capacity. The factory or the labor force may be unable to produce more than a specified maximum number of units. This constraint—that limits how much the company can produce—may be labor hours, machine hours, materials, or square feet of shelf space. (For example, storage may be limited to 50,000 square feet of space in a warehouse.) Constraints vary from company to company. Some companies are constrained by sales. Competition may be stiff, and the business may be able to sell only so many units.

Suppose that Esprit can produce either 20 pairs of slacks *or* 10 shirts per machine-hour, and that the company can sell all the shirts and slacks it produces. Assume the company has 2,000 machine hours of capacity. Which product should it emphasize?

To answer this question, we follow the guiding principle:

> To maximize profits, produce the product with the highest contribution margin *per unit of the constraint.*

In our example, Esprit can sell all the slacks and shirts it makes, so production (machine hours) is the constraint. Thus, Esprit should produce the product with the highest contribution margin per machine hour.

Exhibit 26-7 first determines the contribution margin per machine hour for each product. Slacks have a higher contribution margin per machine hour ($240 = 20 pairs of slacks × $12 per pair) than shirts ($180 = 10 shirts × $18 per shirt). Esprit will earn more profit by producing slacks. Exhibit 26-7 proves this by multiplying the contribution margin per machine hour by the available number of machine hours. Esprit can earn $480,000 of contribution margin by producing slacks, but only $360,000 by producing shirts.

Exhibit 26-7 shows that Esprit should *not* produce the product with the highest contribution margin *per unit* (shirts). The key point is that Esprit will earn more profit if

EXHIBIT 26-7
Product Mix—Which Product to Emphasize

	Product	
	Shirts	**Slacks**
(1) Units that can be produced each hour...........	10	20
(2) Contribution margin per unit........................	× $18	× $12
Contribution margin per hour (1) × (2)	$180	$240
Capacity—number of hours	× 2,000	× 2,000
Total contribution margin at full capacity	$360,000	$480,000

it produces the product with the highest contribution margin per unit of the (machine hours) constraint—slacks. Notice that the analysis in Exhibit 26-7 has once again followed the two guidelines for special business decisions: (1) focus on relevant data (contribution margin in this example, because only sales revenue and variable costs are relevant), and (2) use a contribution margin approach.

Thinking It Over Why are Esprit's fixed expenses irrelevant in the decision whether to produce slacks or shirts?

Answer: Esprit will use the same property, plant, and equipment to make either slacks or shirts. The fixed expenses will be the same whether the company makes slacks or shirts, so the fixed expenses are irrelevant.

Make or Buy

Manufactured goods often include specialized parts. Overhead garage doors, for example, have electronic controls. Genie, the garage-door manufacturer must decide whether to manufacture the control device itself or buy from an outsider. Swaim Furniture may ask, Should we stain and lacquer the furniture we manufacture or hire another company to do the finish work? These make-or-buy decisions are often called **outsourcing** decisions, because managers must decide whether to buy a component product or service, or to produce it in-house. Assuming that quality is unaffected, the heart of these decisions is *how best to use available facilities.*

Outsourcing. A make-or-buy decision, where managers must decide whether to buy a component product or service, or to produce it in-house.

Let's see how make-or-buy decisions are made. Suppose ACDelco's production process uses Part No. 4, which has the following (assumed) manufacturing costs for 250,000 parts:

Part No. 4 Costs	Total Cost (250,000 units)
Direct materials...	$ 40,000
Direct labor...	20,000
Variable overhead.......................................	15,000
Fixed overhead...	50,000
Total manufacturing cost...........................	$125,000
Cost per unit ($125,000 ÷ 250,000)..........	$0.50

Suppose Fram, another company, offers to sell ACDelco the same part for $0.37 per unit. Should ACDelco make Part No. 4 or buy it from Fram? ACDelco's $0.50 unit cost of manufacturing the part is $0.13 higher than the cost of buying it from Fram. At first glance, it appears that ACDelco should purchase Part No. 4. But the correct answer to a make-or-buy question is not so simple. To make the best decision, you must compare the difference in expected future costs between the alternatives. Which costs will differ depending on whether ACDelco makes or buys Part No. 4?

Assume that by purchasing the part, ACDelco can avoid all variable manufacturing costs and reduce its fixed overhead cost by $10,000. (Fixed overhead will decrease to $40,000.) Exhibit 26-8 shows the differences in costs between the make and buy alternatives.

Part No. 4 Costs	Make Part	Buy Part	Difference
Direct materials	$ 40,000	—	$40,000
Direct labor....................................	20,000	—	20,000
Variable overhead	15,000	—	15,000
Fixed overhead..............................	50,000	$ 40,000	10,000
Purchase cost from Fram			
(250,000 × $0.37)......................	—	92,500	(92,500)
Total cost of Part No. 4........................	$125,000	$132,500	$ (7,500)
Cost per unit—250,000 units...............	$0.50	$0.53	$(0.03)

EXHIBIT 26-8
Make or Buy Decision

■ **Daily Exercise 26-11**
■ **Daily Exercise 26-12**

The decision: It would cost less to make the part than to buy it from Fram. The net savings from making 250,000 units of Part No. 4 is $7,500, which works out to $0.03 per unit. This savings exists despite the "make" alternative's $10,000 of incremental fixed overhead cost.

Notice how this example shows that *fixed costs are relevant to a special decision when those fixed costs differ between alternatives.* Exhibit 26-8 also shows that make-or-buy analysis follows our two guidelines for special business decisions: (1) focus on relevant data (variable and fixed manufacturing costs in this case), and (2) use a contribution margin approach that separates variable costs from fixed costs. These guidelines help answer the fundamental question, What difference does the proposed change make?

Best Use of Facilities

■ Daily Exercise 26-13

The cost data in the make-or-buy decision indicate that ACDelco should make Part No. 4. The focus is on making the best use of available facilities. We illustrate this point further with a make-or-buy decision that includes three alternative actions.

Suppose that buying Part No. 4 from an outside supplier will release factory facilities that ACDelco can use to manufacture gasoline filters. Assume the expected annual profit from the gasoline filters is $18,000. ACDelco's managers must decide among three alternatives:

1. Use the facilities to make Part No. 4.
2. Buy Part No. 4 and leave facilities idle.
3. Buy Part No. 4 and use facilities to make gasoline filters.

The alternative with the lowest *net* cost is the best use of ACDelco's facilities. Exhibit 26-9 compares net cost under the three alternatives.

This analysis of net cost indicates that ACDelco should buy Part No. 4 from Fram and use the vacated facilities to make gas filters. If the facilities remain idle, ACDelco will forgo the opportunity to earn $18,000.

Special decisions often include qualitative factors—that is, factors that are difficult to quantify. For example, ACDelco managers may believe they can better control the quality of Part No. 4 by manufacturing it themselves. This argues for ACDelco's making the part. But Fram may be located very close to ACDelco's assembly plant. Fram may be able to achieve a higher on-time delivery rate than ACDelco's own parts plant. This would favor buying the part from Fram. ACDelco's managers should consider these qualitative factors as well as revenue and cost differences in making their final decision.

Sell As Is or Process Further?

■ Daily Exercise 26-14

Should a product be sold as it is, or should the product be processed further into another item? For example, suppose that the Chevron oil company spent $48,000 to produce 50,000 gallons of regular gasoline. Assume Chevron can sell this regular gasoline for $1.20 per gallon, for a total of $60,000. Alternatively, Chevron could further process this regular gasoline into premium-grade gas. Suppose the additional cost to process the gas

EXHIBIT 26-9
Best Use of Facilities

		Buy Parts	
	Make Parts	Facilities Idle	Make Gas Filters
Expected cost of obtaining 250,000 units of Part No. 4 (amounts from Exhibit 26-8).....	$125,000	$132,500	$132,500
Expected profit from the gas filters	—	—	(18,000)
Expected net cost of obtaining 250,000 units of Part No. 4	$125,000	$132,500	$114,500

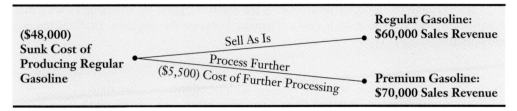

EXHIBIT 26-10
Diagram of Sell As Is or Process
Further Decision

further is $0.11 per gallon, for an additional cost of $5,500 (for 50,000 gallons). Assume the sale price of premium gasoline is $1.40 per gallon, for a total of $70,000.

As in other special business decisions, managers need to know which items are relevant. The $48,000 cost of producing the 50,000 gallons of regular gasoline is *not* relevant to Chevron's sell or process further decision. Why? Because the $48,000 is a **sunk cost**—a past cost that cannot be changed regardless of which future action is taken. Exhibit 26-10 shows that the $48,000 has been incurred whether Chevron sells the regular gasoline as is or processes it further into premium gasoline.

Sunk Cost. A past cost that cannot be changed regardless of which future action is taken.

Exhibits 26-10 and 26-11 show that the relevant items that differ between Chevron's (1) sell as is and (2) process further alternatives are

- Expected revenues
- Expected costs of processing further

The analysis indicates that Chevron should process the gasoline into the premium grade, because the $10,000 extra revenue ($70,000 − $60,000) outweighs the $5,500 cost of the extra processing.

". . . the relevant items that differ between Chevron's (1) sell as is and (2) process further alternatives are

- *Expected revenues*
- *Expected costs of processing further"*

Thinking It Over Some companies have obsolete inventories that cannot be sold at regular prices. How should managers decide whether to sell the units as is or to incur additional manufacturing costs to rework them?

Answer: This is a type of sell or process further decision. Managers should predict the additional costs of reworking the inventory. Then they should forecast the additional revenues after rework. If the additional revenues that can be earned by reworking exceed the additional costs, they should process further. If not, sell the units as is.

Opportunity Cost

We have illustrated six types of special business decisions. For each of the special decisions, managers decided on one course of action—and thereby rejected the opportunity to take alternative actions. When the managers rejected alternatives, their companies incurred an opportunity cost. An **opportunity cost** is the benefit that can be obtained from the next-best course of action. Opportunity cost is *not* an outlay cost that is recorded in accounting. An outlay cost requires a cash disbursement sooner or later, but an opportunity cost does not.

Opportunity Cost. The benefit that can be obtained from the next-best course of action.

EXHIBIT 26-11
Sell As Is or Process Further
Decision

	Sell As Is	Process Further
Expected revenue from selling 50,000 gallons of regular gasoline at $1.20 per gallon	$60,000	
Expected revenue from selling 50,000 gallons of premium gasoline at $1.40 per gallon		$70,000
Additional costs of $0.11 per gallon required to convert 50,000 gallons of regular gasoline into premium gasoline		(5,500)
Total net revenue	$60,000	64,500
Difference in net revenue		$ 4,500

An example of an opportunity cost is the salary forgone by an engineer who may quit his job with IBM to start his own business. Suppose the engineer analyzes his two job opportunities as follows:

Expected Future Event	Open an Independent Business	Remain with IBM
Salary from IBM.............................		$60,000
Sales revenue....................................	$200,000	
Expenses	120,000	
Net income	$ 80,000	$60,000

The opportunity cost of staying with IBM is the forgone $80,000 of net income from the independent business. The opportunity cost of starting a new business is the $60,000 salary from IBM.

How are opportunity costs used in decision making? Consider two examples.

1. *Suppose the IBM engineer has a third job opportunity—employment by Microsoft.* To determine the best alternative, the engineer can compare Microsoft's salary offer with the $80,000 opportunity cost of not opening an independent business. If the engineer's goal is to maximize his personal income, he will accept Microsoft's offer only if it exceeds his $80,000 opportunity cost. (Notice that the IBM salary is irrelevant because opportunity cost is the benefit from the next-best alternative course of action.)

2. *Refer to Exhibit 26-11.* Suppose that Chevron is approached by a customer who needs 50,000 gallons of regular gasoline. The customer is willing to pay more than $1.20 per gallon. Chevron's managers can use the $64,500 ($70,000 – $5,500) opportunity cost of not further processing the gas to determine the sale price that will provide an equivalent income ($64,500 ÷ 50,000 = $1.29). If the customer offers more than Chevron's opportunity cost of $1.29 per gallon, Chevron will be better off selling the regular gasoline. If the customer offers less than $1.29, Chevron will be better off further processing the gas.

We have now completed our discussion of *short-term* special business decisions. Stop for a moment to review the Decision Guidelines feature that summarizes some key points from our discussion. Then work the midchapter summary problems before moving on to *long-term* special business decisions in the second half of the chapter.

DECISION GUIDELINES Short-Term Special Business Decisions

DECISION	GUIDELINE
What information is relevant to a short-term special business decision?	Relevant data: 1. are expected *future* data that 2. *differ* between alternatives.
What are two key guidelines in making short-term special business decisions?	Key guidelines: 1. focus on *relevant* data. 2. use a *contribution margin* approach that separates variable costs from fixed costs.
When will accepting a special sales order increase income?	If the revenue from the order exceeds the extra variable and fixed costs incurred to fill the order, then operating income will increase.
To maximize profit, which product to emphasize when there is a constraining factor?	Emphasize the product with the highest contribution margin per unit of the constraint.
How to decide whether to sell a product as is or process further?	Process further only if the extra sales revenue (from processing further) exceeds the extra costs of additional processing.
How to determine the opportunity cost of a decision?	The opportunity cost of a decision is the benefit foregone by not choosing the next-best course of action.

PROBLEM 1. Aziz, Inc., has two products, a standard model and a deluxe model, with the following data:

	Per Unit	
	Standard	**Deluxe**
Sale price	$20	$30
Variable expenses..........	16	21

The company has 15,000 machine hours of capacity available. Seven units of the standard model can be produced in an hour, compared with three units of the deluxe model. Which product should the company emphasize?

PROBLEM 2. Suppose Toshiba has the following manufacturing costs for 20,000 of its television cabinets:

Direct materials...	$ 20,000
Direct labor..	80,000
Variable overhead...	40,000
Fixed overhead	80,000
Total manufacturing cost	$220,000
Cost per cabinet ($220,000 ÷ 20,000)..........	$11

Another manufacturer has offered to sell Toshiba similar cabinets for $10, a total purchase cost of $200,000. By purchasing the cabinets outside, Toshiba can save $50,000 of fixed overhead cost. The released facilities can be used to manufacture other products that will contribute $60,000 to profits. Identify and analyze the alternatives. What is Toshiba's best course of action?

■ **SOLUTIONS**

PROBLEM 1

	Product	
	Standard	**Deluxe**
Sale price per unit...	$ 20	$ 30
Variable expense per unit	(16)	(21)
Contribution margin per unit.......................................	$ 4	$ 9
Units that can be produced each machine hour	× 7	× 3
Contribution margin per machine hour	$ 28	$ 27
Capacity—number of hours...	× 15,000	× 15,000
Total contribution margin at full capacity	$420,000	$405,000

Decision: Emphasize the standard product because it has the higher contribution margin per unit of the constraint—machine hours.

PROBLEM 2

		Buy Cabinets	
	Make Cabinets	**Facilities Idle**	**Make Other Products**
Relevant costs:			
Direct materials	$ 20,000	—	
Direct labor..	80,000	—	
Variable overhead	40,000	—	
Fixed overhead...	80,000	$ 30,000	$ 30,000
Purchase cost from outsider			
(20,000 × $10)	—	200,000	200,000
Total cost of obtaining cabinets....................	220,000	230,000	230,000
Profit from other products			(60,000)
Net cost of obtaining 20,000 cabinets..........	$220,000	$230,000	$170,000

Decision: Toshiba should buy the television cabinets from the outside supplier and use the released facilities to make other products.

Capital Budgeting

We have seen how managers make short-term special business decisions. Now let's turn to decisions that have long-term effects on business operations.

Think back to the Deer Valley ski resort in the chapter opening story. The owners' decision to spend $13 million to expand Snow Park Lodge will tie up resources for years to come. How did Deer Valley's owners decide that the expansion would be a good investment? The Snow Park Lodge expansion met two conditions:

- First, the investment was part of the company's long-term plan. Director of finance Jim Madsen explained that Deer Valley's long-term plan called for expansion when the resort served a target number of skiers per day and achieved a target level of profits. Thus the Snow Park Lodge expansion was a planned part of Deer Valley's long-term strategy.
- Second, Deer Valley's owners used capital budgeting techniques to analyze the expected financial effects of the investment. **Capital budgeting** is a formal means of analyzing long-term investment decisions. The term describes budgeting for the acquisition of *capital assets*—assets used for a long period of time.

Capital Budgeting. A formal means of analyzing long-term investment decisions. Describes budgeting for the acquisition of capital assets.

Examples of capital budgeting decisions include expanding the Deer Valley resort, building a new plant, or acquiring machinery.

Before proceeding, understand this: Capital budgeting is not an exact science. No matter how precise your calculations, they are based on predictions about an uncertain future. To become a successful decision maker, you must learn how to recognize and cope with uncertainty. Because capital budgeting decisions have effects far into the future, your predictions about the future must consider many uncertain factors, such as changing consumer preferences, competition, and government regulations. The farther into the future the decision extends, the more likely that actual results will differ from predictions. Long-term decisions are thus riskier than short-term decisions.

With this background, we now discuss four popular capital budgeting decision models: payback, accounting rate of return, net present value, and internal rate of return. Three of these models examine the *net cash inflows from operations* generated by each alternative. ◀ Generally accepted accounting principles are based on accrual accounting, but capital budgeting focuses on cash flows. The desirability of a capital asset depends on its ability to generate net cash inflows—that is, cash inflows in excess of cash outflows—over the asset's useful life.

◀▥◀▥◀▥ We discussed cash flows from operating activities, often the primary source of cash, in Chapter 17, page 715.

Payback—Equal Annual Cash Flows

Payback is the length of time it will take to recover, in net cash inflows from operations, the dollars of a capital outlay. When the net cash inflows are equal each year, the payback period can be computed as follows:

Objective 5

Use four capital budgeting models to make longer-term investment decisions

Payback. The length of time it will take to recover, in net cash inflows from operations, the dollars of a capital outlay.

$$\frac{\text{Payback}}{\text{Period}} = \frac{\text{Amount invested}}{\text{Expected annual net cash inflow}}$$

Payback is expressed as a period of time. The payback model measures how quickly managers expect to recover their investment dollars. The shorter the payback period, the more attractive the asset, all else equal.

■ Daily Exercise 26-17
■ Daily Exercise 26-18

To see how payback works, let's suppose that Toshiba Corporation pays $240,000 for an assembling machine with an estimated useful life of six years and zero predicted residual value. Managers expect the machine to generate net cash inflows from operations of $60,000 per year. In general, an increase in cash could result from an increase in revenues, a decrease in expenses, or a combination of the two. In this case, it is a decrease in expenses. Toshiba would compute the machine's payback period as follows:

$$\frac{\text{Payback period for}}{\text{machine 1}} = \frac{\$240,000}{\$60,000} = 4 \text{ years}$$

Exhibit 26-12 verifies that for machine 1, the $240,000 investment is recouped by the end of year 4 when the accumulated net cash inflows total $240,000.

EXHIBIT 26-12
Payback—Equal Annual Net
Cash Inflows

| | | Net Cash Inflows | | | |
| | | Machine 1 | | Machine 2 | |
Year	Amount Invested	Annual	Accumulated	Annual	Accumulated
0	$240,000	—	—	—	—
1	—	$60,000	$ 60,000	$80,000	$ 80,000
2	—	60,000	120,000	80,000	160,000
3	—	60,000	180,000	80,000	240,000
4	—	60,000	240,000		
5	—	60,000	300,000		
6	—	60,000	360,000		

Now suppose that an alternative to the $240,000 machine is a second machine that also costs $240,000 but will save $80,000 per year during its three-year life. The second machine's payback period is computed as follows:

$$\text{Payback period for machine 2} = \frac{\$240,000}{\$80,000} = 3 \text{ years}$$

Once again, Exhibit 26-12 verifies that for machine 2, the $240,000 investment is recouped by the end of year 3 when the accumulated net cash inflows total $240,000. Thus, the payback criterion favors the second machine because it recovers the asset's cost more quickly.

A major criticism of the payback model is that it does not consider profitability. Consequently, the payback technique can lead managers to make unwise decisions. For example, consider the two machines' useful lives. Machine 2's useful life is the same as its payback period—three years. Exhibit 26-12 shows that machine 2 will merely cover its cost and provide no profits. But machine 1 has a useful life of six years. It will continue to generate net cash inflows for two years after its payback period. As Exhibit 26-12 shows, this will give the company an additional net cash inflow of $120,000 ($60,000 × 2 years). Unlike machine 2, machine 1 will be profitable. After considering the assets' useful lives, machine 1 appears to be the better investment.

Payback—Unequal Annual Cash Flows

The payback equation can be used only when net cash inflows are the same for each period. When periodic cash flows are unequal, you must accumulate net cash inflows until the amount invested is recovered. Suppose that machine 1 in our example will produce net cash inflows of $100,000 in Year 1, $80,000 in Year 2, $50,000 in Years 3–5, and $30,000 in Year 6. Exhibit 26-13 shows the payback schedule for these unequal annual cash flows.

By the end of Year 3, we have recovered $230,000. Recovery of the amount invested ($240,000) occurs during Year 4. We can compute that payback occurs in 3.2 years:

$$\text{Payback} = 3 \text{ years} + \frac{\$10,000 \text{ needed to complete recovery in Year 4}}{\$50,000 \text{ net cash inflow in Year 4}} \times 1 \text{ year}$$
$$= 3 \text{ years} + 0.2 \text{ year} = 3.2 \text{ years}$$

EXHIBIT 26-13
Payback—Unequal Annual Net
Cash Inflows

| | | Net Cash Inflow | |
Year	Amount Invested	Periodic	Accumulated
0	$240,000	—	—
1	—	$100,000	$100,000
2	—	80,000	180,000
3	—	50,000	230,000
3.2	—	10,000	240,000
4		40,000	280,000
5		50,000	330,000
6		30,000	360,000

How do managers use the payback model in capital budgeting? Managers often compare the payback period with the asset's useful life. The asset's payback period must be shorter than its useful life. Consider an extreme example. If a machine has a payback period of five years and a useful life of three years, the company will never earn a profit from using the asset. How much shorter than the useful life the payback period must be is a business decision that varies by industry and business conditions. When the business is deciding between two or more assets, the asset with the shortest payback period is better—*if all other factors are the same.*

The payback method highlights cash flows, a key factor in business decisions. And payback is easy to understand. Managers like those at Deer Valley Resort often use the payback method to eliminate proposals that are too risky (projects with long payback periods). However, a major weakness of payback is that it ignores profitability.

Accounting Rate of Return

A primary goal of business is to earn profits. One measure of profitability is the rate of return on investment. The **accounting rate of return** is computed as follows:

$$\text{Accounting rate of return} = \frac{\text{Average annual operating income from asset}}{\text{Average amount invested in asset}}$$

The accounting rate of return focuses on the operating income that an asset generates. Operating income from an asset can be computed as net cash inflow from the asset minus depreciation on the asset. Exhibit 26-14 computes the accounting rate of return for machine 1 in the payback example. Recall that Toshiba's managers expect the machine to generate annual net cash inflows of $60,000. The machine costs $240,000, and has a useful life of six years with no estimated residual value. Annual straight-line depreciation is $40,000 ($240,000 ÷ 6 years). ◀▥ Exhibit 26-14 shows that the average annual operating income from the machine is $20,000 ($60,000 – $40,000).

The accounting rate of return is an *average.* It measures the average rate of return from using the asset over its entire life. First, consider the average annual operating income in the computation. If operating income varies by year (as in the second payback example), compute the *total* operating income over the asset's life. Then divide the total by the number of years of life to find the *average* annual operating income from the asset. Second, consider the average amount invested. The book value of the asset decreases as it is used and depreciated. Thus the company's investment in the asset declines over time. If the asset's residual value is zero, the average investment is half the asset's cost. Exhibit 26-14 shows that the average amount invested in machine 1 in the original payback example is $120,000 ($240,000 ÷ 2).

If the asset's residual value is not zero, the average amount invested is greater than half the asset's cost. For example, assume that the residual value of machine 1 is $30,000. Annual depreciation is $35,000 [($240,000 – $30,000)/6]. The accounting rate of return is

$$\text{Accounting rate of return} = \frac{\$60,000 - \$35,000}{(\$240,000 + \$30,000)/2} = \frac{\$25,000}{\$135,000} = 0.185 = 18.5\%$$

■ **Daily Exercise 26-19**

Accounting Rate of Return. A measure of profitability computed by dividing the average annual operating income from an asset by the average amount invested in the asset.

◀▥ ◀▥ ◀▥ Recall from Chapter 10, page 428, that under straight-line depreciation an equal amount of depreciation expense is assigned to each year of an asset's life.

EXHIBIT 26-14
Accounting Rate of Return

$$\text{Accounting rate of return} = \frac{\text{Average annual operating income from asset*}}{\text{Average amount invested in asset}}$$

$$= \frac{\text{Annual net cash inflow from asset} - \text{Annual depreciation on asset}}{(\text{Amount invested in asset} + \text{Residual value})/2}$$

$$= \frac{\$60,000 - \$40,000^\dagger}{(\$240,000 + \$0)/2}$$

$$= \frac{\$20,000}{\$120,000} = 0.167 = 16.7\%$$

*Operating income can also be computed as revenues minus expenses.

$^\dagger\$40,000 = \dfrac{\$240,000}{6 \text{ years}}$

Companies that use this accounting rate of return model set a minimum required rate of return on their investment projects. They invest only in assets with accounting rates of return equal to or greater than the minimum required rate. Suppose that Toshiba requires a rate of return of at least 20 percent. Would its managers approve an investment in machine 1 in Exhibit 26-14? No, because the machine's average annual return (16.7%) is less than the company's minimum required rate (20%).

Discounted Cash-Flow Models

Chapter 15 introduced the concept of present value. ◀▥ The present value of $1 to be received in the future is less than $1 today. The logic is this: To receive $1 a year from now, we would be willing to pay less than $1 today. Why? Because if we pay $1 now to receive $1 later, we earn no income in the meantime. But if we deposit $1 in a bank and earn interest of, say, $0.06, we will have $1.06 a year from now. We would rather have $1.06 than $1.00. Thus we would rather receive cash earlier than later. The fact that we can earn income by investing money for a period of time is called the **time value of money.** ◀▥

The timing of net cash inflows from operations is important because of the time value of money. Consider two $10,000 investments. Both investments promise future cash inflows of $11,000. Investment 1 will bring in cash of $5,500 at the end of each of the next two years. Investment 2 will return the full $11,000 at the end of the second year. Which investment is better? Investment 1, because it brings in cash sooner. Its $5,500 net cash inflow at the end of the first year can be reinvested right away to earn additional returns.

The accounting rate of return discussed in the previous section measures profitability, but it has a major weakness. It does not recognize the time value of money. Nor does the payback period consider the time value of money. That is, these models consider neither the *timing* of the cash outlay to purchase an asset nor the *timing* of its net cash inflows. *Discounted cash-flow models* overcome this weakness. Discounted cash flow models—the net present value and the internal rate of return—are used by over 85% of large industrial firms in the United States. The chapter opening story indicates that these models are also used by companies that provide services, like Deer Valley Resort.

Net Present Value

Assume that Mitsubishi is considering producing two products, CD players and VCRs. The products require different specialized machines that cost the same amount, $1 million. Each machine is expected to have a five-year life and zero residual value. Suppose the two products have different patterns of predicted net cash inflows:

	Annual Net Cash Inflows	
Year	CD Players	VCRs
1	$ 305,450	$ 500,000
2	305,450	350,000
3	305,450	300,000
4	305,450	250,000
5	305,450	40,000
Total	$1,527,250	$1,440,000

Total net cash inflows are greater if Mitsubishi invests in the CD-player project. However, the VCR project brings in cash sooner. To decide which investment is better, we use **net present value (NPV)** to bring cash inflows and outflows back to a common time period. We say that we *discount* these expected future cash flows to their present value, using a minimum desired rate of return. We then compare the discounted cash inflows with the discounted cash outflows to decide which, if any, projects to undertake.

◀▥ ◀▥ ◀▥ Recall from Chapter 15, page 628, that present value is the amount a person would invest now to receive a greater amount in the future.

◀▥ ◀▥ ◀▥ The time value of money is discussed in the Chapter 15 appendix, page 664.

Time Value of Money. The fact that income can be earned by investing money for a period of time.

Net Present Value (NPV). The decision model that brings cash inflows and outflows back to a common time period by discounting these expected future cash flows to their present value, using a minimum desired rate of return.

EXHIBIT 26-15
Present Value of Annuity of $1

Present Value of Annuity of $1

Period	4%	5%	6%	7%	8%	10%	12%	14%	16%
1	0.962	0.952	0.943	0.935	0.926	0.909	0.893	0.877	0.862
2	1.886	1.859	1.833	1.808	1.783	1.736	1.690	1.647	1.605
3	2.775	2.723	2.673	2.624	2.577	2.487	2.402	2.322	2.246
4	3.630	3.546	3.465	3.387	3.312	3.170	3.037	2.914	2.798
5	4.452	4.329	4.212	4.100	3.993	3.791	3.605	3.433	3.274
6	5.242	5.076	4.917	4.767	4.623	4.355	4.111	3.889	3.685
7	6.002	5.786	5.582	5.389	5.206	4.868	4.564	4.288	4.039
8	6.733	6.463	6.210	5.971	5.747	5.335	4.968	4.639	4.344
9	7.435	7.108	6.802	6.515	6.247	5.759	5.328	4.946	4.607
10	8.111	7.722	7.360	7.024	6.710	6.145	5.650	5.216	4.833
11	8.760	8.306	7.887	7.499	7.139	6.495	5.938	5.453	5.029
12	9.385	8.863	8.384	7.943	7.536	6.814	6.194	5.660	5.197
13	9.986	9.394	8.853	8.358	7.904	7.103	6.424	5.842	5.342
14	10.563	9.899	9.295	8.745	8.244	7.367	6.628	6.002	5.468
15	11.118	10.380	9.712	9.108	8.559	7.606	6.811	6.142	5.575
16	11.652	10.838	10.106	9.447	8.851	7.824	6.974	6.265	5.669
17	12.166	11.274	10.477	9.763	9.122	8.022	7.120	6.373	5.749
18	12.659	11.690	10.828	10.059	9.372	8.201	7.250	6.467	5.818
19	13.134	12.085	11.158	10.336	9.604	8.365	7.366	6.550	5.877
20	13.590	12.462	11.470	10.594	9.818	8.514	7.469	6.623	5.929

Appendix B-2 provides a more comprehensive table for the present value of an annuity of $1.

Discount Rate. Management's minimum desired rate of return on an investment. Also called the **hurdle rate, required rate of return,** and **cost of capital.**

Annuity. A stream of equal periodic amounts.

Management's minimum desired rate of return on an investment is called the **discount rate.** Synonyms are **hurdle rate, required rate of return,** and **cost of capital.** The discount rate varies, depending on the riskiness of investments. The higher the risk, the higher the discount rate. Suppose that Mitsubishi's discount rate for these investments is 14 percent.

Mitsubishi expects the manufacture and sale of CD players to generate $305,450 of net cash inflow each year. A stream of equal periodic amounts is called an **annuity.** The present value of an annuity is computed by multiplying the periodic amount ($305,450) by the present value of an annuity of $1 from Exhibit 26-15. The table indicates that the present value of an annuity of $1 for five years discounted at 14% per year is $3.433. Exhibit 26-16 uses this amount to compute the present value of the net cash inflows of the CD-player project—$1,048,610 (3.433 × $305,450). After subtracting the amount of the investment ($1,000,000), the net present value of the CD-player project is $48,610.

EXHIBIT 26-16
Net Present Value

	Present Value at 14%	Net Cash Inflow	Total Present Value
CD-Player Project			
Present value of annuity of equal annual net cash inflows for 5 years	3.433*	× $305,450 per year =	$ 1,048,610
Investment			(1,000,000)
Net present value of the CD-player project			$ 48,610
VCR Project			
Present value of net cash inflows by year: 1	0.877†	× $500,000 =	$ 438,500
2	0.769	× 350,000 =	269,150
3	0.675	× 300,000 =	202,500
4	0.592	× 250,000 =	148,000
5	0.519	× 40,000 =	20,760
Total present value of net cash inflows			1,078,910
Investment			(1,000,000)
Net present value of the VCR project			$ 78,910

*Present value of annuity of $1 for 5 years at 14%, Exhibit 26-15.
†Present value of $1 in 1 year, 2 years, 3 years, and so on, at 14%, Exhibit 26-17.

In contrast to the CD-player project, the net cash inflows of the VCR project are unequal—$500,000 in Year 1, $350,000 in Year 2, and so on. Because these amounts vary by year, the present value of each amount is computed separately:

Year	Present-Value of $1 from Exhibit 26-17, 14% Column	Net Cash Inflow	Present Value of Net Cash Inflow
1	0.877	× $500,000 =	$438,500
2	0.769	× 350,000 =	269,150

Exhibit 26-16 includes these present-value computations, along with similar computations for years 3–5. The exhibit indicates that the VCR project has a total net present value of $78,910, compared with $48,610 for the CD-player project. Either project, considered alone, is acceptable because its net present value is at least zero. This means that both projects—CD players and VCRs—earn at least the minimum desired rate of return of 14 percent. In contrast, a project with a *negative* net present value would be rejected because it would earn less than the company's 14% required rate of return.

The NPV analysis favors VCRs because an investment in that project will earn the company's required rate of 14% plus an additional $78,910. This expected excess is greater than that of the CD-player project, which also meets the required rate of 14% but returns only an additional $48,610.

This example illustrates an important point about present-value analysis. The CD-player project promises the greater total amount of net cash inflows. But the timing of the VCR cash flows—loaded near the beginning of the project—gives the VCR investment a higher net present value. The VCR project is more attractive because of the time value of money. Its dollars, which are received sooner, are worth more now than the more-distant dollars of the CD-player project.

There is another way to use present-value analysis in capital budgeting. Suppose that Mitsubishi starts the decision-making process by computing the total present values of net cash inflows from the two projects—$1,048,610 for CD players and $1,078,910 for VCRs. The company's managers may ask, What is the most we can invest in the CD-player project and still earn our 14% target rate of return? The answer is $1,048,610. Similarly, the maximum acceptable investment for VCRs is $1,078,910. The $1 million cost of both projects makes them attractive investments.

Present Value of $1

Period	4%	5%	6%	7%	8%	10%	12%	14%	16%
1	0.962	0.952	0.943	0.935	0.926	0.909	0.893	0.877	0.862
2	0.925	0.907	0.890	0.873	0.857	0.826	0.797	0.769	0.743
3	0.889	0.864	0.840	0.816	0.794	0.751	0.712	0.675	0.641
4	0.855	0.823	0.792	0.763	0.735	0.683	0.636	0.592	0.552
5	0.822	0.784	0.747	0.713	0.681	0.621	0.567	0.519	0.476
6	0.790	0.746	0.705	0.666	0.630	0.564	0.507	0.456	0.410
7	0.760	0.711	0.665	0.623	0.583	0.513	0.452	0.400	0.354
8	0.731	0.677	0.627	0.582	0.540	0.467	0.404	0.351	0.305
9	0.703	0.645	0.592	0.544	0.500	0.424	0.361	0.308	0.263
10	0.676	0.614	0.558	0.508	0.463	0.386	0.322	0.270	0.227
11	0.650	0.585	0.527	0.475	0.429	0.350	0.287	0.237	0.195
12	0.625	0.557	0.497	0.444	0.397	0.319	0.257	0.208	0.168
13	0.601	0.530	0.469	0.415	0.368	0.290	0.229	0.182	0.145
14	0.577	0.505	0.442	0.388	0.340	0.263	0.205	0.160	0.125
15	0.555	0.481	0.417	0.362	0.315	0.239	0.183	0.140	0.108
16	0.534	0.458	0.394	0.339	0.292	0.218	0.163	0.123	0.093
17	0.513	0.436	0.371	0.317	0.270	0.198	0.146	0.108	0.080
18	0.494	0.416	0.350	0.296	0.250	0.180	0.130	0.095	0.069
19	0.475	0.396	0.331	0.277	0.232	0.164	0.116	0.083	0.060
20	0.456	0.377	0.312	0.258	0.215	0.149	0.104	0.073	0.051

EXHIBIT 26-17
Present Value of $1

Appendix B-1 provides a more comprehensive table for the present value of $1.

NET PRESENT VALUE OF A PROJECT WITH RESIDUAL VALUE   When management expects the asset to have a residual value at the end of its useful life, that residual value should be considered in the NPV analysis. The residual value is an expected cash inflow at the end of the asset's life. It must be discounted to its present value when determining the total present value of the project's net cash inflows. The residual value is discounted as a single amount—not as an annuity—because it will be received only once, when the asset is sold.

Suppose that the equipment to manufacture CD players is expected to be worth $100,000 at the end of its five-year life. To determine the CD-player project's NPV, we discount $100,000 for five years at 14%—using Exhibit 26-17—and add its present value ($51,900), as shown in Exhibit 26-18.

Compare Exhibits 26-16 and 26-18. The discounted residual value raises the CD-player project's NPV to $100,510, which is higher than that of the VCR project. If Mitsubishi expects the VCR equipment to have zero disposal value, then the CD-player project is now more attractive.

There is great uncertainty surrounding capital budgeting decisions that affect cash flows far into the future. Consequently, Mitsubishi's managers might want to know whether their decision would be affected by:

- Changing the discount rate from 14% to 12% or to 16%
- Changing the net cash flows by 10%
- Changing the residual value of the equipment

Managers can use spreadsheet software to perform these kinds of NPV analyses quickly and easily. After entering the basic information for NPV analysis, managers can perform sensitivity analyses with just a few keystrokes. The computer quickly displays the results.

Working It Out   Suppose Mitsubishi uses a 6% discount rate rather than the 14% discount rate from Exhibit 26-16. Would the net present value of the CD-player project (assuming zero residual value) be higher or lower using the 6% rate than it was using the original 14% rate? Why?

Answer: The higher the discount rate, the lower the present value (today) of dollars to be received in the future. Similarly, the smaller the discount rate, the higher the present value of dollars to be received in the future. Because smaller discount rates lead to higher present values, discounting the cash flows at 6% rather than 14% *increases* the net present value of the CD-player project, as follows:

CD-Player Project	Present Value at 6%	Net Cash Inflow	Total Present Value
Present value of annuity of equal annual net cash inflows for 5 years............................	4.212*	× $305,450 =	$1,286,555
Investment..			(1,000,000)
Net present value at 6%....................................			286,555
Net present value at 14%[†]...............................			(48,610)
Difference...			$ 237,945

*Present value of an annuity of $1 for 5 years at 6%, Exhibit 26-15.
[†]From Exhibit 26-16.

EXHIBIT 26-18
Net Present Value of a Project
with Residual Value

CD-Player Project	Present Value at 14%		Net Cash Inflow		Total Present Value
Present value of annuity of equal annual net cash inflows for 5 years	3.433*	×	$305,450 per year	=	$ 1,048,610
Present value of residual value.....	**0.519[†]**	×	**$100,000**	=	51,900
Total present value of net cash inflows....................................					1,100,510
Investment...					(1,000,000)
Net present value of the CD-player project.........................					$ 100,510

*Present value of an annuity of $1 for 5 years at 14%, Exhibit 26-15.
[†]Present value of $1 in 5 years at 14%, Exhibit 26-17.

Internal Rate of Return

Another discounted cash-flow model for capital budgeting is the internal rate of return. The **internal rate of return (IRR)** is the rate of return (based on discounted cash flows) that a company can expect to earn by investing in the project. The higher the IRR, the more desirable the project. The lower the IRR, the less desirable. The internal rate of return is the discount rate that makes the net present value of the project's cash flows equal to zero.

Exhibit 26-19 shows that Mitsubishi's CD-player project's IRR is 16 percent. The 16 percent rate produces a net present value of zero. To see why, we follow three steps:

1. Identify the expected net cash inflows ($305,450 each year for five years) exactly as in calculating the net present value.

2. Find the discount rate that makes the total present value of the cash inflows equal to the present value of the cash outflows. This is easy when the investment in the project consists of a single immediate cash outflow that is followed by a series of equal cash inflows (an annuity). You can work backwards to find the discount rate that makes the present value of the annuity of cash inflows equal to the amount of the investment by solving the following equation for the annuity present-value (PV) factor:

$$\text{Investment} = \text{Expected annual net cash inflow} \times \text{Annuity PV factor}$$

$$\text{Annuity PV factor} = \frac{\text{Investment}}{\text{Expected annual net cash inflow}}$$

$$= \frac{\$1,000,000}{\$305,450}$$

$$= 3.274$$

3. Turn to the table presenting the present value of an annuity of $1 (Exhibit 26-15). Scan the row corresponding to the project's expected life—period 5, in our example. Choose the column with the number closest to the annuity PV factor that was calculated. The 3.274 annuity factor is in the 16% column. Therefore, the IRR of the CD-player project is 16 percent. Mitsubishi expects the project to earn an annual rate of return of 16% over its life.

To decide whether the project is acceptable, compare the IRR with the minimum desired rate of return. If the IRR is equal to or greater than that minimum rate, the project is acceptable. Otherwise, it is not. If CD players were the only investment under consideration, managers would invest in CD players because their 16% IRR exceeds the 14% discount rate. But recall that the VCR project has a higher net present value than the CD-player project. The VCR investment also has a higher IRR. Because the VCR project has unequal cash inflows, however, computation of the VCR's IRR requires a trial-and-error procedure that is covered in more advanced courses. (Spreadsheet software and even calculators can perform these necessary computations.)

> **Learning Tip:** Remember that payback, net present value, and internal rate of return are all based on *cash inflows and outflows*. Only the accounting rate of return is based on accrual accounting *revenues and expenses*. Also, only net present value and internal rate of return take into account the time value of money.

	Present Value at 16%		Net Cash Inflow		Total Present Value
Present value of annuity of equal annual net cash inflows for 5 years	3.274*	×	$305,450	=	$ 1,000,000[†]
Investment........................					(1,000,000)
Net present value of the CD-player project.....					$　　　0[††]

*Present value of annuity of $1 for 5 years at 16%, Exhibit 26–15.
[†]Slight rounding error.
[††]The zero difference proves that the IRR is 16 percent.

EXHIBIT 26-19
Internal Rate of Return, CD-Player Project

Comparison of the Capital Budgeting Methods

Objective 6

Compare and contrast popular capital budgeting methods

■ Daily Exercise 26-22

How do the NPV and IRR approaches compare? Net present value indicates the amount of the excess (or deficiency) of a project's present value of net cash inflows over (or under) its cost—at a specified discount rate. Net present value, though, does not show the project's unique rate of return. The internal rate of return shows the project's rate but does not indicate the dollar difference between the project's present value and its investment cost. In many cases, the two methods lead to the same investment decision.

The discounted cash-flow methods are superior because they consider both the time value of money and profitability. The time value of money enters the analysis through the discounting of future dollars to present value. Profitability is built into the discounted cash-flow methods because they consider all cash inflows and outflows over the life of a project. In contrast, the payback model considers only the cash flows necessary to recover the initial cash invested.

Exhibit 26-20 summarizes the strengths and weaknesses of payback, accounting rate of return, and the discounted cash-flow methods. In practice, managers often use more than one method to gain different perspectives on risks and returns. For example, Deer Valley's owners could decide to pursue capital projects with positive NPVs, provided that those projects have a payback of four years or less.

Deer Valley's use of both payback and NPV methods is typical of U.S. companies. Surveys have shown that companies headquartered in the United States often use both payback and discounted cash-flow methods (either net present value or internal rate of return). The payback method is most popular in Japan, while discounted cash-flow methods are more popular in Canada, Ireland, and South Korea.

Thinking It Over A pharmaceutical company is considering two research projects. Project A has a net present value of $232,000 and a 3-year payback period. Project B has a net present value of $237,000 and a payback period of 4.5 years. Which project do you think the managers will choose?

Answer: Many managers would accept project A. Net present value is a better guide to decision making than payback period. But managers would consider the 2.2% [($237,000 − $232,000)/ $232,000] difference between the NPVs to be insignificant. In contrast, the 50% [(4.5 years − 3.0 years)/3.0 years] difference between payback periods *is* significant. The uncertainty of receiving operating cash flows increases with each passing year. Managers often forgo small differences in expected cash inflows to decrease the risk of investments.

Take a moment to review the different capital budgeting methods by studying the Decision Guidelines feature. This will help solidify your understanding of capital budgeting before you work the summary review problem.

Concept Highlight

EXHIBIT 26-20
Capital Budgeting Methods

Method	Strengths	Weaknesses
Payback	Easy to understand Based on cash flows Highlights risks	Ignores profitability and the time value of money
Accounting rate of return	Based on profitability	Ignores the time value of money

Discounted cash flow:
  Net present value
  Internal rate of return
	Based on cash flows,
	  profitability, and the
	  time value of money
		Difficult to determine
		  discount rate

DECISION	GUIDELINE

How to decide whether a long-term investment is worthwhile?	Capital budgeting analysis:
	• Payback period
	• Accounting rate of return
	• Discounted cash flow methods:
	  Net present value (NPV)
	  Internal rate of return (IRR)

How to compute the payback period with • Equal annual cash flows?	$\text{Payback period} = \dfrac{\text{Amount invested}}{\text{Expected annual net cash inflow}}$
• Unequal annual cash flows?	Accumulate cash flows until amount of investment is recovered.
How to compute the accounting rate of return?	$\text{Accounting rate of return} = \dfrac{\text{Average annual operating income from asset}}{\text{Average amount invested in asset}}$ $= \dfrac{\text{Average annual net cash inflow from asset} - \text{Annual depreciation on asset}}{(\text{Amount invested in asset} + \text{Residual value})/2}$
How to compute net present value with • Equal annual cash flows?	$\begin{array}{l}\text{Present value of} \\ \textit{annuity} \text{ of \$1} \\ \text{(Exhibit 26-15)}\end{array} \times \begin{array}{l}\text{Annual net cash} \\ \text{inflow or outflow}\end{array}$
• Unequal annual cash flows?	Compute the present value of each year's net cash inflow or outflow (present value of $1 from Exhibit 26-17 × net cash inflow or outflow) and add up yearly present values
How to compute internal rate of return with • Equal annual cash flows?	$\begin{array}{l}\text{Annuity PV factor} \\ \text{(Use Exhibit 26-15)}\end{array} = \dfrac{\text{Investment}}{\text{Expected annual net cash inflow}}$
• Unequal annual cash flows?	Trial and error, computer spreadsheets, or calculator
Which capital budgeting methods are best?	Discounted cash-flow methods (NPV and IRR) are best because they incorporate both profitability and the time value of money.

SUMMARY PROBLEM FOR YOUR REVIEW

The data for a machine are as follows:

Cost of machine	$48,000
Estimated residual value	$ 6,000
Estimated annual net cash inflow	$13,000
Estimated useful life	5 years
Required rate of return	16%

REQUIRED

1. Compute the machine's payback period.
2. Compute the machine's accounting rate of return.
3. Compute the machine's net present value (NPV).
4. Would you decide to buy the machine? Give your reason.

■ **SOLUTION**

REQUIREMENT 1

$$\text{Payback period} = \frac{\text{Amount invested}}{\text{Expected annual net cash inflow}} = \frac{\$48,000}{\$13,000} = 3.7 \text{ years}$$

REQUIREMENT 2

$$\text{Accounting rate of return} = \frac{\text{Average annual operating income}}{\text{Average amount invested in asset}}$$

$$= \frac{\text{Average annual net cash inflow from asset} - \text{Annual depreciation on asset}}{(\text{Amount invested in asset} + \text{Residual value})/2}$$

$$= \frac{\$13,000 - \$8,400^*}{(\$48,000 + \$6,000)/2} = \frac{\$4,600}{\$27,000} = 0.170 = 17\%$$

$$^*\ \frac{\$48,000 - \$6,000}{5 \text{ years}} = \$8,400$$

REQUIREMENT 3

Present value of annuity of equal annual net cash inflows ($13,000 × 3.274†)..	$42,562
Present value of residual value ($6,000 × 0.476‡)	2,856
Total present value of net cash inflows..........................	45,418
Investment...	(48,000)
Net present value	$ (2,582)

†Present value of annuity of $1 for 5 years at 16%, Exhibit 26-15.
‡Present value of $1 in 5 years at 16%, Exhibit 26-17.

REQUIREMENT 4

Decision: Do not buy the machine because it has a negative net present value. The NPV model considers profitability and the time value of money. The other models ignore at least one of those factors.

Summary of Learning Objectives

1. *Identify the relevant information for a special business decision.* To make a decision, managers analyze relevant information. *Relevant information* is expected future data that differ among alternative courses of action. Historical data are irrelevant per se, but they often help managers make predictions about the future.

2. *Make six types of short-term special business decisions.* Two keys to making short-term special business decisions are (1) focusing on relevant items (relevant revenues and relevant costs), and (2) using a contribution margin approach that separates variable costs from fixed costs. Managers use these techniques when deciding whether to accept or reject a special sales order; whether to drop a product, department, or territory; which product to emphasize when a constraint is present; whether to make or buy a part; how to make the best use of facilities; and whether to sell a product as is or to process it further. Managers often select the course of action that is expected to produce the most operating income.

3. *Explain the difference between correct and incorrect analysis of a particular business decision.* Correct analysis of a business decision focuses on differences in revenues and expenses. The conventional absorption costing approach may mislead managers into treating a fixed cost as a variable cost. The contribution margin approach is more useful for decision analysis because it highlights how sales volume affects expenses and income.

4. *Use opportunity costs in decision making. Opportunity cost* is the benefit that can be obtained from the next-best course of

action in a decision. Every business decision has an opportunity cost. Opportunity cost is not an outlay cost, so it is not recorded in the accounting records.

5. *Use four capital budgeting methods to make longer-term investment decisions. Capital budgeting* is a formal means of analyzing long-term investment decisions. Four popular capital budgeting methods are payback, accounting rate of return, net present value, and internal rate of return. *Payback* is the length of time it will take to recover the dollars invested. The *accounting rate of return* is the average annual operating income from an asset divided by the average amount invested in that asset. *Net present value (NPV)* brings the project's cash inflows and outflows back to a common time period. To compute NPV, we discount expected future cash flows by the minimum desired rate of return. Projects with a positive net present value are acceptable. The project's *internal rate of return (IRR)* is the discount rate that makes the net present value of the project's cash flows equal to zero.

6. *Compare and contrast popular capital budgeting methods.* The discounted cash-flow methods—net present value and internal rate of return—are conceptually superior to payback and accounting rate of return. Payback ignores profitability and the time value of money. Accounting rate of return ignores the time value of money. NPV and IRR consider both profitability and the time value of money.

Accounting Vocabulary

Questions

1. How do special decisions differ from ordinary day-to-day business decisions? Give examples of special decisions.
2. Briefly describe how managers use relevant information in making special decisions.
3. Discuss the roles of expected future data and historical data in decision analysis. On which data are special decisions based?
4. Name two key guidelines for making short-term special decisions.
5. Identify two income statement formats. Which is more useful for deciding whether to accept a special sales order? Why?
6. Identify two long-term factors managers should consider in deciding whether to accept a special sales order.
7. What is the similarity between a special sales order decision and a decision to drop a product? The difference?
8. Which cost is more likely to change in a decision situation, a fixed or a variable cost? Can both costs change?
9. Outline how to decide which product to emphasize when there is a constraining factor. Give four examples of constraining factors.
10. Which is relevant to decision analysis, an asset's sunk cost or its residual value? Give your reason, including an explanation of each.
11. What is an opportunity cost? How does it differ from an ordinary accounting cost?
12. Give an example of a decision that is based on opportunity cost. Discuss the role of opportunity cost in making the decision.
13. What is capital budgeting? Are capital budgeting decisions made before or after long-term assets are purchased?
14. Name three capital budgeting decision methods. State the strengths and the weaknesses of each method. Which method is best? Why?
15. Which capital budgeting method is: (a) based on operating income; (b) based on cash flows without regard for their timing or profitability; (c) based on the time value of money.
16. How is the payback period computed for assets that generate equal annual cash inflows? How does the estimated useful life of the asset affect the payback computation?
17. How can managers use the accounting rate of return in capital budgeting decisions?
18. How is the accounting rate of return computed when the annual amounts of operating income vary?
19. Explain why a positive net present value indicates an attractive investment project and a negative net present value indicates an unattractive project.
20. Which capital budgeting strategy is better? (a) Pick the best capital budgeting method and use it exclusively. (b) Use multiple capital budgeting methods. Explain your answer.

Daily Exercises

DE26-1 You are trying to decide whether to trade in your car for a more recent model. Assume that your driving pattern will remain unchanged, and that the old and new cars both get the same gas mileage. Are the following items relevant or irrelevant to your decision?

Identifying relevant data *(Obj. 1)*

a. The price you paid for your old car
b. The price of the new car
c. The trade-in value of the old car
d. Monthly gasoline costs
e. The difference between the insurance cost for the old car and insurance cost for the new car

DE26-2 Consider the ACDelco special sales order example on pages 1123–1126. Suppose that

Accepting or rejecting a special sales order *(Obj. 2)*

a. ACDelco's variable manufacturing cost is $1.35 per oil filter (instead of $1.20).
b. ACDelco would have to buy a special stamping machine that costs $9,000 to mark the customer's logo on the special order oil filters. The machine would be scrapped when the special order is complete.

Use the incremental analysis approach from Exhibit 26-3 to determine whether you would recommend that ACDelco accept the special order under these conditions.

DE26-3 Daniel Green bedroom slippers sell for about $30 per pair. Suppose that the company incurs the following average costs per pair:

Deciding on a special sales order *(Obj. 2)*

Direct materials	$10
Direct labor	3
Variable manufacturing overhead	2
Variable marketing expenses	1
Fixed manufacturing overhead	5*
Total costs	$21

*$500,000 total fixed manufacturing overhead
————————————————————
100,000 pairs of slippers

Green has enough idle capacity to accept a one-time-only special order from Belk Department Store for 20,000 pairs of slippers at $19 per pair. Green will not incur any additional variable marketing expenses for the order.

How would accepting the special order affect Green's operating income?

Deciding on a special sales order (Obj. 2)

DE26-4   Consider the Daniel Green company in Daily Exercise 26-3. In addition to the special order's effect on profits, what other (longer-term qualitative) factors should Daniel Green's managers consider in deciding whether to accept Belk's special order?

Explaining the difference between correct and incorrect analysis for a special sales order (Obj. 2, 3)

DE26-5   Refer to Daily Exercises 26-3 and 26-4. Daniel Green marketing manager Lila Spence argues that Green should not accept Belk's special sales order because Belk's $19 offer price is less than Green's $21 cost to make the slippers. Spence asks you, one of Daniel Green's staff accountants, to write a memo explaining whether her analysis is correct. Use the following format:

Date:	_____
To:	Ms. Lila Spence, Marketing manager
From:	_____
Subject:	Belk special order

Dropping a department (Obj. 2)

DE26-6   Asco Hardware in Baltimore, Maryland operates three departments: Paint, Tools, and Hardware. Asco allocates fixed expenses (building depreciation and utilities) based on the square feet occupied by each department. Departmental operating income data for the third quarter of 1999 are as follows:

	Department			
	Paint	**Tools**	**Hardware**	**Total**
Sales revenue	$75,000	$54,000	$127,000	$256,000
Variable expenses	60,000	35,000	75,000	170,000
Fixed expenses..........................	25,000	15,000	30,000	70,000
Total expenses	85,000	50,000	105,000	240,000
Operating income (loss)...........	($10,000)	$ 4,000	$ 22,000	$ 16,000

Should Asco drop any of the departments? Give your reason. (The store will remain in the same building regardless of the decision.)

Dropping a department; explaining the difference between correct and incorrect analysis (Obj. 2, 3)

DE26-7   Helga Asco is the wife of Jeorg Asco, the owner of Asco Hardware in Daily Exercise 26-6. Helga is concerned. "Look at the Paint Department's results. That department is costing us $10,000 a quarter. We would have had $20,000 more in our retirement fund if you had gotten rid of the Paint Department like I suggested six months ago!"

Help Jeorg reply to Helga. Your response should include an analysis of how dropping the Paint Department would affect Asco's operating income.

Dropping a department (Obj. 2)

DE26-8   Consider Asco Hardware from Daily Exercise 26-6. Assume that the fixed expenses assigned to each department include only

- Salaries of the department's manager
- Cost of advertising directly related to that department

Asco will not incur these fixed expenses if the department is dropped. Under these circumstances, should Asco drop any of the departments? Give your reason.

Determining product mix (Obj. 2)

DE26-9   Each morning, manager Keisha Davis stocks the drink case at Coco's Beach Hut in Venice, California. Coco's has 100 linear feet of refrigerated display space for cold drinks. Each linear foot can hold either six 12-ounce cans or four 20-ounce plastic or glass bottles. Coco's sells three types of cold drinks:

- Coca-Cola Classic in 12-oz cans, for $1.25 per can
- Coca-Cola Classic in 20-oz plastic bottles, for $1.50 per bottle
- Snapple in 20-oz glass bottles, for $2.00 per bottle

Coco's pays its suppliers:

- $0.25 per 12-oz can of Coca-Cola Classic
- $0.30 per 20-oz bottle of Coca-Cola Classic
- $0.70 per 20-oz bottle of Snapple

Coco's monthly fixed expenses include

Hut rental	$ 250
Refrigerator rental............	50
Davis's salary.....................	1,000
Total fixed expenses	$1,300

Coco's can sell all the drinks stocked in the display case each morning.

What is Coco's constraining factor? What should Davis stock in order to maximize profits?

DE26-10 Refer to Daily Exercise 26-9. Suppose Coco's refuses to devote more than 60 linear feet to any individual product. Under this condition, how many linear feet of each drink should Davis stock?

Determining product mix
(Obj. 2)

DE26-11 U.S. Surgical Corporation in Norwalk, Connecticut, manufactures and markets surgical equipment. Lilian Gonzalez manages the company's fleet of 550 automobiles. Gonzalez has been charged with "reengineering" the fleet management function. She has an important decision to make.

Make-or-buy decision for services
(Obj. 1, 2)

- Should she continue to manage the fleet in-house, with the five employees reporting to her? To do so, she will have to acquire new fleet management software to streamline U.S. Surgical's fleet management process.
- Should she outsource the fleet management function to Fleet Management Services, a company that specializes in managing fleets of automobiles for other companies? Fleet Management Services would take over the maintenance, repair, and scheduling of U.S. Surgical's fleet (but U.S. Surgical would retain ownership of its fleet). This alternative would require Gonzalez to lay off her five employees. However, her own job would be secure as she would be U.S. Surgical's liaison with Fleet Management Services.

Assume that Gonzalez's records show the following data concerning U.S. Surgical's fleet:

Book value of U.S. Surgical's autos, with an estimated 5-year life	**$8,250,000**
Annual leasing fee for new fleet management software	**10,000**
Annual maintenance of autos	**275,000**
Fleet supervisor Gonzalez's annual salary	**80,000**
Total annual salaries of U.S. Surgical's five other fleet management employees	**175,000**

Suppose that Fleet Management Services offers to manage U.S. Surgical's fleet for an annual fee of $450,000.

1. Which alternative will maximize U.S. Surgical's short-term operating income?
2. What qualitative factors should Gonzalez consider before making a final decision?

DE26-12 Folsom Electrical Components has been purchasing electric switches for $3 each. Folsom believes that it can make these switches using its excess capacity. No extra equipment or other fixed costs would be required. Folsom estimates that it will need 50,000 switches, and that the cost per switch would include the following:

Make-or-buy decision
(Obj. 1, 2)

Direct materials	**$1.25**
Direct labor	**0.80**
Variable manufacturing overhead	**0.50**
Fixed manufacturing overhead	
(allocated based on machine hours)	**0.75**
Total average cost per switch	**$3.30**

Should Folsom make or buy the switches?

DE26-13 Refer to Folsom Electrical Components in Daily Exercise 26-12. Suppose that

Make or buy; best use of facilities
(Obj. 1, 2)

- Making the switches will require Folsom to hire a new part-time supervisor at a cost of $5,000.
- If Folsom buys the switches, it could rent its idle facilities to another company, Foxfire Products, for $20,000.

Should Folsom make or buy the switches?

DE26-14 Computer Components, Inc., has an inventory of 1,000 obsolete disk drives that are carried in inventory at a manufacturing cost of $200,000. Production supervisor Norman Mangina must decide whether to

Deciding whether to sell as is or process further
(Obj. 1, 2)

- Process the inventory further at a cost of $40,000, with the expectation of selling it for $64,000, or
- Scrap the inventory for a sale price of $17,000

What should Mangina do? Present figures to support your decision.

DE26-15 Computer Components, Inc., from Daily Exercise 26-14 is approached by a customer who wants to buy the 1,000 obsolete disk drives. The customer is willing to pay more than $17,000 for the set of 1,000 disk drives.

Using opportunity costs to make decisions
(Obj. 4)

1. What is Computer Components' opportunity cost of *not* processing the inventory further?
2. How can Mangina use this opportunity cost to set a minimum sale price for the customer? What should be Computer Components' minimum sale price per disk drive?

DE26-16 The concept of opportunity cost applies to all business decisions for which there are alternative courses of action. For example, in Exhibit 26-3, page 1124, the opportunity cost of rejecting the special sales order is the $11,000 of operating income that ACDelco would forego if it rejects the special order.

1. In Exhibit 26-7, page 1128,
   a. What is the opportunity cost of manufacturing the shirts?
   b. What is the opportunity cost of manufacturing the slacks?

DE26-17 Selective Insurance Company of America, a property/casualty insurer based in Branchville, New Jersey, is deciding whether to purchase new payroll software. Assistant vice president Tom DeLuca calculated that the payback period for the $50,000 software package would be 8.37 years.

What are the expected annual cash savings from the new software? Would you recommend that Selective Insurance purchase this software? Give your reason.

DE26-18 Daily Exercises 26-18 through 26-22 consider how Deer Valley Resort (from the chapter opening story) could use capital budgeting methods to decide whether the $13 million Snow Park Lodge expansion would be a good investment.

Assume that Deer Valley's managers developed the following estimates concerning the expansion (all numbers assumed):

Number of additional skiers per day	**100**
Average number of days per year that weather conditions allow	
skiing at Deer Valley	**150**
Useful life of expansion (in years)	**15**
Average cash spent by each skier per day	**$240**
Average variable cost of serving each skier per day	**$85**
Cost of expansion	**$13,000,000**
Discount rate	**12%**

Assume that Deer Valley uses the straight-line depreciation method and expects the lodge expansion to have a residual value of $1 million at the end of its 15-year life.

1. Compute the average annual net cash inflow from the expansion.
2. What is the payback period for the expansion project?

DE26-19 Refer to the Deer Valley Snow Park Lodge expansion project in Daily Exercise 26-18. What is the accounting rate of return?

DE26-20 ◀▥ *Link Back to Chapter 15 (Present-Value Concepts).* Refer to Daily Exercise 26-18. What is the project's net present value?

DE26-21 Refer to Daily Exercise 26-18. *Assume the expansion has zero residual value.* What is the project's internal rate of return?

Evaluating results of different
capital budgeting methods
(Obj. 6)

DE26-22 Use your results from Daily Exercises 26-18 through 26-21 to write a memo to Deer Valley director of finance Jim Madsen. The purpose of your memo is to recommend whether Deer Valley should undertake the expansion. Your memo should cover the strengths and weaknesses of each capital budgeting method cited in your memo. Follow the memo format outlined in Daily Exercise 26-5.

Exercises

E26-1 Suppose the Rock and Roll Hall of Fame in Cleveland, Ohio, has approached Photo-Files, Inc., with a special order. The Hall of Fame wishes to purchase 100,000 celebrity photos for a special promotional campaign and offers $0.75 per photo—a total of $75,000. Photo-Files' total production cost per photo is $1.10, broken down as follows:

Variable costs:	
Direct materials............	$0.18
Direct labor	0.09
Variable overhead	0.33
Fixed overhead	0.50
Total cost.........................	$1.10

Photo-Files has enough excess capacity to handle the special sales order.

REQUIRED

1. Prepare an incremental analysis to determine whether Photo-Files should accept the special sales order.
2. Now assume that the Hall of Fame wants a custom border on the photos. Photo-Files will spend $20,000 to develop this border, which will be useless after the special order is completed. Should Photo-Files accept the special sales order under these circumstances?

E26-2 Top managers of Wuxtry Music are alarmed about their operating losses. They are considering dropping the cassette tape product line. Company accountants have prepared the following analysis to help make this decision:

Keeping or dropping a product line (fixed costs unchanged) (Obj. 1, 2, 3)

	Total	Compact Discs	Cassette Tapes
Sales revenue...	$460,000	$290,000	$170,000
Variable expenses	240,000	140,000	100,000
Contribution margin	220,000	150,000	70,000
Fixed expenses:			
Manufacturing	145,000	70,000	75,000
Marketing and administrative..........	90,000	55,000	35,000
Total fixed expenses.........................	235,000	125,000	110,000
Operating income (loss).....................	$ (15,000)	$ 25,000	$ (40,000)

Total fixed costs will not change if the company stops selling cassette tapes.

Prepare an incremental analysis to show whether Wuxtry should drop the cassette tape product line. Will dropping cassette tapes add $40,000 to operating income? Explain.

E26-3 Refer to Exercise 26-2. Assume that Wuxtry Music can avoid $50,000 of fixed expenses by dropping the cassette tape product line. Prepare an incremental analysis to show whether Wuxtry should stop selling cassette tapes.

Keeping or dropping a product line (fixed costs change) (Obj. 1, 2)

E26-4 Four Seasons Fashions sells both designer and moderately priced women's wear. Top management is deciding which product line to emphasize. Accountants have provided the following data:

Determining product mix (Obj. 1, 2)

	Per Item	
	Designer	Moderately Priced
Average sale price....................................	$200	$80
Average variable expenses	70	24
Average contribution margin....................	130	56
Average fixed expenses (allocated)	20	10
Average operating income	$110	$46

The Four Seasons store in Boca Raton, Florida, has 10,000 square feet of floor space. If it emphasizes moderately priced goods, 500 items can be displayed in the store. In contrast, if it emphasizes designer wear, only 200 designer items can be displayed for sale. These numbers are also the average monthly sales in units.

Prepare an analysis to show which product to emphasize.

Make or buy decision
(Obj. 1, 2, 3)

Determining best use of facilities
(Obj. 1, 2)

Deciding whether to sell or process further; identifying opportunity costs
(Obj. 1, 2, 4)

Computing payback with equal cash flows
(Obj. 5)

Computing payback with unequal cash flows
(Obj. 5)

Determining accounting rate of return
(Obj. 4, 5)

Computing net present value
(Obj. 5)

Computing internal rate of return
(Obj. 5)

Determining product mix
(Obj. 1, 2)

E26-5   Skiptronics Industrial Controls manufactures an electronic control that it uses in its final product. The electronic control has the following manufacturing costs per unit:

Direct materials	$ 5.00
Direct labor	1.00
Variable overhead..........................	1.50
Fixed overhead	4.00
Manufacturing product cost	**$11.50**

Another company has offered to sell Skiptronics the electronic control for $8 per unit. If Skiptronics buys the control from the outside supplier, the manufacturing facilities that will be idled cannot be used for any other purpose. Should Skiptronics make or buy the electronic controls? Explain the difference between correct analysis and incorrect analysis of this decision.

E26-6   Refer to Exercise 26-5. Skiptronics needs 90,000 electronic controls. By purchasing them from the outside supplier, Skiptronics can use its idle facilities to manufacture another product that will contribute $75,000 to operating income. Identify the *incremental* costs that Skiptronics will incur to acquire 90,000 electronic controls under three alternative plans. Which plan makes the best use of Skiptronic's facilities? Support your answer.

E26-7   Garcia Millwork has damaged some custom cabinets, which cost the company $8,000 to manufacture. Owner Luis Garcia is considering two options for disposing of this inventory. One plan is to sell the cabinets as damaged inventory for $1,400. The alternative is to spend an additional $600 to repair the damage and expect to sell the cabinets for $2,200. What should Garcia do? Support your answer with an analysis that shows expected net revenue under each alternative. Identify the opportunity cost of each alternative.

E26-8   Kronos, Inc., is considering acquiring a manufacturing plant. The purchase price is $1,700,000. The owners believe the plant will generate net cash inflows of $485,700 annually. It will have to be replaced in seven years. Use the payback method to determine whether Kronos should purchase this plant.

E26-9   Seco Manufacturing is adding a new product line that will require an investment of $1,262,000. Managers estimate that this investment will generate net cash inflows of $310,000 the first year, $280,000 the second year, and $240,000 each year thereafter. What is the payback period of this investment?

E26-10   Roswell Mills is shopping for new equipment. Managers are considering two investments. Equipment manufactured by Tapistron, Inc., costs $400,000 and will last for five years, with no residual value. The Tapistron equipment is expected to generate annual operating income of $52,000. Equipment manufactured by Johnson Controls is priced at $500,000 and will remain useful for six years. It promises annual operating income of $79,500, and its expected residual value is $30,000.

Which equipment offers the higher accounting rate of return? What is the opportunity cost of purchasing from each manufacturer? How would Roswell Mills managers use the notion of opportunity cost in making their decision?

E26-11   ◄▥ *Link Back to Chapter 15 (Present-Value Concepts).* Use the NPV method to determine whether Earth Products should invest in the following projects:

- *Project A:* Costs $330,000 and offers 8 annual net cash inflows of $75,000. Earth Products requires an annual return of 14% on projects like A.
- *Project B:* Costs $410,000 and offers 9 annual net cash inflows of $75,000. Earth Products demands an annual return of 12% on investments of this nature.

What is the net present value of each project? What is the maximum acceptable price to pay for each project?

E26-12   Refer to Exercise 26-11. Compute the internal rate of return of each project, and use this information to identify the better investment.

CHALLENGE EXERCISE

E26-13   Abex, Inc., produces two types of abdominal exercisers: Regular and Deluxe. Pertinent data follow at the top of the next page.

The exercise craze is such that Abex could use all its available machine hours producing either model. The two models are processed through the same production departments.

Which model should Abex produce? If both models should be produced, compute the mix that will maximize operating income.

	Per Unit	
	Deluxe	**Regular**
Sale price....................................	$130.00	$75.00
Costs:		
Direct materials	$ 33.00	$14.00
Direct labor..................................	15.00	25.00
Variable overhead*........................	37.50	12.50
Fixed overhead*	15.00	5.00
Variable operating expenses	14.00	10.00
Total cost.....................................	114.50	66.50
Operating income............................	$ 15.50	$ 8.50

*Allocated on the basis of machine hours.

Beyond the Numbers

BN26-1 Target is the third largest retailer in the United States, with over 750 stores in 38 states. In 1996, Target stopped selling cigarettes. Cigarettes often have gross margins as high as 20 to 30 percent. Analysts estimate that Target's decision to eliminate the cigarette product line may have cost the company up to $16 million per year in gross margin.

Dropping a product line (Obj. 2)

   Why might Target decide to drop the cigarette product line and give up such a large profit?

BN26-2 Answer the following questions.

Required rate of return (Obj. 5)

1. In discounted cash flow analysis, does a higher discount rate (a higher required rate of return) increase or decrease the present value of the cash flows?

2. When performing discounted cash flow analysis, managers typically use different discount rates for riskier projects than for less risky projects. Would managers use higher or lower discount rates for riskier projects? Why?

3. Chevron Corporation is the second largest oil refiner in the United States, but it is also pursuing an aggressive oil exploration strategy. Would you expect Chevron's managers to use a higher or lower discount rate for oil refining projects than for oil exploration projects? Give your reason.

ETHICAL ISSUE

◀▥ *Link Back to the IMA Ethical Guidelines in Chapter 19.* Pauline Tang is the controller for Acorn Associates, a property management company in San Diego. Each year Tang and payroll clerk Toby Stock meet with the external auditors about payroll accounting. This year, the auditors suggest that Tang consider outsourcing Acorn Associates' payroll accounting to a company specializing in payroll processing services. This would allow Tang and her staff to focus on their primary responsibility, accounting for the properties under management. At present, payroll requires 1.5 employee positions—payroll clerk Toby Stock and a bookkeeper who spends half her time entering payroll data in the system.

Make or buy decision (Obj. 1, 2)

   Tang considers this suggestion, and she lists the following items relating to outsourcing payroll accounting:

a. The current payroll software that was purchased for $4,000 three years ago would not be needed if payroll processing is outsourced.

b. Acorn's bookkeeper would spend half her time preparing the weekly payroll input form that is given to the payroll processing service. She is paid $420 a week.

c. Acorn Associates would no longer need payroll clerk Toby Stock whose annual salary is $32,000.

d. The payroll processing service would charge $2,000 a month.

1. Will outsourcing the payroll function increase or decrease Acorn Associates' operating income?

2. Tang believes that outsourcing payroll would simplify her job, but she does not like the prospect of having to lay off Toby Stock, who has become a close personal friend. She does not believe there is another position available for Stock at his current salary. Can you think of other factors that might support keeping Stock, rather than outsourcing payroll processing? How should each of the factors affect Tang's decision if she wants to do what is best for Acorn and act ethically?

REQUIRED

Problems (GROUP A)

Accepting or rejecting a special sales order
(Obj. 1, 2)

P26-1A Casavas Toy Corporation manufactures toys in Austin, Texas. Casavas's contribution margin income statement for the most recent month contains the following data:

Sales in units...	42,000
Sales revenue	$420,000
Variable expenses:	
Manufacturing	$ 84,000
Marketing and administrative	100,000
Total variable expenses...................	184,000
Contribution margin	236,000
Fixed expenses:	
Manufacturing	116,000
Marketing and administrative	75,000
Total fixed expenses........................	191,000
Operating income	$ 45,000

Harpo Promotions, Inc., wishes to buy 4,000 toys from Casavas. Acceptance of the order will not increase any of Casavas's marketing and administrative expenses. The Casavas plant has unused capacity to manufacture the additional toys. Harpo has offered $7.00 per toy, which is considerably below the normal sale price of $10.

REQUIRED

1. Prepare an incremental analysis to determine whether Casavas should accept this special sales order.

2. Prepare a total analysis to show Casavas's operating income with and without the special sales order.

3. Identify long-term factors that Casavas should consider in deciding whether to accept the special sales order.

Keeping or dropping a product line
(Obj. 1, 2, 3)

P26-2A Members of the board of directors of Acme Alarm Systems, Inc., have received the following operating income data for the year just ended:

	Product Line		
	Industrial Systems	Household Systems	Total
Sales revenue	$419,000	$421,000	$840,000
Cost of goods sold:			
Variable	$ 74,000	$ 55,000	$129,000
Fixed...	241,000	86,000	327,000
Total cost of goods sold	315,000	141,000	456,000
Gross margin	104,000	280,000	384,000
Marketing and administrative expenses:			
Variable	86,000	92,000	178,000
Fixed	58,000	31,000	89,000
Total marketing and administrative			
expenses...	144,000	123,000	267,000
Operating income (loss)	$ (40,000)	$157,000	$117,000

Members of the board are surprised that the industrial systems product line is losing money. They commission a study to determine whether the company should drop the industrial systems product line. Company accountants estimate that dropping industrial systems will decrease fixed cost of goods sold by $95,000 and decrease fixed marketing and administrative expenses by $20,000.

REQUIRED

1. Prepare an incremental analysis to show whether Acme should drop the industrial systems product line.

2. Prepare a total analysis to show Acme's operating income with and without industrial systems. Prepare the income statement in contribution margin format.

3. Explain the difference between correct analysis and incorrect analysis of the decision to keep or drop the industrial systems product line.

P26-3A Drill Tech Corp., located in Pittsburgh, Pennsylvania, produces two lines of electric drills: deluxe and standard models. Because Drill Tech can sell all the drills it can produce, the owners are expanding the plant, and they are deciding which product line to emphasize. To make this decision, they assemble the following data.

Determining product mix *(Obj. 1, 2)*

	Per Unit	
	Deluxe Drill	**Standard Drill**
Sale price	$50	$30
Variable expenses	15	12
Contribution margin...................	$35	$18
Contribution margin ratio..........	70%	60%

After expansion, the factory will have a production capacity of 1,600 machine hours per month. The plant can manufacture either 60 standard drills or 20 deluxe drills per machine hour.

REQUIRED

1. Identify the constraining factor for Drill Tech Corp.
2. Prepare an analysis to show which product line to emphasize.

P26-4A Four Winns manufactures fiberglass boats. Assume that Four Winn's cost of making 1,200 seat covers is

Make or buy; best use of facilities *(Obj. 1, 2)*

Direct materials	$ 7,260
Direct labor..	1,440
Variable overhead	960
Fixed overhead...	2,400
Total manufacturing costs for 1,200 seat covers	**$12,060**

Suppose Nautique Corporation will sell seat covers to Four Winns for $8 each. Four Winns would pay $0.70 per unit to transport the seat covers to its manufacturing plant, where it would add its own Four Winns logo at a cost of $0.16 per seat cover.

REQUIRED

1. Four Winns' accountants predict that purchasing the seat covers from Nautique will enable the company to avoid $900 of fixed overhead. Prepare an analysis to show whether Four Winns should make or buy the seat covers.
2. Assume that the Four Winns facilities freed up by the purchase of seat covers from Nautique can be used to manufacture another product that will contribute $1,500 to profit. Total fixed costs will be the same as if Four Winns had produced the seat covers. Prepare an analysis to show which alternative makes the best use of Four Winns' facilities: (a) make seat covers, (b) buy seat covers and leave facilities idle, or (c) buy seat covers and make another product.

P26-5A Propylene Corporation produces a wide variety of chemical products. Propylene has spent $290,000 to refine 84,000 gallons of acetone, which can be sold for $3.32 a gallon. Alternatively, Propylene can process the acetone further and produce 77,000 gallons of lacquer thinner that can be sold for $4.80 a gallon. The additional processing will cost $0.89 per gallon of lacquer thinner. To sell the lacquer thinner, Propylene must pay a transportation charge of $0.23 a gallon and administrative expenses of $0.16 a gallon.

Deciding whether to sell as is or process further; identifying opportunity costs *(Obj. 1, 2, 4)*

REQUIRED

1. Prepare a diagram of Propylene's decision, using Exhibit 26-10 (page 1131) as a guide.
2. Identify the sunk cost in this situation. Is the sunk cost relevant to Propylene's decision?
3. Prepare an analysis to indicate whether Propylene should sell the acetone or process it into lacquer thinner. Show the expected net revenue difference between the two alternatives.
4. Identify the opportunity cost of each alternative. Explain how managers use the notion of opportunity cost in making their decision.

P26-6A Mesa View Developers, west of Austin in the Texas hill country, is considering purchasing a water park for $1,850,000. Top managers of Mesa View believe the new facility will generate annual net cash inflows of $385,000 for eight years. Architects and engineers estimate that the facility will remain useful for eight years and have a residual value of $600,000. The company uses straight-line depreciation, and its stockholders demand an annual return of 16% on investments of this nature.

Capital budgeting *(Obj. 5, 6)*

REQUIRED

1. Compute the payback period, the accounting rate of return, and the net present value of this investment.
2. Make a recommendation to Mesa View management as to whether the company should invest in this project.

P26-7A NutriLife operates a chain of grocery stores that specialize in health foods. The company is considering two possible expansion plans. Plan A would open eight smaller stores at a cost of $7,396,000. Expected annual net cash inflows are $860,000, with zero residual value at the end of 20 years. Under plan B, NutriLife would open three larger stores at a cost of $6,420,000. This plan is expected to generate net cash inflows of $600,000 per year for 20 years, the estimated life of the store properties. Estimated residual value is $3,000,000. NutriLife uses straight-line depreciation and requires an annual return of 8 percent.

REQUIRED

1. Compute the payback period, the accounting rate of return, and the net present value of these two plans. What are the strengths and weaknesses of these capital budgeting models?
2. Which expansion plan should NutriLife choose? Why?
3. Estimate plan A's internal rate of return (IRR). How does the IRR compare with the company's required rate of return?

Problems (GROUP B)

P26-1B Allied Label Company's contribution margin income statement for the most recent month reports the following:

Sales in units...	760,000
Sales revenue..	$190,000
Variable expenses:	
Manufacturing	$ 38,000
Marketing and administrative	54,000
Total variable expenses....................	92,000
Contribution margin...........................	98,000
Fixed expenses:	
Manufacturing	58,000
Marketing and administrative	16,000
Total fixed expenses	74,000
Operating income	$ 24,000

Empire Abrasive Equipment wants to buy 10,000 labels from Allied. Acceptance of the order will not increase any of Allied's marketing and administrative expenses. Allied's plant has unused capacity to manufacture the additional labels. Empire has offered $0.16 per label, which is considerably below the normal sale price of $0.25.

REQUIRED

1. Prepare an incremental analysis to determine whether Allied should accept this special sales order.
2. Prepare a total analysis to show Allied's operating income with and without the special sales order.
3. Identify long-term factors that Allied should consider in deciding whether to accept the special sales order.

P26-2B The following operating income data of Pasta Bella Company highlights the losses of the fresh pasta product line:

		Product Line	
		Fresh	Dried
	Total	Pasta	Pasta
Sales revenue	$857,500	$227,500	$630,000
Cost of goods sold:			
Variable	$167,500	$ 67,500	$100,000
Fixed..	127,500	37,500	90,000
Total cost of goods sold	295,000	105,000	190,000
Gross margin	562,500	122,500	440,000
Marketing and administrative expenses:			
Variable	375,000	105,000	270,000
Fixed	132,500	52,500	80,000
Total marketing and administrative			
expenses...	507,500	157,500	350,000
Operating income (loss)	$ 55,000	$(35,000)	$ 90,000

Luigi Vito is considering discontinuing the fresh pasta product line. The company's accountants estimate that dropping the fresh pasta line will decrease fixed cost of goods sold by $25,000 and decrease fixed marketing and administrative expenses by $15,000.

REQUIRED

1. Prepare an incremental analysis to show whether Pasta Bella should drop the fresh pasta product line.
2. Prepare a total analysis to show Pasta Bella's operating income with and without the fresh pasta product line. Prepare the income statement in contribution margin format.
3. Explain the difference between correct analysis and incorrect analysis of the decision to keep or drop the fresh pasta product line.

Determining product mix
(Obj. 1, 2)

P26-3B Cody Appliances of Jackson Hole, Wyoming, specializes in washers, dryers and big-screen televisions. Owner Lisa Cody is expanding the store. She is deciding which product line to emphasize. To make this decision, she assembles the following data:

	Per Unit	
	Televisions	**Dryers**
Sale price	$500	$300
Variable expenses	260	162
Contribution margin	$240	$138
Contribution margin ratio	48%	46%

After renovation, the store will have 8,000 square feet of floor space. By devoting the new floor space to dryers, Cody Appliances can display 60 dryers. Alternatively, she could display 30 televisions. She expects monthly sales to equal the maximum number of units displayed.

REQUIRED

1. Identify the constraining factor for Cody Appliances.
2. Prepare an analysis to show which product line to emphasize.

Make or buy; best use of facilities
(Obj. 1, 2)

P26-4B FinCo manufactures swim fins. Cost data for producing 2,000 pairs of fins each year are as follows:

Direct materials	$21,000
Direct labor	15,000
Variable overhead	5,600
Fixed overhead	38,400
Total manufacturing costs	$80,000

Suppose BodyGlove will sell FinCo the fins for $30 per pair. FinCo would pay $1.50 per pair to transport the fins to its warehouse.

REQUIRED

1. FinCo's accountants predict that purchasing the fins from BodyGlove will enable the company to avoid $10,000 of fixed overhead. Prepare an analysis to show whether FinCo should make or buy the fins.
2. Assume that the FinCo facilities freed up by the purchase of the fins from BodyGlove can be used to manufacture swim masks. The masks will contribute $25,000 to profit. Total fixed costs will be the same as if FinCo used the plant to make fins. Prepare an analysis to show which alternative makes the best use of FinCo's facilities: (a) make fins, (b) buy fins and leave facilities idle, or (c) buy fins and make masks.

Deciding whether to sell as is or process further; identifying opportunity costs
(Obj. 1, 2, 4)

P26-5B Phillips Petroleum Company produces a variety of petroleum products. Assume that Phillips has spent $300,000 to refine 60,000 gallons of petroleum distillate. Suppose Phillips can sell the distillate for $5.75 a gallon. Alternatively, Phillips can process the distillate further and produce cleaner for tape heads in cassette decks. Assume that the additional processing will cost another $1.33 a gallon, and that the cleaner can be sold for $7.50 a gallon. To make this sale, Phillips must pay a sales commission of $0.10 a gallon and a transportation charge of $0.15 a gallon.

REQUIRED

1. Prepare a diagram of Phillips' alternatives, using Exhibit 26-10, page 1131, as a guide.
2. Identify the sunk cost in this situation. Is the sunk cost relevant to Philips's decision?
3. Prepare an analysis to indicate whether Phillips should sell the distillate or process it into tape-head cleaner for cassette decks. Show the expected net revenue difference between the two alternatives.
4. Identify the opportunity cost of each option. Explain how managers can use opportunity cost to make this decision.

Capital budgeting
(Obj. 5, 6)

P26-6B Auburn Investments, Inc., operates a resort near Geneva in the Finger Lakes region of New York. The company is considering an expansion. The architectural plan calls for a construction cost of $5,200,000. Top managers of Auburn believe the expansion will generate annual net cash inflows of $700,000 for ten years. Architects and engineers estimate that the new facilities will remain useful for ten years and have a residual value of $2,400,000. The company uses straight-line depreciation, and its stockholders demand an annual return of 12% on investments of this nature.

REQUIRED

1. Compute the payback period, the accounting rate of return, and the net present value of this investment.
2. Make a recommendation to Auburn management as to whether the company should invest in this project.

Capital budgeting
(Obj. 5, 6)

P26-7B Jittery Joe's Java House is considering two possible expansion plans. Plan A is to open eight coffee houses at a cost of $3,220,000. Expected annual net cash inflows are $700,000 with residual value of $420,000 at the end of seven years. Under plan B, Jittery Joe's would open 12 coffee houses at a cost of $4,200,000. This investment is expected to generate net cash inflows of $1,050,000 each year for seven years, which is the estimated useful life of the properties. Estimated residual value of the plan B coffee houses is zero. Jittery Joe's uses straight-line depreciation, and requires an annual return of 14 percent.

REQUIRED

1. Compute the payback period, the accounting rate of return, and the net present value of each plan. What are the strengths and weaknesses of these capital budgeting models?
2. Which expansion plan should Jittery Joe's adopt? Why?
3. Estimate the internal rate of return (IRR) for plan B. How does plan B's IRR compare with Jittery Joe's required rate of return?

Applying Your Knowledge

DECISION CASES

Deciding whether to purchase a new machine
(Obj. 1, 5, 6)

CASE 1. Suppose that Motorola is considering a new computer-controlled machine for etching trenches in the surfaces of silicon wafers. The company processes these wafers into semiconductor chips. The etching machine costs $800,000, and an additional $300,000 would be required for installation. Thus $1,100,000 is the required cash outlay for the investment.

Assume the new etching machine would replace an existing machine that was purchased five years ago for $675,000. That machine has five years of useful life remaining. Motorola must either keep the old machine or replace it with the new machine. The expected useful life of the new machine is five years. Suppose Motorola managers believe that the new machine would save $343,000 per year in cash operating costs. However, annual maintenance cost would be $35,000 higher with the new machine than with the old.

Disposal values of the machines are as follows:

	Old Machine	New Machine
Now.................	$-0-	—
In 5 years..........	-0-	$150,000

Assume Motorola has a minimum desired rate of return of 14% on similar investments.

REQUIRED

1. Is the $675,000 cost of the old machine relevant to the decision of whether to keep or replace the old machine? Why or why not? (*Hint:* What are the requirements for a cost to be relevant?)
2. Which of the four capital budgeting methods is best suited for making this decision? Use that method to decide which course of action is better for Motorola. (*Hint:* Identify the relevant items.)

Analyzing relevant factors in an employment decision
(Obj. 1, 4, 5)

CASE 2. Ted Christensen, a second-year business student at Case Western Reserve University, will graduate in two years with an accounting major and a Spanish minor. Christensen is trying to decide where to work this summer. He has two choices: work full-time for a bottling plant or work part-time in the Accounting Department of a meat-packing plant. He probably will work at the same place next summer as well. He is able to work 12 weeks during the summer.

The bottling plant will pay Christensen $380 per week this year and 7% more next year. At the meat-packing plant, he could work 20 hours per week at $8.75 per hour. By working only part-time, he could take two accounting courses this summer. Tuition is $225 per hour for each of the four-hour courses. Christensen believes that the experience he gains this summer will qualify him for a full-time accounting position with the meat-packing plant next year. That position will pay $550 per week.

Christensen sees two additional benefits of working part-time this year. First, he could reduce his workload during the fall and spring semesters by one course each term. Second, he would have the time to work as a grader in the university's Accounting Department during the 15-week fall term. Grading pays $50 per week.

REQUIRED

1. Suppose that Ted Christensen ignores the time value of money in decisions that cover this short a time period. Suppose also that his sole goal is to make as much money as possible between now and the end of next summer. What should he do? What would *you* do if you were faced with these alternatives?

2. Now suppose that Christensen considers the time value of money for all cash flows that he expects to receive one year or more in the future. Which alternative does this consideration favor? Why?

Team Project

John Menard is the founder and sole owner of Menard, Inc. Analysts have estimated that his chain of 128 home improvement stores scattered around nine midwestern states generate about $3.1 billion in annual sales. But how can Menard compete with giant Home Depot?

Identify relevant data, make or buy, capital budgeting
(Obj. 1, 2, 5)

Suppose Menard is trying to decide whether to invest $45 million in a state-of-the-art manufacturing plant in Eau Claire, Wisconsin. Menard expects the plant would operate for 15 years, after which the plant would have no residual value. The plant would produce Menard's own line of Formica countertops, dog houses, and picnic tables.

Suppose that Menard would incur the following unit costs in producing his own product lines:

	Per Unit		
	Countertops	**Dog Houses**	**Picnic Tables**
Direct materials.....................................	$15	$10	$28
Direct labor...	10	5	20
Variable manufacturing overhead..........	5	2	7

Rather than making these products, assume Menard could buy them from outside suppliers. Suppliers would charge Menard $40 per countertop, $25 per dog house, and $75 per picnic table.

Whether Menard makes or buys these products, assume that he expects the following annual sales:

- Countertops—487,200 at $130 each
- Dog houses—150,000 at $75 each
- Picnic tables—100,000 at $225 each

If "making" is sufficiently more profitable than "buying" these products, then Menard will build the new plant. John Menard has asked your consulting group to recommend whether or not he should build the new plant in Eau Claire. Menard uses a 14% discount rate and the straight-line depreciation method.

REQUIRED

1. Are the following items relevant or irrelevant in Menard's decision to build the new plant that will manufacture his own products?
   a. The $45 million to build the new plant
   b. The unit sale prices of the countertops, dog houses, and picnic tables (the sale prices that Menard charges its customers)
   c. The prices outside suppliers would charge Menard for the three products, if Menard decides to buy the products rather than make them
   d. The direct materials, direct labor, and variable overhead Menard would incur to manufacture the three product lines
   e. Menard's salary

2. Determine whether Menard should make or buy the countertops, dog houses, and picnic tables, *assuming that the company had already built the plant and therefore has the manufacturing capacity to produce these products.* In other words, what is the annual difference in cash flows if Menard decides to make rather than buy each of these three products?

3. In requirement 2, you computed the annual difference in cash flows if Menard decides to make rather than buy the three products. To analyze the investment in the plant relative to the alternative of buying the products, use this *difference* in annual cash flows to compute the following for the investment in the new plant:
   a. Payback period   c. Net present value
   b. Accounting rate of return   d. Internal rate of return
   (*Hint:* Base the benefit side of your computations on the *difference* in annual cash flows you computed in requirement 2, *not* the total expected cash flows from building the plant.)

4. Write a memo giving your recommendation to John Menard. The memo should clearly state your recommendation, along with a brief summary of the reasons for your recommendation. Use the following format for your memo:

Date:	_____
To:	Mr. John Menard, CEO
From:	_____
Subject:	Building new plant in Eau Claire

NIKE, Inc. Annual Report (Excerpts)

FINANCIALS 1997

FINANCIAL HISTORY

(in thousands, except per share data and financial ratios)

YEAR ENDED MAY 31,	1997	1996	1995	1994
Revenues	$9,186,539	$6,470,625	$4,760,834	$3,789,668
Gross margin	3,683,546	2,563,879	1,895,554	1,488,245
Gross margin %	40.1%	39.6%	39.8%	39.3%
Net income	795,822	553,190	399,664	298,794
Net income per common share	2.68	1.88	1.36	0.99
Average number of common and common equivalent shares	297,000	293,608	294,012	301,824
Cash dividends declared per common share	0.38	0.29	0.24	0.20
Cash flow from operations	323,120	339,672	254,913	576,463
Price range of common stock				
High	76.375	52.063	20.156	18.688
Low	47.875	19.531	14.063	10.781
At May 31:				
Cash and equivalents	$ 445,421	$ 262,117	$ 216,071	$ 518,816
Inventories	1,338,640	931,151	629,742	470,023
Working capital	1,964,002	1,259,881	938,393	1,208,444
Total assets	5,361,207	3,951,628	3,142,745	2,373,815
Long-term debt	296,020	9,584	10,565	12,364
Redeemable Preferred Stock	300	300	300	300
Common shareholders' equity	3,155,838	2,431,400	1,964,689	1,740,949
Year-end stock price	57.500	50 .188	19.719	14.750
Market capitalization	16,633,047	14,416,792	5,635,190	4,318,800
Financial Ratios:				
Return on equity	28.5%	25.2%	21.6%	17.7%
Return on assets	17.1%	15.6%	14.5%	13.1%
Inventory turns	4.8	5.0	5.2	4.3
Current ratio at May 31	2.1	1.9	1.8	3.2
Price/Earnings ratio at May 31	21.5	26.6	14.5	14.9
Geographic Revenues:				
United States	$5,529,132	$3,964,662	$ 2,997,864	$2,432,684
Europe	1,833,722	1,334,340	980,444	927,269
Asia/Pacific	1,245,217	735,094	515,652	283,421
Canada, Latin America, and other	578,468	436,529	266,874	146,294
Total Revenues	$9,186,539	$6,470,625	$4,760,834	$3,789,668

All per common share data has been adjusted to reflect the 2-for-1 stock splits paid October 23, 1996, October 30, 1995 and October 5, 1990. The Company's Class B Common Stock is listed on the New York and Pacific Exchanges and trades under the symbol NKE. At May 31, 1997, there were approximately 300,000 shareholders. Years 1993 and prior have been restated to reflect the implementation of Statement of Financial Accounting Standard No. 109 – Accounting for Income Taxes (see Notes 1 and 6 to the Consolidated Financial Statements).

1973 1974 1975 1976 1977 1978 1980 1981 1982 1983 1984 19
2000 2001 2002 2003 2004 2005 2006 2007 2008 2009 20

	1993	1992	1991	1990	1989	1988
	$3,930,984	$3,405,211	$3,003,610	$2,235,244	$1,710,803	$1,203,440
	1,543,991	1,316,122	1,153,080	851,072	635,972	400,060
	39.3%	38.7%	38.4%	38.1%	37.2%	33.2%
	365,016	329,218	287,046	242,958	167,047	101,695
	1.18	1.07	0.94	0.80	0.56	0.34
	308,252	306,408	304,268	302,672	300,576	301,112
	0.19	0.15	0.13	0.10	0.07	0.05
	265,292	435,838	11,122	127,075	169,441	19,019
	22.563	19.344	13.625	10.375	4.969	3.313
	13.750	8.781	6.500	4.750	2.891	1.750
	$ 291,284	$ 260,050	$ 119,804	$ 90,449	$ 85,749	$ 75,357
	592,986	471,202	586,594	309,476	222,924	198,470
	1,165,204	964,291	662,645	561,642	419,599	295,937
	2,186,269	1,871,667	1,707,236	1,093,358	824,216	707,901
	15,033	69,476	29,992	25,941	34,051	30,306
	300	300	300	300	300	300
	1,642,819	1,328,488	1,029,582	781,012	558,597	408,567
	18.125	14.500	9.938	9.813	4.750	3.031
	5,499,273	4,379,574	2,993,020	2,942,679	1,417,381	899,741
	24.5%	27.9%	31.7%	36.3%	34.5%	27.4%
	18.0%	18.4%	20.5%	25.3%	21.8%	16.7%
	4.5	3.9	4.1	5.2	5.1	5.0
	3.6	3.3	2.1	3.1	2.9	2.2
	15.3	13.5	10.5	12.2	8.6	9.0
	$2,528,848	$2,270,880	$2,141,461	$1,755,496	$1,362,148	$ 900,417
	1,085,683	919,763	664,747	334,275	241,380	233,402
	178,196	75,732	56,238	29,332	32,027	21,058
	138,257	138,836	141,164	116,141	75,248	48,563
	$3,930,984	$3,405,211	$3,003,610	$2,235,244	$1,710,803	$1,203,440

Management of NIKE, Inc. is responsible for the information and representations contained in this report. The financial statements have been prepared in conformity with the generally accepted accounting principles we considered appropriate in the circumstances and include some amounts based on our best estimates and judgments. Other financial information in this report is consistent with these financial statements.

The Company's accounting systems include controls designed to reasonably assure that assets are safeguarded from unauthorized use or disposition and which provide for the preparation of financial statements in conformity with generally accepted accounting principles. These systems are supplemented by the selection and training of qualified financial personnel and an organizational structure providing for appropriate segregation of duties.

An Internal Audit department reviews the results of its work with the Audit Committee of the Board of Directors, presently consisting of three outside directors of the Company. The Audit Committee is responsible for recommending to the Board of Directors the appointment of the independent accountants and reviews with the independent accountants, management and the internal audit staff, the scope and the results of the annual examination, the effectiveness of the accounting control system and other matters relating to the financial affairs of the Company as they deem appropriate. The independent accountants and the internal auditors have full access to the Committee, with and without the presence of management, to discuss any appropriate matters.

Portland, Oregon

June 27, 1997

To the Board of Directors and

Shareholders of NIKE, Inc.

In our opinion, the accompanying consolidated balance sheet and the related consolidated statements of income, of cash flows and of shareholders' equity present fairly, in all material respects, the financial position of NIKE, Inc. and its subsidiaries at May 31, 1997 and 1996, and the results of their operations and their cash flows for each of the three years in the period ended May 31, 1997, in conformity with generally accepted accounting principles. These financial statements are the responsibility of the Company's management; our responsibility is to express an opinion on these financial statements based on our audits. We conducted our audits of these statements in accordance with generally accepted auditing standards which require that we plan and perform the audit to obtain reasonable assurance about whether the financial statements are free of material misstatement. An audit includes examining, on a test basis, evidence supporting the amounts and disclosures in the financial statements, assessing the accounting principles used and significant estimates made by management, and evaluating the overall financial statement presentation. We believe that our audits provide a reasonable basis for the opinion expressed above.

Price Waterhouse LLP

NIKE, INC. CONSOLIDATED STATEMENT OF INCOME

(in thousands, except per share data)

YEAR ENDED MAY 31,	1997	1996	1995
Revenues	$9,186,539	$6,470,625	$4,760,834
Costs and expenses:			
Costs of sales	5,502,993	3,906,746	2,865,280
Selling and administrative	2,303,704	1,588,612	1,209,760
Interest expense (Notes 4 and 5)	52,343	39,498	24,208
Other income/expense, net (Notes 1, 9 and 10)	32,277	36,679	11,722
	7,891,317	5,571,535	4,110,970
Income before income taxes	1,295,222	899,090	649,864
Income taxes (Note 6)	499,400	345,900	250,200
Net income	$ 795,822	$ 553,190	$ 399,664
Net income per common share (Note 1)	$ 2.68	$ 1.88	$ 1.36
Average number of common and common equivalent shares (Note 1)	297,000	293,608	294,012

The accompanying notes to consolidated financial statements are an integral part of this statement.

NIKE, INC. CONSOLIDATED BALANCE SHEET

(in thousands)

MAY 31,	1997	1996
Assets		
Current Assets:		
Cash and equivalents	$ 445,421	$ 262,117
Accounts receivable, less allowance for		
doubtful accounts of $57,233 and $43,372	1,754,137	1,346,125
Inventories (Note 2)	1,338,640	931,151
Deferred income taxes (Note 6)	135,663	93,120
Prepaid expenses (Note 1)	157,058	94,427
Total current assets	3,830,919	2,726,940
Property, plant and equipment, net (Notes 3 and 5)	922,369	643,459
Identifiable intangible assets and goodwill (Note 1)	464,191	474,812
Deferred income taxes and other assets (Notes 1 and 6)	143,728	106,417
Total assets	$5,361,207	$3,951,628
Liabilities and Shareholders' Equity		
Current Liabilities:		
Current portion of long-term debt (Note 5)	$ 2,216	$ 7,301
Notes payable (Note 4)	553,153	445,064
Accounts payable (Note 4)	687,121	455,034
Accrued liabilities	570,504	480,407
Income taxes payable	53,923	79,253
Total current liabilities	1,866,917	1,467,059
Long-term debt (Notes 5 and 13)	296,020	9,584
Deferred income taxes and other liabilities (Notes 1 and 6)	42,132	43,285
Commitments and contingencies (Notes 11 and 14)	—	—
Redeemable Preferred Stock (Note 7)	300	300
Shareholders' equity (Note 8):		
Common Stock at stated value:		
Class A convertible – 101,711 and 102,240 shares outstanding	152	153
Class B – 187,559 and 185,018 shares outstanding	2,706	2,702
Capital in excess of stated value	210,650	154,833
Foreign currency translation adjustment	(31,333)	(16,501)
Retained earnings	2,973,663	2,290,213
Total shareholders' equity	3,155,838	2,431,400
Total liabilities and shareholders' equity	$5,361,207	$3,951,628

The accompanying notes to consolidated financial statements are an integral part of this statement.

NIKE, INC. CONSOLIDATED STATEMENT OF CASH FLOWS

(in thousands)

YEAR ENDED MAY 31,	1997	1996	1995
Cash provided (used) by operations:			
Net income	$795,822	$553,190	$399,664
Income charges (credits) not affecting cash:			
Depreciation	138,038	97,179	71,113
Deferred income taxes and purchased tax benefits	(47,146)	(73,279)	(24,668)
Amortization and other	30,291	32,685	14,966
Changes in certain working capital components:			
Increase in inventories	(416,706)	(301,409)	(69,676)
Increase in accounts receivable	(485,595)	(292,888)	(301,648)
Increase in other current assets	(56,928)	(20,054)	(10,276)
Increase in accounts payable, accrued liabilities and income taxes payable	365,344	344,248	175,438
Cash provided by operations	323,120	339,672	254,913
Cash provided (used) by investing activities:			
Additions to property, plant and equipment	(465,908)	(216,384)	(154,125)
Disposals of property, plant and equipment	24,294	12,775	9,011
Increase in other assets	(43,829)	(26,376)	(9,499)
(Decrease) increase in other liabilities	(10,833)	(9,651)	3,239
Acquisition of subsidiaries:			
Identifiable intangible assets and goodwill	—	—	(345,901)
Net assets acquired	—	—	(84,119)
Cash used by investing activities	(496,276)	(239,636)	(581,394)
Cash provided (used) by financing activities:			
Additions to long-term debt	300,500	5,044	2,971
Reductions in long-term debt including current portion	(5,190)	(30,352)	(39,804)
Increase in notes payable	92,926	47,964	263,874
Proceeds from exercise of options	26,282	21,150	6,154
Repurchase of stock	—	(18,756)	(142,919)
Dividends – common and preferred	(100,896)	(78,834)	(65,418)
Cash provided (used) by financing activities	313,622	(53,784)	24,858
Effect of exchange rate changes on cash	(166)	(206)	(1,122)
Effect of May 1996 cash flow activity for certain subsidiaries (Note 1)	43,004	—	—
Net increase (decrease) in cash and equivalents	183,304	46,046	(302,745)
Cash and equivalents, beginning of year	262,117	216,071	518,816
Cash and equivalents, end of year	$445,421	$262,117	$216,071
Supplemental disclosure of cash flow information:			
Cash paid during the year for:			
Interest (net of amount capitalized)	$ 44,000	$ 32,800	$ 20,200
Income taxes	543,100	359,300	285,400

The accompanying notes to consolidated financial statements are an integral part of this statement.

| (in thousands) | Common Stock | | | | Capital In Excess Of Stated Value | Foreign Currency Translation Adjustment | Retained Earnings | Total |
| | Class A | | Class B | | | | | |
	Shares	Amount	Shares	Amount				
Balance at May 31, 1994	26,679	$159	46,521	$2,704	$108,284	$(15,123)	$1,644,925	$1,740,949
Stock options exercised			241	2	8,954			8,956
Conversion to Class B Common Stock	(784)	(4)	784	4				—
Repurchase of Class B Common Stock			(2,130)	(13)	(4,801)		(138,106)	(142,920)
Stock issued pursuant to contractual obligations			134	1	9,999			10,000
Translation of statements of non-U.S. operations						16,708		16,708
Net income							399,664	399,664
Dividends on Redeemable Preferred Stock							(30)	(30)
Dividends on Common Stock							(68,638)	(68,638)
Balance at May 31, 1995	25,895	155	45,550	2,698	122,436	1,585	1,837,815	1,964,689
Stock options exercised			756	3	32,848			32,851
Conversion to Class B Common Stock	(655)	(2)	655	2				—
Repurchase of Class B Common Stock			(200)	(1)	(451)		(18,304)	(18,756)
Two-for-one Stock Split October 30, 1995	25,880		45,748					
Translation of statements of non-U.S. operations						(18,086)		(18,086)
Net income							553,190	553,190
Dividends on Redeemable Preferred Stock							(30)	(30)
Dividends on Common Stock							(82,458)	(82,458)
Balance at May 31, 1996	51,120	153	92,509	2,702	154,833	(16,501)	2,290,213	2,431,400
Stock options exercised			1,475	3	55,817			55,820
Conversion to Class B Common Stock	(279)	(1)	279	1				—
Two-for-one Stock Split October 23, 1996	50,870		93,296					
Translation of statements of non-U.S. operations						(14,832)		(14,832)
Net income							795,822	795,822
Dividends on Redeemable Preferred Stock							(30)	(30)
Dividends on Common Stock							(108,249)	(108,249)
Net income for the month ended May 1996, due to the change in fiscal year-end of certain non-U.S. operations (Note 1)							(4,093)	(4,093)
Balance at May 31, 1997	101,711	$152	187,559	$2,706	$210,650	($31,333)	$2,973,663	$3,155,838

The accompanying notes to consolidated financial statements are an integral part of this statement.

NIKE, INC. NOTES TO CONSOLIDATED FINANCIAL STATEMENTS

NOTE 1 – SUMMARY OF SIGNIFICANT ACCOUNTING POLICIES:

Basis of consolidation:

The consolidated financial statements include the accounts of the Company and its subsidiaries. All significant intercompany trans-actions and balances have been eliminated. Prior to fiscal year 1997, certain of the Company's non-U.S. operations reported their results of operations on a one month lag which allowed more time to compile results. Beginning in the first quarter of fiscal year 1997, the one month lag was eliminated. As a result, the May 1996 charge from operations for these entities of $4,093,000 was recorded to retained earnings in the first quarter of the current year.

Recognition of revenues:

Revenues recognized include sales plus fees earned on sales by licensees.

Advertising:

Advertising production costs are expensed the first time the advertisement is run. Media (TV and print) placement costs are expensed in the month the advertising appears. Total advertising and promotion expenses were $978,251,000, $642,498,000 and $495,006,000 for the years ended May 31, 1997, 1996 and 1995, respectively. Included in prepaid expenses and other assets was $111,925,000 and $69,340,000 at May 31, 1997 and 1996, respectively, relating to prepaid advertising and promotion expenses.

Cash and equivalents:

Cash and equivalents represent cash and short-term, highly liquid investments with original maturities three months or less.

Inventory valuation:

Inventories are stated at the lower of cost or market. Cost is determined using the last-in, first-out (LIFO) method for substantially all U.S. inventories. Non-U.S. inventories are valued on a first-in, first-out (FIFO) basis.

Property, plant and equipment and depreciation:

Property, plant and equipment are recorded at cost. Depreciation for financial reporting purposes is determined on a straight-line basis for buildings and leasehold improvements and principally on a declining balance basis for machinery and equipment, based upon estimated useful lives ranging from two to thirty years.

Identifiable intangible assets and goodwill:

At May 31, 1997 and 1996, the Company had patents, trademarks and other identifiable intangible assets with a value of $219,186,000 and $209,586,000, respectively. The Company's excess of purchase cost over the fair value of net assets of businesses acquired (goodwill) was $326,252,000 and $327,555,000 at May 31, 1997 and 1996, respectively.

Identifiable intangible assets and goodwill are being amortized over their estimated useful lives on a straight-line basis over five to forty years. Accumulated amortization was $81,247,000 and $62,329,000 at May 31, 1997 and 1996, respectively. Amortization expense, which is included in other income/expense, was $19,765,000, $21,772,000 and $13,176,000 for the years ended May 31, 1997, 1996 and 1995, respectively. Intangible assets are periodically reviewed by the Company for impairments where the fair value is less than the carrying value.

Other liabilities:

Other liabilities include amounts with settlement dates beyond one year, and are primarily composed of long-term deferred endorse-ment payments of $15,815,000 and $21,674,000 at May 31, 1997 and 1996, respectively. Deferred payments to endorsers relate to amounts due beyond contract termination, which are discounted at various interest rates and accrued over the contract period.

Endorsement contracts:

Accounting for endorsement contracts is based upon specific contract provisions. Generally, endorsement payments are expensed uniformly over the term of the contract after giving recognition to periodic performance compliance provisions of the contracts. Contracts requiring prepayments are included in prepaid expenses or other assets depending on the length of the contract.

Foreign currency translation:

Adjustments resulting from translating foreign functional currency financial statements into U.S. dollars are included in the foreign currency translation adjustment in shareholders' equity.

Derivatives:

The Company enters into foreign currency contracts in order to reduce the impact of certain foreign currency fluctuations. Firmly committed transactions and the related receivables and payables may be hedged with forward exchange contracts or purchased options. Anticipated, but not yet firmly committed, transactions may be hedged through the use of purchased options. Premiums paid on purchased options and any gains are included in prepaid expenses or accrued liabilities and are recognized in earnings when the transaction being hedged is recognized. Gains and losses arising from foreign currency forward and option contracts, and cross-currency swap transactions are recognized in income or expense as offsets of gains and losses resulting from the underlying hedged transactions. Cash flows from risk management activities are classified in the same category as the cash flows from the related investment, borrowing or foreign exchange activity. See Note 14 for further discussion.

Income taxes:

Income taxes are provided currently on financial statement earnings of non-U.S. subsidiaries expected to be repatriated. The Company intends to determine annually the amount of undistributed non-U.S. earnings to invest indefinitely in its non-U.S. operations.

The Company accounts for income taxes using the asset and liability method. This approach requires the recognition of deferred tax liabilities and assets for the expected future tax consequences of temporary differences between the carrying amounts and the tax bases of other assets and liabilities. See Note 6 for further discussion.

Net income per common share:

Net income per common share is computed based on the weighted average number of common and common equivalent (stock option) shares outstanding for the periods reported.

On October 23, 1996 and October 30, 1995, the Company issued additional shares in connection with two-for-one stock splits effected in the form of a 100% stock dividend on outstanding Class A and Class B common stock. The per common share amounts in the Consolidated Financial Statements and accompanying notes have been adjusted to reflect these stock splits.

Management estimates:

The preparation of financial statements in conformity with generally accepted accounting principles requires management to make estimates, including estimates relating to assumptions that affect the reported amounts of assets and liabilities and disclosure of contingent assets and liabilities at the date of financial statements and the reported amounts of revenues and expenses during the reporting period. Actual results could differ from these estimates.

Reclassifications:

Certain prior year amounts have been reclassified to conform to fiscal 1997 presentation. These changes had no impact on previously reported results of operations or shareholders' equity.

NOTE 2 – INVENTORIES:

Inventories by major classification are as follows:

(in thousands)

MAY 31,	1997	1996
Finished goods	$1,248,401	$874,700
Work-in-progress	50,245	28,940
Raw materials	39,994	27,511
	$1,338,640	$931,151

The excess of replacement cost over LIFO cost was $20,716,000 at May 31, 1997, and $16,023,000 at May 31,1996.

NOTE 3 – PROPERTY, PLANT AND EQUIPMENT:

Property, plant and equipment includes the following:

(in thousands)

MAY 31,	1997	1996
Land	$ 90,792	$ 75,369
Buildings	241,062	246,602
Machinery and equipment	735,739	572,396
Leasehold improvements	206,593	83,678
Construction in process	151,561	69,660
	1,425,747	1,047,705
Less accumulated depreciation	503,378	404,246
	$ 922,369	$ 643,459

Capitalized interest expense was $2,765,000, $858,000 and $261,000 for the fiscal years ended May 31, 1997, 1996 and 1995 respectively.

NOTE 5 – LONG-TERM DEBT:

Long-term debt includes the following:

(in thousands)

MAY 31,	1997	1996
6.375% Medium term notes, payable December 1, 2003	$199,211	$ —
4.30% Japanese yen notes, payable June 26, 2011	92,373	—
9.43% capital warehouse lease	—	7,485
Other	6,652	9,400
Total	298,236	16,885
Less current maturities	2,216	7,301
	$296,020	$ 9,584

In December of 1996, the Company filed a $500 million shelf registration with the Securities and Exhange Commission and issued $200 million seven-year notes, maturing December 1, 2003. The proceeds were subsequently exchanged for Dutch Guilders and loaned to a European subsidiary. Interest on the loan is paid semi-annually. The Company entered into swap transactions reducing the effective interest rate to 5.64% as well as to hedge the foreign currency exposure related to the repayment of the intercompany loan. In June of 1997, the Company issued an additional $100 million medium term notes under this program with maturities of June 16, 2000 and June 17, 2002.

In June of 1996, the Company's Japanese subsidiary borrowed 10.5 billion yen in a private placement with a maturity of June 26, 2011. Interest is paid semi-annually. The agreement provides for early retirement after year ten.

The Company's long-term debt ratings are A+ by Standard and Poor's Corporation and A1 by Moody's Investor Service.

Amounts of long-term maturities in each of the five fiscal years 1998 through 2002, respectively, are $2,216,000, $1,891,000, $2,187,000, $188,000 and $47,000.

NOTE 7 – REDEEMABLE PREFERRED STOCK:

NIAC is the sole owner of the Company's authorized Redeemable Preferred Stock, $1 par value, which is redeemable at the option of NIAC at par value aggregating $300,000. A cumulative dividend of $.10 per share is payable annually on May 31 and no dividends may be declared or paid on the Common Stock of the Company unless dividends on the Redeemable Preferred Stock have been declared and paid in full. There have been no changes in the Redeemable Preferred Stock in the three years ended May 31, 1997. As the holder of the Redeemable Preferred Stock, NIAC does not have general voting rights but does have the right to vote as a separate class on the sale of all or substantially all of the assets of the Company and its subsidiaries, on merger, consolidation, liquidation or dissolution of the Company or on the sale or assignment of the NIKE trademark for athletic footwear sold in the United States.

NOTE 11 – COMMITMENTS AND CONTINGENCIES:

The Company leases space for its offices, warehouses and retail stores under leases expiring from one to twenty years after May 31, 1997. Rent expense aggregated $84,109,000, $52,483,000 and $43,506,000 for the years ended May 31, 1997, 1996 and 1995, respectively. Amounts of minimum future annual rental commitments under non-cancellable operating leases in each of the five fiscal years 1998 through 2002 are $76,319,000, $65,315,000, $53,776,000, $46,125,000, $42,274,000, respectively, and $326,198,000 in later years.

Lawsuits arise during the normal course of business. In the opinion of management, none of the pending lawsuits will result in a significant impact on the consolidated results of operations or financial position.

Present-Value Tables and Future-Value Tables

This appendix provides present-value tables and future-value tables (more complete than those in the Chapter 15 appendix and in Chapter 26).

EXHIBIT B-1
Present Value of $1

Present Value

Periods	1%	2%	3%	4%	5%	6%	7%	8%	9%	10%	12%
1	0.990	0.980	0.971	0.962	0.952	0.943	0.935	0.926	0.917	0.909	0.893
2	0.980	0.961	0.943	0.925	0.907	0.890	0.873	0.857	0.842	0.826	0.797
3	0.971	0.942	0.915	0.889	0.864	0.840	0.816	0.794	0.772	0.751	0.712
4	0.961	0.924	0.888	0.855	0.823	0.792	0.763	0.735	0.708	0.683	0.636
5	0.951	0.906	0.883	0.822	0.784	0.747	0.713	0.681	0.650	0.621	0.567
6	0.942	0.888	0.837	0.790	0.746	0.705	0.666	0.630	0.596	0.564	0.507
7	0.933	0.871	0.813	0.760	0.711	0.665	0.623	0.583	0.547	0.513	0.452
8	0.923	0.853	0.789	0.731	0.677	0.627	0.582	0.540	0.502	0.467	0.404
9	0.914	0.837	0.766	0.703	0.645	0.592	0.544	0.500	0.460	0.424	0.361
10	0.905	0.820	0.744	0.676	0.614	0.558	0.508	0.463	0.422	0.386	0.322
11	0.896	0.804	0.722	0.650	0.585	0.527	0.475	0.429	0.388	0.350	0.287
12	0.887	0.788	0.701	0.625	0.557	0.497	0.444	0.397	0.356	0.319	0.257
13	0.879	0.773	0.681	0.601	0.530	0.469	0.415	0.368	0.326	0.290	0.229
14	0.870	0.758	0.661	0.577	0.505	0.442	0.388	0.340	0.299	0.263	0.205
15	0.861	0.743	0.642	0.555	0.481	0.417	0.362	0.315	0.275	0.239	0.183
16	0.853	0.728	0.623	0.534	0.458	0.394	0.339	0.292	0.252	0.218	0.163
17	0.844	0.714	0.605	0.513	0.436	0.371	0.317	0.270	0.231	0.198	0.146
18	0.836	0.700	0.587	0.494	0.416	0.350	0.296	0.250	0.212	0.180	0.130
19	0.828	0.686	0.570	0.475	0.396	0.331	0.277	0.232	0.194	0.164	0.116
20	0.820	0.673	0.554	0.456	0.377	0.312	0.258	0.215	0.178	0.149	0.104
21	0.811	0.660	0.538	0.439	0.359	0.294	0.242	0.199	0.164	0.135	0.093
22	0.803	0.647	0.522	0.422	0.342	0.278	0.226	0.184	0.150	0.123	0.083
23	0.795	0.634	0.507	0.406	0.326	0.262	0.211	0.170	0.138	0.112	0.074
24	0.788	0.622	0.492	0.390	0.310	0.247	0.197	0.158	0.126	0.102	0.066
25	0.780	0.610	0.478	0.375	0.295	0.233	0.184	0.146	0.116	0.092	0.059
26	0.772	0.598	0.464	0.361	0.281	0.220	0.172	0.135	0.106	0.084	0.053
27	0.764	0.586	0.450	0.347	0.268	0.207	0.161	0.125	0.098	0.076	0.047
28	0.757	0.574	0.437	0.333	0.255	0.196	0.150	0.116	0.090	0.069	0.042
29	0.749	0.563	0.424	0.321	0.243	0.185	0.141	0.107	0.082	0.063	0.037
30	0.742	0.552	0.412	0.308	0.231	0.174	0.131	0.099	0.075	0.057	0.033
40	0.672	0.453	0.307	0.208	0.142	0.097	0.067	0.046	0.032	0.022	0.011
50	0.608	0.372	0.228	0.141	0.087	0.054	0.034	0.021	0.013	0.009	0.003

Present Value

14%	15%	16%	18%	20%	25%	30%	35%	40%	45%	50%	Periods
0.877	0.870	0.862	0.847	0.833	0.800	0.769	0.741	0.714	0.690	0.667	1
0.769	0.756	0.743	0.718	0.694	0.640	0.592	0.549	0.510	0.476	0.444	2
0.675	0.658	0.641	0.609	0.579	0.512	0.455	0.406	0.364	0.328	0.296	3
0.592	0.572	0.552	0.516	0.482	0.410	0.350	0.301	0.260	0.226	0.198	4
0.519	0.497	0.476	0.437	0.402	0.328	0.269	0.223	0.186	0.156	0.132	5
0.456	0.432	0.410	0.370	0.335	0.262	0.207	0.165	0.133	0.108	0.088	6
0.400	0.376	0.354	0.314	0.279	0.210	0.159	0.122	0.095	0.074	0.059	7
0.351	0.327	0.305	0.266	0.233	0.168	0.123	0.091	0.068	0.051	0.039	8
0.308	0.284	0.263	0.225	0.194	0.134	0.094	0.067	0.048	0.035	0.026	9
0.270	0.247	0.227	0.191	0.162	0.107	0.073	0.050	0.035	0.024	0.017	10
0.237	0.215	0.195	0.162	0.135	0.086	0.056	0.037	0.025	0.017	0.012	11
0.208	0.187	0.168	0.137	0.112	0.069	0.043	0.027	0.018	0.012	0.008	12
0.182	0.163	0.145	0.116	0.093	0.055	0.033	0.020	0.013	0.008	0.005	13
0.160	0.141	0.125	0.099	0.078	0.044	0.025	0.015	0.009	0.006	0.003	14
0.140	0.123	0.108	0.084	0.065	0.035	0.020	0.011	0.006	0.004	0.002	15
0.123	0.107	0.093	0.071	0.054	0.028	0.015	0.008	0.005	0.003	0.002	16
0.108	0.093	0.080	0.060	0.045	0.023	0.012	0.006	0.003	0.002	0.001	17
0.095	0.081	0.069	0.051	0.038	0.018	0.009	0.005	0.002	0.001	0.001	18
0.083	0.070	0.060	0.043	0.031	0.014	0.007	0.003	0.002	0.001		19
0.073	0.061	0.051	0.037	0.026	0.012	0.005	0.002	0.001	0.001		20
0.064	0.053	0.044	0.031	0.022	0.009	0.004	0.002	0.001			21
0.056	0.046	0.038	0.026	0.018	0.007	0.003	0.001	0.001			22
0.049	0.040	0.033	0.022	0.015	0.006	0.002	0.001				23
0.043	0.035	0.028	0.019	0.013	0.005	0.002	0.001				24
0.038	0.030	0.024	0.016	0.010	0.004	0.001	0.001				25
0.033	0.026	0.021	0.014	0.009	0.003	0.001					26
0.029	0.023	0.018	0.011	0.007	0.002	0.001					27
0.026	0.020	0.016	0.010	0.006	0.002	0.001					28
0.022	0.017	0.014	0.008	0.005	0.002						29
0.020	0.015	0.012	0.007	0.004	0.001						30
0.005	0.004	0.003	0.001	0.001							40
0.001	0.001	0.001									50

EXHIBIT B-2
Present Value of Annuity of $1

Periods	1%	2%	3%	4%	5%	6%	7%	8%	9%	10%	12%
					Present Value						
1	0.990	0.980	0.971	0.962	0.952	0.943	0.935	0.926	0.917	0.909	0.893
2	1.970	1.942	1.913	1.886	1.859	1.833	1.808	1.783	1.759	1.736	1.690
3	2.941	2.884	2.829	2.775	2.723	2.673	2.624	2.577	2.531	2.487	2.402
4	3.902	3.808	3.717	3.630	3.546	3.465	3.387	3.312	3.240	3.170	3.037
5	4.853	4.713	4.580	4.452	4.329	4.212	4.100	3.993	3.890	3.791	3.605
6	5.795	5.601	5.417	5.242	5.076	4.917	4.767	4.623	4.486	4.355	4.111
7	6.728	6.472	6.230	6.002	5.786	5.582	5.389	5.206	5.033	4.868	4.564
8	7.652	7.325	7.020	6.733	6.463	6.210	5.971	5.747	5.535	5.335	4.968
9	8.566	8.162	7.786	7.435	7.108	6.802	6.515	6.247	5.995	5.759	5.328
10	9.471	8.983	8.530	8.111	7.722	7.360	7.024	6.710	6.418	6.145	5.650
11	10.368	9.787	9.253	8.760	8.306	7.887	7.499	7.139	6.805	6.495	5.938
12	11.255	10.575	9.954	9.385	8.863	8.384	7.943	7.536	7.161	6.814	6.194
13	12.134	11.348	10.635	9.986	9.394	8.853	8.358	7.904	7.487	7.103	6.424
14	13.004	12.106	11.296	10.563	9.899	9.295	8.745	8.244	7.786	7.367	6.628
15	13.865	12.849	11.938	11.118	10.380	9.712	9.108	8.559	8.061	7.606	6.811
16	14.718	13.578	12.561	11.652	10.838	10.106	9.447	8.851	8.313	7.824	6.974
17	15.562	14.292	13.166	12.166	11.274	10.477	9.763	9.122	8.544	8.022	7.120
18	16.398	14.992	13.754	12.659	11.690	10.828	10.059	9.372	8.756	8.201	7.250
19	17.226	15.678	14.324	13.134	12.085	11.158	10.336	9.604	8.950	8.365	7.366
20	18.046	16.351	14.878	13.590	12.462	11.470	10.594	9.818	9.129	8.514	7.469
21	18.857	17.011	15.415	14.029	12.821	11.764	10.836	10.017	9.292	8.649	7.562
22	19.660	17.658	15.937	14.451	13.163	12.042	11.061	10.201	9.442	8.772	7.645
23	20.456	18.292	16.444	14.857	13.489	12.303	11.272	10.371	9.580	8.883	7.718
24	21.243	18.914	16.936	15.247	13.799	12.550	11.469	10.529	9.707	8.985	7.784
25	22.023	19.523	17.413	15.622	14.094	12.783	11.654	10.675	9.823	9.077	7.843
26	22.795	20.121	17.877	15.983	14.375	13.003	11.826	10.810	9.929	9.161	7.896
27	23.560	20.707	18.327	16.330	14.643	13.211	11.987	10.935	10.027	9.237	7.943
28	24.316	21.281	18.764	16.663	14.898	13.406	12.137	11.051	10.116	9.307	7.984
29	25.066	21.844	19.189	16.984	15.141	13.591	12.278	11.158	10.198	9.370	8.022
30	25.808	22.396	19.600	17.292	15.373	13.765	12.409	11.258	10.274	9.427	8.055
40	32.835	27.355	23.115	19.793	17.159	15.046	13.332	11.925	10.757	9.779	8.244
50	39.196	31.424	25.730	21.482	18.256	15.762	13.801	12.234	10.962	9.915	8.305

Present Value

14%	15%	16%	18%	20%	25%	30%	35%	40%	45%	50%	Periods
0.877	0.870	0.862	0.847	0.833	0.800	0.769	0.741	0.714	0.690	0.667	1
1.647	1.626	1.605	1.566	1.528	1.440	1.361	1.289	1.224	1.165	1.111	2
2.322	2.283	2.246	2.174	2.106	1.952	1.816	1.696	1.589	1.493	1.407	3
2.914	2.855	2.798	2.690	2.589	2.362	2.166	1.997	1.849	1.720	1.605	4
3.433	3.352	3.274	3.127	2.991	2.689	2.436	2.220	2.035	1.876	1.737	5
3.889	3.784	3.685	3.498	3.326	2.951	2.643	2.385	2.168	1.983	1.824	6
4.288	4.160	4.039	3.812	3.605	3.161	2.802	2.508	2.263	2.057	1.883	7
4.639	4.487	4.344	4.078	3.837	3.329	2.925	2.598	2.331	2.109	1.922	8
4.946	4.772	4.607	4.303	4.031	3.463	3.019	2.665	2.379	2.144	1.948	9
5.216	5.019	4.833	4.494	4.192	3.571	3.092	2.715	2.414	2.168	1.965	10
5.553	5.234	5.029	4.656	4.327	3.656	3.147	2.752	2.438	2.185	1.977	11
5.660	5.421	5.197	4.793	4.439	3.725	3.190	2.779	2.456	2.197	1.985	12
5.842	5.583	5.342	4.910	4.533	3.780	3.223	2.799	2.469	2.204	1.990	13
6.002	5.724	5.468	5.008	4.611	3.824	3.249	2.814	2.478	2.210	1.993	14
6.142	5.847	5.575	5.092	4.675	3.859	3.268	2.825	2.484	2.214	1.995	15
6.265	5.954	5.669	5.162	4.730	3.887	3.283	2.834	2.489	2.216	1.997	16
6.373	6.047	5.749	5.222	4.775	3.910	3.295	2.840	2.492	2.218	1.998	17
6.467	6.128	5.818	5.273	4.812	3.928	3.304	2.844	2.494	2.219	1.999	18
6.550	6.198	5.877	5.316	4.844	3.942	3.311	2.848	2.496	2.220	1.999	19
6.623	6.259	5.929	5.353	4.870	3.954	3.316	2.850	2.497	2.221	1.999	20
6.687	6.312	5.973	5.384	4.891	3.963	3.320	2.852	2.498	2.221	2.000	21
6.743	6.359	6.011	5.410	4.909	3.970	3.323	2.853	2.498	2.222	2.000	22
6.792	6.399	6.044	5.432	4.925	3.976	3.325	2.854	2.499	2.222	2.000	23
6.835	6.434	6.073	5.451	4.937	3.981	3.327	2.855	2.499	2.222	2.000	24
6.873	6.464	6.097	5.467	4.948	3.985	3.329	2.856	2.499	2.222	2.000	25
6.906	6.491	6.118	5.480	4.956	3.988	3.330	2.856	2.500	2.222	2.000	26
6.935	6.514	6.136	5.492	4.964	3.990	3.331	2.856	2.500	2.222	2.000	27
6.961	6.534	6.152	5.502	4.970	3.992	3.331	2.857	2.500	2.222	2.000	28
6.983	6.551	6.166	5.510	4.975	3.994	3.332	2.857	2.500	2.222	2.000	29
7.003	6.566	6.177	5.517	4.979	3.995	3.332	2.857	2.500	2.222	2.000	30
7.105	6.642	6.234	5.548	4.997	3.999	3.333	2.857	2.500	2.222	2.000	40
7.133	6.661	6.246	5.554	4.999	4.000	3.333	2.857	2.500	2.222	2.000	50

EXHIBIT B-3
Future Value of $1

Future Value

Periods	1%	2%	3%	4%	5%	6%	7%	8%	9%	10%	12%	14%	15%
1	1.010	1.020	1.030	1.040	1.050	1.060	1.070	1.080	1.090	1.100	1.120	1.140	1.150
2	1.020	1.040	1.061	1.082	1.103	1.124	1.145	1.166	1.188	1.210	1.254	1.300	1.323
3	1.030	1.061	1.093	1.125	1.158	1.191	1.225	1.260	1.295	1.331	1.405	1.482	1.521
4	1.041	1.082	1.126	1.170	1.216	1.262	1.311	1.360	1.412	1.464	1.574	1.689	1.749
5	1.051	1.104	1.159	1.217	1.276	1.338	1.403	1.469	1.539	1.611	1.762	1.925	2.011
6	1.062	1.126	1.194	1.265	1.340	1.419	1.501	1.587	1.677	1.772	1.974	2.195	2.313
7	1.072	1.149	1.230	1.316	1.407	1.504	1.606	1.714	1.828	1.949	2.211	2.502	2.660
8	1.083	1.172	1.267	1.369	1.477	1.594	1.718	1.851	1.993	2.144	2.476	2.853	3.059
9	1.094	1.195	1.305	1.423	1.551	1.689	1.838	1.999	2.172	2.358	2.773	3.252	3.518
10	1.105	1.219	1.344	1.480	1.629	1.791	1.967	2.159	2.367	2.594	3.106	3.707	4.046
11	1.116	1.243	1.384	1.539	1.710	1.898	2.105	2.332	2.580	2.853	3.479	4.226	4.652
12	1.127	1.268	1.426	1.601	1.796	2.012	2.252	2.518	2.813	3.138	3.896	4.818	5.350
13	1.138	1.294	1.469	1.665	1.886	2.133	2.410	2.720	3.066	3.452	4.363	5.492	6.153
14	1.149	1.319	1.513	1.732	1.980	2.261	2.579	2.937	3.342	3.798	4.887	6.261	7.076
15	1.161	1.346	1.558	1.801	2.079	2.397	2.759	3.172	3.642	4.177	5.474	7.138	8.137
16	1.173	1.373	1.605	1.873	2.183	2.540	2.952	3.426	3.970	4.595	6.130	8.137	9.358
17	1.184	1.400	1.653	1.948	2.292	2.693	3.159	3.700	4.328	5.054	6.866	9.276	10.76
18	1.196	1.428	1.702	2.026	2.407	2.854	3.380	3.996	4.717	5.560	7.690	10.58	12.38
19	1.208	1.457	1.754	2.107	2.527	3.026	3.617	4.316	5.142	6.116	8.613	12.06	14.23
20	1.220	1.486	1.806	2.191	2.653	3.207	3.870	4.661	5.604	6.728	9.646	13.74	16.37
21	1.232	1.516	1.860	2.279	2.786	3.400	4.141	5.034	6.109	7.400	10.80	15.67	18.82
22	1.245	1.546	1.916	2.370	2.925	3.604	4.430	5.437	6.659	8.140	12.10	17.86	21.64
23	1.257	1.577	1.974	2.465	3.072	3.820	4.741	5.871	7.258	8.954	13.55	20.36	24.89
24	1.270	1.608	2.033	2.563	3.225	4.049	5.072	6.341	7.911	9.850	15.18	23.21	28.63
25	1.282	1.641	2.094	2.666	3.386	4.292	5.427	6.848	8.623	10.83	17.00	26.46	32.92
26	1.295	1.673	2.157	2.772	3.556	4.549	5.807	7.396	9.399	11.92	19.04	30.17	37.86
27	1.308	1.707	2.221	2.883	3.733	4.822	6.214	7.988	10.25	13.11	21.32	34.39	43.54
28	1.321	1.741	2.288	2.999	3.920	5.112	6.649	8.627	11.17	14.42	23.88	39.20	50.07
29	1.335	1.776	2.357	3.119	4.116	5.418	7.114	9.317	12.17	15.86	26.75	44.69	57.58
30	1.348	1.811	2.427	3.243	4.322	5.743	7.612	10.06	13.27	17.45	29.96	50.95	66.21
40	1.489	2.208	3.262	4.801	7.040	10.29	14.97	21.72	31.41	45.26	93.05	188.9	267.9
50	1.645	2.692	4.384	7.107	11.47	18.42	29.46	46.90	74.36	117.4	289.0	700.2	1,084

EXHIBIT B-4
Future Value of Annuity $1

Future Value

Periods	1%	2%	3%	4%	5%	6%	7%	8%	9%	10%	12%	14%	15%
1	1.000	1.000	1.000	1.000	1.000	1.000	1.000	1.000	1.000	1.000	1.000	1.000	1.000
2	2.010	2.020	2.030	2.040	2.050	2.060	2.070	2.080	2.090	2.100	2.120	2.140	2.150
3	3.030	3.060	3.091	3.122	3.153	3.184	3.215	3.246	3.278	3.310	3.374	3.440	3.473
4	4.060	4.122	4.184	4.246	4.310	4.375	4.440	4.506	4.573	4.641	4.779	4.921	4.993
5	5.101	5.204	5.309	5.416	5.526	5.637	5.751	5.867	5.985	6.105	6.353	6.610	6.742
6	6.152	6.308	6.468	6.633	6.802	6.975	7.153	7.336	7.523	7.716	8.115	8.536	8.754
7	7.214	7.434	7.662	7.898	8.142	8.394	8.654	8.923	9.200	9.487	10.09	10.73	11.07
8	8.286	8.583	8.892	9.214	9.549	9.897	10.26	10.64	11.03	11.44	12.30	13.23	13.73
9	9.369	9.755	10.16	10.58	11.03	11.49	11.98	12.49	13.02	13.58	14.78	16.09	16.79
10	10.46	10.95	11.46	12.01	12.58	13.18	13.82	14.49	15.19	15.94	17.55	19.34	20.30
11	11.57	12.17	12.81	13.49	14.21	14.97	15.78	16.65	17.56	18.53	20.65	23.04	24.35
12	12.68	13.41	14.19	15.03	15.92	16.87	17.89	18.98	20.14	21.38	24.13	27.27	29.00
13	13.81	14.68	15.62	16.63	17.71	18.88	20.14	21.50	22.95	24.52	28.03	32.09	34.35
14	14.95	15.97	17.09	18.29	19.60	21.02	22.55	24.21	26.02	27.98	32.39	37.58	40.50
15	16.10	17.29	18.60	20.02	21.58	23.28	25.13	27.15	29.36	31.77	37.28	43.84	47.58
16	17.26	18.64	20.16	21.82	23.66	25.67	27.89	30.32	33.00	35.95	42.75	50.98	55.72
17	18.43	20.01	21.76	23.70	25.84	28.21	30.84	33.75	36.97	40.54	48.88	59.12	65.08
18	19.61	21.41	23.41	25.65	28.13	30.91	34.00	37.45	41.30	45.60	55.75	68.39	75.84
19	20.81	22.84	25.12	27.67	30.54	33.76	37.38	41.45	46.02	51.16	63.44	78.97	88.21
20	22.02	24.30	26.87	29.78	33.07	36.79	41.00	45.76	51.16	57.28	72.05	91.02	102.4
21	23.24	25.78	28.68	31.97	35.72	39.99	44.87	50.42	56.76	64.00	81.70	104.8	118.8
22	24.47	27.30	30.54	34.25	38.51	43.39	49.01	55.46	62.87	71.40	92.50	120.4	137.6
23	25.72	28.85	32.45	36.62	41.43	47.00	53.44	60.89	69.53	79.54	104.6	138.3	159.3
24	26.97	30.42	34.43	39.08	44.50	50.82	58.18	66.76	76.79	88.50	118.2	158.7	184.2
25	28.24	32.03	36.46	41.65	47.73	54.86	63.25	73.11	84.70	98.35	133.3	181.9	212.8
26	29.53	33.67	38.55	44.31	51.11	59.16	68.68	79.95	93.32	109.2	150.3	208.3	245.7
27	30.82	35.34	40.71	47.08	54.67	63.71	74.48	87.35	102.7	121.1	169.4	238.5	283.6
28	32.13	37.05	42.93	49.97	58.40	68.53	80.70	95.34	113.0	134.2	190.7	272.9	327.1
29	33.45	38.79	45.22	52.97	62.32	73.64	87.35	104.0	124.1	148.6	214.6	312.1	377.2
30	34.78	40.57	47.58	56.08	66.44	79.06	94.46	113.3	136.3	164.5	241.3	356.8	434.7
40	48.89	60.40	75.40	95.03	120.8	154.8	199.6	259.1	337.9	442.6	767.1	1,342	1,779
50	64.46	84.58	112.8	152.7	209.3	290.3	406.5	573.8	815.1	1,164	2,400	4,995	7,218

Glossary

Absorption Costing: The costing method that assigns both variable and fixed manufacturing costs to products *(p. 968)*.

Accelerated Depreciation Method: A depreciation method that writes off a relatively larger amount of the asset's cost near the start of its useful life than does the straight-line method *(p. 430)*.

Account Payable: A liability backed by the general reputation and credit standing of the debtor *(p. 13)*.

Account Receivable: A promise to receive cash from customers to whom the business has sold goods or for whom the business has performed services *(p. 13)*.

Account: The detailed record of the changes that have occurred in a particular asset, liability, or owner's equity during a period. The basic summary device of accounting *(p. 44)*.

Accounting Cycle: Process by which companies produce an entity's financial statements for a specific period *(p. 138)*.

Accounting Equation: The most basic tool of accounting, presenting the resources of the business and the claims to those resources: Assets = Liabilities + Owner's Equity *(p. 12)*.

Accounting Information System: The combination of personnel, records, and procedures that a business uses to meet its need for financial data *(p. 246)*.

Accounting: The information system that measures business activities, processes that information into reports, and communicates the results to decision makers *(p. 6)*.

Accounting Rate of Return: A measure of profitability computed by dividing the average annual operating income from an asset by the average amount invested in the asset *(p. 1136)*.

Accounts Receivable Turnover: Ratio of net credit sales to average net accounts receivable. Measures ability to collect cash from credit customers *(p. 788)*.

Accrual-Basis Accounting: Accounting that records the impact of a business event as it occurs, regardless of whether the transaction affected cash *(p. 92)*.

Accrued Expense: An expense that the business has incurred but not yet paid. Also called **accrued liability** *(pp. 102, 469)*.

Accrued Revenue: A revenue that has been earned but not yet received in cash *(p. 103)*.

Accumulated Depreciation: The cumulative sum of all depreciation expense recorded for an asset *(p. 100)*.

Acid-Test Ratio: Ratio of (the sum of cash plus short-term investments plus net current receivables) to total current liabilities. Tells whether the entity could pay all its current liabilities if they came due immediately. Also called the **quick ratio** *(pp. 353, 784)*.

Activity-Based Costing (ABC): A system that focuses on activities as the fundamental cost objects and uses the costs of those activities as building blocks for compiling costs *(p. 1079)*.

Additional Paid-in Capital: The sum of paid-in capital in excess of par—common plus donated capital and other accounts combined for reporting on the balance sheet *(p. 555)*.

Adjusted Trial Balance: A list of all the ledger accounts with their adjusted balances, useful in preparing the financial statements *(p. 106)*.

Adjusting Entry: Entry made at the end of the period to assign revenues to the period in which they are earned and expenses to the period in which they are incurred. Adjusting entries help measure the period's income and bring the related asset and liability accounts to correct balances for the financial statements *(p. 97)*.

Aging of Accounts Receivable: A way to estimate bad debts by analyzing individual accounts receivable according to the length of time they have been receivable from the customer. Also called **balance-sheet approach** *(p. 341)*.

Allowance for Uncollectible Accounts: A contra account, related to accounts receivable, that holds the estimated amount of collection losses. Also called **Allowance for Doubtful Accounts** *(p. 339)*.

Allowance Method: A method of recording collection losses on the basis of estimates, instead of waiting to see which customers the company will not collect from *(p. 339)*.

Amortization: The systematic reduction of a lump-sum amount. Expense that applies to intangible assets in the same way depreciation applies to plant assets and depletion applies to natural resources *(p. 441)*.

Annuity: A stream of equal periodic amounts *(p. 1138)*.

Appraisal Costs: Costs incurred to detect poor-quality goods or services *(p. 1095)*.

Appropriation of Retained Earnings: Restriction of retained earnings that is recorded by a formal journal entry *(p. 595)*.

Asset: An economic resource that is expected to be of benefit in the future *(p. 12)*.

Audit: An examination of a company's financial statements and the accounting systems, controls, and records that produced them *(p. 293)*.

Authorization of Stock: Provision in a corporate charter that gives the state's permission for the corporation to issue—that is, to sell—a certain number of shares of stock *(p. 550)*.

Available-for-Sale Securities: Stock investments other than trading securities in which the investor cannot exercise significant influence over the investee *(p. 675)*.

Balance Sheet: List of an entity's assets, liabilities, and owner's equity as of a specific date. Also called the **statement of financial position** *(p. 20)*.

Bank Collection: Collection of money by the bank on behalf of a depositor *(p. 297)*.

Bank Reconciliation: Document explaining the reasons for the difference between a depositor's cash records and the depositor's cash balance in its bank account *(p. 296)*.

Bank Statement: Document the bank uses to report what it did with the depositor's

cash. Shows the bank account's beginning and ending balances and lists the month's cash transactions conducted through the bank *(p. 295)*.

Batch Processing: Computerized accounting for similar transactions in a group or batch *(p. 250)*.

Benchmarking: The practice of comparing a company to a standard set by other companies, with a view toward improvement *(pp. 779, 1045)*.

Board of Directors: Group elected by the stockholders to set policy for a corporation and to appoint its officers *(p. 545)*.

Bonds Payable: Groups of notes payable (bonds) issued to multiple lenders called bondholders *(p. 626)*.

Book Value: Amount of owners' equity on the company's books for each share of its stock *(p. 560)*.

Book Value (of a Plant Asset): The asset's cost minus accumulated depreciation *(p. 101)*.

Book Value Per Share of Common Stock: Common stockholders' equity divided by the number of shares of common stock outstanding *(p. 793)*.

Brand Names: Distinctive identifications of a product or service *(p. 441)*.

Break-Even Point: The sales level at which operating income is zero: Total revenues equal total expenses *(p. 957)*.

Budget: Quantitative expression of a plan of action that helps managers coordinate and implement the plan *(pp. 309, 818)*.

Bylaws: Constitution for governing a corporation *(p. 545)*.

Callable Bonds: Bonds that the issuer may call or pay off at a specified price whenever the issuer wants *(p. 641)*.

Capital Budgeting: A formal means of analyzing long-term investment decisions. Describes budgeting for the acquisition of capital assets *(p. 1134)*.

Capital Charge: The amount that stockholders and lenders charge a company for the use of their money *(p. 794)*.

Capital Expenditure: Expenditure that increases the capacity or efficiency of an asset or extends its useful life. Capital expenditures are debited to an asset account *(p. 425)*.

Capital Expenditures Budget: A company's plan for purchases of property, plant, equipment, and other long-term assets *(p. 995)*.

Capital Lease: Lease agreement that meets any one of four criteria: (1) The lease transfers title of the leased asset to the lessee. (2) The lease contains a bargain purchase option. (3) The lease term is 75% or more of the estimated useful life of the leased asset. (4) The present value of the lease payments is 90% or more of the market value of the leased asset *(p. 645)*.

Capitalize a Cost: To record a cost as part of an asset's cost, rather than as an expense *(p. 423)*.

Cash-Basis Accounting: Accounting that records transactions only when cash is received or paid *(p. 92)*.

Cash Budget: Details how the business expects to go from the beginning cash balance to the desired ending balance. Also called the statement of budgeted cash receipts and disbursements *(p. 1001)*.

Cash Disbursements Journal: Special journal used to record cash payments by check. Also called the **check register** or **cash payments journal** *(p. 260)*.

Cash Equivalents: Highly liquid short-term investments that can be converted into cash with little delay *(p. 715)*.

Cash Flows: Cash receipts and cash payments (disbursements) *(p. 714)*.

Cash Receipts Journal: Special journal used to record cash receipts *(p. 256)*.

Certified Management Accountant (CMA): A licensed accountant who works for a single company *(p. 8)*.

Certified Public Accountant (CPA): A licensed accountant who serves the general public rather than one particular company *(p. 8)*.

Chairperson: Elected by a corporation's board of directors, usually the most powerful person in the corporations *(p. 545)*.

Chart of Accounts: List of all the accounts and their account numbers in the ledger *(p. 59)*.

Charter: Document that gives the state's permission to form a corporation *(p. 544)*.

Check: Document that instructs a bank to pay the designated person or business a specified amount of money *(p. 295)*.

Closing Entries: Entries that transfer the revenue, expense, and owner withdrawal balances from these respective accounts to the capital account *(p. 146)*.

Closing the Accounts: Step in the accounting cycle at the end of the period that prepares the accounts for recording the transactions of the next period. Closing the accounts consists of journalizing and posting the closing entries to set the balances of the revenue, expense, and owner withdrawal accounts to zero *(p. 145)*.

Common-Size Statement: A financial statement that reports only percentages (no dollar amounts); a type of vertical analysis *(p. 778)*.

Common Stock: The most basic form of capital stock. In a corporation, the common stockholders are the owners of the business *(p. 547)*.

Comprehensive Income: Company's change in total stockholders' equity from all sources other than from the owners of the business *(p. 602)*.

Conservatism: Reporting the least favorable figures in the financial statements *(p. 393)*.

Consignment: Transfer of goods by the owner (consignor) to another business (consignee) that, for a fee, sells the inventory on the owner's behalf. The consignee does not take title to the consigned goods *(p. 384)*.

Consistency Principle: A business should use the same accounting methods and procedures from period to period *(p. 392)*.

Consolidated Statements: Financial statements of the parent company plus those of majority-owned subsidiaries as if the combination were a single legal entity *(p. 682)*.

Constraint: A factor that restricts production or sale of a product *(p. 1128)*.

Contingent Liability: A potential liability that will become an actual liability only if a particular event does occur *(p. 351)*.

Continuous Improvement: A philosophy requiring employees to continually look for ways to improve performance *(p. 836)*.

Contra Account: An account that always has a companion account and whose normal balance is opposite that of the companion account *(p. 100)*.

Contract Interest Rate: Interest rate that determines the amount of cash interest the borrower pays and the investor receives each year. Also called the **stated interest rate** *(p. 628)*.

Contribution Margin: The excess of sales revenue over variable expenses *(p. 954)*.

Contribution Margin Income Statement: Income statement that groups variable and fixed expenses separately, and highlights the contribution margin *(p. 954)*.

Contribution Margin per Unit: Excess of the sales revenue per unit (sale price) over the variable expense per unit *(p. 958)*.

Contribution Margin Ratio: The ratio of contribution margin to sales revenue (*p. 958*).

Control Account: An account whose balance equals the sum of the balances in a group of related accounts in a subsidiary ledger (*p. 256*).

Controller: The chief accounting officer of a company (*p. 291*).

Controlling: Acting to implement planning decisions and then evaluating the performance of operations and employees (*p. 818*).

Conversion Costs: Costs of converting direct materials into finished products, usually direct labor plus manufacturing overhead (*pp. 825, 908*).

Convertible Bonds: Bonds (or notes) that may be converted into the common stock of the issuing company at the option of the investor (*p. 642*).

Convertible Preferred Stock: Preferred stock that may be exchanged by the preferred stockholders, if they choose, for another class of stock in the corporation (*p. 559*).

Copyright: Exclusive right to reproduce and sell a book, musical composition, film, other work of art, or computer program. Issued by the federal government, copyrights extend 50 years beyond the author's life (*p. 441*).

Corporation: A business owned by stockholders; it begins when the state approves its articles of incorporation. A corporation is a legal entity, an "artificial person," in the eyes of the law (*p. 9*).

Cost Behavior: Describes how costs change as a cost driver changes (*p. 950*).

Cost-Benefit Analysis: The weighing of costs against benefits to aid decision making (*p. 819*).

Cost Object: Anything for which a separate measurement of costs is desired (*p. 822*).

Cost of Capital: A weighted average of the returns demanded by a company's stockholders and lenders (*p. 794*).

Cost of Goods Available for Sale: Beginning inventory plus purchases during a period (*p. 383*).

Cost of Goods Manufactured: The (manufacturing) cost of the goods that were (finished)—that is, the cost of the units that completed the production process this period. This is the manufacturer's counterpart to the merchandiser's purchases (*p. 829*).

Cost of Goods Sold: The cost of the inventory that the business has sold to customers, the largest single expense of most merchandising businesses. Also called **cost of sales** (*p. 182*).

Cost-Volume-Profit (CVP) Analysis: Expresses the relationships among costs, volume, and profit or loss (*p. 950*).

Credit Memorandum or Credit Memo: A document issued by a seller to credit a customer's account for returned merchandise (*p. 262*).

Credit: The right side of an account (*p. 47*).

Creditor: The party to a credit transaction who sells goods or a service and obtains a receivable (*p. 336*).

Cumulative Preferred Stock: Preferred stock whose owners must receive all dividends in arrears before the corporation pays dividends to the common stockholders (*p. 558*).

Current Asset: An asset that is expected to be converted to cash, sold, or consumed during the next 12 months, or within the business's normal operating cycle if longer than a year (*p. 150*).

Current Liability: A debt due to be paid with cash or with goods and services within one year or within the entity's operating cycle if the cycle is longer than a year (*p. 150*).

Current Portion of Long-Term Debt: Amount of the principal that is payable within one year. Also called **current maturity** (*p. 468*).

Current Ratio: Total current assets divided by total current liabilities. Measures the ability to pay current liabilities from current assets (*pp. 153, 783*).

Customer Service: Support provided for customers after the sale (*p. 822*).

Database: A computerized storehouse of information (*p. 247*).

Days' Sales in Receivables: Ratio of average net accounts receivable to one day's sales. Tells how many days' sales remain in Accounts Receivable awaiting collection. Also called the **collection period** (*pp. 354, 788*).

Debentures: Unsecured bonds, backed only by the good faith of the borrower (*p. 626*).

Debit Memorandum or Debit Memo: A document issued by a buyer when returning merchandise. The memo informs the seller that the buyer no longer owes the seller for the amount of the returned purchases (*p. 263*).

Debit: The left side of an account (*p. 47*).

Debt Ratio: Ratio of total liabilities to total assets. Tells the proportion of a company's assets that it has financed with debt (*pp. 154, 789*).

Debtor: The party to a credit transaction who makes a purchase and has a payable (*p. 336*).

Deficit: Debit balance in the Retained Earnings account (*p. 548*).

Depletion Expense: The portion of a natural resource's cost that is used up in a particular period. Depletion expense is computed just as units-of-production depreciation is (*p. 440*).

Deposit in Transit: A deposit recorded by the company but not yet by its bank (*p. 297*).

Depreciable Cost: The cost of a plant asset minus its estimated residual value (*p. 427*).

Depreciation: The allocation of a plant asset's cost to expense over its useful life (*p. 99*).

Design: Detailed engineering of products and services, or processes for producing them (*p. 822*).

Direct Cost: A cost that can be specifically traced to a cost object (*p. 822*).

Direct Labor: The compensation of employees who physically convert materials into the company's products; labor costs that are directly traceable to finished products (*p. 824*).

Direct Materials: Materials that become a physical part of a finished product and whose costs are separately and conveniently traceable through the manufacturing process to a finished product (*p. 824*).

Direct Method: Format of the operating activities section of the statement of cash flows that lists the major categories of operating cash receipts (collections from customers and receipts of interest and dividends) and cash disbursements (payments to suppliers, to employees, for interest and income taxes) (*p. 718*).

Direct Write-off Method: A method of accounting for uncollectible receivables, in which the company waits until the credit department decides that a customer's account receivable is uncollectible, and then debits Uncollectible-Account Expense and credits the customer's Account Receivable (*p. 344*).

Disclosure Principle: A business's financial statements must report enough information for outsiders to make knowledgeable decisions about the company (*p. 393*).

Discount (on a Bond): Excess of a bond's maturity (par value) over its issue price. Also called a **bond discount** (*p. 627*).

Discounting a Note Payable: A borrowing arrangement in which the bank subtracts the interest amount from a note's face value. The borrower receives the net amount (*p. 466*).

Discounting a Note Receivable: Selling a note receivable before its maturity date (*p. 350*).

Discount Rate: Management's minimum desired rate of return on an investment. Also called the **Hurdle rate, required rate of return,** and **cost of capital** (*p. 1138*).

Dishonor of a Note: Failure of a note's maker to pay a note receivable at maturity. Also called **default on a note** (*p. 351*).

Dissolution: Ending of a partnership (*p. 508*).

Distribution: Delivery of products or services to customers (*p. 822*).

Dividend Yield: Ratio of dividends per share of stock to the stock's market price per share. Tells the percentage of a stock's market value that the company pays to stockholders as dividends (*p. 792*).

Dividends: Distributions by a corporation to its stockholders (*p. 548*).

Double Taxation: Corporations pay their own income taxes on corporate income. Then, the stockholders pay personal income tax on the cash dividends that they receive from corporations (*p. 545*).

Double-Declining-Balance (DDB) Depreciation Method: An accelerated depreciation method that computes annual depreciation by multiplying the asset's decreasing book value by a constant percentage, which is 2 times the straight-line rate (*p. 430*).

Earnings Per Share (EPS): Amount of a company's net income per share of its outstanding common stock (*pp. 601, 791*).

Economic Value Added (EVA): Combines the concepts of accounting income and corporate finance to measure whether the company's operations have increased stockholder wealth (*p. 794*).

Efficiency Variance: Measures whether the quantity of materials or labor used to make the actual number of outputs is within the standard allowed for that number of outputs. This is computed as the difference in quantities (actual quantity of input used minus standard quantity of input allowed for the actual number of outputs), multiplied by the standard unit price of the input (*p. 1048*).

Efficient Capital Market: A capital market in which market prices fully reflect all information available to the public (*p. 795*).

Electronic Funds Transfer (EFT): System that transfers cash by electronic communication rather than by paper documents (*p. 296*).

Entity: An organization or a section of an organization that, for accounting purposes, stands apart from other organizations and individuals as a separate economic unit (*p. 10*).

Equity Method for Investments: The method used to account for investments in which the investor has 20–50% of the investee's voting stock and can significantly influence the decisions of the investee. The investment account is debited for ownership in the investee's net income and credited for ownership in the investee's dividends (*p. 679*).

Equivalent Units: A measure of the amount of work done during a period, expressed in terms of fully complete units of output. Also called **equivalent units of production** (*p. 909*).

Estimated Residual Value: Expected cash value of an asset at the end of its useful life. Also called scrap value, or salvage value (*p. 427*).

Estimated Useful Life: Length of service that a business expects to get from an asset. May be expressed in years, units of output, miles, or another measure (*p. 427*).

Expense: Decrease in owner's equity that occurs from using assets or increasing liabilities in the course of delivering goods or services to customers (*p. 13*).

External Failure Costs: Costs incurred when poor-quality goods or services are not detected until after delivery to customers (*p. 1095*).

Extraordinary Item: A gain or loss that is both unusual for the company and infrequent. Also called **extraordinary gains and losses** (*p. 599*).

Financial Accounting Standards Board (FASB): The private organization that determines how accounting is practiced in the United States (*p. 8*).

Financial Accounting: The branch of accounting that focuses on information for people outside the firm (*p. 7*).

Financial Budget: Projects cash inflows and outflows, the period-ending balance sheet, and the statement of cash flows (*p. 995*).

Financial Statements: Business documents that report on a business in monetary amounts, providing information to help people make informed business decisions (*p. 6*).

Financing Activities: Activities by which the company gets the cash needed to launch and sustain the business (*p. 356*).

Financing Activity: Activity that obtains the funds from investors and creditors needed to launch and sustain the business; a section of the statement of cash flows (*p. 716*).

Finished Goods Inventory: Completed goods that have not yet been sold (*p. 821*).

First-In, First-Out (FIFO) Inventory Costing Method: Inventory costing method by which the first costs into inventory are the first costs out to cost of goods sold. Ending inventory is based on the costs of the most recent purchases (*p. 386*).

First-In, First-Out (FIFO) Process Costing Method: A process costing method that assigns to each period's equivalent units of production that period's costs per equivalent unit (*p. 917*).

Fixed Asset: Another name for property, plant, and equipment (*p. 150*).

Fixed Cost: Cost that does not change in total despite wide changes in volume (*p. 951*).

Flexible Budget Variance: The difference between what the company actually spent at the actual level of output and what it should have spent to obtain the actual level of output. This is computed as the difference between the actual amount and a flexible budget amount (*p. 1040*).

Flexible Budget: A summarized budget that can easily be computed for several different volume levels. Flexible budgets separate variable costs from fixed costs; it is the variable costs that put the "flex" in the flexible budget (*p. 1036*).

Foreign-Currency Exchange Rate: The measure of one currency against another currency (*p. 687*).

Franchises, Licenses: Privileges granted by a private business or a government to sell a product or service in accordance with specified conditions (*p. 442*).

Full Product Costs: The costs of all resources that are used throughout the value chain for a product (*p. 823*).

General Journal: Journal used to record all transactions that do not fit one of the special journals (*p. 252*).

General Ledger: Ledger of accounts that are reported in the financial statements (*p. 255*).

General Partnership: A form of partnership in which each partner is an owner of the business, with all the privileges and risks of ownership (*p. 510*).

Generally Accepted Accounting Principles (GAAP): Accounting guidelines, formulated by the Financial Accounting Standards Board, that govern how accountants measure, process, and communicate financial information *(p. 10)*.

Goodwill: Excess of the cost of an acquired company over the sum of the market values of its net assets (assets minus liabilities) *(p. 442)*.

Gross Margin: Excess of sales revenue over cost of goods sold. Also called **gross profit** *(pp. 183, 379)*.

Gross Margin Method: A way to estimate inventory on the basis of the cost-of-goods-sold model: Beginning inventory + Net purchases = Cost of goods available for sale. Cost of goods available for sale − Cost of goods sold = Ending inventory. Also called the **gross profit method** *(p. 397)*.

Gross Margin Percentage: Gross margin divided by net sales revenue. A measure of profitability. Also called **gross profit percentage** *(p. 201)*.

Gross Pay: Total amount of salary, wages, commissions, or any other employee compensation before taxes and other deductions *(p. 477)*.

Hardware: Electronic equipment that includes computers, disk drives, monitors, printers, and the network that connects them *(p. 247)*.

Hedging: Protecting oneself from losing money in one transaction by engaging in a counterbalancing transaction *(p. 689)*.

Held-to-Maturity Securities: Investment in bonds, notes, and other debt securities that the investor expects to hold until their maturity date *(p. 683)*.

Horizontal Analysis: Study of percentage changes in comparative financial statements *(p. 773)*.

Imprest System: A way to account for petty cash by maintaining a constant balance in the petty cash account, supported by the fund (cash plus disbursement tickets) totaling the same amount *(p. 308)*.

Income Statement: Summary of an entity's revenues, expenses, and net income or net loss for a specific period. Also called the **statement of operations** or the **statement of earnings** *(p. 19)*.

Income Summary: A temporary "holding tank" account into which revenues and expenses are transferred prior to their final transfer to the capital account *(p. 146)*.

Indirect Cost: A cost that cannot be specifically traced to a cost object *(p. 822)*.

Indirect Labor: Labor costs that are difficult to trace to specific products *(p. 825)*.

Indirect Materials: Materials whose costs cannot conveniently be directly traced to particular finished products *(p. 825)*.

Indirect Method: Format of the operating activities section of the statement of cash flows that starts with net income and shows the reconciliation from net income to operating cash flows. Also called the **reconciliation method** *(p. 718)*.

Intangible Assets: Assets with no physical form. Valuable because of the special rights they carry. Examples are patents and copyrights *(p. 421)*.

Internal Control: Organizational plan and all the related measures adopted by an entity to safeguard assets, and encourage adherence to company policies, promote operational efficiency, and ensure accurate and reliable accounting records *(p. 290)*.

Internal Failure Costs: Costs incurred when the company detects and corrects poor-quality goods or services before delivery to customers *(p. 1095)*.

Internal Rate of Return (IRR): The rate of return (based on discounted cash flows) that a company can expect to earn on a project. The discount rate that makes the net present value of the project's cash flows equal to zero *(p. 1141)*.

Inventoriable Product Costs: All costs of a product that are regarded as an asset for external financial reporting. Must conform to GAAP *(p. 823)*.

Inventory Profit: Difference between gross margin figured on the FIFO basis and gross margin figured on the LIFO basis *(p. 388)*.

Inventory Turnover: Ratio of cost of goods sold to average inventory. Measures the number of times a company sells its average level of inventory during a year *(pp. 201, 786)*.

Investing Activities: Activities that relate to the purchase and sale of a business's long-term assets *(p. 355)*.

Investing Activity: Activity that increases and decreases the long-term assets available to the business; a section of the statement of cash flows *(p. 716)*.

Invoice: A seller's request for cash from the purchaser *(p. 185)*.

Journal: The chronological accounting record of an entity's transactions *(p. 49)*.

Just-In-Time (JIT) Costing: A standard costing system that starts with output completed and then assigns manufacturing costs to units sold and to inventories. Also called **backflush costing** *(p. 1093)*.

Just-In-Time (JIT): A system in which a company schedules production just in time to satisfy needs. Materials are purchased and finished goods are completed only as needed to satisfy customer demand *(p. 834)*.

Last-In, First-Out (LIFO) Inventory Costing Method: Inventory costing method by which the last costs into inventory are the first costs out to cost of goods sold. This method leaves the oldest costs—those of beginning inventory and the earliest purchases of the period—in ending inventory *(p. 386)*.

Lease: Rental agreement in which the tenant (lessee) agrees to make rent payments to the property owner (lessor) to obtain the use of the asset *(p. 644)*.

Ledger: The book of accounts *(p. 44)*.

Legal Capital: The portion of stockholders' equity that cannot be used for dividends *(p. 548)*.

Lessee: Tenant in a lease agreement *(p. 644)*.

Lessor: Property owner in a lease agreement *(p. 644)*.

Liability: An economic obligation (a debt) payable to an individual or an organization outside the business *(p. 12)*.

Life-Cycle Budget: A budget that predicts a product's revenues and costs over its entire life cycle *(p. 1098)*.

LIFO Liquidation: Occurs when the LIFO inventory method is used and inventory quantities fall below the level of the previous period *(p. 389)*.

Limited Liability Partnership: A form of partnership in which each partner's personal liability for the business's debts is limited to a certain amount. Also called **LLPs** *(p. 510)*.

Limited Liability: No personal obligation of a stockholder for corporation debts. A stockholder can lose no more on an investment in a corporation's stock than the cost of the investment *(p. 544)*.

Limited Partnership: A partnership with at least two classes of partners: a general partner and limited partners *(p. 510)*.

Liquidation: The process of going out of business by selling the entity's assets and paying its liabilities. The final step in liquidation of a business is the distribution of any remaining cash to the owner(s) *(p. 523)*.

Liquidity: Measure of how quickly an item can be converted to cash *(p. 150)*.

Long-Term Asset: An asset other than a current asset (p. 150).

Long-Term Investment: A noncurrent asset, a separate asset category reported on the balance sheet between current assets and plant assets (p. 675).

Long-Term Liability: A liability other than a current liability (p. 150).

Long-Term Solvency: Ability to generate enough cash to pay long-term debts as they mature (p. 772).

Lower-of-Cost-or-Market (LCM) Rule: Requires that an asset be reported in the financial statements at whichever is lower—its historical cost or its market value (current replacement cost for inventory) (p. 394).

Major Repair or Extraordinary Repair: Repair work that generates a capital expenditure (p. 425).

Maker of a Note: The person or business that signs the note and promises to pay the amount required by the note agreement; the debtor (p. 349).

Management Accounting: The branch of accounting that focuses on information for internal decision makers of a business, such as top executives (p. 7).

Management by Exception: Directs management's attention to important differences between actual and budgeted amounts (p. 1011).

Manufacturing Company: A company that uses labor, plant, and equipment to convert raw materials into new finished products (p. 820).

Manufacturing Overhead: All manufacturing costs other than direct materials and direct labor. Also called **factory overhead** or **indirect manufacturing cost** (p. 824).

Margin of Safety: Excess of expected sales over break-even sales. Drop in sales a company can absorb before incurring an operating loss (p. 964).

Market Interest Rate: Interest rate that investors demand in order to loan their money. Also called the **effective interest rate** (p. 628).

Market Value: Price for which a person could buy or sell a share of stock (p. 559).

Market-Value Method for Investments: Used to account for all trading investments. These investments are reported at their current market value (p. 675).

Marketing: Promotion of products or services (p. 822).

Master Budget: The set of budgeted financial statements and supporting schedules for the entire organization. This comprehensive budget includes the operating budget, the capital expenditures budget, and the financial budget (p. 995).

Matching Principle: The basis for recording expenses. Directs accountants to identify all expenses incurred during the period, to measure the expenses, and to match them against the revenues earned during that same span of time (p. 95).

Materiality Concept: A company must perform strictly proper accounting only for items and transactions that are significant to the business's financial statements (p. 393).

Materials Inventory: Raw materials for use in the manufacturing process (p. 821).

Menu: A list of options for choosing computer functions (p. 249).

Merchandising Company: A company that buys ready-made inventory for resale to customers (pp. 378, 820).

Method: A depreciation method that writes off a relatively larger amount of the asset's cost near the start of its useful life than does the straight-line method (p. 430).

Minority Interest: A subsidiary company's equity that is held by stockholders other than the parent company (p. 682).

Mixed Cost: Cost that is part variable and part fixed (p. 952).

Module: Separate compatible units of an accounting package that are integrated to function together (p. 251).

Mortgage: Borrower's promise to transfer the legal title to certain assets to the lender if the debt is not paid on schedule (p. 643).

Multi-step Income Statement: Format that contains subtotals to highlight significant relationships. In addition to net income, it presents gross margin and operating income (p. 200).

Mutual Agency: Every partner can bind the business to a contract within the scope of the partnership's regular business operations (p. 508).

Net Income: Excess of total revenues over total expenses. Also called **net earnings** or **net profit** (p. 17).

Net Loss: Excess of total expenses over total revenues (p. 17).

Net Pay: Gross pay minus all deductions. The amount of compensation that the employee actually takes home (p. 477).

Net Present Value (NPV): The decision model that brings cash inflows and outflows back to a common time period by discounting these expected future cash flows to their present value, using a minimum desired rate of return (p. 1137).

Net Purchases: Purchases less purchase discounts and purchase returns and allowances (pp. 204, 229).

Net Sales: Sales revenue less sales discounts and sales returns and allowances (p. 182).

Network: The system of electronic linkages that allows different computers to share the same information (p. 247).

Non-Value-Added Activities: Activities that do not increase customer value (p. 1091).

Nonsufficient Funds (NSF) Check: A "hot" check, one for which the maker's bank account has insufficient money to pay the check (p. 298).

Note Payable: A written promise of future payment (p. 13).

Note Receivable: A written promise for future collection of cash (p. 13).

Off Balance Sheet Financing: Acquisition of assets or services with debt that is not reported on the balance sheet (p. 647).

On-line Processing: Computerized processing of related functions, such as the recording and posting of transactions, on a continuous basis (p. 250).

Operating Activities: Activities that relate to a business's revenue and expense transactions (p. 355).

Operating Activity: Activity that creates revenue or expense in the entity's major line of business; a section of the statement of cash flows. Operating activities affect the income statement (p. 715).

Operating Budget: Sets the expected revenues and expenses—and thus operating income—for the period (p. 995).

Operating Cycle: Time span during which cash is paid for goods and services, which are then sold to customers from whom the business collects cash (p. 150).

Operating Expenses: Expenses, other than cost of goods sold, that are incurred in the entity's major line of business. Examples include rent, depreciation, salaries, wages, utilities, property tax, and supplies expense (p. 198).

Operating Income: Gross margin minus operating expenses plus any other operating revenues. Also called **income from operations** (p. 198).

Operating Lease: Usually a short-term or cancelable rental agreement (p. 645).

Opportunity Cost: The benefit that can be obtained from the next-best course of action (*p. 1131*).

Ordinary Repair: Repair work that creates a revenue expenditure, debited to an expense account (*p. 425*).

Other Expense: Expense that is outside the main operations of a business, such as a loss on the sale of plant assets (*p. 198*).

Other Revenue: Revenue that is outside the main operations of a business, such as a gain on the sale of plant assets (*p. 198*).

Outsourcing: A make-or-buy decision, where managers must decide whether to buy a component product or service, or to produce it in-house (*p. 1129*).

Outstanding Check: A check issued by the company and recorded on its books but not yet paid by its bank (*p. 297*).

Outstanding Stock: Stock in the hands of stockholders (*p. 546*).

Overhead Flexible Budget Variance: The difference between the actual overhead cost and the flexible budget overhead for the actual number of outputs (*p. 1054*).

Owner Withdrawals: Amounts removed from the business by an owner (*p. 13*).

Owner's Equity: The claim of a business owner to the assets of the business. Also called **capital** (*p. 12*).

Paid-in Capital: A corporation's capital from investments by the stockholders. Also called **contributed capital** (*p. 547*).

Par Value: Arbitrary amount assigned to a share of stock (*p. 549*).

Partnership Agreement: The contract between partners that specifies such items as the name, location, and nature of the business; the name, capital investment, and duties of each partner; and the method of sharing profits and losses among the partners. Also called **articles of partnership** (*p. 508*).

Partnership: An association of two or more persons who co-own a business for profit (*pp. 9, 508*).

Patent: A federal government grant giving the holder the exclusive right to produce and sell an invention for 20 years (*p. 441*).

Payback: The length of time it will take to recover, in net cash inflows from operations, the dollars of a capital outlay (*p. 1134*).

Payee of a Note: The person or business to whom the maker of a note promises future payment; the creditor (*p. 349*).

Payroll: A major expense of many businesses. Also called **employee compensation** (*p. 469*).

Pension: Employee compensation that will be received during retirement (*p. 647*).

Percent of Sales Method: A method of estimating uncollectible receivables that calculates uncollectible-account expense. Also called the **income statement approach** (*p. 340*).

Period Costs: Operating costs that are expensed in the period in which they are incurred (*p. 823*).

Periodic Inventory System: An inventory accounting system in which the business does not keep a continuous record of the inventory on hand. Instead, at the end of the period the business makes a physical count of the on-hand inventory and uses this information to prepare the financial statements (*pp. 184, 379*).

Permanent Accounts: Accounts that are not closed at the end of the period—asset, liability, and capital accounts. Also called **real accounts** (*p. 146*).

Perpetual Inventory System: The accounting inventory system in which the business keeps a running record of inventory and cost of goods sold (*pp. 184, 380*).

Petty Cash: Fund containing a small amount of cash that is used to pay for minor expenditures (*p. 307*).

Planning: Choosing goals and deciding how to achieve them (*p. 818*).

Plant Assets: Long-lived tangible assets, such as land, buildings, and equipment, used in the operation of a business. Also called **fixed assets** (*pp. 99, 420*).

Postclosing Trial Balance: List of the ledger accounts (*p. 148*).

Posting: Transferring of amounts from the journal to the ledger (*p. 51*).

Preferred Stock: Stock that gives its owners certain advantages over common stockholders, such as the priority to receive dividends before the common stockholders and the priority to receive assets before the common stockholders if the corporation liquidates (*p. 549*).

Premium: Excess of a bond's issue price over its maturity (par) value. Also called **bond premium** (*p. 627*).

Prepaid Expense: Advance payments of expenses. A category of miscellaneous assets that typically expire or are used up in the near future. Examples include prepaid rent, prepaid insurance, and supplies (*p. 97*).

Present Value: Amount a person would invest now to receive a greater amount at a future date (*p. 628*).

President: Chief operating officer in charge of managing the day-to-day operations of a corporation (*p. 545*).

Prevention Costs: Costs incurred to avoid poor-quality goods or services (*p. 1095*).

Price Variance: Measures how well the business keeps unit prices of material and labor units within standards. This is computed as the difference in prices (actual unit price minus standard unit price) of an input, multiplied by the actual quantity of the input (*p. 1047*).

Price/Earnings Ratio: Ratio of the market price of a share of common stock to the company's earnings per share. Measures the value that the stock market places on $1 of a company's earnings (*p. 792*).

Prime Costs: Direct costs of the manufacturing process, usually direct materials plus direct labor (*p. 825*).

Prior-period Adjustment: A correction to retained earnings for an error of an earlier period (*p. 603*).

Product Life Cycle: The time from research and development through the product's sales and on to the end of customer service (*p. 1097*).

Production Cost Report: Summarizes the operations of a processing department for a period (*p. 922*).

Production or Purchases: Resources used to produce a product or service, or the purchase of finished merchandise (*p. 822*).

Production Volume Variance: The difference between the manufacturing overhead cost in the flexible budget for actual outputs and the standard overhead allocated to production (*p. 1055*).

Proprietorship: A business with a single owner (*p. 9*).

Purchases Journal: Special journal used to record all purchases of inventory, supplies, and other assets on account (*p. 258*).

Rate of Return on Common Stockholders' Equity: Net income minus preferred dividends, divided by average common stockholders' equity. A measure of profitability. Also called **return on stockholders' equity** (*pp. 562, 791*).

Rate of Return on Net Sales: Ratio of net income to net sales. A measure of profitability. Also called **return on sales** (*p. 790*).

Rate of Return on Total Assets: The sum of net income plus interest expense divided by average total assets. This ratio measures the success a company has in using its assets to earn income for the persons who finance the business. Also called **return on assets** (*pp. 562, 790*).

Receivables: Monetary claims against a business or individual (*p. 336*).

Reconciliation Method: Another name for the indirect method (*p. 733*).

Relevant Information: Expected future data that differ among alternative courses of action (*p. 1122*).

Relevant Range: A band of volume in which a specific relationship exists between cost and volume (*p. 953*).

Research and Development (R&D): The process of researching and developing new or improved products or services, or the processes for producing them (*p. 821*).

Responsibility Accounting: A system for evaluating the performance of each responsibility center and its manager (*p. 1009*).

Responsibility Center: A part or subunit of an organization whose manager is accountable for specific activities (*p. 1009*).

Retained Earnings: A corporation's capital that is earned through profitable operation of the business (*p. 547*).

Revenue Expenditure: Expenditure that merely maintains an asset or restores the asset to working order. Revenue expenditures are expensed (matched against revenue) (*p. 425*).

Revenue Principle: The basis for recording revenues; tells accountants when to record revenue and the amount of revenue to record (*p. 94*).

Revenue: Amounts earned by delivering goods or services to customers. Revenues increase owner's equity (*p. 13*).

Reversing Entry: An entry that switches the debit and the credit of a previous adjusting entry. The reversing entry is dated the first day of the period after the adjusting entry (*p. 178*).

S Corporation: A corporation taxed in the same way as a partnership (*p. 511*).

Sales Discount: Reduction in the amount receivable from a customer, offered by the seller as an incentive for the customer to pay promptly. A contra account to Sales Revenue (*p. 191*).

Sales Journal: Special journal used to record credit sales (*p. 253*).

Sales Mix: Combination of products that make up total sales (*p. 965*).

Sales Returns and Allowances: Decreases in the seller's receivable from a customer's return of merchandise or from

granting the customer an allowance from the amount owed to the seller. A contra account to Sales Revenue (*p. 191*).

Sales Revenue: The amount that a merchandiser earns from selling its inventory. Also called **sales** (*p. 182*).

Sales Volume Variance: The difference arising only because the number of units actually sold differs from the number of units expected to be sold according to the static budget. This is computed as the difference between a flexible budget amount and a static budget amount (*p. 1040*).

Segment of the Business: One of various separate divisions of a company (*p. 599*).

Sensitivity Analysis: A what-if technique that asks what a result will be if a predicted amount is not achieved or if an underlying assumption changes (*p. 1005*).

Server: The main computer in a network, where the program and data are stored (*p. 247*).

Service Company: A company that provides intangible services, rather than tangible products (*p. 820*).

Short Presentation: A way to report contingent liabilities in the body of the balance sheet, after total liabilities but with no amount given. An explanatory note accompanies the presentation (*p. 474*).

Short-Term Investment: A current asset; an investment that is readily convertible to cash and that the investor intends either to convert to cash within one year or to use to pay a current liability. Also called a **marketable security** (*p. 675*).

Short-Term Liquidity: Ability to meet current payments as they come due (*p. 772*).

Short-Term Note Payable: Promissory note payable due within one year, a common form of financing (*p. 465*).

Single-Step Income Statement: Format that groups all revenues together and then lists and deducts all expenses together without drawing any subtotals (*p. 200*).

Social Security Tax: Federal Insurance Contributions Act (FICA) tax, which is withheld from employees' pay. Also called **FICA tax** (*p. 478*).

Software: Set of programs or instructions that drive the computer to perform the work desired (*p. 247*).

Special Journal: An accounting journal designed to record one specific type of transaction (*p. 252*).

Specific-Unit-Cost Method: Inventory cost method based on the specific cost of particular units of inventory. Also called

the **specific identification method** (*p. 385*).

Spreadsheet: A computer program that links data by means of formulas and functions; an electronic work sheet (*p. 251*).

Standard Cost: A carefully predetermined cost that usually is expressed on a per-unit basis (*p. 1044*).

Stated Value: Similar to par value (*p. 549*).

Statement of Cash Flows: Reports cash receipts and cash disbursements classified according to the entity's major activities: operating, investing, and financing (*pp. 20, 714*).

Statement of Owner's Equity: Summary of the changes in an entity's owner's equity during a specific period (*p. 20*).

Statement of Stockholders' Equity: Reports the changes in all categories of stockholders' equity during the period (*p. 605*).

Static Budget: The budget prepared for only one level of volume. Also called the **master budget** (*p. 1036*).

Stock Dividend: A proportional distribution by a corporation of its own stock to its stockholders (*p. 585*).

Stock Split: An increase in the number of outstanding shares of stock coupled with a proportionate reduction in the par value of the stock (*p. 588*).

Stock: Shares into which the owners' equity of a corporation is divided (*p. 544*).

Stockholder: A person who owns stock in a corporation. Also called a **shareholder** (*pp. 9, 544*).

Stockholders' Equity: Owners' equity of a corporation (*p. 547*).

Straight-Line (SL) Depreciation Method: Depreciation method in which an equal amount of depreciation expense is assigned to each year (or period) of asset use (*p. 428*).

Strategy: A set of business goals and the tactics to achieve them (*p. 1122*).

Strong Currency: A currency that is rising relative to other nations' currencies (*p. 687*).

Subsidiary Ledger: Book of accounts that provides supporting details on individual balances, the total of which appears in a general ledger account (*p. 255*).

Sunk Cost: A past cost that cannot be changed regardless of which future action is taken (*p. 1131*).

Target Costing: A cost management technique that helps managers set goals for cost savings through product design (*p. 1099*).

Temporary Accounts: The revenue and expense accounts that relate to a particular accounting period and are closed at the end of the period. For a proprietorship, the owner withdrawal account is also temporary. Also called **nominal accounts** (p. 146).

Term Bonds: Bonds that all mature at the same time for a particular issue (p. 626).

Throughput Time: The time between receipt of raw materials and completion of finished products (pp. 834, 1091).

Time-Period Concept: Ensures that accounting information is reported at regular intervals (p. 95).

Times-Interest-Earned Ratio: Ratio of income from operations to interest expense. Measures the number of times that operating income can cover interest expense. Also called the **interest-coverage ratio** (p. 789).

Time Value of Money: The fact that income can be earned by investing money for a period of time (p. 1137).

Total Quality Management (TQM): A philosophy of delighting customers by providing them with superior products and services. Involves improving quality and eliminating defects and waste throughout the value chain (p. 835).

Trademarks, Trade Names, or Brand Names: Distinctive identifications of a product or service (p. 441).

Trading on the Equity: Earning more income on borrowed money than the related interest expense, thereby increasing the earnings for the owners of the business. Also called **leverage** (pp. 644, 791).

Trading Securities: Investments that are to be sold in the very near future with the intent of generating profits on price changes (p. 675).

Transaction: An event that affects the financial position of a particular entity and can be reliably recorded (p. 14).

Transferred-In Costs: Costs incurred in a previous process that are carried forward as part of the product's cost when it moves to the next process (p. 920).

Treasury Stock: A corporation's own stock that it has issued and later reacquired (p. 589).

Trial Balance: A list of all the ledger accounts with their balances (p. 54).

Trigger Points: Points in operations that prompt entries in the accounting records in just-in-time costing (p. 1093).

Uncollectible-Account Expense: Cost to the seller of extending credit. Arises from the failure to collect from credit customers. Also called **doubtful-account expense,** or **bad-debt expense** (p. 339).

Underwriter: Organization that purchases the bonds from an issuing company and resells them to its clients or sells the bonds for a commission, agreeing to buy all unsold bonds (p. 626).

Unearned Revenue: A liability created when a business collects cash from customers in advance of doing work for the customer. The obligation is to provide a product or a service in the future. Also called **deferred revenue** (p. 104).

Unemployment Compensation Tax: Payroll tax paid by employers to the government, which uses the money to pay unemployment benefits to people who are out of work (p. 479).

Units-of-Production (UOP) Depreciation Method: Depreciation method by which a fixed amount of depreciation is assigned to each unit of output produced by a plant asset (p. 428).

Unlimited Personal Liability: When a partnership (or a proprietorship) cannot pay its debts with business assets, the partners (or the proprietor) must use personal assets to meet the debt (p. 509).

Value Chain: Sequence of activities that adds value to a firm's products or services. Includes R&D, design, production, or purchases, marketing, distribution, and customer service (p. 821).

Value Engineering (VE): Designing products that achieve cost targets and meet specified quality and performance standards (p. 1099).

Variable Costing: The costing method that assigns only variable manufacturing costs to products (p. 968).

Variable Costs: Costs that change in total in direct proportion to changes in volume of activity (p. 950).

Variance: The difference between an actual amount and the corresponding budgeted amount. A variance is labeled as favorable if it increases operating income and unfavorable if it decreases operating income (p. 1036).

Vertical Analysis: Analysis of a financial statement that reveals the relationship of each statement item to the total, which is 100 percent (p. 776).

Voucher: Document authorizing a cash disbursement (p. 307).

Weak Currency: A currency that is falling relative to other nations' currencies (p. 687).

Weighted-Average Cost Method: Inventory costing method based on the weighted-average cost of inventory during the period. Weighted-average cost is determined by dividing the cost of goods available for sale by the number of units available. Also called the **average-cost method** (p. 385).

Weighted-Average Process Costing Method: A process costing method that costs all equivalent units of work with a weighted average of that period's and the previous period's costs per equivalent unit (p. 923).

Withheld Income Tax: Income tax deducted from employees' gross pay (p. 478).

Work in Process Inventory: Goods that are partway through the manufacturing process but not yet complete (p. 821).

Work Sheet: A columnar document designed to help move data from the trial balance to the financial statements (p. 138).

Working Capital: Current assets minus current liabilities; measures a business's ability to meet its short-term obligations with its current assets (p. 783).

Company Index

Subject Index

DE14-3	No check figure
DE14-4	1. Total S/E $355,000
DE14-5	1. Total S/E $355,000
DE14-6	No check figure
DE14-7	2. Total S/E $32,100
DE14-8	2. Total S/E $35,300
DE14-9	Report T/S $(1,800)
DE14-10	R/E $116,000; T/S $(24,000)
DE14-11	(a) $3,743,000
DE14-12	No check figure
DE14-13	No check figure
DE14-14	No check figure
DE14-15	Inc. contin. oper. $27,000; Net inc. $21,000
DE14-16	EPS for: Inc. contin. oper. $2.40; Net inc. $1.80
DE14-17	No check figure
DE14-18	Comp. inc. $22,000
DE14-19	R/E 12/31/X5 $478,000
DE14-20	2. $85,000
	3. Sold T/S for $17,000
	4. Mkt. val. of div. $34,000
DE14-21	Net cash inflow from financing $172,000
E14-1	3. Total S/E $363,000
E14-2	2. Total S/E $690,000
E14-3	Total S/E $370,000
E14-4	No check figure
E14-5	Nov. 28 Dr. PIC from T/S Trans. $400 and R/E $400
E14-6	Total S/E $860,000
E14-7	a and b Total S/E $490,000
E14-8	Inc. contin. oper. $42,000: Net inc. $17,600
E14-9	EPS $1.20
E14-10	EPS for: Inc. contin. oper. $2.40, Net inc. $3.42
E14-11	R/E 12/31/X9 $493.8 mil.
E14-12	R/E 12/31/X7 $442 mil.
E14-13	1. $50,000 2. $2.65
E14-14	Total S/E 12/31/X9 $3,352,000
E14-15	2. Total S/E 12/31/X8 $19,100,000
14-1A	Nov. 14 Dr. R/E $1,600; Dec. 22 Cr. PIC from T/S Trans. $2,800
4-2A	2. Total S/E $536,000
-3A	No check figure
4A	2. End. R/E $141,080
	3. Total S/E $566,880
A	Inc. contin. Oper. $48,000; Net inc. $36,400; EPS Net inc. $1.52
	Net inc. $118,000; R/E 6/30/X4 $508,000
	1. EPS for: Inc. contin. oper. $2.91; Net inc. $3.07
	$1.40
	4.10%
	Nov. 8 Cr. PIC from T/S Trans. $3,000; Dec. 13
	Dr. PIC from T/S Trans. $500
	Total S/E $444,100
	No check figure
	End R/E $197,860
	Total S/E $712,680
	contin. oper. $61,000;
	inc. $44,000;
	Net inc. $1.42
	$89,200
	31/X3 $429,200
	for: Inc. contin. oper. $2.06; $1.78
	4.5%
	Cash divs. before and after
	00
ase 1	1. 2-for-1 stock split

Check Figures—Chapter 15

DE15-1	b. $410,500
DE15-2	c. $162.50
DE15-3	No check figure
DE15-4	No check figure
DE15-5	No check figure
DE15-6	b. Interest Exp. $108.33
DE15-7	b. Interest Exp. $193
DE15-8	b. Interest Exp. $148
DE15-9	c. Dr. Interest Pay $163
DE15-10	LT: B/Pay, net $4,715
DE15-11	2. End of period 3 Bond carry. amt. $441,509
DE15-12	1. End of period 5 Bond carry. amt. $500,000;
	2. c. Interest Exp. Yr. 5 $39,260
DE15-13	2. End of period 3 Bond carry. amt. $226,600;
	3. Interest Exp. $6,900
DE15-14	3. EO gain $3,872
DE15-15	2. Cr. PIC in Excess of Par $880,000
DE15-16	EPS: Plan A $2.11; Plan B $1.57
DE15-17	No check figure
DE15-18	Total cur. liab. $84,000
DE15-19	b. Report pension liab. of $500,000
DE15-20	No check figure
E15-1	c. Interest Exp. $2,989
E15-2	c. Interest Exp. $19,812
E15-3	$1,035,000
E15-4	b. Interest Exp. 15,000
E15-5	1. End of period 4 Bond carry. amt. $376,509
E15-6	1. End of period 4 Bond carry. amt. $330,255
E15-7	12/31/X5 Bond carry. amt. $600,000
E15-8	10/1/X5 Dr. EO Loss on Retire of B/Pay $10,625
E15-9	2. $396,400
E15-10	1. Dr. EO Loss on Retire of B/Pay $6,000
	2. Cr. PIC in Excess of Par $127,000
E15-11	EPS: Plan A $7.98; Plan B $4.26
E15-12	1. LT N/Pay. net $514,000
E15-13	1. Dec. 31 Depr. Exp. $6,083; Interest Exp. $5,183
E15-14	4. $27,050,000
	5. 3-31-99 Bond carry. amt. $197,145
E15-15	1. 9/30/98 Interest Exp. $13,445
	2. b. $197,107,000
BN15-1	No check figure
P15-1A	1. d. Interest Exp. $40,000; 3. Current: Interest pay. $40,000; L/T: Bonds pay. $3,000,000
P15-2A	3. c. Interest Exp. $7,650;
	5. Current: Interest pay. $7,750; L/T: N/Pay. net $396,300
P15-3A	2. 9/30/yr. 3 Bond carry. amt. $115,970
	3. Interest exp. $9,146
P15-4A	1. 12/31/X3 Bond carry. amt. $474,920 3. Convert. B/Pay, net $189,968
P15-5A	7/1/X1 Interest Exp. $41,500; 12/31/X1 Depr. Exp. $12,918
P15-6A	No check figure
P15-7A	Total cur. liab. $129,000; Total L/T liab. $493,000
P15-1B	1. d. Interest Exp. $175,000;
	3. Current: Interest pay. $35,000; L/T: Bonds pay. $6,000,000
P15-2B	3. c. Interest Exp. $11,600; 5. Current: Interest pay. $11,333;

	L/T: Bonds pay, net $384,667
P15-3B	2. 9/30/Yr. 3 Bond carry. amt. $162,597
	3. Interest Exp. $12,933
P15-4B	1. 12/31/X3 Bond. carry. amt. $314,688
	3. Convert. B/Pay, net $52,448
P15-5B	7/1/X1 Interest Exp. $16,600; 12/31/X1 Depr. Exp. $16,150
P15-6B	No check figure
P15-7B	Total cur. liab. $43,200
	Total L/T liab. $330,000
Decision Case	EPS: Plan A $6.66; Plan B $6.27; Plan C $6.53
Financial Statement Case 1	1. $393,426,000
P15-A1	1. 5 yrs.: $615,600
	2. 6%: $28,185
P15-A2	1. $10,000,105
	2. $5,640,000
P15-A3	a. $48,110
	b. $112,472
	c. $127,140
P15-A4	1. $284,591
	2. 12/31/X2 Bond carry. amt. $285,629
P15-A5	PV: Nissan Y–4,989,600; Toyota Y–5,197,500
P15-A6	1. $42,740
	2. b. $7,123
	c. $5,238

Check Figures—Chapter 16

DE16-1	b. $49,937.50
DE16-2	No check figure
DE16-3	No check figure
DE16-4	3. Dr. S/T Invest. $4,000
DE16-5	2. 1/27/X9 Loss on Sale of Invest. $1,625
DE16-6	2. 1/16/X7 Gain on Sale of invest. $1,125
DE16-7	19X7 Gain on sale $4,000
DE16-8	2. Gain $1,000
DE16-9	2. Assets: L/T invest. $5,663; S/E: Unrealized loss $(262)
DE16-10	1. Gain on Sale of Invest. $525
DE16-11	3. Bal. of L/T Invest. $101 mil.
DE16-12	Gain $6.5 mil.
DE16-13	No check figure
DE16-14	No check figure
DE16-15	4. $78,000
DE16-16	b. $70,000
	c. $8,000
DE16-17	2. $9,590
DE16-18	May 10 F/C Trans. Gain $200
DE16-19	July 2 F/C Trans. Gain $5,400
DE16-20	No check figure
DE16-21	No check figure
E16-1	1/14/X9 Gain on Sale of Invest. $3,000
E16-2	d. Gain on Sale of Invest. $2,000
E16-3	12/4 Loss on Sale of Invest. $450
E16-4	3. Assets: L/T invest. $242,025; S/E: Unrealized loss $(8,750)
E16-5	No check figure
E16-6	Gain on sale $345,000
E16-7	B/S Assets: L/T invest. $187,200; I/S Other revenue: Equity-meth. invest. rev. $33,600
E16-8	L/T invest. $18,708
E16-9	12/16 F/C Trans. Loss $20
E16-10	Net cash used in investing $(659 mil.)
E16-11	2. Loss on sale $7,313 thou.
E16-12	Dividends rec'd. $9 mil.

Check Figures

Check Figures—Chapter 12

DE12-1	No check figure
DE12-2	No check figure
DE12-3	No check figure
DE12-4	3. Total owner's equity $43 mil.
DE12-5	2. Benz $460,000
	Hanna $95,000
DE12-6	2. $550,000
DE12-7	D $38,000;
	F $22,000;
	G $50,000
DE12-8	L $27,100;
	T $22,900
DE12-9	No check figure
DE12-10	1. No bonus
DE12-11	Bonus to old partners N
	and O $20,000
DE12-12	Total owner's equity $340,000
DE12-13	Bonus to Haenni $30,000
DE12-14	No check figure
DE12-15	c. Cr. G, Cap. $5,000
	I, Cap. $5,000
DE12-16	Dr. G, Cap. $5,000
	I, Cap. $5,000
DE12-17	Cash to: A, $34,000;
	B, $18,000; C, $8,000
DE12-18	Dr.: A, Cap. $34,000; B, Cap. $18,000;
	C, Cap. $8,000
DE12-19	Total assets $228,000
	Total owners' equity $133,000
DE12-20	Net incr. to: T $60,000;
	L $30,000
E12-1	No check figure
E12-2	Cr. G, Cap. $78,900
E12-3	d. Net inc. to: V $37,818
	H $72,182
E12-4	Overall, partnership
	cap. increased $8,000
E12-5	c. K, Cap. $60,000
	B, Cap. $115,000;
	T, Cap. $65,000
E12-6	No check figure
E12-7	1. $50,000
	2. $60,000
E12-8	b. Dr. B. Cap. $48,000;
	G, Cap. $1,200; W, Cap. $800
E12-9	a. M $23,000; N $14,000;
	O $11,000
E12-10	Cash to: P $26,000;
	Q $19,000; R $15,800
E12-11	Sale for $136,000;
	F, Cap. $14,500;
	G, Cap. $42,500;
	H, Cap. $8,000
E12-12	Total assets $276,200;
	J, Cap. $92,600
	G, Cap. $92,300
BN12-1	No check figure
P12-1A	No check figure
P12-2A	2. Total assets $100,000

	T, Cap. $40,450;
	K, Cap. $40,450
P12-3A	3. Cr. N, Cap. $72,000
	4. Cr. N, Cap. $34,000
P12-4A	1. d. Net inc. to:
	Collins $69,750;
	Davis $53,500;
	Chiu $56,750
P12-5A	5. Dr. L, Cap. $38,600
P12-6A	1. a. Cash to:
	M $22,000;
	B $42,000;
	T $44,000
P12-7A	3. Cash to:
	B $4,500;
	P $2,500;
	O $0
P12-1B	No check figure
P12-2B	2. Total assets $119,420
	R, Cap. $48,560
	L, Cap. $48,560
P12-3B	3. Cr. L, Cap. $30,000
	4. Cr. L, Cap. $34,500
P12-4B	1. d. Net inc. to:
	Dewey $35,333
	Karlin $30,333
	DeCastro $25,334
P12-5B	5. Dr. K, Cap. $44,000
P12-6B	1. a. Cash to:
	W $25,800;
	K $73,200;
	I $20,000
P12-7B	3. Cash to:
	R $8,250;
	M $6,750;
	G $9,000
Decision Case	No check figure
Financial Statement Case	2. $999 per hour
	3. $372,825

Check Figures—Chapter 13

DE13-1	No check figure
DE13-2	No check figure
DE13-3	No check figure
DE13-4	No check figure
DE13-5	No check figure
DE13-6	1. Dr. Cash $2,388 mil.
DE13-7	1. $472 mil.
DE13-8	Sum of all dr. to Cash $83,000
DE13-9	All acct. bals. should be the same for
	cases A and B
DE13-10	No check figure
DE13-11	Total S/E $201.2 mil.
DE13-12	c. $323.5 mil.
DE13-13	Total S/E $540,000
DE13-14	R/E incr. by $59,000
DE13-15	4. Pfd. $6,000, Com. $4,000
DE13-16	No check figure
DE13-17	a. $165 b. $46.67
DE13-18	No check figure

DE13-19	No check figure
DE13-20	ROA 24.2%
	ROE 60.5%
DE13-21	2. Net inc. $60,000; Inc. tax pay.
	$32,000; Def. tax liabil. $8,000
E13-1	No check figure
E13-2	2. $116,500
E13-3	2. Total S/E $61,000
E13-4	Cap. in X/S of Par $75,000
E13-5	No check figure
E13-6	Total S/E $179,500
E13-7	Total PIC $990,000
E13-8	Total S/E $427,000
E13-9	Pfd. $18,000
	Com. $42,000
E13-10	Pfd. A $20,000
	Pfd. B $962,000; Com. $118,000
E13-11	BV: Pfd. $60; Com. $21.48
E13-12	BV: Pfd. $68.64; Com. $21.39
E13-13	ROA .088; ROE .075
E13-14	Net inc. $273,000; Inc. tax pay.
	$133,000; Def. tax liabil. $14,000
E13-15	No check figure
BN13-1	No check figure
P13-1A	No check figure
P13-2A	2. Total S/E $421,800
P13-3A	5. Total S/E $292,000
P13-4A	Total S/E: Yankee $709,00_
	Alltell $411,000
P13-5A	No check figure
P13-6A	1. Total assets $420,0_
	$312,000
P13-7A	1. b. Pfd. $35,000
	Com. $180,000
P13-8A	6. BV: Pfd. $52_
P13-9A	1. $200,000
	3. Net inc. $_
P13-1B	No check f_
P13-2B	2. Total _
P13-3B	5. Tota_
P13-4B	Total _
	Hor_
P13-5B	N_
P13-6B	1_
P13-7B	
P13-8F	
P13_	

	$43,000	E20-10	MOH was $90,000 underallocated
E19-4	No check figure	BN20-1	No check figure
E19-5	Total current assets $231,000	BN20-2	No check figure
E19-6	CGM $206,000	**Ethical Issue** No check figure	
E19-7	Net income $43,000	P20-1A	1. April CGS $5,900
E19-8	Gross margin $215,000		4. GM for Job 5: $2,000
E19-9	No check figure	P20-2A	1. CGM $168
E19-10	Net benefits expected from adopting		2. CGS $167.8
	JIT $91,800	P20-3A	3. Ending WIP $197,440
E19-11	No check figure		5. GM House 616: $18,960
E19-12	Ending finished goods inventory	P20-4A	Total job cost $1,619
	$3,300	P20-5A	Operating income $54,746
BN19-1	No check figure	P20-6A	Fee charged to Ying's $3,768.75
BN19-2	No check figure	P20-1B	1. December CGS $4,350
Ethical Issue No check figure			4. GM for Job 4: $100
P19-1A	Total inventoriable product costs	P20-2B	1. CGM $26,200,000
	$35,720		2. CGS $26,500,000
P19-2A	Nite-Glo Neon Nails Manufacturing	P20-3B	3. Ending WIP $181,985
	cost of goods manufactured $64,050		5. GM House 307: $25,075
P19-3A	Operating income $76,000	P20-4B	Total job cost $2,130
P19-4A	Expected value of the benefits exceeds	P20-5B	Operating income $45,242
	cost by $38,572	P20-6B	Fee charged to ELQ $136,000
P19-5A	No check figure	**Decision Case 1** No check figure	
P19-6A	Present value of benefits exceed	**Decision Case 2** Total cost per unit for Job A	
	present value of costs by $343,125		$525
P19-7A	Req. 1 Expected value of benefits is	**Team Project** No check figure	
	$356,895		

P19-8A	No check figure
P19-1B	Total inventoriable product costs $31,610
P19-2B	Bugz-B-Gone Manufacturing cost of goods manufactured $83,350
P19-3B	Beginning finished goods inventory $121,000
P19-4B	Expected value of the benefits exceeds cost by $75,263
P19-5B	No check figure
P19-6B	Present value of costs exceeds present value of benefits by $5,855
P19-7B	Req. 1 Expected value of benefits is $380,398
P19-8B	No check figure
Decision Case No check figure	
Team Project No check figure	

Check Figures—Chapter 20

DE20-1	No check figure
DE20-2	No check figure
DE20-3	Cost/gal. $0.30
DE20-4	No check figure
DE20-5	Ending bal. $315
DE20-6	Balance $1,205
DE20-7	Ending bal. $25,700
DE20-8	Indirect materials $20
DE20-9	No check figure
DE20-10	Balance $188,000
DE20-11	PMOHR $50/MH
DE20-12	Total cost $6,846
DE20-13	Total cost $1,140
DE20-14	Req. 7 MOH is $3,000 underallocated
DE20-15	Ending bal. WIP $9,000
DE20-16	No check figure
DE20-17	MOH is $12,500 overallocated
DE20-18	No check figure
DE20-19	DL traced to client 367: $560
DE20-20	Indirect cost assigned to client 367: $280
E20-1	No check figure
E20-2	CGS $24,100
E20-3	No check figure
E20-4	No check figure
E20-5	GM on job G-65 $14,000
E20-6	MOH is $600 overallocated
E20-7	MOH is $60,000 overallocated
E20-8	Adj. bal. CGS $667,500
E20-9	Bid price $34,188

Check Figures—Chapter 21

DE21-1	No check figure
DE21-2	No check figure
DE21-3	CGS $18
DE21-4	No check figure
DE21-5	Req. 2 Total mixing and injection cost per figurine $0.74
DE21-6	No check figure
DE21-7	2,010 full-time equivalent faculty
DE21-8	100,000 equivalent units of direct materials
DE21-9	50,000 equivalent units of direct materials
DE21-10	40,000 equivalent units of hardening agent
DE21-11	Conversion cost per equivalent unit $1.80
DE21-12	Direct materials cost per equivalent unit $0.50
DE21-13	Ending WIP $14,000
DE21-14	Units started and completed 38,000
DE21-15	38,000 equivalent units of direct materials
DE21-16	77,000 equivalent units of direct materials
DE21-17	Ending WIP $6,965
DE21-18	Cost of goods completed and transferred out $97,420
DE21-19	77,000 equivalent units of direct materials
DE21-20	Ending WIP $6,745
DE21-21	Cost of goods completed and transferred out $97,640
DE21-22	No check figure
E21-1	No check figure
E21-2	No check figure
E21-3	Ending WIP $285
E21-4	Average cost per gallon transferred out $0.75
E21-5	Ending WIP $5,100
E21-6	Ending WIP $1,432.50
E21-7	Average cost per gallon transferred out $2.15
E21-8	Ending WIP $27,280
E21-9	53,200 equivalent units of direct materials
E21-10	82,500 equivalent units of direct materials in Finishing

E21-11	84,500 equivalent units of direct materials in Finishing
E21-12	Ending WIP $106,340
E21-13	Ending WIP $106,106
E21-14	Req. 5 Beginning inventory % completion for conversion work 25%
BN21-1	No check figure
BN21-2	No check figure
Ethical Issue No check figure	
P21-1A	Ending WIP $1,596
P21-2A	Ending WIP $7,660
P21-3A	Ending WIP $1,652
P21-4A	Ending WIP $35,420
P21-5A	No check figure
P21-6A	Ending WIP $3,174
P21-7A	Ending WIP $2,990
P21-1B	Ending WIP $46,624
P21-2B	Ending WIP $1,990
P21-3B	Ending WIP $62.50
P21-4B	Ending WIP $17,847
P21-5B	No check figure
P21-6B	Ending WIP $387,000
P21-7B	Ending WIP $377,000
Decision Case 1	Cost per unit for October production $5.00
Decision Case 2	No check figure
Team Project	Equivalent units of conversion costs in: Chicken & Noodles Dep't: 29,500 Cooking & Shredding Dept: 30,300

Check Figures—Chapter 22

DE22-1	No check figure
DE22-2	No check figure
DE22-3	Req. 1c $48.00
DE22-4	Contribution margin $42,500
DE22-5	No check figure
DE22-6	Fixed manufacturing costs $480,000
DE22-7	2. August operating income $150,000
DE22-8	Breakeven point 5,000 tickets
DE22-9	Breakeven sales $260,000
DE22-10	1. Breakeven point 6,250 round-trips 2. Breakeven point 4,762 round-trips
DE22-11	1. Breakeven point 3,750 round-trips
DE22-12	Contribution margin per car $10,000
DE22-13	Required ticket sales 5,750
DE22-14	Average price per room $85
DE22-15	No check figure
DE22-16	No check figure
DE22-17	Margin of safety: a. 1,000 round-trips c. 16.67%
DE22-18	Margin of safety: a. 700 posters b. $2,450
DE22-19	Break-even point: 350 regular posters 70 large posters
DE22-20	Breakeven point: 2,000 Coach tickets 1,200 Chief tickets
DE22-21	Variable costing income $123,000
DE22-22	No check figure
E22-1	No check figure
E22-2	Increase in operating income $9,000
E22-3	Break-even sales $350,000
E22-4	Break-even point 50,000 units
E22-5	Break-even sales after remodeling $11,000
E22-6	Break-even sales $612,500
E22-7	No check figure
E22-8	Break-even point 1,000,000 tickets

E22-9	Margin of safety 40%
E22-10	Break-even point:
	600 standard T-shirts
	400 fancy T-shirts
E22-11	Absorption costing income $650,000
	Variable costing income $600,000
E22-12	Contribution margin per pair of Pro
	Mountaineers $85
BN22-1	No check figure
BN22-2	No check figure
Ethical Issue	No check figure
P22-1A	No check figure
P22-2A	Contribution margin ratio:
	L 0.600
	N 0.471
P22-3A	Req. 2 Break-even point 40 cruises
	Req. 4 Operating income $231,600
P22-4A	Req. 3 Operating income $120,000
	Req. 4 Break-even sales $1,881,600
P22-5A	Req. 2 Target sales $12,375
	Req. 4 Break-even point 16 tickets
P22-6A	Req. 2 Margin of safety $29,480
	Req. 3 Operating income after sales
	increase $6,700
P22-7A	February operating income:
	Absorption $2,440
	Variable $2,500
P22-1B	No check figure
P22-2B	Contribution margin ratio:
	A 0.586
	C 0.400
P22-3B	Req. 2 Break-even point 57 cruises
	Req. 4 Operating income $23,000
P22-4B	Req. 3 Operating loss ($12,000)
	Req. 4 Break-even point 390,000 boxes
P22-5B	Req. 2 Target sales $14,000
	Req. 4 Break-even point 15 tickets
P22-6B	Req. 2 Margin of safety $110,000
	Req. 3 Operating income after sales
	increase $83,750
P22-7B	November operating income:
	Absorption $32,900
	Variable $33,400
Decision Case 1	Req. 2 Break-even point
	2,000,000
	Req. 3a Break-even point
	1,200,000
Decision Case 2	Annual break-even sales
	$192,000
	Annual target sales $300,000
Team Project 1	Req. 1c Break-even for:
	Phoenix 5,800 belts
	Hermosillo 2,800 belts
	Req. 3 Phoenix operating
	income $60,900
	Req. 4 Hermosillo operating
	income $333,200
Team Project 2	No check figure

Check Figures—Chapter 23

DE23-1	No check figure
DE23-2	No check figure
DE23-3	No check figure
DE23-4	February sales $618,750
DE23-5	No check figure
DE23-6	February purchases $393,250
DE23-7	April–July total $270,000
DE23-8	May purchases $38,400
DE23-9	May cash collections $71,000
DE23-10	May cash disbursements for purchases
	$47,600
DE23-11	February cash collections $500,051.25
DE23-12	Cash deficiency $87,322.50
DE23-13	July interest expense $112.50

DE23-14	No check figure
DE23-15	No check figure
DE23-16	No check figure
DE23-17	No check figure
DE23-18	No check figure
DE23-19	No check figure
DE23-20	Software Department $200,000
DE23-21	No check figure
E23-1	Income is $12,000 higher this year
E23-2	Third quarter purchases $76,300
E23-3	Net income for the year $1,375,089
E23-4	Cash receipt from sale of equipment
	$8,100
E23-5	2. Cash borrowed in Nov. $2,000
E23-6	Ending cash bal. $5,600
E23-7	No check figure
E23-8	Operating income variance for Texas
	$34,000U
E23-9	2. Priming total indirect expense
	$20,300
E23-10	Electronics operating income $46,200
E23-11	June interest expense $55
BN23-1	No check figure
BN23-2	No check figure
Ethical Issue	No check figure
P23-1A	June net income $4,600
P23-2A	June ending cash bal. $21,990
P23-3A	3. Cash available for equipment
	purchases $63,400
P23-4A	Ending cash bal. $23,700
P23-5A	No check figure
P23-6A	New Hampshire operating income
	variance $4,500 F
P23-7A	Custom Travel operating income
	$22,350
P23-1B	September net income $19,000
P23-2B	September ending cash bal. $76,500
P23-3B	Ending cash bal. $24,500
P23-4B	Ending cash bal. before financing
	$10,500
P23-5B	No check figure
P23-6B	Chicago operating income variance
	$17,200 F
P23-7B	Printing operating income $25,065
Decision Case 1	Ending cash bal. -linen, $96
Decision Case 2	2. Total cost per wakeboard
	$220
Team Project	No check figure

Check Figures—Chapter 24

DE24-1	No check figure
DE24-2	9-pool operating income, $16,000
DE24-3	2a. 20-installation operating
	income $8,000
DE24-4	3. August flexible budget total cost,
	$68,000
DE24-5	3. Jan. flexible budget variance, $2,750
	F
DE24-6	Operating income flexible budget
	variance, $12,000 U
DE24-7	Operating income sales volume
	variance, $4,000 F
DE24-8	No check figure
DE24-9	No check figure
DE24-10	No check figure
DE24-11	No check figure
DE24-12	Material price variance, $3,300 U
DE24-13	Ketchup material efficiency variance,
	$2.00 U
DE24-14	Labor price variance, $15,000 F
DE24-15	No check figure
DE24-16	No check figure
DE24-17	Underallocated overhead, $6,000
DE24-18	No check figure

DE24-19	No check figure
DE24-20	No check figure
DE24-21	Operating income, $44,700
E24-1	40,000-level operating income,
	$20,000
E24-2	No check figure
E24-3	Operating income flexible budget
	variance, $17,000 U
E24-4	Sales revenue flexible budget variance,
	$140,000 F
E24-5	Flexible budget variance, $2,275 U
E24-6	Material efficiency variance, $240,000
	U
E24-7	No check figure
E24-8	No check figure
E24-9	Overhead flexible budget variance,
	$300 F
E24-10	Gross margin, $193,500
E24-11	Capacity level, 5100 units
BN24-1	No check figure
BN24-2	No check figure
BN24-3	No check figure
Ethical Issue	No check figure
P24-1A	65,000-unit operating income, $70,350
P24-2A	Operating income sales volume
	variance, $12,500 F
P24-3A	Overhead production volume variance,
	$60,000 F
P24-4A	Actual direct labor hours, 2,950
P24-5A	Material price variance, $7,344 U
P24-6A	Gross margin, $133,588
P24-1B	7,500-unit operating income, $31,125
P24-2B	Total expenses sales volume variance,
	$33,600 U
P24-3B	Overhead production volume variance,
	$700 U
P24-4B	Labor efficiency variance, $600 F
P24-5B	Materials price variance, $1,537 F
P24-6B	Labor price variance, $390 U
Decision Case 1	Flexible budget total receipts,
	$54,050
Decision Case 2	Flexible budget operating
	income, $147,250
Team Project	No check figure

Check Figures—Chapter 25

DE25-1	No check figure
DE25-2	No check figure
DE25-3	No check figure
DE25-4	Total PH overhead, $125
DE25-5	Total aldehyde setup cost, $3,000
DE25-6	Setup cost per lb. of PH, $15
DE25-7	PH gross loss, $69 per lb.
DE25-8	Barron operating income, $900
DE25-9	No check figure
DE25-10	No check figure
DE25-11	Photocopying, $0.10/page
DE25-12	Barron operating income, $1,660
DE25-13	No check figure
DE25-14	Value-added time, 2 hours, 20 min.
DE25-15	No check figure
DE25-16	No check figure
DE25-17	No check figure
DE25-18	No check figure
DE25-19	Total cost of *not* implementing
	program, $215,000
DE25-20	Life-cycle operating contribution,
	$2,375,000
DE25-21	Budgeted life-cycle cost/case, $76.25
DE25-22	Target cost at beginning of production,
	$75.50/case
E25-1	Indirect cost per wheel, $49.20
E25-2	2. Standard model ABC cost, $36.15
E25-3	No check figure

E25-4	No check figure	
E25-5	Conversion cost is $950,000 underallocated	
E25-6	Ending balance FG, $548,000	
E25-7	No check figure	
E25-8	Total cost of *not* implementing program, $160,000	
E25-9	Life-cycle operating contribution, $41,000,000	
E25-10	Target cost, $9,950	
E25-11	Job 103 used 667 parts	
BN25-1	No check figure	
BN25-2	No check figure	
Ethical Issue	No check figure	
P25-1A	Manufacturing product cost, $88.80	
P25-2A	4. Sale price, $102	
P25-3A	2. EZPage ABC unit cost, $20.50	
P25-4A	3. 8/31 bal. RIP, $2,000	
P25-5A	No check figure	
P25-6A	2. Net benefit, $34,000	
P25-7A	3. Target cost at beginning of production, $1,920	
P25-1B	Manufacturing product cost, $129.80	
P25-2B	4. Sale price, $59.20	
P25-3B	2. Travel pack ABC unit cost, $2	
P25-4B	3. 12/31 bal. RIP, $5,000	
P25-5B	No check figure	
P25-6B	2. Net benefit, $4,500	
P25-7B	3. Target cost at beginning of production, $66	
Decision Case 1	Job B ABC costs per unit, $7,300	
Decision Case 2	Target cost at the beginning of production, $21,300	
Team Project 1	Headless Shrimp 2. Original system cost/package	$3.96125

3. ABC cost/package $4.795

Team Project 2   No check figure

Check Figures—Chapter 26

DE26-1	No check figure
DE26-2	Decrease in income, $1,000
DE26-3	Increase in income, $80,000
DE26-4	No check figure
DE26-5	No check figure
DE26-6	No check figure
DE26-7	Decrease in income, $15,000
DE26-8	No check figure
DE26-9	No check figure
DE26-10	Snapple, 40 linear feet
DE26-11	Advantage to outsourcing $10,000 per year
DE26-12	Advantage to making switch, $22,500
DE26-13	Advantage to buying switches and renting out facilities, $2,500
DE26-14	Advantage to processing further, $7,000
DE26-15	Minimum sale price, $24/disk drive
DE26-16	Opportunity cost of slacks, $360,000
DE26-17	Annual cash savings, $5,974
DE26-18	Payback period, 5.59 years
DE26-19	Accounting rate of return, 21.8%
DE26-20	NPV, $3,018,575
DE26-21	IRR, 16%
DE26-22	No check figure
E26-1	2. Decrease in income, $5,000
E26-2	Decrease in income, $70,000
E26-3	Decrease in income, $20,000
E26-4	Total CM at capacity, Moderate, $28,000
E26-5	Advantage to making, $0.50/unit

E26-6	Net cost to buy and use facilities for other product, $645,000
E26-7	Advantage to processing further, $200
E26-8	Payback, 3.5 years
E26-9	Payback, 4.8 years
E26-10	Accounting rate of return, Johnson Controls, 30%
E26-11	NPV of Project B, ($10,400)
E26-12	IRR of Project B, 10–12%
E26-13	No check figure
BN26-1	No check figure
BN26-2	No check figure
Ethical Issue	No check figure
P26-1A	Increase in income, $20,000
P26-2A	Decrease in income, $144,000
P26-3A	Total CM at capacity, Deluxe, $1,120,000
P26-4A	1. Advantage to making, $72
P26-5A	3. Advantage to selling as is, $7,840
P26-6A	NPV, $5,440
P26-7A	3. Plan A's IRR, about 10%
P26-1B	Increase in income, $1,100
P26-2B	Decrease in income, $15,000
P26-3B	Total CM at capacity, Televisions, $7,200
P26-4B	Advantage to making, $11,400
P26-5B	Advantage to processing further, $10,200
P26-6B	NPV, ($472,200)
P26-7B	Plan B's IRR, about 16%
Decision Case 1	NPV, $35,214
Decision Case 2	No check figure
Team Project	IRR, 16%